CUMULATIVE PROBABILITIES FOR THE STANDARD NORMAL DISTRIBUTION

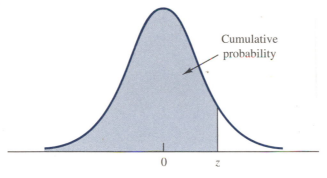

Cumulative probability

D0151694

z	.00	.01	.02	.03	.04	.05	.06	.07	.08	.09
.0	.5000	.5040	.5080	.5120	.5160	.5199	.5239	.5279	.5319	.5359
.1	.5398	.5438	.5478	.5517	.5557	.5596	.5636	.5675	.5714	.5753
.2	.5793	.5832	.5871	.5910	.5948	.5987	.6026	.6064	.6103	.6141
.3	.6179	.6217	.6255	.6293	.6331	.6368	.6406	.6443	.6480	.6517
.4	.6554	.6591	.6628	.6664	.6700	.6736	.6772	.6808	.6844	.6879
.5	.6915	.6950	.6985	.7019	.7054	.7088	.7123	.7157	.7190	.7224
.6	.7257	.7291	.7324	.7357	.7389	.7422	.7454	.7486	.7517	.7549
.7	.7580	.7611	.7642	.7673	.7704	.7734	.7764	.7794	.7823	.7852
.8	.7881	.7910	.7939	.7967	.7995	.8023	.8051	.8078	.8106	.8133
.9	.8159	.8186	.8212	.8238	.8264	.8289	.8315	.8340	.8365	.8389
1.0	.8413	.8438	.8461	.8485	.8508	.8531	.8554	.8577	.8599	.8621
1.1	.8643	.8665	.8686	.8708	.8729	.8749	.8770	.8790	.8810	.8830
1.2	.8849	.8869	.8888	.8907	.8925	.8944	.8962	.8980	.8997	.9015
1.3	.9032	.9049	.9066	.9082	.9099	.9115	.9131	.9147	.9162	.9177
1.4	.9192	.9207	.9222	.9236	.9251	.9265	.9279	.9292	.9306	.9319
1.5	.9332	.9345	.9357	.9370	.9382	.9394	.9406	.9418	.9429	.9441
1.6	.9452	.9463	.9474	.9484	.9495	.9505	.9515	.9525	.9535	.9545
1.7	.9554	.9564	.9573	.9582	.9591	.9599	.9608	.9616	.9625	.9633
1.8	.9641	.9649	.9656	.9664	.9671	.9678	.9686	.9693	.9699	.9706
1.9	.9713	.9719	.9726	.9732	.9738	.9744	.9750	.9756	.9761	.9767
2.0	.9772	.9778	.9783	.9788	.9793	.9798	.9803	.9808	.9812	.9817
2.1	.9821	.9826	.9830	.9834	.9838	.9842	.9846	.9850	.9854	.9857
2.2	.9861	.9864	.9868	.9871	.9875	.9878	.9881	.9884	.9887	.9890
2.3	.9893	.9896	.9898	.9901	.9904	.9906	.9909	.9911	.9913	.9913
2.4	.9918	.9920	.9922	.9925	.9927	.9929	.9931	.9932	.9934	.9936
2.5	.9938	.9940	.9941	.9943	.9945	.9946	.9948	.9949	.9951	.9952
2.6	.9953	.9955	.9956	.9957	.9959	.9960	.9961	.9962	.9963	.9964
2.7	.9965	.9966	.9967	.9968	.9969	.9970	.9971	.9972	.9973	.9974
2.8	.9974	.9975	.9976	.9977	.9977	.9978	.9979	.9979	.9980	.9981
2.9	.9981	.9982	.9982	.9983	.9984	.9984	.9985	.9985	.9986	.9986
3.0	.9987	.9987	.9987	.9988	.9988	.9989	.9989	.9989	.9990	.9990

ESSENTIALS OF MODERN BUSINESS STATISTICS

WITH MICROSOFT® EXCEL, 2e

David R. Anderson
University of Cincinnati

Dennis J. Sweeney
University of Cincinnati

Thomas A. Williams
Rochester Institute of Technology

THOMSON
✳
™
SOUTH-WESTERN

Australia · Canada · Mexico · Singapore · Spain · United Kingdom · United States

Dedicated to
Krista, Justin, Mark, and Colleen
Mark, Linda, Brad, Tim, Scott, and Lisa
Cathy, David, and Kristin

THOMSON
SOUTH-WESTERN

Essentials of Modern Business Statistics with Microsoft® Excel, 2e

David R. Anderson, Dennis J. Sweeney, Thomas A. Williams

Publisher:
Melissa Acuña

Media Developmental Editor:
Chris Wittmer

Cover Design:
Chris A. Miller

Senior Acquisitions Editor:
Charles E. McCormick, Jr.

Media Production Editor:
Amy Wilson

Cover Image:
Digital Vision

Senior Developmental Editor:
Alice C. Denny

Manufacturing Coordinator:
Diane Lohman

Production House and Compositor:
BookMasters, Inc.

Marketing Manager:
Larry Qualls

Internal Design:
Michael H. Stratton/Chris A. Miller

Printer:
Quebecor World—Versailles

Senior Production Editor:
Deanna R. Quinn

Library of Congress Control Number: 2002110226

ISBN 0-324-18452-2

Brief Contents

Contents

Chapter 3
Descriptive Statistics: Numerical Methods 84

Chapter 4
Introduction to Probability 150

Chapter 5
Discrete Probability Distributions 197

Chapter 8
Interval Estimation 313

Chapter 9
Hypothesis Testing 356

Chapter 10
Comparisons Involving Means 411

Chapter 11
Comparisons Involving Proportions and a Test of Independence 475

Chapter 13
Multiple Regression 584

Preface

The purpose of *Essentials of Modern Business Statistics with Microsoft® Excel* is to give students, primarily in the fields of business administration and economics, an introduction to the field of statistics and its many applications. The text is applications oriented and written with the needs of the non-mathematician in mind; the mathematical prerequisite is knowledge of algebra.

Applications of data analysis and statistical methodology are an integral part of the organization and presentation of the text material. The discussion and development of each technique is presented in an application setting, with the statistical results providing insights to decisions and solutions to problems.

Although the book is applications-oriented, we have taken care to provide a sound methodological development and to use notation that is generally accepted for the topic being covered. Students will find that this text provides good preparation for the study of more advanced material. A bibliography to guide further study is included in Appendix A.

USE OF MICROSOFT EXCEL FOR STATISTICAL ANALYSIS

Essentials of Modern Business Statistics with Microsoft® Excel is first and foremost a statistics textbook that emphasizes statistical concepts and applications. However, because most practical problems are too large to be solved using hand calculations, some type of statistical software package is required to solve these problems. There are several excellent statistical packages available today. However, because most students and potential employers value spreadsheet experience, many colleges and universities now use a spreadsheet package in their statistics courses. Microsoft Excel is the most widely used spreadsheet package in business as well as in colleges and universities. We have written *Essentials of Modern Business Statistics with Microsoft® Excel* especially for statistics courses in which Excel is used as the software package.

Excel has been integrated within each of the chapters, and plays an integral part in providing an application orientation. We assume that readers using this text are familiar with Excel basics such as selecting cells, entering formulas, copying, and so on. We build on that familiarity by showing how to use the appropriate Excel statistical functions and data analysis tools.

The discussion of using Excel to perform a statistical procedure appears in a subsection immediately following the discussion of the statistical procedure. We believe that this style enables us to fully integrate the use of Excel throughout the text, but still maintain the primary emphasis on the statistical methodology being discussed. In each of these subsections, we use a standard format for setting up a worksheet for statistical analysis. There are three primary tasks: Enter Data, Enter Functions and Formulas, and Apply Tools. We believe a consistent framework for applying Excel helps users to focus on the statistical methodology without getting bogged down in the details of using the software.

In presenting worksheet figures we often use a nested approach in which the worksheet shown in the background of the figure displays the formulas, and the worksheet shown in the foreground shows the values computed using the formulas. Following is Figure 2.1 from the text, which is displayed to explain use of color in Excel figures. A blue screen is used

FIGURE 2.1 FREQUENCY DISTRIBUTION FOR SOFT DRINK PURCHASES CONSTRUCTED USING EXCEL'S COUNTIF FUNCTION

	A	B	C	D	E
1	**Brand Purchased**		Soft Drink	Frequency	
2	Coke Classic		Coke Classic	=COUNTIF($A$2:$A$51,C2)	
3	Diet Coke		Diet Coke	=COUNTIF($A$2:$A$51,C3)	
4	Pepsi-Cola		Dr. Pepper	=COUNTIF($A$2:$A$51,C4)	
5	Diet Coke		Pepsi-Cola	=COUNTIF($A$2:$A$51,C5)	
6	Coke Classic		Sprite	=COUNTIF($A$2:$A$51,C6)	
7	Coke Classic				
8	Dr. Pepper				
9	Diet Coke				
10	Pepsi-Cola				
45	Pepsi-Cola				
46	Pepsi-Cola				
47	Pepsi-Cola				
48	Coke Classic				
49	Dr. Pepper				
50	Pepsi-Cola				
51	Sprite				
52					

	A	B	C	D	E
1	**Brand Purchased**		Soft Drink	Frequency	
2	Coke Classic		Coke Classic	19	
3	Diet Coke		Diet Coke	8	
4	Pepsi-Cola		Dr. Pepper	5	
5	Diet Coke		Pepsi-Cola	13	
6	Coke Classic		Sprite	5	
7	Coke Classic				
8	Dr. Pepper				
9	Diet Coke				
10	Pepsi-Cola				
45	Pepsi-Cola				
46	Pepsi-Cola				
47	Pepsi-Cola				
48	Coke Classic				
49	Dr. Pepper				
50	Pepsi-Cola				
51	Sprite				
52					

to highlight the data in both worksheets (soft drink purchases in this figure) and a grey screen is used to highlight the cells containing Excel functions and formulas. Dark blue and grey screens are also used in certain figures to highlight material that is printed by Excel as a result of using one of the data analysis tools.

We have provided approximately 180 data sets on the CD-ROM accompanying the text. Many of the data sets are used as examples to illustrate statistical concepts in the text; others contain the data for exercises and case problems. For the data sets used as examples in the text we have also included any worksheets used in the analysis. Students can use these worksheets as templates for solving problems in the text.

CHANGES IN THE SECOND EDITION

We appreciate the acceptance and positive response to the first edition of the text, which was titled *Contemporary Business Statistics with Microsoft® Excel*. The new title better reflects its relationship to *Modern Business Statistics with Microsoft® Excel*, copyright year 2003. Accordingly, in making modifications for this new edition we have maintained the presentation style and readability of the first edition. The significant changes in the second edition are noted here.

Content Revisions

The following list summarizes selected content revisions for this new edition. These changes include:

- A discussion of levels of measurement for data (Chapter 1)
- The introduction of trendlines in the discussion of scatter diagrams (Chapter 2)
- More material on graphical and tabular descriptive statistics (Chapter 2)
- A revision to an earlier discussion of the term *margin of error* and additional information on when to use z and when to use t for interval estimation and hypothesis testing (Chapters 8 though 11)
- The redesign of many worksheets to facilitate their use as templates for similar problems (Chapters 8 through 11)
- More emphasis on computing and interpreting p-values (Chapters 9 through 11)
- A new chapter on multiple regression (Chapter 13).

New Examples and Exercises Based on Real Data

We have added over 200 new examples and exercises based on real data and recent reference sources of statistical information. Using data pulled from sources also used by *The Wall Street Journal, USA Today, Fortune, Barron's,* various Web sites, and a variety of other sources, we have drawn upon actual studies to develop explanations and create exercises that demonstrate many uses of statistics in business and economics. We believe that the use of real data helps generate more student interest in the material and enables the student to learn about both the statistical methodology and its application.

New Chapter on Multiple Regression

Given the importance of regression in applied statistics, we have added a new Chapter 13 entitled Multiple Regression. Simple linear regression remains the topic of Chapter 12. In the new chapter, we cover the multiple regression model, the assumptions, testing for significance and using the estimated regression equation for estimation and prediction. The chapter also includes a section on the use and interpretation of qualitative independent variables.

New Case Problems

We have added six new case problems to this edition, bringing the total number of case problems in the text to twenty-one. The new case problems, which involve larger datasets, appear in the chapters on interval estimation and multiple regression. These case problems provide students with the opportunity to analyze somewhat larger datasets and prepare managerial reports based on the results of their analysis.

New Statistics in Practice

Each chapter begins with a Statistics in Practice article that describes an application of the statistical methodology to be covered in the chapter. Practitioners at companies such as Procter & Gamble, MeadWestvaco, Dollar General, Colgate-Palmolive, Citibank, and others have provided the articles. This edition includes two new Statistics in Practice: Alliance Data Systems (Chapter 12) and International Paper (Chapter 13).

FEATURES AND PEDAGOGY

We have continued many of the features that appeared in the first edition. Some of the more important ones are noted here.

Data Files Accompany the Text

There are approximately 180 data files available and packaged on the CD found in new copies of the text. The data files can be accessed using Excel 97, Excel 2000, and Excel 2002. Data files for all case problems, and for larger data sets in text illustrations and exercises, are included. New for this edition, the Excel files for problems used in text demonstrations include worksheets that can be used as templates to solve the exercises provided in the text.

Margin Annotations and Notes and Comments

Margin annotations that highlight key points and provide additional insights for the student are a key feature of this text. These annotations, which appear in the margins, are designed to provide emphasis and enhance understanding of the terms and concepts being presented in the text.

At the end of many sections, we provide Notes and Comments designed to give the reader additional insights about the statistical methodology and its application. These notes include warnings about limitations of the methodology, recommendations for application, brief descriptions of technical considerations, and other matters.

Methods Exercises and Applications Exercises

The end-of-section exercises are split into two parts: Methods and Applications. The Methods exercises require users to use the formulas and make computations. The Applications exercises require students to apply the chapter material in real-world situations. Thus, students focus on the computational "nuts and bolts" and then move on to the subtleties of statistical applications and the interpretation of the statistical output.

Self-Test Exercises

Certain exercises are identified as self-test exercises. Completely worked-out solutions for these exercises are provided in Appendix D, Self-Test Solutions and Answers to Even-Numbered Exercises, located at the end of the book. Students can attempt the self-text exercises and immediately check the solutions to evaluate their understanding of the concepts presented in the chapter. At the request of professors using our textbooks, we now provide the answers to even-numbered exercises in this same appendix.

ANCILLARY TEACHING AND LEARNING MATERIALS

Several valuable resources are available for students. Both of the printed items are available for direct purchase online at **http://asw.swlearning.com.**

- The *Study Guide* (ISBN: 0-324-18464-6) prepared by John Loucks of St. Edward's University will provide the student with significant supplementary study materials. For each chapter, it contains key concepts, review materials, example problems worked out in full detail, exercises with answers, and self-test questions with answers.

- Another student ancillary is the *Microsoft® Excel Companion for Business Statistics* (ISBN: 0-324-06898-0) by David Eldredge of Murray State University. This printed manual provides step-by-step instructions for using Excel to solve many of the problems included in introductory business statistics.
- *EasyStat: Digital Tutor for Microsoft® Excel,* prepared by the textbook authors, was designed to make it easier for students to learn how to use Excel to perform statistical analysis. In each video, one of the authors demonstrates how Excel can be used to perform a particular statistical procedure. Students may purchase a subscription for this excellent online product at **http://easystat.swlearning.com.**

Instructor support materials are available to adopters. Check Instructor Resources at **http://asw.swlearning.com** for materials that may be downloaded directly. All instructor ancillaries are provided on a single **Instructor's Resource CD-ROM** (ISBN: 0-324-18466-2) and it may be requested from the Academic Resource Center at 800-423-0563. Included in this convenient format are:

- **Solutions Manual**—The *Solutions Manual,* prepared by the text authors, includes solutions for all exercises in the text.
- **Solutions to Case Problems**—The *Solutions to Case Problems,* also prepared by the text authors, contains solutions to all case problems presented in the text.
- **PowerPoint™ Presentation Slides**—Prepared also by John Loucks, the presentation slides contain a teaching outline that incorporates graphics to help instructors create even more stimulating lectures. The slides may be adapted using PowerPoint software to facilitate classroom use.
- **Test Bank** and **ExamView™**—The *Test Bank* includes multiple choice questions and problems for each chapter. ExamView computerized testing software allows instructors to create, edit, store, and print exams.

ACKNOWLEDGMENTS

We would like to acknowledge the work of our reviewers who provided comments and suggestions of ways to continue to improve our text. Thanks to:

Timothy M. Bergquist, Northwest Christian College

Frederick W. Derrick, Loyola College in Maryland

John N. Dyer, Georgia Southern University

Shaomin Huang, Lewis-Clark State College

Mohammad Syed, Miles College

G. Peter Zhang, Georgia State University

We would like to recognize the following individuals who have helped us in the past and continue to influence our writing.

Glen Archibald, University of Mississippi

Mike Bourke, Houston Baptist University

Darl Bien, University of Denver

Thomas W. Bolland, Ohio University

Peter Bryant, University of Colorado

Terri L. Byczkowski, University of Cincinnati

Robert Carver, Stonehill College

Ying Chien, University of Scranton

Robert Cochran, University of Wyoming

Murray Côté, University of Florida

David W. Cravens, Texas Christian University

Tom Dahlstrom, Eastern College

Terry Dielman, Texas Christian University

Ronald Ehresman, Baldwin-Wallace College

Mohammed A. El-Saidi, Ferris State University

Nicholas Farnum, California State University–Fullerton

Abe Feinberg, California State University, Northridge

Michael Ford, Rochester Institute of Technology

Phil Fry, Boise State University

V. Daniel Guide, Duquesne University

Paul Guy, California State University–Chico

Sarai Hedges, University of Cincinnati

Alan Humphrey, University of Rhode Island

Ann Hussein, Philadelphia College of Textiles and Science

Ben Isselhardt, Rochester Institute of Technology

Jeffery Jarrett, University of Rhode Island

Barry Kadets, Bryant College

Kenneth Klassen, California State University, Northridge

David Krueger, St. Cloud State University

June Lapidus, Roosevelt University

Martin S. Levy, University of Cincinnati

Don Marx, University of Alaska, Anchorage

Ka-sing Man, Georgetown University

Tom McCullough, University of California–Berkeley

Mario Miranda, The Ohio State University

Mitchell Muesham, Sam Houston State University

Richard O'Connell, Miami University of Ohio

Alan Olinsky, Bryant College

Lynne Pastor, Carnegie Mellon University

Tom Pray, Rochester Institute of Technology

Harold Rahmlow, St. Joseph's University

Derrick Reagle, Fordham University

Tom Ryan, Case Western Reserve University

Bill Seaver, University of Tennessee

Alan Smith, Robert Morris College

William Struning, Seton Hall University

David Tufte, University of New Orleans

Jack Vaughn, University of Texas–El Paso

Ari Wijetunga, Morehead State University

J. E. Willis, Louisiana State University

Mustafa Yilmaz, Northeastern University

We also send our appreciation to Professor John O. McClain of Cornell University who allowed us to include his PredInt macro on the CD. This macro allows users to develop confidence and prediction intervals for simple linear and multiple regression.

A special thanks is owed to our associates from business and industry that supplied the Statistics in Practice features. We recognize them individually by a credit line in each of the articles. Finally, we are also indebted to our senior acquisitions editor Charles McCormick, Jr., our senior developmental editor Alice Denny, our senior production editor Deanna Quinn, our marketing manager Larry Qualls, and others at Thomson/South-Western for their editorial counsel and support during the preparation of this text.

David R. Anderson
Dennis J. Sweeney
Thomas A. Williams

About the Authors

David R. Anderson. David R. Anderson is Professor of Quantitative Analysis in the College of Business Administration at the University of Cincinnati. Born in Grand Forks, North Dakota, he earned his B.S., M.S., and Ph.D. degrees from Purdue University. Professor Anderson has served as Head of the Department of Quantitative Analysis and Operations Management and as Associate Dean of the College of Business Administration. In addition, he was the coordinator of the College's first Executive Program.

At the University of Cincinnati, Professor Anderson has taught introductory statistics for business students as well as graduate-level courses in regression analysis, multivariate analysis, and management science. He has also taught statistical courses at the Department of Labor in Washington, D.C. He has been honored with nominations and awards for excellence in teaching and excellence in service to student organizations.

Professor Anderson has coauthored ten textbooks in the areas of statistics, management science, linear programming, and production and operations management. He is an active consultant in the field of sampling and statistical methods.

Dennis J. Sweeney. Dennis J. Sweeney is Professor of Quantitative Analysis and Founder of the Center for Productivity Improvement at the University of Cincinnati. Born in Des Moines, Iowa, he earned a B.S.B.A. degree from Drake University and his M.B.A. and D.B.A. degrees from Indiana University where he was an NDEA Fellow. During 1978–79, Professor Sweeney worked in the management science group at Procter & Gamble; during 1981–82, he was a visiting professor at Duke University. Professor Sweeney served as Head of the Department of Quantitative Analysis and as Associate Dean of the College of Business Administration at the University of Cincinnati.

Professor Sweeney has published more than thirty articles and monographs in the area of management science and statistics. The National Science Foundation, IBM, Procter & Gamble, Federated Department Stores, Kroger, and Cincinnati Gas & Electric have funded his research, which has been published in *Management Science*, *Operations Research*, *Mathematical Programming*, *Decision Sciences*, and other journals.

Professor Sweeney has coauthored ten textbooks in the areas of statistics, management science, linear programming, and production and operations management.

Thomas A. Williams. Thomas A. Williams is Professor of Management Science in the College of Business at Rochester Institute of Technology. Born in Elmira, New York, he earned his B.S. degree at Clarkson University. He did his graduate work at Rensselaer Polytechnic Institute, where he received his M.S. and Ph.D. degrees.

Before joining the College of Business at RIT, Professor Williams served for seven years as a faculty member in the College of Business Administration at the University of Cincinnati, where he developed the undergraduate program in Information Systems and then served as its coordinator. At RIT he was the first chairman of the Decision Sciences Department. He teaches courses in management science and statistics, as well as graduate courses in regression and decision analysis.

Professor Williams is the coauthor of eleven textbooks in the areas of management science, statistics, production and operations management, and mathematics. He has been a consultant for numerous *Fortune* 500 companies and has worked on projects ranging from the use of data analysis to the development of large-scale regression models.

CHAPTER 1

Data and Statistics

CONTENTS

Business Week*

NEW YORK, NEW YORK

With a global circulation of more than 1 million, *Business Week* is the most widely read business magazine in the world. More than 200 dedicated reporters and editors in 26 bureaus worldwide deliver a variety of articles of interest to the business and economic community. Along with feature articles on current topics, the magazine contains regular sections on International Business, Economic Analysis, Information Processing, and Science & Technology. Information in the feature articles and the regular sections help readers stay abreast of current developments and assess the impact of those developments on business and economic conditions.

Most issues of *Business Week* provide an in-depth report on a topic of current interest. Often, the in-depth reports contain statistical facts and summaries that help the reader understand the business and/or economic information. For example, the January 8, 2001, issue reported statistical information about the top 25 managers of the year; the March 19, 2001, issue contained a report on the banking crisis in Japan; and the June 18, 2001, issue provided a variety of statistics on the top 100 information technology companies. In addition, the weekly *Business Week Investor* provides statistics about the state of the economy, including production indexes, stock prices, mutual funds, and interest rates.

Business Week also uses statistics and statistical information in managing its own business. For example, an annual survey of subscribers helps the company learn about subscriber demographics, reading habits, likely

Business Week uses statistical facts and summaries in many of its articles. © Deanna Ettinger/South-Western.

purchases, lifestyles, and so on. *Business Week* managers use the statistical summaries from the survey to provide better services to subscribers and advertisers. For instance, a recent North American subscriber survey indicated that 90% of *Business Week* subscribers have a personal computer at home and that 64% of *Business Week* subscribers are involved with computer purchases at work. Such statistics alert *Business Week* managers to subscriber interest in articles about new developments in computers. The results of the survey are also made available to potential advertisers. The high percentage of subscribers using personal computers at home and the high percentage of subscribers involved with computer purchases at work would be an incentive for a computer manufacturer to consider advertising in *Business Week*.

In this chapter, we discuss the types of data that are available for statistical analysis and describe how the data are obtained. We introduce descriptive statistics and statistical inference as ways of converting data into meaningful and easily interpreted statistical information.

---

*The authors are indebted to Charlene Trentham, Research Manager at *Business Week*, for providing this Statistics in Practice.

Frequently, we see the following kinds of statements in newspaper and magazine articles:

- Of the 16,000 foodmakers, just 20 now account for nearly 54% of checkout sales (*Forbes*, April 15, 2002).
- The average price of a movie ticket is $5.60 (*Money*, April 2001).
- E-commerce sites spend an average of $108 to acquire a new customer (*Business 2.0*, March 2000).
- The *Washington Post* reaches 46% of households in the region on weekdays and 61% on Sundays, tops among big city newspapers (*Fortune*, January 10, 2000).
- Stocks account for 75% of the average investor's portfolio (*The Wall Street Journal*, March 27, 2000).
- Nokia, the world's largest and most profitable mobile phone maker, estimated an annual demand for 405 million phones (*Business Week*, June 25, 2001).

The numerical facts in the preceding statements (16,000, 20, 54%, $5.60, $108, 46%, 61%, 75%, and 405 million) are called statistics. Thus, in everyday usage, the term *statistics* refers to numerical facts. However, the field, or subject, of statistics involves much more than numerical facts. In a broad sense, **statistics** is the art and science of collecting, analyzing, presenting, and interpreting data. Particularly in business and economics, a major reason for collecting, analyzing, presenting, and interpreting data is to give managers and decision makers a better understanding of the business and economic environment and thus enable them to make more informed and better decisions. In this text, we emphasize the use of statistics for business and economic decision making.

Chapter 1 begins with some illustrations of the applications of statistics in business and economics. In Section 1.2 we define the term *data* and introduce the concept of a data set. This section also introduces key terms such as *variables* and *observations,* discusses the difference between quantitative and qualitative data, and illustrates the difference between cross-sectional and time series data. Section 1.3 discusses how data can be obtained from existing sources or through survey and experimental studies designed to obtain new data. The important role that the Internet now plays in obtaining data is also highlighted. The use of data in developing descriptive statistics and in making statistical inferences is described in Sections 1.4 and 1.5, and Section 1.6 concludes with an introduction to the use of Microsoft Excel for statistical analysis.

1.1   APPLICATIONS IN BUSINESS AND ECONOMICS

In today's global business and economic environment, vast amounts of statistical information are available. The most successful managers and decision makers are the ones who can understand the information and use it effectively. In this section, we provide examples that illustrate some of the uses of statistics in business and economics.

Accounting

Public accounting firms use statistical sampling procedures when conducting audits for their clients. For instance, suppose an accounting firm wants to determine whether the amount of accounts receivable shown on a client's balance sheet fairly represents the actual amount of accounts receivable. Usually the number of individual accounts receivable is so large that reviewing and validating every account would be too time-consuming and expensive. As common practice in such situations, the audit staff selects a subset of the accounts called a sample. After reviewing the accuracy of the sampled accounts, the auditors draw a conclusion as to whether the accounts receivable amount shown on the client's balance sheet is acceptable.

Finance

Financial analysts use a variety of statistical information to guide their investment recommendations. In the case of stocks, the analysts review a variety of financial data including price/earnings ratios and dividend yields. By comparing the information for an individual stock with information about the stock market averages, a financial analyst can begin to draw a conclusion as to whether an individual stock is over- or undervalued. For example, *Barron's* (January 10, 2000) reported that the average price/earnings ratio for the 30 stocks in the Dow Jones Industrial Average was 24.7. Philip Morris had a price/earnings ratio of 9. In this case, the statistical information on price/earnings ratios showed that Philip Morris had a lower price in comparison to its earnings than the average for the Dow Jones stocks. Therefore, a financial analyst might have concluded that Philip Morris was currently underpriced. This and other information about Philip Morris would help the analyst make buy, sell, or hold recommendations for the stock.

Marketing

Electronic scanners at retail checkout counters collect data for a variety of marketing research applications. For example, data suppliers such as ACNielsen and Information Resources, Inc., purchase point-of-sale scanner data from grocery stores, process the data, and then sell statistical summaries of the data to manufacturers. Manufacturers spent an average of $387,325 per product category to obtain this type of scanner data (Scanner Data User Survey, Mercer Management Consulting, Inc., April 1997). Manufacturers also purchase data and statistical summaries on promotional activities such as special pricing and the use of in-store displays. Brand managers can review the scanner statistics and the promotional activity statistics to gain a better understanding of the relationship between promotional activities and sales. Such analyses are helpful in establishing future marketing strategies for the various products.

Production

With today's emphasis on quality, quality control is an important application of statistics in production. A variety of statistical quality control charts are used to monitor the output of a production process. In particular, an x-bar chart is used to monitor the average output. Suppose, for example, that a machine fills containers with 12 ounces of a soft drink. Periodically, a production worker selects a sample of containers and computes the average number of ounces in the sample. This average, or x-bar value, is plotted on an x-bar chart. A plotted value above the chart's upper control limit indicates overfilling, and a plotted value below the chart's lower control limit indicates underfilling. The process is termed "in control" and allowed to continue as long as the plotted x-bar values fall between the chart's upper and lower control limits. Properly interpreted, an x-bar chart can help determine when adjustments are necessary to correct a production process.

Economics

Economists are frequently asked to provide forecasts about the future of the economy or some aspect of it. They use a variety of statistical information in making such forecasts. For instance, in forecasting inflation rates, economists use statistical information on such indicators as the Producer Price Index, the unemployment rate, and manufacturing capacity utilization. Often these statistical indicators are entered into computerized forecasting models that predict inflation rates.

Applications of statistics such as those described in this section are an integral part of this text. Such examples provide an overview of the breadth of statistical applications. To supplement these examples, practitioners in the fields of business and economics provided chapter-opening Statistics in Practice articles that introduce the material covered in each chapter. The Statistics in Practice applications show the importance of statistics in a wide variety of decision-making situations.

1.2   DATA

Data are the facts and figures collected, analyzed, and summarized for presentation and interpretation. All the data collected in a particular study are referred to as the **data set** for the study. Table 1.1 shows a data set containing information for 25 of the shadow stocks tracked

TABLE 1.1   DATA SET FOR 25 SHADOW STOCKS

Shadow

Company	Exchange	Ticker Symbol	Market Cap ($ millions)	Price/ Earnings Ratio	Gross Profit Margin (%)
DeWolfe Companies	AMEX	DWL	36.4	8.4	36.7
North Coast Energy	OTC	NCEB	52.5	6.2	59.3
Hansen Natural Corp.	OTC	HANS	41.1	14.6	44.8
MarineMax, Inc.	NYSE	HZO	111.5	7.2	23.8
Nanometrics Incorporated	OTC	NANO	228.6	38.0	53.3
TeamStaff, Inc.	OTC	TSTF	92.1	33.5	4.1
Environmental Tectonics	AMEX	ETC	51.1	35.8	35.9
Measurement Specialties	AMEX	MSS	101.8	26.8	37.6
SEMCO Energy, Inc.	NYSE	SEN	193.4	18.7	23.6
Party City Corporation	OTC	PCTY	97.2	15.9	36.4
Embrex, Inc.	OTC	EMBX	136.5	18.9	59.5
Tech/Ops Sevcon, Inc.	AMEX	TO	23.2	20.7	35.7
ARCADIS NV	OTC	ARCAF	173.4	8.8	9.6
Qiao Xing Universal Tele.	OTC	XING	64.3	22.1	30.8
Energy West Incorporated	OTC	EWST	29.1	9.7	16.3
Barnwell Industries, Inc.	AMEX	BRN	27.3	7.4	73.4
Innodata Corporation	OTC	INOD	66.1	11.0	29.6
Medical Action Industries	OTC	MDCI	137.1	26.9	30.6
Instrumentarium Corp.	OTC	INMRY	240.9	3.6	52.1
Petroleum Development	OTC	PETD	95.9	6.1	19.4
Drexler Technology Corp.	OTC	DRXR	233.6	45.6	53.6
Gerber Childrenswear Inc.	NYSE	GCW	126.9	7.9	25.8
Gaiam, Inc.	OTC	GAIA	295.5	68.2	60.7
Artesian Resources Corp.	OTC	ARTNA	62.8	20.5	45.5
York Water Company	OTC	YORW	92.2	22.9	74.2

Source: American Association of Individual Investors Web site, February 2002.

by the American Association of Individual Investors. Shadow stocks are common stocks of smaller companies that are not closely followed by Wall Street analysts.

Elements, Variables, and Observations

Elements are the entities on which data are collected. For the data set in Table 1.1, each individual company's stock is an element. With 25 stocks, the data set contains 25 elements.

A **variable** is a characteristic of interest for the elements. The data set in Table 1.1 has the following five variables:

- *Exchange:* Where the stock is traded—NYSE (New York Stock Exchange), AMEX (American Stock Exchange), and OTC (Over-the-Counter).
- *Ticker Symbol:* The abbreviation used to identify the stock on the exchange listing.
- *Market Cap:* Total value of company (share price multiplied by number of shares outstanding).
- *Price/Earnings Ratio:* Market price per share divided by the most recent 12 months' earnings per share.
- *Gross Profit Margin:* Gross profit as a percent of sales.

Measurements collected on each variable for every element in a study provide the data. The set of measurements obtained for a particular element is called an **observation**. Referring to Table 1.1, we see that the set of measurements for the first observation (DeWolfe Companies) is AMEX, DWL, 36.4, 8.4, and 36.7. The set of measurements for the second observation (North Coast Energy) is OTC, NCEB, 52.5, 6.2, and 59.3; and so on. Because the data set contains 25 elements, it has 25 observations.

Scales of Measurement

Data collection requires one of the following scales of measurement: nominal, ordinal, interval, and ratio. The scale of measurement determines the amount of information contained in the data and indicates the data summarization and statistical analyses that are most appropriate.

The scale of measurement for a variable is a **nominal scale** when the data are labels or names used to identify an attribute of the element. For example, referring to the data in Table 1.1, we see that the scale of measurement for the exchange variable is nominal because NYSE, AMEX, and OTC are labels used to identify where the company's stock is traded. In cases where the scale of measurement is nominal, a numeric code as well as non-numeric labels may be used. For example, to facilitate data collection and to prepare the data for entry into a computer database, we might use a numeric code by letting 1 denote the New York Stock Exchange, 2 denote the American Stock Exchange, and 3 denote over-the-counter. In this case the numeric values 1, 2, and 3 are the labels used to identify where the stock is traded. The scale of measurement is nominal even though the data appear as numeric values.

The scale of measurement for a variable is an **ordinal scale** if the data exhibit the properties of nominal data and the order or rank of the data is meaningful. For example, Eastside Automotive sends customers a questionnaire designed to obtain data on the quality of its automotive repair service. Each customer provides a repair service rating of excellent, good, or poor. Because the data obtained are the labels—excellent, good, or poor—the data have the properties of nominal data. In addition, the data can be ranked, or ordered, with respect to the service quality. Data recorded as excellent indicate the best service, followed by good and then poor. Thus, the scale of measurement is ordinal. Note that the ordinal data can also be recorded using a numeric code. For example, we could use 1 for excellent, 2 for good, and 3 for poor to maintain the properties of ordinal data. Thus, data for an ordinal scale may be either nonnumeric or numeric.

The scale of measurement for a variable is an **interval scale** if the data have the properties of ordinal data and the interval between observations is expressed in terms of a fixed unit of measure. Interval data are always numeric. Scholastic Aptitude Test (SAT) scores are an example of interval-scaled data. For example, three students with SAT scores of 1120, 1050, and 970 can be ranked or ordered in terms of best performance to poorest performance. In addition, the differences between the scores are meaningful. For instance, student 1 scored $1120 - 1050 = 70$ points more than student 2, while student 2 scored $1050 - 970 = 80$ points more than student 3.

The scale of measurement for a variable is a **ratio scale** if the data have all the properties of interval data and the ratio of two values is meaningful. Variables such as distance, height, weight, and time use the ratio scale of measurement. A requirement of this scale is that it must contain a zero value that indicates that nothing exists for the variable at the zero point. For example, consider the cost of an automobile. A zero value for the cost would indicate that the automobile has no cost and is free. In addition, if we compare the cost of $30,000 for one automobile to the cost of $15,000 for a second automobile, the ratio property shows that the first automobile is $30,000/$15,000 = 2 times, or twice, the cost of the second automobile.

Qualitative and Quantitative Data

Qualitative data are often referred to as categorical data.

Data can be further classified as either qualitative or quantitative. **Qualitative data** are labels or names used to identify an attribute of each element. Qualitative data use either the nominal or ordinal scale of measurement and may be nonnumeric or numeric. **Quantitative data** are numeric values that indicate how much or how many. Quantitative data are obtained using either the interval or ratio scale of measurement.

The statistical method appropriate for summarizing data depends upon whether the data are qualitative or quantitative.

A **qualitative variable** is a variable with qualitative data, and a **quantitative variable** is a variable with quantitative data. The statistical analysis appropriate for a particular variable depends upon whether the variable is qualitative or quantitative. If the variable is qualitative, the statistical analysis is rather limited. We can summarize qualitative data by counting the number of observations in each qualitative category or by computing the proportion of the observations in each qualitative category. However, even when the qualitative data use a numeric code, arithmetic operations such as addition, subtraction, multiplication, and division do not provide meaningful results. Section 2.1 discusses ways for summarizing qualitative data.

On the other hand, arithmetic operations often provide meaningful results for a quantitative variable. For example, for a quantitative variable, the data may be added and then divided by the number of observations to compute the average value. This average is usually meaningful and easily interpreted. In general, more alternatives for statistical analysis are possible when the data are quantitative. Section 2.2 and Chapter 3 provide ways of summarizing quantitative data.

Cross-Sectional and Time Series Data

For purposes of statistical analysis, distinguishing between cross-sectional data and time series data is important. **Cross-sectional data** are data collected at the same or approximately the same point in time. The data in Table 1.1 are cross-sectional because they describe the five variables for the 25 shadow stocks at the same point in time. **Time series data** are data collected over several time periods. For example, Figure 1.1 is a graph of the

FIGURE 1.1   U.S. CITY AVERAGE PRICE PER GALLON FOR UNLEADED
REGULAR GASOLINE

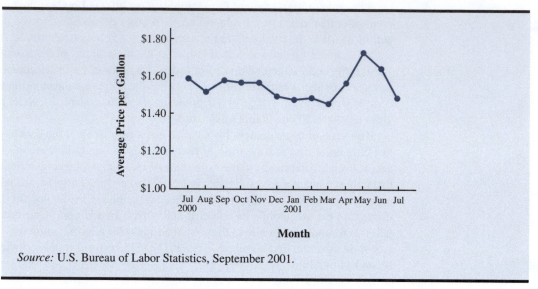

Source: U.S. Bureau of Labor Statistics, September 2001.

U.S. city average price per gallon for unleaded regular gasoline. It shows a rather stable average price per gallon in the $1.45 to $1.60 range over the one-year period with the exception of May–June 2001, when it jumped to $1.73 per gallon. However, by July 2001 it returned to approximately $1.50 per gallon. Most of the statistical methods presented in this text apply to cross-sectional rather than time series data.

NOTES AND COMMENTS

1. An observation is the set of measurements obtained for each element in a data set. Hence, the number of observations is always the same as the number of elements. The number of measurements obtained for each element is equal to the number of variables. Hence, the total number of data items is the number of observations multiplied by the number of variables.

2. Quantitative data may be discrete or continuous. Quantitative data that measure how many are discrete. Quantitative data that measure how much are continuous because they have no separation between the possible data values.

1.3   DATA SOURCES

Data can be collected from existing sources or from surveys and experimental studies designed to obtain new data.

Existing Sources

In some cases, data needed for a particular application may already exist within a firm or organization. All companies maintain a variety of databases about their employees, customers, and business operations. Data on employee salaries, ages, and years of experience can usually be obtained from internal personnel records. Data on sales, advertising expenditures, distribution costs, inventory levels, and production quantities are generally available from other internal records. Most companies also maintain detailed data about their customers. Table 1.2 shows some of the data commonly available from internal company records.

Organizations that specialize in collecting and maintaining data make available substantial amounts of business and economic data. Companies access these external data sources through leasing arrangements or by purchase. Dun & Bradstreet, Bloomberg, and Dow Jones & Company are three firms that provide extensive business database services to clients. ACNielsen and Information Resources, Inc., built successful businesses collecting and processing data that they sell to advertisers and product manufacturers.

Data are also available from a variety of industry associations and special interest organizations. The Travel Industry Association of America maintains travel-related information such as the number of tourists and travel expenditures by states. Such data would be of interest to firms and individuals in the travel industry. The Graduate Management Admission Council maintains data on test scores, student characteristics, and graduate management education programs. Most of the data from these types of sources are available to qualified users at a modest cost.

The Internet continues to grow as an important source of data and statistical information. Almost all companies have Web sites that provide general information about the company as well as data on sales, number of employees, number of products, product prices, and product specifications. In addition, a number of companies now specialize in making information available over the Internet. As a result, one can obtain access to stock quotes, meal prices at restaurants, salary data, and an almost infinite variety of information.

Government agencies are another important source of existing data. For instance, the U.S. Department of Labor maintains considerable data on employment rates, wage rates, size of the labor force, and union membership. Table 1.3 lists selected governmental agencies and some of the data they provide. Most government agencies that collect and process data also make the results available through a Web site. For instance, the U.S. Census Bureau has a wealth of data at its Web site, *www.census.gov*. Figure 1.2 shows the homepage for the U.S. Census Bureau.

TABLE 1.2   EXAMPLES OF DATA AVAILABLE FROM INTERNAL COMPANY RECORDS

Source	Some of the Data Typically Available
Employee records	Name, address, social security number, salary, number of vacation days, number of sick days, and bonus
Production records	Part or product number, quantity produced, direct labor cost, and materials cost
Inventory records	Part or product number, number of units on hand, reorder level, economic order quantity, and discount schedule
Sales records	Product number, sales volume, sales volume by region, and sales volume by customer type
Credit records	Customer name, address, phone number, credit limit, and accounts receivable balance
Customer profile	Age, gender, income level, household size, address, and preferences

TABLE 1.3 EXAMPLES OF DATA AVAILABLE FROM SELECTED
GOVERNMENT AGENCIES

Government Agency	Some of the Data Available
Census Bureau *www.census.gov*	Population data, number of households, and household income
Federal Reserve Board *www.federalreserve.gov*	Data on the money supply, installment credit, exchange rates, and discount rates
Office of Management and Budget *www.whitehouse.gov/omb*	Data on revenue, expenditures, and debt of the federal government
Department of Commerce *www.doc.gov*	Data on business activity, value of shipments by industry, level of profits by industry, and growing and declining industries
Bureau of Labor Statistics *www.bls.gov*	Consumer spending, hourly earnings, unemployment rate, safety records, and international statistics

FIGURE 1.2 U.S. CENSUS BUREAU HOMEPAGE

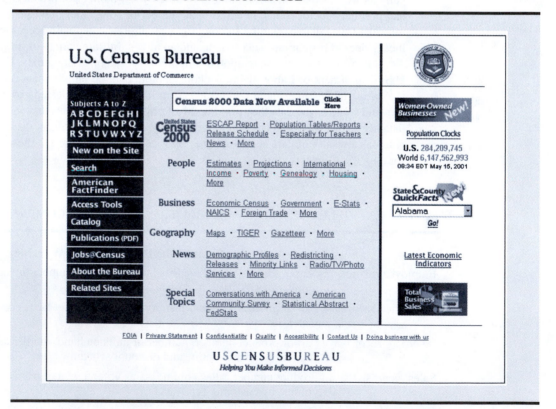

Statistical Studies

Sometimes the data needed for a particular application are not available through existing sources. In such cases, the data can often be obtained by conducting a statistical study. Statistical studies can be classified as either *experimental* or *observational*.

The largest experimental statistical study ever conducted is believed to be the 1954 Public Health Service experiment for the Salk polio vaccine. Nearly 2 million children in grades 1, 2, and 3 were selected from throughout the United States.

In an experimental study, a variable of interest is first identified. Then one or more other variables are identified and controlled so that data can be obtained about how they influence the variable of interest. For example, a pharmaceutical firm might be interested in conducting an experiment to learn about how a new drug affects blood pressure. Blood pressure is the variable of interest in the study. The dosage level of the new drug is another variable that is hoped to have a causal effect on blood pressure. To obtain data about the effect of the new drug, a sample of individuals is selected. The dosage level of the new drug is controlled, with different groups of individuals being given different dosage levels. Data on blood pressure are collected for each group. Statistical analysis of the experimental data can help determine how the new drug affects blood pressure.

Studies of smokers and nonsmokers are observational studies because researchers do not determine or control who will smoke and who will not smoke.

In nonexperimental, or observational, statistical studies, no attempt is made to control the variables of interest. A survey is perhaps the most common type of observational study. For instance, in a personal interview survey, research questions are first identified. Then a questionnaire is designed and administered to a sample of individuals. Some restaurants use observational studies to obtain data about their customers' opinions of the quality of food, service, atmosphere, and so on. A questionnaire used by the Lobster Pot Restaurant in Redington Shores, Florida, is shown in Figure 1.3. Note that the customers completing the questionnaire are asked to provide ratings for five variables: food quality, friendliness of service, promptness of service, cleanliness, and management. The response categories of excellent, good, satisfactory, and unsatisfactory provide data that enable Lobster Pot's managers to assess the quality of the restaurant's operation.

Managers wanting to use data and statistical analyses as an aid to decision making must be aware of the time and cost required to obtain the data. The use of existing data sources is desirable when data must be obtained in a relatively short period of time. If important data are not readily available from an existing source, the additional time and cost involved in obtaining the data must be taken into account. In all cases, the decision maker should consider the contribution of the statistical analysis to the decision-making process. The cost of data acquisition and the subsequent statistical analysis should not exceed the savings generated by using the information to make a better decision.

Data Acquisition Errors

Managers should always be aware of the possibility of data errors in statistical studies. Using erroneous data can be worse than not using any data at all. An error in data acquisition occurs whenever the data value obtained is not equal to the true or actual value that would have been obtained with a correct procedure. Such errors can occur in a number of ways. For example, an interviewer might make a recording error, such as a transposition in writing the age of a 24-year-old person as 42, or the person answering an interview question might misinterpret the question and provide an incorrect response.

Experienced data analysts take great care in collecting and recording data to ensure that errors are not made. Special procedures can be used to check for internal consistency of the data. For instance, such procedures would indicate that the analyst should review the accuracy of data for a respondent who is shown to be 22 years of age but who reports 20 years of work experience. Data analysts also review data with unusually large and small values, called outliers, which are candidates for possible data errors. In Chapter 3 we present some of the methods statisticians use to identify outliers.

FIGURE 1.3 CUSTOMER OPINION QUESTIONNAIRE USED BY THE LOBSTER POT RESTAURANT, REDINGTON SHORES, FLORIDA

The
LOBSTER
Pot
RESTAURANT

We are happy you stopped by the Lobster Pot Restaurant and want to make sure you will come back. So, if you have a little time, we will really appreciate it if you will fill out this card. Your comments and suggestions are extremely important to us. Thank you!

Server's Name _____

	Excellent	Good	Satisfactory	Unsatisfactory
Food Quality	❑	❑	❑	❑
Friendly Service	❑	❑	❑	❑
Prompt Service	❑	❑	❑	❑
Cleanliness	❑	❑	❑	❑
Management	❑	❑	❑	❑

Comments _____

_____

What prompted your visit to us? _____

_____

Please drop in suggestion box at entrance. Thank you.

Errors often occur during data acquisition. Blindly using any data that happen to be available or using data that were acquired with little care can result in misleading information and bad decisions. Thus, taking steps to acquire accurate data can help ensure reliable and valuable decision-making information.

1.4 DESCRIPTIVE STATISTICS

Most of the statistical information in newspapers, magazines, company reports, and other publications consists of data that are summarized and presented in a form that is easy for the reader to understand. Such summaries of data, which may be tabular, graphical, or numerical, are referred to as **descriptive statistics**.

Refer again to the data set in Table 1.1 where data on 25 shadow stocks are presented. Methods of descriptive statistics can be used to provide summaries of the information in this data set. For example, a tabular summary of the data for the qualitative variable Exchange is shown in Table 1.4. A graphical summary of the same data, called a bar graph, is shown in Figure 1.4. These types of tabular and graphical summaries generally make the data easier to interpret. Referring to Table 1.4 and Figure 1.5, we can see easily that the ma-

TABLE 1.4   FREQUENCIES AND PERCENT FREQUENCIES
FOR THE EXCHANGE VARIABLE

Exchange	Frequency	Percent Frequency
New York Stock Exchange (NYSE)	3	12
American Stock Exchange (AMEX)	5	20
Over-the-counter (OTC)	17	68
Totals	25	100

jority of the stocks in the data set are traded over the counter. On a percentage basis, 68% are traded over the counter, 20% are traded on the American Stock Exchange, and 12% are traded on the New York Stock Exchange.

A graphical summary of the data for the quantitative variable Gross Profit Margin for the shadow stocks, called a histogram, is provided in Figure 1.5. From the histogram, it is easy to see that the gross profit margins range from 0.0 to 74.9, with the highest concentrations between 30.0 and 44.9.

In addition to tabular and graphical displays, numerical descriptive statistics are used to summarize data. The most common numerical descriptive statistic is the average, or mean. Using the data on market cap for the shadow stocks in Table 1.1, we can compute the average market cap by adding the market cap for all 25 stocks and dividing the sum by 25. Doing so provides an average market cap of $112.4 million. This average is taken as a measure of the central tendency, or central location, of the data.

FIGURE 1.4   BAR GRAPH FOR THE EXCHANGE VARIABLE

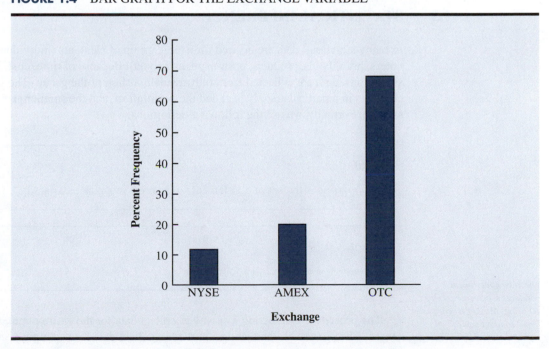

FIGURE 1.5   HISTOGRAM OF GROSS PROFIT MARGIN (%) FOR 25 SHADOW STOCKS

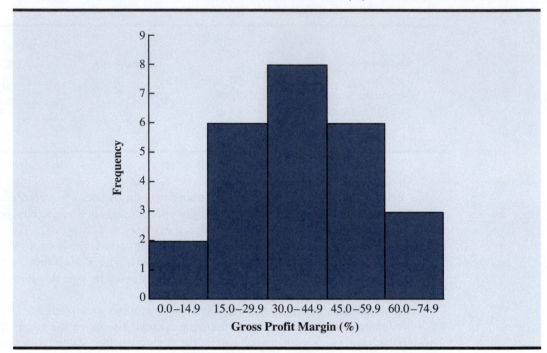

In recent years interest has grown in statistical methods that can be used for developing and presenting descriptive statistics. Chapters 2 and 3 are devoted to the tabular, graphical, and numerical methods of descriptive statistics.

1.5   STATISTICAL INFERENCE

In many situations, data are desired for a large group of elements (individuals, companies, voters, households, products, customers, and so on). Because of time, cost, and other considerations, data are collected from only a small portion of the group. The larger group of elements in a particular study is called the **population**, and the smaller group is called the **sample**. Formally, we use the following definitions.

Population

A *population* is the set of all elements of interest in a particular study.

Sample

A *sample* is a subset of the population.

The U.S. government conducts a census every 10 years. Market research firms conduct sample surveys every day.

The process of conducting a survey to collect data for the entire population is called a census. The process of conducting a survey to collect data for a sample is called a sample survey. A major contribution of statistics is that data from a sample can be used to make estimates and test hypotheses about the characteristics of a population. This process is referred to as **statistical inference**.

As an example of statistical inference, let us consider the study conducted by Norris Electronics. Norris manufactures a high-intensity lightbulb used in a variety of electrical products. In an attempt to increase the useful life of the lightbulb, the product design group has developed a new lightbulb filament. In this case, the population is defined as all lightbulbs that could be produced with the new filament. To evaluate the advantages of the new filament, 200 bulbs with the new filament were manufactured and tested. Data were collected on the number of hours each lightbulb operated before filament burnout. The data from this sample are reported in Table 1.5.

Suppose Norris is interested in using the sample data to make an inference about the average hours of useful life for the population of all lightbulbs that could be produced with the new filament. Adding the 200 values in Table 1.5 and dividing the total by 200 provides the sample average lifetime for the lightbulbs: 76 hours. We can use this sample result to estimate that the average lifetime for the lightbulbs in the population is 76 hours. Figure 1.6 is a graphical summary of the statistical inference process for Norris Electronics.

Whenever statisticians use a sample to estimate population characteristics of interest, they usually provide a statement of the quality, or precision, associated with the estimate. For the Norris example, the statistician might state that the point estimate of the average lifetime for the population of new lightbulbs is 76 hours with a margin of error of ±4 hours. Thus, an interval estimate of the average lifetime for all lightbulbs produced with the new filament is 72 hours to 80 hours. The statistician can also state how confident he or she is that the interval from 72 hours to 80 hours contains the population average.

TABLE 1.5   HOURS UNTIL BURNOUT FOR A SAMPLE OF 200 LIGHTBULBS
FOR THE NORRIS ELECTRONICS EXAMPLE

Norris

107	73	68	97	76	79	94	59	98	57
54	65	71	70	84	88	62	61	79	98
66	62	79	86	68	74	61	82	65	98
62	116	65	88	64	79	78	79	77	86
74	85	73	80	68	78	89	72	58	69
92	78	88	77	103	88	63	68	88	81
75	90	62	89	71	71	74	70	74	70
65	81	75	62	94	71	85	84	83	63
81	62	79	83	93	61	65	62	92	65
83	70	70	81	77	72	84	67	59	58
78	66	66	94	77	63	66	75	68	76
90	78	71	101	78	43	59	67	61	71
96	75	64	76	72	77	74	65	82	86
66	86	96	89	81	71	85	99	59	92
68	72	77	60	87	84	75	77	51	45
85	67	87	80	84	93	69	76	89	75
83	68	72	67	92	89	82	96	77	102
74	91	76	83	66	68	61	73	72	76
73	77	79	94	63	59	62	71	81	65
73	63	63	89	82	64	85	92	64	73

FIGURE 1.6   THE PROCESS OF STATISTICAL INFERENCE FOR THE NORRIS
ELECTRONICS EXAMPLE

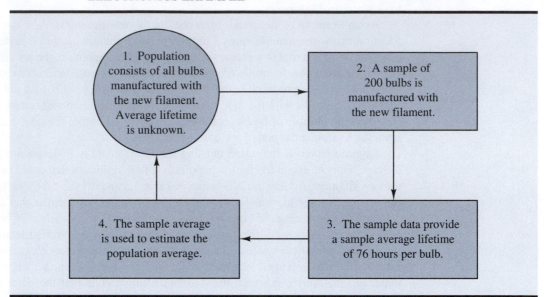

1.6   STATISTICAL ANALYSIS USING MICROSOFT EXCEL

Because statistical analysis typically involves working with large amounts of data, computer software is frequently used to conduct the analysis. Often the data to be analyzed reside in a spreadsheet. Given the data management, data analysis, and presentation capabilities of modern spreadsheet packages, it is now possible to conduct statistical analyses using them. In this book we show how statistical analysis can be performed using Microsoft Excel.

We want to emphasize that this book is about statistics; it is not a book about spreadsheets. Thus our focus is on showing the appropriate statistical procedures for collecting, analyzing, presenting, and interpreting data. Because Excel is widely available in business organizations, you can expect to put the knowledge gained here to use in the setting where you currently, or soon will, work. If in the process of studying this material you become more proficient in Excel, so much the better.

Our focus is on statistical applications. Most sections begin with an application scenario in which a statistical procedure is useful. After showing what the statistical procedure is and how it is used, we turn to showing how to implement the procedure using Excel. Thus, you should gain an understanding of what the procedure is, the situations in which it is useful, and how to implement it using the capabilities of Excel.

Data Sets and Excel Worksheets

Data sets are organized in Excel worksheets in much the same way as the data set for the 25 shadow stocks appears in Table 1.1. Figure 1.7 shows an Excel worksheet for that data set. Note that row 1 and column A contain labels. Cells B1:F1 contain the variable names and cells A2:A26 contain the observation names. Cells B2:F26 contain the data that were collected. A blue screen highlights the data. The data are the focus of the statistical analysis. Excluding the headings in row 1, each row in the worksheet corresponds to an obser-

FIGURE 1.7   EXCEL WORKSHEET FOR THE SHADOW STOCK DATA SET

	A	B	C	D	E	F	G
1	Company	Exchange	Ticker Symbol	Market Cap ($ millions)	Price/Earnings Ratio	Gross Profit Margin (%)	
2	DeWolfe Companies	AMEX	DWL	36.4	8.4	36.7	
3	North Coast Energy	OTC	NCEB	52.5	6.2	59.3	
4	Hansen Natural Corp.	OTC	HANS	41.1	14.6	44.8	
5	MarineMax, Inc.	NYSE	HZO	111.5	7.2	23.8	
6	Nanometrics Incorporated	OTC	NANO	228.6	38.0	53.3	
7	TeamStaff, Inc.	OTC	TSTF	92.1	33.5	4.1	
8	Environmental Tectonics	AMEX	ETC	51.1	35.8	35.9	
9	Measurement Specialties	AMEX	MSS	101.8	26.8	37.6	
10	SEMCO Energy, Inc.	NYSE	SEN	193.4	18.7	23.6	
11	Party City Corporation	OTC	PCTY	97.2	15.9	36.4	
12	Embrex, Inc.	OTC	EMBX	136.5	18.9	59.5	
13	Tech/Ops Sevcon, Inc.	AMEX	TO	23.2	20.7	35.7	
14	ARCADIS NV	OTC	ARCAF	173.4	8.8	9.6	
15	Qiao Xing Universal Tele.	OTC	XING	64.3	22.1	30.8	
16	Energy West Incorporated	OTC	EWST	29.1	9.7	16.3	
17	Barnwell Industries, Inc.	AMEX	BRN	27.3	7.4	73.4	
18	Innodata Corporation	OTC	INOD	66.1	11.0	29.6	
19	Medical Action Industries	OTC	MDCI	137.1	26.9	30.6	
20	Instrumentarium Corp.	OTC	INMRY	240.9	3.6	52.1	
21	Petroleum Development	OTC	PETD	95.9	6.1	19.4	
22	Drexler Technology Corp.	OTC	DRXR	233.6	45.6	53.6	
23	Gerber Childrenswear Inc.	NYSE	GCW	126.9	7.9	25.8	
24	Gaiam, Inc.	OTC	GAIA	295.5	68.2	60.7	
25	Artesian Resources Corp.	OTC	ARTNA	62.8	20.5	45.5	
26	York Water Company	OTC	YORW	92.2	22.9	74.2	
27							

vation and each column corresponds to a variable. For instance, row 2 of the worksheet contains the data for the first observation, DeWolfe Companies, row 3 contains the data for the second observation, North Coast Energy, and so on. Thus, the names in column A provide a convenient way to refer to each of the 25 observations in the study. Note that column 2 of the worksheet contains the data for the variable Exchange, column 3 contains the data for the variable Ticker Symbol, and so on.

Suppose now that we want to use Excel to analyze the Norris Electronics data shown in Table 1.5. The data in Table 1.5 are organized into 10 columns with 20 data values in each column so that it would fit nicely on a single page of the text. Even though the table has several columns, it shows data for only one variable (hours until burnout). In statistical worksheets, it is customary to put all the data for each variable in a single column. Refer to the Excel worksheet shown in Figure 1.8. To make it easier to identify each observation in the data set, we entered the heading Observation into cell A1 and the numbers 1–200 into cells A2:A201. The heading Hours Until Burnout has been entered into cell B1, and the data for the 200 observations have been entered into cells B2:B201. Displaying a worksheet with this many rows on a single page of a textbook is not practical. In such cases we will hide selected rows to conserve space. In the Excel worksheet for the Norris

FIGURE 1.8   EXCEL WORKSHEET FOR THE NORRIS ELECTRONICS DATA SET

Note: Rows 7–195 are hidden.

	A	B	C
1	Observation	Hours Until Burnout	
2	1	107	
3	2	54	
4	3	66	
5	4	62	
6	5	74	
196	195	45	
197	196	75	
198	197	102	
199	198	76	
200	199	65	
201	200	73	
202			

Electronics problem we have hidden rows 7 through 195 (observations 6 through 194) to conserve space.*

Using Excel for Statistical Analysis

In this text, we are careful to separate the discussion of a statistical procedure from the discussion of using Excel to implement the procedure. The material that discusses the use of Excel will be set apart in sections with headings such as Using Excel's COUNTIF Function to Construct a Frequency Distribution, Using Excel's Chart Wizard to Construct Bar Graphs and Pie Charts, and so on. In using Excel for statistical analysis, three tasks may be needed: Enter Data; Enter Functions and Formulas; and Apply Tools.

Enter Data: Select cell locations for the data and enter the data along with appropriate descriptive labels.

Enter Functions and Formulas: Select cell locations, enter Excel functions and formulas, and provide descriptive material to identify the results.

Apply Tools: Use Excel's tools for data management, data analysis, and presentation.

Our approach will be to describe how these tasks are performed each time we use Excel to implement a statistical procedure. It will always be necessary to enter data. But, depending upon the complexity of the statistical analysis, only one of the last two tasks may be needed.

To illustrate how the discussion of using Excel will appear throughout the book, we will show how to use Excel's AVERAGE function to compute the average lifetime for the 200 burnout times in Table 1.5. Refer to Figure 1.9 as we describe the tasks involved. The worksheet shown in the foreground of Figure 1.9 displays the data for the problem and shows the results of the analysis. It is called a **value worksheet**. The worksheet shown in the background displays the Excel formula used to compute the average lifetime and is called the **formula worksheet.** A blue screen is used to highlight the data in both worksheets. In

___
*To hide rows 7 through 195 in the Excel worksheet, first select rows 7 through 195. Then, right click and choose the Hide option. To redisplay rows 7 through 195, just select rows 6 and 196, right click, and select the Unhide option.

FIGURE 1.9   COMPUTING THE AVERAGE LIFETIME OF LIGHTBULBS FOR NORRIS ELECTRONICS USING EXCEL'S AVERAGE FUNCTION

	A	B	C	D	E	F
1	Observation	Hours Until Burnout				
2	1	107		Average Lifetime	=AVERAGE(B2:B201)	
3	2	54				
4	3	66				
5	4	62				
6	5	74				
196	195	45				
197	196	75				
198	197	102				
199	198	76				
200	199	65				
201	200	73				
202						

	A	B	C	D	E	F
1	Observation	Hours Until Burnout				
2	1	107		Average Lifetime	76	
3	2	54				
4	3	66				
5	4	62				
6	5	74				
196	195	45				
197	196	75				
198	197	102				
199	198	76				
200	199	65				
201	200	73				
202						

Note: Rows 7–195 are hidden.

addition, a grey screen is used to highlight functions and formulas in the formula worksheet and the corresponding results in the value worksheet.

Enter Data: The labels Observation and Hours Until Burnout are entered into cells A1:B1. The numbers 1–200 are entered into cells A2:A201 to identify each of the observations, and the data showing the hours until burnout for each observation are entered into cells B2:B201 of the worksheet.

Enter Functions and Formulas: Excel's AVERAGE function can be used to compute the average lifetime for the 200 lightbulbs. We can compute the average lifetime by entering the following formula into cell E2:

=AVERAGE(B2:B201)

To identify the result, the label Average Lifetime is entered into cell D2. Note that for this problem, the Apply Tools task was not required. The value worksheet shows that the value computed using the AVERAGE function is 76 hours.

SUMMARY

Statistics is the art and science of collecting, analyzing, presenting, and interpreting data. Nearly every college student majoring in business or economics is required to take a course in statistics. We began the chapter by describing typical statistical applications for business and economics.

Data are the facts and figures that are collected and analyzed. Four scales of measurement are used to obtain data on a particular variable: nominal, ordinal, interval, and ratio.

The scale of measurement for a variable is nominal when the data are labels or names used to identify an attribute of an element. The scale is ordinal if the data have the properties of nominal data and the order or rank of the data is meaningful. The scale is interval if the data have the properties of ordinal data and the interval between observations is expressed in terms of a fixed unit of measure. Finally, the scale of measurement is ratio if the data have all the properties of interval data and the ratio of two values is meaningful.

For purposes of statistical analysis, data can be classified as qualitative or quantitative. Qualitative data are labels or names used to identify an attribute of each element. Qualitative data use either the nominal or ordinal scale of measurement and may be nonnumeric or numeric. Quantitative data are numeric values that indicate how much or how many. Quantitative data use either the interval or ratio scale of measurement. Ordinary arithmetic operations are meaningful only if the data are quantitative. Therefore, statistical computations used for quantitative data are not always appropriate for qualitative data.

In Sections 1.4 and 1.5 we introduced the topics of descriptive statistics and statistical inference. Descriptive statistics are the tabular, graphical, and numerical methods used to summarize data. Statistical inference is the process of using data obtained from a sample to make estimates or test hypotheses about the characteristics of a population.

In the last section of the chapter we provided an introduction to the use of Excel for statistical analysis. We showed that data sets are organized in Excel worksheets in much the same way as the data set for the shadow stocks presented in Table 1.1. That is, the columns in the worksheet correspond to variables in the data set and the rows correspond to observations. We also introduced the approach that will be used throughout the text to describe the use of Excel for statistical analysis. Three tasks may be needed: Enter Data; Enter Functions and Formulas; and Apply Tools. As an illustration, we showed how Excel's AVERAGE function could be used to compute the average lifetime for the 200 observations in the Norris Electronics data set.

GLOSSARY

Statistics   The art and science of collecting, analyzing, presenting, and interpreting data.

Data   The facts and figures collected, analyzed, and summarized for presentation and interpretation.

Data set   All the data collected in a particular study.

Elements   The entities on which data are collected.

Variable   A characteristic of interest for the elements.

Observation   The set of measurements obtained for a particular element.

Nominal scale   The scale of measurement for a variable when the data are labels or names used to identify an attribute of an element. Nominal data may be nonnumeric or numeric.

Ordinal scale   The scale of measurement for a variable if the data exhibit the properties of nominal data and the order or rank of the data is meaningful. Ordinal data may be nonnumeric or numeric.

Interval scale   The scale of measurement for a variable if the data have the properties of ordinal data and the interval between observations is expressed in terms of a fixed unit of measure. Interval data are always numeric.

Ratio scale   The scale of measurement for a variable if the data have all the properties of interval data and the ratio of two values is meaningful. Ratio data are always numeric.

Qualitative data   Labels or names used to identify an attribute of each element. Qualitative data use either the nominal or ordinal scale of measurement and may be nonnumeric or numeric.

Quantitative data   Numeric values that indicate how much or how many of something. Quantitative data are obtained using either the interval or ratio scale of measurement.

Qualitative variable   A variable with qualitative data.

Quantitative variable   A variable with quantitative data.

Cross-sectional data   Data collected at the same or approximately the same point in time.

Time series data   Data collected over several time periods.

Descriptive statistics   Tabular, graphical, and numerical summaries of data.

Population   The set of all elements of interest in a particular study.

Sample   A subset of the population.

Statistical inference   The process of using data obtained from a sample to make estimates or test hypotheses about the characteristics of a population.

Value worksheet   A worksheet that displays the data for the problem and shows the results of the analysis.

Formula worksheet   A worksheet that displays the Excel formulas used to create the results shown in the value worksheet.

SUPPLEMENTARY EXERCISES

1. Discuss the differences between statistics as numerical facts and statistics as a discipline or field of study.

2. Condé Nast Traveler conducts an annual poll of subscribers in order to determine the best places to stay throughout the world. Table 1.6 is a sample of nine European hotels from one of their polls. The price of a standard double room during the hotel's high season ranges from $ (lowest price) to $$$$ (highest price). The overall score includes

TABLE 1.6   RATINGS FOR NINE PLACES TO STAY IN EUROPE

Hotel

Name of Property	Country	Room Rate	Number of Rooms	Overall Score
Graveteye Manor	England	$$	18	83.6
Villa d'Este	Italy	$$$$	166	86.3
Hotel Prem	Germany	$	54	77.8
Hotel d'Europe	France	$$	47	76.8
Palace Luzern	Switzerland	$$	326	80.9
Royal Crescent Hotel	England	$$$	45	73.7
Hotel Sacher	Austria	$$$	120	85.5
Duc de Bourgogne	Belgium	$	10	76.9
Villa Gallici	France	$$	22	90.6

Source: Condé Nast Traveler, January 2000.

subscriber's evaluations of each hotel's rooms, service, restaurants, location/atmosphere, and public areas; a higher overall score corresponds to a higher level of satisfaction.
   a. How many elements are in this data set?
   b. How many variables are in this data set?
   c. Which variables are qualitative and which variables are quantitative?
   d. What type of measurement scale is used for each of the variables?

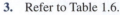

3. Refer to Table 1.6.
   a. What is the average number of rooms for the nine hotels?
   b. Compute the average overall score.
   c. What is the percentage of hotels located in England?
   d. What is the percentage of hotels with a room rate of $$?

4. All-in-one sound systems, called minisystems, typically include an AM/FM tuner, a dual-cassette tape deck, and a CD changer in a book-sized box with two separate speakers. The data in Table 1.7 show the retail price, sound quality, CD capacity, FM tuning sensitivity and selectivity, and the number of tape decks for a sample of 10 minisystems (*Consumer Reports Buying Guide 2002*).
   a. How many elements are in this data set?
   b. What is the population?
   c. Compute the average price for the sample.
   d. Using the results in part (c), estimate the average price for the population.

5. Consider the data set for the sample of 10 minisystems in Table 1.7.
   a. How many variables are in the data set?
   b. Which of the variables are quantitative and which are qualitative?
   c. What is the average CD capacity for the sample?
   d. What percentage of the minisystems provides an FM tuning rating of very good or excellent?
   e. What percentage of the minisystems includes two tape decks?

6. Columbia House provides CDs to its mail-order club members. A Columbia House Music Survey asked new club members to complete an 11-question survey. Some of the questions asked were:
   a. How many CDs have you bought in the last 12 months?
   b. Are you currently a member of a national mail-order book club? (Yes or No)
   c. What is your age?

TABLE 1.7   A SAMPLE OF 10 MINISYSTEMS

Brand & Model	Price ($)	Sound Quality	CD Capacity	FM Tuning	Tape Decks
Aiwa NSX-AJ800	250	Good	3	Fair	2
JVC FS-SD1000	500	Good	1	Very Good	0
JVC MX-G50	200	Very Good	3	Excellent	2
Panasonic SC-PM11	170	Fair	5	Very Good	1
RCA RS 1283	170	Good	3	Poor	0
Sharp CD-BA2600	150	Good	3	Good	2
Sony CHC-CL1	300	Very Good	3	Very Good	1
Sony MHC-NX1	500	Good	5	Excellent	2
Yamaha GX-505	400	Very Good	3	Excellent	1
Yamaha MCR-E100	500	Very Good	1	Excellent	0

    d.   Including yourself, how many people (adults and children) are in your household?

    e.   What kind of music are you interested in buying? (15 categories were listed, including hard rock, soft rock, adult contemporary, heavy metal, rap, and country.)

Comment on whether each question provides qualitative or quantitative data.

7. A *Barron's* subscriber survey (September 15, 2000) asked subscribers to indicate their employment status. The data were recorded with 1 denoting employed full-time, 2 denoting employed part-time, 3 denoting retired, and 4 denoting unemployed (homemaker, student, etc.).

    a.   The variable is employment status. Is it a qualitative or quantitative variable?

    b.   What type of measurement scale is being used for this variable?

8. The Gallup organization conducted telephone surveys with a randomly selected national sample of 1005 adults, 18 years and older. The poll asked the respondents, "How would you describe your own physical health at this time?" (*www.gallup.com,* February 7, 2002). Response categories were Excellent, Good, Only Fair, Poor, and No opinion.

    a.   What was the sample size for this survey?

    b.   Are the data qualitative or quantitative?

    c.   Would it make more sense to use averages or percentages as a summary of the data for this question?

    d.   Of the respondents, 29% said their personal health was excellent. How many individuals provided this response?

9. The Commerce Department reported receiving the following applications for the Malcolm Baldrige National Quality Award: 23 from large manufacturing firms, 18 from large service firms, and 30 from small businesses.

    a.   Is type of business a qualitative or quantitative variable?

    b.   What percentage of the applications came from small businesses?

10. State whether each of the following variables is qualitative or quantitative and indicate its measurement scale.

    a.   Age

    b.   Gender

    c.   Class rank

    d.   Make of automobile

    e.   Number of people favoring the death penalty

11. State whether each of the following variables is qualitative or quantitative and indicate its measurement scale.

    a.   Annual sales

    b.   Soft-drink size (small, medium, large)

    c.   Employee classification (GS1 through GS18)

    d.   Earnings per share

    e.   Method of payment (cash, check, credit card)

12. The Hawaii Visitors Bureau collects data on visitors to Hawaii. The following questions were among 16 asked in a questionnaire handed out to passengers during incoming airline flights in June 2001.

    •   This trip to Hawaii is my: 1st, 2nd, 3rd, 4th, etc.

    •   The primary reason for this trip is: (10 categories including vacation, convention, honeymoon)

    •   Where I plan to stay: (11 categories including hotel, apartment, relatives, camping)

    •   Total days in Hawaii

    a.   What is the population being studied?

    b.   Is the use of a questionnaire a good way to reach the population of passengers on incoming airline flights?

    c.   Comment on each of the four questions in terms of whether it will provide qualitative or quantitative data.

13. Figure 1.10 provides a bar graph summarizing the actual and projected earnings for Volkswagen for the years 1997 to 2002 (*Business Week,* July 23, 2001).
   a. Are the data qualitative or quantitative?
   b. Are the data times series or cross-sectional?
   c. What is the variable of interest?
   d. Comment on the trend in Volkswagen's earnings over time. Would you expect to see an increase or decrease in 2003?

14. The Recording Industry of America keeps track of recorded music sales by type of music, format, and age group. The following data show the percentage of music sales by type (*The New York Times 2002 Almanac*).

Music

Type	1996	1997	1998	1999	2000
Rock	32.6	32.5	25.7	25.2	24.8
Country	12.1	11.2	12.8	10.8	10.7
R&B	12.1	11.2	12.8	10.5	9.7
Pop	9.3	9.4	10.0	10.3	11.0
Rap	8.9	10.1	9.7	10.8	12.9
Gospel	4.3	4.5	6.3	5.1	4.8
Classical	3.4	2.8	3.3	3.5	2.7
Jazz	3.3	2.8	1.9	3.0	2.9
Other	14.0	15.5	17.5	20.8	20.5

   a. Is the type of music a qualitative or quantitative variable?
   b. Construct a graph of rock music sales over the 5-year period; use the horizontal axis to display the year and the vertical axis to display the percentage of music sales. Is this graph based on cross-sectional data or time series data?
   c. Construct a bar graph for type of music sales in 1998. Is this graph based on cross-sectional data or time series data?

15. Refer again to the data in Table 1.7 for the minisystems. Are they cross-sectional or time series data? Why?

FIGURE 1.10   EARNINGS FOR VOLKSWAGEN

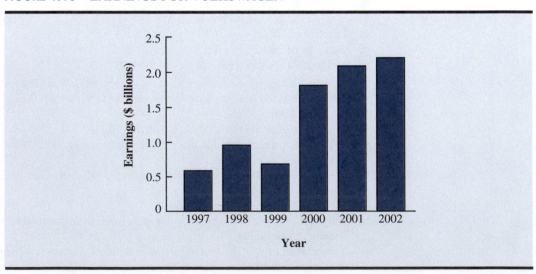

16. The marketing group at your company developed a new diet soft drink that it claims will capture a large share of the young adult market.

    a. What data would you want to see before deciding to invest substantial funds in introducing the new product into the marketplace?

    b. How would you expect the data mentioned in part (a) to be obtained?

17. A manager of a large corporation recommends a $10,000 raise be given to keep a valued subordinate from moving to another company. What internal and external sources of data might be used to decide whether such a salary increase is appropriate?

18. In a recent study of causes of death in men 60 years of age and older, a sample of 120 men indicated that 48 died as a result of some form of heart disease.

    a. Develop a descriptive statistic that can be used as an estimate of the percentage of men 60 years of age or older who die from some form of heart disease.

    b. Are the data on cause of death qualitative or quantitative?

    c. Discuss the role of statistical inference in this type of medical research.

19. A *Business Week* North American subscriber study collected data from a sample of 2861 subscribers. Fifty-nine percent of the respondents indicated that their annual income was $75,000 or more, and 50% reported having an American Express credit card.

    a. What is the population of interest in this study?

    b. Is annual income a qualitative or quantitative variable?

    c. Is ownership of an American Express card a qualitative or quantitative variable?

    d. Does this study involve cross-sectional or time series data?

    e. Describe any statistical inferences *Business Week* might make on the basis of the survey.

20. A Scanner Data User Survey of 50 companies provided the following findings (Mercer Management Consulting, Inc., April 24, 1997):

    • ACNielsen earned 56% of the dollar-share of the market.

    • The average amount spent on scanner data per category of consumer goods was $387,325.

    • On a scale of 1 (very dissatisfied) to 5 (very satisfied), the average level of overall satisfaction with scanner data was 3.73.

    a. Cite two descriptive statistics.

    b. Make an inference of the overall satisfaction in the population of all users of scanner data.

    c. Make an inference about the average amount spent per category for scanner data for consumer goods.

21. A seven-year medical research study reported that women whose mothers took the drug DES during pregnancy were *twice* as likely to develop tissue abnormalities that might lead to cancer as were women whose mothers did not take the drug.

    a. This study involved the comparison of two populations. What were the populations?

    b. Do you suppose the data were obtained in a survey or an experiment?

    c. For the population of women whose mothers took the drug DES during pregnancy, a sample of 3980 women showed 63 developed tissue abnormalities that might lead to cancer. Provide a descriptive statistic that could be used to estimate the number of women out of 1000 in this population who have tissue abnormalities.

    d. For the population of women whose mothers did not take the drug DES during pregnancy, what is the estimate of the number of women out of 1000 who would be expected to have tissue abnormalities?

    e. Medical studies often use a relatively large sample (in this case, 3980). Why?

22. A firm is interested in testing the advertising effectiveness of a new television commercial. As part of the test, the commercial is shown on a 6:30 P.M. local news program in Denver,

Colorado. Two days later, a market research firm conducts a telephone survey to obtain information on recall rates (percentage of viewers who recall seeing the commercial) and impressions of the commercial.

a. What is the population for this study?

b. What is the sample for this study?

c. Why would a sample be used in this situation? Explain.

23. ACNielsen conducts weekly surveys of television viewing throughout the United States. The ACNielsen statistical ratings indicate the size of the viewing audience for each major network television program. Rankings of the television programs and of the viewing audience market shares for each network are published each week.

a. What is the ACNielsen organization attempting to measure?

b. What is the population?

c. Why would a sample be used for this situation?

d. What kinds of decisions or actions are based on the ACNielsen studies?

24. A sample of midterm grades for five students showed the following results: 72, 65, 82, 90, 76. Which of the following statements are correct, and which should be challenged as being too generalized?

a. The average midterm grade for the sample of five students is 77.

b. The average midterm grade for all students who took the exam is 77.

c. An estimate of the average midterm grade for all students who took the exam is 77.

d. More than half of the students who take this exam will score between 70 and 85.

e. If five other students are included in the sample, their grades will be between 65 and 90.

CHAPTER 2

Descriptive Statistics: Tabular and Graphical Methods

CONTENTS

STATISTICS IN PRACTICE

Colgate-Palmolive Company*

NEW YORK, NEW YORK

The Colgate-Palmolive Company started as a small soap and candle shop in New York City in 1806. Today, Colgate-Palmolive is a $9 billion company whose products can be found in more than 200 countries and territories around the world. Although best known for its brand names of Colgate, Palmolive, Ajax, and Fab, the company also markets Mennen, Hill's Science Diet, and Hill's Prescription Diet products.

The Colgate-Palmolive Company uses statistics in its quality assurance program for home laundry detergent products. One concern is customer satisfaction with the quantity of detergent in a carton. Every carton in each size category is filled with the same amount of detergent by weight, but the volume of detergent is affected by the density of the detergent powder. For instance, if the powder density is on the heavy side, a smaller volume of detergent is needed to reach the carton's specified weight. As a result, the carton may appear to be underfilled when opened by the consumer.

To control the problem of heavy detergent powder, limits are placed on the acceptable range of powder density. Statistical samples are taken periodically, and the density of each powder sample is measured. Data summaries are then provided for operating personnel so that corrective action can be taken if necessary to keep the density within the desired quality specifications.

A frequency distribution for the densities of 150 samples taken over a one-week period and a histogram are shown in the accompanying table and figure. Density levels above .40 are unacceptably high. The frequency distribution and histogram show that the operation is meeting its quality guidelines with all of the densities less than or equal to .40. Managers viewing these statistical summaries would be pleased with the quality of the detergent production process.

In this chapter, you will learn about tabular and graphical methods of descriptive statistics such as fre-

*The authors are indebted to William R. Fowle, Manager of Quality Assurance, Colgate-Palmolive Company, for providing this Statistics in Practice.

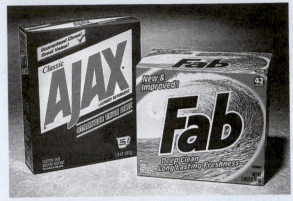

Statistical summaries help maintain the quality of these Colgate-Palmolive products. © Joe Higgins/South-Western.

quency distributions, bar graphs, histograms, stem-and-leaf displays, crosstabulations, and others. The goal of these methods is to summarize data so that they can be easily understood and interpreted.

Frequency Distribution of Density Data

Density	Frequency
.29–.30	30
.31–.32	75
.33–.34	32
.35–.36	9
.37–.38	3
.39–.40	1
Total	150

Histogram of Density Data

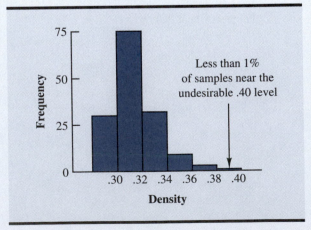

As indicated in Chapter 1, data can be classified as either qualitative or quantitative. **Qualitative data** are labels or names used to identify categories of like items. **Quantitative data** are numerical values that indicate how much or how many.

The purpose of this chapter is to introduce tabular and graphical methods commonly used to summarize both qualitative and quantitative data. Tabular and graphical summaries of data can be found in annual reports, newspaper articles, and research studies. Everyone is exposed to these types of presentations. Hence, it is important to understand how they are prepared and how they should be interpreted. We begin with tabular and graphical methods for summarizing data concerning a single variable. The last section introduces methods for summarizing data when the relationship between two variables is of interest.

Excel's wide variety of functions and tools for descriptive statistics are used extensively in this chapter. The Chart Wizard and PivotTable tool are two Excel tools that are extremely valuable in summarizing and presenting data. The Chart Wizard has extensive capabilities for developing graphical presentations and the PivotTable tool is useful in preparing crosstabulations for data sets involving more than one variable.

2.1   SUMMARIZING QUALITATIVE DATA

Frequency Distribution

We begin the discussion of how tabular and graphical methods can be used to summarize qualitative data with the definition of a **frequency distribution**.

> **Frequency Distribution**
>
> A frequency distribution is a tabular summary of data showing the number (frequency) of items in each of several nonoverlapping classes.

Let us use the following example to demonstrate the construction and interpretation of a frequency distribution for qualitative data. According to *Beverage Digest*, Coke Classic, Diet Coke, Dr. Pepper, Pepsi-Cola, and Sprite are the five top-selling soft drinks (*The Wall Street Journal Almanac*, 1998). Assume that the data in Table 2.1 show the soft drinks selected in a sample of 50 soft drink purchases.

To develop a frequency distribution for these data, we count the number of times each soft drink appears in Table 2.1. Coke Classic appears 19 times, Diet Coke appears 8 times, Dr. Pepper appears 5 times, Pepsi-Cola appears 13 times, and Sprite appears 5 times. These counts are summarized in the frequency distribution in Table 2.2.

This frequency distribution provides a summary of how the 50 soft drink purchases are distributed across the five soft drinks. This summary provides more insight than the original data shown in Table 2.1. Viewing the frequency distribution, we see that Coke Classic is the leader, Pepsi-Cola is second, Diet Coke is third, and Sprite and Dr. Pepper are tied for fourth. The frequency distribution has provided information about the relative popularity of the five best-selling soft drinks.

Counting the number of times each soft drink appears in the data was not too difficult for the sample of 50 soft drink purchases. However, the effort needed to develop an accurate count for each soft drink would have been greater had the sample size been larger. Let

TABLE 2.1   DATA FROM A SAMPLE OF 50 SOFT DRINK PURCHASES

SoftDrink

Coke Classic	Sprite	Pepsi-Cola
Diet Coke	Coke Classic	Coke Classic
Pepsi-Cola	Diet Coke	Coke Classic
Diet Coke	Coke Classic	Coke Classic
Coke Classic	Diet Coke	Pepsi-Cola
Coke Classic	Coke Classic	Dr. Pepper
Dr. Pepper	Sprite	Coke Classic
Diet Coke	Pepsi-Cola	Diet Coke
Pepsi-Cola	Coke Classic	Pepsi-Cola
Pepsi-Cola	Coke Classic	Pepsi-Cola
Coke Classic	Coke Classic	Pepsi-Cola
Dr. Pepper	Pepsi-Cola	Pepsi-Cola
Sprite	Coke Classic	Coke Classic
Coke Classic	Sprite	Dr. Pepper
Diet Coke	Dr. Pepper	Pepsi-Cola
Coke Classic	Pepsi-Cola	Sprite
Coke Classic	Diet Coke	

TABLE 2.2

FREQUENCY
DISTRIBUTION OF
SOFT DRINK
PURCHASES

Soft Drink	Frequency
Coke Classic	19
Diet Coke	8
Dr. Pepper	5
Pepsi-Cola	13
Sprite	5
Total	50

*Appendix E provides help
in identifying and using the
statistical functions
available in Excel.*

us now see how Excel can be used to count the frequencies and construct a frequency distribution for the soft drink data in Table 2.1.

Using Excel's COUNTIF Function to Construct a Frequency Distribution

Two tasks are involved in using Excel's COUNTIF function to construct a frequency distribution: Enter Data and Enter Functions and Formulas. Refer to Figure 2.1 as we describe the tasks involved. The formula worksheet is in the background; the value worksheet is in the foreground.

Enter Data: The label "Brand Purchased" and the data for the 50 soft drink purchases are entered into cells A1:A51.

Enter Functions and Formulas: Excel's COUNTIF function can be used to count the number of times each soft drink appears in cells A2:A51. We first entered a label and the soft drink names into cells C1:C6 and D1. Then, to count the number of times that Coke Classic appears, we entered the following formula into cell D2:

$$=COUNTIF(\$A\$2:\$A\$51,C2)$$

To count the number of times the other soft drinks appear, we copied the same formula into cells D3:D6.

The value worksheet, in the foreground of Figure 2.1, shows the values computed using these cell formulas; we see that the Excel worksheet shows the same frequency distribution that we developed in Table 2.2.

FIGURE 2.1   FREQUENCY DISTRIBUTION FOR SOFT DRINK PURCHASES
CONSTRUCTED USING EXCEL'S COUNTIF FUNCTION

	A	B	C	D	E
1	Brand Purchased		Soft Drink	Frequency	
2	Coke Classic		Coke Classic	=COUNTIF($A$2:$A$51,C2)	
3	Diet Coke		Diet Coke	=COUNTIF($A$2:$A$51,C3)	
4	Pepsi-Cola		Dr. Pepper	=COUNTIF($A$2:$A$51,C4)	
5	Diet Coke		Pepsi-Cola	=COUNTIF($A$2:$A$51,C5)	
6	Coke Classic		Sprite	=COUNTIF($A$2:$A$51,C6)	
7	Coke Classic				
8	Dr. Pepper				
9	Diet Coke				
10	Pepsi-Cola				
45	Pepsi-Cola				
46	Pepsi-Cola				
47	Pepsi-Cola				
48	Coke Classic				
49	Dr. Pepper				
50	Pepsi-Cola				
51	Sprite				
52					

Note: Rows 11–44
are hidden.

	A	B	C	D	E
1	Brand Purchased		Soft Drink	Frequency	
2	Coke Classic		Coke Classic	19	
3	Diet Coke		Diet Coke	8	
4	Pepsi-Cola		Dr. Pepper	5	
5	Diet Coke		Pepsi-Cola	13	
6	Coke Classic		Sprite	5	
7	Coke Classic				
8	Dr. Pepper				
9	Diet Coke				
10	Pepsi-Cola				
45	Pepsi-Cola				
46	Pepsi-Cola				
47	Pepsi-Cola				
48	Coke Classic				
49	Dr. Pepper				
50	Pepsi-Cola				
51	Sprite				
52					

Relative Frequency and Percent Frequency Distributions

A frequency distribution shows the number (frequency) of items in each of several nonoverlapping classes. However, we are often interested in the proportion, or percentage, of items in each class. The *relative frequency* of a class is the fraction or proportion of items belonging to a class. For a data set with n observations, the relative frequency of each class is as follows:

Relative Frequency

$$\text{Relative Frequency of a Class} = \frac{\text{Frequency of the Class}}{n} \qquad (2.1)$$

The *percent frequency* of a class is the relative frequency multiplied by 100.

A **relative frequency distribution** is a tabular summary of data showing the relative frequency for each class. A **percent frequency distribution** is a tabular summary of data showing the percent frequency for each class. Table 2.3 shows a relative frequency distribution and a percent frequency distribution for the soft drink data. In Table 2.3 we see that the relative frequency for Coke Classic is 19/50 = .38, the relative frequency for Diet Coke is 8/50 = .16, and so on. From the percent frequency distribution, we see that 38% of the purchases were Coke Classic, 16% of the purchases were Diet Coke, and so on. We can also note that 38% + 26% + 16% = 80% of the purchases were of the top three soft drinks.

Using Excel to Construct Relative Frequency and Percent Frequency Distributions

Extending the worksheet shown in Figure 2.1, we can develop the relative frequency and percent frequency distributions shown in Table 2.3. Refer to Figure 2.2 as we describe the tasks involved. The formula worksheet is in the background; the value worksheet is in the foreground.

Enter Data: The label "Brand Purchased" and the data for the 50 soft drink purchases are entered into cells A1:A51.

Enter Functions and Formulas: The information in cells C1:D6 is the same as in Figure 2.1. Excel's SUM function is used in cell D7 to compute the sum of the frequencies in cells D2:D6. The resulting value of 50 is the number of observations in the data set. To compute the relative frequency for Coke Classic using Equation (2.1), we entered the formula =D2/$D$7 into cell E2; the result, 0.38, is the relative frequency for Coke Classic. Copying cell E2 to cells E3:E6 computes the relative frequencies for each of the other soft drinks.

To compute the percent frequency for Coke Classic we entered the formula =E2*100 into cell F2. The result, 38, indicates that 38% of the soft drink purchases were Coke Classic. Copying cell F2 to cells F3:F6 computes the percent frequencies for each of the other soft drinks. Finally, copying cell D7 to cells E7:F7 computes the total of the relative frequencies (1.00) and the total of the percent frequencies (100).

Bar Graphs and Pie Charts

A **bar graph** is a graphical device for depicting qualitative data that have been summarized in a frequency, relative frequency, or percent frequency distribution. On one axis of the graph (usually the horizontal axis), we specify the labels that are used for the classes

TABLE 2.3   RELATIVE AND PERCENT FREQUENCY DISTRIBUTIONS OF SOFT DRINK PURCHASES

Soft Drink	Relative Frequency	Percent Frequency
Coke Classic	.38	38
Diet Coke	.16	16
Dr. Pepper	.10	10
Pepsi-Cola	.26	26
Sprite	.10	10
Total	1.00	100

FIGURE 2.2   RELATIVE FREQUENCY AND PERCENT FREQUENCY DISTRIBUTIONS OF SOFT DRINK PURCHASES CONSTRUCTED USING EXCEL

	A	B	C	D	E	F	G
1	Brand Purchased		Soft Drink	Frequency	Relative Frequency	Percent Frequency	
2	Coke Classic		Coke Classic	=COUNTIF($A$2:$A$51,C2)	=D2/$D$7	=E2*100	
3	Diet Coke		Diet Coke	=COUNTIF($A$2:$A$51,C3)	=D3/$D$7	=E3*100	
4	Pepsi-Cola		Dr. Pepper	=COUNTIF($A$2:$A$51,C4)	=D4/$D$7	=E4*100	
5	Diet Coke		Pepsi-Cola	=COUNTIF($A$2:$A$51,C5)	=D5/$D$7	=E5*100	
6	Coke Classic		Sprite	=COUNTIF($A$2:$A$51,C6)	=D6/$D$7	=E6*100	
7	Coke Classic		Total	=SUM(D2:D6)	=SUM(E2:E6)	=SUM(F2:F6)	
8	Dr. Pepper						
9	Diet Coke						
10	Pepsi-Cola						
45	Pepsi-Cola						
46	Pepsi-Cola						
47	Pepsi-Cola						
48	Coke Classic						
49	Dr. Pepper						
50	Pepsi-Cola						
51	Sprite						
52							

Note: Rows 11–44 are hidden.

	A	B	C	D	E	F	G
1	Brand Purchased		Soft Drink	Frequency	Relative Frequency	Percent Frequency	
2	Coke Classic		Coke Classic	19	0.38	38	
3	Diet Coke		Diet Coke	8	0.16	16	
4	Pepsi-Cola		Dr. Pepper	5	0.1	10	
5	Diet Coke		Pepsi-Cola	13	0.26	26	
6	Coke Classic		Sprite	5	0.1	10	
7	Coke Classic		Total	50	1.00	100	
8	Dr. Pepper						
9	Diet Coke						
10	Pepsi-Cola						
45	Pepsi-Cola						
46	Pepsi-Cola						
47	Pepsi-Cola						
48	Coke Classic						
49	Dr. Pepper						
50	Pepsi-Cola						
51	Sprite						
52							

In quality control applications, bar graphs are used to identify the most important causes of problems. When the bars are arranged in descending order of height from left to right with the most frequently occurring cause appearing first, the bar graph is called a pareto diagram. *This diagram is named for its founder, Vilfredo Pareto, an Italian economist.*

(categories) of data. A frequency, relative frequency, or percent frequency scale can be used for the other axis of the graph (usually the vertical axis). Then, using a bar of fixed width drawn above each class label, we extend the length of the bar until we reach the frequency, relative frequency, or percent frequency of the class. For qualitative data, the bars should be separated to emphasize the fact that each class (category) is separate. Figure 2.3 is a bar graph of the frequency distribution for the 50 soft drink purchases. Note how the graphical presentation shows Coke Classic, Pepsi-Cola, and Diet Coke to be the most preferred brands.

The **pie chart** is another graphical device for presenting relative frequency and percent frequency distributions for qualitative data. To construct a pie chart, we first draw a circle to represent all of the data. Then we use the relative frequencies to subdivide the circle into sectors, or parts, that correspond to the relative frequency for each class. For example, because a circle has 360 degrees and Coke Classic has a relative frequency of .38, the sector of the pie chart labeled Coke Classic consists of .38(360) = 136.8 degrees. The sector of the pie chart labeled Diet Coke consists of .16(360) = 57.6 degrees. Similar calculations for the other classes yield the pie chart in Figure 2.4. The numerical values shown for each sector can be frequencies, relative frequencies, or percent frequencies.

FIGURE 2.3   BAR GRAPH OF SOFT DRINK PURCHASES

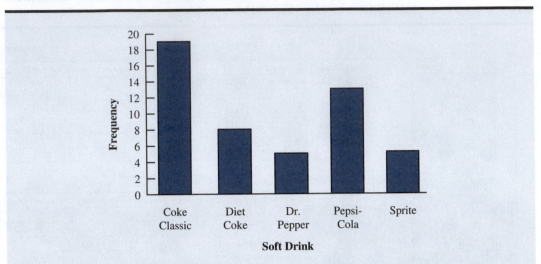

Using Excel's Chart Wizard to Construct Bar Graphs and Pie Charts

Excel's Chart Wizard provides a general tool for constructing a variety of graphical displays, including bar graphs and pie charts. We will illustrate the use of Excel's Chart Wizard by showing how to construct the bar graph for soft drink purchases. The Chart Wizard tool allows us to go beyond what can be done with functions and formulas alone. When such tools are used, a third task is needed for worksheet construction: Apply Tools.

The same data and functions and formulas that were used in Figure 2.1 are used here. Thus, the chart we are going to develop is an extension of that worksheet. Refer to Fig-

FIGURE 2.4   PIE CHART OF SOFT DRINK PURCHASES

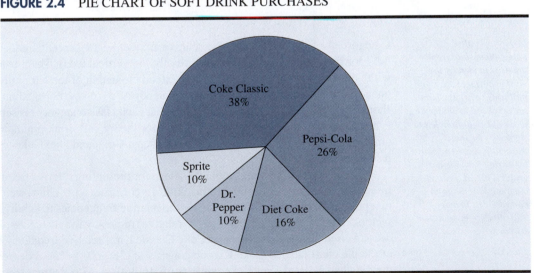

ure 2.5 as we describe the Apply Tools task. The value worksheet is in the background; the chart developed using the Excel Chart Wizard is in the foreground.

Enter Data: Same as in Figure 2.1.

Enter Functions and Formulas: Same as in Figure 2.1.

Apply Tools: The following steps describe how to use Excel's Chart Wizard to construct a bar graph for the soft drink data using the frequency distribution appearing in cells C1:D6.

Step 1. Select cells C1:D6

Step 2. Click the **Chart Wizard** button on the Standard toolbar (or select the **Insert** menu and choose the **Chart** option)

Step 3. When the **Chart Wizard–Step 1 of 4–Chart Type** dialog box appears:
Choose **Column** in the **Chart type** list
Choose **Clustered Column** from the **Chart sub-type** display
Click **Next >**

Step 4. When the **Chart Wizard–Step 2 of 4–Chart Source Data** dialog box appears:
Click **Next >**

FIGURE 2.5   BAR GRAPH OF SOFT DRINK PURCHASES CONSTRUCTED USING EXCEL'S CHART WIZARD

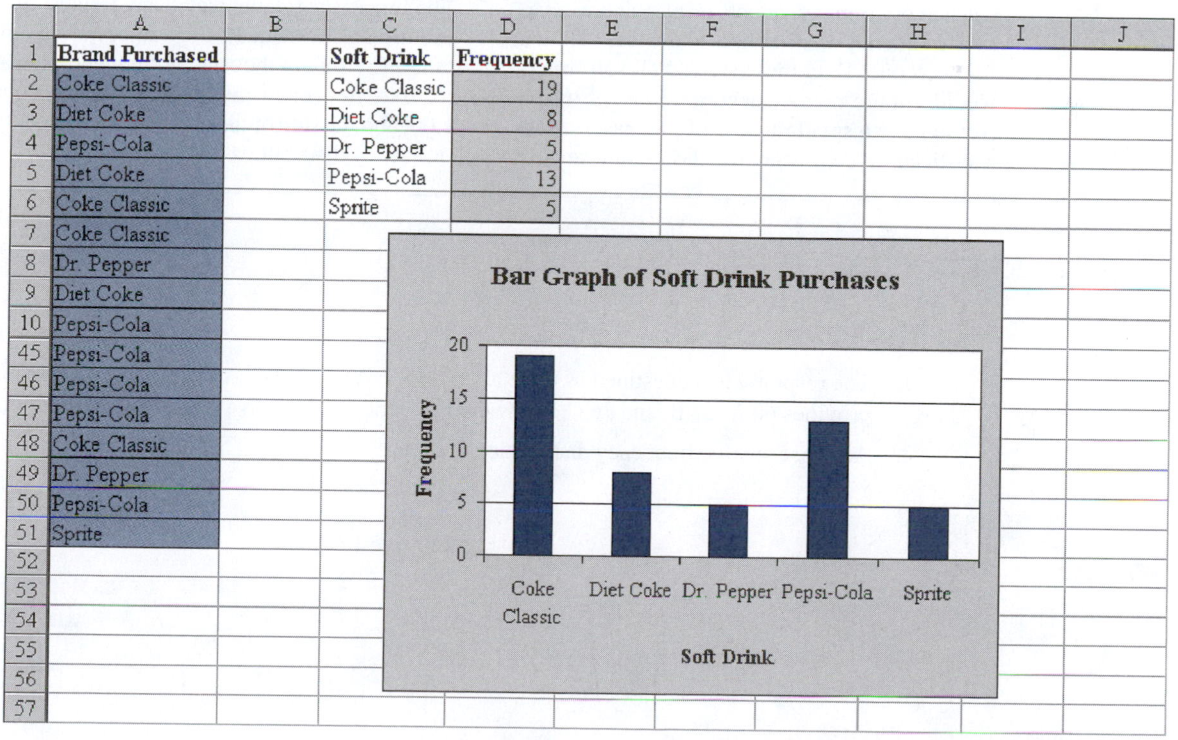

Step 5. When the **Chart Wizard–Step 3 of 4–Chart Options** dialog box appears:

Select the **Titles** tab and then

Type **Bar Graph of Soft Drink Purchases** in the **Chart title** box

Type **Soft Drink** in the **Category (X)** axis box

Type **Frequency** in the **Value (Y)** axis box

Select the **Legend** tab and then

Remove the check in the **Show legend** Box

Click **Next >**

Step 6. When the **Chart Wizard–Step 4 of 4–Chart Location** dialog box appears:

Specify a location for the new chart (we used the default setting of the current worksheet)

Click **Finish**

The resulting bar graph (chart) is shown in Figure 2.5.* A dark blue screen is used to highlight the chart provided.

Excel's Chart Wizard can produce a pie chart for the soft drink data in a similar fashion. The major difference is that in step 3 we would choose Pie in the Chart type list.

NOTES AND COMMENTS

1. Often the number of classes in a frequency distribution is the same as the number of categories found in the data, as is the case for the soft drink purchase data in this section. The data involve only five soft drinks, and a separate frequency distribution class was defined for each one. Data that included all soft drinks would require many categories, most of which would have a small number of purchases. Most statisticians recommend that classes with smaller frequencies be grouped into an aggregate class called "other." Classes with frequencies of 5 percent or less would most often be treated in this fashion.

2. The sum of the frequencies in any frequency distribution always equals the number of observations. The sum of the relative frequencies in any relative frequency distribution always equals 1.00, and the sum of the percentages in a percent frequency distribution always equals 100.

EXERCISES

Methods

1. The response to a question has three alternatives: A, B, and C. A sample of 120 responses provides 60 A, 24 B, and 36 C. Show the frequency and relative frequency distributions.

2. A partial relative frequency distribution is given.

Class	Relative Frequency
A	.22
B	.18
C	.40
D	

---

*The bar graph in Figure 2.5 is slightly larger than what was provided by Excel after selecting **Finish**. Resizing an Excel chart is not difficult. First, select the chart. Small black squares, called sizing handles, will appear on the chart border. Click on the sizing handles and drag them to resize the figure to your preference.

    a. What is the relative frequency of class D?
    b. The total sample size is 200. What is the frequency of class D?
    c. Show the frequency distribution.
    d. Show the percent frequency distribution.

3. A questionnaire provides 58 yes, 42 no, and 20 no-opinion answers.
    a. In the construction of a pie chart, how many degrees would be in the section of the pie showing the yes answers?
    b. How many degrees would be in the section of the pie showing the no answers?
    c. Construct a pie chart.
    d. Construct a bar graph.

Applications

4. According to Nielsen Media Research, the top four TV shows at 8:00 P.M., April 6, 2000, were Millionaire, Frasier, Chicago Hope, and Charmed (*USA Today*, April 13, 2000). Data for a sample of 50 viewers follow.

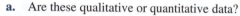

Millionaire	Millionaire	Millionaire	Frasier	Charmed
Frasier	Frasier	Millionaire	Millionaire	Frasier
Frasier	Millionaire	Millionaire	Chicago Hope	Millionaire
Charmed	Millionaire	Frasier	Chicago Hope	Millionaire
Chicago Hope	Charmed	Frasier	Frasier	Millionaire
Millionaire	Frasier	Millionaire	Millionaire	Chicago Hope
Frasier	Millionaire	Millionaire	Charmed	Chicago Hope
Chicago Hope	Millionaire	Millionaire	Millionaire	Millionaire
Frasier	Frasier	Millionaire	Frasier	Frasier
Millionaire	Millionaire	Chicago Hope	Millionaire	Frasier

    a. Are these qualitative or quantitative data?
    b. Provide frequency and percent frequency distributions.
    c. Construct a bar graph and a pie chart.
    d. On the basis of the sample, which show has the largest market share? Which one is second?

5. In alphabetical order, the six most common last names in the United States are Brown, Davis, Johnson, Jones, Smith, and Williams (*Time Almanac 2001*). Assume that a sample of 50 individuals with one of these last names provided the following data.

Brown	Williams	Williams	Williams	Brown
Smith	Jones	Smith	Johnson	Smith
Davis	Smith	Brown	Williams	Johnson
Johnson	Smith	Smith	Johnson	Brown
Williams	Davis	Johnson	Williams	Johnson
Williams	Johnson	Jones	Smith	Brown
Johnson	Smith	Smith	Brown	Jones
Jones	Jones	Smith	Smith	Davis
Davis	Jones	Williams	Davis	Smith
Jones	Johnson	Brown	Johnson	Davis

Summarize the data by constructing the following:
    a. Relative and percent frequency distributions
    b. A bar graph
    c. A pie chart
    d. Based on these data, what are the three most common last names?

6. The eight best-selling paperback business books in February 2000 are listed in Table 2.4 (*Business Week*, April 3, 2000). Suppose a sample of book purchases in the Denver, Colorado, area provided the following data for these eight books.

CD file

BwBooks

7 Habits	Dad	7 Habits	Millionaire	Millionaire	WSJ Guide
Motley	Millionaire	Tax Guide	7 Habits	Dad	Dummies
Millionaire	Motley	Dad	Dad	Parachute	Dad
Dad	7 Habits	WSJ Guide	WSJ Guide	WSJ Guide	7 Habits
Motley	WSJ Guide	Millionaire	7 Habits	Millionaire	Millionaire
Millionaire	7 Habits	Millionaire	7 Habits	Motley	Motley
Motley	7 Habits	Dad	Dad	Dad	Dad
7 Habits	WSJ Guide	Tax Guide	Millionaire	Motley	Tax Guide
Motley	Motley	Millionaire	Millionaire	Dad	Dummies
Millionaire	Millionaire	Millionaire	Dad	Millionaire	Dad

a. Construct frequency and percent frequency distributions for the data. Group any books with a frequency of 5% or less in an "other" category.
b. Rank the best-selling books.
c. What percentage of the sales are represented by *The Millionaire Next Door* and *Rich Dad, Poor Dad*?

SELF test

7. Leverock's Waterfront Steakhouse in Maderia Beach, Florida, uses a questionnaire to ask customers how they rate the server, food quality, cocktails, prices, and atmosphere at the restaurant. Each characteristic is rated on a scale of outstanding (O), very good (V), good (G), average (A), and poor (P). Use descriptive statistics to summarize the following data collected on food quality. What is your feeling about the food quality ratings at the restaurant?

G	O	V	G	A	O	V	O	V	G	O	V	A
V	O	P	V	O	G	A	O	O	O	G	O	V
V	A	G	O	V	P	V	O	O	G	O	O	V
O	G	A	O	V	O	O	G	V	A	G		

TABLE 2.4

THE EIGHT BEST-SELLING PAPERBACK BUSINESS BOOKS

- *The 7 Habits of Highly Effective People*
- *Investing for Dummies*
- *The Ernst & Young Tax Guide 2000*
- *The Millionaire Next Door*
- *The Motley Fool Investment Guide*
- *Rich Dad, Poor Dad*
- *The Wall Street Journal Guide to Understanding Money and Investing*
- *What Color Is Your Parachute? 2000*

8. Data for a sample of 55 members of the Baseball Hall of Fame in Cooperstown, New York, are shown here. Each observation indicates the primary position played by the Hall of Famers: pitcher (P), catcher (H), 1st base (1), 2nd base (2), 3rd base (3), shortstop (S), left field (L), center field (C), and right field (R).

L	P	C	H	2	P	R	1	S	S	1	L	P	R	P
P	P	P	R	C	S	L	R	P	C	C	P	P	R	P
2	3	P	H	L	P	1	C	P	P	P	S	1	L	R
R	1	2	H	S	3	H	2	L	P					

a. Use frequency and relative frequency distributions to summarize the data.
b. What position provides the most Hall of Famers?
c. What position provides the fewest Hall of Famers?
d. What outfield position (L, C, or R) provides the most Hall of Famers?
e. Compare infielders (1, 2, 3, and S) to outfielders (L, C, and R).

9. The flextime system at Electronics Associates allows employees to begin their working day at 7:00, 7:30, 8:00, 8:30, or 9:00 A.M. The following data represent a sample of the starting times selected by the employees.

7:00	8:30	9:00	8:00	7:30	7:30	8:30	8:30	7:30	7:00
8:30	8:30	8:00	8:00	7:30	8:30	7:00	9:00	8:30	8:00

Summarize the data by constructing the following:

a. A frequency distribution
b. A percent frequency distribution
c. A bar graph
d. A pie chart
e. What do the summaries tell you about employee preferences in the flextime system?

10. A 2001 Merrill Lynch Client Satisfaction Survey asked clients to indicate how satisfied they were with their financial consultant. Client responses were coded 1 to 7, with 1 indicating "not at all satisfied" and 7 indicating "extremely satisfied." Assume that the following data are from a sample of 60 responses for a particular financial consultant.

Client

5	7	6	6	7	5	5	7	3	6
7	7	6	6	6	5	5	6	7	7
6	6	4	4	7	6	7	6	7	6
5	7	5	7	6	4	7	5	7	6
6	5	3	7	7	6	6	6	6	5
5	6	6	7	7	5	6	4	6	6

a. Comment on why these are qualitative data.
b. Provide a frequency distribution and a relative frequency distribution for the data.
c. Provide a bar graph.
d. On the basis of your summaries, comment on the clients' overall evaluation of the financial consultant.

2.2   SUMMARIZING QUANTITATIVE DATA

Frequency Distribution

As defined in Section 2.1, a frequency distribution is a tabular summary of data showing the number (frequency) of items in each of several nonoverlapping classes. This definition holds for quantitative as well as qualitative data. However, with quantitative data we have to be more careful in defining the nonoverlapping classes to be used in the frequency distribution.

TABLE 2.5

YEAR-END AUDIT TIMES (IN DAYS)

12	14	19	18
15	15	18	17
20	27	22	23
22	21	33	28
14	18	16	13

For example, consider the quantitative data in Table 2.5. These data show the time in days required to complete year-end audits for a sample of 20 clients of Sanderson and Clifford, a small public accounting firm; the data have been rounded to the nearest day. The three steps necessary to define the classes for a frequency distribution with quantitative data are:

1. Determine the number of nonoverlapping classes.
2. Determine the width of each class.
3. Determine the class limits.

Let us demonstrate these steps by developing a frequency distribution for the audit time data in Table 2.5.

Audit

Number of Classes.   Classes are formed by specifying ranges that will be used to group the data. As a general guideline, we recommend using between 5 and 20 classes. For a small number of data items, as few as five or six classes may be used to summarize the data. For a larger number of data items, a larger number of classes is usually required. The goal is to use enough classes to show the variation in the data, but not so many classes that some contain only a few data items. Because the number of data items in Table 2.5 is relatively small ($n = 20$), we chose to develop a frequency distribution with five classes.

Width of the Classes.   The second step in constructing a frequency distribution for quantitative data is to choose a width for the classes. As a general guideline, we recommend that the width be the same for each class. Thus the choices of the number of classes and the width

Making the classes the same width reduces the chance of inappropriate interpretations by the user.

of classes are not independent decisions. A larger number of classes means a smaller class width, and vice versa. To determine an approximate class width, we begin by identifying the largest and smallest data values. Then, once the desired number of classes has been specified, we can use the following expression to determine the approximate class width.

$$\text{Approximate Class Width} = \frac{\text{Largest Data Value} - \text{Smallest Data Value}}{\text{Number of Classes}} \quad (2.2)$$

The approximate class width given by Equation (2.2) can be rounded to a more convenient value based on the preference of the person developing the frequency distribution. For example, an approximate class width of 9.28 might be rounded to 10 simply because 10 is a more convenient class width to use in presenting a frequency distribution.

For the data involving the year-end audit times, the largest value is 33 and the smallest value is 12. Because we decided to summarize the data with five classes, using Equation (2.2) provides an approximate class width of $(33 - 12)/5 = 4.2$. We therefore decided to round up and use a class width of five days in the frequency distribution.

No single frequency distribution is best for a data set. Different people may construct different, but equally acceptable, frequency distributions. The goal is to reveal the natural grouping and variation in the data.

In practice, the number of classes and the appropriate class width are determined by trial and error. Once a possible number of classes is chosen, Equation (2.2) is used to find the approximate class width. The process can be repeated for a different number of classes. Ultimately, the analyst uses judgment to determine the combination of the number of classes and class width that provides the best frequency distribution for summarizing the data.

For the audit time data in Table 2.5, after deciding to use five classes, each with a width of five days, the next task is to specify the class limits for each of the classes.

Class Limits. Class limits must be chosen so that each data item belongs to one and only one class. The *lower class limit* identifies the smallest possible data value assigned to the class. The *upper class limit* identifies the largest possible data value assigned to the class. In developing frequency distributions for qualitative data, we did not need to specify class limits because each data item naturally fell into a separate class (category). But with quantitative data, such as the audit times in Table 2.5, class limits are necessary to determine where each data value belongs.

Using the audit time data in Table 2.5, we selected 10 days as the lower class limit and 14 days as the upper class limit for the first class. This class is denoted 10–14 in Table 2.6. The smallest data value, 12, is included in the 10–14 class. We then selected 15 days as the lower class limit and 19 days as the upper class limit of the next class. We continued defining the lower and upper class limits to obtain a total of five classes: 10–14, 15–19, 20–24, 25–29, and 30–34. The largest data value, 33, is included in the 30–34 class. The difference between the lower class limits of adjacent classes is the class width. Using the first two lower class limits of 10 and 15, we see that the class width is $15 - 10 = 5$.

Once the number of classes, class width, and class limits have been determined, a frequency distribution can be obtained by counting the number of data values belonging to each class. For example, the data in Table 2.5 show that four values—12, 14, 14, and 13—belong to the 10–14 class. Thus, the frequency for the 10–14 class is 4. Continuing this counting process for the 15–19, 20–24, 25–29, and 30–34 classes provides the frequency distribution in Table 2.6. Using this frequency distribution, we can observe that:

1. The most frequently occurring audit times are in the class of 15–19 days. Eight of the 20 audit times belong to this class.
2. Only one audit required 30 or more days.

Other conclusions are possible, depending on the interests of the person viewing the frequency distribution. The value of a frequency distribution is that it provides insights about the data that are not easily obtained by viewing the data in their original unorganized form.

TABLE 2.6

FREQUENCY DISTRIBUTION FOR THE AUDIT TIME DATA

Audit Time (days)	Frequency
10–14	4
15–19	8
20–24	5
25–29	2
30–34	1
Total	20

Class Midpoint.   In some applications, we want to know the midpoints of the classes in a frequency distribution for quantitative data. The **class midpoint** is the value halfway between the lower and upper class limits. For the audit time data, the five class midpoints are 12, 17, 22, 27, and 32.

Using Excel's FREQUENCY Function to Construct a Frequency Distribution

Constructing a frequency distribution for quantitative data using Excel's COUNTIF function is cumbersome. Here we show how to use Excel's FREQUENCY function to construct a frequency distribution for quantitative data. The FREQUENCY function involves the use of array formulas that provide multiple values (in this case the class frequencies) as output. Refer to Figure 2.6 as we describe the tasks involved. The formula worksheet is in the background; the value worksheet is in the foreground.

FIGURE 2.6   FREQUENCY DISTRIBUTION FOR AUDIT TIME DATA CONSTRUCTED USING EXCEL'S FREQUENCY FUNCTION

	A	B	C	D	E
1	Audit Time		Audit Time	Frequency	
2	12		10-14	=FREQUENCY(A2:A21,{14,19,24,29,34})	
3	15		15-19	=FREQUENCY(A2:A21,{14,19,24,29,34})	
4	20		20-24	=FREQUENCY(A2:A21,{14,19,24,29,34})	
5	22		25-29	=FREQUENCY(A2:A21,{14,19,24,29,34})	
6	14		30-34	=FREQUENCY(A2:A21,{14,19,24,29,34})	
7	14				
8	15				
9	27				
10	21				
11	18				
12	19				
13	18				
14	22				
15	33				
16	16				
17	18				
18	17				
19	23				
20	28				
21	13				
22					

	A	B	C	D	E
1	Audit Time		Audit Time	Frequency	
2	12		10-14	4	
3	15		15-19	8	
4	20		20-24	5	
5	22		25-29	2	
6	14		30-34	1	
7	14				
8	15				
9	27				
10	21				
11	18				
12	19				
13	18				
14	22				
15	33				
16	16				
17	18				
18	17				
19	23				
20	28				
21	13				
22					

Enter Data: The label Audit Time and the data for the 20 audit times have been entered into cells A1:A21.

Enter Functions and Formulas: Descriptive labels have been entered into cells C1 and D1 and the class limits 10–14, 15–19, and so on, have been entered using text format into cells C2:C6. Unlike simple Excel functions, the FREQUENCY function is capable of providing multiple values. In this case, the multiple values are the class frequencies. A formula that can return multiple values is called an array formula and must be entered in a special way. The following steps describe how to create and enter an array formula that uses the FREQUENCY function to calculate the frequencies for the audit time data.

You must hold down Ctrl and Shift while pressing Enter to enter an array formula.

Step 1. Select cells D2:D6, the cells in which we want the frequencies to appear
Step 2. Type the following formula:
　　　=FREQUENCY(A2:A21,{14,19,24,29,34})
Step 3. Press CTRL + SHIFT + ENTER and the array formula will be entered into each of the cells D2:D6

The results are shown in Figure 2.6. Because we entered an array formula into cells D2:D6, the formula that Excel displays in each of these cells is the same. But, the values calculated are not. They are the frequencies for each class (see Table 2.6). The class upper limits in the second argument of the FREQUENCY function (between the braces in step 2) tell Excel which frequency to put in each cell within the range of the array formula. The frequency for the class with an upper limit of 14 is placed in the first cell (D2), the frequency for the class with an upper limit of 19 is placed in the second cell (D3), and so on.

Relative Frequency and Percent Frequency Distributions

We define the relative frequency and percent frequency distributions for quantitative data in the same manner as for qualitative data. First, recall that the relative frequency is simply the proportion of the observations belonging to a class. With n observations,

$$\text{Relative Frequency of Class} = \frac{\text{Frequency of the Class}}{n}$$

The percent frequency of a class is the relative frequency multiplied by 100.

Based on the class frequencies in Table 2.6 and with $n = 20$, Table 2.7 shows the relative frequency distribution and percent frequency distribution for the audit time data. Note that .40 of the audits, or 40%, required from 15 to 19 days. Only .05 of the audits, or 5%, required 30 or more days. Again, additional interpretations and insights can be obtained by using Table 2.7.

Histogram

A common graphical presentation of quantitative data is a **histogram**. This graphical summary can be prepared for data previously summarized in either a frequency, relative frequency, or percent frequency distribution. A histogram is constructed by placing the variable of interest on the horizontal axis and the frequency, relative frequency, or percent frequency on the vertical axis. The frequency, relative frequency, or percent frequency of each class is shown by drawing a rectangle whose base is the class interval on the horizontal axis and whose height is the corresponding frequency, relative frequency, or percent frequency.

TABLE 2.7   RELATIVE AND PERCENT FREQUENCY DISTRIBUTIONS FOR THE AUDIT
TIME DATA

Audit Time (days)	Relative Frequency	Percent Frequency
10–14	.20	20
15–19	.40	40
20–24	.25	25
25–29	.10	10
30–34	.05	5
Total	1.00	100

Figure 2.7 is a histogram for the audit time data. Note that the class with the greatest frequency is shown by the rectangle appearing above the class of 15–19 days. The height of the rectangle shows that the frequency of this class is 8. A histogram for the relative or percent frequency distribution of this data would look the same as the histogram in Figure 2.7 with the exception that the vertical axis would be labeled with relative or percent frequency values.

As Figure 2.7 shows, the adjacent rectangles of a histogram touch one another. Unlike a bar graph, a histogram has no natural separation between the rectangles of adjacent classes. This format is the usual convention for histograms. Because the classes for the audit time data are stated as 10–14, 15–19, 20–24, 25–29, and 30–34, one-unit intervals of 14 to 15, 19 to 20, 24 to 25, and 29 to 30 appear between the classes. These spaces are eliminated by drawing the vertical lines of the histogram halfway between the class limits. The vertical lines separating the classes for the histogram in Figure 2.7 are located at 14.5, 19.5, 24.5, and 29.5. The first class starts at 9.5 and the last class ends at 34.5 to show all classes have a class width of five. This minor adjustment to eliminate the spaces between classes in a histogram helps show that, even though the data are rounded, all values between the lower limit of the first class and the upper limit of the last class are possible.

FIGURE 2.7   HISTOGRAM FOR THE AUDIT TIME DATA

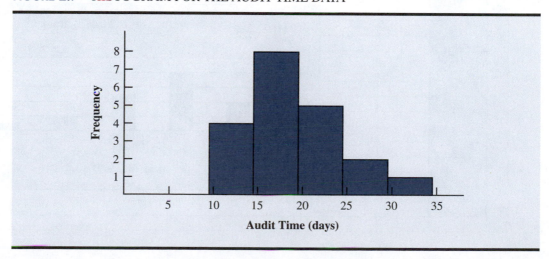

Using Excel's Chart Wizard to Construct a Histogram

We can use Excel's Chart Wizard to construct a histogram for the audit time data. Refer to Figures 2.8 to 2.10 as we describe the tasks involved.

Enter Data: Same as in Figure 2.6.

Enter Functions and Formulas: Same as in Figure 2.6.

Apply Tools: The following steps describe how to use Excel's Chart Wizard to produce a histogram for the audit time data using the frequency distribution appearing in cells C2:D6 of the worksheet shown in Figure 2.8.

Step 1. Select cells C1:D6
Step 2. Click the **Chart Wizard** button on the Standard toolbar (or select the **Insert** menu and choose the **Chart** option)
Step 3. When the **Chart Wizard–Step 1 of 4–Chart Type** dialog box appears:
    Choose **Column** in the **Chart type** list
    Choose **Clustered Column** from the **Chart sub-type** display
    Click **Next >**
Step 4. When the **Chart Wizard–Step 2 of 4–Chart Source Data** dialog box appears:
    Click **Next >**
Step 5. When the **Chart Wizard–Step 3 of 4–Chart Options** dialog box appears:
    Select the **Titles** tab and then
        Type **Histogram for Audit Time Data** in the **Chart title** box

FIGURE 2.8   INITIAL HISTOGRAM CONSTRUCTED USING EXCEL FOR THE AUDIT TIME DATA

	A	B	C	D	E	F	G	H	I	J
1	Audit Time		Audit Time	Frequency						
2	12		10-14	4						
3	15		15-19	8						
4	20		20-24	5						
5	22		25-29	2						
6	14		30-34	1						
7	14									
8	15									
9	27									
10	21									
11	18									
12	19									
13	18									
14	22									
15	33									
16	16									
17	18									
18	17									
19	23									
20	28									
21	13									
22										

> Type **Audit Time in Days** in the **Category (X)** axis box
> Type **Frequency** in the **Value (Y)** axis box
> > Select the **Legend** tab and then
> > > Remove the check in the **Show legend** Box
> > Click **Next >**
> Step 6. When the **Chart Wizard–Step 4 of 4–Chart Location** dialog box appears:
> > Specify a location for the chart (we used the default setting of the current worksheet)
> > Click **Finish**

The worksheet displayed in Figure 2.8 shows the column chart produced by Excel. Note the gaps between the rectangles. Because the adjacent rectangles in a histogram must touch, we need to edit the chart in order to eliminate the gap between each of the rectangles. The following steps describe this process. Refer to Figure 2.9 as we describe the steps.

> Step 1. Right click on any rectangle in the column chart to produce a list of options
> Step 2. Select the **Format Data Series** option
> Step 3. When the **Format Data Series** dialog box appears:
> > Select the **Options** tab and then
> > > Enter **0** in the **Gap width** box
> > > Click **OK**

Figure 2.10 displays the histogram produced by Excel. With the exception of the labels on the horizontal axis, it is the same histogram that we developed earlier in Figure 2.7. The size of the chart can now be adjusted to suit user preference.

Cumulative Distributions

A variation of the frequency distribution that provides another tabular summary of quantitative data is the **cumulative frequency distribution**. The cumulative frequency distribution uses the number of classes, class widths, and class limits that were developed for the frequency distribution. However, rather than showing the frequency of each class, the cumulative frequency distribution shows the number of data items with values *less than or equal to the upper class limit* of each class. The first two columns of Table 2.8 provide the cumulative frequency distribution for the audit time data.

To understand how the cumulative frequencies are determined, consider the class with the description "less than or equal to 24." The cumulative frequency for this class is simply the sum of the frequencies for all classes with data values less than or equal to 24. For the frequency distribution in Table 2.6, the sum of the frequencies for classes 10–14, 15–19, and 20–24 indicates that $4 + 8 + 5 = 17$ data values are less than or equal to 24. Hence, the cumulative frequency for this class is 17. In addition, the cumulative frequency distribution in Table 2.8 shows that four audits were completed in 14 days or less and 19 audits were completed in 29 days or less.

As a final point, we note that a **cumulative relative frequency distribution** shows the proportion of data items, and a **cumulative percent frequency distribution** shows the percentage of data items with values less than or equal to the upper limit of each class. The cumulative relative frequency distribution can be computed either by summing the relative frequencies in the relative frequency distribution or by dividing the cumulative frequencies by the total number of items. Using the latter approach, we found the cumulative relative frequencies in column 3 of Table 2.8 by dividing the cumulative frequencies in column 2 by the total number of items ($n = 20$). The cumulative percent frequencies were again computed by multiplying the relative frequencies by 100. The cumulative relative and percent

FIGURE 2.9   REMOVING THE GAPS BETWEEN CLASSES TO DISPLAY A HISTOGRAM
FOR THE AUDIT TIME DATA

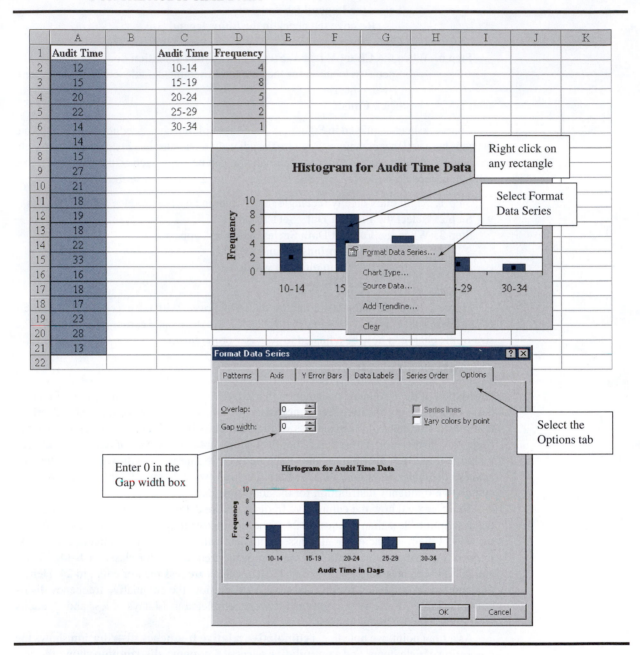

FIGURE 2.10   FINAL HISTOGRAM CONSTRUCTED USING EXCEL FOR THE AUDIT TIME DATA

	A	B	C	D	E	F	G	H	I	J
1	Audit Time		Audit Time	Frequency						
2	12		10-14	4						
3	15		15-19	8						
4	20		20-24	5						
5	22		25-29	2						
6	14		30-34	1						
7	14									
8	15									
9	27									
10	21									
11	18									
12	19									
13	18									
14	22									
15	33									
16	16									
17	18									
18	17									
19	23									
20	28									
21	13									
22										

Histogram for Audit Time Data

frequency distributions show that .85 of the audits, or 85%, were completed in 24 days or less, .95 of the audits, or 95%, were completed in 29 days or less, and so on.

Ogive

A graph of a cumulative distribution is called an **ogive**. The data values are shown on the horizontal axis and either the cumulative frequencies, the cumulative relative frequencies, or the cumulative percent frequencies are shown on the vertical axis. Figure 2.11 is the ogive for the cumulative frequencies of the audit time data in Table 2.8.

TABLE 2.8   CUMULATIVE FREQUENCY, CUMULATIVE RELATIVE FREQUENCY, AND CUMULATIVE PERCENT FREQUENCY DISTRIBUTIONS FOR THE AUDIT TIME DATA

Audit Time (days)	Cumulative Frequency	Cumulative Relative Frequency	Cumulative Percent Frequency
Less than or equal to 14	4	.20	20
Less than or equal to 19	12	.60	60
Less than or equal to 24	17	.85	85
Less than or equal to 29	19	.95	95
Less than or equal to 34	20	1.00	100

FIGURE 2.11   OGIVE FOR THE AUDIT TIME DATA

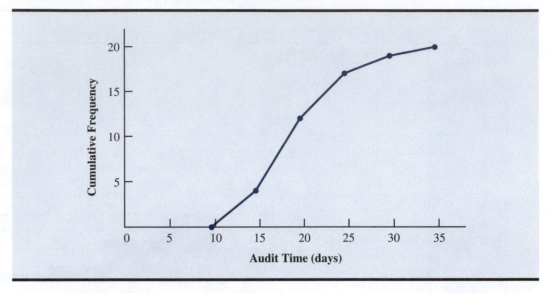

The ogive is constructed by plotting a point corresponding to the cumulative frequency of each class. Because the classes for the audit time data are 10–14, 15–19, 20–24, and so on, one-unit gaps appear from 14 to 15, 19 to 20, and so on. As with the histogram, these gaps are eliminated by plotting points halfway between the class limits. Thus, 14.5 is used for the 10–14 class, 19.5 is used for the 15–19 class, and so on. The "less than or equal to 14" class with a cumulative frequency of 4 is shown on the ogive in Figure 2.11 by the point located at 14.5 on the horizontal axis and 4 on the vertical axis. The "less than or equal to 19" class with a cumulative frequency of 12 is shown by the point located at 19.5 on the horizontal axis and 12 on the vertical axis. Note that one additional point is plotted at the left end of the ogive. This point starts the ogive by showing that no data values fall below the 10–14 class. It is plotted at 9.5 on the horizontal axis and 0 on the vertical axis. The plotted points are connected by straight lines to complete the ogive.

NOTES AND COMMENTS

1. A bar graph and a histogram are essentially the same thing; both are graphical presentations of the data in a frequency distribution. A histogram is just a bar graph with no separation between bars. The separation between bars is appropriate for qualitative data because the data are discrete; no intermediate values are possible. For some quantitative data, a separation between bars is appropriate. Consider, for example, the number of classes in which a college student is enrolled. The data may only assume integer values. Intermediate values such as 1.5, 2.73, and so on are not possible. With continuous quantitative data, such as the audit times in Table 2.5, a separation between bars is not appropriate.

2. The appropriate values for the class limits with quantitative data depend on the level of accuracy of the data. For instance, with the audit time data of Table 2.5 the limits used were integer values because the data had been rounded to the nearest day. If the data were rounded to the nearest tenth of a day (e.g., 12.3, 14.4, and so on), then the limits would have been stated in tenths of days. For instance, the first class would have been 10.0–14.9. If the data were rounded to the nearest hundredth of a day (e.g., 12.34, 14.45, and so on), the limits would have been stated in hundredths of days. For instance, the first class would have been 10.00–14.99.

3. An *open-end* class is one that has only a lower class limit or an upper class limit. For example, in the audit time data of Table 2.5, suppose two of the audits had taken 58 and 65 days. Rather than continue with the classes of width 5 with classes 35–39, 40–44, 45–49, and so on, we could simplify the frequency distribution to show an open-end class of "35 or more." This class would have a frequency of 2. Most often the open-end class appears at the upper end of the distribution. Sometimes an open-end class appears at the lower end of the distribution, and occasionally such classes appear at both ends.

4. The last entry in a cumulative frequency distribution is always the total number of observations. The last entry in a cumulative relative frequency distribution is always 1.00 and the last entry in a cumulative percent frequency distribution is always 100.

5. In addition to the FREQUENCY function to construct a frequency distribution for quantitative data, and the Chart Wizard for constructing a histogram, Excel has a Histogram tool in its Data Analysis add-in. It can be used to construct both a frequency distribution and a histogram in one series of steps. We show how it can be used to construct a frequency distribution and histogram for the audit time data in Appendix 2.1. We note there the advantages and disadvantages to the use of this tool. Other tools in the Data Analysis add-in will be introduced in Chapter 3.

EXERCISES

Methods

11. Consider the following data.

14	21	23	21	16
19	22	25	16	16
24	24	25	19	16
19	18	19	21	12
16	17	18	23	25
20	23	16	20	19
24	26	15	22	24
20	22	24	22	20

  a. Develop a frequency distribution using classes of 12–14, 15–17, 18–20, 21–23, and 24–26.

  b. Develop a relative frequency distribution and a percent frequency distribution using the classes in part (a).

12. Consider the following frequency distribution.

Class	Frequency
10–19	10
20–29	14
30–39	17
40–49	7
50–59	2

Construct a cumulative frequency distribution and a cumulative relative frequency distribution.

13. Construct a histogram and an ogive for the data in Exercise 12.

14. Consider the following data.

8.9	10.2	11.5	7.8	10.0	12.2	13.5	14.1	10.0	12.2
6.8	9.5	11.5	11.2	14.9	7.5	10.0	6.0	15.8	11.5

a. Construct a frequency distribution.
b. Construct a percent frequency distribution.

Applications

15. A doctor's office staff studied the waiting times for patients who arrive at the office with a request for emergency service. The following data were collected over a one-month period (the waiting times are in minutes).

2	5	10	12	4	4	5	17	11	8	9	8	12	21	6	8	7	13	18	3

Use classes of 0–4, 5–9, and so on in the following:
a. Show the frequency distribution.
b. Show the relative frequency distribution.
c. Show the cumulative frequency distribution.
d. Show the cumulative relative frequency distribution.
e. What proportion of patients needing emergency service wait 9 minutes or less?

16. A sample of 25 computer hardware companies taken from the *Stock Invester Pro* database is shown in Table 2.9.
a. Develop tabular summaries and a histogram for the stock price data. Comment on typical stock prices and the distribution of stock prices.
b. Develop tabular summaries and a histogram for the earnings per share data. Comment on your results.

17. Mendelsohn Media Research provided survey data on the annual amount of household purchases by families with an annual income of $75,000 or more (*Money*, 2001). Assume that the following data from a sample of 25 households show the dollars spent in the past year on books and magazines.

280	496	382	202	287
266	119	10	385	135
475	255	379	267	24
42	25	283	110	423
160	123	16	243	363

a. Construct a frequency distribution and relative frequency distribution for the data.
b. Provide a histogram.
c. Comment on the annual spending on books and magazines for families in the sample.

18. Wageweb conducts surveys of salary data and presents summaries on its Web site. Using salary data as of January 1, 2000, Wageweb reported that salaries of marketing vice presidents ranged from $85,090 to $190,054 (*Wageweb.com*, April 12, 2000). Assume the following data are a sample of the annual salaries for 50 marketing vice presidents. Data are in thousands of dollars.

145	95	148	112	132
140	162	118	170	144
145	127	148	165	138
173	113	104	141	142
116	178	123	141	138
127	143	134	136	137
155	93	102	154	142
134	165	123	124	124
138	160	157	138	131
114	135	151	138	157

TABLE 2.9   DATA SET FOR 25 COMPUTER HARDWARE COMPANIES

Stocks

Company	Stock Price	Institutional Ownership (%)	Price/Book Value	Earnings per Share (Annual $)
Amdahl	12.31	45.4	2.49	−2.49
Auspex Systems	11.00	66.1	2.22	0.85
Compaq Computer	65.50	83.0	6.84	2.01
Data General	35.94	91.5	4.25	1.15
Digi International	15.00	33.4	2.04	−0.89
Digital Equipment Corp.	43.00	58.8	1.92	−2.93
En Pointe Technologies	14.25	11.8	3.47	0.80
Equitrac	16.25	20.9	2.38	0.76
Franklin Electronic Pbls.	12.88	30.8	1.41	0.82
Gateway 2000	39.13	36.0	6.45	1.74
Hewlett-Packard	61.50	50.2	4.35	2.64
Ingram Micro	28.75	14.4	4.53	1.01
Maxwell Technologies	30.50	26.5	8.07	0.46
MicroAge	27.19	76.6	2.16	1.25
Micron Electronics	16.31	18.8	4.48	1.06
Network Computing Devices	11.88	39.8	3.34	0.15
Pomeroy Computer Resource	33.00	56.9	3.29	1.81
Sequent Computer Systems	28.19	57.0	2.65	0.36
Silicon Graphics	27.44	63.0	3.01	0.44
Southern Electronics	15.13	41.9	2.46	0.99
Stratus Computer	55.50	77.2	2.48	2.52
Sun Microsystems	48.00	59.3	7.50	1.67
Tandem Computers	34.25	61.3	3.61	1.02
Tech Data	38.94	82.3	3.80	1.50
Unisys	11.31	34.8	16.64	0.08

Source: Stock Investor Pro, American Association of Individual Investors, August 31, 1997.

a. What are the lowest and highest salaries?
b. Use a class width of $15,000 and prepare tabular summaries of the annual salary data.
c. What proportion of the annual salaries are $135,000 or less?
d. What percentage of the annual salaries are more than $150,000?
e. Prepare a histogram.

19. The data for the numbers of units produced by a production employee during the most recent 20 days are shown here.

160	170	181	156	176
148	198	179	162	150
162	156	179	178	151
157	154	179	148	156

Summarize the data by constructing the following:
a. A frequency distribution
b. A relative frequency distribution
c. A cumulative frequency distribution
d. A cumulative relative frequency distribution
e. An ogive

20. The U.S. Census Bureau publishes a variety of information on the U.S. population. Shown here is the percent frequency distribution of the U.S. population by age as of July 1, 2000 (*The World Almanac and Book of Facts 2000*).

Age	Percent Frequency
0–13	20.0
14–17	5.7
18–24	9.6
25–34	13.6
35–44	16.3
45–54	13.5
55–64	8.7
65 or over	12.6
	100.0

a. What percentage of the population is 34 years old or younger?
b. What percentage of the population is older than 34 years old?
c. What percentage of the population is between 25 and 54 years old inclusively?
d. The total population is 275 million. How many people are younger than 25 years old?
e. Suppose you believe that half the people in the 55–64 class are retired and that approximately all of the people 65 or older are retired. Estimate the number of retired people in the population.

Computer

21. The *Nielsen Home Technology Report* provided information about home technology and its usage by persons aged 12 and older. The following data are the hours of personal computer usage during one week for a sample of 50 persons.

4.1	1.5	10.4	5.9	3.4	5.7	1.6	6.1	3.0	3.7
3.1	4.8	2.0	14.8	5.4	4.2	3.9	4.1	11.1	3.5
4.1	4.1	8.8	5.6	4.3	3.3	7.1	10.3	6.2	7.6
10.8	2.8	9.5	12.9	12.1	0.7	4.0	9.2	4.4	5.7
7.2	6.1	5.7	5.9	4.7	3.9	3.7	3.1	6.1	3.1

Summarize the data by constructing the following:
a. A frequency distribution (use a class width of three hours)
b. A relative frequency distribution
c. A histogram
d. An ogive
e. Comment on what the data indicate about personal computer usage at home.

2.3   EXPLORATORY DATA ANALYSIS: THE STEM-AND-LEAF DISPLAY

The techniques of **exploratory data analysis** consist of simple arithmetic and easy-to-draw graphs that can be used to summarize data quickly. One technique—referred to as a **stem-and-leaf display**—can be used to show both the rank order and shape of a data set simultaneously.

To illustrate the use of a stem-and-leaf display, consider the data in Table 2.10. These data are the result of a 150-question aptitude test given to 50 individuals who were recently interviewed for a position at Haskens Manufacturing. The data values indicate the number of questions answered correctly.

TABLE 2.10   NUMBER OF QUESTIONS ANSWERED CORRECTLY ON AN APTITUDE TEST

ApTest

112	72	69	97	107
73	92	76	86	73
126	128	118	127	124
82	104	132	134	83
92	108	96	100	92
115	76	91	102	81
95	141	81	80	106
84	119	113	98	75
68	98	115	106	95
100	85	94	106	119

To develop a stem-and-leaf display, we first arrange the leading digits of each data value to the left of a vertical line. To the right of the vertical line, we record the last digit for each data value as we pass through the observations in the order they were recorded. The last digit for each data value is placed on the line corresponding to its first digit as follows:

```
 6 | 9  8
 7 | 2  3  6  3  6  5
 8 | 6  2  3  1  1  0  4  5
 9 | 7  2  2  6  2  1  5  8  8  5  4
10 | 7  4  8  0  2  6  6  0  6
11 | 2  8  5  9  3  5  9
12 | 6  8  7  4
13 | 2  4
14 | 1
```

With this organization of the data, sorting the digits on each line into rank order is simple. Doing so leads to the stem-and-leaf display shown here.

```
 6 | 8  9
 7 | 2  3  3  5  6  6
 8 | 0  1  1  2  3  4  5  6
 9 | 1  2  2  2  4  5  5  6  7  8  8
10 | 0  0  2  4  6  6  6  7  8
11 | 2  3  5  5  8  9  9
12 | 4  6  7  8
13 | 2  4
14 | 1
```

The numbers to the left of the vertical line (6, 7, 8, 9, 10, 11, 12, 13, and 14) form the *stem,* and each digit to the right of the vertical line is a *leaf.* For example, consider the first row with a stem value of 6 and leaves of 8 and 9.

$$6 \mid 8 \quad 9$$

It indicates that two data values have a first digit of six. The leaves show that the data values are 68 and 69. Similarly, the second row

$$7 \mid 2 \quad 3 \quad 3 \quad 5 \quad 6 \quad 6$$

indicates that six data values have a first digit of seven. The leaves show that the data values are 72, 73, 73, 75, 76, and 76.

To focus on the shape indicated by the stem-and-leaf display, let us use a rectangle to contain the leaves of each stem. Doing so, we obtain the following.

```
 6 | 8  9
 7 | 2  3  3  5  6  6
 8 | 0  1  1  2  3  4  5  6
 9 | 1  2  2  2  4  5  5  6  7  8  8
10 | 0  0  2  4  6  6  6  7  8
11 | 2  3  5  5  8  9  9
12 | 4  6  7  8
13 | 2  4
14 | 1
```

Rotating this page counterclockwise onto its side provides a picture of the data that is similar to a histogram with classes of 60–69, 70–79, 80–89, and so on.

Although the stem-and-leaf display may appear to offer the same information as a histogram, it has two primary advantages.

1. The stem-and-leaf display is easier to construct by hand.
2. Within a class interval, the stem-and-leaf display provides more information than the histogram because the stem-and-leaf shows the actual data values.

In a stretched stem-and-leaf display, whenever a stem value is stated twice, the first value corresponds to leaf values of 0–4, and the second value corresponds to leaf values of 5–9.

Just as a frequency distribution or histogram has no absolute number of classes, neither does a stem-and-leaf display have an absolute number of rows or stems. If we believe that our original stem-and-leaf display has condensed the data too much, we can easily stretch the display by using two or more stems for each leading digit. For example, to use two stems for each leading digit, we would place all data values ending in 0, 1, 2, 3, and 4 in one row and all values ending in 5, 6, 7, 8, and 9 in a second row. The following stretched stem-and-leaf display illustrates this approach.

```
 6 | 8  9
 7 | 2  3  3
 7 | 5  6  6
 8 | 0  1  1  2  3  4
 8 | 5  6
 9 | 1  2  2  2  4
 9 | 5  5  6  7  8  8
10 | 0  0  2  4
10 | 6  6  6  7  8
11 | 2  3
11 | 5  5  8  9  9
12 | 4
12 | 6  7  8
13 | 2  4
13 |
14 | 1
```

Note that values 72, 73, and 73 have leaves in the 0–4 range and are shown with the first stem value of 7. The values 75, 76, and 76 have leaves in the 5–9 range and are shown with the second stem value of 7. This stretched stem-and-leaf display is similar to a frequency distribution with intervals of 65–69, 70–74, 75–79, and so on.

The preceding example showed a stem-and-leaf display for data having up to three digits. Stem-and-leaf displays for data with more than three digits are possible. For example, consider the following data on the number of hamburgers sold by a fast-food restaurant for each of 15 weeks.

| 1565 | 1852 | 1644 | 1766 | 1888 | 1912 | 2044 | 1812 |
| 1790 | 1679 | 2008 | 1852 | 1967 | 1954 | 1733 | |

A stem-and-leaf display of these data follows.

Leaf Unit = 10

```
15 | 6
16 | 4  7
17 | 3  6  9
18 | 1  5  5  8
19 | 1  5  6
20 | 0  4
```

A single digit is used to define each leaf in a stem-and-leaf display. The leaf unit indicates how to multiply the stem-and-leaf numbers in order to approximate the original data. Leaf units may be 100, 10, 1, 0.1, and so on.

Note that a single digit is used to define each leaf and that only the first three digits of each observation have been used to construct the display. At the top of the display we have specified Leaf Unit = 10. To illustrate how to interpret the values in the display, consider the first stem, 15, and its associated leaf, 6. Combining these numbers, we obtain 156. To reconstruct an approximation of the original observation, we must multiply this number by 10, the value of the *leaf unit*. Thus, $156 \times 10 = 1560$ is an approximation of the original observation used to construct the stem-and-leaf display. Although it is not possible to reconstruct the exact data from this stem-and-leaf display, the convention of using a single digit for each leaf enables stem-and-leaf displays to be constructed for data having a large number of digits. For stem-and-leaf displays where the leaf unit is not shown, the leaf unit is assumed to equal 1.

EXERCISES

Methods

22. Construct a stem-and-leaf display for the following data.

70	72	75	64	58	83	80	82
76	75	68	65	57	78	85	72

23. Construct a stem-and-leaf display for the following data.

11.3	9.6	10.4	7.5	8.3	10.5	10.0
9.3	8.1	7.7	7.5	8.4	6.3	8.8

24. Construct a stem-and-leaf display for the following data. Use a leaf unit of 10.

1161	1206	1478	1300	1604	1725	1361	1422
1221	1378	1623	1426	1557	1730	1706	1689

Applications

25. A psychologist developed a new test of adult intelligence. The test was administered to 20 individuals, and the following data were obtained.

114	99	131	124	117	102	106	127	119	115
98	104	144	151	132	106	125	122	118	118

Construct a stem-and-leaf display for the data.

26. The earnings per share data for a sample of 20 companies from the *Business Week* Corporate Scoreboard follow (*Business Week*, November 17, 1997):

Company	Earnings per Share ($)	Company	Earnings per Share ($)
Barnes & Noble	0.78	Hershey Foods	1.97
Citicorp	7.10	Hewlett-Packard	2.82
Compaq Computer	2.16	Humana	0.89
Dana	3.42	Microsoft	2.66
Dell Computer	2.03	Procter & Gamble	2.53
Digital Equipment	1.28	Quaker State	0.41
General Dynamics	4.82	Sara Lee	2.08
Goodyear	0.94	Snap-On Tools	2.38
Harley-Davidson	1.11	Sunstrand	2.53
Heinz	0.98	Xerox	3.95

Develop a stem-and-leaf display for the data. Use a leaf unit of 0.1. Comment on what you learned about the earnings per share for these companies.

27. In a study of job satisfaction, a series of tests was administered to 50 subjects. The following data were obtained; higher scores represent greater dissatisfaction.

JobSat

87	76	67	58	92	59	41	50	90	75	80	81	70
73	69	61	88	46	85	97	50	47	81	87	75	60
65	92	77	71	70	74	53	43	61	89	84	83	70
46	84	76	78	64	69	76	78	67	74	64		

Construct a stem-and-leaf display for the data.

28. Periodically *Barron's* publishes earnings forecasts for the companies listed in the Dow Jones Industrial Average. The following are the 2000 forecasts of price/earnings (P/E) ratios for these companies implied by *Barron's* earnings forecasts (*Barron's*, February 14, 2000).

PEforecast

Company	2000 P/E Forecast	Company	2000 P/E Forecast
AT&T	23	Honeywell	13
Alcoa	15	IBM	28
American Express	25	Intel	37
Boeing	16	International Paper	14
Caterpillar	13	Johnson & Johnson	23
Citigroup	17	McDonald's	23
Coca-Cola	39	Merck	25
Disney	47	Microsoft	60
Dupont	18	Minnesota Mining	19
Eastman Kodak	11	J. P. Morgan	11
Exxon/Mobil	22	Philip Morris	5
General Electric	37	Procter & Gamble	26
General Motors	8	SBC Comm.	19
Hewlett-Packard	36	United Technologies	14
Home Depot	48	Wal-Mart	40

a. Develop a stem-and-leaf display for the data.
b. Use the results of the stem-and-leaf display to develop a frequency distribution and percent frequency distribution.

2.4   CROSSTABULATIONS AND SCATTER DIAGRAMS

Crosstabulations and scatter diagrams are used to summarize data in a way that reveals the relationship between two variables.

Thus far in this chapter, we focused on tabular and graphical methods used to summarize the data for *one variable at a time*. Often a manager or decision maker is interested in tabular and graphical methods that will assist in the understanding of the *relationship between two variables*. Crosstabulation and scatter diagrams are two such methods.

Crosstabulation

A **crosstabulation** is a tabular summary of data for two variables. Let us illustrate the use of a crosstabulation by considering the following application. Zagat's Restaurant Review is a service that provides data on restaurants located throughout the world. Data on a variety of variables such as the restaurant's quality rating and typical meal price are reported. Quality rating is a qualitative variable with rating categories of good, very good, and excellent. Meal price is a quantitative variable that generally ranges from $10 to $49. The quality rating and the meal price data were collected for a sample of 300 restaurants located in the Los Angeles area. Table 2.11 shows the data for the first 10 restaurants.

TABLE 2.11   QUALITY RATING AND MEAL PRICE FOR 300 LOS ANGELES RESTAURANTS

Restaurant

Restaurant	Quality Rating	Meal Price ($)
1	Good	18
2	Very Good	22
3	Good	28
4	Excellent	38
5	Very Good	33
6	Good	28
7	Very Good	19
8	Very Good	11
9	Very Good	23
10	Good	13
.	.	.
.	.	.
.	.	.

A crosstabulation of the data for this application is shown in Table 2.12. The left and top margin labels define the classes for the two variables. In the left margin, the row labels (good, very good, and excellent) correspond to the three classes of the quality rating variable. In the top margin, the column labels ($10–19, $20–29, $30–39, and $40–49) correspond to the four classes of the meal price variable. Each restaurant in the sample provides a quality rating and a meal price. Thus, each restaurant in the sample is associated with a cell appearing in one of the rows and one of the columns of the crosstabulation. For example, restaurant 5 is identified as having a very good quality rating and a meal price of $33. This restaurant belongs to the cell in row 2 and column 3 of Table 2.12. In constructing a crosstabulation, we simply count the number of restaurants that belong to each of the cells in the crosstabulation table.

In reviewing Table 2.12, we see that the greatest number of restaurants in the sample (64) have a very good rating and a meal price in the $20–29 range. Only two restaurants have an excellent rating and a meal price in the $10–19 range. Similar interpretations of the other frequencies can be made. In addition, note that the right and bottom margins of the crosstabulation provide the frequency distributions for quality rating and meal price separately. From the frequency distribution in the right margin, we see that data on quality ratings show 84 good restaurants, 150 very good restaurants, and 66 excellent restaurants. Similarly, the bottom margin shows the frequency distribution for the meal price variable.

TABLE 2.12   CROSSTABULATION OF QUALITY RATING AND MEAL PRICE FOR 300 LOS ANGELES RESTAURANTS

Quality Rating	Meal Price $10–19	$20–29	$30–39	$40–49	Total
Good	42	40	2	0	84
Very Good	34	64	46	6	150
Excellent	2	14	28	22	66
Total	78	118	76	28	300

The value of a crosstabulation is that it provides insight about the relationship between the variables. From the results in Table 2.12, higher meal prices appear to be associated with the higher quality restaurants and the lower meal prices appear to be associated with the lower quality restaurants.

Converting the entries in the table into row percentages or column percentages can afford additional insight about the relationship between the variables. For row percentages, the results of dividing each frequency in Table 2.12 by its corresponding row total are shown in Table 2.13. For example, the percentage in the first row and first column, 50.0, is calculated by dividing 42 by 84 and multiplying by 100 ($42/84 \times 100 = 50.0\%$). Of the restaurants with the lowest (good) quality rating, we see that the greatest percentages are for the less expensive restaurants (50.0% have \$10–19 meal prices and 47.6% have \$20–29 meal prices). Of the restaurants with the highest (excellent) quality rating, we see that the greatest percentages are for the more expensive restaurants (42.4% have \$30–39 meal prices and 33.4% have \$40–49 meal prices). Thus, we continue to see that the more expensive meals are associated with the higher quality restaurants.

Crosstabulation is widely used for examining the relationship between two variables. In practice, final reports for many statistical surveys include a large number of crosstabulation tables. In the Los Angeles restaurant sample, the crosstabulation is based on one qualitative variable (quality rating) and one quantitative variable (meal price). Crosstabulations can also be developed when both variables are qualitative and when both variables are quantitative.

Using Excel's PivotTable Report to Construct a Crosstabulation

Excel's PivotTable Report provides a general tool for summarizing the data for two or more variables simultaneously. We will illustrate the use of Excel's PivotTable Report by showing how to develop a crosstabulation of quality ratings and meal prices for the sample of 300 restaurants located in the Los Angeles area.

Enter Data: The labels "Restaurant," "Quality Rating," and "Meal Price (\$)" have been entered into cells A1:C1 of the worksheet shown in Figure 2.12. The data for each of the 300 restaurants in the sample has been entered into cells B2:C301.

Enter Functions and Formulas: No functions and formulas are needed.

Apply Tools: The crosstabulation shown in Table 2.12 has three rows under the heading Quality Rating, corresponding to the three quality categories, Good, Very Good, and Excellent. Unless we specify differently, the PivotTable Report will order the labels alphabetically causing the quality ratings to be listed in the order Excellent, Good, and Very Good. Because we want the quality ratings in the order Good, Very Good, Excellent, we must change the default order for the PivotTable Report. The following steps will do so:

Step 1. Select the **Tools** menu
Step 2. Choose **Options**

TABLE 2.13   ROW PERCENTAGES FOR EACH QUALITY RATING CATEGORY

	Meal Price				
Quality Rating	\$10–19	\$20–29	\$30–39	\$40–49	Total
Good	50.0	47.6	2.4	0.0	100
Very Good	22.7	42.7	30.6	4.0	100
Excellent	3.0	21.2	42.4	33.4	100

FIGURE 2.12   EXCEL WORKSHEET CONTAINING RESTAURANT DATA

CD file

Restaurant

Note: Rows 12–291 are hidden.

	A	B	C	D
1	Restaurant	Quality Rating	Meal Price ($)	
2	1	Good	18	
3	2	Very Good	22	
4	3	Good	28	
5	4	Excellent	38	
6	5	Very Good	33	
7	6	Good	28	
8	7	Very Good	19	
9	8	Very Good	11	
10	9	Very Good	23	
11	10	Good	13	
292	291	Very Good	23	
293	292	Very Good	24	
294	293	Excellent	45	
295	294	Good	14	
296	295	Good	18	
297	296	Good	17	
298	297	Good	16	
299	298	Good	15	
300	299	Very Good	38	
301	300	Very Good	31	
302				

Step 3. When the Options dialog box appears (see Figure 2.13):
Select the **Custom Lists** tab
In the **List entries:** box, type **Good** and press Enter; type **Very Good** and press Enter; and type **Excellent**
Click **Add**
Click **OK**

We are now ready to use the PivotTable Report to construct a crosstabulation of the data for quality rating and meal price. Starting with the worksheet in Figure 2.12, the following steps are necessary:

Step 1. Select the **Data** menu
Step 2. Choose **PivotTable and PivotChart Report**
Step 3. When the **PivotTable and PivotChart Wizard–Step 1 of 3** dialog box appears:
Choose **Microsoft Excel list or database**
Choose **PivotTable**
Click **Next >**
Step 4. When the **PivotTable and PivotChart Wizard–Step 2 of 3** dialog box appears:
Enter A1:C301 in the **Range:** box
Click **Next >**
Step 5. When the **PivotTable and PivotChart Wizard–Step 3 of 3** dialog box appears:
Select **New Worksheet**
Click **Layout**

FIGURE 2.13   DIALOG BOX FOR CHANGING SORT ORDER IN EXCEL

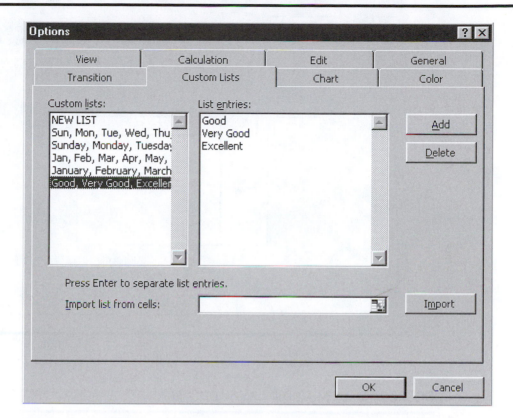

When the **PivotTable and PivotChart Wizard–Layout** diagram appears (See Figure 2.14):

Drag the **Quality Rating** field button to the **ROW** section of the diagram

Drag the **Meal Price ($)** field button to the **COLUMN** section of the diagram

Drag the **Restaurant** field button to the **DATA** section of the diagram

Double click the **Sum of Restaurant** field button in the data section

When the **PivotTable Field** dialog box appears:

Choose **Count** under **Summarize by:**

Click **OK** (Figure 2.15 shows the completed layout diagram)

Click **OK**

When the **PivotTable and PivotChart Wizard–Step 3 of 3** dialog box reappears:

Click **Finish>**

A portion of the output generated by Excel is shown in Figure 2.16. Note that the output that appears in columns D through AK has been hidden so the results can be shown in a reasonably sized figure. The row labels (Good, Very Good, and Excellent) and row totals (84, 150, 66, and 300) that appear in Figure 2.16 are the same as the row labels and row totals shown in Table 2.12. But, in Figure 2.16, one column is designated for each possible

FIGURE 2.14 PivotTable AND PivotChart WIZARD-LAYOUT DIAGRAM

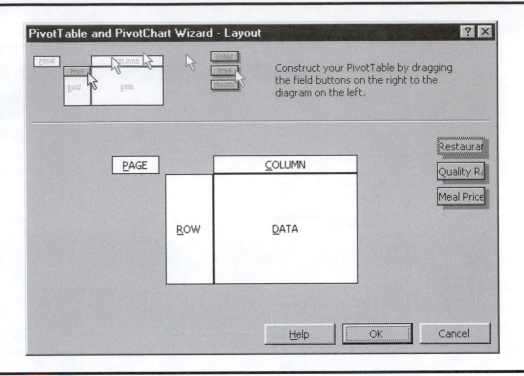

FIGURE 2.15 COMPLETED LAYOUT DIAGRAM

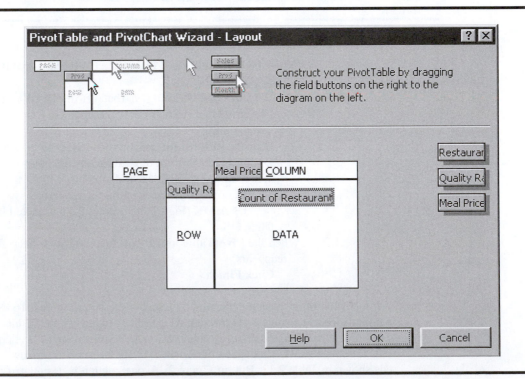

FIGURE 2.16   INITIAL PivotTable REPORT OUTPUT (COLUMNS D:AK ARE HIDDEN.)

	A	B	C	AL	AM	AN	AO
1							
2							
3	Count of Restaurant	Meal Price ($) ▾					
4	Quality Rating ▾	10	11	47	48	Grand Total	
5	Good	6	4			84	
6	Very Good	1	4		1	150	
7	Excellent			2	2	66	
8	Grand Total	7	8	2	3	300	
9							
10							

value of meal price. For example, column B contains a count of restaurants with a $10 meal price, column C contains a count of restaurants with an $11 meal price, and so on. To view the PivotTable Report in a form similar to that shown in Table 2.12, we must group the columns into four price categories: $10–19, $20–29, $30–39, and $40–49. The steps necessary to group the columns for the worksheet shown in Figure 2.16 follow.

*In Excel 2002 **Group and Outline** is replaced by **Group and Show Detail**.*

Step 1. Right click on Meal Price ($) in cell B3 to produce a list of options

Step 2. Choose the **Group and Outline** option and then choose **Group** from the list that appears

Step 3. When the **Grouping** dialog box appears
  Check **Starting at:** and type 10 in the corresponding box
  Check **Ending at:** and type 49 in the corresponding box
  Type 10 in the **By** box
  Click **OK**

The revised PivotTable output is shown in Figure 2.17. It is the final PivotTable. Note that it provides the same information as the crosstabulation shown in Table 2.12.

FIGURE 2.17   FINAL PivotTable REPORT FOR RESTAURANT DATA

	A	B	C	D	E	F	G
1							
2							
3	Count of Restaurant	Meal Price ($) ▾					
4	Quality Rating ▾	10-19	20-29	30-39	40-49	Grand Total	
5	Good	42	40	2		84	
6	Very Good	34	64	46	6	150	
7	Excellent	2	14	28	22	66	
8	Grand Total	78	118	76	28	300	
9							
10							

Scatter Diagram and Trendline

A **scatter diagram** is a graphical presentation of the relationship between two quantitative variables, and a **trendline** is a line that provides an approximation of the relationship. As an illustration, consider the advertising/sales relationship for a stereo and sound equipment store in San Francisco. On 10 occasions during the past three months, the store used weekend television commercials to promote sales at its stores. The managers want to investigate whether a relationship exists between the number of commercials shown and sales at the store during the following week. Sample data for the 10 weeks with sales in hundreds of dollars are shown in Table 2.14.

Figure 2.18 shows the scatter diagram and the trendline* for the data in Table 2.14. The number of commercials (x) is shown on the horizontal axis and the sales (y) are shown on the vertical axis. For week 1, $x = 2$ and $y = 50$. A point with those coordinates is plotted on the scatter diagram. Similar points are plotted for the other nine weeks. Note that during two of the weeks one commercial was shown, on two of the weeks two commercials were shown, and so on.

The completed scatter diagram in Figure 2.18 indicates a positive relationship between the number of commercials and sales. Higher sales are associated with a higher number of commercials. The relationship is not perfect in that all points are not on a straight line. However, the general pattern of the points and the trendline suggest that the overall relationship is positive.

Some general scatter diagram patterns and the types of relationships they suggest are shown in Figure 2.19. The top left panel depicts a positive relationship similar to the one for the number of commercials and sales example. In the top right panel, the scatter diagram shows no apparent relationship between the variables. The bottom panel depicts a negative relationship where y tends to decrease as x increases.

Using Excel's Chart Wizard to Construct a Scatter Diagram and a Trendline

We can use Excel's Chart Wizard to construct a scatter diagram and a trendline for the stereo and sound equipment store data. Refer to Figures 2.20 and 2.21 as we describe the tasks involved.

TABLE 2.14 SAMPLE DATA FOR THE STEREO AND SOUND EQUIPMENT STORE

Week	Number of Commercials x	Sales ($100s) y
1	2	50
2	5	57
3	1	41
4	3	54
5	4	54
6	1	38
7	5	63
8	3	48
9	4	59
10	2	46

*The equation of the trendline is $y = 4.95x + 36.15$. The slope of the trendline is 4.95 and the y-intercept (the point where the line intersects the y axis) is 36.15. We will discuss in detail the interpretation of the slope and y-intercept for a linear trendline in Chapter 12 when we study simple linear regression.

FIGURE 2.18   SCATTER DIAGRAM AND TRENDLINE FOR THE STEREO AND SOUND EQUIPMENT STORE

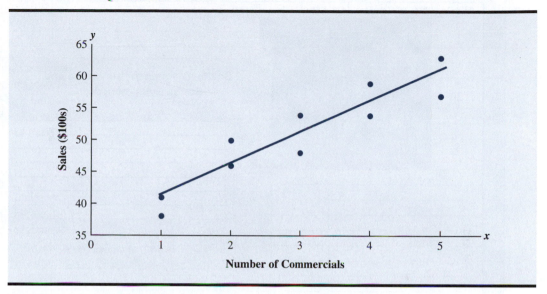

FIGURE 2.19   TYPES OF RELATIONSHIPS DEPICTED BY SCATTER DIAGRAMS

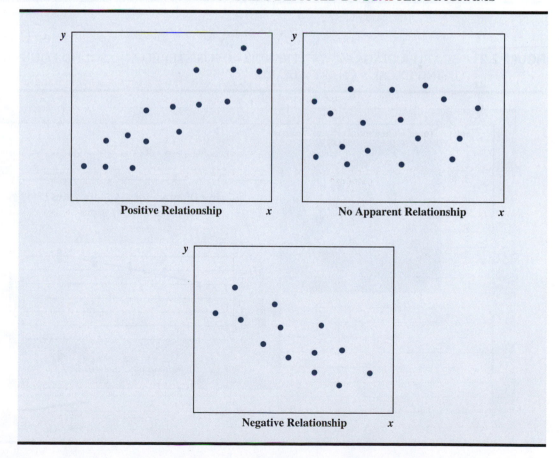

FIGURE 2.20 SCATTER DIAGRAM FOR STEREO AND SOUND EQUIPMENT STORE USING EXCEL'S CHART WIZARD

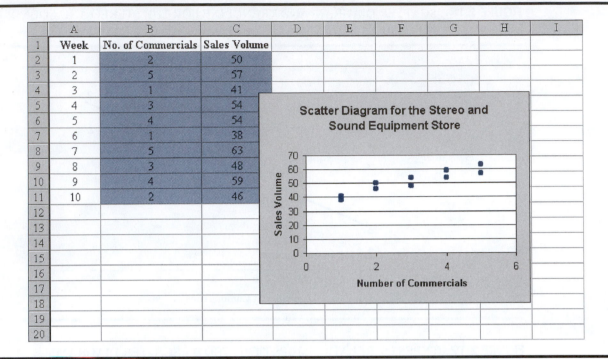

FIGURE 2.21 SCATTER DIAGRAM AND TRENDLINE FOR STEREO AND SOUND EQUIPMENT STORE USING EXCEL'S CHART WIZARD

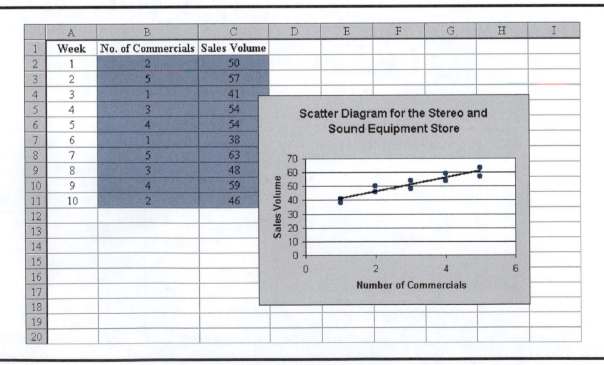

Enter Data: Appropriate labels and the sample data have been entered into cells A1:C11 of the worksheet shown in Figure 2.20.

Enter Functions and Formulas: No functions and formulas are needed.

Apply Tools: The following steps describe how to use Excel's Chart Wizard to produce a scatter diagram from the data in the worksheet.

Step 1. Select cells B1:C11

Step 2. Click the **Chart Wizard** button on the standard toolbar (or select the **Insert** menu and choose the **Chart** option)

Step 3. When the **Chart Wizard–Step 1 of 4–Chart Type** dialog box appears:
   Choose **XY (Scatter)** in the **Chart type** list
   Choose **Scatter** from the **Chart sub-type** display
   Click **Next >**

Step 4. When the **Chart Wizard–Step 2 of 4–Chart Source Data** dialog box appears:
   Click **Next >**

Step 5. When the **Chart Wizard–Step 3 of 4–Chart Options** dialog box appears:
   Select the **Titles** tab and then
     Type **Scatter Diagram for the Stereo and Sound Equipment Store**
      in the **Chart title:** box
     Type **Number of Commercials** in the **Value (X) axis:** box
     Type **Sales Volume** in the **Value (Y) axis:** box
   Select the **Legend** tab and then
     Remove the check in the **Show legend** box
     Click **Next >**

Step 6. When the **Chart Wizard–Step 4 of 4–Chart Location** dialog box appears:
   Specify a location for the chart (we used the default setting of the current worksheet)
   Click **Finish**

The worksheet displayed in Figure 2.20 shows the scatter diagram produced by Excel. (We enlarged the scatter diagram slightly.) The following steps describe how to add a trendline.

Step 1. Position the mouse pointer over any data point in the scatter diagram and right click to display a list of options

Step 2. Choose **Add Trendline**

Step 3. When the Add Trendline dialog box appears:
   Select the **Type** tab and then
     Choose **Linear** from the **Trend/Regression type** display
     Click **OK**

The worksheet displayed in Figure 2.21 shows the scatter diagram with the trendline added.

EXERCISES

Methods

29. The following data are for 30 observations on two qualitative variables, x and y. The categories for x are A, B, and C; the categories for y are 1 and 2.

Crosstab

Observation	x	y	Observation	x	y
1	A	1	16	B	2
2	B	1	17	C	1
3	B	1	18	B	1
4	C	2	19	C	1
5	B	1	20	B	1
6	C	2	21	C	2
7	B	1	22	B	1
8	C	2	23	C	2
9	A	1	24	A	1
10	B	1	25	B	1
11	A	1	26	C	2
12	B	1	27	C	2
13	C	2	28	A	1
14	C	2	29	B	1
15	C	2	30	B	2

a. Develop a crosstabulation for the data, with x in the rows and y in the columns.
b. Compute the row percentages.
c. Compute column percentages.
d. What is the relationship, if any, between x and y?

30. The following 20 observations are for two quantitative variables, x and y.

Scatter

Observation	x	y	Observation	x	y
1	−22	22	11	−37	48
2	−33	49	12	34	−29
3	2	8	13	9	−18
4	29	−16	14	−33	31
5	−13	10	15	20	−16
6	21	−28	16	−3	14
7	−13	27	17	−15	18
8	−23	35	18	12	17
9	14	−5	19	−20	−11
10	3	−3	20	−7	−22

a. Develop a scatter diagram for the relationship between x and y.
b. What is the relationship, if any, between x and y?

Applications

31. Compute column percentages for the restaurant data in Table 2.12. What is the relationship between quality rating and meal price?

32. Table 2.15 provides financial data for a sample of 36 companies whose stock is traded on the New York Stock Exchange (*Investor's Business Daily*, April 7, 2000). The data on Sales/Margins/ROE is a composite rating based on a company's sales growth rate, its profit margins, and its return on equity (ROE). EPS Rating is a measure of growth in earnings per share for the company.
    a. Prepare a crosstabulation of the data on Sales/Margins/ROE (rows) and EPS Rating (columns). Use classes of 0–19, 20–39, 40–59, 60–79, and 80–99 for EPS Rating.
    b. Compute row percentages and comment on any relationship between the variables.

TABLE 2.15   FINANCIAL DATA FOR A SAMPLE OF 36 COMPANIES

CD file

IBD

Company	EPS Rating	Relative Price Strength	Industry Group Relative Strength	Sales/Margins/ ROE
Advo	81	74	B	A
Alaska AirGp	58	17	C	B
Alliant Tech	84	22	B	B
Atmos Engy	21	9	C	E
Bank of Am.	87	38	C	A
Bowater PLC	14	46	C	D
Callaway Golf	46	62	B	E
Central Parking	76	18	B	C
Dean Foods	84	7	B	C
Dole Food	70	54	E	C
Elec. Data Sys	72	69	A	B
Fed. Dept. Stor.	79	21	D	B
Gateway	82	68	A	A
Goodyear	21	9	E	D
Hanson PLC	57	32	B	B
ICN Pharm.	76	56	A	D
Jefferson plt	80	38	D	C
Kroger	84	24	D	A
Mattel	18	20	E	D
McDermott	6	6	A	C
Monaco	97	21	D	A
Murphy Oil	80	62	B	B
Nordstrom	58	57	B	C
NYMAGIC	17	45	D	D
Office Depot	58	40	B	B
Payless Shoes	76	59	B	B
Praxair	62	32	C	B
Reebok	31	72	C	E
Safeway	91	61	D	A
Teco Energy	49	48	D	B
Texaco	80	31	D	C
US West	60	65	B	A
United Rental	98	12	C	A
Wachovia	69	36	E	B
Winnebago	83	49	D	A
York Intl.	28	14	D	B

Source: Investor's Business Daily, April 7, 2000.

33. Refer to the data in Table 2.15.
   a. Prepare a crosstabulation of the data on Sales/Margins/ROE and Industry Group Relative Strength.
   b. Prepare a frequency distribution for the data on Sales/Margins/ROE.
   c. Prepare a frequency distribution for the data on Industry Group Relative Strength.
   d. How has the crosstabulation helped in preparing the frequency distributions in parts (b) and (c)?

34. Refer to the data in Table 2.15.
   a. Prepare a scatter diagram of the data on EPS Rating and Relative Price Strength.
   b. Comment on the relationship, if any, between the variables. (The meaning of the EPS Rating is described in Exercise 32. Relative Price Strength is a measure of the change in the stock's price over the past 12 months. Higher values indicate greater strength.)

35. The National Football League rates prospects position by position on a scale that ranges from 5 to 9. The ratings are interpreted as follows: 8–9 should start the first year; 7.0–9.0 should start; 6.0–6.9 will make the team as a backup; and 5.0–5.9 can make the club and contribute. The following table shows the position, weight, speed (seconds for 40 yards), and ratings for 40 NFL prospects (*USA Today*, April 14, 2000).

NFL

Observation	Name	Position	Weight	Speed	Rating
1	Peter Warrick	Wide receiver	194	4.53	9
2	Plaxico Burress	Wide receiver	231	4.52	8.8
3	Sylvester Morris	Wide receiver	216	4.59	8.3
4	Travis Taylor	Wide receiver	199	4.36	8.1
5	Laveranues Coles	Wide receiver	192	4.29	8
6	Dez White	Wide receiver	218	4.49	7.9
7	Jerry Porter	Wide receiver	221	4.55	7.4
8	Ron Dugans	Wide receiver	206	4.47	7.1
9	Todd Pinkston	Wide receiver	169	4.37	7
10	Dennis Northcutt	Wide receiver	175	4.43	7
11	Anthony Lucas	Wide receiver	194	4.51	6.9
12	Darrell Jackson	Wide receiver	197	4.56	6.6
13	Danny Farmer	Wide receiver	217	4.6	6.5
14	Sherrod Gideon	Wide receiver	173	4.57	6.4
15	Trevor Gaylor	Wide receiver	199	4.57	6.2
16	Cosey Coleman	Guard	322	5.38	7.4
17	Travis Claridge	Guard	303	5.18	7
18	Kaulana Noa	Guard	317	5.34	6.8
19	Leander Jordan	Guard	330	5.46	6.7
20	Chad Clifton	Guard	334	5.18	6.3
21	Manula Savea	Guard	308	5.32	6.1
22	Ryan Johanningmeir	Guard	310	5.28	6
23	Mark Tauscher	Guard	318	5.37	6
24	Blaine Saipaia	Guard	321	5.25	6
25	Richard Mercier	Guard	295	5.34	5.8
26	Damion McIntosh	Guard	328	5.31	5.3
27	Jeno James	Guard	320	5.64	5
28	Al Jackson	Guard	304	5.2	5
29	Chris Samuels	Offensive tackle	325	4.95	8.5
30	Stockar McDougle	Offensive tackle	361	5.5	8
31	Chris McIngosh	Offensive tackle	315	5.39	7.8
32	Adrian Klemm	Offensive tackle	307	4.98	7.6
33	Todd Wade	Offensive tackle	326	5.2	7.3
34	Marvel Smith	Offensive tackle	320	5.36	7.1
35	Michael Thompson	Offensive tackle	287	5.05	6.8
36	Bobby Williams	Offensive tackle	332	5.26	6.8
37	Darnell Alford	Offensive tackle	334	5.55	6.4
38	Terrance Beadles	Offensive tackle	312	5.15	6.3
39	Tutan Reyes	Offensive tackle	299	5.35	6.1
40	Greg Robinson-Ran	Offensive tackle	333	5.59	6

a. Prepare a crosstabulation of the data on Position (rows) and Speed (columns). Use classes of 4.00–4.49, 4.50–4.99, 5.00–5.49, and 5.50–5.99 for speed.

b. Comment on the relationship between Position and Speed based upon the crosstabulation developed in part (a).

c. Develop a scatter diagram of the data on Speed and Rating. Use the vertical axis for Rating.

d. Comment on the relationship, if any, between Speed and Rating.

SUMMARY

A set of data, even if modest in size, is often difficult to interpret directly in the form in which it is gathered. Tabular and graphical methods provide procedures for organizing and summarizing data so that patterns are revealed and the data are more easily interpreted. Frequency distributions, relative frequency distributions, percent frequency distributions, bar graphs, and pie charts were presented as tabular and graphical procedures for summarizing qualitative data. Frequency distributions, relative frequency distributions, percent frequency distributions, histograms, cumulative frequency distributions, cumulative relative frequency distributions, cumulative percent frequency distributions, and ogives were presented as ways of summarizing quantitative data. A stem-and-leaf display provides an exploratory data analysis technique that can be used to summarize quantitative data. Crosstabulation was presented as a tabular method for summarizing data for two variables. The scatter diagram was introduced as a graphical method for showing the relationship between two quantitative variables. Figure 2.22 shows the tabular and graphical methods presented in this chapter.

For most of the statistical methods introduced, we showed how they can be implemented using Excel. The COUNTIF and FREQUENCY functions can be used to construct frequency distributions for a single variable, and the PivotTable Report can be used to prepare a

FIGURE 2.22   TABULAR AND GRAPHICAL METHODS FOR SUMMARIZING DATA

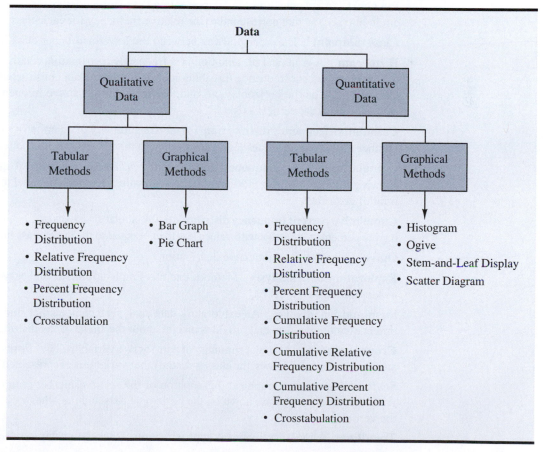

crosstabulation for a two-variable data set. The Chart Wizard provides extensive graphical presentations. We showed how it can be used to construct bar graphs, pie charts, histograms, and scatter diagrams. In the chapter appendix, we show how to use the Histogram tool as an alternative for constructing a frequency distribution and histogram for quantitative data.

If you have trouble recalling which Excel function to use in a particular situation, or have difficulty using a function, Excel's Insert Function Dialog Box has been designed to provide help. We describe how to use it in Appendix E: Using Excel Functions.

GLOSSARY

Qualitative data   Labels or names used to identify categories of like items.

Quantitative data   Numerical values that indicate how much or how many.

Frequency distribution   A tabular summary of data showing the number (frequency) of items in each of several nonoverlapping classes.

Relative frequency distribution   A tabular summary of data showing the fraction or proportion of data items in each of several nonoverlapping classes.

Percent frequency distribution   A tabular summary of data showing the percentage of items in each of several nonoverlapping classes.

Bar graph   A graphical device for depicting qualitative data that have been summarized in a frequency, relative frequency, or percent frequency distribution.

Pie chart   A graphical device for presenting data summaries based on subdivision of a circle into sectors that correspond to the relative frequency for each class.

Class midpoint   The value halfway between the lower and upper class limits.

Histogram   A graphical presentation of a frequency distribution, relative frequency distribution, or percent frequency distribution of quantitative data constructed by placing the class intervals on the horizontal axis and the frequencies, relative frequencies, or percent frequencies on the vertical axis.

Cumulative frequency distribution   A tabular summary of quantitative data showing the number of items with values less than or equal to the upper class limit of each class.

Cumulative relative frequency distribution   A tabular summary of quantitative data showing the fraction or proportion of items with values less than or equal to the upper class limit of each class.

Cumulative percent frequency distribution   A tabular summary of quantitative data showing the percentage of items with values less than or equal to the upper class limit of each class.

Ogive   A graph of a cumulative distribution.

Exploratory data analysis   Methods that use simple arithmetic and easy-to-draw graphs to summarize data quickly.

Stem-and-leaf display   An exploratory data analysis technique that simultaneously rank orders quantitative data and provides insight about the shape of the distribution.

Crosstabulation   A tabular summary of data for two variables. The classes for one variable are represented by the rows; the classes for the other variable are represented by the columns.

Scatter diagram   A graphical presentation of the relationship between two quantitative variables. One variable is shown on the horizontal axis and the other variable is shown on the vertical axis.

Trendline   A line that provides an approximation of the relationship between two variables.

KEY FORMULAS

Relative Frequency

$$\frac{\text{Frequency of the Class}}{n} \tag{2.1}$$

Approximate Class Width

$$\frac{\text{Largest Data Value} - \text{Smallest Data Value}}{\text{Number of Classes}} \tag{2.2}$$

SUPPLEMENTARY EXERCISES

36. *Autodata* and *USA Today* research provided data on the best-selling vehicle models for March 2000 (*USA Today*, April 4, 2000). Among those listed were Chevrolet Silverado/C/K pickup, Ford F-Series pickup, Ford Taurus, Honda Accord, and Toyota Camry. Data from a sample of 50 vehicle purchases are presented in Table 2.16.

TABLE 2.16   DATA FOR 50 VEHICLE PURCHASES

Vehicles

Silverado	Taurus	Accord	F-Series	Silverado
F-Series	Accord	Silverado	Camry	Taurus
Silverado	F-Series	Camry	Silverado	F-Series
Taurus	F-Series	Taurus	F-Series	Camry
Taurus	F-Series	F-Series	Accord	Camry
Silverado	Silverado	Silverado	Silverado	Taurus
Camry	Silverado	Accord	F-Series	F-Series
Taurus	F-Series	Accord	Camry	Accord
F-Series	Silverado	F-Series	F-Series	Taurus
Camry	Silverado	F-Series	F-Series	F-Series

a. Develop a frequency and percent frequency distribution.
b. What are the two top-selling vehicles?
c. Show a pie chart.

37. Each of the *Fortune* 1000 companies belongs to one of several industry classifications (*Fortune*, April 17, 2000). A sample of 20 companies with their corresponding industry classification follows.

Company	Industry Classification	Company	Industry Classification
IBP	Food	Borden	Food
Intel	Electronics	McDonnell Douglas	Aerospace
Coca-Cola	Beverage	Morton International	Chemicals
Union Carbide	Chemicals	Quaker Oats	Food
General Electric	Electronics	PepsiCo	Beverage
Motorola	Electronics	Maytag	Electronics
Kellogg	Food	Textron	Aerospace
Dow Chemical	Chemicals	Sara Lee	Food
Campbell Soup	Food	Harris	Electronics
Ralston Purina	Food	Eaton	Electronics

a.   Provide a frequency distribution showing the number of companies in each industry.
b.   Provide a percent frequency distribution.
c.   Provide a bar graph for the data.

38. *Golf Magazine*'s Top 100 Teachers were asked the question, "What is the most critical area that prevents golfers from reaching their potential?" The possible responses were lack of accuracy, poor approach shots, poor mental approach, lack of power, limited practice, poor putting, poor short game, and poor strategic decisions. The data obtained follow (*Golf Magazine*, February 2002):

Golf

Mental approach	Mental approach	Short game	Short game	Short game
Practice	Accuracy	Mental approach	Accuracy	Putting
Power	Approach shots	Accuracy	Short game	Putting
Accuracy	Mental approach	Mental approach	Accuracy	Power
Accuracy	Accuracy	Short game	Power	Short game
Accuracy	Putting	Mental approach	Strategic decisions	Accuracy
Short game	Power	Mental approach	Approach shots	Short game
Practice	Practice	Mental approach	Power	Power
Mental approach	Short game	Mental approach	Short game	Strategic decisions
Accuracy	Short game	Accuracy	Mental approach	Short game
Mental approach	Putting	Mental approach	Mental approach	Putting
Practice	Putting	Practice	Short game	Putting
Power	Mental approach	Short game	Practice	Strategic decisions
Accuracy	Short game	Accuracy	Practice	Putting
Accuracy	Short game	Accuracy	Short game	Putting
Accuracy	Approach shots	Short game	Mental approach	Practice
Short game	Short game	Strategic decisions	Short game	Short game
Practice	Practice	Short game	Practice	Strategic decisions
Mental approach	Strategic decisions	Strategic decisions	Power	Short game
Accuracy	Practice	Practice	Practice	Accuracy

a.   Develop a frequency and percent frequency distribution.
b.   Which four critical areas most often prevent golfers from reaching their potential?

39. The data in Table 2.17 represent sales in millions of dollars for 20 companies in the health care services industry during the third quarter of 1997 (*Business Week*, November 17, 1997).
a.   Construct a frequency distribution to summarize the data. Use a class width of 500.
b.   Develop a relative frequency distribution.
c.   Construct a cumulative frequency distribution.

TABLE 2.17   SALES IN HEALTH CARE SERVICES FOR THE THIRD QUARTER, 1997

Beverly Ent.	805	Novacare	357
Coventry	307	Phycor	284
Express Scripts	320	Quest Diag.	374
Healthsouth	748	Quorum Health	393
Horizon	445	Sun Healthcare	486
Humana	1968	Tenet Healthcare	2331
Int. Health	472	U. Wisconsin	389
Lab. Corp. Am.	377	Univ. Health	362
Manor Care	274	Vencor	845
Medpartners	1614	Wellpoint	1512

Source: Business Week, November 17, 1997.

      d.   Construct a cumulative relative frequency distribution.

      e.   Construct a histogram as a graphical representation of the data.

40. The closing prices of 40 common stocks follow (*Barron's*, September 3, 2001).

Comstock

29.63	34.00	43.25	8.75	37.88	8.63	7.63	30.38	35.25	19.38
9.25	16.50	38.00	53.38	16.63	1.25	48.38	18.00	9.38	9.25
10.00	25.02	18.00	8.00	28.50	24.25	21.63	18.50	33.63	31.13
32.25	29.63	79.38	11.38	38.88	11.50	52.00	14.00	9.00	33.50

      a.   Construct frequency and relative frequency distributions.

      b.   Construct cumulative frequency and cumulative relative frequency distributions.

      c.   Construct a histogram.

      d.   Using your summaries, make comments and observations about the price of common stock.

41. Ninety-four new shadow stocks were reported by the American Association of Individual Investors (*AAII Journal*, February 1997). The term *shadow* indicates stocks for small to medium-sized firms not followed closely by the major brokerage houses. Information on where the stock was traded—New York Stock Exchange (NYSE), American Stock Exchange (AMEX), and over-the-counter (OTC)—the earnings per share, and the price/earnings ratio was provided for the following sample of 20 shadow stocks.

Shadow

Stock	Exchange	Earnings per Share ($)	Price/ Earnings Ratio
Chemi-Trol	OTC	.39	27.30
Candie's	OTC	.07	36.20
TST/Impreso	OTC	.65	12.70
Unimed Pharm.	OTC	.12	59.30
Skyline Chili	AMEX	.34	19.30
Cyanotech	OTC	.22	29.30
Catalina Light.	NYSE	.15	33.20
DDL Elect.	NYSE	.10	10.20
Euphonix	OTC	.09	49.70
Mesa Labs	OTC	.37	14.40
RCM Tech.	OTC	.47	18.60
Anuhco	AMEX	.70	11.40
Hello Direct	OTC	.23	21.10
Hilite Industries	OTC	.61	7.80
Alpha Tech.	OTC	.11	34.60
Wegener Group	OTC	.16	24.50
U.S. Home & Garden	OTC	.24	8.70
Chalone Wine	OTC	.27	44.40
Eng. Support Sys.	OTC	.89	16.70
Int. Remote Imaging	AMEX	.86	4.70

      a.   Provide frequency and relative frequency distributions for the exchange data. Where are most shadow stocks listed?

      b.   Provide frequency and relative frequency distributions for the earnings per share and price/earnings ratio data. Use classes of 0.00–0.19, 0.20–0.39, and so on, for the earnings per share data and classes of 0.0–9.9, 10.0–19.9, and so on for the price/ earnings ratio data. What observations and comments can you make about the shadow stocks?

42. A state-by-state listing of per capita personal income for 1998 follows (Bureau of Economic Analysis, *Current Population Survey*, March 2000).

Income

Ala.	21,500	Ky.	21,551	N.D.	21,708
Alaska	25,771	La.	21,385	Ohio	25,239
Ariz.	23,152	Maine	23,002	Okla.	21,056
Ark.	20,393	Md.	30,023	Ore.	24,775
Calif.	27,579	Mass.	32,902	Penn.	26,889
Colo.	28,821	Mich.	25,979	R.I.	26,924
Conn.	37,700	Minn.	27,667	S.C.	21,387
Del.	29,932	Miss.	18,998	S.D.	22,201
D.C.	37,325	Mo.	24,447	Tenn.	23,615
Fla.	25,922	Mont.	20,427	Texas	25,028
Ga.	25,106	Neb.	24,786	Utah	21,096
Hawaii	26,210	Nev.	27,360	Vt.	24,217
Idaho	21,080	N.H.	29,219	Va.	27,489
Ill.	28,976	N.J.	33,953	Wash.	28,066
Ind.	24,302	N.M.	20,008	W. Va.	19,373
Iowa	24,007	N.Y.	31,679	Wis.	25,184
Kan.	25,049	N.C.	24,122	Wyo.	23,225

Develop a frequency distribution, a relative frequency distribution, and a histogram.

43. The conclusion from a 40-state poll conducted by the Joint Council on Economic Education is that students do not learn enough economics. The findings were based on test results from 11th- and 12th-grade students who took a 46-question, multiple-choice test on basic economic concepts such as profit and the law of supply and demand. The following table gives sample data on the number of questions answered correctly.

12	10	16	24	12	14	18	23
31	14	15	19	17	9	19	28
24	16	21	13	20	12	22	18
22	18	30	16	26	18	16	14
8	25	22	15	33	24	17	19

Summarize these data using the following:
a. Stem-and-leaf display
b. Frequency distribution
c. Relative frequency distribution
d. Cumulative frequency distribution
e. On the basis of these data, do you agree with the claim that students are not learning enough economics? Explain.

44. The daily high and low temperatures for 20 cities follow (*USA Today*, May 9, 2000).

HighLow

City	High	Low	City	High	Low
Athens	75	54	Havana	86	68
Bangkok	92	74	Hong Kong	81	72
Cairo	84	57	Johannesburg	61	50
Copenhagen	64	39	London	73	48
Dublin	64	46	Manila	93	75

City	High	Low	City	High	Low
Melbourne	66	50	Seoul	64	50
Montreal	64	52	Singapore	90	75
Paris	77	55	Sydney	68	55
Rio de Janeiro	80	61	Tokyo	79	59
Rome	81	54	Vancouver	57	43

   a. Prepare a stem-and-leaf display for the high temperatures.
   b. Prepare a stem-and-leaf display for the low temperatures.
   c. Compare the stem-and-leaf displays from parts (a) and (b), and make some comments about the differences between daily high and low temperatures.
   d. Use the stem-and-leaf display from part (a) to determine the number of cities having a high temperature of 80 degrees or above.
   e. Provide frequency distributions for both high and low temperature data.

45. Refer to the data set for high and low temperatures for 20 cities in Exercise 44.
   a. Develop a scatter diagram to show the relationship between the two variables, high temperature and low temperature.
   b. Comment on the relationship between high and low temperature.

46. A study of job satisfaction was conducted for four occupations. Job satisfaction was measured using an 18-item questionnaire with each question receiving a response score of 1 to 5 with higher scores indicating greater satisfaction. The sum of the 18 scores provides the job satisfaction score for each individual in the sample. The data are as follow.

CD file

OccupSat

Occupation	Satisfaction Score	Occupation	Satisfaction Score	Occupation	Satisfaction Score
Lawyer	42	Physical Therapist	78	Systems Analyst	60
Physical Therapist	86	Systems Analyst	44	Physical Therapist	59
Lawyer	42	Systems Analyst	71	Cabinetmaker	78
Systems Analyst	55	Lawyer	50	Physical Therapist	60
Lawyer	38	Lawyer	48	Physical Therapist	50
Cabinetmaker	79	Cabinetmaker	69	Cabinetmaker	79
Lawyer	44	Physical Therapist	80	Systems Analyst	62
Systems Analyst	41	Systems Analyst	64	Lawyer	45
Physical Therapist	55	Physical Therapist	55	Cabinetmaker	84
Systems Analyst	66	Cabinetmaker	64	Physical Therapist	62
Lawyer	53	Cabinetmaker	59	Systems Analyst	73
Cabinetmaker	65	Cabinetmaker	54	Cabinetmaker	60
Lawyer	74	Systems Analyst	76	Lawyer	64
Physical Therapist	52				

   a. Provide a crosstabulation of occupation and job satisfaction score.
   b. Compute the row percentages for your crosstabulation in part (a).
   c. What observations can you make concerning the level of job satisfaction for these occupations?

47. Do larger companies generate more revenue? The following data show the number of employees and annual revenue for a sample of 20 *Fortune* 1000 companies (*Fortune*, April 17, 2000).

RevEmps

Company	Employees	Revenue ($ millions)	Company	Employees	Revenue ($ millions)
Sprint	77,600	19,930	American Financial	9,400	3,334
Chase Manhattan	74,801	33,710	Fluor	53,561	12,417
Computer Sciences	50,000	7,660	Phillips Petroleum	15,900	13,852
Wells Fargo	89,355	21,795	Cardinal Health	36,000	25,034
Sunbeam	12,200	2,398	Borders Group	23,500	2,999
CBS	29,000	7,510	MCI Worldcom	77,000	37,120
Time Warner	69,722	27,333	Consolidated Edison	14,269	7,491
Steelcase	16,200	2,743	IBP	45,000	14,075
Georgia-Pacific	57,000	17,796	Super Value	50,000	17,421
Toro	1,275	4,673	H&R Block	4,200	1,669

a. Prepare a scatter diagram to show the relationship between the variables Revenue and Employees.
b. Comment on any relationship between the variables.

48. A survey of commercial buildings served by the Cincinnati Gas & Electric Company was concluded in 1992 (CG&E Commercial Building Characteristics Survey, November 25, 1992). One question asked what main heating fuel was used and another asked the year the commercial building was constructed. A partial crosstabulation of the findings follows.

Year Constructed	Fuel Type				
	Electricity	Natural Gas	Oil	Propane	Other
1973 or before	40	183	12	5	7
1974–1979	24	26	2	2	0
1980–1986	37	38	1	0	6
1987–1991	48	70	2	0	1

a. Complete the crosstabulation by showing the row totals and column totals.
b. Show the frequency distributions for year constructed and for fuel type.
c. Prepare a crosstabulation showing column percentages.
d. Prepare a crosstabulation showing row percentages.
e. Comment on the relationship between year constructed and fuel type.

49. Table 2.18 contains a portion of the data on the file named Fortune on the CD ROM at the back of the book. It provides data on stockholders' equity, market value, and profits for a sample of 50 *Fortune* 500 companies (*Fortune*, April 26, 1999).
a. Prepare a crosstabulation for the variables Stockholders' Equity and Profit. Use classes of 0–200, 200–400, . . . ,1000–1200 for Profit, and classes of 0–1200, 1200–2400, . . . , 4800–6000 for Stockholders' Equity.
b. Compute the row percentages for your crosstabulation in part (a)
c. What relationship, if any, do you notice between Profit and Stockholders' Equity?

TABLE 2.18   DATA FOR A SAMPLE OF 50 *FORTUNE* 500 COMPANIES

Fortune

Company	Stockholders' Equity ($1000s)	Market Value ($1000s)	Profit ($1000s)
AGCO	982.1	372.1	60.6
AMP	2698.0	12017.6	2.0
Apple Computer	1642.0	4605.0	309.0
Baxter International	2839.0	21743.0	315.0
Bergen Brunswick	629.1	2787.5	3.1
Best Buy	557.7	10376.5	94.5
Charles Schwab	1429.0	35340.6	348.5
.	.	.	.
.	.	.	.
.	.	.	.
Walgreen	2849.0	30324.7	511.0
Westvaco	2246.4	2225.6	132.0
Whirlpool	2001.0	3729.4	325.0
Xerox	5544.0	35603.7	395.0

50. Refer to the data set in Table 2.18.
   a. Prepare a crosstabulation for the variables Market Value and Profit.
   b. Compute the row percentages for your crosstabulation in part (a).
   c. Comment on any relationship between the variables.

51. Refer to the data set in Table 2.18.
   a. Prepare a scatter diagram to show the relationship between the variables Profit and Stockholders' Equity.
   b. Comment on any relationship between the variables.

52. Refer to the data set in Table 2.18.
   a. Prepare a scatter diagram to show the relationship between the variables Market Value and Stockholders' Equity.
   b. Comment on any relationship between the variables.

Case Problem   CONSOLIDATED FOODS

Consolidated Foods operates a chain of supermarkets in New Mexico, Arizona, and California. A promotional campaign advertised the chain's credit card policy offering its customers the option of paying for their purchases with credit cards, such as Visa and MasterCard, in addition to the usual options of cash or personal check. The policy is being implemented on a trial basis with the hope that the credit card option will encourage customers to make larger purchases.

After the first month of operation, a random sample of 100 customers was selected over a one-week period. Data were collected on the method of payment and how much was spent by each of the 100 customers. A portion of the sample data are shown in Table 2.19. Prior to the new credit card policy, approximately 50% of Consolidated Foods' customers paid in cash and approximately 50% paid by personal check.

TABLE 2.19 PURCHASE AMOUNT AND METHOD OF PAYMENT FOR A SAMPLE
OF 100 CONSOLIDATED FOODS CUSTOMERS

Consolid

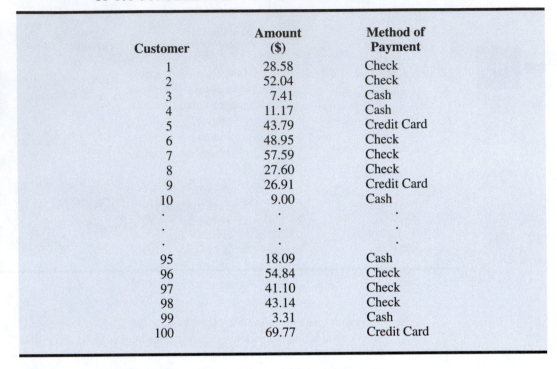

Customer	Amount ($)	Method of Payment
1	28.58	Check
2	52.04	Check
3	7.41	Cash
4	11.17	Cash
5	43.79	Credit Card
6	48.95	Check
7	57.59	Check
8	27.60	Check
9	26.91	Credit Card
10	9.00	Cash
.	.	.
.	.	.
.	.	.
95	18.09	Cash
96	54.84	Check
97	41.10	Check
98	43.14	Check
99	3.31	Cash
100	69.77	Credit Card

Managerial Report

Use the tabular and graphical methods of descriptive statistics to summarize the sample data
in the data set named Consolid. Your report should contain summaries such as the following.

1. A frequency and relative frequency distribution for the method of payment.
2. A bar graph or pie chart for the method of payment.
3. Frequency and relative frequency distributions for the amount spent in each method
   of payment.
4. Histograms and/or stem-and-leaf plots for the amount spent in each method of
   payment.
5. A crosstabulation for the variables method of payment and amount spent.

What preliminary insights do you have about the amounts spent and method of payment at
Consolidated Foods?

Appendix 2.1   USING EXCEL'S HISTOGRAM TOOL TO CONSTRUCT
A FREQUENCY DISTRIBUTION AND HISTOGRAM

In illustrating how to use Excel to summarize quantitative data, we used the FREQUENCY
function to construct a frequency distribution and the Chart Wizard to construct a histogram. Microsoft Excel also provides a set of data analysis tools that can be accessed through
the Tools pull-down menu. The data analysis tool for constructing frequency distributions
and histograms is the Histogram tool. It can save steps when both a frequency distribution

and a histogram are desired. Here we show how it is used by constructing a frequency distribution and a histogram for the audit time data in Table 2.5. As we did in section 2.2, we will use five classes, each with a width of five days.

Enter Data: The label Audit Time and the data for the 20 audit times have been entered into cells A1:A21 of the worksheet shown in Figure 2.23.

Enter Functions and Formulas: No functions and formulas are needed.

Apply Tools: Excel's Histogram tool requires the identification of what are called *bins* for each class in the frequency distribution using the class upper limits. Hence, five bins with upper limits of 14, 19, 24, 29, and 34 are needed for the audit time data. The bin upper limits must be entered in ascending order in a column or row of the worksheet. We have entered the bin upper limits into cells C10:C14 and the label Audit Time into cell C9 of the worksheet in Figure 2.23.

Note: If the **Data Analysis** *option does not appear when you select the* **Tools** *menu, choose* **Add-Ins**, *and check* **Analysis ToolPak** *to install it.*

The following steps describe how to use the Histogram tool to produce a frequency distribution and a histogram consisting of five classes, or bins, for the audit time data.

Step 1. Select the **Tools** menu
Step 2. Choose the **Data Analysis** option
Step 3. Choose **Histogram** from the list of Analysis Tools

FIGURE 2.23   WORKSHEET FOR AUDIT TIME DATA AFTER CREATING BINS USING CLASS UPPER LIMITS

	A	B	C	D
1	**Audit Time**			
2	12			
3	15			
4	20			
5	22			
6	14			
7	14			
8	15			
9	27		**Audit Time**	
10	21		14	
11	18		19	
12	19		24	
13	18		29	
14	22		34	
15	33			
16	16			
17	18			
18	17			
19	23			
20	28			
21	13			
22				

Step 4. When the **Histogram** dialog box appears (see Figure 2.24):

>>>Enter A1:A21 in the **Input Range** box
>>>Enter C9:C14 in the **Bin Range** box
>>>Select **Labels**
>>>Select **Output Range**
>>>Enter C1 in the **Output Range** box (it tells Excel where to display the frequency distribution)
>>>Select **Chart Output** (to request a histogram)
>>>Click **OK**

The worksheet shown in Figure 2.25 displays the frequency distribution and the histogram created using these steps. The frequency distribution is displayed in cells C1:D6. Note that Excel added a row to the frequency distribution with a label of "More" in order to provide for the possibility that we might have entered too few bin values. You can simply delete this row. Also, the histogram produced using the Histogram tool contains gaps between the rectangles. We encountered this same situation when using the Chart Wizard to construct a histogram. We can remove the gaps the same way we did then (see Figure 2.9).

As we have just seen, the Histogram tool can be used to construct both a frequency distribution and histogram in one series of steps. In the chapter, we showed how to use the FREQUENCY function and the Chart Wizard to accomplish the same thing. The advantage of using the FREQUENCY function and Chart Wizard is that the results remain linked to the data. Thus, a change in the data will prompt an automatic update of the frequency distribution and histogram. With the Histogram tool, the results are not linked to the data so a change in the data requires that we reconstruct the frequency distribution and histogram.

FIGURE 2.24   DIALOG BOX FOR HISTOGRAM TOOL

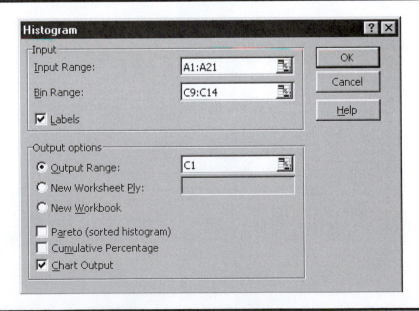

FIGURE 2.25   FREQUENCY DISTRIBUTION AND HISTOGRAM CONSTRUCTED USING HISTOGRAM TOOL

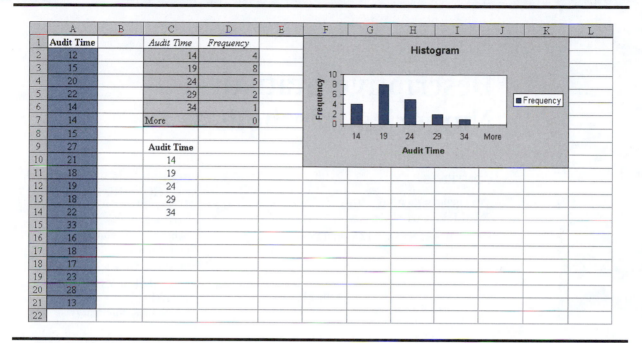

CHAPTER 3

Descriptive Statistics: Numerical Methods

CONTENTS

Small Fry Design*

SANTA ANA, CALIFORNIA

Founded in 1997, Small Fry Design is a toy and accessory company that designs and imports products for infants. The company's product line includes teddy bears, mobiles, musical toys, rattles, and security blankets, and features high-quality soft toy designs with an emphasis on color, texture, and sound. The products are designed in the United States and manufactured in China.

Small Fry Design uses independent representatives to sell the products to infant furnishing retailers, children's accessory and apparel stores, gift shops, upscale department stores, and major catalog companies. Currently, Small Fry Design products are distributed in more than 1000 retail outlets throughout the United States.

Cash flow management is one of the most critical activities in the day-to-day operation of this company. Ensuring sufficient incoming cash to meet both current and ongoing debt obligations can mean the difference between business success and failure. A critical factor in cash flow management is the analysis and control of accounts receivable. By measuring the average age and dollar value of outstanding invoices, management can predict cash availability and monitor changes in the status of accounts receivable. The company set the following goals: the average age for outstanding invoices should not exceed 45 days, and the dollar value of invoices more than 60 days old should not exceed 5% of the dollar value of all accounts receivable.

In a recent summary of accounts receivable status, the following descriptive statistics were provided for the age of outstanding invoices:

Some of the Small Fry Design products. © Photo courtesy of Small Fry Design.

Mean	40 days
Median	35 days
Mode	31 days

Interpretation of these statistics shows that the mean or average age of an invoice is 40 days. The median shows that half of the invoices have been outstanding 35 days or more. The mode of 31 days is the most frequent invoice age indicating that the most common length of time an invoice has been outstanding is 31 days. The statistical summary also showed that only 3% of the dollar value of all accounts receivable was more than 60 days old. Based on the statistical information, management was satisfied that accounts receivable and incoming cash flow were under control.

In this chapter, you will learn how to compute and interpret some of the statistical measures used by Small Fry Design. In addition to the mean, median, and mode, you will learn about other descriptive statistics such as the range, variance, standard deviation, percentiles, and correlation. These numerical measures will assist in the understanding and interpretation of data.

*The authors are indebted to John A. McCarthy, president of Small Fry Design, for providing this Statistics in Practice.

In Chapter 2 we discussed tabular and graphical methods used to summarize data. In this chapter, we present several numerical methods of descriptive statistics that provide additional alternatives for summarizing data.

We start by developing numerical summaries for data sets consisting of a single variable. When a data set contains more than one variable, the same numerical summaries can be computed separately for each variable. However, in the two-variable case, we will also develop measures of the relationship between the variables.

Several numerical measures of location, dispersion, and association are introduced. If the measures are computed for data from a sample, they are called **sample statistics**. If the measures are computed for data from a population, they are called **population parameters**. In statistical inference, a sample statistic is referred to as the **point estimator** of the corresponding population parameter. In Chapter 7 we will discuss in more detail the process of point estimation.

Several more of Excel's statistical functions are introduced in this chapter. In most cases we introduce them with little digression from the flow of the statistical material. But, at the end of Section 3.2, we pause to show how Excel's Descriptive Statistics tool can be used to perform the work of several functions by providing a summary of the most commonly used descriptive statistics. If you experience trouble using any of the statistical functions, recall that Excel's Insert Function dialog box is designed to provide help (see Appendix E: Using Excel Functions).

3.1   MEASURES OF LOCATION

Mean

Perhaps the most important measure of location is the **mean**, or average value, for a variable. The mean provides a measure of central location for the data. If the data are from a sample, the mean is denoted by $\bar{x}$; if the data are from a population, the mean is denoted by the Greek letter μ.

In statistical formulas, it is customary to denote the value of variable x for the first observation by x_1, the value of variable x for the second observation by x_2, and so on. In general, the value of variable x for the ith observation is denoted by x_i. For a sample with n observations, the formula for the sample mean is as follows.

The sample mean $\bar{x}$ is a sample statistic.

> **Sample Mean**
>
> $$\bar{x} = \frac{\Sigma x_i}{n} \qquad (3.1)$$

In the preceding formula, the numerator is the sum of the values of the n observations. That is,

$$\Sigma x_i = x_1 + x_2 + \cdots + x_n$$

The Greek letter Σ is the summation sign.

To illustrate the computation of a sample mean, let us consider the following class size data for a sample of five college classes.

$$46 \quad 54 \quad 42 \quad 46 \quad 32$$

We use the notation x_1, x_2, x_3, x_4, x_5 to represent the number of students in each of the five classes.

$$x_1 = 46 \qquad x_2 = 54 \qquad x_3 = 42 \qquad x_4 = 46 \qquad x_5 = 32$$

Hence, to compute the sample mean, we can write

$$\bar{x} = \frac{\Sigma x_i}{n} = \frac{x_1 + x_2 + x_3 + x_4 + x_5}{5} = \frac{46 + 54 + 42 + 46 + 32}{5} = 44$$

The sample mean class size is 44 students.

Another illustration of the computation of a sample mean is given in the following situation. Suppose that a college placement office sent a questionnaire to a sample of business school graduates requesting information on monthly starting salaries. Table 3.1 shows the collected data. The mean monthly starting salary for the sample of 12 business college graduates is computed as

$$\bar{x} = \frac{\Sigma x_i}{n} = \frac{x_1 + x_2 + \cdots + x_{12}}{12}$$
$$= \frac{2850 + 2950 + \cdots + 2880}{12}$$
$$= \frac{35,280}{12} = 2940$$

Equation (3.1) shows how the mean is computed for a sample with n observations. The formula for computing the mean of a population is the same, but we use different notation to indicate that we are working with the entire population. The number of observations in a population is denoted by N and the symbol for a population mean is μ.

The sample mean $\bar{x}$ is the point estimator of the population mean μ.

Population Mean

$$\mu = \frac{\Sigma x_i}{N} \tag{3.2}$$

TABLE 3.1   MONTHLY STARTING SALARIES FOR A SAMPLE OF 12 BUSINESS SCHOOL GRADUATES

Salary

Graduate	Monthly Starting Salary ($)	Graduate	Monthly Starting Salary ($)
1	2850	7	2890
2	2950	8	3130
3	3050	9	2940
4	2880	10	3325
5	2755	11	2920
6	2710	12	2880

Median

The **median** is another measure of central location for a variable. The median is the value in the middle when the data are arranged in ascending order (smallest value to largest value). With an odd number of observations, the median is the middle value. An even number of observations has no single middle value. In this case, we follow the convention of defining the median to be the average of the values for the middle two observations. For convenience the definition of the median is restated as follows.

Median

Arrange the data in ascending order (smallest value to largest value).

   (a) For an odd number of observations the median is the middle value.
   (b) For an even number of observations, the median is the average of the two middle values.

Let us apply this definition to compute the median class size for the sample of five college classes. Arranging the data in ascending order provides the following list.

32   42   46   46   54

Because $n = 5$ is odd, the median is the middle value. Thus the median class size is 46 students. Even though this data set has two observations with values of 46, each observation is treated separately when we arrange the data in ascending order.

Suppose we also compute the median starting salary for 12 business college graduates. We first arrange the data in Table 3.1 in ascending order.

2710   2755   2850   2880   2880   2890   2920   2940   2950   3050   3130   3325

Middle Two Values

Because $n = 12$ is even, we identify the middle two values: 2890 and 2920. The median is the average of these values.

$$\text{Median} = \frac{2890 + 2920}{2} = 2905$$

The median is the measure of location most often reported for annual income and property value data because a few extremely large incomes or property values can inflate the mean. In such cases, the median is a better measure of central location.

Although the mean is the more commonly used measure of central location, in some situations the median is preferred. The mean is influenced by extremely small and large data values. For instance, suppose that one of the graduates (see Table 3.1) had a starting salary of $10,000 per month (maybe the individual's family owns the company). If we change the highest monthly starting salary in Table 3.1 from $3325 to $10,000 and recompute the mean, the sample mean changes from $2940 to $3496. The median of $2905, however, is unchanged, because $2890 and $2920 are still the middle two values. With the extremely high starting salary included, the median provides a better measure of central location than the mean. We can generalize to say that whenever a data set contains extreme values, the median is often the preferred measure of central location.

Mode

A third measure of location is the **mode**. The mode is defined as follows.

Mode

The mode is the value that occurs with greatest frequency.

To illustrate the identification of the mode, consider the sample of five class sizes. The only value that occurs more than once is 46. Because this value, occurring with a frequency of 2, has the greatest frequency, it is the mode. As another illustration, consider the sample of starting salaries for the business school graduates. The only monthly starting salary that occurs more than once is $2880. Because this value has the greatest frequency, it is the mode.

Situations can arise for which the greatest frequency occurs at two or more different values. In these instances more than one mode exists. If the data have exactly two modes, we say that the data are *bimodal*. If data have more than two modes, we say that the data are *multimodal*. In multimodal cases the mode is almost never reported because listing three or more modes would not be particularly helpful in describing a location for the data.

The mode is an important measure of location for qualitative data. For example, the qualitative data set in Table 2.2 resulted in the following frequency distribution for soft drink purchases.

Soft Drink	Frequency
Coke Classic	19
Diet Coke	8
Dr. Pepper	5
Pepsi-Cola	13
Sprite	5
Total	50

The mode, or most frequently purchased soft drink, is Coke Classic. For this type of data it obviously makes no sense to speak of the mean or median. The mode provides the information of interest, the most frequently purchased soft drink.

Using Excel to Compute the Mean, Median, and Mode

Excel provides functions for computing the mean, median, and mode. We illustrate the use of these Excel functions by computing the mean, median, and mode for the starting salary data in Table 3.1. Refer to Figure 3.1 as we describe the tasks involved. The formula worksheet is in the background; the value worksheet is in the foreground.

Enter Data: Labels and the starting salary data are entered into cells A1:B13 of the worksheet.

Enter Functions and Formulas: Excel's AVERAGE function can be used to compute the mean by entering the following formula into cell E1:

$$=\text{AVERAGE(B2:B13)}$$

FIGURE 3.1   EXCEL WORKSHEET USED TO COMPUTE THE MEAN, MEDIAN, AND MODE FOR STARTING SALARIES

	A	B	C	D	E	F
1	Graduate	Starting Salary		Mean	=AVERAGE(B2:B13)	
2	1	2850		Median	=MEDIAN(B2:B13)	
3	2	2950		Mode	=MODE(B2:B13)	
4	3	3050				
5	4	2880				
6	5	2755				
7	6	2710				
8	7	2890				
9	8	3130				
10	9	2940				
11	10	3325				
12	11	2920				
13	12	2880				
14						

	A	B	C	D	E	F
1	Graduate	Starting Salary		Mean	2940	
2	1	2850		Median	2905	
3	2	2950		Mode	2880	
4	3	3050				
5	4	2880				
6	5	2755				
7	6	2710				
8	7	2890				
9	8	3130				
10	9	2940				
11	10	3325				
12	11	2920				
13	12	2880				
14						

If the data are bimodal or multimodal, Excel's MODE function will incorrectly identify a single mode.

Similarly, the formulas =MEDIAN(B2:B13) and =MODE(B2:B13) are entered into cells E2 and E3, respectively, to compute the median and the mode. The labels Mean, Median, and Mode are entered into cells D1:D3 to identify the output.

The formulas in cells E1:E3 are displayed in the formula worksheet in the background of Figure 3.1. The worksheet in the foreground shows the values computed using the Excel functions. Note that the mean (2940), median (2905), and mode (2880) are the same as we computed earlier.

Percentiles

A **percentile** provides information about how the data are spread over the interval from the smallest value to the largest value. For data that do not have numerous repeated values, the pth percentile divides the data into two parts. Approximately p percent of the observations have values less than the pth percentile; approximately $(100 - p)$ percent of the observations have values greater than the pth percentile. The pth percentile is formally defined as follows.

Percentile

The pth percentile is a value such that *at least p* percent of the observations are less than or equal to this value and *at least* $(100 - p)$ percent of the observations are greater than or equal to this value.

Colleges and universities frequently report admission test scores in terms of percentiles. For instance, suppose an applicant obtains a raw score of 54 on the verbal portion of an admission test. How this student performed in relation to other students taking the same test may not be readily apparent. However, if the raw score of 54 corresponds to the 70th percentile, we know that approximately 70% of the students scored lower than this individual and approximately 30% of the students scored higher than this individual.

The following procedure can be used to compute the pth percentile.

Following these steps makes it easy to calculate percentiles.

Calculating the pth Percentile

Step 1. Arrange the data in ascending order (smallest value to largest value).
Step 2. Compute an index i

$$i = \left(\frac{p}{100}\right)n$$

where p is the percentile of interest and n is the number of observations.

Step 3. (a) If i *is not an integer, round up.* The next integer *greater* than i denotes the position of the pth percentile.
(b) If i *is an integer,* the pth percentile is the average of the values in positions i and $i + 1$.

As an illustration of this procedure, let us determine the 85th percentile for the starting salary data in Table 3.1.

Step 1. Arrange the data in ascending order.

2710   2755   2850   2880   2880   2890   2920   2940   2950   3050   3130   3325

Step 2.

$$i = \left(\frac{p}{100}\right)n = \left(\frac{85}{100}\right)12 = 10.2$$

Step 3. Because i is not an integer, *round up.* The position of the 85th percentile is the next integer greater than 10.2, the 11th position.

Returning to the data, we see that the 85th percentile is the data value in the 11th position, or 3130.

As another illustration of this procedure, let us consider the calculation of the 50th percentile for the starting salary data. Applying step 2, we obtain

$$i = \left(\frac{50}{100}\right)12 = 6$$

Because i is an integer, step 3(b) states that the 50th percentile is the average of the sixth and seventh data values; thus the 50th percentile is $(2890 + 2920)/2 = 2905$. Note that the *50th percentile is also the median.*

Quartiles

Quartiles are just specific percentiles; thus, the steps for computing percentiles can be applied directly in the computation of quartiles.

It is often desirable to divide data into four parts, with each part containing approximately one-fourth, or 25% of the observations. Figure 3.2 shows a data set divided into four parts. The division points are referred to as the **quartiles** and are defined as

Q_1 = first quartile, or 25th percentile

Q_2 = second quartile, or 50th percentile (also the median)

Q_3 = third quartile, or 75th percentile.

The starting salary data are again arranged in ascending order. Q_2, the second quartile (median), has already been identified as 2905.

2710   2755   2850   2880   2880   2890   2920   2940   2950   3050   3130   3325

The computations of quartiles Q_1 and Q_3 require the use of the rule for finding the 25th and 75th percentiles. These calculations follow.

For Q_1,

$$i = \left(\frac{p}{100}\right)n = \left(\frac{25}{100}\right)12 = 3$$

Because i is an integer, step 3(b) indicates that the first quartile, or 25th percentile, is the average of the third and fourth data values; thus, $Q_1 = (2850 + 2880)/2 = 2865$.

For Q_3,

$$i = \left(\frac{p}{100}\right)n = \left(\frac{75}{100}\right)12 = 9$$

Again, because i is an integer, step 3(b) indicates that the third quartile, or 75th percentile, is the average of the ninth and tenth data values; thus, $Q_3 = (2950 + 3050)/2 = 3000$.

The quartiles divide the starting salary data into four parts, with each part containing 25% of the observations.

FIGURE 3.2   LOCATION OF THE QUARTILES

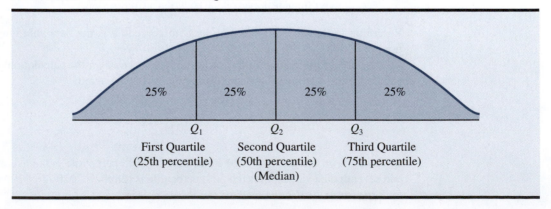

$$2710 \quad 2755 \quad 2850 \quad \bigg| \quad 2880 \quad 2880 \quad 2890 \quad \bigg| \quad 2920 \quad 2940 \quad 2950 \quad \bigg| \quad 3050 \quad 3130 \quad 3325$$

$$Q_1 = 2865 \qquad\qquad Q_2 = 2905 \qquad\qquad Q_3 = 3000$$
$$\text{(Median)}$$

We defined the quartiles as the 25th, 50th, and 75th percentiles. Thus, we computed the quartiles in the same way as percentiles. However, other conventions are sometimes used to compute quartiles, and the actual values reported for quartiles may vary slightly depending on the convention used. Nevertheless, the objective of all procedures for computing quartiles is to divide the data into four equal parts.

Using Excel to Sort Data and to Compute Percentiles and Quartiles

Excel provides functions for computing percentiles and quartiles. However, for small data sets (such as the starting salary data), these functions do not always provide results that strictly satisfy the definition of a percentile. We show here how to use Excel to compute percentiles another way. We first sort the data and then select the appropriate percentile from its position in the data set. This procedure also provides quartiles and the median because they are also percentiles. We will illustrate this approach to computing the 25th, 50th, 75th, and 85th percentiles for the starting salary data in Table 3.1. Refer to Figure 3.3 as we present the steps involved. The worksheet containing the original starting salary data is in the background; the worksheet obtained after sorting the data is in the foreground.

FIGURE 3.3   EXCEL WORKSHEET USED TO COMPUTE PERCENTILES AND QUARTILES FOR STARTING SALARIES

	A	B	C	D	E
1	Graduate	Starting Salary			
2	1	2850			
3	2	2950			
4	3	3050			
5	4	2880			
6	5	2755			
7	6	2710			
8	7	2890			
9	8	3130			
10	9	2940			
11	10	3325			
12	11	2920			
13	12	2880			
14					

	A	B	C	D	E
1	Graduate	Starting Salary			
2	6	2710			
3	5	2755			
4	1	2850		$Q_1 = 2865$	
5	4	2880			
6	12	2880			
7	7	2890		$Q_2 = 2905$	
8	11	2920			
9	9	2940			
10	2	2950		$Q_3 = 3000$	
11	3	3050			
12	8	3130		85th percentile = 3130	
13	10	3325			
14					

Enter Data: Labels and the starting salary data are entered into cells A1:B13.

Enter Functions and Formulas: No functions and formulas are needed.

Apply Tools: The following steps will sort the data into ascending order.

Step 1. Select any cell containing data in column B
Step 2. Select the **Data** menu
Step 3. Choose the **Sort** option
Step 4. When the **Sort** dialog box appears:

> In the **Sort by** box, make sure that **Starting Salary** appears and that **Ascending** is selected
>
> Click **OK** (the sorted data appear in the worksheet shown in the foreground of Figure 3.3)

In the previous subsection, we showed how to calculate the pth percentile by first arranging the data in ascending order and then computing an index that can be used to identify the position of the pth percentile. Recall that for the starting salary data the 25th percentile (Q_1) was the average of the 3rd and 4th values, the 50th percentile (Q_2 and the median) was the average of the 6th and 7th values, the 75th percentile (Q_3) was the average of the 9th and 10th values, and the 85th percentile was the 11th data value. Using the sorted data shown in Figure 3.3, it is easy to identify the position of these values in the data (the row number minus one) and hence compute the percentile values by hand.

NOTES AND COMMENTS

It is better to use the median than the mean as a measure of central location when a data set contains extreme values. Another measure, sometimes used when extreme values are present, is the *trimmed mean*. It is obtained by deleting a percentage of the smallest and largest values from a data set and then computing the mean of the remaining values. For example, the 5% trimmed mean is obtained by removing the smallest 5% and the largest 5% of the data values and then computing the mean of the remaining values. Using the sample with $n = 12$ starting salaries, $0.05(12) = 0.6$. Rounding this value to 1 indicates that the 5% trimmed mean would remove the 1 smallest data value and the 1 largest data value. The 5% trimmed mean using the 10 remaining observations is 2924.50.

EXERCISES

Methods

1. Consider a sample with data values of 10, 20, 12, 17, and 16. Compute the mean and median.

2. Consider a sample with data values of 10, 20, 21, 17, 16, and 12. Compute the mean and median.

3. Consider a sample with data values of 27, 25, 20, 15, 30, 34, 28, and 25. Compute the 20th, 25th, 65th, and 75th percentiles.

4. Consider a sample with data values of 53, 55, 70, 58, 64, 57, 53, 69, 57, 68, and 53. Compute the mean, median, and mode.

Applications

5. According to a salary survey conducted by the National Association of Colleges and Employers, bachelor's degree candidates in accounting received starting offers averaging $34,500 per year (Bureau of Labor Statistics, *Occupational Outlook Handbook*, 2000–01

Edition). A sample of 30 students who graduated in 2000 with a bachelor's degree in accounting resulted in the following starting salaries. Data are in thousands of dollars.

AcctSal

36.8	34.9	35.2	37.2	36.2
35.8	36.8	36.1	36.7	36.6
37.3	38.2	36.3	36.4	39.0
38.3	36.0	35.0	36.7	37.9
38.3	36.4	36.5	38.4	39.4
38.8	35.4	36.4	37.0	36.4

a. What is the mean starting salary?
b. What is the median starting salary?
c. What is the mode?
d. What is the first quartile?
e. What is the third quartile?

6. More and more investors are turning to discount brokers to save money when buying and selling shares of stock. The American Association of Individual Investors conducts an annual survey of discount brokers. The commissions charged by a sample of 20 discount brokers for two types of trades, 500 shares at $50 per share and 1000 shares at $5 per share, are shown in Table 3.2.
   a. Compute the mean, median, and mode for the commission charged on a trade of 500 shares at $50 per share.
   b. Compute the mean, median, and mode for the commission charged on a trade of 1000 shares at $5 per share.
   c. Which costs the most: trading 500 shares at $50 per share or trading 1000 shares at $5 per share?
   d. Does the cost of a transaction seem to be related to the amount of the transaction?

TABLE 3.2   COMMISSIONS CHARGED BY DISCOUNT BROKERS

Discount

Broker	500@$50	1000@$5
AcuTrade	38.00	48.00
Bank of San Francisco	140.00	79.50
Burke Christensen & Lewis	34.00	34.00
Bush Burns Securities	35.00	35.00
Charles Schwab	155.00	90.00
Downstate Discount	55.00	60.00
Dreyfus Lion Account	154.50	88.50
First Union Brokerage	140.00	90.00
Levitt & Levitt	35.00	70.00
Max Ule	195.00	70.00
Mongerson & Co	95.00	66.00
Quick & Reilly	119.50	60.50
Scottsdale Securities, Inc.	50.00	63.00
Seaport Securities Corp.	50.00	70.00
St. Louis Discount	66.00	64.00
Summit Financial Services	95.00	60.50
T. Rowe Price Brokerage	134.00	80.00
Unified Financial Services	154.00	90.00
Wall Street Access	45.00	45.00
Your Discount Broker	55.00	70.00

Source: AAII Journal, January 2000.

7. The average person spends 45 minutes a day listening to recorded music (*Des Moines Register*, December 5, 1997). The following data were obtained for the number of minutes spent listening to recorded music for a sample of 30 individuals.

Music

88.3	4.3	4.6	7.0	9.2
0.0	99.2	34.9	81.7	0.0
85.4	0.0	17.5	45.0	53.3
29.1	28.8	0.0	98.9	64.5
4.4	67.9	94.2	7.6	56.6
52.9	145.6	70.4	65.1	63.6

a. Compute the mean.
b. Do these data appear to be consistent with the average reported by the newspaper?
c. Compute the median.
d. Compute the first and third quartiles.
e. Compute and interpret the 40th percentile.

8. Millions of Americans get up each morning and telecommute to work from offices in their home. Following is a sample of age data for individuals working at home.

18	54	20	46	25	48	53	27	26	37
40	36	42	25	27	33	28	40	45	25

a. Compute the mean and mode.
b. The median age of the population of all adults is 35.5 years (*The New York Times Almanac*, 2001). Use the median age of the preceding data to comment on whether the at-home workers tend to be younger or older than the population of all adults.
c. Compute the first and third quartiles.
d. Compute and interpret the 32nd percentile.

9. Media Matrix collected data showing the most popular Web sites when browsing at home and at work (*Business 2.0*, January 2000). The following data show the number of unique visitors (thousands) for the top 25 Web sites when browsing at home.

Websites

Web Site	Unique Visitors (1000s)
about.com	5538
altavista.com	7391
amazon.com	7986
angelfire.com	8917
aol.com	23863
bluemountainarts.com	6786
ebay.com	8296
excite.com	10479
geocities.com	15321
go.com	14330
hotbot.com	5760
hotmail.com	11791
icq.com	5052
looksmart.com	5984
lycos.com	9950
microsoft.com	15593
msn.com	23505
netscape.com	14470

Web Site	Unique Visitors (1000s)
passport.com	11299
real.com	6785
snap.com	5730
tripod.com	7970
xoom.com	5652
yahoo.com	26796
zdnet.com	5133

a. Compute the mean and median.
b. Do you think it would be better to use the mean or the median as the measure of central tendency for these data? Explain.
c. Compute the first and third quartiles.
d. Compute and interpret the 85th percentile.

10. The *Los Angeles Times* regularly reports the air quality index for various areas of Southern California. Index ratings of 0–50 are considered good, 51–100 moderate, 101–200 unhealthy, 201–275 very unhealthy, and over 275 hazardous. Recent air quality indexes for Pomona were 28, 42, 58, 48, 45, 55, 60, 49, and 50.
    a. Compute the mean, median, and mode for the data. Should the Pomona air quality index be considered good?
    b. Compute the 25th percentile and 75th percentile for the Pomona air quality data.

11. In automobile mileage and gasoline-consumption testing, 13 automobiles were road tested for 300 miles in both city and highway driving conditions. The following data were recorded for miles-per-gallon performance.

City: 16.2 16.7 15.9 14.4 13.2 15.3 16.8 16.0 16.1 15.3 15.2 15.3 16.2
Highway: 19.4 20.6 18.3 18.6 19.2 17.4 17.2 18.6 19.0 21.1 19.4 18.5 18.7

Use the mean, median, and mode to make a statement about the difference in performance for city and highway driving.

12. Because of recent technological advances, today's digital cameras produce better-looking pictures than their predecessors did a year ago. The following data show the street price, maximum picture capacity, and battery life (minutes) for 20 of the latest models (*PC World*, January 2000).

CD file

Cameras

Camera	Price ($)	Maximum Picture Capacity	Battery Life (minutes)
Agfa Ephoto CL30	349	36	25
Canon PowerShot A50	499	106	75
Canon PowerShot Pro70	999	96	118
Epson PhotoPC 800	699	120	99
Fujifilm DX-10	299	30	229
Fujifilm MX-2700	699	141	124
Fujifilm MX-2900 Zoom	899	141	88
HP PhotoSmart C200	299	80	68

(continued)

Camera	Price ($)	Maximum Picture Capacity	Battery Life (minutes)
Kodak DC215 Zoom	399	54	159
Kodak DC265 Zoom	899	180	186
Kodak DC280 Zoom	799	245	143
Minolta Dimage EX Zoom 1500	549	105	38
Nikon Coolpix 950	999	32	88
Olympus D-340R	299	122	161
Olympus D-450 Zoom	499	122	62
Richo RDC-500	699	99	56
Sony Cybershot DSC-F55	699	63	69
Sony Mavica MVC-FD73	599	40	186
Sony Mavica MVC-FD88	999	40	88
Toshiba PDR-M4	599	124	142

a. Compute the mean price.
b. Compute the mean maximum picture capacity.
c. Compute the mean battery life.
d. If you had to select one camera from this list, what camera would you choose? Explain.

3.2   MEASURES OF VARIABILITY

In addition to measures of location, it is often desirable to consider measures of variability, or dispersion. For example, suppose that you are a purchasing agent for a large manufacturing firm and that you regularly place orders with two different suppliers. After several months of operation, you find that the mean number of days required to fill orders is 10 days for both of the suppliers. The histograms summarizing the number of working days required to fill orders from the suppliers are shown in Figure 3.4. Although the mean number of days

FIGURE 3.4   HISTORICAL DATA SHOWING THE NUMBER OF DAYS REQUIRED TO FILL ORDERS

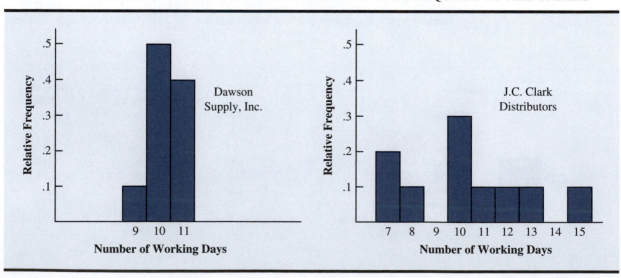

is 10 for both suppliers, do the two suppliers have the same degree of reliability in terms of making deliveries on schedule? Note the dispersion, or variability, in delivery times indicated by the histograms. Which supplier would you prefer?

For most firms, receiving materials and supplies on schedule is important. The seven- or eight-day deliveries shown for J. C. Clark Distributors might be viewed favorably; however, a few of the slow 13- to 15-day deliveries could be disastrous in terms of keeping a workforce busy and production on schedule. This example illustrates a situation in which the variability in the delivery times may be an overriding consideration in selecting a supplier. For most purchasing agents, the lower variability shown for Dawson Supply, Inc., would make Dawson the preferred supplier.

We turn now to a discussion of some commonly used measures of variability

Range

The simplest measure of variability is the **range**.

Range

$$\text{Range} = \text{Largest Value} - \text{Smallest Value}$$

Let us refer to the data on starting salaries for business school graduates in Table 3.1. The largest starting salary is 3325 and the smallest is 2710. The range is $3325 - 2710 = 615$.

Although the range is the easiest of the measures of variability to compute, it is seldom used as the only measure. The reason is that the range is based on only two of the observations and thus is highly influenced by extreme values. Suppose one of the graduates had a starting salary of $10,000 per month. In this case, the range would be $10,000 - 2710 = 7290$ rather than 615. This large value for the range would not be especially descriptive of the variability in the data because 11 of the 12 starting salaries are closely grouped between 2710 and 3130.

Interquartile Range

A measure of variability that overcomes the dependency on extreme values is the **interquartile range** (IQR). This measure of variability is simply the difference between the third quartile, Q_3, and the first quartile, Q_1. In other words, the interquartile range is the range for the middle 50% of the data.

Interquartile Range

$$\text{IQR} = Q_3 - Q_1 \tag{3.3}$$

For the data on monthly starting salaries, the quartiles are $Q_3 = 3000$ and $Q_1 = 2865$. Thus, the interquartile range is $3000 - 2865 = 135$.

Variance

The **variance** is a measure of variability that utilizes all the data. The variance is based on the difference between the value of each observation (x_i) and the mean. The difference between each x_i and the mean ($\bar{x}$ for a sample, μ for a population) is called a *deviation about the mean*. For a sample, a deviation about the mean is written ($x_i - \bar{x}$); for a population, it is written ($x_i - \mu$). In the computation of the variance, the deviations about the mean are *squared*.

If the data are for a population, the average of the squared deviations is called the *population variance*. The population variance is denoted by the Greek symbol σ^2. For a population of N observations and with μ denoting the population mean, the definition of the population variance is as follows.

Population Variance

$$\sigma^2 = \frac{\Sigma(x_i - \mu)^2}{N} \qquad (3.4)$$

In most statistical applications, the data being analyzed are for a sample. When we compute a sample variance, we are often interested in using it to estimate the population variance σ^2. Although a detailed explanation is beyond the scope of this text, it can be shown that if the sum of the squared deviations about the sample mean is divided by $n - 1$, and not n, the resulting sample variance provides an unbiased estimate of the population variance. For this reason, the *sample variance,* denoted by s^2, is defined as follows.

The sample variance s^2 is the point estimator of the population variance σ^2.

Sample Variance

$$s^2 = \frac{\Sigma(x_i - \bar{x})^2}{n - 1} \qquad (3.5)$$

To illustrate the computation of the sample variance, we will use the data on class size for the sample of five college classes as presented in Section 3.1. A summary of the data, including the computation of the deviations about the mean and the squared deviations about the mean, is shown in Table 3.3. The sum of squared deviations about the mean is $\Sigma(x_i - \bar{x})^2 = 256$. Hence, with $n - 1 = 4$, the sample variance is

$$s^2 = \frac{\Sigma(x_i - \bar{x})^2}{n - 1} = \frac{256}{4} = 64$$

TABLE 3.3 COMPUTATION OF DEVIATIONS AND SQUARED DEVIATIONS ABOUT THE MEAN FOR THE CLASS SIZE DATA

Number of Students in Class (x_i)	Mean Class Size ($\bar{x}$)	Deviation About the Mean ($x_i - \bar{x}$)	Squared Deviation About the Mean ($x_i - \bar{x}$)^2
46	44	2	4
54	44	10	100
42	44	−2	4
46	44	2	4
32	44	−12	144
		0	256
		$\Sigma(x_i - \bar{x})$	$\Sigma(x_i - \bar{x})^2$

Before moving on, let us note that the units associated with the sample variance often cause confusion. Because the values being summed in the variance calculation, $(x_i - \bar{x})^2$, are squared, the units associated with the sample variance are also *squared*. For instance, the sample variance for the class size data is $s^2 = 64$ (students)^2. The squared units associated with variance make it difficult to obtain an intuitive understanding and interpretation of the numerical value of the variance. We recommend that you think of the variance as a measure useful in comparing the amount of variability for two or more variables. In a comparison of the variables, the one with the larger variance has the most variability. Further interpretation of the value of the variance may not be necessary.

The variance is useful in comparing the variability of two or more variables.

As another illustration of computing a sample variance, consider the starting salaries listed in Table 3.1 for the 12 business school graduates. In Section 3.1, we showed that the sample mean starting salary was 2940. A summary of the data, including the computation of the deviations about the mean and the squared deviations about the mean, is shown in Figure 3.5. The worksheet in the background shows the Excel formulas used to compute the results shown in the value worksheet in the foreground. The sum of the squared deviations about the mean is $\Sigma(x_i - \bar{x})^2 = 301{,}850$ (see cell E14). Hence, with $n - 1 = 11$, the sample variance is

$$s^2 = \frac{\Sigma(x_i - \bar{x})^2}{n - 1} = \frac{301{,}850}{11} = 27{,}440.91$$

Using the definition to compute the sample variance helps us to realize that the variance measures variability as a function of the squared deviations about the mean.

The method we used for computing the sample variance for starting salaries is the same method that we used to compute the sample variance for the class size data (see Table 3.3). We used the definition as given by equation (3.5). The only difference is that this time we use an Excel worksheet to ease the computational burden. Later we will see that Excel provides a function for obtaining the sample variance directly without entering all the formulas needed to compute the sum of the squared deviations about the mean.

Note that in Table 3.3 and Figure 3.5 we show both the sum of the deviations about the mean and the sum of the squared deviations about the mean. For any data set, the sum of the deviations about the mean will *always equal zero*. Note that in Table 3.3 and Figure 3.5, $\Sigma(x_i - \bar{x}) = 0$. The positive deviations and negative deviations cancel each other, causing the sum of the deviations about the mean to equal zero.

Standard Deviation

The **standard deviation** is defined to be the positive square root of the variance. Following the notation we adopted for a sample variance and a population variance, we use s to denote the sample standard deviation and σ to denote the population standard deviation. The standard deviation is derived from the variance in the following way.

The sample standard deviation s is the point estimator of the population standard deviation σ.

Standard Deviation

$$\text{Sample Standard Deviation} = s = \sqrt{s^2} \tag{3.6}$$

$$\text{Population Standard Deviation} = \sigma = \sqrt{\sigma^2} \tag{3.7}$$

FIGURE 3.5   EXCEL WORKSHEET USED TO COMPUTE THE DEVIATIONS AND SQUARED DEVIATIONS ABOUT THE MEAN FOR THE STARTING SALARIES

	A	B	C	D	E	F
1	Graduate	Starting Salary	Sample Mean	Deviation about the Mean	Squared Deviation about the Mean	
2	1	2850	=AVERAGE($B$2:$B$13)	=B2-C2	=D2^2	
3	2	2950	=AVERAGE($B$2:$B$13)	=B3-C3	=D3^2	
4	3	3050	=AVERAGE($B$2:$B$13)	=B4-C4	=D4^2	
5	4	2880	=AVERAGE($B$2:$B$13)	=B5-C5	=D5^2	
6	5	2755	=AVERAGE($B$2:$B$13)	=B6-C6	=D6^2	
7	6	2710	=AVERAGE($B$2:$B$13)	=B7-C7	=D7^2	
8	7	2890	=AVERAGE($B$2:$B$13)	=B8-C8	=D8^2	
9	8	3130	=AVERAGE($B$2:$B$13)	=B9-C9	=D9^2	
10	9	2940	=AVERAGE($B$2:$B$13)	=B10-C10	=D10^2	
11	10	3325	=AVERAGE($B$2:$B$13)	=B11-C11	=D11^2	
12	11	2920	=AVERAGE($B$2:$B$13)	=B12-C12	=D12^2	
13	12	2880	=AVERAGE($B$2:$B$13)	=B13-C13	=D13^2	
14				=SUM(D2:D13)	=SUM(E2:E13)	
15						

	A	B	C	D	E	F
1	Graduate	Starting Salary	Sample Mean	Deviation about the Mean	Squared Deviation about the Mean	
2	1	2850	2940	-90	8100	
3	2	2950	2940	10	100	
4	3	3050	2940	110	12100	
5	4	2880	2940	-60	3600	
6	5	2755	2940	-185	34225	
7	6	2710	2940	-230	52900	
8	7	2890	2940	-50	2500	
9	8	3130	2940	190	36100	
10	9	2940	2940	0	0	
11	10	3325	2940	385	148225	
12	11	2920	2940	-20	400	
13	12	2880	2940	-60	3600	
14				0	301850	
15						

The standard deviation is easier to interpret than the variance because the standard deviation is measured in the same units as the data.

Recall that the sample variance for the sample of class sizes in five college classes is $s^2 = 64$. Thus the sample standard deviation is $s = \sqrt{64} = 8$. For the data on starting salaries, the sample standard deviation is $s = \sqrt{27,440.91} = 165.65$.

What is gained by converting the variance to its corresponding standard deviation? Recall that the units associated with the variance are squared. For example, the sample variance for the starting salary data of business school graduates is $s^2 = 27,440.91$ (dollars)^2. Because the standard deviation is the square root of the variance, the units of the variance, dollars squared, are converted to dollars in the standard deviation. Thus, the standard deviation of the starting salary data is $165.65. In other words, the standard deviation is measured in the same units as the original data. For this reason the standard deviation is more easily compared to the mean and other statistics that are measured in the same units as the original data.

Using Excel to Compute the Sample Variance and Sample Standard Deviation

Excel provides functions for computing the sample variance and sample standard deviation, which we will illustrate using the starting salary data. Refer to Figure 3.6 as we describe the steps involved. Figure 3.6 is an extension of Figure 3.1 where we showed how to use Excel functions to compute the mean, median, and mode. The formula worksheet is in the background; the value worksheet is in the foreground.

Enter Data: Labels and the starting salary data are entered into cells A1:B13 of the worksheet.

Enter Functions and Formulas: The Excel AVERAGE, MEDIAN, and MODE functions are entered into cells E1:E3 as described earlier. Excel's VAR function can be used to compute the sample variance by entering the following formula into cell E4:

$$=VAR(B2:B13)$$

Similarly, the formula =STDEV(B2:B13) is entered into cell E5 to compute the sample standard deviation. Appropriate labels are entered into cells D1:D5 to identify the output.

The value worksheet, in the foreground, shows the values computed using the Excel functions. Note that the sample variance and sample standard deviation are the same as we computed earlier using the definitions.

FIGURE 3.6   EXCEL WORKSHEET USED TO COMPUTE THE SAMPLE VARIANCE AND THE SAMPLE STANDARD DEVIATION FOR STARTING SALARIES

	A	B	C	D	E	F
1	Graduate	Starting Salary		Mean	=AVERAGE(B2:B13)	
2	1	2850		Median	=MEDIAN(B2:B13)	
3	2	2950		Mode	=MODE(B2:B13)	
4	3	3050		Variance	=VAR(B2:B13)	
5	4	2880		Standard Deviation	=STDEV(B2:B13)	
6	5	2755				
7	6	2710				
8	7	2890				
9	8	3130				
10	9	2940				
11	10	3325				
12	11	2920				
13	12	2880				
14						

	A	B	C	D	E	F
1	Graduate	Starting Salary		Mean	2940	
2	1	2850		Median	2905	
3	2	2950		Mode	2880	
4	3	3050		Variance	27440.91	
5	4	2880		Standard Deviation	165.65	
6	5	2755				
7	6	2710				
8	7	2890				
9	8	3130				
10	9	2940				
11	10	3325				
12	11	2920				
13	12	2880				
14						

Coefficient of Variation

In some situations we may be interested in a descriptive statistic that indicates how large the standard deviation is relative to the mean. This measure is called the **coefficient of variation** and is computed as follows.

Coefficient of Variation

$$\frac{\text{Standard Deviation}}{\text{Mean}} \times 100 \qquad\qquad (3.8)$$

For the class size data, we found a sample mean of 44 and a sample standard deviation of 8. The coefficient of variation is $(8/44) \times 100 = 18.2$. In words, the coefficient of variation tells us that the sample standard deviation is 18.2% of the value of the sample mean. For the starting salary data with a sample mean of 2940 and a sample standard deviation of 165.65, the coefficient of variation, $(165.65/2940) \times 100 = 5.6$, tells us the sample standard deviation is only 5.6% of the value of the sample mean. In general, the coefficient of variation is a useful statistic for comparing the variability of variables that have different standard deviations and different means.

Using Excel's Descriptive Statistics Tool

As we have seen, Excel provides statistical functions to compute descriptive statistics for a data set. These functions can be used to compute one statistic at a time (e.g., mean, variance, etc.). Excel also provides a variety of Data Analysis Tools. One of these, called Descriptive Statistics, allows the user to compute a variety of descriptive statistics at once. We show here how it can be used to compute descriptive statistics for the starting salary data in Table 3.1. Refer to Figures 3.7 and 3.8 as we describe the steps involved.

Enter Data: Labels and the starting salary data are entered into cells A1:B13 of the worksheet.

Enter Functions and Formulas: No functions and formulas are needed.

Apply Analysis Tools: The following steps describe how to use Excel's descriptive statistics tool for these data:

Step 1. Select the **Tools** menu
Step 2. Choose the **Data Analysis** option
Step 3. Choose **Descriptive Statistics** from the list of Analysis Tools
Step 4. When the **Descriptive Statistics** dialog box appears (see Figure 3.7):
      Enter B1:B13 in the **Input Range** box
      Select **Grouped By Columns**
      Select **Labels in First Row**
      Select **Output Range**
      Enter D1 in the **Output Range** box (to identify the upper left corner of the section of the worksheet where the descriptive statistics will appear)
      Select **Summary Statistics**
      Click **OK**

Cells D1:E15 of Figure 3.8 show the descriptive statistics provided by Excel. A grey screen is used to highlight the results. The boldfaced entries are the descriptive statistics we have covered. The descriptive statistics that are not boldfaced are either covered subsequently in the text or discussed in more advanced texts.

FIGURE 3.7   DESCRIPTIVE STATISTICS DIALOG BOX FOR THE STARTING
SALARY DATA

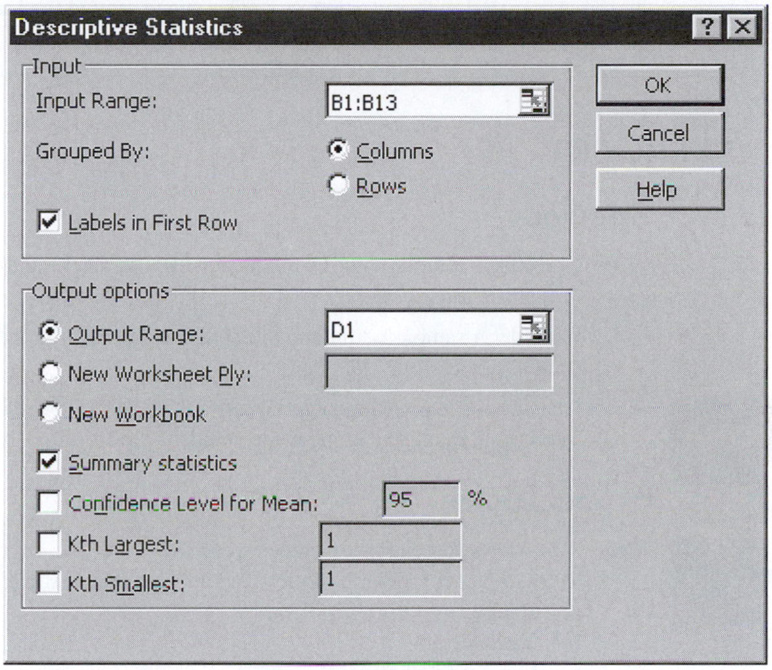

FIGURE 3.8   USING EXCEL TO COMPUTE DESCRIPTIVE STATISTICS
FOR STARTING SALARIES

	A	B	C	D	E	F
1	Graduate	Starting Salary		*Starting Salary*		
2	1	2850				
3	2	2950		Mean	2940	
4	3	3050		Standard Error	47.8199	
5	4	2880		Median	2905	
6	5	2755		Mode	2880	
7	6	2710		Standard Deviation	165.653	
8	7	2890		Sample Variance	27440.91	
9	8	3130		Kurtosis	1.718884	
10	9	2940		Skewness	1.091109	
11	10	3325		Range	615	
12	11	2920		Minimum	2710	
13	12	2880		Maximum	3325	
14				Sum	35280	
15				Count	12	
16						

NOTES AND COMMENTS

The standard deviation is a commonly used measure of the risk associated with investing in stock and stock funds (*Business Week*, January 17, 2000). It provides a measure of how monthly returns fluctuate around the long-run average return.

EXERCISES

Methods

13. Consider a sample with data values of 10, 20, 12, 17, and 16. Compute the range and interquartile range.

14. Consider a sample with data values of 10, 20, 12, 17, and 16. Compute the variance and standard deviation.

15. Consider a sample with data values of 27, 25, 20, 15, 30, 34, 28, and 25. Compute the range, interquartile range, variance, and standard deviation.

Applications

16. A bowler's scores for six games were 182, 168, 184, 190, 170, and 174. Using these data as a sample, compute the following descriptive statistics.
    a. Range
    b. Variance
    c. Standard deviation
    d. Coefficient of variation

17. *PC World* provided ratings for 15 notebook PCs (*PC World*, February 2000). A 100-point scale was used to provide an overall rating for each notebook. A score in the 90s is exceptional, while one in the 70s is above average. The overall ratings for the 15 notebooks are shown here.

Notebook

Notebook	Overall Rating
AMS Tech Roadster 15CTA380	67
Compaq Armada M700	78
Compaq Prosignia Notebook 150	79
Dell Inspiron 3700 C466GT	80
Dell Inspiron 7500 R500VT	84
Dell Latitude Cpi A366XT	76
Enpower ENP-313 Pro	77
Gateway Solo 9300LS	92
HP Pavillion Notebook PC	83
IBM ThinkPad I Series 1480	78
Micro Express NP7400	77
Micron TransPort NX PII-400	78
NEC Versa SX	78
Sceptre Soundx 5200	73
Sony VAIO PCG-F340	77

Compute the range, interquartile range, variance, and standard deviation for this sample of notebook PCs.

18. The Hawaii Visitors Bureau collects data on the number of visitors to the islands. The following data are a representative sample of visitors (in thousands) for several days in November.

From the mainland, Canada, and Europe:

| 108.70 | 112.25 | 94.01 | 144.03 | 162.44 | 161.61 | 76.20 |
| 102.11 | 110.87 | 79.36 | 129.04 | 95.16 | 114.16 | 121.88 |

From Asia and the Pacific:

| 29.89 | 41.13 | 40.67 | 40.41 | 43.07 | 24.86 |
| 31.61 | 21.60 | 27.34 | 64.57 | 32.98 | 41.31 |

   a. Compute the mean and median number of daily visitors from the two sources.
   b. Compute the range, the standard deviation, and the coefficient of variation for the two sources of visitors.
   c. What comparisons can you make between the numbers of visitors from the two sources?

19. The *Los Angeles Times* regularly reports the air quality index for various areas of Southern California. A sample of air quality index values for Pomona provided the following data: 28, 42, 58, 48, 45, 55, 60, 49, and 50.
   a. Compute the range and interquartile range.
   b. Compute the sample variance and sample standard deviation.
   c. A sample of air quality index readings for Anaheim provided a sample mean of 48.5, a sample variance of 136, and a sample standard deviation of 11.66. What comparisons can you make between the air quality in Pomona and that in Anaheim on the basis of these descriptive statistics?

20. Assume that the following data were used to construct the histograms of the number of days required to fill orders for Dawson Supply, Inc., and J.C. Clark Distributors (see Figure 3.4).

| *Dawson Supply Days for Delivery:* | 11 | 10 | 9 | 10 | 11 | 11 | 10 | 11 | 10 | 10 |
| *Clark Distributors Days for Delivery:* | 8 | 10 | 13 | 7 | 10 | 11 | 10 | 7 | 15 | 12 |

   Use the range and standard deviation to support the previous observation that Dawson Supply provides the more consistent and reliable delivery times.

21. Police records show the following numbers of daily crime reports for a sample of days during the winter months and a sample of days during the summer months.

Winter	Summer
18	28
20	18
15	24
16	32
21	18
20	29
12	23
16	38
19	28
20	18

   a. Compute the range and interquartile range for each period.
   b. Compute the variance and standard deviation for each period.
   c. Compute the coefficient of variation for each period.
   d. Compare the variability of the two periods.

CD file

Discount

22. The American Association of Individual Investors conducts an annual survey of discount brokers (*AAII Journal*, January 2000). The commissions charged by a sample of 20 discount brokers for two types of trades, 500 shares at $50 per share and 1000 shares at $5 per share, are shown in Table 3.2.
    a. Compute the range and interquartile range for each type of trade.
    b. Compute the variance and standard deviation for each type of trade.
    c. Compute the coefficient of variation for each type of trade.
    d. Compare the variability of cost for the two types of trades.

23. A production department uses a sampling procedure to test the quality of newly produced items. The department employs the following decision rule at an inspection station: If a sample of 14 items has a variance of more than .005, the production line must be shut down for repairs. Suppose the following data have just been collected:

3.43	3.45	3.43	3.48	3.52	3.50	3.39
3.48	3.41	3.38	3.49	3.45	3.51	3.50

Should the production line be shut down? Why or why not?

24. The following times were recorded by the quarter-mile and mile runners of a university track team (times are in minutes).

Quarter-mile Times:	.92	.98	1.04	.90	.99
Mile Times:	4.52	4.35	4.60	4.70	4.50

After viewing this sample of running times, one of the coaches commented that the quarter-milers turned in the more consistent times. Use the standard deviation and the coefficient of variation to summarize the variability in the data. Does the use of the coefficient of variation indicate that the coach's statement should be qualified?

3.3 MEASURES OF RELATIVE LOCATION AND DETECTING OUTLIERS

We have described several measures of location and variability for data. The mean is the most widely used measure of location, whereas the standard deviation and variance are the most widely used measures of variability. Using the mean and the standard deviation together, we also can learn about the relative location of observations in a data set.

z-Scores

By using both the mean and standard deviation, we can determine the relative location of any observation. Suppose we have a sample of *n* observations, with the values denoted by $x_1, x_2, \ldots, x_n$. In addition, assume that the sample mean, $\bar{x}$, and the sample standard deviation, *s*, have been computed. Associated with each value, x_i, is another value called its **z-score.** Equation (3.9) shows how the z-score is computed for each x_i.

Excel's STANDARDIZE function can be used to compute the z-score. But it is just as easy to enter a cell formula to compute z_i.

z-Score

$$z_i = \frac{x_i - \bar{x}}{s} \qquad (3.9)$$

where

$$z_i = \text{the } z\text{-score for } x_i$$
$$\bar{x} = \text{the sample mean}$$
$$s = \text{the sample standard deviation}$$

The z-score is often called the *standardized value*. The z-score, z_i, can be interpreted as the *number of standard deviations x_i is from the mean $\bar{x}$*. For example, $z_1 = 1.2$ would indicate that x_1 is 1.2 standard deviations greater than the sample mean. Similarly, $z_2 = -.5$ would indicate that x_2 is .5, or 1/2, standard deviation less than the sample mean. A z-score greater than zero occurs for observations with a value greater than the mean, and a z-score less than zero occurs for observations with a value less than the mean. A z-score of zero indicates that the value of the observation is equal to the mean.

The z-score for any observation can be interpreted as a measure of the relative location of the observation in a data set. Thus, observations in two different data sets with the same z-score can be said to have the same relative location in terms of being the same number of standard deviations from the mean.

The z-scores for the class size data are computed in Table 3.4. Recall the previously computed sample mean, $\bar{x} = 44$, and sample standard deviation, $s = 8$. The z-score of -1.50 for the fifth observation shows it is farthest from the mean; it is 1.50 standard deviations below the mean.

Chebyshev's Theorem

Chebyshev's theorem enables us to make statements about the proportion of data values that must be within a specified number of standard deviations of the mean.

Chebyshev's Theorem

At least $(1 - 1/z^2)$ of the data values must be within z standard deviations of the mean, where z is any value greater than 1.

TABLE 3.4 z-SCORES FOR THE CLASS SIZE DATA

The calculations in this table can be easily made in an Excel worksheet.

Number of Students in Class (x_i)	Deviation About the Mean ($x_i - \bar{x}$)	z-score $\left(\dfrac{x_i - \bar{x}}{s}\right)$
46	2	2/8 = .25
54	10	10/8 = 1.25
42	−2	−2/8 = −.25
46	2	2/8 = .25
32	−12	−12/8 = −1.50

Some of the implications of this theorem, with $z = 2$, 3, and 4 standard deviations, follow.

- At least .75, or 75%, of the data values must be within $z = 2$ standard deviations of the mean.
- At least .89, or 89%, of the data values must be within $z = 3$ standard deviations of the mean.
- At least .94, or 94%, of the data values must be within $z = 4$ standard deviations of the mean.

For an example using Chebyshev's theorem, suppose that the midterm test scores for 100 students in a college business statistics course had a mean of 70 and a standard deviation of 5. How many students had test scores between 60 and 80? How many students had test scores between 58 and 82?

For the test scores between 60 and 80, we note that 60 is two standard deviations below the mean and 80 is two standard deviations above the mean. Using Chebyshev's theorem, we see that at least .75, or at least 75%, of the observations must have values within two standard deviations of the mean. Thus, at least 75% of the students must have scored between 60 and 80.

Chebyshev's theorem requires z > 1; but z need not be an integer.

For the test scores between 58 and 82, we see that $(58 - 70)/5 = -2.4$ indicates 58 is 2.4 standard deviations below the mean and that $(82 - 70)/5 = +2.4$ indicates 82 is 2.4 standard deviations above the mean. Applying Chebyshev's theorem with $z = 2.4$, we have

$$\left(1 - \frac{1}{z^2}\right) = \left[1 - \frac{1}{(2.4)^2}\right] = .826$$

At least 82.6% of the students must have test scores between 58 and 82.

Empirical Rule

The empirical rule is based on the normal probability distribution, which will be discussed in Chapter 6. The normal distribution is used extensively throughout the text.

One of the advantages of Chebyshev's theorem is that it applies to any data set regardless of the shape of the distribution of the data. In practical applications, however, many data sets exhibit a mound-shaped or bell-shaped distribution like the one shown in Figure 3.9. When the data are believed to approximate this distribution, the **empirical rule** can be used to determine the percentage of data values that must be within a specified number of standard deviations of the mean.

Empirical Rule

For data having a bell-shaped distribution:

- Approximately 68% of the data values will be within one standard deviation of the mean.
- Approximately 95% of the data values will be within two standard deviations of the mean.
- Almost all of the data values will be within three standard deviations of the mean.

FIGURE 3.9   A MOUND-SHAPED OR BELL-SHAPED DISTRIBUTION

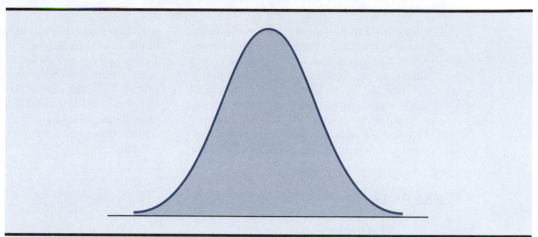

For example, liquid detergent cartons are filled automatically on a production line. Filling weights frequently have a bell-shaped distribution. If the mean filling weight is 16 ounces and the standard deviation is .25 ounces, we can use the empirical rule to draw the following conclusions.

- Approximately 68% of the filled cartons will have weights between 15.75 and 16.25 ounces (that is, within one standard deviation of the mean).
- Approximately 95% of the filled cartons will have weights between 15.50 and 16.50 ounces (that is, within two standard deviations of the mean).
- Almost all filled cartons will have weights between 15.25 and 16.75 ounces (that is, within three standard deviations of the mean).

Detecting Outliers

Sometimes a data set will have one or more observations with unusually large or unusually small values. Extreme values such as these are called **outliers**. Experienced statisticians take steps to identify outliers and then review each one carefully. An outlier may be a data value that has been incorrectly recorded. If so, it can be corrected before further analysis. An outlier may also be from an observation that was incorrectly included in the data set; if so, it can be removed. Finally, an outlier may be an unusual data value that has been recorded correctly and belongs in the data set. In such cases it should remain.

It is a good idea to check for outliers before making decisions based on data analysis. Errors are often made in recording data and entering data into the computer. Outliers should not necessarily be deleted, but their accuracy and appropriateness should be verified.

Standardized values (z-scores) can be used to identify outliers. Recall that the empirical rule allows us to conclude that for data with a bell-shaped distribution, almost all the data values will be within three standard deviations of the mean. Hence, in using z-scores to identify outliers, we recommend treating any data value with a z-score less than -3 or greater than $+3$ as an outlier. Such data values can then be reviewed for accuracy and to determine whether they belong in the data set.

Refer to the z-scores for the class size data in Table 3.4. The z-score of -1.50 shows the fifth class size is farthest from the mean. However, this standardized value is well within the -3 to $+3$ guideline for outliers. Thus, the z-scores do not indicate that outliers are present in the class size data.

NOTES AND COMMENTS

1. Chebyshev's theorem is applicable for any data set and can be used to state the minimum number of data values that will be within a certain number of standard deviations of the mean. If the data are known to be approximately bell-shaped, more can be said. For instance, the empirical rule allows us to say that *approximately* 95% of the data values will be within two standard deviations of the mean; Chebyshev's theorem allows us to conclude only that at least 75% of the data values will be in that interval.

2. Before analyzing a data set, statisticians usually make a variety of checks to ensure the validity of data. In a large study it is not uncommon for errors to be made in recording data values or in entering the values into a computer. Identifying outliers is one tool used to check the validity of the data.

EXERCISES

Methods

25. Consider a sample with data values of 10, 20, 12, 17, and 16. Compute the z-score for each of the five observations.

26. Consider a sample with a mean of 500 and a standard deviation of 100. What are the z-scores for the following data values: 520, 650, 500, 450, and 280?

27. Consider a sample with a mean of 30 and a standard deviation of 5. Use Chebyshev's theorem to determine the percentage of the data within each of the following ranges.
    a. 20 to 40
    b. 15 to 45
    c. 22 to 38
    d. 18 to 42
    e. 12 to 48

28. Suppose the data have a bell-shaped distribution with a mean of 30 and a standard deviation of 5. Use the empirical rule to determine the percentage of data within each of the following ranges.
    a. 20 to 40
    b. 15 to 45
    c. 25 to 35

Applications

29. The results of a national survey of 1154 adults showed that on average, adults sleep 6.9 hours per day during the workweek (2000 Omnibus Sleep in America Poll). Suppose that the standard deviation is 1.2 hours.
    a. Use Chebyshev's theorem to calculate the percentage of individuals who sleep between 4.5 and 9.3 hours per day.
    b. Use Chebyshev's theorem to calculate the percentage of individuals who sleep between 3.9 and 9.9 hours per day.
    c. Assume that the number of hours of sleep follows a bell-shaped distribution. Use the empirical rule to calculate the percentage of individuals who sleep between 4.5 and 9.3 hours per day. How does this result compare to the value that you obtained using Chebyshev's theorem in part (a)?

30. According to Nielsen Media Research, kids aged 12 to 17 watched an average of 3 hours of television per day for the broadcast year that ended in August (*Barron's*, November 8, 1999). Suppose that the standard deviation is 1 hour and that the distribution of the time spent watching television has a bell-shaped distribution.

a. What percentage of kids aged 12 to 17 watches television between 2 and 3 hours per day?

b. What percentage of kids aged 12 to 17 watches television between 1 and 4 hours per day?

c. What percentage of kids aged 12 to 17 watches television more than 4 hours per day?

31. Suppose that IQ scores have a bell-shaped distribution with a mean of 100 and a standard deviation of 15.

a. What percentage of people should have an IQ score between 85 and 115?

b. What percentage of people should have an IQ score between 70 and 130?

c. What percentage of people should have an IQ score of more than 130?

d. A person with an IQ score greater than 145 is considered a genius. Does the empirical rule support this statement? Explain.

32. The average labor cost for color TV repair in Chicago is $90.06 (*The Wall Street Journal*, January 2, 1998). Suppose the standard deviation is $20.00.

a. What is the z-score for a repair job with a labor cost of $71.00?

b. What is the z-score for a repair job with a labor cost of $168.00?

c. Interpret the z-scores in parts (a) and (b). Comment on whether either should be considered an outlier.

33. Wageweb conducts surveys of salary data and presents summaries on its Web site. Using salary data as of January 1, 2000, Wageweb reported that salaries of benefits managers ranged from $50,935 to $79,577 (Wageweb.com, April 12, 2000). Assume the following data are a sample of the annual salaries for 30 benefits managers (data are in thousands of dollars).

57.7	64.4	62.1	59.1	71.1
63.0	64.7	61.2	66.8	61.8
64.2	63.3	62.2	61.2	59.4
63.0	66.7	60.3	74.0	62.8
68.7	63.8	59.2	60.3	56.6
59.3	69.5	61.7	58.9	63.1

a. Compute the mean and standard deviation for the sample data.

b. Using the mean and standard deviation computed in part (a) as estimates of the mean and standard deviation of salary for the population of benefits managers, use Chebyshev's theorem to determine the percentage of benefits managers with an annual salary between $55,000 and $71,000.

c. Develop a histogram for the sample data. Does it appear reasonable to assume that the distribution of annual salary can be approximated by a bell-shaped distribution?

d. Assume that the distribution of annual salary is bell-shaped. Using the mean and standard deviation computed in part (a) as estimates of the mean and standard deviation of salary for the population of benefits managers, use the empirical rule to determine the percentage of benefits managers with an annual salary between $55,000 and $71,000. Compare your answer with the value computed in part (b).

e. Do the sample data contain any outliers?

34. A sample of 10 National Basketball Association (NBA) scores provided the following data (*USA Today*, April 14, 2000).

Winning Team	Points Scored	Losing Team	Points Scored	Winning Margin
Philadelphia	93	Washington	84	9
Charlotte	119	Atlanta	87	32

(continued)

Winning Team	Points Scored	Losing Team	Points Scored	Winning Margin
Milwaukee	101	Cleveland	100	1
Indiana	77	Toronto	73	4
Seattle	110	Minnesota	83	27
Boston	95	Orlando	91	4
Detroit	90	Miami	73	17
New York	91	New Jersey	89	2
Utah	102	L.A. Clippers	93	9
Phoenix	122	Vancouver	116	6

a. Compute the mean and standard deviation for the points scored by the winning teams.

b. Assume that the points scored by the winning teams for all NBA games are bell-shaped. Using the mean and standard deviation computed in part (a) as estimates of the mean and standard deviation of the points scored for the population of all NBA games, estimate the percentage of all NBA games in which the winning team will score 100 or more points. Estimate the percentage of games in which the winning team will score more than 114 points.

c. Compute the mean and standard deviation for the winning margin. Do the winning margin data contain outliers? Explain.

35. *Consumer Review* posts reviews and ratings of a variety of products on the Internet. The following is a sample of 20 speaker systems and the ratings posted on January 2, 1998 (see *www.audioreview.com*). The ratings are on a scale of 1 to 5, with 5 being best.

Speakers

Speaker	Rating	Speaker	Rating
Infinity Kappa 6.1	4.00	ACI Sapphire III	4.67
Allison One	4.12	Bose 501 Series	2.14
Cambridge Ensemble II	3.82	DCM KX-212	4.09
Dynaudio Contour 1.3	4.00	Eosone RSF1000	4.17
Hsu Rsch. HRSW12V	4.56	Joseph Audio RM7si	4.88
Legacy Audio Focus	4.32	Martin Logan Aerius	4.26
Mission 73li	4.33	Omni Audio SA 12.3	2.32
PSB 400i	4.50	Polk Audio RT12	4.50
Snell Acoustics D IV	4.64	Sunfire True Subwoofer	4.17
Thiel CS1.5	4.20	Yamaha NS-A636	2.17

a. Compute the mean and the median.

b. Compute the first and third quartiles.

c. Compute the standard deviation.

d. What are the *z*-scores associated with Allison One and Omni Audio?

e. Do the data contain any outliers? Explain.

3.4   EXPLORATORY DATA ANALYSIS

In Chapter 2 we introduced the stem-and-leaf display as a technique of exploratory data analysis. Recall that exploratory data analysis enables us to use simple arithmetic and easy-to-draw pictures to summarize data. In this section we continue exploratory data analysis by considering five-number summaries and box plots.

Five-Number Summary

In a **five-number summary**, the following five numbers are used to summarize the data.

1. Smallest value
2. First quartile (Q_1)
3. Median (Q_2)
4. Third quartile (Q_3)
5. Largest value

In Section 3.1, we showed how Excel can be used to put the starting salary data in ascending order.

The easiest way to develop a five-number summary is to first place the data in ascending order. Then it is easy to identify the smallest value, the three quartiles, and the largest value. The monthly starting salaries shown in Table 3.1 for a sample of 12 business school graduates are repeated here in ascending order.

$$2710 \quad 2755 \quad 2850 \ \bigg| \ 2880 \quad 2880 \quad 2890 \ \bigg| \ 2920 \quad 2940 \quad 2950 \ \bigg| \ 3050 \quad 3130 \quad 3325$$

$$Q_1 = 2865 \qquad\qquad Q_2 = 2905 \qquad\qquad Q_3 = 3000$$
$$\text{(Median)}$$

The median of 2905 and the quartiles $Q_1 = 2865$ and $Q_3 = 3000$ were computed in Section 3.1. Reviewing the data shows a smallest value of 2710 and a largest value of 3325. Thus the five-number summary for the salary data is 2710, 2865, 2905, 3000, 3325. Approximately one-fourth, or 25%, of the observations are between adjacent numbers in a five-number summary.

Box Plot

A **box plot** is a graphical summary of data that is based on a five-number summary. A key to the development of a box plot is the computation of the median and the quartiles, Q_1 and Q_3. The interquartile range, IQR = $Q_3 - Q_1$, is also used. Figure 3.10 is the box plot for the monthly starting salary data. The steps used to construct the box plot follow.

Box plots provide another way to identify outliers. But they do not necessarily identify the same values as those with a z-score less than −3 or greater than +3. Either, or both, procedures may be used.

1. A box is drawn with the ends of the box located at the first and third quartiles. For the salary data, $Q_1 = 2865$ and $Q_3 = 3000$. This box contains the middle 50% of the data.
2. A vertical line is drawn in the box at the location of the median (2905 for the salary data).
3. By using the interquartile range, IQR = $Q_3 - Q_1$, *limits* are located. The limits for the box plot are 1.5(IQR) below Q_1 and 1.5(IQR) above Q_3. For the salary data, IQR = $Q_3 - Q_1 = 3000 - 2865 = 135$. Thus, the limits are $2865 - 1.5(135) = 2662.5$ and $3000 + 1.5(135) = 3202.5$. Data outside these limits are considered *outliers*.
4. The dashed lines in Figure 3.10 are called *whiskers*. The whiskers are drawn from the ends of the box to the smallest and largest values *inside the limits* computed in step 3. Thus the whiskers end at salary values of 2710 and 3130.
5. Finally, the location of each outlier is shown with the symbol *. In Figure 3.10 we see one outlier, 3325.

In Figure 3.10 we included lines showing the location of the upper and lower limits. These lines were drawn to show how the limits are computed and where they are located for the salary data. Although the limits are always computed, generally they are not drawn on the box plots. Figure 3.11 shows the usual appearance of a box plot for the salary data.

FIGURE 3.10   BOX PLOT OF THE STARTING SALARY DATA WITH LINES SHOWING
THE LOWER AND UPPER LIMITS

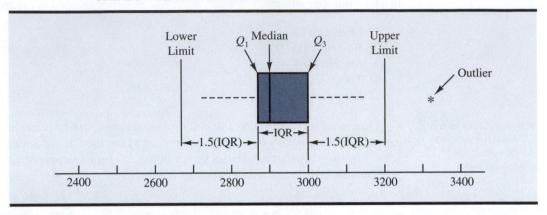

FIGURE 3.11   BOX PLOT OF THE STARTING SALARY DATA

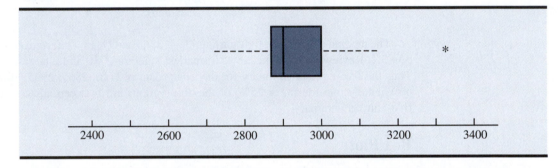

NOTES AND COMMENTS

1. When using a box plot, we may or may not identify the same outliers as the ones we select when using z-scores less than -3 and greater than $+3$. However, the objective of both approaches is simply to identify extreme data values that should be reviewed to ensure the validity of the data. Outliers identified by either procedure should be reviewed.

2. An advantage of the exploratory data analysis procedures is that they are easy to use; few numerical calculations are necessary. We simply sort the data values into ascending order and identify the five-number summary. The box plot can then be constructed. It is not necessary to compute the mean and the standard deviation for the data.

3. The basic Excel package does not contain a tool for constructing box plots. The Chart Wizard can be used for this purpose, but it is rather awkward and probably not worth the effort.

EXERCISES

Methods

36. Consider a sample with data values of 27, 25, 20, 15, 30, 34, 28, and 25. Provide the five-number summary for the data.

37. Show the box plot for the data in Exercise 36.

38. Show the five-number summary and the box plot for the following data: 5, 15, 18, 10, 8, 12, 16, 10, 6.

39. A data set has a first quartile of 42 and a third quartile of 50. Compute the lower and upper limits for the corresponding box plot. Should a data value of 65 be considered an outlier?

Applications

40. A goal of management is to help their company earn as much as possible relative to the capital invested. One measure of success is return on equity—the ratio of net income to stockholders' equity. Shown here are return on equity percentages for 25 companies (*Standard & Poor's Stock Reports*, November 1997).

ReEquity

9.0	19.6	22.9	41.6	11.4
15.8	52.7	17.3	12.3	5.1
17.3	31.1	9.6	8.6	11.2
12.8	12.2	14.5	9.2	16.6
5.0	30.3	14.7	19.2	6.2

  a. Provide a five-number summary.
  b. Compute the lower and upper limits.
  c. Do the data contain any outliers? How would this information be helpful to a financial analyst?
  d. Show a box plot.

41. Annual sales, in millions of dollars, for 21 pharmaceutical companies follow.

8408	1374	1872	8879	2459	11413
608	14138	6452	1850	2818	1356
10498	7478	4019	4341	739	2127
3653	5794	8305			

  a. Provide a five-number summary.
  b. Compute the lower and upper limits.
  c. Do the data contain any outliers?
  d. Johnson & Johnson's sales are the largest on the list at $14,138 million. Suppose a data entry error (a transposition) had been made and the sales had been entered as $41,138 million. Would the method of detecting outliers in part (c) identify this problem and allow for correction of the data entry error?
  e. Show a box plot.

42. Corporate share repurchase programs are often touted as a benefit for shareholders. But, Robert Gabele, director of insider research for First Call/Thomson Financial, notes that many companies undertake these programs solely to acquire stock to use for incentive options for top managers. Across all companies, existing stock options in 1998 represented 6.2 percent of all common shares outstanding. The following data show the number of shares covered by option grants and the number of shares outstanding for 15 companies. *Bloomberg* identified these companies as the ones that would need to repurchase the highest percentage of outstanding shares to cover their option grants (*Bloomberg Personal Finance*, January/February 2000).

Options

Company	Shares Covered by Options Grants (millions)	Common Shares Outstanding (millions)
Adobe Systems	20.3	61.8
Apple Computer	52.7	160.9
Applied Materials	109.1	375.4
		(*continued*)

Company	Shares Covered by Options Grants (millions)	Common Shares Outstanding (millions)
Autodesk	15.7	58.9
Best Buy	44.2	203.8
Cendant	183.3	718.1
Dell Computer	720.8	2540.9
Fruit of the Loom	14.2	66.9
ITT Industries	18.0	87.9
Merrill Lynch	89.9	365.5
Novell	120.2	335.0
Parametric Technology	78.3	269.3
Reebok International	12.8	56.1
Silicon Graphics	52.6	188.8
Toys R Us	54.8	247.6

     a.   What are the mean and median number of shares covered by option grants?
     b.   What are the first and third quartiles for the number of shares covered by option grants?
     c.   Do the number of shares covered by option grants show any outliers? Show a box plot.
     d.   For each company, compute the percentage of shares outstanding that are covered by option grants. How does the mean of this percentage compare to the 1998 percentage of 6.2 reported for all companies?

43. The Highway Loss Data Institute's Injury and Collision Loss Experience report rates car models on the basis of the number of insurance claims filed after accidents. Index ratings near 100 are considered average. Lower ratings are better, indicating a safer car model. Shown are ratings for 20 midsize cars and 20 small cars.

Injury

Midsize cars:	81	91	93	127	68	81	60	51	58	75
	100	103	119	82	128	76	68	81	91	82
Small cars:	73	100	127	100	124	103	119	108	109	113
	108	118	103	120	102	122	96	133	80	140

Summarize the data for the midsize and small cars separately.
     a.   Provide a five-number summary for midsize cars and for small cars.
     b.   Show the box plots.
     c.   Make a statement about what your summaries indicate about the safety of midsize cars in comparison to small cars.

44. Birinyi Associates, Inc., conducted a survey of stock markets around the world to assess their performance during 1997. Table 3.5 summarizes the findings for a sample of 30 countries.
     a.   What are the mean and median percentage changes for these countries?
     b.   What are the first and third quartiles?
     c.   Do the data contain any outliers? Show a box plot.
     d.   What percentile would you report for the United States?

3.5   MEASURES OF ASSOCIATION BETWEEN TWO VARIABLES

Thus far we examined numerical methods used to summarize the data for *one variable at a time.* Often a manager or decision maker is interested in the *relationship between two variables.* In this section we present covariance and correlation as descriptive measures of the relationship between two variables.

TABLE 3.5   PERCENT CHANGE IN VALUE FOR WORLD STOCK MARKETS

CD file
World

Country	Percent Change	Country	Percent Change
Argentina	24.70	India	18.60
Australia	7.91	Israel	27.91
Bahrain	49.67	Japan	−21.19
Barbados	48.29	Lithuania	16.82
Bermuda	51.92	Mexico	54.92
Brazil	44.84	Namibia	6.52
Chile	12.80	Nigeria	−7.97
Colombia	69.60	Panama	59.40
Croatia	−1.07	Poland	2.27
Czech Republic	−3.25	Russia	125.89
Ecuador	5.37	Slovenia	18.71
Estonia	62.34	Sri Lanka	15.49
Finland	32.31	Taiwan	18.08
Germany	47.11	Turkey	254.45
Greece	59.19	United States	22.64

Source: The Wall Street Journal, January 2, 1998.

We begin by reconsidering the application concerning a stereo and sound equipment store in San Francisco as presented in Section 2.4. The store's manager wants to determine the relationship between the number of weekend television commercials shown and the sales at the store during the following week. Sample data with sales expressed in hundreds of dollars are provided in Table 3.6. It shows 10 observations ($n = 10$), one for each week. The scatter diagram in Figure 3.12 shows a positive relationship, with higher sales (y) associated with a greater number of commercials (x). In fact, the scatter diagram suggests that a straight line could be used as an approximation of the relationship. In the following discussion, we introduce **covariance** as a descriptive measure of the linear association between two variables.

TABLE 3.6   SAMPLE DATA FOR THE STEREO AND SOUND EQUIPMENT STORE

CD file
Stereo

Week	Number of Commercials x	Sales Volume ($100s) y
1	2	50
2	5	57
3	1	41
4	3	54
5	4	54
6	1	38
7	5	63
8	3	48
9	4	59
10	2	46

FIGURE 3.12   SCATTER DIAGRAM FOR THE STEREO AND SOUND EQUIPMENT STORE

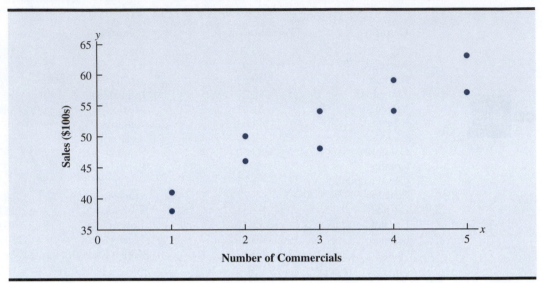

Covariance

For a sample of size n with the observations (x_1, y_1), (x_2, y_2), and so on, the sample covariance is defined as follows:

Sample Covariance

$$s_{xy} = \frac{\Sigma(x_i - \bar{x})(y_i - \bar{y})}{n - 1} \qquad (3.10)$$

This formula pairs each x_i with a y_i. We then sum the products obtained by multiplying the deviation of each x_i from its sample mean $\bar{x}$ by the deviation of the corresponding y_i from its sample mean $\bar{y}$; this sum is then divided by $n - 1$.

To measure the strength of the linear relationship between the number of commercials x and the sales volume y in the stereo and sound equipment store problem, we use equation (3.10) to compute the sample covariance. The calculations in Table 3.7 show the computation of $\Sigma(x_i - \bar{x})(y_i - \bar{y})$. Note that $\bar{x} = 30/10 = 3$ and $\bar{y} = 510/10 = 51$. Using equation (3.10), we obtain a sample covariance of

$$s_{xy} = \frac{\Sigma(x_i - \bar{x})(y_i - \bar{y})}{n - 1} = \frac{99}{9} = 11$$

The formula for computing the covariance of a population of size N is similar to equation (3.10), but we use different notation to indicate that we are working with the entire population.

Population Covariance

$$\sigma_{xy} = \frac{\Sigma(x_i - \mu_x)(y_i - \mu_y)}{N} \tag{3.11}$$

In equation (3.11) we use the notation μ_x for the population mean of the variable x and μ_y for the population mean of the variable y. The population covariance σ_{xy} is defined for a population of size N.

Interpretation of the Covariance

To aid in the interpretation of the sample covariance, consider Figure 3.13. It is the same as the scatter diagram of Figure 3.12 with a vertical dashed line at $\bar{x} = 3$ and a horizontal dashed line at $\bar{y} = 51$. Four quadrants have been identified on the graph. Points in quadrant I correspond to x_i greater than $\bar{x}$ and y_i greater than $\bar{y}$, points in quadrant II correspond to x_i less than $\bar{x}$ and y_i greater than $\bar{y}$, and so on. Thus, the value of $(x_i - \bar{x})(y_i - \bar{y})$ must be positive for points in quadrant I, negative for points in quadrant II, positive for points in quadrant III, and negative for points in quadrant IV.

The covariance is a measure of the linear association between two variables.

If the value of s_{xy} is positive, the points that have had the greatest influence on s_{xy} must be in quadrants I and III. Hence, a positive value for s_{xy} is indicative of a positive linear association between x and y; that is, as the value of x increases, the value of y increases. If the value of s_{xy} is negative, however, the points that have had the greatest influence on s_{xy} are in quadrants II and IV. Hence, a negative value for s_{xy} indicates a negative linear association between x and y; that is, as the value of x increases, the value of y decreases. Finally, if the points are evenly distributed across all four quadrants, the value of s_{xy} will be close to zero, indicating no linear association between x and y. Figure 3.14 shows the values of s_{xy} that can be expected with three different types of scatter diagrams.

Referring again to Figure 3.13, we see that the scatter diagram for the stereo and sound equipment store follows the pattern in the top panel of Figure 3.14. As we should expect, the value of the sample covariance indicates a positive linear relationship with $s_{xy} = 11$.

TABLE 3.7   CALCULATIONS FOR THE SAMPLE COVARIANCE

The calculations in this table can be easily made in an Excel worksheet.

	x_i	y_i	$x_i - \bar{x}$	$y_i - \bar{y}$	$(x_i - \bar{x})(y_i - \bar{y})$
	2	50	-1	-1	1
	5	57	2	6	12
	1	41	-2	-10	20
	3	54	0	3	0
	4	54	1	3	3
	1	38	-2	-13	26
	5	63	2	12	24
	3	48	0	-3	0
	4	59	1	8	8
	2	46	-1	-5	5
Totals	30	510	0	0	99

$$s_{xy} = \frac{\Sigma(x_i - \bar{x})(y_i - \bar{y})}{n - 1} = \frac{99}{10 - 1} = 11$$

FIGURE 3.13   PARTITIONED SCATTER DIAGRAM FOR THE STEREO AND SOUND EQUIPMENT STORE

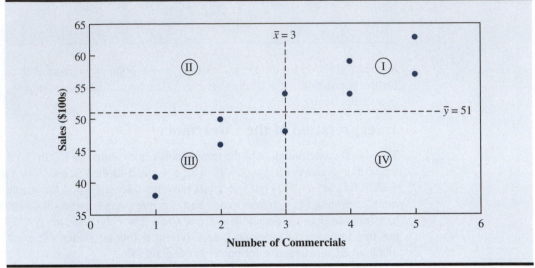

From the preceding discussion, it might appear that a large positive value for the covariance indicates a strong positive linear relationship and that a large negative value indicates a strong negative linear relationship. However, one problem with using covariance as a measure of the strength of the linear relationship is that the value of the covariance depends on the units of measurement for x and y. For example, suppose we are interested in the relationship between height x and weight y for individuals. Clearly the strength of the relationship should be the same whether we measure height in feet or inches. When height is measured in inches, however, we have much larger numerical values for $(x_i - \bar{x})$ than we have when height is measured in feet. Thus, with height measured in inches, we would obtain a larger value for the numerator $\Sigma(x_i - \bar{x})(y_i - \bar{y})$ in equation (3.10)—and hence a larger covariance—when in fact the relationship does not change. A measure of the relationship between two variables that avoids this difficulty is the **correlation coefficient**.

Correlation Coefficient

For sample data, the Pearson product moment correlation coefficient is defined as follows.

Pearson Product Moment Correlation Coefficient: Sample Data

$$r_{xy} = \frac{s_{xy}}{s_x s_y} \tag{3.12}$$

where

$$
\begin{aligned}
r_{xy} &= \text{sample correlation coefficient} \\
s_{xy} &= \text{sample covariance} \\
s_x &= \text{sample standard deviation of } x \\
s_y &= \text{sample standard deviation of } y
\end{aligned}
$$

FIGURE 3.14   INTERPRETATION OF SAMPLE COVARIANCE

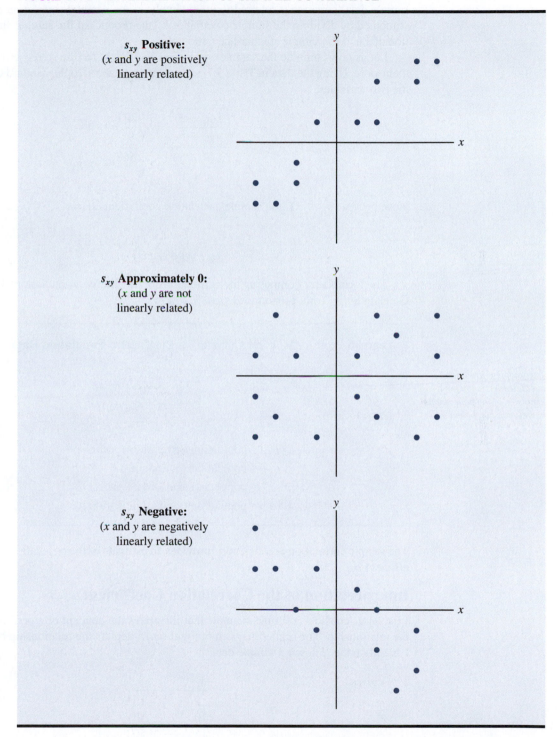

Equation (3.12) shows that the Pearson product moment correlation coefficient for sample data (commonly referred to more simply as the *sample correlation coefficient*) is computed by dividing the sample covariance by the product of the sample standard deviation of x and the sample standard deviation of y.

Let us now compute the sample correlation coefficient for the stereo and sound equipment store. Using the data in Table 3.7, we can compute the sample standard deviations for the two variables.

$$s_x = \sqrt{\frac{\Sigma(x_i - \bar{x})^2}{n - 1}} = \sqrt{\frac{20}{9}} = 1.49$$

$$s_y = \sqrt{\frac{\Sigma(y_i - \bar{y})^2}{n - 1}} = \sqrt{\frac{566}{9}} = 7.93$$

Now, because $s_{xy} = 11$, the sample correlation coefficient equals

$$r_{xy} = \frac{s_{xy}}{s_x s_y} = \frac{11}{(1.49)(7.93)} = +.93$$

The formula for computing the correlation coefficient for a population, denoted by the Greek letter ρ_{xy} (rho, pronounced "row"), follows.

The sample correlation coefficient r_{xy} is the point estimator of the population correlation coefficient ρ_{xy}.

Pearson Product Moment Correlation Coefficient: Population Data

$$\rho_{xy} = \frac{\sigma_{xy}}{\sigma_x \sigma_y} \tag{3.13}$$

where

ρ_{xy} = population correlation coefficient
σ_{xy} = population covariance
σ_x = population standard deviation for x
σ_y = population standard deviation for y

The sample correlation coefficient r_{xy} provides an estimate of the population correlation coefficient ρ_{xy}.

Interpretation of the Correlation Coefficient

First let us consider a simple example that illustrates the concept of a perfect positive linear relationship. The scatter diagram in Figure 3.15 depicts the relationship between x and y based on the following sample data.

x_i	y_i
5	10
10	30
15	50

The straight line drawn through each of the three points shows a perfect linear relationship between x and y. In order to apply equation (3.12) to compute the sample correla-

FIGURE 3.15   SCATTER DIAGRAM DEPICTING A PERFECT POSITIVE
LINEAR RELATIONSHIP

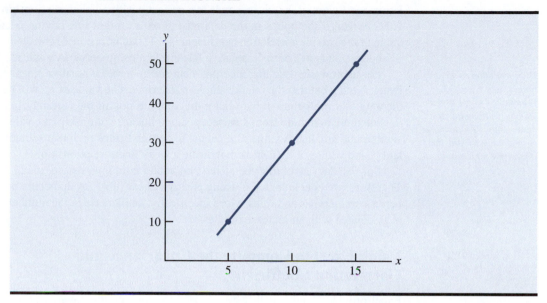

tion we must first compute s_{xy}, s_x, and s_y. Some of the necessary computations are contained in Table 3.8. Using the results in Table 3.8, we find

$$s_{xy} = \frac{\Sigma(x_i - \bar{x})(y_i - \bar{y})}{n - 1} = \frac{200}{2} = 100$$

$$s_x = \sqrt{\frac{\Sigma(x_i - \bar{x})^2}{n - 1}} = \sqrt{\frac{50}{2}} = 5$$

$$s_y = \sqrt{\frac{\Sigma(y_i - \bar{y})^2}{n - 1}} = \sqrt{\frac{800}{2}} = 20$$

$$r_{xy} = \frac{s_{xy}}{s_x s_y} = \frac{100}{5(20)} = 1$$

Thus, we see that the value of the sample correlation coefficient is 1.

TABLE 3.8   COMPUTATIONS USED IN CALCULATING THE SAMPLE
CORRELATION COEFFICIENT

	x_i	y_i	$x_i - \bar{x}$	$(x_i - \bar{x})^2$	$y_i - \bar{y}$	$(y_i - \bar{y})^2$	$(x_i - \bar{x})(y_i - \bar{y})$
	5	10	−5	25	−20	400	100
	10	30	0	0	0	0	0
	15	50	5	25	20	400	100
Totals	30	90	0	50	0	800	200

$\bar{x} = 10$ $\bar{y} = 30$

In general, it can be shown that if all the points in a data set fall on a positively sloped straight line, the value of the sample correlation coefficient is $+1$; that is, a sample correlation coefficient of $+1$ corresponds to a perfect positive linear relationship between x and y. Moreover, if the points in the data set fall on a straight line having negative slope, the value of the sample correlation coefficient is -1; that is, a sample correlation coefficient of -1 corresponds to a perfect negative linear relationship between x and y.

The correlation coefficient ranges from -1 to $+1$. Values close to -1 or $+1$ indicate a strong linear relationship. The closer the correlation is to zero, the weaker the relationship.

Let us now suppose that a certain data set indicates a positive linear relationship between x and y but that the relationship is not perfect. The value of r_{xy} will be less than 1, indicating that the points in the scatter diagram are not all on a straight line. As the points deviate more and more from a perfect positive linear relationship, the value of r_{xy} becomes smaller and smaller. A value of r_{xy} equal to zero indicates no linear relationship between x and y, and values of r_{xy} near zero indicate a weak linear relationship.

For the data involving the stereo and sound equipment store, recall that $r_{xy} = +.93$. Therefore, we conclude that a strong positive linear relationship occurs between the number of commercials and sales. More specifically, an increase in the number of commercials is associated with an increase in sales.

Using Excel to Compute the Covariance and Correlation Coefficient

Excel's COVAR function is designed for a population and Excel's CORREL function is designed for a sample.

Excel provides functions that can be used to compute the covariance and correlation coefficient. But, you must be careful when using these functions because the covariance function treats the data as a population and the correlation function treats the data as a sample. Thus, the result obtained using Excel's covariance function must be adjusted to provide the sample covariance. We show here how these functions can be used to compute the sample covariance and the sample correlation coefficient for the stereo and sound equipment store data. Refer to Figure 3.16 as we present the steps involved. The formula worksheet is in the background; the value worksheet is in the foreground.

FIGURE 3.16   EXCEL WORKSHEET USED TO COMPUTE THE COVARIANCE AND
CORRELATION COEFFICIENT

	A	B	C	D	E	F	G
1	Week	Commercials	Sales		Population Covariance	=COVAR(B2:B11,C2:C11)	
2	1	2	50		Sample Correlation	=CORREL(B2:B11,C2:C11)	
3	2	5	57				
4	3	1	41				
5	4	3	54				
6	5	4	54				
7	6	1	38				
8	7	5	63				
9	8	3	48				
10	9	4	59				
11	10	2	46				
12							

	A	B	C	D	E	F	G
1	Week	Commercials	Sales		Population Covariance	9.9	
2	1	2	50		Sample Correlation	0.9305	
3	2	5	57				
4	3	1	41				
5	4	3	54				
6	5	4	54				
7	6	1	38				
8	7	5	63				
9	8	3	48				
10	9	4	59				
11	10	2	46				
12							

Enter Data: Labels and data on commercials and sales are entered into cells A1:C11 of the worksheet.

Enter Functions and Formulas: Excel's covariance function, COVAR, can be used to compute the population covariance by entering the following formula into cell F1:

$$=COVAR(B2:B11,C2:C11)$$

Similarly, the formula =CORREL(B2:B11,C2:C11) is entered into cell F2 to compute the sample correlation coefficient. The labels Population Covariance and Sample Correlation are entered into cells E1 and E2 to identify the output.

The formulas in cells F1:F2 are displayed in the worksheet in the background of Figure 3.16. The worksheet in the foreground shows the values computed using the Excel functions. Note that, except for rounding, the value of the sample correlation coefficient (.9305) is the same as we computed earlier using equation (3.12). However, the result provided by the COVAR function, 9.9, was obtained by treating the data as a population. Thus, we must adjust the Excel result of 9.9 to obtain the sample covariance. The adjustment is rather simple. First, note that the formula for the population covariance, equation (3.11), requires dividing by the total number of observations in the data set. But, the formula for the sample covariance, equation (3.10), requires dividing by the total number of observations minus 1. So to use the Excel result of 9.9 to compute the sample covariance, we simply multiply 9.9 by $n/(n-1)$. With $n = 10$, we obtain

$$s_{xy} = \left(\frac{10}{9}\right)9.9 = 11$$

Thus, the sample covariance for the stereo and sound equipment data is 11.

EXERCISES

Methods

45. Five observations taken for two variables follow.

x_i	4	6	11	3	16
y_i	50	50	40	60	30

     a. Develop a scatter diagram with x on the horizontal axis.
     b. What does the scatter diagram developed in part (a) indicate about the relationship between the two variables?
     c. Compute and interpret the sample covariance.
     d. Compute and interpret the sample correlation coefficient.

46. Five observations taken for two variables follow.

x_i	6	11	15	21	27
y_i	6	9	6	17	12

     a. Develop a scatter diagram for these data.
     b. What does the scatter diagram indicate about a relationship between x and y?
     c. Compute and interpret the sample covariance.
     d. Compute and interpret the sample correlation coefficient.

Applications

47. A high school guidance counselor collected the following data about the grade point averages (GPA) and the SAT mathematics test scores for six seniors.

GPA	2.7	3.5	3.7	3.3	3.6	3.0
SAT	450	560	700	620	640	570

a. Develop a scatter diagram for the data with GPA on the horizontal axis.
b. Is any relationship evident between the GPA and the SAT mathematics test score? Explain.
c. Compute and interpret the sample covariance.
d. Compute the sample correlation coefficient. What does this value tell us about the relationship between the two variables?

48. A department of transportation's study on driving speed and mileage for midsize automobiles resulted in the following data.

Driving Speed	30	50	40	55	30	25	60	25	50	55
Mileage	28	25	25	23	30	32	21	35	26	25

Compute and interpret the sample correlation coefficient.

49. *PC World* provided ratings for 15 notebook PCs (*PC World*, February 2000). The performance score is a measure of how fast a PC can run a mix of common business applications as compared to a baseline machine. For example, a PC with a performance score of 200 is twice as fast as the baseline machine. A 100-point scale was used to provide an overall rating for each notebook tested in the study. A score in the 90s is exceptional, while one in the 70s is above average. Table 3.9 shows the performance scores and the overall ratings for the 15 notebooks.
a. Compute the sample correlation coefficient.
b. What does the sample correlation coefficient tell about the relationship between the performance score and the overall rating?

TABLE 3.9   PERFORMANCE SCORES AND OVERALL RATINGS FOR 15 NOTEBOOK PCs

CD file
PCs

Notebook	Performance Score	Overall Rating
AMS Tech Roadster 15CTA380	115	67
Compaq Armada M700	191	78
Compaq Prosignia Notebook 150	153	79
Dell Inspiron 3700 C466GT	194	80
Dell Inspiron 7500 R500VT	236	84
Dell Latitude Cpi A366XT	184	76
Enpower ENP-313 Pro	184	77
Gateway Solo 9300LS	216	92
HP Pavilion Notebook PC	185	83
IBM ThinkPad I Series 1480	183	78
Micro Express NP7400	189	77
Micron TransPort NX PII-400	202	78
NEC Versa SX	192	78
Sceptre Soundx 5200	141	73
Sony VAIO PCG-F340	187	77

50. The Dow Jones Industrial Average (DJIA) and the Standard & Poor's (S&P) 500 Index are both used as measures of overall movement in the stock market. The DJIA is based on the price movements of 30 large companies; the S&P 500 is an index composed of 500 stocks. Some say the S&P 500 is a better measure of stock market performance because it is broader based. The closing price for the DJIA and the S&P 500 for 10 weeks, beginning with February 11, 2000, are shown (*Barron's*, April 17, 2000).

DowS&P

Date	Dow Jones	S&P 500
February 11	10425	1387
February 18	10220	1346
February 25	9862	1333
March 3	10367	1409
March 10	9929	1395
March 17	10595	1464
March 24	11113	1527
March 31	10922	1499
April 7	11111	1516
April 14	10306	1357

a. Compute the sample correlation coefficient for these data.
b. Are they poorly correlated, or do they have a close association?

51. The daily high and low temperatures for 20 cities follow (*USA Today*, May 9, 2000).

HighLow

City	High	Low
Athens	75	54
Bangkok	92	74
Cairo	84	57
Copenhagen	64	39
Dublin	64	46
Havana	86	68
Hong Kong	81	72
Johannesburg	61	50
London	73	48
Manila	93	75
Melbourne	66	50
Montreal	64	52
Paris	77	55
Rio de Janeiro	80	61
Rome	81	54
Seoul	64	50
Singapore	90	75
Sydney	68	55
Tokyo	79	59
Vancouver	57	43

What is the correlation between the high and low temperatures?

3.6   THE WEIGHTED MEAN AND WORKING WITH GROUPED DATA

In Section 3.1, we presented the mean as one of the most important measures of central location. The formula for the mean of a sample with n observations is restated as follows.

$$\bar{x} = \frac{\Sigma x_i}{n} = \frac{x_1 + x_2 + \cdots + x_n}{n} \qquad (3.14)$$

In this formula, each x_i is given equal importance or weight. Although this practice is most common, in some instances, the mean is computed by giving each observation a weight that reflects its importance. A mean computed in this manner is referred to as a **weighted mean**.

Weighted Mean

The weighted mean is computed as follows:

Weighted Mean

$$\bar{x} = \frac{\Sigma w_i x_i}{\Sigma w_i} \qquad (3.15)$$

where

$$x_i = \text{value of observation } i$$
$$w_i = \text{weight for observation } i$$

When the data are from a sample, equation (3.15) provides the weighted sample mean. When the data are from a population, μ replaces $\bar{x}$ and equation (3.15) provides the weighted population mean.

As an example of the need for a weighted mean, consider the following sample of five purchases of a raw material over the past three months.

Purchase	Cost per Pound ($)	Number of Pounds
1	3.00	1200
2	3.40	500
3	2.80	2750
4	2.90	1000
5	3.25	800

Note that the cost per pound has varied from $2.80 to $3.40 and the quantity purchased has varied from 500 to 2750 pounds. Suppose that a manager has asked for information about the mean cost per pound of the raw material. Because the quantities ordered vary, we must use the formula for a weighted mean. The five cost-per-pound data values are $x_1 = 3.00$, $x_2 = 3.40$, $x_3 = 2.80$, $x_4 = 2.90$, and $x_5 = 3.25$. The weighted mean cost per pound is found by weighting each cost by its corresponding quantity. For this example, the weights are

$w_1 = 1200$, $w_2 = 500$, $w_3 = 2750$, $w_4 = 1000$, and $w_5 = 800$. Using equation (3.15), the weighted mean is calculated as follows:

$$\bar{x} = \frac{1200(3.00) + 500(3.40) + 2750(2.80) + 1000(2.90) + 800(3.25)}{1200 + 500 + 2750 + 1000 + 800}$$

$$= \frac{18,500}{6250} = 2.96$$

Thus, the weighted mean computation shows that the mean cost per pound for the raw material is $2.96. Note that using equation (3.14) rather than the weighted mean formula would have provided misleading results. In this case, the mean of the five cost-per-pound values is $(3.00 + 3.40 + 2.80 + 2.90 + 3.25)/5 = 15.35/5 = \$3.07$, which overstates the actual mean cost per pound purchased.

Computing a grade point average is a good example of the use of a weighted mean.

The choice of weights for a particular weighted mean computation depends upon the application. An example that is well known to college students is the computation of a grade point average (GPA). In this computation, the data values generally used are 4 for an A grade, 3 for a B grade, 2 for a C grade, 1 for a D grade, and 0 for an F grade. The weights are the number of credits hours earned for each grade. Exercise 54 at the end of this section provides an example of this weighted mean computation. In other weighted mean computations, quantities such as pounds, dollars, and/or volume are frequently used as weights. In any case, when observations vary in importance, the analyst must choose the weight that best reflects the importance of each observation in the determination of the mean.

Grouped Data

In most cases, measures of location and variability are computed by using the individual data values. Sometimes, however, data are available only in a grouped or frequency distribution form. In the following discussion, we show how the weighted mean formula can be used to obtain approximations of the mean, variance, and standard deviation for **grouped data**.

In Section 2.2 we provided a frequency distribution of the time in days required to complete year-end audits for the public accounting firm of Sanderson and Clifford. The frequency distribution of audit times based on a sample of 20 clients is shown again in Table 3.10. Based on this frequency distribution, what is the sample mean audit time?

To compute the mean using only the grouped data, we treat the midpoint of each class as being representative of the items in the class. Let M_i denote the midpoint for class i and let f_i denote the frequency of class i. The weighted mean formula (3.15) is then used with

TABLE 3.10   FREQUENCY DISTRIBUTION OF AUDIT TIMES

Audit Time (days)	Frequency
10–14	4
15–19	8
20–24	5
25–29	2
30–34	1
Total	20

the data values denoted as M_i and the weights given by the frequencies f_i. In this case, the denominator of equation (3.15) is the sum of the frequencies, which is the sample size n. That is, $\Sigma f_i = n$. Thus, the equation for the sample mean for grouped data is as follows.

Sample Mean for Grouped Data

$$\bar{x} = \frac{\Sigma f_i M_i}{n} \qquad (3.16)$$

where

$$M_i = \text{the midpoint for class } i$$
$$f_i = \text{the frequency for class } i$$
$$n = \text{the sample size}$$

With the class midpoints, M_i, halfway between the class limits, the first class of 10–14 in Table 3.10 has a midpoint at $(10 + 14)/2 = 12$. The five class midpoints and the weighted mean computation for the audit time data are summarized in Table 3.11. As can be seen, the sample mean audit time is 19 days.

To compute the variance for grouped data, we use a slightly altered version of the formula for the variance provided in equation (3.5). In equation (3.5), the squared deviations of the data about the sample mean $\bar{x}$ were written $(x_i - \bar{x})^2$. However, with grouped data, the values are not known. In this case, we treat the class midpoint, M_i, as being representative of the x_i values in the corresponding class. Thus the squared deviations about the sample mean, $(x_i - \bar{x})^2$, are replaced by $(M_i - \bar{x})^2$. Then, just as we did with the sample mean calculations for grouped data, we weight each value by the frequency of the class, f_i. The sum of the squared deviations about the mean for all the data is approximated by $\Sigma f_i(M_i - \bar{x})^2$. The term $n - 1$ rather than n appears in the denominator in order to make the sample variance the estimate of the population variance. Thus, the following formula is used to obtain the sample variance for grouped data.

TABLE 3.11   COMPUTATION OF THE SAMPLE MEAN AUDIT TIME FOR GROUPED DATA

The calculations in this table can be easily made in an Excel worksheet.

Audit Time (days)	Class Midpoint (M_i)	Frequency (f_i)	$f_i M_i$
10–14	12	4	48
15–19	17	8	136
20–24	22	5	110
25–29	27	2	54
30–34	32	1	32
		20	380

$$\text{Sample mean } \bar{x} = \frac{\Sigma f_i M_i}{n} = \frac{380}{20} = 19 \text{ days}$$

Sample Variance for Grouped Data

$$s^2 = \frac{\sum f_i (M_i - \bar{x})^2}{n - 1} \qquad (3.17)$$

The calculation of the sample variance for audit times based on the grouped data from Table 3.10 is shown in Table 3.12. As can be seen, the sample variance is 30.

The standard deviation for grouped data is simply the square root of the variance for grouped data. For the audit time data, the sample standard deviation is $s = \sqrt{30} = 5.48$.

Before closing this section on computing measures of location and dispersion for grouped data, we note that formulas (3.16) and (3.17) are for a sample. Population summary measures are computed similarly. The grouped data formulas for a population mean and variance follow.

Population Mean for Grouped Data

$$\mu = \frac{\sum f_i M_i}{N} \qquad (3.18)$$

Population Variance for Grouped Data

$$\sigma^2 = \frac{\sum f_i (M_i - \mu)^2}{N} \qquad (3.19)$$

TABLE 3.12   COMPUTATION OF THE SAMPLE VARIANCE OF AUDIT TIMES FOR GROUPED DATA (SAMPLE MEAN $\bar{x} = 19$)

The calculations in this table can be easily made in an Excel worksheet.

Audit Time (days)	Class Midpoint (M_i)	Frequency (f_i)	Deviation ($M_i - \bar{x}$)	Squared Deviation ($M_i - \bar{x})^2$	$f_i(M_i - \bar{x})^2$
10–14	12	4	−7	49	196
15–19	17	8	−2	4	32
20–24	22	5	3	9	45
25–29	27	2	8	64	128
30–34	32	1	13	169	169
		20			570

$$\sum f_i (M_i - \bar{x})^2$$

$$\text{Sample variance } s^2 = \frac{\sum f_i (M_i - \bar{x})^2}{n - 1} = \frac{570}{19} = 30$$

NOTES AND COMMENTS

In computing descriptive statistics for grouped data, the class midpoints are used to approximate the data values in each class. As a result, the descriptive statistics for grouped data approximate the descriptive statistics that would result from using the original data directly. We therefore recommend computing descriptive statistics from the original data rather than from grouped data whenever possible.

EXERCISES

Methods

52. Consider the following data and corresponding weights.

x_i	Weight (w_i)
3.2	6
2.0	3
2.5	2
5.0	8

a. Compute the weighted mean.
b. Compute the sample mean of the four data values without weighting. Note the difference in the results provided by the two computations.

53. Consider the sample data in the following frequency distribution.

Class	Midpoint	Frequency
3–7	5	4
8–12	10	7
13–17	15	9
18–22	20	5

a. Compute the sample mean.
b. Compute the sample variance and sample standard deviation.

Applications

54. The grade point average for college students is based on a weighted mean computation. For most colleges, the grades are given the following data values: A (4), B (3), C (2), D (1), and F (0). After 60 credit hours of course work, a student at State University has earned 9 credit hours of A, 15 credit hours of B, 33 credit hours of C, and 3 credit hours of D.
a. Compute the student's grade point average.
b. Students at State University must have a 2.5 grade point average for their first 60 credit hours of course work in order to be admitted to the business college. Will this student be admitted?

55. *Bloomberg Personal Finance* (July/August 2001) included the following companies in its recommended investment portfolio. For a portfolio value of $25,000, the recommended dollar amounts allocated to each stock are shown.

Company	Portfolio	Estimated Growth Rate	Dividend Yield
Citigroup	$3000	15%	1.21%
General Electric	5500	14	1.48
Kimberly-Clark	4200	12	1.72
Oracle	3000	25	0.00
Pharmacia	3000	20	0.96
SBC Communications	3800	12	2.48
WorldCom	2500	35	0.00

    a. Using the portfolio dollar amounts as the weights, what is the weighted average estimated growth rate for the portfolio?

    b. What is the weighted average dividend yield for the portfolio?

56. A service station recorded the following frequency distribution for the number of gallons of gasoline sold per car in a sample of 680 cars.

Gasoline (gallons)	Frequency
0–4	74
5–9	192
10–14	280
15–19	105
20–24	23
25–29	6
Total	680

Compute the mean, variance, and standard deviation for these grouped data. If the service station expects to service about 120 cars on a given day, estimate the total number of gallons of gasoline that will be sold.

57. A survey of subscribers to *Fortune* magazine asked the following question: "How many of the last four issues have you read or looked through?" Suppose that the following frequency distribution summarizes 500 responses.

Number Read	Frequency
0	15
1	10
2	40
3	85
4	350
Total	500

    a. What is the mean number of issues read by a *Fortune* subscriber?

    b. What is the standard deviation of the number of issues read?

SUMMARY

In this chapter we introduced several descriptive statistics that can be used to summarize the location and variability of data. Unlike the tabular and graphical procedures introduced in Chapter 2, the measures introduced in this chapter summarize the data in terms of numerical values. When the numerical values obtained are for a sample, they are called sample statistics. When the numerical values obtained are for a population, they are called population parameters. Some of the notation used for sample statistics and population parameters follow.

	Sample Statistic	Population Parameter
Mean	$\bar{x}$	μ
Variance	s^2	σ^2
Standard deviation	s	σ
Covariance	s_{xy}	σ_{xy}
Correlation	r_{xy}	ρ_{xy}

In statistical inference, the sample statistic is referred to as the point estimator of the population parameter.

As measures of central location, we defined the mean, median, and mode. Then the concept of percentiles was used to describe other locations in the data set. Next, we presented the range, interquartile range, variance, standard deviation, and coefficient of variation as measures of variability or dispersion. We then described how the mean and standard deviation could be used, applying Chebyshev's theorem and the empirical rule, to provide more information about the distribution of data and to identify outliers.

In Section 3.4 we showed how to develop a five-number summary and a box plot to provide simultaneous information about the location, variability, and shape of the distribution. In Section 3.5 we introduced covariance and the correlation coefficient as measures of association between two variables. In the final section, we showed how to compute a weighted mean and how to calculate a mean, variance, and standard deviation for grouped data.

Most of the descriptive statistics discussed in the chapter can be computed using the functions and tools available in Excel. We showed how to use many of these functions as well as the Descriptive Statistics tool.

GLOSSARY

Sample statistic   A numerical value used as a summary measure for a sample (e.g., the sample mean, $\bar{x}$, the sample variance, s^2, and the sample standard deviation, s).

Population parameter   A numerical value used as a summary measure for a population (e.g., the population mean, μ, the population variance, σ^2, and the population standard deviation, σ).

Point estimator   The sample statistic, such as $\bar{x}$, s^2, and s, used to estimate the corresponding population parameter.

Mean   A measure of central location. It is computed by summing the data values and dividing by the number of observations.

Median   A measure of central location. It is the value in the middle when the data are arranged in ascending order.

Mode   A measure of location, defined as the value that occurs with greatest frequency.

Percentile   A value such that at least p percent of the observations are less than or equal to this value and at least $(100 - p)$ percent of the observations are greater than or equal to this value. The 50th percentile is the median.

Quartiles   The 25th, 50th, and 75th percentiles are the first quartile, the second quartile (median), and third quartile, respectively. The quartiles can be used to divide a data set into four parts, with each part containing approximately 25% of the data.

Range   A measure of variability, defined to be the largest value minus the smallest value.

Interquartile range (IQR)   A measure of variability, defined to be the difference between the third and first quartiles.

Variance   A measure of variability based on the squared deviations of the data values about the mean.

Standard deviation   A measure of variability computed by taking the positive square root of the variance.

Coefficient of variation   A measure of relative variability computed by dividing the standard deviation by the mean and multiplying by 100.

z-score   A value computed by dividing the deviation about the mean $(x_i - \bar{x})$ by the standard deviation s. A z-score is referred to as a standardized value and denotes the number of standard deviations x_i is from the mean.

Chebyshev's theorem   A theorem that can be used to make statements about the proportion of data values that must be within a specified number of standard deviations of the mean.

Empirical rule   A rule that can be used to compute the percentage of data values that must be within one, two, and three standard deviations of the mean for data having a bell-shaped distribution.

Outlier   An unusually small or unusually large data value.

Five-number summary   An exploratory data analysis technique that uses five numbers to summarize the data: smallest value, first quartile, median, third quartile, and largest value.

Box plot   A graphical summary of data based on a five-number summary.

Covariance   A measure of linear association between two variables. Positive values indicate a positive relationship; negative values indicate a negative relationship.

Correlation coefficient   A measure of linear association between two variables that takes on values between -1 and $+1$. Values near $+1$ indicate a strong positive linear relationship, values near -1 indicate a strong negative linear relationship, and values near zero indicate the lack of a linear relationship.

Weighted mean   The mean obtained by assigning each observation a weight that reflects its importance.

Grouped data   Data available in class intervals as summarized by a frequency distribution. Individual values of the original data are not available.

KEY FORMULAS

Sample Mean

$$\bar{x} = \frac{\Sigma x_i}{n} \tag{3.1}$$

Population Mean

$$\mu = \frac{\Sigma x_i}{N} \tag{3.2}$$

Interquartile Range

$$IQR = Q_3 - Q_1 \qquad (3.3)$$

Population Variance

$$\sigma^2 = \frac{\Sigma(x_i - \mu)^2}{N} \qquad (3.4)$$

Sample Variance

$$s^2 = \frac{\Sigma(x_i - \bar{x})^2}{n - 1} \qquad (3.5)$$

Standard Deviation

$$\text{Sample Standard Deviation} = s = \sqrt{s^2} \qquad (3.6)$$

$$\text{Population Standard Deviation} = \sigma = \sqrt{\sigma^2} \qquad (3.7)$$

Coefficient of Variation

$$\frac{\text{Standard Deviation}}{\text{Mean}} \times 100 \qquad (3.8)$$

z-score

$$z_i = \frac{x_i - \bar{x}}{s} \qquad (3.9)$$

Sample Covariance

$$s_{xy} = \frac{\Sigma(x_i - \bar{x})(y_i - \bar{y})}{n - 1} \qquad (3.10)$$

Population Covariance

$$\sigma_{xy} = \frac{\Sigma(x_i - \mu_x)(y_i - \mu_y)}{N} \qquad (3.11)$$

Pearson Product Moment Correlation Coefficient: Sample Data

$$r_{xy} = \frac{s_{xy}}{s_x s_y} \qquad (3.12)$$

Pearson Product Moment Correlation Coefficient: Population Data

$$\rho_{xy} = \frac{\sigma_{xy}}{\sigma_x \sigma_y} \qquad (3.13)$$

Weighted Mean

$$\bar{x} = \frac{\Sigma w_i x_i}{\Sigma w_i} \tag{3.15}$$

Sample Mean for Grouped Data

$$\bar{x} = \frac{\Sigma f_i M_i}{n} \tag{3.16}$$

Sample Variance for Grouped Data

$$s^2 = \frac{\Sigma f_i (M_i - \bar{x})^2}{n - 1} \tag{3.17}$$

Population Mean for Grouped Data

$$\mu = \frac{\Sigma f_i M_i}{N} \tag{3.18}$$

Population Variance for Grouped Data

$$\sigma^2 = \frac{\Sigma f_i (M_i - \mu)^2}{N} \tag{3.19}$$

SUPPLEMENTARY EXERCISES

58. The average American spends $65.88 per month dining out (*The Des Moines Register*, December 5, 1997). A sample of young adults provided the following dining out expenditures (in dollars) over the past month.

CD file

Eat

253	101	245	467	131	0	225
80	113	69	198	95	129	124
11	178	104	161	0	118	151
55	152	134	169			

   a. Compute the mean, median, and mode.
   b. Considering your results in part (a), do these young adults seem to spend about the same as an average American eating out?
   c. Compute the first and third quartiles.
   d. Compute the range and interquartile range.
   e. Compute the variance and standard deviation.
   f. Do the data contain any outliers?

59. The total annual compensation for a board member at one of the nation's 100 biggest public companies is based in part on the cash retainer, an annual payment for serving on the board. In addition to the cash retainer, a board member may receive a stock retainer, a stock grant, a stock option, and a fee for attending board meetings. The total compensation can easily exceed $100,000 even with an annual retainer as low as $15,000. The following data show the cash retainer (in $1000s) for a sample of 20 of the nation's biggest public companies (*USA Today*, April 17, 2000).

Retainer

Company	Cash Retainer
American Express	64
Bank of America	36
Boeing	26
Chevron	35
Dell Computer	40
DuPont	35
ExxonMobil	40
Ford Motor	30
General Motors	60
International Paper	36
Kroger	28
Lucent Technologies	50
Motorola	20
Procter & Gamble	55
Raytheon	40
Sears Roebuck	30
Texaco	15
United Parcel Service	55
Wal-Mart Stores	25
Xerox	40

Compute the following descriptive statistics.
a. Mean, median, and mode
b. The first and third quartiles
c. The range and interquartile range
d. The variance and the standard deviation
e. Coefficient of variation

60. A survey conducted to assess the ability of computer manufacturers to handle problems quickly obtained the following results (*PC Computing*, November 1997).

Company	Days to Resolve Problems	Company	Days to Resolve Problems
Compaq	13	Gateway	21
Packard Bell	27	Digital	27
Quantex	11	IBM	12
Dell	14	Hewlett-Packard	14
NEC	14	AT&T	20
AST	17	Toshiba	37
Acer	16	Micron	17

a. What are the mean and median number of days needed to resolve problems?
b. What are the variance and standard deviation?
c. Which manufacturer holds the best record?
d. What is the z-score for Packard Bell?
e. What is the z-score for IBM?
f. Do the data contain any outliers?

61. According to Forrester Research, Inc., approximately 19% of Internet users play games online. The following data show the number of unique users (in thousands) for the month of March for 10 game sites (*The Wall Street Journal*, April 17, 2000).

Site	Unique Users
AOLGames.aol	9416
extremelotto.com	3955
freelotto.com	12901
gamesville.com	4844
iwin.com	7410
prizecentral.com	4899
shockwave.com	5582
speedyclick.com	6628
uproar.com	8821
webstakes.com	7499

Using these data, compute the mean, median, variance, and standard deviation.

62. The typical household income for a sample of 20 cities follow (*Places Rated Almanac*, 2000). Data are in thousands of dollars.

Income

City	Income
Akron, OH	74.1
Atlanta, GA	82.4
Birmingham, AL	71.2
Bismark, ND	62.8
Cleveland, OH	79.2
Columbia, SC	66.8
Danbury, CT	132.3
Denver, CO	82.6
Detroit, MI	85.3
Fort Lauderdale, FL	75.8
Hartford, CT	89.1
Lancaster, PA	75.2
Madison, WI	78.8
Naples, FL	100.0
Nashville, TN	77.3
Philadelphia, PA	87.0
Savannah, GA	67.8
Toledo, OH	71.2
Trenton, NJ	106.4
Washington, DC	97.4

a. Compute the mean and standard deviation for the sample data.
b. Using the mean and standard deviation computed in part (a) as estimates of the mean and standard deviation of household income for the population of all cities, use Chebyshev's theorem to determine the range within which 75% of the household incomes for the population of all cities must fall.

c. Assume that the distribution of household income is bell-shaped. Using the mean and standard deviation computed in part (a) as estimates of the mean and standard deviation of household income for the population of all cities, use the empirical rule to determine the range within which 95% of the household incomes for the population of all cities must fall. Compare your answer with the value in part (b).

d. Do the sample data contain any outliers?

63. Public transportation and the automobile are two methods an employee can use to get to work each day. Samples of times recorded for each method are shown. Times are in minutes.

| Public Transportation: | 28 | 29 | 32 | 37 | 33 | 25 | 29 | 32 | 41 | 34 |
| Automobile: | 29 | 31 | 33 | 32 | 34 | 30 | 31 | 32 | 35 | 33 |

a. Compute the sample mean time to get to work for each method.
b. Compute the sample standard deviation for each method.
c. On the basis of your results from parts (a) and (b), which method of transportation should be preferred? Explain.
d. Develop a box plot for each method. Does a comparison of the box plots support your conclusion in part (c)?

64. The typical household income and typical home price for a sample of 20 cities follow (*Places Rated Almanac*, 2000). Data are in thousands of dollars.

Cities

City	Income	Home Price
Bismark, ND	62.8	92.8
Columbia, SC	66.8	116.7
Savannah, GA	67.8	108.1
Birmingham, AL	71.2	130.9
Toledo, OH	71.2	101.1
Akron, OH	74.1	114.9
Lancaster, PA	75.2	125.9
Fort Lauderdale, FL	75.8	145.3
Nashville, TN	77.3	125.9
Madison, WI	78.8	145.2
Cleveland, OH	79.2	135.8
Atlanta, GA	82.4	126.9
Denver, CO	82.6	161.9
Detroit, MI	85.3	145.0
Philadelphia, PA	87.0	151.5
Hartford, CT	89.1	162.1
Washington, DC	97.4	191.9
Naples, FL	100.0	173.6
Trenton, NJ	106.4	168.1
Danbury, CT	132.3	234.1

a. What is the value of the sample covariance? Does it indicate a positive or a negative linear relationship?
b. What is the sample correlation coefficient?

65. The following data show the media expenditures ($ millions) and shipments in millions of barrels (bbls.) for 10 major brands of beer (*Superbrands '98*, October 20, 1997).

Beer

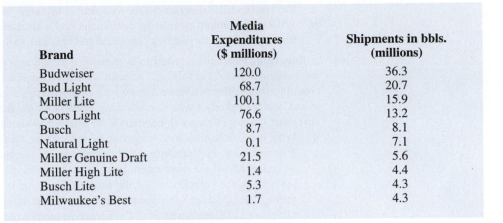

Brand	Media Expenditures ($ millions)	Shipments in bbls. (millions)
Budweiser	120.0	36.3
Bud Light	68.7	20.7
Miller Lite	100.1	15.9
Coors Light	76.6	13.2
Busch	8.7	8.1
Natural Light	0.1	7.1
Miller Genuine Draft	21.5	5.6
Miller High Lite	1.4	4.4
Busch Lite	5.3	4.3
Milwaukee's Best	1.7	4.3

a.   What is the sample covariance? Does it indicate a positive or negative relationship?

b.   What is the sample correlation coefficient?

66.   *Road & Track* provided the following sample of the tire ratings and load-carrying capacity of automobiles tires.

Tire Rating	Load-Carrying Capacity
75	853
82	1047
85	1135
87	1201
88	1235
91	1356
92	1389
93	1433
105	2039

a.   Develop a scatter diagram for the data with tire rating on the *x*-axis.

b.   What is the sample correlation coefficient, and what does it tell you about the relationship between tire rating and load-carrying capacity?

67.   The following data show the trailing 52-weeks primary share earnings and book values as reported by 10 companies (*The Wall Street Journal*, March 13, 2000).

Company	Book Value	Earnings
Am Elec	25.21	2.69
Columbia En	23.20	3.01
Con Ed	25.19	3.13
Duke Energy	20.17	2.25
Edison Int'l	13.55	1.79
Enron Cp.	7.44	1.27
Peco	13.61	3.15
Pub Sv Ent	21.86	3.29
Southn Co.	8.77	1.86
Unicom	23.22	2.74

   a. Develop a scatter diagram for the data with book value on the *x*-axis.
   b. What is the sample correlation coefficient, and what does it tell you about the relationship between the earnings per share and the book value?

68. A forecasting technique referred to as moving averages uses the average or mean of the most recent *n* periods to forecast the next value for time series data. With a three-period moving average, the most recent three periods of data are used in the forecast computation. Consider a product with the following demand for the first three months of the current year: January (800 units), February (750 units), and March (900 units).
   a. What is the three-month moving average forecast for April?
   b. A variation of this forecasting technique is called weighted moving averages. The weighting allows the more recent time series data to receive more weight or more importance in the computation of the forecast. For example, a weighted three-month moving average might give a weight of 3 to data one month old, a weight of 2 to data two months old, and a weight of 1 to data three months old. Use the data given to provide a three-month weighted moving average forecast for April.

69. The days to maturity for a sample of five money market funds are shown here. The dollar amounts invested in the funds are provided. Use the weighted mean to determine the mean number of days to maturity for dollars invested in these five money market funds.

Days to Maturity	Dollar Value ($ millions)
20	20
12	30
7	10
5	15
6	10

70. Automobiles traveling on a road that has a posted speed limit of 55 miles per hour are checked for speed by a state police radar system. Following is a frequency distribution of speeds.

Speed (miles per hour)	Frequency
45–49	10
50–54	40
55–59	150
60–64	175
65–69	75
70–74	15
75–79	10
Total	475

   a. What is the mean speed of the automobiles traveling on this road?
   b. Compute the variance and the standard deviation.

71. Dinner check amounts at La Maison French Restaurant show the following frequency distribution. Compute the mean, variance, and standard deviation.

Dinner Check ($)	Frequency
25–34	2
35–44	6
45–54	4
55–64	4
65–74	2
75–84	2
Total	20

Case Problem 1   CONSOLIDATED FOODS, INC.

Consolidated Foods, Inc., operates a chain of supermarkets in New Mexico, Arizona, and California. Data showing the dollar amounts and method of payment were collected for a sample of 100 customers. A portion of the data is shown in Table 3.13. The complete data set is available on the data disk in the file named Consolid. Consolidated's managers requested the sample be taken to learn about payment practices of the store's customers. In

TABLE 3.13   PURCHASE AMOUNT AND METHOD OF PAYMENT FOR A SAMPLE
OF 100 CONSOLIDATED FOODS CUSTOMERS

Customer	Amount ($)	Method of Payment
1	28.58	Check
2	52.04	Check
3	7.41	Cash
4	11.17	Cash
5	43.79	Credit Card
6	48.95	Check
7	57.59	Check
8	27.60	Check
9	26.91	Credit Card
10	9.00	Cash
.	.	.
.	.	.
.	.	.
95	18.09	Cash
96	54.84	Check
97	41.10	Check
98	43.14	Check
99	3.31	Cash
100	69.77	Credit Card

particular, managers wanted to learn about how a new credit card payment option is related to the customers' purchase amounts.

Managerial Report

Use the methods of descriptive statistics presented in Chapter 3 to summarize the sample data. Provide summaries of the dollar purchase amounts for cash customers, personal check customers, and credit card customers separately. Your report should contain the following summaries and discussions.

1. A comparison and interpretation of means and medians.
2. A comparison and interpretation of measures of variability such as the range and standard deviation.
3. The identification and interpretation of the five-number summaries for each method of payment.

Use the summary section of your report to provide a discussion of what you learned about the method of payment and the amounts of payments for Consolidated Foods' customers.

Case Problem 2   NATIONAL HEALTH CARE ASSOCIATION

The National Health Care Association is concerned about the shortage of nurses the health care profession is projecting for the future. To learn the current degree of job satisfaction among nurses, the association sponsored a study of hospital nurses throughout the country. As part of this study, 50 nurses in a sample indicated their degree of satisfaction with their work, their pay, and their opportunities for promotion. Each of the three aspects of satisfaction was measured on a scale from 0 to 100, with larger values indicating higher degrees of satisfaction. The data collected also showed the type of hospital employing the nurses. The types of hospitals were Private, Veterans Administration (VA), and University. A portion of the data is shown in Table 3.14. The complete data set can be found on the data disk in the file named Health.

Managerial Report

Use methods of descriptive statistics to summarize the data. Present the summaries that will be beneficial in communicating the results to others. Discuss your findings. Specifically, comment on the following questions.

1. On the basis of the entire data set and the three job satisfaction variables, what aspect of the job is most satisfying for the nurses? What appears to be the least satisfying? In what area(s), if any, do you feel improvements should be made? Discuss.
2. On the basis of descriptive measures of variability, what measure of job satisfaction appears to generate the greatest difference of opinion among the nurses? Explain.
3. What can be learned about the types of hospitals? Does any particular type of hospital seem to have better levels of job satisfaction than the other types? Do your results suggest any recommendations for learning about and/or improving job satisfaction? Discuss.
4. What additional descriptive statistics and insights can you use to learn about and possibly improve job satisfaction?

TABLE 3.14   SATISFACTION SCORE DATA FOR A SAMPLE OF 50 NURSES

Health

Nurse	Hospital	Work	Pay	Promotion
1	Private	74	47	63
2	VA	72	76	37
3	University	75	53	92
4	Private	89	66	62
5	University	69	47	16
6	Private	85	56	64
7	University	89	80	64
8	Private	88	36	47
9	University	88	55	52
10	Private	84	42	66
.	.	.	.	.
.	.	.	.	.
.	.	.	.	.
45	University	79	59	41
46	University	84	53	63
47	University	87	66	49
48	VA	84	74	37
49	VA	95	66	52
50	Private	72	57	40

Case Problem 3   BUSINESS SCHOOLS OF ASIA-PACIFIC

The pursuit of a higher education degree in business is now international. A survey shows that more and more Asians choose the Master of Business Administration degree route to corporate success (*Asia, Inc.*, September 1997). The number of applicants for MBA courses at Asia-Pacific schools has been increasing about 30 percent a year. In 1997, the 74 business schools in the Asia-Pacific region reported a record 170,000 applications for the 11,000 full-time MBA degrees to be awarded in 1999. A main reason for the surge in demand is that an MBA can greatly enhance earning power.

Across the region, thousands of Asians show an increasing willingness to temporarily shelve their careers and spend two years in pursuit of a theoretical business qualification. Courses in these schools are notoriously tough and include economics, banking, marketing, behavioral sciences, labor relations, decision making, strategic thinking, business law, and more. *Asia, Inc.* provided the data set in Table 3.15, which shows some of the characteristics of the leading Asia-Pacific business schools.

Asian

Managerial Report

Use the methods of descriptive statistics to summarize the data in Table 3.15. Discuss your findings.

1. Include a summary for each variable in the data set. Make comments and interpretations based on maximums and minimums, as well as the appropriate means and proportions. What new insights do these descriptive statistics provide concerning Asia-Pacific business schools?

TABLE 3.15 DATA FOR 25 ASIA-PACIFIC BUSINESS SCHOOLS

Business School	Full-Time Enrollment	Students per Faculty	Local Tuition ($)	Foreign Tuition ($)	Age	%Foreign	GMAT	English Test	Work Experience	Starting Salary ($)
Melbourne Business School	200	5	24,420	29,600	28	47	Yes	No	Yes	71,400
University of New South Wales (Sydney)	228	4	19,993	32,582	29	28	Yes	No	Yes	65,200
Indian Institute of Management (Ahmedabad)	392	5	4,300	4,300	22	0	No	No	No	7,100
Chinese University of Hong Kong	90	5	11,140	11,140	29	10	Yes	No	No	31,000
International University of Japan (Niigata)	126	4	33,060	33,060	28	60	Yes	No	No	87,000
Asian Institute of Management (Manila)	389	5	7,562	9,000	25	50	Yes	No	Yes	22,800
Indian Institute of Management (Bangalore)	380	5	3,935	16,000	23	1	Yes	No	No	7,500
National University of Singapore	147	6	6,146	7,170	29	51	Yes	Yes	Yes	43,300
Indian Institute of Management (Calcutta)	463	8	2,880	16,000	23	0	No	No	No	7,400
Australian National University (Canberra)	42	2	20,300	20,300	30	80	Yes	Yes	Yes	46,600
Nanyang Technological University (Singapore)	50	5	8,500	8,500	32	20	Yes	No	Yes	49,300
University of Queensland (Brisbane)	138	17	16,000	22,800	32	26	No	No	Yes	49,600
Hong Kong University of Science and Technology	60	2	11,513	11,513	26	37	Yes	No	Yes	34,000
Macquarie Graduate School of Management (Sydney)	12	8	17,172	19,778	34	27	No	No	Yes	60,100
Chulalongkorn University (Bangkok)	200	7	17,355	17,355	25	6	Yes	No	Yes	17,600
Monash Mt. Eliza Business School (Melbourne)	350	13	16,200	22,500	30	30	Yes	Yes	Yes	52,500
Asian Institute of Management (Bangkok)	300	10	18,200	18,200	29	90	No	Yes	Yes	25,000
University of Adelaide	20	19	16,426	23,100	30	10	No	No	Yes	66,000
Massey University (Palmerston North, New Zealand)	30	15	13,106	21,625	37	35	No	Yes	Yes	41,400
Royal Melbourne Institute of Technology Business Graduate School	30	7	13,880	17,765	32	30	No	Yes	Yes	48,900
Jammalal Bajaj Institute of Management Studies (Bombay)	240	9	1,000	1,000	24	0	No	No	Yes	7,000
Curtin Institute of Technology (Perth)	98	15	9,475	19,097	29	43	Yes	No	Yes	55,000
Lahore University of Management Sciences	70	14	11,250	26,300	23	2.5	No	No	No	7,500
Universiti Sains Malaysia (Penang)	30	5	2,260	2,260	32	15	No	Yes	Yes	16,000
De La Salle University (Manila)	44	17	3,300	3,600	28	3.5	Yes	No	Yes	13,100

2. Summarize the data to compare the following:
   a. Any difference between local and foreign tuition costs.
   b. Any difference between mean starting salaries for schools requiring and not requiring work experience.
   c. Any difference between starting salaries for schools requiring and not requiring English tests.
3. Do starting salaries appear to be related to tuition?
4. Present any additional graphical and numerical summaries that will be beneficial in communicating the data in Table 3.15 to others.

CHAPTER 4

Introduction to Probability

CONTENTS

Morton International*

CHICAGO, ILLINOIS

Morton International is a company with businesses in salt, household products, rocket motors, and specialty chemicals. Carstab Corporation, a subsidiary of Morton International, produces specialty chemicals and offers a variety of chemicals designed to meet the unique specifications of its customers. For one particular customer, Carstab produced an expensive catalyst used in chemical processing. Some, but not all, of the lots produced by Carstab met the customer's specifications for the product.

Carstab's customer agreed to test each lot after receiving it and determine whether the catalyst would perform the desired function. Lots that did not pass the customer's test would be returned to Carstab. Over time, Carstab found that the customer was accepting 60% of the lots and returning 40%. In probability terms, each Carstab shipment to the customer had a .60 probability of being accepted and a .40 probability of being returned.

Neither Carstab nor its customer was pleased with these results. In an effort to improve service, Carstab explored the possibility of duplicating the customer's test prior to shipment. However, the high cost of the special testing equipment made that alternative infeasible. Carstab's chemists then proposed a new, relatively low-cost test designed to indicate whether a lot would pass the customer's test. The probability ques-

Morton Salt: "When It Rains It Pours." © Joe Higgins/ South-Western.

tion of interest was: What is the probability that a lot will pass the customer's test if it has passed the new Carstab test?

A sample of lots was produced and subjected to the new Carstab test. Only lots that passed the new test were sent to the customer. Probability analysis of the data indicated that if a lot passed the Carstab test, it had a .909 probability of passing the customer's test and being accepted. Alternatively, if a lot passed the Carstab test, it had only a .091 probability of being returned. The probability analysis provided key supporting evidence for the adoption and implementation of the new testing procedure at Carstab. The new test resulted in an immediate improvement in customer service and a substantial reduction in shipping and handling costs for returned lots.

The probability of a lot being accepted by the customer after passing the new Carstab test is called a conditional probability. In this chapter, you will learn how to compute this and other probabilities that are helpful in decision making.

*The authors are indebted to Michael Haskell of Morton International for providing this Statistics in Practice.

Managers often base their decisions on an analysis of uncertainties such as the following:

1. What are the chances that sales will decrease if we increase prices?
2. What is the likelihood a new assembly method will increase productivity?
3. How likely is it that the project will be finished on time?
4. What is the chance that a new investment will be profitable?

Some of the earliest work on probability originated in a series of letters between Pierre de Fermat and Blaise Pascal in the 1650s.

Probability is a numerical measure of the likelihood that an event will occur. Thus, probabilities could be used as measures of the degree of uncertainty associated with the four events previously listed. If probabilities were available, we could determine the likelihood of each event occurring.

Probability values are always assigned on a scale from 0 to 1. A probability near zero indicates an event is unlikely to occur; a probability near 1 indicates an event is almost certain to occur. Other probabilities between 0 and 1 represent degrees of likelihood that an event will occur. For example, if we consider the event "rain tomorrow," we understand that when the weather report indicates "a near-zero probability of rain," it means almost no chance of rain. However, if a .90 probability of rain is reported, we know that rain is likely to occur. A .50 probability indicates that rain is just as likely to occur as not. Figure 4.1 depicts the view of probability as a numerical measure of the likelihood of an event occurring.

4.1   EXPERIMENTS, COUNTING RULES, AND ASSIGNING PROBABILITIES

In discussing probability, we define an **experiment** as a process that generates well-defined outcomes. On any single repetition of an experiment, one and only one of the possible experimental outcomes will occur. Several examples of experiments and their associated outcomes follow.

Experiment	Experimental Outcomes
Toss a coin	Head, tail
Select a part for inspection	Defective, nondefective
Conduct a sales call	Purchase, no purchase
Roll a die	1, 2, 3, 4, 5, 6
Play a football game	Win, lose, tie

FIGURE 4.1   PROBABILITY AS A NUMERICAL MEASURE OF THE LIKELIHOOD OF AN EVENT OCCURRING

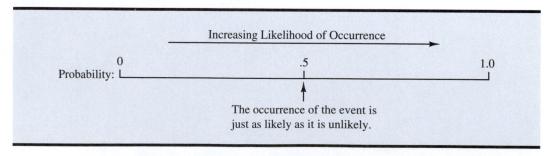

By specifying all possible experimental outcomes, we identify the **sample space** for an experiment.

Sample Space

The sample space for an experiment is the set of all experimental outcomes.

Experimental outcomes are also called sample points.

An experimental outcome is also called a **sample point** to identify it as an element of the sample space.

Consider the first experiment in the preceding table—tossing a coin. The upward face of the coin—a head or a tail—determines the experimental outcomes (sample points). If we let S denote the sample space, we can use the following notation to describe the sample space.

$$S = \{Head, Tail\}$$

The sample space for the second experiment in the table—selecting a part for inspection—can be described as follows:

$$S = \{Defective, Nondefective\}$$

Both of the experiments just described have two experimental outcomes (sample points). However, suppose we consider the fourth experiment listed in the table—rolling a die. The possible experimental outcomes, defined as the number of dots appearing on the upward face of the die, are the six points in the sample space for this experiment.

$$S = \{1, 2, 3, 4, 5, 6\}$$

Counting Rules, Combinations, and Permutations

Being able to identify and count the experimental outcomes is a necessary step in assigning probabilities. We now discuss three useful counting rules.

Multiple-Step Experiments.   The first counting rule applies to multiple-step experiments. Consider the experiment of tossing two coins. Let the experimental outcomes be defined in terms of the pattern of heads and tails appearing on the upward faces of the two coins. How many experimental outcomes are possible for this experiment? The experiment of tossing two coins can be thought of as a two-step experiment in which step 1 is the tossing of the first coin and step 2 is the tossing of the second coin. If we use H to denote a head and T to denote a tail, (H, H) indicates the experimental outcome with a head on the first coin and a head on the second coin. Continuing this notation, we can describe the sample space (S) for this coin-tossing experiment as follows:

$$S = \{(H, H), (H, T), (T, H), (T, T)\}$$

Thus, we see that four experimental outcomes are possible. In this case, we can easily list all of the experimental outcomes.

The counting rule for multiple-step experiments makes it possible to determine the number of experimental outcomes without listing them.

A Counting Rule for Multiple-Step Experiments

If an experiment can be described as a sequence of k steps with n_1 possible outcomes on the first step, n_2 possible outcomes on the second step, and so on, then the total number of experimental outcomes is given by $(n_1)(n_2) \ldots (n_k)$.

Viewing the experiment of tossing two coins as a sequence of first tossing one coin ($n_1 = 2$) and then tossing the other coin ($n_2 = 2$), we can see from the counting rule that there are $(2)(2) = 4$ distinct experimental outcomes. As shown, they are $S = \{(H, H), (H, T), (T, H), (T, T)\}$. The number of experimental outcomes in an experiment involving tossing six coins is $(2)(2)(2)(2)(2)(2) = 64$.

Without the tree diagram, one might think only three experimental outcomes are possible for two tosses of a coin: 0 heads, 1 head, and 2 heads.

A **tree diagram** is a graphical representation that helps in visualizing a multiple-step experiment. Figure 4.2 shows a tree diagram for the experiment of tossing two coins. The sequence of steps moves from left to right through the tree. Step 1 corresponds to tossing the first coin, and Step 2 corresponds to tossing the second coin. For each step, the two possible outcomes are head or tail. Note that for each possible outcome at step 1 two branches correspond to the two possible outcomes at step 2. Each of the points on the right end of the tree corresponds to an experimental outcome. Each path through the tree from the leftmost node to one of the nodes at the right side of the tree corresponds to a unique sequence of outcomes.

Let us now see how the counting rule for multiple-step experiments can be used in the analysis of a capacity expansion project for the Kentucky Power & Light Company (KP&L). KP&L is starting a project designed to increase the generating capacity of one of its plants in northern Kentucky. The project is divided into two sequential stages or steps: stage 1 (design) and stage 2 (construction). Even though each stage will be scheduled and controlled as closely

FIGURE 4.2   TREE DIAGRAM FOR THE EXPERIMENT OF TOSSING TWO COINS

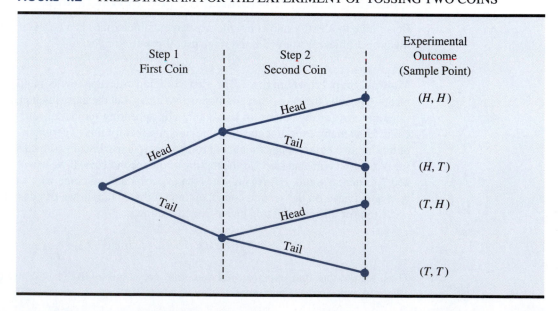

TABLE 4.1 EXPERIMENTAL OUTCOMES (SAMPLE POINTS) FOR THE KP&L PROJECT

Completion Time (months)

Stage 1 Design	Stage 2 Construction	Notation for Experimental Outcome	Total Project Completion Time (months)
2	6	(2, 6)	8
2	7	(2, 7)	9
2	8	(2, 8)	10
3	6	(3, 6)	9
3	7	(3, 7)	10
3	8	(3, 8)	11
4	6	(4, 6)	10
4	7	(4, 7)	11
4	8	(4, 8)	12

as possible, management cannot predict beforehand the exact time required to complete each stage of the project. An analysis of similar construction projects revealed possible completion times for the design stage of 2, 3, or 4 months and possible completion times for the construction stage of 6, 7, or 8 months. In addition, because of the critical need for additional electrical power, management set a goal of 10 months for the completion of the entire project.

Because this project has three possible completion times for the design stage (step 1) and three possible completion times for the construction stage (step 2), the counting rule for multiple-step experiments can be applied here to determine a total of (3)(3) = 9 experimental outcomes. To describe the experimental outcomes, we use a two-number notation; for instance, (2, 6) indicates that the design stage is completed in 2 months and the construction stage is completed in 6 months. This experimental outcome results in a total of 2 + 6 = 8 months to complete the entire project. Table 4.1 summarizes the nine experimental outcomes for the KP&L problem. The tree diagram in Figure 4.3 shows how the nine outcomes (sample points) occur.

The counting rule and tree diagram help the project manager identify the experimental outcomes and determine the possible project completion times. From the information in Figure 4.3, we see that the project will be completed in 8 to 12 months, with six of the nine experimental outcomes providing the desired completion time of 10 months or less. Even though identifying the experimental outcomes may be helpful, we need to consider how probability values can be assigned to the experimental outcomes before making an assessment of the probability that the project will be completed within the desired 10 months.

Combinations. A second useful counting rule allows one to count the number of experimental outcomes when the experiment involves selecting n objects from a (usually larger) set of N objects. It is called the counting rule for combinations.

Counting Rule for Combinations

The number of combinations of N objects taken n at a time is

$$C_n^N = \binom{N}{n} = \frac{N!}{n!(N-n)!} \qquad (4.1)$$

FIGURE 4.3   TREE DIAGRAM FOR THE KP&L PROJECT

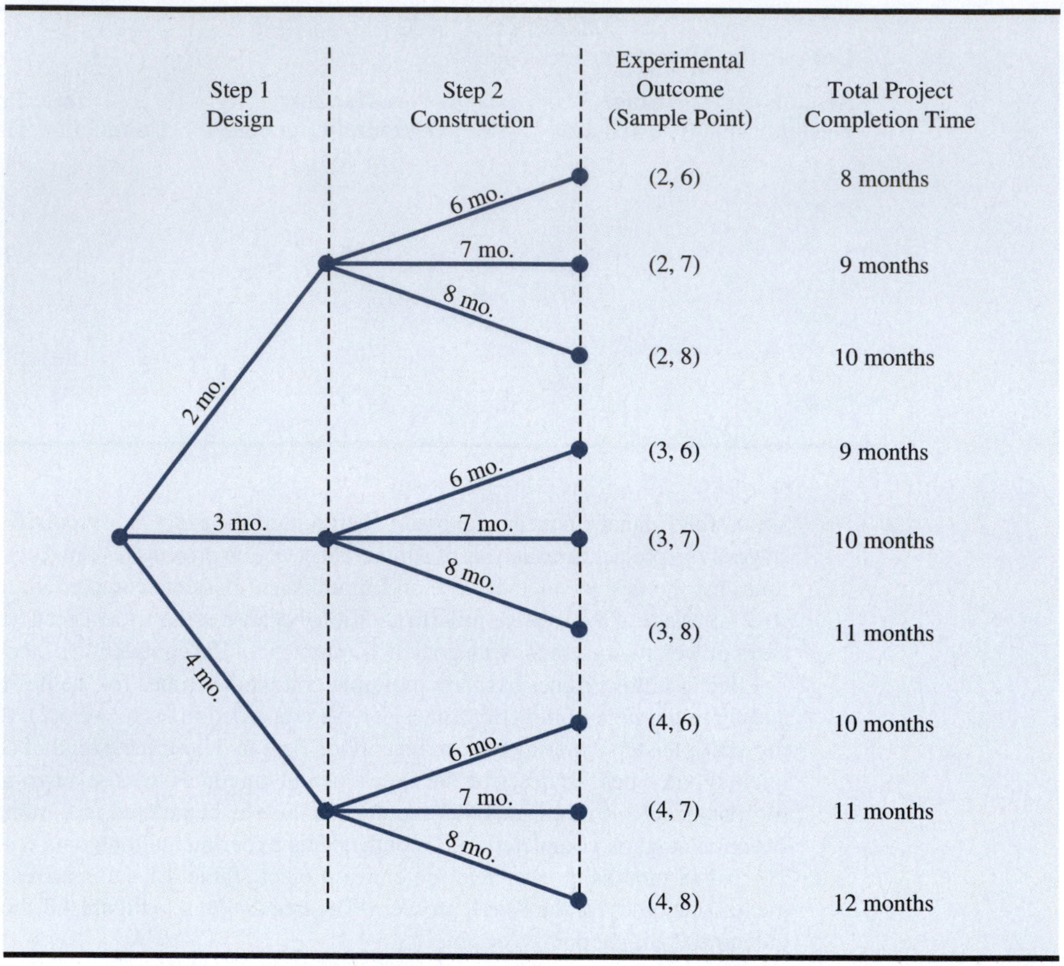

Step 1 Design	Step 2 Construction	Experimental Outcome (Sample Point)	Total Project Completion Time
	6 mo.	(2, 6)	8 months
2 mo.	7 mo.	(2, 7)	9 months
	8 mo.	(2, 8)	10 months
	6 mo.	(3, 6)	9 months
3 mo.	7 mo.	(3, 7)	10 months
	8 mo.	(3, 8)	11 months
	6 mo.	(4, 6)	10 months
4 mo.	7 mo.	(4, 7)	11 months
	8 mo.	(4, 8)	12 months

where
$$N! = N(N-1)(N-2) \cdots (2)(1)$$
$$n! = n(n-1)(n-2) \cdots (2)(1)$$

and, by definition,
$$0! = 1$$

The notation ! means *factorial;* for example, 5 factorial is $5! = (5)(4)(3)(2)(1) = 120$.

As an illustration of the counting rule for combinations, consider a quality control procedure in which an inspector randomly selects two of five parts to test for defects. In a group of five parts, how many combinations of two parts can be selected? The counting rule in equation (4.1) shows that with $N = 5$ and $n = 2$, we have

In sampling from a finite population of size N, the counting rule for combinations is used to find the number of different samples of size n that can be selected.

$$C_2^5 = \binom{5}{2} = \frac{5!}{2!(5-2)!} = \frac{(5)(4)(3)(2)(1)}{(2)(1)(3)(2)(1)} = \frac{120}{12} = 10$$

Thus, 10 outcomes are possible for the experiment of randomly selecting two parts from a group of five. If we label the five parts as A, B, C, D, and E, the 10 combinations or experimental outcomes can be identified as AB, AC, AD, AE, BC, BD, BE, CD, CE, and DE.

As another example, consider that the Ohio lottery system uses the random selection of six integers from a group of 47 to determine the weekly lottery winner. The counting rule for combinations, equation (4.1), can be used to determine the number of ways six different integers can be selected from a group of 47.

$$\binom{47}{6} = \frac{47!}{6!(47-6)!} = \frac{47!}{6!41!} = \frac{(47)(46)(45)(44)(43)(42)}{(6)(5)(4)(3)(2)(1)} = 10{,}737{,}573$$

The counting rule for combinations shows that the chance of winning the lottery is very unlikely.

The counting rule for combinations tells us that more than 10 million experimental outcomes are possible in the lottery drawing. An individual who buys a lottery ticket has 1 chance in 10,737,573 of winning.

Permutations.   A third counting rule that is sometimes useful is the counting rule for permutations. It allows one to compute the number of experimental outcomes when n objects are to be selected from a set of N objects where the order of selection is important. The same n objects selected in a different order is considered a different experimental outcome.

Counting Rule for Permutations

The number of permutations of N objects taken n at a time is given by

$$P_n^N = n!\binom{N}{n} = \frac{N!}{(N-n)!} \tag{4.2}$$

The counting rule for permutations closely relates to the one for combinations; however, an experiment results in more permutations than combinations for the same number of objects because every selection of n objects can be ordered in $n!$ different ways.

As an example, consider again the quality control process in which an inspector selects two of five parts to inspect for defects. How many permutations may be selected? The counting rule in equation (4.2) shows that with $N = 5$ and $n = 2$, we have

$$P_2^5 = \frac{5!}{(5-2)!} = \frac{5!}{3!} = \frac{(5)(4)(3)(2)(1)}{(3)(2)(1)} = \frac{120}{6} = 20$$

Thus, 20 outcomes are possible for the experiment of randomly selecting two parts from a group of five when the order of selection must be taken into account. If we label the parts A, B, C, D, and E, the 20 permutations are AB, BA, AC, CA, AD, DA, AE, EA, BC, CB, BD, DB, BE, EB, CD, DC, CE, EC, DE, and ED.

Assigning Probabilities

Now let us see how probabilities can be assigned to experimental outcomes. The three approaches most frequently used are the classical, relative frequency, and subjective methods. Regardless of the method used, two **basic requirements for assigning probabilities** must be met.

Basic Requirements for Assigning Probabilities

1. The probability assigned to each experimental outcome must be between 0 and 1, inclusively. If we let E_i denote the ith experimental outcome and $P(E_i)$ its probability, then this requirement can be written as

$$0 \leq P(E_i) \leq 1 \text{ for all } i \qquad (4.3)$$

2. The sum of the probabilities for all the experimental outcomes must equal 1. For n experimental outcomes, this requirement can be written as

$$P(E_1) + P(E_2) + \cdots + P(E_n) = 1 \qquad (4.4)$$

The **classical method** of assigning probabilities is appropriate when all the experimental outcomes are equally likely. If n experimental outcomes are possible, a probability of $1/n$ is assigned to each experimental outcome. When using this approach, the two basic requirements for assigning probabilities are automatically satisfied.

For an example, consider the experiment of tossing a fair coin; the two experimental outcomes—head and tail—are equally likely. Because one of the two equally likely outcomes is a head, the probability of observing a head is 1/2, or .50. Similarly, the probability of observing a tail is also 1/2, or .50.

As another example, consider the experiment of rolling a die. It would seem reasonable to conclude that the six possible outcomes are equally likely, and hence each outcome is assigned a probability of 1/6. If $P(1)$ denotes the probability that one dot appears on the upward face of the die, then $P(1) = 1/6$. Similarly, $P(2) = 1/6$, $P(3) = 1/6$, $P(4) = 1/6$, $P(5) = 1/6$, and $P(6) = 1/6$. Note that these probabilities satisfy the two basic requirements of equations (4.3) and (4.4) because each of the probabilities is greater than or equal to zero and they sum to one.

The **relative frequency method** of assigning probabilities is appropriate when data are available to estimate the proportion of the time the experimental outcome will occur if the experiment is repeated a large number of times. As an example consider a study of waiting times in the X-ray department for a local hospital. A clerk recorded the number of patients waiting for service at 9:00 A.M. on 20 successive days, and obtained the following results.

Number Waiting	Number of Days Outcome Occurred
0	2
1	5
2	6
3	4
4	3
Total	20

These data show that on 2 of the 20 days, zero patients were waiting for service; on 5 of the days, one patient was waiting for service; and so on. Using the relative frequency method, we would assign a probability of 2/20 = .10 to the experimental outcome of zero patients waiting for service, 5/20 = .25 to the experimental outcome of one patient waiting, 6/20 = .30 to two patients waiting, 4/20 = .20 to three patients waiting, and 3/20 = .15 to four patients waiting. As with the classical method, using the relative frequency method automatically satisfies the two basic requirements of equations (4.3) and (4.4).

The **subjective method** of assigning probabilities is most appropriate when one cannot realistically assume that the experimental outcomes are equally likely and when little relevant data are available. When the subjective method is used to assign probabilities to the experimental outcomes, we may use any information available, such as our experience or intuition. After considering all available information, a probability value that expresses our *degree of belief* (on a scale from 0 to 1) that the experimental outcome will occur is specified. Because subjective probability expresses a person's degree of belief, it is personal. Using the subjective method, different people can be expected to assign different probabilities to the same experimental outcome.

The subjective method requires extra care to ensure that the two basic requirements of equations (4.3) and (4.4) are satisfied. Regardless of a person's degree of belief, the probability value assigned to each experimental outcome must be between 0 and 1, inclusive, and the sum of all the probabilities for the experimental outcomes must equal one.

Consider the case in which Tom and Judy Elsbernd make an offer to purchase a house. Two outcomes are possible:

$$E_1 = \text{their offer is accepted}$$
$$E_2 = \text{their offer is rejected}$$

Judy believes that the probability their offer will be accepted is .8; thus, Judy would set $P(E_1) = .8$ and $P(E_2) = .2$. Tom, however, believes that the probability that their offer will be accepted is .6; hence, Tom would set $P(E_1) = .6$ and $P(E_2) = .4$. Note that Tom's probability estimate for E_1 reflects a greater pessimism that their offer will be accepted.

Bayes' theorem (see Section 4.5) provides a means for combining subjectively determined prior probabilities with probabilities obtained by other means to obtain revised, or posterior, probabilities.

Both Judy and Tom assigned probabilities that satisfy the two basic requirements. The fact that their probability estimates are different emphasizes the personal nature of the subjective method.

Even in business situations where either the classical or the relative frequency approach can be applied, managers may want to provide subjective probability estimates. In such cases, the best probability estimates often are obtained by combining the estimates from the classical or relative frequency approach with subjective probability estimates.

Probabilities for the KP&L Project

To perform further analysis on the KP&L project, we must develop probabilities for each of the nine experimental outcomes listed in Table 4.1. On the basis of experience and judgment, management concluded that the experimental outcomes were not equally likely. Hence, the classical method of assigning probabilities could not be used. Management then decided to conduct a study of the completion times for similar projects undertaken by KP&L over the past three years. The results of a study of 40 similar projects are summarized in Table 4.2.

After reviewing the results of the study, management decided to employ the relative frequency method of assigning probabilities. Management could have provided subjective probability estimates, but felt that the current project was quite similar to the 40 previous projects. Thus, the relative frequency method was judged best.

In using the data in Table 4.2 to compute probabilities, we note that outcome (2, 6)—stage 1 completed in 2 months and stage 2 completed in 6 months—occurred six times in

TABLE 4.2 COMPLETION RESULTS FOR 40 KP&L PROJECTS

Completion Time (months)			Number of Past Projects Having These
Stage 1 Design	Stage 2 Construction	Sample Point	Completion Times
2	6	(2, 6)	6
2	7	(2, 7)	6
2	8	(2, 8)	2
3	6	(3, 6)	4
3	7	(3, 7)	8
3	8	(3, 8)	2
4	6	(4, 6)	2
4	7	(4, 7)	4
4	8	(4, 8)	6
		Total	40

the 40 projects. We can use the relative frequency method to assign a probability of $6/40 = .15$ to this outcome. Similarly, outcome (2, 7) also occurred in six of the 40 projects, providing a $6/40 = .15$ probability. Continuing in this manner, we obtain the probability assignments for the sample points of the KP&L project shown in Table 4.3. Note that $P(2, 6)$ represents the probability of the sample point (2, 6), $P(2, 7)$ represents the probability of the sample point (2, 7), and so on.

TABLE 4.3 PROBABILITY ASSIGNMENTS FOR THE KP&L PROJECT BASED ON THE RELATIVE FREQUENCY METHOD

Sample Point	Project Completion Time	Probability of Sample Point
(2, 6)	8 months	$P(2, 6) = 6/40 =$ .15
(2, 7)	9 months	$P(2, 7) = 6/40 =$ .15
(2, 8)	10 months	$P(2, 8) = 2/40 =$ .05
(3, 6)	9 months	$P(3, 6) = 4/40 =$ .10
(3, 7)	10 months	$P(3, 7) = 8/40 =$ .20
(3, 8)	11 months	$P(3, 8) = 2/40 =$ .05
(4, 6)	10 months	$P(4, 6) = 2/40 =$ .05
(4, 7)	11 months	$P(4, 7) = 4/40 =$ .10
(4, 8)	12 months	$P(4, 8) = 6/40 =$ .15
	Total	1.00

NOTES AND COMMENTS

1. In statistics, the notion of an experiment differs somewhat from the notion of an experiment in the physical sciences. In the physical sciences, researchers usually conduct an experiment in a laboratory or a controlled environment in order to learn about cause and effect. In statistical experiments, probability determines outcomes. Even though the experiment is repeated

in exactly the same way, an entirely different outcome may occur. Because of this influence of probability on the outcome, the experiments of statistics are sometimes called *random experiments.*

2. When drawing a random sample without replacement from a population of size N, the counting rule for combinations is used to find the number of different samples of size n that can be selected.

EXERCISES

Methods

1. An experiment has three steps with three outcomes possible for the first step, two outcomes possible for the second step, and four outcomes possible for the third step. How many experimental outcomes exist for the entire experiment?

2. How many ways can three items be selected from a group of six items? Use the letters A, B, C, D, E, and F to identify the items, and list each of the different combinations of three items.

3. How many permutations of three items can be selected from a group of six? Use the letters A, B, C, D, E, and F to identify the items, and list each of the permutations of items B, D, and F.

4. Consider the experiment of tossing a coin three times.
   a. Develop a tree diagram for the experiment.
   b. List the experimental outcomes.
   c. What is the probability for each experimental outcome?

5. Suppose an experiment has five equally likely outcomes: E_1, E_2, E_3, E_4, E_5. Assign probabilities to each outcome and show that the conditions in equations (4.3) and (4.4) are satisfied. What method did you use?

6. An experiment with three outcomes has been repeated 50 times, and it was learned that E_1 occurred 20 times, E_2 occurred 13 times, and E_3 occurred 17 times. Assign probabilities to the outcomes. What method did you use?

7. A decision maker subjectively assigned the following probabilities to the four outcomes of an experiment: $P(E_1) = .10$, $P(E_2) = .15$, $P(E_3) = .40$, and $P(E_4) = .20$. Are these probability assignments valid? Explain.

Applications

8. In the city of Milford, applications for zoning changes go through a two-step process: a review by the planning commission and a final decision by the city council. At step 1 the planning commission reviews the zoning change request and makes a positive or negative recommendation concerning the change. At step 2 the city council reviews the planning commission's recommendation and then votes to approve or to disapprove the zoning change. Suppose the developer of an apartment complex submits an application for a zoning change. Consider the application process as an experiment.
   a. How many sample points are there for this experiment? List the sample points.
   b. Construct a tree diagram for the experiment.

9. Simple random sampling uses a sample of size n from a population of size N to obtain data that can be used to make inferences about the characteristics of a population. Suppose we have a population of 50 bank accounts and want to take a random sample of four accounts in order to learn about the population. How many different random samples of four accounts are possible?

10. The availability of venture capital provided a big boost in funds available to companies in recent years. According to Venture Economics (*Investor's Business Daily,* April 28, 2000), 2374 venture capital disbursements were made in 1999. Of these, 1434 were to companies in California, 390 were to companies in Massachusetts, 217 were to companies in New York, and 112 were to companies in Colorado. Twenty-two percent of the companies receiving funds were in the early stages of development and 55% of the companies were in an expansion stage.

Suppose you want to randomly choose one of these companies to learn about how they used the funds.

  a. What is the probability the company chosen will be from California?

  b. What is the probability the company chosen will not be from one of the four states mentioned?

  c. What is the probability the company will not be in the early stages of development?

  d. Assuming the companies in the early stages of development were evenly distributed across the country, how many Massachusetts companies receiving venture capital funds were in their early stages of development?

  e. The total amount of funds invested was $32.4 billion. Estimate the amount that went to Colorado.

11. Strom Construction made bids on two contracts. The owner identified the possible outcomes and subjectively assigned the following probabilities.

Experimental Outcome	Obtain Contract 1	Obtain Contract 2	Probability
1	Yes	Yes	.15
2	Yes	No	.15
3	No	Yes	.30
4	No	No	.25

  a. Are these valid probability assignments? Why or why not?

  b. What would have to be done to make the probability assignments valid?

12. The Powerball lottery is played twice each week in 21 states and the District of Columbia. To play Powerball a participant must purchase a ticket for $1 and then select five numbers from the digits 1 through 49 and a Powerball number from the digits 1 through 42. To determine the winning numbers for each game, lottery officials draw five white balls out of a drum with 49 white balls, and one red ball out of a drum with 42 red balls. To win the jackpot, a participant's numbers must match the numbers on the five white balls in any order and the number on the red Powerball. In August 2001, four winners shared a jackpot of $295 million by matching the numbers 8-17-22-42-47 plus the Powerball number of 21. In addition to the jackpot, a variety of other prizes are awarded each time the game is played. For instance, a prize of $100,000 is paid if the participant's five numbers match the numbers on the five white balls (*www.powerball.com,* August 31, 2001).

  a. Compute the number of ways the first five numbers can be selected.

  b. What is the probability of winning a prize of $100,000 by matching the numbers on the five white balls?

  c. What is the probability of winning the Powerball jackpot?

13. A company that manufactures toothpaste is studying five different package designs. Assuming that one design is just as likely to be selected by a consumer as any other design, what selection probability would you assign to each of the package designs? In an actual experiment, 100 consumers were asked to pick the design they preferred. The following data were obtained. Do the data confirm the belief that one design is just as likely to be selected as another? Explain.

Design	Number of Times Preferred
1	5
2	15
3	30
4	40
5	10

4.2   EVENTS AND THEIR PROBABILITIES

In the introduction to this chapter we used the term *event* much as it would be used in everyday language. Then, in Section 4.1 we introduced the concept of an experiment and its associated experimental outcomes or sample points. Sample points and events provide the foundation for the study of probability. As a result, we must now introduce the formal definition of an **event** as it relates to sample points. Doing so will provide the basis for determining the probability of an event.

Event

An event is a collection of sample points.

For an example, let us return to the KP&L project and assume that the project manager is interested in the event that the entire project can be completed in 10 months or less. Referring to Table 4.3, we see that six sample points—(2, 6), (2, 7), (2, 8), (3, 6), (3, 7), and (4, 6)—provide a project completion time of 10 months or less. Let C denote the event that the project is completed in 10 months or less; we write

$$C = \{(2, 6), (2, 7), (2, 8), (3, 6), (3, 7), (4, 6)\}$$

Event C is said to occur if *any one* of these six sample points appears as the experimental outcome.

Other events that might be of interest to KP&L management include the following.

L = The event that the project is completed in *less* than 10 months
M = The event that the project is completed in *more* than 10 months

Using the information in Table 4.3, we see that these events consist of the following sample points.

$$L = \{(2, 6), (2, 7), (3, 6)\}$$
$$M = \{(3, 8), (4, 7), (4, 8)\}$$

A variety of additional events can be defined for the KP&L project, but in each case the event must be identified as a collection of sample points for the experiment.

Given the probabilities of the sample points shown in Table 4.3, we can use the following definition to compute the probability of any event that KP&L management might want to consider.

Probability of an Event

The probability of any event is equal to the sum of the probabilities of the sample points in the event.

Using this definition, we calculate the probability of a particular event by adding the probabilities of the sample points (experimental outcomes) that make up the event. We can now compute the probability that the project will take 10 months or less to complete. Because this event is given by $C = \{(2, 6), (2, 7), (2, 8), (3, 6), (3, 7), (4, 6)\}$, the probability of event C, denoted $P(C)$, is given by

$$P(C) = P(2, 6) + P(2, 7) + P(2, 8) + P(3, 6) + P(3, 7) + P(4, 6)$$

Refer to the sample point probabilities in Table 4.3; we have

$$P(C) = .15 + .15 + .05 + .10 + .20 + .05 = .70$$

Similarly, because the event that the project is completed in less than 10 months is given by $L = \{(2, 6), (2, 7), (3, 6)\}$, the probability of this event is given by

$$P(L) = P(2, 6) + P(2, 7) + P(3, 6)$$
$$= .15 + .15 + .10 = .40$$

Finally, for the event that the project is completed in more than 10 months, we have $M = \{(3, 8), (4, 7), (4, 8)\}$ and thus

$$P(M) = P(3, 8) + P(4, 7) + P(4, 8)$$
$$= .05 + .10 + .15 = .30$$

Using these probability results, we can now tell KP&L management that there is a .70 probability that the project will be completed in 10 months or less, a .40 probability that the project will be completed in less than 10 months, and a .30 probability that the project will be completed in more than 10 months. This procedure of computing event probabilities can be repeated for any event of interest to the KP&L management.

Any time that we can identify all the sample points of an experiment and assign probabilities to each, we can compute the probability of an event using the definition. However, in many experiments the large number of sample points makes the identification of the sample points, as well as the determination of their associated probabilities, extremely cumbersome, if not impossible. In the remaining sections of this chapter, we present some basic probability relationships that can be used to compute the probability of an event without knowledge of all the sample point probabilities.

NOTES AND COMMENTS

1. The sample space, S, is an event. Because it contains all the experimental outcomes, it has a probability of 1; that is, $P(S) = 1$.
2. When the classical method is used to assign probabilities, the assumption is that the experimental outcomes are equally likely. In such cases, the probability of an event can be computed by counting the number of experimental outcomes in the event and dividing the result by the total number of experimental outcomes.

EXERCISES

Methods

14. An experiment has four equally likely outcomes: E_1, E_2, E_3, and E_4.
    a. What is the probability that E_2 occurs?
    b. What is the probability that any two of the outcomes occur (e.g., E_1 or E_3)?
    c. What is the probability that any three of the outcomes occur (e.g., E_1 or E_2 or E_4)?

 15. Consider the experiment of selecting a playing card from a deck of 52 playing cards. Each card corresponds to a sample point with a 1/52 probability.
    a. List the sample points in the event an ace is selected.
    b. List the sample points in the event a club is selected.
    c. List the sample points in the event a face card (jack, queen, or king) is selected.
    d. Find the probabilities associated with each of the events in (a), (b), and (c).

16. Consider the experiment of rolling a pair of dice. Suppose that we are interested in the sum of the face values showing on the dice.
    a. How many sample points are possible? (Hint: Use the counting rule for multiple-step experiments.)
    b. List the sample points.
    c. What is the probability of obtaining a value of 7?
    d. What is the probability of obtaining a value of 9 or greater?
    e. Because each roll has six possible even values (2, 4, 6, 8, 10, and 12) and only five possible odd values (3, 5, 7, 9, and 11), the dice should show even values more often than odd values. Do you agree with this statement? Explain.
    f. What method did you use to assign the probabilities requested?

Applications

 17. Refer to the KP&L sample points and sample point probabilities in Tables 4.2 and 4.3.
    a. The design stage (stage 1) will run over budget if it takes 4 months to complete. List the sample points in the event the design stage is over budget.
    b. What is the probability that the design stage is over budget?
    c. The construction stage (stage 2) will run over budget if it takes 8 months to complete. List the sample points in the event the construction stage is over budget.
    d. What is the probability that the construction stage is over budget?
    e. What is the probability that both stages are over budget?

18. Suppose that a manager of a large apartment complex provides the following subjective probability estimates about the number of vacancies that will exist next month.

Vacancies	Probability
0	.05
1	.15
2	.35
3	.25
4	.10
5	.10

List the sample points in each of the following events and provide the probability of the event.
a. No vacancies
b. At least four vacancies
c. Two or fewer vacancies

19. The manager of a furniture store sells from 0 to 4 china hutches each week. On the basis of past experience, the following probabilities are assigned to sales of 0, 1, 2, 3, or 4 hutches: $P(0) = .08$; $P(1) = .18$; $P(2) = .32$; $P(3) = .30$; and $P(4) = .12$.
a. Are these valid probability assignments? Why or why not?
b. Let A be the event that 2 or fewer are sold in one week. Find $P(A)$.
c. Let B be the event that 4 or more are sold in one week. Find $P(B)$.

20. *Fortune* magazine publishes an annual issue containing information on *Fortune* 500 companies. The following data show the six states with the largest number of *Fortune* 500 companies as well as the number of companies headquartered in those states (*Fortune*, April 17, 2000).

State	Number of Companies
New York	56
California	53
Texas	43
Illinois	37
Ohio	28
Pennsylvania	28

Suppose a *Fortune* 500 company is chosen for a follow-up questionnaire. What are the probabilities of the following events?
a. Let N be the event the company is headquartered in New York. Find $P(N)$.
b. Let T be the event the company is headquartered in Texas. Find $P(T)$.
c. Let B be the event the company is headquartered in one of these six states. Find $P(B)$.

21. A survey of 50 students at Tarpon Springs College about the number of extracurricular activities resulted in the data shown.

Number of Activities	Frequency
0	8
1	20

Number of Activities	Frequency
2	12
3	6
4	3
5	1

a. Let A be the event that a student participates in at least 1 activity. Find $P(A)$.
b. Let B be the event that a student participates in 3 or more activities. Find $P(B)$.
c. What is the probability that a student participates in exactly 2 activities?

4.3 SOME BASIC RELATIONSHIPS OF PROBABILITY

Complement of an Event

Given an event A, the **complement of** A is defined to be the event consisting of all sample points that are *not* in A. The complement of A is denoted by A^c. Figure 4.4 is a diagram, known as a **Venn diagram**, which illustrates the concept of a complement. The rectangular area represents the sample space for the experiment and as such contains all possible sample points. The circle represents event A and contains only the sample points that belong to A. The shaded region of the rectangle contains all sample points not in event A, and is by definition the complement of A.

In any probability application, either event A or its complement A^c must occur. Therefore, we have

$$P(A) + P(A^c) = 1$$

Solving for $P(A)$, we obtain the following result.

Computing Probability Using the Complement
$$P(A) = 1 - P(A^c) \tag{4.5}$$

FIGURE 4.4   COMPLEMENT OF EVENT A IS SHADED

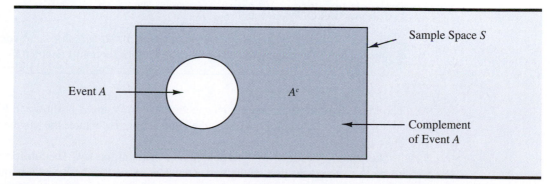

Equation (4.5) shows that the probability of an event A can be computed easily if the probability of its complement, $P(A^c)$, is known.

As an example, consider the case of a sales manager who, after reviewing sales reports, states that 80% of new customer contacts result in no sale. By allowing A to denote the event of a sale and A^c to denote the event of no sale, the manager is stating that $P(A^c) = .80$. Using equation (4.5), we see that

$$P(A) = 1 - P(A^c) = 1 - .80 = .20$$

We can conclude that a new customer contact has a .20 probability of resulting in a sale.

In another example, a purchasing agent states a .90 probability that a supplier will send a shipment that is free of defective parts. Using the complement, we can conclude that there is a $1 - .90 = .10$ probability that the shipment will contain defective parts.

Addition Law

The addition law is helpful when we are interested in knowing the probability that at least one of two events occurs. That is, with events A and B we are interested in knowing the probability that event A or event B or both occur.

Before we present the addition law, we need to discuss two concepts related to the combination of events: the *union* of events and the *intersection* of events. Given two events A and B, the **union of A and B** is defined as follows.

Union of Two Events

The *union* of A and B is the event containing *all* sample points belonging to *A or B or both*. The union is denoted by $A \cup B$.

The Venn diagram in Figure 4.5 depicts the union of events A and B. Note that the two circles contain all the sample points in event A as well as all the sample points in event B. The fact that the circles overlap indicates that some sample points are contained in both A and B.

The definition of the **intersection of A and B** follows.

Intersection of Two Events

Given two events A and B, the *intersection* of A and B is the event containing the sample points belonging to *both A and B*. The intersection is denoted by $A \cap B$.

The Venn diagram depicting the intersection events A and B is shown in Figure 4.6. The area where the two circles overlap is the intersection; it contains the sample points that are in both A and B.

Let us now continue with a discussion of the addition law. The **addition law** provides a way to compute the probability that event A or event B or both occur. In other words, the

FIGURE 4.5   UNION OF EVENTS *A* AND *B* IS SHADED

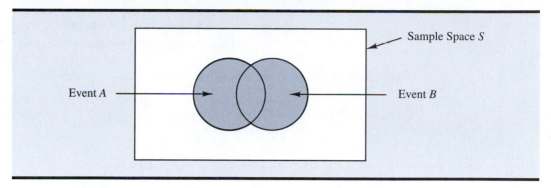

addition law is used to compute the probability of the union of two events. The addition law is written as follows.

Addition Law

$$P(A \cup B) = P(A) + P(B) - P(A \cap B) \qquad (4.6)$$

To understand the addition law intuitively, note that the first two terms in the addition law, $P(A) + P(B)$, account for all the sample points in $A \cup B$. However, because the sample points in the intersection $A \cap B$ are in both A and B, when we compute $P(A) + P(B)$, we are in effect counting each of the sample points in $A \cap B$ twice. We correct for this over-counting by subtracting $P(A \cap B)$.

As an example of an application of the addition law, let us consider the case of a small assembly plant with 50 employees. Each worker is expected to complete work assignments on time and in such a way that the assembled product will pass a final inspection. On occasion, some of the workers fail to meet the performance standards by completing work late and/or assembling a defective product. At the end of a performance evaluation period, the production manager found that 5 of the 50 workers completed work late, 6 of the 50 workers assembled a defective product, and 2 of the 50 workers both completed work late *and* assembled a defective product.

FIGURE 4.6   INTERSECTION OF EVENTS *A* AND *B* IS SHADED

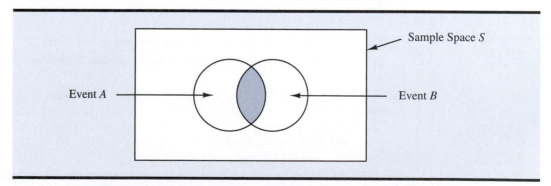

Let

$$L = \text{the event that the work is completed late}$$
$$D = \text{the event that the assembled product is defective}$$

The relative frequency information leads to the following probabilities.

$$P(L) = \frac{5}{50} = .10$$

$$P(D) = \frac{6}{50} = .12$$

$$P(L \cap D) = \frac{2}{50} = .04$$

After reviewing the performance data, the production manager decided to assign a poor performance rating to any employee whose work was either late or defective; thus the event of interest is $L \cup D$. What is the probability that the production manager assigned an employee a poor performance rating?

Note that the probability question is about the union of two events. Specifically, we want to know $P(L \cup D)$. Using equation (4.6), we have

$$P(L \cup D) = P(L) + P(D) - P(L \cap D)$$

Knowing values for the three probabilities on the right side of this expression, we can write

$$P(L \cup D) = .10 + .12 - .04 = .18$$

This calculation tells us that there is a .18 probability that a randomly selected employee received a poor performance rating.

As another example of the addition law, consider a recent study conducted by the personnel manager of a major computer software company. The study showed that 30% of the employees who left the firm within two years did so primarily because they were dissatisfied with their salary, 20% left because they were dissatisfied with their work assignments, and 12% of the former employees indicated dissatisfaction with *both* their salary and their work assignments. What is the probability that an employee who leaves within two years does so because of dissatisfaction with salary, dissatisfaction with the work assignment, or both?

Let

$$S = \text{the event that the employee leaves because of salary}$$
$$W = \text{the event that the employee leaves because of work assignment}$$

We have $P(S) = .30$, $P(W) = .20$, and $P(S \cap W) = .12$. Using equation (4.6), the addition law, we have

$$P(S \cup W) = P(S) + P(W) - P(S \cap W) = .30 + .20 - .12 = .38.$$

We find a .38 probability that an employee leaves for salary or work assignment reasons.

FIGURE 4.7   MUTUALLY EXCLUSIVE EVENTS

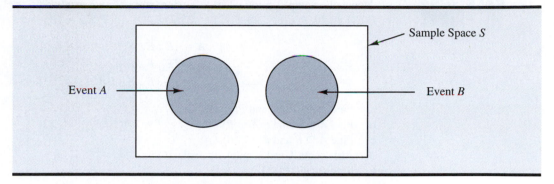

Before we conclude our discussion of the addition law, let us consider a special case that arises for **mutually exclusive events**.

Mutually Exclusive Events

Two events are said to be mutually exclusive if the events have no sample points in common.

Events A and B are mutually exclusive if, when one event occurs, the other cannot occur. Thus, a requirement for A and B to be mutually exclusive is that their intersection must contain no sample points. The Venn diagram depicting two mutually exclusive events A and B is shown in Figure 4.7. In this case $P(A \cap B) = 0$ and the addition law can be written as follows.

Addition Law for Mutually Exclusive Events

$$P(A \cup B) = P(A) + P(B)$$

EXERCISES

Methods

22. Suppose that we have a sample space with five equally likely experimental outcomes: E_1, E_2, E_3, E_4, E_5. Let

$$A = \{E_1, E_2\}$$
$$B = \{E_3, E_4\}$$
$$C = \{E_2, E_3, E_5\}$$

a. Find $P(A)$, $P(B)$, and $P(C)$.
b. Find $P(A \cup B)$. Are A and B mutually exclusive?
c. Find A^c, C^c, $P(A^c)$, and $P(C^c)$.
d. Find $A \cup B^c$ and $P(A \cup B^c)$.
e. Find $P(B \cup C)$.

23. Suppose that we have a sample space $S = \{E_1, E_2, E_3, E_4, E_5, E_6, E_7\}$, where $E_1, E_2, \ldots, E_7$ denote the sample points. The following probability assignments apply: $P(E_1) = .05$, $P(E_2) = .20$, $P(E_3) = .20$, $P(E_4) = .25$, $P(E_5) = .15$, $P(E_6) = .10$, and $P(E_7) = .05$. Let

$$A = \{E_1, E_4, E_6\}$$
$$B = \{E_2, E_4, E_7\}$$
$$C = \{E_2, E_3, E_5, E_7\}$$

a. Find $P(A)$, $P(B)$, and $P(C)$.
b. Find $A \cup B$ and $P(A \cup B)$.
c. Find $A \cap B$ and $P(A \cap B)$.
d. Are events A and C mutually exclusive?
e. Find B^c and $P(B^c)$.

Applications

24. Clarkson University surveyed alumni to learn more about what they think of Clarkson. One part of the survey asked respondents to indicate whether their overall experience at Clarkson fell short of expectations, met expectations, or surpassed expectations. The results showed that 4% of the respondents did not provide a response, 26% said that their experience fell short of expectations, and 65% of the respondents said that their experience met expectations (*Clarkson Magazine*, Summer 2001).
a. If we chose an alumnus at random, what is the probability that he or she would say their experience surpassed expectations?
b. If we chose an alumnus at random, what is the probability that he or she would say their experience met or surpassed expectations?

25. Data on the 30 largest bond funds provides 1-year and 5-year percentage returns for the period ending March 31, 2000 (*The Wall Street Journal*, April 10, 2000). Suppose we consider a 1-year return in excess of 2% to be high and a 5-year return in excess of 44% to be high. One-half of the funds had a 1-year return in excess of 2%, 12 of the funds had a 5-year return in excess of 44%, and six of the funds had a 1-year return in excess of 2% and a 5-year return in excess of 44%.
a. Find the probability of a fund having a high 1-year return, the probability of a fund having a high 5-year return, and the probability of a fund having both a high 1-year return and a high 5-year return.
b. What is the probability that a fund has a high 1-year return or a high 5-year return or both?
c. What is the probability that a fund has neither a high 1-year return nor a high 5-year return?

26. Data on the 30 largest stock and balanced funds provided 1-year and 5-year percentage returns for the period ending March 31, 2000 (*The Wall Street Journal*, April 10, 2000). Suppose we consider a 1-year return in excess of 50% to be high and a 5-year return in excess of 300% to be high. Nine of the funds had 1-year returns in excess of 50%, seven of the funds had 5-year returns in excess of 300%, and five of the funds had both 1-year returns in excess of 50% and 5-year returns in excess of 300%.
a. What is the probability of a high 1-year return, and what is the probability of a high 5-year return?
b. What is the probability of both a high 1-year return and a high 5-year return?
c. What is the probability of neither a high 1-year return nor a high 5-year return?

27. A 2001 preseason NCAA football poll asked respondents to answer the question, "Will the Big Ten or the Pac-10 have a team in this year's national championship game, the Rose Bowl? Of the 13,429 respondents, 2961 said the Big Ten would, 4494 said the Pac-10 would, and 6823 said neither the Big Ten nor the Pac-10 would have a team in the Rose Bowl (*www.yahoo.com*, August 30, 2001).

a. What is the probability that a respondent said neither the Big Ten nor the Pac-10 will have a team in the Rose Bowl?

b. What is the probability that a respondent said either the Big Ten or the Pac-10 will have a team in the Rose Bowl?

c. Find the probability that a respondent said both the Big Ten and the Pac-10 would have a team in the Rose Bowl.

28. A survey of magazine subscribers showed that 45.8% rented a car during the past 12 months for business reasons, 54% rented a car during the past 12 months for personal reasons, and 30% rented a car during the past 12 months for both business and personal reasons.

a. What is the probability that a subscriber rented a car during the past 12 months for business or personal reasons?

b. What is the probability that a subscriber did not rent a car during the past 12 months for either business or personal reasons?

29. High school seniors with strong academic records apply to the nation's most selective colleges in greater numbers each year. Because the number of slots remains relatively stable, some colleges reject more early applicants. The University of Pennsylvania received 2851 applications for early admission. Of this group, it admitted 1033 students, rejected 854 outright, and deferred 964 to the regular admissions pool. Penn admitted about 18% of the applicants in the regular admissions pool for a total class size (number of early admissions plus number of regular admissions) of 2375 students (*USA Today,* January 24, 2001). Let E, R, and D represent the events that a student who applies for early admission is admitted, rejected outright, or deferred to the regular admissions pool; and let A represent the event that a student in the regular admissions pool is admitted.

a. Use the data to estimate $P(E)$, $P(R)$, and $P(D)$.

b. Are events E and D mutually exclusive? Find $P(E \cap D)$.

c. For the 2375 students admitted to Penn, what is the probability that a randomly selected student was accepted for early admission?

d. Are events E and A mutually exclusive?

e. Suppose a student applies to Penn for early admission. What is the probability the student will be admitted for early admission or be accepted for admission in the regular admissions pool?

4.4   CONDITIONAL PROBABILITY

Often, the probability of an event is influenced by whether a related event already occurred. Suppose we have an event A with probability $P(A)$. If we obtain new information and learn that a related event, denoted by B, already occurred, we will want to take advantage of this information by calculating a new probability for event A. This new probability of event A is called a **conditional probability** and is written $P(A \mid B)$. We use the notation | to indicate that we are considering the probability of event A *given* the condition that event B has occurred. Hence, the notation $P(A \mid B)$ reads "the probability of A given B."

As an illustration of the application of conditional probability, consider the situation of the promotion status of male and female officers of a major metropolitan police force in the eastern United States. The police force consists of 1200 officers, 960 men and 240 women. Over the past two years, 324 officers on the police force received promotions. The specific breakdown of promotions for male and female officers is shown in Table 4.4.

After reviewing the promotion record, a committee of female officers raised a discrimination case on the basis that 288 male officers had received promotions but only 36 female officers had received promotions. The police administration argued that the relatively low number of promotions for female officers was due not to discrimination, but to the fact that

TABLE 4.4   PROMOTION STATUS OF POLICE OFFICERS OVER THE PAST TWO YEARS

	Men	Women	Totals
Promoted	288	36	324
Not Promoted	672	204	876
Totals	960	240	1200

relatively few females are members of the police force. Let us show how conditional proba-bility could be used to analyze the discrimination charge.

Let

$$M = \text{event an officer is a man}$$
$$W = \text{event an officer is a woman}$$
$$A = \text{event an officer is promoted}$$
$$A^c = \text{event an officer is not promoted}$$

Dividing the data values in Table 4.4 by the total of 1200 officers enables us to summarize the available information with the following probability values.

$P(M \cap A) = 288/1200 = .24 =$ probability that a randomly selected officer is a man *and* is promoted

$P(M \cap A^c) = 672/1200 = .56 =$ probability that a randomly selected officer is a man *and* is not promoted

$P(W \cap A) = 36/1200 = .03 =$ probability that a randomly selected officer is a woman *and* is promoted

$P(W \cap A^c) = 204/1200 = .17 =$ probability that a randomly selected officer is a woman *and* is not promoted

Because each of these values gives the probability of the intersection of two events, the probabilities are called **joint probabilities**. Table 4.5, which provides a summary of the probability information for the police officer promotion situation, is referred to as a *joint probability table*.

TABLE 4.5   JOINT PROBABILITY TABLE FOR PROMOTIONS

Joint probabilities appear in the body of the table.	Men (*M*)	Women (*W*)	Totals
Promoted (*A*)	.24	.03	.27
Not Promoted (*A^c*)	.56	.17	.73
Totals	.80	.20	1.00

Marginal probabilities appear in the margins of the table.

The values in the margins of the joint probability table provide the probabilities of each event separately. That is, $P(M) = .80$, $P(W) = .20$, $P(A) = .27$, and $P(A^c) = .73$. These probabilities are referred to as **marginal probabilities** because of their location in the margins of the joint probability table. We note that the marginal probabilities are found by summing the joint probabilities in the corresponding row or column of the joint probability table. For instance, the marginal probability of being promoted is $P(A) = P(M \cap A) + P(W \cap A) = .24 + .03 = .27$. From the marginal probabilities, we see that 80% of the force is male, 20% of the force is female, 27% of all officers received promotions, and 73% were not promoted.

Let us begin the conditional probability analysis by computing the probability that an officer is promoted given that the officer is a man. In conditional probability notation, we are attempting to determine $P(A \mid M)$. To calculate $P(A \mid M)$, we first realize that this notation simply means that we are considering the probability of the event A (promotion) given that the condition designated as event M (the officer is a man) is known to exist. Thus $P(A \mid M)$ tells us that we are now concerned only with the promotion status of the 960 male officers. Because 288 of the 960 male officers received promotions, the probability of being promoted given that the officer is a man is 288/960 = .30. In other words, given that an officer is a man, that officer has a 30% chance of receiving a promotion over the past two years.

This procedure was easy to apply because the values in Table 4.4 show the number of officers in each category. We now want to demonstrate how conditional probabilities such as $P(A \mid M)$ can be computed directly from related event probabilities rather than the frequency data of Table 4.4.

We have shown that $P(A \mid M) = 288/960 = .30$. Let us now divide both the numerator and denominator of this fraction by 1200, the total number of officers in the study.

$$P(A \mid M) = \frac{288}{960} = \frac{288/1200}{960/1200} = \frac{.24}{.80} = .30$$

We now see that the conditional probability $P(A \mid M)$ can be computed as .24/.80. Refer to the joint probability table (Table 4.5). Note in particular that .24 is the joint probability of A and M; that is, $P(A \cap M) = .24$. Also note that .80 is the marginal probability that a randomly selected officer is a man; that is, $P(M) = .80$. Thus, the conditional probability $P(A \mid M)$ can be computed as the ratio of the joint probability $P(A \cap M)$ to the marginal probability $P(M)$.

$$P(A \mid M) = \frac{P(A \cap M)}{P(M)} = \frac{.24}{.80} = .30$$

The fact that conditional probabilities can be computed as the ratio of a joint probability to a marginal probability provides the following general formula for conditional probability calculations for two events A and B.

Conditional Probability

$$P(A \mid B) = \frac{P(A \cap B)}{P(B)} \tag{4.7}$$

or

$$P(B \mid A) = \frac{P(A \cap B)}{P(A)} \qquad (4.8)$$

The Venn diagram in Figure 4.8 is helpful in obtaining an intuitive understanding of conditional probability. The circle on the right shows that event B has occurred; the portion of the circle that overlaps with event A denotes the event $(A \cap B)$. We know that once event B has occurred, the only way that we can also observe event A is for the event $(A \cap B)$ to occur. Thus, the ratio $P(A \cap B)/P(B)$ provides the conditional probability that we will observe event A given that event B has already occurred.

Let us return to the issue of discrimination against the female officers. The marginal probability in row 1 of Table 4.5 shows that the probability of promotion of an officer is $P(A) = .27$ (regardless of whether that officer is male or female). However, the critical issue in the discrimination case involves the two conditional probabilities $P(A \mid M)$ and $P(A \mid W)$. That is, what is the probability of a promotion *given* that the officer is a man, and what is the probability of a promotion *given* that the officer is a woman? If these two probabilities are equal, a discrimination argument has no basis because the chances of a promotion are the same for male and female officers. However, a difference in the two conditional probabilities will support the position that male and female officers are treated differently in promotion decisions.

We already determined that $P(A \mid M) = .30$. Let us now use the probability values in Table 4.5 and the basic relationship of conditional probability in equation (4.7) to compute the probability that an officer is promoted given that the officer is a woman; that is, $P(A \mid W)$. Using equation (4.7), with W replacing B, we obtain

$$P(A \mid W) = \frac{P(A \cap W)}{P(W)} = \frac{.03}{.20} = .15$$

What conclusion do you draw? The probability of a promotion given that the officer is a man is .30, twice the .15 probability of a promotion given that the officer is a woman. Al-

FIGURE 4.8   CONDITIONAL PROBABILITY $P(A \mid B) = P(A \cap B)/P(B)$

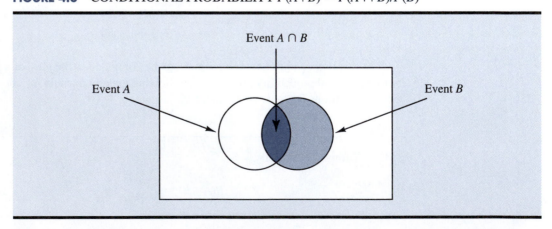

though the use of conditional probability does not in itself prove that discrimination exists in this case, the conditional probability values support the argument presented by the female officers.

Independent Events

In the preceding illustration, $P(A) = .27$, $P(A \mid M) = .30$, and $P(A \mid W) = .15$. We see that the probability of a promotion (event A) is affected or influenced by whether the officer is a man or a woman. Particularly, because $P(A \mid M) \neq P(A)$, we would say that events A and M are dependent events. That is, the probability of event A (promotion) is altered or affected by knowing that event M (the officer is a man) exists. Similarly, with $P(A \mid W) \neq P(A)$, we would say that events A and W are *dependent events*. However, if the probability of event A is not changed by the existence of event M—that is, $P(A \mid M) = P(A)$—we would say that events A and M are **independent events**. This situation leads to the following definition of the independence of two events.

Independent Events

Two events A and B are independent if

$$P(A \mid B) = P(A) \tag{4.9}$$

or

$$P(B \mid A) = P(B) \tag{4.10}$$

Otherwise, the events are dependent.

Multiplication Law

Whereas the addition law of probability is used to compute the probability of a union of two events, the multiplication law is used to compute the probability of the intersection of two events. The multiplication law is based on the definition of conditional probability. Using equations (4.7) and (4.8) and solving for $P(A \cap B)$, we obtain the **multiplication law**.

Multiplication Law

$$P(A \cap B) = P(B)P(A \mid B) \tag{4.11}$$

or

$$P(A \cap B) = P(A)P(B \mid A) \tag{4.12}$$

To illustrate the use of the multiplication law, consider a newspaper circulation department where it is known that 84% of the households in a particular neighborhood subscribe to the daily edition of the paper. If we let D denote the event that a household subscribes to the daily edition, $P(D) = .84$. In addition, it is known that the probability that a household who already holds a daily subscription also subscribes to the Sunday edition (event S) is

.75; that is, $P(S \mid D) = .75$. What is the probability that a household subscribes to both the Sunday and daily editions of the newspaper? Using the multiplication law, we compute the desired $P(S \cap D)$ as

$$P(S \cap D) = P(D)P(S \mid D) = .84(.75) = .63$$

We now know that 63% of the households subscribe to both the Sunday and daily editions.

Before concluding this section, let us consider the special case of the multiplication law when the events involved are independent. Recall that events A and B are independent whenever $P(A \mid B) = P(A)$ or $P(B \mid A) = P(B)$. Hence, using equations (4.11) and (4.12) for the special case of independent events, we obtain the following multiplication law.

Multiplication Law for Independent Events

$$P(A \cap B) = P(A)P(B) \tag{4.13}$$

To compute the probability of the intersection of two independent events, we simply multiply the corresponding probabilities. Note that the multiplication law for independent events provides another way to determine whether A and B are independent. That is, if $P(A \cap B) = P(A)P(B)$, then A and B are independent; if $P(A \cap B) \neq P(A)P(B)$, then A and B are dependent.

As an application of the multiplication law for independent events, consider the situation of a service station manager who knows from past experience that 80% of the customers use a credit card when they purchase gasoline. What is the probability that the next two customers purchasing gasoline will each use a credit card? If we let

$A =$ the event that the first customer uses a credit card

$B =$ the event that the second customer uses a credit card

then the event of interest is $A \cap B$. Given no other information, we can reasonably assume that A and B are independent events. Thus,

$$P(A \cap B) = P(A)P(B) = (.80)(.80) = .64$$

To summarize this section, we note that our interest in conditional probability is motivated by the fact that events are often related. In such cases, we say the events are dependent and the conditional probability formulas in equations (4.7) and (4.8) must be used to compute the event probabilities. If two events are not related, they are independent; in this case neither event's probability is affected by whether the other event occurred.

NOTES AND COMMENTS

Do not confuse the notion of mutually exclusive events with that of independent events. Two events with nonzero probabilities cannot be both mutually exclusive and independent. If one mutually exclusive event is known to occur, the other cannot occur; thus, the probability of the other event occurring is reduced to zero. They are therefore dependent.

EXERCISES

Methods

30. Suppose that we have two events, A and B, with $P(A) = .50$, $P(B) = .60$, and $P(A \cap B) = .40$.
  a. Find $P(A \mid B)$.
  b. Find $P(B \mid A)$.
  c. Are A and B independent? Why or why not?

31. Assume that we have two events, A and B, that are mutually exclusive. Assume further that we know $P(A) = .30$ and $P(B) = .40$.
  a. What is $P(A \cap B)$?
  b. What is $P(A \mid B)$?
  c. A student in statistics argues that the concepts of mutually exclusive events and independent events are really the same, and that if events are mutually exclusive they must be independent. Do you agree with this statement? Use the probability information in this problem to justify your answer.
  d. What general conclusion would you make about mutually exclusive and independent events given the results of this problem?

Applications

32. A Daytona Beach nightclub has the following data on the age and marital status of 140 customers.

		Marital Status	
		Single	**Married**
Age	**Under 30**	77	14
	30 or Over	28	21

  a. Develop a joint probability table for these data.
  b. Use the marginal probabilities to comment on the age of customers attending the club.
  c. Use the marginal probabilities to comment on the marital status of customers attending the club.
  d. What is the probability of finding a customer who is single and under the age of 30?
  e. If a customer is under 30, what is the probability that he or she is single?
  f. Is marital status independent of age? Explain, using probabilities.

33. In a survey of MBA students, the following data were obtained on "students' first reason for application to the school in which they matriculated."

		Reason for Application			
		School Quality	**School Cost or Convenience**	**Other**	**Totals**
Enrollment Status	**Full Time**	421	393	76	890
	Part Time	400	593	46	1039
	Totals	821	986	122	1929

    a. Develop a joint probability table for these data.

    b. Use the marginal probabilities of school quality, school cost or convenience, and other to comment on the most important reason for choosing a school.

    c. If a student goes full time, what is the probability that school quality is the first reason for choosing a school?

    d. If a student goes part time, what is the probability that school quality is the first reason for choosing a school?

    e. Let A denote the event that a student is full time and let B denote the event that the student lists school quality as the first reason for applying. Are events A and B independent? Justify your answer.

34. The following table shows the distribution of blood types in the general population (Hoxworth Blood Center, Cincinnati, Ohio).

	A	B	AB	O
Rh+	34%	9%	4%	38%
Rh−	6%	2%	1%	6%

    a. What is the probability a person will have type O blood?

    b. What is the probability a person will be Rh−?

    c. What is the probability a married couple will both be Rh−?

    d. What is the probability a married couple will both have type AB blood?

    e. What is the probability a person will be Rh− given she or he has type O blood?

    f. What is the probability a person will have type B blood given he or she is Rh+?

35. "Since 1950, the January Barometer has predicted the annual course of the stock market with amazing accuracy" (*1998 Stock Trader's Almanac*). Over the 48 years from 1950 through 1997, the stock market has been up in January 31 times; it has been up for the year 36 times; and it has been up for the year and up for January 29 times.

    a. Estimate the probability the stock market will be up in January.

    b. Estimate the probability the stock market will be up for the year.

    c. What is the probability the stock market will be up for the year given it is up in January?

    d. Do the probabilities suggest that the stock market's January performance and its annual performance are independent events? Explain.

36. A study of job satisfaction was conducted for four occupations: cabinetmaker, lawyer, physical therapist, and systems analyst. Job satisfaction was measured on a scale of 0–100. The data obtained are summarized in the following crosstabulation.

	Satisfaction Score				
Occupation	**Under 50**	**50–59**	**60–69**	**70–79**	**80–89**
Cabinetmaker	0	2	4	3	1
Lawyer	6	2	1	1	0
Physical Therapist	0	5	2	1	2
Systems Analyst	2	1	4	3	0

    a. Develop a joint probability table.

    b. What is the probability one of the participants studied received a satisfaction score in the 80s?

    c. What is the probability of a satisfaction score in the 80s given the study participant was a physical therapist?

    d. What is the probability one of the participants studied was a lawyer?

    e. What is the probability one of the participants was a lawyer and received a score under 50?

    f. What is the probability of receiving a satisfaction score under 50 given a person is a lawyer?

    g. What is the probability of a satisfaction score of 70 or higher?

37. A purchasing agent placed rush orders for a particular raw material with two different suppliers, A and B. If neither order arrives in four days, the production process must be shut down until at least one of the orders arrives. The probability that supplier A can deliver the material in four days is .55. The probability that supplier B can deliver the material in four days is .35.

    a. What is the probability that both suppliers will deliver the material in four days? Because two separate suppliers are involved, we are willing to assume independence.

    b. What is the probability that at least one supplier will deliver the material in four days?

    c. What is the probability that the production process will be shut down in four days because of a shortage of raw material (that is, both orders are late)?

38. A survey of 1035 workers by the Institute for the Future and the Gallup Organization found that workers are being inundated by messages (*The Cincinnati Enquirer*, November 2, 1998). The study indicated that each worker gets an average of 190 messages per day. The following table shows the breakdown by type of message.

Source	Daily Messages	Source	Daily Messages
Telephone	52	E-mail	30
Voice mail	22	Interoffice mail	18
U.S. mail	18	Fax	15
Post-it note	11	Phone msg. slip	10
Pager	4	Overnight courier	4
Cellular phone	3	U.S. Express mail	3

    a. For any particular worker, what is the probability the next message will be on the telephone?

    b. For the next two messages, what is the probability the first will be via e-mail and the second will be via fax?

    c. What is the probability the next message received will be via telephone call or interoffice mail?

4.5   BAYES' THEOREM

In the discussion of conditional probability, we indicated that revising probabilities when new information is obtained is an important phase of probability analysis. Often, we begin the analysis with initial or **prior probability** estimates for specific events of interest. Then, from sources such as a sample, a special report, or a product test, we obtain additional information about the events. Given this new information, we update the prior probability values by calculating revised probabilities, referred to as **posterior probabilities**. **Bayes' theorem** provides a means for making these probability calculations. The steps in this probability revision process are shown in Figure 4.9.

    As an application of Bayes' theorem, consider a manufacturing firm that receives shipments of parts from two different suppliers. Let A_1 denote the event that a part is from

FIGURE 4.9   PROBABILITY REVISION USING BAYES' THEOREM

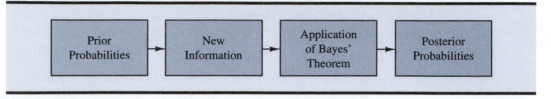

supplier 1 and A_2 denote the event that a part is from supplier 2. Currently, 65% of the parts purchased by the company are from supplier 1 and the remaining 35% are from supplier 2. Hence, if a part is selected at random, we would assign the prior probabilities $P(A_1) = .65$ and $P(A_2) = .35$.

The quality of the purchased parts varies with the source of supply. Historical data suggest that the quality ratings of the two suppliers are as shown in Table 4.6. If we let G denote the event that a part is good and B denote the event that a part is bad, the information in Table 4.6 provides the following conditional probability values.

$$P(G \mid A_1) = .98 \quad P(B \mid A_1) = .02$$
$$P(G \mid A_2) = .95 \quad P(B \mid A_2) = .05$$

The tree diagram in Figure 4.10 depicts the process of the firm receiving a part from one of the two suppliers and then discovering that the part is good or bad as a two-step experiment. We see that four experimental outcomes are possible; two correspond to the part being good and two correspond to the part being bad.

Each of the experimental outcomes is the intersection of two events, so we can use the multiplication rule to compute the probabilities. For instance,

$$P(A_1, G) = P(A_1 \cap G) = P(A_1)P(G \mid A_1)$$

The process of computing these joint probabilities can be depicted in what is called a probability tree (see Figure 4.11). From left to right through the tree, the probabilities for each branch at step 1 are prior probabilities and the probabilities for each branch at step 2 are conditional probabilities. To find the probabilities of each experimental outcome, we simply multiply the probabilities on the branches leading to the outcome. Each of these joint probabilities is shown in Figure 4.11 along with the known probabilities for each branch.

Suppose now that the parts from the two suppliers are used in the firm's manufacturing process and that a machine breaks down because it attempts to process a bad part. Given the information that the part is bad, what is the probability that it came from supplier 1 and what is the probability that it came from supplier 2? With the information in the probability tree (Figure 4.11), Bayes' theorem can be used to answer these questions.

TABLE 4.6   HISTORICAL QUALITY LEVELS OF TWO SUPPLIERS

	Percentage Good Parts	Percentage Bad Parts
Supplier 1	98	2
Supplier 2	95	5

FIGURE 4.10   TREE DIAGRAM FOR TWO-SUPPLIER EXAMPLE

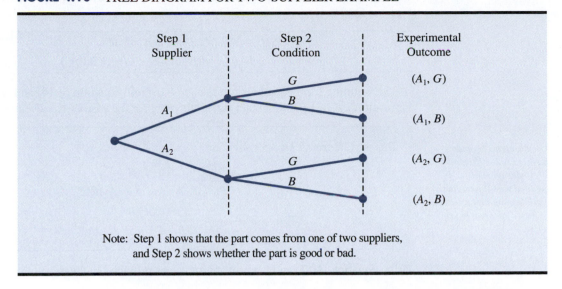

Note: Step 1 shows that the part comes from one of two suppliers,
and Step 2 shows whether the part is good or bad.

Letting B denote the event that the part is bad, we are looking for the posterior probabilities $P(A_1 \mid B)$ and $P(A_2 \mid B)$. From the law of conditional probability, we know that

$$P(A_1 \mid B) = \frac{P(A_1 \cap B)}{P(B)} \qquad (4.14)$$

Referring to the probability tree, we see that

$$P(A_1 \cap B) = P(A_1)P(B \mid A_1) \qquad (4.15)$$

FIGURE 4.11   PROBABILITY TREE FOR TWO-SUPPLIER EXAMPLE

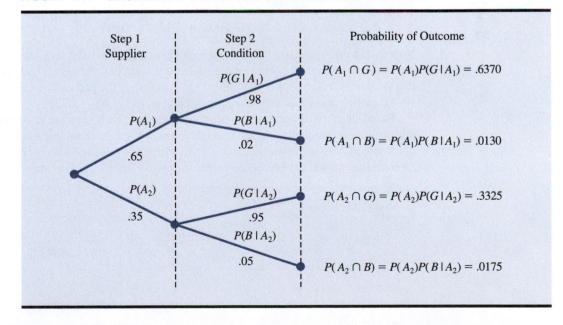

To find $P(B)$, we note that event B can occur in only two ways: $(A_1 \cap B)$ and $(A_2 \cap B)$. Therefore, we have

$$
\begin{aligned}
P(B) &= P(A_1 \cap B) + P(A_2 \cap B) \\
&= P(A_1)P(B \mid A_1) + P(A_2)P(B \mid A_2)
\end{aligned}
\tag{4.16}
$$

Substituting from equations (4.15) and (4.16) into equation (4.14) and writing a similar result for $P(A_2 \mid B)$, we obtain Bayes' theorem for the case of two events.

The Reverend Thomas Bayes (1702–1761), a Presbyterian minister, is credited with the original work leading to the version of Bayes' theorem in use today.

Bayes' Theorem (Two-Event Case)

$$
P(A_1 \mid B) = \frac{P(A_1)P(B \mid A_1)}{P(A_1)P(B \mid A_1) + P(A_2)P(B \mid A_2)}
\tag{4.17}
$$

$$
P(A_2 \mid B) = \frac{P(A_2)P(B \mid A_2)}{P(A_1)P(B \mid A_1) + P(A_2)P(B \mid A_2)}
\tag{4.18}
$$

Using equation (4.17) and the probability values provided in the example, we have

$$
\begin{aligned}
P(A_1 \mid B) &= \frac{P(A_1)P(B \mid A_1)}{P(A_1)P(B \mid A_1) + P(A_2)P(B \mid A_2)} \\
&= \frac{(.65)(.02)}{(.65)(.02) + (.35)(.05)} = \frac{.0130}{.0130 + .0175} \\
&= \frac{.0130}{.0305} = .4262
\end{aligned}
$$

In addition, using equation (4.18), we find $P(A_2 \mid B)$.

$$
\begin{aligned}
P(A_2 \mid B) &= \frac{(.35)(.05)}{(.65)(.02) + (.35)(.05)} \\
&= \frac{.0175}{.0130 + .0175} = \frac{.0175}{.0305} = .5738
\end{aligned}
$$

Note that in this application we started with a probability of .65 that a part selected at random was from supplier 1. However, given information that the part is bad, the probability that the part is from supplier 1 drops to .4262. In fact, if the part is bad, it has better than a 50–50 chance that it came from supplier 2; that is, $P(A_2 \mid B) = .5738$.

Bayes' theorem is applicable when the events for which we want to compute posterior probabilities are mutually exclusive and their union is the entire sample space.* For the case of n mutually exclusive events $A_1, A_2, \ldots, A_n$, whose union is the entire sample space, Bayes' theorem can be used to compute any posterior probability $P(A_i \mid B)$ as shown below.

Bayes' Theorem

$$
P(A_i \mid B) = \frac{P(A_i)P(B \mid A_i)}{P(A_1)P(B \mid A_1) + P(A_2)P(B \mid A_2) + \cdots + P(A_n)P(B \mid A_n)}
\tag{4.19}
$$

---

*If the union of events is the entire sample space, the events are said to be *collectively exhaustive*.

With prior probabilities $P(A_1)$, $P(A_2)$, ..., $P(A_n)$ and the appropriate conditional probabilities $P(B \mid A_1)$, $P(B \mid A_2)$, ..., $P(B \mid A_n)$, equation (4.19) can be used to compute the posterior probability of the events $A_1, A_2, \ldots, A_n$.

Tabular Approach

A tabular approach is helpful in conducting the Bayes' theorem calculations. Such an approach is shown in Table 4.7 for the parts supplier problem. The computations shown there are done in the following steps.

Step 1. Prepare the following three columns:
  Column 1—The mutually exclusive events A_i for which posterior probabilities are desired.
  Column 2—The prior probabilities $P(A_i)$ for the events.
  Column 3—The conditional probabilities $P(B \mid A_i)$ of the new information B given each event.

Step 2. In column 4, compute the joint probabilities $P(A_i \cap B)$ for each event and the new information B by using the multiplication law. These joint probabilities are found by multiplying the prior probabilities in column 2 by the corresponding conditional probabilities in column 3; that is, $P(A_i \cap B) = P(A_i)P(B \mid A_i)$.

Step 3. Sum the joint probabilities in column 4. The sum is the probability of the new information, $P(B)$. Thus we see in Table 4.7 that there is a .0130 probability that the part came from supplier 1 and is bad and a .0175 probability that the part came from supplier 2 and is bad. Because these are the only two ways in which a bad part can be obtained, the sum .0130 + .0175 shows an overall probability of .0305 of finding a bad part from the combined shipments of the two suppliers.

Step 4. In column 5, compute the posterior probabilities using the basic relationship of conditional probability.

$$P(A_i \mid B) = \frac{P(A_i \cap B)}{P(B)}$$

Note that the joint probabilities $P(A_i \cap B)$ are in column 4 and the probability $P(B)$ is the sum of column 4.

TABLE 4.7   TABULAR APPROACH TO BAYES' THEOREM CALCULATIONS FOR THE TWO-SUPPLIER PROBLEM

(1) Events A_i	(2) Prior Probabilities $P(A_i)$	(3) Conditional Probabilities $P(B \mid A_i)$	(4) Joint Probabilities $P(A_i \cap B)$	(5) Posterior Probabilities $P(A_i \mid B)$
A_1	.65	.02	.0130	.0130/.0305 = .4262
A_2	.35	.05	.0175	.0175/.0305 = .5738
	1.00		$P(B) = .0305$	1.0000

FIGURE 4.12 EXCEL WORKSHEET FOR COMPUTING POSTERIOR PROBABILITIES

	A	B	C	D	E	F
1		Prior	Conditional	Joint	Posterior	
2	Events	Probabilities	Probabilities	Probabilities	Probabilities	
3	A1	0.65	0.02	=B3*C3	=D3/$D$5	
4	A2	0.35	0.05	=B4*C4	=D4/$D$5	
5		=SUM(B3:B4)		=SUM(D3:D4)	=SUM(E3:E4)	
6						

	A	B	C	D	E	F
1		Prior	Conditional	Joint	Posterior	
2	Events	Probabilities	Probabilities	Probabilities	Probabilities	
3	A1	0.65	0.02	0.0130	0.4262	
4	A2	0.35	0.05	0.0175	0.5738	
5		1		0.0305	1.0000	
6						

Using Excel to Compute Posterior Probabilities

The tabular approach to Bayes' Theorem can be easily implemented within an Excel worksheet. In this subsection we show how the Bayes' theorem calculations shown in Table 4.7 can be made. Refer to Figure 4.12 as we describe the tasks involved. The formula worksheet is in the background; the value worksheet is in the foreground.

Enter Data: Labels are placed in rows 1 and 2 and the two mutually exclusive events are identified in cells A3:A4. The prior probabilities were entered into cells B3:B4 and the conditional probabilities were entered into cells C3:C4.

Enter Functions and Formulas: The formulas in cells D3:D4 show that the joint probabilities are the product of the prior probabilities in column B and the conditional probabilities in column C. The results, shown in cells D3:D4 of the value worksheet, are the same as those shown in Table 4.7. The sum in cell D5 shows that the probability of finding a bad part is .0305. This probability is the denominator in Bayes' theorem. The formulas in cells E3:E4 provide the posterior probabilities. From the value worksheet we see that they are the same as the posterior probabilities in Table 4.7.

Note that the same worksheet could be used to find the posterior probabilities of the two suppliers given a good part is found. The prior probabilities in cells B3:B4 would not change. But, we would replace the conditional probabilities in cells C3:C4 with the values .98 and .95 respectively. Doing so would provide $P(A_1 \mid G) = .6570$ and $P(A_2 \mid G) = .3430$ in cells E3:E4.

This worksheet can also be modified to handle Bayes' theorem calculations for more than two events. Just add a row for each additional event and move the sum row down.

NOTES AND COMMENTS

1. Bayes' theorem is used extensively in decision analysis. The prior probabilities are often subjective estimates provided by a decision maker. Sample information is obtained and posterior probabilities are computed for use in choosing the best decision.

2. An event and its complement are mutually exclusive, and their union is the entire sample space. Thus, Bayes' theorem is always applicable for computing posterior probabilities of an event and its complement.

EXERCISES

Methods

39. The prior probabilities for events A_1 and A_2 are $P(A_1) = .40$ and $P(A_2) = .60$. It is also known that $P(A_1 \cap A_2) = 0$. Suppose $P(B \mid A_1) = .20$ and $P(B \mid A_2) = .05$.
    a. Are A_1 and A_2 mutually exclusive? Explain.
    b. Compute $P(A_1 \cap B)$ and $P(A_2 \cap B)$.
    c. Compute $P(B)$.
    d. Apply Bayes' theorem to compute $P(A_1 \mid B)$ and $P(A_2 \mid B)$.

40. The prior probabilities for events A_1, A_2, and A_3 are $P(A_1) = .20$, $P(A_2) = .50$, and $P(A_3) = .30$. The conditional probabilities of event B given A_1, A_2, and A_3 are $P(B \mid A_1) = .50$, $P(B \mid A_2) = .40$, and $P(B \mid A_3) = .30$.
    a. Compute $P(B \cap A_1)$, $P(B \cap A_2)$, and $P(B \cap A_3)$.
    b. Apply Bayes' theorem, equation (4.19), to compute the posterior probability $P(A_2 \mid B)$.
    c. Use the tabular approach to applying Bayes' theorem to compute $P(A_1 \mid B)$, $P(A_2 \mid B)$, and $P(A_3 \mid B)$.

Applications

41. A consulting firm submitted a bid for a large research project. The firm's management initially felt they had a 50–50 chance of getting the project. However, the agency to which the bid was submitted subsequently requested additional information on the bid. Past experience indicates that for 75% of the successful bids and 40% of the unsuccessful bids the agency requested additional information.
    a. What is the prior probability of the bid being successful (that is, prior to the request for additional information)?
    b. What is the conditional probability of a request for additional information given that the bid will ultimately be successful?
    c. Compute the posterior probability that the bid will be successful given a request for additional information.

42. A local bank reviewed its credit card policy with the intention of recalling some of its credit cards. In the past approximately 5% of cardholders defaulted, leaving the bank unable to collect the outstanding balance. Hence, management established a prior probability of .05 that any particular cardholder will default. The bank also found that the probability of missing a monthly payment is .20 for customers who do not default. Of course, the probability of missing a monthly payment for those who default is 1.
    a. Given that a customer missed a monthly payment, compute the posterior probability that the customer will default.
    b. The bank would like to recall its card if the probability that a customer will default is greater than .20. Should the bank recall its card if the customer misses a monthly payment? Why or why not?

43. Small cars get better gas mileage, but they are not as safe as bigger cars. Small cars accounted for 18% of the vehicles on the road, but accidents involving small cars led to 11,898 fatalities during a recent year (*Reader's Digest*, May 2000). Assume the probability a small car is involved in an accident is .18. The probability of an accident involving a small car leading to a fatality is .128 and the probability of an accident not involving a small car leading to a fatality is .05. Suppose you learn of an accident involving a fatality. What is the probability a small car was involved?

44. A city's professional basketball team plays at home, and its professional hockey team plays away on the same night. A professional basketball team has a .641 probability of winning

a home game and a professional hockey team has a .462 probability of winning an away game. Historically, when both teams play on the same night, the chance that the next morning's leading sports story will be about the basketball game is 60% and the chance that it will be about the hockey game is 40%. Suppose that on the morning after these games the newspaper's leading sports story begins with the headline "We Win!!" What is the probability that the story is about the basketball team?

45. In an article about investment growth, *Money* magazine reported that drug stocks show powerful long-term trends and offer investors unparalleled potential for strong and steady gains. The federal Health Care Financing Administration supports this conclusion through its forecast that annual prescription drug expenditures will reach $366 billion by 2010, up from $117 billion in 2000. Many individuals age 65 and older rely heavily on prescription drugs. For this group, 82% take prescription drugs regularly, 55% take three or more prescriptions regularly, and 40% currently use five or more prescriptions. In contrast, 49% of people under age 65 take prescriptions regularly, with 17% taking three or more prescriptions regularly and 28% using five or more prescriptions (*Money*, September 2001). The U.S. Census Bureau reports that of the 281,421,906 people in the United States, 34,991,753 are age 65 years and older (*U.S. Census Bureau*, Census 2000).

   a. Compute the probability that a person in the United States is age 65 or older.
   b. Compute the probability that a person takes prescription drugs regularly.
   c. Compute the probability that a person is age 65 or older and takes five or more prescriptions.
   d. Given a person uses five or more prescriptions, compute the probability that the person is age 65 or older.

SUMMARY

In this chapter we introduced basic probability concepts and illustrated how probability analysis can be used to provide helpful information for decision making. We described how probability can be interpreted as a numerical measure of the likelihood that an event will occur. In addition, we saw that the probability of an event can be computed either by summing the probabilities of the experimental outcomes (sample points) comprising the event or by using the relationships established by the addition, conditional probability, and multiplication laws of probability. For cases in which additional information is available, we showed how Bayes' theorem can be used to obtain revised or posterior probabilities.

GLOSSARY

Probability   A numerical measure of the likelihood that an event will occur.

Experiment   A process that generates well-defined outcomes.

Sample space   The set of all experimental outcomes.

Sample point   An element of the sample space. A sample point represents an experimental outcome.

Tree diagram   A graphical representation that helps in visualizing a multiple-step experiment.

Basic requirements for assigning probabilities   Two requirements that restrict the manner in which probability assignments can be made: (1) for each experimental outcome E_i we must have $0 \le P(E_i) \le 1$; (2) considering all experimental outcomes, we must have $P(E_1) + P(E_2) + \cdots + P(E_n) = 1$.

Classical method   A method of assigning probabilities that is appropriate when all the experimental outcomes are equally likely.

Relative frequency method   A method of assigning probabilities that is appropriate when data are available to estimate the proportion of the time the experimental outcome will occur if the experiment is repeated a large number of times.

Subjective method   A method of assigning probabilities on the basis of judgment.

Event   A collection of sample points.

Complement of A   The event consisting of all sample points that are not in A.

Venn diagram   A graphical representation for showing symbolically the sample space and operations involving events in which the sample space is represented by a rectangle and events are represented as circles within the sample space.

Union of A and B   The event containing all sample points belonging to A or B or both. The union is denoted $A \cup B$.

Intersection of A and B   The event containing the sample points belonging to both A and B. The intersection is denoted $A \cap B$.

Addition law   A probability law used to compute the probability of the union of two events. It is $P(A \cup B) = P(A) + P(B) - P(A \cap B)$. For mutually exclusive events, $P(A \cap B) = 0$; in this case the addition law reduces to $P(A \cup B) = P(A) + P(B)$.

Mutually exclusive events   Events that have no sample points in common; that is, $A \cap B$ is empty and $P(A \cap B) = 0$.

Conditional probability   The probability of an event given that another event already occurred. The conditional probability of A given B is $P(A \mid B) = P(A \cap B)/P(B)$.

Joint probability   The probability of two events both occurring; that is, the probability of the intersection of two events.

Marginal probability   The values in the margins of a joint probability table that provide the probabilities of each event separately.

Independent events   Two events A and B where $P(A \mid B) = P(A)$ or $P(B \mid A) = P(B)$; that is, the events have no influence on each other.

Multiplication law   A probability law used to compute the probability of the intersection of two events. It is $P(A \cap B) = P(B)P(A \mid B)$ or $P(A \cap B) = P(A)P(B \mid A)$. For independent events it reduces to $P(A \cap B) = P(A)P(B)$.

Prior probabilities   Initial estimates of the probabilities of events.

Posterior probabilities   Revised probabilities of events based on additional information.

Bayes' theorem   A method used to compute posterior probabilities.

KEY FORMULAS

Counting Rule for Combinations

$$C_n^N = \binom{N}{n} = \frac{N!}{n!(N - n)!} \tag{4.1}$$

Counting Rule for Permutations

$$P_n^N = n!\binom{N}{n} = \frac{N!}{(N - n)!} \tag{4.2}$$

Computing Probability Using the Complement

$$P(A) = 1 - P(A^c) \tag{4.5}$$

Addition Law

$$P(A \cup B) = P(A) + P(B) - P(A \cap B) \tag{4.6}$$

Conditional Probability

$$P(A \mid B) = \frac{P(A \cap B)}{P(B)} \tag{4.7}$$

$$P(B \mid A) = \frac{P(A \cap B)}{P(A)} \tag{4.8}$$

Multiplication Law

$$P(A \cap B) = P(B)P(A \mid B) \tag{4.11}$$

$$P(A \cap B) = P(A)P(B \mid A) \tag{4.12}$$

Multiplication Law for Independent Events

$$P(A \cap B) = P(A)P(B) \tag{4.13}$$

Bayes' Theorem

$$P(A_i \mid B) = \frac{P(A_i)P(B \mid A_i)}{P(A_1)P(B \mid A_1) + P(A_2)P(B \mid A_2) + \cdots + P(A_n)P(B \mid A_n)} \tag{4.19}$$

SUPPLEMENTARY EXERCISES

46. In a *Business Week*/Harris Poll, 1035 adults were asked about their attitudes toward business (*Business Week*, September 11, 2000). One question asked: "How would you rate large U.S. companies on making good products and competing in a global environment?" The responses were: excellent—18%, pretty good—50%, only fair—26%, poor—5%, and don't know/no answer—1%.
   a. What is the probability that a respondent rated U.S. companies pretty good or excellent?
   b. How many respondents rated U.S. companies poor?
   c. How many respondents did not know or did not answer?

47. A financial manager made two new investments—one in the oil industry and one in municipal bonds. After a one-year period, each of the investments will be classified as either successful or unsuccessful. Consider the making of the two investments as an experiment.
   a. How many sample points exist for this experiment?
   b. Show a tree diagram and list the sample points.
   c. Let O = the event that the oil industry investment is successful and M = the event that the municipal bond investment is successful. List the sample points in O and in M.
   d. List the sample points in the union of the events ($O \cup M$).
   e. List the sample points in the intersection of the events ($O \cap M$).
   f. Are events O and M mutually exclusive? Explain.

48. A survey of American opinion asked adults: Are you satisfied or dissatisfied with the state of the U.S. economy today? (*The Wall Street Journal*, June 27, 1997). The following table provides the responses for all adults and the distribution by age groups.

	Satisfied (%)	Dissatisfied (%)	Other (%)
All Adults	61	37	2
18–34	64	35	1
35–49	58	41	1
50–64	57	40	3
65+	70	26	4

    a.   What is the probability a respondent is satisfied?

    b.   Which age groups report a higher level of satisfaction than the average for all adults?

    c.   What is the probability a respondent 65 or over did not indicate they were satisfied?

49. A study of 31,000 hospital admissions in New York State found that 4% of the admissions led to treatment-caused injuries. One-seventh of these treatment-caused injuries resulted in death, and one-fourth were caused by negligence. Malpractice claims were filed in one out of 7.5 cases involving negligence, and payments were made in one out of every two claims.

    a.   What is the probability a person admitted to the hospital will suffer a treatment-caused injury due to negligence?

    b.   What is the probability a person admitted to the hospital will die from a treatment-caused injury?

    c.   In the case of a negligent treatment-caused injury, what is the probability a malpractice claim will be paid?

50. A telephone survey to determine viewer response to a new television show obtained the following data.

Rating	Frequency
Poor	4
Below average	8
Average	11
Above average	14
Excellent	13

    a.   What is the probability that a randomly selected viewer will rate the new show as average or better?

    b.   What is the probability that a randomly selected viewer will rate the new show below average or worse?

51. *Business Week* surveyed its subscribers concerning the number of cars they owned or leased. Responses were obtained to three questions: How many cars do you own? How many cars do you lease? How many cars do you have (owned or leased)? Table 4.8 contains the results obtained from 932 households (*Business Week* 1996 Worldwide Subscriber Study). In interpreting the table note that the third row shows that 401 households own 2 cars, 47 households lease 2 cars, and 447 households have 2 cars (owned and/or leased).

    a.   What is the probability a household leases 1 car?

    b.   What is the probability a household owns 2 or fewer cars?

    c.   What is the probability a household has 3 or more cars?

    d.   What is the probability a household does not own or lease a car?

TABLE 4.8 NUMBER OF CARS OWNED OR LEASED, AND TOTAL NUMBER OF CARS PER HOUSEHOLD

	Number of Households		
Cars	Own	Lease	Have
0	65	708	19
1	242	168	168
2	401	47	447
3	149	9	186
4 or more	75	0	112
Total	932	932	932

52. A GMAC MBA new-matriculants survey provided the following data for 2018 students.

		Applied to More Than One School	
		Yes	No
	23 and under	207	201
	24–26	299	379
Age Group	27–30	185	268
	31–35	66	193
	36 and over	51	169

a. For a randomly selected MBA student, prepare a joint probability table for the experiment consisting of observing the student's age and whether the student applied to one or more schools.
b. What is the probability that a randomly selected applicant is 23 or under?
c. What is the probability that a randomly selected applicant is older than 26?
d. What is the probability that a randomly selected applicant applied to more than one school?

53. Refer again to the data from the GMAC new-matriculants survey in Exercise 52.
a. Given that a person applied to more than one school, what is the probability that the person is 24–26 years old?
b. Given that a person is in the 36-and-over age group, what is the probability that the person applied to more than one school?
c. What is the probability that a person is 24–26 years old or applied to more than one school?
d. Suppose a person is known to have applied to only one school. What is the probability that the person is 31 or more years old?
e. Is the number of schools applied to independent of age? Explain.

54. An IBD/TIPP poll was conducted to learn about attitudes toward investment and retirement (*Investor's Business Daily*, May 5, 2000). One question asked male and female respondents how important they felt level of of risk was in choosing a retirement investment. The following joint probability table was constructed from the data provided. Important means the respondent said level of risk was either important or very important.

	Male	Female	Total
Important	.22	.27	.49
Not Important	.28	.23	.51
Total	.50	.50	1.00

a. What is the probability a survey respondent will say level of risk is important?
b. What is the probability a male respondent will say level of risk is important?
c. What is the probability a female respondent will say level of risk is important?
d. Is the level of risk independent of the gender of the respondent? Why or why not?
e. Do male and female attitudes toward risk differ?

55. A large consumer goods company has been running a television advertisement for one of its soap products. On the basis of a survey that was conducted, probabilities were assigned to the following events.

$$B = \text{individual purchased the product}$$
$$S = \text{individual recalls seeing the advertisement}$$
$$B \cap S = \text{individual purchased the product and recalls seeing the advertisement}$$

The probabilities assigned were $P(B) = .20$, $P(S) = .40$, and $P(B \cap S) = .12$.
a. What is the probability of an individual's purchasing the product given that the individual recalls seeing the advertisement? Does seeing the advertisement increase the probability that the individual will purchase the product? As a decision maker, would you recommend continuing the advertisement (assuming that the cost is reasonable)?
b. Assume that individuals who do not purchase the company's soap product buy from its competitors. What would be your estimate of the company's market share? Would you expect that continuing the advertisement will increase the company's market share? Why or why not?
c. The company also tested another advertisement and assigned it values of $P(S) = .30$ and $P(B \cap S) = .10$. What is $P(B \mid S)$ for this other advertisement? Which advertisement seems to have had the bigger effect on customer purchases?

56. Cooper Realty is a small real estate company located in Albany, New York, specializing primarily in residential listings. They recently became interested in determining the likelihood of one of their listings being sold within a certain number of days. An analysis of company sales of 800 homes in previous years produced the following data.

		Days Listed Until Sold			
		Under 30	31–90	Over 90	Total
	Under $150,000	50	40	10	100
Initial Asking Price	**$150,000–$199,999**	20	150	80	250
	$200,000–$250,000	20	280	100	400
	Over $250,000	10	30	10	50
	Total	100	500	200	800

a. If A is defined as the event that a home is listed for more than 90 days before being sold, estimate the probability of A.
b. If B is defined as the event that the initial asking price is under $150,000, estimate the probability of B.
c. What is the probability of $A \cap B$?
d. Assuming that a contract just signed to list a home has an initial asking price of less than $150,000, what is the probability that the home will take Cooper Realty more than 90 days to sell?
e. Are events A and B independent?

57. A company studied the number of lost-time accidents occurring at its Brownsville, Texas, plant. Historical records show that 6% of the employees suffered lost-time accidents last year. Management believes that a special safety program will reduce such accidents to 5% during the current year. In addition, it estimates that 15% of employees who had lost-time accidents last year will experience a lost-time accident during the current year.
a. What percentage of the employees will experience lost-time accidents in both years?
b. What percentage of the employees will suffer at least one lost-time accident over the two-year period?

58. The Dallas IRS auditing staff, concerned with identifying potentially fraudulent tax returns, believes that the probability of finding a fraudulent return given that the return contains deductions for contributions exceeding the IRS standard is .20. Given that the deductions for contributions do not exceed the IRS standard, the probability of a fraudulent return decreases to .02. If 8% of all returns exceed the IRS standard for deductions due to contributions, what is the best estimate of the percentage of fraudulent returns?

59. An oil company purchased an option on land in Alaska. Preliminary geologic studies assigned the following prior probabilities.

$$P(\text{high-quality oil}) = .50$$
$$P(\text{medium-quality oil}) = .20$$
$$P(\text{no oil}) = .30$$

a. What is the probability of finding oil?
b. After 200 feet of drilling on the first well, a soil test is taken. The probabilities of finding the particular type of soil identified by the test follow.

$$P(\text{soil} \mid \text{high-quality oil}) = .20$$
$$P(\text{soil} \mid \text{medium-quality oil}) = .80$$
$$P(\text{soil} \mid \text{no oil}) = .20$$

How should the firm interpret the soil test? What are the revised probabilities, and what is the new probability of finding oil?

60. A Bayesian approach can be used to revise probabilities that a prospect field will produce oil. In one case, geological assessment indicates a 25% chance that the field will produce oil. Further, there is an 80% chance that a particular well will produce oil given that oil is present in the prospect field.
a. Suppose that one well is drilled on the field and it comes up dry. What is the probability that the prospect field will produce oil?
b. If two wells come up dry, what is the probability that the field will produce oil?
c. The oil company would like to keep looking as long as the chances of finding oil are greater than 1%. How many dry wells must be drilled before the field will be abandoned?

Case Problem   HAMILTON COUNTY JUDGES

Hamilton County judges try thousands of cases per year. In an overwhelming majority of the cases disposed, the verdict stands as rendered. However, some cases are appealed, and of those appealed, some of the cases are reversed. Kristen DelGuzzi of *The Cincinnati Enquirer* conducted a study of cases handled by Hamilton County judges over the years 1994 through 1996 (*The Cincinnati Enquirer*, January 11, 1998). Shown in Table 4.9 are the results for 182,908 cases handled (disposed) by 38 judges in Common Pleas Court, Domestic Relations Court, and Municipal Court. Two of the judges (Dinkelacker and Hogan) did not serve in the same court for the entire three-year period.

The purpose of the newspaper's study was to evaluate the performance of the judges. Appeals are often the result of mistakes made by judges, and the newspaper wanted to know which judges were doing a good job and which were making too many mistakes. You have been called in to assist in the data analysis. Use your knowledge of probability and conditional probability to help with the ranking of the judges. You also may be able to analyze the likelihood of appeal and reversal for cases handled by different courts.

Managerial Report

Prepare a report with your rankings of the judges. Also, include an analysis of the likelihood of appeal and case reversal in the three courts. At a minimum, your report should include the following:

1. The probability of cases being appealed and reversed in the three different courts.
2. The probability of a case being appealed for each judge.
3. The probability of a case being reversed for each judge.
4. The probability of reversal given an appeal for each judge.
5. Rank the judges within each court. State the criteria you used and provide a rationale for your choice.

Common Pleas Court

Judge	Total Cases Disposed	Appealed Cases	Reversed Cases
Fred Cartolano	3037	137	12
Thomas Crush	3372	119	10
Patrick Dinkelacker	1258	44	8
Timothy Hogan	1954	60	7
Robert Kraft	3138	127	7
William Mathews	2264	91	18
William Morrissey	3032	121	22
Norbert Nadel	2959	131	20
Arthur Ney, Jr.	3219	125	14
Richard Niehaus	3353	137	16
Thomas Nurre	3000	121	6
John O'Connor	2969	129	12
Robert Ruehlman	3205	145	18
J. Howard Sundermann	955	60	10
Ann Marie Tracey	3141	127	13
Ralph Winkler	3089	88	6
Total	43945	1762	199

Domestic Relations Court

Judge	Total Cases Disposed	Appealed Cases	Reversed Cases
Penelope Cunningham	2729	7	1
Patrick Dinkelacker	6001	19	4
Deborah Gaines	8799	48	9
Ronald Panioto	12970	32	3
Total	30499	106	17

Municipal Court

Judge	Total Cases Disposed	Appealed Cases	Reversed Cases
Mike Allen	6149	43	4
Nadine Allen	7812	34	6
Timothy Black	7954	41	6
David Davis	7736	43	5
Leslie Isaiah Gaines	5282	35	13
Karla Grady	5253	6	0
Deidra Hair	2532	5	0
Dennis Helmick	7900	29	5
Timothy Hogan	2308	13	2
James Patrick Kenney	2798	6	1
Joseph Luebbers	4698	25	8
William Mallory	8277	38	9
Melba Marsh	8219	34	7
Beth Mattingly	2971	13	1
Albert Mestemaker	4975	28	9
Mark Painter	2239	7	3
Jack Rosen	7790	41	13
Mark Schweikert	5403	33	6
David Stockdale	5371	22	4
John A. West	2797	4	2
Total	108464	500	104

CD file

Judge

CHAPTER 5

Discrete Probability Distributions

CONTENTS

STATISTICS IN PRACTICE

Citibank*

LONG ISLAND CITY, NEW YORK

Citibank, a division of Citigroup, makes available a wide range of financial services, including checking and savings accounts, loans and mortgages, insurance, and investment services, within the framework of a unique strategy for delivering those services called Citibanking. Citibanking entails a consistent brand identity all over the world, consistent product offerings, and high-level customer service. Citibanking lets you manage your money anytime, anywhere, anyway you choose. Whether you need to save for the future or borrow for today, you can do it all at Citibank.

Citibanking's state-of-the art automatic teller machines (ATMs) located in Citicard Banking Centers (CBCs), let customers do all their banking in one place with the touch of a finger, 24 hours a day, 7 days a week. More than 150 different banking functions from deposits to managing investments can be performed with ease. Citibanking ATMs are so much more than just cash machines that customers today use them for 80% of their transactions.

Each Citibank CBC operates as a waiting line system with randomly arriving customers seeking service at one of the ATMs. If all ATMs are busy, the arriving customers wait in line. Periodic CBC capacity studies are used to analyze customer waiting times and to determine whether additional ATMs are needed.

Data collected by Citibank showed that the random customer arrivals followed a probability distribution known as the Poisson probability distribution. Using the Poisson probability distribution, Citibank can compute

A Citibank ATM in Manhattan © PhotoDisc, Inc.

probabilities for the number of customers arriving at a CBC during any time period and make decisions concerning the number of ATMs needed. For example, let x = the number of customers arriving during a one-minute period. Assuming that a particular CBC has a mean arrival rate of two customers per minute, the following table shows the probabilities for the number of customers arriving during a one-minute period.

x	Probability
0	.1353
1	.2707
2	.2707
3	.1804
4	.0902
5 or more	.0527

Discrete probability distributions, such as the one used by Citibank, are the topic of this chapter. In addition to the Poisson probability distribution, you will learn about the binomial and hypergeometric probability distributions and how they can be used to provide helpful probability information.

---

*The authors are indebted to Ms. Stacey Karter, Citibank, for providing this Statistics in Practice.

In this chapter we continue the study of probability by introducing the concepts of random variables and probability distributions. The focus of this chapter is discrete probability distributions. Three special discrete probability distributions—the binomial, Poisson, and hypergeometric—are covered.

5.1 RANDOM VARIABLES

In Chapter 4 we defined the concept of an experiment and its associated experimental outcomes. A random variable provides a means for describing experimental outcomes using numerical values. Random variables must assume numerical values.

Random variables must assume numerical values.

> **Random Variable**
>
> A **random variable** is a numerical description of the outcome of an experiment.

In effect, a random variable associates a numerical value with each possible experimental outcome. The particular numerical value of the random variable depends on the outcome of the experiment. A random variable can be classified as being either *discrete* or *continuous* depending on the numerical values it assumes.

Discrete Random Variables

A random variable that may assume either a finite number of values or an infinite sequence of values such as 0, 1, 2, . . . is referred to as a **discrete random variable**. For example, consider the experiment of an accountant taking the certified public accountant (CPA) examination. The examination has four parts. We can define a random variable as $x =$ the number of parts of the CPA examination passed. It is a discrete random variable because it may assume the finite number of values 0, 1, 2, 3, or 4.

As another example of a discrete random variable, consider the experiment of cars arriving at a tollbooth. The random variable of interest is $x =$ the number of cars arriving during a one-day period. The possible values for x come from the sequence of integers 0, 1, 2, and so on. Hence, x is a discrete random variable assuming one of the values in this infinite sequence.

Although many experiments have outcomes that are naturally described by numerical values, others do not. For example, a survey question might ask an individual to recall the message in a recent television commercial. This experiment would have two possible outcomes: the individual cannot recall the message and the individual can recall the message. We can still describe these experimental outcomes numerically by defining the discrete random variable x as follows: let $x = 0$ if the individual cannot recall the message and $x = 1$ if the individual can recall the message. The numerical values for this random variable are arbitrary (we could have used 5 and 10), but they are acceptable in terms of the definition of a random variable—namely, x is a random variable because it provides a numerical description of the outcome of the experiment.

TABLE 5.1   EXAMPLES OF DISCRETE RANDOM VARIABLES

Experiment	Random Variable (x)	Possible Values for the Random Variable
Contact five customers	Number of customers who place an order	0, 1, 2, 3, 4, 5
Inspect a shipment of 50 radios	Number of defective radios	0, 1, 2, $\cdots$, 49, 50
Operate a restaurant for one day	Number of customers	0, 1, 2, 3, $\cdots$
Sell an automobile	Gender of the customer	0 if male; 1 if female

Table 5.1 provides some additional examples of discrete random variables. Note that in each example the discrete random variable assumes a finite number of values or an infinite sequence of values such as 0, 1, 2, ... Discrete random variables such as these are discussed in detail in this chapter.

Continuous Random Variables

A random variable that may assume any numerical value in an interval or collection of intervals is called a **continuous random variable**. Experimental outcomes based on measurement scales such as time, weight, distance, and temperature can be described by continuous random variables. For example, consider an experiment of monitoring incoming telephone calls to the claims office of a major insurance company. Suppose the random variable of interest is x = the time between consecutive incoming calls in minutes. This random variable may assume any value in the interval $x \geq 0$. Actually, an infinite number of values are possible for x, including values such as 1.26 minutes, 2.751 minutes, 4.3333 minutes, and so on. As another example, consider a 90-mile section of interstate highway I-75 north of Atlanta, Georgia. For an emergency ambulance service located in Atlanta, we might define the random variable as x = number of miles to the location of the next traffic accident along this section of I-75. In this case, x would be a continuous random variable assuming any value in the interval $0 \leq x \leq 90$. Additional examples of continuous random variables are listed in Table 5.2. Note that each example describes a random variable that

TABLE 5.2   EXAMPLES OF CONTINUOUS RANDOM VARIABLES

Experiment	Random Variable (x)	Possible Values for the Random Variable
Operate a bank	Time between customer arrivals in minutes	$x \geq 0$
Fill a soft drink can (max = 12.1 ounces)	Number of ounces	$0 \leq x \leq 12.1$
Construct a new library	Percentage of project complete after six months	$0 \leq x \leq 100$
Test a new chemical process	Temperature when the desired reaction takes place (min 150° F; max 212° F)	$150 \leq x \leq 212$

may assume any value in an interval of values. Continuous random variables and their probability distributions will be the topic of Chapter 6.

NOTES AND COMMENTS

One way to determine whether a random variable is discrete or continuous is to think of the values of the random variable as points on a line segment. Choose two points representing values of the random variable. If the entire line segment between the two points also represents possible values for the random variable, then the random variable is continuous.

EXERCISES

Methods

1. Consider the experiment of tossing a coin twice.
   a. List the experimental outcomes.
   b. Define a random variable that represents the number of heads occurring on the two tosses.
   c. Show what value the random variable would assume for each of the experimental outcomes.
   d. Is this random variable discrete or continuous?

2. Consider the experiment of a worker assembling a product.
   a. Define a random variable that represents the time in minutes required to assemble the product.
   b. What values may the random variable assume?
   c. Is the random variable discrete or continuous?

Applications

3. Three students scheduled interviews for summer employment at the Brookwood Institute. In each case the interview results in either an offer for a position or no offer. Experimental outcomes are defined in terms of the results of the three interviews.
   a. List the experimental outcomes.
   b. Define a random variable that represents the number of offers made. Is the random variable continuous?
   c. Show the value of the random variable for each of the experimental outcomes.

4. Suppose we know home mortgage rates for 12 Florida lending institutions. Assume that the random variable of interest is the number of lending institutions in this group that offers a 30-year fixed rate of 8.5% or less. What values may this random variable assume?

5. To perform a certain type of blood analysis, lab technicians must perform two procedures. The first procedure requires either 1 or 2 separate steps, and the second procedure requires either 1, 2, or 3 steps.
   a. List the experimental outcomes associated with performing the blood analysis.
   b. If the random variable of interest is the total number of steps required to do the complete analysis (both procedures), show what value the random variable will assume for each of the experimental outcomes.

6. Listed is a series of experiments and associated random variables. In each case, identify the values that the random variable can assume and state whether the random variable is discrete or continuous.

Experiment	Random Variable (x)
a. Take a 20-question examination	Number of questions answered correctly
b. Observe cars arriving at a tollbooth for 1 hour	Number of cars arriving at tollbooth
c. Audit 50 tax returns	Number of returns containing errors
d. Observe an employee's work	Number of nonproductive hours in an 8-hour workday
e. Weigh a shipment of goods	Number of pounds

5.2   DISCRETE PROBABILITY DISTRIBUTIONS

The **probability distribution** for a random variable describes how probabilities are distributed over the values of the random variable. For a discrete random variable x, the probability distribution is defined by a **probability function**, denoted by $f(x)$. The probability function provides the probability for each value of the random variable.

As an illustration of a discrete random variable and its probability distribution, consider the sales of automobiles at DiCarlo Motors in Saratoga, New York. Over the past 300 days of operation, sales data show 54 days with no automobiles sold, 117 days with 1 automobile sold, 72 days with 2 automobiles sold, 42 days with 3 automobiles sold, 12 days with 4 automobiles sold, and 3 days with 5 automobiles sold. Suppose we consider the experiment of selecting a day of operation at DiCarlo Motors and define the random variable of interest as $x =$ the number of automobiles sold during a day. From historical data, we know x is a discrete random variable that can assume the values 0, 1, 2, 3, 4, or 5. In probability function notation, $f(0)$ provides the probability of 0 automobiles sold, $f(1)$ provides the probability of 1 automobile sold, and so on. Because historical data show 54 of 300 days with 0 automobiles sold, we assign the value $54/300 = .18$ to $f(0)$, indicating that the probability of 0 automobiles being sold during a day is .18. Similarly, because 117 of 300 days had 1 automobile sold, we assign the value $117/300 = .39$ to $f(1)$, indicating that the probability of exactly 1 automobile being sold during a day is .39. Continuing in this way for the other values of the random variable, we compute the values for $f(2)$, $f(3)$, $f(4)$, and $f(5)$ as shown in Table 5.3, the probability distribution for the number of automobiles sold during a day at DiCarlo Motors.

TABLE 5.3   PROBABILITY DISTRIBUTION FOR THE NUMBER OF AUTOMOBILES SOLD DURING A DAY AT DICARLO MOTORS

x	$f(x)$
0	.18
1	.39
2	.24
3	.14
4	.04
5	.01
Total	1.00

A primary advantage of defining a random variable and its probability distribution is that once the probability distribution is known, it is relatively easy to determine the probability of a variety of events that may be of interest to a decision maker. For example, using the probability distribution for DiCarlo Motors as shown in Table 5.3, we see that the most probable number of automobiles sold during a day is 1 with a probability of $f(1) = .39$. In addition, there is an $f(3) + f(4) + f(5) = .14 + .04 + .01 = .19$ probability of selling 3 or more automobiles during a day. These probabilities, plus others the decision maker may ask about, provide information that can help the decision maker understand the process of selling automobiles at DiCarlo Motors.

In the development of a probability function for any discrete random variable, the following two conditions must be satisfied.

These conditions are the analogs to the two basic requirements for assigning probabilities to experimental outcomes presented in Chapter 4.

Required Conditions for a Discrete Probability Function

$$f(x) \geq 0 \tag{5.1}$$

$$\Sigma f(x) = 1 \tag{5.2}$$

Table 5.3 shows that the probabilities for the random variable x satisfy equation (5.1); $f(x)$ is greater than or equal to 0 for all values of x. In addition, because the probabilities sum to 1, equation (5.2) is satisfied. Thus, the DiCarlo Motors probability function is a valid discrete probability function.

We can also present probability distributions graphically. In Figure 5.1 the values of the random variable x for DiCarlo Motors are shown on the horizontal axis and the probability associated with these values is shown on the vertical axis.

In addition to tables and graphs, a formula that gives the probability function, $f(x)$, for every value of x is often used to describe probability distributions. The simplest example of

FIGURE 5.1   GRAPHICAL REPRESENTATION OF THE PROBABILITY DISTRIBUTION FOR THE NUMBER OF AUTOMOBILES SOLD DURING A DAY AT DICARLO MOTORS

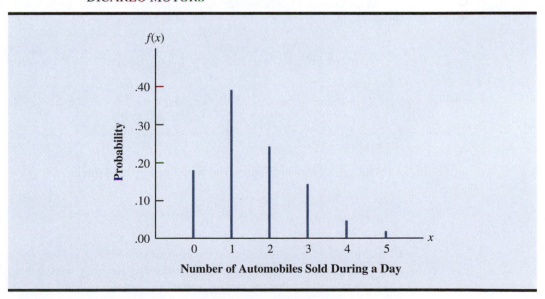

a discrete probability distribution given by a formula is the **discrete uniform probability distribution**. Its probability function is defined by equation (5.3).

Discrete Uniform Probability Function

$$f(x) = 1/n \qquad\qquad (5.3)$$

where

$$n = \text{the number of values the random variable may assume}$$

For example, suppose that for the experiment of rolling a die we define the random variable x to be the number of dots on the upward face. There are $n = 6$ possible values for the random variable; $x = 1, 2, 3, 4, 5, 6$. Thus, the probability function for this random variable is

$$f(x) = 1/6 \qquad x = 1, 2, 3, 4, 5, 6$$

The possible values of the random variable and the associated probabilities are shown.

x	$f(x)$
1	1/6
2	1/6
3	1/6
4	1/6
5	1/6
6	1/6

Note that the values of the random variable are equally likely.

As another example, consider the random variable x with the following discrete probability distribution.

x	$f(x)$
1	1/10
2	2/10
3	3/10
4	4/10

This probability distribution can be defined by the formula

$$f(x) = \frac{x}{10} \qquad \text{for } x = 1, 2, 3, \text{ or } 4$$

Evaluating $f(x)$ for a given value of the random variable will provide the associated probability. For example, using the preceding probability function, we see that $f(2) = 2/10$ provides the probability that the random variable assumes a value of 2.

The more widely used discrete probability distributions generally are specified by formulas. Three important cases are the binomial, Poisson, and hypergeometric probability distributions; they are discussed later in the chapter.

EXERCISES

Methods

7. The probability distribution for the random variable x follows.

x	$f(x)$
20	.20
25	.15
30	.25
35	.40

   a. Is this probability distribution valid? Explain.
   b. What is the probability that $x = 30$?
   c. What is the probability that x is less than or equal to 25?
   d. What is the probability that x is greater than 30?

Applications

8. The following data were collected by counting the number of operating rooms in use at Tampa General Hospital over a 20-day period: On 3 of the days only 1 operating room was used, on 5 of the days 2 were used, on 8 of the days 3 were used, and on 4 days all 4 of the hospital's operating rooms were used.
   a. Use the relative frequency approach to construct a probability distribution for the number of operating rooms in use on any given day.
   b. Draw a graph of the probability distribution.
   c. Show that your probability distribution satisfies the required conditions for a valid discrete probability distribution.

9. Nationally, 38% of fourth-graders cannot read an age-appropriate book. The following data show the number of children, by age, identified as learning disabled under special education. Most of these children have reading problems that should be identified and corrected before third grade. Current federal law prohibits most children from receiving extra help from special education programs until they fall behind by approximately two years' worth of learning, and that typically means third grade or later (*USA Today*, September 6, 2001).

Age	Number of Children
6	37,369
7	87,436
8	160,840
9	239,719
10	286,719
11	306,533
12	310,787
13	302,604
14	289,168

Suppose that we want to select a sample of children identified as learning disabled under special education for a special program designed to improve reading ability. Let x be a random variable indicating the age of one randomly selected child.

   a. Use the data to develop a probability distribution for x. Specify the values for the random variable and the corresponding values for the probability function $f(x)$.

   b. Draw a graph of the probability distribution.

   c. Show that the probability distribution satisfies equations (5.1) and (5.2).

10. Table 5.4 shows the percent frequency distributions of job satisfaction scores for a sample of information systems (IS) senior executives and IS middle managers (*Computerworld*, May 26, 1997). The scores range from a low of 1 (very dissatisfied) to a high of 5 (very satisfied).

   a. Develop a probability distribution for the job satisfaction score of a senior executive.

   b. Develop a probability distribution for the job satisfaction score of a middle manager.

   c. What is the probability a senior executive will report a job satisfaction score of 4 or 5?

   d. What is the probability a middle manager is very satisfied?

   e. Compare the overall job satisfaction of senior executives and middle managers.

11. A technician services mailing machines at companies in the Phoenix area. Depending on the type of malfunction, the service call can take 1, 2, 3, or 4 hours. The different types of malfunctions occur at about the same frequency.

   a. Develop a probability distribution for the duration of a service call.

   b. Draw a graph of the probability distribution.

   c. Show that your probability distribution satisfies the conditions required for a discrete probability function.

   d. What is the probability a service call will take 3 hours?

   e. A service call has just come in, but the type of malfunction is unknown. It is 3:00 P.M. and service technicians usually get off at 5:00 P.M. What is the probability the service technician will have to work overtime to fix the machine today?

12. The director of admissions at Lakeville Community College subjectively assessed a probability distribution for x, the number of entering students, as follows.

x	$f(x)$
1000	.15
1100	.20
1200	.30
1300	.25
1400	.10

TABLE 5.4 PERCENT FREQUENCY DISTRIBUTION OF JOB SATISFACTION SCORES FOR INFORMATION SYSTEMS EXECUTIVES AND MIDDLE MANAGERS

Job Satisfaction Score	IS Senior Executives (%)	IS Middle Managers (%)
1	5	4
2	9	10
3	3	12
4	42	46
5	41	28

a. Is this probability distribution valid? Explain.

b. What is the probability of 1200 or fewer entering students?

13. A psychologist determined that the number of hours required to obtain the trust of a new patient is either 1, 2, or 3. Let x be a random variable indicating the time in hours required to gain the patient's trust. The following probability function has been proposed.

$$f(x) = \frac{x}{6} \qquad \text{for } x = 1, 2, \text{ or } 3$$

a. Is this probability function valid? Explain.

b. What is the probability that it takes exactly 2 hours to gain the patient's trust?

c. What is the probability that it takes at least 2 hours to gain the patient's trust?

14. The following table is a partial probability distribution for the MRA Company's projected profits (x = profit in $1000s) for the first year of operation (the negative value denotes a loss).

x	$f(x)$
−100	.10
0	.20
50	.30
100	.25
150	.10
200	

a. What is the proper value for $f(200)$? What is your interpretation of this value?

b. What is the probability that MRA will be profitable?

c. What is the probability that MRA will make at least $100,000?

5.3   EXPECTED VALUE AND VARIANCE

Expected Value

The **expected value**, or mean, of a random variable is a measure of the central location for the random variable. The formula for the expected value of a discrete random variable x follows.

The expected value is a weighted average of the values the random variable may assume. The weights are the probabilities.

Expected Value of a Discrete Random Variable

$$E(x) = \mu = \Sigma x f(x) \qquad (5.4)$$

Both the notations $E(x)$ and μ are used to denote the expected value of a random variable.

Equation (5.4) shows that to compute the expected value of a discrete random variable, we must multiply each value of the random variable by the corresponding probability $f(x)$ and then add the resulting products. Using the DiCarlo Motors automobile sales example from Section 5.2, we show the calculation of the expected value for the number of automobiles sold during a day in Table 5.5. The sum of the entries in the $xf(x)$ column shows that the expected value is 1.50 automobiles per day. We therefore know that although sales

The expected value does not have to be a value the random variable can assume.

TABLE 5.5   CALCULATION OF THE EXPECTED VALUE FOR THE NUMBER OF AUTOMOBILES SOLD DURING A DAY AT DICARLO MOTORS

x	$f(x)$	$xf(x)$
0	.18	$0(.18) = $ .00
1	.39	$1(.39) = $ .39
2	.24	$2(.24) = $ .48
3	.14	$3(.14) = $ .42
4	.04	$4(.04) = $ .16
5	.01	$5(.01) = $ .05
		1.50

$$E(x) = \mu = \Sigma xf(x)$$

of 0, 1, 2, 3, 4, or 5 automobiles are possible on any one day, over time DiCarlo can anticipate selling an average of 1.50 automobiles per day. Assuming 30 days of operation during a month, we can use the expected value of 1.50 to forecast average monthly sales of $30(1.50) = 45$ automobiles.

Variance

Even though the expected value provides the mean value for the random variable, we often need a measure of variability, or dispersion. Just as we used the **variance** in Chapter 3 to summarize the variability in data, we now use variance to summarize the variability in the values of a random variable. The formula for the variance of a discrete random variable follows.

The variance is a weighted average of the squared deviations of a random variable from its mean. The weights are the probabilities.

Variance of a Discrete Random Variable

$$\text{Var}(x) = \sigma^2 = \Sigma(x - \mu)^2 f(x) \tag{5.5}$$

As equation (5.5) shows, an essential part of the variance formula is the deviation, $x - \mu$, which measures how far a particular value of the random variable is from the expected value, or mean, μ. In computing the variance of a random variable, the deviations are squared and then weighted by the corresponding value of the probability function. The sum of these weighted squared deviations for all values of the random variable is referred to as the *variance*. The notations $\text{Var}(x)$ and σ^2 are both used to denote the variance of a random variable.

The calculation of the variance for the probability distribution of the number of automobiles sold during a day at DiCarlo Motors is summarized in Table 5.6. We see that the variance is 1.25. The **standard deviation**, σ, is defined as the positive square root of the variance. Thus, the standard deviation for the number of automobiles sold during a day is

$$\sigma = \sqrt{1.25} = 1.118$$

The standard deviation is measured in the same units as the random variable ($\sigma = 1.118$ automobiles) and therefore is often preferred in describing the variability of a random variable. The variance σ^2 is measured in squared units and is thus more difficult to interpret.

TABLE 5.6   CALCULATION OF THE VARIANCE FOR THE NUMBER OF AUTOMOBILES
SOLD DURING A DAY AT DICARLO MOTORS

x	$x - \mu$	$(x - \mu)^2$	$f(x)$	$(x - \mu)^2 f(x)$
0	$0 - 1.50 = -1.50$	2.25	.18	$2.25(.18) = .4050$
1	$1 - 1.50 = -.50$	.25	.39	$.25(.39) = .0975$
2	$2 - 1.50 = .50$	.25	.24	$.25(.24) = .0600$
3	$3 - 1.50 = 1.50$	2.25	.14	$2.25(.14) = .3150$
4	$4 - 1.50 = 2.50$	6.25	.04	$6.25(.04) = .2500$
5	$5 - 1.50 = 3.50$	12.25	.01	$12.25(.01) = .1225$
				1.2500

$$\sigma^2 = \Sigma(x - \mu)^2 f(x)$$

Using Excel to Compute the Expected Value, Variance, and Standard Deviation

The calculations involved in computing the expected value and variance for a discrete random variable can easily be made in an Excel worksheet. One approach is to enter the formulas necessary to make the calculations in Tables 5.5 and 5.6. An easier way, however, is to make use of Excel's SUMPRODUCT function. In this section we show how to use the SUMPRODUCT function to compute the expected value and variance for daily automobile sales at DiCarlo Motors. Refer to Figure 5.2 as we describe the tasks involved. The formula worksheet is in the background; the value worksheet is in the foreground.

Enter Data: The data needed are the values for the random variable and the corresponding probabilities. Labels, values for the random variable, and the corresponding probabilities are entered in cells A1:B7.

FIGURE 5.2   EXCEL WORKSHEET FOR EXPECTED VALUE, VARIANCE, AND STANDARD DEVIATION

	A	B	C	D
1	Sales	Probability	Sq Dev from Mean	
2	0	0.18	=(A2-$B$9)^2	
3	1	0.39	=(A3-$B$9)^2	
4	2	0.24	=(A4-$B$9)^2	
5	3	0.14	=(A5-$B$9)^2	
6	4	0.04	=(A6-$B$9)^2	
7	5	0.01	=(A7-$B$9)^2	
8				
9	Mean	=SUMPRODUCT(A2:A7,B2:B7)		
10				
11	Variance	=SUMPRODUCT(C2:C7,B2:B7)		
12				
13	Std Deviation	=SQRT(B11)		
14				

	A	B	C	D
1	Sales	Probability	Sq Dev from Mean	
2	0	0.18	2.25	
3	1	0.39	0.25	
4	2	0.24	0.25	
5	3	0.14	2.25	
6	4	0.04	6.25	
7	5	0.01	12.25	
8				
9	Mean	1.5		
10				
11	Variance	1.25		
12				
13	Std Deviation	1.118034		
14				

Enter Functions and Formulas: The SUMPRODUCT function multiplies each value in one range by the corresponding value in another range, and sums the products. To use the SUMPRODUCT function to compute the expected value of daily automobile sales at Di-Carlo Motors, we entered the following formula into cell B9:

$$=\text{SUMPRODUCT(A2:A7,B2:B7)}$$

Note that the first range, A2:A7, contains the values for the random variable, daily automobile sales. The second range, B2:B7, contains the corresponding probabilities. Thus, the SUMPRODUCT function in cell B9 is computing A2*B2 + A3*B3 + A4*B4 + A5*B5 + A6*B6 + A7*B7; hence, it is applying the formula in equation (5.4) to compute the expected value. The result, shown in cell B9 of the value worksheet, is 1.5.

The formulas in cells C2:C7 are used to compute the squared deviations from the expected value or mean of 1.5 (the mean is in cell B9). The results, shown in the value worksheet, are the same as the results shown in Table 5.6. The formula necessary to compute the variance for daily automobile sales was entered into cell B11. It uses the SUMPRODUCT function to multiply each value in the range C2:C7 by each corresponding value in the range B2:B7, and sums the products. The result, shown in the value worksheet, is 1.25. Because the standard deviation is the square root of the variance, we entered the formula =SQRT(B11) into cell B13 to compute the standard deviation for daily automobile sales. The result, shown in the value worksheet, is 1.118034.

EXERCISES

Methods

15.   The following table provides a probability distribution for the random variable x.

x	$f(x)$
3	.25
6	.50
9	.25

   a.   Compute $E(x)$, the expected value of x.
   b.   Compute σ^2, the variance of x.
   c.   Compute σ, the standard deviation of x.

16.   The following table provides a probability distribution for the random variable y.

y	$f(y)$
2	.20
4	.30
7	.40
8	.10

   a.   Compute $E(y)$.
   b.   Compute Var(y) and σ.

Applications

17. A volunteer ambulance service handles 0 to 5 service calls on any given day. The probability distribution for the number of service calls is as follows.

Number of Service Calls	Probability
0	.10
1	.15
2	.30
3	.20
4	.15
5	.10

  a. What is the expected number of service calls?
  b. What is the variance in the number of service calls? What is the standard deviation?

18. The *Statistical Abstract of the United States*, 1997, shows that the average number of television sets per household is 2.3. Assume that the probability distribution for the number of television sets per household in New Orleans is as shown in the following table.

x	f(x)
0	.01
1	.23
2	.41
3	.20
4	.10
5	.05

  a. Compute the expected value of the number of television sets per household and compare it with the average reported in the *Statistical Abstract*.
  b. What are the variance and standard deviation of the number of television sets per household?

19. The actual shooting records of four basketball teams showed the probability of making a 2-point basket was .50 and the probability of making a 3-point basket was .39.
  a. What is the expected value of a 2-point shot for these teams?
  b. What is the expected value of a 3-point shot for these teams?
  c. If the probability of making a 2-point basket is greater than the probability of making a 3-point basket, why do coaches allow some players to shoot the 3-point shot if they have the opportunity? Use expected value to explain your answer.

20. The probability distribution for damage claims paid by the Newton Automobile Insurance Company on collision insurance follows.

Payment ($)	Probability
0	.90
400	.04
1000	.03
2000	.01
4000	.01
6000	.01

    a. Use the expected collision payment to determine the collision insurance premium that would enable the company to break even.

    b. The insurance company charges an annual rate of $260 for the collision coverage. What is the expected value of the collision policy for a policyholder? (Hint: It is the expected payments from the company minus the cost of coverage.) Why does the policyholder purchase a collision policy with this expected value?

21. The following probability distributions of job satisfaction scores for a sample of information systems (IS) senior executives and IS middle managers range from a low of 1 (very dissatisfied) to a high of 5 (very satisfied) (*Computerworld*, May 26, 1997).

Job Satisfaction Score	Probability IS Senior Executives	Probability IS Middle Managers
1	.05	.04
2	.09	.10
3	.03	.12
4	.42	.46
5	.41	.28

    a. What is the expected value of the job satisfaction score for senior executives?
    b. What is the expected value of the job satisfaction score for middle managers?
    c. Compute the variance of job satisfaction scores for executives and middle managers.
    d. Compute the standard deviation of job satisfaction scores for both probability distributions.
    e. Compare the overall job satisfaction of senior executives and middle managers.

22. The demand for a product of Carolina Industries varies greatly from month to month. The probability distribution in the following table, based on the past two years of data, shows the company's monthly demand.

Unit Demand	Probability
300	.20
400	.30
500	.35
600	.15

    a. If the company bases monthly orders on the expected value of the monthly demand, what should Carolina's monthly order quantity be for this product?
    b. Assume that each unit demanded generates $70 in revenue and that each unit ordered costs $50. How much will the company gain or lose in a month if it places an order based on your answer to part (a) and the actual demand for the item is 300 units?

23. According to a survey, 95% of subscribers to *The Wall Street Journal Interactive Edition* have a computer at home. For those households, the probability distributions for the number of laptop and desktop computers are given (*The Wall Street Journal Interactive Edition Subscriber Study*, 1999).

	Probability	
Number of Computers	Laptop	Desktop
0	.47	.06
1	.45	.56
2	.06	.28
3	.02	.10

    a. What is the expected value of the number of computers per household for each type of computer?

    b. What is the variance of the number of computers per household for each type of computer?

    c. Make some comparisons between the number of laptops and the number of desktops owned by the *Journal*'s subscribers.

24. The J. R. Ryland Computer Company is considering a plant expansion that will enable the company to begin production of a new computer product. The company's president must determine whether to make the expansion a medium- or large-scale project. An uncertainty is the demand for the new product, which for planning purposes may be low demand, medium demand, or high demand. The probability estimates for demand are .20, .50, and .30, respectively. Letting x and y indicate the annual profit in thousands of dollars, the firm's planners have developed the following profit forecasts for the medium- and large-scale expansion projects.

		Medium-Scale Expansion Profit		Large-Scale Expansion Profit	
		x	$f(x)$	y	$f(y)$
	Low	50	.20	0	.20
Demand	Medium	150	.50	100	.50
	High	200	.30	300	.30

    a. Compute the expected value for the profit associated with the two expansion alternatives. Which decision is preferred for the objective of maximizing the expected profit?

    b. Compute the variance for the profit associated with the two expansion alternatives. Which decision is preferred for the objective of minimizing the risk or uncertainty?

5.4   BINOMIAL PROBABILITY DISTRIBUTION

The binomial probability distribution is a discrete probability distribution that has many applications. It is associated with a multiple-step experiment that we call the binomial experiment.

A Binomial Experiment

A **binomial experiment** has the following four properties.

Properties of a Binomial Experiment

1. The experiment consists of a sequence of n identical trials.
2. Two outcomes are possible on each trial. We refer to one outcome as a *success* and the other outcome as a *failure*.
3. The probability of a success, denoted by p, does not change from trial to trial. Consequently, the probability of a failure, denoted by $1 - p$, does not change from trial to trial.
4. The trials are independent.

Jakob Bernoulli (1654–1705), the first of the Bernoulli family of Swiss mathematicians, published a treatise on probability that contained the theory of permutations and combinations, as well as the Binomial Theorem.

If properties 2, 3, and 4 are present, we say the trials are generated by a Bernoulli process. If, in addition, property 1 is present, we say we have a binomial experiment. Figure 5.3 depicts one possible sequence of successes and failures for a binomial experiment involving eight trials.

In a binomial experiment, our interest is in the *number of successes occurring in the n trials*. If we let x denote the number of successes occurring in the n trials, we see that x can assume the values of 0, 1, 2, 3, . . . , n. Because the number of values is finite, x is a *discrete* random variable. The probability distribution associated with this random variable is called the **binomial probability distribution**. For example, consider the experiment of tossing a coin five times and on each toss observing whether the coin lands with a head or a tail on its upward face. Suppose we are interested in counting the number of heads appearing over the five tosses. Does this experiment have the properties of a binomial experiment? What is the random variable of interest? Note that:

1. The experiment consists of five identical trials; each trial involves the tossing of one coin.
2. Two outcomes are possible for each trial: a head or a tail. We can designate head a success and tail a failure.
3. The probability of a head and the probability of a tail are the same for each trial, with $p = .5$ and $1 - p = .5$.
4. The trials or tosses are independent because the outcome on any one trial is not affected by what happens on other trials or tosses.

Thus, the properties of a binomial experiment are satisfied. The random variable of interest is x = the number of heads appearing in the five trials. In this case, x can assume the values of 0, 1, 2, 3, 4, or 5.

As another example, consider an insurance salesperson who visits 10 randomly selected families. The outcome associated with each visit is classified as a success if the family purchases an insurance policy and a failure if the family does not. From past experience, the salesperson knows the probability that a randomly selected family will purchase an insurance policy is .10. Checking the properties of a binomial experiment, we observe that:

1. The experiment consists of 10 identical trials; each trial involves contacting one family.
2. Two outcomes are possible on each trial: the family purchases a policy (success) or the family does not purchase a policy (failure).

FIGURE 5.3   ONE POSSIBLE SEQUENCE OF SUCCESSES AND FAILURES
FOR AN EIGHT-TRIAL BINOMIAL EXPERIMENT

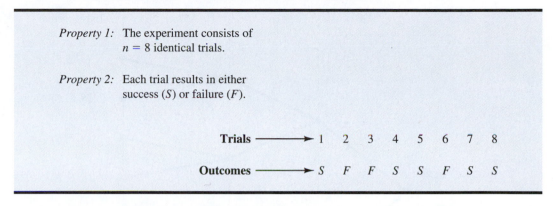

Property 1:   The experiment consists of
$n = 8$ identical trials.

Property 2:   Each trial results in either
success (S) or failure (F).

Trials ⟶ 1   2   3   4   5   6   7   8

Outcomes ⟶   S   F   F   S   S   F   S   S

3. The probabilities of a purchase and a nonpurchase are assumed to be the same for each sales call, with $p = .10$ and $1 - p = .90$.
4. The trials are independent because the families are randomly selected.

Because the four assumptions are satisfied, this example is a binomial experiment. The random variable of interest is the number of sales obtained in contacting the 10 families. In this case, x can assume the values of 0, 1, 2, 3, 4, 5, 6, 7, 8, 9, and 10.

Property 3 of the binomial experiment is called the *stationarity assumption* and is sometimes confused with property 4, independence of trials. To see how they differ, consider again the case of the salesperson calling on families to sell insurance policies. If, as the day wore on, the salesperson got tired and lost enthusiasm, the probability of success (selling a policy) might drop to .05, for example, by the tenth call. In such a case, property 3 (stationarity) would not be satisfied, and we would not have a binomial experiment. Even if property 4 held—that is, the purchase decisions of each family were made independently— it would not be a binomial experiment if property 3 was not satisfied.

In applications involving binomial experiments, a special mathematical formula, called the **binomial probability function**, can be used to compute the probability of x successes in the n trials. Using probability concepts introduced in Chapter 4, we will show in the context of an illustrative problem how the formula can be developed.

Martin Clothing Store Problem

Let us consider the purchase decisions of the next three customers who enter the Martin Clothing Store. On the basis of past experience, the store manager estimates the probability that any one customer will make a purchase is .30. What is the probability that two of the next three customers will make a purchase?

Using a tree diagram (Figure 5.4), we can see that the experiment of observing the three customers each making a purchase decision has eight possible outcomes. Using S to denote success (a purchase) and F to denote failure (no purchase), we are interested in experimental outcomes involving two successes in the three trials (purchase decisions). Next, let us verify that the experiment involving the sequence of three purchase decisions can be viewed as a binomial experiment. Checking the four requirements for a binomial experiment, we note that:

1. The experiment can be described as a sequence of three identical trials, one trial for each of the three customers who will enter the store.
2. Two outcomes—the customer makes a purchase (success) or the customer does not make a purchase (failure)—are possible for each trial.

FIGURE 5.4   TREE DIAGRAM FOR THE MARTIN CLOTHING STORE PROBLEM

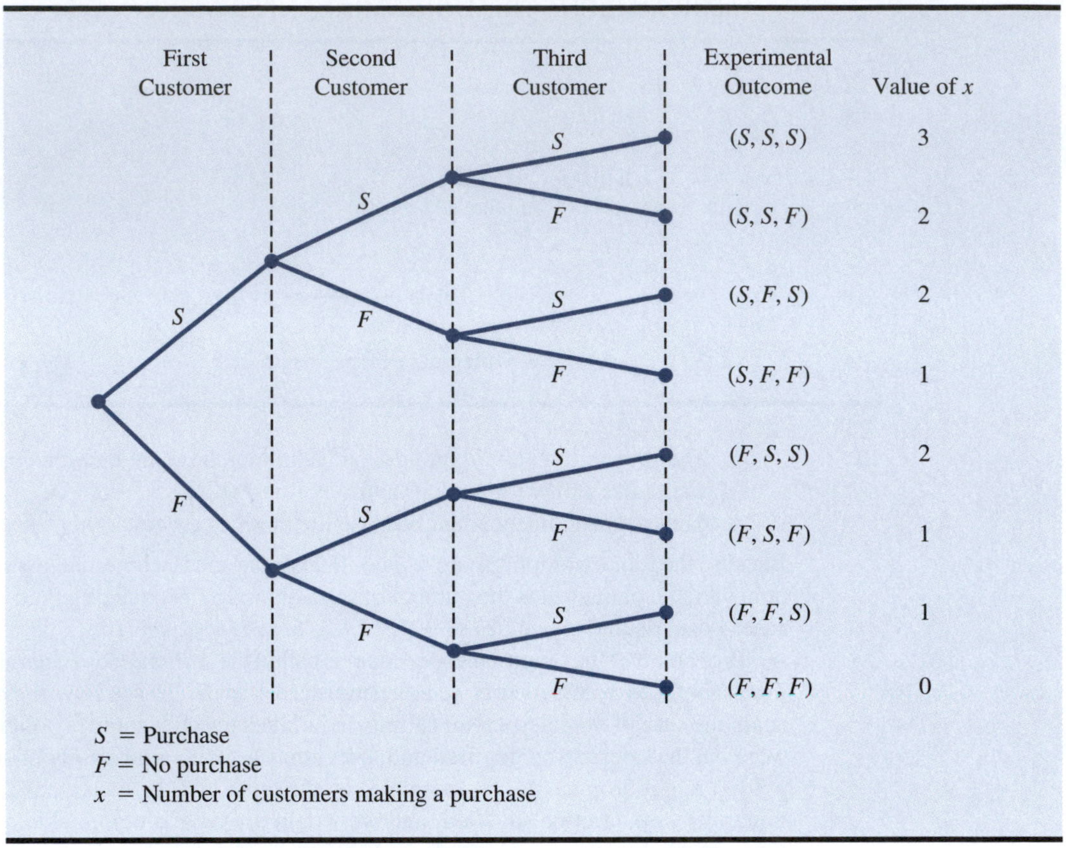

First Customer	Second Customer	Third Customer	Experimental Outcome	Value of x
		S	(S, S, S)	3
	S	F	(S, S, F)	2
S	F	S	(S, F, S)	2
		F	(S, F, F)	1
	S	S	(F, S, S)	2
F		F	(F, S, F)	1
	F	S	(F, F, S)	1
		F	(F, F, F)	0

S = Purchase
F = No purchase
x = Number of customers making a purchase

3. The probability that the customer will make a purchase (.30) or will not make a purchase (.70) is assumed to be the same for all customers.
4. The purchase decision of each customer is independent of the decisions of the other customers.

Hence, the properties of a binomial experiment are present.

The number of experimental outcomes resulting in exactly x successes in n trials can be computed using the following formula.*

Number of Experimental Outcomes Providing Exactly x Successes in n Trials

$$\binom{n}{x} = \frac{n!}{x!(n-x)!} \qquad (5.6)$$

---

*This formula, introduced in Chapter 4, determines the number of combinations of n objects selected x at a time. For the binomial experiment, this combinatorial formula provides the number of experimental outcomes (sequences of n trials) resulting in x successes.

where

$$n! = n(n - 1)(n - 2) \cdots (2)(1)$$

and, by definition,

$$0! = 1$$

Now let us return to the Martin Clothing Store experiment involving three customer purchase decisions. Equation (5.6) can be used to determine the number of experimental outcomes involving two purchases; that is, the number of ways of obtaining $x = 2$ successes in the $n = 3$ trials. From (5.6) we have

$$\binom{n}{x} = \binom{3}{2} = \frac{3!}{2!(3 - 2)!} = \frac{(3)(2)(1)}{(2)(1)(1)} = \frac{6}{2} = 3$$

Equation (5.6) shows that three of the experimental outcomes yield two successes. From Figure 5.4 we see these three outcomes are denoted by (S, S, F), (S, F, S), and (F, S, S).

Using equation (5.6) to determine how many experimental outcomes have three successes (purchases) in the three trials, we obtain

$$\binom{n}{x} = \binom{3}{3} = \frac{3!}{3!(3 - 3)!} = \frac{3!}{3!0!} = \frac{(3)(2)(1)}{3(2)(1)(1)} = \frac{6}{6} = 1$$

From Figure 5.4 we see that the one experimental outcome with three successes is identified by (S, S, S).

We know that equation (5.6) can be used to determine the number of experimental outcomes that result in x successes. But, if we are to determine the probability of x successes in n trials, we must also know the probability associated with each of these experimental outcomes. Because the trials of a binomial experiment are independent, we can simply multiply the probabilities associated with each trial outcome to find the probability of a particular sequence of successes and failures.

The probability of purchases by the first two customers and no purchase by the third customer, denoted (S, S, F), is given by

$$pp(1 - p)$$

With a .30 probability of a purchase on any one trial, the probability of a purchase on the first two trials and no purchase on the third is given by

$$(.30)(.30)(.70) = (.30)^2(.70) = .063$$

Two other experimental outcomes also result in two successes and one failure. The probabilities for all three experimental outcomes involving two successes follow.

| Trial Outcomes | | | | |
1st Customer	2nd Customer	3rd Customer	Experimental Outcome	Probability of Experimental Outcome
Purchase	Purchase	No purchase	(S, S, F)	$pp(1-p) = p^2(1-p)$ $= (.30)^2(.70) = .063$
Purchase	No purchase	Purchase	(S, F, S)	$p(1-p)p = p^2(1-p)$ $= (.30)^2(.70) = .063$
No purchase	Purchase	Purchase	(F, S, S)	$(1-p)pp = p^2(1-p)$ $= (.30)^2(.70) = .063$

Observe that all three experimental outcomes with two successes have exactly the same probability. This observation holds in general. In any binomial experiment, all sequences of trial outcomes yielding x successes in n trials have the *same probability* of occurrence. The probability of each sequence of trials yielding x successes in n trials follows.

$$\text{Probability of a Particular Sequence of Trial Outcomes} = p^x(1-p)^{(n-x)} \qquad (5.7)$$
with x Successes in n Trials

For the Martin Clothing Store, this formula shows that any experimental outcome with two successes has a probability of $p^2(1-p)^{(3-2)} = p^2(1-p)^1 = (.30)^2(.70)^1 = .063$.

Because equation (5.6) shows the number of outcomes in a binomial experiment with x successes and equation (5.7) gives the probability for each sequence involving x successes, we combine equations (5.6) and (5.7) to obtain the following **binomial probability function**.

Binomial Probability Function

$$f(x) = \binom{n}{x} p^x(1-p)^{(n-x)} \qquad (5.8)$$

where

$f(x) = $ the probability of x successes in n trials

$n = $ the number of trials

$\binom{n}{x} = \dfrac{n!}{x!(n-x)!}$

$p = $ the probability of a success on any one trial

$1 - p = $ the probability of a failure on any one trial

In the Martin Clothing Store example, let us compute the probability that no customer makes a purchase, exactly one customer makes a purchase, exactly two customers make a

TABLE 5.7   PROBABILITY DISTRIBUTION FOR THE NUMBER OF CUSTOMERS
MAKING A PURCHASE

x	$f(x)$
0	$\dfrac{3!}{0!3!}(.30)^0(.70)^3 = .343$
1	$\dfrac{3!}{1!2!}(.30)^1(.70)^2 = .441$
2	$\dfrac{3!}{2!1!}(.30)^2(.70)^1 = .189$
3	$\dfrac{3!}{3!0!}(.30)^3(.70)^0 = \underline{.027}$
	1.000

purchase, and all three customers make a purchase. The calculations are summarized in
Table 5.7, which gives the probability distribution of the number of customers making a
purchase. Figure 5.5 is a graph of this probability distribution.

The binomial probability function can be applied to *any* binomial experiment. If we are
satisfied that a situation has the properties of a binomial experiment and if we know the values of n, p, and $(1 - p)$, we can use equation (5.8) to compute the probability of x successes
in the n trials.

If we consider variations of the Martin experiment, such as 10 customers rather than
three entering the store, the binomial probability function given by equation (5.8) is still

FIGURE 5.5   GRAPHICAL REPRESENTATION OF THE PROBABILITY DISTRIBUTION
FOR THE NUMBER OF CUSTOMERS MAKING A PURCHASE

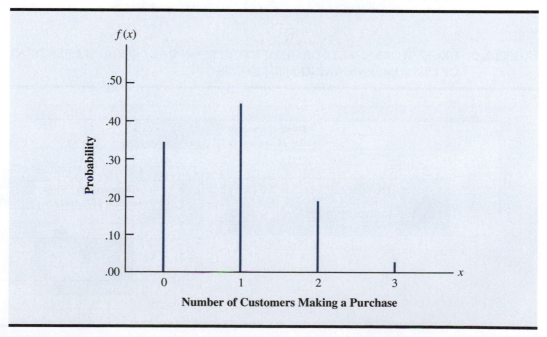

applicable. Suppose we have a binomial experiment with $n = 10$, $x = 4$, and $p = .30$. The probability of making exactly four sales to 10 potential customers entering the store is

$$f(4) = \frac{10!}{4!6!}(.30)^4(.70)^6 = .2001$$

Using Excel to Compute Binomial Probabilities

For many probability functions that can be specified as formulas, Excel provides functions for computing probabilities and cumulative probabilities. In this section, we show how Excel's BINOMDIST function can be used to compute binomial probabilities and cumulative binomial probabilities. We begin by showing how to compute the binomial probabilities for the Martin Clothing Store example shown in Table 5.7. Refer to Figure 5.6 as we describe the tasks involved. The formula worksheet is in the background; the value worksheet is in the foreground.

Enter Data: In order to compute a binomial probability we must know the number of trials (n), the probability of success (p), and the value of the random variable (x). For the Martin Clothing Store example, the number of trials is 3; this value has been entered into cell D1. The probability of success is .3; this value has been entered into cell D2. Because we want to compute the probability for $x = 0$, 1, 2, and 3, these values were entered into cells B5:B8.

Enter Functions and Formulas: The BINOMDIST function has four arguments: the first is the value of x, the second is the value of n, the third is the value of p, and the fourth is FALSE or TRUE. We choose FALSE for the fourth argument if a probability is desired and TRUE if a cumulative probability is desired. The formula =BINOMDIST(B5,$D$1,$D$2,FALSE) has been entered into cell C5 to compute the probability of 0 successes in 3 trials. Note in the value worksheet that the probability computed for $f(0)$, .343, is the same as that shown in Table 5.7. The formula in cell C5 is copied to cells C6:C8 to compute the probabilities for $x = 1$, 2, and 3 successes, respectively.

FIGURE 5.6 EXCEL WORKSHEET FOR COMPUTING BINOMIAL PROBABILITIES OF NUMBER OF CUSTOMERS MAKING A PURCHASE

	A	B	C	D	E
1			Number of Trials (*n*)	3	
2			Probability of Success (*p*)	0.3	
3					
4		*x*	*f*(*x*)		
5		0	=BINOMDIST(B5,$D$1,$D$2,FALSE)		
6		1	=BINOMDIST(B6,$D$1,$D$2,FALSE)		
7		2	=BINOMDIST(B7,$D$1,$D$2,FALSE)		
8		3	=BINOMDIST(B8,$D$1,$D$2,FALSE)		
9					

	A	B	C	D	E
1		Number of Trials (*n*)		3	
2		Probability of Success (*p*)		0.3	
3					
4		*x*	*f*(*x*)		
5		0	0.343		
6		1	0.441		
7		2	0.189		
8		3	0.027		
9					

We can also compute cumulative probabilities using Excel's BINOMDIST function. To illustrate, let us consider the case of 10 customers entering the Martin Clothing Store and compute the probabilities and cumulative probabilities for the number of customers making a purchase. Recall that the cumulative probability for $x = 1$ is the probability of 1 or fewer purchases, the cumulative probability for $x = 2$ is the probability of 2 or fewer purchases, and so on. So, the cumulative probability for $x = 10$ is 1. Refer to Figure 5.7 as we describe the tasks involved in computing these cumulative probabilities. The formula worksheet is in the background; the value worksheet is in the foreground.

Enter Data: We entered the number of trials (10) into cell D1, the probability of success (.3) into cell D2, and the values for the random variable into cells B5:B15.

Enter Functions and Formulas: The binomial probabilities for each value of the random variable are computed in column C and the cumulative probabilities are computed in column D. We entered the formula =BINOMDIST(B5,$D$1,$D$2,FALSE) into cell C5 to compute the probability of 0 successes in 10 trials. Note that we used FALSE as the fourth argument in the BINOMDIST function. The probability (.0282) is shown in cell C5 of the value worksheet. The formula in cell C5 is simply copied to cells C6:C15 to compute the remaining probabilities.

To compute the cumulative probabilities we start by entering the formula =BINOMDIST (B5,$D$1,$D$2,TRUE) into cell D5. Note that we used TRUE as the fourth argument in the BINOMDIST function. The formula in cell D5 is then copied to cells D6:D15 to compute the remaining cumulative probabilities. In cell D5 of the value worksheet we see that the cumulative probability for $x = 0$ is the same as the probability for $x = 0$. Each of the remaining cumulative probabilities is the sum of the previous cumulative probability and the individual probability in column C. For instance, the cumulative probability for $x = 4$ is given by .6496 + .2001 = .8497. Note also that the cumulative probability for $x = 10$ is 1.

FIGURE 5.7   EXCEL WORKSHEET FOR COMPUTING PROBABILITIES AND CUMULATIVE PROBABILITIES FOR NUMBER OF PURCHASES WITH 10 CUSTOMERS

	A	B	C	D	E
1			Number of Trials (n)	10	
2			Probability of Success (p)	0.3	
3					
4		x	$f(x)$	Cum Prob	
5		0	=BINOMDIST(B5,$D$1,$D$2,FALSE)	=BINOMDIST(B5,$D$1,$D$2,TRUE)	
6		1	=BINOMDIST(B6,$D$1,$D$2,FALSE)	=BINOMDIST(B6,$D$1,$D$2,TRUE)	
7		2	=BINOMDIST(B7,$D$1,$D$2,FALSE)	=BINOMDIST(B7,$D$1,$D$2,TRUE)	
8		3	=BINOMDIST(B8,$D$1,$D$2,FALSE)	=BINOMDIST(B8,$D$1,$D$2,TRUE)	
9		4	=BINOMDIST(B9,$D$1,$D$2,FALSE)	=BINOMDIST(B9,$D$1,$D$2,TRUE)	
10		5	=BINOMDIST(B10,$D$1,$D$2,FALSE)	=BINOMDIST(B10,$D$1,$D$2,TRUE)	
11		6	=BINOMDIST(B11,$D$1,$D$2,FALSE)	=BINOMDIST(B11,$D$1,$D$2,TRUE)	
12		7	=BINOMDIST(B12,$D$1,$D$2,FALSE)	=BINOMDIST(B12,$D$1,$D$2,TRUE)	
13		8	=BINOMDIST(B13,$D$1,$D$2,FALSE)	=BINOMDIST(B13,$D$1,$D$2,TRUE)	
14		9	=BINOMDIST(B14,$D$1,$D$2,FALSE)	=BINOMDIST(B14,$D$1,$D$2,TRUE)	
15		10	=BINOMDIST(B15,$D$1,$D$2,FALSE)	=BINOMDIST(B15,$D$1,$D$2,TRUE)	
16					

	A	B	C	D	E
1		Number of Trials (n)		10	
2		Probability of Success (p)		0.3	
3					
4		x	$f(x)$	Cum Prob	
5		0	0.0282	0.0282	
6		1	0.1211	0.1493	
7		2	0.2335	0.3828	
8		3	0.2668	0.6496	
9		4	0.2001	0.8497	
10		5	0.1029	0.9527	
11		6	0.0368	0.9894	
12		7	0.0090	0.9984	
13		8	0.0014	0.9999	
14		9	0.0001	1.0000	
15		10	0.0000	1.0000	
16					

The cumulative probability of $x = 9$ is also 1 because the probability of $x = 10$ is zero (to 4 decimal places of accuracy).

Expected Value and Variance for the Binomial Probability Distribution

In Section 5.3 we provided formulas for computing the expected value and variance of a discrete random variable. In the special case where the random variable has a binomial probability distribution with a known number of trials n and a known probability of success p, the general formulas for the expected value and variance can be simplified. The results follow.

Expected Value and Variance for the Binomial Probability Distribution

$$E(x) = \mu = np \tag{5.9}$$

$$\text{Var}(x) = \sigma^2 = np(1 - p) \tag{5.10}$$

For the Martin Clothing Store problem with three customers, we can use equation (5.9) to compute the expected number of customers who will make a purchase.

$$E(x) = np = 3(.30) = .9$$

Suppose that for the next month the Martin Clothing Store forecasts 1000 customers will enter the store. What is the expected number of customers who will make a purchase? The answer is $\mu = np = (1000)(.3) = 300$. Thus, to increase the expected number of purchases, Martin's must induce more customers to enter the store and/or somehow increase the probability that any individual customer will make a purchase after entering.

For the Martin Clothing Store problem with three customers, we see that the variance and standard deviation for the number of customers who will make a purchase are

$$\sigma^2 = np(1 - p) = 3(.3)(.7) = .63$$
$$\sigma = \sqrt{.63} = .79$$

The np chart and lot acceptance sampling are quality control procedures that are excellent examples of the use of the binomial distribution. These procedures are discussed in Chapter 14, Statistical Methods for Quality Control.

For the next 1000 customers entering the store, the variance and standard deviation for the number of customers who will make a purchase are

$$\sigma^2 = np(1 - p) = 1000(.3)(.7) = 210$$
$$\sigma = \sqrt{210} = 14.49$$

NOTES AND COMMENTS

Statisticians have developed tables that give probabilities and cumulative probabilities for a binomial random variable. These tables can be found in some statistics textbooks. With modern calculators and the capability of the BINOMDIST function in Microsoft Excel, such tables are unnecessary.

EXERCISES

Methods

25. Consider a binomial experiment with two trials and $p = .4$.
    a. Draw a tree diagram for this experiment (see Figure 5.4).
    b. Compute the probability of one success, $f(1)$.
    c. Compute $f(0)$.
    d. Compute $f(2)$.
    e. Compute the probability of at least one success.
    f. Compute the expected value, variance, and standard deviation.

26. Consider a binomial experiment with $n = 10$ and $p = .10$.
    a. Compute $f(0)$.
    b. Compute $f(2)$.
    c. Compute $P(x \leq 2)$.
    d. Compute $P(x \geq 1)$.
    e. Compute $E(x)$.
    f. Compute $\text{Var}(x)$ and σ.

27. Consider a binomial experiment with $n = 20$ and $p = .70$.
    a. Compute $f(12)$.
    b. Compute $f(16)$.
    c. Compute $P(x \geq 16)$.
    d. Compute $P(x \leq 15)$.
    e. Compute $E(x)$.
    f. Compute $\text{Var}(x)$ and σ.

Applications

28. The 1999 Youth and Money Survey, sponsored by the American Savings Education Council, the Employee Benefit Research Institute, and Matthew Greenwald & Associates, talked to 1000 students ages 16–22 about personal finance. The survey found that 33% of the students have their own credit card.
    a. In a sample of six students, what is the probability that two will have their own credit card?
    b. In a sample of six students, what is the probability that at least two will have their own credit card?
    c. In a sample of 10 students, what is the probability that none will have their own credit card?

29. According to a *Business Week*/Harris Poll of 1035 adults, 40% of those surveyed agreed strongly with the proposition that business has too much power over American life (*Business Week*, September 11, 2000). Assume this percentage is representative of the American population and that a sample of 20 individuals has been taken from a cross-section of the American population to learn about the role of business in their lives. What is the probability that at least five of these individuals will feel that business has too much power over American life?

30. When a new machine is functioning properly, only 3% of the items produced are defective. Assume that we will randomly select two parts produced on the machine and that we are interested in the number of defective parts found.
    a. Describe the conditions under which this situation would be a binomial experiment.
    b. Draw a tree diagram similar to Figure 5.4 showing this problem as a two-trial experiment.
    c. How many experimental outcomes result in exactly one defect being found?
    d. Compute the probabilities associated with finding no defects, exactly one defect, and two defects.

31. Five percent of American truck drivers are women (*Statistical Abstract of the United States*, 1997). Suppose 10 truck drivers are selected randomly to be interviewed about quality of work conditions.
  a. Is the selection of the 10 drivers a binomial experiment? Explain.
  b. What is the probability that two of the drivers will be women?
  c. What is the probability that none will be women?
  d. What is the probability that at least one will be a woman?

32. Military radar and missile detection systems are designed to warn a country against enemy attacks. A reliability question is whether a detection system will be able to identify an attack and issue a warning. Assume that a particular detection system has a .90 probability of detecting a missile attack. Use the binomial probability distribution to answer the following questions.
  a. What is the probability that a single detection system will detect an attack?
  b. If two detection systems are installed in the same area and operate independently, what is the probability that at least one of the systems will detect the attack?
  c. If three systems are installed, what is the probability that at least one of the systems will detect the attack?
  d. Would you recommend that multiple detection systems be used? Explain.

33. Fifty percent of Americans think we are in a recession, even though technically we have not had two straight quarters of negative growth (*Business Week*, July 30, 2001). For a sample of 20 Americans, make the following calculations.
  a. Compute the probability that exactly 12 people think we are in a recession.
  b. Compute the probability that no more than five people think we are in a recession.
  c. How many people would you expect to say we are in a recession?
  d. Compute the variance and standard deviation of the number of people who think we are in a recession.

34. Forty percent of business travelers carry either a cell phone or a laptop (*USA Today*, September 12, 2000). For a sample of 15 business travelers, make the following calculations.
  a. Compute the probability that three of the travelers have a cell phone or laptop.
  b. Compute the probability that 12 of the travelers have neither a cell phone nor a laptop.
  c. Compute the probability that at least three of the travelers have a cell phone or a laptop.

35. A university found that 20% of its students withdraw without completing the introductory statistics course. Assume that 20 students registered for the course this quarter.
  a. Compute the probability that two or fewer will withdraw.
  b. Compute the probability that exactly four will withdraw.
  c. Compute the probability that more than three will withdraw.
  d. Compute the expected number of withdrawals.

36. For the special case of a binomial random variable, we stated that the variance could be computed using the formula $\sigma^2 = np(1 - p)$. For the Martin Clothing Store problem data in Table 5.7, we found $\sigma^2 = np(1 - p) = .63$. Use the general definition of variance for a discrete random variable, equation (5.5), and the data in Table 5.7 to verify that the variance is in fact .63.

37. Twenty-nine percent of lawyers and judges are women (*Statistical Abstract of the United States*, 1997). In a jurisdiction with 30 lawyers and judges, what is the expected number of women? What are the variance and standard deviation?

5.5   POISSON PROBABILITY DISTRIBUTION

In this section we consider a discrete random variable that is often useful in estimating the number of occurrences over a specified interval of time or space. For example, the random variable of interest might be the number of arrivals at a car wash in one hour, the number

The Poisson probability distribution is often used to model arrival rates in waiting line situations.

of repairs needed in 10 miles of highway, or the number of leaks in 100 miles of pipeline. If the following two properties are satisfied, the number of occurrences is a random variable described by the **Poisson probability distribution**.

Properties of a Poisson Experiment

1. The probability of an occurrence is the same for any two intervals of equal length.
2. The occurrence or nonoccurrence in any interval is independent of the occurrence or nonoccurrence in any other interval.

The **Poisson probability function** is defined by equation (5.11).

Poisson Probability Function

Siméon Poisson taught mathematics at the Ecole Polytechnique in Paris from 1802 to 1808. In 1837, he published a work entitled, "Researches on the Probability of Criminal and Civil Verdicts," which includes a discussion of what later became known as the Poisson distribution.

$$f(x) = \frac{\mu^x e^{-\mu}}{x!} \tag{5.11}$$

where

$$f(x) = \text{the probability of } x \text{ occurrences in an interval}$$
$$\mu = \text{expected value or mean number of occurrences}$$
$$\text{in an interval}$$
$$e = 2.71828$$

Before we consider a specific example to see how the Poisson distribution can be applied, note that the number of occurrences, x, has no upper limit. It is a discrete random variable that may assume an infinite sequence of values ($x = 0, 1, 2, \ldots$).

An Example Involving Time Intervals

Bell Labs uses the Poisson distribution to model the arrival of phone calls.

Suppose that we are interested in the number of arrivals at the drive-up teller window of a bank during a 15-minute period on weekday mornings. If we can assume that the probability of a car arriving is the same for any two time periods of equal length and that the arrival or nonarrival of a car in any time period is independent of the arrival or nonarrival in any other time period, the Poisson probability function is applicable. Suppose these assumptions are satisfied and an analysis of historical data shows that the average number of cars arriving in a 15-minute period of time is 10; in this case, the following probability function applies.

$$f(x) = \frac{10^x e^{-10}}{x!}$$

The random variable here is x = number of cars arriving in any 15-minute period.

If management wanted to know the probability of exactly five arrivals in 15 minutes, we would set $x = 5$ and thus obtain

$$\text{Probability of Exactly} \atop \text{5 Arrivals in 15 Minutes} = f(5) = \frac{10^5 e^{-10}}{5!} = .0378$$

This probability was determined by using a calculator to evaluate the probability function with $\mu = 10$ and $x = 5$. Microsoft Excel also provides a function, called POISSON, for computing Poisson probabilities and cumulative probabilities. This function is easier to use when numerous probabilities and/or cumulative probabilities are desired. We show how to compute these probabilities with Excel at the end of this section.

Our illustration involves a 15-minute period, but other time periods can be used. Suppose we want to compute the probability of one arrival in a three-minute period. Because 10 is the expected number of arrivals in a 15-minute period, we see that $10/15 = 2/3$ is the expected number of arrivals in a one-minute period and that $(2/3)(3 \text{ minutes}) = 2$ is the expected number of arrivals in a three-minute period. Thus, the probability of x arrivals in a three-minute time period with $\mu = 2$ is given by the following Poisson probability function.

$$f(x) = \frac{2^x e^{-2}}{x!}$$

Suppose now we want to compute the probability of one arrival in a three-minute period.

$$\text{Probability of Exactly} \atop \text{1 Arrival in 3 Minutes} = f(1) = \frac{2^1 e^{-2}}{1!} = .2707$$

An Example Involving Length or Distance Intervals

Let us illustrate an application not involving time intervals in which the Poisson probability distribution is useful. Suppose we are concerned with the occurrence of major defects in a highway one month after resurfacing. We will assume that the probability of a defect is the same for any two highway intervals of equal length and that the occurrence or nonoccurrence of a defect in any one interval is independent of the occurrence or nonoccurrence of a defect in any other interval. Hence, the Poisson probability distribution can be applied.

Suppose we learn that major defects one month after resurfacing occur at the average rate of two per mile. Let us find the probability of no major defects in a particular three-mile section of the highway. Because we are interested in an interval with a length of three miles, $\mu = (2 \text{ defects/mile})(3 \text{ miles}) = 6$ represents the expected number of major defects over the three-mile section of highway. Using equation (5.11), the probability of no major defects is $f(0) = 6^0 e^{-6}/0! = .0025$. Thus, it is unlikely that no major defects will occur in the three-mile section. In fact, this example indicates a $1 - .0025 = .9975$ probability of at least one major defect in the three-mile highway section.

Using Excel to Compute Poisson Probabilities

The Excel function for computing Poisson probabilities and cumulative probabilities is called POISSON. It works in much the same way as the Excel function for computing binomial probabilities. Here we show how to use it to compute Poisson probabilities and cumulative probabilities. To illustrate, we use the example introduced earlier in this section; cars arrive at a bank drive-up teller window at the mean rate of 10 per 15-minute time interval. Refer to Figure 5.8 as we describe the tasks involved.

Enter Data: In order to compute a Poisson probability we must know the mean number of occurrences (μ) per time period and the number of occurrences for which we want to compute the probability (x). For the drive-up teller window example, the occurrences of interest are the arrivals of cars. The mean arrival rate is 10, which has been entered in cell D1. Earlier in this section, we computed the probability of 5 arrivals. But, suppose now we want

FIGURE 5.8   EXCEL WORKSHEET FOR COMPUTING POISSON PROBABILITIES

	A	B	C	D	E
1			Mean No. of Occurrences	10	
2					
3	No. of Arrivals (x)	f(x)			
4	0	=POISSON(A4,$D$1,FALSE)			
5	1	=POISSON(A5,$D$1,FALSE)			
6	2	=POISSON(A6,$D$1,FALSE)			
7	3	=POISSON(A7,$D$1,FALSE)			
8	4	=POISSON(A8,$D$1,FALSE)			
9	5	=POISSON(A9,$D$1,FALSE)			
10	6	=POISSON(A10,$D$1,FALSE)			
11	7	=POISSON(A11,$D$1,FALSE)			
12	8	=POISSON(A12,$D$1,FALSE)			
13	9	=POISSON(A13,$D$1,FALSE)			
14	10	=POISSON(A14,$D$1,FALSE)			
15	11	=POISSON(A15,$D$1,FALSE)			
16	12	=POISSON(A16,$D$1,FALSE)			
17	13	=POISSON(A17,$D$1,FALSE)			
18	14	=POISSON(A18,$D$1,FALSE)			
19	15	=POISSON(A19,$D$1,FALSE)			
20	16	=POISSON(A20,$D$1,FALSE)			
21	17	=POISSON(A21,$D$1,FALSE)			
22	18	=POISSON(A22,$D$1,FALSE)			
23	19	=POISSON(A23,$D$1,FALSE)			
24	20	=POISSON(A24,$D$1,FALSE)			
25					

	A	B	C	D	E	F	G	H	I	J
1		Mean No. of Occurrences		10						
2										
3	No. of Arrivals (x)	f(x)								
4	0	0.0000								
5	1	0.0005								
6	2	0.0023								
7	3	0.0076								
8	4	0.0189								
9	5	0.0378								
10	6	0.0631								
11	7	0.0901								
12	8	0.1126								
13	9	0.1251								
14	10	0.1251								
15	11	0.1137								
16	12	0.0948								
17	13	0.0729								
18	14	0.0521								
19	15	0.0347								
20	16	0.0217								
21	17	0.0128								
22	18	0.0071								
23	19	0.0037								
24	20	0.0019								
25										

Poisson Probabilities chart (Probability vs. No. of Arrivals)

to compute the probability of zero up through 20 arrivals.* To do so, we enter the values 0, 1, 2, . . . , 20 into cells A4:A24.

Enter Functions and Formulas: The POISSON function has three arguments: the first is the value of x, the second is the value of μ, and the third is FALSE or TRUE. We choose FALSE for the third argument if a probability is desired. The formula =POISSON(A4, $D$1,FALSE) has been entered into cell B4 to compute the probability of 0 arrivals in a 15-minute period. See the formula worksheet in the background of Figure 5.8. The value worksheet in the foreground shows that the probability of 0 arrivals is 0.0000. The formula in cell B4 is copied to cells B5:B24 to compute the probabilities for 1 through 20 arrivals. Note, in cell B9 of the value worksheet, that the probability of 5 arrivals is .0378. This result is the same as we calculated earlier in the text.

Notice how easy it was to compute all the probabilities for 0 through 20 arrivals using the Excel function. These calculations would take quite a bit of work using a calculator. We have also used Excel's Chart Wizard to develop a graph of the Poisson probability distribution of arrivals. See the value worksheet in Figure 5.8. This chart gives a nice graphical presentation of the probabilities for the various number of arrival possibilities in a 15-minute interval. We can quickly see that the most likely number of arrivals is 9 or 10 and that the probabilities fall off rather smoothly for smaller and larger values.

Let us now see how cumulative probabilities are generated using Excel's POISSON function. It is really a simple extension of what we have already done. We again use the

Instructions for using the Chart Wizard are in Chapter 2.

---

*The Poisson probabilities for $x > 20$ are very close to zero and not shown.

example of arrivals at a drive-up teller window. Refer to Figure 5.9 as we describe the tasks involved.

Enter Data: To compute cumulative Poisson probabilities we must provide the mean number of occurrences (μ) per time period and the values of x that we are interested in. The mean arrival rate (10) has been entered into cell D1. Suppose we want to compute the cumulative probabilities for a number of arrivals ranging from zero up through 20. To do so, we enter the values 0, 1, 2, . . . , 20 into cells A4:A24.

Enter Functions and Formulas: Refer to the formula worksheet in the background of Figure 5.8. The formulas we enter into cells B4:B24 of Figure 5.9 are the same as in Figure 5.8 with one exception. Instead of FALSE for the third argument we enter the word TRUE to obtain cumulative probabilities. After entering these formulas into cells B4:B24 of the worksheet in Figure 5.9 the cumulative probabilities shown were obtained.

Note, in Figure 5.9, that the probability of 5 or fewer arrivals is .0671 and that the probability of 4 or fewer arrivals is .0293. Thus, the probability of exactly 5 arrivals is the difference in these two numbers: $f(5) = .0671 - .0293 = .0378$. We computed this probability earlier in this section and in Figure 5.8. Using these cumulative probabilities it is easy to compute the probability that a random variable lies within a certain interval. For instance,

FIGURE 5.9   EXCEL WORKSHEET FOR COMPUTING CUMULATIVE POISSON PROBABILITIES

	A	B	C	D	E
1			Mean No. of Occurrences	10	
2					
3	No. of Arrivals (x)	Cum Prob			
4	0	=POISSON(A4,$D$1,TRUE)			
5	1	=POISSON(A5,$D$1,TRUE)			
6	2	=POISSON(A6,$D$1,TRUE)			
7	3	=POISSON(A7,$D$1,TRUE)			
8	4	=POISSON(A8,$D$1,TRUE)			
9	5	=POISSON(A9,$D$1,TRUE)			
10	6	=POISSON(A10,$D$1,TRUE)			
11	7	=POISSON(A11,$D$1,TRUE)			
12	8	=POISSON(A12,$D$1,TRUE)			
13	9	=POISSON(A13,$D$1,TRUE)			
14	10	=POISSON(A14,$D$1,TRUE)			
15	11	=POISSON(A15,$D$1,TRUE)			
16	12	=POISSON(A16,$D$1,TRUE)			
17	13	=POISSON(A17,$D$1,TRUE)			
18	14	=POISSON(A18,$D$1,TRUE)			
19	15	=POISSON(A19,$D$1,TRUE)			
20	16	=POISSON(A20,$D$1,TRUE)			
21	17	=POISSON(A21,$D$1,TRUE)			
22	18	=POISSON(A22,$D$1,TRUE)			
23	19	=POISSON(A23,$D$1,TRUE)			
24	20	=POISSON(A24,$D$1,TRUE)			
25					

	A	B	C	D	E
1		Mean No. of Occurrences		10	
2					
3	No. of Arrivals (x)	Cum Prob			
4	0	0.0000			
5	1	0.0005			
6	2	0.0028			
7	3	0.0103			
8	4	0.0293			
9	5	0.0671			
10	6	0.1301			
11	7	0.2202			
12	8	0.3328			
13	9	0.4579			
14	10	0.5830			
15	11	0.6968			
16	12	0.7916			
17	13	0.8645			
18	14	0.9165			
19	15	0.9513			
20	16	0.9730			
21	17	0.9857			
22	18	0.9928			
23	19	0.9965			
24	20	0.9984			
25					

suppose we wanted to know the probability of more than 5 and fewer than 16 arrivals. We would just find the cumulative probability of 15 arrivals and subtract from that the cumulative probability for 5 arrivals. Referring to Figure 5.9 to obtain the appropriate probabilities, we obtain .9513 − .0671 = .8842. With such a high probability, we could conclude that 6 to 15 cars will arrive in most 15-minute intervals. Using the cumulative probability for 20 arrivals, we can also conclude that the probability of more than 20 arrivals in a 15-minute period is 1 − .9984 = .0016; thus, there is almost no chance of more than 20 cars arriving.

EXERCISES

Methods

38. Consider a Poisson probability distribution with $\mu = 3$.
   a. Write the appropriate Poisson probability function.
   b. Compute $f(2)$.
   c. Compute $f(1)$.
   d. Compute $P(x \geq 2)$.

39. Consider a Poisson probability distribution with an average number of occurrences per time period of two.
   a. Write the appropriate Poisson probability function.
   b. What is the average number of occurrences in three time periods?
   c. Write the appropriate Poisson probability function to determine the probability of x occurrences in three time periods.
   d. Compute the probability of two occurrences in one time period.
   e. Compute the probability of six occurrences in three time periods.
   f. Compute the probability of five occurrences in two time periods.

Applications

40. Phone calls arrive at the rate of 48 per hour at the reservation desk for Regional Airways.
   a. Compute the probability of receiving three calls in a five-minute interval of time.
   b. Compute the probability of receiving exactly 10 calls in 15 minutes.
   c. Suppose no calls are currently on hold. If the agent takes five minutes to complete the current call, how many callers do you expect to be waiting by that time? What is the probability that none will be waiting?
   d. If no calls are currently being processed, what is the probability that the agent can take three minutes for personal time without being interrupted by a call?

41. During the period of time phone-in registrations are being taken at a local university, calls come in at the rate of one every two minutes.
   a. What is the expected number of calls in one hour?
   b. What is the probability of three calls in five minutes?
   c. What is the probability of no calls in a five-minute period?

42. More than 50 million guests stayed at bed and breakfasts (B&Bs) last year. The Web site for the Bed and Breakfast Inns of North America (*www.bestInns.net*), which averages approximately seven visitors per minute, enables many B&Bs to attract guests without waiting years to be mentioned in guidebooks (*Time*, September 2001).
   a. Compute the probability of no Web site visitors in a 1-minute period.
   b. Compute the probability of two or more Web site visitors in a 1-minute period.
   c. Compute the probability of one or more Web site visitors in a 30-second period.
   d. Compute the probability of five or more Web site visitors in a 1-minute period.

43. Airline passengers arrive randomly and independently at the passenger-screening facility at a major international airport. The mean arrival rate is 10 passengers per minute.
   a. Compute the probability of no arrivals in a 1-minute period.
   b. Compute the probability that three or fewer passengers arrive in a 1-minute period.
   c. Compute the probability of no arrivals in a 15-second period.
   d. Compute the probability of at least one arrival in a 15-second period.

44. Investment activities for subscribers to *The Wall Street Journal Interactive Edition* show that the average number of security transactions per year is approximately 15 (*The Wall Street Journal* Subscriber Study, 1999). Assume that a particular investor makes transactions at this rate. Furthermore, assume that the probability of a transaction for this investor is the same for any two months and transactions in one month are independent of transactions in any other month.
   a. Compute the mean number of transactions per month.
   b. Compute the probability of no transactions during a month.
   c. Compute the probability of exactly one transaction during a month.
   d. Compute the probability of more than one transaction during a month.

45. The National Safety Council reported that air bag-related fatalities dropped to 18 in the year 2000 (*www.nsc.org*).
   a. Compute the average number of air bag-related fatalities per month.
   b. Compute the probability of no air bag-related fatalities in a typical month.
   c. Compute the probability of two or more air bag-related fatalities in a typical month.

5.6   HYPERGEOMETRIC PROBABILITY DISTRIBUTION

The hypergeometric probability distribution is closely related to the binomial probability distribution. The two probability distributions differ in two key ways. With the hypergeometric distribution, the trials are not independent; and, the probability of success changes from trial to trial.

In the usual notation for the hypergeometric probability distribution, r denotes the number of elements in the population of size N labeled success, and $N - r$ denotes the number of elements in the population labeled failure. The **hypergeometric probability function** is used to compute the probability that in a random selection of n elements, selected without replacement, we obtain x elements labeled success and $n - x$ elements labeled failure. For this outcome to occur, we must obtain x successes from the r successes in the population and $n - x$ failures from the $N - r$ failures. The following hypergeometric probability function provides $f(x)$, the probability of obtaining x successes in a sample of size n.

Hypergeometric Probability Function

$$f(x) = \frac{\binom{r}{x}\binom{N-r}{n-x}}{\binom{N}{n}} \qquad \text{for } 0 \leq x \leq r \qquad (5.12)$$

where

$$f(x) = \text{probability of } x \text{ successes in } n \text{ trials}$$
$$n = \text{number of trials}$$
$$N = \text{number of elements in the population}$$
$$r = \text{number of elements in the population labeled success}$$

Note that $\binom{N}{n}$ represents the number of ways a sample of size n can be selected from a population of size N; $\binom{r}{x}$ represents the number of ways that x successes can be selected from a total of r successes in the population; and $\binom{N-r}{n-x}$ represents the number of ways that $n - x$ failures can be selected from a total of $N - r$ failures in the population.

To illustrate the computations involved in using equation (5.12), let us consider the problem of selecting two people from a five-member committee to send to a Las Vegas convention. Assume that the five-member committee consists of three women and two men. To determine the probability of randomly selecting two women, we can use equation (5.12) with $n = 2$, $N = 5$, $r = 3$, and $x = 2$.

$$f(2) = \frac{\binom{3}{2}\binom{2}{0}}{\binom{5}{2}} = \frac{\left(\frac{3!}{2!1!}\right)\left(\frac{2!}{2!0!}\right)}{\left(\frac{5!}{2!3!}\right)} = \frac{3}{10} = .30$$

Suppose we learn later that three committee members will be allowed to make the trip. If we use $n = 3$, $N = 5$, $r = 3$, and $x = 2$, the probability that exactly two of the three members will be women is

$$f(2) = \frac{\binom{3}{2}\binom{2}{1}}{\binom{5}{3}} = \frac{\left(\frac{3!}{2!1!}\right)\left(\frac{2!}{1!1!}\right)}{\left(\frac{5!}{3!2!}\right)} = \frac{6}{10} = .60$$

As another illustration, suppose a population consists of 10 items, four of which are classified as defective and six of which are classified as nondefective. What is the probability that a random selection of three will provide two defective items? For this problem we can think of obtaining a defective item as a "success." Using equation (5.12) with $n = 3$, $N = 10$, $r = 4$, and $x = 2$, we can compute $f(2)$ as follows.

$$f(2) = \frac{\binom{4}{2}\binom{6}{1}}{\binom{10}{3}} = \frac{\left(\frac{4!}{2!2!}\right)\left(\frac{6!}{1!5!}\right)}{\left(\frac{10!}{3!7!}\right)} = \frac{36}{120} = .30$$

Using Excel to Compute Hypergeometric Probabilities

The Excel function for computing hypergeometric probabilities is called HYPGEOMDIST. It only computes probabilities; not cumulative probabilities. The HYPGEOMDIST function has four arguments: x, n, r, N. It is fairly straightforward to use so we dispense with showing a worksheet figure and just show the formula. Let us reconsider the example of three women and two men on a five-person committee. Two people are to be chosen at random to send to a Las Vegas convention. We want to compute the probability that the two persons chosen are women. In this case, $x = 2$, $n = 2$, $r = 3$, and $N = 5$. So the appropriate formula to place in a cell of an Excel worksheet would be =HYPGEOMDIST(2,2,3,5). Placing this formula in a cell of an Excel worksheet provides a hypergeometric probability of .30.

If 3 people are selected to go to Las Vegas, we have $x = 2$, $n = 3$, $r = 3$, and $N = 5$. So using the HYPGEOMDIST function to compute the probability of randomly selecting two women, we would enter the following formula into a cell of the worksheet: =HYPGEOMDIST(2,3,3,5). The probability computed is .6.

EXERCISES

Methods

46. Suppose $N = 10$ and $r = 3$. Compute the hypergeometric probabilities for the following values of n and x.
  a. $n = 4, x = 1$.
  b. $n = 2, x = 2$.
  c. $n = 2, x = 0$.
  d. $n = 4, x = 2$.

47. Suppose $N = 15$ and $r = 4$. What is the probability of $x = 3$ for $n = 10$?

Applications

48. According to *Beverage Digest,* Coke Classic and Pepsi ranked number one and number two in sales (*The Wall Street Journal Almanac,* 1998). Assume that in a group of 10 individuals, six preferred Coke Classic and four preferred Pepsi. A random sample of three of these individuals is selected.
  a. What is the probability that exactly two preferred Coke Classic?
  b. What is the probability that the majority (either two or three) preferred Pepsi?

49. Blackjack, or twenty-one as it is frequently called, is a popular gambling game played in Las Vegas casinos. A player is dealt two cards. Face cards (jacks, queens, and kings) and tens have a point value of 10. Aces have a point value of 1 or 11. A 52-card deck has 16 cards with a point value of 10 (jacks, queens, kings, and tens) and four aces.
  a. What is the probability that both cards dealt are aces or 10-point cards?
  b. What is the probability that both of the cards are aces?
  c. What is the probability that both of the cards have a point value of 10?
  d. A blackjack is a 10-point card and an ace for a value of 21. Use your answers to parts (a), (b), and (c) to determine the probability that a player is dealt blackjack. (Hint: Part (d) is not a hypergeometric problem. Develop your own logical relationship as to how the hypergeometric probabilities from parts (a), (b), and (c) can be combined to answer this question.)

50. Axline Computers manufactures personal computers at two plants, one in Texas and the other in Hawaii. The Texas plant has 40 employees; the Hawaii plant has 20. A random sample of 10 employees is to be asked to fill out a benefits questionnaire.

    a. What is the probability that none of the employees in the sample work at the plant in Hawaii?

    b. What is the probability that one of the employees in the sample works at the plant in Hawaii?

    c. What is the probability that two or more of the employees in the sample work at the plant in Hawaii?

    d. What is the probability that nine of the employees in the sample work at the plant in Texas?

51. Of the 25 students (14 boys and 11 girls) in the sixth-grade class at St. Andrew School, five students were absent Thursday.

    a. What is the probability that two of the absent students were girls?

    b. What is the probability that two of the absent students were boys?

    c. What is the probability that all of the absent students were boys?

    d. What is the probability that none of the absent students were boys?

52. A shipment of 10 items has two defective and eight nondefective items. In the inspection of the shipment, a sample of items will be selected and tested. If a defective item is found, the shipment of 10 items will be rejected.

    a. If a sample of three items is selected, what is the probability that the shipment will be rejected?

    b. If a sample of four items is selected, what is the probability that the shipment will be rejected?

    c. If a sample of five items is selected, what is the probability that the shipment will be rejected?

    d. If management would like a .90 probability of rejecting a shipment with two defective and eight nondefective items, how large a sample would you recommend?

SUMMARY

A random variable provides a numerical description of the outcome of an experiment. The probability distribution for a random variable describes how the probabilities are distributed over the values the random variable can assume. For any discrete random variable x, the probability distribution is defined by a probability function, denoted by $f(x)$, which provides the probability associated with each value of the random variable. Once the probability function is defined, we can compute the expected value, variance, and standard deviation for the random variable.

The binomial probability distribution can be used to determine the probability of x successes in n trials whenever the experiment has the following properties:

1. The experiment consists of a sequence of n identical trials.
2. Two outcomes are possible on each trial, one called success and the other failure.
3. The probability of a success p does not change from trial to trial. Consequently, the probability of failure, $1 - p$, does not change from trial to trial.
4. The trials are independent.

When the four properties hold, the binomial probability function can be used to determine the probability of obtaining x successes in n trials. Formulas were also presented for the mean and variance of the binomial probability distribution.

The Poisson probability distribution is used when it is desirable to determine the probability of obtaining x occurrences over an interval of time or space. The following assumptions are necessary for the Poisson distribution to be applicable.

1. The probability of an occurrence of the event is the same for any two intervals of equal length.
2. The occurrence or nonoccurrence of the event in any interval is independent of the occurrence or nonoccurrence of the event in any other interval.

A third discrete probability distribution, the hypergeometric, was introduced in Section 5.6. Like the binomial, it is used to compute the probability of x successes in n trials. But, in contrast to the binomial, the probability of success changes from trial to trial.

GLOSSARY

Random variable   A numerical description of the outcome of an experiment.

Discrete random variable   A random variable that may assume either a finite number of values or an infinite sequence of values.

Continuous random variable   A random variable that may assume any numerical value in an interval or collection of intervals.

Probability distribution   A description of how the probabilities are distributed over the values of the random variable.

Probability function   A function, denoted by $f(x)$, that provides the probability that x assumes a particular value for a discrete random variable.

Discrete uniform probability distribution   A probability distribution for which each possible value of the random variable has the same probability.

Expected value   A measure of the central location of a random variable.

Variance   A measure of the variability, or dispersion, of a random variable.

Standard deviation   The positive square root of the variance.

Binomial experiment   An experiment having the four properties stated at the beginning of Section 5.4.

Binomial probability distribution   A probability distribution showing the probability of x successes in n trials of a binomial experiment.

Binomial probability function   The function used to compute binomial probabilities.

Poisson probability distribution   A probability distribution showing the probability of x occurrences of an event over a specified interval of time or space.

Poisson probability function   The function used to compute Poisson probabilities.

Hypergeometric probability function   The function used to compute the probability of x successes in n trials when the probability of success changes from trial to trial.

KEY FORMULAS

Discrete Uniform Probability Function

$$f(x) = 1/n \qquad (5.3)$$

where

$n =$ the number of values the random variable may assume

Expected Value of a Discrete Random Variable

$$E(x) = \mu = \Sigma x f(x) \tag{5.4}$$

Variance of a Discrete Random Variable

$$\text{Var}(x) = \sigma^2 = \Sigma(x - \mu)^2 f(x) \tag{5.5}$$

Number of Experimental Outcomes Providing Exactly x Successes in n Trials

$$\binom{n}{x} = \frac{n!}{x!(n-x)!} \tag{5.6}$$

Binomial Probability Function

$$f(x) = \binom{n}{x} p^x (1-p)^{(n-x)} \tag{5.8}$$

Expected Value for the Binomial Probability Distribution

$$E(x) = \mu = np \tag{5.9}$$

Variance for the Binomial Probability Distribution

$$\text{Var}(x) = \sigma^2 = np(1-p) \tag{5.10}$$

Poisson Probability Function

$$f(x) = \frac{\mu^x e^{-\mu}}{x!} \tag{5.11}$$

Hypergeometric Probability Function

$$f(x) = \frac{\binom{r}{x}\binom{N-r}{n-x}}{\binom{N}{n}} \quad \text{for } 0 \le x \le r \tag{5.12}$$

SUPPLEMENTARY EXERCISES

53. A *Wall Street Journal*/NBC News poll asked 2004 adults how they felt about their opportunities for career advancement (*The Wall Street Journal*, September 19, 1997). Twenty-three percent indicated they were very satisfied; 38% indicated they were somewhat satisfied; 3% indicated they were not sure; 18% indicated they were somewhat dissatisfied; and 18% indicated they were very dissatisfied. Let x be a random variable representing level of satisfaction with opportunities for career advancement. We let $x = 5$ for very satisfied, $x = 4$ for somewhat satisfied, $x = 3$ for not sure, $x = 2$ for somewhat dissatisfied, and $x = 1$ for very dissatisfied.
    a. Develop a probability distribution for level of satisfaction with opportunities for career advancement.
    b. Compute the expected value for level of satisfaction. Does a higher score indicate more or less satisfaction?
    c. Compute the variance and standard deviation for the level of satisfaction.

54. An opinion survey of 1009 adults was conducted by Louis Harris & Associates, Inc. (*Business Week*, December 29, 1997). Table 5.8 shows the probability distribution of responses to a question concerning the stock market's valuation.
    a. Show that the probability distribution in Table 5.8 satisfies the properties of all probability distributions.
    b. What are the expected value and variance of the probability distribution of opinions?
    c. Comment on whether people think the stock market is overvalued.

55. The budgeting process for a midwestern college resulted in expense forecasts for the coming year (in $ millions) of $9, $10, $11, $12, and $13. Because the actual expenses are unknown, the following respective probabilities are assigned: .3, .2, .25, .05, and .2.
    a. Show the probability distribution for the expense forecast.
    b. What is the expected value of the expense forecast for the coming year?
    c. What is the variance of the expense forecast for the coming year?
    d. If income projections for the year are estimated at $12 million, comment on the financial position of the college.

56. Kristen DelGuzzi conducted a study of Hamilton County judges and courts over a three-year period (*The Cincinnati Enquirer*, January 11, 1998). One finding was that 4% of the cases decided in Common Pleas Court were appealed.
    a. If 20 cases are heard on a particular day, what is the probability that 3 will be appealed?
    b. If 20 cases are heard on a particular day, what is the probability none will be appealed?
    c. It is not unusual for 1200 cases to be heard in a month. What is the expected number of appeals?
    d. If 1200 cases are heard in a month, what are the variance and standard deviation of the number of appeals?

57. A company is planning to interview Internet users to learn how its proposed Web site will be received by different age groups. According to the Bureau of the Census, 40% of individuals aged 18 to 54, and 12% of individuals aged 55 and over use the Internet (*Statistical Abstract of the United States*, 2000).
    a. How many people from the 18–54 age group must be contacted to find an expected number of at least 10 Internet users?
    b. How many people from the age group 55 and over must be contacted to find an expected number of at least 10 Internet users?
    c. If you contact the number of 18- to 54-year-old people suggested in part (a), what is the standard deviation of the number who will be Internet users?
    d. If you contact the number of people aged 55 and older suggested in part (b), what is the standard deviation of the number who will be Internet users?

TABLE 5.8   PROBABILITY DISTRIBUTION OF RESPONSES CONCERNING STOCK MARKET'S VALUATION

Market Valuation	Random Variable (x)	Probability $f(x)$
Very undervalued	1	0.02
Somewhat undervalued	2	0.06
Fairly valued	3	0.28
Somewhat overvalued	4	0.54
Very overvalued	5	0.10

58. Many companies use a quality control technique called *acceptance sampling* to monitor incoming shipments of parts, raw materials, and so on. In the electronics industry, component parts are commonly shipped from suppliers in large lots. Inspection of a sample of *n* components can be viewed as the *n* trials of a binomial experiment. The outcome for each component tested (trial) will be that the component is classified as good or defective. Reynolds Electronics accepts a lot from a particular supplier if the defective components in the lot do not exceed 1%. Suppose a random sample of five items from a recent shipment is tested.
    a. Assume that 1% of the shipment is defective. Compute the probability that no items in the sample are defective.
    b. Assume that 1% of the shipment is defective. Compute the probability that exactly one item in the sample is defective.
    c. What is the probability of observing one or more defective items in the sample if 1% of the shipment is defective?
    d. Would you feel comfortable accepting the shipment if one item were found to be defective? Why or why not?

59. The unemployment rate is 4.1% (*Barron's*, September 4, 2000). Assume that 100 employable people are selected randomly.
    a. What is the expected number of people who are unemployed?
    b. What is the variance and standard deviation of the number of people who are unemployed?

60. In December 1997, the U.S. Department of Justice issued an injunction against Microsoft Corporation for bundling its Internet Explorer® Web browser with its Windows 95® operating system (*Fortune*, February 2, 1998). Public opinion was divided on whether Microsoft was a monopoly. In a *Fortune* poll, 41% of respondents agreed with the statement, "Microsoft is a monopoly." Suppose a sample of 800 people is taken.
    a. How many would you expect to agree that Microsoft is a monopoly?
    b. What is the standard deviation of the number of respondents who believe Microsoft is a monopoly?
    c. What is the standard deviation of the number of respondents who do not believe Microsoft is a monopoly?

61. Cars arrive at a car wash randomly and independently; the probability of an arrival is the same for any two time intervals of equal length. The mean arrival rate is 15 cars per hour. What is the probability that 20 or more cars will arrive during any given hour of operation?

62. A new automated production process averages 1.5 breakdowns per day. Because of the cost associated with a breakdown, management is concerned about the possibility of having three or more breakdowns during a day. Assume that breakdowns occur randomly, that the probability of a breakdown is the same for any two time intervals of equal length, and that breakdowns in one period are independent of breakdowns in other periods. What is the probability of having three or more breakdowns during a day?

63. A regional director responsible for business development in the state of Pennsylvania is concerned about the number of small business failures. If the mean number of small business failures per month is 10, what is the probability that exactly four small businesses will fail during a given month? Assume that the probability of a failure is the same for any two months and that the occurrence or nonoccurrence of a failure in any month is independent of failures in any other month.

64. Customer arrivals at a bank are random and independent; the probability of an arrival in any one-minute period is the same as the probability of an arrival in any other one-minute period. Answer the following questions, assuming a mean arrival rate of three customers per minute.
    a. What is the probability of exactly three arrivals in a one-minute period?
    b. What is the probability of at least three arrivals in a one-minute period?

65. A deck of playing cards contains 52 cards, four of which are aces. What is the probability that the deal of a five-card hand provides:
  a. A pair of aces?
  b. Exactly one ace?
  c. No aces?
  d. At least one ace?

66. Through the week ending September 16, 2001, Tiger Woods was the leading money winner on the PGA Tour, with total earnings of $5,517,777. Of the top 10 money winners, seven players used a Titleist brand golf ball (*www.pgatour.com*). Suppose that we randomly select two of the top 10 money winners.
  a. What is the probability that exactly one uses a Titleist golf ball?
  b. What is the probability that both use Titleist golf balls?
  c. What is the probability that neither uses a Titleist golf ball?

CHAPTER 6

Continuous Probability Distributions

CONTENTS

STATISTICS IN PRACTICE

Procter & Gamble*

CINCINNATI, OHIO

Procter & Gamble (P&G) is in the consumer products business worldwide. P&G produces and markets such products as detergents, disposable diapers, over-the-counter pharmaceuticals, dentifrices, bar soaps, mouthwashes, and paper towels. It has the leading brand in more categories than any other consumer products company.

As a leader in the application of statistical methods in decision making, P&G employs people with diverse academic backgrounds: engineering, statistics, operations research, and business. The major quantitative technologies for which these people provide support are probabilistic decision and risk analysis, advanced simulation, quality improvement, and quantitative methods (e.g., linear programming, regression analysis, probability analysis).

The Industrial Chemicals Division of P&G is a major supplier of fatty alcohols derived from natural substances such as coconut oil and from petroleum-based derivatives. Because it wanted to know the economic risks and opportunities of expanding its fatty-alcohol production facilities, the division called in P&G's experts in probabilistic decision and risk analysis to help. After structuring and modeling the problem, they determined that the key to profitability was the cost difference between the petroleum- and coconut-based raw materials. Future costs were unknown, but the analysts were able to represent them with the following continuous random variables.

$$x = \text{the coconut oil price per pound of fatty alcohol}$$

and

$$y = \text{the petroleum raw material price per pound of fatty alcohol}$$

Some of Procter & Gamble's many well-known products. Photo © Joe Higgins/South-Western.

Because the key to profitability was the difference between these two random variables, a third random variable, $d = x - y$, was used in the analysis. Experts were interviewed to determine the probability distribution for x and y. In turn, this information was used to develop a probability distribution for the difference in prices d. This continuous probability distribution showed a .90 probability that the price difference would be $.0655 or less and a .50 probability that the price difference would be $.035 or less. In addition, there was only a .10 probability that the price difference would be $.0045 or less.[†]

The Industrial Chemicals Division thought that being able to quantify the impact of raw material price differences was key to reaching a consensus. The probabilities obtained were used in a sensitivity analysis of the raw material price difference. The analysis yielded sufficient insight to form the basis for a recommendation to management.

The use of continuous random variables and their probability distributions was helpful to P&G in analyzing the economic risks associated with its fatty-alcohol production. In this chapter, you will gain an understanding of continuous random variables and their probability distributions including one of the most important probability distributions in statistics, the normal distribution.

*The authors are indebted to Joel Kahn of Procter & Gamble for providing this Statistics in Practice.

[†]The price differences stated here have been modified to protect proprietary data.

In the preceding chapter we discussed discrete random variables and their probability distributions. In this chapter we turn to the study of continuous random variables. Specifically, we discuss three continuous probability distributions: the uniform, the normal, and the exponential.

A fundamental difference separates discrete and continuous random variables in terms of how probabilities are computed. For a discrete random variable, the probability function $f(x)$ provides the probability that the random variable assumes a particular value. With continuous random variables, the counterpart of the probability function is the **probability density function**, also denoted by $f(x)$. The difference is that the probability density function does not directly provide probabilities. However, the area under the graph of $f(x)$ corresponding to a given interval does provide the probability that the continuous random variable x assumes a value in that interval. So when we compute probabilities for continuous random variables we are computing the probability that the random variable assumes any value in an interval.

One of the implications of the definition of probability for continuous random variables is that the probability of any particular value of the random variable is zero, because the area under the graph of $f(x)$ at any particular point is zero. In Section 6.1 we demonstrate these concepts for a continuous random variable that has a uniform probability distribution.

Much of the chapter is devoted to describing and showing applications of the normal probability distribution. The normal probability distribution is of major importance; it is used extensively in statistical inference. The chapter closes with a discussion of the exponential probability distribution.

6.1   UNIFORM PROBABILITY DISTRIBUTION

Whenever the probability is proportional to the length of the interval, the random variable is uniformly distributed.

Consider the random variable x representing the flight time of an airplane traveling from Chicago to New York. Suppose that, for normal operating conditions, the flight time will be in the interval from 120 minutes to 140 minutes. Because the flight time can be any value in that interval, the random variable x is a continuous rather than a discrete random variable. Let us assume that sufficient actual flight data are available to conclude that the probability of a flight time within any one-minute interval is the same as the probability of a flight time within any other one-minute interval. With every one-minute interval being equally likely, the random variable x is said to have a **uniform probability distribution**. The probability density function, which defines the uniform probability distribution for x, the flight-time random variable, is

$$f(x) = \begin{cases} 1/20 & \text{for } 120 \leq x \leq 140 \\ 0 & \text{elsewhere} \end{cases}$$

Figure 6.1 is a graph of this probability density function. In general, the uniform probability density function for a random variable x is defined by the following formula.

Uniform Probability Density Function

$$f(x) = \begin{cases} \dfrac{1}{b-a} & \text{for } a \leq x \leq b \\ 0 & \text{elsewhere} \end{cases} \tag{6.1}$$

For the flight-time random variable, $a = 120$ and $b = 140$.

FIGURE 6.1   UNIFORM PROBABILITY DENSITY FUNCTION FOR FLIGHT TIME

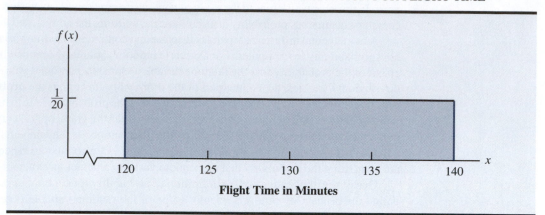

As noted in the introduction, for a continuous random variable, we consider probability only in terms of the likelihood that a random variable assumes a value within a specified interval. In the flight-time example, an acceptable probability question is: What is the probability that the flight time is between 120 and 130 minutes? That is, what is $P(120 \leq x \leq 130)$? Because the flight time must be between 120 and 140 minutes and because the probability is described as being uniform over this interval, we feel comfortable saying $P(120 \leq x \leq 130) = .50$. In the following subsection we show that this probability can be computed as the area under the graph of $f(x)$ from 120 to 130 (see Figure 6.2).

Area as a Measure of Probability

Let us make an observation about the graph in Figure 6.2. Consider the area under the graph of $f(x)$ in the interval from $x = 120$ to $x = 130$. The area is rectangular, and the area of a rectangle is simply its width multiplied by its height. With the width of the interval equal to $130 - 120 = 10$ and the height equal to the value of the probability density function $f(x) = 1/20$, we have area = width × height = $10(1/20) = 10/20 = .50$.

What observation can you make about the area under the graph of $f(x)$ and probability? They are identical! Indeed, this observation is valid for all continuous random variables.

FIGURE 6.2   AREA PROVIDES PROBABILITY OF FLIGHT TIME BETWEEN 120 AND 130 MINUTES

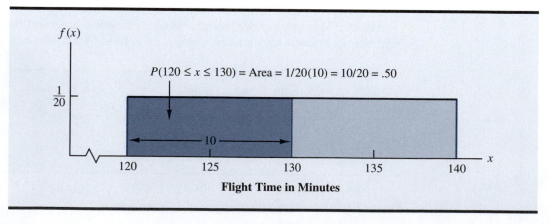

Once a probability density function $f(x)$ has been identified, the probability that x takes a value between some lower value x_1 and some higher value x_2 can be found by computing the area under the graph of $f(x)$ over the interval from x_1 to x_2.

Given the uniform probability distribution for flight time and using the interpretation of area as probability, we can answer any number of probability questions about flight times. For example, what is the probability of a flight time between 128 and 136 minutes? The width of the interval is $136 - 128 = 8$. With the uniform height of $f(x) = 1/20$, we see that $P(128 \leq x \leq 136) = 8(1/20) = .40$.

Note that $P(120 \leq x \leq 140) = 20(1/20) = 1$. That is, the total area under the graph of $f(x)$ is equal to 1. This property holds for all continuous probability distributions and is the analog of the condition that the sum of the probabilities must equal 1 for a discrete probability function. For a continuous probability density function, we must also require that $f(x) \geq 0$ for all values of x. This requirement is the analog of the requirement that $f(x) \geq 0$ for discrete probability functions.

Two major differences stand out between the treatment of continuous random variables and the treatment of their discrete counterparts.

1. We no longer talk about the probability of the random variable assuming a particular value. Instead, we talk about the probability of the random variable assuming a value within some given interval.

2. The probability of the random variable assuming a value within some given interval from x_1 to x_2 is defined to be the area under the graph of the probability density function between x_1 and x_2. It implies that the probability of a continuous random variable assuming any particular value exactly is zero, because the area under the graph of $f(x)$ at a single point is zero.

To see that the probability of any single point is 0, refer to Figure 6.2 and compute the probability of a single point, say, $x = 125$. $P(x = 125) = P(125 \leq x \leq 125) = 0(1/20) = 0$.

The calculation of the expected value and variance for a continuous random variable is analogous to that for a discrete random variable. However, because the computational procedure involves integral calculus, we leave the derivation of the appropriate formulas to more advanced texts.

For the uniform continuous probability distribution introduced in this section, the formulas for the expected value and variance are

$$E(x) = \frac{a + b}{2}$$

$$Var(x) = \frac{(b - a)^2}{12}$$

In these formulas, a is the smallest value and b is the largest value that the random variable may assume.

Applying these formulas to the uniform probability distribution for flight times from Chicago to New York, we obtain

$$E(x) = \frac{(120 + 140)}{2} = 130$$

$$Var(x) = \frac{(140 - 120)^2}{12} = 33.33$$

The standard deviation of flight times can be found by taking the square root of the variance. Thus, $\sigma = 5.77$ minutes.

NOTES AND COMMENTS

1. For a continuous random variable the probability of any particular value is zero; thus, $P(a \le x \le b) = P(a < x < b)$. This means that the probability of a random variable assuming a value in any interval is the same whether or not the endpoints are included.

2. To see more clearly why the height of a probability density function is not a probability, think about a random variable with the following uniform probability distribution.

$$f(x) = \begin{cases} 2 & \text{for } 0 \le x \le .5 \\ 0 & \text{elsewhere} \end{cases}$$

The height of the probability density function, $f(x)$, is 2 for values of x between 0 and .5. However, we know probabilities can never be greater than 1. Thus, we see that $f(x)$ cannot be interpreted as the probability of x.

EXERCISES

Methods

1. The random variable x is known to be uniformly distributed between 1.0 and 1.5.
   a. Show the graph of the probability density function.
   b. Compute $P(x = 1.25)$.
   c. Compute $P(1.0 \le x \le 1.25)$.
   d. Compute $P(1.20 < x < 1.5)$.

2. The random variable x is known to be uniformly distributed between 10 and 20.
   a. Show the graph of the probability density function.
   b. Compute $P(x < 15)$.
   c. Compute $P(12 \le x \le 18)$.
   d. Compute $E(x)$.
   e. Compute $\text{Var}(x)$.

Applications

3. Delta Airlines quotes a flight time of 2 hours, 5 minutes for its flights from Cincinnati to Tampa. Suppose we believe that actual flight times are uniformly distributed between 2 hours and 2 hours, 20 minutes.
   a. Show the graph of the probability density function for flight time.
   b. What is the probability that the flight will be no more than five minutes late?
   c. What is the probability that the flight will be more than 10 minutes late?
   d. What is the expected flight time?

4. Most computer languages have a function that can be used to generate random numbers. In Excel, the RAND function can be used to generate random numbers between 0 and 1. If we let x denote a random number generated using RAND, then x is a continuous random variable with the following probability density function.

$$f(x) = \begin{cases} 1 & \text{for } 0 \le x \le 1 \\ 0 & \text{elsewhere} \end{cases}$$

   a. Graph the probability density function.
   b. What is the probability of generating a random number between .25 and .75?

    c. What is the probability of generating a random number with a value less than or equal to .30?

    d. What is the probability of generating a random number with a value greater than .60?

5. The driving distance for the top 60 women golfers on the LPGA tour is between 238.9 and 261.2 yards (*Golfweek*, December 6, 1997). Assume that the driving distance for these women is uniformly distributed over this interval.

    a. Give a mathematical expression for the probability density function of driving distance.

    b. What is the probability the driving distance for one of these women is less than 250 yards?

    c. What is the probability the driving distance for one of these women is at least 255 yards?

    d. What is the probability the driving distance for one of these women is between 245 and 260 yards?

    e. How many of these women drive the ball at least 250 yards?

6. The label on a bottle of liquid detergent shows contents to be 12 ounces per bottle. The production operation fills the bottle uniformly according to the following probability density function.

$$f(x) = \begin{cases} 8 & \text{for } 11.975 \le x \le 12.100 \\ 0 & \text{elsewhere} \end{cases}$$

    a. What is the probability that a bottle will be filled with between 12 and 12.05 ounces?

    b. What is the probability that a bottle will be filled with 12.02 or more ounces?

    c. Quality control accepts a bottle that is filled to within .02 ounces of the number of ounces shown on the container label. What is the probability that a bottle of this liquid detergent will fail to meet the quality control standard?

7. Suppose we are interested in bidding on a piece of land and we know there is one other bidder.* The seller announces that the highest bid in excess of $10,000 will be accepted. Assume that the competitor's bid x is a random variable that is uniformly distributed between $10,000 and $15,000.

    a. Suppose you bid $12,000. What is the probability that your bid will be accepted?

    b. Suppose you bid $14,000. What is the probability that your bid will be accepted?

    c. What amount should you bid to maximize the probability that you get the property?

    d. Suppose you know someone who is willing to pay you $16,000 for the property. Would you consider bidding less than the amount in part (c)? Why or why not?

6.2   NORMAL PROBABILITY DISTRIBUTION

The most important probability distribution for describing a continuous random variable is the **normal probability distribution**. The normal probability distribution has been used in a wide variety of practical applications in which the random variables are heights and weights of people, test scores, scientific measurements, amounts of rainfall, and so on. It is also widely used in statistical inference, which is the major topic of the remainder of this book. In such applications, the normal probability distribution provides a description of the likely results obtained through sampling.

---

*This exercise is based on a problem suggested to us by Professor Roger Myerson of Northwestern University.

FIGURE 6.3   BELL-SHAPED CURVE FOR THE NORMAL PROBABILITY
DISTRIBUTION

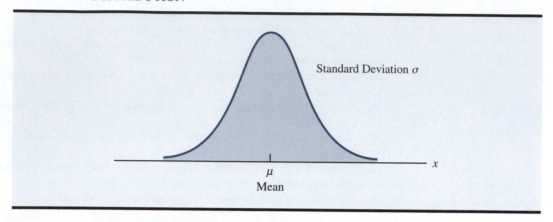

Normal Curve

Abraham de Moivre, a French mathematician, published The Doctrine of Chances *in 1733. He derived the normal probability distribution.*

The form, or shape, of the normal probability distribution is illustrated by the bell-shaped normal curve in Figure 6.3. The probability density function that defines the normal curve of the normal probability distribution follows.

Normal Probability Density Function

$$f(x) = \frac{1}{\sigma\sqrt{2\pi}}\, e^{-(x-\mu)^2/2\sigma^2} \qquad (6.2)$$

where

μ = mean
σ = standard deviation
π = 3.14159
e = 2.71828

We make several observations about the characteristics of the normal probability distribution.

The normal probability distribution has two parameters, μ and σ. They determine the location and shape of the normal curve.

1. There is an entire family of normal probability distributions; each is uniquely identified by its mean μ and its standard deviation σ.
2. The highest point on the normal curve is at the mean, which is also the median and mode of the distribution.
3. The mean of the distribution can be any numerical value: negative, zero, or positive. Three normal distributions with the same standard deviation but three different means (-10, 0, and 20) are shown here.

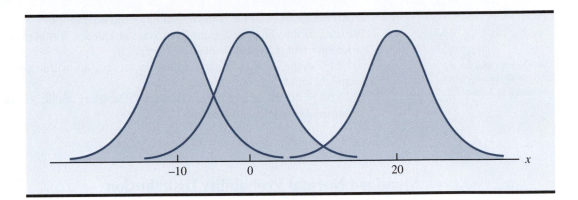

4. The normal probability distribution is symmetric, with the shape of the normal curve to the left of the mean a mirror image of the shape of the normal curve to the right of the mean. The tails of the normal curve extend to infinity in both directions and theoretically never touch the horizontal axis.

5. The standard deviation determines how flat and wide the normal curve is. Larger values of the standard deviation result in wider, flatter curves, showing more variability in the data. Two normal distributions with the same mean but with different standard deviations are shown here.

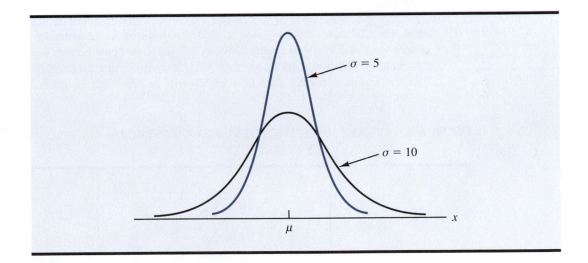

6. Probabilities for the normal random variable are given by areas under the normal curve. The total area under the curve for the normal probability distribution is 1, which is true for all continuous probability distributions. Because the normal probability distribution is symmetric, the total area under the normal curve to the left of the mean is .50 and the total area under the normal curve to the right of the mean is .50.

7. The percentage of values in some commonly used intervals are:
   a. 68.26% of the values of a normal random variable are within plus or minus one standard deviation of its mean.
   b. 95.44% of the values of a normal random variable are within plus or minus two standard deviations of its mean.
   c. 99.72% of the values of a normal random variable are within plus or minus three standard deviations of its mean.

These percentages are the basis for the empirical rule introduced in Section 3.3.

Figure 6.4 shows properties (a), (b), and (c) graphically.

Standard Normal Probability Distribution

A random variable that has a normal probability distribution with a mean of zero and a standard deviation of one is said to have a **standard normal probability distribution**. The letter z is commonly used to designate this particular normal random variable. Figure 6.5 is the graph of the standard normal probability density function. It has the same general appearance as other normal distributions, but with the special properties of $\mu = 0$ and $\sigma = 1$.

For the uniform distribution, the height of the probability density function is constant, so it is easy to compute the area under the curve. For the normal probability density function, the height of the curve varies and calculus is required to compute the areas that represent probability.

As with other continuous random variables, probability calculations with any normal probability distribution are made by computing areas under the graph of the probability density function. Thus, to find the probability that a normal random variable is within any specific interval, we must compute the area under the normal curve over that interval. For the standard normal probability distribution, areas under the normal curve have been computed and are available in tables that can be used in computing probabilities. Table 6.1 is such a table; it is also available as Table 1 of Appendix B and inside the front cover of this text.

Given a z value, we use the standard normal table to find the appropriate probability (an area under the curve).

To see how the table of areas under the curve for the standard normal probability distribution (Table 6.1) can be used to find probabilities, let us consider some examples. Later, we will see how this same table can be used to compute probabilities for any normal distribution. To begin, let us see how we can compute the probability that the z value for the standard normal random variable will be less than or equal to 1.00; that is,

FIGURE 6.4   AREAS UNDER THE CURVE FOR ANY NORMAL PROBABILITY DISTRIBUTION

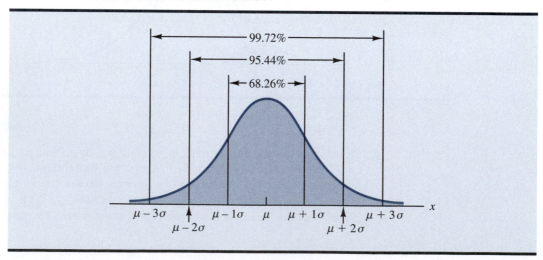

FIGURE 6.5   THE STANDARD NORMAL PROBABILITY DISTRIBUTION

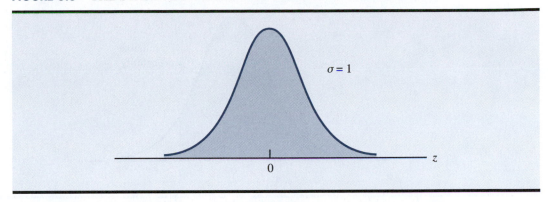

$P(z \leq 1.00)$. This is a cumulative probability; it is represented by the darkly shaded region in the following graph.

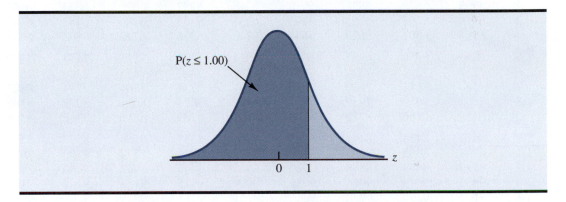

The probabilities in Table 6.1 are also cumulative probabilities so we just find the entry in the table corresponding to $z = 1.00$. First we find 1.0 in the left column of the table and then find .00 in the top row of the table. By looking in the body of the table, we find that the 1.0 row and the .00 column intersect at the value of .8413. Thus, $P(z \leq 1.00) = .8413$. A portion of Table 6.1 showing these steps follows.

z	.00	.01	.02
.			
.			
.			
.9	.8159	.8186	.8212
1.0	.8413	.8438	.8461
1.1	.8643	.8665	.8686
1.2	.8849	.8869	.8888
.			
.			
.			

$P(z \leq 1.00)$

TABLE 6.1   CUMULATIVE PROBABILITIES FOR THE STANDARD NORMAL DISTRIBUTION

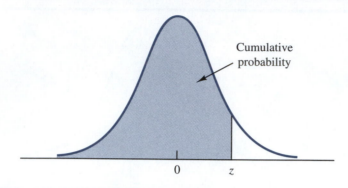

z	.00	.01	.02	.03	.04	.05	.06	.07	.08	.09
.0	.5000	.5040	.5080	.5120	.5160	.5199	.5239	.5279	.5319	.5359
.1	.5398	.5438	.5478	.5517	.5557	.5596	.5636	.5675	.5714	.5753
.2	.5793	.5832	.5871	.5910	.5948	.5987	.6026	.6064	.6103	.6141
.3	.6179	.6217	.6255	.6293	.6331	.6368	.6406	.6443	.6480	.6517
.4	.6554	.6591	.6628	.6664	.6700	.6736	.6772	.6808	.6844	.6879
.5	.6915	.6950	.6985	.7019	.7054	.7088	.7123	.7157	.7190	.7224
.6	.7257	.7291	.7324	.7357	.7389	.7422	.7454	.7486	.7517	.7549
.7	.7580	.7611	.7642	.7673	.7704	.7734	.7764	.7794	.7823	.7852
.8	.7881	.7910	.7939	.7967	.7995	.8023	.8051	.8078	.8106	.8133
.9	.8159	.8186	.8212	.8238	.8264	.8289	.8315	.8340	.8365	.8389
1.0	.8413	.8438	.8461	.8485	.8508	.8531	.8554	.8577	.8599	.8621
1.1	.8643	.8665	.8686	.8708	.8729	.8749	.8770	.8790	.8810	.8830
1.2	.8849	.8869	.8888	.8907	.8925	.8944	.8962	.8980	.8997	.9015
1.3	.9032	.9049	.9066	.9082	.9099	.9115	.9131	.9147	.9162	.9177
1.4	.9192	.9207	.9222	.9236	.9251	.9265	.9279	.9292	.9306	.9319
1.5	.9332	.9345	.9357	.9370	.9382	.9394	.9406	.9418	.9429	.9441
1.6	.9452	.9463	.9474	.9484	.9495	.9505	.9515	.9525	.9535	.9545
1.7	.9554	.9564	.9573	.9582	.9591	.9599	.9608	.9616	.9625	.9633
1.8	.9641	.9649	.9656	.9664	.9671	.9678	.9686	.9693	.9699	.9706
1.9	.9713	.9719	.9726	.9732	.9738	.9744	.9750	.9756	.9761	.9767
2.0	.9772	.9778	.9783	.9788	.9793	.9798	.9803	.9808	.9812	.9817
2.1	.9821	.9826	.9830	.9834	.9838	.9842	.9846	.9850	.9854	.9857
2.2	.9861	.9864	.9868	.9871	.9875	.9878	.9881	.9884	.9887	.9890
2.3	.9893	.9896	.9898	.9901	.9904	.9906	.9909	.9911	.9913	.9913
2.4	.9918	.9920	.9922	.9925	.9927	.9929	.9931	.9932	.9934	.9936
2.5	.9938	.9940	.9941	.9943	.9945	.9946	.9948	.9949	.9951	.9952
2.6	.9953	.9955	.9956	.9957	.9959	.9960	.9961	.9962	.9963	.9964
2.7	.9965	.9966	.9967	.9968	.9969	.9970	.9971	.9972	.9973	.9974
2.8	.9974	.9975	.9976	.9977	.9977	.9978	.9979	.9979	.9980	.9981
2.9	.9981	.9982	.9982	.9983	.9984	.9984	.9985	.9985	.9986	.9986
3.0	.9987	.9987	.9987	.9988	.9988	.9989	.9989	.9989	.9990	.9990

Now suppose we want to compute the probability that the standard normal random variable will be between .00 and 1.00; that is, $P(.00 \leq z \leq 1.00)$. The darkly shaded region in the following graph shows this area, or probability.

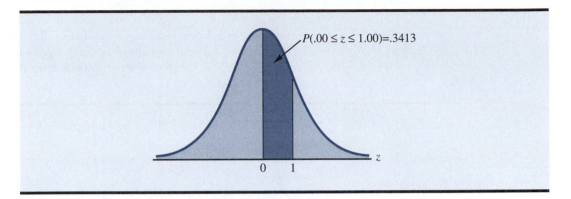

We just found $P(z \leq 1.00) = .8413$. To find $P(.00 \leq z \leq 1.00)$, we must now subtract the area under the curve to the left of $z = .00$. This area is .50. Thus, $P(.00 \leq z \leq 1.00) = P(z \leq 1.00) - P(z \leq .00) = .8413 - .5000 = .3413$.

Using the same approach, we can find $P(.00 \leq z \leq 1.25)$. By first locating the 1.2 row and then moving across to the .05 column, we find $P(z \leq 1.25) = .8944$. Subtracting the area under the curve to the left of the mean, we obtain $P(0.00 \leq z \leq 1.25) = P(z \leq 1.25) - P(z \leq 0.00) = .8944 - .5000 = .3944$.

As another example of the use of the table of cumulative probabilities for the standard normal distribution, we compute the probability of obtaining a z value between $z = -1.00$ and $z = 1.00$; that is, $P(-1.00 \leq z \leq 1.00)$. We have already shown that the probability of a z value between $z = .00$ and $z = 1.00$ is .3413. Now recall that the normal probability distribution is symmetric. Thus, the probability of a z value between $z = .00$ and $z = -1.00$ is the same as the probability of a z value between $z = .00$ and $z = +1.00$. Hence, the probability of a z value between $z = -1.00$ and $z = +1.00$ is

$$P(-1.00 \leq z \leq .00) + P(.00 \leq z \leq 1.00) = .3413 + .3413 = .6826$$

This area is shown graphically in the following figure.

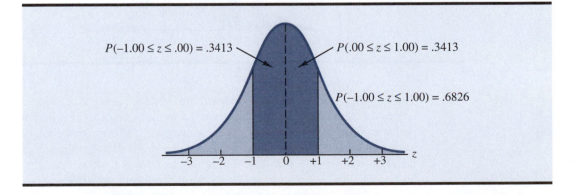

In a similar manner, we can use the values in Table 6.1 to show that the probability of a z value between -2.00 and $+2.00$ is $.4772 + .4772 = .9544$ and that the probability of a

z value between -3.00 and $+3.00$ is $.4986 + .4986 = .9972$. Because we know that the total probability or total area under the curve for any continuous random variable must be 1.0000, the probability $.9972$ tells us that the value of z will almost always be between -3.00 and $+3.00$.

Next, we compute the probability of obtaining a z value of at least 1.58; that is, $P(z \geq 1.58)$. First, we use the $z = 1.5$ row and the $.08$ column of Table 6.1 to find that $P(z < 1.58) = .9429$. Now, because the total area under the curve equals 1, $P(z \geq 1.58) = 1 - P(z < 1.58) = 1 - .9429 = .0571$. This probability is shown in the following figure.

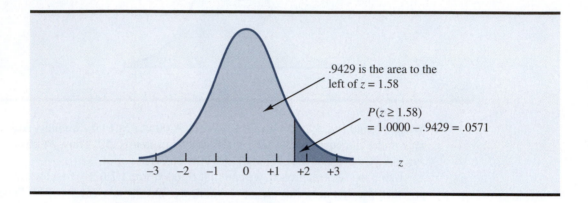

As another illustration, let us compute the probability that the random variable z assumes a value of at most $-.50$; that is, $P(z \leq -.50)$. We are interested in the area under the normal curve to the left of $z = -.50$. The following graph shows this area.

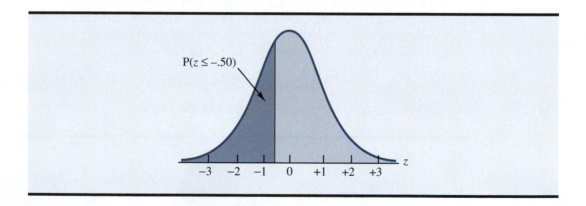

The cumulative probabilities in Table 6.1 are only for nonnegative values of z. So we must take advantage of the symmetric nature of the normal probability distribution to compute this probability. Because of the symmetry, the area under the curve to the left of $z = -.50$ is the same as the area under the curve to the right of $z = .50$. That is, $P(z \leq -.50) = P(z \geq .50)$. But, $P(z \geq .50) = 1 - P(z < .50)$. Referring to Table 6.1, we see that $P(z < .50) = .6915$. So we have $P(z \leq -.50) = 1 - P(z < .50) = 1 - .6915 = .3085$.

As a final illustration, let us find a z value such that the probability of obtaining a larger z value is $.10$. The following figure shows this situation graphically.

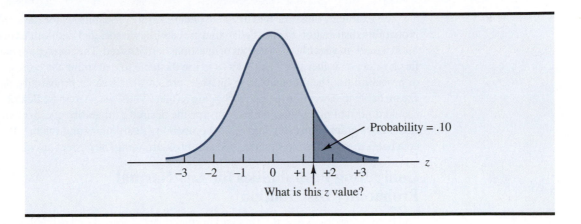

What is this z value?

Given a probability, we can use the standard normal table in an inverse fashion to find the corresponding z value.

This problem is the inverse of those in the preceding examples. Previously, we specified the z value of interest and then found the corresponding probability, or area. In this example, we are given the probability, or area, and asked to find the corresponding z value. To do so, we use the table of areas for the standard normal probability distribution (Table 6.1) somewhat differently.

Recall that the body of Table 6.1 gives the area under the curve to the left of a particular z value. We have been given the information that the area in the upper tail of the curve is .10. Hence, the area under the curve to the left of the unknown z value must equal .9000. Scanning the body of the table, we find .8997 is the cumulative probability value closest to .9000. The section of the table providing this result follows.

z	.06	.07	.08	.09
.				
.				
.				
1.0	.8554	.8577	.8599	.8621
1.1	.8770	.8790	.8810	.8830
1.2	.8962	.8980	.8997	.9015
1.3	.9131	.9147	.9162	.9177
1.4	.9279	.9292	.9306	.9319
.				
.				

Cumulative probability value closest to .9000

Reading the z value from the left-most column and the top row of the table, we find that the corresponding z value is 1.28. Thus, an area of approximately .9000 (actually .8997) will be to the left of $z = 1.28$.* In terms of the question originally asked, there is an approximately .10 probability of a z value larger than 1.28.

_____

*We could use interpolation in the body of the table to get a better approximation of the z value that corresponds to an area of .9000. Doing so to provide one more decimal place of accuracy would yield a z value of 1.282. However, in most practical situations, sufficient accuracy is obtained by simply using the table value closest to the desired probability.

The examples illustrate that the table of cumulative probabilities for the standard normal probability distribution can be used to find probabilities associated with values of the standard normal random variable z. Two types of questions can be asked. The first type of question specifies a value, or values, for z and asks us to use the table to determine the corresponding areas or probabilities. The second type of question provides an area, or probability, and asks us to use the table to determine the corresponding z value. Thus, we need to be flexible in using the standard normal probability table to answer the desired probability question. In most cases, sketching a graph of the standard normal probability distribution and shading the appropriate area helps to visualize the situation and aids in determining the correct answer.

Computing Probabilities for Any Normal Probability Distribution

The reason for discussing the standard normal distribution so extensively is that probabilities for all normal distributions are computed by using the standard normal distribution. That is, when we have a normal distribution with any mean μ and any standard deviation σ, we answer probability questions about the distribution by first converting to the standard normal distribution. Then we can use Table 6.1 and the appropriate z values to find the desired probabilities. The formula used to convert any normal random variable x with mean μ and standard deviation σ to the standard normal random variable z follows.

The formula for the standard normal random variable is similar to the formula we introduced in Chapter 3 for computing z-scores for a data set.

Converting to the Standard Normal Distribution

$$z = \frac{x - \mu}{\sigma} \tag{6.3}$$

A value of x equal to its mean μ results in $z = (\mu - \mu)/\sigma = 0$. Thus, we see that a value of x equal to its mean μ corresponds to a value of z at its mean 0. Now suppose that x is one standard deviation above its mean; that is, $x = \mu + \sigma$. Applying equation (6.3), we see that the corresponding z value is $z = [(\mu + \sigma) - \mu]/\sigma = \sigma/\sigma = 1$. Thus, an x value that is one standard deviation above its mean corresponds to $z = 1$. In other words, we can interpret z as the number of standard deviations that the normal random variable x is from its mean μ.

To see how this conversion enables us to compute probabilities for any normal distribution, suppose we have a normal distribution with $\mu = 10$ and $\sigma = 2$. What is the probability that the random variable x is between 10 and 14? Using equation (6.3) we see that at $x = 10$, $z = (x - \mu)/\sigma = (10 - 10)/2 = 0$ and that at $x = 14$, $z = (14 - 10)/2 = 4/2 = 2$. Thus, the answer to our question about the probability of x being between 10 and 14 is given by the equivalent probability that z is between 0 and 2 for the standard normal distribution. In other words, the probability that we are seeking is the probability that the random variable x is between its mean and two standard deviations above the mean. Using $z = 2.00$ and Table 6.1, we see that $P(z \leq 2) = .9772$. And with $P(z \leq 0) = .5000$, we can compute $P(.00 \leq z \leq 2.00) = P(z \leq 2) - P(z \leq 0) = .9772 - .5000 = .4772$. Hence the probability that x is between 10 and 14 is .4772.

Grear Tire Company Problem

We turn now to an application of the normal probability distribution. Suppose the Grear Tire Company developed a new steel-belted radial tire to be sold through a national chain of discount stores. Because the tire is a new product, Grear's managers believe that the mileage guarantee offered with the tire will be an important factor in the acceptance of the product. Before finalizing the tire mileage guarantee policy, Grear's managers want probability information about x = number of miles the tires will last.

From actual road tests with the tires, Grear's engineering group estimated that the mean tire mileage is μ = 36,500 miles and that the standard deviation is σ = 5000. In addition, the data collected indicate that a normal distribution is a reasonable assumption. What percentage of the tires can be expected to last more than 40,000 miles? In other words, what is the probability that the tire mileage, x, will exceed 40,000? This question can be answered by finding the area of the darkly shaded region in Figure 6.6.

At x = 40,000, we have

$$z = \frac{x - \mu}{\sigma} = \frac{40,000 - 36,500}{5000} = \frac{3500}{5000} = .70$$

Refer now to the bottom of Figure 6.6. We see that a value of x = 40,000 on the Grear Tire normal distribution corresponds to a value of z = .70 on the standard normal distribution. Using Table 6.1, we see that the area under the standard normal curve to the left of z = .70 is .7580. Thus, $1.000 - .7580 = .2420$ is the probability that z will exceed .70 and hence x will exceed 40,000. We can conclude that about 24.2% of the tires will exceed 40,000 in mileage.

Let us now assume that Grear is considering a guarantee that will provide a discount on replacement tires if the original tires do not provide the guaranteed mileage. What should the guarantee mileage be if Grear wants no more than 10% of the tires to be eligible for the discount guarantee? This question is interpreted graphically in Figure 6.7.

According to Figure 6.7, the area under the curve to the left of the unknown guarantee mileage must be .10. So, we must first find the z-value that cuts off an area of .10 in the left tail of a standard normal distribution. Table 6.1 does not provide negative z-values, so we must take advantage of the symmetry of the normal curve and look for the z-value that cuts off an area of .10 in the upper tail. The negative of that z-value will cut off an area of .10 in the lower tail. The z-value that cuts off an area of .10 in the upper tail is the same as the

FIGURE 6.6   GREAR TIRE COMPANY MILEAGE DISTRIBUTION

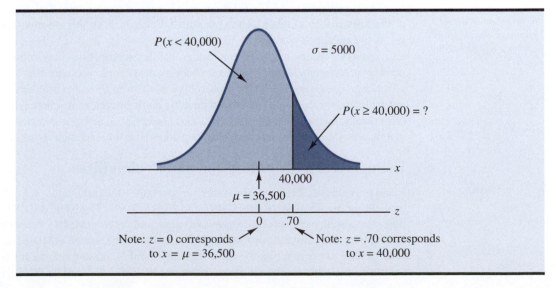

FIGURE 6.7   GREAR'S DISCOUNT GUARANTEE

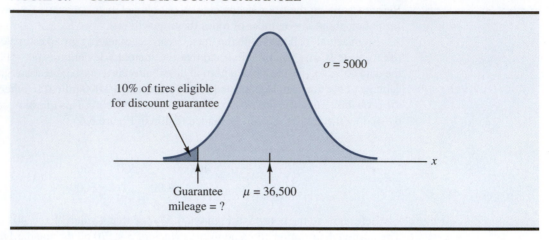

z-value that provides a cumulative probability of .90. Looking to Table 6.1 we see that a z-value of approximately 1.28 provides a cumulative probability of .90. Therefore, $z = -1.28$ cuts off an area of .10 in the lower tail. Hence, $z = -1.28$ is the value of the standard normal random variable corresponding to the desired mileage guarantee on the Grear Tire normal distribution. To find the value of x corresponding to $z = -1.28$, we have

The guarantee mileage we need to find is 1.28 standard deviations below the mean. Thus, $x = \mu - 1.28\sigma$.

$$z = \frac{x - \mu}{\sigma} = -1.28$$

$$x - \mu = -1.28\sigma$$

$$x = \mu - 1.28\sigma$$

With $\mu = 36,500$ and $\sigma = 5000$,

$$x = 36,500 - 1.28(5000) = 30,100$$

With the guarantee set at 30,000 miles, the actual percentage eligible for the guarantee will be 9.68%.

Thus, a guarantee of 30,100 miles will meet the requirement that approximately 10% of the tires will be eligible for the guarantee. Perhaps, with this information, the firm will set its tire mileage guarantee at 30,000 miles.

Again, we see the important role that probability distributions play in providing decision-making information. Namely, once a probability distribution is established for a particular application, it can be used to obtain probability information about the problem. Probability does not make a decision recommendation directly, but it provides information that helps the decision maker better understand the risks and uncertainties associated with the problem. Ultimately, this information may assist the decision maker in reaching a good decision.

Using Excel to Compute Normal Probabilities

Excel provides two functions for computing probabilities and z values for a standard normal probability distribution: NORMSDIST and NORMSINV. The NORMSDIST function computes the cumulative probability given a z value, and the NORMSINV function computes the z value given a cumulative probability. Two similar functions, NORMDIST and NORMINV, are available for computing the cumulative probability and the x value for any normal distribution. We begin by showing how to use the NORMSDIST and NORMSINV functions.

The letter S that appears in the name of the NORMSDIST and NORMSINV functions reminds us that these functions relate to the standard normal probability distribution.

The NORMSDIST function provides the area under the standard normal curve to the left of a given z value. For nonnegative z values, the NORMSDIST function provides the same cumulative probability we would obtain if we used Table 6.1. Using the NORMSDIST function is just like having the computer look up cumulative normal probabilities for you. But, unlike Table 6.1, the NORMSDIST function provides cumulative probabilities for negative z values as well. The NORMSINV function is the inverse of the NORMSDIST function; it takes a cumulative probability as input and provides the z value corresponding to that cumulative probability.

Let's see how both of these functions work by computing the probabilities and z values obtained earlier in this section using Table 6.1. Refer to Figure 6.8 as we describe the tasks involved. The formula worksheet is in the background; the value worksheet is in the foreground.

Enter Data: No data are entered in the worksheet. We will simply enter the appropriate z values and probabilities directly into the formulas as needed.

Enter Functions and Formulas: The NORMSDIST function has one argument: the z value for which we want to obtain the cumulative probability. To illustrate the use of the NORMSDIST function we compute the six probabilities shown in cells D3:D8 of Figure 6.8.

To compute the cumulative probability to the left of a given z value (area in lower tail), we simply evaluate NORMSDIST at the z value. For instance, to compute $P(z \leq 1)$ we entered the formula =NORMSDIST(1) into cell D3. The result, .8413, is the same as obtained using Table 6.1. The cumulative probability in cell D8, $P(z \leq -.50)$, is computed in a similar fashion.

The probability in cell D6, 0.6827, differs from what we computed earlier (.6826) due to rounding.

To compute the probability of z being in an interval we compute the value of NORMSDIST at the upper endpoint of the interval and subtract the value of NORMSDIST at the lower endpoint of the interval. For instance, to find $P(.00 \leq z \leq 1.00)$, we enter the formula =NORMSDIST(1)-NORMSDIST(0) into cell D4. The interval probabilities in cells D5 and D6 are computed in a similar fashion.

To compute the probability to the right of a given z value (upper tail area), we must subtract the cumulative probability represented by the area under the curve below the

FIGURE 6.8   EXCEL WORKSHEET FOR COMPUTING PROBABILITIES AND z VALUES FOR THE STANDARD NORMAL DISTRIBUTION

	A	B	C	D	E
1			Probabilities: Standard Normal Distribution		
2					
3			$P (z <= 1)$	=NORMSDIST(1)	
4			$P (0.00 <= z <= 1.00)$	=NORMSDIST(1)-NORMSDIST(0)	
5			$P (0.00 <= z <= 1.25)$	=NORMSDIST(1.25)-NORMSDIST(0)	
6			$P (-1.00 <= z <= 1.00)$	=NORMSDIST(1)-NORMSDIST(-1)	
7			$P (z >= 1.58)$	=1-NORMSDIST(1.58)	
8			$P (z <= -.50)$	=NORMSDIST(-0.5)	
9					
10			Finding z Values Given Probabilities		
11					
12			z value with .10 in upper tail	=NORMSINV(0.9)	
13			z value with .025 in upper tail	=NORMSINV(0.975)	
14			z value with .025 in lower tail	=NORMSINV(0.025)	
15					

	A	B	C	D	E
1	Probabilities: Standard Normal Distribution				
2					
3			$P (z <= 1)$	0.8413	
4			$P (0.00 <= z <= 1.00)$	0.3413	
5			$P (0.00 <= z <= 1.25)$	0.3944	
6			$P (-1.00 <= z <= 1.00)$	0.6827	
7			$P (z >= 1.58)$	0.0571	
8			$P (z <= -.50)$	0.3085	
9					
10		Finding z Values Given Probabilities			
11					
12			z value with .10 in upper tail	1.28	
13			z value with .025 in upper tail	1.96	
14			z value with .025 in lower tail	-1.96	
15					

z value (lower tail area) from 1. For example, to compute $P(z \geq 1.58)$ we entered the formula =1-NORMSDIST(1.58) into Cell D7.

To compute the z value for a given cumulative probability (lower tail area), we use the NORMSINV function. To find the z value corresponding to an upper tail probability of .10, we enter the formula =NORMSINV(0.9) into cell D12. Actually, NORMSINV(0.9) gives us the z value providing a cumulative probability (lower tail area) of .9. But, that is also the z value associated with an upper tail area of .10.

Two other z values are computed in Figure 6.8. These z values will be used extensively in succeeding chapters. To compute the z value corresponding to an upper tail probability of .025, we entered the formula =NORMSINV(0.975) into cell D13. To compute the z value corresponding to a lower tail probability of .025, we entered the formula =NORMSINV(0.025) into cell D14. We see that $z = 1.96$ corresponds to an upper tail probability of .025 and $z = -1.96$ corresponds to a lower tail probability of .025.

Let us now turn to the Excel functions for computing cumulative probabilities and x values for any normal distribution. The NORMDIST function provides the area under the normal curve to the left of a given value of the random variable x. It provides cumulative probabilities. The NORMINV function is the inverse of the NORMDIST function; it takes a cumulative probability as input and provides the value of x corresponding to that cumulative probability. The NORMDIST and NORMINV functions do the same thing for any normal distribution that the NORMSDIST and NORMSINV functions do for the standard normal distribution.

Let's see how both of these functions work by computing probabilities and x values for the Grear Tire Company example introduced earlier in this section. Recall that the lifetime of a Grear tire has a mean of 36,500 miles and a standard deviation of 5000 miles. Refer to Figure 6.9 as we describe the tasks involved. The formula worksheet is in the background; the value worksheet is in the foreground.

FIGURE 6.9 EXCEL WORKSHEET FOR COMPUTING PROBABILITIES AND x VALUES FOR THE NORMAL DISTRIBUTION

	A	B	C	D	E	F
1				**Probabilities: Normal Distribution**		
2						
3			**P (x <= 20000)**	=NORMDIST(20000,36500,5000,TRUE)		
4			**P (20000 <= x <= 40000)**	=NORMDIST(40000,36500,5000,TRUE)-NORMDIST(20000,36500,5000,TRUE)		
5			**P (x >= 40000)**	=1-NORMDIST(40000,36500,5000,TRUE)		
6						
7				**Finding x values Given Probabilities**		
8						
9			**x value with .10 in lower tail**	=NORMINV(0.1,36500,5000)		
10			**x value with .025 in upper tail**	=NORMINV(0.975,36500,5000)		
11						

	A	B	C	D	E
1	**Probabilities: Normal Distribution**				
2					
3			**P (x <= 20000)**	0.0005	
4			**P (20000 <= x <= 40000)**	0.7576	
5			**P (x >= 40000)**	0.2420	
6					
7	**Finding x values Given Probabilities**				
8					
9			**x value with .10 in lower tail**	30092.25	
10			**x value with .025 in upper tail**	46299.81	
11					

Enter Data: No data are entered in the worksheet. We simply enter the appropriate x values and probabilities directly into the formulas as needed.

Enter Functions and Formulas: The NORMDIST function has four arguments: (1) the x value we want to compute the cumulative probability for, (2) the mean, (3) the standard deviation, and (4) a value of TRUE or FALSE. For the fourth argument, we enter TRUE if a cumulative probability is desired, and we enter FALSE if the height of the curve is desired. Because we will always be using NORMDIST to compute cumulative probabilities, we will always choose TRUE for the fourth argument.

To compute the cumulative probability to the left of a given x value (lower tail area), we simply evaluate NORMDIST at the x value. For instance, to compute the probability that a Grear tire will not last more than 20,000 miles we entered the formula =NORMDIST(20000,36500,5000, TRUE) into cell D3. The value worksheet shows that this cumulative probability is .0005. So, we can conclude that almost all Grear tires will last at least 20,000 miles.

To compute the probability of x being in an interval we compute the value of NORMDIST at the upper endpoint of the interval and subtract the value of NORMDIST at the lower endpoint of the interval. The formula in cell D4 provides the probability that a tire's lifetime is between 20,000 and 40,000 miles, $P(20{,}000 \leq x \leq 40{,}000)$. In the value worksheet, we see that this probability is .7576.

To compute the probability to the right of a given x value (upper tail area), we must subtract the cumulative probability represented by the area under the curve below the x value (lower tail area) from 1. The formula in cell D5 computes the probability that a Grear tire will last for at least 40,000 miles. We see that this probability is .2420.

To compute the x value for a given cumulative probability, we use the NORMINV function. The NORMINV function has only three arguments. The first argument is the cumulative probability; the second and third arguments are the mean and standard deviation. For instance, to compute the tire mileage corresponding to a lower tail area of .1 for Grear Tire, we enter the formula =NORMINV(0.1,36500,5000) into cell D9. From the value worksheet, we see that 10% of the Grear tires will not last more than 30,092.25 miles.

To compute the minimum tire mileage for the top 2.5% of Grear tires, we want to find the value of x corresponding to an area of .025 in the upper tail. This calculation is the same as finding the x value that provides a cumulative probability of .975. Thus we entered the formula =NORMINV(0.975,36500,5000) into cell D10 to compute this tire mileage. From the value worksheet, we see that 2.5% of the Grear tires will last at least 46,299.81 miles.

EXERCISES

Methods

8. Using Figure 6.4 as a guide, sketch a normal curve for a random variable x that has a mean of $\mu = 100$ and a standard deviation of $\sigma = 10$. Label the horizontal axis with values of 70, 80, 90, 100, 110, 120, and 130.

9. A random variable is normally distributed with a mean of $\mu = 50$ and a standard deviation of $\sigma = 5$.
    a. Sketch a normal curve for the probability density function. Label the horizontal axis with values of 35, 40, 45, 50, 55, 60, and 65. Figure 6.4 shows that the normal curve almost touches the horizontal axis at three standard deviations below and at three standard deviations above the mean (in this case at 35 and 65).
    b. What is the probability the random variable will assume a value between 45 and 55?
    c. What is the probability the random variable will assume a value between 40 and 60?

10. Draw a graph for the standard normal distribution. Label the horizontal axis at values of $-3, -2, -1, 0, 1, 2,$ and 3. Then use the table of probabilities for the standard normal distribution to compute the following probabilities.
    a. $P(z \leq 1.5)$
    b. $P(z \leq 1)$
    c. $P(1 \leq z \leq 1.5)$
    d. $P(0 < z < 2.5)$

11. Given that z is a standard normal random variable, compute the following probabilities.
    a. $P(z \geq -1)$
    b. $P(z \leq -1.0)$
    c. $P(z \geq -1.5)$
    d. $P(-2.5 \leq z)$
    e. $P(-3 < z \leq 0)$

12. Given that z is a standard normal random variable, compute the following probabilities.
    a. $P(0 \leq z \leq .83)$
    b. $P(-1.57 \leq z \leq 0)$
    c. $P(z > .44)$
    d. $P(z \geq -.23)$
    e. $P(z < 1.20)$
    f. $P(z \leq -.71)$

 13. Given that z is a standard normal random variable, compute the following probabilities.
    a. $P(-1.98 \leq z \leq .49)$
    b. $P(.52 \leq z \leq 1.22)$
    c. $P(-1.75 \leq z \leq -1.04)$

14. Given that z is a standard normal random variable, find z for each situation.
    a. The area to the left of z is .9750.
    b. The area between 0 and z is .4750.
    c. The area to the left of z is .7291.
    d. The area to the right of z is .1314.
    e. The area to the left of z is .6700.
    f. The area to the right of z is .3300.

 15. Given that z is a standard normal random variable, find z for each situation.
    a. The area to the left of z is .2119.
    b. The area between $-z$ and z is .9030.
    c. The area between $-z$ and z is .2052.
    d. The area to the left of z is .9948.
    e. The area to the right of z is .6915.

16. Given that z is a standard normal random variable, find z for each situation.
    a. The area to the right of z is .01.
    b. The area to the right of z is .025.
    c. The area to the right of z is .05.
    d. The area to the right of z is .10.

Applications

17. The average amount parents and children spent per child on back-to-school clothes in Autumn 2001 was $527 (CNBC, September 5, 2001). Assume the standard deviation is $160 and that the amount spent is normally distributed.

a. What is the probability that the amount spent is more than $700?
b. What is the probability that the amount spent is less than $100?
c. What is the probability that the amount spent is between $450 and $700?
d. What is the probability that the amount spent is no more than $300?

18. The average time a subscriber spends reading *The Wall Street Journal* is 49 minutes (*The Wall Street Journal* Subscriber Study, 1996). Assume the standard deviation is 16 minutes and that the times are normally distributed.
    a. What is the probability a subscriber will spend at least 1 hour reading the *Journal*?
    b. What is the probability a subscriber will spend no more than 30 minutes reading the *Journal*?
    c. For the 10% who spend the most time reading the *Journal*, how much time do they spend?

19. The average amount of precipitation in Dallas, Texas, during the month of April is 3.5 inches (*The World Almanac*, 2000). Assume that a normal distribution applies and that the standard deviation is .8 inches.
    a. What percentage of the time does the amount of rainfall in April exceed 5 inches?
    b. What percentage of the time is the amount of rainfall in April less than 3 inches?
    c. A month is classified as extremely wet if the amount of rainfall is in the upper 10% for that month. How much precipitation must fall before a month of April is classified as extremely wet?

20. According to a survey, subscribers to *The Wall Street Journal Interactive Edition* spend an average of 27 hours per week using the computer at work (*wsj.com* Subscriber Study, 1999). Assume the normal distribution applies and that the standard deviation is 8 hours.
    a. What is the probability a randomly selected subscriber spends less than 11 hours using the computer at work?
    b. What percentage of the subscribers spends more than 40 hours per week using the computer at work?
    c. A person is classified as a heavy user if he or she is in the upper 20% in terms of hours of usage. How many hours must a subscriber use the computer in order to be classified as a heavy user?

21. A person must score in the upper 2% of the population on an IQ test to qualify for membership in Mensa, the international high-IQ society (*US Airways Attaché*, September 2000). If IQ scores are normally distributed with a mean of 100 and a standard deviation of 15, what score must a person get to qualify for Mensa?

22. According to the Bureau of Labor Statistics, the average weekly pay for a U.S. production worker was $441.84 in 1998 (*The World Almanac*, 2000). Assume that available data indicate that wages are normally distributed with a standard deviation of $90.
    a. What is the probability that a worker earns between $400 and $500?
    b. How much does a production worker have to earn to be in the top 20% of wage earners?
    c. For a randomly selected production worker, what is the probability the worker earns less than $250 per week?

23. The time needed to complete a final examination in a particular college course is normally distributed with a mean of 80 minutes and a standard deviation of 10 minutes. Answer the following questions.
    a. What is the probability of completing the exam in one hour or less?
    b. What is the probability that a student will complete the exam in more than 60 minutes but less than 75 minutes?
    c. Assume that the class has 60 students and that the examination period is 90 minutes in length. How many students do you expect will be unable to complete the exam in the allotted time?

24. The daily trading volumes (millions of shares) for stocks traded on the New York Stock Exchange for 12 days in August and September are shown here (*Barron's*, August 7, 2000, September 4, 2000, and September 11, 2000).

917	983	1,046
944	723	783
813	1,057	766
836	992	973

The probability distribution of trading volume is approximately normal.
  a. Compute the mean and standard deviation for the daily trading volume to use as estimates of the population mean and standard deviation.
  b. What is the probability that on a particular day the trading volume will be less than 800 million shares?
  c. What is the probability that trading volume will exceed 1 billion shares?
  d. If the exchange wants to issue a press release on the top 5% of trading days, what volume will trigger a release?

25. The average ticket price for a Washington Redskins football game was $81.89 for the 2001 season (*USA Today*, September 6, 2001). With the additional costs of parking, food, drinks, and souvenirs, the average cost for a family of four to attend a game was $442.54. Assume the normal distribution applies and that the standard deviation is $65.
  a. What is the probability that a family of four will spend more than $400?
  b. What is the probability that a family of four will spend $300 or less?
  c. What is the probability that a family of four will spend between $400 and $500?

6.3 EXPONENTIAL PROBABILITY DISTRIBUTION

A continuous probability distribution that is useful in describing the time it takes to complete a task is the **exponential probability distribution**. The exponential random variable can be used to describe such things as the time between arrivals at a car wash, the time required to load a truck, the distance between major defects in a highway, and so on. The exponential probability density function is defined by equation (6.4).

Exponential Probability Density Function

$$f(x) = \frac{1}{\mu} e^{-x/\mu} \qquad \text{for } x \geq 0, \mu > 0 \qquad (6.4)$$

where

$$\mu = \text{mean}$$
$$e = 2.71828$$

As an example of the exponential probability distribution, suppose that $x =$ loading time for a truck at the Schips loading dock follows such a distribution. If the mean, or average, time to load a truck is 15 minutes ($\mu = 15$), the appropriate probability density function is

$$f(x) = \frac{1}{15} e^{-x/15}$$

The blue line in Figure 6.10 is the graph of this probability density function.

FIGURE 6.10   EXPONENTIAL PROBABILITY DISTRIBUTION FOR THE SCHIPS
LOADING DOCK EXAMPLE

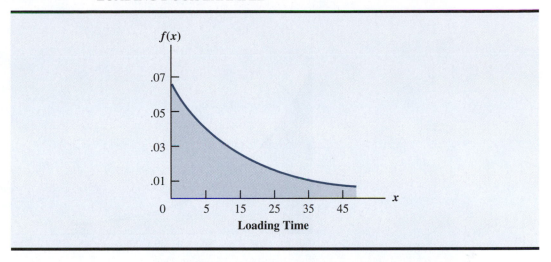

Computing Probabilities for the Exponential Distribution

In waiting line applications, the exponential distribution is often used for service time.

As with any continuous probability distribution, the area under the curve corresponding to an interval provides the probability that the random variable assumes a value in that interval. In the Schips loading dock example, the probability that loading a truck will take 6 minutes or less ($x \leq 6$) is defined to be the area under the curve in Figure 6.10 from $x = 0$ to $x = 6$. Similarly, the probability that loading a truck will take 18 minutes or less ($x \leq 18$) is the area under the curve from $x = 0$ to $x = 18$. Note also that the probability that loading a truck will take between 6 minutes and 18 minutes ($6 \leq x \leq 18$) is given by the area under the curve from $x = 6$ to $x = 18$.

To compute exponential probabilities such as those just described, we use the following formula. It provides the cumulative probability of obtaining a value for the exponential random variable of less than or equal to some specific value of x, denoted by x_0.

Exponential Distribution: Cumulative Probabilities

$$P(x \leq x_0) = 1 - e^{-x_0/\mu} \qquad\qquad (6.5)$$

For the Schips loading dock example, x = loading time and $\mu = 15$. So, we have

$$P(x \leq x_0) = 1 - e^{-x_0/15}$$

Hence, the probability that loading a truck will take 6 minutes or less is

$$P(x \leq 6) = 1 - e^{-6/15} = .3297$$

Figure 6.11 shows the area or probability for a loading time of 6 minutes or less.

FIGURE 6.11   PROBABILITY OF A LOADING TIME OF SIX MINUTES OR LESS

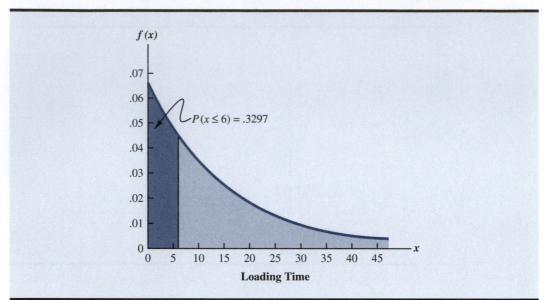

Using equation (6.5), the probability of loading a truck in 18 minutes or less $P(x \leq 18)$ is

$$P(x \leq 18) = 1 - e^{-18/15} = .6988$$

Thus, the probability that loading a truck will take between 6 minutes and 18 minutes is equal to .6988 − .3297 = .3691. Probabilities for any other interval can be computed similarly.

Relationship Between the Poisson and Exponential Distributions

In Section 5.5 we introduced the Poisson distribution as a discrete probability distribution that is often useful in examining the number of occurrences of an event over a specified interval of time or space. Recall that the Poisson probability function is

$$f(x) = \frac{\mu^x e^{-\mu}}{x!}$$

where

$$x = \text{number of occurrences over a specified interval}$$
$$\mu = \text{expected value or mean number of}$$
$$\text{occurrences over a specified interval}$$

The continuous exponential probability distribution is related to the discrete Poisson distribution. If the Poisson distribution provides an appropriate description of the number of occurrences per interval, the exponential distribution provides a description of the length of the interval between occurrences.

If arrivals follow a Poisson distribution, the time between arrivals must follow an exponential distribution.

To illustrate this relationship, suppose the number of cars that arrive at a car wash during one hour is described by a Poisson probability distribution with a mean of 10 cars per hour. The Poisson probability function that gives the probability of x arrivals per hour is

$$f(x) = \frac{10^x e^{-10}}{x!}$$

Because the average number of arrivals is 10 cars per hour, the average time between cars arriving is

$$\frac{1 \text{ hour}}{10 \text{ cars}} = .1 \text{ hour/car}$$

Thus, the corresponding exponential distribution that describes the time between the arrivals has a mean of $\mu = .1$ hour per car; as a result, the appropriate exponential probability density function is

$$f(x) = \frac{1}{.1} e^{-x/.1} = 10e^{-10x}$$

Using Excel to Compute Exponential Probabilities

The EXPONDIST function can be used to compute exponential probabilities. We will illustrate by computing probabilities associated with the time it takes to load a truck at the Schips loading dock. This example was introduced at the beginning of this section. Refer to Figure 6.12 as we describe the tasks involved. The formula worksheet is in the background; the value worksheet is in the foreground.

Enter Data: No data are entered in the worksheet. We simply enter the appropriate values for the exponential random variable into the formulas as needed. The random variable is x = loading time.

Enter Functions and Formulas: The EXPONDIST function has three arguments: the first is the value of x, the second is $1/\mu$, and the third is TRUE or FALSE. We choose TRUE for the third argument if a cumulative probability is desired and FALSE if the height of the probability density function is desired. We will always use TRUE because we will always be computing cumulative probabilities.

FIGURE 6.12   EXCEL WORKSHEET FOR COMPUTING PROBABILITIES FOR THE EXPONENTIAL PROBABILITY DISTRIBUTION

	A	B	C	D	E	F	G
1				Probabilities: Exponential Distribution			
2							
3			$P(x \leq 18)$	=EXPONDIST(18,1/15,TRUE)			
4			$P(6 \leq x \leq 18)$	=EXPONDIST(18,1/15,TRUE)-EXPONDIST(6,1/15,TRUE)			
5			$P(x \geq 8)$	=1-EXPONDIST(8,1/15,TRUE)			
6							

	A	B	C	D	E
1		Probabilities: Exponential Distribution			
2					
3			$P(x \leq 18)$	0.6988	
4			$P(6 \leq x \leq 18)$	0.3691	
5			$P(x \geq 8)$	0.5866	
6					

The first probability we compute is the probability that the loading time is 18 minutes or less. For the Schips problem, $1/\mu = 1/15$, so we enter the formula =EXPONDIST(18,1/15,TRUE) into cell D3 to compute the desired cumulative probability. From the value worksheet, we see that the probability of loading a truck in 18 minutes or less is .6988.

The second probability we compute is the probability that the loading time is between 6 and 18 minutes. To find this probability we first compute the cumulative probability for the upper endpoint of the time interval and subtract the cumulative probability for the lower endpoint of the interval. The formula we have entered into cell D4 calculates this probability. The value worksheet shows that this probability is .3691.

The last probability we calculate is the probability that the loading time is at least 8 minutes. Because the EXPONDIST function only computes cumulative (lower tail) probabilities, we compute this probability by entering the formula =1-EXPONDIST(8,1/15,TRUE) into cell D5. The value worksheet shows that the probability of a loading time of 8 minutes or more is .5866.

EXERCISES

Methods

26. Consider the following exponential probability density function.

$$f(x) = \frac{1}{8} e^{-x/8} \qquad \text{for } x \geq 0$$

    a. Compute $P(x \leq 6)$.
    b. Compute $P(x \leq 4)$.
    c. Compute $P(x \geq 6)$.
    d. Compute $P(4 \leq x \leq 6)$.

27. Consider the following exponential probability density function.

$$f(x) = \frac{1}{3} e^{-x/3} \qquad \text{for } x \geq 0$$

    a. Write the formula for $P(x \leq x_0)$.
    b. Compute $P(x \leq 2)$.
    c. Compute $P(x \geq 3)$.
    d. Compute $P(x \leq 5)$.
    e. Compute $P(2 \leq x \leq 5)$.

Applications

28. *Internet Magazine* monitors Internet service providers (ISPs) and provides statistics on their performance. The average time to download a Web page for free ISPs is approximately 20 seconds for European Web pages (*Internet Magazine*, January 2000). Assume the time to download a Web page follows an exponential distribution.
    a. What is the probability it will take less than 10 seconds to download a Web page?
    b. What is the probability it will take more than 30 seconds to download a Web page?
    c. What is the probability it will take between 10 and 30 seconds to download a Web page?

29. The time between arrivals of vehicles at a particular intersection follows an exponential probability distribution with a mean of 12 seconds.

    a. Sketch this exponential probability distribution.
    b. What is the probability that the time between vehicle arrivals is 12 seconds or less?
    c. What is the probability that the time between vehicle arrivals is 6 seconds or less?
    d. What is the probability of 30 or more seconds between vehicle arrivals?

30. The lifetime (hours) of an electronic device is a random variable with the following exponential probability density function.

$$f(x) = \frac{1}{50} e^{-x/50} \qquad \text{for } x \geq 0$$

    a. What is the mean lifetime of the device?
    b. What is the probability that the device will fail in the first 25 hours of operation?
    c. What is the probability that the device will operate 100 or more hours before failure?

31. Sparagowski & Associates conducted a study of service times at the drive-up window of fast-food restaurants. The average time between placing an order and receiving the order at McDonald's restaurants was 2.78 minutes (*The Cincinnati Enquirer*, July 9, 2000). Waiting times, such as these, frequently follow an exponential distribution.
    a. What is the probability that a customer's service time is less than 2 minutes?
    b. What is the probability that a customer's service time is more than 5 minutes?
    c. What is the probability that a customer's service time is more than 2.78 minutes?

32. According to *Barron's 1998 Primary Reader Survey*, the average annual number of investment transactions for a subscriber is 30 (*www.barronsmag.com*, July 28, 2000). Suppose the number of transactions in a year follows the Poisson probability distribution.
    a. Show the probability distribution for the time between investment transactions.
    b. What is the probability of no transactions during the month of January for a particular subscriber?
    c. What is the probability that the next transaction will occur within the next half-month for a particular subscriber?

SUMMARY

This chapter extended the discussion of probability distributions to the case of continuous random variables. The major conceptual difference between discrete and continuous probability distributions involves the method of computing probabilities. With discrete distributions, the probability function $f(x)$ provides the probability that the random variable x assumes various values. With continuous probability distributions, the probability density function $f(x)$ does not provide probability values directly. Instead, probabilities are given by areas under the curve or graph of the probability density function $f(x)$. Because the area under the curve above a single point is zero, we observe that the probability of any particular value is zero for a continuous random variable.

Three continuous probability distributions—the uniform, normal, and exponential distributions—were treated in detail. The normal probability distribution is used widely in statistical inference and will be used extensively throughout the remainder of the text.

GLOSSARY

Probability density function   A function used to compute probabilities for a continuous random variable. Unlike the probability function for discrete random variables, it does not provide probabilities directly. The area under the graph of a probability density function over an interval represents probability.

Uniform probability distribution   A continuous probability distribution for which the probability that the random variable will assume a value in any interval is the same for all intervals of equal length.

Normal probability distribution   A continuous probability distribution. Its probability density function is bell shaped and determined by its mean μ and standard deviation σ.

Standard normal probability distribution   A normal probability distribution with a mean of zero and a standard deviation of one.

Exponential probability distribution   A continuous probability distribution that is useful in computing probabilities for the time it takes to complete a task.

KEY FORMULAS

Uniform Probability Density Function

$$f(x) = \begin{cases} \dfrac{1}{b-a} & \text{for } a \leq x \leq b \\ 0 & \text{elsewhere} \end{cases} \tag{6.1}$$

Normal Probability Density Function

$$f(x) = \frac{1}{\sigma\sqrt{2\pi}}\, e^{-(x-\mu)^2/2\sigma^2} \tag{6.2}$$

Converting to the Standard Normal Distribution

$$z = \frac{x-\mu}{\sigma} \tag{6.3}$$

Exponential Probability Density Function

$$f(x) = \frac{1}{\mu}\, e^{-x/\mu} \qquad \text{for } x \geq 0,\ \mu > 0 \tag{6.4}$$

Exponential Distribution: Cumulative Probabilities

$$P(x \leq x_0) = 1 - e^{-x_0/\mu} \tag{6.5}$$

SUPPLEMENTARY EXERCISES

33.   A business manager, transferred from Chicago to Atlanta, needs to sell her house in Chicago quickly. The manager's employer offered to buy the house for $210,000, but the offer expires at the end of the week. The manager does not currently have a better offer, but can afford to leave the house on the market for another month. From conversations with her realtor, the manager believes the price she will get by leaving the house on the market for another month is uniformly distributed between $200,000 and $225,000.

    a.   If she leaves the house on the market for another month, what is the mathematical expression for the probability density function of the sales price?

    b.   If she leaves it on the market for another month, what is the probability she will get at least $215,000 for the house?

    c.   If she leaves it on the market for another month, what is the probability she will get less than $210,000?

    d.   Should the manager leave the house on the market for another month? Why or why not?

34.   Sixty-eight percent of the debt owed by American families is home mortgage or equity credit (*Federal Reserve Bulletin*, January 1997). The median amount of mortgage debt for families with the head of the household under 35 years old is $63,000. Assume the amount of mortgage debt for this group is normally distributed and the standard deviation is $15,000.

    a.   What is the mean amount of mortgage debt for this group?

    b.   How much mortgage debt do the 10% with the smallest debt have?

    c. What percent of these families have mortgage debt in excess of $80,000?

    d. The upper 5% of mortgage debt is in excess of what amount?

35. Motorola uses the normal distribution to determine the probability of defects and the number of defects expected in a production process (*APICS—The Performance Advantage*, July 1991). Assume a production process produces units with a mean weight of 10 ounces. Calculate the probability of a defect and the expected number of defects for a 1000-unit production run in the following situations.

    a. The process standard deviation is .15, and the process control is set at plus or minus one standard deviation. Units with weights less than 9.85 or greater than 10.15 ounces will be classified as defects.

    b. Through process design improvements, the process standard deviation can be reduced to .05. Assume the process control remains the same, with weights less than 9.85 or greater than 10.15 ounces being classified as defects.

    c. What is the advantage of reducing process variation, thereby setting process control limits at a greater number of standard deviations from the mean?

36. The average annual amount American households spend on daily transportation is $6312 (*Money*, August 2001). Assume that the amount spent is normally distributed.

    a. Suppose you learn that 5% of American households spend less than $1000 annually on daily transportation. What is the standard deviation of the amount spent?

    b. What is the probability that a household spends between $4000 and $6000?

    c. What is the annual amount spent by the 3% of households with the highest daily transportation cost?

37. The sales of High-Brite Toothpaste are believed to be approximately normally distributed, with a mean of 10,000 tubes per week and a standard deviation of 1500 tubes per week.

    a. What is the probability that more than 12,000 tubes will be sold in any given week?

    b. To have a .95 probability that the company will have sufficient stock to cover the weekly demand, how many tubes should be produced?

38. Ward Doering Auto Sales is considering offering a special service contract that will cover the total cost of any service work required on leased vehicles. From experience, the company manager estimates that yearly service costs are approximately normally distributed, with a mean of $150 and a standard deviation of $25.

    a. If the company offers the service contract to customers for a yearly charge of $200, what is the probability that any one customer's service costs will exceed the contract price of $200?

    b. What is Ward's expected profit per service contract?

39. The Asian currency crisis of late 1997 and early 1998 was expected to lead to substantial job losses in the United States as inexpensive imports flooded markets. California was expected to be especially hard hit. The Economic Policy Institute estimated that the mean number of job losses in California would be 126,681 (*St. Petersburg Times*, January 24, 1998). Assume the number of jobs lost is normally distributed with a standard deviation of 30,000.

    a. What is the probability the number of lost jobs is between 80,000 and 150,000?

    b. What is the probability the number of lost jobs will be less than 50,000?

    c. What cutoff value will provide a .95 probability that the number of lost jobs will not exceed the value?

40. Assume that the test scores from a college admissions test are normally distributed, with a mean of 450 and a standard deviation of 100.

    a. What percentage of the people taking the test score between 400 and 500?

    b. Suppose someone receives a score of 630. What percentage of the people taking the test score better? What percentage score worse?

    c. If a particular university will not admit anyone scoring below 480, what percentage of the persons taking the test would be accepted at the university?

41. According to *Advertising Age*, the average base salary for women working as copywriters in advertising firms is higher than the average base salary for men. The average base salary for women is $67,000, and the average base salary for men is $65,500 (*Working Woman*, July/August 2000). Assume salaries are normally distributed and that the standard deviation is $7000 for both men and women.
    a. What is the probability of a woman receiving a salary in excess of $75,000?
    b. What is the probability of a man receiving a salary in excess of $75,000?
    c. What is the probability of a woman receiving a salary below $50,000?
    d. How much would a woman have to make to have a higher salary than 99% of her male counterparts?

42. A machine fills containers with a particular product. The standard deviation of filling weights is known from past data to be .6 ounce. If only 2% of the containers hold less than 18 ounces, what is the mean filling weight for the machine? That is, what must μ equal? Assume the filling weights have a normal distribution.

43. The time in minutes for which a student uses a computer terminal at the computer center of a major university follows an exponential probability distribution with a mean of 36 minutes. Assume a student arrives at the terminal just as another student is beginning to work on the terminal.
    a. What is the probability that the wait for the second student will be 15 minutes or less?
    b. What is the probability that the wait for the second student will be between 15 and 45 minutes?
    c. What is the probability that the second student will have to wait an hour or more?

44. The Web site for the Bed and Breakfast Inns of North America (*www.bestInns.net*) gets approximately seven visitors per minute (*Time*, September 2001). Suppose the number of Web site visitors per minute follows a Poisson probability distribution.
    a. What is the mean time between visits to the Web site?
    b. Show the exponential probability density function for the time between Web site visits.
    c. What is the probability no one will access the Web site in a 1-minute period?
    d. What is the probability no one will access the Web site in a 12-second period?

45. The average travel time to work for New York City residents is 36.5 minutes (*Time Almanac, 2001*).
    a. Assume the exponential probability distribution applies and show the probability density function for the travel time to work for a typical New Yorker.
    b. What is the probability it will take a typical New Yorker between 20 and 40 minutes to travel to work?
    c. What is the probability it will take a typical New Yorker more than 40 minutes to travel to work?

46. The time (in minutes) between telephone calls at an insurance claims office has the following exponential probability distribution.

$$f(x) = .50e^{-.50x} \qquad \text{for } x \geq 0$$

    a. What is the mean time between telephone calls?
    b. What is the probability of having 30 seconds or less between telephone calls?
    c. What is the probability of having 1 minute or less between telephone calls?
    d. What is the probability of having 5 or more minutes without a telephone call?

CHAPTER 7

Sampling and Sampling Distributions

CONTENTS

STATISTICS IN PRACTICE

MeadWestvaco Corporation*

STAMFORD, CONNECTICUT

MeadWestvaco Corporation is a leading producer of packaging, coated and specialty papers, consumer and office products, and specialty chemicals. Its more than 30,000 employees work at its worldwide operations located in 33 countries. MeadWestvaco holds a leading position in paper production, with an annual capacity of 1.8 million tons that serves customers in 98 countries. MeadWestvaco's internal consulting group uses sampling to provide a variety of information that enables the company to obtain significant productivity benefits and remain competitive.

For example, MeadWestvaco maintains large woodland holdings, which provide the trees that are the raw material for many of the company's products. Managers need reliable and accurate information about the timberlands and forests to evaluate the company's ability to meet its future raw material needs. What is the present volume in the forests? What is the past growth of the forests? What is the projected future growth of the forests? With answers to these important questions, MeadWestvaco's managers can develop plans for the future, including long-term planting and harvesting schedules for the trees.

How does MeadWestvaco obtain the information it needs about its vast forest holdings? Data collected from sample plots throughout the forests provide the basis for learning about the population of trees owned by the company. To identify the sample plots, the timberland holdings are first divided into three sections based on location and types of trees. Using maps and random num-

Random sampling of its forest holdings enables Mead-Westvaco Corporation to meet future raw material needs. © Gaetano/CORBIS.

bers, MeadWestvaco analysts identify random samples of 1/5- to 1/7-acre plots in each section of the forest. MeadWestvaco foresters collect data and learn about the forest population from these sample plots.

Foresters throughout the organization participate in the field data collection process. Periodically, two-person teams gather information on each tree in every sample plot. The sample data are entered into the company's continuous forest inventory (CFI) computer system. Reports from the CFI system include a number of frequency distribution summaries containing statistics on types of trees, present forest volume, past forest growth rates, and projected future forest growth and volume. Sampling and the associated statistical summaries of the sample data provide the reports essential for the effective management of MeadWestvaco's forests and timberlands.

In this chapter you will learn about simple random sampling and the sample selection process. In addition, you will learn how statistics such as the sample mean and sample proportion are used to estimate the population mean and population proportion. The important concept of a sampling distribution is also introduced.

*The authors are indebted to Dr. Edward P. Winkofsky for providing this Statistics in Practice.

In Chapter 1, we defined a *population* and a *sample* as two important aspects of a statistical study. The definitions are restated here.

1. A *population* is the set of all the elements of interest in a particular study.
2. A *sample* is a subset of the population.

The purpose of *statistical inference* is to develop estimates and test hypotheses about the characteristics of a population using information contained in a sample. Let us begin by citing two situations in which sampling is conducted to give a manager or decision maker information about a population.

1. A tire manufacturer developed a new tire designed to provide an increase in mileage over the firm's current line of tires. To estimate the mean number of miles provided by the new tires, the manufacturer selected a sample of 120 new tires for testing. The test results provided a sample mean of 36,500 miles. Hence, an estimate of the mean tire mileage for the population of new tires was 36,500 miles.
2. Members of a political party were considering supporting a particular candidate for election to the U.S. Senate, and party leaders wanted an estimate of the proportion of registered voters favoring the candidate. The time and cost associated with contacting every individual in the population of registered voters were prohibitive. Hence, a sample of 400 registered voters was selected and 160 of the 400 voters indicated a preference for the candidate. An estimate of the proportion of the population of registered voters favoring the candidate was 160/400 = .40.

The preceding examples show how sampling and the sample results can be used to develop estimates of population characteristics. Note that in the tire mileage example, collecting the data on tire life involves wearing out each tire tested. Clearly it is not feasible to test every tire in the population; a sample is the only realistic way to obtain the desired tire mileage data. In the example involving the election, contacting every registered voter in the population is theoretically possible, but the time and cost in doing so are prohibitive; thus, a sample of registered voters is preferred.

A sample mean provides an estimate of a population mean, and a sample proportion provides an estimate of a population proportion. With estimates such as these, some sampling error can be expected. A key point in this chapter is that statistical methods can be used to make probability statements about the size of the sampling error.

The examples illustrate some of the reasons for using samples. However, it is important to realize that sample results provide only *estimates* of the values of the population characteristics. That is, we do not expect the sample mean of 36,500 miles to exactly equal the mean mileage for all tires in the population, nor do we expect exactly 40% of the population of registered voters to favor the candidate. The reason is simply that the sample contains only a portion of the population. With proper sampling methods, the sample results will provide "good" estimates of the population characteristics. But how good can we expect the sample results to be? Fortunately, statistical procedures are available for answering this question.

In this chapter we show how simple random sampling can be used to select a sample from a population. We then show how data obtained from a simple random sample can be used to compute estimates of a population mean, a population standard deviation, and a population proportion. In addition, we introduce the important concept of a sampling distribution. As we show, knowledge of the appropriate sampling distribution is what enables us to make statements about the goodness of the sample results. The last section discusses some alternatives to simple random sampling that are often employed in practice.

7.1   THE ELECTRONICS ASSOCIATES SAMPLING PROBLEM

The director of personnel for Electronics Associates, Inc. (EAI), wants to develop a profile of the company's 2500 managers. The characteristics to be identified include the mean annual salary for the managers and the proportion of managers who participated in the company's management training program.

EAI

Using the 2500 managers as the population for this study, we can find the annual salary and the training program status for each individual by referring to the firm's personnel records. The data file containing this information for all 2500 managers in the population is on the disk at the back of the book.

Using the EAI data set and the formulas presented in Chapter 3, we computed the population mean and the population standard deviation for the annual salary data.

$$\text{Population mean:} \quad \mu = \$51,800$$
$$\text{Population standard deviation:} \quad \sigma = \$4000$$

The data for the training program status show that 1500 of the 2500 managers completed the training program. Letting p denote the proportion of the population that participated in the training program, we see that $p = 1500/2500 = .60$.

A **parameter** is a numerical measure of a population characteristic. The population mean annual salary ($\mu = \$51,800$), the population standard deviation of annual salary ($\sigma = \$4000$), and the population proportion having completed the training program ($p = .60$) are parameters of the population of EAI managers.

Now, suppose that the necessary information on all the EAI managers was not readily available in the company's database. Employee records for recent hires might not be on the computer. Perhaps only the salary information (and not the training program status) is in the employee records. Or, maybe the employee records at some locations are on the computer, but records at other locations are not. For whatever reason, it is often the case that it is not possible, or is perhaps too costly, to collect and process information on all elements of a population. In such cases, information from a sample can often be used to develop estimates of the population parameters of interest.

The cost of collecting information from a sample is usually substantially less than from a population, especially when personal interviews must be conducted to collect the information.

The question we now consider is how the firm's director of personnel can obtain estimates of the population parameters of interest by using a sample of managers rather than all 2500 managers in the population. A sample of 30 managers will be used. Clearly, the time and the cost of developing a profile would be substantially less for 30 managers than for the entire population. If the personnel director could be assured that a sample of 30 managers would provide adequate information about the population of 2500 managers, working with a sample would be preferable to working with the entire population. Let us explore the possibility of using a sample for the EAI study by first considering how we can identify a sample of 30 managers.

7.2   SIMPLE RANDOM SAMPLING

Several methods can be used to select a sample from a population; one of the most common is **simple random sampling**. The definition of a simple random sample and the process of selecting a simple random sample depend on whether the population is *finite* or *infinite*. Because the EAI sampling problem involves a finite population of 2500 managers, we first consider sampling from a finite population.

Sampling from a Finite Population

A simple random sample of size n from a finite population of size N is defined as follows.

Simple Random Sample (Finite Population)

A simple random sample of size n from a finite population of size N is a sample selected such that each possible sample of size n has the same probability of being selected.

One procedure for selecting a simple random sample from a finite population is to choose the elements for the sample one at a time in such a way that each of the elements remaining in the population has the same probability of being selected. Sampling *n* elements in this way will satisfy the definition of a simple random sample from a finite population.

To use this procedure for selecting a simple random sample from the finite population of EAI managers, one approach is to first assign each of the 2500 EAI managers a number. For instance, we can number them from 1 to 2500 in the order that their names appear in EAI personnel files. Next, we refer to the table of random numbers shown in Table 7.1.[1] Referring to the first row of the table, each digit, 6, 3, 2, . . . , is a random digit having an equal chance of occurring. Because the largest number in the population list of EAI managers, 2500, has four digits, we will select random numbers from the table in sets or groups of four digits. We may start anywhere in the table and move systematically in a direction of our choice. We choose to use the first row of Table 7.1 and move from left to right. The first seven four-digit random numbers are

6327   1599   8671   7445   1102   1514   1807

Because the numbers in the table are random, these four-digit numbers are equally probable or equally likely.

TABLE 7.1   RANDOM NUMBERS

The random numbers are shown in groups of 5 for readability.

63271	59986	71744	51102	15141	80714	58683	93108	13554	79945
88547	09896	95436	79115	08303	01041	20030	63754	08459	28364
55957	57243	83865	09911	19761	66535	40102	26646	60147	15702
46276	87453	44790	67122	45573	84358	21625	16999	13385	22782
55363	07449	34835	15290	76616	67191	12777	21861	68689	03263
69393	92785	49902	58447	42048	30378	87618	26933	40640	16281
13186	29431	88190	04588	38733	81290	89541	70290	40113	08243
17726	28652	56836	78351	47327	18518	92222	55201	27340	10493
36520	64465	05550	30157	82242	29520	69753	72602	23756	54935
81628	36100	39254	56835	37636	02421	98063	89641	64953	99337
84649	48968	75215	75498	49539	74240	03466	49292	36401	45525
63291	11618	12613	75055	43915	26488	41116	64531	56827	30825
70502	53225	03655	05915	37140	57051	48393	91322	25653	06543
06426	24771	59935	49801	11082	66762	94477	02494	88215	27191
20711	55609	29430	70165	45406	78484	31639	52009	18873	96927
41990	70538	77191	25860	55204	73417	83920	69468	74972	38712
72452	36618	76298	26678	89334	33938	95567	29380	75906	91807
37042	40318	57099	10528	09925	89773	41335	96244	29002	46453
53766	52875	15987	46962	67342	77592	57651	95508	80033	69828
90585	58955	53122	16025	84299	53310	67380	84249	25348	04332
32001	96293	37203	64516	51530	37069	40261	61374	05815	06714
62606	64324	46354	72157	67248	20135	49804	09226	64419	29457
10078	28073	85389	50324	14500	15562	64165	06125	71353	77669
91561	46145	24177	15294	10061	98124	75732	00815	83452	97355
13091	98112	53959	79607	52244	63303	10413	63839	74762	50289

---

[1]Tables of random numbers are available in a variety of handbooks such as The Rand Corporation's *A Million Random Digits with 100,000 Normal Deviates* (New York: The Free Press, 1983).

We can now use these four-digit random numbers to give each manager in the population an equal chance of being included in the random sample. The first number, 6327, is greater than 2500. It does not correspond to one of the numbered managers in the population, and hence is discarded. The second number, 1599, is between 1 and 2500. Thus the first manager selected for the random sample is number 1599 in the list of EAI managers. Continuing this process, we ignore the numbers 8671 and 7445 before identifying manager numbers 1102, 1514, and 1807 to be included in the random sample. This process continues until the simple random sample of 30 EAI managers has been obtained.

In implementing this simple random sample selection process, it is possible that a random number used previously may appear again in the table before the sample of 30 EAI managers has been selected. Because we do not want to select a manager more than one time, any previously used random numbers are ignored because the corresponding manager is already included in the sample. Selecting a sample in this manner is referred to as **sampling without replacement**. If we had selected the sample such that previously used random numbers were acceptable and specific managers could be included in the sample two or more times, we would be **sampling with replacement**. Sampling without replacement is the procedure used most often, so when we refer to simple random sampling, we will assume that the sampling is without replacement.

Now consider another approach to selecting a simple random sample using random numbers. This approach often takes longer when selecting a sample by hand, but it is efficient when using a computer to select the sample. We first assign a random number to each of the 2500 EAI managers. Then, we select the 30 managers with the smallest random numbers as the simple random sample. Because each of the 2500 managers has the same probability of being assigned one of the 30 smallest random numbers, this procedure provides a simple random sample of 30 EAI managers. Using this approach, we do not have to worry about any managers being included twice.[2] We now describe how this approach is implemented using Excel.

Using Excel to Select a Simple Random Sample

Excel can be used to select a simple random sample without replacement. The method for doing so is based on random numbers generated by Excel's RAND function. The RAND function generates random numbers in the interval from 0 to 1. Because the numbers generated are random, any number in the interval is equally likely; the random numbers are actually values of a uniformly distributed random variable.

To select a simple random sample of 30 EAI managers without replacement from the population of 2500 EAI managers, we begin by generating 2500 random numbers, one for each manager in the population. Then we choose the 30 managers corresponding to the 30 smallest random numbers as our sample. Refer to Figure 7.1 as we describe the steps involved.

Enter Data: The first three columns of the worksheet in the background show the annual salary data and training program status for the first 30 managers in the population of 2500 EAI managers. (The complete worksheet contains all 2500 managers.)

Enter Functions and Formulas: In the background worksheet, the label **Random Numbers** has been entered into cell D1 and the formula =RAND() has been entered into cells D2:D2501 to generate a random number between 0 and 1 for each of the 2500 EAI managers. The random number generated for the first manager is 0.613872, the random number generated for the second manager is 0.473204, and so on.

---

[2]It is possible for a tie to occur for the 30th smallest random number. But, the tie can be broken by including tied managers in the sample in the order in which they appear in the list of managers.

FIGURE 7.1   USING EXCEL TO SELECT A SIMPLE RANDOM SAMPLE WITHOUT REPLACEMENT

	A	B	C	D
	Manager	Annual Salary	Training Program	Random Numbers
2	1	55769.50	No	0.613872
3	2	50823.00	Yes	0.473204
4	3	48408.20	No	0.549011
5	4	49787.50	No	0.047482
6	5	52801.60	Yes	0.531085
7	6	51767.70	No	0.994296
8	7	58346.60	Yes	0.189065
9	8	46670.20	No	0.020714
10	9	50246.80	Yes	0.647318
11	10	51255.00	No	0.524341
12	11	52546.60	No	0.764998
13	12	49512.50	Yes	0.255244
14	13	51753.00	Yes	0.010923
15	14	53547.10	No	0.238003
16	15	48052.20	No	0.635675
17	16	44652.50	Yes	0.177294
18	17	51764.90	Yes	0.415097
19	18	45187.80	Yes	0.883440
20	19	49867.50	Yes	0.476824
21	20	53706.30	Yes	0.101065
22	21	52039.50	Yes	0.775323
23	22	52973.60	No	0.011729
24	23	53372.50	No	0.762026
25	24	54592.00	Yes	0.066344
26	25	55738.10	Yes	0.776766
27	26	52975.10	Yes	0.828493
28	27	52386.20	Yes	0.841532
29	28	51051.60	Yes	0.899427
30	29	52095.60	Yes	0.486284
31	30	44956.50	No	0.264628

The formula in cells D2:D2501 is =RAND().

Note: Rows 32–2501 are not shown.

	A	B	C	D
	Manager	Annual Salary	Training Program	Random Numbers
2	812	49094.30	Yes	0.000193
3	1411	53263.90	Yes	0.000484
4	1795	49643.50	Yes	0.002641
5	2095	49894.90	Yes	0.002763
6	1235	47621.60	No	0.002940
7	744	55924.00	Yes	0.002977
8	470	49092.30	Yes	0.003182
9	1606	51404.40	Yes	0.003448
10	1744	50957.70	Yes	0.004203
11	179	55109.70	Yes	0.005293
12	1387	45922.60	Yes	0.005709
13	1782	57268.40	No	0.005729
14	1006	55688.80	Yes	0.005796
15	278	51564.70	No	0.005966
16	1850	56188.20	No	0.006250
17	844	51766.00	Yes	0.006708
18	2028	52541.30	No	0.007767
19	1654	44980.00	Yes	0.008095
20	444	51932.60	Yes	0.009686
21	556	52973.00	Yes	0.009711
22	2449	45120.90	Yes	0.010595
23	13	51753.00	Yes	0.010923
24	2187	54391.80	No	0.011364
25	1633	50164.20	No	0.011603
26	22	52973.60	No	0.011729
27	1530	50241.30	No	0.013570
28	820	52793.90	No	0.013669
29	1258	50979.40	Yes	0.014042
30	2349	55860.90	Yes	0.014532
31	1698	57309.10	No	0.014539

Apply Tools: All that remains is to find the managers associated with the 30 smallest random numbers. To do so we sort the data in columns A through D into ascending order by the random numbers in column D.

Step 1. Select cells A2:D2501

Step 2. Select the **Data** menu

Step 3. Choose the **Sort** option

Step 4. When the **Sort** dialog box appears
       Choose **Random Numbers** in the **Sort by** text box
       Choose **Ascending**
       Click **OK**

After completing these steps we obtain the worksheet shown in the foreground of Figure 7.1.[3] The managers listed in rows 2–31 are the ones corresponding to the smallest 30 random numbers that were generated. Hence, this group of 30 managers is a simple random sample. Note that the random numbers shown in the foreground of Figure 7.1 are in ascending order, and that the managers are not in their original order. For instance, manager 812 in the population is associated with the smallest random number and is the first element in the sample, and manager 13 in the population (see row 14 of the background worksheet) has been included as the 22nd observation in the sample (row 23 of the foreground worksheet).

Sampling from an Infinite Population

In practice, a population being studied is usually considered infinite if it involves an ongoing process that makes listing or counting every element in the population impossible.

Many sampling situations in business and economics involve finite populations, but in some situations the population is either infinite or so large that for practical purposes it must be treated as infinite. In sampling from an infinite population, we must use a different definition of a simple random sample. In addition, because the elements in an infinite population cannot be listed and numbered, we must use a different process for selecting the sample.

Suppose we want to estimate the average time between placing an order and receiving food for customers at a fast-food restaurant during the 11:30 A.M. to 1:30 P.M. lunch period. If we consider the population as being all possible customer visits, we see that it would not be feasible to specify a finite limit on the number of possible visits or to list the possible visitors. In fact, if we define the population as being all customer visits that could conceivably occur during the lunch period, we can consider the population as being infinite. Our task is to select a simple random sample of *n* customers from this population. The definition of a simple random sample from an infinite population follows.

Simple Random Sample (Infinite Population)

A simple random sample from an infinite population is a sample selected such that the following conditions are satisfied.

1. Each element selected comes from the same population.
2. Each element is selected independently.

For the problem of selecting a simple random sample of customer visits at a fast-food restaurant, the first condition in the definition is satisfied by any customer visit occurring during the 11:30 A.M. to 1:30 P.M. lunch period while the restaurant is operating with its

---

[3]In order to show the same random numbers in the foreground worksheet, we turned off the automatic recalculation option for the worksheet prior to sorting. This is not a necessary step in selecting a sample. But, it allowed us to show, in the foreground worksheet, that the sample was, indeed, associated with the 30 smallest random numbers.

For infinite populations, a sample selection procedure must be specially devised to select the items independently and thus avoid a selection bias that gives higher selection probabilities to certain types of elements.

regular staff under "normal" operating conditions. The second condition is satisfied by ensuring that the selection of a particular customer does not influence the selection of any other customer. That is, the customers are selected independently.

A well-known fast-food restaurant implemented a simple random sampling procedure for just such a situation. The sampling procedure is based on the fact that some customers present discount coupons for special prices on sandwiches, drinks, french fries, and so on. Whenever a customer presents a discount coupon, the next customer served is selected for the sample. Because the customers present discount coupons randomly and independently, the firm is satisfied that the sampling plan satisfies the two conditions in the definition of a simple random sample from an infinite population. We note that the customers presenting the coupons were not selected for the sample because their purchase behavior may not be the same as the rest of the customers.

NOTES AND COMMENTS

1. Excel has a sampling tool that can be accessed by selecting the **Tools** menu and choosing the **Data Analysis** option. It selects a simple random sample with replacement. However, as we stated previously, most practical applications involve sampling without replacement.

2. Finite populations are often defined by lists such as organization membership rosters, student enrollment records, credit card account lists, inventory product numbers, and so on. Infinite populations are often defined by an ongoing process whereby the elements of the population consist of items generated as though the process would operate indefinitely under the same conditions. In such cases, it is impossible to obtain a list of all elements in the population. For example, populations consisting of all possible parts to be manufactured, all possible customer visits, all possible bank transactions, and so on are classified as infinite populations.

3. The number of different simple random samples of size n that can be selected from a finite population of size N is

$$\frac{N!}{n!(N-n)!}$$

In this formula, $N!$ and $n!$ are the factorial computations discussed in Chapter 4. For the EAI problem with $N = 2500$ and $n = 30$, this expression can be used to show that approximately 2.75×10^{69} different simple random samples of 30 EAI managers are possible.

EXERCISES

Methods

1. Consider a finite population with five elements labeled A, B, C, D, and E. Ten possible simple random samples of size 2 can be selected.
   a. List the 10 possible samples. Hint: Two are AB and AC.
   b. Using simple random sampling, what is the probability that each sample of size 2 is selected?
   c. Assign the number 1 to A, the number 2 to B, and so on. List the simple random sample of size 2 that will be selected by using the random digits 8 0 5 7 5 3 2.

2. Assume a finite population has 350 elements. Use the last three digits of each of the following five-digit random numbers. Move from left to right to select the first four elements of a simple random sample.

   98601   73022   83448   02147   34229   27553   84147   93289   14209

Applications

3. *Fortune* publishes data on sales, profits, assets, stockholders' equity, market value, and earnings per share for the 500 largest U.S. industrial corporations (*Fortune* 500, 2000). Assume that you want to select a simple random sample of 10 corporations from the *Fortune* 500 list. Use the last three digits in column 9 of Table 7.1, beginning with 554. Read down the column and identify the numbers of the 10 corporations that would be selected.

4. Ten companies with widely held stocks are shown here (*USA Today*, September 6, 2000).

AT&T	IBM
America Online	Johnson & Johnson
Cisco Systems	Microsoft
General Electric	Motorola
Intel	Pfizer

     a. Assume that a simple random sample of five of these companies will be selected for an in-depth study of common business practices in large corporations. Beginning with the first random digit in Table 7.1 and reading down the column, use the single-digit random numbers to sequentially select a simple random sample of five companies to be used in the study.

     b. Assign one of the first 10 random digits in column one of Table 7.1 to each of the companies. Select a simple random sample of five companies by choosing the ones with the smallest random numbers.

     c. According to the third point in Notes and Comments, how many different simple random samples of size five can be selected from the list of 10 companies?

     d. Use Excel to select a simple random sample of five companies.

5. A student government organization is interested in estimating the proportion of students who favor a mandatory "pass-fail" grading policy for elective courses. A list of names and addresses of the 645 students enrolled during the current quarter is available from the registrar's office.

     a. Using three-digit random numbers in row 10 of Table 7.1, and moving across the row from left to right, identify the first 10 students who would be selected using simple random sampling. The three-digit random numbers begin with 816, 283, and 610.

     b. Describe how Excel could be used to select a simple random sample of 50 students.

6. The *County and City Data Book*, published by the Bureau of the Census, lists information on 3139 counties throughout the United States. Assume that a national study will collect data from 30 randomly selected counties. Use four-digit random numbers from the last column of Table 7.1 to identify the numbers corresponding to the first five counties selected for the sample. Ignore the first digits and begin with the four-digit random numbers 9945, 8364, 5702, and so on.

EAI

7. In this section we showed how Excel can be used to select a simple random sample of 30 EAI managers. Use this procedure to select a simple random sample of 50 EAI managers.

8. The following table provides the NCAA football top 25 teams at the beginning of the 2000 season (*Sports Illustrated*, August 14, 2000).

CD file

Football

1. Nebraska	8. Clemson
2. Florida State	9. Texas
3. Alabama	10. Miami
4. Michigan	11. Florida
5. Wisconsin	12. Virginia Tech
6. Kansas State	13. Washington
7. Georgia	14. Tennessee

15. TCU	21. Illinois
16. Purdue	22. Ohio State
17. Mississippi	23. Oklahoma
18. USC	24. Colorado State
19. Penn State	25. Colorado
20. Southern Miss	

a. Use column 9 of the random numbers in Table 7.1 beginning with 13554, to select a simple random sample of six football teams. Begin with 13 and use the first two digits in each row of column 9 for your selection process. Using this sequential one-at-a-time procedure, how many random numbers were needed and which six teams were selected?

b. Use Excel to select the six teams with the smallest random numbers. How many random numbers were needed and which six teams were selected?

9. *Business Week* provided performance data and annual ratings for 895 mutual funds (*Business Week*, February 3, 1997). Assume that a simple random sample of 12 of the 895 mutual funds will be selected for a follow-up study on the performance of mutual funds. Use column 4 of the random numbers in Table 7.1, beginning with 51102, to select the simple random sample of 12 mutual funds. Begin with mutual fund 511 and use the first three digits in each row of column 4 for your selection process. What are the numbers of the 12 mutual funds in the simple random sample?

10. Indicate whether the following populations should be considered finite or infinite.
a. All registered voters in the state of California.
b. All television sets that could be produced by the Allentown, Pennsylvania, plant of the TV-M Company.
c. All orders that could be processed by a mail-order firm.
d. All emergency telephone calls that could come into a local police station.
e. All components that Fibercon, Inc., produced on the second shift on May 17.

7.3   POINT ESTIMATION

We have already selected a simple random sample for the EAI problem. The simple random sample of 30 managers selected in Figure 7.1 and the corresponding data on annual salary and management training program participation are as shown in Table 7.2. The notation x_1, x_2, and so on is used to denote the annual salary of the first manager in the sample, the annual salary of the second manager in the sample, and so on. Participation in the management training program is indicated by Yes in the management training program column.

A parameter is a numerical measure of a population characteristic.

To estimate the value of a population parameter, we compute a corresponding characteristic of the sample, referred to as a **sample statistic**. For example, to estimate the population mean μ and the population standard deviation σ for the annual salary of EAI managers, we simply use the data in Table 7.2 to calculate the corresponding sample statistics: the sample mean $\bar{x}$ and the sample standard deviation s. Using the formulas for a sample mean and a sample standard deviation presented in Chapter 3, the sample mean is

$$\bar{x} = \frac{\Sigma x_i}{n} = \frac{1,554,420}{30} = \$51,814.00$$

and the sample standard deviation is

$$s = \sqrt{\frac{\Sigma(x_i - \bar{x})^2}{n-1}} = \sqrt{\frac{325,009,260}{29}} = \$3347.72$$

In addition, by computing the proportion of managers in the sample who participated in the management training program, we can estimate the proportion of managers in the population

TABLE 7.2   ANNUAL SALARY AND TRAINING PROGRAM STATUS FOR A SIMPLE
RANDOM SAMPLE OF 30 EAI MANAGERS

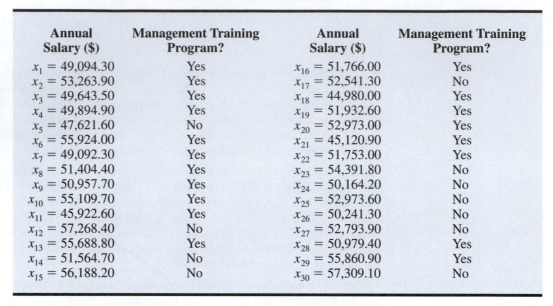

Annual Salary ($)	Management Training Program?	Annual Salary ($)	Management Training Program?
$x_1 = 49{,}094.30$	Yes	$x_{16} = 51{,}766.00$	Yes
$x_2 = 53{,}263.90$	Yes	$x_{17} = 52{,}541.30$	No
$x_3 = 49{,}643.50$	Yes	$x_{18} = 44{,}980.00$	Yes
$x_4 = 49{,}894.90$	Yes	$x_{19} = 51{,}932.60$	Yes
$x_5 = 47{,}621.60$	No	$x_{20} = 52{,}973.00$	Yes
$x_6 = 55{,}924.00$	Yes	$x_{21} = 45{,}120.90$	Yes
$x_7 = 49{,}092.30$	Yes	$x_{22} = 51{,}753.00$	Yes
$x_8 = 51{,}404.40$	Yes	$x_{23} = 54{,}391.80$	No
$x_9 = 50{,}957.70$	Yes	$x_{24} = 50{,}164.20$	No
$x_{10} = 55{,}109.70$	Yes	$x_{25} = 52{,}973.60$	No
$x_{11} = 45{,}922.60$	Yes	$x_{26} = 50{,}241.30$	No
$x_{12} = 57{,}268.40$	No	$x_{27} = 52{,}793.90$	No
$x_{13} = 55{,}688.80$	Yes	$x_{28} = 50{,}979.40$	Yes
$x_{14} = 51{,}564.70$	No	$x_{29} = 55{,}860.90$	Yes
$x_{15} = 56{,}188.20$	No	$x_{30} = 57{,}309.10$	No

CD file

EAI

who participated in the management training program. Table 7.2 shows that 19 of the 30 managers in the sample participated in the training program. Thus, the sample proportion, denoted by $\bar{p}$, is given by

$$\bar{p} = \frac{19}{30} = .63$$

This value is used as an estimate of the population proportion p.

By making the preceding computations, we performed the statistical procedure called point estimation. In point estimation we use the data from the sample to compute the value of a sample statistic that serves as an estimate of a population parameter. Using the terminology of point estimation, we refer to $\bar{x}$ as the **point estimator** of the population mean μ, s as the point estimator of the population standard deviation σ, and $\bar{p}$ as the point estimator of the population proportion p. The actual numerical value obtained for $\bar{x}$, s, or $\bar{p}$ in a particular sample is called the **point estimate** of the parameter. Thus, for the sample of 30 EAI managers, \$51,814.00 is the point estimate of μ, \$3347.72 is the point estimate of σ, and .63 is the point estimate of p. Table 7.3 summarizes the sample results and compares the point estimates to the actual values of the population parameters.

Sampling error is the result of using a subset of the population (the sample), and not the entire population to develop estimates.

As Table 7.3 shows, none of the point estimates exactly equal the corresponding population parameters. The differences are to be expected because only a sample and not a census of the entire population is being used to develop the estimates. The absolute value of the difference between an unbiased point estimate and the corresponding population parameter is called the **sampling error**. For a sample mean and sample proportion, the sampling errors are $|\bar{x} - \mu|$ and $|\bar{p} - p|$, respectively.[4] Thus, for the EAI sample, the sampling

---

[4]Technically the difference between the point estimate and the population parameter is called *sampling error* only when the point estimator is unbiased. A point estimator is unbiased if the mean of its sampling distribution (see Sections 7.4–7.6) is equal to the population parameter being estimated. The point estimators $\bar{x}$ and $\bar{p}$ are unbiased. While s^2 is an unbiased estimate of σ^2, s is a biased estimator of σ. So, the difference between s and σ, $|s - \sigma|$ includes some bias as well as sampling error.

TABLE 7.3 SUMMARY OF POINT ESTIMATES OBTAINED FROM A SIMPLE RANDOM SAMPLE OF 30 EAI MANAGERS

Population Parameter	Parameter Value	Point Estimator	Point Estimate
μ = Population mean annual salary	$51,800.00	$\bar{x}$ = Sample mean annual salary	$51,814.00
σ = Population standard deviation for annual salary	$4000.00	s = Sample standard deviation for annual salary	$3347.72
p = Population proportion having completed the management training program	.60	$\bar{p}$ = Sample proportion having completed the management training program	.63

errors are $|\$51,814 - \$51,800| = \$14$ for the sample mean and $|.63 - .60| = .03$ for the sample proportion.

We were able to compute the sampling errors here because the population parameters were known. However, in an actual sampling application we will not be able to calculate the sampling error exactly because the value of the population parameter will not be known. We will show how statisticians analyze the sample data in order to make probability statements about the size of the sampling error.

NOTES AND COMMENTS

In our discussion of point estimators, we use $\bar{x}$ to denote a sample mean and $\bar{p}$ to denote a sample proportion. Our use of $\bar{p}$ is based on the fact that the sample proportion is also a *sample mean*. Suppose that in a sample of size n with data values $x_1, x_2, \ldots, x_n$, we let $x_i = 1$ when a characteristic of interest is present for the ith observation and $x_i = 0$ when the characteristic is not present. Then the sample pro-

portion is computed by $\Sigma x_i / n$, which is the formula for a sample mean. We also like the consistency of using the bar over the letter to remind the reader that the sample proportion $\bar{p}$ estimates the population proportion just as the sample mean $\bar{x}$ estimates the population mean. Some texts use $\hat{p}$ instead of $\bar{p}$ to denote the sample proportion.

EXERCISES

Methods

11. The following data are from a simple random sample.

$$5 \quad 8 \quad 10 \quad 7 \quad 10 \quad 14$$

    a. What is the point estimate of the population mean?
    b. What is the point estimate of the population standard deviation?

12. A survey question for a simple random sample of 150 individuals yielded 75 Yes responses, 55 No responses, and 20 No Opinions.
    a. What is the point estimate of the proportion in the population that would respond Yes?
    b. What is the point estimate of the proportion in the population that would respond No?

Applications

13. A simple random sample of five months of sales data provided the following information:

Month:	1	2	3	4	5
Units Sold:	94	100	85	94	92

   a. What is the point estimate of the population mean number of units sold per month?
   b. What is the point estimate of the population standard deviation?

14. A sample of 784 children ages 9 to 14 were asked about cash provided by their parents (*Consumer Reports*, January 1997). The responses were as follow.

Source of Cash	Frequency
Allowance only	149
Handouts & chores plus an allowance	219
Handouts & chores but no allowance	251
Nothing	165
Total	784

   a. What is the point estimate of the proportion of children who receive an allowance as their only source of cash?
   b. What is the point estimate of the proportion of children who receive cash as handouts and for chores, but nothing in the form of an allowance?
   c. Considering all sources, what is the point estimate of the proportion of children who receive at least some cash from their parents?

15. *Appliance Magazine* provided estimates of the life expectancy of household appliances (*USA Today*, September 5, 2000). A simple random sample of 10 VCRs shows the following useful life in years.

$$6.5 \quad 8.0 \quad 6.2 \quad 7.4 \quad 7.0 \quad 8.4 \quad 9.5 \quad 4.6 \quad 5.0 \quad 7.4$$

   a. What is the point estimate of the population mean life expectancy for VCRs?
   b. What is the point estimate of the population standard deviation for life expectancy of VCRs?

16. The U.S. Department of Transportation reports statistics on how frequently major airline flights arrive at or before their scheduled arrival times (*Associated Press,* September 2000). Assume that the estimated proportion of flights arriving on time for an airline is based on a simple random sample of 1400 flights. If 1117 of the flights arrive on time, what is the point estimate of the proportion of all flights that arrive on time?

17. A Louis Harris poll used a survey of 1008 adults to learn how people feel about the economy (*Business Week*, August 7, 2000). Responses were as follow:

595 adults	The economy is growing.
332 adults	The economy is staying about the same.
81 adults	The economy is shrinking.

Develop the point estimate of the following population parameters.
   a. The proportion of all adults who feel the economy is growing.
   b. The proportion of all adults who feel the economy is staying about the same.
   c. The proportion of all adults who feel the economy is shrinking.

18. In this section we showed how a simple random sample of 30 EAI managers can be used to develop point estimates of the population mean annual salary, the population standard deviation for annual salary, and the population proportion having completed the management training program.

    a. Use Excel to select a simple random sample of 50 EAI managers.
    b. Develop a point estimate of the mean annual salary.
    c. Develop a point estimate of the population standard deviation for annual salary.
    d. Develop a point estimate of the population proportion having completed the management training program.

7.4   INTRODUCTION TO SAMPLING DISTRIBUTIONS

In the preceding section we used a simple random sample of 30 EAI managers to develop point estimates of the mean and standard deviation of annual salary for the population of all EAI managers as well as the proportion of the managers in the population who have completed the company's management training program. Suppose we select another simple random sample of 30 EAI managers, and an analysis of the data from the second sample provides the following information.

$$\text{Sample Mean } \bar{x} = \$52{,}669.70$$
$$\text{Sample Standard Deviation } s = \$4239.07$$
$$\text{Sample Proportion } \bar{p} = .70$$

The concept of a sampling distribution is one of the most important topics in this chapter. The ability to understand the material in subsequent chapters depends heavily on the ability to understand and use the sampling distributions presented in this chapter.

These results show that the second sample provided different values of $\bar{x}$, s, and $\bar{p}$. In general, a second simple random sample will not contain the same elements as the first. Let us imagine carrying out the same process of selecting a new simple random sample of 30 managers over and over again, each time computing values of $\bar{x}$, s, and $\bar{p}$. In this way we could begin to identify the variety of values that these point estimators can assume. To illustrate, we repeated the simple random sampling process for the EAI problem until we obtained 500 samples of 30 managers each and the corresponding $\bar{x}$, s, and $\bar{p}$ values. A portion of the results is shown in Table 7.4. Table 7.5 gives the frequency and relative frequency distributions for the 500 $\bar{x}$ values. Figure 7.2 is the relative frequency histogram for the $\bar{x}$ values.

TABLE 7.4   VALUES OF $\bar{x}$, s, AND $\bar{p}$ FROM 500 SIMPLE RANDOM SAMPLES OF 30 EAI MANAGERS

Sample Number	Sample Mean ($\bar{x}$)	Sample Standard Deviation (s)	Sample Proportion ($\bar{p}$)
1	51,814.00	3,347.72	.63
2	52,669.70	4,239.07	.70
3	51,780.30	4,433.43	.67
4	51,587.90	3,985.32	.53
.	.	.	.
.	.	.	.
.	.	.	.
500	51,752.00	3,857.82	.50

TABLE 7.5   FREQUENCY AND RELATIVE FREQUENCY DISTRIBUTION OF $\bar{x}$
FROM 500 SIMPLE RANDOM SAMPLES OF 30 EAI MANAGERS

Sample Mean ($\bar{x}$)	Frequency	Relative Frequency
49,500.00–49,999.99	2	.004
50,000.00–50,499.99	16	.032
50,500.00–50,999.99	52	.104
51,000.00–51,499.99	101	.202
51,500.00–51,999.99	133	.266
52,000.00–52,499.99	110	.220
52,500.00–52,999.99	54	.108
53,000.00–53,499.99	26	.052
53,500.00–53,999.99	6	.012
Totals	500	1.000

Recall that in Chapter 5 we defined a random variable as a numerical description of the outcome of an experiment. If we consider the process of selecting a simple random sample as an experiment, the sample mean $\bar{x}$ is a numerical description of the outcome of the experiment. Thus, the sample mean $\bar{x}$ is a random variable. Just like other random variables, $\bar{x}$ has a mean or expected value, a variance, and a probability distribution. Because the various possible values of $\bar{x}$ result from different simple random samples, the probability distribution of $\bar{x}$ is called the *sampling distribution* of $\bar{x}$. Knowledge of this sampling distribution

FIGURE 7.2   RELATIVE FREQUENCY HISTOGRAM OF $\bar{x}$ VALUES FROM 500 SIMPLE
RANDOM SAMPLES OF SIZE 30 EACH

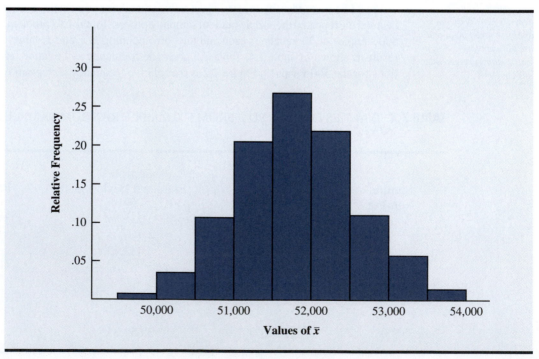

and its properties enable us to make probability statements about how close the sample mean $\bar{x}$ is to the population mean μ.

Let us consider Figure 7.2. We would need to enumerate every possible sample of 30 managers and compute each sample mean to completely determine the sampling distribution of $\bar{x}$. However, the histogram of 500 $\bar{x}$ values gives an approximation of this sampling distribution. From the approximation we observe the bell-shaped appearance of the distribution. We note that the estimate of the population mean provided by $\bar{x}$ varies quite a bit. But we also note that the largest concentration of the $\bar{x}$ values and the mean of the 500 $\bar{x}$ values is near the population mean $\mu = \$51,800$. We will describe the properties of the sampling distribution of $\bar{x}$ more fully in the next section.

The 500 values of the sample standard deviation s and the 500 values of the sample proportion $\bar{p}$ are summarized by the relative frequency histograms in Figures 7.3 and 7.4. As in the case of $\bar{x}$, both s and $\bar{p}$ are random variables that provide numerical descriptions of the outcome of a simple random sample. If every possible sample of size 30 were selected from the population and if a value of s and a value of $\bar{p}$ were computed for each sample, the resulting probability distributions would be called the sampling distribution of s and the sampling distribution of $\bar{p}$, respectively. The relative frequency histograms of the 500 sample values, Figures 7.3 and 7.4, provide an approximation of these two sampling distributions.

In practice, we select only one simple random sample from the population. We repeated the sampling process 500 times in this section simply to illustrate that many different samples are possible and that the different samples generate a variety of values for the sample statistics $\bar{x}$, s, and $\bar{p}$. The probability distribution of any particular sample statistic is called the **sampling distribution** of the statistic. In Section 7.5 we show the characteristics of the sampling distribution of $\bar{x}$. In Section 7.6 we show the characteristics of the sampling distribution of $\bar{p}$.

FIGURE 7.3   RELATIVE FREQUENCY HISTOGRAM OF s VALUES FROM 500 SIMPLE RANDOM SAMPLES OF SIZE 30 EACH

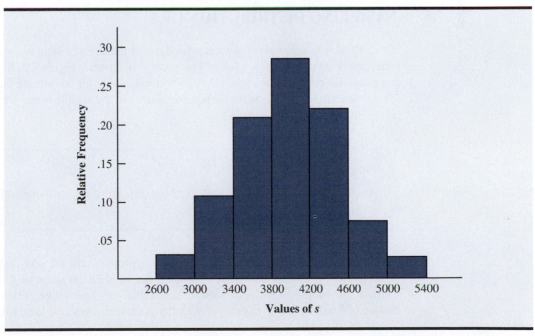

FIGURE 7.4   RELATIVE FREQUENCY HISTOGRAM OF $\bar{p}$ VALUES FROM 500 SIMPLE
RANDOM SAMPLES OF SIZE 30 EACH

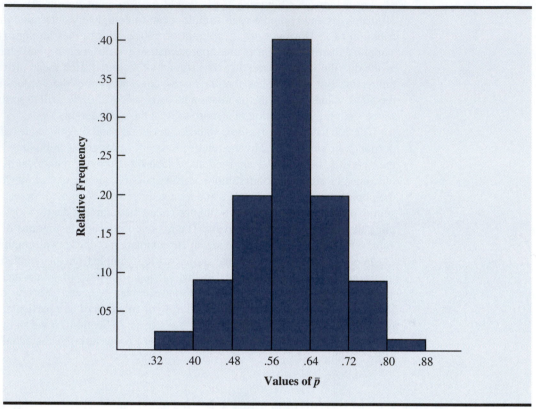

7.5   SAMPLING DISTRIBUTION OF $\bar{x}$

One of the most common statistical procedures is the use of a sample mean $\bar{x}$ to make inferences about a population mean μ. This process is shown in Figure 7.5. If the process were repeated, we could anticipate obtaining a different value for the sample mean $\bar{x}$ each time. The probability distribution for all possible values of the sample mean $\bar{x}$ is called the sampling distribution of the sample mean $\bar{x}$.

> **Sampling Distribution of $\bar{x}$**
>
> The sampling distribution of $\bar{x}$ is the probability distribution of all possible values of the sample mean, $\bar{x}$.

The purpose of this section is to describe the properties of the sampling distribution of $\bar{x}$, including the expected value or mean of $\bar{x}$, the standard deviation of $\bar{x}$, and the shape or form of the sampling distribution itself. As we shall see, knowledge of the sampling distribution of $\bar{x}$ will enable us to make probability statements about the sampling error involved

FIGURE 7.5   THE STATISTICAL PROCESS OF USING A SAMPLE MEAN TO MAKE INFERENCES ABOUT A POPULATION MEAN

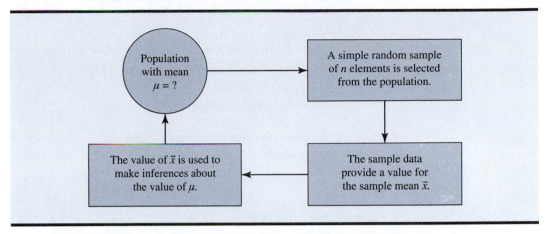

when $\bar{x}$ is used to estimate μ. Let us begin by considering the mean of all possible $\bar{x}$ values, which is referred to as the expected value of $\bar{x}$.

Expected Value of $\bar{x}$

In the EAI sampling problem we saw that different simple random samples result in a variety of values for the sample mean $\bar{x}$. Because many different values of the random variable $\bar{x}$ are possible, we are often interested in the mean of all possible values of $\bar{x}$ that can be generated by the various simple random samples. The mean of the $\bar{x}$ random variable is the expected value of $\bar{x}$. Let $E(\bar{x})$ represent the expected value of $\bar{x}$ and μ represent the mean of the population from which we are sampling. It can be shown that with simple random sampling, $E(\bar{x})$ and μ are equal.

The expected value of $\bar{x}$ equals the mean of the population from which the sample is drawn.

Expected Value of $\bar{x}$

$$E(\bar{x}) = \mu \qquad (7.1)$$

where

$$E(\bar{x}) = \text{the expected value of } \bar{x}$$
$$\mu = \text{the population mean}$$

This result shows that with simple random sampling, the expected value or mean of $\bar{x}$ is equal to the mean of the population from which we are sampling. In Section 7.1 we saw that the mean annual salary for the population of EAI managers is $\mu = \$51,800$. Thus, according to equation (7.1), the mean of all possible sample means for the EAI study is also $\$51,800$.

When the expected value of a point estimator is equal to the population parameter, we say the point estimator is **unbiased**. Thus, equation (7.1) shows that $\bar{x}$ is an unbiased estimator of the population mean μ. Unbiasedness is a desirable property of point estimators.

Standard Deviation of $\bar{x}$

Let us define the standard deviation of the sampling distribution of $\bar{x}$. We will use the following notation.

$$\sigma_{\bar{x}} = \text{the standard deviation of the sampling distribution of } \bar{x}$$
$$\sigma = \text{the standard deviation of the population}$$
$$n = \text{the sample size}$$
$$N = \text{the population size}$$

It can be shown that with simple random sampling, the standard deviation of $\bar{x}$ depends on whether the population is finite or infinite. The two formulas for the standard deviation of $\bar{x}$ follow.

Standard Deviation of $\bar{x}$

Finite Population	*Infinite Population*	
$$\sigma_{\bar{x}} = \sqrt{\frac{N-n}{N-1}}\left(\frac{\sigma}{\sqrt{n}}\right)$$	$$\sigma_{\bar{x}} = \frac{\sigma}{\sqrt{n}}$$	(7.2)

In comparing the two formulas in equation (7.2), we see that the factor $\sqrt{(N-n)/(N-1)}$ is required for the finite population case but not for the infinite population case. This factor is commonly referred to as the **finite population correction factor**. In many practical sampling situations, we find that the population involved, although finite, is "large," whereas the sample size is relatively "small." In such cases the finite population correction factor $\sqrt{(N-n)/(N-1)}$ is close to 1. As a result, the difference between the values of the standard deviation of $\bar{x}$ for the finite and infinite population cases becomes negligible. With a finite population correction factor so close to 1, $\sigma_{\bar{x}} = \sigma/\sqrt{n}$ becomes a good approximation to the standard deviation of $\bar{x}$ even though the population is finite. This observation leads to the following general guideline, or rule of thumb, for computing the standard deviation of $\bar{x}$.

Use the Following Formula to Calculate the Standard Deviation of $\bar{x}$

$$\sigma_{\bar{x}} = \frac{\sigma}{\sqrt{n}} \qquad (7.3)$$

whenever

1. The population is infinite; or
2. The population is finite *and* the sample size is less than or equal to 5% of the population size; that is, $n/N \le .05$.

Problem 21 shows that when $n/N \le .05$, the finite population correction factor has little effect on the value of $\sigma_{\bar{x}}$.

In cases where $n/N > .05$, the finite population version of equation (7.2) should be used to compute $\sigma_{\bar{x}}$. Unless otherwise noted, throughout the text we will assume that the population size is "large," $n/N \le .05$, and equation (7.3) can be used to compute $\sigma_{\bar{x}}$.

Now let us return to the EAI study and compute the standard deviation for the sampling distribution of $\bar{x}$. In Section 7.1 we saw that the population standard deviation for the annual salary data is $\sigma = 4000$. In this case the population is finite, with $N = 2500$. However, with a sample size of 30, we have $n/N = 30/2500 = .012$. Following the rule of thumb given in equation (7.3), we can ignore the finite population correction factor and use equation (7.3) to compute the standard deviation of $\bar{x}$.

$$\sigma_{\bar{x}} = \frac{\sigma}{\sqrt{n}} = \frac{4000}{\sqrt{30}} = 730.30$$

The standard error is, itself, a standard deviation. Standard error is a term used for the standard deviation of a point estimator.

Later we will see that the value of $\sigma_{\bar{x}}$ is helpful in determining how far the sample mean may be from the population mean. Because of the role that $\sigma_{\bar{x}}$ plays in computing possible sampling errors when $\bar{x}$ is used as an estimate of μ, $\sigma_{\bar{x}}$ is referred to as the **standard error of the mean**.

Central Limit Theorem

The final step in identifying the characteristics of the sampling distribution of $\bar{x}$ is to determine the form of the probability distribution of $\bar{x}$. We consider two cases: one in which the form of the population distribution is unknown and one in which the population distribution is known to be normally distributed.

When the population distribution is unknown, we rely on one of the most important theorems in statistics—the **central limit theorem**. A statement of the central limit theorem as it applies to the sampling distribution of $\bar{x}$ follows.

Central Limit Theorem

In selecting simple random samples of size n from a population, the sampling distribution of the sample mean $\bar{x}$ can be approximated by a *normal probability distribution* as the sample size becomes large.

Figure 7.6 shows how the central limit theorem works for three different populations; each column refers to one of the populations. The top panel shows the probability distributions for the populations. In each case the population clearly is not normal. However, note what happens to the sampling distribution of $\bar{x}$ as the sample size increases. When the samples are of size 2 (see the second panel), we see that the sampling distribution of $\bar{x}$ begins to take on an appearance different from that of the population distribution. For samples of size 5, we see all three sampling distributions beginning to take on a bell-shaped appearance. Finally, the samples of size 30 show all three sampling distributions to be approximately normal. Thus, for sufficiently large samples, the sampling distribution of $\bar{x}$ can be approximated by a normal probability distribution. However, how large must the sample size be before we can assume that the central limit theorem applies? General statistical practice is to assume that for most applications, the sampling distribution of $\bar{x}$ can be approximated by a normal probability distribution whenever the sample size is 30 or more. In effect, a sample size of 30 or more is assumed to satisfy

FIGURE 7.6   ILLUSTRATION OF THE CENTRAL LIMIT THEOREM FOR THREE
POPULATIONS

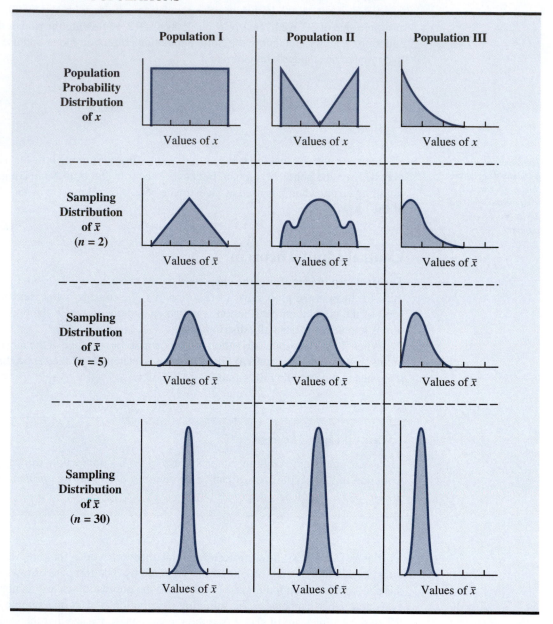

the large-sample condition of the central limit theorem. This observation is so important
that we restate it.

> The sampling distribution of $\bar{x}$ can be approximated by a normal probability distribu-
> tion whenever the sample size is large. The large-sample condition can be assumed
> for simple random samples of size 30 or more.

The central limit theorem applies to any population. Thus, when the sample size is large, it can be used to describe the sampling distribution of $\bar{x}$ even when the form of the population distribution is unknown.

The central limit theorem is the key to identifying the appropriate form of the sampling distribution of $\bar{x}$ whenever the form of the population distribution is unknown. However, we may encounter some sampling situations in which the population is assumed or believed to have a normal probability distribution. When this condition occurs, the following result identifies the form of the sampling distribution of $\bar{x}$.

> Whenever the population has a normal probability distribution, the sampling distribution of $\bar{x}$ has a normal probability distribution for any sample size.

In summary, if we use a large ($n \geq 30$) simple random sample, the central limit theorem enables us to conclude that the sampling distribution of $\bar{x}$ can be approximated by a normal probability distribution. When the simple random sample is small ($n < 30$), the sampling distribution of $\bar{x}$ can be considered normal only if we are willing to assume that the population has a normal probability distribution.

Sampling Distribution of $\bar{x}$ for the EAI Problem

For the EAI study we showed that $E(\bar{x}) = 51{,}800$ and $\sigma_{\bar{x}} = 730.30$. Because we are using a simple random sample of 30 managers, the central limit theorem enables us to conclude that the sampling distribution of $\bar{x}$ is approximately normal as shown in Figure 7.7.

Practical Value of the Sampling Distribution of $\bar{x}$

Whenever a simple random sample is selected and the value of the sample mean $\bar{x}$ is used to estimate the value of the population mean μ, we cannot expect the sample mean to exactly equal the population mean. As stated earlier, the absolute value of the difference between the value of the sample mean $\bar{x}$ and the value of the population mean μ, $|\bar{x} - \mu|$, is called the sampling error. The practical reason for our interest in the sampling distribution

FIGURE 7.7   SAMPLING DISTRIBUTION OF $\bar{x}$ FOR A SIMPLE RANDOM SAMPLE OF 30 EAI MANAGERS

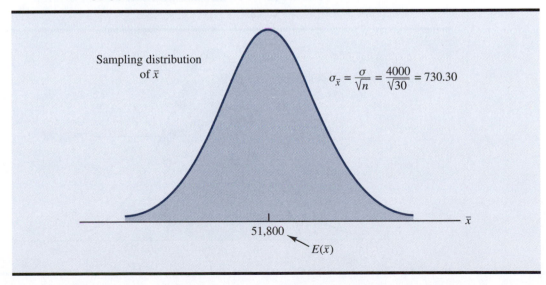

Sampling distribution of $\bar{x}$

$$\sigma_{\bar{x}} = \frac{\sigma}{\sqrt{n}} = \frac{4000}{\sqrt{30}} = 730.30$$

51,800

$E(\bar{x})$

of $\bar{x}$ is that it can be used to provide probability information about the size of the sampling error. To demonstrate this use, let us return to the EAI problem.

Suppose the personnel director believes the sample mean will be an acceptable estimate of the population mean if the sample mean is within $500 of the population mean. However, it is not possible to *guarantee* that the sample mean will be within $500 of the population mean. Indeed, Table 7.5 and Figure 7.2 show that some of the 500 sample means differed by more than $2000 from the population mean. So we must think of the personnel director's request in probability terms. That is, the personnel director is concerned with the following question: What is the probability that the sample mean computed using a simple random sample of 30 EAI managers will be within $500 of the population mean?

Since we identified the properties of the sampling distribution of $\bar{x}$ (see Figure 7.7), we can use this distribution to answer the probability question. Refer to the sampling distribution of $\bar{x}$ shown again in Figure 7.8. The personnel director wants to know the probability that the sample mean falls between $51,300 and $52,300. If the value of the sample mean $\bar{x}$ is in this interval, the value of $\bar{x}$ will be within $500 of the population mean. The appropriate probability is given by the darkly shaded area of the sampling distribution shown in Figure 7.8. Because the sampling distribution is normal we can compute this probability using the table for the standard normal probability distribution. We first calculate the z value at the upper endpoint of the interval (52,300) and use the table to find the area under the curve to the left of that point (left tail area). Then we compute the z value at the lower endpoint of the interval (51,300) and use the table to find the area under the curve to the left of that point (another left tail area). Subtracting the second tail area from the first gives us the desired probability.

At $\bar{x}$ = 52,300, we have

$$z = \frac{52,300 - 51,800}{730.30} = .68$$

Referring to the standard normal probability distribution table, we find a cumulative probability (area to the left of z = .68) of .7517.

FIGURE 7.8   PROBABILITY OF A SAMPLE MEAN BEING WITHIN $500 OF THE POPULATION MEAN WHEN A SIMPLE RANDOM SAMPLE OF 30 EAI MANAGERS IS USED

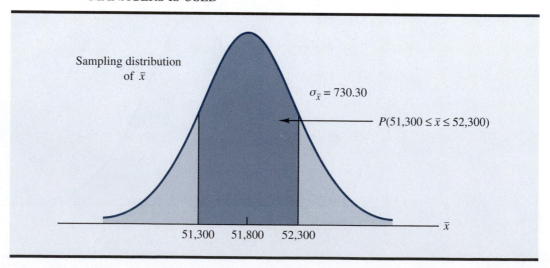

At $\bar{x} = 51{,}300$, we have

$$z = \frac{51{,}300 - 51{,}800}{730.30} = -.68$$

By symmetry, the area under the curve to the left of $z = -.68$ is the same as the area under the curve to the right of $z = .68$. So $P(z \leq -.68) = 1 - P(z \leq .68) = 1 - .7517 = .2483$. Therefore, $P(51{,}300 \leq \bar{x} \leq 52{,}300) = P(z \leq .68) - P(z \leq -.68) = .7517 - .2483 = .5034$.

Using Excel's NORMDIST function is easier and provides more accurate results than the tables.

The desired probability can also be computed using Excel's NORMDIST function. The advantage of using the NORMDIST function is that we do not have to make a separate computation of the z value. Evaluating the NORMDIST function at the upper endpoint of the interval provides the area under the curve to the left of 52,300. Entering the formula =NORMDIST(52300,51800,730.30,TRUE) into a cell of an Excel worksheet provides .7532 for this cumulative probability. Evaluating the NORMDIST function at the lower endpoint of the interval provides the area under the curve to the left of 51,300. Entering the formula =NORMDIST(51300,51800,730.30,TRUE) into a cell of an Excel worksheet provides .2468 for this cumulative probability. The probability of $\bar{x}$ being in the interval from 51,300 to 52,300 is then given by $.7532 - .2468 = .5064$. We note that this result is slightly different from the probability obtained using the tables, because in using the normal tables we rounded to two decimal places of accuracy when computing the z value. The result obtained using NORMDIST is thus more accurate.

The sampling distribution of $\bar{x}$ can be used to provide probability information about how close the sample mean $\bar{x}$ is to the population mean μ.

The preceding computations show that a simple random sample of 30 EAI managers has a .5064 probability of providing a sample mean $\bar{x}$ that is within $500 of the population mean. Thus, there is a $1 - .5064 = .4936$ probability that the sampling error will be more than $500. In other words, a simple random sample of 30 EAI managers has roughly a 50-50 chance of providing a sample mean within the allowable $500. Perhaps a larger sample size should be considered. Let us explore this possibility by considering the relationship between the sample size and the sampling distribution of $\bar{x}$.

Relationship Between the Sample Size and the Sampling Distribution of $\bar{x}$

Suppose that in the EAI sampling problem we select a simple random sample of 100 EAI managers instead of the 30 originally considered. Intuitively, it would seem that with more data provided by the larger sample size, the sample mean based on $n = 100$ should provide a better estimate of the population mean than the sample mean based on $n = 30$. To see how much better, let us consider the relationship between the sample size and the sampling distribution of $\bar{x}$.

First note that $E(\bar{x}) = \mu$ regardless of the sample size. Thus, the mean of all possible values of $\bar{x}$ is equal to the population mean μ regardless of the sample size n. However, note that the standard error of the mean, $\sigma_{\bar{x}} = \sigma/\sqrt{n}$, is related to the square root of the sample size. Whenever the sample size is increased, the standard error of the mean $\sigma_{\bar{x}}$ is decreased. With $n = 30$, the standard error of the mean for the EAI problem is 730.30. However, with the increase in the sample size to $n = 100$, the standard error of the mean is decreased to

$$\sigma_{\bar{x}} = \frac{\sigma}{\sqrt{n}} = \frac{4000}{\sqrt{100}} = 400$$

The sampling distributions of $\bar{x}$ with $n = 30$ and $n = 100$ are shown in Figure 7.9. Because the sampling distribution with $n = 100$ provides a smaller standard error, the values of $\bar{x}$ vary less and tend to be grouped closer around the population mean than the values of $\bar{x}$ with $n = 30$.

FIGURE 7.9   COMPARISON OF THE SAMPLING DISTRIBUTIONS OF $\bar{x}$ FOR SIMPLE
RANDOM SAMPLES OF $n = 30$ AND $n = 100$ EAI MANAGERS

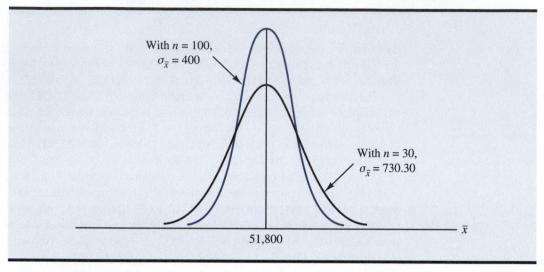

With $n = 100$,
$\sigma_{\bar{x}} = 400$

With $n = 30$,
$\sigma_{\bar{x}} = 730.30$

51,800

$\bar{x}$

We can use the sampling distribution of $\bar{x}$ for the case with $n = 100$ to compute the probability that a simple random sample of 100 EAI managers will provide a sample mean that is within $500 of the population mean. In this case the sampling distribution is normal with a mean of 51,800 and a standard deviation of 400 (see Figure 7.10). Again, we could compute the appropriate z values and use the standard normal probability distribution table to make this probability calculation. However, Excel's NORMDIST function is easier to use and provides more accurate results. Entering the formula =NORMDIST(52300,51800,400,TRUE)

FIGURE 7.10   PROBABILITY OF A SAMPLE MEAN BEING WITHIN $500
OF THE POPULATION MEAN FOR A SIMPLE RANDOM SAMPLE
OF 100 EAI MANAGERS

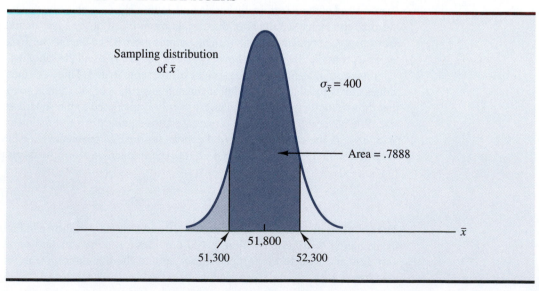

Sampling distribution
of $\bar{x}$

$\sigma_{\bar{x}} = 400$

Area = .7888

51,800

51,300

52,300

$\bar{x}$

into a cell of an Excel worksheet provides the cumulative probability corresponding to $\bar{x} = 52{,}300$. The value provided by Excel is .8944. Entering the formula =NORMDIST (51300,51800,400,TRUE) into a cell of an Excel worksheet provides the cumulative probability corresponding to $\bar{x} = 51{,}300$. The value provided by Excel is .1056. Thus, the probability of $\bar{x}$ being in the interval from 51,300 to 52,300 is given by $.8944 - .1056 = .7888$. By increasing the sample size from 30 to 100 EAI managers, we increase the probability that the sampling error will be $500 or less; that is, the probability of obtaining a sample mean within $500 of the population mean increases from .5064 to .7888.

The important point in this discussion is that as the sample size increases, the standard error of the mean decreases. As a result, a larger sample size will provide a higher probability that the sample mean falls within a specified distance of the population mean.

NOTES AND COMMENTS

1. In presenting the sampling distribution of $\bar{x}$ for the EAI problem, we took advantage of the fact that the population mean $\mu = 51{,}800$ and the population standard deviation $\sigma = 4000$ were known. However, usually the values of the population mean μ and the population standard deviation σ that are needed to determine the sampling distribution of $\bar{x}$ will be unknown. In Chapter 8 we will show how the sample mean $\bar{x}$ and the sample standard deviation s are used when μ and σ are unknown.

2. The theoretical proof of the central limit theorem requires independent observations in the sample. This condition is met for infinite populations and for finite populations where sampling is done with replacement. Although the central limit theorem does not directly address sampling without replacement from finite populations, general statistical practice has been to apply the findings of the central limit theorem in this situation when the population size is large.

EXERCISES

Methods

19. In a population with a mean of 200 and a standard deviation of 50, suppose a simple random sample of size 100 is selected and $\bar{x}$ is used to estimate μ.
   a. What is the probability that the sample mean will be within ± 5 of the population mean?
   b. What is the probability that the sample mean will be within ± 10 of the population mean?

20. Assume the population standard deviation is $\sigma = 25$. Compute the standard error of the mean, $\sigma_{\bar{x}}$, for sample sizes of 50, 100, 150, and 200. What can you say about the size of the standard error of the mean as the sample size is increased?

21. Suppose a simple random sample of size 50 is selected from a population with $\sigma = 10$. Find the value of the standard error of the mean in each of the following cases (use the finite population correction factor if appropriate).
   a. The population size is infinite.
   b. The population size is $N = 50{,}000$.
   c. The population size is $N = 5000$.
   d. The population size is $N = 500$.

22. In a population with a mean of 400 and a standard deviation of 50, the probability distribution of the population is unknown.

   a. A researcher will use simple random samples of either 10, 20, 30, or 40 items to collect data about the population. With which of these sample-size alternatives will we be able to use a normal probability distribution to describe the sampling distribution of $\bar{x}$? Explain.

   b. Show the sampling distribution of $\bar{x}$ for the instances in which the normal probability distribution is appropriate.

23. In a large population with a mean of 100 and a standard deviation of 16, what is the probability that a sample mean will be within ± 2 of the population mean for each of the following sample sizes?

   a. $n = 50$

   b. $n = 100$

   c. $n = 200$

   d. $n = 400$

   e. What is the advantage of a larger sample size?

Applications

24. Refer to the EAI sampling problem. Suppose a simple random sample of 60 managers is used.

   a. Sketch the sampling distribution of $\bar{x}$ when simple random samples of size 60 are used.

   b. What happens to the sampling distribution of $\bar{x}$ if simple random samples of size 120 are used?

   c. What general statement can you make about what happens to the sampling distribution of $\bar{x}$ as the sample size is increased? Does this generalization seem logical? Explain.

25. In the EAI sampling problem (see Figure 7.8), we showed that for $n = 30$, there was .5064 probability of obtaining a sample mean within $\pm\$500$ of the population mean.

   a. What is the probability that $\bar{x}$ is within $500 of the population mean if a sample of size 60 is used?

   b. Answer part (a) for a sample of size 120.

26. The mean price per gallon of regular gasoline sold in the United States is $1.20 (*The Energy Information Administration*, March 3, 1997). Assume the population mean price per gallon is $\mu = 1.20$, and the population standard deviation is $\sigma = .10$. Suppose that a random sample of 50 gasoline stations will be selected, and a sample mean price per gallon will be computed for data collected from the 50 gasoline stations.

   a. Show the sampling distribution of the sample mean $\bar{x}$ where $\bar{x}$ is the sample mean price per gallon for the 50 gasoline stations.

   b. What is the probability that the simple random sample will provide a sample mean within 2 cents or .02 of the population mean?

   c. What is the probability that the simple random sample will provide a sample mean within 1 cent or .01 of the population mean?

27. The College Board American College Testing Program reported a population mean SAT score of $\mu = 1017$ (*The New York Times*, 2000 Almanac). Assume that the population standard deviation is $\sigma = 100$.

   a. What is the probability that a random sample of 75 students will provide a sample mean SAT score within 10 of the population mean?

   b. What is the probability that a random sample of 75 students will provide a sample mean SAT score within 20 of the population mean?

28. The mean annual starting salary for marketing majors is $34,000 (*Time*, May 8, 2000). Assume that for the population of graduates with a marketing major, the mean annual starting salary is $\mu = 34{,}000$, and the standard deviation is $\sigma = 2000$.

   a. What is the probability that a simple random sample of marketing majors will have a sample mean within $\pm\$250$ of the population mean for each of the following sample sizes: 30, 50, 100, 200, and 400?

   b. What is the advantage of a larger sample size when attempting to estimate the population mean?

29. The mean monthly rental rate for a two-bedroom apartment in Atlanta is $982 (*Elle*, September 1998). Assume that the population mean is $982 and the population standard deviation is $210.

   a. What is the probability that a simple random sample of 40 two-bedroom apartments will provide a sample mean monthly rental rate within $\pm\$100$ of the population mean?

   b. What is the probability that a simple random sample of 40 two-bedroom apartments will provide a sample mean monthly rental rate within $\pm\$25$ of the population mean?

   c. Discuss the results in parts (a) and (b).

30. The population mean for the price of a new one-family home is $166,500 (U.S. Bureau of the Census, *New One-Family Houses Sold*, 1997). Assume that the population standard deviation is $42,000 and that a sample of 100 new one-family homes will be selected.

   a. Show the sampling distribution of the sample mean price for new homes based on the sample of 100.

   b. What is the probability that the sample mean for the 100 new homes will be within $10,000 of the population mean?

   c. Repeat part (b) for values of $5000, $2500, and $1000.

   d. To estimate the population mean price to within $\pm\$2500$ or $\pm\$1000$, what would you recommend?

31. *Money* magazine reported that the average price per gallon of gasoline in the United States during the first quarter of 2001 was $1.46 (*Money*, August 2001). Assume the price reported by *Money* is the population mean and the population standard deviation is $\sigma = \$.15$.

   a. What is the probability that the mean price per gallon for a simple random sample of 30 gas stations is within $.03 of the population mean?

   b. What is the probability that the mean price per gallon for a simple random sample of 50 gas stations is within $.03 of the population mean?

   c. What is the probability that the mean price per gallon for a simple random sample of 100 gas stations is within $.03 of the population mean?

   d. Would you recommend a sample size of 30, 50, or 100 to have at least a .95 probability that the sample mean price per gallon is within $.03 of the population mean?

32. To estimate the mean age for a population of 4000 employees, a simple random sample of 40 employees is selected.

   a. Would you use the finite population correction factor in calculating the standard error of the mean? Explain.

   b. If the population standard deviation is $\sigma = 8.2$ years, compute the standard error both with and without using the finite population correction factor. What is the rationale for ignoring the finite population correction factor whenever $n/N \leq .05$?

   c. What is the probability that the sample mean age of the employees will be within ± 2 years of the population mean age?

7.6   SAMPLING DISTRIBUTION OF $\bar{p}$

In many situations in business and economics, we use the sample proportion $\bar{p}$ to make statistical inferences about the population proportion p. This process is depicted in Figure 7.11. On each repetition of the process, we can anticipate obtaining a different value for the sample proportion $\bar{p}$. The probability distribution for all possible values of the sample proportion $\bar{p}$ is called the sampling distribution of the sample proportion $\bar{p}$.

Sampling Distribution of $\bar{p}$

The sampling distribution of $\bar{p}$ is the probability distribution of all possible values of the sample proportion $\bar{p}$.

To determine how close the sample proportion $\bar{p}$ is to the population proportion p, we need to understand the properties of the sampling distribution of $\bar{p}$: the expected value of $\bar{p}$, the standard deviation of $\bar{p}$, and the shape or form of the sampling distribution of $\bar{p}$.

Expected Value of $\bar{p}$

The expected value of $\bar{p}$, denoted $E(\bar{p})$, is the mean of all possible values of $\bar{p}$. Equation (7.4) shows that the mean of all possible $\bar{p}$ values is equal to the population proportion p. Thus, the point estimator $\bar{p}$ is an unbiased estimator of the population proportion, p.

Expected Value of $\bar{p}$

$$E(\bar{p}) = p \qquad (7.4)$$

where

$$E(\bar{p}) = \text{the expected value of } \bar{p}$$
$$p = \text{the population proportion}$$

FIGURE 7.11   THE STATISTICAL PROCESS OF USING A SAMPLE PROPORTION TO MAKE INFERENCES ABOUT A POPULATION PROPORTION

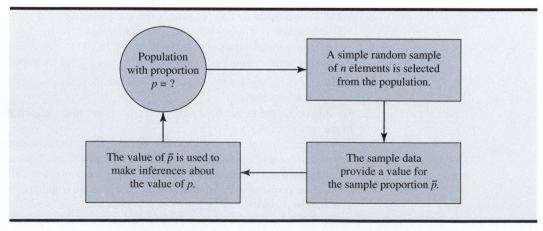

Recall that in Section 7.1 we noted that $p = .60$ for the EAI population, where p is the proportion of the population of managers who had participated in the company's management training program. Equation (7.4) shows that the expected value of $\bar{p}$ for the EAI sampling problem is .60.

Standard Deviation of $\bar{p}$

The standard deviation of $\bar{p}$, denoted $\sigma_{\bar{p}}$, is referred to as the *standard error of the proportion*. Just as we found for the sample mean $\bar{x}$, the standard deviation of $\bar{p}$ depends on whether the population is finite or infinite. The two formulas for computing the standard deviation of $\bar{p}$ follow.

Standard Deviation of $\bar{p}$

$$\text{Finite Population} \qquad\qquad \text{Infinite Population}$$

$$\sigma_{\bar{p}} = \sqrt{\frac{N-n}{N-1}}\sqrt{\frac{p(1-p)}{n}} \qquad\qquad \sigma_{\bar{p}} = \sqrt{\frac{p(1-p)}{n}} \qquad\qquad (7.5)$$

Comparing the two formulas in equation (7.5), we see that the only difference is the use of the finite population correction factor $\sqrt{(N-n)/(N-1)}$.

As was the case with the sample mean $\bar{x}$, the difference between the values obtained using the expressions for the finite population and the infinite population becomes negligible if the size of the finite population is large in comparison to the sample size. We follow the same rule of thumb that we recommended for the sample mean. That is, if the population is finite with $n/N \le .05$, we will use $\sigma_{\bar{p}} = \sqrt{p(1-p)/n}$. However, if the population is finite and if $n/N > .05$, the finite population correction factor should be used. Again, unless specifically noted, throughout the text we will assume that the population size is large in relation to the sample size and thus the finite population correction factor is unnecessary.

For the EAI study we know that the population proportion of managers who participated in the management training program is $p = .60$. With $n/N = 30/2500 = .012$, we can ignore the finite population correction factor when we compute the standard deviation of $\bar{p}$. For the simple random sample of 30 managers, $\sigma_{\bar{p}}$ is

$$\sigma_{\bar{p}} = \sqrt{\frac{p(1-p)}{n}} = \sqrt{\frac{.60(1-.60)}{30}} = .0894$$

Form of the Sampling Distribution of $\bar{p}$

Now that we know the mean and standard deviation of $\bar{p}$, we want to consider the form of the sampling distribution of $\bar{p}$. Applying the central limit theorem as it relates to $\bar{p}$ produces the following result.

The sampling distribution of $\bar{p}$ can be approximated by a normal probability distribution whenever the sample size is large.

These criteria are slightly different from the $n \geq 30$ criteria we used for the large sample case for $\bar{x}$. The reason is that small values of p or $(1 - p)$ can cause the sampling distribution to be skewed even with $n \geq 30$.

With $\bar{p}$, the sample size can be considered large[5] whenever the following two conditions are satisfied.

$$np \geq 5$$
$$n(1 - p) \geq 5$$

Recall that for the EAI sampling problem we know that the population proportion of managers who participated in the training program is $p = .60$. With a simple random sample of size 30, we have $np = 30(.60) = 18$ and $n(1 - p) = 30(.40) = 12$. Thus, the sampling distribution of $\bar{p}$ can be approximated by a normal probability distribution as shown in Figure 7.12.

Practical Value of the Sampling Distribution of $\bar{p}$

Whenever a simple random sample is selected and the value of the sample proportion $\bar{p}$ is used to estimate the value of the population proportion p, we anticipate some sampling error. In this case, the sampling error is the absolute value of the difference between the value of the sample proportion $\bar{p}$ and the value of the population proportion p. The practical value of the sampling distribution of $\bar{p}$ is that it can be used to provide probability information about the sampling error.

Suppose, in the EAI problem, the personnel director wants to know the probability of obtaining a value of $\bar{p}$ that is within .05 of the population proportion of EAI managers who

FIGURE 7.12   SAMPLING DISTRIBUTION OF $\bar{p}$ FOR THE PROPORTION
OF EAI MANAGERS WHO PARTICIPATED IN THE MANAGEMENT
TRAINING PROGRAM

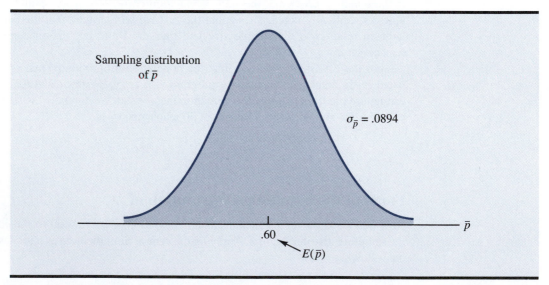

---

[5]For values of p near .50, sample sizes as small as 10 permit a normal approximation. But, with very small, or large, values of p, much larger samples are needed.

participated in the training program. That is, what is the probability of obtaining a sample with a sample proportion $\bar{p}$ between .55 and .65? The darkly shaded area in Figure 7.13 shows this probability. Using the fact that the sampling distribution of $\bar{p}$ can be approximated by a normal probability distribution with a mean of .60 and a standard error of $\sigma_{\bar{p}} = .0894$, we can use Excel's NORMDIST function to make this calculation. Entering the formula =NORMDIST(.65,.60,.0894,TRUE) into a cell of an Excel worksheet provides the cumulative probability corresponding to $\bar{p} = .65$. The value calculated by Excel is .7120. Entering the formula =NORMDIST(.55,.60,.0894,TRUE) into a cell of an Excel worksheet provides the cumulative probability corresponding to $\bar{p} = .55$. The value calculated by Excel is .2880. Thus, the probability of $\bar{p}$ being in the interval from .55 to .65 is given by .7120 − .2880 = .4240.

If we consider increasing the sample size to $n = 100$, the standard error of the proportion becomes

$$\sigma_{\bar{p}} = \sqrt{\frac{.60(1 - .60)}{100}} = .0490$$

With a sample size of 100 EAI managers, the probability of the sample proportion having a value within .05 of the population proportion can now be computed. Because the sampling distribution is approximately normal, with mean .60 and standard deviation .0490, we can use Excel's NORMDIST function to make this calculation. Entering the formula =NORMDIST(.65,.60,.0490,TRUE) into a cell of an Excel worksheet provides the cumulative probability corresponding to $\bar{p} = .65$. The value calculated by Excel is .8462. Entering the formula =NORMDIST(.55,.60,.0490,TRUE) into a cell of an Excel worksheet provides the cumulative probability corresponding to $\bar{p} = .55$. The value calculated by Excel is .1538. Thus, the probability of $\bar{p}$ being in the interval from .55 to .65 is given by .8462 − .1538 = .6924. Increasing the sample size increases the probability that the sampling error will be less than or equal to .05 by .2684 (from .4240 to .6924).

FIGURE 7.13   SAMPLING DISTRIBUTION OF $\bar{p}$ FOR THE EAI SAMPLING PROBLEM

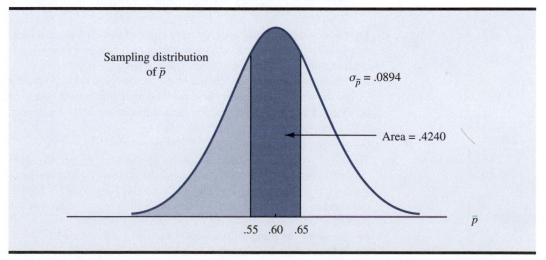

EXERCISES

Methods

33. A simple random sample of size 100 is selected from a population with $p = .40$.
    a. What is the expected value of $\bar{p}$?
    b. What is the standard deviation of $\bar{p}$?
    c. Show the sampling distribution of $\bar{p}$.
    d. What does the sampling distribution of $\bar{p}$ show?

34. A population proportion is .40. A simple random sample of size 200 will be taken and the sample proportion $\bar{p}$ will be used to estimate the population proportion.
    a. What is the probability that the sample proportion will be within $\pm.03$ of the population proportion?
    b. What is the probability that the sample proportion will be within $\pm.05$ of the population proportion?

35. Assume that the population proportion is .55. Compute the standard error of the proportion, $\sigma_{\bar{p}}$, for sample sizes of 100, 200, 500, and 1000. What can you say about the size of the standard error of the proportion as the sample size increases?

36. The population proportion is .30. What is the probability that a sample proportion will be within $\pm.04$ of the population proportion for each of the following sample sizes?
    a. $n = 100$
    b. $n = 200$
    c. $n = 500$
    d. $n = 1000$
    e. What is the advantage of a larger sample size?

Applications

37. The president of Doerman Distributors, Inc., believes that 30% of the firm's orders come from first-time customers. A simple random sample of 100 orders will be used to estimate the proportion of first-time customers.
    a. Assume that the president is correct and $p = .30$. What is the sampling distribution of $\bar{p}$ for this study?
    b. What is the probability that the sample proportion $\bar{p}$ will be between .20 and .40?
    c. What is the probability that the sample proportion will be within $\pm.05$ of the population proportion $p = .30$?

38. The Grocery Manufacturers of America reported that 76% of consumers read the ingredients listed on a product's label. Assume the population proportion is $p = .76$ and a simple random sample of 400 consumers is selected from the population.
    a. Show the sampling distribution of the sample proportion $\bar{p}$ where $\bar{p}$ is the proportion of the sampled consumers who read the ingredients listed on a product's label.
    b. What is the probability that the sample proportion will be within $\pm.03$ of the population proportion?
    c. Answer part (b) for a sample of 750 consumers.

39. *Time*/CNN voter polls monitored public opinion for the presidential candidates during the 2000 presidential election campaign. One *Time*/CNN poll conducted by Yankelovich Partners, Inc., used a sample of 589 likely voters (*Time*, June 26, 2000). Assume the population proportion in favor of a presidential candidate is $p = .50$. Let $\bar{p}$ be the sample proportion of likely voters favoring the presidential candidate.
    a. Show the sampling distribution of $\bar{p}$.
    b. What is the probability the *Time*/CNN poll will provide a sample proportion within $\pm.04$ of the population proportion?

c. What is the probability the *Time*/CNN poll will provide a sample proportion within ±.03 of the population proportion?

d. What is the probability the *Time*/CNN poll will provide a sample proportion within ±.02 of the population proportion?

40. Even though most people believe breakfast is the most important meal of the day, 25% of adults skip breakfast (*U.S. News & World Report*, November 10, 1997). Assume the population proportion is $p = .25$, and $\bar{p}$ is the sample proportion of adults who skip breakfast based on a sample of 200 adults.

    a. Show the sampling distribution of $\bar{p}$.

    b. What is the probability that the sample proportion will be within ±.03 of the population proportion?

    c. What is the probability that the sample proportion will be within ±.05 of the population proportion?

41. The *Democrat and Chronicle* reported that 25% of the flights arriving at the San Diego airport during the first five months of 2001 were late (*Democrat and Chronicle*, July 23, 2001). From this information, assume the population proportion is $p = .25$.

    a. Show the sampling distribution of $\bar{p}$, the proportion of late flights in a sample of 1000 flights.

    b. What is the probability that the sample proportion will be within ±.03 of the population proportion if a sample of size 1000 is selected?

    c. Answer part (b) for a sample of 500 flights.

42. Assume that 15% of the parts produced in an assembly line operation are defective, but that the firm's production manager is not aware of this situation. Assume further that 50 parts are tested by the quality assurance department to determine the quality of the assembly operation. Let $\bar{p}$ be the sample proportion found defective by the quality assurance test.

    a. Show the sampling distribution for $\bar{p}$.

    b. What is the probability that the sample proportion will be within ±.03 of the population proportion that is defective?

    c. If the test shows $\bar{p} = .10$ or more, the assembly line operation will be shut down to check for the cause of the defects. What is the probability that the sample of 50 parts will lead to the conclusion that the assembly line should be shut down?

43. The Food Marketing Institute shows that 17% of households spend more than $100 per week on groceries. Assume the population proportion is $p = .17$ and a simple random sample of 800 households will be selected from the population.

    a. Show the sampling distribution of $\bar{p}$, the sample proportion of households spending more than $100 per week on groceries.

    b. What is the probability that the sample proportion will be within ±.02 of the population proportion?

    c. Answer part (b) for a sample of 1600 households.

7.7   SAMPLING METHODS

This section provides a brief introduction to sampling methods other than simple random sampling.

We described the simple random sampling procedure and discussed the properties of the sampling distributions of $\bar{x}$ and $\bar{p}$ when simple random sampling is used. However, simple random sampling is not the only sampling method available. Such methods as stratified random sampling, cluster sampling, and systematic sampling provide alternatives that in some situations offer advantages over simple random sampling. In this section we briefly introduce some of these alternative sampling methods.

FIGURE 7.14   DIAGRAM FOR STRATIFIED RANDOM SAMPLING

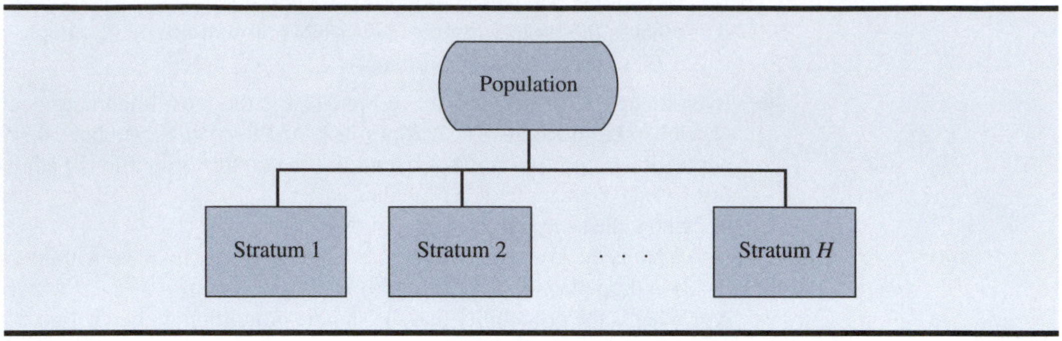

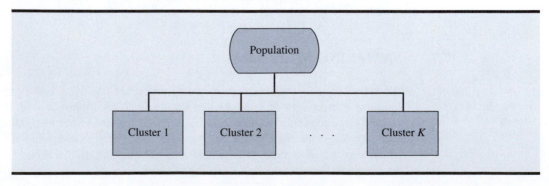

Stratified Random Sampling

In **stratified random sampling**, the elements in the population are first divided into groups called strata, such that each element in the population belongs to one and only one stratum. The basis for forming the strata, such as department, location, age, industry type, and so on, is at the discretion of the designer of the sample. However, the best results are obtained when the elements within each stratum are as much alike (homogeneous) as possible. Figure 7.14 is a diagram of a population divided into H strata.

Stratified random sampling works best when the elements in each stratum are similar.

After the strata are formed, a simple random sample is taken from each stratum. Formulas are available for combining the results for the individual stratum samples into one estimate of the population parameter of interest. The value of stratified random sampling depends on how homogeneous the elements are within the strata. If elements within strata are alike, the strata will have low variances. Thus relatively small sample sizes can be used to obtain good estimates of the strata characteristics. If strata are homogeneous, the stratified random sampling procedure will provide results just as precise as those of simple random sampling by using a smaller total sample size.

Cluster Sampling

Cluster sampling works best when each cluster provides a small-scale representation of the population.

In **cluster sampling,** the elements in the population are first divided into separate groups of elements called clusters. Each element of the population belongs to one and only one cluster (see Figure 7.15). A simple random sample of the clusters is then taken. All elements within each sampled cluster form the sample. Cluster sampling tends to provide the best re-

FIGURE 7.15   DIAGRAM FOR CLUSTER SAMPLING

sults when the elements within the clusters are not alike (heterogeneous). In the ideal case, each cluster is a representative small-scale version of the entire population. The value of cluster sampling depends on how representative each cluster is of the entire population. If all clusters are alike in this regard, sampling a small number of clusters will provide good estimates of the population parameters.

One of the primary applications of cluster sampling is area sampling, where clusters are city blocks or other well-defined areas. Cluster sampling generally requires a larger total sample size than either simple random sampling or stratified random sampling. However, it can result in cost savings when, for example, an interviewer is sent to a sampled cluster (e.g., a city-block location) and can obtain many sample observations in a relatively short time. Hence, a larger sample size may be obtainable with a significantly lower total cost.

Systematic Sampling

In some sampling situations, especially those with large populations, it is time-consuming to select a simple random sample by first finding a random number and then counting or searching through a list of the population elements until the corresponding element is found. An alternative to simple random sampling is **systematic sampling**. For example, if a sample size of 50 is desired from a population containing 5000 elements, we will sample one element for every $5000/50 = 100$ elements in the population. A systematic sample for this case involves selecting randomly one of the first 100 elements from the population list. Other sample elements are identified by starting with the first sampled element and then selecting every 100th element that follows in the population list. In effect, the sample of 50 is identified by moving systematically through the population and identifying every 100th element after the first randomly selected element. The sample of 50 usually will be easier to identify in this way than it would be if simple random sampling were used. Because the first element selected is a random choice, a systematic sample is usually assumed to have the properties of a simple random sample. This assumption is especially applicable when the list of elements in the population is a random ordering of the elements in the population (e.g., a telephone book).

Convenience Sampling

The sampling methods discussed thus far are referred to as *probability sampling* techniques. Elements selected from the population have a known probability of being included in the sample. The advantage of probability sampling is that the sampling distribution of the appropriate sample statistic generally can be identified. Formulas such as the ones for simple random sampling presented in this chapter can be used to determine the properties of the sampling distribution. Then the sampling distribution can be used to make probability statements about the sampling error associated with the results.

Convenience sampling is a *nonprobability sampling* technique. As the name implies, the sample is identified primarily by convenience. Elements are included in the sample without prespecified or known probabilities of being selected. For example, a professor conducting research at a university may use student volunteers to constitute a sample simply because they are readily available and will participate as subjects for little or no cost. Similarly, an inspector may sample a shipment of oranges by selecting oranges haphazardly from among several crates. Labeling each orange and using a probability method of sampling would be impractical. Samples such as wildlife captures and volunteer panels for consumer research are also convenience samples.

Convenience samples provide the advantage of relatively easy sample selection and data collection; however, it is impossible to evaluate the "goodness" of the sample in terms of its representativeness of the population. A convenience sample may provide good results or it may not; no statistically justified procedure allows a probability analysis and inference about the quality of the sample results. Sometimes researchers apply statistical methods designed for probability samples to a convenience sample, arguing that the convenience sample can be treated as though it were a probability sample. However, this argument cannot be supported, and we should be cautious in interpreting the results of convenience samples that are used to make inferences about populations.

Judgment Sampling

One additional nonprobability sampling technique is **judgment sampling**. In this approach, the person most knowledgeable on the subject of the study selects elements of the population that he or she feels are most representative of the population. Often this method is a relatively easy way of selecting a sample. For example, a reporter may sample two or three senators, judging that those senators reflect the general opinion of all senators. However, the quality of the sample results depends on the judgment of the person selecting the sample. Again, great caution is warranted in drawing conclusions based on judgment samples used to make inferences about populations.

NOTES AND COMMENTS

We recommend using probability sampling methods: simple random sampling, stratified random sampling, cluster sampling, or systematic sampling. For these methods, formulas are available for evaluating the "goodness" of the sample results in terms of the closeness of the results to the popula-tion characteristics being estimated. An evaluation of the goodness cannot be made with convenience or judgment sampling. Thus, great care should be used in interpreting the results when nonprobability sampling methods are used.

SUMMARY

In this chapter we presented the concepts of simple random sampling and sampling distributions. We demonstrated how a simple random sample can be selected and how the data collected for the sample can be used to develop point estimates of population parameters. Because different simple random samples provide a variety of different values for the point estimators, point estimators such as $\bar{x}$ and $\bar{p}$ are random variables. The probability distribution of such a random variable is called a sampling distribution. In particular, we described the sampling distributions of the sample mean $\bar{x}$ and the sample proportion $\bar{p}$.

In considering the characteristics of the sampling distributions of $\bar{x}$ and $\bar{p}$, we stated that $E(\bar{x}) = \mu$ and $E(\bar{p}) = p$. These results allow us to conclude that $\bar{x}$ and $\bar{p}$ are unbiased point estimators. After developing the standard deviation or standard error formulas for these point estimators, we showed how the central limit theorem provided the basis for using a normal probability distribution to approximate these sampling distributions in the large-sample case. Rules of thumb were given for determining when large-sample conditions were satisfied. Other sampling methods including stratified random sampling, cluster sampling, systematic sampling, convenience sampling, and judgment sampling were discussed.

GLOSSARY

Parameter   A numerical measure of a population characteristic, such as a population mean μ, a population standard deviation σ, a population proportion p, and so on.

Simple random sampling   Finite population: a sample selected such that each possible sample of size n has the same probability of being selected. Infinite population: a sample selected such that each element comes from the same population and the elements are selected independently.

Sampling without replacement   Once an element has been included in the sample, it is removed from the population and cannot be selected a second time.

Sampling with replacement   Once an element has been included in the sample, it is returned to the population. A previously selected element can be selected again and therefore may appear in the sample more than once.

Sample statistic   A sample characteristic, such as a sample mean $\bar{x}$, a sample standard deviation s, a sample proportion $\bar{p}$, and so on. The value of the sample statistic is used to estimate the value of the population parameter.

Point estimator   The sample statistic, such as $\bar{x}$, s, or $\bar{p}$, that provides the point estimate of the population parameter.

Point estimate   A single numerical value used as an estimate of a population parameter.

Sampling error   The absolute value of the difference between an unbiased point estimator and the corresponding population parameter.

Sampling distribution   A probability distribution consisting of all possible values of a sample statistic.

Unbiased   A property of a point estimator. If the expected value of a point estimator is equal to the population parameter it estimates, then the point estimator is unbiased.

Finite population correction factor   The term $\sqrt{(N - n)/(N - 1)}$ that is used in the formulas for $\sigma_{\bar{x}}$ and $\sigma_{\bar{p}}$ whenever a finite population, rather than an infinite population, is being sampled. The generally accepted rule of thumb is to ignore the finite population correction factor whenever $n/N \leq .05$.

Standard error   The standard deviation of a point estimator.

Central limit theorem   A theorem that enables one to use the normal probability distribution to approximate the sampling distribution of $\bar{x}$ and $\bar{p}$ whenever the sample size is large.

Stratified random sampling   A probability sampling method in which the population is first divided into strata and a simple random sample is then taken from each stratum.

Cluster sampling   A probability sampling method in which the population is first divided into clusters and then a simple random sample of the clusters is taken.

Systematic sampling   A probability sampling method in which we randomly select one of the first k elements and then select every kth element thereafter.

Convenience sampling   A nonprobability method of sampling whereby elements are selected for the sample on the basis of convenience.

Judgment sampling   A nonprobability method of sampling whereby elements are selected for the sample based on the judgment of the person doing the study.

KEY FORMULAS

Expected Value of $\bar{x}$

$$E(\bar{x}) = \mu \tag{7.1}$$

Standard Deviation of $\bar{x}$

      Finite Population   *Infinite Population*

$$\sigma_{\bar{x}} = \sqrt{\frac{N-n}{N-1}}\left(\frac{\sigma}{\sqrt{n}}\right) \qquad\qquad \sigma_{\bar{x}} = \frac{\sigma}{\sqrt{n}} \tag{7.2}$$

Expected Value of $\bar{p}$

$$E(\bar{p}) = p \tag{7.4}$$

Standard Deviation of $\bar{p}$

      Finite Population   *Infinite Population*

$$\sigma_{\bar{p}} = \sqrt{\frac{N-n}{N-1}}\sqrt{\frac{p(1-p)}{n}} \qquad\qquad \sigma_{\bar{p}} = \sqrt{\frac{p(1-p)}{n}} \tag{7.5}$$

SUPPLEMENTARY EXERCISES

44. *Business Week's* Corporate Scoreboard provides quarterly data on sales, profits, net income, return on equity, price/earnings ratio, and earning per share for 899 companies (*Business Week*, August 14, 2000). The companies can be numbered 1 to 899 in the order they appear on the Corporate Scoreboard list. Begin at the bottom of column 2 of random digits in Table 7.1. Ignoring the first two digits in each group and using the three-digit random numbers beginning with 112, read *up* the column to identify the first eight companies to be included in a simple random sample.

45. The mean television viewing time for teens is 3 hours per day (*Barron's*, November 8, 1999). Assume the population mean is $\mu = 3$ and the population standard deviation is $\sigma = 1.2$ hours. Suppose a sample of 50 teens will be used to monitor television viewing time. Let $\bar{x}$ denote the sample mean viewing time.
  a. Show the sampling distribution of $\bar{x}$.
  b. What is the probability the sample mean will be within $\pm.25$ hours of the population mean?

46. The mean travel time to work for individuals in Chicago is 31.5 minutes (*1998 Information Please Almanac*). Assume the population mean is $\mu = 31.5$ minutes and the population standard deviation is $\sigma = 12$ minutes. A sample of 50 Chicago residents is selected.
  a. Show the sampling distribution of $\bar{x}$ where $\bar{x}$ is the sample mean travel time to work for the 50 Chicago residents.
  b. What is the probability that the sample mean will be within ±1 minute of the population mean?
  c. What is the probability that the sample mean will be within ±3 minutes of the population mean?

47. The U.S. Bureau of Labor Statistics reported the mean hourly wage rate for individuals in executive, administrative, and managerial occupations is $24.07 (*The Wall Street Journal Almanac 1998*). Assume the population mean is $\mu = \$24.07$ and the population standard deviation is $\sigma = \$4.80$. A simple random sample of 120 individuals in executive, administrative, and managerial occupations will be selected.
   a. What is the probability that the sample mean will be within $\pm\$0.50$ of the population mean?
   b. What is the probability that the sample mean will be within $\pm\$1.00$ of the population mean?

48. The average annual salary for federal government employees in Indiana during 1999 was $41,979 (*The World Almanac 2001*). Use this figure as the population mean and assume the standard deviation is $\sigma = \$5000$. Suppose that a simple random sample of 50 federal government employees will be selected from the population.
   a. What is the value of the standard error of the mean?
   b. What is the probability that the sample mean will be more than $41,979?
   c. What is the probability the sample mean will be within $1000 of the population mean?
   d. How would the probability in part (c) change if the sample size increases to 100?

49. Three firms have inventories that differ in size. Firm A has an inventory of 2000 items, firm B has an inventory of 5000 items, and firm C has an inventory of 10,000 items. The population standard deviation for the cost of the items in each firm's inventory is $\sigma = 144$. A statistical consultant recommends that each firm take a sample of 50 items from its inventory to provide statistically valid estimates of the average cost per item. Managers of the small firm state that because it has the smallest population, it should be able to obtain the data from a much smaller sample than that required by the larger firms. However, the consultant states that to obtain the same standard error and thus the same precision in the sample results, all firms should use the same sample size regardless of population size.
   a. Using the finite population correction factor, compute the standard error for each of the three firms given a sample of size 50.
   b. What is the probability that for each firm the sample mean $\bar{x}$ will be within ± 25 of the population mean μ?

50. A researcher reports survey results by stating that the standard error of the mean is 20. The population standard deviation is 500.
   a. How large was the sample used in this survey?
   b. What is the probability that the point estimate was within ± 25 of the population mean?

51. A production process is checked periodically by a quality control inspector. The inspector selects simple random samples of 30 finished products and computes the sample mean product weights $\bar{x}$. If test results over a long period of time show that 5% of the $\bar{x}$ values are over 2.1 pounds and 5% are under 1.9 pounds, what are the mean and the standard deviation for the population of products produced with this process?

52. As of June 13, 2001, 30.5% of individual investors were bullish on the stock market short term (*AAII Journal*, July 2001). Answer the following questions assuming a simple random sample of 200 individual investors will be surveyed.
   a. Show the sampling distribution of $\bar{p}$, the sample proportion of individual investors who are bullish on the market short term.
   b. What is the probability that the sample proportion will be within $\pm.04$ of the population proportion?
   c. What is the probability that the sample proportion will be within $\pm.02$ of the population proportion?

53. A market research firm conducts telephone surveys with a 40% historical response rate. What is the probability that in a new sample of 400 telephone numbers, at least 150 individuals will cooperate and respond to the questions? In other words, what is the probability that the sample proportion will be at least 150/400 = .375?

54. According to ORC International, 71% of Internet users connect their computers to the Internet by normal telephone lines (*USA Today*, January 18, 2000). Assume a population proportion $p = .71$.
   a. What is the probability that a sample proportion from a simple random sample of 350 Internet users will be within ±.05 of the population proportion?
   b. What is the probability that a sample proportion from a simple random sample of 350 Internet users will be .75 or greater?

55. The proportion of individuals insured by the All-Driver Automobile Insurance Company who received at least one traffic ticket during a five-year period is .15.
   a. Show the sampling distribution of $\bar{p}$ if a random sample of 150 insured individuals is used to estimate the proportion having received at least one ticket.
   b. What is the probability that the sample proportion will be within ±.03 of the population proportion?

56. Lori Jeffrey is a successful sales representative for a major publisher of college textbooks. Historically, Lori obtains a book adoption on 25% of her sales calls. Viewing her sales calls for one month as a sample of all possible sales calls, assume that a statistical analysis of the data yields a standard error of the proportion of .0625.
   a. How large was the sample used in this analysis? That is, how many sales calls did Lori make during the month?
   b. Let $\bar{p}$ indicate the sample proportion of book adoptions obtained during the month. Show the sampling distribution of $\bar{p}$.
   c. Using the sampling distribution of $\bar{p}$, compute the probability that Lori will obtain book adoptions on 30% or more of her sales calls during a one-month period.

CHAPTER 8

Interval Estimation

CONTENTS

STATISTICS IN PRACTICE

Dollar General Corporation*

GOODLETTSVILLE, TENNESSEE

Dollar General Corporation was founded in 1939 as a dry goods wholesale company. After World War II, the company began opening retail locations in rural south-central Kentucky. Today Dollar General Corporation operates more than 4300 stores across the middle and southeastern United States. Emphasizing small-store convenience, Dollar General markets health and beauty aids, cleaning supplies, housewares, stationery, apparel, shoes, and domestic items at everyday low prices.

Being in an inventory-intense business with more than 20,000 products, Dollar General made the decision to adopt the LIFO (last-in, first-out) method of inventory valuation. This method matches current costs against current revenues, which minimizes the effect of radical price changes on profit and loss results. In addition, the LIFO method reduces net income and thereby income taxes during periods of inflation. LIFO also brings disposable cash generated from sales in line with income and allows for the replacement of inventory at current costs.

Accounting practices require that a LIFO index be established for inventory under the LIFO method of valuation. For example, a LIFO index of 1.028 indicates that the company's inventory value at current costs reflects a 2.8% increase due to inflation over the most recent one-year period.

The establishment of a LIFO index requires that the year-end inventory count for each product be valued at the current year-end cost and at the preceding year-end cost. To avoid counting the inventory of every product

This store in Bedford, Indiana, is one of more than 4300 Dollar General Stores. © Darren Wright/South-Western.

in more than 4300 retail locations, a random sample of 800 products is selected from 100 retail locations and three warehouses. Physical inventories for the sampled products are taken at the end of the year. Accounting personnel then provide the current-year and preceding-year costs needed to construct the LIFO index.

For a recent year, the LIFO index was 1.030. However, because this index is a sample estimate of the population's LIFO index, a statement about the precision of the estimate was required. On the basis of the sample results and a 95% confidence level, the margin of error was computed to be .006. Thus, the interval from 1.024 to 1.036 provides the 95% confidence interval estimate of the population LIFO index. This precision was judged to be good.

In this chapter you will learn how to compute the margin of error associated with a sample mean and a sample proportion. Then, you will learn how to use this information to construct and interpret confidence interval estimates of a population mean and a population proportion. You will also learn how to determine the sample size needed to ensure that the margin of error will be within acceptable limits.

*The authors are indebted to Robert S. Knaul, Controller, Dollar General Corporation, for providing this Statistics in Practice.

In Chapter 7 we stated that a point estimator is a sample statistic used to estimate a population parameter. For instance, the sample mean $\bar{x}$ is a point estimator of the population mean μ, and the sample proportion $\bar{p}$ is a point estimator of the population proportion p. Because a point estimator does not provide information about how close the estimate is to the population parameter, statisticians usually prefer to construct an **interval estimate** by subtracting and adding a value, called the **margin of error**, to a point estimate.

$$\text{Point Estimate} \pm \text{Margin of Error}$$

The focus in this chapter will be on developing interval estimates for a population mean μ and a population proportion p. An interval estimate of the population mean is

$$\bar{x} \pm \text{Margin of Error}$$

and an interval estimate of a population proportion is

$$\bar{p} \pm \text{Margin of Error}$$

The inclusion of the margin of error term in an interval estimate provides a measure of the precision associated with the estimate. As we shall see, much of the work in constructing an interval estimate is in determining a value for the margin of error that will provide the desired precision. The sampling distribution of $\bar{x}$ and the sampling distribution of $\bar{p}$ presented in Chapter 7 play important roles in this regard.

In Section 8.1 we show how to develop interval estimates of a population mean for the large-sample case ($n \geq 30$). We begin with this case because the majority of applications in practice involve large samples. Large-sample interval estimation procedures are applicable regardless of the form of the population from which the sample is taken (parent population). Small-sample interval estimation procedures, however, require knowledge of the form of the parent population. In Section 8.2 we show how interval estimates can be developed for the small-sample case when the parent population has a normal probability distribution. In Section 8.3 we show how to determine the sample size required to develop an interval estimate of a population mean with a desired margin of error. In Section 8.4 we discuss interval estimation of a population proportion; only large-sample procedures are discussed in this section because large samples are almost always required to control the margin of error when developing interval estimates of a population proportion.

8.1   INTERVAL ESTIMATION OF A POPULATION MEAN: LARGE-SAMPLE CASE

An assumption about the form of the parent population is not required to use the methods of this section.

In this section we show how a simple random sample can be used to develop an interval estimate of a population mean in the large-sample case ($n \geq 30$). We begin with a situation in which the population standard deviation σ can be assumed *known*. We then consider the case where it cannot be; in this case σ is estimated by the sample standard deviation s.

CJW Problem

The development of an interval estimate of a population mean can be illustrated by considering the monthly customer service survey conducted by CJW, Inc. CJW provides a Web site for accepting customer orders and providing follow-up service over the Internet. The company prides itself on providing easy online ordering, timely delivery, and prompt response to customer inquiries. Good customer service is critical to the ongoing success of the company.

CJW's quality assurance team uses a customer survey to measure satisfaction with its Web site and online customer service. Each month, a questionnaire is sent to a random sample of customers who placed an order or requested service during the previous month. Customers are asked to rate their satisfaction with such things as ease of placing orders, timely delivery, accurate order filling, and technical advice. Each customer's questionnaire is summarized by an overall satisfaction score x that ranges from 0 (worst possible score) to 100 (best possible score). A sample mean customer satisfaction score $\bar{x}$ is then computed.

The sample mean satisfaction score is used as a point estimate of the mean satisfaction score μ for the population of all CJW customers for the month. With this timely measure of customer service, CJW can promptly take corrective action if a low customer satisfaction score is obtained. The company has been conducting this satisfaction survey for a number of months and has consistently obtained an estimate near 20 for the standard deviation of satisfaction scores. Based on this historical data, they now assume a known value of $\sigma = 20$ for the population standard deviation.

During the month of May, the quality assurance team has surveyed 100 customers ($n = 100$), and a sample mean satisfaction score of $\bar{x} = 82$ has been obtained. This sample mean satisfaction score provides a point estimate of the population mean satisfaction score for the month of May. In the discussion that follows, we will show how to compute a margin of error for this estimate and hence develop an interval estimate.

Margin of Error and the Interval Estimate   As previously stated, CJW assumes that the population standard deviation of customer satisfaction scores is $\sigma = 20$. With a sample size of $n = 100$, the central limit theorem, introduced in Chapter 7, enables us to conclude that the sampling distribution of $\bar{x}$ can be approximated by a normal probability distribution with an unknown mean of μ and a standard error of $\sigma_{\bar{x}} = \sigma/\sqrt{n} = 20/\sqrt{100} = 2$. The sampling distribution of $\bar{x}$ is shown in Figure 8.1. It shows how the values of $\bar{x}$ are distributed around μ, and hence provides information about the possible difference between $\bar{x}$ and μ. As noted in Chapter 7 the absolute value of the difference between the sample mean and the population mean, denoted $|\bar{x} - \mu|$, is called the **sampling error**.

The standard error is the standard deviation of the sampling distribution. The standard deviation of x is σ, and the standard deviation of $\bar{x}$ is the standard error $\sigma_{\bar{x}} = \sigma/\sqrt{n}$.

FIGURE 8.1   SAMPLING DISTRIBUTION OF THE SAMPLE MEAN SATISFACTION SCORE FOR SIMPLE RANDOM SAMPLES OF 100 CUSTOMERS

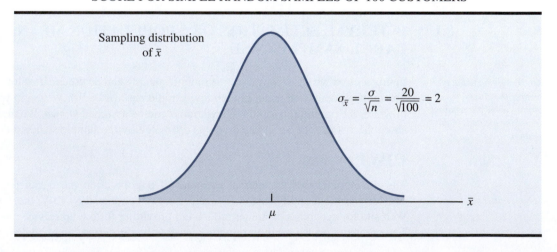

Using the table of areas for the standard normal probability distribution, we find that 95% of the values of any normally distributed random variable are within ± 1.96 standard deviations of the mean. Because the sampling distribution of $\bar{x}$ can be approximated by a normal probability distribution, 95% of all $\bar{x}$ values must be within ± 1.96 standard errors of the population mean μ. In the CJW case, $1.96\sigma_{\bar{x}} = 1.96(2) = 3.92$, so we know that 95% of the sample means that could be obtained using a sample of size $n = 100$ must be within ± 3.92 of the population mean.

The location of the sample means that differ from μ by 3.92 or less is shown in Figure 8.2. Note that if a sample mean is in the region denoted "95% of all $\bar{x}$ values," it provides a sampling error of 3.92 or less. However, if a sample mean is in either the lower tail or the upper tail of the distribution, the sampling error, $|\bar{x} - \mu|$, will be greater than 3.92. Therefore we can make the following probability statement about the sampling error for the CJW problem.

There is a .95 probability that the sample mean will provide a sampling error of 3.92 or less.

This probability statement about the sampling error is a **precision statement** telling CJW about the likely size of the sampling error when a simple random sample of 100 customers is used to estimate the population mean satisfaction score.

An interval estimate for a population mean, μ, is of the form:

$$\bar{x} \pm \text{Margin of Error} \tag{8.1}$$

If we select $1.96\sigma_{\bar{x}} = 1.96(2) = 3.92$ as the margin of error in the CJW case, we can then construct an interval estimate of the population mean satisfaction score μ by subtracting 3.92 from $\bar{x}$ and adding 3.92 to $\bar{x}$; that is, we compute $\bar{x} \pm 3.92$. It follows from the preceding precision statement that there is .95 probability this interval estimate will contain

FIGURE 8.2   SAMPLING DISTRIBUTION OF $\bar{x}$ SHOWING THE LOCATION OF SAMPLE
MEANS THAT PROVIDE A SAMPLING ERROR OF 3.92 OR LESS

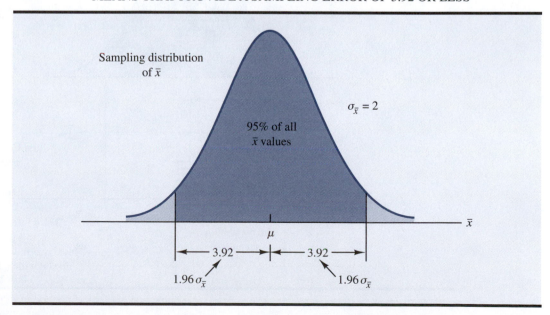

the population mean μ. Recall that for the month of May, a sample of 100 customers provided a sample mean satisfaction score of $\bar{x} = 82$. With $\bar{x} = 82$ and a margin of error of 3.92, the interval estimate of the population mean satisfaction score is 82 ± 3.92, or $82 - 3.92 = 78.08$ to $82 + 3.92 = 85.92$.

σ Assumed Known

We have just developed an interval estimate for the population mean satisfaction score for the specific case of the CJW problem. Let us now develop a general procedure for interval estimates in the large-sample case ($n \geq 30$) when σ is assumed known.

In actual practice, only one sample is selected to develop an interval estimate. But, in order to show how to correctly interpret the interval estimate of μ, let us return to the CJW example and suppose that three *different* random samples of 100 customers were taken. We will refer to the value of the first sample mean as $\bar{x}_1$, the value of the second sample mean as $\bar{x}_2$, and the value of the third sample mean as $\bar{x}_3$. Figure 8.3 shows the resulting interval estimates. We obtained three different interval estimates, but each has the same margin of error (3.92).

As Figure 8.3 shows, the interval formed using $\bar{x}_1$ includes the population mean μ. Although the interval formed using $\bar{x}_2$ is different, it also includes μ. However, the interval

FIGURE 8.3   INTERVALS FORMED FROM SELECTED SAMPLE MEANS AT LOCATIONS $\bar{x}_1, \bar{x}_2,$ AND $\bar{x}_3$

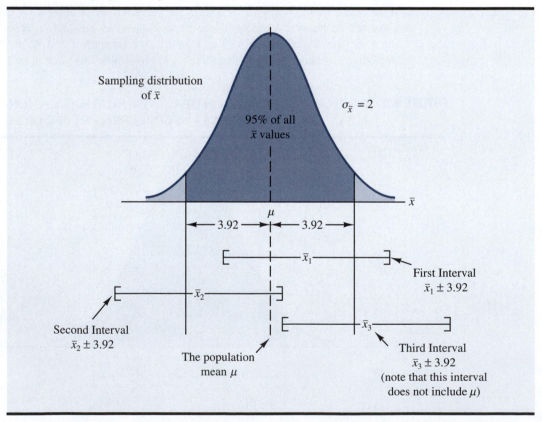

formed using $\bar{x}_3$ does not include μ; the reason is that $\bar{x}_3$ is in the upper tail of the sampling distribution of $\bar{x}$ and is farther than 3.92 from μ.

Any sample mean, $\bar{x}$, that is within the darkly shaded region of Figure 8.3 will provide an interval estimate that contains the population mean μ. Because 95% of the sample means are within this region, 95% of all intervals formed by subtracting 3.92 from $\bar{x}$ and adding 3.92 to $\bar{x}$ will include μ. Thus, the probability that an interval estimate generated using this procedure will contain the population mean, μ, is .95. Statisticians would say that we are 95% confident that the population mean satisfaction score μ is contained in an interval constructed from $\bar{x} - 3.92$ to $\bar{x} + 3.92$. Using common statistical terminology, we refer to the interval $\bar{x} \pm 3.92$ as a **confidence interval**. Because 95% of the sample means will result in a confidence interval that includes the population mean μ, we say that the confidence interval is established at the 95% **confidence level**. The value .95 is referred to as the *confidence coefficient*.

Although a 95% confidence level is frequently used in developing an interval estimate, other confidence levels such as 90% and 99% can be used. For instance, using the standard normal probability distribution table, we find that 90% of the $\bar{x}$ values are within ± 1.645 standard deviations of μ. Thus, if we choose a margin of error of $1.645\sigma_{\bar{x}}$, we can conclude that 90% of the interval estimates generated of the form $\bar{x} \pm 1.645\sigma_{\bar{x}}$ will contain the population mean. Thus, an interval of the form $\bar{x} \pm 1.645\sigma_{\bar{x}}$ is a 90% confidence interval. In CJW's case $\sigma_{\bar{x}} = 2$, so the margin of error for a 90% confidence interval would be $1.645(2) = 3.29$, and a 90% confidence interval would be given by $\bar{x} \pm 3.29$. Similarly, because 99% of the $\bar{x}$ values are within 2.576 standard deviations[1] of μ, a 99% confidence interval would be constructed by choosing a margin of error of $2.576\sigma_{\bar{x}}$. In CJW's case, $2.576\sigma_{\bar{x}} = 2.576(2) = 5.15$. Hence, a 99% confidence interval estimate of μ is $\bar{x} \pm 5.15$.

Another term sometimes associated with an interval estimate is the **level of significance**. The level of significance associated with an interval estimate is denoted by the Greek letter α. The level of significance and the confidence coefficient are related as follows:

$$\alpha = \text{Level of Significance} = 1 - \text{Confidence Coefficient}$$

The level of significance is the probability that the interval estimation procedure will generate an interval that does not contain μ. For example, the level of significance corresponding to a .95 confidence coefficient is $\alpha = 1 - .95 = .05$. In CJW's case, the level of significance ($\alpha = .05$) is the probability of drawing a sample, computing the sample mean, and finding that $\bar{x}$ lies in one of the tails of the sampling distribution (see $\bar{x}_3$ in Figure 8.3). When that happens (and it will 5% of the time), the confidence interval generated will not contain μ.

Let us generalize the procedure we used to develop an interval estimate of a population mean in the large-sample case with σ assumed known. First, recall that in Chapter 6 we stated that the letter z is commonly used to designate values for the standard normal random variable. For instance, using the table of areas for the standard normal probability distribution, we know that the probability of obtaining a z value between $z = -1.96$ and $z = 1.96$ is .95. Thus, we used a z value of 1.96 to compute the margin of error for a 95% confidence interval estimate of the population mean μ for the CJW problem. Because a z

---

[1]The standard normal probability table provides z values with two decimal places. However, for the common confidence levels of 90%, 95%, and 99%, it is common practice to use three decimal places of accuracy for the three values (1.645, 1.960, and 2.576).

value of 1.96 corresponds to an area of .025 in the upper tail of the standard normal probability distribution, the z value corresponding to a 95% confidence interval is denoted $z_{.025}$; that is, $z_{.025} = 1.96$.

The level of significance α is used to determine the z value corresponding to a particular confidence coefficient. Let $z_{\alpha/2}$ denote the z value corresponding to an area of $\alpha/2$ in the upper tail of the standard normal probability distribution. For instance, to develop a 90% confidence interval estimate of the population mean μ we must determine the z value corresponding to an area of $\alpha/2 = .10/2 = .05$ in the upper tail of the standard normal probability distribution. Thus, we must determine the value of $z_{\alpha/2} = z_{.10/2} = z_{.05}$. Using the table of areas for the standard normal probability distribution, we find that $z_{.05} = 1.645$. Hence, the 90% confidence interval is $\bar{x} \pm z_{\alpha/2}\sigma_{\bar{x}} = \bar{x} \pm 1.645\sigma_{\bar{x}}$.

Using the fact that $\sigma_{\bar{x}} = \sigma/\sqrt{n}$, we can now state that the margin of error for an interval estimate of a population mean for the large-sample case ($n \geq 30$) with σ assumed known is as follows:

$$z_{\alpha/2}\frac{\sigma}{\sqrt{n}}$$

The corresponding interval estimate is shown below.

In expression (8.2), the standard error of the mean is $\sigma_{\bar{x}} = \sigma/\sqrt{n}$.

Interval Estimate of a Population Mean: Large-Sample Case ($n \geq 30$) with σ Assumed Known

$$\bar{x} \pm z_{\alpha/2}\frac{\sigma}{\sqrt{n}} \tag{8.2}$$

where $1 - \alpha$ is the confidence coefficient and $z_{\alpha/2}$ is the z value providing an area of $\alpha/2$ in the upper tail of the standard normal probability distribution.

The values of $z_{\alpha/2}$ and the margins of error for the most commonly used confidence levels are given in Table 8.1.

σ Estimated by s

A difficulty in using expression (8.2) to compute an interval estimate is that in most applications the value of the population standard deviation σ is unknown. In the large-sample case ($n \geq 30$), we simply use the value of the sample standard deviation, s, as the point es-

TABLE 8.1   VALUES OF $z_{\alpha/2}$ AND MARGINS OF ERROR FOR THE MOST COMMONLY USED CONFIDENCE LEVELS

Confidence Level	α	$\alpha/2$	$z_{\alpha/2}$	Margin of Error
90%	.10	.05	1.645	$1.645\sigma_{\bar{x}}$
95%	.05	.025	1.960	$1.960\sigma_{\bar{x}}$
99%	.01	.005	2.576	$2.576\sigma_{\bar{x}}$

timate of the population standard deviation σ in computing the margin of error. The following interval estimate is obtained.[2]

Interval Estimate of a Population Mean: Large-Sample Case ($n \geq 30$) with σ Estimated by s

In expression (8.3), $s/\sqrt{n}$ is used as an estimate of the standard error of the mean $\sigma_{\bar{x}}$.

$$\bar{x} \pm z_{\alpha/2} \frac{s}{\sqrt{n}} \tag{8.3}$$

where s is the sample standard deviation, $1 - \alpha$ is the confidence coefficient, and $z_{\alpha/2}$ is the z value providing an area of $\alpha/2$ in the upper tail of the standard normal probability distribution.

To illustrate this interval estimation procedure, let us consider a sampling study designed to estimate the credit card debt of U.S. households. A sample of 85 households provided the credit card balances shown in Table 8.2. With $n = 85$, we have the large-sample case. And, with no prior information about the standard deviation of credit card balances, we will use the sample standard deviation s as an estimate of σ. Thus, it is appropriate to use expression (8.3) to develop an interval estimate. Let us develop a 95% confidence interval estimate of the population mean credit card balance per household.

Using the data in Table 8.2, we find $\bar{x} = \$5900$ and $s = \$3058$. At 95% confidence, $z_{\alpha/2} = z_{.025} = 1.96$. With a sample size of $n = 85$, expression (8.3) provides the following interval estimate:

$$5900 \pm 1.96 \frac{3058}{\sqrt{85}}$$

$$5900 \pm 650.11$$

TABLE 8.2   CREDIT CARD BALANCES FOR A SAMPLE OF 85 HOUSEHOLDS

Balance

9619	5994	3344	7888	7581	9980
5364	4652	13627	3091	12545	8718
8348	5376	968	943	7959	8452
7348	5998	4714	8762	2563	4935
381	7530	4334	1407	6787	5938
2998	3678	4911	6644	5071	5266
1686	3581	1920	7644	9536	10658
1962	5625	3780	11169	4459	3910
4920	5619	3478	7979	8047	7503
5047	9032	6185	3258	8083	1582
6921	13236	1141	8660	2153	
5759	4447	7577	7511	8003	
8047	609	4667	14442	6795	
3924	414	5219	4447	5915	
3470	7636	6416	6550	7164	

---

[2]The theoretical justification for using this interval estimate in the large-sample case is based on both the central limit theorem and the fact that s^2 converges to σ^2 as the sample size increases. Use of expression (8.3) does not require knowledge of the form of the population probability distribution.

Rounding to the nearest dollar, the margin of error is $650 and the 95% confidence interval estimate of the population mean is 5900 − 650 = 5250 to 5900 + 650 = 6550. Thus, we can be 95% confident that the population mean credit card balance for all U.S. households is between $5250 and $6550.

Using Excel to Construct a Confidence Interval

We will use the credit card balance data in Table 8.2 to illustrate how Excel can be used to construct confidence intervals for the population mean in the large-sample case. Because σ is unknown, s and the sample size n are used to estimate the standard error. The margin of error is computed as the product of the z value and the estimated standard error. Then by subtracting and adding the margin of error to the point estimate (the sample mean) we obtain the confidence interval. Refer to Figure 8.4 as we describe the tasks involved. The formula worksheet is in the background; the value worksheet is in the foreground.

Enter Data: A label and the credit card balances for the 85 households have been entered into cells A1:A86.

Enter Functions and Formulas: The descriptive statistics we need are provided in cells D4:D6. Excel's COUNT, AVERAGE, and STDEV functions were used to compute the sample size, sample mean, and sample standard deviation for the data in cells A2:A86. The value worksheet shows $n = 85$, $\bar{x} = 5900$, and $s = 3058$.

FIGURE 8.4   EXCEL WORKSHEET FOR 95% CONFIDENCE INTERVAL ESTIMATE OF THE POPULATION MEAN HOUSEHOLD CREDIT CARD BALANCE

	A	B	C	D	E	F
1	Balance		**Interval Estimate of a Population Mean**			
2	9619		**Using the Standard Normal Distribution (z)**			
3	5364					
4	8348		Sample Size	=COUNT(A2:A86)		
5	7348		Mean	=AVERAGE(A2:A86)		
6	381		Standard Deviation	=STDEV(A2:A86)		
7	2998					
8	1686		Confidence Coefficient	0.95		
9	1962		Level of Significance (alpha)	=1-D8		
10	4920		z Value	=NORMSINV(1-D9/2)		
11	5047					
12	6921		Standard Error	=D6/SQRT(D4)		
13	5759		Margin of Error	=D10*D12		
14	8047					
15	3924		Point Estimate	=D5		
16	3470		Lower Limit	=D15-D13		
17	5994		Upper Limit	=D15+D13		
18	4652					
84	3910					
85	7503					
86	1582					
87						

Note: Rows 19–83 are hidden.

This and future worksheets in this chapter can be used as templates for interval estimation problems.

	A	B	C	D	E	F	G
1	Balance		**Interval Estimate of a Population Mean**				
2	9619		**Using the Standard Normal Distribution (z)**				
3	5364						
4	8348		Sample Size	85			
5	7348		Mean	5900			
6	381		Standard Deviation	3058			
7	2998						
8	1686		Confidence Coefficient	0.95			
9	1962		Level of Significance (alpha)	0.05			
10	4920		z Value	1.960			
11	5047						
12	6921		Standard Error	331.69			
13	5759		Margin of Error	650			
14	8047						
15	3924		Point Estimate	5900			
16	3470		Lower Limit	5250			
17	5994		Upper Limit	6550			
18	4652						
84	3910						
85	7503						
86	1582						
87							

Cells D8:D10 are used to compute the appropriate z value. The confidence coefficient has been entered into cell D8 and the level of significance (α) has been computed in cell D9 by entering the formula =1-D8. The z value corresponding to an upper tail area of $\alpha/2$ has been computed in cell D10 by using the NORMSINV function. Recall from Chapter 6 that the form of the NORMSINV function is =NORMSINV(cumulative probability). We use a cumulative probability as input, and the function provides the corresponding z value. If we want an area of $\alpha/2$ in the upper tail, the appropriate cumulative probability is $1 - \alpha/2$. Thus, we entered the formula =NORMSINV(1-D9/2) into cell D10. The value worksheet shows that the z value obtained is $z_{.025} = 1.960$.

Cells D12:D13 provide the estimate of the standard error of the mean and the margin of error. In cell D12, we entered the formula =D6/SQRT(D4) to estimate the standard error of the mean. The formula =D10*D12, entered into cell D13, computes the margin of error associated with a 95% confidence interval. The resulting value of 650 is the margin of error associated with the interval estimate of the population mean household credit card balance.

Cells D15:D17 provide the point estimate and the lower and upper limits for the confidence interval. Because the point estimate is just the sample mean, the formula =D5 has been entered into cell D15. To compute the lower limit of the 95% confidence interval, $\bar{x} -$ (margin of error), we entered the formula =D15-D13 into cell D16. To compute the upper limit of the 95% confidence interval, $\bar{x} +$ (margin of error), we entered the formula =D15+D13 into cell D17. The value worksheet shows a lower limit of 5250 and an upper limit of 6550. In other words, the 95% confidence interval for the population mean is from $5250 to $6550.

We note that once a worksheet is set up to compute a confidence interval, other confidence intervals can easily be computed. For instance, a 90% confidence interval can be computed by simply changing the confidence coefficient in cell D8 to .90. Doing so, we would obtain a 90% confidence interval of $5354 to $6446. As expected the 90% confidence interval is slightly narrower than the 95% confidence interval.

In the credit card balance problem we just worked with, s is used as an estimate of σ. To use this worksheet as a template for another problem of this type, we must first enter the new problem data in column A. Then the ranges for the formulas in the descriptive statistics cells (D4:D6) would be revised to correspond to the new data. After doing so, the point estimate and a 95% confidence interval will be displayed in cells D15:D17. If a confidence interval with a different confidence coefficient is desired, we simply change the value in cell D8.

This worksheet can also be used as a template for large-sample interval estimation when σ is assumed known. In this type of situation, we type the value of the assumed standard deviation in cell D6 and proceed as before. We can also use this worksheet as a template for text exercises in which the sample mean, the sample standard deviation, and the sample size are given. In this type of situation we simply replace the formulas in cells D4:D6 with the given values for the sample size, the sample mean, and the sample standard deviation.

NOTES AND COMMENTS

1. In developing an interval estimate of the population mean, we specify the desired confidence coefficient $(1 - \alpha)$ before selecting the sample. Thus, prior to selecting the sample, we conclude that there is a $1 - \alpha$ probability that the confidence interval we eventually compute will contain the population mean μ and an α probability that it will not. However, once the sample is taken, the sample mean $\bar{x}$ is computed, and the particular interval estimate is determined, the

resulting interval may or may not contain μ. If $1 - \alpha$ is reasonably large, we can be confident that the resulting interval will contain μ because we know that if we use this procedure repeatedly, $100(1 - \alpha)$ percent of all possible intervals developed in this way will contain μ.

2. In practical applications, the population standard deviation σ is rarely known, and s is used to estimate σ. However, in some cases it makes sense to assume a known value of σ. For instance, in quality control applications the variance of an in-control process can often be assumed known. And, in situations where a substantial amount of historical data is available (e.g., standardized test scores), it is often rea-

sonable to use the standard deviation for the historical data as the known value of σ.

3. The sample size n appears in the denominator of the margin of error term in the interval estimation expressions (8.2) and (8.3). Thus, if a particular sample size provides too wide an interval to be of any practical use, we may want to consider increasing the sample size. With n in the denominator, a larger sample size will provide a smaller margin of error, a narrower interval, and greater precision. The procedure for determining the size of a simple random sample necessary to obtain a desired precision is discussed in Section 8.3.

EXERCISES

Methods

1. A simple random sample of 40 items resulted in a sample mean of 25. The population standard deviation is $\sigma = 5$.
   a. What is the standard error of the mean, $\sigma_{\bar{x}}$?
   b. At 95% confidence, what is the margin of error?

2. A simple random sample of 50 items resulted in a sample mean of 32 and a sample standard deviation of 6.
   a. Provide a 90% confidence interval for the population mean.
   b. Provide a 95% confidence interval for the population mean.
   c. Provide a 99% confidence interval for the population mean.

3. A sample of 60 items resulted in a sample mean of 80 and a sample standard deviation of 15.
   a. Compute the 95% confidence interval for the population mean.
   b. Assume that the same sample mean and sample standard deviation were obtained from a sample of 120 items. Provide a 95% confidence interval for the population mean.
   c. What is the effect of a larger sample size on the interval estimate of a population mean?

4. A 95% confidence interval for a population mean was reported to be 122 to 130. If the sample mean is 126 and the sample standard deviation is 16.07, what sample size was used in this study?

Applications

5. In an effort to estimate the mean amount spent per customer for dinner at a major Atlanta restaurant, data were collected for a sample of 49 customers.
   a. Assume a population standard deviation of $5. What is the standard error of the mean?
   b. At a 95% confidence level, what is the margin of error?
   c. If the sample mean is $34.80, what is the 95% confidence interval for the population mean?

Service

6. *The New York Times 1998 Almanac* reported mean weekly earnings of individuals working in various industries. The mean weekly earnings for individuals in the service industry was $369. Suppose that a follow-up study of 250 service employees resulted in the weekly salaries contained in the data set Service.
   a. Use the sample data to develop a point estimate of the mean weekly salary for the population of service employees.
   b. What is the sample standard deviation?
   c. Develop a 95% confidence interval estimate of the mean weekly salary for the population of service employees.

7. The mean undergraduate grade point average (GPA) for students admitted to the top graduate business schools was 3.37 (*Best Graduate Schools, U.S. News and World Report*, 2001 Edition). Assume this estimate was based on a sample of 120 students admitted to the top schools. Using past years' data, the population standard deviation can be assumed known with $\sigma = .28$. What is the 95% confidence interval estimate of the mean undergraduate GPA for students admitted to the top graduate business schools?

8. The National Association of Independent Colleges and Universities reported that students in public colleges and universities graduate with an average debt of $12,000 (*Kiplinger's Personal Finance Magazine*, November 1998). Assume that this average or mean amount is based on a sample of 245 students and that, based on past studies, the population standard deviation for the debt upon graduation is $2200.
   a. Develop a 90% confidence interval estimate of the population mean.
   b. Develop a 95% confidence interval estimate of the population mean.
   c. Develop a 99% confidence interval estimate of the population mean.
   d. Discuss what happens to the width of the confidence interval as the confidence level is increased. Does this result seem reasonable? Explain.

USWorkers

9. The U.S. Bureau of Labor Statistics collects information on hourly wages and number of hours worked for U.S. production workers. The mean number of weekly hours worked in 2000 was 34.5 (*The World Almanac and Book of Facts*, 2002). A representative sample of hourly wages for 60 workers in 2000 is contained in the data set USWorkers.
   a. Use the USWorkers data set to develop a point estimate of the mean hourly pay rate of the population of production workers.
   b. What is the sample standard deviation?
   c. Using the data in the sample develop a 95% confidence interval for the mean hourly pay rate for the population of production workers.

10. Nielsen Media Research reports the household mean television viewing time during the 8 P.M. to 11 P.M. time period is 7.75 hours per week (*The World Almanac 2000*). Assuming a sample size of 180 households and a sample standard deviation of 3.45 hours, what is the 95% confidence interval estimate of the mean television viewing time per week during the 8 P.M. to 11 P.M. time period?

11. The International Air Transport Association surveys business travelers to develop quality ratings for transatlantic gateway airports. The maximum possible rating is 10. Suppose a simple random sample of 50 business travelers is selected and each traveler is asked to provide a rating for the Miami International Airport. The ratings obtained from the sample of 50 follow.

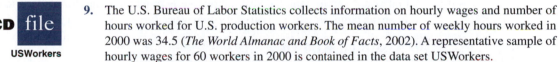

6	4	6	8	7	7	6	3	3	8	10	4	8
7	8	7	5	9	5	8	4	3	8	5	5	4
4	4	8	4	5	6	2	5	9	9	8	4	8
9	9	5	9	7	8	3	10	8	9	6		

Miami

Develop a 95% confidence interval estimate of the population mean rating for Miami.

12. Thirty fast-food restaurants including Wendy's, McDonald's, and Burger King were visited during the summer of 2000 (*The Cincinnati Enquirer*, July 9, 2000). During each visit, the customer went to the drive-through window and ordered a basic meal such as a "combo" meal or a sandwich, fries, and shake. The elapsed time between a customer pulling up to the message board and receiving a filled order was recorded. The times in minutes for 30 visits are as follow:

0.9	1.0	1.2	2.2	1.9	3.6	2.8	5.2	1.8	2.1
6.8	1.3	3.0	4.5	2.8	2.3	2.7	5.7	4.8	3.5
2.6	3.3	5.0	4.0	7.2	9.1	2.8	3.6	7.3	9.0

FastFood

a. Provide a point estimate of the population mean drive-through time at fast-food restaurants.
b. At 95% confidence, what is the margin of error?
c. Develop a 95% confidence interval estimate of the population mean.

8.2   INTERVAL ESTIMATION OF A POPULATION MEAN: SMALL-SAMPLE CASE

The sampling distribution of $\bar{x}$ depends on the probability distribution of the population from which the sample was drawn. In the large sample case ($n \geq 30$) the central limit theorem allows us to conclude that the sampling distribution is approximately normally distributed and the methodology of Section 8.1 is applicable. In the small-sample case ($n < 30$), we cannot draw such a conclusion.

The methodology presented in this section is based on the assumption that the population has a normal probability distribution.

If the population has a normal probability distribution, the methodology presented in this section can be used to develop a confidence interval for a population mean in the small-sample case. However, if the assumption of a normal probability distribution for the population is not appropriate, the best alternative is to increase the sample size to $n \geq 30$ and rely on the large-sample interval estimation procedures given by expressions (8.2) and (8.3).

σ Assumed Known

We begin by making the assumption that the population has a normal distribution and that the population standard deviation σ is assumed known. Under these conditions, and regardless of the sample size, the sampling distribution of $\bar{x}$ is exactly normal with mean μ and standard deviation $\sigma_{\bar{x}} = \sigma/\sqrt{n}$. Thus, given that the sampling distribution of $\bar{x}$ is a normal distribution, the small-sample interval estimation procedure with σ assumed known is identical to the large-sample interval estimation procedure presented in Section 8.1.

Interval Estimate of a Population Mean: Small-Sample Case ($n < 30$) with σ Assumed Known

Assumption: The population has a normal distribution.

When using Excel to develop an interval estimate using expression (8.4), the worksheet in Figure 8.4 can be used as a template.

$$\bar{x} \pm z_{\alpha/2} \frac{\sigma}{\sqrt{n}} \tag{8.4}$$

where $(1 - \alpha)$ is the confidence coefficient and $z_{\alpha/2}$ is the z-value providing an area $\alpha/2$ in the upper tail of the standard normal probability distribution

---

With σ assumed known and $z_{\alpha/2}$ selected based on the desired confidence level, the selection of a sample of size n and the computation of the sample mean $\bar{x}$ will provide the information necessary to use expression (8.4) to compute the margin of error and the interval estimate of the population mean. Because this computation is identical to the computations made in Section 8.1, we shall not present a new numerical example here.

σ Estimated by s

William Sealy Gosset, writing under the name "Student," developed the t distribution. Gosset, an Oxford graduate in mathematics, worked for the Guinness Brewery in Dublin, Ireland. He developed a new small-sample theory of statistics while doing work involving temperature experiments in the brewery.

We start by again making the assumption that the population has a normal distribution. If the situation provides no basis for assuming that the population standard deviation σ is known, the sample standard deviation s is used to estimate σ. Under these conditions, the interval estimation procedure is based on a probability distribution known as the **t distribution**.

The t distribution is a family of similar probability distributions, with each individual t distribution's shape depending on a parameter known as the **degrees of freedom**. The t distribution with one degree of freedom is unique, as is the t distribution with two degrees of freedom, with three degrees of freedom, and so on. As the number of degrees of freedom increases, the difference between the t distribution and the standard normal probability distribution becomes smaller and smaller. Figure 8.5 shows t distributions with 10 and 20 degrees of freedom and their relationship to the standard normal probability distribution. Note that a t distribution with more degrees of freedom has less variability and more closely resembles the standard normal probability distribution. Also note that the means of both the standard normal and all the t distributions are zero.

We will place a subscript on t to indicate the area in the upper tail of the t distribution. For example, just as we used $z_{.025}$ to indicate the z value providing a .025 area in the upper tail of a standard normal probability distribution, we will use $t_{.025}$ to indicate a .025 area in the upper tail of a t distribution. In general, we will use the notation $t_{\alpha/2}$ to represent a t value with an area of $\alpha/2$ in the upper tail of the t distribution. See Figure 8.6.

Table 8.3 is a table for the t distribution. This table is also shown inside the front cover of this book. Note, for example, that for a t distribution with 10 degrees of freedom, $t_{.025} = 2.228$. Similarly, for a t distribution with 20 degrees of freedom, $t_{.025} = 2.086$. As the degrees of freedom continue to increase, $t_{.025}$ approaches $z_{.025} = 1.96$.

FIGURE 8.5 COMPARISON OF THE STANDARD NORMAL DISTRIBUTION WITH t DISTRIBUTIONS HAVING 10 AND 20 DEGREES OF FREEDOM

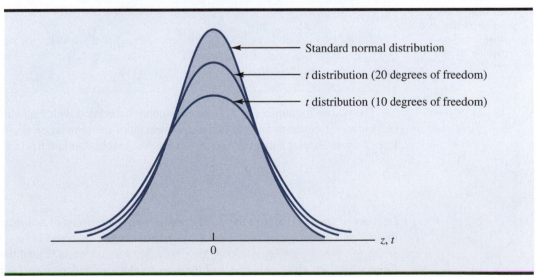

Standard normal distribution

t distribution (20 degrees of freedom)

t distribution (10 degrees of freedom)

z, t

0

FIGURE 8.6 t DISTRIBUTION WITH AN AREA OR PROBABILITY OF $\alpha/2$ IN THE UPPER TAIL

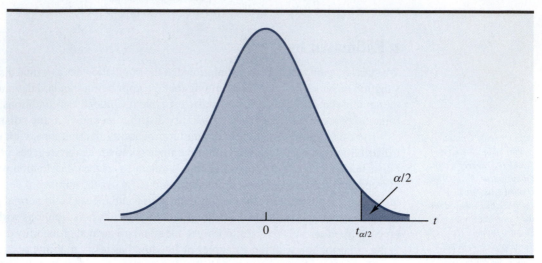

Now that we have an idea of what the t distribution is, let us see how it is used to develop an interval estimate of a population mean. Assume that the population has a normal probability distribution and that the sample standard deviation s is used to estimate the population standard deviation σ. With a confidence coefficient of $1 - \alpha$, the margin of error is given by $t_{\alpha/2}\dfrac{s}{\sqrt{n}}$ and the interval estimation procedure is given by expression (8.5).

The t distribution is based on the assumption that the population has a normal probability distribution. However, research indicates that confidence intervals based on the t distribution provide good approximations even when the population deviates from normality.

Interval Estimate of a Population Mean: Small-Sample Case ($n < 30$) with σ Estimated by s

Assumption: The population has a normal distribution.

$$\bar{x} \pm t_{\alpha/2}\frac{s}{\sqrt{n}} \tag{8.5}$$

where s is the sample standard deviation, $(1 - \alpha)$ is the confidence coefficient, and $t_{\alpha/2}$ is the t value providing an area of $\alpha/2$ in the upper tail of the t distribution with $n - 1$ degrees of freedom.

The reason the number of degrees of freedom associated with the t value in expression (8.5) is $n - 1$ concerns the use of s as an estimate of the population standard deviation σ. Recall from Chapter 3 that the expression for the sample standard deviation is

$$s = \sqrt{\frac{\Sigma(x_i - \bar{x})^2}{n - 1}}$$

Degrees of freedom refer to the number of independent pieces of information that go into the computation of $\Sigma(x_i - \bar{x})^2$. The n pieces of information involved in computing $\Sigma(x_i - \bar{x})^2$ are as follows: $x_1 - \bar{x}, x_2 - \bar{x}, \ldots, x_n - \bar{x}$. In Section 3.2 we indicated that $\Sigma(x_i - \bar{x}) = 0$ for any data set. Thus, only $n - 1$ of the $x_i - \bar{x}$ values are independent; that is, if we know

TABLE 8.3 t DISTRIBUTION TABLE FOR AREAS IN THE UPPER TAIL.
EXAMPLE: WITH 10 DEGREES OF FREEDOM, $t_{.025} = 2.228$

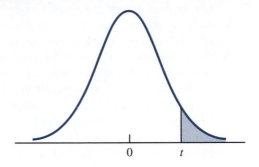

As the degrees of freedom increase, the t distribution approaches the standard normal distribution. In fact, standard normal distribution z values can be found in the infinite degrees of freedom row of this t distribution table.

Degrees of Freedom	Upper-Tail Area (Shaded)				
	.10	**.05**	**.025**	**.01**	**.005**
1	3.078	6.314	12.706	31.821	63.657
2	1.886	2.920	4.303	6.965	9.925
3	1.638	2.353	3.182	4.541	5.841
4	1.533	2.132	2.776	3.747	4.604
5	1.476	2.015	2.571	3.365	4.032
6	1.440	1.943	2.447	3.143	3.707
7	1.415	1.895	2.365	2.998	3.499
8	1.397	1.860	2.306	2.896	3.355
9	1.383	1.833	2.262	2.821	3.250
10	1.372	1.812	**2.228**	2.764	3.169
11	1.363	1.796	2.201	2.718	3.106
12	1.356	1.782	2.179	2.681	3.055
13	1.350	1.771	2.160	2.650	3.012
14	1.345	1.761	2.145	2.624	2.977
15	1.341	1.753	2.131	2.602	2.947
16	1.337	1.746	2.120	2.583	2.921
17	1.333	1.740	2.110	2.567	2.898
18	1.330	1.734	2.101	2.552	2.878
19	1.328	1.729	2.093	2.539	2.861
20	1.325	1.725	2.086	2.528	2.845
21	1.323	1.721	2.080	2.518	2.831
22	1.321	1.717	2.074	2.508	2.819
23	1.319	1.714	2.069	2.500	2.807
24	1.318	1.711	2.064	2.492	2.797
25	1.316	1.708	2.060	2.485	2.787
26	1.315	1.706	2.056	2.479	2.779
27	1.314	1.703	2.052	2.473	2.771
28	1.313	1.701	2.048	2.467	2.763
29	1.311	1.699	2.045	2.462	2.756
30	1.310	1.697	2.042	2.457	2.750
40	1.303	1.684	2.021	2.423	2.704
60	1.296	1.671	2.000	2.390	2.660
120	1.289	1.658	1.980	2.358	2.617
∞	1.282	1.645	1.960	2.326	2.576

$n - 1$ of the values, the remaining value can be determined exactly by using the condition that the sum of the $x_i - \bar{x}$ values must be 0. Thus, $n - 1$ is the number of degrees of freedom associated with $\Sigma(x_i - \bar{x})^2$ and hence the t distribution used in expression (8.5).

Let us demonstrate the small-sample interval estimation procedure by considering the training program evaluation conducted by Scheer Industries. Scheer's director of manufacturing is interested in a computer-assisted program that can be used to train the firm's maintenance employees for machine-repair operations. The expectation is that the computer-assisted method will reduce the time needed to train employees. To evaluate the training method, the director of manufacturing has requested an estimate of the mean training time required for the computer-assisted program.

Suppose management has agreed to train 15 employees with the new approach. The data on training days required for each employee in the sample are listed in Table 8.4. The sample mean and sample standard deviation for these data follow.

$$\bar{x} = \frac{\Sigma x_i}{n} = \frac{808}{15} = 53.87 \text{ days}$$

$$s = \sqrt{\frac{\Sigma(x_i - \bar{x})^2}{n - 1}} = \sqrt{\frac{651.73}{14}} = 6.82 \text{ days}$$

The point estimate of the mean training time for the population of employees is 53.87 days. We can obtain information about the precision of this estimate by computing the margin of error and developing an interval estimate of the population mean. Because the population standard deviation is unknown, we will use the sample standard deviation $s = 6.82$ days. With the small sample size, $n = 15$, we will use expression (8.5) to develop an interval estimate of the population mean at 95% confidence. With the assumption that the population of training times has a normal probability distribution, the t distribution with $n - 1 = 14$ degrees of freedom is the appropriate probability distribution for the interval estimation procedure. We see from Table 8.3 that with 14 degrees of freedom, $t_{\alpha/2} = t_{.025} = 2.145$. Using expression (8.5), we have

$$\bar{x} \pm t_{.025} \frac{s}{\sqrt{n}}$$

$$53.87 \pm 2.145 \left(\frac{6.82}{\sqrt{15}} \right)$$

$$53.87 \pm 3.78$$

Thus, the margin of error is 3.78, and the 95% confidence interval estimate of the population mean training time is 50.09 days to 57.65 days.

TABLE 8.4   TRAINING TIME IN DAYS FOR THE COMPUTER-ASSISTED PROGRAM AT SCHEER INDUSTRIES

Employee	Time	Employee	Time	Employee	Time
1	52	6	59	11	54
2	44	7	50	12	58
3	55	8	54	13	60
4	44	9	62	14	62
5	45	10	46	15	63

Using Excel to Construct a Confidence Interval With σ Estimated by s

Excel can be used to construct a 95% confidence interval for the population mean training time at Scheer Industries. Excel's TINV function is used to compute the appropriate t value. Because σ is unknown, s and the sample size n are used to estimate the standard error. The margin of error is computed as the product of the t value and the estimated standard error. Then by subtracting and adding the margin of error to the point estimate (the sample mean), we obtain the confidence interval. Refer to Figure 8.7 as we describe the tasks involved. The formula worksheet is in the background; the value worksheet is in the foreground.

Enter Data: A label and the training time data for the 15 employees are entered into cells A1:A16.

Enter Functions and Formulas: The descriptive statistics we need are provided in cells D4:D6. Excel's COUNT, AVERAGE, and STDEV functions compute the sample size, sample mean, and sample standard deviation for the data in cells A2:A16. The value worksheet shows $n = 15$, $\bar{x} = 53.87$, and $s = 6.82$.

Cells D8:D11 are used to compute the appropriate t value. The confidence coefficient (.95) has been entered into cell D8 and the level of significance (α) has been computed in cell D9 by entering the formula =1-D8. We entered the formula =D4-1 into cell D10 to compute the degrees of freedom as the (sample size) − 1. Next, the t value corresponding to an upper tail area of $\alpha/2$, $t_{\alpha/2}$, is computed by using the TINV function. The form of the TINV function is TINV(level of significance, degrees of freedom). Because the level of significance (α) is in cell D9 and the degrees of freedom ($n - 1$) are in cell D10, the formula =TINV(D9, D10) is entered into cell D11. The value worksheet shows that $t_{.025} = 2.145$.

Cells D13:D14 provide the estimate of the standard error and the margin of error. In cell D13, we entered the formula =D6/SQRT(D4) to estimate the standard error of the mean. The formula =D11*D13 entered into cell D14 computes the margin of error associated with a 95%

FIGURE 8.7 EXCEL WORKSHEET FOR SCHEER INDUSTRIES

	A	B	C	D	E	F
1	Training Time		Interval Estimate of a Population Mean			
2	52		Using the *t* Distribution			
3	44					
4	55		Sample size	=COUNT(A2:A16)		
5	44		Mean	=AVERAGE(A2:A16)		
6	45		Standard Deviation	=STDEV(A2:A16)		
7	59					
8	50		Confidence Coefficient	0.95		
9	54		Level of Significance (alpha)	=1-D8		
10	62		Degrees of Freedom	=D4-1		
11	46		*t* Value	=TINV(D9,D10)		
12	54					
13	58		Standard Error	=D6/SQRT(D4)		
14	60		Margin of Error	=D11*D13		
15	62					
16	63		Point Estimate	=D5		
17			Lower Limit	=D16-D14		
18			Upper Limit	=D16+D14		
19						

	A	B	C	D	E	F
1	Training Time		Interval Estimate of a Population Mean			
2	52		Using the *t* Distribution			
3	44					
4	55		Sample size	15		
5	44		Mean	53.87		
6	45		Standard Deviation	6.82		
7	59					
8	50		Confidence Coefficient	0.95		
9	54		Level of Significance (alpha)	0.05		
10	62		Degrees of Freedom	14		
11	46		*t* Value	2.145		
12	54					
13	58		Standard Error	1.76		
14	60		Margin of Error	3.78		
15	62					
16	63		Point Estimate	53.87		
17			Lower Limit	50.09		
18			Upper Limit	57.65		
19						

confidence interval. The resulting value of 3.78 is the margin of error associated with the 95% interval estimate of the population mean training time for Scheer Industries employees.

Cells D16:D18 provide the point estimate and the lower and upper limits for the confidence interval. Because the point estimate is just the sample mean, the formula =D5 is entered into cell D16. To compute the lower limit of the 95% confidence interval, $\bar{x}$ − (margin of error), we entered the formula =D16-D14 into cell D17. To compute the upper limit of the 95% confidence interval, $\bar{x}$ + (margin of error), we entered the formula =D16+D14 into cell D18. The value worksheet shows a lower limit of 50.09 and an upper limit of 57.65. In other words the 95% confidence interval for the population mean training time is 50.09 to 57.65 days.

The worksheet in Figure 8.7 can be used as a template for developing confidence intervals in the small sample ($n < 30$) case when s is used to estimate σ. The Scheer Industries problem is one in which s is used as an estimate of σ. To use this worksheet as a template for another problem of this type, we must first enter the new problem data in column A. Then the ranges for the formulas in the descriptive statistics cells (D4:D6) would be revised to correspond to the new data. After doing so, the point estimate and a 95% confidence interval will be displayed in cells D16:D18. If a confidence interval with a different confidence coefficient is desired, we simply change the value in cell D8.

The Role of the Population Distribution

An important consideration in developing an interval estimate of a population mean requires determining what is known about the population distribution. The large-sample interval estimation procedures in Section 8.1 make no assumption about the population distribution and can be applied to a population having any distribution. The small-sample interval estimation procedures in Section 8.2 are based on the assumption that the population has a normal distribution and can be applied to a population having a normal, or near-normal, distribution.

In practice, if the sample size is large ($n \geq 30$) and the form of the population distribution is unknown, we rely on the procedures in Section 8.1. In this case, an interval estimate of a population mean can be constructed as follows:

σ assumed known

$$\bar{x} \pm z_{\alpha/2} \frac{\sigma}{\sqrt{n}} \tag{8.2}$$

σ estimated by s

$$\bar{x} \pm z_{\alpha/2} \frac{s}{\sqrt{n}} \tag{8.3}$$

The important thing to note is that the large-sample theory supports the use of expressions (8.2) and (8.3) for a population having *any distribution.*

If the population has a normal distribution, the procedures in Section 8.2 apply. In this case we can develop an interval estimate of a population mean as follows:

σ assumed known

$$\bar{x} \pm z_{\alpha/2} \frac{\sigma}{\sqrt{n}} \tag{8.4}$$

σ estimated by s

$$\bar{x} \pm t_{\alpha/2} \frac{s}{\sqrt{n}} \tag{8.5}$$

In fact, if the population has a normal distribution, expressions (8.4) and (8.5) can be used to develop an interval estimate of a population mean in both the large-sample and small-sample cases.

In most practical applications, the form of the population distribution is unknown. Because expressions (8.2) and (8.3) apply to a population with any distribution, we make no assumption about the form of the population distribution and use (8.2) or (8.3) provided the sample size is large ($n \geq 30$). Thus, the only time it is necessary to address the assumption that the population has a normal distribution and consider using expressions (8.4) or (8.5) is when the sample size is small ($n < 30$). Figure 8.8 summarizes the interval estimation procedures we covered and provides a practical guide for computing an interval estimate of a population mean.

Excel can be used to implement the interval estimation procedures summarized in Figure 8.8. For the intervals involving a $z_{\alpha/2}$ value, the worksheet in Figure 8.4 can be used as a template. For the intervals involving a $t_{\alpha/2}$ value, the worksheet in Figure 8.7 can be used as a template.

FIGURE 8.8 SUMMARY OF INTERVAL ESTIMATION PROCEDURES FOR A POPULATION MEAN

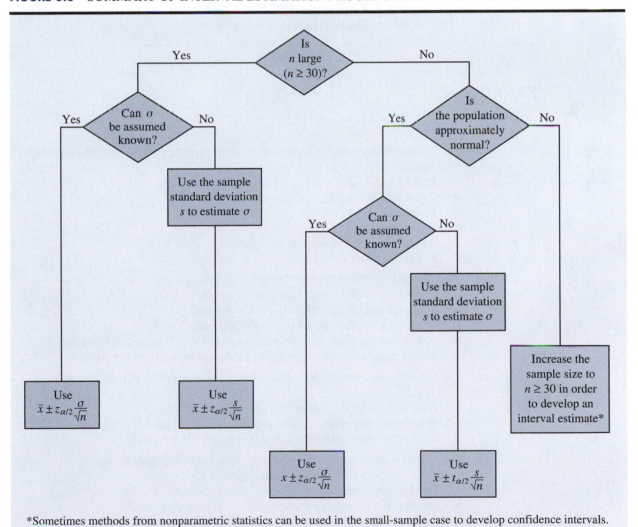

*Sometimes methods from nonparametric statistics can be used in the small-sample case to develop confidence intervals.

NOTES AND COMMENTS

1. To develop an interval estimate of μ in the small-sample case, the population must have a normal or approximately normal probability distribution. Determining normality for the small-sample case is difficult, and all that can usually be done is to apply good judgment. If in your judgment the population is roughly mound shaped and approximately symmetric, then the normality assumption and the use of the t distribution are appropriate.

2. Excel's Descriptive Statistics tool (see Chapter 3) can also be used to compute the margin of error when the t distribution is used to develop a confidence interval estimate of a population mean. For instance, suppose we wanted to compute descriptive statistics and the margin of error for a 95% confidence interval for the

Scheer Industries training time data. Starting with a worksheet containing the data in column A of Figure 8.7, select the **Tools** pull-down menu, choose the **Data Analysis** option, and then choose **Descriptive Statistics** from the list of analysis tools. When the Descriptive Statistics dialog box appears, complete it as shown in Figure 8.9. Note that we have provided the usual information needed to compute descriptive statistics plus we have checked the **Confidence Level for Mean:** box and entered **95** as the confidence level. After clicking **OK,** the information shown in Figure 8.10 will be generated. Note that the margin of error is contained in cell D16. Using the margin of error and the sample mean in cell D3 it is easy to now compute the confidence interval.

EXERCISES

Methods

13. For a t distribution with 12 degrees of freedom, find the area, or probability, that is in each region.
    a. To the left of 1.782.
    b. To the right of -1.356.
    c. To the right of 2.681.
    d. To the left of -1.782.
    e. Between -2.179 and $+2.179$.
    f. Between -1.356 and $+1.782$.

14. Find the t value(s) for each of the following cases.
    a. Upper tail area of .05 with 18 degrees of freedom.
    b. Lower tail area of .10 with 22 degrees of freedom.
    c. Upper tail area of .01 with 5 degrees of freedom.
    d. 90% of the area is between these two t values with 14 degrees of freedom.
    e. 95% of the area is between these two t values with 28 degrees of freedom.

15. The following data were collected for a sample from a normal population: 10, 8, 12, 15, 13, 11, 6, 5.
    a. What is the point estimate of the population mean?
    b. What is the point estimate of the population standard deviation?
    c. What is the 95% confidence interval for the population mean?

16. A simple random sample of 20 observations from a normal population resulted in a sample mean of 17.25 and a sample standard deviation of 3.3.
    a. Develop a 90% confidence interval for the population mean.
    b. Develop a 95% confidence interval for the population mean.
    c. Develop a 99% confidence interval for the population mean.

FIGURE 8.9   EXCEL'S DESCRIPTIVE STATISTICS DIALOG BOX

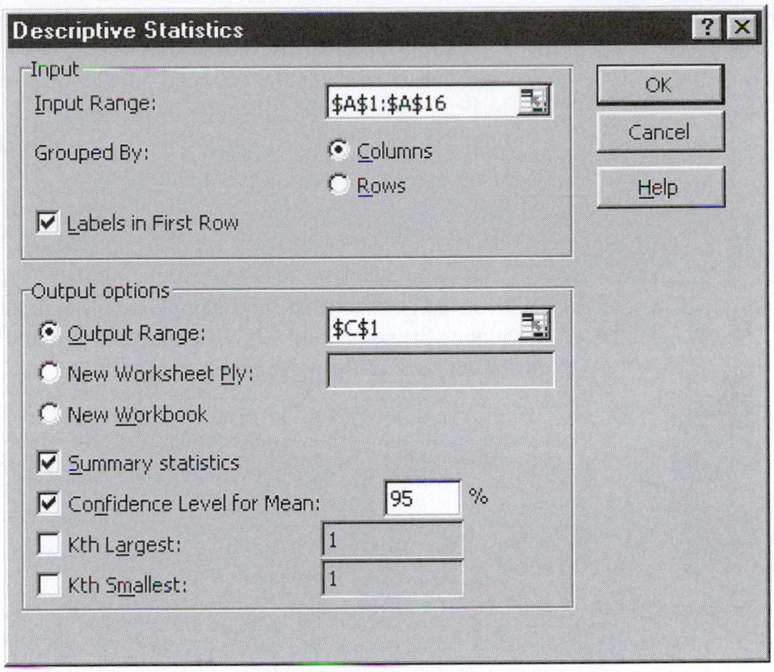

FIGURE 8.10   DESCRIPTIVE STATISTICS AND MARGIN OF ERROR
FOR SCHEER INDUSTRIES

	A	B	C	D	E	F	G
1	**Training Time**		*Training Time*				
2	52						
3	44		**Mean**	53.86667			
4	55		Standard Error	1.761673			
5	44		Median	54			
6	45		Mode	44			
7	59		Standard Deviation	6.822931			
8	50		Sample Variance	46.55238			
9	54		Kurtosis	-1.37004			
10	62		Skewness	-0.23179			
11	46		Range	19			
12	54		Minimum	44			
13	58		Maximum	63			
14	60		Sum	808			
15	62		Count	15		The value of the	
16	63		**Confidence Level(95.0%)**	3.778416		margin of error appears in cell D16.	
17							
18							

Applications

17. To test a new production method, 18 employees were selected randomly and asked to try the new method. The sample mean production rate for the 18 employees was 80 parts per hour and the sample standard deviation was 10 parts per hour. Provide 90% and 95% confidence intervals for the population mean production rate for the new method, assuming the population has a normal probability distribution.

18. A *USA Today* study of rental car gasoline prices found the following prices per gallon at 12 major airports (*USA Today*, April 4, 2000).

1.58   1.53   . 1.60   1.55   1.80   1.75   1.58   1.62   1.69   1.21   1.50   1.55

  a. What is the point estimate of the population mean price per gallon?
  b. What is the point estimate of the population standard deviation?
  c. Assuming the population follows a normal distribution, develop a 95% confidence interval estimate of the population mean price per gallon.

TVtime

19. The American Association of Advertising Agencies records data on nonprogram minutes during half-hour prime-time television shows. Representative data in minutes for a sample of 20 prime-time shows on major networks at 8:30 P.M. follows.

6.0	6.6	5.8
7.0	6.3	6.2
7.2	5.7	6.4
7.0	6.5	6.2
6.0	6.5	7.2
7.3	7.6	6.8
6.0	6.2	

Provide a point estimate and a 95% confidence interval for the mean number of nonprogram minutes during half-hour, prime-time television shows at 8:30 P.M. Assume the population has a normal distribution.

20. Sales personnel for Skillings Distributors are required to submit weekly reports listing the customer contacts made during the week. A sample of 61 weekly contact reports showed a mean of 22.4 customer contacts per week for the sales personnel. The sample standard deviation was 5 contacts.

  a. Use the large-sample case and expression (8.3) to develop a 95% confidence interval for the mean number of weekly customer contacts for the population of sales personnel.
  b. Assume that the population of weekly contact data has a normal distribution. Use the *t* distribution with 60 degrees of freedom to develop a 95% confidence interval for the mean number of weekly customer contacts.
  c. Compare your answers for parts (a) and (b). Comment on why in the large-sample case it is permissible to develop interval estimates using the procedure in part (a) even though the *t* distribution may also be applicable.

21. Due to constituents' complaints to their representatives about rising prescription drug prices, the U.S. Congress considered laws that would force pharmaceutical companies to offer prescription discounts to senior citizens. The House Government Reform Committee provided data on the prescription cost for some of the most widely used drugs (*Newsweek*, May 8, 2000). Assume the following data show a sample of the prescription cost (in dollars) for Zocor, a drug used to lower cholesterol.

     110   112   115   99   100   98   104   126

Assuming a normally distributed population, develop a 95% confidence interval estimate of the population mean cost for a prescription of Zocor.

Sleep

22. The number of hours Americans sleep each night varies considerably with 12% of the population sleeping fewer than six hours to 3% sleeping more than eight hours (*The Macmillan Visual Almanac*, 1996). The following sample of 25 individuals reports the hours of sleep per night.

6.9	7.6	6.5	6.2	5.3
7.8	7.0	5.5	7.6	6.7
7.3	6.6	7.1	6.9	6.0
6.8	6.5	7.2	5.8	8.6
7.6	7.1	6.0	7.2	7.7

a. What is the point estimate of the population mean number of hours of sleep each night?
b. Assuming that the population has a normal distribution, develop a 95% confidence interval for the population mean number of hours of sleep each night.

8.3   DETERMINING THE SAMPLE SIZE

In the large-sample case with σ known, the quantity $z_{\alpha/2}\,(\sigma/\sqrt{n})$ is the margin of error for an interval estimate with a confidence coefficient of $1 - \alpha$. The values of $z_{\alpha/2}$, σ, and the sample size n combine to determine the margin of error. Given values for $z_{\alpha/2}$ and σ, we can determine the sample size n needed to provide any desired margin of error. Development of the formula used to compute the required sample size n follows.

Let E = the desired margin of error

$$E = z_{\alpha/2}\frac{\sigma}{\sqrt{n}}$$

If a desired margin of error E is selected prior to sampling, the procedures in this section can be used to determine the sample size necessary to satisfy the margin of error requirement.

Solving for $\sqrt{n}$, we have

$$\sqrt{n} = \frac{z_{\alpha/2}\sigma}{E}$$

Squaring both sides of this equation, we obtain the following formula for the sample size.

Sample Size for an Interval Estimate of a Population Mean

$$n = \frac{(z_{\alpha/2})^2\sigma^2}{E^2} \tag{8.6}$$

This sample size will provide the desired margin of error at the chosen confidence level.

In equation (8.6) E is the margin of error that the user is willing to accept, and the value of $z_{\alpha/2}$ follows directly from the confidence level to be used in developing the interval estimate. Although user preference must be considered, 95% confidence is the most frequently chosen value ($z_{.025} = 1.96$).

Finally, equation (8.6) requires a value for the population standard deviation σ. In most cases, σ will be unknown. However, we can still use equation (8.6) if we have a

A planning value for the population standard deviation σ must be specified before the sample size can be determined. Three methods of obtaining a planning value for σ are discussed here.

preliminary or *planning value* for σ. In practice, one of the following procedures can be used.

1. Use the sample standard deviation from a previous study of the same or similar elements.
2. Use a pilot study to select a preliminary sample. The sample standard deviation from the preliminary sample can be used as the planning value for σ.
3. Use judgment or a "best guess" for the value of σ. For example, we might begin by estimating the largest and smallest data values in the population. The difference between the largest and smallest values provides an estimate of the range for the data. Finally, the range divided by four is often suggested as a rough approximation of the standard deviation and thus an acceptable planning value for σ.

Let us demonstrate the use of equation (8.6) to determine the sample size by considering the following example. A previous study that investigated the cost of renting automobiles in the United States found that the cost of renting a medium-sized automobile ranged from $36 per day in Oakland, California, to $73.50 per day in Hartford, Connecticut (*USA Today*, October 16, 1998). Suppose that the organization that conducted this study would like to conduct a new study in order to estimate the current population mean daily rental cost for a medium-sized automobile in the United States. In designing the new study, let us also suppose that the project director wanted to develop a 95% confidence interval for the population mean daily rental cost with a margin of error of $2.

The project director specified a desired margin of error of $E = 2$ and the 95% level of confidence indicates $z_{.025} = 1.96$. Thus, we only need a planning value for the population standard deviation σ in order to compute the required sample size. At this point, an analyst reviewed the sample data from the previous study and found that the sample standard deviation for the daily rental cost was $9.65. Using 9.65 as the planning value for σ, we obtain

Equation (8.6) provides the minimum sample size needed to satisfy the desired margin of error requirement. If the computed sample size is not an integer, rounding up to the next integer value will provide a margin of error slightly smaller than required.

$$n = \frac{(z_{\alpha/2})^2 \sigma^2}{E^2} = \frac{(1.96)^2 (9.65)^2}{2^2} = 89.43$$

Thus, the sample size for the new study needs to be at least 89.43 medium-sized automobile rentals in order to satisfy the project director's $2 margin-of-error requirement. In cases where the computed n is not an integer, we round up to the next integer value; hence, the recommended sample size is 90 medium-sized automobile rentals.

EXERCISES

Methods

23. How large a sample should be selected to provide a 95% confidence interval with a margin of error of 5? Assume that the population standard deviation is 25.

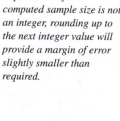

24. The range for a set of data is estimated to be 36.
   a. What is the planning value for the population standard deviation?
   b. Using a 95% confidence level, how large a sample should be used to provide a margin of error of 3?
   c. Using a 95% confidence level, how large a sample should be used to provide a margin of error of 2?

Applications

25. Refer to the Scheer Industries example in Section 8.2. Use $\sigma = 6.82$ as a planning value for the population standard deviation.
    a. Assuming a 95% confidence level, what sample size would be required to obtain a margin of error of 1.5 days?
    b. If the precision statement was made with a 90% confidence level, what sample size would be required to obtain a margin of error of 2 days?

26. *Bride's* magazine reported that the mean cost of a wedding is $19,000 (*USA Today*, April 17, 2000). Assume that the population standard deviation is $9,400. *Bride's* plans to use an annual survey to monitor the cost of a wedding. Use 95% confidence.
    a. What is the recommended sample size if the desired margin of error is $1000?
    b. What is the recommended sample size if the desired margin of error is $500?
    c. What is the recommended sample size if the desired margin of error is $200?

27. Annual starting salaries for college graduates with business administration degrees are believed to have a standard deviation of approximately $2000. Assume that a 95% confidence interval estimate of the mean annual starting salary is desired. How large a sample should be taken if the margin of error is
    a. $500?   b. $200?   c. $100?

28. RealFacts, a real estate research firm, provides monthly mean apartment rental costs for Los Angeles County (*Los Angeles Times*, August 1, 1999). Assume the population standard deviation of rental cost is $220 and that the desired margin of error is $50.
    a. What is the recommended sample size for a 90% confidence interval estimate of the population mean rental cost?
    b. What is the recommended sample size for a 95% confidence interval?
    c. What is the recommended sample size for a 99% confidence interval?
    d. If the desired margin of error is fixed, what happens to the sample size as the confidence level is increased?

29. The travel-to-work time for residents of the 15 largest cities in the United States is reported in the *1998 Information Please Almanac*. Suppose that a preliminary simple random sample of residents of San Francisco is used to develop a planning value of 6.25 minutes for the population standard deviation.
    a. If we want to estimate the population mean travel-to-work time for San Francisco residents with a margin of error of 2 minutes, what sample size should be used? Assume a 95% confidence level.
    b. If we want to estimate the population mean travel-to-work time for San Francisco residents with a margin of error of 1 minute, what sample size should be used? Assume a 95% confidence level.

30. The sample standard deviation of P/E ratios for stocks listed on the New York Stock Exchange is $s = 7.8$ (*The Wall Street Journal*, January 20, 2000). Assume that we are now interested in estimating the population mean P/E ratio for all stocks listed on the New York Stock Exchange in July 2003. How many stocks should be included in the sample if we want a margin of error of 2? Use a 95% confidence level.

8.4 INTERVAL ESTIMATION OF A POPULATION PROPORTION

In Chapter 7 we showed that the sample proportion $\bar{p}$ is used as a point estimator of a population proportion p and that for large samples the sampling probability distribution of $\bar{p}$ can be approximated by a normal probability distribution, as shown in Figure 8.11. Recall that the use of the normal distribution as an approximation of the sampling distribution of $\bar{p}$ is

FIGURE 8.11　NORMAL APPROXIMATION OF THE SAMPLING DISTRIBUTION OF $\bar{p}$
WHEN $np \geq 5$ AND $n(1 - p) \geq 5$

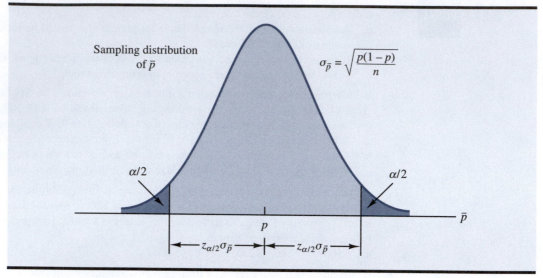

based on the condition that both np and $n(1 - p)$ are 5 or more. We will be using the sampling distribution of $\bar{p}$ to make probability statements about the sampling error whenever a sample proportion $\bar{p}$ is used to estimate a population proportion p. In this case, the sampling error is defined as the absolute value of the difference between $\bar{p}$ and p, written $|\bar{p} - p|$.

When the sample size is large enough to assume the sampling distribution of $\bar{p}$ is normally distributed, the following statement can be made about the sampling error.

> There is a $1 - \alpha$ probability that the value of the sample proportion will provide a sampling error of $z_{\alpha/2}\sigma_{\bar{p}}$ or less.

Hence, for a proportion, the quantity $z_{\alpha/2}\sigma_{\bar{p}}$ is the margin of error.

Once we know the margin of error, $z_{\alpha/2}\sigma_{\bar{p}}$, we can subtract and add this value to $\bar{p}$ to obtain an interval estimate of the population proportion. Such an interval estimate is given by

$$\bar{p} \pm z_{\alpha/2}\sigma_{\bar{p}} \tag{8.7}$$

where $1 - \alpha$ is the confidence coefficient. Because the standard error of the proportion is $\sigma_{\bar{p}} = \sqrt{p(1 - p)/n}$, we can rewrite (8.7) as

$$\bar{p} \pm z_{\alpha/2}\sqrt{\frac{p(1 - p)}{n}} \tag{8.8}$$

To use expression (8.8) to develop an interval estimate of a population proportion p, the value of p would have to be known. But the value of p is what we are trying to estimate, so we simply substitute the sample proportion $\bar{p}$ for p. The resulting general expression for a confidence interval estimate of a population proportion follows.[3]

---

[3]An unbiased estimate of $\sigma_{\bar{p}}^2$ is $\bar{p}(1 - \bar{p})/(n - 1)$, which suggests that $\sqrt{\bar{p}(1 - \bar{p})/(n - 1)}$ should be used in place of $\sqrt{\bar{p}(1 - \bar{p})/n}$ in expression (8.9). However, the bias introduced by using n in the denominator does not cause any difficulty because a large sample is generally used in making estimates about population proportions. In such cases the numerical difference between the results obtained by using n and those obtained by using $n - 1$ is negligible.

Interval Estimate of a Population Proportion

When developing confidence intervals for proportions, the quantity $z_{\alpha/2}\sqrt{\bar{p}(1-\bar{p})/n}$ provides the margin of error.

$$\bar{p} \pm z_{\alpha/2} \sqrt{\frac{\bar{p}(1-\bar{p})}{n}} \qquad (8.9)$$

where $1 - \alpha$ is the confidence coefficient and $z_{\alpha/2}$ is the z value providing an area of $\alpha/2$ in the upper tail of the standard normal probability distribution.

Let us use the following example to illustrate the computation of the margin of error and an interval estimate for a population proportion. In 1997, Ferrell Calvillo Communications conducted a national survey of 902 women golfers to learn how women golfers view themselves as being treated at golf courses in the United States (*USA Today*, June 3, 1997). The survey found that 397 of the women golfers were satisfied with the availability of tee times. Thus, a point estimate of the proportion of the population of women golfers who are satisfied with the availability of tee times is 397/902 = .4401. Using expression (8.9) and a 95% confidence level, we have

$$\bar{p} \pm z_{\alpha/2} \sqrt{\frac{\bar{p}(1-\bar{p})}{n}}$$

$$.4401 \pm 1.96 \sqrt{\frac{.4401(1 - .4401)}{902}}$$

$$.4401 \pm .0324$$

Thus, at 95% confidence, the margin of error is .0324 and the interval estimate of the population proportion is .4077 to .4725. Using percentages, the survey results enable us to state with 95% confidence that between 40.77% and 47.25% of all women golfers are satisfied with the availability of tee times.

Using Excel to Construct a Confidence Interval

Golfer

Excel can be used to construct an interval estimate of the population proportion of women golfers who are satisfied with the availability of tee times. Suppose that the responses in the Ferrell Calvillo survey had been recorded as a Yes or No for each woman surveyed. Refer to Figure 8.12 as we describe the tasks involved in constructing a 95% confidence interval. The formula worksheet is in the background; the value worksheet is in the foreground.

Enter Data: A label and the Yes-No data for the 902 women golfers are entered into cells A1:A903.

Enter Functions and Formulas: The descriptive statistics we need are provided in cells D3:D6. Because Excel's COUNT function only works with numerical data, we used the COUNTA function in cell D3 to compute the sample size. The response for which we want to develop an interval estimate, Yes or No, is entered into cell D4. Figure 8.12 shows that Yes has been entered into cell D4, indicating that we want to develop an interval estimate of the population proportion of women golfers who are satisfied with the availability of tee times. If we had wanted to develop an interval estimate of the population proportion of women golfers who are not satisfied with the availability of tee times, we would have entered No in cell D4. With Yes entered in cell D4, the COUNTIF function in cell D5 counts

FIGURE 8.12   EXCEL WORKSHEET FOR THE SURVEY OF WOMEN GOLFERS

	A	B	C	D	E
1	Response		**Interval Estimate of a Population Proportion**		
2	Yes				
3	No		Sample Size	=COUNTA(A2:A903)	
4	Yes		Response of Interest	Yes	
5	Yes		Count for Response	=COUNTIF(A2:A903,D4)	
6	No		Sample Proportion	=D5/D3	
7	No				
8	No		Confidence Coefficient	0.95	
9	Yes		Level of Significance (alpha)	=1-D8	
10	Yes		z Value	=NORMSINV(1-D9/2)	
11	Yes				
12	No		Standard Error	=SQRT(D6*(1-D6)/D3)	
13	No		Margin of Error	=D10*D12	
14	Yes				
15	No		Point Estimate	=D6	
16	No		Lower Limit	=D15-D13	
17	Yes		Upper Limit	=D15+D13	
18	No				
901	Yes				
902	No				
903	Yes				
904					

Note: Rows 19–900 are hidden.

	A	B	C	D	E	F	G
1	Response		**Interval Estimate of a Population Proportion**				
2	Yes						
3	No		Sample Size	902		Enter Yes as the	
4	Yes		Response of Interest	Yes		Response of Interest	
5	Yes		Count for Response	397			
6	No		Sample Proportion	0.4401			
7	No						
8	No		Confidence Coefficient	0.95			
9	Yes		Level of Significance (alpha)	0.05			
10	Yes		z Value	1.960			
11	Yes						
12	No		Standard Error	0.0165			
13	No		Margin of Error	0.0324			
14	Yes						
15	No		Point Estimate	0.4401			
16	No		Lower Limit	0.4077			
17	Yes		Upper Limit	0.4725			
18	No						
901	Yes						
902	No						
903	Yes						
904							

the number of Yes responses in the sample. The sample proportion is then computed in cell D6 by dividing the number of Yes responses in cell D5 by the sample size in cell D3.

Cells D8:D10 are used to compute the appropriate z value. The confidence coefficient (0.95) is entered into cell D8 and the level of significance (α) is computed in cell D9 by entering the formula =1-D8. The z value corresponding to an upper tail area of $\alpha/2$ is computed by entering the formula =NORMSINV(1-D9/2) into cell D10. The value worksheet shows that $z_{.025} = 1.960$.

Cells D12:D13 provide the estimate of the standard error and the margin of error. In cell D12, we entered the formula =SQRT(D6*(1-D6)/D3) to compute the standard error using the sample proportion and the sample size as inputs. The formula =D10*D12 is entered into cell D13 to compute the margin of error.

Cells D15:D17 provide the point estimate and the lower and upper limits for a confidence interval. The point estimate in cell D15 is the sample proportion. The lower and upper limits in cells D16 and D17 are obtained by subtracting and adding the margin of error to the point estimate. We note that the 95% confidence interval for the proportion of women golfers who are satisfied with the availability of tee times is .4077 to .4725.

The worksheet in Figure 8.12 can be used as a template for developing confidence intervals about a population proportion p. To use this worksheet for another problem of this type, we must first enter the new problem data in column A. The response of interest would then be typed in cell D4 and the ranges for the formulas in cells D3 and D5 would be revised to correspond to the new data. After doing so, the point estimate and a 95% confidence interval will be displayed in cells D15:D17. If a confidence interval with a different confidence coefficient is desired, we simply change the value in cell D8.

Determining the Sample Size

Let us consider the question of how large the sample size should be to obtain an estimate of a population proportion at a specified level of precision. The rationale for the sample size determination in developing interval estimates of p is similar to the rationale used in Section 8.3 to determine the sample size for estimating a population mean.

Previously in this section we pointed out that the margin of error associated with an estimate of a population proportion is $z_{\alpha/2}\sigma_{\bar{p}}$. With $\sigma_{\bar{p}} = \sqrt{p(1-p)/n}$ the size of the margin of error is based on the values of $z_{\alpha/2}$, the population proportion p, and the sample size n. For a confidence coefficient of $1 - \alpha$, $z_{\alpha/2}$ is known. Then, for a specified value of the population proportion p, the size of the margin of error is determined by the sample size n. Larger sample sizes provide a smaller margin of error and better precision.

Let E = the desired margin of error

$$E = z_{\alpha/2}\sqrt{\frac{p(1-p)}{n}}$$

Solving this equation for n provides the following formula for the sample size.

Sample Size for an Interval Estimate of a Population Proportion

$$n = \frac{(z_{\alpha/2})^2 p(1-p)}{E^2} \tag{8.10}$$

In equation (8.10), an acceptable size for the desired margin of error is usually specified by the user; in most cases, $E = .10$ or less is chosen. User preference also determines the confidence level and thus the corresponding value of $z_{\alpha/2}$. Finally, because the value of p will not be known in practice, use of equation (8.10) requires a planning value for the population proportion p. The planning value can be chosen by one of the following procedures.

Because the population proportion p is what we are attempting to estimate from the sample, a planning value for p must be available in order to use equation (8.10). Four ways to obtain this planning value are provided here.

1. Use the sample proportion from a previous study of the same or similar elements.
2. Use a pilot study to select a preliminary sample. The sample proportion from this sample can be used as the planning value for p.
3. Use judgment or a "best guess" for the value of p.
4. If none of the preceding alternatives apply, use a planning value of $p = .50$.

Let us return to the Ferrell Calvillo Communications survey of women golfers and assume that the company is interested in conducting a new survey to estimate the current proportion of the population of women golfers who are satisfied with the availability of tee times. How large should the sample be if the survey director wants the new study to be able to estimate the population proportion with a margin of error of .025 at a 95% confidence level? With $E = .025$ and $z_{\alpha/2} = 1.96$, we need a planning value of p to answer the sample size question. Using the 1997 survey result of $\bar{p} = .4401$ as the planning value for p, equation (8.10) shows that

$$n = \frac{(z_{\alpha/2})^2 p(1-p)}{E^2} = \frac{(1.96)^2(.4401)(1-.4401)}{(.025)^2} = 1514.5861$$

Thus, the sample size must be at least 1514.5861 women golfers to satisfy the margin of error requirement. Rounding up to the next integer value indicates that a sample of 1515 women golfers is recommended.

TABLE 8.5   SOME POSSIBLE VALUES FOR $p(1 - p)$

p	$p(1 - p)$	
.10	$(.10)(.90) = .09$	
.30	$(.30)(.70) = .21$	
.40	$(.40)(.60) = .24$	
.50	$(.50)(.50) = .25$	← Largest value for $p(1 - p)$
.60	$(.60)(.40) = .24$	
.70	$(.70)(.30) = .21$	
.90	$(.90)(.10) = .09$	

Surveys containing questions about several proportions are often designed by using a planning value of $p = .50$ for the sample size computation. Using this planning value gives a sample size that guarantees that all estimates of proportions will meet their margin of error requirements.

The fourth alternative suggested for selecting a planning value for p is to use $p = .50$. This value of p is frequently used when no other information is available. To understand why, note that the numerator of equation (8.10) shows that the sample size is proportional to the quantity $p(1 - p)$. A larger value for the quantity $p(1 - p)$ will result in a larger sample size. Table 8.5 gives some possible values of $p(1 - p)$. Note that the largest value of $p(1 - p)$ occurs when $p = .50$. Thus, any uncertainty about an appropriate planning value for p can be eased by using $p = .50$ because it provides the largest sample size recommendation. In effect, we are being on the safe or conservative side in recommending the largest possible sample size. If the proportion turns out to be different from the .50 planning value, the precision statement will be better than anticipated. Thus, in using $p = .50$, we are guaranteeing that the sample size will be sufficient to obtain the desired margin of error.

In the survey of women golfers example, a planning value of $p = .50$ would have provided the sample size

$$n = \frac{(z_{\alpha/2})^2 p(1 - p)}{E^2} = \frac{(1.96)^2(.50)(1 - .50)}{(.025)^2} = 1536.64$$

Thus a slightly larger sample size of 1537 women golfers is recommended.

NOTES AND COMMENTS

The margin of error for estimating a population proportion is almost always .10 or less. In national public opinion polls conducted by organizations such as Gallup and Harris, a .03 or .04 margin of error is generally reported. With such margins of error [E in equation (8.10)] the sample size formula will almost always provide a sample size that is large enough to satisfy the large sample requirements of $np \geq 5$ and $n(1 - p) \geq 5$.

EXERCISES

Methods

31. A simple random sample of 400 individuals provided 100 Yes responses.
   a. What is the point estimate of the proportion of the population that would provide Yes responses?
   b. What is the standard error of the proportion, $\sigma_{\bar{p}}$?
   c. Compute the 95% confidence interval for the population proportion.

32. A simple random sample of 800 elements generates a sample proportion $\bar{p} = .70$.
   a. Provide a 90% confidence interval for the population proportion.
   b. Provide a 95% confidence interval for the population proportion.

33. In a survey, the planning value for the population proportion p is .35. How large a sample should be taken to provide a 95% confidence interval with a margin of error of .05?

34. Using a 95% confidence level, how large a sample should be taken to obtain a margin of error for the estimation of a population proportion of .03? Assume that past data are not available for developing a planning value for p.

Applications

35. A *Time*/CNN poll asked 814 adults to respond to a series of questions about their feelings toward the state of affairs within the United States. A total of 562 adults responded Yes to the question: Do you feel things are going well in the United States these days? (*Time*, August 11, 1997).
   a. What is the point estimate of the proportion of the adult population who feel things are going well in the United States?
   b. At a 90% confidence level, what is the margin of error?
   c. What is the 90% confidence interval for the proportion of the adult population who feel things are going well in the United States?

36. A survey by the Society for Human Resource Management asked 346 job seekers why employees change jobs so frequently (*The Wall Street Journal*, March 28, 2000). The answer selected most (152 times) was "higher compensation elsewhere."
   a. What is the point estimate of the proportion of job seekers who would select "higher compensation elsewhere" as the reason for changing jobs?
   b. What is the 95% confidence interval estimate of the population proportion?

Attitude

37. A survey by Wirthlin Worldwide collected data on attitudes toward the quality of customer service in retail stores. The percentage of Americans who believe that customer service is better today than it was two years ago was reported (*USA Today*, January 20, 1998). Suppose that a sample of 650 adults resulted in the data contained in the data set Attitude. A response of Yes indicates that the individual surveyed believes that customer service is better. Develop a 95% confidence interval for the proportion of the population of adults who believe that customer service is better today than it was two years ago.

38. Audience profile data collected at the ESPN SportsZone Web site showed that 26% of the users were women (*USA Today*, January 21, 1998). Assume that this percentage was based on a sample of 400 users.
   a. What is the margin of error associated with a 95% confidence interval for the proportion of users who are women?
   b. What is the 95% confidence interval for the population proportion of ESPN SportsZone Web site users who are women?
   c. How large a sample should be taken if the desired margin of error is .03?

39. An Employee Benefit Research Institute survey explored the reasons small business employers offer a retirement plan to their employees (*USA Today*, April 4, 2000). The reason "competitive advantage in recruitment/retention" was mentioned 33% of the time.
   a. What sample size is recommended if a survey goal is to estimate the proportion of small business employers who offer a retirement plan primarily for "competitive advantage in recruitment/retention" with a margin of error of .03? Use 95% confidence.
   b. Repeat part (a) using 99% confidence.

40. An Associated Press poll of 1018 adults found 255 adults planned to spend less money on gifts during the 1998 holiday season compared to the previous year (ICR Media survey, November 13–17, 1998).
   a. What is the point estimate of the proportion of all adults who planned to spend less money on gifts during the 1998 holiday season?
   b. At the 95% confidence level, what is the margin of error associated with this estimate?

41. An American Express retail survey found that 16% of U.S. consumers used the Internet to buy gifts during the 1999 holiday season (*USA Today*, January 18, 2000). If 1285 customers participated in the survey, what is the margin of error and what is the interval estimate of the population proportion of customers using the Internet to buy gifts? Use 95% confidence.

42. A *USA Today*/CNN/Gallup poll for the 2000 presidential campaign sampled 491 potential voters in June (*USA Today*, June 9, 2000). A primary purpose of the poll was to obtain an estimate of the proportion of potential voters who favored each candidate.

   Closer to the November election, better precision and smaller margins of error are desired. Assume a planning value for the population proportion of $p = .50$ and that a 95% confidence level is desired. Determine the recommended sample size for each of the following surveys.

Survey	Margin of Error
September	.04
October	.03
Early November	.02
Pre-Election Day	.01

43. The League of American Theatres and Producers uses an ongoing audience tracking survey that provides up-to-date information about Broadway theater audiences (*Playbill*, Winter 1997). Every week, the League distributes a one-page survey on random theater seats at a rotation roster of Broadway shows. The survey questionnaire takes only five minutes to complete and enables audiences to communicate their views about the theater industry.
   a. How large a sample should be taken if the desired margin of error on any population proportion is .04? Use a 95% confidence level and a planning value of $p = .50$.
   b. Assume that the sample size recommended in part (a) is implemented and that during one week 445 theatergoers indicated that they do not live in New York City. What is the point estimate of the proportion of Broadway audiences that do not live in New York City?
   c. Using the data in part (b), what is the 95% confidence interval for the population proportion of Broadway audiences that do not live in New York City?

SUMMARY

In this chapter we presented methods for developing a confidence interval for a population mean μ and a population proportion p. The purpose of developing a confidence interval is to give the user a better understanding of the margin of error that may be present. A wide confidence interval indicates poor precision; in such cases, the sample size can be increased to reduce the width of the confidence interval and improve the precision of the estimate.

   The expression used to compute an interval estimate of a population mean depends on whether the sample size is large ($n \geq 30$) or small ($n < 30$); whether the population standard deviation can be assumed known or is estimated using the sample standard deviation; and in some cases whether the form of the population is a normal or approximately normal probability distribution. If the sample size is large, no assumption is required about the form of the distribution of the population, and $z_{\alpha/2}$ is used in the computation of the interval estimate. If the sample size is small, the population must have a normal or approximately normal probability distribution in order to develop an interval estimate of μ. For a normal probability distribution, $z_{\alpha/2}$ is used in the computation of the interval estimate when σ is assumed known, whereas $t_{\alpha/2}$ is used when σ is estimated by the sample standard deviation s. Finally, if the sample size is small and the assumption of a normally distributed population is inappropriate, we recommend increasing the sample size to $n \geq 30$ to develop a large-sample interval estimate of the population mean.

In practice, the sample sizes required for interval estimates of a population proportion are generally large. Hence, we only provided the large-sample interval estimation formulas for a population proportion where both $np \geq 5$ and $n(1 - p) \geq 5$. In addition, we showed how to determine the sample size so that interval estimates of μ and p would have a desired margin of error.

We showed how to implement all of the interval estimation procedures using an Excel worksheet. The worksheet in Figure 8.4 can be used as a template to develop interval estimates of a population mean involving a $z_{\alpha/2}$ value, and the worksheet in Figure 8.7 can be used as a template for interval estimates of a population mean involving a $t_{\alpha/2}$ value. The worksheet in Figure 8.12 can be used as a template for using Excel to develop interval estimates of a population proportion.

GLOSSARY

Interval estimate   An estimate of a population parameter that provides an interval believed to contain the value of the parameter. It is of the form: Point Estimator $\pm$ Margin of Error.

Margin of error   The $\pm$ value added to and subtracted from a point estimate in order to develop a confidence interval.

Sampling error   The absolute value of the difference between an unbiased point estimator, such as the sample mean $\bar{x}$, and the population parameter it estimates, such as the population mean μ. In the case of a population mean, the sampling error is $|\bar{x} - \mu|$. In the case of a population proportion, the sampling error is $|\bar{p} - p|$.

Precision statement   A probability statement about the size of the sampling error.

Confidence interval   Another term for an interval estimate.

Confidence level   The confidence associated with an interval estimate. For example, if an interval estimation procedure provides intervals such that 95% of the intervals formed using the procedure will include the population parameter, the interval estimate is said to be constructed at the 95% confidence level.

Level of significance   The probability that an interval estimation procedure will generate an interval that does not contain the population parameter.

t distribution   A family of probability distributions that can be used to develop interval estimates of a population mean whenever the population standard deviation is estimated by the sample standard deviation and the population has a normal or near-normal probability distribution.

Degrees of freedom   A parameter of the t distribution. When the t distribution is used in the computation of an interval estimate of a population mean, the appropriate t distribution has $n - 1$ degrees of freedom, where n is the size of the simple random sample.

KEY FORMULAS

General Form of an Interval Estimate for a Population Mean

$$\bar{x} \pm \text{Margin of Error} \tag{8.1}$$

Interval Estimate of a Population Mean: Large-Sample Case ($n \geq 30$) with σ Assumed Known

$$\bar{x} \pm z_{\alpha/2} \frac{\sigma}{\sqrt{n}} \tag{8.2}$$

Interval Estimate of a Population Mean: Large-Sample Case ($n \geq 30$) with σ Estimated by s

$$\bar{x} \pm z_{\alpha/2} \frac{s}{\sqrt{n}} \tag{8.3}$$

Interval Estimate of a Population Mean: Small-Sample Case ($n < 30$) with σ Assumed Known

$$\bar{x} \pm z_{\alpha/2} \frac{\sigma}{\sqrt{n}} \tag{8.4}$$

Interval Estimate of a Population Mean: Small-Sample Case ($n < 30$) with σ Estimated by s

$$\bar{x} \pm t_{\alpha/2} \frac{s}{\sqrt{n}} \tag{8.5}$$

Sample Size for an Interval Estimate of a Population Mean

$$n = \frac{(z_{\alpha/2})^2 \sigma^2}{E^2} \tag{8.6}$$

Interval Estimate of a Population Proportion

$$\bar{p} \pm z_{\alpha/2} \sqrt{\frac{\bar{p}(1 - \bar{p})}{n}} \tag{8.9}$$

Sample Size for an Interval Estimate of a Population Proportion

$$n = \frac{(z_{\alpha/2})^2 p(1 - p)}{E^2} \tag{8.10}$$

SUPPLEMENTARY EXERCISES

44. A survey of first-time home buyers found that the mean of annual household income was $50,000 (*CNBC.com*, July 11, 2000). Assume the survey used a sample of 400 first-time home buyers and that the sample standard deviation in income was $20,500.
   a. Using 95% confidence, what is the margin of error for this study?
   b. Develop a 95% confidence interval for the population mean annual household income for first-time home buyers.

Vacation

45. A survey conducted by the American Automobile Association showed that a family of four spends an average of $215.60 per day while on vacation. Suppose a sample of 64 families of four vacationing at Niagara Falls resulted in the daily expenditures contained in the data set Vacation.

a. Develop a 95% confidence interval estimate of the mean amount spent per day by a family of four visiting Niagara Falls.

b. Using the confidence interval from part (a), does it appear that the population mean amount spent per day by families visiting Niagara Falls is different from the mean reported by the American Automobile Association? Explain.

ActTemps

46. A survey by Accountemps asked a sample of 200 executives to provide data on the number of minutes per day office workers waste trying to locate mislabeled, misfiled, or misplaced items (*Astounding Averages*, by D.D. Dauphinais and K. Droste, 1995). Data consistent with this survey are contained in the data set ActTemps.

a. Use ActTemps to develop a point estimate of the number of minutes per day office workers waste trying to locate mislabeled, misfiled, or misplaced items.

b. What is the sample standard deviation?

c. What is the 95% confidence interval for the mean number of minutes wasted per day?

Mail

47. Arthur D. Little, Inc., estimates that approximately 70% of mail received by a household is advertisements (*Time*, July 14, 1997). A sample of 20 households shows the following data for the number of advertisements received and the total number of pieces of mail received during one week.

Household	Advertisements	Total Mail	Household	Advertisements	Total Mail
1	24	35	11	13	19
2	9	14	12	16	28
3	18	30	13	20	27
4	9	12	14	17	22
5	15	28	15	21	24
6	23	33	16	21	33
7	13	20	17	15	25
8	17	20	18	15	24
9	20	23	19	18	24
10	20	25	20	12	16

a. What is the point estimate of the mean number of advertisements received per week? What is the 95% confidence interval for the population mean?

b. What is the point estimate of the mean number of pieces of mail received per week? What is the 95% confidence interval for the population mean?

c. Use the point estimates in parts (a) and (b). Are these estimates in agreement with the statement that approximately 70% of mailings are advertisements?

48. The Money & Investing section of *The Wall Street Journal* contains a summary of daily investment performance for stock exchanges, overseas markets, options, commodities, futures, and so on. In the New York Stock Exchange section, information is provided on each stock's 52-week high price per share, 52-week low price per share, dividend rate, yield, P/E ratio, daily volume, daily high price per share, daily low price per share, closing price per share, and daily net change. The P/E (price/earnings) ratio for each stock is determined by dividing the price of a share of stock by the earnings per share reported by the company for the most recent four quarters. A sample of 10 stocks taken from *The Wall Street Journal* (September 29, 2000) provided the following data on P/E ratios: 5, 7, 9, 10, 14, 23, 20, 15, 3, 26.

a. What is the point estimate of the mean P/E ratio for the population of all stocks listed on the New York Stock Exchange?

b. What is the point estimate of the standard deviation of the P/E ratios for the population of all stocks listed on the New York Stock Exchange?

c. At 95% confidence, what is the interval estimate of the mean P/E ratio for the population of all stocks listed on the New York Stock Exchange? Assume that the population has a normal distribution.

d. Comment on the precision of the results.

49. Many Americans who work in large offices also work at home or in the office on weekends (*USA Today*, June 18, 1997). How large a sample should be taken to estimate the population mean amount of time worked on weekends with a margin of error of 10 minutes. Use a 95% confidence level and assume that the planning value for the population standard deviation is 45 minutes.

50. Mileage tests are conducted for a particular model of automobile. If the desired precision is a 98% confidence interval with a margin of error of 1 mile per gallon, how many automobiles should be used in the test? Assume that preliminary mileage tests indicate the standard deviation to be 2.6 miles per gallon.

51. In developing patient appointment schedules, a medical center wants an estimate of the mean time that a staff member spends with each patient. How large a sample should be taken if the margin of error is to be 2 minutes at a 95% level of confidence? How large a sample should be taken for a 99% level of confidence? Use a planning value for the population standard deviation of 8 minutes.

52. Annual salary plus bonus data for chief executive officers were presented in the *Business Week* 47th Annual Pay Survey (*Business Week*, April 21, 1997). A preliminary sample showed that the standard deviation is $675 with data provided in thousands of dollars. How many chief executive officers should be in a sample if we want to estimate the population mean annual salary plus bonus with a margin of error of $100,000? (Note: The margin of error would be $E = 100$ because the data are in thousands of dollars.) Use a 95% confidence interval.

Work

53. The National Center for Education Statistics conducted a survey to determine the percentage of college students who work to pay for tuition and living expenses (*The Tampa Tribune*, January 22, 1997). The data set Work provides results consistent with the survey for a sample of 450 college students. A response of Yes indicates that the student works to pay for tuition and living expenses.

a. Provide a 95% confidence interval for the population proportion of college students who work to pay for tuition and living expenses.

b. Provide a 99% confidence interval for the population proportion of college students who work to pay for tuition and living expenses.

c. What happens to the margin of error as the confidence is increased from 95% to 99%?

54. A *USA Today*/CNN Gallup survey of 369 working parents found 200 who said they spend too little time with their children because of work commitments (*USA Today*, April 10, 1995).

a. What is the point estimate of the proportion of the population of working parents who feel they spend too little time with their children because of work commitments?

b. At a 95% confidence level, what is the margin of error?

c. What is the 95% confidence interval estimate of the population proportion of working parents who feel they spend too little time with their children because of work commitments?

55. A *Time*/CNN poll of 1400 American adults asked, "Where would you rather go in your spare time?" The top response by 504 adults was a shopping mall.

a. What is the point estimate of the proportion of American adults who would prefer going to a shopping mall in their spare time?

b. At a 95% confidence level, what is the margin of error associated with this estimate?

56. A well-known bank credit card firm is interested in estimating the proportion of credit card-holders who carry a nonzero balance at the end of the month and incur an interest charge. Assume that the desired margin of error is .03 at a 98% confidence level.

   a. How large a sample should be selected if it is anticipated that roughly 70% of the firm's cardholders carry a nonzero balance at the end of the month?

   b. How large a sample should be selected if no planning value for the population proportion could be specified?

57. In a survey, 200 people were asked to identify their major source of news information; 110 stated that their major source was television news.

   a. Construct a 95% confidence interval for the proportion of people in the population who consider television their major source of news information.

   b. How large a sample would be necessary to estimate the population proportion with a margin of error of .05 at a 95% confidence level?

58. A Roper Starch survey asked employees ages 18 to 29 if they would prefer better health insurance or a raise in salary (*USA Today*, September 5, 2000). Answer the following questions assuming that 340 of the 500 employees surveyed said they would prefer better health insurance over a raise.

   a. What is the point estimate of the proportion of all employees ages 18 to 29 who would prefer better health insurance?

   b. What is the 95% confidence interval estimate of the population proportion?

59. The *1997 Statistical Abstract of the United States* reports the percentage of people 18 years of age and older who smoke. Suppose that a study is being designed to collect new data on smokers and nonsmokers. The best preliminary estimate of the population proportion who smoke is .30.

   a. How large a sample should be taken to estimate the proportion of smokers in the population with a margin of error of .02? Use a 95% confidence level.

   b. Assume that the study uses your sample size recommendation in part (a) and finds 520 smokers. What is the point estimate of the proportion of smokers in the population?

   c. What is the 95% confidence interval for the proportion of smokers in the population?

60. Although airline schedules and cost are important factors for business travelers when choosing an airline carrier, a *USA Today* survey found that business travelers list an airline's frequent flyer program as the most important factor (*USA Today*, April 11, 1995). From a sample of $n = 1993$ business travelers who responded to the survey, 618 listed a frequent flyer program as the most important factor.

   a. What is the point estimate of the proportion of the population of business travelers who believe a frequent flyer program is the most important factor when choosing an airline carrier?

   b. Develop a 95% confidence interval estimate of the population proportion.

   c. How large a sample would be required to report the margin of error of .01 at a 95% confidence level? Would you recommend that *USA Today* attempt to provide this degree of precision? Why or why not?

Case Problem 1   BOCK INVESTMENT SERVICES

Lisa Rae Bock started Bock Investment Services (BIS) in 1994 with the goal of making BIS the leading money market advisory service in South Carolina. To provide better service for her present clients and to attract new clients, she developed a weekly newsletter. Lisa is considering adding a new feature to the newsletter that will report the results of a weekly telephone survey of fund managers. To investigate the feasibility of offering this service and to determine what type of information to include in the newsletter, Lisa selected a simple random sample of 45 money market funds. A portion of the data obtained is shown in Table 8.6,

TABLE 8.6   DATA FOR BOCK INVESTMENT SERVICES

Bock

Money Market Fund	Assets ($ millions)	7-Day Yield (%)	30-Day Yield (%)
Amcore	103.9	4.10	4.08
Alger	156.7	4.79	4.73
Arch MM/Trust	496.5	4.17	4.13
BT Instit Treas	197.8	4.37	4.32
Benchmark Div	2755.4	4.54	4.47
Bradford	707.6	3.88	3.83
Capital Cash	1.7	4.29	4.22
Cash Mgt Trust	2707.8	4.14	4.04
Composite	122.8	4.03	3.91
Cowen Standby	694.7	4.25	4.19
Cortland	217.3	3.57	3.51
Declaration	38.4	2.67	2.61
Dreyfus	4832.8	4.01	3.89
Elfun	81.7	4.51	4.41
FFB Cash	506.2	4.17	4.11
Federated Master	738.7	4.41	4.34
Fidelity Cash	13272.8	4.51	4.42
Flex-fund	172.8	4.60	4.48
Fortis	105.6	3.87	3.85
Franklin Money	996.8	3.97	3.92
Freedom Cash	1079.0	4.07	4.01
Galaxy Money	801.4	4.11	3.96
Government Cash	409.4	3.83	3.82
Hanover Cash	794.3	4.32	4.23
Heritage Cash	1008.3	4.08	4.00
Infinity/Alpha	53.6	3.99	3.91
John Hancock	226.4	3.93	3.87
Landmark Funds	481.3	4.28	4.26
Liquid Cash	388.9	4.61	4.64
MarketWatch	10.6	4.13	4.05
Merrill Lynch Money	27005.6	4.24	4.18
NCC Funds	113.4	4.22	4.20
Nationwide	517.3	4.22	4.14
Overland	291.5	4.26	4.17
Pierpont Money	1991.7	4.50	4.40
Portico Money	161.6	4.28	4.20
Prudential MoneyMart	6835.1	4.20	4.16
Reserve Primary	1408.8	3.91	3.86
Schwab Money	10531.0	4.16	4.07
Smith Barney Cash	2947.6	4.16	4.12
Stagecoach	1502.2	4.18	4.13
Strong Money	470.2	4.37	4.29
Transamerica Cash	175.5	4.20	4.19
United Cash	323.7	3.96	3.89
Woodward Money	1330.0	4.24	4.21

Source: Barron's, October 3, 1994.

which reports fund assets and 7-day and 30-day yields. Before calling the money market fund managers to obtain additional data, Lisa decided to do some preliminary analysis of the data already collected.

Managerial Report

1. Use appropriate descriptive statistics to summarize the data on assets and yields for the money market funds.
2. Develop a 95% confidence interval estimate of the mean assets, mean 7-day yield, and mean 30-day yield for the population of money market funds. Provide a managerial interpretation of each interval estimate.
3. Discuss the implications of your findings in terms of how Lisa could use this type of information in preparing her weekly newsletter.
4. What other information would you recommend that Lisa gather to provide the most useful information to her clients?

Case Problem 2   GULF REAL ESTATE PROPERTIES

Gulf Real Estate Properties, Inc., is a real estate firm located in Southwest Florida. The company, which advertises itself as "expert in the real estate market," monitors condominium sales by collecting data on location, list price, sale price, and number of days it takes to sell each unit. Each condominium is classified as *Gulf View* if it is located directly on the Gulf of Mexico or *No Gulf View* if it is located on the bay or a golf course, near but not on the Gulf. Sample data from the multiple listing service in Naples, Florida, provided sales data for 40 Gulf View condominiums and 18 No Gulf-View condominiums.* The data are shown in Table 8.7. Prices are in thousands of dollars.

Managerial Report

1. Use appropriate descriptive statistics to summarize each of the three variables for the 40 Gulf View condominiums.
2. Use appropriate descriptive statistics to summarize each of the three variables for the 18 No Gulf View condominiums.
3. Compare your summary results. Discuss any specific statistical results that would help a real estate agent understand the condominium market.
4. Develop a 95% confidence interval estimate for the mean sales price and mean number of days to sell a Gulf View condominium. Interpret your results.
5. Develop a 95% confidence interval estimate for the mean sales price and mean number of days to sell a No Gulf View condominium. Interpret your results.
6. Assume the branch manager requested estimates of the mean selling price of Gulf View condominiums with a margin of error of $40,000 and the mean selling price of No Gulf View condominiums with a margin of error of $15,000. Using 95% confidence, how large should the sample sizes be?
7. Gulf Real Estate Properties just signed contracts for two new listings: a Gulf View condominium with a list price of $589,000 and a No Gulf View condominium with a list price of $285,000. What is your estimate of the final selling price and number of days required to sell each of these units?

---

*Data based on condominium sales reported in the Naples MLS (Coldwell Banker, June 2000).

TABLE 8.7   SALES DATA FOR GULF REAL ESTATE PROPERTIES

CD file

GulfProp

Gulf View Condominiums			No Gulf View Condominiums		
List Price	Sale Price	Days to Sell	List Price	Sale Price	Days to Sell
495.0	475.0	130	217.0	217.0	182
379.0	350.0	71	148.0	135.5	338
529.0	519.0	85	186.5	179.0	122
552.5	534.5	95	239.0	230.0	150
334.9	334.9	119	279.0	267.5	169
550.0	505.0	92	215.0	214.0	58
169.9	165.0	197	279.0	259.0	110
210.0	210.0	56	179.9	176.5	130
975.0	945.0	73	149.9	144.9	149
314.0	314.0	126	235.0	230.0	114
315.0	305.0	88	199.8	192.0	120
885.0	800.0	282	210.0	195.0	61
975.0	975.0	100	226.0	212.0	146
469.0	445.0	56	149.9	146.5	137
329.0	305.0	49	160.0	160.0	281
365.0	330.0	48	322.0	292.5	63
332.0	312.0	88	187.5	179.0	48
520.0	495.0	161	247.0	227.0	52
425.0	405.0	149			
675.0	669.0	142			
409.0	400.0	28			
649.0	649.0	29			
319.0	305.0	140			
425.0	410.0	85			
359.0	340.0	107			
469.0	449.0	72			
895.0	875.0	129			
439.0	430.0	160			
435.0	400.0	206			
235.0	227.0	91			
638.0	618.0	100			
629.0	600.0	97			
329.0	309.0	114			
595.0	555.0	45			
339.0	315.0	150			
215.0	200.0	48			
395.0	375.0	135			
449.0	425.0	53			
499.0	465.0	86			
439.0	428.5	158			

Case Problem 3   METROPOLITAN RESEARCH, INC.

Metropolitan Research, Inc., is a consumer research organization that conducts surveys designed to evaluate a wide variety of products and services available to consumers. In one particular study, Metropolitan was interested in learning about consumer satisfaction with the performance of automobiles produced by a major Detroit manufacturer. A questionnaire sent to owners of one of the manufacturer's full-sized cars revealed several complaints about early transmission problems. To learn more about the transmission failures, Metropolitan used a sample of actual transmission repairs provided by a transmission repair firm in the Detroit area. The following data show the actual number of miles that 50 vehicles had been driven at the time of transmission failure.

85,092	32,609	59,465	77,437	32,534	64,090	32,464	59,902
39,323	89,641	94,219	116,803	92,857	63,436	65,605	85,861
64,342	61,978	67,998	59,817	101,769	95,774	121,352	69,568
74,276	66,998	40,001	72,069	25,066	77,098	69,922	35,662
74,425	67,202	118,444	53,500	79,294	64,544	86,813	116,269
37,831	89,341	73,341	85,288	138,114	53,402	85,586	82,256
77,539	88,798						

Managerial Report

1. Use appropriate descriptive statistics to summarize the transmission failure data.
2. Develop a 95% confidence interval for the mean number of miles driven until transmission failure for the population of automobiles that experienced transmission failure. Provide a managerial interpretation of the interval estimate.
3. Discuss the implications of your statistical finding in terms of the belief that some owners of the automobiles experienced early transmission failures.
4. How many repair records should be sampled if the research firm wants the population mean number of miles driven until transmission failure to be estimated with a margin of error of 5000 miles? Use a 95% confidence level.
5. What other information would you like to gather to evaluate the transmission failure problem more fully?

CHAPTER 9

Hypothesis Testing

CONTENTS

STATISTICS IN PRACTICE

Harris Corporation*

MELBOURNE, FLORIDA

Harris Corporation, a communications equipment company, provides products and services for worldwide markets, including wireless, broadcast, government, and network support systems. The company operates sales and service facilities in more than 80 countries. Many of the Harris products require medium- to high-volume production operations, including printed circuit assembly, final product assembly, and testing.

One of the company's high-volume products consists of an assembly called an RF deck. Each RF deck consists of 16 electronic components soldered to a machined casting that forms the plated surface of the deck. During a manufacturing run, a problem developed in the soldering process; the flow of solder onto the deck did not meet the quality criteria established for the product. After considering a variety of factors that might affect the soldering process, an engineer made the preliminary determination that the soldering problem was most likely due to defective platings.

The engineer wondered whether the proportion of defective platings in the Harris inventory exceeded the level set by the supplier's design specifications. With p indicating the proportion of defective platings in the Harris inventory and p_0 indicating the proportion of defective platings set by the supplier's design specifications, the following hypotheses were formulated.

$$H_0: p \le p_0$$
$$H_a: p > p_0$$

H_0 indicates that the Harris inventory has a defective plating proportion less than or equal to the supplier's de-

Harris Corporation used hypothesis testing to solve a problem in the soldering process for one of its circuit boards. © CORBIS.

sign specifications. Such a proportion would be judged acceptable, and the engineer would need to look for other causes of the soldering problem. However, H_a indicates that the Harris inventory has a defective plating proportion greater than the supplier's design specifications. In that case, excessive defective platings may well be the cause of the soldering problem and action should be taken to determine why the defective proportion in inventory is so high.

Tests made on a sample of platings from the Harris inventory resulted in the rejection of H_0. The conclusion was that H_a was true and that the proportion of defective platings in inventory exceeded that set by the supplier's design specifications. Further investigation of the inventory storage area led to the conclusion that the underlying problem was shelf contamination during storage. By altering the storage environment, the engineer was able to solve the problem.

In this chapter you will learn how to formulate hypotheses about a population mean and a population proportion. Through the analysis of sample data, you will be able to determine whether a hypothesis should or should not be rejected. Appropriate conclusions and actions will be demonstrated for testing research hypotheses, testing the validity of a claim, and decision making.

*The authors are indebted to Richard A. Marshall of the Harris Corporation for providing this Statistics in Practice.

In Chapters 7 and 8 we showed how a sample could be used to develop point and interval estimates of population parameters. In this chapter we continue the discussion of statistical inference by showing how *hypothesis testing* can be used to determine whether a statement about the value of a population parameter should or should not be rejected.

In hypothesis testing we begin by making a tentative assumption about a population parameter. This tentative assumption is called the **null hypothesis** and is denoted by H_0. We then define another hypothesis, called the **alternative hypothesis**, which is the opposite of what is stated in the null hypothesis. The alternative hypothesis is denoted by H_a. The hypothesis testing procedure involves using data from a sample to test the two competing statements indicated by H_0 and H_a.

This chapter describes the hypothesis testing procedure and shows how hypothesis tests can be conducted about a population mean and a population proportion. We begin by providing examples that illustrate approaches to developing null and alternative hypotheses.

9.1 DEVELOPING NULL AND ALTERNATIVE HYPOTHESES

Learning to formulate hypotheses correctly will take practice. Expect some initial confusion over the proper choice of hypotheses H_0 and H_a. The examples in this section show a variety of forms for H_0 and H_a depending upon the application.

In some applications it may not be obvious how the null and alternative hypotheses should be formulated. Care must be taken to be sure the hypotheses are structured appropriately so that the hypothesis testing conclusion provides the information the researcher or decision maker wants. Guidelines for establishing the null and alternative hypotheses will be given for three types of situations in which hypothesis testing procedures are commonly employed.

Testing Research Hypotheses

Consider a particular automobile model that currently attains an average fuel efficiency of 24 miles per gallon. A product research group developed a new fuel injection system specifically designed to increase the miles-per-gallon rating. To evaluate the new system, several will be manufactured, installed in automobiles, and subjected to research-controlled driving tests. Here the product research group is looking for evidence to conclude that the new system *increases* the mean miles-per-gallon rating. In this case, the research hypothesis is that the new fuel injection system will provide a mean miles-per-gallon rating exceeding 24; that is, $\mu > 24$. As a general guideline, a research hypothesis should be stated as the *alternative hypothesis*. Hence, the appropriate null and alternative hypotheses for the study are:

$$H_0: \mu \le 24$$
$$H_a: \mu > 24$$

Hypothesis testing is proof by contradiction. Thus, the research hypothesis is the alternative hypothesis. The conclusion that the research hypothesis is true can be made if the sample data contradicts the null hypothesis.

If the sample results indicate that H_0 cannot be rejected, researchers cannot conclude that the new fuel injection system is better. Perhaps more research and subsequent testing should be conducted. However, if the sample results indicate that H_0 can be rejected, researchers can make the inference that $H_a: \mu > 24$ is true. With this conclusion, the researchers have the statistical support necessary to state that the new system increases the mean number of miles per gallon. Action to begin production with the new fuel injection system may be undertaken.

In research studies such as these, the null and alternative hypotheses should be formulated so that the rejection of H_0 supports the conclusion and action being sought. The research hypothesis therefore should be expressed as the alternative hypothesis.

Testing the Validity of a Claim

As an illustration of testing the validity of a claim, consider the situation of a manufacturer of soft drinks who states that two-liter containers of its products are filled with an average of at least 67.6 fluid ounces. A sample of two-liter containers will be selected, and the contents will be measured to test the manufacturer's claim. In this type of hypothesis testing situation, we generally assume that the manufacturer's claim is true unless the sample evidence is contradictory. Using this approach for the soft-drink example, we would state the null and alternative hypotheses as follows.

$$H_0: \mu \geq 67.6$$
$$H_a: \mu < 67.6$$

A manufacturer's claim is usually given the benefit of the doubt and stated as the null hypothesis. The conclusion that the claim is false can be made if the null hypothesis is rejected.

If the sample results indicate H_0 cannot be rejected, the manufacturer's claim will not be challenged. However, if the sample results indicate H_0 can be rejected, the inference will be made that $H_a: \mu < 67.6$ is true. With this conclusion, statistical evidence indicates that the manufacturer's claim is incorrect and that the soft drink containers are being filled with a mean less than the claimed 67.6 ounces. Appropriate action against the manufacturer may be considered.

In any situation that involves testing the validity of a claim, the null hypothesis is generally based on the assumption that the claim is true. The alternative hypothesis is then formulated so that rejection of H_0 will provide statistical evidence that the stated assumption is incorrect. Action to correct the claim should be considered whenever H_0 is rejected.

Testing in Decision-Making Situations

In testing research hypotheses or testing the validity of a claim, action is taken if H_0 is rejected. In many instances, however, action must be taken both when H_0 cannot be rejected and when H_0 can be rejected. In general, this type of situation occurs when a decision maker must choose between two courses of action, one associated with the null hypothesis and another associated with the alternative hypothesis. For example, on the basis of a sample of parts from a shipment just received, a quality control inspector must decide whether to accept the shipment or to return the shipment to the supplier because it does not meet specifications. Assume that specifications for a particular part require a mean length of two inches per part. If the mean length is greater or less than the 2-inch standard, the parts will cause quality problems in the assembly operation. In this case, the null and alternative hypotheses would be formulated as follows.

$$H_0: \mu = 2$$
$$H_a: \mu \neq 2$$

If the sample results indicate H_0 cannot be rejected, the quality control inspector will have no reason to doubt that the shipment meets specifications, and the shipment will be accepted. However, if the sample results indicate H_0 should be rejected, the conclusion will be that the parts do not meet specifications. In this case, the quality control inspector will have sufficient evidence to return the shipment to the supplier. Thus, we see that for these types of situations, action is taken both when H_0 cannot be rejected and when H_0 can be rejected.

Summary of Forms for Null and Alternative Hypotheses

The three possible forms of hypotheses H_0 and H_a are shown here. Note that the equality always appears in the null hypothesis H_0.

The hypothesis tests in this chapter involve two population parameters: the population mean and the population proportion. The situation determines which form the hypothesis tests about a population parameter may take: Two of the forms use inequalities in the null hypothesis; the third form uses an equality in the null hypothesis. For hypothesis tests involving a population mean, we let μ_0 denote the hypothesized value, and we choose one of the following three forms for the hypothesis test.

$$H_0: \mu \geq \mu_0 \qquad H_0: \mu \leq \mu_0 \qquad H_0: \mu = \mu_0$$
$$H_a: \mu < \mu_0 \qquad H_a: \mu > \mu_0 \qquad H_a: \mu \neq \mu_0$$

For reasons that will be clear later, the first two forms are called one-tailed tests. The third form is called a two-tailed test.

In many situations, the choice of H_0 and H_a is not obvious and judgment is necessary to select the proper form. However, as the preceding forms show, the equality part of the expression (either $\geq$, $\leq$, or $=$) *always* appears in the null hypothesis. In selecting the proper form of H_0 and H_a, keep in mind that the alternative hypothesis is often what the test is attempting to establish. Hence, asking whether the user is looking for evidence to support $\mu < \mu_0, \mu > \mu_0$, or $\mu \neq \mu_0$ will help determine H_a. The following exercises are designed to provide practice in choosing the proper form for a hypothesis test involving a population mean.

EXERCISES

1. The manager of the Danvers-Hilton Resort Hotel stated that the mean guest bill for a weekend is $600 or less. A member of the hotel's accounting staff noticed that the total charges for guest bills have been increasing in recent months. The accountant will use a sample of weekend guest bills to test the manager's claim.
   a. Which form of hypothesis test should be used to test the manager's claim? Explain.

$$H_0: \mu \geq 600 \qquad H_0: \mu \leq 600 \qquad H_0: \mu = 600$$
$$H_a: \mu < 600 \qquad H_a: \mu > 600 \qquad H_a: \mu \neq 600$$

   b. What conclusion is appropriate when H_0 cannot be rejected?
   c. What conclusion is appropriate when H_0 can be rejected?

2. The manager of an automobile dealership is considering a new bonus plan designed to increase sales volume. Currently, the mean sales volume is 14 automobiles per month. The manager wants to conduct a research study to see whether the new bonus plan increases sales volume. To collect data on the plan, a sample of sales personnel will be allowed to sell under the new bonus plan for a 1-month period.
   a. Develop the null and alternative hypotheses that are most appropriate for this research situation.
   b. Comment on the conclusion when H_0 cannot be rejected.
   c. Comment on the conclusion when H_0 can be rejected.

3. A production line operation is designed to fill cartons with laundry detergent to a mean weight of 32 ounces. A sample of cartons is periodically selected and weighed to determine whether underfilling or overfilling is occurring. If the sample data lead to a conclusion of underfilling or overfilling, the production line will be shut down and adjusted to obtain proper filling.
   a. Formulate the null and alternative hypotheses that will help in deciding whether to shut down and adjust the production line.
   b. Comment on the conclusion and the decision when H_0 cannot be rejected.
   c. Comment on the conclusion and the decision when H_0 can be rejected.

4. Because of high production-changeover time and costs, a director of manufacturing must convince management that a proposed manufacturing method reduces costs before the new method can be implemented. The current production method operates with a mean cost of $220 per hour. A research study is to be conducted in which the cost of the new method will be measured over a sample production period.

    a. Develop the null and alternative hypotheses that are most appropriate for this study.

    b. Comment on the conclusion when H_0 cannot be rejected.

    c. Comment on the conclusion when H_0 can be rejected.

9.2   TYPE I AND TYPE II ERRORS

The null and alternative hypotheses are competing statements about the population. Either the null hypothesis H_0 is true or the alternative hypothesis H_a is true, but not both. Ideally the hypothesis testing procedure should lead to the acceptance of H_0 when H_0 is true and the rejection of H_0 when H_a is true. Unfortunately, correct conclusions are not always obtained. Because hypothesis tests are based on sample information, we must allow for the possibility of errors. Table 9.1 illustrates the two kinds of errors that can be made in hypothesis testing.

The first row of Table 9.1 shows what can happen when the conclusion is to accept H_0. If H_0 is true, this conclusion is correct. However, if H_a is true, we have made a **Type II error**; that is, we have accepted H_0 when it is false. The second row of Table 9.1 shows what can happen when the conclusion is to reject H_0. If H_0 is true, we have made a **Type I error**; that is, we have rejected H_0 when it is true. However, if H_a is true, rejecting H_0 is correct.

Recall the hypothesis testing illustration discussed in Section 9.1 in which an automobile product research group developed a new fuel injection system designed to increase the miles-per-gallon rating of a particular automobile. With the current model obtaining an average of 24 miles per gallon, the hypothesis test was formulated as follows.

$$H_0: \mu \leq 24$$
$$H_a: \mu > 24$$

The alternative hypothesis, $H_a: \mu > 24$, indicates that the researchers are looking for sample evidence that will support the conclusion that the population mean miles per gallon is greater than 24.

In this application, the Type I error of rejecting H_0 when it is true corresponds to concluding that the new fuel injection system improves the miles-per-gallon rating ($\mu > 24$) when in fact the new fuel injection system is not any better than the current system. In contrast,

TABLE 9.1   ERRORS AND CORRECT CONCLUSIONS IN HYPOTHESIS TESTING

		Population Condition	
		H_0 True	H_a True
	Accept H_0	Correct Conclusion	Type II Error
Conclusion			
	Reject H_0	Type I Error	Correct Conclusion

the Type II error of accepting H_0 when it is false corresponds to the researchers' conclusion that the new fuel injection system is not any better than the current system ($\mu \leq 24$) when in fact the new fuel injection system improves the miles-per-gallon rating.

In practice, the person conducting the hypothesis test specifies the maximum allowable probability of making a Type I error, called the **level of significance** for the test. The level of significance is denoted α. Common choices for the level of significance are $\alpha = .05$ and $\alpha = .01$. Referring to the second row of Table 9.1, note that the conclusion to *reject H_0* indicates that either a Type I error or a correct conclusion has been made. Thus, if the probability of making a Type I error is controlled for by selecting a small value for the level of significance, we have a high degree of confidence that the conclusion to reject H_0 is correct. In such cases, we have statistical support for concluding that H_0 is false and H_a is true. Any action suggested by the alternative hypothesis H_a is appropriate.

If the sample data are consistent with the null hypothesis H_0, we will follow the practice of concluding "do not reject H_0." This conclusion is preferred over "accept H_0," when we have not controlled for the probability of making a Type II error.

Although most applications of hypothesis testing control for the probability of making a Type I error, they do not always control for the probability of making a Type II error. Hence, if we decide to accept H_0, we cannot determine how confident we can be with that decision. Because of the uncertainty associated with making a Type II error, statisticians often recommend that we use the statement "do not reject H_0" instead of "accept H_0." Using the statement "do not reject H_0" carries the recommendation to withhold both judgment and action. In effect, by never directly accepting H_0, the statistician avoids the risk of making a Type II error. Whenever the probability of making a Type II error has not been determined and controlled, we will not make the conclusion to accept H_0. In such cases, only two conclusions are possible: *do not reject H_0 or reject H_0*.

Controlling for a Type II error in hypothesis testing is not common, but it can be done. More advanced texts describe procedures for determining and controlling the probability of making a Type II error.* If proper controls have been established for this error, action based on an "accept H_0" conclusion can be appropriate.

NOTES AND COMMENTS

Many applications of hypothesis testing have a decision-making goal. The conclusion *reject H_0* provides the statistical support to conclude that H_a is true and to take whatever action is appropriate. The statement "do not reject H_0", although inconclusive, often forces managers to behave as though H_0 is true. In this case, managers need to be aware of the fact that such action may result in a Type II error.

EXERCISES

5. Americans spend an average of 8.6 minutes per day reading newspapers (*USA Today*, April 10, 1995). A researcher believes that individuals in management positions spend more than the national average time per day reading newspapers. A sample of individuals in management positions will be selected by the researcher. Data on newspaper reading times will be used to test the following null and alternative hypotheses.

$$H_0: \mu \leq 8.6$$
$$H_a: \mu > 8.6$$

---

*See, for example, *Statistics for Business and Economics*, 8th ed. Anderson, D. R., D. J. Sweeney, and T. A. Williams, Cincinnati, OH: South-Western, 2002.

a. What is the Type I error in this situation? What are the consequences of making this error?

b. What is the Type II error in this situation? What are the consequences of making this error?

6. The label on a 3-quart carton of orange juice claims that the orange juice contains an average of 1 gram of fat or less. Answer the following questions for a hypothesis test that could be used to test the claim on the label.

   a. Develop the appropriate null and alternative hypotheses.

   b. What is the Type I error in this situation? What are the consequences of making this error?

   c. What is the Type II error in this situation? What are the consequences of making this error?

7. Carpetland salespersons averaged $8000 per week in sales. Steve Contois, the firm's vice president, proposed a compensation plan with new selling incentives. Steve hopes that the results of a trial selling period will enable him to conclude that the compensation plan increases the average sales per salesperson.

   a. Develop the appropriate null and alternative hypotheses.

   b. What is the Type I error in this situation? What are the consequences of making this error?

   c. What is the Type II error in this situation? What are the consequences of making this error?

8. Suppose a new production method will be implemented if a hypothesis test supports the conclusion that the new method reduces the mean operating cost per hour.

   a. State the appropriate null and alternative hypotheses if the mean cost for the current production method is $220 per hour.

   b. What is the Type I error in this situation? What are the consequences of making this error?

   c. What is the Type II error in this situation? What are the consequences of making this error?

9.3 ONE-TAILED TESTS ABOUT A POPULATION MEAN: LARGE-SAMPLE CASE

In practice, the majority of hypothesis testing applications involve large samples.

In this section we describe how one-tailed hypothesis tests about a population mean are conducted when a large sample is available. For hypothesis tests involving a population mean, we follow the guideline that a sample size of $n \geq 30$ allows us to employ the large-sample procedures.

The Federal Trade Commission (FTC) periodically conducts studies designed to test the claims manufacturers make about their products. For example, the label on a large can of Hilltop Coffee states that the can contains at least 3 pounds of coffee. Suppose we want to check this claim by collecting a sample and conducting a hypothesis test.

The first step is to develop the null and alternative hypotheses. We begin by tentatively assuming that the manufacturer's claim is correct. If the population of coffee cans has a mean weight of 3 or more pounds per can, Hilltop's claim about its product is correct. However, if the population of coffee cans has a mean weight less than 3 pounds per can, Hilltop's claim is incorrect.

With μ denoting the mean weight of cans for the population, the null and the alternative hypotheses are as follows.

$$H_0: \mu \geq 3$$
$$H_a: \mu < 3$$

If the sample data indicate that H_0 cannot be rejected, the statistical evidence does not support the conclusion that a label violation has occurred. Hence, no action would be taken against Hilltop. However, if sample data indicate that H_0 can be rejected, we will conclude that the alternative hypothesis, $H_a: \mu < 3$, is true. In that case, a conclusion of underfilling and a charge of a label violation will be justified.

Suppose a random sample of 36 cans of coffee is selected. Note that if the mean filling weight, $\bar{x}$, for the sample of 36 cans is less than 3 pounds, the sample results will begin to cast doubt on the null hypothesis $H_0: \mu \geq 3$. But how much less than 3 pounds must $\bar{x}$ be before we would be willing to risk making a Type I error and falsely accuse the company of a label violation?

To answer this question, let us tentatively assume that the null hypothesis is true with $\mu = 3$. From the study of sampling distributions in Chapter 7, we know that whenever the sample size is large ($n \geq 30$), the sampling distribution of $\bar{x}$ can be approximated by a normal probability distribution. Figure 9.1 shows the sampling distribution of $\bar{x}$ when the null hypothesis is true at $\mu = 3$.

The value of $z = (\bar{x} - 3)/\sigma_{\bar{x}}$ is the number of standard errors $\bar{x}$ is from $\mu = 3$. For large-sample hypothesis tests about a population mean, we will use z as a **test statistic** to determine whether $\bar{x}$ deviates enough from $\mu = 3$ to justify rejecting the null hypothesis. Note that a value of $z = -1$ means that $\bar{x}$ is 1 standard error below $\mu = 3$, a value of $z = -2$ means that $\bar{x}$ is 2 standard errors below $\mu = 3$, and so on. Obtaining a value of $z < -3$ is unlikely if the null hypothesis is true. The key question is: How small must the test statistic z be before we have enough evidence to reject the null hypothesis?

Figure 9.2 shows that the probability of observing a value for $\bar{x}$ of more than 1.645 standard errors below the mean of $\mu = 3$ is .05. Hence, if we were to reject the null hypothesis whenever the value of the test statistic $z = (\bar{x} - 3)/\sigma_{\bar{x}}$ is less than -1.645, the probability of making a Type I error would be .05. If the FTC considered .05 to be an acceptable probability of making a Type I error, we would reject the null hypothesis whenever the test statistic indicates that the sample mean is more than 1.645 standard errors below $\mu = 3$. Thus, we would reject H_0 if $z < -1.645$.

The methodology of hypothesis testing requires that we specify the maximum allowable probability of a Type I error. As noted in the preceding section, this maximum probability is called the level of significance for the test. The level of significance is denoted by

Recall that the standard error is the name used for the standard deviation of a point estimator ($\bar{x}$ in this case).

FIGURE 9.1   SAMPLING DISTRIBUTION OF $\bar{x}$ FOR THE HILLTOP COFFEE STUDY WHEN THE NULL HYPOTHESIS IS TRUE ($\mu = 3$)

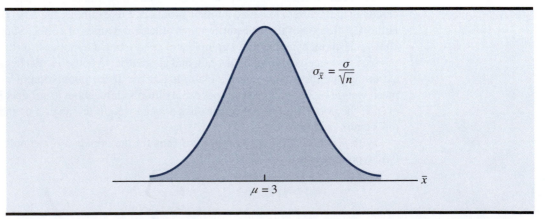

α and it represents the probability of making a Type I error when the null hypothesis is true as an equality. The manager making the decision must specify the level of significance. If the cost of making a Type I error is high, a small value should be chosen for the level of significance. If the cost is not high, a larger value may be appropriate.

In the Hilltop Coffee study, the director of the FTC's testing program has made the following statement: "If the company is meeting its weight specifications exactly ($\mu = 3$), I would like a 99% chance of not taking any action against the company. While I do not want to accuse the company wrongly of underfilling its product, I am willing to risk a 1% chance of making this error."

The director's choice of $\alpha = .01$ implies a high cost of the Type I error of falsely accusing Hilltop of mislabeling.

From the director's statement, the maximum probability of a Type I error is .01. Hence, the level of significance for the hypothesis test is $\alpha = .01$. Figure 9.3 shows the sampling distributions of both $\bar{x}$ and $z = (\bar{x} - \mu)/\sigma_{\bar{x}}$ for the Hilltop Coffee example. Note that when the null hypothesis is true at $\mu = 3$, the probability is .01 that $\bar{x}$ is more than 2.33 standard errors below the mean of 3. Therefore, we establish the following rejection rule.

$$\text{Reject } H_0 \text{ if } z = \frac{\bar{x} - \mu}{\sigma_{\bar{x}}} < -2.33$$

If the value of $\bar{x}$ is such that the test statistic z is in the **rejection region** ($z < -2.33$), we reject H_0 and conclude that H_a is true. If the value of $\bar{x}$ is such that the test statistic z is not in the rejection region, we cannot reject H_0. Note that the rejection region in Figure 9.3 is in only one tail of the sampling distribution. In such cases, we say the test is a **one-tailed hypothesis test**.

σ Assumed Known

We are now ready to return to the Hilltop Coffee study and to use the sample results to draw the hypothesis testing conclusion. Two methods can be used: one based on the observed value of the test statistic, and one based on the *p*-value criterion. We begin by using the test statistic.

FIGURE 9.2   PROBABILITY THAT $\bar{x}$ IS MORE THAN 1.645 STANDARD ERRORS BELOW THE MEAN OF $\mu = 3$

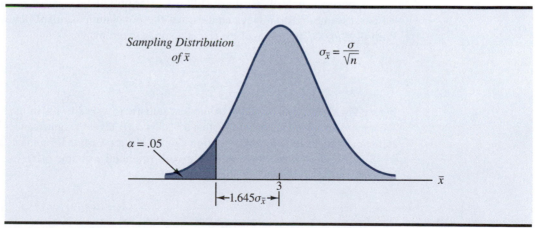

FIGURE 9.3 HILLTOP COFFEE REJECTION RULE HAS A LEVEL OF SIGNIFICANCE OF $\alpha = .01$

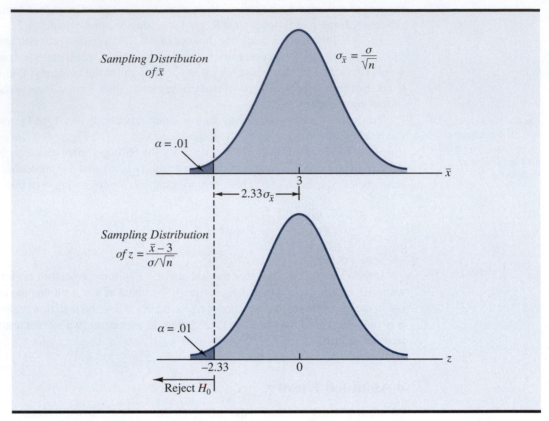

Using the Test Statistic In the large-sample case with the population standard deviation σ assumed known, the test statistic is given by

$$z = \frac{\bar{x} - \mu_0}{\sigma/\sqrt{n}} \qquad (9.1)$$

Suppose a sample of 36 cans of Hilltop Coffee provides a mean of $\bar{x} = 2.92$ pounds and we can assume from previous studies that the population standard deviation is $\sigma = .18$. With $\sigma_{\bar{x}} = \sigma/\sqrt{n}$, the value of the test statistic is given by

$$z = \frac{\bar{x} - \mu}{\sigma/\sqrt{n}} = \frac{2.92 - 3}{.18/\sqrt{36}} = -2.67$$

Figure 9.4 shows that the value of the test statistic ($z = -2.67$) is in the rejection region. We are now justified in concluding that $\mu < 3$ at a .01 level of significance. The director has statistical justification for taking action against Hilltop Coffee for underfilling its product.

Suppose, however, the sample of 36 cans provided a sample mean of $\bar{x} = 2.97$. In this case, the value of the test statistic would be

$$z = \frac{\bar{x} - 3}{\sigma/\sqrt{n}} = \frac{2.97 - 3}{.18/\sqrt{36}} = -1.00$$

FIGURE 9.4 VALUE OF THE TEST STATISTIC ($z = -2.67$) FOR $\bar{x} = 2.92$ IS
IN THE REJECTION REGION

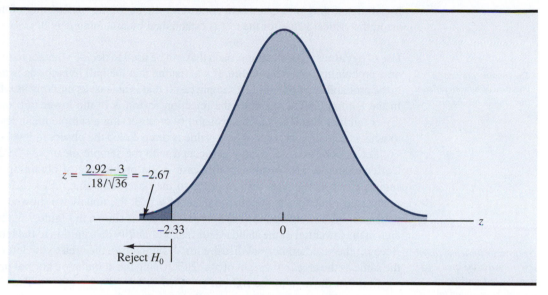

Because $z = -1.00$ is greater than -2.33, the value of the test statistic is not in the rejection region (see Figure 9.5). Hence we cannot reject the null hypothesis. Thus, with a sample mean of $\bar{x} = 2.97$, the statistical evidence is not sufficient to take action against Hilltop Coffee.

The value $z = -2.33$ establishes the boundary of the rejection region and is called the **critical value**. In establishing the critical value, we tentatively assume the null hypothesis is true. For Hilltop Coffee, the null hypothesis is true whenever $\mu \geq 3$; however, we considered only the case when $\mu = 3$. What about the case when $\mu > 3$? If $\mu > 3$, the probability

FIGURE 9.5 VALUE OF THE TEST STATISTIC ($z = -1.00$) FOR $\bar{x} = 2.97$ IS NOT
IN THE REJECTION REGION

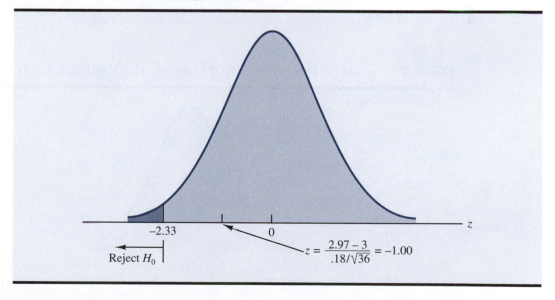

of making a Type I error will be less than it is when $\mu = 3$; that is, we are even less likely to find a value of the test statistic that is in the rejection region. Because the objective of the hypothesis testing procedure is to control for the maximum probability of making a Type I error, the critical value for the test is established by assuming $\mu = 3$.

Use of p-Values Another approach that can be used to decide whether to reject H_0 is based on a probability called a **p-value**. If we assume that the null hypothesis is true, the p-value is the probability of obtaining a sample result that is at least as unlikely as what is observed. In the Hilltop Coffee example, the rejection region is in the lower tail; the p-value for a lower tail hypothesis test is the probability of observing a sample mean less than or equal to what is actually observed. The p-value is often called the observed level of significance.

> *The p-value provides a measure of how significant the sample results are.*

Let us compute the p-value associated with the sample mean $\bar{x} = 2.92$ in the Hilltop Coffee example. The p-value in this case is the probability of obtaining a value for the sample mean that is less than or equal to the observed value of $\bar{x} = 2.92$, given the hypothesized value for the population mean of $\mu = 3$. Previously we showed that the test statistic $z = -2.67$ corresponded to $\bar{x} = 2.92$. Thus, as shown in Figure 9.6, the p-value is the area in the lower tail of the standard normal probability distribution to the left of $z = -2.67$. Because the standard normal distribution is symmetric, the area to the left of $z = -2.67$ is the same as the area to the right of $z = 2.67$. Using the cumulative normal probability table, we find that the area to the right of $z = 2.67$ is $1 - .9962 = .0038$. The p-value is therefore .0038. This p-value shows a small probability of obtaining a sample mean as small as $\bar{x} = 2.92$ when sampling from a population with $\mu = 3$.

> *The p-value for a one-tailed test is always the area from the test statistic toward the rejection tail of the distribution. With a lower tail test, it is the cumulative probability to the left of the test statistic.*

The p-value can be used to make the decision in a hypothesis test by noting that if the p-value is *less than the level of significance* α, the value of the test statistic is in the rejection region. Similarly, if the p-value is *greater than or equal to* α, the value of the test statistic is not in the rejection region. For the Hilltop Coffee example, the fact that the p-value of .0038 is less than the level of significance, $\alpha = .01$, indicates that the null hypothesis should be rejected. Given the level of significance α, the decision of whether to reject H_0 can be made as follows.

---

p-Value Criterion for Hypothesis Testing

Reject H_0 if p-value $< \alpha$

FIGURE 9.6 *p*-VALUE FOR THE HILLTOP COFFEE STUDY WHEN $\bar{x} = 2.92$ AND $z = -2.67$

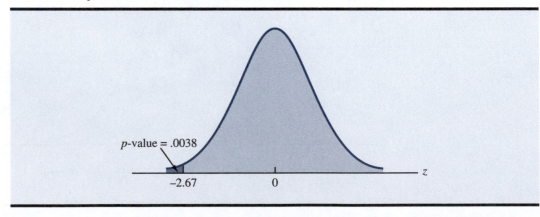

Using the p-value, or the corresponding test statistic, will always provide the same hypothesis testing conclusion. When the rejection region is in the lower tail of the sampling distribution, the p-value is the area under the curve less than or equal to the test statistic (a cumulative probability). When the rejection region is in the upper tail of the sampling distribution, the p-value is the area under the curve greater than or equal to the test statistic. For continuous sampling distributions, the p-value for an upper tail rejection region is 1 minus the p-value for a lower tail rejection region.

A small p-value indicates a sample result that is unusual given the assumption that H_0 is true. Small p-values lead to rejection of H_0, whereas large p-values indicate that the null hypothesis cannot be rejected.

Sometimes a researcher may simply report the p-value for a particular sample result. The user of the research findings can select any level of significance, α, he or she is willing to tolerate. Depending on that choice, some may reject H_0; others may not.

Steps of Hypothesis Testing

In conducting the Hilltop Coffee hypothesis test, we carried out the steps that can be used for any hypothesis test. In the summary that follows, note that either the test statistic or the p-value may be used to draw the hypothesis testing conclusion.

Steps of Hypothesis Testing

1. Develop the null and alternative hypotheses.
2. Specify the level of significance α.
3. Select the test statistic that will be used to test the hypothesis.

Using the Test Statistic:

4. Use the level of significance to determine the critical value(s) for the test statistic and state the rejection rule for H_0.
5. Collect the sample data and compute the value of the test statistic.
6. Use the value of the test statistic and the rejection rule to determine whether to reject H_0.

Using the p-Value:

4. Collect the sample data and compute the value of the test statistic.
5. Use the value of the test statistic to compute the p-value.
6. Reject H_0 if p-value $< \alpha$.

σ Estimated by s

In the Hilltop Coffee study the test statistic used to make the hypothesis testing decision was

$$z = \frac{\bar{x} - \mu_0}{\sigma/\sqrt{n}} \tag{9.1}$$

To compute the value of z corresponding to a particular sample mean $\bar{x}$, we had to know the value of the population standard deviation. A difficulty in using equation (9.1) is that in most applications the population standard deviation σ is unknown. In the large-sample case ($n \geq 30$), we simply use the value of the sample standard deviation, s, as the point estimate of the population standard deviation σ in computing the test statistic. The following test statistic is obtained.

$$z = \frac{\bar{x} - \mu_0}{s/\sqrt{n}} \tag{9.2}$$

As an illustration of the hypothesis testing procedure when σ is estimated by s, let us consider a problem facing ComSpeed, Inc., a firm that provides high-speed Internet access throughout the Northeast. As a marketing strategy, management is considering opening kiosks in shopping malls to attract new customers. Before committing to this strategy, ComSpeed decided to try it for one weekend at a sample of 30 shopping malls. For each mall, the random variable of interest is the number of people who sign up for the ComSpeed service. To justify the cost incurred for leasing space and hiring additional employees, management decided that the mean number of customers who sign up at each mall must be greater than 100. If the sample results enable management to conclude that the population mean is greater than 100, ComSpeed plans to start using this approach at each of the malls in its service area.

Let us see how a hypothesis test can be conducted to determine whether ComSpeed should expand the mall kiosk strategy to its entire service area. For the population of all shopping malls, μ is the mean number of customers who sign up for the ComSpeed service. Because ComSpeed wants to take action if the mean number of customers is greater than 100, the appropriate null and alternative hypotheses for the study are:

$$H_0: \mu \leq 100$$
$$H_a: \mu > 100$$

Suppose the maximum probability of a Type I error that management is willing to accept is .05. Hence, the level of significance for the hypothesis test is $\alpha = .05$.

With $n = 30$ (large-sample case) and the value of the population standard deviation σ unknown, equation (9.2) can be used to compute the value of the test statistic z. Because the alternative hypothesis is greater than ($>$), the rejection region is placed in the upper tail of the sampling distribution. The key question is: How large must the test statistic z be before we have enough evidence to reject the null hypothesis? Using the standard normal probability distribution, we know that the z value corresponding to an upper tail probability of .05 is $z = 1.645$. Therefore, we establish the following rejection rule.

$$\text{Reject } H_0 \text{ if } z = \frac{\bar{x} - \mu}{s/\sqrt{n}} > 1.645$$

Figure 9.7 shows the sampling distribution of z and the rejection region for the ComSpeed problem.

The data obtained for the sample of 30 malls are shown in Table 9.2. The sample mean is $\bar{x} = 109$, and the sample standard deviation is $s = 23.0022$. Thus, the value of the test statistic is given by

$$z = \frac{\bar{x} - \mu}{s/\sqrt{n}} = \frac{109 - 100}{23.0022/\sqrt{30}} = 2.1431$$

Because the value of the test statistic ($z = 2.1431$) is greater than the critical value (1.645), at the .05 level of significance we can reject the null hypothesis and conclude that the mean

FIGURE 9.7   REJECTION REGION FOR THE COMSPEED UPPER TAIL HYPOTHESIS TEST

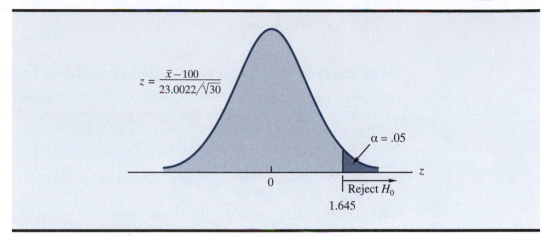

number of customers that sign up for the ComSpeed service is greater than 100. Management of ComSpeed has statistical justification for opening kiosks in all the shopping malls in their service area.

The p-value approach can also be used to make the hypothesis testing decision for ComSpeed. The p-value in this case is the probability of obtaining a value for the sample mean that is greater than or equal to the observed value of $\bar{x} = 109$, given the hypothesized value for the population mean of $\mu = 100$. Previously, we showed that the test statistic is $z = 2.1431$. Thus, the p-value is the area in the upper tail of the standard normal probability distribution to the right of $z = 2.1431$. Using the cumulative normal probability table, we find that the area to the right of $z = 2.14$ is $1 - .9838 = .0162$. Thus, the p-value is .0162. Recall that when using the p-value approach to hypothesis testing, the decision of whether to reject H_0 at the level of significance α is made as follows:

$$\text{Reject } H_0 \text{ if } p\text{-value} < \alpha$$

TABLE 9.2   COMSPEED DATA FOR A SAMPLE OF 30 MALLS

CD file

ComSpeed

Mall	Number of Customers	Mall	Number of Customers	Mall	Number of Customers
1	86	11	97	21	118
2	97	12	79	22	124
3	159	13	103	23	125
4	92	14	104	24	129
5	146	15	104	25	132
6	138	16	105	26	98
7	101	17	105	27	88
8	87	18	102	28	68
9	151	19	112	29	135
10	69	20	116	30	100

Thus, for the ComSpeed study, we reject H_0 at the .05 level of significance because the p-value $= .0162$ is less than $\alpha = .05$; as a result, we can conclude that the mean number of customers that sign up for the ComSpeed service is greater than 100.

Using Excel to Conduct a One-Tailed Hypothesis Test

Excel can be used to conduct a hypothesis test for the ComSpeed problem. We show how to compute the p-value. The user can then choose α and draw a conclusion. Refer to Figure 9.8 as we describe the tasks involved. The formula worksheet is in the background; the value worksheet is in the foreground.

Enter Data: Column A shows the number of people who signed up for the ComSpeed service at each of the 30 malls.

Enter Functions and Formulas: The descriptive statistics needed are provided in cells D4:D6. Excel's COUNT, AVERAGE, and STDEV functions compute the sample size, sample mean, and sample standard deviation, respectively.

The hypothesized value of the population mean (100) is entered into cell D8. Using the sample standard deviation as an estimate of the population standard deviation, an estimate of the standard error is obtained in cell D10 by dividing the sample standard deviation in cell D6 by the square root of the sample size in cell D4. The formula $=(D5-D8)/D10$ entered into cell D11 computes the test statistic z (2.1431). Finally, the NORMSDIST function

FIGURE 9.8   EXCEL WORKSHEET FOR COMSPEED ONE-TAILED HYPOTHESIS TEST

Note: Rows 18–28 are hidden.

used in cell D13 computes the p-value corresponding to $z = 2.1431$. Because the ComSpeed problem involves an upper tail test, we use 1-NORMSDIST(D11) to find the area in the upper tail as the p-value; the result is .0161.

We can reject H_0 at the .05 level of significance because the p-value $= .0161$ is less than the level of significance. We conclude that the mean number of customers who sign up for the ComSpeed service is greater than 100.

In the ComSpeed problem, the alternative hypothesis is H_a: $\mu > 100$. Thus, the rejection region is located in the upper tail of the sampling distribution of $\bar{x}$. In the Hilltop Coffee study the alternative hypothesis was H_a: $\mu < 3$, and thus the rejection region was located in the lower tail of the sampling distribution. To use the Excel procedure that we just described for hypothesis tests in which the rejection region is in the lower tail, we will modify the ComSpeed worksheet in Figure 9.8 by computing two p-values: a p-value (Lower Tail) and a p-value (Upper Tail). If the hypothesis test we are conducting has a rejection region in the lower tail, we compare the p-value (Lower Tail) to α to make the rejection decision. If the hypothesis test we are conducting has a rejection region in the upper tail, we compare the p-value (Upper Tail) to α to make the rejection decision.

The worksheet in Figure 9.9 shows the extension we described. Cell D13 provides the p-value for a lower tail test using the ComSpeed data, and cell D14 provides the p-value for an upper tail test using the ComSpeed data. In the background worksheet we see that the formula in cell D13 is =NORMSDIST(D11), and the formula in cell D14 is =1-NORMSDIST(D11). As in Figure 9.8, the p-value for the upper tail test (cell D14) is .0161. The p-value for the lower tail test (cell D13) is .9839. For a given value of the test statistic, the p-value for the upper tail test is just one minus the p-value for a lower

FIGURE 9.9 MODIFIED WORKSHEET FOR COMSPEED ONE-TAILED HYPOTHESIS TEST

	A	B	C	D	E	F
1	Customers		Hypothesis Test about a Population Mean			
2	86		Using the Standard Normal Distribution (z)			
3	97					
4	159		Sample Size	=COUNT(A2:A31)		
5	92		Mean	=AVERAGE(A2:A31)		
6	146		Standard Deviation	=STDEV(A2:A31)		
7	138					
8	101		Hypothesized value	100		
9	87					
10	151		Standard Error	=D6/SQRT(D4)		
11	69		Test Statistic	=(D5-D8)/D10		
12	97					
13	79		p-value (Lower Tail)	=NORMSDIST(D11)		
14	103		p-value (Upper Tail)	=1-NORMSDIST(D11)		
15	104					
16	104					
17	105					
29	68					
30	135					
31	100					
32						

	A	B	C	D	E	F	G
1	Customers		Hypothesis Test about a Population Mean				
2	86		Using the Standard Normal Distribution (z)				
3	97						
4	159		Sample Size	30			
5	92		Mean	109			
6	146		Standard Deviation	23.0022			
7	138						
8	101		Hypothesized value	100			
9	87						
10	151		Standard Error	4.1996			
11	69		Test Statistic	2.1431			
12	97						
13	79		p-value (Lower Tail)	0.9839			
14	103		p-value (Upper Tail)	0.0161			
15	104						
16	104						
17	105						
29	68						
30	135						
31	100						
32							

Note: Rows 18–28 are hidden.

tail test. The cell formulas required for both the lower and upper tail cases are summarized here:

	Rejection Region in Lower Tail	Rejection Region in Upper Tail
p-value	=NORMSDIST(D11)	=1-NORMSDIST(D11)

The worksheet in Figure 9.9 can be used as a template for one-tailed hypothesis tests of a population mean in the large-sample case. To use it for a different data set, one would need to insert the new data in column A, modify the ranges for the descriptive statistics in cells D4:D6, and place the hypothesized value for μ_0 into cell D8. The p-value corresponding to a lower tail hypothesis test is computed in cell D13, and the p-value corresponding to an upper tail hypothesis test is computed in cell D14. For a hypothesis test with the rejection region in the lower tail, the p-value in cell D13 can be compared with α to make the rejection decision. For a hypothesis test with the rejection region in the upper tail, the p-value in cell D14 can be compared with α to make the rejection decision.

This worksheet can also be used as a template for exercises in which n, $\bar{x}$, and s or σ are given. Just ignore the data section in column A and type the known values for the descriptive statistics in cells D4:D6. Then type the appropriate hypothesized value for μ_0 into cell D8. The p-values corresponding to lower and upper tail hypothesis tests will then appear in cells D13 and D14.

To illustrate, suppose that we wanted to use the worksheet in Figure 9.9 as a template for the Hilltop Coffee hypothesis test. The sample size was $n = 36$, the sample mean was $\bar{x} = 2.92$, and the population standard deviation was assumed known with $\sigma = .18$. The hypothesized value was $\mu_0 = 3$. Figure 9.10 shows the worksheet obtained by entering

FIGURE 9.10 WORKSHEET FOR HILLTOP COFFEE ONE-TAILED HYPOTHESIS TEST

Note: Rows 18–28 are hidden.

these values in the appropriate cells of the worksheet in Figure 9.9. Note in the background worksheet that the formulas in cells D4:D6 have been replaced with numerical values, and the hypothesized value in cell D8 has been changed to 3. The values of the standard error and the test statistic are .03 and -2.6667 (the same values calculated earlier). Because the Hilltop Coffee hypothesis test has a rejection region in the lower tail, the p-value in cell D13 (.0038) is the one we want to use. Thus, for $\alpha = .01$, we would reject the null hypothesis.

Summary: One-Tailed Tests About a Population Mean

Let us generalize the hypothesis testing procedure for one-tailed tests about a population mean in the large-sample case ($n \geq 30$). The general form of a lower tail test, where μ_0 is a hypothesized value for the population mean, follows.

One-Tailed Test: Large-Sample Case ($n \geq 30$) with the Rejection Region in the Lower Tail

$$H_0: \mu \geq \mu_0$$
$$H_a: \mu < \mu_0$$

Test Statistic: σ Assumed Known

$$z = \frac{\bar{x} - \mu_0}{\sigma/\sqrt{n}} \tag{9.1}$$

In most applications the sample standard deviation s is used in the computation of the test statistic because the population standard deviation σ is unknown.

Test Statistic: σ Estimated by s

$$z = \frac{\bar{x} - \mu_0}{s/\sqrt{n}} \tag{9.2}$$

Rejection Rule

Using Test Statistic: Reject H_0 if $z < -z_\alpha$

Using p-Value: Reject H_0 if p-value $< \alpha$

The general form of the upper tail test, where μ_0 is a hypothesized value for the population mean, follows.

One-Tailed Test: Large-Sample Case ($n \geq 30$) with the Rejection Region in the Upper Tail

$$H_0: \mu \leq \mu_0$$
$$H_a: \mu > \mu_0$$

Test Statistic: σ Assumed Known

$$z = \frac{\bar{x} - \mu_0}{\sigma/\sqrt{n}} \tag{9.1}$$

Test Statistic: σ Estimated by s

$$z = \frac{\bar{x} - \mu_0}{s/\sqrt{n}} \qquad (9.2)$$

Rejection Rule

Using Test Statistic: Reject H_0 if $z > z_\alpha$

Using p-Value: Reject H_0 if p-value $< \alpha$

NOTES AND COMMENTS

The p-value, the observed level of significance, is a measure of the likelihood of the sample results when the null hypothesis is assumed to be true at $\mu = \mu_0$. The smaller the p-value, the less likely it is that the sample results came from a population where the null hypothesis is true.

EXERCISES

Note to Student: Some of the hypothesis testing exercises that follow will ask you to compare the value of the test statistic to the critical value and other exercises will ask you to compare the p-value to α. Both methods will provide the same hypothesis testing conclusion. We provided exercises with both methods to allow practice using both. In an actual application, you may select either method based on personal preference.

Methods

9. Consider the following hypothesis test.

$$H_0: \mu \geq 10$$
$$H_a: \mu < 10$$

A sample with $n = 50$ provides a sample mean of 9.46 and sample standard deviation of 2.

  a. At $\alpha = .05$, what is the critical value for z? What is the rejection rule?
  b. Compute the value of the test statistic z. What is your conclusion?

10. Consider the following hypothesis test.

$$H_0: \mu \leq 15$$
$$H_a: \mu > 15$$

A sample size of 40 provides a sample mean of 16.5 and sample standard deviation of 7.

  a. At $\alpha = .02$, what is the critical value for z, and what is the rejection rule?
  b. Compute the value of the test statistic z.
  c. What is the p-value?
  d. What is your conclusion?

11.   Consider the following hypothesis test.

$$H_0: \mu \geq 25$$
$$H_a: \mu < 25$$

A sample of 100 is used, and the population standard deviation is 12. Provide the value of the test statistic z and your conclusion for each of the following sample results. Use $\alpha = .05$.

a. $\bar{x} = 22.0$
b. $\bar{x} = 24.0$
c. $\bar{x} = 23.5$
d. $\bar{x} = 22.8$

12.   Consider the following hypothesis test.

$$H_0: \mu \leq 5$$
$$H_a: \mu > 5$$

For each of the following test statistics, compute the corresponding p-values and make the appropriate conclusions based on $\alpha = .05$.

a. $z = 1.82$
b. $z = .45$
c. $z = 1.50$
d. $z = 3.30$
e. $z = -1.00$

Applications

13.   Individuals filing federal income tax returns prior to March 31 had an average refund of $1056. Consider the population of "last-minute" filers who mail their returns during the last five days of the income tax period (typically April 10 to April 15).

a.   A researcher suggests that one of the reasons individuals wait until the last five days to file their returns is that on average those individuals have a lower refund than early filers. Develop appropriate hypotheses such that rejection of H_0 will support the re-searcher's contention.
b.   Using $\alpha = .05$, what is the critical value for the test statistic, and what is the rejection rule?
c.   For a sample of 400 individuals who filed a return between April 10 and April 15, the sample mean refund was $910 and the sample standard deviation was $1600. Compute the value of the test statistic.
d.   What is your conclusion?
e.   What is the p-value for the test?

14.   A Nielsen survey estimated the mean number of hours of television viewing per household at 7.25 hours per day (*New York Daily News*, November 2, 1997). Assume that the Nielsen survey involved 200 households and that the sample standard deviation was 2.5 hours per day. Ten years ago the population mean number of hours of television viewing per household was reported to be 6.70 hours. Letting μ = the population mean number of hours of television viewing per household in 1997, test the hypotheses $H_0: \mu \leq 6.70$ and $H_a: \mu > 6.70$. Use $\alpha = .01$.

a.   What is the critical value of the test statistic, and what is the rejection rule?
b.   Compute the value of the test statistic.
c.   What is your conclusion?

Auto

15. According to the National Automobile Dealers Association, the mean price for used cars is $10,192. A manager of a Kansas City used car dealership selected a sample of 100 recent used car sales at the dealership. The sample data are contained in the data set Auto. Letting μ denote the population mean price for used cars at the Kansas City dealership, test H_0: $\mu \geq 10{,}192$ and H_a: $\mu < 10{,}192$ at a .05 level of significance.
    a. What is the hypothesis testing conclusion?
    b. What is the p-value?
    c. What information does the hypothesis test result provide for the manager of the Kansas City dealership? What follow-up action might the manager want to consider?

Miles

16. New tires manufactured by a company in Findlay, Ohio, are designed to provide a mean of at least 28,000 miles. Tests with 30 randomly selected tires resulted in the data set Miles. Using a .05 level of significance, test whether the data provide sufficient evidence to reject the claim of a mean of at least 28,000 miles. What is the p-value?

17. Media Metrix, Inc., tracks Internet users in seven countries: Australia, Great Britain, Canada, France, Germany, Japan, and the United States. According to recent measurement figures, American home users rank first in Internet usage with a mean of 13 hours per month (*The Washington Post*, August 4, 2000). Assume that in a follow-up study involving a sample of 145 Canadian Internet users, the sample mean was 10.8 hours per month and the sample standard deviation was 9.2 hours.
    a. Formulate the null and alternative hypotheses that can be used to determine whether the sample data support the conclusion that Canadian Internet users have a population mean less than the U.S. mean of 13 hours per month.
    b. Using $\alpha = .01$, what is the critical value for the test statistic? State the rejection rule.
    c. What is the value of the test statistic?
    d. What is your conclusion?

18. A Channel One Network study reported that teens spend a mean of $5.72 per visit to fast-food restaurants such as McDonald's, Burger King, and Wendy's (*USA Today*, October 5, 1998). In a follow-up study, a sample of 102 teen visits to fast-food restaurants in Chicago provided a sample mean of $5.98 and a sample standard deviation of $1.24.
    a. Formulate the null and alternative hypotheses that can be used to determine whether the sample data support the conclusion that teens in Chicago have a population mean expenditure of more than $5.72 per visit to fast-food restaurants.
    b. What is the value of the test statistic?
    c. What is the p-value?
    d. Using $\alpha = .05$, what is your conclusion?

19. The national mean sales price for new one-family homes is $181,900 (*The New York Times Almanac 2000*). A sample of 40 one-family home sales in the South showed a sample mean of $166,400 and a sample standard deviation of $33,500.
    a. Formulate the null and alternative hypotheses that can be used to determine whether the sample data support the conclusion that the population mean sales price for new one-family homes in the South is less than the national mean of $181,900.
    b. What is the value of the test statistic?
    c. What is the p-value?
    d. Using $\alpha = .01$, what is your conclusion?

20. According to the National Association of Colleges and Employers, the 2000 mean annual salary of business degree graduates in accounting was $37,000 (*Time*, May 8, 2000). In a follow-up study in June 2001, a sample of 48 graduating accounting majors provided a sample mean of $38,100 and a sample standard deviation of $5,200.
    a. Formulate the null and alternative hypotheses that can be used to determine whether the sample data support the conclusion that June 2001 graduates in accounting have a mean salary greater than the 2000 mean annual salary of $37,000.

b. What is the value of the test statistic?

c. What is the *p*-value?

d. Using $\alpha = .05$, what is your conclusion?

9.4   TWO-TAILED TESTS ABOUT A POPULATION MEAN: LARGE-SAMPLE CASE

Two-tailed hypothesis tests differ from one-tailed tests in that the rejection region is divided between the lower and the upper tails of the sampling distribution. Let us introduce an example to show why and how two-tailed tests are conducted.

The United States Golf Association (USGA) established rules that manufacturers of golf equipment must meet if their products are to be acceptable for use in USGA events. One of the rules for the manufacture of golf balls states: "A brand of golf ball, when tested on apparatus approved by the USGA on the outdoor range at the USGA Headquarters . . . shall not cover an average distance in carry and roll exceeding 280 yards." Suppose Superflight, Inc., recently developed a high-technology manufacturing method that can produce golf balls having an average distance in carry and roll of 280 yards.

Superflight realizes, however, that if the new manufacturing process goes out of adjustment, the process may produce golf balls for which the average distance is either less than 280 yards or greater than 280 yards. In the former case, sales may decline as a result of marketing an inferior product, and in the latter case the golf balls may be rejected by the USGA.

Superflight's management instituted a quality control program to monitor the manufacturing process. Periodically, a hypothesis test will be used to determine whether the manufacturing process is out of adjustment. In formulating the null and alternative hypotheses, we will begin by assuming that the manufacturing process is functioning correctly, with the golf balls having the desired mean distance of 280 yards. The null and alternative hypotheses are as follow:

$$H_0: \mu = 280$$
$$H_a: \mu \neq 280$$

If the sample data indicate that H_0 cannot be rejected, no action will be taken to adjust the manufacturing process. However, if the sample data indicate that H_0 should be rejected, we can conclude that the golf balls do not have the desired mean distance of 280 yards; in this case corrective action should be taken to adjust the manufacturing process and return it to its desired state.

The quality control team selected $\alpha = .05$ as the level of significance for the hypothesis test. Let us assume that Superflight will use a large sample each time the quality control test is performed. As a result the test statistics are

$$z = \frac{\bar{x} - \mu_0}{\sigma/\sqrt{n}}$$

if σ is assumed known, and

$$z = \frac{\bar{x} - \mu_0}{s/\sqrt{n}}$$

The test statistics are the same as those used for one-tailed tests in Section 9.3.

if σ is estimated by *s*.

As usual, we make the tentative assumption that the null hypothesis is true. We want to reject H_0: $\mu = 280$ when the test statistic z indicates that the sample mean distance $\bar{x}$ is significantly less than 280 yards or significantly greater than 280 yards. Thus, H_0 may be rejected for values of z in either the lower tail or upper tail of the sampling distribution. Therefore, the test is called a **two-tailed hypothesis test**.

Figure 9.11 shows the sampling distribution of z with the two-tailed rejection region for $\alpha = .05$. With two-tailed hypothesis tests, we always determine the rejection region by placing an area or probability of $\alpha/2$ in each tail of the distribution. The values of z that provide an area of .025 in each tail can be found from the cumulative normal probability table. We see in Figure 9.11 that $-z_{.025} = -1.96$ identifies an area of .025 in the lower tail and $z_{.025} = +1.96$ identifies an area of .025 in the upper tail. Referring to Figure 9.11, we can establish the following rejection rule.

Reject H_0 if $z < -1.96$ or if $z > 1.96$

Suppose that a simple random sample of 36 golf balls provided the data in Table 9.3. For these data we obtain a sample mean of $\bar{x} = 278.5$ yards and a sample standard deviation of $s = 12$ yards. Using $\mu_0 = 280$ from the null hypothesis and the sample standard deviation of $s = 12$ as an estimate of the population standard deviation σ, the value of the test statistic is

$$z = \frac{\bar{x} - \mu_0}{s/\sqrt{n}} = \frac{278.5 - 280}{12/\sqrt{36}} = -.75$$

According to the rejection rule, H_0 cannot be rejected. The sample results provide no reason to doubt the assumption that the manufacturing process is producing golf balls with a population mean distance of 280 yards.

FIGURE 9.11   REJECTION REGION FOR THE TWO-TAILED HYPOTHESIS TEST
FOR SUPERFLIGHT, INC.

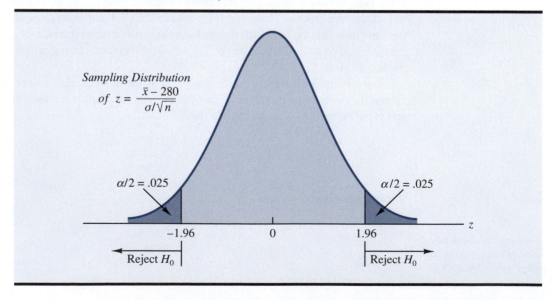

TABLE 9.3   DISTANCE DATA FOR SIMPLE RANDOM SAMPLE OF 36 SUPERFLIGHT
GOLF BALLS

Distance

Ball	Yards	Ball	Yards	Ball	Yards
1	269	13	296	25	272
2	300	14	265	26	285
3	268	15	271	27	293
4	278	16	279	28	281
5	282	17	284	29	269
6	263	18	260	30	299
7	301	19	275	31	263
8	295	20	282	32	264
9	288	21	260	33	273
10	278	22	266	34	291
11	276	23	270	35	274
12	286	24	293	36	277

p-Values for Two-Tailed Tests

Let us compute the *p*-value for the Superflight golf ball example. The sample mean of $\bar{x} = 278.5$ has a corresponding *z* value of $-.75$. Because the standard normal probability distribution is symmetric, the area to the left of $z = -.75$ is the same as the area to the right of $z = .75$. Using the cumulative normal probability table, we find that the area to the right of $z = .75$ is $1 - .7734 = .2266$. Thus, the area in the lower tail is also .2266. Looking at Figure 9.11, we see that the lower tail portion of the rejection region has an area or probability of $\alpha/2 = .05/2 = .025$. Thus, with $.2266 > .025$, the test statistic is not in the rejection region, and the null hypothesis cannot be rejected.

In a two-tailed test, the p-value is found by doubling the area in the tail of the sampling distribution. The doubling of the area is done so that the p-value can be compared directly to α. As a result the same rejection rule can be used for both one-tailed and two-tailed tests.

One question remains: What value should we report as the *p*-value for the two-tailed test? At first glance, you may be inclined to say the *p*-value is .2266. If that is your choice, you will have to remember two different rules: one for the one-tailed test, which is to reject H_0 if the *p*-value $< \alpha$, and another for the two-tailed test, which is to reject H_0 if the *p*-value $< \alpha/2$. Alternatively, suppose we define the *p*-value for a two-tailed test as *double* the area found in the tail of the sampling distribution. Thus, for the Superflight example, we would define the *p*-value to be $2(.2266) = .4532$. The advantage of this definition of the *p*-value for a two-tailed test is that the *p*-value can be compared directly to the level of significance α. Hence, with $.4532 > .05$, we see that the null hypothesis cannot be rejected. By remembering that the *p*-value for a two-tailed test is simply double the area found in the tail of the sampling distribution, the previous rule to reject H_0 if the *p*-value $< \alpha$ can be used for all hypothesis tests (lower tail, upper tail, and two-tailed).

Using Excel to Conduct a Two-Tailed Hypothesis Test

Excel can be used to conduct a hypothesis test for the Superflight study. The worksheet is similar to the one in Figure 9.10 for the one-tailed test. We simply add the *p*-value for a two-tailed test. Refer to Figure 9.12 as we describe the tasks involved. The formula worksheet is in the background; the value worksheet is in the foreground.

FIGURE 9.12   EXCEL WORKSHEET FOR THE SUPERFLIGHT TWO-TAILED HYPOTHESIS TEST

	A	B	C	D	E	F
1	Yards		**Hypothesis Test about a Population Mean**			
2	269		**Using the Standard Normal Distribution (z)**			
3	300					
4	268		Sample Size	=COUNT(A2:A37)		
5	278		Mean	=AVERAGE(A2:A37)		
6	282		Standard Deviation	=STDEV(A2:A37)		
7	263					
8	301		Hypothesized value	280		
9	295					
10	288		Standard Error	=D6/SQRT(D4)		
11	278		Test Statistic	=(D5-D8)/D10		
12	276					
13	286		p-value (Lower Tail)	=NORMSDIST(D11)		
14	296		p-value (Upper Tail)	=1-NORMSDIST(D11)		
15	265		p-value (Two Tail)	=2*MIN(D13,D14)		
16	271					
34	273					
35	291					
36	274					
37	277					
38						

	A	B	C	D	E	F	G
1	Yards		**Hypothesis Test about a Population Mean**				
2	269		**Using the Standard Normal Distribution (z)**				
3	300						
4	268		Sample Size	36			
5	278		Mean	278.5			
6	282		Standard Deviation	12.0012			
7	263						
8	301		Hypothesized value	280			
9	295						
10	288		Standard Error	2.0002			
11	278		Test Statistic	-0.7499			
12	276						
13	286		p-value (Lower Tail)	0.2266			
14	296		p-value (Upper Tail)	0.7734			
15	265		p-value (Two Tail)	0.4533			
16	271						
34	273						
35	291						
36	274						
37	277						
38							

Note: Rows 17–33 are hidden.

Enter Data: Column A shows the distance in carry and roll for each of the 36 golf balls.

Enter Functions and Formulas: The descriptive statistics needed are provided in cells D4:D6. Excel's COUNT, AVERAGE, and STDEV functions compute the sample size, sample mean, and sample standard deviation, respectively.

The hypothesized value of the population mean (280) is entered into cell D8. Using the sample standard deviation as an estimate of the population standard deviation, an estimate of the standard error is obtained in cell D10 by dividing the sample standard deviation in cell D6 by the square root of the sample size in cell D4. The formula =(D5-D8)/D10 entered into cell D11 computes the test statistic z ($-.7499$).

We then use the test statistic to compute three p-values. The formula =NORMSDIST(D11) entered into cell D13 computes the p-value corresponding to a hypothesis test with the rejection region in the lower tail. Then, the formula =1-NORMSDIST(D11) entered into cell D14 computes the p-value corresponding to a hypothesis test with the rejection region in the upper tail. Finally, the p-value corresponding to a two-tailed hypothesis test is then computed in cells D15 as 2 times the minimum of the p-values in cells D13 and D14; the result is p-value (Two Tail) = .4533. We cannot reject H_0 at the .05 level of significance because the p-value (Two Tail) = .4533 is greater than $\alpha = .05$. Thus, the quality control manager has no reason to doubt the assumption that the manufacturing process is producing golf balls with a population mean distance of 280 yards.

Summary: Two-Tailed Tests About a Population Mean

Let μ_0 represent the hypothesized value of the population mean. The general form of the two-tailed hypothesis test about a population mean follows.

Two-Tailed Test: Large-Sample Case ($n \geq 30$)

$$H_0: \mu = \mu_0$$
$$H_a: \mu \neq \mu_0$$

Test Statistic: σ Assumed Known

$$z = \frac{\bar{x} - \mu_0}{\sigma/\sqrt{n}} \tag{9.1}$$

Test Statistic: σ Estimated by s

$$z = \frac{\bar{x} - \mu_0}{s/\sqrt{n}} \tag{9.2}$$

Rejection Rule

Using Test Statistic: Reject H_0 if $z < -z_{\alpha/2}$ or if $z > z_{\alpha/2}$

Using p-Value: Reject H_0 if p-value $< \alpha$ $\tag{9.3}$

Relationship Between Interval Estimation and Hypothesis Testing

In Chapter 8 we showed how to develop a confidence interval estimate of a population mean. In the large-sample case, the confidence interval estimate of a population mean corresponding to a $1 - \alpha$ confidence coefficient is given by

$$\bar{x} \pm z_{\alpha/2}\frac{\sigma}{\sqrt{n}} \tag{9.4}$$

when σ is assumed known and

$$\bar{x} \pm z_{\alpha/2}\frac{s}{\sqrt{n}} \tag{9.5}$$

when σ is estimated by s.

Conducting a hypothesis test requires us first to develop competing hypotheses about the value of a population parameter. In the case of the population mean, the two-tailed hypothesis test has the form

$$H_0: \mu = \mu_0$$
$$H_a: \mu \neq \mu_0$$

where μ_0 is the hypothesized value for the population mean. Using the rejection rule provided by expression (9.3), we see that the region over which we do not reject H_0 includes all values of the sample mean $\bar{x}$ that are within $-z_{\alpha/2}$ and $+z_{\alpha/2}$ standard errors of μ_0. Thus, the do-not-reject region for the sample mean $\bar{x}$ in a two-tailed hypothesis test is given by

$$\mu_0 \pm z_{\alpha/2}\frac{\sigma}{\sqrt{n}} \tag{9.6}$$

when σ is assumed known and

$$\mu_0 \pm z_{\alpha/2}\frac{s}{\sqrt{n}} \qquad\qquad (9.7)$$

when σ is estimated by s.

The plus-or-minus value is called the margin of error in interval estimation.

A close look at expressions (9.4) and (9.6) provides insight about the relationship between the estimation and hypothesis testing approaches to statistical inference. Note in particular that both procedures require the computation of the values $z_{\alpha/2}$ and $\sigma/\sqrt{n}$. Focusing on α, we see that a confidence coefficient of $(1 - \alpha)$ for interval estimation corresponds to a level of significance of α in hypothesis testing. For example, a 95% confidence interval corresponds to a .05 level of significance for hypothesis testing. Furthermore, expressions (9.4) and (9.6) show that because $z_{\alpha/2}(\sigma/\sqrt{n})$ is the plus-or-minus value for both expressions, if $\bar{x}$ is in the do-not-reject region defined by expression (9.6), the hypothesized value μ_0 will be in the confidence interval defined by expression (9.4). Conversely, if the hypothesized value μ_0 is in the confidence interval defined by expression (9.4), the sample mean $\bar{x}$ will be in the do-not-reject region for the hypothesis $H_0: \mu = \mu_0$ as defined by expression (9.6). These observations lead to the following procedure for using confidence interval results to draw hypothesis testing conclusions.

A Confidence Interval Approach to Hypothesis Testing: Large-Sample Case

Form of Hypotheses:

$$H_0: \mu = \mu_0$$
$$H_a: \mu \neq \mu_0$$

1. Select a simple random sample from the population and use the value of the sample mean $\bar{x}$ to develop the confidence interval for the population mean μ. If σ is assumed known, compute the interval estimate using

$$\bar{x} \pm z_{\alpha/2}\frac{\sigma}{\sqrt{n}}$$

   If σ is estimated by s, compute the interval estimate using

$$\bar{x} \pm z_{\alpha/2}\frac{s}{\sqrt{n}}$$

2. If the confidence interval contains the hypothesized value μ_0, do not reject H_0. Otherwise, reject H_0.

For a two-tailed hypothesis test, the null hypothesis can be rejected if the confidence interval for the population mean does not include μ_0.

Let us return to the Superflight golf ball study and the following two-tailed test.

$$H_0: \mu = 280$$
$$H_a: \mu \neq 280$$

To test this hypothesis with a level of significance of $\alpha = .05$, we sampled 36 golf balls and found a sample mean of $\bar{x} = 278.5$ yards and a sample standard deviation of $s = 12$ yards.

Using these results with $z_{.025} = 1.96$, we find that the 95% confidence interval estimate of the population mean becomes

$$\bar{x} \pm z_{.025} \frac{s}{\sqrt{n}}$$

$$278.5 \pm 1.96 \frac{12}{\sqrt{36}}$$

$$278.5 \pm 3.92$$

or

$$274.58 \text{ to } 282.42$$

This finding enables the quality control manager to conclude with 95% confidence that the mean distance for the population of golf balls is between 274.58 and 282.42 yards. Because the hypothesized value for the population mean, $\mu_0 = 280$, is in this interval, the hypothesis testing conclusion is that the null hypothesis, $H_0: \mu = 280$, cannot be rejected.

Note that this discussion and example pertain to two-tailed hypothesis tests about a population mean. However, the same confidence interval and hypothesis testing relationship exists for other two-tailed tests about population parameters. In addition, the relationship can be extended to make one-tailed tests about population parameters. Doing so, however, requires the development of one-sided confidence intervals.

NOTES AND COMMENTS

1. The p-value depends on the sample outcome and whether the hypothesis test is one-tailed or two-tailed. For a lower tail hypothesis test, the p-value is the area under the curve to the left of the test statistic; for an upper tail hypothesis test, the p-value is the area under the curve to the right of the test statistic. For a two-tailed test, we first determine which tail of the sampling distribution the test statistic is in. The p-value is then twice the tail area cut off by the test statistic.

2. The interval estimation approach to hypothesis testing helps to highlight the role of the sample size. From expression (9.4) we can see that larger sample sizes lead to narrower confidence intervals. Thus, for a given level of significance α, a larger sample is less likely to lead to an interval containing μ_0 when the null hypothesis is false. That is, the larger sample size will provide a higher probability of rejecting H_0 when H_0 is false.

EXERCISES

Methods

21. Consider the following hypothesis test.

$$H_0: \mu = 10$$
$$H_a: \mu \neq 10$$

A sample of 36 provides a sample mean of 11 and sample standard deviation of 2.5.
a. At $\alpha = .05$, what is the rejection rule?
b. Compute the value of the test statistic z. What is your conclusion?

22. Consider the following hypothesis test.

$$H_0: \mu = 15$$
$$H_a: \mu \neq 15$$

A sample of 50 gives a sample mean of 14.2 and sample standard deviation of 5.
  a. At $\alpha = .02$, what is the rejection rule?
  b. Compute the value of the test statistic z.
  c. What is the p-value?
  d. What is your conclusion?

23. Consider the following hypothesis test.

$$H_0: \mu = 25$$
$$H_a: \mu \neq 25$$

A sample of 80 is used and the population standard deviation is 10. Use $\alpha = .05$. Compute the value of the test statistic z and specify your conclusion for each of the following sample results.
  a. $\bar{x} = 22.0$
  b. $\bar{x} = 27.0$
  c. $\bar{x} = 23.5$
  d. $\bar{x} = 28.0$

24. Consider the following hypothesis test.

$$H_0: \mu = 5$$
$$H_a: \mu \neq 5$$

For each of the following test statistics, compute the corresponding p-values and specify your conclusions based on $\alpha = .05$.
  a. $z = 1.80$
  b. $z = -.45$
  c. $z = 2.05$
  d. $z = -3.50$
  e. $z = -1.00$

Applications

25. The mean length of a work week for the population of workers is reported to be 39.2 hours (*Investor's Business Daily*, September 11, 2000). Suppose a sample of 112 workers in a particular county showed a sample mean of 38.5 hours and a sample standard deviation of 4.8 hours. Test the hypotheses: $H_0: \mu = 39.2$ and $H_a: \mu \neq 39.2$, with $\alpha = .05$.
  a. What are the critical values for the test statistic, and what is the rejection rule?
  b. What is the value of the test statistic?
  c. Can the null hypothesis be rejected? What is your conclusion?
  d. What is the p-value?

26. CNN and ActMedia provided a television channel that showed news, features, and ads, and was targeted to individuals waiting in grocery checkout lines. The television programs were designed with an 8-minute cycle on the assumption that the population mean time a shopper stands in line at a grocery store checkout is 8 minutes. (*Astounding Averages*,

1995). A sample of 120 shoppers at a major grocery store showed a sample mean waiting time of 7.5 minutes with a sample standard deviation of 3.2 minutes.

a. Test $H_0: \mu = 8$ and $H_a: \mu \neq 8$. Use a .05 level of significance. Does the population mean waiting time at the grocery store differ from the 8-minute waiting time assumption?

b. What is the p-value for the test?

27. A production line operates with a mean filling weight of 16 ounces per container. Overfilling or underfilling presents a serious problem, and the production line should be shut down if either occurs. From past data, σ is known to be .8 ounces. A quality control inspector samples 30 items every 2 hours and at that time makes the decision of whether to shut the line down for adjustment.

a. With a .05 level of significance, what is the rejection rule?

b. If a sample mean of $\bar{x} = 16.32$ ounces were found, what action would you recommend?

c. If $\bar{x} = 15.82$ ounces, what action would you recommend?

d. What is the p-value for parts (b) and (c)?

Assembly

28. An automobile assembly line operation has a scheduled mean completion time of 2.2 minutes. Because of the effect of completion time on both preceding and subsequent assembly operations, it is important to maintain the 2.2-minute mean completion time. A random sample of 45 assemblies resulted in the completion times shown in the data set Assembly. Use a .02 level of significance and test whether the operation is meeting its 2.2-minute mean completion time.

29. Historically, evening long-distance phone calls from a particular city averaged 15.2 minutes per call. In a random sample of 35 calls, the sample mean time was 14.3 minutes per call, with a sample standard deviation of 5 minutes. Use this sample information to test for any change in the mean duration of long-distance phone calls. Use a .05 level of significance. What is the p-value?

30. A Gallup survey found the mean charitable contribution on federal tax returns was $1075 (*USA Today*, April 10, 2000). Assume a sample of April 2001 tax returns is used to conduct a hypothesis test designed to determine whether any change occurred in the mean charitable contributions.

a. Formulate the null and alternative hypotheses.

b. Assume that a sample of 200 tax returns shows a sample mean of $1160 and a sample standard deviation of $840. What is the value of the test statistic?

c. What is the p-value?

d. Using $\alpha = .05$, what is your conclusion?

9.5   TESTS ABOUT A POPULATION MEAN: SMALL-SAMPLE CASE

The procedures for conducting hypothesis tests about a population mean discussed in Sections 9.3 and 9.4 were based on the central limit theorem and large-sample theory. In this section, we consider tests about a population mean using a small sample ($n < 30$). In this case the central limit theorem is not applicable; the hypothesis testing procedures for the small-sample case require the assumption that the population has a normal probability distribution. If this assumption is appropriate, the methodology presented in this section can be used. However, if this assumption is not appropriate, the best alternative is to increase the sample size to $n > 30$ and rely on the large-sample hypothesis testing procedures presented in Sections 9.3 and 9.4.

The methodology presented in this section is based on the assumption that the population has a normal distribution.

When $\bar{x}$ follows a normal distribution, z follows a standard normal distribution.

If the population can be assumed to have a normal distribution, the sampling distribution of $\bar{x}$ is normally distributed with mean μ and standard deviation $\sigma_{\bar{x}} = \sigma/\sqrt{n}$, for any sample size. If, based on historical data or other considerations, σ can also be assumed known, then the small-sample hypothesis testing procedures are identical to the large-sample hypothesis testing procedures presented in Sections 9.3 and 9.4. In this case, the test statistic is

$$z = \frac{\bar{x} - \mu_0}{\sigma/\sqrt{n}} \tag{9.7}$$

Because the hypothesis testing computations are identical to the computations made previously, we shall not present a new numerical example at this time.

The small-sample hypothesis testing procedure with σ estimated by s is based on the same theory used for the small-sample interval estimation procedure with σ estimated by s presented in Section 8.2. Both use a normal population assumption and the t distribution.

Next, consider the situation in which the sample size is small ($n < 30$), the population is assumed to have a normal distribution, and the population standard deviation σ is estimated by the sample standard deviation s. In this case, the t distribution should be used to make inferences about the value of the population mean. The test statistic is

$$t = \frac{\bar{x} - \mu_0}{s/\sqrt{n}} \tag{9.8}$$

This test statistic has a t distribution with $n - 1$ degrees of freedom.

One-Tailed Test

CD file

Heathrow

Let us consider an example of a one-tailed hypothesis test about a population mean for the small-sample case. The International Air Transport Association surveys business travelers to develop ratings of transatlantic gateway airports. The maximum possible rating is 10. A magazine devoted to business travel decided to classify airports according to the rating they receive. Airports with a population mean rating higher than 7 will be designated as providing superior service. Suppose a simple random sample of 12 business travelers were asked to rate London's Heathrow airport, and that the 12 ratings obtained were 7, 8, 10, 8, 6, 9, 6, 7, 7, 8, 9, and 8. The sample mean is $\bar{x} = 7.75$ and the sample standard deviation is $s = 1.2154$. Assuming that the population of ratings can be approximated by a normal probability distribution, should Heathrow be designated as providing superior service?

Using a .05 level of significance, we need a test to determine whether the population mean rating for the Heathrow airport is greater than 7. The null and alternative hypotheses follow.

$$H_0: \mu \leq 7$$
$$H_a: \mu > 7$$

The Heathrow airport will be designated as providing superior service if H_0 can be rejected. The rejection region is in the upper tail of the sampling distribution. With $n - 1 = 12 - 1 = 11$ degrees of freedom, Table 2 of Appendix B shows that the critical value is $t_{.05} = 1.796$. Thus, the rejection rule is

$$\text{Reject } H_0 \text{ if } t > 1.796$$

Using equation (9.8) with $\bar{x} = 7.75$ and $s = 1.2154$, we calculate the following value for the test statistic.

$$t = \frac{\bar{x} - \mu_0}{s/\sqrt{n}} = \frac{7.75 - 7}{1.2154/\sqrt{12}} = 2.1376$$

Because 2.1376 is greater than 1.796, the null hypothesis is rejected. At the .05 level of significance, we can conclude that the population mean rating for the Heathrow airport is greater than 7. Thus, Heathrow can be designated as providing superior service. Figure 9.13 shows that the value of the test statistic is in the rejection region.

In the Heathrow Airport study, the rejection region was located in the upper tail of the sampling distribution. The general form of an upper tail test about a population mean for the small-sample case is the same as in the large-sample case. With μ_0 denoting the stated value for the population mean, we would state the null and alternative hypotheses as follows:

$$H_0: \mu \leq \mu_0$$
$$H_a: \mu > \mu_0$$

The test statistic is

$$t = \frac{\bar{x} - \mu_0}{s/\sqrt{n}}$$

and the rejection rule at a level of significance α is

$$\text{Reject } H_0 \text{ if } t > t_\alpha$$

A second form of the one-tailed test for the small-sample case rejects the null hypothesis when the test statistic is in the lower tail of the sampling distribution. In this case, the general form of the test is as follows:

$$H_0: \mu \geq \mu_0$$
$$H_a: \mu < \mu_0$$

FIGURE 9.13   VALUE OF THE TEST STATISTIC ($t = 2.1376$) FOR THE HEATHROW AIRPORT HYPOTHESIS TEST IS IN THE REJECTION REGION

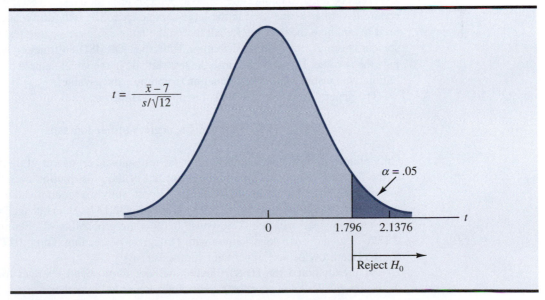

The test statistic for the upper tail case is the same as for the lower tail case, given by equation (9.8). The only change is that the rejection rule now becomes

$$\text{Reject } H_0 \text{ if } t < -t_\alpha$$

p-Values and the *t* Distribution

Let us consider the *p*-value for the Heathrow airport hypothesis test. The usual rule applies: If the *p*-value is less than the level of significance α, the null hypothesis can be rejected. Unfortunately, the format of the *t* distribution table provided in most statistics textbooks does not have sufficient detail to determine the exact *p*-value for the test. However, we can still use the *t* distribution table to narrow the range of possible values. For example, the *t* distribution used in the Heathrow airport hypothesis test has 11 degrees of freedom. Referring to Table 2 of Appendix B, we see that row 11 provides the following information about a *t* distribution with 11 degrees of freedom.

Area in Upper Tail	.10	.05	.025	.01	.005
t Value	1.363	1.796	2.201	2.718	3.106

The p-values are difficult to obtain directly from a table of the t distribution. Generally, the best that can be done with the table is to specify a range for the p-value such as between .05 and .025. With Excel we can compute the exact p-value.

The computed test statistic for the hypothesis test was $t = 2.1376$. The *p*-value is the area in the upper tail corresponding to $t = 2.1376$. From row 11 of the *t* table, we see 2.1376 is between 1.796 and 2.201. Thus, although we cannot determine the exact *p*-value associated with $t = 2.1376$, we do know that the *p*-value must be between .05 and .025. With a level of significance of $\alpha = .05$, we know that the *p*-value must be less than .05; thus, the null hypothesis is rejected.

Using Excel to Conduct a One-Tailed Hypothesis Test: Small-Sample Case

Excel can be used to conduct one-tailed hypothesis tests for the small-sample case. The procedure is similar to that used in the large-sample case. The only difference is the function used to compute the *p*-value. Recall that in the large-sample case, the test statistic *z* has a standard normal probability distribution. Thus, the NORMSDIST function was used to compute the *p*-value. However, because the test statistic in the small-sample case has a *t* distribution, we must use the TDIST function to compute the *p*-value.

The general form of the TDIST function is as follows:

TDIST(test statistic,degrees of freedom,tails)

Only nonnegative values are allowed for the test statistic argument. If the value of tails is 1, the function returns the area in the upper tail of the *t* distribution corresponding to the value of the test statistic. In the Heathrow Airport study we found a value for the test statistic of $t = 2.1376$. If we enter the function =TDIST(2.1376,11,1) into an Excel worksheet, the value obtained will be .0279. Thus, .0279 is the probability of obtaining a *t* value of 2.1376 or greater for a *t* distribution with 11 degrees of freedom. Thus, .0279 is the *p*-value for the Heathrow Airport upper tail hypothesis test.

As already noted, the TDIST function will not allow negative values for the test statistic argument. We know that the *p*-value for a lower tail hypothesis test is the cumulative probability associated with the value of the test statistic; that is, the p-value is the area under the curve for the t distribution to the left of the value of the test statistic. We also know that the p-value for an upper tail hypothesis test is the area under the curve to the right of the value of the test statistic. So, as with hypothesis tests involving the normal probability distribution, the p-value for an upper tail test involving the t distribution is one minus the p-value for a lower tail test. These points are the keys to how we compute p-values for the t distribution. We first find the value of the test statistic. To determine the p-value for a lower tail test, we compute the area under the curve to the left of the test statistic. Then, we subtract the p-value we computed for a lower tail test from one to obtain the p-value for an upper tail test. Finally, the p-value for a two-tailed test is just 2 times the smaller of the two tail areas, in other words, the p-value for a two-tailed test is just two times the minimum of the two one-tailed p-values.

We show an example of a two-tailed test in the next subsection.

Let us develop a general formula for using the TDIST function to compute lower tail areas. It involves using Excel's IF function to first determine whether the value of the test statistic is positive or negative. If the test statistic is negative, we use TDIST in one way to compute the p-value. If the test statistic is nonnegative, we use TDIST in another way to compute the p-value. The general form of the IF function for computing lower tail p-values for the t distribution is IF(test statistic < 0,formula1,formula2). If the test statistic is negative, formula1 is used to compute the p-value. If the test statistic is nonnegative, formula2 is used to compute the p-value.

formula1 = TDIST(-test statistic, degrees of freedom, 1)
formula2 = 1-TDIST(test statistic, degrees of freedom, 1)

As noted, once p-value (Lower Tail) has been computed, p-value (Upper Tail) can be easily computed by subtracting p-value (Lower Tail) from 1.

Let us now construct an Excel worksheet to conduct the upper tail hypothesis test for the Heathrow Airport rating study. Refer to Figure 9.14 as we describe the tasks involved. The formula worksheet is in the background; the value worksheet is in the foreground.

FIGURE 9.14 EXCEL WORKSHEET FOR THE HEATHROW AIRPORT HYPOTHESIS TEST

	A	B	C	D	E
1	Rating		Hypothesis Tests about a Population Mean		
2	7		Using the *t* Distribution		
3	8				
4	10		Sample Size	=COUNT(A2:A13)	
5	8		Mean	=AVERAGE(A2:A13)	
6	6		Standard Deviation	=STDEV(A2:A13)	
7	9				
8	6		Hypothesized value	7	
9	7				
10	7		Standard Error	=D6/SQRT(D4)	
11	8		Test Statistic	=(D5-D8)/D10	
12	9		Degrees of Freedom	=D4-1	
13	8				
14			*p*-value (Lower Tail)	=IF(D11<0,TDIST(-D11,D12,1),1-TDIST(D11,D12,1))	
15			*p*-value (Upper Tail)	=1-D14	
16			*p*-value (Two Tail)	=2*MIN(D14,D15)	
17					

	A	B	C	D	E	F	G
1	Rating		Hypothesis Tests about a Population Mean				
2	7		Using the *t* Distribution				
3	8						
4	10		Sample Size	12			
5	8		Mean	7.75			
6	6		Standard Deviation	1.2154			
7	9						
8	6		Hypothesized value	7			
9	7						
10	7		Standard Error	0.3509			
11	8		Test Statistic	2.1376			
12	9		Degrees of Freedom	11			
13	8						
14			*p*-value (Lower Tail)	0.9721			
15			*p*-value (Upper Tail)	0.0279			
16			*p*-value (Two Tail)	0.0558			
17							

Enter Data: Column A shows the rating provided by each of the 12 travelers.

Enter Functions and Formulas: The descriptive statistics needed are provided in cells D4:D6. Excel's COUNT, AVERAGE, and STDEV functions compute the sample size, sample mean, and sample standard deviation.

The hypothesized value of the population mean (7) is entered into cell D8. Using the sample standard deviation as an estimate of the population standard deviation, an estimate of the standard error is obtained in cell D10 by dividing the sample standard deviation in cell D6 by the square root of the sample size in cell D4. The formula =(D5-D8)/D10 is entered into cell D11 to compute the test statistic t (2.1376). The degrees of freedom are computed in cell D12 as the sample size in cell D4 minus 1.

To compute the p-value for a lower tail test, we entered the formula

$$=IF(D11<0,TDIST(-D11,D12,1),1-TDIST(D11,D12,1))$$

into cell D14. The p-value for an upper tail test is then computed in cell D15 as 1 minus the p-value for the lower tail test. Finally, the p-value for a two-tailed test is computed in cell D16 as 2 times the minimum of the two one-tailed p-values.

In the Heathrow Airport study we want to conduct an upper tail hypothesis test, so we want to compare the p-value (Upper Tail) with the level of significance. Because the p-value (Upper Tail) = .0279 in cell D15 is less than $\alpha = .05$, we reject the null hypothesis and conclude that the mean rating for the Heathrow airport is greater than 7.

The worksheet developed in Figure 9.14 can be used for any hypothesis test involving the t distribution. If a lower tail test is required, compare the p-value (Lower Tail) with α to make the rejection decision. If an upper tail test is required, compare the p-value (Upper Tail) with α to make the rejection decision. And, if a two-tailed test is required, compare the p-value (Two Tail) with α to make the rejection decision. Let us now see an example involving a two-tailed hypothesis test.

Two-Tailed Test

As an example of a two-tailed hypothesis test about a population mean using a small sample, consider the following production problem. A production process is designed to fill containers with a mean filling weight of $\mu = 16$ ounces. If the process underfills containers, the consumer will not receive the amount of product indicated on the container label. If the process overfills containers, the firm loses money because more product is placed in a container than is required. To monitor the process, quality assurance personnel periodically select a simple random sample of eight containers and test the following two-tailed hypotheses.

$$H_0: \mu = 16$$
$$H_a: \mu \neq 16$$

Weight

If H_0 is rejected, the production process will be stopped and the mechanism for regulating filling weights will be readjusted to ensure a mean filling weight of 16 ounces. Suppose a sample yields data values of 16.02, 16.22, 15.82, 15.92, 16.22, 16.32, 16.12, and 15.92 ounces. The sample mean is $\bar{x} = 16.07$, and the sample standard deviation is .1773. Assume that the population of filling weights is normally distributed. At the .05 level of significance, what action should be taken?

With a two-tailed test and a level of significance of $\alpha = .05$, the value of $-t_{.025}$ and the value of $t_{.025}$ are the critical values for the test. Using the table for the t distribution, we find that with $n - 1 = 8 - 1 = 7$ degrees of freedom, $-t_{.025} = -2.365$ and $t_{.025} = +2.365$. Thus, the rejection rule is

$$\text{Reject } H_0 \text{ if } t < -2.365 \text{ or if } t > 2.365$$

Using $\bar{x} = 16.07$ and $s = .1773$, we have

$$t = \frac{\bar{x} - \mu_0}{s/\sqrt{n}} = \frac{16.07 - 16}{.1773/\sqrt{8}} = 1.117$$

Because $t = 1.117$ is not in the rejection region, the null hypothesis cannot be rejected. The evidence is not sufficient to stop the production process.

Using Table 2 of Appendix B and the row for seven degrees of freedom, we see that the computed t value of 1.117 has an upper tail area of *more than* .10. Although the format of the t distribution table prevents us from being more specific, we can at least conclude that the two-tailed p-value is greater than 2(.10) = .20. Because this value is greater than the .05 level of significance, we see that the p-value leads to the same conclusion; that is, do not reject H_0.

Using Excel to Conduct a Two-Tailed Hypothesis Test: Small-Sample Case

Excel can be used to conduct the two-tailed hypothesis test for the container filling production problem. Refer to Figure 9.15 as we describe the tasks involved. The formula worksheet is in the background; the value worksheet is in the foreground.

Enter Data: Column A shows the weight in ounces for each of the eight containers.

Enter Functions and Formulas: The descriptive statistics needed are provided in cells D4:D6. Excel's COUNT, AVERAGE, and STDEV functions compute the sample size, sample mean, and sample standard deviation.

The hypothesized value of the population mean (16) is entered into cell D8. Using the sample standard deviation as an estimate of the population standard deviation, an estimate

FIGURE 9.15 EXCEL WORKSHEET FOR THE CONTAINER-FILLING HYPOTHESIS TEST

	A	B	C	D	E
1	Weight		Hypothesis Tests about a Population Mean		
2	16.02		Using the *t* Distribution		
3	16.22				
4	15.82		Sample Size	=COUNT(A2:A9)	
5	15.92		Mean	=AVERAGE(A2:A9)	
6	16.22		Standard Deviation	=STDEV(A2:A9)	
7	16.32				
8	16.12		Hypothesized value	16	
9	15.92				
10			Standard Error	=D6/SQRT(D4)	
11			Test Statistic	=(D5-D8)/D10	
12			Degrees of Freedom	=D4-1	
13					
14			*p*-value (Lower Tail)	=IF(D11<0,TDIST(-D11,D12,1),1-TDIST(D11,D12,1))	
15			*p*-value (Upper Tail)	=1-D14	
16			*p*-value (Two Tail)	=2*MIN(D14,D15)	
17					

	A	B	C	D	E	F	G
1	Weight		Hypothesis Tests about a Population Mean				
2	16.02		Using the *t* Distribution				
3	16.22						
4	15.82		Sample Size	8			
5	15.92		Mean	16.07			
6	16.22		Standard Deviation	0.1773			
7	16.32						
8	16.12		Hypothesized value	16			
9	15.92						
10			Standard Error	0.0627			
11			Test Statistic	1.1168			
12			Degrees of Freedom	7			
13							
14			*p*-value (Lower Tail)	0.8495			
15			*p*-value (Upper Tail)	0.1505			
16			*p*-value (Two Tail)	0.3009			
17							

of the standard error is obtained in cell D10 by dividing the sample standard deviation in cell D6 by the square root of the sample size in cell D4. The formula =(D5 − D8)/D10 is entered into cell D11 to compute the test statistic t (1.1168). The degrees of freedom are computed in cell D12 as the sample size in cell D4 minus 1.

To compute the p-value (Lower Tail), we entered the formula

$$=\text{IF(D11<0,TDIST(-D11,D12,1),1-TDIST(D11,D12,1))}$$

into cell D14. Then, the p-value (Upper Tail) is computed in cell D15 as $1 - p$-value (Lower Tail). Finally, the p-value (Two Tail) is computed in cell D16 as 2 times the minimum of the two one-tailed p-values.

In the container-filling study we want to conduct a two-tailed hypothesis test, so we want to compare the two-tailed p-value with the level of significance. Because the p-value (Two Tail) = .3009 in cell D16 is greater than $\alpha = .05$, we cannot reject the null hypothesis. We conclude that the sample data do not provide sufficient evidence to stop the production process.

EXERCISES

Methods

31. Consider the following hypothesis test.

$$H_0: \mu \leq 10$$
$$H_a: \mu > 10$$

A sample of 16 items provides a sample mean of 11 and sample standard deviation of 3.
   a. With $\alpha = .05$, what is the rejection rule?
   b. Compute the value of the test statistic t. What is your conclusion?

32. Consider the following hypothesis test.

$$H_0: \mu = 20$$
$$H_a: \mu \neq 20$$

Data from a sample of six items are 18, 20, 16, 19, 17, 18.
   a. Compute the sample mean.
   b. Compute the sample standard deviation.
   c. With $\alpha = .05$, what is the rejection rule?
   d. Compute the value of the test statistic t.
   e. What is your conclusion?

33. Consider the following hypothesis test.

$$H_0: \mu \geq 15$$
$$H_a: \mu < 15$$

A sample of size 22 is used, and the sample standard deviation is 8. Use $\alpha = .05$. Provide the value of the test statistic t and your conclusion for each of the following sample results.
   a. $\bar{x} = 13.0$
   b. $\bar{x} = 11.5$
   c. $\bar{x} = 15.0$
   d. $\bar{x} = 19.0$

34.   Consider the following hypothesis test.

$$H_0: \mu \leq 50$$
$$H_a: \mu > 50$$

Assume a sample of 16 items provided the following test statistics. What can you say about the *p*-values in each case? What are your conclusions based on $\alpha = .05$?

a. $t = 2.602$
b. $t = 1.341$
c. $t = 1.960$
d. $t = 1.055$
e. $t = 3.261$

Applications

35.   The population mean earnings per share for financial services corporations including American Express, E*Trade Group, Goldman Sachs, and Merrill Lynch was \$3 (*Business Week*, August 14, 2000). In 2001, a sample of 10 financial services corporations provided the following earnings per share data:

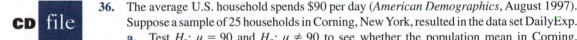

| 1.92 | 2.16 | 3.63 | 3.16 | 4.02 | 3.14 | 2.20 | 2.34 | 3.05 | 2.38 |

a.   Formulate the null and alternative hypotheses that can be used to determine whether population mean earnings per share in 2001 differs from the \$3 per share reported in 2000.
b.   Using $\alpha = .05$, what are the critical values for the test statistic, and what is the rejection rule?
c.   Compute the sample mean.
d.   Compute the sample standard deviation.
e.   Compute the value of the test statistic.
f.   What is your conclusion?
g.   What is the *p*-value?

36.   The average U.S. household spends \$90 per day (*American Demographics*, August 1997). Suppose a sample of 25 households in Corning, New York, resulted in the data set DailyExp.

CD file

DailyExp

a.   Test $H_0: \mu = 90$ and $H_a: \mu \neq 90$ to see whether the population mean in Corning, New York, differs from the U.S. mean. Use a .05 level of significance. What is your conclusion?
b.   What is the *p*-value?

37.   On the average, a stay-at-home mom with a husband and two children is estimated to work 55 hours or less per week on household-related activities. The hours worked during a week for a sample of eight stay-at-home moms are 58, 52, 64, 63, 59, 62, 62, and 55.

a.   Use $\alpha = .05$ to test $H_0: \mu \leq 55$, $H_a: \mu > 55$. What is your conclusion about the mean number of hours worked per week?
b.   What is the *p*-value?

38.   The cost of a one-carat VS2 clarity, H color diamond from the Diamond Source USA is \$4000 (*www.diasource.com*, July 2000). A midwestern jeweler makes calls to contacts in the diamond district of New York City to see whether the mean price of similar diamonds differs from \$4000. The jeweler collects cost data from 14 New York City contacts.

a.   Formulate the null and alternative hypotheses that can be used to determine whether the mean price in New York City differs from \$4000.
b.   Using $\alpha = .05$, what are the critical values for the test, and what is the rejection rule?

   c.   Assume the sample of 14 New York City contacts provides a sample mean price of $4120 and a sample standard deviation of $275. Compute the value of the test statistic.

   d.   What is your conclusion?

   e.   What is the p-value?

39. Callaway Golf Company's new forged titanium ERC driver has been described as "illegal" because it promised driving distances that exceeded the USGA's standard. *Golf Digest* compared actual driving distances with the ERC driver and a USGA-approved driver with a population mean driving distance of 280 yards. Using nine test drives, the mean driving distance by the ERC driver was 286.9 yards. (*Golf Digest*, May 12, 2000). Answer the following questions assuming a population standard deviation driving distance of 10 yards.

   a.   Formulate the null and alternative hypotheses that can be used to determine whether the new ERC driver has a population mean driving distance greater than 280 yards.

   b.   On average, how many yards farther did the golf ball travel with the ERC driver?

   c.   Using $\alpha = .05$, what is the critical value for the test statistic, and what is the rejection rule?

   d.   Compute the value of the test statistic.

   e.   What is your conclusion?

   f.   What is the p-value?

40. Joan's Nursery specializes in custom-designed landscaping for residential areas. The estimated labor cost associated with a particular landscaping proposal is based on the number of plantings of trees, shrubs, and so on to be used for the project. For cost-estimating purposes, managers use 2 hours of labor time for the planting of a mediumsized tree. Actual times from a sample of 10 plantings during the past month follow (times in hours).

1.9	1.7	2.8	2.4	2.6	2.5	2.8	3.2	1.6	2.5

Using a .05 level of significance, test whether the mean tree-planting time exceeds 2 hours. What is your conclusion, and what recommendations would you consider making to the managers?

9.6   TESTS ABOUT A POPULATION PROPORTION

With p denoting the population proportion and p_0 denoting a particular hypothesized value for the population proportion, the three forms for a hypothesis test about a population proportion are as follows.

$$H_0: p \geq p_0 \qquad H_0: p \leq p_0 \qquad H_0: p = p_0$$
$$H_a: p < p_0 \qquad H_a: p > p_0 \qquad H_a: p \neq p_0$$

The first two forms are one-tailed tests, whereas the third form is a two-tailed test. The specific form used depends on the application.

    Hypothesis tests about a population proportion are based on the difference between the sample proportion $\bar{p}$ and the hypothesized population proportion p_0. The methods used to conduct the tests are similar to the procedures used for hypothesis tests about a population mean. The only difference is that we use the sample proportion $\bar{p}$ and its standard error $\sigma_{\bar{p}}$ in developing the test statistic. We begin by formulating null and alternative hypotheses about the value of the population proportion. Then, using the value of the sample proportion $\bar{p}$ and its standard error $\sigma_{\bar{p}}$, we compute a value for the test statistic z. Comparing the value of the test statistic to the critical value or comparing the p-value to α enables us to determine whether the null hypothesis should be rejected.

Let us illustrate hypothesis testing for a population proportion by considering the situation faced by Pine Creek golf course. Over the past few months, 20% of the players at Pine Creek have been women. In an effort to increase the proportion of women playing, Pine Creek is now using a special promotion to attract women golfers. After one week, a random sample of 400 players showed 300 men and 100 women. Course managers would like to determine whether the data support the conclusion that the population proportion of women playing at Pine Creek has increased.

To determine whether the promotion actually increased the population proportion of women golfers, we state the following null and alternative hypotheses.

$$H_0: p \leq .20$$
$$H_a: p > .20$$

As usual, we begin the hypothesis testing procedure by assuming that H_0 is true with $p = .20$. Using the sample proportion $\bar{p}$ to estimate p, we next consider the sampling distribution of $\bar{p}$. From Chapter 7, we know that the mean of the sampling distribution of $\bar{p}$ is $p = .20$, and the standard deviation of $\bar{p}$ (the standard error) is given by

The standard error of $\bar{p}$ is the standard deviation of the sampling distribution of $\bar{p}$.

$$\sigma_{\bar{p}} = \sqrt{\frac{p(1 - p)}{n}}$$

With the assumed value of $p = .20$ and a sample size of $n = 400$, the standard error of $\bar{p}$ is

$$\sigma_{\bar{p}} = \sqrt{\frac{.20(1 - .20)}{400}} = .02$$

In Chapter 7 we saw that the sampling distribution of $\bar{p}$ can be approximated by a normal probability distribution in the large-sample case. With population proportions, the rule of thumb is that both np and $n(1 - p)$ must be greater than or equal to 5. In the Pine Creek case, $np = 400(.20) = 80$ and $n(1 - p) = 400(.80) = 320$; thus, the normal probability distribution approximation is appropriate. The sampling distribution of $\bar{p}$ is shown in Figure 9.16.

FIGURE 9.16   SAMPLING DISTRIBUTION OF $\bar{p}$ FOR THE PROPORTION OF WOMEN GOLFERS AT PINE CREEK GOLF COURSE

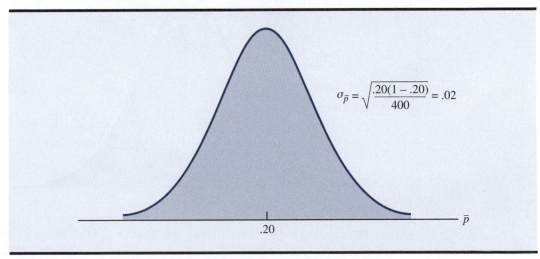

When the sampling distribution of $\bar{p}$ is approximately normal, the following test statistic can be used.

Test Statistic for Hypothesis Tests About a Population Proportion

$$z = \frac{\bar{p} - p_0}{\sigma_{\bar{p}}} \tag{9.9}$$

where

$$\sigma_{\bar{p}} = \sqrt{\frac{p_0(1 - p_0)}{n}} \tag{9.10}$$

In hypothesis testing, a value of the population proportion, p_0, is assumed in H_0. Therefore, when H_0 is true, $\sigma_{\bar{p}}$ can be computed by using p_0 as shown in (9.10). The sample proportion, $\bar{p}$, is not used in the computation of $\sigma_{\bar{p}}$.

Suppose that $\alpha = .05$ has been selected as the level of significance for the test. With $z_{.05} = 1.645$, the upper tail rejection region for the hypothesis test (see Figure 9.17) provides the following rejection rule.

$$\text{Reject } H_0 \text{ if } z > 1.645$$

Because 100 of the 400 players during the promotion were women, we obtain $\bar{p} = 100/400 = .25$. With $\sigma_{\bar{p}} = .02$, the value of the test statistic is

$$z = \frac{\bar{p} - p_0}{\sigma_{\bar{p}}} = \frac{.25 - .20}{.02} = 2.5$$

Because $z = 2.5 > 1.645$, we can reject H_0. The Pine Creek managers can conclude that the population proportion of women players has increased.

FIGURE 9.17   REJECTION REGION FOR THE PINE CREEK GOLF COURSE HYPOTHESIS TEST

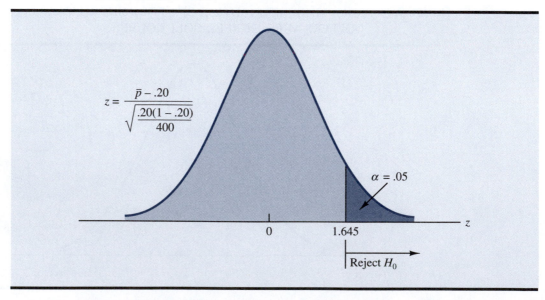

The *p*-value approach can also be used to determine whether the null hypothesis should be rejected. Using the cumulative normal probability table, we find that the area to the right of $z = 2.5$ is $1 - .9938 = .0062$. Thus, the *p*-value for the test is .0062. Because the *p*-value is less than α, the null hypothesis can be rejected.

We see that hypothesis tests about a population proportion and a population mean are similar; the primary difference is that the test statistic is based on the sampling distribution of $\bar{x}$ when the hypothesis test involves a population mean and on the sampling distribution of $\bar{p}$ when the hypothesis test involves a population proportion. The tentative assumption that the null hypothesis is true, the use of the level of significance to establish the critical value, and the comparison of the test statistic to the critical value are identical in the two testing procedures. Figure 9.18 summarizes the decision rules for hypothesis tests about a population proportion. We assume the large-sample case, $np \geq 5$ and $n(1 - p) \geq 5$, where the normal probability distribution can be used to approximate the sampling distribution of $\bar{p}$.

Using Excel to Conduct Hypothesis Tests About a Population Proportion

CD file

Golf

As we stated in the preceding paragraph, the primary difference between hypothesis tests about a population proportion and a population mean is that the test statistic is based on the sampling distribution of $\bar{x}$ when the hypothesis test involves a population mean and on the sampling distribution of $\bar{p}$ when the hypothesis test involves a population proportion. But, in the large-sample case, the test statistic z for both tests can be approximated by a normal probability distribution. Thus, although different formulas are used to compute the test statistic needed to make the hypothesis testing decision, the computations of the critical value and the *p*-value for the tests are identical. We will illustrate the procedure by showing how Excel can be used to conduct the hypothesis test for the Pine Creek golf course study. Refer to Figure 9.19 as we describe the tasks involved. The value worksheet is in the foreground; the formula worksheet is in the background.

Enter Data: Column A identifies the gender of each golfer in the sample of size 400.

Enter Functions and Formulas: The descriptive statistics needed are provided in cells D4:D7. Because the data are not numeric, Excel's COUNTA function, not the COUNT function, is used in cell D4 to determine the sample size. We typed Female in cell D5 to identify the response for which we wish to compute a proportion. The COUNTIF function is then used in cell D6 to determine the number of responses of the type identified in cell D5. The sample proportion is then computed in cell D7 by dividing the response count by the sample size.

The hypothesized value of the population proportion (.2) is entered into cell D9. The standard error is obtained in cell D11 by entering the formula =SQRT(D9*(1-D9)/D4). The formula =(D7-D9)/D11 entered into cell D12 computes the test statistic z (2.5). Finally, the NORMSDIST function in cells D14 and D15 computes the lower tail and upper tail *p*-values, respectively. Although we didn't need it for this application, the two-tailed *p*-value is also computed in cell D16 as 2 times the minimum of the one-tailed *p*-values.

The Pine Creek hypothesis test has an upper tail rejection region, so the *p*-value we want to use is found in cell D15 [*p*-value (Upper Tail) = .0062]. At the $\alpha = .05$ level of significance we reject the null hypothesis that the population proportion is .20 or less. Indeed, with this *p*-value we would reject the null hypothesis for any level of significance greater than .0062.

The worksheet in Figure 9.19 can be used as a template for hypothesis tests about a population proportion in the large-sample case. Just enter the appropriate data in column A, adjust the ranges for the formulas in cells D4 and D6, type the appropriate response in cell D5, and enter the hypothesized value in cell D9. The standard error, the test statistic,

FIGURE 9.18   SUMMARY OF REJECTION RULES FOR HYPOTHESIS TESTS ABOUT A
POPULATION PROPORTION (LARGE-SAMPLE CASE: $np \geq 5$ and $n(1-p) \geq 5$)

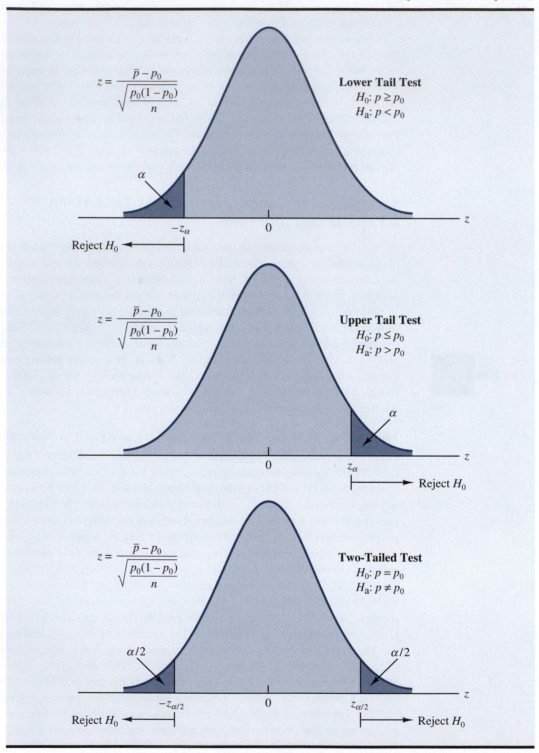

FIGURE 9.19   EXCEL WORKSHEET FOR PINE CREEK GOLF COURSE HYPOTHESIS TEST

	A	B	C	D	E	F	G
1	Gender		Hypothesis Test about a Population Proportion				
2	Male		Using the Standard Normal Distribution (z)				
3	Male						
4	Female		Sample Size	=COUNTA(A2:A401)			
5	Female		Response of Interest	Female			
6	Female		Count of Response	=COUNTIF(A2:A401,D5)			
7	Male		Sample Proportion	=D6/D4			
8	Female						
9	Male		Hypothesized value	0.2			
10	Male						
11	Male		Standard Error	=SQRT(D9*(1-D9)/D4)			
12	Male		Test Statistic	=(D7-D9)/D11			
13	Male						
14	Male		p-value (Lower Tail)	=NORMSDIST(D12)			
15	Male		p-value (Upper Tail)	=1-NORMSDIST(D12)			
16	Female		p-value (Two Tail)	=2*MIN(D14,D15)			
17	Female						
399	Male						
400	Male						
401	Male						
402							

	A	B	C	D	E	F	G	H
1	Gender		Hypothesis Test about a Population Proportion					
2	Male		Using the Standard Normal Distribution (z)					
3	Male							
4	Female		Sample Size	400				
5	Female		Response of Interest	Female				
6	Female		Count of Response	100				
7	Male		Sample Proportion	0.25				
8	Female							
9	Male		Hypothesized value	0.2				
10	Male							
11	Male		Standard Error	0.0200				
12	Male		Test Statistic	2.5000				
13	Male							
14	Male		p-value (Lower Tail)	0.9938				
15	Male		p-value (Upper Tail)	0.0062				
16	Female		p-value (Two Tail)	0.0124				
17	Female							
399	Male							
400	Male							
401	Male							
402								

Note: Rows 18–398 are hidden.

and the three p-values will then appear. Depending on the form of the hypothesis test (lower tail, upper tail, or two-tailed), we can then choose the appropriate p-value to make the rejection decision.

NOTES AND COMMENTS

We have not shown the procedure for small-sample hypothesis tests involving population proportions. In the small-sample case, the sampling distribution of $\bar{p}$ follows the binomial distribution and hence the normal approximation is not applicable. More advanced texts show how hypothesis tests are conducted for this situation. However, in practice large samples are almost always used to estimate a population proportion.

EXERCISES

Methods

41. Consider the following hypothesis test.

$$H_0: p \leq .50$$
$$H_a: p > .50$$

A sample of 200 items provided a sample proportion $\bar{p} = .57$.
  a. At $\alpha = .05$, what is the rejection rule?
  b. Compute the value of the test statistic z. What is your conclusion?

42. Consider the following hypothesis test.

$$H_0: p = .20$$
$$H_a: p \neq .20$$

A sample of 400 items provided a sample proportion of $\bar{p} = .175$.
a. At $\alpha = .05$, what is the rejection rule?
b. Compute the value of the test statistic z.
c. What is the p-value?
d. What is your conclusion?

43. Consider the following hypothesis test.

$$H_0: p \geq .75$$
$$H_a: p < .75$$

A sample of 300 items is selected. Use $\alpha = .05$. Provide the value of the test statistic z, the p-value, and your conclusion for each of the following sample results.
a. $\bar{p} = .68$
b. $\bar{p} = .72$
c. $\bar{p} = .70$
d. $\bar{p} = .77$

Applications

44. The Heldrich Center for Workforce Development found that 40% of Internet users received more than 10 email messages per day (*USA Today*, May 7, 2000). In 2001, a similar study on the use of email was repeated. The purpose of the study was to see whether the use of email increased.
a. Formulate the null and alternative hypotheses to determine whether an *increase* occurred in the proportion of Internet users receiving more than 10 emails message per day.
b. Using $\alpha = .05$, what is the critical value for the test, and what is the rejection rule?
c. If a sample of 420 Internet users found 188 receiving more than 10 email messages per day, what is the sample proportion, and what is the value of the test statistic?
d. What is your conclusion?

45. A study by *Consumer Reports* showed that 64% of supermarket shoppers believed supermarket brands to be as good as national name brands in terms of product quality. To investigate whether this result applies to its own product, the manufacturer of a national name-brand ketchup product asked 100 supermarket shoppers whether they believed the supermarket brand of ketchup was as good as the national name-brand ketchup. Suppose that 52 of the shoppers in the sample indicated that the supermarket brand was as good as the national name brand. Test $H_0: p \geq .64$ and $H_a: p < .64$. Use a .05 level of significance. What is your conclusion?

46. Burger King sponsored what it believed to be the biggest product giveaway in fast-food history when it initiated "FreeFryDay" on Friday, January 2, 1998. Anyone who stopped at one of Burger King's 7400 restaurants received a small order of the new Burger

King fries free of charge. A national taste test comparing the new Burger King fries to McDonald's fries was the basis for the launch of the Burger King promotion. Of the 500 customers who participated in the taste test, 285 expressed a taste preference for the Burger King fries (*USA Today*, December 10, 1997). Let p = the population proportion that favors the Burger King fries. Consider the following hypothesis test:

$$H_0: p \leq .50$$
$$H_a: p > .50$$

a.   What is the point estimate of the population proportion that favors the Burger King fries?
b.   What is your conclusion? Use a .01 level of significance.
c.   Do you believe that the national taste test statistics helped Burger King's management decide to implement the "FreeFryDay" campaign? Discuss.

Students

47.   A magazine claims that 25% of its readers are college students. A random sample of 200 readers resulted in the data set Students. A response of Yes indicates that the reader is a college student. Use a .10 level of significance to test $H_0: p = .25$ and $H_a: p \neq .25$. What is the p-value?

48.   Shell Oil office workers were asked which work schedule appealed most: working five 8-hour days or four 10-hour days (*USA Today*, September 11, 2000). Let p equal the proportion of office workers preferring the schedule with four 10-hour days. Test the hypotheses $H_0: p = .50$ and $H_a: p \neq .50$ at $\alpha = .01$. A sample of 105 office workers showed that 67 prefer the four 10-hour day schedule.
a.   What is the sample proportion preferring four 10-hour days?
b.   What is the value of the test statistic?
c.   What is the p-value?
d.   What is your conclusion? Is a statistically significant preference indicated between the two alternatives?

49.   Drugstore.com was the first e-commerce company to offer Internet drugstore retailing. Drugstore.com customers could buy health, beauty, personal care, wellness, and pharmaceutical replenishment products over the Internet. At the end of 10 months of operation, the company reported that 44% of orders were from repeat customers (*Drugstore.com Annual Report*, January 2, 2000). Assume that Drugstore.com will use a sample of customer orders each quarter to determine whether the proportion of orders from repeat customers has changed from the initial $p = .44$.
a.   Formulate the null and alternative hypotheses.
b.   During the first quarter, a sample of 500 orders showed 205 repeat customers. What is the p-value? What is your conclusion using $\alpha = .05$?
c.   During the second quarter, a sample of 500 orders showed 245 repeat customers. What is the p-value? What is your conclusion using $\alpha = .05$?

50.   Microsoft Outlook is believed to be the most widely used e-mail manager. A Microsoft executive claims that Microsoft Outlook is used by at least 75% of Internet users. A Merrill Lynch study reported 72% use Microsoft Outlook (CNBC, June 2000). Test the following hypotheses: $H_0: p \geq .75$, $H_a: p < 75$ at $\alpha = .05$.
a.   Assuming the Merrill Lynch sample size was 300 users, compute the value of the test statistic.
b.   What is the p-value?
c.   Should the executive's claim of at least 75% be rejected?

51. Based on rates of errors, third base is the most difficult position to play in professional baseball. Considering all third basemen, an error occurs on 4.7% of fielding chances (*ESPN The Magazine*, July 12, 1999). A sample of games played by all-star third baseman Brooks Robinson showed that he had 35 errors in 1182 fielding chances. Does the sample support the conclusion that Brooks Robinson makes fewer errors than the typical third baseman? Use $\alpha = .01$.

    a. What are the appropriate null and alternative hypotheses?

    b. What is the sample proportion error percentage for Brooks Robinson?

    c. Compute the value of the test statistic.

    d. What is the *p*-value?

    e. What is your conclusion?

SUMMARY

Hypothesis testing is a statistical procedure that uses sample data to determine whether a statement about the value of a population parameter should be rejected. The hypotheses, which come from a variety of sources, are two competing statements about a population parameter: a null hypothesis H_0 and an alternative hypothesis H_a. In some applications it is not obvious how the null and alternative hypotheses should be formulated. We suggested guidelines for developing hypotheses in the three types of situations most frequently encountered.

Figure 9.20 summarizes the test statistics used in hypothesis tests about a population mean and provides a practical guide for selecting the hypothesis testing procedure. The figure shows that the test statistic depends on whether the sample size is large, whether the population standard deviation is assumed known, and in some cases whether the population has a normal or approximately normal probability distribution. If the sample size is large, ($n \geq 30$), the z test statistic is used to conduct the hypothesis test. If the sample size is small, ($n < 30$), the population must have a normal or approximately normal probability distribution to conduct a hypothesis test about the value of μ. If that is the case, the z test statistic is used if σ is assumed known, whereas the t test statistic is used if σ is estimated by the sample standard deviation s. Finally, note that if the sample size is small and the assumption of a normal probability distribution for the population is inappropriate, we recommend increasing the sample size to $n \geq 30$.

Hypothesis tests about a population proportion were developed for the large-sample case where both $np \geq 5$ and $n(1 - p) \geq 5$. The test statistic used is

$$z = \frac{\bar{p} - p_0}{\sqrt{\dfrac{p_0(1 - p_0)}{n}}}$$

We did not consider the small-sample case for proportions because, in practice, hypothesis tests for proportions almost always involve large samples.

The rejection rule for all the hypothesis testing procedures involves comparing the value of the test statistic with a critical value. For lower tail tests, the null hypothesis is rejected if the value of the test statistic is less than the critical value. For upper tail tests, the null hypothesis is rejected if the test statistic is greater than the critical value. For two-tailed tests, the null hypothesis is rejected for values of the test statistic in either tail of the sampling distribution.

FIGURE 9.20   SUMMARY OF THE TEST STATISTICS TO BE USED IN A HYPOTHESIS TEST ABOUT
A POPULATION MEAN

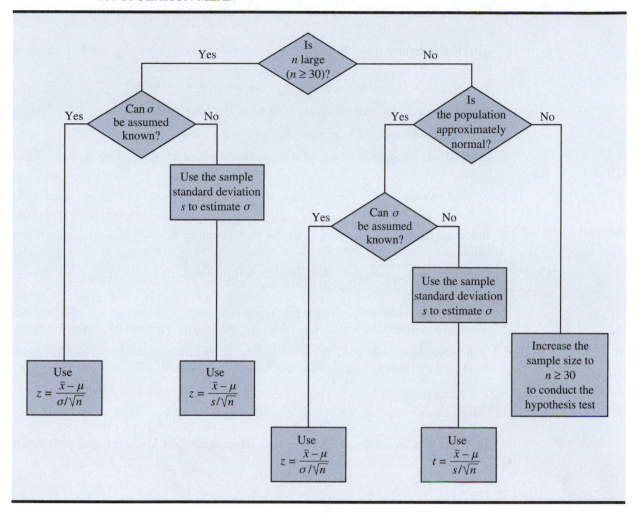

We also saw that p-values could be used for hypothesis testing. The p-value is the probability, when the null hypothesis is true, of obtaining a sample result that is at least as unlikely as what is observed. When p-values are used to conduct a hypothesis test, the rejection rule calls for rejecting the null hypothesis whenever the p-value is less than α. The p-value is often called the observed level of significance. The p-value for a lower tail test is the area under the curve to the left of the test statistic, and the p-value for an upper tail test is the area under the curve to the right of the test statistic. The p-value for a two-tailed test is twice the minimum of the one-tailed p-values.

We showed how to implement the hypothesis testing procedures presented using Excel. The worksheet in Figure 9.12 can be used for any hypothesis test about a population mean involving the test statistic z from a normal probability distribution. The worksheet in Figure 9.14 can be used as a template for any hypothesis test about a population mean using a test statistic t from the t distribution. And, the worksheet in Figure 9.19 can be used for hypothesis tests about a population proportion.

GLOSSARY

Null hypothesis The hypothesis tentatively assumed true in the hypothesis testing procedure.

Alternative hypothesis The hypothesis concluded to be true if the null hypothesis is rejected.

Type I error The error of rejecting H_0 when it is true.

Type II error The error of accepting H_0 when it is false.

Level of significance The maximum allowable probability of a Type I error.

Test statistic A statistic whose value is used to determine whether the null hypothesis can be rejected.

Critical value A value that is compared with the test statistic to determine whether H_0 should be rejected.

Rejection region The range of values for the test statistic that will lead to rejection of the null hypothesis.

One-tailed hypothesis test A hypothesis test in which the rejection region is in only one tail of the sampling distribution.

_p_-value The probability, when the null hypothesis is true, of obtaining a sample result that is at least as unlikely as what is observed. It is often called the observed level of significance.

Two-tailed hypothesis test A hypothesis test in which rejection of the null hypothesis occurs for values of the test statistic in either tail of the sampling distribution.

KEY FORMULAS

Test Statistics for a Large-Sample ($n \geq 30$) Hypothesis Test About a Population Mean

$$\sigma \text{ assumed known} \qquad z = \frac{\bar{x} - \mu_0}{\sigma/\sqrt{n}} \tag{9.1}$$

$$\sigma \text{ estimated by } s \qquad z = \frac{\bar{x} - \mu_0}{s/\sqrt{n}} \tag{9.2}$$

Test Statistics for a Small-Sample ($n < 30$) Hypothesis Test About a Population Mean

$$\sigma \text{ assumed known} \qquad z = \frac{\bar{x} - \mu_0}{\sigma/\sqrt{n}} \tag{9.7}$$

$$\sigma \text{ estimated by } s \qquad t = \frac{\bar{x} - \mu_0}{s/\sqrt{n}} \tag{9.8}$$

Test Statistic for Hypothesis Tests About a Population Proportion

$$z = \frac{\bar{p} - p_0}{\sigma_{\bar{p}}} \tag{9.9}$$

where

$$\sigma_{\bar{p}} = \sqrt{\frac{p_0(1 - p_0)}{n}} \tag{9.10}$$

SUPPLEMENTARY EXERCISES

52. The population mean annual salary for public school teachers in the state of New York is $45,250. The mean annual salary of public school teachers in New York City is $47,000 (*Time*, April 3, 2000). Assume the New York City results are based on a sample of 95 teachers and the sample standard deviation was $6,300.

    a. Formulate the null and alternative hypotheses that can be used to determine whether the sample data support the conclusion that public school teachers in New York City have a higher mean annual salary than the public school teachers in the state of New York.

    b. What is the value of the test statistic?

    c. What is the *p*-value?

    d. Using $\alpha = .01$, what is your conclusion?

53. The Buick LeSabre is listed as having a highway fuel efficiency average of 30 miles per gallon (U.S. Dept. of Energy, Model Year 2001, Fuel Economy Guide). A consumer interest group conducts automobile mileage tests seeking statistical evidence to show that automobile manufacturers overstate the miles per gallon ratings for particular models. In the case of the Buick LeSabre, hypotheses for the test would be stated H_0: $\mu \geq 30$ and H_a: $\mu < 30$. In a sample of 50 mileage tests with Buick LeSabre, the consumer interest group finds a sample mean highway mileage rating of 29.5 miles per gallon and a sample standard deviation of 1.8 miles per gallon. What conclusion should be drawn from the sample results? Use a .01 level of significance.

54. The chamber of commerce of a Florida Gulf Coast community advertises that area residential property is available at a mean cost of $25,000 or less per lot. Using a .05 level of significance, test the validity of this claim. Suppose a sample of 32 properties provided a sample mean of $26,000 per lot and a sample standard deviation of $2500. What is the *p*-value?

55. A bath soap manufacturing process is designed to produce a mean of 120 bars of soap per batch. Quantities over or under the standard are undesirable. A sample of 10 batches shows the following numbers of bars of soap. The population is assumed to be normally distributed.

108	118	120	122	119	113	124	122	120	123

Using a .05 level of significance, test to see whether the sample results indicate that the manufacturing process is functioning properly.

56. The monthly rent for a two-bedroom apartment in a particular city is reported to average $550. Suppose we want to test H_0: $\mu = 550$ versus H_a: $\mu \neq 550$. A sample of 36 two-bedroom apartments is selected. The sample mean is $\bar{x} = \$562$ and the sample standard deviation is $s = \$40$.

    a. Conduct this hypothesis test with a .05 level of significance.

    b. Compute the *p*-value.

    c. Use the sample results to construct a 95% confidence interval for the population mean. What hypothesis testing conclusion would you draw from the confidence interval result?

IdleTime

57. In making bids on building projects, Sonneborn Builders, Inc., assumes construction workers are idle no more than 15% of the time. Hence, for a normal 8-hour shift, the mean idle time per worker should be 72 minutes or less per day. A sample of 30 construction workers resulted in the idle times shown in the data set IdleTime. Suppose a hypothesis test is to be designed to test the validity of the company's assumption.

    a. What is the *p*-value associated with the sample result?

    b. Using a .05 level of significance and the *p*-value approach, test H_0: $\mu \leq 72$. What is your conclusion?

58. The Immigration and Naturalization service reported that 79% of foreign travelers visiting the United States stated that the primary purpose of their visit was to enjoy a vacation. In a follow-up study conducted in 2001, suppose a sample of 500 foreign visitors is selected and that 360 say that their primary reason for visiting the United States is to enjoy a vacation. Is the proportion of foreign travelers vacationing in the United States in 2001 less than the proportion previously reported? Support your conclusion with a statistical test using a .05 level of significance.

CD file

CoWorker

59. In a comprehensive study of workplace communications conducted by Pitney Bowes, 72% of the workers surveyed said they regularly work with coworkers who are not in the office, which made face-to-face meetings or voice-to-voice phone conversations more difficult to schedule and conduct (*ORMS Today*, August 1998). A related study of 400 workers was conducted at Trident Manufacturing. The data collected are shown in the data set CoWorker. A response of Yes indicates that the worker regularly works with coworkers not in the office. Conduct a statistical test to determine whether the proportion of workers who regularly work with coworkers not in the office is greater at Trident Manufacturing than the percentage reported by Pitney Bowes. Use a .05 level of significance.

60. The Gallup Organization conducted a survey of 1350 people for the National Occupational Information Coordinating Committee, a panel Congress created to improve the use of job information. A research question related to the study was: Do individuals hold jobs that they had planned to hold or do they hold jobs for such reasons as chance or lack of choice? Let p indicate the population proportion of individuals who hold jobs that they had planned to hold.

    a. If the hypotheses are stated H_0: $p \geq .50$ and H_a: $p < .50$, discuss the research hypothesis H_a in terms of what the researcher is investigating.

    b. The Gallup poll found that 41% of the respondents hold jobs they planned to hold. What is your conclusion at a .01 level of significance? Discuss.

61. A well-known doctor hypothesized that 75% of women wear shoes that are too small. A study of 356 women by the American Orthopedic Foot and Ankle Society found 313 women who wore shoes that were at least one size too small. Test H_0: $p = .75$ and H_a: $p \neq .75$ at $\alpha = .01$. What is your conclusion?

62. An airline promotion to business travelers was based on the assumption that approximately two-thirds of business travelers use a laptop computer on overnight business trips. Test this assumption by testing the hypotheses H_0: $p = .67$ and H_a: $p \neq .67$ at $\alpha = .05$. Use the sample results from an American Express online survey, which found 355 of 546 business travelers use a laptop computer on overnight business trips (*The Cincinnati Enquirer*, August 31, 1998).

    a. What is the sample proportion?

    b. Compute the value of the test statistic.

    c. What is the p-value?

    d. Can the claim of two-thirds be rejected? Discuss.

63. The Department of Transportation reported Amtrack trains had a 78% on-time arrival record over the previous 12 months (*USA Today*, November 23, 1998). Assume that in 2001, a study found 330 of 400 Amtrack trains arrived on time. Does the sample indicate the Amtrack arrival rate has changed? Test H_0: $p = .78$ and H_a: $p \neq .78$ at $\alpha = .05$.

    a. What is the sample proportion of Amtrack trains arriving on time?

    b. Compute the value of the test statistic.

    c. What is the p-value?

    d. What is your conclusion?

64. Environmental health indicators include air quality, water quality, and food quality. Over twenty-five years ago, 47% of U.S. food samples contained pesticide residues (*U.S. News*

& World Report, April 17, 2000). In a recent study, 44 of 125 food samples contained pesticide residues.

a. What is the sample proportion?

b. Compute the value of the test statistic.

c. What is the p-value?

d. Has the proportion of foods containing pesticides declined? Using $\alpha = .01$, what is your conclusion?

Case Problem 1   UNEMPLOYMENT STUDY

Each month the U.S. Bureau of Labor Statistics publishes a variety of unemployment statistics, including the number of individuals who are unemployed and the mean length of time the individuals have been unemployed. For November 1998, the Bureau of Labor Statistics reported that the national mean length of time of unemployment was 14.6 weeks.

The mayor of Philadelphia requested a study on the status of unemployment in the Philadelphia area. A sample of 50 unemployed residents of Philadelphia included data on the age and the number of weeks without a job. The data collected in November 1998 are available in the data set BLS.

Managerial Report

1. Use descriptive statistics to summarize the data.
2. Develop a 95% confidence interval estimate of the mean age of unemployed individuals in Philadelphia.
3. Conduct a hypothesis test to determine whether the mean duration of unemployment in Philadelphia is greater than the national mean duration of 14.6 weeks. Use a .01 level of significance. What is your conclusion?
4. Can a relationship between the age of an unemployed individual and the number of weeks of unemployment be identified? Explain.

Case Problem 2   QUALITY ASSOCIATES, INC.

Quality Associates, Inc., is a consulting firm that advises its clients about sampling and statistical procedures that can be used to control manufacturing processes. In one particular application, a client provided Quality Associates with a sample of 800 observations that were taken during a time in which the client's process was operating satisfactorily. The sample standard deviation for these data was .21; hence, with so much data, the population standard deviation was assumed to be .21. Quality Associates then suggested that random samples of size 30 be taken periodically to monitor the process on an ongoing basis. By analyzing the new samples, the client could quickly learn whether the process was operating satisfactorily. When the process was not operating satisfactorily, corrective action could be taken to eliminate the problem. The design specification indicated the mean for the process should be 12. The hypothesis test suggested by Quality Associates follows.

$$H_0: \mu = 12$$
$$H_a: \mu \neq 12$$

Corrective action will be taken any time H_0 is rejected.

The following four samples were collected during the first day of operation of the new statistical process control procedure. These data are available in the data set Quality.

Quality

Sample 1	Sample 2	Sample 3	Sample 4
11.55	11.62	11.91	12.02
11.62	11.69	11.36	12.02
11.52	11.59	11.75	12.05
11.75	11.82	11.95	12.18
11.90	11.97	12.14	12.11
11.64	11.71	11.72	12.07
11.80	11.87	11.61	12.05
12.03	12.10	11.85	11.64
11.94	12.01	12.16	12.39
11.92	11.99	11.91	11.65
12.13	12.20	12.12	12.11
12.09	12.16	11.61	11.90
11.93	12.00	12.21	12.22
12.21	12.28	11.56	11.88
12.32	12.39	11.95	12.03
11.93	12.00	12.01	12.35
11.85	11.92	12.06	12.09
11.76	11.83	11.76	11.77
12.16	12.23	11.82	12.20
11.77	11.84	12.12	11.79
12.00	12.07	11.60	12.30
12.04	12.11	11.95	12.27
11.98	12.05	11.96	12.29
12.30	12.37	12.22	12.47
12.18	12.25	11.75	12.03
11.97	12.04	11.96	12.17
12.17	12.24	11.95	11.94
11.85	11.92	11.89	11.97
12.30	12.37	11.88	12.23
12.15	12.22	11.93	12.25

Managerial Report

1. Conduct the hypothesis test for each sample at the .01 level of significance and determine what action, if any, should be taken. Provide the test statistic and *p*-value for each test.
2. Consider the standard deviation for each of the four samples. Does the assumption of .21 for the population standard deviation appear reasonable?
3. Compute limits for the sample mean $\bar{x}$ around $\mu = 12$ such that, as long as a new sample mean is within those limits, the process will be considered to be operating satisfactorily. If $\bar{x}$ exceeds the upper limit or if $\bar{x}$ is below the lower limit, corrective action will be taken. These limits are referred to as upper and lower control limits for quality control purposes.
4. Discuss the implications of changing the level of significance to a larger value. What mistake or error could increase if the level of significance were changed?

CHAPTER 10

Comparisons Involving Means

CONTENTS

STATISTICS IN PRACTICE

Fisons Corporation*

ROCHESTER, NEW YORK

Fisons Corporation, Rochester, New York, is a unit of Fisons Plc., UK. Fisons opened its U.S. operations in 1966.

Fisons' Pharmaceutical Division uses extensive statistical procedures to test and develop new drugs. The testing process in the pharmaceutical industry usually consists of three stages: (1) preclinical testing, (2) testing for long-term usage and safety, and (3) clinical efficacy testing. At each successive stage, the chance that a drug will pass the rigorous tests decreases; however, the cost of further testing increases dramatically. Industry surveys indicate that on average the research and development for one new drug costs $250 million and takes 12 years. Hence, it is important to eliminate unsuccessful new drugs in the early stages of the testing process, as well as identify promising ones for further testing.

Statistics plays a major role in pharmaceutical research, where government regulations are stringent and rigorously enforced. In preclinical testing, a two- or three-population statistical study typically is used to determine whether a new drug should continue in the long-term usage and safety program. The populations may consist of one using the new drug, one used as a control, and one using a standard drug. The preclinical testing process begins when a new drug is sent to the pharmacology group for evaluation of efficacy—the capacity of the drug to produce the desired effects. As part of the process, a statistician designs an experiment that can be used to test the new drug. The design must specify the sample size and the statistical methods of analysis. In a two-population study, one sample is used to obtain data on the efficacy of the new drug (population 1) and a second sample is used to obtain data on the efficacy of a standard drug (population 2). Depending on the intended use, the new and standard drugs are tested in such disciplines as neurology,

Statistical methods are used to test and develop new drugs.
© Mark Richards/PhotoEdit, Inc.

cardiology, and immunology. In most studies, the statistical method involves hypothesis testing for the difference between the means of the population using the new drug and the population using the standard drug. If a new drug lacks efficacy or produces undesirable effects in comparison with the standard drug, the new drug is withdrawn from further testing. Only new drugs that show promising comparisons with standard drugs move forward to the long-term usage and safety testing program.

Further data collection and multipopulation studies are conducted in the long-term usage and safety testing program and in the clinical testing programs. The Food and Drug Administration (FDA) requires that statistical methods be defined prior to such testing to avoid data-related biases. In addition, to avoid human biases, some of the clinical trials are double or triple blind. That is, neither the subject nor the investigator knows what drug is administered to whom. If the new drug meets all requirements in relation to the standard drug, a new drug application is filed with the FDA. The application is rigorously scrutinized by statisticians and scientists at the agency.

In this chapter you will learn how to make statistical inferences about means of two or more populations. Techniques will be presented for analyzing independent random samples as well as matched samples.

*The authors are indebted to Dr. M. C. Trivedi for providing this Statistics in Practice.

In Chapters 8 and 9 we showed how to develop interval estimates and conduct hypothesis tests for situations involving one population mean. In this chapter we continue our discussion of statistical inference by showing how interval estimates and hypothesis tests can be developed for situations involving two or more populations. For example, we may want to develop an interval estimate of the difference between the mean starting salary for a population of men and the mean starting salary for a population of women or test a hypothesis that the mean number of hours between breakdowns is the same for four machines. We begin our discussion by showing how an interval estimate of the difference between the means of two populations can be developed for a sampling study conducted by Greystone Department Stores, Inc. As usual, when a new procedure is introduced, we also show how it can be implemented using Excel.

10.1   ESTIMATION OF THE DIFFERENCE BETWEEN THE MEANS OF TWO POPULATIONS: INDEPENDENT SAMPLES

Greystone Department Stores, Inc., operates two stores in Buffalo, New York; one is in the inner city and the other is in a suburban shopping center. The regional manager noticed that products that sell well in one store do not always sell well in the other. The manager believes this situation may be attributable to differences in customer demographics at the two locations. Customers differ in age, education, income, and so on. Suppose the manager asks us to investigate the difference between the mean ages of the customers who shop at the two stores.

Let us define population 1 as all customers who shop at the inner-city store and population 2 as all customers who shop at the suburban store.

$$\mu_1 = \text{mean of population 1 (i.e., the mean age of all customers}$$
$$\text{who shop at the inner-city store)}$$

$$\mu_2 = \text{mean of population 2 (i.e., the mean age of all customers}$$
$$\text{who shop at the suburban store)}$$

The difference between the two population means is $\mu_1 - \mu_2$.

To estimate $\mu_1 - \mu_2$, we select a simple random sample of n_1 customers from population 1 and a simple random sample of n_2 customers from population 2. Because the simple random sample of n_1 customers is selected independently of the simple random sample of n_2 customers, they are **independent simple random samples.**

$$\bar{x}_1 = \text{sample mean age for the simple random sample of } n_1 \text{ inner-city customers}$$
$$\bar{x}_2 = \text{sample mean age for the simple random sample of } n_2 \text{ suburban customers}$$

Because $\bar{x}_1$ is a point estimator of μ_1 and $\bar{x}_2$ is a point estimator of μ_2, the point estimator of the difference between the two population means is expressed as follows.

Point Estimator of the Difference Between the Means of Two Populations

$$\bar{x}_1 - \bar{x}_2 \tag{10.1}$$

Thus, we see that the point estimator of the difference between the two population means is the difference between the sample means of the two independent simple random samples. Figure 10.1 provides an overview of the process used to estimate the difference between two population means based on two independent simple random samples.

FIGURE 10.1 ESTIMATING THE DIFFERENCE BETWEEN THE MEANS OF TWO POPULATIONS

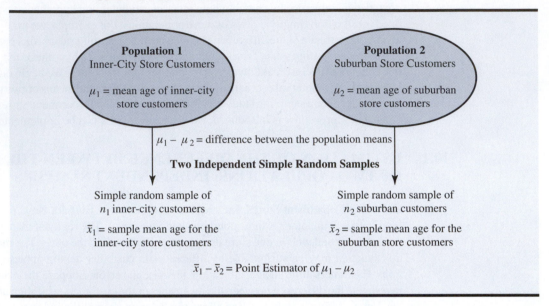

To estimate the difference between the mean ages of the two populations of Greystone Department Store customers, a simple random sample of 36 inner-city customers and a simple random sample of 49 suburban customers were selected. The data obtained are shown in Table 10.1; summary statistics are given in Table 10.2. Using expression (10.1), we find that a point estimate of the difference between the mean ages of the two populations is $\bar{x}_1 - \bar{x}_2 = 40 - 35 = 5$ years. Thus, we are led to believe that the customers at the inner-city store have a mean age 5 years greater than the mean age of the suburban store customers. However, as with all point estimates, we know that 5 years is only one of many possible estimates of the difference between the mean ages of the two populations. If Greystone selected another simple random sample of 36 inner-city customers and another simple

TABLE 10.1 DATA SET FOR THE GREYSTONE DEPARTMENT STORES STUDY

CD file

Greystone

Inner-City Customers				Suburban Customers				
39	35	43	34	28	33	46	39	25
44	41	21	39	36	40	43	38	47
28	41	34	52	41	50	38	46	35
20	49	37	26	14	13	18	37	24
39	45	45	48	39	35	22	16	17
42	57	46	58	57	40	34	35	19
37	43	41		36	35	40	29	45
37	41	53		36	41	39	37	23
34	45	42		38	29	35	36	54
38	44	22		36	42	44	35	

TABLE 10.2   SAMPLE STATISTICS FOR GREYSTONE DEPARTMENT STORES

Store	Number of Customers Sampled	Sample Mean Age	Sample Standard Deviation
Inner City	$n_1 = 36$	$\bar{x}_1 = 40$ years	$s_1 = 9$ years
Suburban	$n_2 = 49$	$\bar{x}_2 = 35$ years	$s_2 = 10$ years

random sample of 49 suburban customers, the difference between the two new sample means would probably not equal 5 years. The sampling distribution of $\bar{x}_1 - \bar{x}_2$ is the probability distribution of the difference in sample means for all possible sets of two independent simple random samples.

Sampling Distribution of $\bar{x}_1 - \bar{x}_2$

We can use the sampling distribution of $\bar{x}_1 - \bar{x}_2$ to develop an interval estimate of the difference between the two population means in much the same way as we used the sampling distribution of $\bar{x}$ for interval estimation with a single population mean. The sampling distribution of $\bar{x}_1 - \bar{x}_2$ has the following properties.

Sampling Distribution of $\bar{x}_1 - \bar{x}_2$

The standard deviation of the sampling distribution of $\bar{x}_1 - \bar{x}_2$ is also referred to as the standard error of the point estimator $\bar{x}_1 - \bar{x}_2$.

$$\text{Expected Value:} \quad E(\bar{x}_1 - \bar{x}_2) = \mu_1 - \mu_2 \tag{10.2}$$

$$\text{Standard Deviation:} \quad \sigma_{\bar{x}_1 - \bar{x}_2} = \sqrt{\frac{\sigma_1^2}{n_1} + \frac{\sigma_2^2}{n_2}} \tag{10.3}$$

where

$\sigma_1 = $ standard deviation of population 1

$\sigma_2 = $ standard deviation of population 2

$n_1 = $ sample size for the simple random sample from population 1

$n_2 = $ sample size for the simple random sample from population 2

Distribution form: If the sample sizes are both *large* ($n_1 \geq 30$ and $n_2 \geq 30$), the sampling distribution of $\bar{x}_1 - \bar{x}_2$ can be approximated by a normal probability distribution.

Figure 10.2 shows the sampling distribution of $\bar{x}_1 - \bar{x}_2$ and its relationship to the individual sampling distributions of $\bar{x}_1$ and $\bar{x}_2$.

Let us now develop an interval estimate of the difference between the means of two populations. We consider two cases, one in which the sample sizes are large ($n_1 \geq 30$ and $n_2 \geq 30$) and another in which one or both sample sizes are small ($n_1 < 30$ and/or $n_2 < 30$). We consider the large-sample case first.

FIGURE 10.2   SAMPLING DISTRIBUTION OF $\bar{x}_1 - \bar{x}_2$ AND ITS RELATIONSHIP
TO THE INDIVIDUAL SAMPLING DISTRIBUTION OF $\bar{x}_1$ AND $\bar{x}_2$

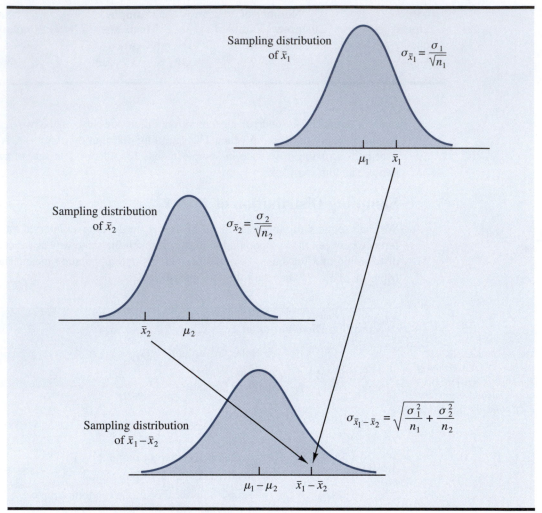

Large-Sample Case

In the large-sample case, the central limit theorem is applicable and thus the sampling distribution of $\bar{x}_1 - \bar{x}_2$ can be approximated by a normal probability distribution. With this approximation we can use the following expression to develop an interval estimate of the difference between the means of the two populations.

**Interval Estimate of the Difference Between the Means of Two Populations:
Large-Sample Case ($n_1 \geq 30$ and $n_2 \geq 30$) with σ_1 and σ_2 Assumed Known**

$$\bar{x}_1 - \bar{x}_2 \pm z_{\alpha/2}\sigma_{\bar{x}_1-\bar{x}_2} \tag{10.4}$$

where $1 - \alpha$ is the confidence coefficient.

Note that to use expression (10.4) to develop an interval estimate of the difference between the means of two populations, we must know the value of $\sigma_{\bar{x}_1 - \bar{x}_2}$, the standard error of the point estimator $\bar{x}_1 - \bar{x}_2$. However, equation (10.3) shows that the value of $\sigma_{\bar{x}_1 - \bar{x}_2}$ depends on the values of σ_1 and σ_2, the standard deviations of each of the populations. If the population standard deviations are unknown, we use the sample standard deviations as estimates of the population standard deviations and estimate $\sigma_{\bar{x}_1 - \bar{x}_2}$ as follows.

Point Estimator of $\sigma_{\bar{x}_1 - \bar{x}_2}$

$$s_{\bar{x}_1 - \bar{x}_2} = \sqrt{\frac{s_1^2}{n_1} + \frac{s_2^2}{n_2}} \qquad (10.5)$$

Thus when σ_1 and σ_2 are estimated by s_1 and s_2, we can use $s_{\bar{x}_1 - \bar{x}_2}$ to develop the following confidence interval estimate of the difference between the two population means in the large-sample case.

Interval Estimate of the Difference Between the Means of Two Populations: Large-Sample Case ($n_1 \geq 30$ and $n_2 \geq 30$) with σ_1 and σ_2 Estimated by s_1 and s_2

$$\bar{x}_1 - \bar{x}_2 \pm z_{\alpha/2} s_{\bar{x}_1 - \bar{x}_2} \qquad (10.6)$$

where $1 - \alpha$ is the confidence coefficient.

Let us use expression (10.6) to develop a confidence interval estimate of the difference between the mean ages of the two customer populations in the Greystone Department Store study. Recall that the sample mean age and sample standard deviation for the simple random sample of 36 inner-city customers are $\bar{x}_1 = 40$ years and $s_1 = 9$ years, respectively; the sample mean and sample standard deviation for the simple random sample of 49 suburban customers are $\bar{x}_2 = 35$ years and $s_2 = 10$ years, respectively. Using equation (10.5) to estimate $\sigma_{\bar{x}_1 - \bar{x}_2}$ we have

$$s_{\bar{x}_1 - \bar{x}_2} = \sqrt{\frac{(9)^2}{36} + \frac{(10)^2}{49}} = 2.07$$

With $z_{\alpha/2} = z_{.025} = 1.96$, expression (10.6) provides the following 95% confidence interval.

$$5 \pm (1.96)(2.07)$$

or

$$5 \pm 4.06$$

Thus, at a 95% level of confidence, the margin of error is 4.06 years and the interval estimate of the difference between the mean ages of the two Greystone populations is .94 years to 9.06 years.

Using Excel: Large-Sample Case

Excel can be used to develop an interval estimate of the difference between the population means in the Greystone Department Stores study. Except for the fact that we are working with two samples, the procedure is similar to the approach used to develop an interval estimate for a single population mean described in Chapter 8. Refer to Figure 10.3 as we describe the tasks involved. The formula worksheet is in the background; the value worksheet is in the foreground.

Enter Data: Column A contains the age data for the simple random sample of 36 inner-city customers, and column B contains the age data for the simple random sample of 49 suburban customers.

Enter Functions and Formulas: The descriptive statistics needed are provided in cells E5:F7. The confidence coefficient is entered into cell E9 (.95) and the corresponding level of significance is computed in cell E10. In cell E11 we use the NORMSINV function to compute the z value needed for the interval estimate.

Using the two sample standard deviations and sample sizes, $s_{\bar{x}_1 - \bar{x}_2}$ is computed by entering the following formula into cell E13:

$$=\text{SQRT(E7\^{}2/E5+F7\^{}2/F5)}$$

This cell formula is the Excel equivalent of equation (10.5). The margin of error computed in cell E14 multiplies the z value times the estimate of the standard error.

In cell E16 the difference in the sample means is used to compute the point estimate of the difference in the two population means. The lower limit of the confidence interval computed in cell E17 (.94) and the upper limit computed in cell E18 (9.06) provide the 95% confidence interval estimate of the difference in the two population means of .94 to 9.06.

FIGURE 10.3 EXCEL WORKSHEET FOR THE GREYSTONE DEPARTMENT STORES STUDY

	A	B	C	D	E	F	G
1	Inner City	Suburban		Interval Estimate: Difference in Population Means			
2	39	28		Using the Standard Normal Distribution (z)			
3	44	36					
4	28	41			Inner City	Suburban	
5	20	14		Sample Size	=COUNT(A2:A37)	=COUNT(B2:B50)	
6	39	39		Mean	=AVERAGE(A2:A37)	=AVERAGE(B2:B50)	
7	42	57		Standard Deviation	=STDEV(A2:A37)	=STDEV(B2:B50)	
8	37	36					
9	37	36		Confidence Coefficient	0.95		
10	34	38		Level of Significance (alpha)	=1-E9		
11	38	36		z Value	=NORMSINV(1-E10/2)		
12	35	33					
13	41	40		Standard Error	=SQRT(E7^2/E5+F7^2/F5)		
14	41	50		Margin of Error	=E11*E13		
15	49	13					
16	45	35		Point Estimate of Difference	=E6-F6		
17	57	40		Lower Limit	=E16-E14		
18	43	35		Upper Limit	=E16+E14		
36	48	16					
37	58	35					
49		23					
50		54					
51							

	A	B	C	D	E	F	G	H
1	Inner City	Suburban		Interval Estimate: Difference in Population Means				
2	39	28		Using the Standard Normal Distribution (z)				
3	44	36						
4	28	41			Inner City	Suburban		
5	20	14		Sample Size	36	49		
6	39	39		Mean	40	35		
7	42	57		Standard Deviation	9.00	10		
8	37	36						
9	37	36		Confidence Coefficient	0.95			
10	34	38		Level of Significance (alpha)	0.05			
11	38	36		z Value	1.960			
12	35	33						
13	41	40		Standard Error	2.07			
14	41	50		Margin of Error	4.06			
15	49	13						
16	45	35		Point Estimate of Difference	5			
17	57	40		Lower Limit	0.94			
18	43	35		Upper Limit	9.06			
36	48	16						
37	58	35						
49		23						
50		54						
51								

Note: Rows 19–35 and 38–48 are hidden.

Small-Sample Case

Let us now consider the interval estimation procedure for the difference between the means of two populations whenever one or both sample sizes are less than 30; that is, $n_1 < 30$ and/or $n_2 < 30$, which will be referred to as the small-sample case.

In Chapter 8, we presented the small-sample interval estimation procedures for a population mean. Recall that the small-sample case required the assumption that the population has a normal probability distribution. If the population standard deviation σ can be assumed known, the standard normal distribution z is used to develop the interval estimate. However, if the population standard deviation σ is estimated by the sample standard deviation s, we use the t distribution to develop the interval estimate.

When σ_1 and σ_2 are estimated by s_1 and s_2, the t distribution is used to develop the small-sample interval estimate of the difference between two population means.

In developing a small-sample interval estimate of the difference between two population means, we make the assumption that both populations have a normal probability distribution. If the population standard deviations σ_1 and σ_2 are assumed known, the large-sample interval estimation procedure provided by expression (10.4) can be used for the small-sample case. However, if the population standard deviations σ_1 and σ_2 are estimated by the sample standard deviations s_1 and s_2, the t distribution is required to develop a small-sample interval estimate of the difference between two population means. The details of this procedure and an example follow. We begin by making the following assumptions:

1. Both populations have normal probability distributions.
2. The variances of the populations are equal ($\sigma_1^2 = \sigma_2^2 = \sigma^2$).

If the sample sizes are equal, the procedure in this section provides acceptable results even if the population variances are not equal. Thus, whenever possible, a researcher should use equal sample sizes.

Given these assumptions, the sampling distribution of $\bar{x}_1 - \bar{x}_2$ is normally distributed regardless of the sample sizes. The expected value of $\bar{x}_1 - \bar{x}_2$ is $\mu_1 - \mu_2$. Because of the equal variances assumption, equation (10.3) can be written

$$\sigma_{\bar{x}_1 - \bar{x}_2} = \sqrt{\frac{\sigma^2}{n_1} + \frac{\sigma^2}{n_2}} = \sqrt{\sigma^2\left(\frac{1}{n_1} + \frac{1}{n_2}\right)} \qquad (10.7)$$

The sampling distribution of $\bar{x}_1 - \bar{x}_2$ is shown in Figure 10.4.

FIGURE 10.4   SAMPLING DISTRIBUTION OF $\bar{x}_1 - \bar{x}_2$ WHEN THE POPULATIONS HAVE NORMAL DISTRIBUTIONS WITH EQUAL VARIANCES

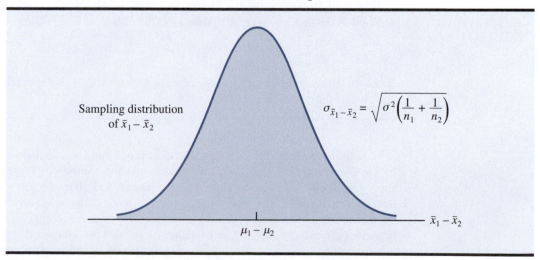

Sampling distribution of $\bar{x}_1 - \bar{x}_2$

$\sigma_{\bar{x}_1 - \bar{x}_2} = \sqrt{\sigma^2\left(\frac{1}{n_1} + \frac{1}{n_2}\right)}$

$\mu_1 - \mu_2$

$\bar{x}_1 - \bar{x}_2$

Because equation (10.7) is based on the assumption that $\sigma_1^2 = \sigma_2^2 = \sigma^2$, we do not need separate estimates of σ_1^2 and σ_2^2. In fact, we can combine the data from the two samples to provide a single estimate of σ^2. The process of combining the results of two independent simple random samples to provide one estimate of σ^2 is referred to as *pooling*. The **pooled variance** estimator of σ^2, denoted by s^2, is a weighted average of the two sample variances s_1^2 and s_2^2. The formula for the pooled estimator of σ^2 follows.

Pooled Variance Estimator of σ^2

$$s^2 = \frac{(n_1 - 1)s_1^2 + (n_2 - 1)s_2^2}{n_1 + n_2 - 2} \qquad (10.8)$$

With s^2 as the pooled estimator of σ^2, we can substitute s^2 into equation (10.7) to obtain the following estimator of $\sigma_{\bar{x}_1 - \bar{x}_2}$.

Point Estimator of $\sigma_{\bar{x}_1 - \bar{x}_2}$ When $\sigma_1^2 = \sigma_2^2 = \sigma^2$

$$s_{\bar{x}_1 - \bar{x}_2} = \sqrt{s^2 \left(\frac{1}{n_1} + \frac{1}{n_2} \right)} \qquad (10.9)$$

The t distribution can now be used to compute an interval estimate of the difference between the means of the two populations. Because $n_1 - 1$ degrees of freedom are associated with the sample from population 1 and $n_2 - 1$ degrees of freedom are associated with the sample from population 2, the t distribution will have $n_1 + n_2 - 2$ degrees of freedom. The interval estimator is as follows.

Interval Estimate of the Difference Between the Means of Two Populations: Small-Sample Case ($n_1 < 30$ and/or $n_2 < 30$) with σ_1 and σ_2 Estimated by s_1 and s_2

$$\bar{x}_1 - \bar{x}_2 \pm t_{\alpha/2} s_{\bar{x}_1 - \bar{x}_2} \qquad (10.10)$$

where the t value is based on a t distribution with $n_1 + n_2 - 2$ degrees of freedom and $1 - \alpha$ is the confidence coefficient.

Let us demonstrate the interval estimation procedure for a sampling study conducted by the Clearview National Bank. Independent random samples of checking account balances for 12 customers at the Cherry Grove branch and 10 customers at the Beechmont Branch were selected. The data obtained and summary statistics appear in Table 10.3.

Let us use these sample results to develop a 90% confidence interval for the difference between the mean checking account balances at the two branch banks. Suppose that checking account balances are normally distributed at both branches and that the variances of

TABLE 10.3   CHECKING ACCOUNT BALANCE DATA AND SUMMARY STATISTICS FOR THE CLEARVIEW NATIONAL BANK STUDY

CD file

Clearview

	Cherry Grove	Beechmont
	1208	1081
	983	971
	1037	1032
	836	886
	978	958
	915	1043
	996	734
	699	747
	1223	906
	1085	842
	1119	
	921	

Summary Statistics

Sample Size	$n_1 = 12$	$n_2 = 10$
Sample Mean	$\bar{x}_1 = 1000$	$\bar{x}_2 = 920$
Sample Standard Deviation	$s_1 = 150$	$s_2 = 120$

checking account balances at the branches are equal. Using equation (10.8), the pooled estimate of the population variance becomes

$$s^2 = \frac{(n_1 - 1)s_1^2 + (n_2 - 1)s_2^2}{n_1 + n_2 - 2} = \frac{(11)(150)^2 + (9)(120)^2}{12 + 10 - 2} = 18{,}855$$

Using equation (10.9), the corresponding estimate of $\sigma_{\bar{x}_1 - \bar{x}_2}$ is

$$s_{\bar{x}_1 - \bar{x}_2} = \sqrt{s^2\left(\frac{1}{n_1} + \frac{1}{n_2}\right)} = \sqrt{18{,}855\left(\frac{1}{12} + \frac{1}{10}\right)} = 58.79$$

The appropriate t distribution for the interval estimation procedure has $n_1 + n_2 - 2 = 12 + 10 - 2 = 20$ degrees of freedom. With $\alpha = .10$, $t_{\alpha/2} = t_{.05} = 1.725$. Thus, using expression (10.10), the interval estimate is

$$\bar{x}_1 - \bar{x}_2 \pm t_{.05}\, s_{\bar{x}_1 - \bar{x}_2}$$
$$1000 - 920 \pm (1.725)(58.79)$$
$$80 \pm 101.41$$

At a 90% confidence level, the margin of error is $101.41 and the interval estimate of the difference between the mean account balances at the two branch banks is −$21.41 to $181.41. The fact that the interval includes a negative range of values indicates that the actual difference between the two means, $\mu_1 - \mu_2$, may be negative. Thus, μ_2 could actually be larger than μ_1, indicating that the population mean balance could be greater for the Beechmont branch even though the results show a greater sample mean balance at the Cherry Grove branch. The fact that the confidence interval contains the value 0 can be interpreted as indicating that we do not have sufficient evidence to conclude that the population mean account balances differ between the two branches.

Using Excel: Small-Sample Case

Excel can be used to develop an interval estimate of the difference between the population means at the two branches of the Clearview National Bank. Refer to Figure 10.5 as we describe the tasks involved. The formula worksheet is in the background; the value worksheet is in the foreground.

Enter Data: Column A contains the data for the simple random sample of 12 Cherry Grove customers, and column B contains the data for the simple random sample of 10 Beechmont customers.

Enter Functions and Formulas: The descriptive statistics needed to compute the interval estimate are provided in cells E5:F7. The confidence coefficient is entered into cell E9 (.90) and the corresponding level of significance is computed in cell E10. The degrees of freedom is computed in cell E11, and the TINV function used in cell E12 computes the t value needed to develop the interval estimate.

Using the two sample standard deviations and sample sizes, the pooled variance estimate of the population variance is computed by entering the following formula into cell E14:

=((E5−1)*E7^2+(F5−1)*F7^2)/E11

This cell formula is the Excel equivalent of equation (10.8).

A point estimate of $\sigma_{\bar{x}_1-\bar{x}_2}$, the standard error of the point estimator $\bar{x}_1 - \bar{x}_2$, is computed by entering the following formula into cell E15:

=SQRT(E14*(1/E5+1/F5))

This cell formula is the Excel equivalent of equation (10.9). The margin of error computed in cell E16 multiplies the t value times the standard error.

FIGURE 10.5 EXCEL WORKSHEET FOR THE CLEARVIEW NATIONAL BANK STUDY

	A	B	C	D	E	F	G
1	Cherry Grove	Beechmont		Interval Estimate: Difference in Population Means			
2	1208	1081		Using the *t* Distribution			
3	983	971					
4	1037	1032			Cherry Grove	Beechmont	
5	836	886		Sample Size	=COUNT(A2:A13)	=COUNT(B2:B11)	
6	978	958		Mean	=AVERAGE(A2:A13)	=AVERAGE(B2:B11)	
7	915	1043		Standard Deviation	=STDEV(A2:A13)	=STDEV(B2:B11)	
8	996	734					
9	699	747		Confidence Coefficient	0.9		
10	1223	906		Level of Significance (alpha)	=1-E9		
11	1085	842		Degrees of Freedom	=E5+F5-2		
12	1119			*t* Value	=TINV(E10,E11)		
13	921						
14				Pooled Estimate of Variance	=((E5-1)*E7^2+(F5-1)*F7^2)/E11		
15				Standard Error	=SQRT(E14*(1/E5+1/F5))		
16				Margin of Error	=E12*E15		
17							
18				Point Estimate of Difference	=E6-F6		
19				Lower Limit	=E18-E16		
20				Upper Limit	=E18+E16		
21							

	A	B	C	D	E	F
1	Cherry Grove	Beechmont		Interval Estimate: Difference in Population Means		
2	1208	1081		Using the *t* Distribution		
3	983	971				
4	1037	1032			Cherry Grove	Beechmont
5	836	886		Sample Size	12	10
6	978	958		Mean	1000	920
7	915	1043		Standard Deviation	150	120
8	996	734				
9	699	747		Confidence Coefficient	0.9	
10	1223	906		Level of Significance (alpha)	0.1	
11	1085	842		Degrees of Freedom	20	
12	1119			*t* Value	1.725	
13	921					
14				Pooled Estimate of Variance	18855	
15				Standard Error	58.79	
16				Margin of Error	101.40	
17						
18				Point Estimate of Difference	80	
19				Lower Limit	-21.40	
20				Upper Limit	181.40	
21						

In cell E18 the difference in the sample means is used to compute the point estimate of the difference in the two population means. The lower limit of the confidence interval computed in cell E19 (−21.40) and the upper limit computed in cell E20 (181.40) provide the 90% confidence interval estimate of the difference in the two population means: −21.40 to 181.40.*

NOTES AND COMMENTS

1. The use of the t distribution in the small-sample case is based on the assumptions that both populations have normal probability distributions and $\sigma_1^2 = \sigma_2^2$. Fortunately, this procedure is a *robust* statistical procedure, meaning that it is relatively insensitive to these assumptions. For instance, if $\sigma_1^2 \neq \sigma_2^2$ the procedure provides acceptable results if n_1 and n_2 are approximately equal.

2. The t distribution is not restricted to the small-sample situation; it is applicable whenever both populations are normally distributed and the variances of the populations are equal. However, expressions (10.4) and (10.6) show how to compute an interval estimate of the difference between the means of two populations when the sample sizes are large. Thus, in the large-sample case, use of the t distribution and its corresponding normality assumption is not required. We therefore do not refer to the t distribution until we have a small-sample case.

EXERCISES

Methods

1. Consider the following results for two independent random samples taken from two populations.

Sample 1	Sample 2
$n_1 = 50$	$n_2 = 35$
$\bar{x}_1 = 13.6$	$\bar{x}_2 = 11.6$
$s_1 = 2.2$	$s_2 = 3.0$

    a. What is the point estimate of the difference between the two population means?
    b. Provide a 90% confidence interval for the difference between the two population means.
    c. Provide a 95% confidence interval for the difference between the two population means.

2. Consider the following results for two independent simple random samples taken from two populations.

Sample 1	Sample 2
$n_1 = 10$	$n_2 = 8$
$\bar{x}_1 = 22.5$	$\bar{x}_2 = 20.1$
$s_1 = 2.5$	$s_2 = 2.0$

    a. What is the point estimate of the difference between the two population means?
    b. What is the pooled estimate of the population variance?
    c. Develop a 95% confidence interval for the difference between the two population means.

---

*This interval differs by .01 from the interval obtained earlier (−21.41 to 181.41), because the t value generated using Excel is more accurate.

3. Consider the following data for two independent simple random samples taken from two populations.

Sample 1		Sample 2	
10	7	8	7
12	7	8	4
9	9	6	9

   a. Compute the two sample means.
   b. Compute the two sample standard deviations.
   c. What is the point estimate of the difference between the two population means?
   d. What is the pooled estimate of the population variance?
   e. Develop a 95% confidence interval for the difference between the two population means.

Applications

4. Gasoline prices increased substantially from 1999 to 2000. The American Automobile Association provided information on the mean cost per gallon for self-serve regular unleaded gasoline over the two years (*AAA Going Places,* May/June 2000). Assume the following results were obtained from independent samples of locations throughout the country.

2000 Cost	1999 Cost
$\bar{x}_1 = \$1.58$	$\bar{x}_2 = \$0.98$
$s_1 = \$0.12$	$s_2 = \$0.08$
$n_1 = 50$	$n_2 = 42$

   a. What is the point estimate of the increase in the mean cost per gallon from 1999 to 2000?
   b. What is the 95% confidence interval estimate of the increase in the mean cost per gallon from 1999 to 2000?

Miles

5. Data gathered by the U.S. Department of Transportation show the number of miles that residents of the 75 largest metropolitan areas travel per day in a car. Suppose that a simple random sample of 50 Buffalo residents and an independent simple random sample of 100 Boston residents resulted in the miles traveled data shown in the data set named Miles.
   a. What is the point estimate of the difference between the mean number of miles that Buffalo residents travel per day and the mean number of miles that Boston residents travel per day?
   b. What is the 95% confidence interval for the difference between the two population means?

6. The International Air Transport Association surveyed business travelers to determine ratings of various international airports. The maximum possible rating score was 10. Suppose 50 business travelers were asked to rate the Miami airport, and 50 other business travelers were asked to rate the Los Angeles airport. The rating scores follow.

Airport

Miami

6	4	6	8	7	7	6	3	3	8	10	4	8
7	8	7	5	9	5	8	4	3	8	5	5	4
4	4	8	4	5	6	2	5	9	9	8	4	8
9	9	5	9	7	8	3	10	8	9	6		

Los Angeles

10	9	6	7	8	7	9	8	10	7	6	5	7
3	5	6	8	7	10	8	4	7	8	6	9	9
5	3	1	8	9	6	8	5	4	6	10	9	8
3	2	7	9	5	3	10	3	5	10	8		

Develop a 95% confidence interval estimate of the difference between the mean ratings of the Miami and Los Angeles airports.

7. A Cornell University study of wage differentials between men and women reported that one of the reasons wages for men are higher than wages for women is that men tend to have more years of work experience than women (*Business Week*, August 28, 2000). Assume the following sample summaries show the years of experience for each group.

Men	Women
$\bar{x}_1 = 14.9$ years	$\bar{x}_2 = 10.3$ years
$s_1 = 5.2$ years	$s_2 = 3.8$ years
$n_1 = 100$	$n_2 = 85$

a. What is the point estimate of the difference between the two population means?
b. At 95% confidence, what is the margin of error?
c. What is the 95% confidence interval estimate of the difference between the two population means?

8. An urban planning group wants to estimate the difference between the mean household incomes for two neighborhoods in a large metropolitan area. Independent random samples of households in the neighborhoods provide the following results.

Neighborhood 1	Neighborhood 2
$n_1 = 8$	$n_2 = 12$
$\bar{x}_1 = \$45,700$	$\bar{x}_2 = \$44,500$
$s_1 = \$700$	$s_2 = \$850$

a. Develop a point estimate of the difference between the mean incomes in the two neighborhoods.
b. Develop a 95% confidence interval for the difference between the mean incomes in the two neighborhoods.
c. What assumptions were made to compute the interval estimates in part (b)?

9. The National Association of Home Builders provided data on the cost of the most popular home remodeling projects (*USA Today*, June 17, 1997). Sample data on the cost (in thousands of dollars) for two types of remodeling projects follow.

Kitchen	Master Bedroom
25.2	18.0
17.4	22.9

(continued)

Kitchen	Master Bedroom
22.8	26.4
21.9	24.8
19.7	26.9
23.0	17.8
19.7	24.6
16.9	21.0
21.8	
23.6	

a. Develop a point estimate of the difference between the population mean remodeling costs for the two types of projects.
b. Develop a 90% confidence interval for the difference between the two population means.

10. Suppose independent random samples of 15 unionized women and 20 nonunionized women in manufacturing provided the following hourly wage rates.

Union Workers

22.40	18.90	16.70	14.05	16.20	20.00	16.10	16.30	19.10
16.50	18.50	19.80	17.00	14.30	17.20			

Nonunion Workers

17.60	14.40	16.60	15.00	17.65	15.00	17.55	13.30	11.20
15.90	19.20	11.85	16.65	15.20	15.30	17.00	15.10	14.30
13.90	14.50							

a. What is the point estimate of the difference between the hourly wages for the two populations?
b. What is the pooled estimate of the population variance?
c. Develop a 95% confidence interval estimate of the difference between the two population means.
d. Does there appear to be any difference in the mean wage rate for these two groups? Explain.

10.2 HYPOTHESIS TESTS ABOUT THE DIFFERENCE BETWEEN THE MEANS OF TWO POPULATIONS: INDEPENDENT SAMPLES

In this section we present procedures that can be used to test hypotheses about the difference between the means of two populations. The methodology is again divided into large-sample ($n_1 \geq 30$ and $n_2 \geq 30$) and small-sample ($n_1 < 30$ and/or $n_2 < 30$) cases.

Large-Sample Case

As part of a study to evaluate differences in educational quality between two training centers, a standardized examination is given to individuals who are trained at the two centers.

The examination scores are a major factor in assessing quality differences between the centers. The population means for the two centers follow.

$$\mu_1 = \text{the mean examination score for all individuals trained at center A}$$

$$\mu_2 = \text{the mean examination score for all individuals trained at center B}$$

We begin with the tentative assumption that no difference exists in the training quality provided at the two centers. Hence, in terms of the mean examination scores, the null hypothesis is that $\mu_1 - \mu_2 = 0$. If sample evidence leads to the rejection of this hypothesis, we will conclude that the mean examination scores differ for the two populations. This conclusion indicates a quality differential between the two centers and that a follow-up study investigating the reasons for the differential may be warranted. The null and alternative hypotheses are written as follows.

$$H_0: \mu_1 - \mu_2 = 0$$
$$H_a: \mu_1 - \mu_2 \neq 0$$

Following the hypothesis testing procedure from Chapter 9, we make the tentative assumption that H_0 is true. Using the difference between the sample means as the point estimator of the difference between the population means, we base the hypothesis test on the sampling distribution of $\bar{x}_1 - \bar{x}_2$ when H_0 is true. For the large-sample case, this distribution is as shown in Figure 10.6. Because the sampling distribution of $\bar{x}_1 - \bar{x}_2$ can be approximated by a normal probability distribution, the following test statistic is used.

$$z = \frac{(\bar{x}_1 - \bar{x}_2) - (\mu_1 - \mu_2)}{\sqrt{\sigma_1^2/n_1 + \sigma_2^2/n_2}} \qquad (10.11)$$

FIGURE 10.6   SAMPLING DISTRIBUTION OF $\bar{x}_1 - \bar{x}_2$ WITH $H_0: \mu_1 - \mu_2 = 0$

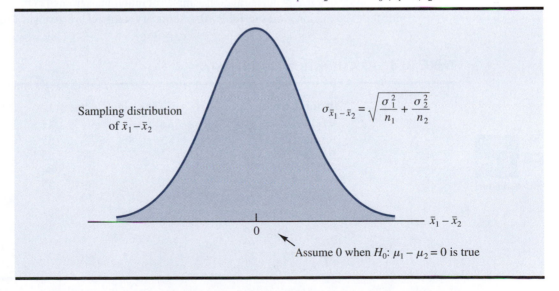

FIGURE 10.7   REJECTION REGION FOR THE TWO-TAILED HYPOTHESIS TEST WITH $\alpha = .05$ AND $H_0: \mu_1 - \mu_2 = 0$

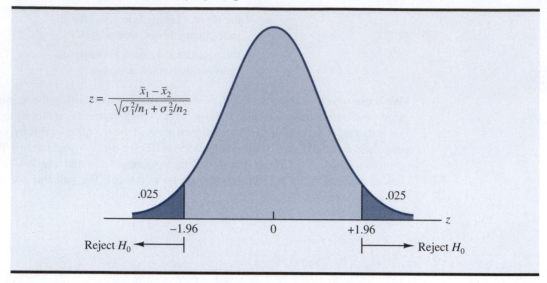

$$z = \frac{\bar{x}_1 - \bar{x}_2}{\sqrt{\sigma_1^2/n_1 + \sigma_2^2/n_2}}$$

.025   .025

−1.96   0   +1.96 z

Reject H_0 Reject H_0

Whenever $n_1 \geq 30$, $n_2 \geq 30$, and σ_1^2 and σ_2^2 are unknown, we will use s_1^2 and s_2^2 as estimates of σ_1^2 and σ_2^2 to compute the test statistic.

The value of z given by equation (10.11) can be interpreted as the number of standard errors $\bar{x}_1 - \bar{x}_2$ is from the value of $\mu_1 - \mu_2$ specified in H_0. For $\alpha = .05$ and thus $z_{\alpha/2} = z_{.025} = 1.96$, the rejection region for the two-tailed hypothesis test is shown in Figure 10.7. The rejection rule is as follows:

Using test statistic: Reject H_0 if $z < -1.96$ or if $z > +1.96$
Using p-value: Reject H_0 if p-value $< .05$

Suppose that independent random samples of individuals trained at the two centers provide the examination scores in Table 10.4; summary statistics are given in Table 10.5. Using

TABLE 10.4   EXAMINATION SCORE DATA

CD file

ExamData

Training Center A			Training Center B			
97	83	91	64	66	91	84
90	84	87	85	83	78	85
94	76	73	72	74	87	85
79	82	92	64	70	93	84
78	85	64	74	82	89	59
87	85	74	93	82	79	62
83	91	88	70	75	84	91
89	72	88	79	78	65	83
76	86	74	79	99	78	80
84	70	73	75	57	66	76

TABLE 10.5   DESCRIPTIVE STATISTICS FOR TWO INDEPENDENT SIMPLE RANDOM SAMPLES OF EXAMINATION SCORES

Training Center A	Training Center B
$n_1 = 30$	$n_2 = 40$
$\bar{x}_1 = 82.5$	$\bar{x}_2 = 78$
$s_1 = 8$	$s_2 = 10$

s_1^2 and s_2^2 to estimate σ_1^2 and σ_2^2, we find that the test statistic z given by equation (10.11) for the null hypothesis $H_0: \mu_1 - \mu_2 = 0$ becomes

$$z = \frac{(82.5 - 78) - 0}{\sqrt{(8)^2/30 + (10)^2/40}} = 2.09$$

Because $z = 2.09 > 1.96$, the conclusion is to reject H_0. Thus, we can conclude that μ_1 and μ_2 are not equal and that the two centers differ in terms of educational quality.

In a two-tailed test, the p-value is computed by doubling the area in the tail.

With $z = 2.09$, the standard normal probability distribution table can be used to compute the p-value for this two-tailed test. Using the cumulative standard normal probability table, we find that the area to the right of $z = 2.09$ is $1 - .9817 = .0183$. Thus, the p-value is $2(.0183) = .0366$. Because the p-value is less than $\alpha = .05$, the p-value approach also results in the rejection of H_0.

In this hypothesis test, we wanted to determine whether the means of the two populations are different. If we have no prior belief that one mean might be greater than or less than the other, then the hypotheses $H_0: \mu_1 - \mu_2 = 0$ and $H_a: \mu_1 - \mu_2 \neq 0$ are appropriate. In other hypothesis tests about the difference between the means of two populations, we may want to find out whether one mean is greater than or perhaps less than the other mean. In these cases, a one-tailed hypothesis test would be appropriate. The two forms of a one-tailed hypothesis test about the difference between two population means follow.

$$H_0: \mu_1 - \mu_2 \leq 0 \qquad H_0: \mu_1 - \mu_2 \geq 0$$
$$H_a: \mu_1 - \mu_2 > 0 \qquad H_a: \mu_1 - \mu_2 < 0$$

In the large-sample case, these hypotheses are tested by using the test statistic z given by equation (10.11). The rejection region for the first test is in the upper tail and the rejection region for the second test is in the lower tail.

Using Excel: Large-Sample Case

Excel's z-Test: Two Sample for Means tool can be used to conduct a hypothesis test about the difference between the population means in the training center study. Refer to the Excel worksheet shown in Figure 10.8 and the dialog box in Figure 10.9 as we describe the tasks involved. Only two formulas are used, so we will not show the formula worksheet in the background.

Enter Data: Column A contains the examination score data for the simple random sample of 30 individuals trained at center A, and column B contains the examination score data for the simple random sample of 40 individuals trained at center B.

Enter Functions and Formulas: To use Excel's z-Test: Two Sample for Means tool we must first compute the sample variance for both samples. To compute the sample variance

FIGURE 10.8 EXCEL WORKSHEET FOR THE TRAINING CENTER STUDY

	A	B	C	D	E	F	G	H	I
1	Center A	Center B			Center A	Center B			
2	97	64		**Sample Variance**	64.0517	100		Formula: =VAR(B2:B41)	
3	90	85							
4	94	72		z-Test: Two Sample for Means					
5	79	64						Formula: =VAR(A2:A31)	
6	78	74			Center A	Center B			
7	87	93		Mean	82.5	78			
8	83	70		Known Variance	64.0517	100			
9	89	79		Observations	30	40			
10	76	79		Hypothesized Mean Difference	0				
11	84	75		z	2.09				
12	83	66		P(Z<=z) one-tail	0.0183				
13	84	83		z Critical one-tail	1.645				
14	76	74		P(Z<=z) two-tail	0.0366				
15	82	70		z Critical two-tail	1.960				
16	85	82							
17	85	82							
29	88	65							
30	74	78							
31	73	66							
32		84							
40		80							
41		76							
42									

Note: Rows 18–28 and 33–39 are hidden.

for the 30 individuals trained at center A, we enter the formula =VAR(A2:A31) into cell E2. Then, to compute the sample variance for the 40 individuals trained at center B we enter the formula =VAR(B2:B41) into cell F2. We see that the sample variance for center A is 64.0517 and that the sample variance for center B is 100.

Apply Tools: The following steps describe how to use Excel's z-Test: Two Sample for Means tool to conduct the hypothesis test about the difference between the population means in the training center study.

Step 1. Select the **Tools** menu
Step 2. Choose the **Data Analysis** option
Step 3. Choose **z-Test: Two Sample for Means** from the list of Analysis Tools
Step 4. When the **z-Test: Two Sample for Means** dialog box appears (see Figure 10.9):
    Enter A1:A31 in the **Variable 1 Range** box
    Enter B1:B41 in the **Variable 2 Range** box
    Type 0 in the **Hypothesized Mean Difference** box
    Type 64.0517 in the **Variable 1 Variance (known)*** box

---

*Excel is asking for a known variance (σ_1^2) here. But, in the large-sample case, we can substitute s_1^2. Note, however, that Excel will not accept a reference to cell E2 here. The same is true for the variance of variable 2 on the next line.

FIGURE 10.9   DIALOG BOX FOR EXCEL'S z-TEST: TWO SAMPLE FOR MEANS

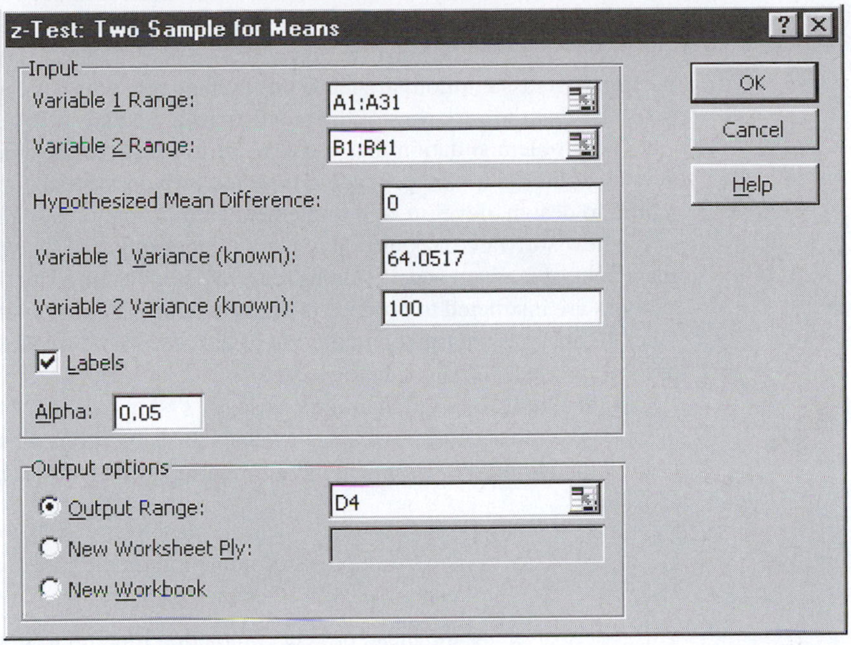

Type 100 in the **Variable 2 Variance (known)** box
Select **Labels**
Enter .05 in the **Alpha** box
Select **Output Range**
Enter D4 in the **Output Range** box (to identify the upper left corner of the section of the worksheet where the output will appear)
Click **OK**

The results are shown in cells D4:F15 of the worksheet shown in Figure 10.8. Descriptive statistics for the two samples are shown in cells E7:F9. The value of the test statistic, 2.09, is shown in cell E11. The critical value 1.96, labeled z Critical two-tail, is shown in cell E15. Because $z = 2.09$ is in the rejection region, we can conclude that the population means are not equal. Alternatively, we can use the p-value to make the hypothesis testing decision. The p-value for the test, labeled P(Z <= z) two-tail, is shown in cell E14. Because the p-value, 0.0366, is less than the level of significance, $\alpha = .05$, we have sufficient statistical evidence to reject the null hypothesis and conclude that the population means are not equal.

The same procedure can also be used to conduct one-tailed hypothesis tests. The value of the test statistic z is identical to the two-tailed case. The only changes required to make the hypothesis testing decision are that we need to use the critical value for a one-tailed test, labeled z Critical one-tail (see Cell E13), or the p-value for a one-tailed test, labeled P(Z <= z) one-tail (see Cell E12).

Excel's z-Test: Two Sample For Means tool assumes a known variance for each population. But, as we have shown, it can also be used when s_1^2 and s_2^2 are substituted for σ_1^2 and σ_2^2 in the large-sample case. The small-sample case is discussed next.

Small-Sample Case

Let us now consider hypothesis tests about the difference between the means of two populations for the small-sample case; that is, where $n_1 < 30$ and/or $n_2 < 30$. The procedure we will use is based on the t distribution with $n_1 + n_2 - 2$ degrees of freedom. As discussed in Section 10.1, assumptions are made that both populations have normal probability distributions and that the variances of the populations are equal.

The problem situation that we will use to illustrate the small-sample case involves a new computer software package developed to help systems analysts reduce the time required to design, develop, and implement an information system. To evaluate the benefits of the new software package, a simple random sample of 24 systems analysts is selected. Each analyst is given specifications for a hypothetical information system. Then 12 of the analysts are instructed to produce the information system by using current technology. The other 12 analysts are trained in the use of the new software package and then instructed to use it to produce the information system.

In this study, one population consists of systems analysts using the current technology and the other consists of systems analysts using the new software package. In terms of the time required to complete the information system project, the population means are as follow.

μ_1 = the mean project completion time for systems analysts using the current technology

μ_2 = the mean project completion time for systems analysts using the new software package

The researcher in charge of the new software evaluation project hopes to show that the new software package will provide a shorter mean project completion time. Thus, the researcher seeks evidence to conclude that μ_2 is less than μ_1; in this case, the difference between the two population means, $\mu_1 - \mu_2$, will be greater than zero. The research hypothesis $\mu_1 - \mu_2 > 0$ is stated as the alternative hypothesis.

$$H_0: \mu_1 - \mu_2 \leq 0$$
$$H_a: \mu_1 - \mu_2 > 0$$

Suppose that the 24 analysts complete the study with the results shown in Table 10.6. Under the assumption that the variances of the populations are equal, equation (10.8) is used to compute the pooled estimate of σ^2.

$$s^2 = \frac{(n_1 - 1)s_1^2 + (n_2 - 1)s_2^2}{n_1 + n_2 - 2} = \frac{11(40)^2 + 11(44)^2}{12 + 12 - 2} = 1768$$

The test statistic for the small-sample case is

$$t = \frac{(\bar{x}_1 - \bar{x}_2) - (\mu_1 - \mu_2)}{\sqrt{s^2\left(\frac{1}{n_1} + \frac{1}{n_2}\right)}} \tag{10.12}$$

In the case of two independent random samples of sizes n_1 and n_2, the t distribution will have $n_1 + n_2 - 2$ degrees of freedom. For $\alpha = .05$, the t distribution table shows that with

TABLE 10.6   COMPLETION TIME DATA AND SUMMARY STATISTICS
FOR THE SOFTWARE TESTING STUDY

Software

	Current Technology	New Software
	300	276
	280	222
	344	310
	385	338
	372	200
	360	302
	288	317
	321	260
	376	320
	290	312
	301	334
	283	265
Summary Statistics		
Sample size	$n_1 = 12$	$n_2 = 12$
Sample mean	$\bar{x}_1 = 325$	$\bar{x}_2 = 288$
Sample standard deviation	$s_1 = 40$	$s_2 = 44$

$12 + 12 - 2 = 22$ degrees of freedom, the critical value is $t_{.05} = 1.717$. Thus, the rejection region for the one-tailed test is as follows:

Using test statistic: Reject H_0 if $t > 1.717$

Using p-value: Reject H_0 if p-value $< .05$

The sample data and equation (10.12) provide the following value for the test statistic.

$$t = \frac{(325 - 288) - 0}{\sqrt{1768\left(\dfrac{1}{12} + \dfrac{1}{12}\right)}} = 2.16$$

Checking the rejection region, we see that $t = 2.16 > 1.717$ allows the rejection of H_0 at the .05 level of significance. Thus, the sample results enable the researcher to conclude that $\mu_1 - \mu_2 > 0$ and that the new software package provides a smaller mean completion time.

Using Excel: Small-Sample Case

Excel's t-Test: Two Sample Assuming Equal Variances tool can be used to conduct a hypothesis test about the difference between the population means for the software training study. Refer to the Excel worksheet shown in Figure 10.10 and the dialog box in Figure 10.11 as we describe the tasks involved. No functions or formulas are used so no background worksheet is shown.

Enter Data: Column A contains the completion time data for the simple random sample of 12 projects completed using the current technology, and column B contains the completion time data for the simple random sample of 12 projects completed using the new software package.

FIGURE 10.10 EXCEL WORKSHEET FOR THE SOFTWARE TRAINING STUDY

	A	B	C	D	E	F	G
1	**Current**	**New**		t-Test: Two-Sample Assuming Equal Variances			
2	300	276					
3	280	222			*Current*	*New*	
4	344	310		Mean	325	288	
5	385	338		Variance	1600	1936	
6	372	200		Observations	12	12	
7	360	302		Pooled Variance	1768		
8	288	317		Hypothesized Mean Difference	0		
9	321	260		df	22		
10	376	320		t Stat	2.16		
11	290	312		P(T<=t) one-tail	0.0212		
12	301	334		t Critical one-tail	1.717		
13	283	265		P(T<=t) two-tail	0.0423		
14				t Critical two-tail	2.074		
15							

Apply Tools: The following steps describe how to use Excel's t-Test: Two Sample Assuming Equal Variances tool.

Step 1. Select the **Tools** menu
Step 2. Choose the **Data Analysis** option
Step 3. Choose **t-Test: Two-Sample Assuming Equal Variances** from the list of Analysis Tools

FIGURE 10.11 DIALOG BOX FOR EXCEL'S t-TEST: TWO-SAMPLE ASSUMING EQUAL VARIANCES

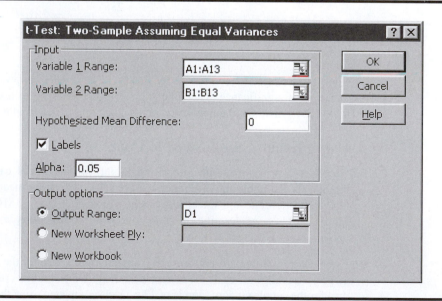

Step 4. When the t-Test: Two-Sample Assuming Equal Variances dialog box appears (see Figure 10.11):

Enter A1:A13 in the **Variable 1 Range** box

Enter B1:B13 in the **Variable 2 Range** box

Type 0 in the **Hypothesized Mean Difference** box

Select **Labels**

Enter .05 in the **Alpha** box

Select **Output Range**

Enter D1 in the **Output Range** box (to identify the upper left corner of the section of the worksheet where the output will appear)

Click **OK**

The results are shown in cells D1:F14 of the worksheet shown in Figure 10.10. Descriptive statistics for the completion times using the two software packages are shown in cells E4:F6 and the pooled variance estimate is shown in cell E7.

The value of the test statistic, $t = 2.16$, is shown in cell E10. The critical value 1.717, labeled t Critical one-tail, is shown in cell E12. Because $t = 2.16$ is in the rejection region $(2.16 > 1.717)$, we can conclude that the new software package provides a smaller mean completion time. Alternatively, we can use the p-value to make the hypothesis testing decision. The p-value for the test, labeled $P(T <= t)$ one-tail, is shown in cell E11. Because the p-value, 0.0212, is less than the level of significance, $\alpha = .05$, we have sufficient statistical evidence to reject the null hypothesis and conclude that the new software package provides a smaller mean completion time.

The same procedure can also be used to conduct two-tailed hypothesis tests in the small-sample case. The value of the test statistic t is identical to the one-tailed case. The only changes required to make the hypothesis testing decision are that we need to use the critical value for a two-tailed test, labeled t Critical two-tail (see Cell E14), and the p-value for a two-tailed test, labeled $P(T <= t)$ two-tail (see Cell E13).

NOTES AND COMMENTS

In hypothesis tests about the difference between the means of two populations, the null hypothesis typically contains the assumption of no difference between the means. Hence, the following null hypotheses are possible choices.

$$H_0: \mu_1 - \mu_2 = 0$$
$$H_0: \mu_1 - \mu_2 \leq 0$$
$$H_0: \mu_1 - \mu_2 \geq 0$$

In some instances, we may want to determine whether there is a nonzero difference D_0 between the population means. The specific value chosen for D_0 depends on the application under study. However, in this case, the null hypothesis may be of the following forms.

$$H_0: \mu_1 - \mu_2 = D_0$$
$$H_0: \mu_1 - \mu_2 \leq D_0$$
$$H_0: \mu_1 - \mu_2 \geq D_0$$

The hypothesis testing computations remain the same with the exception that D_0 is used for the value of $\mu_1 - \mu_2$ in equations (10.11) and (10.12).

EXERCISES

Methods

11. Consider the following hypothesis test.

$$H_0: \mu_1 - \mu_2 \leq 0$$
$$H_a: \mu_1 - \mu_2 > 0$$

The following results are for two independent simple random samples taken from the two populations.

Sample 1	Sample 2
$n_1 = 40$	$n_2 = 50$
$\bar{x}_1 = 25.2$	$\bar{x}_2 = 22.8$
$s_1 = 5.2$	$s_2 = 6.0$

a. Using $\alpha = .05$, what is your hypothesis testing conclusion?
b. What is the p-value?

12. Consider the following hypothesis test.

$$H_0: \mu_1 - \mu_2 = 0$$
$$H_a: \mu_1 - \mu_2 \neq 0$$

The following results are for two independent simple random samples taken from the two populations.

Sample 1	Sample 2
$n_1 = 80$	$n_2 = 70$
$\bar{x}_1 = 104$	$\bar{x}_2 = 106$
$s_1 = 8.4$	$s_2 = 7.6$

a. Using $\alpha = .05$, what is your hypothesis testing conclusion?
b. What is the p-value?

13. Consider the following hypothesis test.

$$H_0: \mu_1 - \mu_2 = 0$$
$$H_a: \mu_1 - \mu_2 \neq 0$$

The following results are for two independent simple random samples taken from the two populations. Using $\alpha = .05$, what is your hypothesis testing conclusion?

Sample 1	Sample 2
$n_1 = 8$	$n_2 = 7$
$\bar{x}_1 = 1.4$	$\bar{x}_2 = 1.0$
$s_1 = 0.4$	$s_2 = 0.6$

Applications

14. Coastal areas of the United States, including Cape Cod, the Outer Banks, the Carolinas, and the Gulf Coast, experienced relatively high population growth rates during the 1990s. Data were collected on residents living in the coastal communities as well as on residents living in noncoastal areas throughout the United States (*USA Today*, July 21, 2000). Assume that the following sample results were obtained on the ages of individuals in the two populations:

Coastal Areas	Noncoastal Areas
$\bar{x}_1 = 39.3$ years	$\bar{x}_2 = 35.4$ years
$s_1 = 16.8$ years	$s_2 = 15.2$ years
$n_1 = 150$	$n_2 = 175$

Conduct a hypothesis test to determine whether the mean ages of the two populations differ. Use $\alpha = .05$.

a. Formulate the null and alternative hypotheses.
b. What is the rejection rule?
c. What is the value of the test statistic?
d. What is your conclusion?
e. What is the p-value?

Airport

15. Refer to Exercise 6 in which two independent random samples of business travelers rated the Miami and Los Angeles airports. The data for this problem are in the data set Airport. Is the population mean rating for the Los Angeles airport greater than the population mean rating for the Miami airport? Support your conclusion with a statistical test using a .05 level of significance.

SELF test

16. The Greystone Department Store study in Section 10.1 supplied the following data on customer ages from independent random samples taken at two store locations (see Table 10.2).

Inner-City Store	Suburban Store
$n_1 = 36$	$n_2 = 49$
$\bar{x}_1 = 40$ years	$\bar{x}_2 = 35$ years
$s_1 = 9$ years	$s_2 = 10$ years

Using $\alpha = .05$, test $H_0: \mu_1 - \mu_2 = 0$ against the alternative $H_a: \mu_1 - \mu_2 \neq 0$. What is your conclusion about the mean ages of the populations of customers at the two stores?

17. A firm is studying the delivery times of two raw material suppliers. The firm is basically satisfied with supplier A and is prepared to stay with that supplier if the mean delivery time is the same as or less than that of supplier B. However, if the firm finds that the mean delivery time of supplier B is less than that of supplier A, it will begin making raw material purchases from supplier B.

a. What are the null and alternative hypotheses for this situation?
b. Assume that independent simple random samples show the following delivery time characteristics for the two suppliers.

Supplier A	Supplier B
$n_1 = 50$	$n_2 = 30$
$\bar{x}_1 = 14$ days	$\bar{x}_2 = 12.5$ days
$s_1 = 3$ days	$s_2 = 2$ days

Using $\alpha = .05$, what is your conclusion for the hypotheses from part (a)? What action do you recommend in terms of supplier selection?

Wages

18. In a wage discrimination case involving male and female employees, independent samples of 44 male and 32 female employees with 5 years' experience or more provided the data shown in the data set Wages. The null hypothesis is that male employees have a mean hourly wage less than or equal to that of the female employees. Rejection of H_0 leads to the conclusion that male employees have a mean hourly wage exceeding that of the female employees. Test the hypothesis using $\alpha = .01$. Does wage discrimination appear to be present in this case?

19. Starting annual salaries for individuals entering the public accounting and financial planning professions were presented in *Fortune*, June 26, 1995. The starting salaries for a sample of 12 public accountants and a sample of 14 financial planners follow, with data in thousands of dollars.

Starting

Public Accountant	Financial Planner
30.6	31.6
31.2	26.6
28.9	25.5
35.2	25.0
25.1	25.9
33.2	32.9
31.3	26.9
35.3	25.8
31.0	27.5
30.1	29.6
29.9	23.9
24.4	26.9
	24.4
	25.5

a. Using $\alpha = .05$, test for any difference between the population mean starting annual salaries for the two professions. What is your conclusion?

b. What is the point estimate of the difference between the two population means? Which profession has the higher mean annual starting salary?

20. Arnold Palmer and Tiger Woods are two of the best golfers ever to play the game. The question was raised as to how these two golfers would have compared if both were playing at the top of their game. The following sample data show 18-hole average scores during one year of PGA tour competition. Palmer's scores are from his 1960 season, while Wood's scores are from his 1999 season (*Golf Magazine*, February 2000).

Palmer, 1960	Woods, 1999
$\bar{x}_1 = 69.95$	$\bar{x}_2 = 69.56$
$n_1 = 112$	$n_2 = 84$

Use the sample results to test the hypothesis of no difference between the population mean 18-hole scores for the two golfers.

a. Assuming a population standard deviation of 2.5 for both golfers, what is the value of the test statistic?

b. What is the p-value?

c. Using $\alpha = .01$, what is your conclusion?

21. The mean time to locate flight information on Internet Web sites of the major airline companies is generally 2 to 3 minutes (*USA Today*, September 11, 2000). Sample results representative of the times for Delta Airlines and Northwest Airlines are as follows:

Delta	Northwest
$\bar{x}_1 = 2.5$ minutes	$\bar{x}_2 = 2.1$ minutes
$s_1 = .8$ minutes	$s_2 = 1.1$ minutes
$n_1 = 22$	$n_2 = 20$

a. Formulate the hypotheses if the purpose is to test for a significant difference between the mean times for the two airlines.
b. Using $\alpha = .05$, what is the rejection rule?
c. Compute the value of the test statistic.
d. What is your conclusion?
e. What is the *p*-value?

22. Periodically, Merrill Lynch asks its customers to evaluate its financial consultants and services (2000 Merrill Lynch Client Satisfaction Survey). Higher ratings on the client satisfaction survey indicate better service with 7 as the maximum service rating. Independent samples of service ratings for two financial consultants are summarized here. Consultant A has 10 years of experience while consultant B has 1 year of experience. Using $\alpha = .05$, test to see whether the consultant with more experience achieves the higher population mean service rating.

Consultant A	Consultant B
$\bar{x}_1 = 6.82$	$\bar{x}_2 = 6.25$
$s_1 = .64$	$s_2 = .75$
$n_1 = 16$	$n_2 = 10$

a. Formulate the null and alternative hypotheses.
b. What is your hypothesis testing decision?

10.3   INFERENCES ABOUT THE DIFFERENCE BETWEEN THE MEANS OF TWO POPULATIONS: MATCHED SAMPLES

Suppose a manufacturing company is considering two methods by which employees can perform a production task. To maximize production output, the company wants to identify the method with the shortest mean completion time. Let μ_1 denote the mean completion time for production method 1 and μ_2 denote the mean completion time for production method 2. With no preliminary indication of the preferred production method, we begin by tentatively assuming that the two production methods have the same mean completion time. Thus, the null hypothesis is $H_0: \mu_1 - \mu_2 = 0$. If this hypothesis is rejected, we can conclude that the mean completion times differ. In this case, the method providing the shorter mean completion time would be recommended. The null and alternative hypotheses are written as follows.

$$H_0: \mu_1 - \mu_2 = 0$$
$$H_a: \mu_1 - \mu_2 \neq 0$$

In choosing the sampling procedure that will be used to collect production time data and test the hypotheses, we consider two alternative designs. One is based on **independent samples,** and the other is based on **matched samples.**

1. *Independent sample design:* A simple random sample of workers is selected and each worker in the sample uses method 1. A second independent simple random sample of workers is selected and each worker in this sample uses method 2. The test of the difference between means is based on the procedures in Section 10.2.
2. *Matched sample design:* One simple random sample of workers is selected. Each worker first uses one method and then uses the other method. The order of the two methods is assigned randomly to the workers, with some workers performing method 1 first and others performing method 2 first. Each worker provides a pair of completion time values, one value for method 1 and another value for method 2.

In the matched sample design the two production methods are tested under similar conditions (i.e., with the same worker); hence this design often leads to a smaller sampling error than the independent sample design. The primary reason is that in a matched sample design, variation between workers is eliminated as a source of sampling error.

Let us demonstrate the analysis of a matched sample design by using it to test the difference between mean completion times for the two production methods. A random sample of six workers is used. The data on completion times for the six workers are given in Table 10.7. Note that each worker provides a pair of completion time values, one for each production method. The last column contains the difference in completion times d_i for each worker in the sample.

The key to the analysis of the matched sample data is to realize that we consider only the column of differences. We therefore have six values (.6, $-.2$, .5, .3, .0, and .6) that will be used to analyze the difference between the means of the two production methods.

Let μ_d = the mean of the *difference* values for the population of workers. With this notation, the null and alternative hypotheses are rewritten as follows.

$$H_0: \mu_d = 0$$
$$H_a: \mu_d \neq 0$$

If H_0 can be rejected, we can conclude that the mean completion times differ.

The d notation is a reminder that the matched sample provides *difference* data. The sample mean and sample standard deviation for the six difference values in Table 10.7 follow.

Other than the use of the d notation, the formulas for the sample mean and sample standard deviation are the same as those used in Chapter 3.

$$\bar{d} = \frac{\Sigma d_i}{n} = \frac{1.8}{6} = .30$$

$$s_d = \sqrt{\frac{\Sigma(d_i - \bar{d})^2}{n - 1}} = \sqrt{\frac{.56}{5}} = .3347$$

In Chapter 9 we stated that if the population can be assumed to be normally distributed, the t distribution with $n - 1$ degrees of freedom can be used to test the null hypothesis about a population mean. Assuming that the population of difference data is normally distributed, the test statistic becomes

$$t = \frac{\bar{d} - \mu_d}{s_d/\sqrt{n}} \qquad (10.13)$$

TABLE 10.7   TASK COMPLETION TIMES FOR A MATCHED SAMPLE DESIGN

Worker	Completion Time for Method 1 (minutes)	Completion Time for Method 2 (minutes)	Difference in Completion Times (d_i)
1	6.0	5.4	.6
2	5.0	5.2	−.2
3	7.0	6.5	.5
4	6.2	5.9	.3
5	6.0	6.0	.0
6	6.4	5.8	.6

CD file

Matched

Using $\alpha = .05$ and $n - 1 = 5$ degrees of freedom ($t_{.025} = 2.571$), the rejection rule for the two-tailed test is as follows:

Using test statistic: Reject H_0 if $t < -2.571$ or if $t > 2.571$

Using p-value: Reject H_0 if p-value $< .05$

With $\bar{d} = .30$, $s_d = .3347$, and $n = 6$, the value of the test statistic for the null hypothesis $H_0: \mu_d = 0$ is

$$t = \frac{\bar{d} - \mu_d}{s_d/\sqrt{n}} = \frac{.30 - 0}{.3347/\sqrt{6}} = 2.20$$

Because $t = 2.20$ is not in the rejection region, the sample data do not provide sufficient evidence to conclude that the mean completion times differ.

For 5 degrees of freedom, the t distribution table shows that $t = 2.20$ is between $t_{.025} = 2.571$ and $t_{.05} = 2.015$. Thus, the one-tailed area associated with $t = 2.20$ is between .025 and .05. For a two-tailed test, we know the p-value is between $2(.025) = .05$ and $2(.05) = .10$. Because this p-value is greater than $\alpha = .05$, H_0 is not rejected. In the next subsection we will show that using Excel provides the exact p-value $= .0795$.

We can obtain an interval estimate of the difference between the two population means by applying the single population methodology of Chapter 8 to the difference data. The calculation follows.

Once the difference data have been computed, the t distribution interval estimation procedure for matched samples is the same as for the one-population procedure described in Chapter 8.

$$\bar{d} \pm t_{\alpha/2}\frac{s_d}{\sqrt{n}}$$

$$0.3 \pm 2.571\left(\frac{.3347}{\sqrt{6}}\right)$$

$$0.3 \pm .35$$

Thus, the 95% confidence interval for the difference between the mean completion times of the two production methods is −.05 minutes to .65 minutes. Note that because the confidence interval includes the value of zero, it confirms our hypothesis testing decision; that is, the sample data do not provide sufficient evidence to reject H_0.

Using Excel

Excel's t-Test: Paired Two Sample for Means tool can be used to conduct a hypothesis test about the difference between the population means for the two production methods. Refer to the Excel worksheet shown in Figure 10.12 and the dialog box in Figure 10.13 as we describe the tasks involved.

Enter Data: Column A is used to identify each of the six workers who participated in the study. Column B contains the completion time data for each worker using method 1, and column C contains the completion time data for each worker using method 2.

Apply Tools: The following steps describe how to use Excel's t-Test: Paired Two Sample for Means tool to conduct the hypothesis test about the difference between the means of the two production methods

Step 1. Select the **Tools** menu
Step 2. Choose the **Data Analysis** option
Step 3. Choose **t-Test: Paired Two Sample for Means** from the list of Analysis Tools
Step 4. When the t-Test: Paired Two Sample for Means dialog box appears (see Figure 10.13):

   Enter B1:B7 in the **Variable 1 Range** box
   Enter C1:C7 in the **Variable 2 Range** box
   Type 0 in the **Hypothesized Mean Difference** box
   Select **Labels**
   Enter .05 in the **Alpha** box
   Select **Output Range**
   Enter E1 in the **Output Range** box (to identify the upper left corner of the section of the worksheet where the output will appear)
   Click **OK**

The results are shown in cells E1:E14 of the worksheet shown in Figure 10.12. The value of the test statistic, $t = 2.196$, is shown in cell F10. The critical value 2.571, labeled t Critical

FIGURE 10.12   EXCEL WORKSHEET FOR THE MATCHED SAMPLES STUDY

	A	B	C	D	E	F	G	H
1	Worker	Method 1	Method 2		t-Test: Paired Two Sample for Means			
2	1	6	5.4					
3	2	5	5.2			Method 1	Method 2	
4	3	7	6.5		Mean	6.1	5.8	
5	4	6.2	5.9		Variance	0.428	0.212	
6	5	6	6		Observations	6	6	
7	6	6.4	5.8		Pearson Correlation	0.8764		
8					Hypothesized Mean Difference	0		
9					df	5		
10					t Stat	2.196		
11					P(T<=t) one-tail	0.0398		
12					t Critical one-tail	2.015		
13					P(T<=t) two-tail	0.0795		
14					t Critical two-tail	2.571		
15								

FIGURE 10.13   DIALOG BOX FOR EXCEL'S t-TEST: PAIRED TWO SAMPLE FOR MEANS

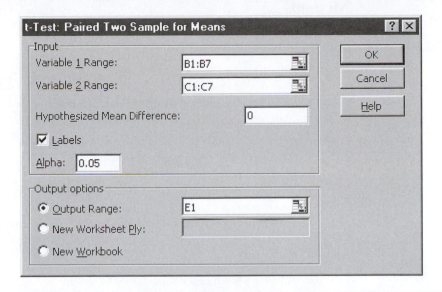

two-tail, is shown in cell F14. Because $t = 2.196$ is not in the rejection region ($2.196 \leq 2.571$), the sample data do not provide sufficient evidence to reject H_0. Alternatively, we can use the p-value to make the hypothesis testing decision. The p-value for the test, labeled P(T <= t) two-tail, is shown in cell F13. Because the p-value, 0.0795, is greater than the level of significance, $\alpha = .05$, we cannot reject the null hypothesis that the mean completion times are equal.

The same procedure can also be used to conduct one-tailed hypothesis tests. The value of the test statistic t is identical to the two-tailed case. The only changes required to make the hypothesis testing decision are that we need to use the critical value for a one-tailed test, labeled t Critical one-tail (see cell F12), and the p-value for a one-tailed test, labeled P(T <= t) one-tail (see cell F11).

NOTES AND COMMENTS

1. In the example presented in this section, workers performed the production task with first one method and then the other method. This example illustrates a matched sample design in which each sampled element (worker) provides a pair of data values. It is also possible to use different but "similar" elements to provide the pair of data values. For example, a worker at one location could be matched with a similar worker at another location (similarity based on age, education, sex, experience, etc.). The pairs of workers would provide the difference data that could be used in the matched sample analysis.

2. Because a matched sample procedure for inferences about two population means generally provides better precision than the independent sample approach, it is the recommended design. However, in some applications the matching cannot be achieved, or perhaps the time and cost associated with matching are excessive. In such cases, the independent sample design should be used.

3. The example presented in this section had a sample size of six workers and thus was a small-sample case. The t distribution was used in both the hypothesis test and interval estimation computations. If the sample size is large ($n \geq 30$), use of the t distribution is unnecessary; in such cases, statistical inferences can be based on the z values of the standard normal probability distribution.

EXERCISES

Methods

23. Consider the following hypothesis test.

$$H_0: \mu_d \leq 0$$
$$H_a: \mu_d > 0$$

The following data are from matched samples taken from two populations.

		Population	
Element		**1**	**2**
1		21	20
2		28	26
3		18	18
4		20	20
5		26	24

     a. Compute the difference value for each element.
     b. Compute $\bar{d}$.
     c. Compute the standard deviation s_d.
     d. Test the hypothesis using $\alpha = .05$. What is your conclusion?

24. The following data are from matched samples taken from two populations.

		Population	
Element		**1**	**2**
1		11	8
2		7	8
3		9	6
4		12	7
5		13	10
6		15	15
7		15	14

     a. Compute the difference value for each element.
     b. Compute $\bar{d}$.
     c. Compute the standard deviation s_d.
     d. What is the point estimate of the difference between the two population means?
     e. Provide a 95% confidence interval for the difference between the two population means.

Applications

25. A market research firm used a sample of individuals to rate the purchase potential of a particular product before and after the individuals saw a new television commercial about the product. The purchase potential ratings were based on a 0 to 10 scale, with higher values indicating a higher purchase potential. The null hypothesis stated that the mean rating "after" would be less than or equal to the mean rating "before." Rejection of this hypothesis would show that the commercial improved the mean purchase potential rating. Use $\alpha = .05$ and the following data to test the hypothesis and comment on the value of the commercial.

| | Purchase Rating | | | | Purchase Rating | |
Individual	After	Before	Individual	After	Before
1	6	5	5	3	5
2	6	4	6	9	8
3	7	7	7	7	5
4	4	3	8	6	6

26. A sample of 10 international telephone calls provided the Sprint and WorldCom calling rates per minute for calls from the United States (*World Traveler*, July 2000).

Traveler

Country	Sprint	WorldCom
Australia	.46	.26
Belgium	.69	.40
Brazil	.92	.53
Colombia	.55	.53
Denmark	.50	.26
France	.46	.26
Germany	.46	.26
Hong Kong	.92	.40
Japan	.69	.40
United Kingdom	.46	.26

Provide a 95% confidence interval estimate of the difference between the two population means.

27. The cost of transportation from the airport to the downtown area depends on the method of transportation. One-way costs for taxi and shuttle bus transportation for a sample of 10 major cities follow. Provide a 95% confidence interval for the mean cost increase associated with taxi transportation.

City	Taxi ($)	Shuttle Bus ($)	City	Taxi ($)	Shuttle Bus ($)
Atlanta	15.00	7.00	Minneapolis	16.50	7.50
Chicago	22.00	12.50	New Orleans	18.00	7.00
Denver	11.00	5.00	New York (LaGuardia)	16.00	8.50
Houston	15.00	4.50	Philadelphia	20.00	8.00
Los Angeles	26.00	11.00	Washington, D.C.	10.00	5.00

28. Rental car gasoline prices per gallon were sampled at eight major airports. Data for Hertz and National car rental companies follow (*USA Today*, April 4, 2000).

Airport	Hertz	National
Boston Logan	1.55	1.56
Chicago O'Hare	1.62	1.59
Los Angeles	1.72	1.78

(continued)

Airport	Hertz	National
Miami	1.65	1.49
New York (JFK)	1.72	1.51
New York (LaGuardia)	1.67	1.50
Orange County, CA	1.68	1.77
Washington (Dulles)	1.52	1.41

Use $\alpha = .05$ to test the hypothesis of no difference between the population mean prices per gallon for the two companies.

29. A survey was made of Book-of-the-Month Club members to ascertain whether members spend more time watching television than they do reading. Assume a sample of 15 respondents provided the following data on weekly hours of television watching and weekly hours of reading. Using a .05 level of significance, can you conclude that Book-of-the-Month Club members spend more hours per week watching television than reading?

CD file

TVRead

Respondent	Television	Reading	Respondent	Television	Reading
1	10	6	9	4	7
2	14	16	10	8	8
3	16	8	11	16	5
4	18	10	12	5	10
5	15	10	13	8	3
6	14	8	14	19	10
7	10	14	15	11	6
8	12	14			

30. A manufacturer produces both a deluxe and a standard model of an automatic sander designed for home use. Selling prices obtained from a sample of retail outlets follow.

	Model Price ($)			Model Price ($)	
Retail Outlet	Deluxe	Standard	Retail Outlet	Deluxe	Standard
1	39	27	5	40	30
2	39	28	6	39	34
3	45	35	7	35	29
4	38	30			

a. The manufacturer's suggested retail prices for the two models show a $10 price differential. Using a .05 level of significance, test that the mean difference between the prices of the two models is $10.

b. What is the 95% confidence interval for the difference between the mean prices of the two models?

31. The 1997 price/earnings ratios and estimated 1998 price/earnings ratios for a sample of 12 stocks are shown here (*Kiplinger's Personal Finance Magazine,* November 1997).

PERatio

Stock	1997 P/E Ratio	Est. 1998 P/E Ratio
Coca-Cola	40	32
Walt Disney	33	23
Du Pont	24	16
Eastman Kodak	21	13
General Electric	30	23
General Mills	25	19
IBM	19	14
Merck	29	21
McDonald's	20	17
Motorola	35	20
Philip Morris	17	13
Xerox	20	17

 a. Use $\alpha = .05$ and test for any change in the population mean price/earnings ratios for the two-year period.
 b. Provide a 95% confidence interval for the change in the population mean price/earnings ratios for the two-year period. What is your conclusion?

10.4 INTRODUCTION TO ANALYSIS OF VARIANCE

In Section 10.2 we showed how a hypothesis test can be conducted to determine whether the means of two populations are equal based upon two independent simple random samples. In this section, we introduce a statistical technique called **analysis of variance** (ANOVA) which can be used to test the hypothesis that the means of three or more populations are equal. We begin our discussion of analysis of variance by considering a problem facing National Computer Products, Inc.

National Computer Products, Inc. (NCP), manufactures printers and fax machines at plants located in Atlanta, Dallas, and Seattle. To measure how much employees at these plants know about total quality management, a random sample of six employees was selected from each plant and given a quality awareness examination. The examination scores obtained for these 18 employees are listed in Table 10.8. The sample means, sample variances, and sample standard deviations for each group are also provided. Managers want to use these data to test the hypothesis that the population mean examination score is the same for all three plants.

We will define population 1 as all employees at the Atlanta plant, population 2 as all employees at the Dallas plant, and population 3 as all employees at the Seattle plant. Let

$$\mu_1 = \text{mean examination score for population 1}$$
$$\mu_2 = \text{mean examination score for population 2}$$
$$\mu_3 = \text{mean examination score for population 3}$$

TABLE 10.8   EXAMINATION SCORES FOR 18 EMPLOYEES

NCP

Observation	Plant 1 Atlanta	Plant 2 Dallas	Plant 3 Seattle
1	85	71	59
2	75	75	64
3	82	73	62
4	76	74	69
5	71	69	75
6	85	82	67
Sample mean	79	74	66
Sample variance	34	20	32
Sample standard deviation	5.83	4.47	5.66

Although we will never know the actual values of μ_1, μ_2, and μ_3, we want to use the sample results to test the following hypotheses.

$$H_0: \mu_1 = \mu_2 = \mu_3$$
$$H_a: \text{Not all population means are equal}$$

If H_0 is rejected, we cannot conclude that all population means are different. Rejecting H_0 implies that at least two population means have different values.

As we will demonstrate shortly, analysis of variance is a statistical procedure that can be used to determine whether the observed differences in the three sample means are large enough to reject H_0.

The two variables in the NCP example are plant location and score on the quality awareness examination. Because the objective is to determine whether the mean examination score is the same for plants located in Atlanta, Dallas, and Seattle, examination score is referred to as the dependent or **response variable** and plant location as the independent variable or **factor.** In general, the values of a factor selected for investigation are referred to as the levels of the factor or **treatments.** Thus, in the NCP example the three treatments are Atlanta, Dallas, and Seattle. These three treatments define the populations of interest in the NCP example. For each treatment or plant location, the response variable is the examination score.

Assumptions for Analysis of Variance

Three assumptions are required to use analysis of variance.

If the sample sizes are equal, analysis of variance is not sensitive to departures from the assumption of normally distributed populations.

1. *For each population, the response variable is normally distributed.* Implication: In the NCP example, the examination scores (response variable) must be normally distributed at each plant.
2. *The variance of the response variable, denoted σ^2, is the same for all of the populations.* Implication: In the NCP example, the variance of examination scores must be the same for all three plants.
3. *The observations must be independent.* Implication: In the NCP example, the examination score for each employee must be independent of the examination score for any other employee.

Conceptual Overview

If the three population means are equal, we would expect the three sample means to be close together. In fact, the closer the three sample means are to one another, the more evidence we have for the conclusion that the population means are equal. Alternatively, the more the sample means differ, the more evidence we have for the conclusion that the population means are not equal. In other words, if the variability among the sample means is "small," it supports H_0; if the variability among the sample means is "large," it supports H_a.

If the null hypothesis, $H_0: \mu_1 = \mu_2 = \mu_3$, is true, we can use the variability among the sample means to develop an estimate of σ^2. First, note that if the assumptions for analysis of variance are satisfied, each sample will have come from the same normal probability distribution with mean μ and variance σ^2. Recall from Chapter 7 that the sampling distribution of the sample mean $\bar{x}$ for a simple random sample of size n from a normal population will be normally distributed with mean μ and variance σ^2/n. Figure 10.14 illustrates such a sampling distribution.

Thus, if the null hypothesis is true, we can think of each of the three sample means, $\bar{x}_1 = 79$, $\bar{x}_2 = 74$, and $\bar{x}_3 = 66$, from Table 10.8 as values drawn at random from the sampling distribution shown in Figure 10.14. In this case, the mean and variance of the three $\bar{x}$ values can be used to estimate the mean and variance of the sampling distribution. When the sample sizes are equal, as in the NCP example, the best estimate of the mean of the sampling distribution of $\bar{x}$ is the mean or average of the sample means. Thus, in the NCP example, an estimate of the mean of the sampling distribution of $\bar{x}$ is $(79 + 74 + 66)/3 = 73$. We refer to this estimate as the *overall sample mean*. An estimate of the variance of the sampling distribution of $\bar{x}$ is provided by the variance of the three sample means.

$$s_{\bar{x}}^2 = \frac{(79 - 73)^2 + (74 - 73)^2 + (66 - 73)^2}{3 - 1} = \frac{86}{2} = 43$$

Because $\sigma_{\bar{x}}^2 = \sigma^2/n$, solving for σ^2 gives

$$\sigma^2 = n\sigma_{\bar{x}}^2$$

FIGURE 10.14   SAMPLING DISTRIBUTION OF $\bar{x}$ GIVEN H_0 IS TRUE

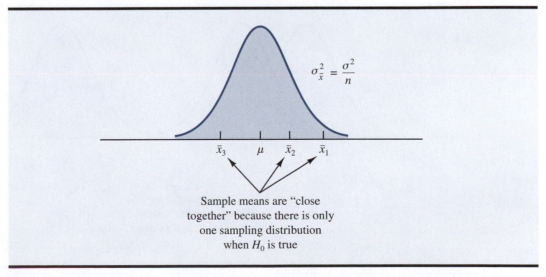

Hence,

$$\text{Estimate of } \sigma^2 = n \, (\text{Estimate of } \sigma_{\bar{x}}^2) = ns_{\bar{x}}^2 = 6(43) = 258$$

The result, $ns_{\bar{x}}^2 = 258$, is referred to as the *between-treatments* estimate of σ^2.

The between-treatments estimate of σ^2 is based on the assumption that the null hypothesis is true. In this case, each sample comes from the same population, and there is only one sampling distribution of $\bar{x}$. To illustrate what happens when H_0 is false, suppose the population means all differ. Note that because the three samples are from normal populations with different means, they will result in three different sampling distributions. Figure 10.15 shows that in this case, the sample means are not as close together as they were when H_0 was true. Thus, $s_{\bar{x}}^2$ will be larger, causing the between-treatments estimate of σ^2 to be larger. In general, when the population means are not equal, the between-treatments estimate will overestimate the population variance σ^2.

The variation within each of the samples also has an effect on the conclusion we reach in analysis of variance. When a simple random sample is selected from each population, each of the sample variances provides an unbiased estimate of σ^2. Hence, we can combine or pool the individual estimates of σ^2 into one overall estimate. The estimate of σ^2 obtained in this way is called the *pooled* or *within-treatments* estimate of σ^2. Because each sample variance provides an estimate of σ^2 based only on the variation within each sample, the within-treatments estimate of σ^2 is not affected by whether the population means are equal. When the sample sizes are equal, the within-treatments estimate of σ^2 can be obtained by computing the average of the individual sample variances. For the NCP example we obtain

$$\text{Within-Treatments Estimate of } \sigma^2 = \frac{34 + 20 + 32}{3} = \frac{86}{3} = 28.67$$

In the NCP example, the between-treatments estimate of σ^2 (258) is much larger than the within-treatments estimate of σ^2 (28.67). In fact, the ratio of these two estimates is $258/28.67 = 9.00$. Recall, however, that the between-treatments approach provides a good

FIGURE 10.15   SAMPLING DISTRIBUTION FOR $\bar{x}$ GIVEN H_0 IS FALSE

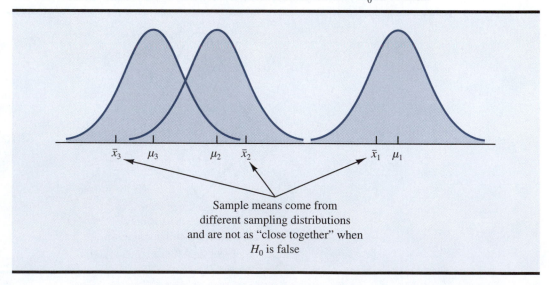

Sample means come from
different sampling distributions
and are not as "close together" when
H_0 is false

estimate of σ^2 only if the null hypothesis is true; if the null hypothesis is false, the between-treatments approach overestimates σ^2. The within-treatments approach provides a good estimate of σ^2 in either case. Thus, if the null hypothesis is true, the two estimates will be similar and their ratio will be close to 1. If the null hypothesis is false, the between-treatments estimate will be larger than the within-treatments estimate, and their ratio will be large. In the next section we will show how large this ratio must be to reject H_0.

In summary, the logic behind ANOVA is based on the development of two independent estimates of the common population variance σ^2. One estimate of σ^2 is based on the variability among the sample means themselves, and the other estimate of σ^2 is based on the variability of the data within each sample. By comparing these two estimates of σ^2, we will be able to determine whether the population means are equal.

NOTES AND COMMENTS

1. In Sections 10.2 and 10.3 we presented statistical methods for testing the hypothesis that the means of two populations are equal. ANOVA can also be used to test the hypothesis that the means of two populations are equal. In practice, however, analysis of variance is only used when dealing with three or more population means.

2. In Section 10.2 we discussed how to test for the equality of two population means whenever one or both sample sizes are less than 30 (the small-sample case). As part of that discussion we illustrated the process of combining the results of two independent random samples to provide one estimate of σ^2; that process was referred to as pooling, and the resulting sample variance was referred to as the pooled estimator of σ^2. In analysis of variance, the within-treatments estimate of σ^2 is simply the generalization of that concept to the case of more than two samples, which is why we also refer to the within-treatments estimator in ANOVA as the pooled estimator of σ^2.

10.5   ANALYSIS OF VARIANCE: TESTING FOR THE EQUALITY OF k POPULATION MEANS

Analysis of variance can be used to test for the equality of k population means. The general form of the hypothesis test is

$$H_0: \mu_1 = \mu_2 = \cdots = \mu_k$$
$$H_a: \text{Not all population means are equal}$$

where

$$\mu_j = \text{mean of the } j\text{th population}$$

We assume that a simple random sample of size n_j has been selected from each of the k populations or treatments. For the resulting sample data, let

$$x_{ij} = \text{value of observation } i \text{ for treatment } j$$
$$n_j = \text{number of observations for treatment } j$$
$$\bar{x}_j = \text{sample mean for treatment } j$$
$$s_j^2 = \text{sample variance for treatment } j$$
$$s_j = \text{sample standard deviation for treatment } j$$

The formulas for the sample mean and sample variance for treatment j are as follow.

$$\bar{x}_j = \frac{\sum\limits_{i=1}^{n_j} x_{ij}}{n_j} \qquad (10.14)$$

$$s_j^2 = \frac{\sum\limits_{i=1}^{n_j} (x_{ij} - \bar{x}_j)^2}{n_j - 1} \qquad (10.15)$$

The overall sample mean, denoted $\bar{\bar{x}}$, is the sum of all the observations divided by the total number of observations. That is,

$$\bar{\bar{x}} = \frac{\sum\limits_{j=1}^{k} \sum\limits_{i=1}^{n_j} x_{ij}}{n_T} \qquad (10.16)$$

where

$$n_T = n_1 + n_2 + \cdots + n_k \qquad (10.17)$$

If the size of each sample is n, $n_T = kn$; in this case equation (10.16) reduces to

$$\bar{\bar{x}} = \frac{\sum\limits_{j=1}^{k} \sum\limits_{i=1}^{n_j} x_{ij}}{nk} = \frac{\sum\limits_{j=1}^{k} \sum\limits_{i=1}^{n_j} x_{ij}/n}{k} = \frac{\sum\limits_{j=1}^{k} \bar{x}_j}{k} \qquad (10.18)$$

In other words, whenever the sample sizes are the same, the overall sample mean is just the average of the k sample means.

Because each sample in the NCP example consists of $n = 6$ observations, the overall sample mean can be computed by using equation (10.18). For the data in Table 10.8 we obtained the following result.

$$\bar{\bar{x}} = \frac{79 + 74 + 66}{3} = 73$$

If the null hypothesis is true ($\mu_1 = \mu_2 = \mu_3 = \mu$), the overall sample mean of 73 is the best estimate of the population mean μ.

Between-Treatments Estimate of Population Variance

In the preceding section, we introduced the concept of a between-treatments estimate of σ^2 and showed how to compute it when the sample sizes were equal. This estimate of σ^2 is called the *mean square due to treatments* and is denoted MSTR. The general formula for computing MSTR is

$$\text{MSTR} = \frac{\sum\limits_{j=1}^{k} n_j(\bar{x}_j - \bar{\bar{x}})^2}{k - 1} \tag{10.19}$$

The numerator in equation (10.19) is called the *sum of squares due to treatments* and is denoted SSTR. The denominator, $k - 1$, represents the degrees of freedom associated with SSTR. Hence, the mean square due to treatments can be computed by the following formula.

Mean Square Due to Treatments

$$\text{MSTR} = \frac{\text{SSTR}}{k - 1} \tag{10.20}$$

where

$$\text{SSTR} = \sum_{j=1}^{k} n_j(\bar{x}_j - \bar{\bar{x}})^2 \tag{10.21}$$

If H_0 is true, MSTR provides an unbiased estimate of σ^2. However, if the means of the k populations are not equal, MSTR is not an unbiased estimate of σ^2; in fact, in that case, MSTR should overestimate σ^2.

For the NCP data in Table 10.8, we obtain the following results.

$$\text{SSTR} = \sum_{j=1}^{k} n_j(\bar{x}_j - \bar{\bar{x}})^2 = 6(79 - 73)^2 + 6(74 - 73)^2 + 6(66 - 73)^2 = 516$$

$$\text{MSTR} = \frac{\text{SSTR}}{k - 1} = \frac{516}{2} = 258$$

Within-Treatments Estimate of Population Variance

In the preceding section we introduced the concept of a within-treatments estimate of σ^2 and showed how to compute it when the sample sizes were equal. This estimate of σ^2 is called the *mean square due to error* and is denoted MSE. The general formula for computing MSE is

$$\text{MSE} = \frac{\sum\limits_{j=1}^{k} (n_j - 1)s_j^2}{n_T - k} \tag{10.22}$$

The numerator in equation (10.22) is called the *sum of squares due to error* and is denoted SSE. The denominator of MSE is referred to as the degrees of freedom associated with SSE. Hence, the formula for MSE can also be stated as follows.

Mean Square Due to Error

$$\text{MSE} = \frac{\text{SSE}}{n_T - k} \tag{10.23}$$

where

$$SSE = \sum_{j=1}^{k} (n_j - 1)s_j^2 \tag{10.24}$$

Note that MSE is based on the variation within each of the treatments; it is not influenced by whether the null hypothesis is true. Thus, MSE always provides an unbiased estimate of σ^2.

For the NCP data in Table 10.8 we obtain the following results.

$$SSE = \sum_{j=1}^{k} (n_j - 1)s_j^2 = (6 - 1)34 + (6 - 1)20 + (6 - 1)32 = 430$$

$$MSE = \frac{SSE}{n_T - k} = \frac{430}{18 - 3} = \frac{430}{15} = 28.67$$

Comparing the Variance Estimates: The *F* Test

Let us assume that the null hypothesis is true. In that case, MSTR and MSE provide two independent, unbiased estimates of σ^2. For normal populations, the sampling distribution of the ratio of two independent estimates of σ^2 follows an *F* distribution. Hence, if the null hypothesis is true and the ANOVA assumptions are valid, the sampling distribution of MSTR/MSE is an *F* distribution with numerator degrees of freedom equal to $k - 1$ and denominator degrees of freedom equal to $n_T - k$.

If the means of the k populations are not equal, the value of MSTR/MSE will be inflated because MSTR overestimates σ^2. Hence, we will reject H_0 if the resulting value of MSTR/MSE appears to be too large to have been selected at random from an *F* distribution with degrees of freedom $k - 1$ in the numerator and $n_T - k$ in the denominator. The value of $F = MSTR/MSE$ that will cause us to reject H_0 depends on α, the level of significance. Once α is selected, a critical value can be determined. Figure 10.16 shows the sampling dis-

FIGURE 10.16   SAMPLING DISTRIBUTION OF $F = MSTR/MSE$; THE CRITICAL VALUE FOR REJECTING THE NULL HYPOTHESIS OF EQUALITY OF MEANS IS F_α

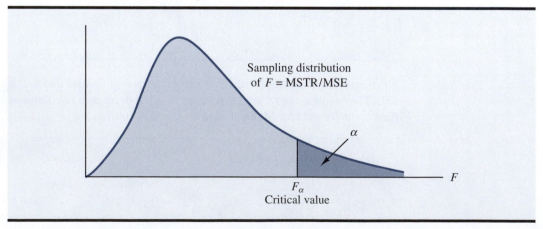

tribution of $F = \text{MSTR}/\text{MSE}$ and the rejection region associated with a level of significance equal to α, where F_α denotes the critical value.

Suppose the manager responsible for making the decision in the National Computer Products example was willing to accept a probability of making a Type I error of $\alpha = .05$. From Table 4 of Appendix B we can determine the critical F value by locating the value corresponding to numerator degrees of freedom equal to $k - 1 = 3 - 1 = 2$ and denominator degrees of freedom equal to $n_T - k = 18 - 3 = 15$. Thus, we obtain the critical value $F_{.05} = 3.68$. Note that this means that if the null hypothesis is true, we will observe a value greater than 3.68 only 5% of the time. Moreover, the theory behind the analysis of variance tells us that if the null hypothesis is true, the ratio of MSTR/MSE is a value from this F distribution. Hence, the appropriate rejection rule for the NCP example is written

Using test statistic: Reject H_0 if $F = \text{MSTR}/\text{MSE} > 3.68$
Using p-value: Reject H_0 if p-value $< .05$

Recall that $\text{MSTR} = 258$ and $\text{MSE} = 28.67$. Because $F = \text{MSTR}/\text{MSE} = 258/28.67 = 9.00$ is greater than the critical value, $F_{.05} = 3.68$, we have sufficient evidence to reject the null hypothesis that the means of the three populations are equal. In other words, analysis of variance supports the conclusion that the population mean examination scores at the three NCP plants are not equal.

The p-value criterion can also be used for this hypothesis test. The usual rejection rule applies: Reject H_0 if p-value $< \alpha$. Excel makes computing the p-value easy. For example, for the NCP example, simply enter $=\text{FDIST}(9,2,15)$ in any cell of a worksheet; the result, .0027, is the p-value associated with the test statistic $F = 9.00$. With a p-value $= .0027 < \alpha = .05$, the null hypothesis that the means of the three populations are equal can be rejected. A summary of the overall procedure for testing for the equality of k population means follows.

Test for the Equality of k Population Means

$$H_0: \mu_1 = \mu_2 = \cdots = \mu_k$$
$$H_a: \text{Not all population means are equal}$$

Test Statistic

$$F = \frac{\text{MSTR}}{\text{MSE}} \tag{10.25}$$

Rejection Rule

Using test statistic: Reject H_0 if $F > F_\alpha$
Using p-value: Reject H_0 if p-value $< \alpha$

where the value of F_α is based on an F distribution with $k - 1$ numerator degrees of freedom and $n_T - k$ denominator degrees of freedom.

ANOVA Table

The results of the preceding calculations can be displayed conveniently in a table referred to as the analysis of variance or **ANOVA table.** Table 10.9 is the analysis of variance table for the National Computer Products example. The sum of squares associated with the source

TABLE 10.9   ANALYSIS OF VARIANCE TABLE FOR THE NCP EXAMPLE

Source of Variation	Sum of Squares	Degrees of Freedom	Mean Square	F
Treatments	516	2	258.00	9.00
Error	430	15	28.67	
Total	946	17		

of variation referred to as "Total" is called the *total sum of squares (SST)*. Note that the results for the NCP example suggest that SST = SSTR + SSE, and that the degrees of freedom associated with this total sum of squares is the sum of the degrees of freedom associated with the between-treatments estimate of σ^2 and the within-treatments estimate of σ^2.

We point out that SST divided by its degrees of freedom $n_T - 1$ is nothing more than the overall sample variance that would be obtained if we treated the entire set of 18 observations as one data set. With the entire data set as one sample, the formula for computing the total sum of squares, SST, is

$$SST = \sum_{j=1}^{k}\sum_{i=1}^{n_j}(x_{ij} - \bar{\bar{x}})^2 \tag{10.26}$$

It can be shown that the results we observed for the analysis of variance table for the NCP example also apply to other problems. That is,

$$SST = SSTR + SSE \tag{10.27}$$

Analysis of variance can be thought of as a statistical procedure for partitioning the total sum of squares into separate components.

In other words, SST can be partitioned into two sums of squares: the sum of squares due to treatments and the sum of squares due to error. Note also that the degrees of freedom corresponding to SST, $n_T - 1$, can be partitioned into the degrees of freedom corresponding to SSTR, $k - 1$, and the degrees of freedom corresponding to SSE, $n_T - k$. Thus, the analysis of variance can be viewed as the process of **partitioning** the total sum of squares and the degrees of freedom into their corresponding sources: treatments and error. Dividing the sum of squares by the appropriate degrees of freedom provides the variance estimates and the F value used to test the hypothesis of equal population means.

Using Excel's Anova: Single Factor Tool

Excel's Anova: Single Factor tool can be used to conduct a hypothesis test about the difference between the population means for the National Computer Products example. Refer to the Excel worksheet shown in Figure 10.17 and the dialog box in Figure 10.18 as we describe the tasks involved.

Enter Data: Column A is used to identify the observations at each of the plants. Columns B, C, and D contain the examination scores for the three plants.

FIGURE 10.17   EXCEL ANOVA OUTPUT FOR THE NCP EXAMPLE

	A	B	C	D	E	F	G	H
1	Observation	Atlanta	Dallas	Seattle				
2	1	85	71	59				
3	2	75	75	64				
4	3	82	73	62				
5	4	76	74	69				
6	5	71	69	75				
7	6	85	82	67				
8								
9	Anova: Single Factor							
10								
11	SUMMARY							
12	*Groups*	*Count*	*Sum*	*Average*	*Variance*			
13	Atlanta	6	474	79	34			
14	Dallas	6	444	74	20			
15	Seattle	6	396	66	32			
16								
17								
18	ANOVA							
19	*Source of Variation*	*SS*	*df*	*MS*	*F*	*P-value*	*F crit*	
20	Between Groups	516	2	258	9	0.0027	3.68	
21	Within Groups	430	15	28.6667				
22								
23	Total	946	17					
24								

FIGURE 10.18   DIALOG BOX FOR ANOVA: SINGLE FACTOR

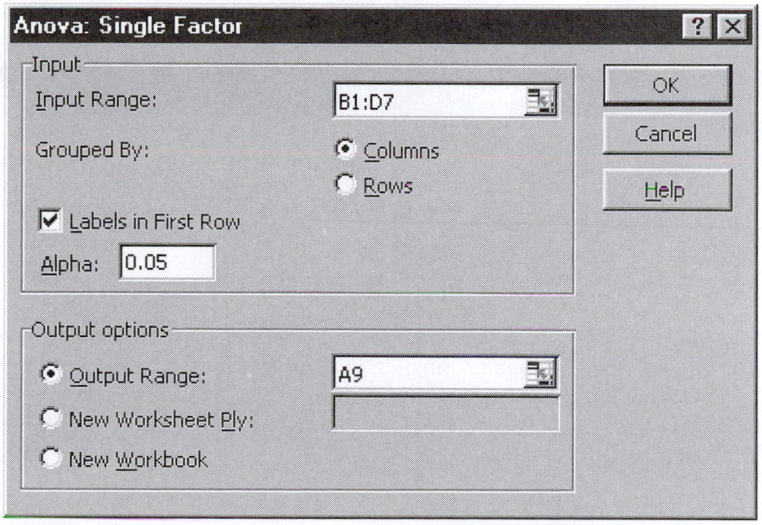

Apply Tools: The following steps describe how to use Excel's Anova: Single Factor tool to test the hypothesis that the mean examination score is the same for all three plants.

Step 1. Select the **Tools** menu
Step 2. Choose the **Data Analysis** option
Step 3. Choose **Anova: Single Factor** from the list of Analysis Tools
Step 4. When the Anova: Single Factor dialog box appears (see Figure 10.18):
>   Enter B1:D7 in the **Input Range** box
>   Select Grouped By **Columns**
>   Select **Labels in First Row**
>   Enter .05 in the **Alpha** box
>   Select **Output Range**
>   Enter A9 in the **Output Range** box (to identify the upper left corner of the section of the worksheet where the output will appear)
>   Click **OK**

The output, titled *Anova: Single Factor*, appears in cells A9:G23 of the worksheet in Figure 10.17. Cells A11:E15 provide a summary of the data. Note that the sample mean and sample variance for each plant is the same as shown in Table 10.8. The ANOVA table, shown in cells A18:G23, is basically the same as the ANOVA table shown in Table 10.9. Excel identifies the Treatments source of variation using the label *Between Groups* and the Error source of variation using the label *Within Groups*. In addition, the Excel output provides the p-value associated with the test as well as the critical F value.

We can make the hypothesis testing decision by comparing the computed F value shown in cell E20, $F = 9$, to the critical F value shown in cell G20, $F_{.05} = 3.68$. Because $F = 9$ is greater than $F_{.05} = 3.68$, we can reject the null hypothesis and conclude that the population mean examination scores at the three NCP plants are not equal.

Alternatively, we can use the p-value shown in cell F20, 0.0027, to make the hypothesis testing decision. Thus, at the $\alpha = .05$ level of significance, we reject H_0 because the p-value $= 0.0027 < \alpha = .05$. Hence, using the p-value approach we still conclude that the mean examination scores differ among the three plants.

NOTES AND COMMENTS

1. The overall sample mean can also be computed as a weighted average of the k sample means.

$$\bar{\bar{x}} = \frac{n_1\bar{x}_1 + n_2\bar{x}_2 + \cdots + n_k\bar{x}_k}{n_T}$$

In problems where the sample means are provided, this formula is simpler than equation (10.16) for computing the overall mean.

2. If each sample consists of n observations, equation (10.19) can be written as

$$MSTR = \frac{n\sum_{j=1}^{k}(\bar{x}_j - \bar{\bar{x}})^2}{k - 1} = n\left[\frac{\sum_{j=1}^{k}(\bar{x}_j - \bar{\bar{x}})^2}{k - 1}\right]$$

$$= ns_{\bar{x}}^2$$

Note that this result is the same as presented in Section 10.4 when we introduced the concept of the between-treatments estimate of σ^2. Equation (10.19) is simply a generalization of this result to the unequal sample-size case.

3. If each sample has n observations, $n_T = kn$; thus, $n_T - k = k(n - 1)$, and equation (10.22) can be rewritten as

$$\text{MSE} = \frac{\sum\limits_{j=1}^{k}(n - 1)s_j^2}{k(n - 1)} = \frac{(n - 1)\sum\limits_{j=1}^{k}s_j^2}{k(n - 1)} = \frac{\sum\limits_{j=1}^{k}s_j^2}{k}$$

In other words, if the sample sizes are the same, MSE is just the average of the k sample variances. Note that it is the same result we used in

Section 10.4 when we introduced the concept of the within-treatments estimate of σ^2.

4. Confidence interval estimates for each of the k population means can be developed using

$$\bar{x} \pm t_{\alpha/2}\frac{\sqrt{\text{MSE}}}{\sqrt{n}}$$

The degrees of freedom for the t value are the degrees of freedom associated with the within-treatments estimate of σ^2.

EXERCISES

Methods

32. Simple random samples of five observations were selected from each of three populations. The data obtained follow.

	Sample 1	Sample 2	Sample 3
	32	44	33
	30	43	36
	30	44	35
	26	46	36
	32	48	40
Sample mean	30	45	36
Sample variance	6.00	4.00	6.50

a. Compute the between-treatments estimate of σ^2.
b. Compute the within-treatments estimate of σ^2.
c. At the $\alpha = .05$ level of significance, can we reject the null hypothesis that the means of the three populations are equal?
d. Set up the ANOVA table for this problem.

33. Simple random samples of four observations were selected from each of three populations. The data obtained follow.

	Sample 1	Sample 2	Sample 3
	165	174	169
	149	164	154
	156	180	161
	142	158	148
Sample mean	153	169	158
Sample variance	96.67	97.33	82.00

    a. Compute the between-treatments estimate of σ^2.
    b. Compute the within-treatments estimate of σ^2.
    c. At the $\alpha = .05$ level of significance, can we reject the null hypothesis that the three population means are equal? Explain.
    d. Set up the ANOVA table for this problem.

34. Simple random samples were selected from three populations. The data obtained follow.

	Sample 1	Sample 2	Sample 3
	93	77	88
	98	87	75
	107	84	73
	102	95	84
		85	75
		82	
$\bar{x}_j$	100	85	79
s_j^2	35.33	35.60	43.50

    a. Compute the between-treatments estimate of σ^2.
    b. Compute the within-treatments estimate of σ^2.
    c. At the $\alpha = .05$ level of significance, can we reject the null hypothesis that the three population means are equal? Explain.
    d. Set up the ANOVA table for this problem.

35. Random samples of 16 observations were selected from each of four populations. A portion of the ANOVA table follows.

Source of Variation	Sum of Squares	Degrees of Freedom	Mean Square	F
Treatments			400	
Error				
Total	1500			

    a. Provide the missing entries for the ANOVA table.
    b. At the $\alpha = .05$ level of significance, can we reject the null hypothesis that the means of the four populations are equal?

36. Random samples of 25 observations were selected from each of three populations. For these data, SSTR = 120 and SSE = 216.
    a. Set up the ANOVA table for this problem.
    b. At the $\alpha = .05$ level of significance, what is the critical F value?
    c. At the $\alpha = .05$ level of significance, can we reject the null hypothesis that the three population means are equal?

Applications

37. To test whether the mean time needed to mix a batch of material is the same for machines produced by three manufacturers, the Jacobs Chemical Company obtained the following data on the time (in minutes) needed to mix the material. Use these data to test whether the population mean times for mixing a batch of material differ for the three manufacturers. Use $\alpha = .05$.

Manufacturer		
1	**2**	**3**
20	28	20
26	26	19
24	31	23
22	27	22

38. Managers at all levels of an organization need adequate information to perform their respective tasks. One study investigated the effect the source has on the dissemination of information. In this particular study the sources of information were a superior, a peer, and a subordinate. In each case, a measure of dissemination was obtained, with higher values indicating greater dissemination of information. Using $\alpha = .05$ and the following data, test whether the source of information significantly affects dissemination. What is your conclusion, and what does it suggest about the use and dissemination of information?

Superior	Peer	Subordinate
8	6	6
5	6	5
4	7	7
6	5	4
6	3	3
7	4	5
5	7	7
5	6	5

39. A study investigated the perception of corporate ethical values among individuals specializing in marketing. Using $\alpha = .05$ and the following data (higher scores indicate higher ethical values), test for significant differences in perception among the three groups of specialists.

Marketing Managers	Marketing Research	Advertising
6	5	6
5	5	7
4	4	6
5	4	5
6	5	6
4	4	6

40. A study reported in the *Journal of Small Business Management* concluded that self-employed individuals experience higher job stress than individuals who are not self-employed. In this study job stress was assessed with a 15-item scale designed to measure various aspects of ambiguity and role conflict. Ratings for each of the 15 items were made using a scale with 1–5 response options ranging from strong agreement to strong disagreement. The sum of the ratings for the 15 items for each individual surveyed is between 15 and 75, with higher values indicating a higher degree of job stress (*Journal of Small*

Business Management, October 1997). Suppose that a similar approach, using a 20-item scale with 1–5 response options, was used to measure the job stress of individuals for 15 randomly selected real estate agents, 15 architects, and 15 stockbrokers. The results obtained follow.

Stress

Real Estate Agent	Architect	Stockbroker
81	43	65
48	63	48
68	60	57
69	52	91
54	54	70
62	77	67
76	68	83
56	57	75
61	61	53
65	80	71
64	50	54
69	37	72
83	73	65
85	84	58
75	58	58

Using $\alpha = .05$, test for any significant difference in job stress among the three professions.

41. The *Business Week* Global 1000 ranks companies on the basis of their market value (*Business Week*, July 7, 1997). The following table shows the price/earnings ratios for 29 companies classified as being in the finance economic sector. An industry code of 1 indicates a banking firm, a code of 2 a financial services firm, and a code of 3 an insurance firm. At the .05 level of significance, test whether the mean price/earnings ratio is the same for these three groups of financial firms.

MktValue

Company	Industry Code	P/E	Company	Industry Code	P/E
Citicorp	1	15	MBNA	2	24
NationsBank	1	14	Cincinnati Financial	2	19
Wells Fargo	1	25	Franklin Resources	2	22
First Union	1	13	Fannie Mae	2	17
KeyCorp	1	14	American International	3	21
Chase Manhattan	1	12	Group		
Fifth Third Bancorp	1	23	Allstate	3	14
Bank of New York	1	17	Marsh & McLennan	3	20
First Chicago NBD	1	13	American General	3	16
Mellon Bank	1	16	Cigna	3	12
Fleet Financial Group	1	15	Lincoln National	3	13
First Bank System	1	16	AFLAC	3	21
American Express	2	19	Equitable	3	11
Travelers	2	15	Chubb	3	20
Merrill Lynch	2	12	General Re	3	15

SUMMARY

In this chapter we discussed procedures for developing interval estimates and conducting hypothesis tests involving two or more population means. First, we showed how to make inferences about the difference between the means of two populations when independent simple random samples are selected. We considered both the large- and small-sample cases. The z values from the standard normal probability distribution are used for inferences about the difference between two population means when the sample sizes are large. In the small-sample case, if the populations are normally distributed with assumed equal variances, the t distribution is used for inferences.

Inferences about the difference between the means of two populations were then discussed for the matched sample design. In the matched sample design each element provides a pair of data values, one from each population. The difference between the paired data values is then used in the statistical analysis. The matched sample design is generally preferred to the independent sample design because the matched sample procedure often reduces the sampling error and improves the precision of the estimate.

Finally, we showed how analysis of variance can be used to test for differences among means of several populations. We showed that the basis for the statistical tests used in analysis of variance is the development of two independent estimates of the population variance, σ^2. By computing the ratio of these two estimates (the F statistic), we developed a rejection rule for determining whether to reject the null hypothesis that the population means are equal.

We showed how Excel can be used to develop the interval estimates and conduct the hypothesis tests discussed in the chapter. Many of the worksheets can be used as templates to solve problems encountered in practice as well as the exercises and case problems found in the text.

GLOSSARY

Independent samples   Samples selected from two populations in such a way that the elements making up one sample are chosen independently of the elements making up the other sample.

Pooled variance   An estimate of the population variance based on a weighted average of two sample variances. The pooled variance estimate is appropriate whenever the variances of two populations are assumed equal.

Matched samples   Samples in which each data value of one sample is matched with a corresponding data value of the other sample.

Analysis of variance (ANOVA)   A statistical technique that can be used to test the hypothesis that the means of several populations are equal.

Response variable   Another word for the dependent variable of interest.

Factor   Another word for the independent variable of interest.

Treatment   Different levels of a factor.

ANOVA table   A table used to summarize the analysis of variance computations and results. It contains columns showing the source of variation, the sum of squares, the degrees of freedom, the mean square, and the F value(s).

Partitioning   The process of allocating the total sum of squares and degrees of freedom to the various components.

KEY FORMULAS

Point Estimator of the Difference Between the Means of Two Populations

$$\bar{x}_1 - \bar{x}_2 \tag{10.1}$$

Expected Value of $\bar{x}_1 - \bar{x}_2$

$$E(\bar{x}_1 - \bar{x}_2) = \mu_1 - \mu_2 \tag{10.2}$$

Standard Deviation of $\bar{x}_1 - \bar{x}_2$ (Independent Samples)

$$\sigma_{\bar{x}_1 - \bar{x}_2} = \sqrt{\frac{\sigma_1^2}{n_1} + \frac{\sigma_2^2}{n_2}} \tag{10.3}$$

Interval Estimate of the Difference Between the Means of Two Populations: Large-Sample Case ($n_1 \geq 30$ and $n_2 \geq 30$) with σ_1 and σ_2 Assumed Known

$$\bar{x}_1 - \bar{x}_2 \pm z_{\alpha/2}\sigma_{\bar{x}_1 - \bar{x}_2} \tag{10.4}$$

Point Estimator of $\sigma_{\bar{x}_1 - \bar{x}_2}$

$$s_{\bar{x}_1 - \bar{x}_2} = \sqrt{\frac{s_1^2}{n_1} + \frac{s_2^2}{n_2}} \tag{10.5}$$

Interval Estimate of the Difference Between the Means of Two Populations: Large-Sample Case ($n_1 \geq 30$ and $n_2 \geq 30$) with σ_1 and σ_2 Estimated by s_1 and s_2

$$\bar{x}_1 - \bar{x}_2 \pm z_{\alpha/2}s_{\bar{x}_1 - \bar{x}_2} \tag{10.6}$$

Standard Deviation of $\bar{x}_1 - \bar{x}_2$ When $\sigma_1^2 = \sigma_2^2 = \sigma^2$

$$\sigma_{\bar{x}_1 - \bar{x}_2} = \sqrt{\frac{\sigma^2}{n_1} + \frac{\sigma^2}{n_2}} = \sqrt{\sigma^2\left(\frac{1}{n_1} + \frac{1}{n_2}\right)} \tag{10.7}$$

Pooled Variance Estimator of σ^2

$$s^2 = \frac{(n_1 - 1)s_1^2 + (n_2 - 1)s_2^2}{n_1 + n_2 - 2} \tag{10.8}$$

Point Estimator of $\sigma_{\bar{x}_1 - \bar{x}_2}$ When $\sigma_1^2 = \sigma_2^2 = \sigma^2$

$$s_{\bar{x}_1 - \bar{x}_2} = \sqrt{s^2\left(\frac{1}{n_1} + \frac{1}{n_2}\right)} \tag{10.9}$$

Interval Estimate of the Difference Between the Means of Two Populations: Small-Sample Case ($n_1 < 30$ and/or $n_2 < 30$) with σ_1 and σ_2 Estimated by s_1 and s_2

$$\bar{x}_1 - \bar{x}_2 \pm t_{\alpha/2}s_{\bar{x}_1 - \bar{x}_2} \tag{10.10}$$

Test Statistic for Hypothesis Tests About the Difference Between the Means of Two Populations: Large-Sample Case

$$z = \frac{(\bar{x}_1 - \bar{x}_2) - (\mu_1 - \mu_2)}{\sqrt{\sigma_1^2/n_1 + \sigma_2^2/n_2}} \tag{10.11}$$

Test Statistic for Hypothesis Tests About the Difference Between the Means of Two Populations: Small-Sample Case

$$t = \frac{(\bar{x}_1 - \bar{x}_2) - (\mu_1 - \mu_2)}{\sqrt{s^2\left(\dfrac{1}{n_1} + \dfrac{1}{n_2}\right)}} \qquad (10.12)$$

Sample Mean for Matched Samples

$$\bar{d} = \frac{\Sigma d_i}{n}$$

Sample Standard Deviation for Matched Samples

$$s_d = \sqrt{\frac{\Sigma(d_i - \bar{d})^2}{n - 1}}$$

Test Statistic for Matched Samples

$$t = \frac{\bar{d} - \mu_d}{s_d/\sqrt{n}} \qquad (10.13)$$

Sample Mean for Treatment j

$$\bar{x}_j = \frac{\displaystyle\sum_{i=1}^{n_j} x_{ij}}{n_j} \qquad (10.14)$$

Sample Variance for Treatment j

$$s_j^2 = \frac{\displaystyle\sum_{i=1}^{n_j}(x_{ij} - \bar{x}_j)^2}{n_j - 1} \qquad (10.15)$$

Overall Sample Mean

$$\bar{\bar{x}} = \frac{\displaystyle\sum_{j=1}^{k}\sum_{i=1}^{n_j} x_{ij}}{n_T} \qquad (10.16)$$

$$n_T = n_1 + n_2 + \cdots + n_k \qquad (10.17)$$

Mean Square Due to Treatments

$$\text{MSTR} = \frac{\text{SSTR}}{k - 1} \qquad (10.20)$$

Sum of Squares Due to Treatments

$$\text{SSTR} = \sum_{j=1}^{k} n_j(\bar{x}_j - \bar{\bar{x}})^2 \qquad (10.21)$$

Mean Square Due to Error

$$\text{MSE} = \frac{\text{SSE}}{n_T - k} \qquad (10.23)$$

Sum of Squares Due to Error

$$SSE = \sum_{j=1}^{k}(n_j - 1)s_j^2 \qquad (10.24)$$

Test for the Equality of k Population Means

$$F = \frac{MSTR}{MSE} \qquad (10.25)$$

Total Sum of Squares

$$SST = \sum_{j=1}^{k}\sum_{i=1}^{n_j}(x_{ij} - \bar{\bar{x}})^2 \qquad (10.26)$$

Partition of Sum of Squares

$$SST = SSTR + SSE \qquad (10.27)$$

SUPPLEMENTARY EXERCISES

42. Starting annual salaries for individuals with master's and bachelor's degrees were collected in two independent random samples. Use the following data to develop a 90% confidence interval estimate of the increase in starting salary that can be expected upon completion of a master's program.

Master's Degree	Bachelor's Degree
$n_1 = 60$	$n_2 = 80$
$\bar{x}_1 = \$45,000$	$\bar{x}_2 = \$35,000$
$s_1 = \$4000$	$s_2 = \$3500$

43. Safegate Foods, Inc., is redesigning the checkout lanes in its supermarkets throughout the country. For the two designs suggested, tests on customer checkout times were conducted at two stores where the new systems were already installed. The data collected are in the data set Safegate. Test at the .05 level of significance to determine whether the mean checkout times of the two systems differ. Which system is preferred?

44. Mutual funds are classified as *load* or *no-load* funds. Load funds require an investor to pay an initial fee based on a percentage of the amount invested in the fund. The no-load funds do not require this initial fee. Some financial advisors argue that the load mutual funds may be worth the extra fee because these funds provide a higher mean rate of return than the no-load mutual funds. A sample of 30 load mutual funds and a sample of 30 no-load mutual funds were selected from *Barron's Lipper Mutual Funds Quarterly*, January 12, 1998. Data were collected on the annual return for the funds over a five-year period. The data are contained in the data set Mutual. The data for the first five load and first five no-load mutual funds follow.

Mutual Funds—Load	Return	Mutual Funds—No Load	Return
American National Growth	15.51	Amana Income Fund	13.24
Arch Small Cap Equity	14.57	Berger One Hundred	12.13
Bartlett Cap Basic	17.73	Columbia International Stock	12.17
Calvert World International	10.31	Dodge & Cox Balanced	16.06
Colonial Fund A	16.23	Evergreen Fund	17.61

a. Formulate H_0 and H_a such that rejection of H_0 leads to the conclusion that the load mutual funds have a higher mean annual return over the five-year period.
b. Use the 60 mutual funds in the data set Mutual to conduct the hypothesis test. Using $\alpha = .05$, what is your conclusion?
c. What is the p-value?

45. Figure Perfect, Inc., is a women's figure salon that specializes in weight reduction programs. Weights for a sample of clients before and after a 6-week introductory program are shown here.

	Weight	
Client	Before	After
1	140	132
2	160	158
3	210	195
4	148	152
5	190	180
6	170	164

Using $\alpha = .05$, test to determine whether the introductory program provides a statistically significant weight loss. What is your conclusion?

46. The Asian economy faltered during the last few months of 1997. Investors anticipated that the downturn in the Asian economy would have a negative effect on the earnings of companies in the United States during the fourth quarter of 1997. The following sample data show the earnings per share for the fourth quarter of 1996 and the fourth quarter of 1997 (*The Wall Street Journal*, January 28, 1998).

Company	Earnings 1996	Earnings 1997
Atlantic Richfield	1.16	1.17
Balchem Corp.	0.16	0.13
Black & Decker Corp.	0.97	1.02
Dial Corp.	0.18	0.23
DSC Communications	0.15	−0.32
Eastman Chemical	0.77	0.36
Excel Communications	0.28	−0.14
Federal Signal	0.40	0.29
Ford Motor Company	0.97	1.45
GTE Corp	0.81	0.73
ITT Industries	0.59	0.60
Kimberly-Clark	0.61	−0.27
Minnesota Mining & Mfr.	0.91	0.89
Procter & Gamble	0.63	0.71

a. Formulate H_0 and H_a such that rejection of H_0 leads to the conclusion that the mean earnings per share for the fourth quarter of 1997 are less than for the fourth quarter of 1996.
b. Use the data in the file Asia to conduct the hypothesis test. Using $\alpha = .05$, what is your conclusion?

47. A simple random sample of the asking prices ($1000s) of four houses currently for sale in each of two residential areas resulted in the following data.

Area 1	Area 2
92	90
89	102
98	96
105	88

a. Use the procedure developed in Section 10.2 to test whether the mean asking price is the same in both areas. Use $\alpha = .05$.

b. Use the ANOVA procedure to test whether the mean asking price is the same. Compare your analysis with part (a). Use $\alpha = .05$.

c. Suppose that data were collected for another residential area. The asking prices for the simple random sample from the third area were $81,000, $86,000, $75,000, and $90,000. Is the mean asking price the same for all three areas? Use $\alpha = .05$.

48. Buyers of sport utility vehicles (SUVs) and pickup trucks find a wide choice in today's marketplace. One of the factors that is important to many buyers is the resale value of the vehicle. The following table shows the resale value (%) after two years for 10 SUVs, 10 small pickup trucks, and 10 full-size pickup trucks (*Kiplinger's New Cars & Trucks 2000 Buyer's Guide*).

Trucks

Sport Utility	Resale Value	Small Pickup	Resale Value
Chevrolet Blazer LS	55	Chevrolet S-10 Extended Cab	46
Ford Explorer Sport	57	Dodge Dakota Club Cab Sport	53
GMC Yukon XL 1500	67	Ford Ranger XLT Regular Cab	48
Honda CR-V	65	Ford Ranger XLT Supercab	55
Isuzu VehiCross	62	GMC Sonoma Regular Cab	44
Jeep Cherokee Limited	57	Isuzu Hombre Spacecab	41
Mercury Mountaineer	59	Mazda B4000 SE Cab Plus	51
Nissan Pathfinder XE	54	Nissan Frontier XE Regular Cab	51
Toyota 4Runner	55	Toyota Tacoma Xtracab	49
Toyota RAV4	55	Toyota Tacoma Xtracab V6	50

Full-Size Pickup	Resale Value
Chevrolet K2500	60
Chevrolet Silverado 2500 Ext	64
Dodge Ram 1500	54
Dodge Ram Quad Cab 2500	63
Dodge Ram Regular Cab 2500	59
Ford F150 XL	58
Ford F-350 Super Duty Crew Cab XL	64
GMC New Sierra 1500 Ext Cab	68
Toyota Tundra Access Cab Limited	53
Toyota Tundra Regular Cab	58

At the $\alpha = .05$ level of significance, test for any significant difference in the mean resale value for the three types of vehicles.

49. The following data show the age of 12 top executives for major marketers of food, retail, and personal care products (*Advertising Age,* December 1, 1997).

AgeExec

Company	Category	Executive	Age
Campbell Soup Co.	Food	Dale F. Morrison	48
General Mills	Food	Stephen W. Sanger	51
Kellogg Co.	Food	Arnold G. Langbo	59
RJR Nabisco	Food	Stephen F. Goldstone	51
Estee Lauder Cos.	Personal Care	Leonard A. Lauder	64
Gillette Co.	Personal Care	Alfred M. Zeien	67
Procter & Gamble Co.	Personal Care	John E. Pepper	59
Unilever	Personal Care	Morris Tabaksblat	59
Federated Department Stores	Retail	James W. Zimmerman	53
J.C. Penney Co.	Retail	James E. Oesterreicher	55
Sears Roebuck & Co.	Retail	Arthur C. Martinez	57
Kmart Corp.	Retail	Floyd Hall	58

At the $\alpha = .05$ level of significance, is there a significant difference in the mean age of executives for the three categories of companies?

50. A study reported in the *Journal of Small Business Management* concluded that self-employed individuals do not experience higher job satisfaction than individuals who are not self-employed. In this study, job satisfaction is measured using 18 items, each of which is rated using a Likert-type scale with 1–5 response options ranging from strong agreement to strong disagreement. A higher score on this scale indicates a higher degree of job satisfaction. The sum of the ratings for the 18 items, ranging from 18–90, is used as the measure of job satisfaction (*Journal of Small Business Management*, October 1997). Suppose that this approach was used to measure the job satisfaction for lawyers, physical therapists, cabinetmakers, and systems analysts. The results obtained for a sample of 10 individuals from each profession follow.

SatisJob

Lawyer	Physical Therapist	Cabinetmaker	Systems Analyst
44	55	54	44
42	78	65	73
74	80	79	71
42	86	69	60
53	60	79	64
50	59	64	66
45	62	59	41
48	52	78	55
64	55	84	76
38	50	60	62

At the $\alpha = .05$ level of significance, test for any difference in the job satisfaction among the four professions.

51. Crown Plaza Hotels and Resorts offered special weekend rates at hotels and resorts nationwide. A sample of 30 properties from three regions of the country provided the following room rates (*USA Today*, April 14, 2000).

CD file

Resorts

West	Rate ($)	South	Rate ($)	Northeast	Rate ($)
Albuquerque	89	Atlanta	105	Albany	89
Irvine	79	Dallas	80	Boston	139
Las Vegas	119	Greenville	79	Hartford	85
Los Angeles	99	Houston	79	New York	159
Palo Alto	109	Jackson	69	Philadelphia	99
Phoenix	149	Macon	69	Pittsfield	99
Portland	79	Miami	89	Providence	149
San Francisco	139	Orlando	119	Washington	159
San Jose	99	Richmond	109	White Plains	109
Seattle	119	Tampa	119	Worchester	124

At the $\alpha = .05$ level of significance, test whether the mean rates are the same for the three regions.

52. According to the sixth annual survey of ad agency employees conducted by the accounting firm Altschuler, Melvoin & Glasser, ad agency employees can expect another banner year in compensation (*Advertising Age*, December 1, 1997). To investigate whether the annual compensation for art directors differs by region, suppose that a sample of 10 art directors was selected from each of four regions: West, South, North Central, and Northeast. The base salary ($1000s) for each of the individuals sampled follows.

CD file

ArtDir

West	South	North Central	Northeast
60.9	50.8	49.5	65.9
45.9	39.6	42.3	58.6
62.1	44.2	35.5	49.3
66.6	40.0	49.1	52.9
68.0	53.9	56.7	48.5
65.0	45.4	41.4	52.9
49.4	61.1	51.3	52.4
62.3	42.3	49.4	48.1
62.6	38.4	42.1	46.5
57.2	38.3	55.7	45.9

At the $\alpha = .05$ level of significance, test whether the mean base salary for art directors is the same for each of the four regions.

53. The National Football League rates prospects position by position on a scale that ranges from 5 to 9. The ratings are interpreted as follows: 8–9 should start the first year; 7.0–7.9 should start; 6.0–6.9 will make the team as backup; and 5.0–5.9, can make the club and contribute. The following table shows the ratings for three positions for 40 NFL prospects (*USA Today*, April 14, 2000). Does there appear to be any significant effect on the rating due to the player's position?

NFL

Wide Receiver		Guard		Offensive Tackle	
Name	**Rating**	**Name**	**Rating**	**Name**	**Rating**
Peter Warrick	9.0	Cosey Coleman	7.4	Chris Samuels	8.5
Plaxico Burress	8.8	Travis Claridge	7.0	Stockar McDougle	8.0
Sylvester Morris	8.3	Kaulana Noa	6.8	Chris McIngosh	7.8
Travis Taylor	8.1	Leander Jordan	6.7	Adrian Klemm	7.6
Laveranues Coles	8.0	Chad Clifton	6.3	Todd Wade	7.3
Dez White	7.9	Manula Savea	6.1	Marvel Smith	7.1
Jerry Porter	7.4	Ryan Johanningmeir	6.0	Michael Thompson	6.8
Ron Dugans	7.1	Mark Tauscher	6.0	Bobby Williams	6.8
Todd Pinkston	7.0	Blaine Saipaia	6.0	Darnell Alford	6.4
Dennis Northcutt	7.0	Richard Mercier	5.8	Terrance Beadles	6.3
Anthony Lucas	6.9	Damion McIntosh	5.3	Tutan Reyes	6.1
Darrell Jackson	6.6	Jeno James	5.0	Greg Robinson-Ran	6.0
Danny Farmer	6.5	Al Jackson	5.5		
Sherrod Gideon	6.4				
Trevor Gaylor	6.2				

54. Each month *Internet Magazine* accesses more than 100 Internet Service Providers (ISPs) in order to check the availability of the ISP and test the speed of the connection by measuring the time (seconds) it takes to download a number of popular Web pages. The following data show the download time for 22 free ISPs for Web sites located in the United Kingdom, United States, and Europe (*Internet Magazine*, January 2000).

ISP

ISP Name	U.K.	U.S.	Europe
Abel Gratis	10.62	14.64	17.08
Breathe	11.67	14.14	19.86
btclick.com	12.12	16.43	21.30
Bun	11.13	14.09	15.83
Cable & Wireless Life	9.99	13.07	18.43
conX	12.63	15.97	22.12
Freebeeb	11.71	15.52	19.57
Free-Online	13.77	13.98	23.35
Freeserve	10.65	13.62	25.56
FreeUK	12.20	14.96	18.95
Icom-Web	9.62	11.66	15.91
IPNet	13.82	16.70	22.86
I-way Soho	14.86	12.86	19.32
LineOne	12.01	17.82	21.88
Madasafish	13.38	15.59	19.61
NetDirect Online	11.71	15.52	19.57
Netscape Online	10.84	12.66	16.52
Screaming.net (BT Line)	13.23	15.91	23.08
Telinco Internet Services	12.83	15.34	18.76
UK Online	10.39	13.28	21.04
UKPeople	13.79	19.82	19.76
Virgin Net	12.17	15.47	21.94

At $\alpha = .05$, is there a significant difference in the mean download time for Web sites located in the three countries?

Case Problem 1   PAR, INC.

Par, Inc., is a major manufacturer of golf equipment. Management believes that Par's market share could be increased with the introduction of a cut-resistant, longer-lasting golf ball. Therefore, the research group at Par has been investigating a new golf ball coating designed to resist cuts and provide a more durable ball. The tests with the coating have been promising.

One of the researchers voiced concern about the effect of the new coating on driving distances. Par would like the new cut-resistant ball to offer driving distances comparable to those of its current-model golf ball. To compare the driving distances for the two balls, 40 balls of each type were subjected to distance tests. The testing was performed with a mechanical hitting machine so that any difference between the mean distances for the two models could be attributed to a difference in the design. The results of the tests, with distances measured to the nearest yard, follow. These data are available on the data disk in the data set Golf.

Golf

\multicolumn{2}{c}{Model}		\multicolumn{2}{c}{Model}		\multicolumn{2}{c}{Model}		\multicolumn{2}{c}{Model}	
Current	New	Current	New	Current	New	Current	New
264	277	270	272	263	274	281	283
261	269	287	259	264	266	274	250
267	263	289	264	284	262	273	253
272	266	280	280	263	271	263	260
258	262	272	274	260	260	275	270
283	251	275	281	283	281	267	263
258	262	265	276	255	250	279	261
266	289	260	269	272	263	274	255
259	286	278	268	266	278	276	263
270	264	275	262	268	264	262	279

Managerial Report

1. Provide descriptive statistical summaries of the data for each model.
2. Formulate and present the rationale for a hypothesis test that Par could use to compare the driving distances of the current and new golf balls.
3. Analyze the data to provide the hypothesis testing conclusion. What is the *p*-value for your test? What is your recommendation for Par, Inc.?
4. Do you see a need for larger sample sizes and more testing with the golf balls? Discuss.

Case Problem 2   WENTWORTH MEDICAL CENTER

As part of a long-term study of individuals 65 years of age or older, sociologists and physicians at the Wentworth Medical Center in upstate New York investigated the relationship between geographic location and depression. They selected a sample of 60 individuals, all in reasonably good health: 20 individuals were residents of Florida, 20 were residents of New York, and 20 were residents of North Carolina. The researchers gave each of the individuals sampled a standardized test to measure depression. The data collected follow; higher test scores indicate higher levels of depression. These data are available on the data disk in the file Medical1.

A second part of the study considered the relationship between geographic location and depression for individuals 65 years of age or older who had a chronic health condition such as arthritis, hypertension, and/or heart ailment. The researchers identified a sample of 60 individuals with such conditions. Again, 20 were residents of Florida, 20 were residents of New York, and 20 were residents of North Carolina. The levels of depression recorded for this study follow. These data are available on the data disk in the file Medical2.

| | Data from Medical1 | | | Data from Medical2 | |
Florida	New York	North Carolina	Florida	New York	North Carolina
3	8	10	13	14	10
7	11	7	12	9	12
7	9	3	17	15	15
3	7	5	17	12	18
8	8	11	20	16	12
8	7	8	21	24	14
8	8	4	16	18	17
5	4	3	14	14	8
5	13	7	13	15	14
2	10	8	17	17	16
6	6	8	12	20	18
2	8	7	9	11	17
6	12	3	12	23	19
6	8	9	15	19	15
9	6	8	16	17	13
7	8	12	15	14	14
5	5	6	13	9	11
4	7	3	10	14	12
7	7	8	11	13	13
3	8	11	17	11	11

CD file
Medical1

CD file
Medical2

Managerial Report

1. Use descriptive statistics to summarize the data from the two studies. What are your preliminary observations about the depression scores?
2. Use analysis of variance on both data sets. State the hypotheses being tested in each case. What are your conclusions?
3. Use inferences about individual treatment means where appropriate. What are your conclusions?
4. Discuss extensions of this study or other analyses that you feel might be helpful.

Case Problem 3   COMPENSATION FOR ID PROFESSIONALS

For 10 years, *Industrial Distribution* tracked compensation of industrial distribution (ID) professionals. Results for the 358 respondents in the 1997 Annual Salary Survey showed that 27% of the respondents work for companies with sales over $40 million, with the typical ID professional working for a $12 million firm. Those who work for small to mid-sized companies (between $6 million and $20 million) report higher earnings than those in larger firms. The lowest paid employees work for firms with sales of less than $1 million. The typical outside salesperson made $50,000 in 1996, and the typical inside salesperson earned just $30,000 (*Industrial Distribution*, November 1997). Suppose that a local chapter of ID professionals in the greater San Francisco area conducted a survey of its membership to study the relationship, if any, between the years of experience and salary for individuals employed in outside and inside sales positions. On the survey, respondents were asked to specify one of three levels of years of experience: low (1–10 years); medium (11–20 years); and high (21 or more years). A portion of the data obtained follow. The complete data set, consisting of 120 observations, is available on the data disk in the file IDSalary.

IDSalary

Observation	Salary $	Position	Experience
1	28938	Inside	Medium
2	27694	Inside	Medium
3	45515	Outside	Low
4	27031	Inside	Medium
5	37283	Outside	Low
6	32718	Inside	Low
7	54081	Outside	High
8	23621	Inside	Low
9	47835	Outside	High
10	29768	Inside	Medium
.	.	.	.
.	.	.	.
.	.	.	.
115	33080	Inside	High
116	53702	Outside	Medium
117	58131	Outside	Medium
118	32788	Inside	High
119	28070	Inside	Medium
120	35259	Outside	Low

Managerial Report

1. Use descriptive statistics to summarize the data.
2. Develop a 95% confidence interval estimate of the mean annual salary for all salespersons, regardless of years of experience and type of position.
3. Develop a 95% confidence interval estimate of the mean salary for outside salespersons. Compare your results with the national value reported by *Industrial Distribution*.
4. Develop a 95% confidence interval estimate of the mean salary for inside salespersons. Compare your results with the national value reported by *Industrial Distribution*.
5. Ignoring the years of experience, develop a 95% confidence interval estimate of the mean difference between the annual salary for outside salespersons and the mean annual salary for inside salespersons. What is your conclusion?
6. Use analysis of variance to test for any significant differences due to position. Use a .05 level of significance, and for now, ignore the effect of years of experience.
7. Use analysis of variance to test for any significant differences due to years of experience. Use a .05 level of significance, and for now, ignore the effect of position.

CHAPTER 11

Comparisons Involving Proportions and a Test of Independence

CONTENTS

STATISTICS IN PRACTICE

United Way*

ROCHESTER, NEW YORK

United Way of Greater Rochester is a nonprofit organization dedicated to improving the quality of life for all people in the seven counties it serves by meeting the community's most important human care needs.

The annual United Way/Red Cross fund-raising campaign, conducted each spring, funds hundreds of programs offered by more than 200 service providers. These providers meet a wide variety of human needs—physical, mental, and social—and serve people of all ages, backgrounds, and economic means. Because of enormous volunteer involvement, United Way of Greater Rochester is able to hold its operating costs at just 8 cents of every dollar raised.

The United Way of Greater Rochester decided to conduct a survey to learn more about community perceptions of charities. Focus group interviews were held with professional, service, and general worker groups to get preliminary information on perceptions. The information obtained was then used to help develop the questionnaire for the survey. The questionnaire was pretested, modified, and distributed to 440 individuals; 323 completed questionnaires were received.

A variety of descriptive statistics, including frequency distributions and crosstabulations, were provided from the data collected. An important part of the analysis involved the use of contingency tables and chi-square tests of independence. One use of such statistical tests was to determine whether perceptions of administrative expenses were independent of occupation.

The hypotheses for the test of independence were:

H_0: Perception of United Way administrative expenses is independent of the occupation of the respondent.

Statistical surveys help United Way adjust its programs to better meet the needs of the people it serves. © Tony Freeman/PhotoEdit, Inc.

H_a: Perception of United Way administrative expenses is not independent of the occupation of the respondent.

Two questions in the survey provided the data for the statistical test. One question obtained data on perceptions of the percentage of funds going to administrative expenses (up to 10%, 11–20%, and 21% or more). The other question asked for the occupation of the respondent.

The chi-square test at a 5% level of significance led to rejection of the null hypothesis of independence and to the conclusion that perceptions of United Way's administrative expenses did vary by occupation. Actual administrative expenses were less than 9%, but 35% of the respondents perceived that administrative expenses were 21% or more. Hence, many had inaccurate perceptions of administrative expenses. In this group, production-line, clerical, sales, and professional-technical employees had more inaccurate perceptions than other groups.

The community perceptions study helped United Way of Rochester to develop adjustments to its program and fund-raising activities.

In this chapter, you will learn how a statistical test of independence, such as that described here, is conducted.

---

*The authors are indebted to Dr. Philip R. Tyler, Marketing Consultant to the United Way, for providing this Statistics in Practice.

In many statistical applications it is of interest to compare population proportions. In Section 11.1, we will describe statistical inferences that can be made concerning differences in the proportions for two populations. Two samples are required, one from each population, and the statistical inference is based on a comparison of the two sample proportions. The second section is concerned with a hypothesis test involving the proportions of a single multinomial population. One sample from the multinomial population is used and the hypothesis test is based on comparing the sample proportions with those stated in the null hypothesis. In the last section of the chapter, we show how contingency tables are used to test for the independence of two variables. The Statistics in Practice described how the Rochester United Way applied such a test. One sample is used for the test of independence, but measures on two variables are required for each sampled element. Both Sections 11.2 and 11.3 rely on the use of a chi-square statistical test.

11.1   INFERENCES ABOUT THE DIFFERENCE BETWEEN THE PROPORTIONS OF TWO POPULATIONS

Let us begin with an example involving a tax preparation firm that is interested in comparing the quality of work at two of its regional offices. By selecting simple random samples of tax returns prepared at each office and having the sample returns verified for accuracy, the firm will be able to estimate the proportion of erroneous returns prepared at each office. Of particular interest is the difference between these proportions. Let

The methods of this section are appropriate for independent random samples from two populations.

p_1 = proportion of erroneous returns for population 1 (office 1)

p_2 = proportion of erroneous returns for population 2 (office 2)

$\bar{p}_1$ = sample proportion for a simple random sample from population 1

$\bar{p}_2$ = sample proportion for a simple random sample from population 2

The difference between the two population proportions is $p_1 - p_2$. The point estimator of $p_1 - p_2$ is the difference between the two sample proportions.

Point Estimator of the Difference Between the Proportions of Two Populations

$$\bar{p}_1 - \bar{p}_2 \tag{11.1}$$

Sampling Distribution of $\bar{p}_1 - \bar{p}_2$

In the study of the difference between two population proportions, $\bar{p}_1 - \bar{p}_2$ is the point estimator of interest. The sampling distribution of a point estimator provides the basis for developing interval estimates and in testing hypotheses about parameters of interest. The properties of the sampling distribution of $\bar{p}_1 - \bar{p}_2$ follow.

Sampling Distribution of $\bar{p}_1 - \bar{p}_2$

The standard deviation of the sampling distribution of $\bar{p}_1 - \bar{p}_2$ is also referred to as the standard error of the point estimator $\bar{p}_1 - \bar{p}_2$.

Expected Value: $E(\bar{p}_1 - \bar{p}_2) = p_1 - p_2 \tag{11.2}$

Standard Deviation: $\sigma_{\bar{p}_1 - \bar{p}_2} = \sqrt{\dfrac{p_1(1 - p_1)}{n_1} + \dfrac{p_2(1 - p_2)}{n_2}} \tag{11.3}$

---

where

$$n_1 = \text{sample size for the simple random sample from population 1}$$
$$n_2 = \text{sample size for the simple random sample from population 2}$$

Distribution form: If the sample sizes are large—i.e., if $n_1 p_1$, $n_1(1 - p_1)$, $n_2 p_2$, and $n_2(1 - p_2)$ are all greater than or equal to 5—the sampling distribution of $\bar{p}_1 - \bar{p}_2$ can be approximated by a normal probability distribution.

Figure 11.1 shows the sampling distribution of $\bar{p}_1 - \bar{p}_2$.

Interval Estimation of $p_1 - p_2$

Suppose that independent simple random samples of tax returns from the two offices provide the following information.

Taxes

Office 1	Office 2
$n_1 = 250$	$n_2 = 300$
Number of returns with errors $= 35$	Number of returns with errors $= 27$

The sample proportions for the two offices are as follows:

$$\bar{p}_1 = \frac{35}{250} = .14$$

$$\bar{p}_2 = \frac{27}{300} = .09$$

FIGURE 11.1   SAMPLING DISTRIBUTION OF $\bar{p}_1 - \bar{p}_2$

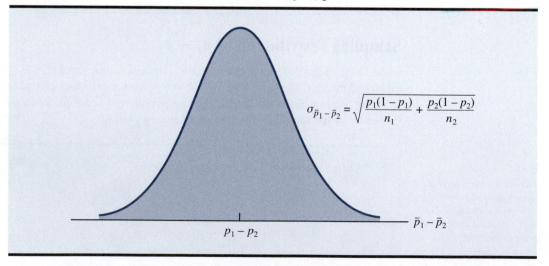

$$\sigma_{\bar{p}_1 - \bar{p}_2} = \sqrt{\frac{p_1(1 - p_1)}{n_1} + \frac{p_2(1 - p_2)}{n_2}}$$

$p_1 - p_2$

$\bar{p}_1 - \bar{p}_2$

The point estimate of the difference between the proportions of erroneous tax returns for the two populations is $\bar{p}_1 - \bar{p}_2 = .14 - .09 = .05$. Thus, we estimate that office 1 has a .05 greater error rate than office 2.

Before developing a confidence interval for the difference between population proportions, we must estimate $\sigma_{\bar{p}_1-\bar{p}_2}$. Note that equation (11.3) cannot be used directly because p_1 and p_2 are unknown. The approach taken is to substitute $\bar{p}_1$ as an estimator of p_1 and $\bar{p}_2$ as an estimator of p_2 in equation (11.3). Doing so provides the point estimator of $\sigma_{\bar{p}_1-\bar{p}_2}$ given by equation (11.4).

$s_{\bar{p}_1-\bar{p}_2}$ is the point estimator of $\sigma_{\bar{p}_1-\bar{p}_2}$, the standard error of the point estimator $\bar{p}_1 - \bar{p}_2$.

Point Estimator of $\sigma_{\bar{p}_1-\bar{p}_2}$

$$s_{\bar{p}_1-\bar{p}_2} = \sqrt{\frac{\bar{p}_1(1-\bar{p}_1)}{n_1} + \frac{\bar{p}_2(1-\bar{p}_2)}{n_2}} \qquad (11.4)$$

Using equation (11.4), the following expression provides an interval estimate of the difference between the proportions of the two populations in the large-sample case.

The use of $z_{\alpha/2}$ in equation (11.5) is due in part to the fact that we can assume a normal sampling distribution for $\bar{p}_1 - \bar{p}_2$ in the large-sample case.

Interval Estimate of the Difference Between the Proportions of Two Populations: Large-Sample Case with n_1p_1, $n_1(1-p_1)$, n_2p_2, and $n_2(1-p_2) \geq 5$

$$\bar{p}_1 - \bar{p}_2 \pm z_{\alpha/2}\, s_{\bar{p}_1-\bar{p}_2} \qquad (11.5)$$

where $1 - \alpha$ is the confidence coefficient.

Let us now use expression (11.5) to develop an interval estimate of the difference between the population proportions for the two tax preparation offices in our example. Using equation (11.4), we find

$$s_{\bar{p}_1-\bar{p}_2} = \sqrt{\frac{.14(.86)}{250} + \frac{.09(.91)}{300}} = .0275$$

With a 90% confidence interval, we have $z_{\alpha/2} = z_{.05} = 1.645$, and a margin of error of $1.645(.0275) = .0452$. Thus, the interval estimate is

$$(.14 - .09) \pm 1.645(.0275) = .05 \pm .0452$$

Hence, the 90% confidence interval for the difference in error rates at the two offices is .0048 to .0952.

Using Excel to Develop an Interval Estimate of $p_1 - p_2$

Excel can be used to develop an interval estimate of the difference between the proportions of erroneous tax returns at the two offices of the tax preparation firm. Refer to Figure 11.2 as we describe the tasks involved. The formula worksheet is in the background; the value worksheet is in the foreground.

Enter Data: Columns A and B contain Yes or No labels that indicate which of the tax returns from each office contain an error.

FIGURE 11.2   EXCEL WORKSHEET FOR INTERVAL ESTIMATE OF THE DIFFERENCE
BETWEEN TWO POPULATION PROPORTIONS

	A	B	C	D	E	F	G
1	Return?			Interval Estimate: Difference in Population Proportions			
2	Office 1	Office 2		Using the Standard Normal Distribution (z)			
3	No	Yes					
4	No	No			Office 1	Office 2	
5	No	No		Sample Size	=COUNTA(A3:A252)	=COUNTA(B3:B302)	
6	Yes	No		Response of Interest	Yes	Yes	
7	No	No		Count for Response	=COUNTIF(A3:A252,E6)	=COUNTIF(B3:B302,F6)	
8	No	No		Sample Proportion	=E7/E5	=F7/F5	
9	No	No					
10	Yes	No		Confidence Coefficient	0.9		
11	No	No		Level of Significance (alpha)	=1-E10		
12	No	No		z Value	=NORMSINV(1-E11/2)		
13	No	No					
14	No	Yes		Standard Error	=SQRT(E8*(1-E8)/E5+F8*(1-F8)/F5)		
15	No	Yes		Margin of Error	=E12*E14		
16	No	No					
17	No	No		Point Estimate of Difference	=E8-F8		
18	Yes	No		Lower Limit	=E17-E15		
19	No	No		Upper Limit	=E17+E15		
250	Yes	No					
251	No	No					
252	No	No					
301		No					
302		No					
303							

*Note: Rows 20–249 and
253–300 are hidden.*

	A	B	C	D	E	F	G	H	I
1	Erroneous Return?			Interval Estimate: Difference in Population Proportions					
2	Office 1	Office 2		Using the Standard Normal Distribution (z)					
3	No	Yes							
4	No	No			Office 1	Office 2			
5	No	No		Sample Size	250	300			
6	Yes	No		Response of Interest	Yes	Yes			
7	No	No		Count for Response	35	27			
8	No	No		Sample Proportion	0.14	0.09			
9	No	No							
10	Yes	No		Confidence Coefficient	0.9				
11	No	No		Level of Significance (alpha)	0.1				
12	No	No		z Value	1.645				
13	No	No							
14	No	Yes		Standard Error	0.0275				
15	No	Yes		Margin of Error	0.0452				
16	No	No							
17	No	No		Point Estimate of Difference	0.05				
18	Yes	No		Lower Limit	0.0048				
19	No	No		Upper Limit	0.0952				
250	Yes	No							
251	No	No							
252	No	No							
301		No							
302		No							
303									

Enter Functions and Formulas: The descriptive statistics needed to compute the interval estimate are provided in cells E5:F8. Note that Excel's COUNTA function is used in cells E5 and F5 to count the number of observations for each of the samples. The value worksheet indicates 250 returns in the sample from office 1 and 300 returns in the sample from office 2. In cells E6 and F6, we type Yes to indicate the response of interest. Excel's COUNTIF function is used in cells E7 and F7 to count the number of erroneous returns from each office. Formulas entered into cells E8 and F8 compute the sample proportions. The confidence coefficient entered into cell E10 (.9) is used to compute the corresponding level of significance in cell E11. In cell E12 we use the NORMSINV function to compute the z value needed to develop the interval estimate.

The formula in cell E14 provides a point estimate of $\sigma_{\bar{p}_1 - \bar{p}_2}$, the standard error of the point estimator $\bar{p}_1 - \bar{p}_2$.

A point estimate of $\sigma_{\bar{p}_1 - \bar{p}_2}$, the standard error of the point estimator $\bar{p}_1 - \bar{p}_2$, is computed based on the two sample proportions and sample sizes by entering the following formula into cell E14

$$=\text{SQRT}(E8*(1-E8)/E5+F8*(1-F8)/F5)$$

This cell formula is the Excel equivalent of equation (11.4). The margin of error is computed in cell E15 by multiplying the z value times the standard error.

The point estimate of the difference in the two population proportions is computed by entering the formula =E8-F8 into cell E17; the result, shown in the value worksheet, is 0.05. To compute the lower limit of the confidence interval, the formula =E17-E15 is entered into cell E18. The upper limit of the confidence interval is computed by entering the formula =E17 + E15 into cell E19. The 90% confidence interval estimate of the difference in the two population proportions is .0048 to .0952.

Hypotheses Tests About $p_1 - p_2$

As an example of a hypothesis test concerning the difference between two population proportions, let us reconsider the example concerning the error rates at two offices of the tax preparation firm. Suppose the firm was simply interested in whether the two offices experienced a significant difference in error rates. The appropriate null and alternative hypotheses then are

$$H_0\colon p_1 - p_2 = 0$$
$$H_a\colon p_1 - p_2 \neq 0$$

Figure 11.3 shows the sampling distribution of $\bar{p}_1 - \bar{p}_2$. If H_0 is true, there is no difference between the population proportions and $p_1 - p_2 = 0$. In the large-sample case, the sampling distribution is approximately normally distributed and the test statistic for the difference between two population proportions is

$$z = \frac{(\bar{p}_1 - \bar{p}_2) - (p_1 - p_2)}{\sigma_{\bar{p}_1 - \bar{p}_2}} \tag{11.6}$$

Using $\alpha = .10$ and $z_{\alpha/2} = z_{.05} = 1.645$, the rejection rule is as follows:

Using test statistic: Reject H_0 if $z < -1.645$ or if $z > 1.645$
Using p-value: Reject H_0 if p-value $< .10$

The computation of z in equation (11.6) requires a value for $\sigma_{\bar{p}_1 - \bar{p}_2}$, the standard error of the point estimator $\bar{p}_1 - \bar{p}_2$. As in the case of interval estimation, it will be necessary to estimate $\sigma_{\bar{p}_1 - \bar{p}_2}$ using $s_{\bar{p}_1 - \bar{p}_2}$ because p_1 and p_2 will not be known in practice. But for the special case of a null hypothesis stating no difference in the proportions (i.e., either $H_0\colon p_1 - p_2 = 0$, $H_0\colon p_1 - p_2 \leq 0$, or $H_0\colon p_1 - p_2 \geq 0$), equation (11.4) is modified to reflect the fact that when we assume H_0 to be true at the equality, we are assuming $p_1 = p_2 = p$. When this assumption is made, we combine or *pool* the two sample proportions to provide one estimate of p given by $\bar{p}$.

$$\bar{p} = \frac{n_1 \bar{p}_1 + n_2 \bar{p}_2}{n_1 + n_2} \tag{11.7}$$

FIGURE 11.3   SAMPLING DISTRIBUTION OF $\bar{p}_1 - \bar{p}_2$ WITH $H_0: p_1 - p_2 = 0$

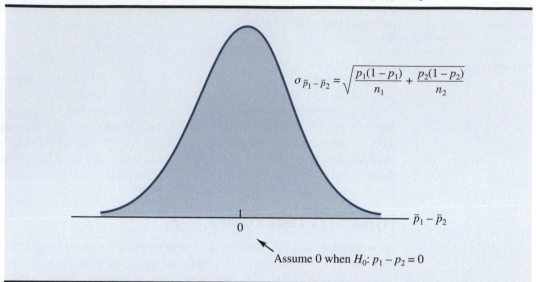

$$\sigma_{\bar{p}_1 - \bar{p}_2} = \sqrt{\frac{p_1(1 - p_1)}{n_1} + \frac{p_2(1 - p_2)}{n_2}}$$

$\bar{p}_1 - \bar{p}_2$

0

Assume 0 when $H_0: p_1 - p_2 = 0$

With $\bar{p}$ used in place of both $\bar{p}_1$ and $\bar{p}_2$, equation (11.4) is revised to

$$s_{\bar{p}_1 - \bar{p}_2} = \sqrt{\bar{p}(1 - \bar{p})\left(\frac{1}{n_1} + \frac{1}{n_2}\right)} \tag{11.8}$$

Using equations (11.7) and (11.8), we can now proceed with a hypothesis test for the tax preparation firm example.

$$\bar{p} = \frac{250(.14) + 300(.09)}{550} = \frac{62}{550} = .113$$

$$s_{\bar{p}_1 - \bar{p}_2} = \sqrt{(.113)(.887)\left(\frac{1}{250} + \frac{1}{300}\right)} = .0271$$

The value of the test statistic is

$$z = \frac{(\bar{p}_1 - \bar{p}_2) - (p_1 - p_2)}{s_{\bar{p}_1 - \bar{p}_2}} = \frac{(.14 - .09) - 0}{.0271} = 1.85$$

Because $1.85 > 1.645$, the null hypothesis is rejected at the .10 level of significance. The sample evidence indicates a difference between the error proportions at the two offices.

The p-value approach can also be used to make the hypothesis testing decision for the tax preparation firm example. The table for the standard normal probability distribution shows that the area in the upper tail of the standard normal probability distribution for $z = 1.85$ is $1 - .9678 = .0322$. Because it is a two-tailed hypothesis test, the p-value is found by doubling the area in the tail. Thus, the p-value is $2(.0322) = .0644$. With $.0644 < \alpha = .10$, the null hypothesis is rejected.

As we saw with hypothesis tests about differences between two population means in Chapter 10, one-tailed tests can also be developed for the difference between two population proportions. The one-tailed rejection regions are established in a manner similar to the one-tailed hypothesis testing procedures for a single population proportion.

Using Excel to Conduct a Hypothesis Test About $p_1 - p_2$

Excel can be used to conduct a hypothesis test about the difference between the proportions of erroneous tax returns at the two offices of the tax preparation firm. Refer to Figure 11.4 as we describe the tasks involved. The formula worksheet is in the background; the value worksheet is in the foreground.

FIGURE 11.4 EXCEL WORKSHEET FOR HYPOTHESIS TEST OF NO DIFFERENCE BETWEEN POPULATION PROPORTIONS

	A	B	C	D	E	F	G
1	Erroneous Return?			Hyptothesis Test: Difference in Population Proportions			
2	Office 1	Office 2		Using the Standard Normal distribution (z)			
3	No	Yes					
4	No	No			Office 1	Office 2	
5	No	No		Sample Size	=COUNTA(A3:A252)	=COUNTA(B3:B302)	
6	Yes	No		Response of Interest	Yes	Yes	
7	No	No		Count for Response	=COUNTIF(A3:A252,E6)	=COUNTIF(B3:B302,F6)	
8	No	No		Sample Proportion	=E7/E5	=F7/F5	
9	No	No					
10	Yes	No		Hypothesized Value	0		
11	No	No		Point Estimate of Difference	=E8-F8		
12	No	No					
13	No	No		Pooled Estimate of *p*	=(E5*E8+F5*F8)/(E5+F5)		
14	No	Yes		Standard Error	=SQRT(E13*(1-E13)*(1/E5+1/F5))		
15	No	Yes		Test Statistic	=(E11-E10)/E14		
16	No	No					
17	No	No		*p*-value (Lower Tail)	=NORMSDIST(E15)		
18	Yes	No		*p*-value (Upper Tail)	=1-NORMSDIST(E15)		
19	No	No		*p*-value (Two Tail)	=2*MIN(E17,E18)		
250	Yes	No					
251	No	No					
252	No	No					
301		No					
302		No					
303							

	A	B	C	D	E	F	G	H	I
1	Erroneous Return?			Hyptothesis Test: Difference in Population Proportions					
2	Office 1	Office 2		Using the Standard Normal distribution (z)					
3	No	Yes							
4	No	No			Office 1	Office 2			
5	No	No		Sample Size	250	300			
6	Yes	No		Response of Interest	Yes	Yes			
7	No	No		Count for Response	35	27			
8	No	No		Sample Proportion	0.14	0.09			
9	No	No							
10	Yes	No		Hypothesized Value	0				
11	No	No		Point Estimate of Difference	0.05				
12	No	No							
13	No	No		Pooled Estimate of *p*	0.1127				
14	No	Yes		Standard Error	0.0271				
15	No	Yes		Test Statistic	1.8462				
16	No	No							
17	No	No		*p*-value (Lower Tail)	0.9676				
18	Yes	No		*p*-value (Upper Tail)	0.0324				
19	No	No		*p*-value (Two Tail)	0.0649				
250	Yes	No							
251	No	No							
252	No	No							
301		No							
302		No							
303									

Note: Rows 20–249 and 253–300 are hidden.

Enter Data: Columns A and B contain Yes or No labels that indicate which of the tax returns from each office have errors.

Enter Functions and Formulas: The descriptive statistics needed to perform the hypothesis test are provided in cells E5:F8. They are the same as the ones used for an interval estimate (see Figure 11.2).

The hypothesized value of the difference in the two population proportions (0) is entered into cell E10. In cell E11 the difference in the sample proportions is used to compute a point estimate of the difference in the two population proportions. Using the two sample proportions and sample sizes, a pooled estimate of the population proportion p is computed by entering the following formula into cell E13:

$$=(E5*E8+F5*F8)/(E5+F5)$$

Then, using the pooled estimate of p, $s_{\bar{p}_1-\bar{p}_2}$ is computed by entering the following formula into cell E14:

$$=SQRT(E13*(1-E13)*(1/E5+1/F5)$$

This cell formula is the Excel equivalent of equation (11.8).

The formula $=(E11-E10)/E14$ entered into cell E15 computes the test statistic z (1.8462). The NORMSDIST function is then used to compute the p-value (Lower Tail) and the p-value (Upper Tail) in cells E17 and E18. The p-value (Two Tail) is computed in cell E19 as twice the minimum of the two one-tailed p-values. The value worksheet shows that p-value (Two Tail) = .0649. Because the p-value = .0649 is less than the level of significance, $\alpha = .10$, we have sufficient evidence to reject the null hypothesis and conclude that the population proportions are not equal.

The p-value here (.0649) differs from the one we found using the cumulative normal probability tables (.0644) due to rounding.

This worksheet can be used as a template for hypothesis testing problems involving a difference of zero in population proportions. The new data can be entered into columns A and B. The ranges for the new data and the response of interest need to be revised in cells E5:F7. The remainder of the worksheet will then be updated as needed to conduct the hypothesis test.

To use this worksheet for exercises in which the sample statistics are given, just type in the given values for cells E5:F5 and E7:F8. The remainder of the worksheet will then be updated as needed to conduct the hypothesis test.

EXERCISES

Methods

1. Consider the following results for two independent simple random samples taken from two populations.

Sample 1	Sample 2
$n_1 = 400$	$n_2 = 300$
$\bar{p}_1 = .48$	$\bar{p}_2 = .36$

a. What is the point estimate of the difference between the two population proportions?
b. Develop a 90% confidence interval for the difference between the two population proportions.
c. Develop a 95% confidence interval for the difference between the two population proportions.

2. Consider the following hypothesis test:

$$H_0: p_1 - p_2 \leq 0$$
$$H_a: p_1 - p_2 > 0$$

The following results are for two independent simple random samples taken from the two populations.

Sample 1	Sample 2
$n_1 = 200$	$n_2 = 300$
$\bar{p}_1 = .22$	$\bar{p}_2 = .16$

a. Using $\alpha = .05$, what is your hypothesis testing conclusion?

b. What is the p-value?

Applications

3. A *Business Week*/Harris survey asked senior executives at large corporations their opinions about the economic outlook for the future (*Business Week*, June 16, 1997). One question was "Do you think that there will be an increase in the number of full-time employees at your company over the next 12 months?" In May 1997, 220 of 400 executives answered yes, while in December 1996, 192 of 400 executives had answered yes. Provide a 95% confidence interval estimate for the difference between the proportions at the two points in time. What is your interpretation of the interval estimate?

4. A CNN/*USA Today* poll evaluated the popularity of major league baseball after the Mark McGwire and Sammy Sosa record-setting home-run chase during the 1998 season. A sample of 1082 found 682 people responding yes to the question "Are you a fan of major league baseball?" (*USA Today*, September 17, 1998). During the baseball strike of April 1995, a sample of 1008 found only 413 people responding yes to the same question.

a. Use the sample proportions to estimate the fan support for major league baseball in 1998 and in 1995. What is the point estimate of the increase in major league baseball fan support from the strike in 1995 to the McGwire/Sosa home-run chase of 1998?

b. Develop a 95% confidence interval estimate of the increase in fan support.

5. The women and family issues committee of the American Institute of Certified Public Accountants (AICPA) mailed surveys asking about family-friendly policies and women's upward mobility to 5300 firms of all sizes (excluding sole practitioners). Of the 1710 responses, 57% were from firms with five or fewer AICPA members, 26% were from firms with six to 10 members, 9% were from firms with 11 to 20 members, and 8% were from firms with more than 20 members. For the firms with fewer than five AICPA members, 58% of the hires within the previous three years were women and 42% were men. In contrast, firms with more than 20 AICPA members hired 43% women and 57% men (*Journal of Accountancy*, October 1994). Develop a 95% confidence interval estimate of the difference between the proportion of women hired by firms with fewer than five AICPA members and the proportion of women hired by firms with more than 20 AICPA members.

6. *Fortune* enlisted Yankelovich Partners to poll 600 adults on their ideas about marriage, divorce, and the contribution of the corporate wife to her executive husband (*Fortune*, February 2, 1998). In response to the statement, "In a divorce in a long-term marriage where the husband works outside the home and the wife is not employed for pay, the wife should be entitled to half the assets accumulated during the marriage," 279 of 300 women agreed and 255 of 300 men agreed.

a. What are the sample proportions for the two populations, women and men?

b. Test the hypothesis $H_0: p_1 - p_2 = 0$, using $\alpha = .05$. What is your conclusion?

c. Provide a 95% confidence interval for the difference between the population proportions.

7. A sample of 1545 men and an independent sample of 1691 women were used to compare the amount of housework done by women and men in dual-earner marriages. The study showed that 67.5% of the men felt the division of housework was fair and 60.8% of the women felt the division of housework was fair (*American Journal of Sociology*, September 1994). Is the proportion of men who felt the division of housework was fair greater than the proportion of women who felt the division of housework was fair? Support your conclusion with a statistical test using a .05 level of significance.

Survey

8. A survey firm conducts door-to-door surveys on a variety of issues. Some individuals cooperate with the interviewer and complete the interview questionnaire, and others do not. A recent survey of 200 men and 300 women resulted in the data set Survey. A response of Yes means that the respondent completed the questionnaire.
   a. Using $\alpha = .05$, test the hypothesis that the response rate is the same for both men and women.
   b. Compute a 95% confidence interval for the difference between the proportions of men and women who completed the questionnaire.

TVAdv

9. In a test of the quality of two television commercials, each commercial was shown in a separate test area six times over a 1-week period. The following week a telephone survey was conducted to identify individuals who had seen the commercials. The individuals who had seen the commercials were asked to state the primary message in the commercials. The results obtained for 150 individuals who saw commercial A and 200 individuals who saw commercial B are in the data set TVAdv. A response of Yes indicates that the individual recalled the primary message.
   a. Using $\alpha = .05$, test the hypothesis of no difference in the recall proportions for the two commercials.
   b. Compute a 95% confidence interval for the difference between the recall proportions for the two populations.

10. The stock market declined in early 2000 with many stocks dropping below their 1997 highs. In fact, 81.5% of New York Stock Exchange (NYSE) stocks and 72.4% of NASDAQ stocks were trading below their 1997 highs (*Barron's*, May 22, 2000). If the data were based on 232 NYSE stocks and 210 NASDAQ stocks, test the hypothesis $H_0: p_1 - p_2 = 0$ with $\alpha = .05$. What is the *p*-value? What is your conclusion?

11. *Yahoo! Internet Life* sponsored surveys in several metropolitan areas to estimate the proportion of adults using the Internet at work (*USA Today*, May 7, 2000). Results showed 40% of Washington, D.C., adults use the Internet at work, while 32% of San Francisco adults use the Internet at work. If the sample sizes are 240 and 250 respectively, do the sample results indicate that the population proportion of adults using the Internet at work in Washington, D.C., is greater than the population proportion in San Francisco? What is the *p*-value? Using $\alpha = .05$, what is your conclusion?

11.2   HYPOTHESIS TEST FOR PROPORTIONS OF A MULTINOMIAL POPULATION

In this section, we consider hypothesis tests concerning the proportion of elements in a population belonging to each of several classes or categories. In contrast to the preceding section, we will be dealing with a single population: a **multinomial population.** The parameters of the multinomial population are the proportion of elements belonging to each category; the hypothesis tests we describe concern the value of those parameters.

The assumptions for the multinomial experiment parallel those for the binomial experiment with the exception that the multinomial experiment has three or more outcomes per trial.

The multinomial probability distribution can be thought of as an extension of the binomial distribution to the case of three or more categories of outcomes. On each trial of a multinomial experiment, one and only one of the outcomes occurs. Each trial of the experiment is assumed to be independent, and the probabilities of the outcomes stay the same for each trial.

As an example, consider the market share study being conducted by Scott Marketing Research. Over the past year market shares have stabilized at 30% for company A, 50% for company B, and 20% for company C. Recently company C developed a "new and improved" product to replace its current entry in the market. Company C retained Scott Marketing Research to determine whether the new product will alter market shares.

In this example, the population of interest is a multinomial population; each customer is classified as buying from company A, company B, or company C. Thus, we have a multinomial population with three classifications or categories. Let us use the following notation for the proportions.

$$p_A = \text{market share for company A}$$
$$p_B = \text{market share for company B}$$
$$p_C = \text{market share for company C}$$

Scott Marketing Research will conduct a sample survey and compute the proportion of respondents preferring each company's product. A hypothesis test will then be conducted to see whether the new product caused a change in market shares. Assuming that company C's new product will not alter the market shares, the null and alternative hypotheses are stated as follows.

$$H_0: p_A = .30, p_B = .50, \text{ and } p_C = .20$$
$$H_a: \text{The population proportions are not}$$
$$p_A = .30, p_B = .50, \text{ and } p_C = .20$$

If the sample results lead to the rejection of H_0, Scott Marketing Research will have evidence that the introduction of the new product affected the market shares.

Let us assume that the market research firm used a consumer panel of 200 customers for the study. Each individual was asked to specify a purchase preference among the three alternatives: company A's product, company B's product, and company C's new product. The 200 responses are summarized here.

The consumer panel of 200 customers in which each individual is asked to select one of three alternatives is equivalent to a multinomial experiment consisting of 200 trials.

	Observed Frequency	
Company A's Product	**Company B's Product**	**Company C's New Product**
48	98	54

We now can perform a **goodness of fit test** that will determine whether the sample of 200 customer purchase preferences is consistent with the null hypothesis. The goodness of fit test is based on a comparison of the sample of *observed* results with the *expected* results under the assumption that the null hypothesis is true. Hence, the next step is to compute expected purchase preferences for the 200 customers under the assumption that $p_A = .30$, $p_B = .50$, and $p_C = .20$. Doing so provides the expected results.

	Expected Frequency	
Company A's Product	**Company B's Product**	**Company C's New Product**
200(.30) = 60	200(.50) = 100	200(.20) = 40

Thus, we see that the expected frequency for each category is found by multiplying the sample size of 200 by the hypothesized proportion for the category.

The goodness of fit test now focuses on the differences between the observed frequencies and the expected frequencies. Large differences between observed and expected frequencies cast doubt on the assumption that the hypothesized proportions or market shares are correct. Whether the differences between the observed and expected frequencies are "large" or "small" is a question answered with the aid of the following test statistic.

Test Statistic for Goodness of Fit

$$\chi^2 = \sum_{i=1}^{k} \frac{(f_i - e_i)^2}{e_i}$$

(11.9)

where

f_i = observed frequency for category i

e_i = expected frequency for category i

k = the number of categories

Note: The test statistic has a chi-square distribution with $k - 1$ degrees of freedom provided that the expected frequencies are 5 *or more* for all categories.

Let us return to the market share data for the three companies. Because the expected frequencies are all 5 or more, we can proceed with the computation of the chi-square test statistic. The calculations necessary to compute the chi-square test statistic for the Scott Marketing Research market share study are shown in Table 11.1. We see that the value of the test statistic is $\chi^2 = 7.34$.

The test for goodness of fit is always a one-tailed test with the rejection region in the upper tail of the chi-square distribution.

Suppose we test the null hypothesis that the multinomial population has the proportions of $p_A = .30$, $p_B = .50$, and $p_C = .20$ at the $\alpha = .05$ level of significance. Because we will reject the null hypothesis if the differences between the observed and expected frequencies are *large*, we will place a rejection area of .05 in the upper tail of the chi-square distribution. Checking the chi-square distribution table (Table 3 of Appendix B), we find that with $k - 1 = 3 - 1 = 2$ degrees of freedom, $\chi^2_{.05} = 5.99$. With $7.34 > 5.99$, we reject H_0. In re-

TABLE 11.1   COMPUTATION OF THE CHI-SQUARE TEST STATISTIC FOR THE SCOTT MARKETING RESEARCH MARKET SHARE STUDY

Category	Hypothesized Proportion	Observed Frequency (f_i)	Expected Frequency (e_i)	Difference ($f_i - e_i$)	Squared Difference ($f_i - e_i)^2$	Squared Difference Divided by Expected Frequency ($f_i - e_i)^2/e_i$
Company A	.30	48	60	−12	144	2.40
Company B	.50	98	100	−2	4	0.04
Company C	.20	54	40	14	196	4.90
Total		200				7.34

The p-value criterion can also be used for the goodness of fit test.

jecting H_0 we are concluding that the introduction of the new product by company C will alter the current market share structure.

Computer software packages such as Excel can greatly simplify the computations needed to perform a goodness of fit test for a multinomial population. In the next subsection we will show how Excel was used to compute a p-value of .0255 for the Scott Marketing Research hypothesis test. Using the p-value, the decision of whether to reject H_0 at a given level of significance α is

$$\text{Reject } H_0 \text{ if the } p\text{-value} < \alpha$$

Because the p-value = .0255 < α = .05, we reject H_0 and conclude that the introduction of the new product will alter the current market share structure.

Although no further statistical conclusions can be made as a result of the hypothesis test, we can compare the observed and expected frequencies informally to obtain an idea of how the market share structure may change. Considering company C, we find that the observed frequency of 54 is larger than the expected frequency of 40. Because the expected frequency was based on current market shares, the larger observed frequency suggests that the new product will have a positive effect on company C's market share. Comparisons of the observed and expected frequencies for the other two companies indicate that company C's gain in market share will hurt company A more than company B.

Let us summarize the general steps that can be used to conduct a goodness of fit test for any hypothesized multinomial population distribution.

Multinomial Distribution Goodness of Fit Test: A Summary

1. State the null and alternative hypotheses.

   H_0: The population follows a multinomial probability distribution with specified probabilities for each of the k categories

   H_a: The population does not follow a multinomial probability distribution with the specified probabilities for each of the k categories

2. Select a random sample and record the observed frequencies f_i for each category.
3. Assuming the null hypothesis is true, determine the expected frequency e_i in each category by multiplying the category probability by the sample size.
4. Compute the value of the test statistic.

$$\chi^2 = \sum_{i=1}^{k} \frac{(f_i - e_i)^2}{e_i}$$

5. Rejection rule

   Using test statistic: Reject H_0 if $\chi^2 > \chi_\alpha^2$

   Using p-value: Reject H_0 if p-value < α

   where α is the level of significance for the test and $k - 1$ is the degrees of freedom.

Using Excel to Conduct a Goodness of Fit Test

CD file

Research

Excel can be used to conduct a goodness of fit test for the Scott Marketing Research Study. Refer to Figure 11.5 as we describe the tasks involved. The formula worksheet is in the background; the value worksheet is in the foreground.

Enter Data: Column A is used to identify each of the 200 customers who made up the consumer panel in the study. Column B shows the purchase preference (A, B, or C) for each customer. The hypothesized proportions, 0.3, 0.5, and 0.2, are entered into cells E4:E6.

Enter Functions and Formulas: Excel's COUNTIF function is used to count the number of customers who preferred company A's product by entering the following formula into cell F4:

$$=COUNTIF(B2:B201,``A")$$

The COUNTIF function is also used in cells F5 and F6 to count the number of customers who preferred company B's product and company C's product, respectively. The SUM function used in cell F7 computes the total frequency. To compute the expected frequency for company A, the formula =E4*F7 is entered into cell G4; similar formulas are entered into cells G5 and G6 to compute the expected frequencies for company B and company C, respectively.

    The difference between the observed frequency and the expected frequency for company A is computed by entering the formula =F4-G4 into cell H4. The squared difference for company A is computed by entering the formula =H4^2 into cell I4, and the squared difference divided by the expected frequency is computed by entering the formula =I4/G4 into cell J4. The formulas in cells H4:J4 copied into cells H5:J6 make the same computation for company B and company C. Finally, the formula =SUM(J4:J6) entered into cell J7 computes the value of the test statistic (7.34). Note that the worksheet computations in Figure 11.5 parallel the computations shown in Table 11.1.

FIGURE 11.5   EXCEL WORKSHEET FOR THE SCOTT MARKETING RESEARCH MARKET SHARE STUDY

	A	B	C	D	E	F	G	H	I	J	K
1	Customer	Product								Squared Diff.	
2	1	B			Hyp.	Obs.	Exp.		Squared	Divided by	
3	2	A		Category	Proportion	Freq.	Freq.	Diff.	Diff.	Exp. Freq.	
4	3	C		Company A	0.3	=COUNTIF(B2:B201,"A")	=E4*F7	=F4-G4	=H4^2	=I4/G4	
5	4	C		Company B	0.5	=COUNTIF(B2:B201,"B")	=E5*F7	=F5-G5	=H5^2	=I5/G5	
6	5	C		Company C	0.2	=COUNTIF(B2:B201,"C")	=E6*F7	=F6-G6	=H6^2	=I6/G6	
7	6	A			Total	=SUM(F4:F6)				=SUM(J4:J6)	
8	7	A									
9	8	A		Number of Categories	3						
10	9	C									
11	10	A		Test Statistic	=J7						
12	11	C		Degrees of Freedom	=F9-1						
13	12	B									
14	13	C		p-value	=CHIDIST(F11,F12)						
15	14	A									
200	199	C									
201	200	C									
202											

Note: Rows 16–199 are hidden.

	A	B	C	D	E	F	G	H	I	J
1	Customer	Product								Squared Diff.
2	1	B			Hyp.	Obs.	Exp.		Squared	Divided by
3	2	A		Category	Proportion	Freq.	Freq.	Diff.	Diff.	Exp. Freq.
4	3	C		Company A	0.3	48	60	-12	144	2.4
5	4	C		Company B	0.5	98	100	-2	4	0.04
6	5	C		Company C	0.2	54	40	14	196	4.9
7	6	A			Total	200				7.34
8	7	A								
9	8	A		Number of Categories	3					
10	9	C								
11	10	A		Test Statistic	7.34					
12	11	C		Degrees of Freedom	2					
13	12	B								
14	13	C		p-value	0.0255					
15	14	A								
200	199	C								
201	200	C								
202										

The number of categories, 3, is entered into cell F9. The test statistic computed in cell J7 is displayed in cell F11 by entering the formula =J7, and the degrees of freedom for the test is computed in cell F12 by entering the formula =F9-1. Finally, Excel's CHIDIST function computes the p-value in cell F14. The form of the CHIDIST function is CHIDIST(test statistic, degrees of freedom); the value returned by the function is the upper tail probability associated with the test statistic. Because the rejection region for a goodness of fit test is always in the upper tail, the value provided by the CHIDIST function is the p-value. Thus, to compute the p-value for the Scott Marketing Research goodness of fit test we entered the following formula into cell F14:

$$=CHIDIST(F11,F12)$$

The value worksheet shows that the resulting p-value is 0.0255. The decision of whether to reject H_0 at a given level of significance α, is:

$$\text{Reject } H_0 \text{ if the } p\text{-value} < \alpha$$

Thus, with $\alpha = .05$ and the p-value = 0.0255, we reject H_0 and conclude that the introduction of the new product by company C will alter the current market share structure.

NOTES AND COMMENTS

1. For χ^2 goodness of fit tests the rejection region is always in the upper tail. The differences between observed and expected frequencies are squared, and larger differences lead to larger values for χ^2.
2. Many applications of the goodness of fit test involve choosing a sample and observing the category to which each sampled item belongs. In such cases one must take care to choose a random sample. Otherwise, the independence assumption will not be satisfied.

EXERCISES

Methods

12. Test the following hypotheses using the χ^2 goodness of fit test.

$$H_0: p_A = .40, p_B = .40, \text{ and } p_C = .20$$

$$H_a: \text{The population proportions are not } \\ p_A = .40, p_B = .40, \text{ and } p_C = .20$$

A sample of size 200 yielded 60 in category A, 120 in category B, and 20 in category C. Use $\alpha = .01$ and test to see whether the proportions are as stated in H_0.

13. Suppose we have a multinomial population with four categories: A, B, C, and D. The null hypothesis is that the proportion of items is the same in every category. The null hypothesis is

$$H_0: p_A = p_B = p_C = p_D = .25$$

A sample of size 300 yielded the following results.

A: 85   B: 95   C: 50   D: 70

Use $\alpha = .05$ to determine whether H_0 should be rejected.

Applications

M&MCandy

14. During the first 13 weeks of the television season, the Saturday evening 8:00 P.M. to 9:00 P.M. audience proportions were recorded as ABC 29%, CBS 28%, NBC 25%, and others 18%. A sample of 300 homes two weeks after a Saturday night schedule revision yielded the following viewing audience data: ABC 95 homes, CBS 70 homes, NBC 89 homes, and others 46 homes. Test with $\alpha = .05$ to determine whether the viewing audience proportions changed.

15. M&M/MARS, makers of M&M® Chocolate Candies, conducted a national poll in which more than 10 million people indicated their preference for a new color. The tally of this poll resulted in the replacement of tan-colored M&Ms with a new blue color. In the brochure "Colors," made available by M&M/MARS Consumer Affairs, the distribution of colors for the plain candies is as follows:

Brown	Yellow	Red	Orange	Green	Blue
30%	20%	20%	10%	10%	10%

In a study reported in *Chance* (no. 4, 1996), samples of 1-pound bags were used to determine whether the reported percentages were indeed valid. The results obtained for a sample of 506 plain candies are shown in the data set M&MCandy. Use $\alpha = .05$ to determine whether these data support the percentages reported by the company.

16. One of the questions on the *Business Week* 1996 Subscriber Study was, "When making investment purchases, do you use full service or discount brokerage firms?" Survey results showed that 264 respondents use full service brokerage firms only, 255 use discount brokerage firms only, and 229 use both full service and discount firms. Use $\alpha = .10$ to determine whether there are any differences in preference among the three service choices.

17. Negative appeals are recognized as an effective method of persuasion in advertising. A study in *The Journal of Advertising* (Summer 1997) reported the results of a content analysis of guilt advertisements in 24 magazines. The number of ads with guilt appeals that appeared in selected magazine types follow.

Magazine Type	Number of Ads with Guilt Appeals
News and opinion	20
General editorial	15
Family-oriented	30
Business/financial	22
Female-oriented	16
African-American	12

Using $\alpha = .10$, test to see whether the proportion of ads with guilt appeals among the six types of magazines differs.

18. Consumer panel preferences for three proposed store displays follow.

Display A	Display B	Display C
43	53	39

Use $\alpha = .05$ and test to see whether there is a difference in preference among the three display designs.

19. How well do airline companies serve their customers? A study showed the following customer ratings: 3% excellent, 28% good, 45% fair, and 24% poor (*Business Week*, September 11, 2000). In a similar study of service by telephone companies, assume that a sample of 400 adults found the following customer ratings: 24 excellent, 124 good, 172 fair, and 80 poor. Is the distribution of the customer ratings for telephone companies different from the distribution of customer ratings for airline companies? Test with $\alpha = .01$. What is your conclusion?

11.3   TEST OF INDEPENDENCE: CONTINGENCY TABLES

Another important application of the chi-square distribution involves using sample data to test for the independence of two variables. Let us illustrate the test of independence by considering the study conducted by the Alber's Brewery of Tucson, Arizona. Alber's manufactures and distributes three types of beer: light, regular, and dark. In an analysis of the market segments for the three beers, the firm's market research group has raised the question of whether preferences for the three beers differ among male and female beer drinkers. If beer preference is independent of the gender of the beer drinker, one advertising campaign will be initiated for all of Alber's beers. However, if beer preference depends on the gender of the beer drinker, the firm will tailor its promotions to different target markets.

A test of independence addresses the question of whether the beer preference (light, regular, or dark) is independent of the gender of the beer drinker (male, female). The hypotheses for this test of independence are:

H_0: Beer preference is independent of the gender of the beer drinker

H_a: Beer preference is not independent of the gender of the beer drinker

To test whether two variables are independent, one sample is selected and crosstabulation is used to summarize the data for the two variables simultaneously.

Table 11.2 can be used to describe the situation being studied. After identification of the population as all male and female beer drinkers, a sample can be selected and each individual asked to state his or her preference for the three Alber's beers. Every individual in the sample will be classified in one of the six cells in the table. For example, an individual may be a male preferring regular beer (cell (1,2)), a female preferring light beer (cell (2,1)),

TABLE 11.2   CONTINGENCY TABLE FOR BEER PREFERENCE AND GENDER OF BEER DRINKER

	Beer Preference		
Gender	**Light**	**Regular**	**Dark**
Male	cell(1,1)	cell(1,2)	cell(1,3)
Female	cell(2,1)	cell(2,2)	cell(2,3)

TABLE 11.3   SAMPLE RESULTS FOR BEER PREFERENCES OF MALE AND FEMALE BEER DRINKERS (OBSERVED FREQUENCIES)

Gender	Beer Preference			Total
	Light	Regular	Dark	
Male	20	40	20	80
Female	30	30	10	70
Total	50	70	30	150

a female preferring dark beer (cell (2,3)), and so on. Because we listed all possible combinations of beer preference and gender or, in other words, listed all possible contingencies, Table 11.2 is called a **contingency table.** The test of independence uses the contingency table format and for that reason is sometimes referred to as a *contingency table test.*

Suppose a simple random sample of 150 beer drinkers is selected. After tasting each beer, the individuals in the sample state their preference or first choice. The crosstabulation in Table 11.3 summarizes the responses for the study. As we see, the data for the test of independence are collected in terms of counts or frequencies for each cell or category. Of the 150 individuals in the sample, 20 were men who favored light beer, 40 were men who favored regular beer, 20 were men who favored dark beer, and so on.

The data in Table 11.3 are the observed frequencies for the six classes or categories. If we can determine the expected frequencies under the assumption of independence between beer preference and gender of the beer drinker, we can use the chi-square distribution to determine whether there is a significant difference between observed and expected frequencies.

Expected frequencies for the cells of the contingency table are based on the following rationale. First we assume that the null hypothesis of independence between beer preference and gender of the beer drinker is true. Then we note that in the entire sample of 150 beer drinkers, a total of 50 prefer light beer, 70 prefer regular beer, and 30 prefer dark beer. In terms of fractions we conclude that $\frac{50}{150} = \frac{1}{3}$ of the beer drinkers prefer light beer, $\frac{70}{150} = \frac{7}{15}$ prefer regular beer, and $\frac{30}{150} = \frac{1}{5}$ prefer dark beer. If the *independence* assumption is valid, we argue that these fractions must be applicable to both male and female beer drinkers. Thus, under the assumption of independence, we would expect the sample of 80 male beer drinkers to show that $(\frac{1}{3})80 = 26.67$ prefer light beer, $(\frac{7}{15})80 = 37.33$ prefer regular beer, and $(\frac{1}{5})80 = 16$ prefer dark beer. Application of the same fractions to the 70 female beer drinkers provides the expected frequencies shown in Table 11.4.

Let e_{ij} denote the expected frequency for the contingency table category in row i and column j. With this notation, let us reconsider the expected frequency calculation for males (row

TABLE 11.4   EXPECTED FREQUENCIES IF BEER PREFERENCE IS INDEPENDENT OF THE GENDER OF THE BEER DRINKER

Gender	Beer Preference			Total
	Light	Regular	Dark	
Male	26.67	37.33	16.00	80
Female	23.33	32.67	14.00	70
Total	50.00	70.00	30.00	150

$i = 1$) who prefer regular beer (column $j = 2$); that is, expected frequency e_{12}. Following the preceding argument for the computation of expected frequencies, we can show that

$$e_{12} = (\tfrac{7}{15})80 = 37.33$$

This expression can be written slightly differently as

$$e_{12} = (\tfrac{7}{15})80 = (\tfrac{70}{150})80 = \frac{(80)(70)}{150} = 37.33$$

Note that 80 in the expression is the total number of males (row 1 total), 70 is the total number of individuals preferring regular beer (column 2 total), and 150 is the total sample size. Hence, we see that

$$e_{12} = \frac{(\text{Row 1 Total})(\text{Column 2 Total})}{\text{Sample Size}}$$

Generalization of the expression shows that the following formula provides the expected frequencies for a contingency table in the test of independence.

Expected Frequencies for Contingency Tables Under the Assumption of Independence

$$e_{ij} = \frac{(\text{Row } i \text{ Total})(\text{Column } j \text{ Total})}{\text{Sample Size}} \tag{11.10}$$

Using the formula for male beer drinkers who prefer dark beer, we find an expected frequency of $e_{13} = (80)(30)/150 = 16.00$, as shown in Table 11.4. Use equation (11.10) to verify the other expected frequencies shown in Table 11.4.

The test procedure for comparing the observed frequencies of Table 11.3 with the expected frequencies of Table 11.4 is similar to the goodness of fit calculations made in Section 11.2. Specifically, the χ^2 value based on the observed and expected frequencies is computed as follows.

Test Statistic for Independence

$$\chi^2 = \sum_i \sum_j \frac{(f_{ij} - e_{ij})^2}{e_{ij}} \tag{11.11}$$

where

f_{ij} = observed frequency for contingency table category in row i and column j

e_{ij} = expected frequency for contingency table category in row i and column j based on the assumption of independence

Note: With n rows and m columns in the contingency table, the test statistic has a chi-square distribution with $(n - 1)(m - 1)$ degrees of freedom provided that the expected frequencies are five or more for all categories.

The double summation in equation (11.11) is used to indicate that the calculation must be made for all the cells in the contingency table.

By reviewing the expected frequencies in Table 11.4, we see that the expected frequencies are five or more for each category. We therefore proceed with the computation of the chi-square test statistic. The calculations necessary to compute the chi-square test statistic for determining whether beer preference is independent of the gender of the beer drinker are shown in Table 11.5. We see that the value of the test statistic is $\chi^2 = 6.13$.

The number of degrees of freedom for the appropriate chi-square distribution is computed by multiplying the number of rows minus 1 by the number of columns minus 1. With two rows and three columns, we have $(2 - 1)(3 - 1) = (1)(2) = 2$ degrees of freedom for the test of independence of beer preference and gender of the beer drinker. With $\alpha = .05$ for the level of significance of the test, Table 3 of Appendix B shows an upper-tail χ^2 value of $\chi^2_{.05} = 5.99$. Note that we are again using the upper tail value because we will reject the null hypothesis only if the differences between observed and expected frequencies provide a large χ^2 value. In our example, $\chi^2 = 6.13$ is greater than the critical value of $\chi^2_{.05} = 5.99$. Thus, we reject the null hypothesis of independence and conclude that beer preference is not independent of the gender of the beer drinker.

The test for independence is always a one-tailed test with the rejection region in the upper tail of the chi-square distribution.

Computer software packages such as Excel can greatly simplify the computations needed to perform a test of independence and to provide the *p*-value for the test. In the next subsection we will show how Excel was used to compute a *p*-value of .0468 for the Alber's Brewery test of independence. Because the *p*-value = .0468 < α = .05, we reject H_0 and conclude that beer preference is not independent of the gender of the beer drinker.

Although no further statistical conclusions can be made as a result of the test, we can compare the observed and expected frequencies informally to obtain an idea about the dependence between beer preference and gender. Refer to Tables 11.3 and 11.4. We see that male beer drinkers have higher observed than expected frequencies for both regular and dark beers, whereas female beer drinkers have a higher observed than expected frequency only for light beer. These observations give us insight about the beer preference differences between male and female beer drinkers.

Let us summarize the steps in a contingency table test of independence.

Test of Independence: A Summary

1. State the null and alternative hypotheses.

   H_0: The column variable is independent of the row variable
   H_a: The column variable is not independent of the row variable

2. Select a random sample and record the observed frequencies for each cell of the contingency table.
3. Use equation (11.10) to compute the expected frequency for each cell.
4. Use equation (11.11) to compute the value of the χ^2 test statistic.
5. Rejection rule

   Using test statistic: Reject H_0 if $\chi^2 > \chi^2_\alpha$
   Using *p*-value: Reject H_0 if *p*-value < α

   where α is the level of significance; with *n* rows and *m* columns, the degrees of freedom is $(n - 1)(m - 1)$.

TABLE 11.5   COMPUTATION OF THE CHI-SQUARE TEST STATISTIC FOR DETERMINING WHETHER BEER PREFERENCE IS INDEPENDENT OF THE GENDER OF THE BEER DRINKER

Gender	Beer Preference	Observed Frequency (f_{ij})	Expected Frequency (e_{ij})	Difference $(f_{ij} - e_{ij})$	Squared Difference $(f_{ij} - e_{ij})^2$	Squared Difference Divided by Expected Frequency $(f_{ij} - e_{ij})^2/e_{ij}$
Male	Light	20	26.67	−6.67	44.49	1.67
Male	Regular	40	37.33	2.67	7.13	0.19
Male	Dark	20	16.00	4.00	16.00	1.00
Female	Light	30	23.33	6.67	44.49	1.91
Female	Regular	30	32.67	−2.67	7.13	0.22
Female	Dark	10	14.00	−4.00	16.00	1.14
	Total	150				6.13

Using Excel to Conduct a Test of Independence

CD file

Alber's

Excel can be used to conduct a test of independence for the Alber's Brewery example. Refer to Figure 11.6 as we describe the tasks involved. The formula worksheet is in the background; the value worksheet is in the foreground.

Enter Data: Column A is used to identify each of the 150 individuals in the study. Column B shows the gender and column C shows the beer preference (Light, Regular, or Dark for each individual).

Apply Tools: Using Excel's PivotTable tool (see Section 2.4 for details regarding how to use this tool), we developed the crosstabulation shown in cells E3:I7. The values in cells F5:H6 are the observed frequencies for the Alber's Brewery study.

Enter Functions and Formulas: To compute the expected frequencies for the Alber's Brewery contingency table under the assumption of independence, we use equation (11.10). Thus, to compute the expected number of male drinkers who prefer light beer we enter the formula =F7*I5/I7 into cell F11. To compute the expected number of male drinkers who prefer regular beer we enter the formula =G7*I5/I7 into cell G11, and to compute the expected number of male drinkers who prefer dark beer we enter the formula =H7*I5/I7 into cell H11. Similar formulas entered into cells F12:H12 compute the expected frequencies for the females in the study.

Cells F5:H6 contain the observed frequencies, and cells F11:H12 contain the expected frequencies for the Alber's Brewery study. Although a cell formula could be written to compute equation (11.11), the χ^2 test statistic for independence, it is simpler to use Excel's CHITEST function to compute the p-value for the test. To compute the p-value associated with this goodness of fit test, we entered the following function into cell H15:

$$=\text{CHITEST(F5:H6,F11:H12)}$$

The value worksheet shows that the resulting p-value is 0.0468. The decision of whether to reject H_0 at a given level of significance α is

Reject H_0 if the p-value $< \alpha$

Thus, with $\alpha = .05$ and the p-value $= 0.0468$, we reject H_0 and conclude that beer preference is not independent of the gender of the beer drinker.

In using the Excel approach it was not necessary for us to compute the value of the test statistic; Excel did this calculation automatically as part of its procedure for computing the

FIGURE 11.6 EXCEL WORKSHEET FOR THE ALBER'S BREWERY TEST OF INDEPENDENCE

	A	B	C	D	E	F	G	H	I	J
1	**Individual**	**Gender**	**Preference**							
2	1	Female	Light							
3	2	Female	Regular		Count of Individual	Preference				
4	3	Male	Regular		Gender	Light	Regular	Dark	Grand Total	
5	4	Female	Light		Male	20	40	20	80	
6	5	Female	Light		Female	30	30	10	70	
7	6	Female	Regular		Grand Total	50	70	30	150	
8	7	Male	Regular							
9	8	Female	Dark		**Expected Frequencies**					
10	9	Female	Regular			Light	Regular	Dark		
11	10	Male	Dark		Male	=F7*I5/I7	=G7*I5/I7	=H7*I5/I7		
12	11	Male	Regular		Female	=F7*I6/I7	=G7*I6/I7	=H7*I6/I7		
13	12	Male	Regular							
14	13	Female	Regular				**chi-square**	=CHIINV(H15,2)		
15	14	Female	Regular				***p*-value**	=CHITEST(F5:H6,F11:H12)		
16	15	Male	Light							
149	148	Male	Regular							
150	149	Female	Light							
151	150	Female	Regular							
152										

	A	B	C	D	E	F	G	H	I	J
1	**Individual**	**Gender**	**Preference**							
2	1	Female	Light							
3	2	Female	Regular		Count of Individual	Preference				
4	3	Male	Regular		Gender	Light	Regular	Dark	Grand Total	
5	4	Female	Light		Male	20	40	20	80	
6	5	Female	Light		Female	30	30	10	70	
7	6	Female	Regular		Grand Total	50	70	30	150	
8	7	Male	Regular							
9	8	Female	Dark		**Expected Frequencies**					
10	9	Female	Regular			Light	Regular	Dark		
11	10	Male	Dark		Male	26.6667	37.3333	16		
12	11	Male	Regular		Female	23.3333	32.6667	14		
13	12	Male	Regular							
14	13	Female	Regular				**chi-square**	6.1225		
15	14	Female	Regular				***p*-value**	0.0468		
16	15	Male	Light							
149	148	Male	Regular							
150	149	Female	Light							
151	150	Female	Regular							
152										

Note: Rows 17–148 are hidden.

p-value. But, because the sampling distribution of the test statistic for the test of independence is a chi-square distribution, we can use Excel's CHIINV function to look up the value of the test statistic for independence corresponding to the *p*-value of 0.0468. In the previous section we indicated that the CHIINV function has two arguments: the upper tail area and the degrees of freedom. The upper tail area corresponds to the *p*-value of 0.0468 and the degrees of freedom are $(n - 1)(m - 1) = (2 - 1)(3 - 1) = 2$. Thus, in cell H14 we enter the following function in order to compute the test statistic:

=CHIINV(H15,2)

The value spreadsheet shows that the test statistic is 6.1225. The slight difference between 6.1225 and the value that we computed in Table 11.5 (6.13) using equation (11.11) is simply due to the additional accuracy Excel used in making the computation.

NOTES AND COMMENTS

The test statistic for the chi-square tests in this chapter requires an expected frequency of five for each category. When a category has fewer than five, it is often appropriate to combine two adjacent categories to obtain an expected frequency of five or more in each category.

EXERCISES

Methods

20. The following 2×3 contingency table contains observed frequencies for a sample of 200. Test for independence of the row and column variables using the χ^2 test with $\alpha = .025$.

| | Column Variable | | |
Row Variable	A	B	C
P	20	44	50
Q	30	26	30

21. The following 3×3 contingency table contains observed frequencies for a sample of 240. Test for independence of the row and column variables using the χ^2 test with $\alpha = .05$.

| | Column Variable | | |
Row Variable	A	B	C
P	20	30	20
Q	30	60	25
R	10	15	30

Applications

22. One of the questions on the *Business Week* 1996 Subscriber Study was, "In the past 12 months, when traveling for business, what type of airline ticket did you purchase most often?" The data obtained are shown in the following contingency table.

| | Type of Flight | |
Type of Ticket	Domestic Flights	International Flights
First class	29	22
Business/executive class	95	121
Full fare economy/coach class	518	135

Using $\alpha = .05$, test for the independence of type of flight and type of ticket. What is your conclusion?

23. In a study of brand loyalty in the automotive industry, new-car customers were asked whether the make of their new car was the same as the make of their previous car (*Business Week*, May 8, 2000). The breakdown of 600 responses shows the brand loyalty for domestic, European, and Asian cars.

| | Manufacturer | | |
Purchased	Domestic	European	Asian
Same Make	125	55	68
Different Make	140	105	107

a. Test a hypothesis to determine whether brand loyalty is independent of the manufacturer. Use $\alpha = .05$. What is your conclusion?

b. If a significant difference is found, which manufacturer appears to have the greatest brand loyalty?

24. Starting positions for business and engineering graduates are classified by industry as shown in the following table.

	Industry			
Major	Oil	Chemical	Electrical	Computer
Business	30	15	15	40
Engineering	30	30	20	20

Use $\alpha = .01$ and test for independence of major and industry type.

Gifts

25. The results of a study conducted by Marist Institute for Public Opinion showed who men and women say is the most difficult person for them to buy holiday gifts for (*USA Today*, December 15, 1997). Suppose that a follow-up study consisting of 100 men and 100 women was conducted. The data collected are shown in the data set Gifts. Use $\alpha = .05$ and test for independence of gender and the most difficult person to buy for. What is your conclusion?

26. Negative appeals have been recognized as an effective method of persuasion in advertising. A study in *The Journal of Advertising* (Summer 1997) reported the results of a content analysis of guilt and fear advertisements in 24 magazines. The number of ads with guilt and fear appeals that appeared in selected magazine types follows.

	Type of Appeal	
Magazine Type	Number of Ads with Guilt Appeals	Number of Ads with Fear Appeals
News and opinion	20	10
General editorial	15	11
Family-oriented	30	19
Business/financial	22	17
Female-oriented	16	14
African-American	12	15

Use the chi-square test of independence with a .01 level of significance to analyze the data. What is your conclusion?

27. Businesses are increasingly placing orders online. The Performance Measurement Group collected data on the rates of correctly filled electronic orders by industry (*Investor's Business Daily*, May 8, 2000). Assume a sample of 700 electronic orders provided the following results.

	Industry			
Order	Pharmaceutical	Consumer	Computers	Telecommunications
Correct	207	136	151	178
Incorrect	3	4	9	12

    a. Test a hypothesis to determine whether correctness of order fulfillment is independent of industry. Use $\alpha = .05$. What is your conclusion?

    b. Which industry has the highest percentage of correctly filled orders?

28. Three suppliers provide the following data on defective parts.

Supplier	Part Quality		
	Good	Minor Defect	Major Defect
A	90	3	7
B	170	18	7
C	135	6	9

Use $\alpha = .05$ and test for independence between supplier and part quality. What does the result of your analysis tell the purchasing department?

29. A study of educational levels of voters and their political party affiliations yielded the following results.

Educational Level	Party Affiliation		
	Democratic	Republican	Independent
Did not complete high school	40	20	10
High school degree	30	35	15
College degree	30	45	25

Use $\alpha = .01$ and determine whether party affiliation is independent of the educational level of the voters.

30. On the syndicated Siskel and Ebert television show the hosts often created the impression that they strongly disagreed about which movies were best. An article in *Chance* (no. 2, 1997) reported the results of ratings of 160 movies by Siskel and Ebert. Each review is categorized as Pro ("thumbs up"), Con ("thumbs down"), or Mixed.

Siskel Rating	Ebert Rating		
	Con	Mixed	Pro
Con	24	8	13
Mixed	8	13	11
Pro	10	9	64

Use the chi-square test of independence with a .01 level of significance to analyze the data. What is your conclusion?

SUMMARY

In this chapter, we described statistical procedures for comparisons involving proportions and the contingency table test for independence of two variables. In the first section, we focused on comparing a proportion for one population with the same proportion from another population. We described how to construct an interval estimate of the difference between the proportions and how to conduct a hypothesis test to learn whether the difference between the proportions is statistically significant.

In the second section, we showed how to conduct hypothesis tests to determine whether the sample proportions for the categories of a multinomial population are significantly different from the hypothesized values. The chi-square goodness of fit test was used to make the comparison.

The final section looked at tests of independence for two variables. A test of independence for two variables extends the methodology employed in the goodness of fit test for a multinomial population. A contingency table is used to determine the observed and expected frequencies. Then a chi-square value is computed. Large chi-square values, caused by large differences between observed and expected frequencies, lead to the rejection of the null hypothesis of independence.

GLOSSARY

Multinomial population   A population in which each element belongs to one and only one of several categories. The multinomial probability distribution can be thought of as an extension of the binomial probability distribution to the case of three or more categories of outcomes.

Goodness of fit test   A statistical test that uses the differences between observed and expected frequencies to determine whether to reject a hypothesized probability distribution for a population.

Contingency table   A crosstabulation table used to summarize observed and expected frequencies for a test of independence.

KEY FORMULAS

Point Estimator of the Difference Between the Proportions of Two Populations

$$\bar{p}_1 - \bar{p}_2 \tag{11.1}$$

Expected Value of $\bar{p}_1 - \bar{p}_2$

$$E(\bar{p}_1 - \bar{p}_2) = p_1 - p_2 \tag{11.2}$$

Standard Deviation of $\bar{p}_1 - \bar{p}_2$

$$\sigma_{\bar{p}_1-\bar{p}_2} = \sqrt{\frac{p_1(1 - p_1)}{n_1} + \frac{p_2(1 - p_2)}{n_2}} \tag{11.3}$$

Point Estimator of $\sigma_{\bar{p}_1-\bar{p}_2}$

$$s_{\bar{p}_1-\bar{p}_2} = \sqrt{\frac{\bar{p}_1(1 - \bar{p}_1)}{n_1} + \frac{\bar{p}_2(1 - \bar{p}_2)}{n_2}} \tag{11.4}$$

Interval Estimate of the Difference Between the Proportions of Two Populations: Large-Sample Case With n_1p_1, $n_1(1 - p_1)$, n_2p_2, and $n_2(1 - p_2) \geq 5$

$$\bar{p}_1 - \bar{p}_2 \pm z_{\alpha/2}s_{\bar{p}_1-\bar{p}_2} \tag{11.5}$$

Test Statistic for the Difference Between Two Population Proportions

$$z = \frac{(\bar{p}_1 - \bar{p}_2) - (p_1 - p_2)}{\sigma_{\bar{p}_1 - \bar{p}_2}}$$ (11.6)

Pooled Estimator of the Population Proportion

$$\bar{p} = \frac{n_1 \bar{p}_1 + n_2 \bar{p}_2}{n_1 + n_2}$$ (11.7)

Point Estimator of $\sigma_{\bar{p}_1 - \bar{p}_2}$ When $p_1 = p_2 = p$

$$s_{\bar{p}_1 - \bar{p}_2} = \sqrt{\bar{p}(1 - \bar{p})\left(\frac{1}{n_1} + \frac{1}{n_2}\right)}$$ (11.8)

Test Statistic for Goodness of Fit

$$\chi^2 = \sum_{i=1}^{k} \frac{(f_i - e_i)^2}{e_i}$$ (11.9)

Expected Frequencies for Contingency Tables Under the Assumption of Independence

$$e_{ij} = \frac{(\text{Row } i \text{ Total})(\text{Column } j \text{ Total})}{\text{Sample Size}}$$ (11.10)

Test Statistic for Independence

$$\chi^2 = \sum_i \sum_j \frac{(f_{ij} - e_{ij})^2}{e_{ij}}$$ (11.11)

SUPPLEMENTARY EXERCISES

CD file

Cable

31. A cable television firm is considering submitting bids for rights to operate in two regions of the state of Florida. Surveys were conducted of the two regions to obtain data on customer acceptance of the cable television service. The data obtained are shown in the data set Cable. A response of Yes indicates that the customer surveyed indicated an intent to purchase the cable television service. Develop a 99% confidence interval for the difference between the population proportions of customer acceptance in the two regions.

32. A *Business Week*/Harris poll asked 1035 adults how well U.S. companies competed in the global economy; 704 respondents answered good/excellent (*Business Week*, September 11, 2000). In a similar poll of 1004 adults in 1996, 582 respondents answered good/excellent. Can the sample results be used to conclude that the population proportion of adults responding good/excellent *increased* over the four years from 1996 to 2000?

a. State the null and alternative hypotheses.

b. Compute the *p*-value.

c. Using $\alpha = .01$, what is your conclusion?

33. A large automobile company selected samples of single and married male policyholders and recorded the number who made an insurance claim over the preceding three-year period.

Single Policyholders	Married Policyholders
$n_1 = 400$	$n_2 = 900$
Number making claims = 76	Number making claims = 90

   a. Using $\alpha = .05$, test to determine whether the claim rates differ between single and married male policyholders.
   b. Provide a 95% confidence interval for the difference between the proportions for the two populations.

34. Medical tests were conducted to learn about drug-resistant tuberculosis. Of 142 cases tested in New Jersey, nine were found to be drug-resistant. Of 268 cases tested in Texas, five were found to be drug-resistant. Do these data suggest a statistically significant difference between the proportions of drug-resistant cases in the two states? Test $H_0: p_1 - p_2 = 0$ at the .02 level of significance. What is the p-value, and what is your conclusion?

35. In July 2001 the Harris Ad Track Research Service conducted a survey to evaluate the effectiveness of a major advertising campaign for Kodak cameras (*USA Today*, August 27, 2001). In a sample of 430 respondents, 38% thought the ads were "very effective." In a separate sample of 285 respondents, 23% thought the ads in other ad campaigns were "very effective."
   a. Estimate the number of respondents who thought the Kodak ads were "very effective" and the number of respondents who felt the other ads were "very effective."
   b. Provide a 95% confidence interval for the difference in proportions.
   c. On the basis of your results in part (b), do you believe the Kodak advertising campaign is more effective than most advertising campaigns?

36. In June 2001, 38% of fund managers surveyed believed that the core inflation rate would be higher in one year. One month later a similar survey revealed that 22% of fund managers expected the core inflation rate to be higher in one year (*Global Research Highlights*, Merrill Lynch, July 20, 2001). Assume that the sample size was 200 in each the June and July surveys.
   a. Develop a point estimate of the difference between the June and July proportions of fund managers who felt the core inflation rate would be higher in one year.
   b. Develop hypotheses such that rejection of the null hypothesis will allow us to conclude that inflation expectations diminished between June and July.
   c. Conduct a test of the hypotheses in part (b) using $\alpha = .01$. What is your conclusion?

37. In setting sales quotas, a marketing manager makes the assumption that order potentials are the same for each of four sales territories. A sample of 200 sales follows. Should the manager's assumption be rejected? Use $\alpha = .05$.

Sales Territories			
I	II	III	IV
60	45	59	36

38. Seven percent of mutual fund investors rate corporate stocks "very safe," 58% rate them "somewhat safe," 24% rate them "not very safe," 4% rate them "not at all safe," and 7% are "not sure." A *Business Week*/Harris poll asked 529 mutual fund investors how they would rate corporate bonds on safety. The responses are as follows.

Safety Rating	Frequency
Very safe	48
Somewhat safe	323
Not very safe	79
Not at all safe	16
Not sure	63

Do mutual fund investors' attitudes toward corporate bonds differ from their attitudes toward corporate stocks? Support your conclusion with a statistical test using $\alpha = .01$.

Park

39. A community park is to be opened soon. A sample of 140 individuals has been asked to state their preference for when they would most like to visit the park. The sample results are shown in the data set Park. In developing a staffing plan, should the park manager plan on the same number of individuals visiting the park each day? Support your conclusion with a statistical test using $\alpha = .05$.

40. A regional transit authority is concerned about the number of riders on one of its bus routes. In setting up the route, the assumption is that the number of riders is the same on every day from Monday through Friday. Using the following data, conduct a statistical test using $\alpha = .05$ to determine whether the transit authority's assumption is correct.

Day	Number of Riders
Monday	13
Tuesday	16
Wednesday	28
Thursday	17
Friday	16

41. The results of *Computerworld's* Annual Job Satisfaction Survey showed that 28% of Information Systems (IS) managers are very satisfied with their job, 46% are somewhat satisfied, 12% are neither satisfied or dissatisfied, 10% are somewhat dissatisfied, and 4% are very dissatisfied (*Computerworld*, May 26, 1997). Suppose that a sample of 500 computer programmers yielded the following results.

Category	Number of Respondents
Very satisfied	105
Somewhat satisfied	235
Neither	55
Somewhat dissatisfied	90
Very dissatisfied	15

Using $\alpha = .05$, conduct a statistical test to determine whether the job satisfaction for computer programmers is different from the job satisfaction for IS managers.

42. A sample of parts provided the following contingency table data on part quality by production shift.

	Part Quality	
Shift	Number Good	Number Defective
First	368	32
Second	285	15
Third	176	24

Use $\alpha = .05$ and test the hypothesis that part quality is independent of the production shift. What is your conclusion?

43. *The Wall Street Journal* 1996 Subscriber Study showed data on the employment status of subscribers. Sample results corresponding to subscribers of the eastern and western editions are shown here.

	Region	
Employment Status	Eastern Edition	Western Edition
Full-time	1105	574
Part-time	31	15
Self-employed/consultant	229	186
Not employed	485	344

Using $\alpha = .05$, test the hypothesis that employment status is independent of the region. What is your conclusion?

44. A lending institution supplied the following data on loan approvals by four loan officers. Use $\alpha = .05$ and test to determine whether the loan approval decision is independent of the loan officer reviewing the loan application.

	Loan Approval Decision	
Loan Officer	Approved	Rejected
Miller	24	16
McMahon	17	13
Games	35	15
Runk	11	9

45. Data on the marital status of men and women ages 20 to 29 were obtained as part of a national survey. The results from a sample of 350 men and 400 women follow. These data are representative of results published in the *U.S. Current Population Report* (*The Statistical Abstract of the United States*, 1999).

Gender	Marital Status		
	Never Married	Married	Divorced
Men	234	106	10
Women	216	168	16

a. Using $\alpha = .01$, test for independence between marital status and gender. What is your conclusion?

b. Summarize the percent in each marital status category for men and for women.

46. The following crosstabulation shows industry type and P/E ratio for 100 companies in the consumer products and banking industries.

Industry	P/E Ratio					Total
	5–9	10–14	15–19	20–24	25–29	
Consumer	4	10	18	10	8	50
Banking	14	14	12	6	4	50
Total	18	24	30	16	12	100

Does there appear to be a relationship between industry type and P/E ratio? Support your conclusion with a statistical test using $\alpha = .05$.

47. The following data were collected on the number of emergency ambulance calls for an urban county and a rural county in Virginia.

County	Day of Week							Total
	Sun	Mon	Tue	Wed	Thur	Fri	Sat	
Urban	61	48	50	55	63	73	43	393
Rural	7	9	16	13	9	14	10	78
Total	68	57	66	68	72	87	53	471

Conduct a test for independence using $\alpha = .05$. What is your conclusion?

48. The office occupancy rates were reported for four California metropolitan areas. Do the following data suggest that the office vacancies were independent of metropolitan area? Use a .05 level of significance. What is your conclusion?

Occupancy Status	Los Angeles	San Diego	San Francisco	San Jose
Occupied	160	116	192	174
Vacant	40	34	33	26

Case Problem   A BIPARTISAN AGENDA FOR CHANGE

In a study conducted by Zogby International for the *Democrat and Chronicle*, more than 700 New Yorkers were polled to determine whether the New York state government works. Respondents surveyed were asked questions involving pay cuts for state legislators, restrictions on lobbyists, terms limits for legislators, and whether state citizens should be able to put matters directly on the state ballot for a vote (*Democrat and Chronicle*, December 7, 1997). The results regarding several proposed reforms had broad support, crossing all demographic and political lines.

Suppose that a follow-up survey of 100 individuals who live in the western region of New York was conducted. The party affiliation (Democrat, Independent, Republican) of each individual surveyed was recorded, as well as their responses to the following three questions.

1. Should legislative pay be cut for every day the state budget is late?
   Yes _____   No _____
2. Should there be more restrictions on lobbyists?
   Yes _____   No _____
3. Should there be term limits requiring that legislators serve a fixed number of years?
   Yes _____   No _____

CD file

NYReform

The responses were coded using 1 for a *yes* response and 2 for a *no* response. The complete data set is available on the data disk in the data set named NYReform.

Managerial Report

1. Use descriptive statistics to summarize the data from this study. What are your preliminary conclusions about the independence of the response (yes or no) and party affiliation for each of the three questions in the survey?
2. With regard to question 1, test for the independence of the response (yes and no) and party affiliation. Use $\alpha = .05$.
3. With regard to question 2, test for the independence of the response (yes and no) and party affiliation. Use $\alpha = .05$.
4. With regard to question 3, test for the independence of the response (yes and no) and party affiliation. Use $\alpha = .05$.
5. Does it appear that there is broad support for change across political lines? Explain.

CHAPTER 12

Simple Linear Regression

CONTENTS

Alliance Data Systems*

DALLAS, TEXAS

Alliance Data Systems (ADS) provides transaction processing, credit services, and marketing services for clients in the rapidly growing customer relationship management (CRM) industry. ADS clients are concentrated in four industries: retail, petroleum/convenience stores, utilities, and transportation. In 1983, Alliance began offering end-to-end credit processing services to the retail, petroleum, and casual dining industries; today they employ more than 6500 employees who provide services to clients around the world. Operating more than 140,000 point-of-sale terminals in the United States alone, ADS processes in excess of 2.5 billion transactions annually. The company ranks second in the United States in private label credit services by representing 49 private label programs with nearly 72 million cardholders. In 2001, ADS made an initial public offering and is now listed on the New York Stock Exchange.

As one of its marketing services, ADS designs direct mail campaigns and promotions. With its database containing information on the spending habits of more than 100 million consumers, ADS can target those consumers most likely to benefit from a direct mail promotion. The Analytical Development Group uses regression analysis to build models that measure and predict the responsiveness of consumers to direct market campaigns. Some regression models predict the probability of purchase for individuals receiving a promotion, and others predict the amount spent by those consumers making a purchase.

For one particular campaign, a retail store chain wanted to attract new customers. To predict the effect of the campaign, ADS analysts selected a sample from the consumer database, sent the sampled individuals promotional materials, and then collected transaction data on the consumers' response. Sample data were collected on the amount of purchase made by the consumers responding to the campaign, as well as a variety of

Alliance Data analysts discuss use of a regression model to predict sales for a direct marketing campaign. Courtesy of Alliance Data Systems.

consumer-specific variables thought to be useful in predicting sales. The consumer-specific variable that contributed most to predicting the amount purchased was the total amount of credit purchases at related stores over the past 39 months. ADS analysts developed an estimated regression equation relating the amount of purchase to the amount spent at related stores:

$$\hat{y} = 26.7 + 0.00205x$$

where

$$\hat{y} = \text{amount of purchase}$$
$$x = \text{amount spent at related stores}$$

Using this equation, we could predict that someone spending $10,000 over the past 39 months would spend $47.20 when responding to the direct mail promotion. In this chapter, you will learn how to develop estimated regression equations such as this.

The final model developed by ADS analysts also included several other variables that increased the predictive power of the preceding equation. Some of these variables included the absence/presence of a bank credit card, estimated income, and the average amount spent per trip at a selected store. In the following chapter, we will learn how such additional variables can be incorporated into a multiple regression model.

*The authors are indebted to Philip Clemance, Director of Analytical Development at Alliance Data Systems, for providing this Statistics in Practice.

Managers often base decisions on the relationship between two or more variables. For example, after considering the relationship between advertising expenditures and sales, a marketing manager might attempt to predict sales for a given level of advertising expenditures. In another case, a public utility might use the relationship between the daily high temperature and the demand for electricity to predict electricity usage on the basis of next month's anticipated daily high temperatures. Sometimes a manager relies on intuition to judge how two variables are related. However, if data can be obtained, a statistical procedure called *regression analysis* can be used to develop an equation showing how the variables are related.

The statistical methods used in studying the relationship between two variables were first employed by Sir Francis Galton (1822–1911). Galton studied the relationship between a father's height and the son's height. Galton's disciple, Karl Pearson (1857–1936), analyzed the relationship between the father's height and the son's height for 1078 pairs of subjects.

In regression terminology, the variable being predicted is called the **dependent variable**. The variable or variables being used to predict the value of the dependent variable are called the **independent variables**. For example, in analyzing the effect of advertising expenditures on sales, a marketing manager's desire to predict sales would suggest making sales the dependent variable. Advertising expenditure would be the independent variable used to help predict sales. In statistical notation, y denotes the dependent variable and x denotes the independent variable.

The simplest type of regression analysis involving one independent variable and one dependent variable, in which the relationship between the variables is approximated by a straight line, is called **simple linear regression**. Regression analysis involving two or more independent variables is called multiple regression analysis; multiple regression is covered in Chapter 13.

12.1   SIMPLE LINEAR REGRESSION MODEL

Armand's Pizza Parlors operates Italian food restaurants located in a five-state area. Armand's most successful restaurants are located near college campuses. The managers believe that quarterly sales for these restaurants (denoted by y) are related positively to the size of the student population (denoted by x); that is, restaurants near campuses with a large student population tend to generate more sales than those located near campuses with a small population. Using regression analysis, we can develop an equation showing how the dependent variable y is related to the independent variable x.

Regression Model and Regression Equation

In the Armand's Pizza Parlors example, every restaurant is associated with a value of x (student population) and a corresponding value of y (quarterly sales). The equation that describes how y is related to x and an error term is called the *regression model*. The regression model used in simple linear regression follows.

Simple Linear Regression Model

$$y = \beta_0 + \beta_1 x + \epsilon \tag{12.1}$$

In the **simple linear regression model**, y is a linear function of x (the $\beta_0 + \beta_1 x$ part) plus ϵ. β_0 and β_1 are referred to as the parameters of the model, and ϵ (the Greek letter epsilon) is a random variable referred to as the error term. The error term accounts for the variability in y that cannot be explained by the linear relationship between x and y.

In Section 12.4 we will discuss the assumptions for the simple linear regression model and ϵ. One of the assumptions is that the mean or expected value of ϵ is zero. A consequence of this assumption is that the mean or expected value of y, denoted $E(y)$, is equal to $\beta_0 + \beta_1 x$; in other words, the mean value of y is a linear function of x. The equation that describes how the mean value of y is related to x is called the regression equation. The regression equation for simple linear regression follows.

Simple Linear Regression Equation

$$E(y) = \beta_0 + \beta_1 x \qquad (12.2)$$

The graph of the **simple linear regression equation** is a straight line; β_0 is the y intercept of the regression line, β_1 is the slope, and $E(y)$ is the mean or expected value of y for a given value of x. Examples of possible regression lines for simple linear regression are shown in Figure 12.1. The regression line in panel A of the figure shows that the mean value of y is related positively to x, with larger values of $E(y)$ associated with larger values of x. The regression line in panel B shows that the mean value of y is related negatively to x, with smaller values of $E(y)$ associated with larger values of x. The regression line in panel C shows that the mean value of y is not related to x; that is, the mean value of y is the same for every value of x.

Estimated Regression Equation

If the values of the parameters β_0 and β_1 were known, we could use equation (12.2) to compute the mean value of y for a known value of x. Unfortunately, the parameter values are not known in practice and must be estimated by using sample data. Sample statistics (denoted b_0 and b_1) are computed as estimates of the parameters β_0 and β_1. Substituting the

FIGURE 12.1 POSSIBLE REGRESSION LINES FOR SIMPLE LINEAR REGRESSION

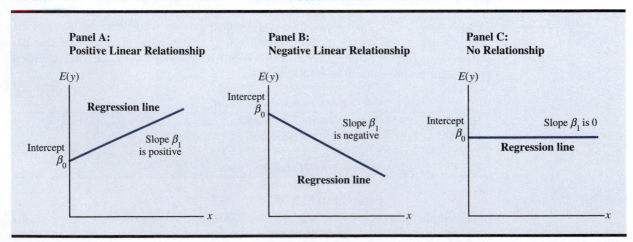

values of the sample statistics b_0 and b_1 for β_0 and β_1 in the regression equation, we obtain the **estimated simple linear regression equation.**

Estimated Simple Linear Regression Equation

$$\hat{y} = b_0 + b_1x \tag{12.3}$$

The graph of the estimated simple linear regression equation is called the *estimated regression line*; b_0 is the y intercept, b_1 is the slope, and $\hat{y}$ (pronounced y hat) is the estimated value of y for a given value of x. In the next section, we show how data from a sample can be used to compute the values of b_0 and b_1 in the estimated regression equation. Figure 12.2 is a summary of the estimation process for simple linear regression.

NOTES AND COMMENTS

Regression analysis *cannot* be interpreted as a procedure for establishing a *cause-and-effect* relationship between variables. It can only indicate how or to what extent variables are *associated* with each other. Any conclusions about cause and effect must be based on the *judgment* of the individual or individuals most knowledgeable about the application.

FIGURE 12.2   THE ESTIMATION PROCESS FOR SIMPLE LINEAR REGRESSION

The estimation of β_0 and β_1 is a statistical process much like the estimation of μ discussed in Chapter 7. β_0 and β_1 are the unknown parameters of interest, and b_0 and b_1 are the sample statistics used to estimate the parameters.

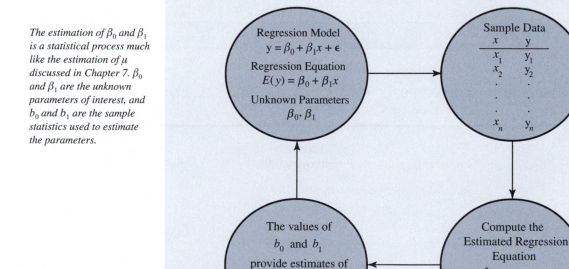

12.2 LEAST SQUARES METHOD

In simple linear regression, each observation consists of two values: one for the independent variable and one for the dependent variable.

The **least squares method** is a procedure for using sample data to compute an estimated regression equation. To illustrate the least squares method, suppose we collected data from a sample of 10 Armand's Pizza Parlor restaurants located near college campuses. For the *i*th observation or restaurant in the sample, x_i is the size of the student population (in thousands) and y_i is the quarterly sales (in thousands of dollars). Table 12.1 summarizes the values of x_i and y_i for the 10 restaurants in the sample. We see that restaurant 1, with $x_1 = 2$ and $y_1 = 58$, is near a campus with 2000 students and has quarterly sales of $58,000. Restaurant 2, with $x_2 = 6$ and $y_2 = 105$, is near a campus with 6000 students and has quarterly sales of $105,000. The largest sales value is for restaurant 10, which is near a campus with 26,000 students and has quarterly sales of $202,000.

Scatter diagrams were first introduced in Chapter 2.

Figure 12.3 shows a scatter diagram of the data in Table 12.1. The size of the student population is shown on the horizontal axis and the value of quarterly sales is shown on the vertical axis. **Scatter diagrams** for regression analysis are constructed with values of the independent variable *x* on the horizontal axis and values of the dependent variable *y* on the vertical axis. The scatter diagram enables us to observe the data graphically and to draw preliminary conclusions about the possible relationship between the variables.

What preliminary conclusions can be drawn from Figure 12.3? Quarterly sales appear to be higher at campuses with larger student populations. In addition, for these data the relationship between the size of the student population and quarterly sales appears to be approximated by a straight line; indeed, there seems to be a positive linear relationship between *x* and *y*. We therefore choose the simple linear regression model to represent the relationship between quarterly sales and student population. Given that choice, we next use the sample data in Table 12.1 to determine the values of b_0 and b_1 in the estimated simple linear regression equation. For the *i*th restaurant, the estimated regression equation is

$$\hat{y}_i = b_0 + b_1 x_i \tag{12.4}$$

TABLE 12.1 STUDENT POPULATION AND QUARTERLY SALES DATA FOR 10 ARMAND'S PIZZA PARLORS

CD file

Armand's

Restaurant i	Student Population (1000s) x_i	Quarterly Sales ($1000s) y_i
1	2	58
2	6	105
3	8	88
4	8	118
5	12	117
6	16	137
7	20	157
8	20	169
9	22	149
10	26	202

FIGURE 12.3   SCATTER DIAGRAM OF STUDENT POPULATION AND QUARTERLY
SALES FOR ARMAND'S PIZZA PARLORS

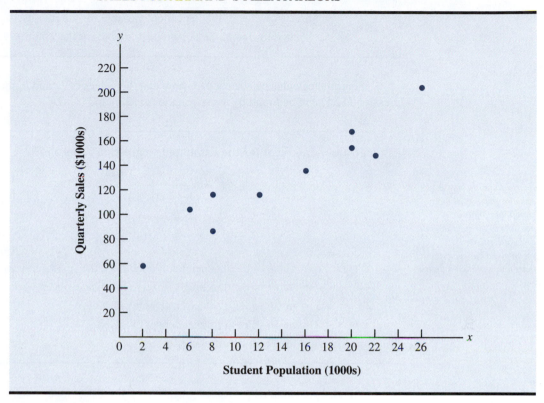

where

$\hat{y}_i$ = estimated value of quarterly sales ($1000s) for the ith restaurant

b_0 = the y intercept of the estimated regression line

b_1 = the slope of the estimated regression line

x_i = size of the student population (1000s) for the ith restaurant

With y_i denoting the observed (actual) quarterly sales for restaurant i and $\hat{y}_i$ in equation (12.4) representing the estimated value of quarterly sales for restaurant i, every restaurant in the sample will provide an observed value of quarterly sales y_i and an estimated value of quarterly sales $\hat{y}_i$. For the estimated regression line to provide a good fit to the data, we want the differences between the observed values and the estimated values to be small.

The least squares method uses the sample data to provide the values of b_0 and b_1 that minimize the *sum of the squares of the deviations* between the observed values of the dependent variable y_i and the estimated values of the dependent variable $\hat{y}_i$. The criterion for the least squares method is given by expression (12.5).

*Carl Friedrich Gauss
(1777–1855) proposed the
least squares method.*

Least Squares Criterion

$$\min \Sigma(y_i - \hat{y}_i)^2 \qquad\qquad (12.5)$$

where

$$y_i = \text{observed value of the dependent variable for the } i\text{th observation}$$
$$\hat{y}_i = \text{estimated value of the dependent variable for the } i\text{th observation}$$

Differential calculus can be used to show that the values of b_0 and b_1 that minimize expression (12.5) can be found by using equations (12.6) and (12.7).

Slope and y-Intercept for the Estimated Regression Equation*

$$b_1 = \frac{\Sigma(x_i - \bar{x})(y_i - \bar{y})}{\Sigma(x_i - \bar{x})^2} \tag{12.6}$$

$$b_0 = \bar{y} - b_1\bar{x} \tag{12.7}$$

In computing b_1 with a calculator, carry as many significant digits as possible in the intermediate calculations. We recommend carrying at least four significant digits.

where

$x_i = $ value of the independent variable for the ith observation
$y_i = $ value of the dependent variable for the ith observation
$\bar{x} = $ mean value for the independent variable
$\bar{y} = $ mean value for the dependent variable
$n = $ total number of observations

Some of the calculations necessary to develop the least squares estimated regression equation for Armand's Pizza Parlors appear in Table 12.2. The sample of 10 restaurants gives us $n = 10$ observations. Because equations (12.6) and (12.7) require $\bar{x}$ and $\bar{y}$, we begin the calculations by computing $\bar{x}$ and $\bar{y}$.

$$\bar{x} = \frac{\Sigma x_i}{n} = \frac{140}{10} = 14$$

$$\bar{y} = \frac{\Sigma y_i}{n} = \frac{1300}{10} = 130$$

Using equations (12.6) and (12.7), and the information in Table 12.2, we can compute the slope and intercept of the estimated regression equation for Armand's Pizza Parlors. The calculation of the slope (b_1) proceeds as follows.

$$b_1 = \frac{\Sigma(x_i - \bar{x})(y_i - \bar{y})}{\Sigma(x_i - \bar{x})^2}$$

$$= \frac{2840}{568}$$

$$= 5$$

---

*An alternate formula for b_1 is

$$b_1 = \frac{\Sigma x_i y_i - (\Sigma x_i \Sigma y_i)/n}{\Sigma x_i^2 - (\Sigma x_i)^2/n}$$

This form of equation (12.6) is often recommended when using a calculator to compute b_1.

TABLE 12.2 CALCULATIONS FOR THE LEAST SQUARES ESTIMATED REGRESSION EQUATION FOR ARMAND'S PIZZA PARLORS

Restaurant i	x_i	y_i	$x_i - \bar{x}$	$y_i - \bar{y}$	$(x_i - \bar{x})(y_i - \bar{y})$	$(x_i - \bar{x})^2$
1	2	58	−12	−72	864	144
2	6	105	−8	−25	200	64
3	8	88	−6	−42	252	36
4	8	118	−6	−12	72	36
5	12	117	−2	−13	26	4
6	16	137	2	7	14	4
7	20	157	6	27	162	36
8	20	169	6	39	234	36
9	22	149	8	19	152	64
10	26	202	12	72	864	144
Totals	140	1300			2840	568
	Σx_i	Σy_i			$\Sigma(x_i - \bar{x})(y_i - \bar{y})$	$\Sigma(x_i - \bar{x})^2$

The calculations in this table can be easily made in an Excel worksheet.

The calculation of the y intercept (b_0) follows.

$$b_0 = \bar{y} - b_1\bar{x}$$
$$= 130 - 5(14)$$
$$= 60$$

Thus, the estimated regression equation is

$$\hat{y} = 60 + 5x$$

Figure 12.4 shows the graph of this equation on the scatter diagram.

The slope of the estimated regression equation ($b_1 = 5$) is positive, implying that as student population increases, quarterly sales increase. In fact, we can conclude (because quarterly sales are measured in $1000s and student population in 1000s) that an increase in the student population of 1000 is associated with an increase of $5000 in expected quarterly sales; that is, quarterly sales are expected to increase by $5 per student.

If we believe the least squares estimated regression equation adequately describes the relationship between x and y, it would seem reasonable to use the estimated regression equation to predict the value of y for a given value of x. For example, if we wanted to predict sales for a restaurant to be located near a campus with 16,000 students, we would compute

$$\hat{y} = 60 + 5(16) = 140$$

Using the estimated regression equation to make predictions outside the range of the values of the independent variable should be done with caution, because outside that range we cannot be sure that the same relationship is valid.

Hence, we would predict quarterly sales of $140,000 for this restaurant. In the following sections we will discuss methods for assessing the appropriateness of using the estimated regression equation for prediction.

Using Excel to Develop a Scatter Diagram and Compute the Estimated Regression Equation

In Section 2.4 we showed how Excel's Chart Wizard could be used to construct a scatter diagram. Once a scatter diagram has been developed, Excel's Chart menu provides options for computing the estimated regression equation and displaying the graph of the estimated

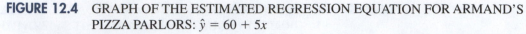

FIGURE 12.4   GRAPH OF THE ESTIMATED REGRESSION EQUATION FOR ARMAND'S
PIZZA PARLORS: $\hat{y} = 60 + 5x$

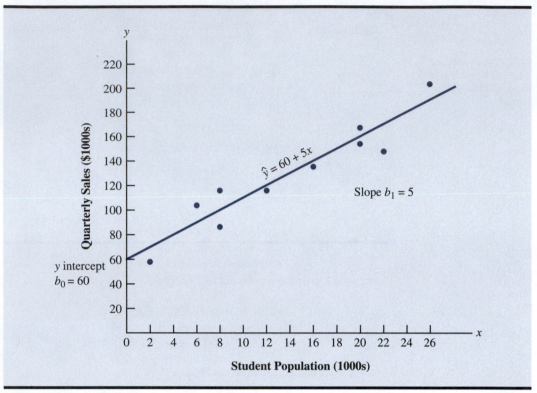

regression equation. We will demonstrate these capabilities using the Armand's Pizza Parlor data appearing in Table 12.1. Refer to Figure 12.5 as we describe the tasks involved.

Enter Data: The labels Restaurant, Population, and Sales are entered into cells A1:C1 of
the worksheet. To identify each of the 10 observations, we enter the numbers 1 through 10
into cells A2:A11. The sample data are entered into cells B2:C11.

Apply Tools: We will first use Excel's Chart Wizard to produce a scatter diagram. We
will then show how options available can be used to compute the estimated regression equation and to display the estimated regression line.

Step 1. Select cells B1:C11
Step 2. Select the **Chart Wizard** (or select the **Insert** menu and choose the **Chart**
option)
Step 3. When the **Chart Wizard—Step 1 of 4—Chart Type** dialog box appears:
     Choose **XY (Scatter)** in the **Chart type** list
     Choose **Scatter** from the **Chart sub-type** display
     Click **Next >**
Step 4. When the **Chart Wizard—Step 2 of 4—Chart Source Data** dialog box appears:
     Click **Next >**
Step 5. When the **Chart Wizard—Step 3 of 4—Chart Options** dialog box appears:
     Select the **Titles** tab and then
        Delete **Sales** in the Chart title box

FIGURE 12.5   SCATTER DIAGRAM, ESTIMATED REGRESSION EQUATION, AND THE ESTIMATED
REGRESSION LINE FOR ARMAND'S PIZZA PARLORS

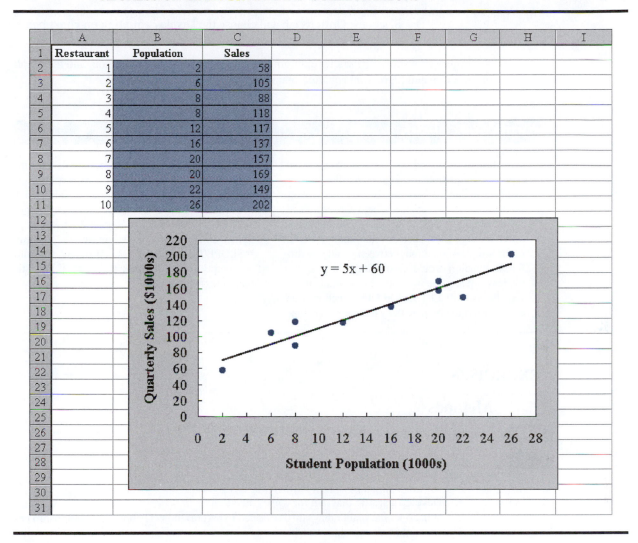

Type **Student Population (1000s)** in the **Value (X)** axis box

Type **Quarterly Sales ($1000s)** in the **Value (Y)** axis box

Select the **Legend** tab and then

Remove the check in the **Show Legend** box

Click **Next >**

Step 6. When the **Chart Wizard—Step 4 of 4—Chart Location** dialog box appears:

Specify a location for the new chart (we used the default setting of the current worksheet)

Click **Finish** to display the scatter diagram

Step 7. Position the mouse pointer over any data point and right click to display a list of options

Step 8. Choose the **Add Trendline** option

Step 9. When the Add Trendline dialog box appears:

Select the **Type** tab and choose **Linear** from the **Trend/Regression type** display

Select the **Options** tab and choose the **Display equation on chart** box

Click **OK**

Figure 12.5 shows the scatter diagram, the estimated regression equation, and the graph of the estimated regression equation obtained.

NOTES AND COMMENTS

1. The least squares method provides an estimated regression equation that minimizes the sum of squared deviations between the observed values of the dependent variable y_i and the estimated values of the dependent variable $\hat{y}_i$. If some other criterion were used, such as minimizing the sum of the absolute deviations between y_i and $\hat{y}_i$, a different equation would be obtained. In practice, the least squares method is the most widely used.

2. Excel's INTERCEPT and SLOPE functions can also be used to compute the y intercept and slope

of the estimated regression equation. For instance, for the Armand's data shown in columns B and C of Figure 12.5, the formula =INTERCEPT (C2:C11,B2:B11) can be entered into any empty cell of the worksheet to compute the y intercept of the estimated regression line, and the formula =SLOPE(C2:C11,B2:B11) can be entered into any empty cell to compute the slope of the estimated regression line.

EXERCISES

Methods

1. Given are five observations for two variables, x and y.

x_i	1	2	3	4	5
y_i	3	7	5	11	14

  a. Develop a scatter diagram for these data.

  b. What does the scatter diagram developed in part (a) indicate about the relationship between the two variables?

  c. Try to approximate the relationship between x and y by drawing a straight line through the data.

  d. Develop the estimated regression equation by computing the values of b_0 and b_1 using equations (12.6) and (12.7).

  e. Use the estimated regression equation to predict the value of y when $x = 4$.

2. Given are five observations for two variables, x and y.

x_i	2	3	5	1	8
y_i	25	25	20	30	16

  a. Develop a scatter diagram for these data.

  b. What does the scatter diagram developed in part (a) indicate about the relationship between the two variables?

  c. Try to approximate the relationship between x and y by drawing a straight line through the data.

   d. Develop the estimated regression equation by computing the values of b_0 and b_1 using
equations (12.6) and (12.7).
   e. Use the estimated regression equation to predict the value of y when $x = 6$.

3. Given are five observations collected in a regression study with two variables.

x_i	2	4	5	7	8
y_i	2	3	2	6	4

   a. Develop a scatter diagram for these data.
   b. Develop the estimated regression equation for these data.
   c. Use the estimated regression equation to predict the value of y when $x = 4$.

Applications

4. The following data were collected on the height (inches) and weight (pounds) of women
swimmers.

Height	68	64	62	65	66
Weight	132	108	102	115	128

   a. Develop a scatter diagram for these data with height as the independent variable.
   b. What does the scatter diagram developed in part (a) indicate about the relationship between the two variables?
   c. Try to approximate the relationship between height and weight by drawing a straight
line through the data.
   d. Develop the estimated regression equation by computing the values of b_0 and b_1 using
equations (12.6) and (12.7).
   e. If a swimmer's height is 63 inches, what would you estimate her weight to be?

5. The following data show the media expenditures (millions of dollars) and the case sales
(millions) for seven major brands of soft drinks (*Superbrands '98*, October 20, 1997).

Brand	Media Expenditures ($)	Case Sales
Coca-Cola Classic	131.3	1929.2
Pepsi-Cola	92.4	1384.6
Diet Coke	60.4	811.4
Sprite	55.7	541.5
Dr. Pepper	40.2	536.9
Mountain Dew	29.0	535.6
7-Up	11.6	219.5

   a. Develop a scatter diagram for these data with media expenditures as the independent
variable.
   b. What does the scatter diagram developed in part (a) indicate about the relationship between the two variables?
   c. Draw a straight line through the data to approximate a linear relationship between
media expenditures and case sales.
   d. Use the least squares method to develop the estimated regression equation.
   e. Provide an interpretation for the slope of the estimated regression equation.
   f. Predict the case sales for a brand with a media expenditure of $70 million.

6. Airline performance data for U.S. airlines were reported in *The Wall Street Journal Almanac 1998*. Data on the percentage of flights arriving on time and the number of complaints per 100,000 passengers follow.

Airline	Percentage on Time	Complaints
Southwest	81.8	0.21
Continental	76.6	0.58
Northwest	76.6	0.85
US Airways	75.7	0.68
United	73.8	0.74
American	72.2	0.93
Delta	71.2	0.72
America West	70.8	1.22
TWA	68.5	1.25

a. Develop a scatter diagram for these data with percentage on time as the independent variable.
b. What does the scatter diagram developed in part (a) indicate about the relationship between the two variables?
c. Develop the estimated regression equation showing how the number of complaints per 100,000 passengers is related to the percentage of flights arriving on time.
d. Provide an interpretation for the slope of the estimated regression equation.
e. What is the estimated number of complaints per 100,000 passengers if the percentage of flights arriving on time is 80%?

7. Both the Dow Jones Industrial Average (DJIA) and the Standard & Poor's 500 (S&P) indexes measure overall movement in the stock market. The DJIA is based on the price movements of 30 large companies; the S&P 500 is an index composed of 500 stocks. Some say the S&P 500 provides a better measure of stock market performance because it is broader based. The closing prices for the DJIA and the S&P 500 for 10 weeks, beginning February 11, 2000, follow (*Barron's*, April 17, 2000).

DowS&P

Date	DJIA	S&P
February 11	10425	1387
February 18	10220	1346
February 25	9862	1333
March 3	10367	1409
March 10	9929	1395
March 17	10595	1464
March 24	11113	1527
March 31	10922	1499
April 7	11111	1516
April 14	10306	1357

a. Develop a scatter diagram for these data with DJIA as the independent variable.
b. Develop the least squares estimated regression equation.
c. Suppose the closing price for the DJIA is 11,000. Estimate the closing price for the S&P 500.

8. Mountain bikes that cost less than $1000 now contain many of the high-quality components that until recently were only available on high-cost models. Today, even sub-$1000 models often offer supple suspensions, clipless pedals, and highly engineered frames. An interesting question is whether higher price still buys a higher level of handling, as measured by the bike's sidetrack capability. To measure sidetrack capability, *Outside Magazine* used a rating scale from 1 to 5, with 1 representing an average rating and 5 representing an excellent rating. The sidetrack capability and the price for 10 mountain bikes tested by *Outside Magazine* follow (*Outside Magazine Buyer's Guide*, 2001).

MtnBikes

Manufacturer and Model	Sidetrack Capability	Price ($)
Raleigh M80	1	600
Marin Bear Valley Feminina	1	649
GT Avalanche 2.0	2	799
Kona Jake the Snake	1	899
Schwinn Moab 2	3	950
Giant XTC NRS 3	4	1100
Fisher Paragon Genesisters	4	1149
Jamis Dakota XC	3	1300
Trek Fuel 90	5	1550
Specialized Stumpjumper M4	4	1625

a. Develop a scatter diagram for these data with sidetrack capability as the independent variable.
b. Does it appear that higher priced models have a higher level of handling? Explain.
c. Develop the least squares estimated regression equation.
d. What is the estimated price for a mountain bike if it has a sidetrack capability rating of 4?

9. A sales manager has collected the following data on years of experience and annual sales.

Salesperson	Years of Experience	Annual Sales ($1000s)
1	1	80
2	3	97
3	4	92
4	4	102
5	6	103
6	8	111
7	10	119
8	10	123
9	11	117
10	13	136

a. Develop a scatter diagram for these data with years of experience as the independent variable.
b. Develop an estimated regression equation that can be used to predict annual sales given the years of experience.
c. Use the estimated regression equation to predict annual sales for a salesperson with nine years of experience.

10. *PC World* provided ratings for the top 15 notebook PCs (*PC World*, February 2000). The performance score is a measure of how fast a PC can run a mix of common business applications as compared to how fast a baseline machine can run them. For example, a PC with a performance score of 200 is twice as fast as the baseline machine. A 100-point scale was used to provide an overall rating for each notebook tested in the study. A score in the 90s is exceptional, while one in the 70s is above average. The performance scores and the overall ratings for the 15 notebooks follow.

PCs

Notebook	Performance Score	Overall Rating
AMS Tech Roadster 15CTA380	115	67
Compaq Armada M700	191	78
Compaq Prosignia Notebook 150	153	79
Dell Inspiron 3700 C466GT	194	80
Dell Inspiron 7500 R500VT	236	84
Dell Latitude Cpi A366XT	184	76
Enpower ENP-313 Pro	184	77
Gateway Solo 9300LS	216	92
HP Pavilion Notebook PC	185	83
IBM ThinkPad I Series 1480	183	78
Micro Express NP7400	189	77
Micron TransPort NX PII-400	202	78
NEC Versa SX	192	78
Sceptre Soundx 5200	141	73
Sony VAIO PCG-F340	187	77

a. Develop a scatter diagram for these data with performance score as the independent variable.
b. Develop the least squares estimated regression equation.
c. Estimate the overall rating for a new PC with a performance score of 225.

11. The following data show the hotel revenue and the gaming revenue, in millions of dollars, for 10 Las Vegas casino hotels (*Cornell Hotel And Restaurant Administration Quarterly*, October 1997).

Casino

Company	Hotel Revenue ($)	Gaming Revenue ($)
Boyd Gaming	303.5	548.2
Circus Circus Enterprises	664.8	664.8
Grand Casinos	121.0	270.7
Hilton Corp. Gaming Div.	429.6	511.0
MGM Grand, Inc.	373.1	404.7
Mirage Resorts	670.9	782.8
Primadonna Resorts	66.4	130.7
Rio Hotel & Casino	105.8	105.5
Sahara Gaming	102.4	148.7
Station Casinos	135.8	358.5

a. Develop a scatter diagram for these data with hotel revenue as the independent variable.
b. Is there a linear relationship between the two variables?

c. Develop the estimated regression equation relating the gaming revenue to the hotel revenue.

d. Suppose that the hotel revenue was $500 million. What is an estimate of the gaming revenue?

12. The following table gives the number of employees and the revenue (millions of dollars) for 20 companies (*Fortune,* April 17, 2000).

EmpRev

Company	Employees	Revenue ($ millions)
Sprint	77,600	19,930
Chase Manhattan	74,801	33,710
Computer Sciences	50,000	7,660
Wells Fargo	89,355	21,795
Sunbeam	12,200	2,398
CBS	29,000	7,510
Time Warner	69,722	27,333
Steelcase	16,200	2,743
Georgia-Pacific	57,000	17,796
Toro	1,275	4,673
American Financial	9,400	3,334
Fluor	53,561	12,417
Phillips Petroleum	15,900	13,852
Cardinal Health	36,000	25,034
Borders Group	23,500	2,999
MCI Worldcom	77,000	37,120
Consolidated Edison	14,269	7,491
IBP	45,000	14,075
Super Value	50,000	17,421
H&R Block	4,200	1,669

a. Develop a scatter diagram for these data with number of employees as the independent variable.

b. What does the scatter diagram developed in part (a) indicate about the relationship between the number of employees and revenue?

c. Develop the estimated regression equation for these data.

d. Use the estimated regression equation to predict the revenue for a firm with 75,000 employees.

13. To the Internal Revenue Service, the reasonableness of total itemized deductions depends on the taxpayer's adjusted gross income. Large deductions, which include charity and medical deductions, are more reasonable for taxpayers with large adjusted gross incomes. If a taxpayer claims larger than average itemized deductions for a given level of income, the chances of an IRS audit increase. Data on adjusted gross income and the average amount of itemized deductions follow (Money, October 1994). The data are in thousands of dollars.

Adjusted Gross Income ($1000s)	Total Itemized Deductions ($1000s)
22	9.6
27	9.6
32	10.1

(continued)

Adjusted Gross Income ($1000s)	Total Itemized Deductions ($1000s)
48	11.1
65	13.5
85	17.7
120	25.5

a. Develop a scatter diagram for these data with adjusted gross income as the independent variable.

b. Develop the estimated regression equation.

c. Predict a reasonable level of total itemized deductions for a taxpayer with an adjusted gross income of $52,500. If this taxpayer claimed total itemized deductions of $20,400, would the IRS agent's request for an audit appear justified? Explain.

14. The following data report the occupancy rates (%) and room rates ($) for the largest U.S. hotel markets (*The Wall Street Journal Almanac 1998*).

Hotel

Market	Average Room Rate ($)	Occupancy Rate (%)
Los Angeles–Long Beach	75.91	67.9
Chicago	92.04	72.0
Washington	94.42	68.4
Atlanta	81.69	67.7
Dallas	74.76	69.5
San Diego	80.86	68.7
Anaheim–Santa Ana	70.04	69.5
San Francisco	106.47	78.7
Houston	66.11	62.0
Miami–Hialeah	85.83	71.2
Oahu Island	107.11	80.7
Phoenix	95.34	71.4
Boston	105.51	73.5
Tampa–St. Petersburg	67.45	63.4
Detroit	64.79	68.7
Philadelphia	83.56	70.1
Nashville	70.12	67.1
Seattle	82.60	73.4
Minneapolis–St. Paul	73.64	69.8
New Orleans	99.00	70.6

a. Develop a scatter diagram for these data with average room rate as the independent variable.

b. Develop the estimated regression equation relating the occupancy rate to the average room rate.

c. Predict the occupancy rate for a hotel with an average room rate of $80.

12.3 COEFFICIENT OF DETERMINATION

For the Armand's Pizza Parlors example, we developed the estimated regression equation $\hat{y} = 60 + 5x$ to approximate the linear relationship between the size of the student population x and quarterly sales y. A question now is: How well does the estimated regression equation fit the data? In this section, we show that the **coefficient of determination** provides a measure of the goodness of fit for the estimated regression equation.

For the ith observation, the difference between the observed value of the dependent variable, y_i, and the estimated value of the dependent variable, $\hat{y}_i$, is called the **ith residual**. The ith residual represents the error in using $\hat{y}_i$ to estimate y_i. Thus, for the ith observation, the residual is $y_i - \hat{y}_i$. The sum of squares of these residuals or errors is the quantity that is minimized by the least squares method. This quantity, also known as the *sum of squares due to error*, is denoted by SSE.

Sum of Squares Due to Error

$$SSE = \Sigma(y_i - \hat{y}_i)^2 \tag{12.8}$$

The value of SSE is a measure of the error in using the estimated regression equation to estimate the values of the dependent variable in the sample.

In Table 12.3 we show the calculations required to compute the sum of squares due to error for the Armand's Pizza Parlors example. For instance, for restaurant 1 the values of the independent and dependent variables are $x_1 = 2$ and $y_1 = 58$. Using the estimated regression equation, we find that the estimated value of quarterly sales for restaurant 1 is $\hat{y}_1 = 60 + 5(2) = 70$. Thus, the error (residual) in using $\hat{y}_1$ to estimate y_1 for restaurant 1 is $y_1 - \hat{y}_1 = 58 - 70 = -12$. The squared error, $(-12)^2 = 144$, is shown in the last column of Table 12.3. After computing and squaring the residuals (errors) for each restaurant in the sample, we sum them to obtain SSE = 1530. Thus, SSE = 1530 measures the error in using the estimated regression equation $\hat{y} = 60 + 5x$ to predict quarterly sales.

Now suppose we are asked to develop an estimate of quarterly sales without knowledge of the size of the student population. Without knowledge of any related variables, we would use the sample mean as an estimate of quarterly sales at any given restaurant. We earlier computed the mean value of quarterly sales for the sample of 10 Armand's restaurants as

TABLE 12.3 CALCULATION OF SSE FOR ARMAND'S PIZZA PARLORS

Restaurant i	x_i = Student Population (1000s)	y_i = Quarterly Sales ($1000s)	$\hat{y}_i = 60 + 5x_i$	$y_i - \hat{y}_i$	$(y_i - \hat{y}_i)^2$
1	2	58	70	-12	144
2	6	105	90	15	225
3	8	88	100	-12	144
4	8	118	100	18	324
5	12	117	120	-3	9
6	16	137	140	-3	9
7	20	157	160	-3	9
8	20	169	160	9	81
9	22	149	170	-21	441
10	26	202	190	12	144
					SSE = 1530

TABLE 12.4   CALCULATION OF SST FOR ARMAND'S PIZZA PARLORS

Restaurant i	x_i = Student Population (1000s)	y_i = Quarterly Sales ($1000s)	$y_i - \bar{y}$	$(y_i - \bar{y})^2$
1	2	58	−72	5,184
2	6	105	−25	625
3	8	88	−42	1,764
4	8	118	−12	144
5	12	117	−13	169
6	16	137	7	49
7	20	157	27	729
8	20	169	39	1,521
9	22	149	19	361
10	26	202	72	5,184
				SST = 15,730

$\bar{y} = \Sigma y_i/n = 1300/10 = 130$. In Table 12.4 we show the sum of squared deviations obtained by using the sample mean $\bar{y} = 130$ to estimate quarterly sales for each restaurant in the sample. For the ith restaurant in the sample, the difference $y_i - \bar{y}$ provides a measure of the error involved if we had used $\bar{y}$ to estimate y_i. The corresponding sum of squares, called the *total sum of squares,* is denoted SST.

SST *is the numerator of the formula for sample variance shown in Chapter 3.*

Total Sum of Squares

$$SST = \Sigma(y_i - \bar{y})^2 \qquad (12.9)$$

The sum at the bottom of the last column in Table 12.4 is the total sum of squares for Armand's Pizza Parlors; it is SST = 15,730.

In Figure 12.6 we show the estimated regression line $\hat{y} = 60 + 5x$ and the line corresponding to $\bar{y} = 130$. Note that the points cluster more closely around the estimated regression line than they do about the line $\bar{y} = 130$. For example, for the 10th restaurant in the sample we see that the error is much larger when $\bar{y} = 130$ is used as an estimate of y_{10} than when $\hat{y}_{10} = 60 + 5(26) = 190$ is used. We can think of SST as a measure of how well the observations cluster about the $\bar{y}$ line and SSE as a measure of how well the observations cluster about the $\hat{y}$ line found using the least squares method.

To measure how much the $\hat{y}$ values on the estimated regression line deviate from $\bar{y}$, another sum of squares is computed. This sum of squares, called the *sum of squares due to regression,* is denoted SSR.

Sum of Squares Due to Regression

$$SSR = \Sigma(\hat{y}_i - \bar{y})^2 \qquad (12.10)$$

FIGURE 12.6   DEVIATIONS ABOUT THE ESTIMATED REGRESSION LINE AND FROM THE LINE $y = \bar{y}$ FOR ARMAND'S PIZZA PARLORS

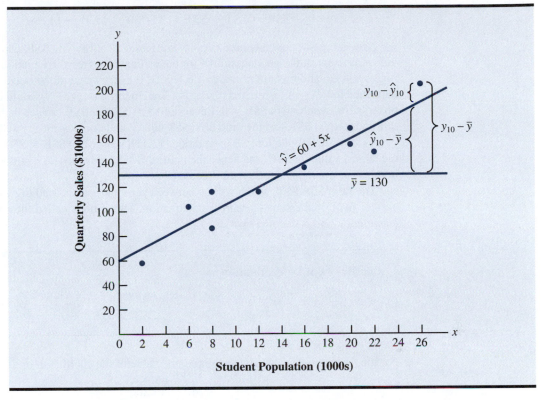

From the preceding discussion, we should expect that SST, SSR, and SSE are related. Indeed, the relationship among these three sums of squares provides one of the most important results in statistics.

SSR can be thought of as the explained portion of SST, and SSE can be thought of as the unexplained portion of SST.

Relationship Among SST, SSR, and SSE

$$SST = SSR + SSE \qquad (12.11)$$

where

$$SST = \text{total sum of squares}$$
$$SSR = \text{sum of squares due to regression}$$
$$SSE = \text{sum of squares due to error}$$

Equation (12.11) shows that the total sum of squares can be partitioned into two components, the sum of squares due to regression and the sum of squares due to error. Hence, if the values of any two of these sums of squares are known, the third sum of squares can be computed easily. For instance, in the Armand's Pizza Parlors example, we already know that SSE = 1530 and SST = 15,730; therefore, solving for SSR in equation (12.11), we find that the sum of squares due to regression is

$$SSR = SST - SSE = 15,730 - 1530 = 14,200$$

Now let us see how the three sums of squares, SST, SSR, and SSE, can be used to provide a measure of the goodness of fit for the estimated regression equation. The estimated regression equation would provide a perfect fit if every value of the dependent variable y_i happened to lie on the estimated regression line. In this case, $y_i - \hat{y}_i$ would be zero for each observation, resulting in SSE = 0. Because SST = SSR + SSE, we see that for a perfect fit SSR must equal SST, and the ratio SSR/SST must equal one. Poorer fits will result in larger values for SSE. Solving for SSE in equation (12.11), we see that SSE = SST − SSR. Hence, the largest value for SSE (and hence the poorest fit) occurs when SSR = 0 and SSE = SST; in this case the ratio SSR/SST must equal 0.

The ratio SSR/SST, which will be between zero and one, is used to evaluate the goodness of fit for the estimated regression equation. This ratio is called the *coefficient of determination* and is denoted by r^2.

Coefficient of Determination

$$r^2 = \frac{SSR}{SST} \tag{12.12}$$

For the Armand's Pizza Parlors example, the value of the coefficient of determination is

$$r^2 = \frac{SSR}{SST} = \frac{14,200}{15,730} = .9027$$

The least squares method finds the estimated regression equation that maximizes r^2.

When we express the coefficient of determination as a percentage, r^2 can be interpreted as the percentage of the total sum of squares that can be explained by using the estimated regression equation. For Armand's Pizza Parlors, we can conclude that 90.27% of the total sum of squares can be explained by using the estimated regression equation $\hat{y} = 60 + 5x$ to predict quarterly sales. In other words, 90.27% of the variability in quarterly sales can be explained by the linear relationship between the size of the student population and quarterly sales. We should be pleased to find such a good fit for the estimated regression equation.

Using Excel to Compute the Coefficient of Determination

In Section 12.2 we used Excel's Chart Wizard to construct a scatter diagram for the Armand's Pizza Parlors data. We then showed how options available could be used to compute the estimated regression equation and display its graph. We will now describe how to compute the coefficient of determination.

Step 1. Position the mouse pointer over any data point in the scatter diagram and right click to display a list of options
Step 2. Choose the **Add Trendline** option
Step 3. When the Add Trendline dialog box appears:
         Select the **Options** tab and choose the **Display R-squared value on chart** box
         Click **OK**

FIGURE 12.7 USING EXCEL TO COMPUTE THE COEFFICIENT OF DETERMINATION

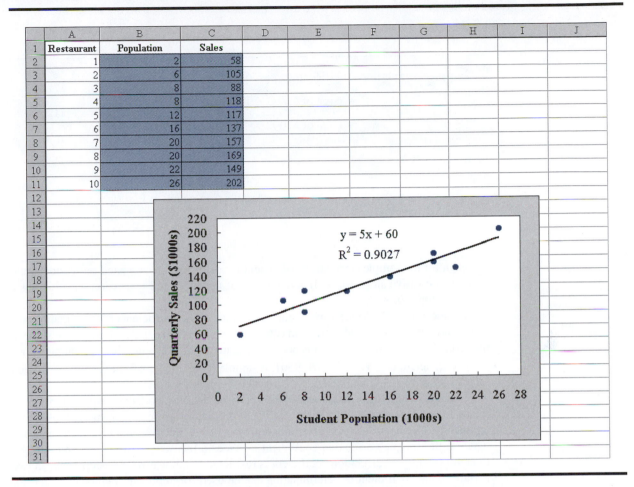

Figure 12.7 displays the scatter diagram, the estimated regression equation, the graph of the estimated regression equation, and the coefficient of determination for the Armand's Pizza Parlors data. We see that $r^2 = .9027$.

Correlation Coefficient

In Chapter 3 we introduced the **correlation coefficient** as a descriptive measure of the strength of linear association between two variables, x and y. Values of the correlation coefficient are always between -1 and $+1$. A value of $+1$ indicates that the two variables x and y are perfectly related in a positive linear sense. That is, all data points are on a straight line that has a positive slope. A value of -1 indicates that x and y are perfectly related in a negative linear sense, with all data points on a straight line that has a negative slope. Values of the correlation coefficient close to zero indicate that x and y are not linearly related.

In Section 3.5 we presented the equation for computing the sample correlation coefficient. If a regression analysis has already been performed and the coefficient of determination r^2 has been computed, the sample correlation coefficient can be computed as follows.

Sample Correlation Coefficient

$$r_{xy} = (\text{sign of } b_1)\sqrt{\text{Coefficient of Determination}}$$

$$= (\text{sign of } b_1)\sqrt{r^2}$$

(12.13)

where

$$b_1 = \text{the slope of the estimated regression equation } \hat{y} = b_0 + b_1x$$

The sign for the sample correlation coefficient is positive if the estimated regression equation has a positive slope ($b_1 > 0$) and negative if the estimated regression equation has a negative slope ($b_1 < 0$).

For the Armand's Pizza Parlor example, the value of the coefficient of determination corresponding to the estimated regression equation $\hat{y} = 60 + 5x$ is .9027. Because the slope of the estimated regression equation is positive, equation (12.13) shows that the sample correlation coefficient is $+\sqrt{.9027} = +.9501$. A sample correlation coefficient of $r_{xy} = +.9501$ indicates a strong positive linear association between x and y.

In the case of a linear relationship between two variables, both the coefficient of determination and the sample correlation coefficient provide measures of the strength of the relationship. The coefficient of determination provides a measure between zero and one whereas the sample correlation coefficient provides a measure between -1 and $+1$. Although the sample correlation coefficient is restricted to a linear relationship between two variables, the coefficient of determination can be used for nonlinear relationships and for relationships that have two or more independent variables. In that sense, the coefficient of determination has a wider range of applicability.

NOTES AND COMMENTS

1. In developing the least squares estimated regression equation we conducted no statistical tests for the significance of the relationship between x and y. Larger values of r^2 simply imply that the least squares line provides a better fit to the data; that is, the observations are more closely grouped about the least squares line. But, using only r^2, we can draw no conclusion about whether the relationship between x and y is statistically significant. Such a conclusion must be based on considerations that involve the sample size and the properties of the appropriate sampling distributions of the least squares estimators.

2. As a practical matter, for typical data found in the social sciences, values of r^2 as low as .25 are often considered useful. For data in the physical and life sciences, r^2 values of .60 or greater are often found; in fact, in some cases, r^2 values greater than .90 can be found. In business applications, r^2 values vary greatly, depending on the unique characteristics of each application.

EXERCISES

Methods

15. The data from Exercise 1 follow.

x_i	1	2	3	4	5
y_i	3	7	5	11	14

The estimated regression equation for these data is $\hat{y} = .20 + 2.60x$.
a.   Compute SSE, SST, and SSR using equations (12.8), (12.9), and (12.10).
b.   Compute the coefficient of determination r^2. Comment on the goodness of fit.
c.   Compute the sample correlation coefficient.

16. The data from Exercise 2 follow.

x_i	2	3	5	1	8
y_i	25	25	20	30	16

The estimated regression equation for these data is $\hat{y} = 30.33 + 1.88x$.
a.   Compute SSE, SST, and SSR.
b.   Compute the coefficient of determination r^2. Comment on the goodness of fit.
c.   Compute the sample correlation coefficient.

17. The data from Exercise 3 follow.

x_i	2	4	5	7	8
y_i	2	3	2	6	4

The estimated regression equation for these data is $\hat{y} = .75 + .51x$. What percentage of the total sum of squares can be accounted for by the estimated regression equation? What is the value of the sample correlation coefficient?

Applications

18. The following data are the grade point averages x and the monthly salaries y for students who obtained a bachelor's degree in business administration with a major in information systems. The estimated regression equation for these data is $\hat{y} = 1790.5 + 581.1x$.

GPA	Monthly Salary ($)
2.6	3300
3.4	3600
3.6	4000
3.2	3500
3.5	3900
2.9	3600

a.   Compute SST, SSR, and SSE.
b.   Compute the coefficient of determination r^2. Comment on the goodness of fit.
c.   What is the value of the sample correlation coefficient?

19. The data from Exercise 7 follow.

CD file

DowS&P

Date	x = DJIA	y = S&P
February 11	10425	1387
February 18	10220	1346
February 25	9862	1333
March 3	10367	1409
March 10	9929	1395
March 17	10595	1464
March 24	11113	1527
March 31	10922	1499
April 7	11111	1516
April 14	10306	1357

The estimated regression equation for these data is $\hat{y} = -137.63 + .1489x$. What percentage of the total sum of squares can be accounted for by the estimated regression equation? Comment on the goodness of fit. What is the sample correlation coefficient?

20. The typical household income and typical home price for a sample of 18 cities follow (*Places Rated Almanac*, 2000). Data are in thousands of dollars.

CD file

Cities

City	Income	Home Price
Akron, OH	74.1	114.9
Atlanta, GA	82.4	126.9
Birmingham, AL	71.2	130.9
Bismarck, ND	62.8	92.8
Cleveland, OH	79.2	135.8
Columbia, SC	66.8	116.7
Denver, CO	82.6	161.9
Detroit, MI	85.3	145.0
Fort Lauderdale, FL	75.8	145.3
Hartford, CT	89.1	162.1
Lancaster, PA	75.2	125.9
Madison, WI	78.8	145.2
Naples, FL	100.0	173.6
Nashville, TN	77.3	125.9
Philadelphia, PA	87.0	151.5
Savannah, GA	67.8	108.1
Toledo, OH	71.2	101.1
Washington, DC	97.4	191.9

a. Use these data to develop an estimated regression equation that could be used to estimate the typical home price for a city given the typical household income.

b. Compute r^2. Would you feel comfortable using this estimated regression equation to estimate the typical home price for a city?

c. Estimate the typical home price for a city with typical household income of $95,000.

21. An important application of regression analysis in accounting is the estimation of cost. By collecting data on production volume and cost and using the least squares method to develop an estimated regression equation relating volume and cost, an accountant can estimate the cost associated with a particular manufacturing operation. Consider the following sample of production volumes and total cost data for a manufacturing operation.

Production Volume (units)	Total Cost ($)
400	4000
450	5000
550	5400
600	5900
700	6400
750	7000

    a. Use these data to develop an estimated regression equation that could be used to predict the total cost for a given production volume.

    b. What is the variable, or additional, cost per unit produced?

    c. Compute the coefficient of determination. What percentage of the variation in total cost can be explained by production volume?

    d. The company's production schedule shows 500 units must be produced next month. What is the estimated total cost for this operation?

22. Are company presidents and chief executive officers paid according to the profit performance of the company? The following table lists corporate data on percentage change in return on equity over a two-year period and percentage change in the pay of presidents and chief executive officers immediately after the two-year period (*Business Week*, April 21, 1997).

Company	Two-Year Change in Return on Equity (%)	Change in Executive Compensation (%)
Dow Chemical	201.3	18
Rohm & Haas	146.5	28
Morton International	76.7	10
Union Carbide	158.2	28
Praxair	−34.9	15
Air Products & Chemicals	73.2	−9
Eastman Chemical	−7.9	−20

    a. Develop the estimated regression equation with the two-year percentage change in return on equity as the independent variable.

    b. Compute r^2. Would you feel comfortable using the percentage change in return on equity over a two-year period to predict the percentage change in the pay of presidents and chief executive officers? Discuss.

    c. What is the sample correlation coefficient? Does it reflect a strong or weak relationship between return on equity and executive compensation?

12.4   MODEL ASSUMPTIONS

In regression analysis, we begin by making an assumption about the appropriate model for the relationship between the dependent variable and the independent variable. In the case of simple linear regression, the assumed regression model is

$$y = \beta_0 + \beta_1 x + \epsilon$$

Then, the least squares method is used to develop values for b_0 and b_1, the estimates of the model parameters β_0 and β_1, respectively. The resulting estimated regression equation is

$$\hat{y} = b_0 + b_1 x$$

We saw that the value of the coefficient of determination (r^2) is a measure of the goodness of fit of the estimated regression equation. However, even with a large value of r^2, the estimated regression equation should not be used until further analysis of the appropriateness of the assumed model is conducted. An important step in determining whether the assumed model is appropriate involves testing for the significance of the relationship. The tests of significance in regression analysis are based on the following assumptions about the error term ϵ.

Assumptions About the Error Term ϵ in the Regression Model

$$y = \beta_0 + \beta_1 x + \epsilon$$

1. The error term ϵ is a random variable with a mean or expected value of zero; that is, $E(\epsilon) = 0$.
   Implication: Because β_0 and β_1 are constants, $E(\beta_0) = \beta_0$ and $E(\beta_1) = \beta_1$; thus, for a given value of x, the mean or expected value of y is

$$E(y) = \beta_0 + \beta_1 x \qquad (12.14)$$

   As we indicated previously, equation (12.14) is referred to as the regression equation.
2. The variance of ϵ, denoted by σ^2, is the same for all values of x.
   Implication: The variance of y at a given value of x equals σ^2 and is the same for all values of x.
3. The values of ϵ are independent.
   Implication: The value of ϵ for a particular value of x is not related to the value of ϵ for any other value of x; thus, the value of y for a particular value of x is not related to the value of y for any other value of x.
4. The error term ϵ is a normally distributed random variable.
   Implication: Because y is a linear function of ϵ, y is also a normally distributed random variable.

Figure 12.8 is an illustration of the model assumptions and their implications; note that in this graphical interpretation, the value of $E(y)$ changes according to the specific value of x considered. However, regardless of the x value, the probability distribution of ϵ and hence the probability distributions of y are normally distributed, each with the same variance. The specific value of the error ϵ at any particular point depends on whether the actual value of y is greater than or less than $E(y)$.

At this point, we must keep in mind that we are also making an assumption or hypothesis about the form of the relationship between x and y; that is, we assume that a straight line represented by $\beta_0 + \beta_1 x$ is the basis for the relationship between the variables. We must not lose sight of the fact that some other model, for instance $y = \beta_0 + \beta_1 x^2 + \epsilon$, may turn out to be a better model for the underlying relationship.

FIGURE 12.8   ASSUMPTIONS FOR THE REGRESSION MODEL

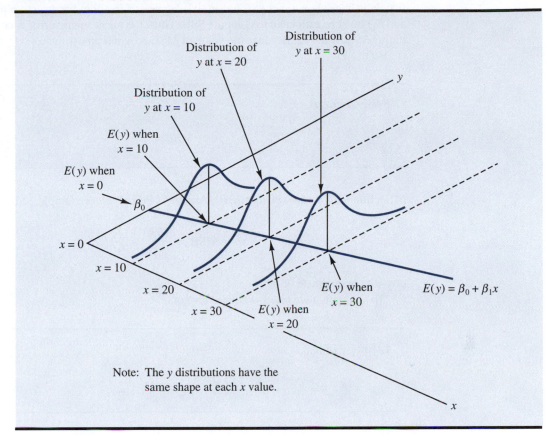

Note: The y distributions have the
same shape at each x value.

12.5   TESTING FOR SIGNIFICANCE

In a simple linear regression equation the mean or expected value of y is a linear function of x: $E(y) = \beta_0 + \beta_1 x$. If the value of β_1 is zero, $E(y) = \beta_0 + (0)x = \beta_0$. In this case, the mean value of y does not depend on the value of x and hence we would conclude that x and y are not linearly related. Alternatively, if the value of β_1 is not equal to zero, we would conclude that the two variables are related. Thus, to test for a significant regression relationship, we conduct a hypothesis test to determine whether the value of β_1 is zero. The tests used require an estimate of σ^2, the variance of ϵ.

Estimate of σ^2

From the regression model and its assumptions, we can conclude that σ^2, the variance of ϵ, also represents the variance of the y values about the regression line. Recall that the deviations of the y values about the estimated regression line are called *residuals*. Thus, SSE, the sum of squared residuals, is a measure of the variability of the y values about the estimated regression line. The **mean square error** (MSE) provides the estimate of σ^2; it is SSE divided by its degrees of freedom.

With $\hat{y}_i = b_0 + b_1 x_i$, SSE can be written as

$$SSE = \Sigma(y_i - \hat{y}_i)^2 = \Sigma(y_i - b_0 - b_1 x_i)^2$$

Every sum of squares has associated with it a number called its degrees of freedom. Statisticians have shown that SSE has $n - 2$ degrees of freedom because two parameters (β_0 and β_1) must be estimated to compute SSE. Thus, the mean square error is computed by dividing SSE by $n - 2$. Because the value of MSE provides an estimate of σ^2, the notation s^2 is also used.

Estimate of σ^2

$$s^2 = \text{MSE} = \frac{\text{SSE}}{n - 2} \tag{12.15}$$

In Section 12.3 we showed that for the Armand's Pizza Parlors example, SSE = 1530; hence,

$$s^2 = \text{MSE} = \frac{1530}{8} = 191.25$$

provides an estimate of σ^2.

To estimate σ we take the square root of s^2.

Estimate of σ

$$s = \sqrt{\text{MSE}} = \sqrt{\frac{\text{SSE}}{n - 2}} \tag{12.16}$$

For the Armand's Pizza Parlors example, $s = \sqrt{\text{MSE}} = \sqrt{191.25} = 13.829$. In the following discussion, we use s to conduct tests for a significant relationship between x and y.

t Test

The simple linear regression model is $y = \beta_0 + \beta_1 x + \epsilon$. If x and y are linearly related, we must have $\beta_1 \neq 0$. The t test uses the sample data to conduct the following hypothesis test about β_1.

$$H_0: \beta_1 = 0$$
$$H_a: \beta_1 \neq 0$$

If H_0 is rejected, we will conclude that $\beta_1 \neq 0$ and that the two variables have a statistically significant relationship. However, if H_0 cannot be rejected, we will have insufficient evidence to conclude that a significant relationship exists. The properties of the sampling distribution of b_1, the least squares estimator of β_1, provide the basis for the hypothesis test.

First, let us consider what would happen if we used a different random sample for the same regression study. For example, suppose that Armand's Pizza Parlors used the quarterly sales data for a different sample of 10 restaurants. A regression analysis of this new sample might result in an estimated regression equation similar to our previous estimated regression equation $\hat{y} = 60 + 5x$. However, it is doubtful that we would obtain exactly the same equation (with an intercept of exactly 60 and a slope of exactly 5). Indeed, b_0 and b_1, the least squares estimators, are sample statistics that have their own sampling distributions. The properties of the sampling distribution of b_1 follow.

Sampling Distribution of b_1

The standard deviation of b_1 is also referred to as the standard error of b_1.

Expected Value

$$E(b_1) = \beta_1$$

Standard Deviation

$$\sigma_{b_1} = \frac{\sigma}{\sqrt{\Sigma(x_i - \bar{x})^2}} \qquad (12.17)$$

Distribution Form

Normal

Note that the expected value of b_1 is equal to β_1, so b_1 is an unbiased estimator of β_1.

Because we do not know the value of σ, we develop an estimate of σ_{b_1}, denoted s_{b_1}, by estimating σ with s in equation (12.17). Thus, we obtain the following estimate of σ_{b_1}.

Estimated Standard Deviation of b_1

s_{b_1} provides an estimate of the standard error of b_1.

$$s_{b_1} = \frac{s}{\sqrt{\Sigma(x_i - \bar{x})^2}} \qquad (12.18)$$

For Armand's Pizza Parlors, $s = 13.829$ and $\Sigma(x_i - \bar{x})^2 = 568$ (see Table 12.2). Thus, we have

$$s_{b_1} = \frac{13.829}{\sqrt{568}} = .5803$$

as the estimated standard deviation of b_1.

The t test for a significant relationship is based on the fact that the test statistic

$$\frac{b_1 - \beta_1}{s_{b_1}}$$

follows a t distribution with $n - 2$ degrees of freedom. If the null hypothesis is true, then $\beta_1 = 0$ and $t = b_1/s_{b_1}$. With b_1/s_{b_1} as the test statistic, the steps of the t test for a significant relationship are as follows.

---

t Test for Significance in Simple Linear Regression

$$H_0: \beta_1 = 0$$
$$H_a: \beta_1 \neq 0$$

t Test Statistic

$$t = \frac{b_1}{s_{b_1}}$$
(12.19)

Rejection Rule

Using test statistic: Reject H_0 if $t < -t_{\alpha/2}$ or if $t > t_{\alpha/2}$

Using p-value: Reject H_0 if p-value $< \alpha$

where $t_{\alpha/2}$ is based on a t distribution with $n - 2$ degrees of freedom.

Let us conduct this test of significance for Armand's Pizza Parlors at the $\alpha = .01$ level of significance. The value of the test statistic (12.19) is

$$t = \frac{b_1}{s_{b_1}} = \frac{5}{.5803} = 8.62$$

From Table 2 of Appendix B we find that the two-tailed t value corresponding to $\alpha = .01$ and $n - 2 = 10 - 2 = 8$ degrees of freedom is $t_{.005} = 3.355$. With $8.62 > 3.355$, we reject H_0 and conclude at the .01 level of significance that β_1 is not equal to zero. The statistical evidence is sufficient to conclude that we have a significant relationship between student population and sales.

The p-value criterion can also be used for this hypothesis test. The two-tailed p-value associated with the test statistic $t = 8.62$ is .0000255. With $.0000255 < \alpha = .01$ we would reject H_0 and conclude that we have a significant relationship between student population and sales. In the next section, we will see that the p-value for this hypothesis test is computed automatically as part of the output when we use Excel's regression tool.

Excel's TDIST function can also be used to compute the p-value (see Chapter 9).

Confidence Interval for β_1

The form of a confidence interval for β_1 is as follows:

$$b_1 \pm t_{\alpha/2}s_{b_1}$$

The point estimator is b_1 and the margin of error is $t_{\alpha/2}s_{b_1}$. The confidence coefficient associated with this interval is $1 - \alpha$, and $t_{\alpha/2}$ is the t value providing an area of $\alpha/2$ in the upper tail of a t distribution with $n - 2$ degrees of freedom. For example, suppose that we wanted to develop a 99% confidence interval estimate of β_1 for Armand's Pizza Parlors. From Table 2 of Appendix B we find that the t value corresponding to $\alpha = .01$ and $n - 2 = 10 - 2 = 8$ degrees of freedom is $t_{.005} = 3.355$. Thus, the 99% confidence interval estimate of β_1 is

$$b_1 \pm t_{\alpha/2}s_{b_1} = 5 \pm 3.355(.5803) = 5 \pm 1.95$$

or 3.05 to 6.95.

In using the t test for significance, the hypotheses tested were

$$H_0: \beta_1 = 0$$
$$H_a: \beta_1 \neq 0$$

At the $\alpha = .01$ level of significance, we can use the 99% confidence interval as an alternative for drawing the hypothesis testing conclusion for the Armand's data. Because 0, the hypothesized value of β_1, is not included in the confidence interval (3.05 to 6.95), we can reject H_0 and conclude that a significant statistical relationship exists between student population and sales. In general, a confidence interval can be used to test any two-sided hypothesis about β_1. If the hypothesized value of β_1 is contained in the confidence interval, do not reject H_0. Otherwise, reject H_0.

F Test

An *F* test, based on the *F* probability distribution, can also be used to test for significance in regression. With only one independent variable, the *F* test will provide the same conclusion as the *t* test; that is, if the *t* test indicates $\beta_1 \neq 0$ and hence a significant relationship, the *F* test will also indicate a significant relationship. But with more than one independent variable, only the *F* test can be used to test for an overall significant relationship.

The logic behind the use of the *F* test for determining whether the regression relationship is statistically significant is based on the development of two independent estimates of σ^2. We see that MSE provides an estimate of σ^2. If the null hypothesis $H_0: \beta_1 = 0$ is true, the sum of squares due to regression, SSR, divided by its degrees of freedom provides another independent estimate of σ^2. This estimate is called the *mean square due to regression*, or simply the *mean square regression*, and is denoted MSR. In general,

$$\text{MSR} = \frac{\text{SSR}}{\text{Regression Degrees of Freedom}}$$

For the models we consider in this text, the regression degrees of freedom is always equal to the number of independent variables; thus,

$$\text{MSR} = \frac{\text{SSR}}{\text{Number of Independent Variables}} \tag{12.20}$$

Because only one independent variable is used in the Armand's Pizza Parlors example, we have MSR = SSR/1 = SSR. Hence, for Armand's Pizza Parlors, MSR = SSR = 14,200.

If the null hypothesis ($H_0: \beta_1 = 0$) is true, MSR and MSE are two independent estimates of σ^2 and the sampling distribution of MSR/MSE follows an *F* distribution with numerator degrees of freedom equal to one and denominator degrees of freedom equal to $n - 2$. Therefore, when $\beta_1 = 0$, the value of MSR/MSE should be close to one. However, if the null hypothesis is false ($\beta_1 \neq 0$), MSR will overestimate σ^2 and the value of MSR/MSE will be inflated; thus, large values of MSR/MSE lead to the rejection of H_0 and the conclusion that the relationship between x and y is statistically significant. A summary of how the *F* test is used to test for a significant relationship follows.

F Test for Significance

$$H_0: \beta_1 = 0$$
$$H_a: \beta_1 \neq 0$$

F Test Statistic

$$F = \frac{\text{MSR}}{\text{MSE}} \tag{12.21}$$

Rejection Rule

Using test statistic: Reject H_0 if $F > F_\alpha$

Using p-value: Reject H_0 if p-value $< \alpha$

where F_α is based on an F distribution with 1 degree of freedom in the numerator and $n - 2$ degrees of freedom in the denominator

Let us conduct the F test for the Armand's Pizza Parlors example at the $\alpha = .01$ level of significance. The test statistic is

$$F = \frac{\text{MSR}}{\text{MSE}} = \frac{14{,}200}{191.25} = 74.25$$

The F test and the t test provide identical results for simple linear regression.

From Table 4 of Appendix B we find that the F value corresponding to $\alpha = .01$ with one degree of freedom in the numerator and $n - 2 = 10 - 2 = 8$ degrees of freedom in the denominator is $F_{.01} = 11.26$. With $74.25 > 11.26$, we reject H_0 and conclude at the .01 level of significance that β_1 is not equal to zero. The F test provides the statistical evidence necessary to conclude a significant relationship exists between student population and sales.

We stated at the beginning of this subsection that, for simple linear regression, the F test would provide the same hypothesis testing conclusion as the t test. The p-value associated with $F = 74.25$ is .0000255. This p-value is the same as found for the t test in the previous subsection and confirms our earlier comment that the F test and the t test lead to the same conclusion. In the next section, we will see that the p-value for the F test is computed automatically as part of the output when we use Excel's regression tool.

Excel's FDIST function can also be used to compute the p-value.

In Chapter 10 we covered analysis of variance (ANOVA) and showed how an **ANOVA table** could be used to provide a convenient summary of the computational aspects of analysis of variance. A similar ANOVA table can be used to summarize the results of the F test for significance in regression. Table 12.5 is the general form of the ANOVA table for regression studies involving one independent variable. Regression, Error, and Total are listed as the three sources of variation, with SSR, SSE, and SST appearing as the corresponding sum of squares in column two. The degrees of freedom, 1 for Regression, $n - 2$ for Error, and $n - 1$ for Total, are shown in column three. Column 4 contains the values of MSR and

TABLE 12.5   GENERAL FORM OF THE ANOVA TABLE FOR SIMPLE LINEAR REGRESSION

In every analysis of variance table the total sum of squares is the sum of the regression sum of squares and the error sum of squares; in addition, the total degrees of freedom is the sum of the regression degrees of freedom and the error degrees of freedom.

Source of Variation	Sum of Squares	Degrees of Freedom	Mean Square	F
Regression	SSR	1	$\text{MSR} = \dfrac{\text{SSR}}{1}$	$F = \dfrac{\text{MSR}}{\text{MSE}}$
Error	SSE	$n - 2$	$\text{MSE} = \dfrac{\text{SSE}}{n - 2}$	
Total	SST	$n - 1$		

TABLE 12.6   ANOVA TABLE FOR THE ARMAND'S PIZZA PARLORS PROBLEM

Source of Variation	Sum of Squares	Degrees of Freedom	Mean Square	F
Regression	14,200	1	$\dfrac{14,200}{1} = 14,200$	$\dfrac{14,200}{191.25} = 74.25$
Error	1,530	8	$\dfrac{1530}{8} = 191.25$	
Total	15,730	9		

MSE, and column 5 contains the value of $F =$ MSR/MSE. Table 12.6 is the ANOVA table with the F test computations just performed for Armand's Pizza Parlors.

Some Cautions About the Interpretation of Significance Tests

Regression analysis, which can be used to identify how variables are associated with one another, cannot be used as evidence of a cause-and-effect relationship.

Rejecting the null hypothesis H_0: $\beta_1 = 0$ and concluding that the relationship between x and y is significant does not enable us to conclude that a cause-and-effect relationship is present between x and y. Concluding that a cause-and-effect relationship exists is warranted only if the analyst can show theoretical justification that the relationship is in fact causal. In the Armand's Pizza Parlors example, we can conclude that a significant relationship exists between the size of the student population x and quarterly sales y; moreover, the estimated regression equation $\hat{y} = 60 + 5x$ provides the least squares estimate of the relationship. We cannot, however, conclude that changes in student population x cause changes in quarterly sales y just because we have identified a statistically significant relationship. The appropriateness of such a cause-and-effect conclusion depends on the amount of supporting theoretical justification and on good judgment on the part of the analyst. In this case, Armand's managers had good reason to believe that increases in the student population were a likely cause of increased quarterly sales. Thus, the result of the significance test enabled them to conclude that a cause-and-effect relationship was present.

In addition, just because we are able to reject H_0: $\beta_1 = 0$ and demonstrate statistical significance does not enable us to conclude that the relationship between x and y is linear. We can state only that x and y are related and that a linear relationship explains a significant portion of the variability in y over the range of values for x observed in the sample. Figure 12.9 illustrates this situation. The test for significance leads to the rejection of the null hypothesis H_0: $\beta_1 = 0$ and to the conclusion that x and y are significantly related, but the figure shows that the actual relationship between x and y is not linear. Although the linear approximation provided by $\hat{y} = b_0 + b_1x$ is good over the range of x values observed in the sample, it becomes poor for x values outside that range.

Given a significant relationship, we should feel confident in using the estimated regression equation for predictions corresponding to x values within the range of the x values observed in the sample. For Armand's Pizza Parlors, this range corresponds to values of x between 2 and 26. But unless reasons indicate that the model is valid beyond this range, predictions outside the range of the independent variable should be made with caution. For Armand's Pizza Parlors, because the regression relationship is significant at the .01 level, we should feel confident using it to predict quarterly sales for restaurants where the associated student population is between 2000 and 26,000.

FIGURE 12.9   EXAMPLE OF A LINEAR APPROXIMATION OF A NONLINEAR RELATIONSHIP

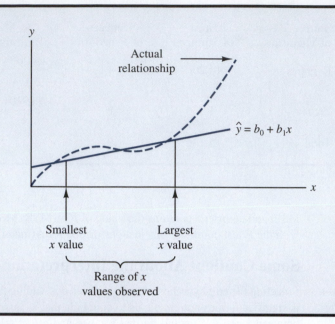

NOTES AND COMMENTS

1. The assumptions made about the error term (Section 12.4) allow for the tests of statistical significance in this section. The properties of the sampling distribution of b_1 and the subsequent t and F tests follow directly from these assumptions.

2. Do not confuse statistical significance with practical significance. With very large sample sizes, statistically significant results can be obtained for small values of b_1; in such cases, one must exercise care in concluding that the relationship has practical significance.

3. A test of significance for a linear relationship between x and y can also be performed by using

the sample correlation coefficient r_{xy}. With ρ_{xy} denoting the population correlation coefficient, the hypotheses are as follows.

$$H_0: \rho_{xy} = 0$$
$$H_a: \rho_{xy} \neq 0$$

A significant relationship can be concluded if H_0 is rejected. However, the t and F tests presented previously in this section give the same result as the test for significance using the correlation coefficient. Conducting a test for significance using the correlation coefficient therefore is not necessary if a t or F test has already been conducted.

EXERCISES

Methods

23. The data from Exercise 1 follow.

x_i	1	2	3	4	5
y_i	3	7	5	11	14

a. Compute the mean square error using equation (12.15).
b. Compute the estimate of σ using equation (12.16).

c. Compute the estimated standard deviation of b_1 using equation (12.18).
d. Use the t test to test the following hypotheses ($\alpha = .05$):

$$H_0: \beta_1 = 0$$
$$H_a: \beta_1 \neq 0$$

e. Use the F test to test the hypotheses in part (d) at a .05 level of significance. Present the results in the analysis of variance table format (see Table 12.5).

24. The data from Exercise 2 follow.

x_i	2	3	5	1	8
y_i	25	25	20	30	16

a. Compute the mean square error using equation (12.15).
b. Compute the estimate of σ using equation (12.16).
c. Compute the estimated standard deviation of b_1 using equation (12.18).
d. Use the t test to test the following hypotheses ($\alpha = .05$):

$$H_0: \beta_1 = 0$$
$$H_a: \beta_1 \neq 0$$

e. Use the F test to test the hypotheses in part (d) at a .05 level of significance. Present the results in the analysis of variance table format.

25. The data from Exercise 3 follow.

x_i	2	4	5	7	8
y_i	2	3	2	6	4

a. Compute the estimate of σ.
b. Test for a significant relationship by using the t test. Use $\alpha = .05$.
c. Use the F test to test for a significant relationship. Use $\alpha = .05$. What is your conclusion?

Applications

26. In Exercise 18 the data on grade point average and monthly salary were as follows.

GPA	Monthly Salary ($)	GPA	Monthly Salary ($)
2.6	3300	3.2	3500
3.4	3600	3.5	3900
3.6	4000	2.9	3600

a. Does the t test indicate a significant relationship between grade point average and monthly salary? What is your conclusion? Use $\alpha = .05$.
b. Test for a significant relationship using the F test. What is your conclusion? Use $\alpha = .05$.
c. Show the ANOVA table.

27. *Outside Magazine* tested 10 different models of day hikers and backpacking boots. The following data show the upper support and price for each model tested. Upper support was measured using a rating from 1 to 5, with a rating of 1 denoting average upper support and a rating of 5 denoting excellent upper support (*Outside Magazine Buyer's Guide*, 2001).

Boots

Manufacturer and Model	Upper Support	Price
Salomon Super Raid	2	120
Merrell Chameleon Prime	3	125
Teva Challenger	3	130
Vasque Fusion GTX	3	135
Boreal Maigmo	3	150
L.L. Bean GTX Super Guide	5	189
Lowa Kibo	5	190
Asolo AFX 520 GTX	4	195
Raichle Mt. Trail GTX	4	200
Scarpa Delta SL M3	5	220

a. Use these data to develop an estimated regression equation to estimate the price of a day hiker and backpacking boot given the upper support rating.
b. At the .05 level of significance, determine whether upper support and price are related.
c. Would you feel comfortable using the estimated regression equation developed in part (a) to estimate the price for a day hiker or backpacking boot given the upper support rating?
d. Estimate the price for a day hiker with an upper support rating of 4.

28. Refer to Exercise 10, where an estimated regression equation relating the performance score and the overall rating for notebook PCs was developed. At the .05 level of significance, test whether these two variables are related. Show the ANOVA table. What is your conclusion?

29. Refer to Exercise 21, where data on production volume and cost were used to develop an estimated regression equation relating production volume and cost for a particular manufacturing operation. Using $\alpha = .05$, test whether the production volume is significantly related to the total cost. Show the ANOVA table. What is your conclusion?

30. Refer to Exercise 22, where the following data were used to determine whether company presidents and chief executive officers are paid on the basis of company profit performance (*Business Week*, April 21, 1997).

Company	Two-Year Change in Return on Equity (%)	Change in Executive Compensation (%)
Dow Chemical	201.3	18
Rohm & Haas	146.5	28
Morton International	76.7	10
Union Carbide	158.2	28
Praxair	−34.9	15
Air Products & Chemicals	73.2	−9
Eastman Chemical	−7.9	−20

Do these data indicate a significant relationship between the two variables? Conduct the appropriate statistical test and state your conclusion. Use $\alpha = .05$.

31. Refer to Exercise 20, where an estimated regression equation was developed relating typical household income and typical home price. Test whether the typical household income for a city and the typical home price are related at the .01 level of significance.

12.6   EXCEL'S REGRESSION TOOL

In previous sections of this chapter we showed how Excel can be used to perform various tasks in a regression analysis separately. Excel also offers a more comprehensive Regression tool. In this section we will illustrate how Excel's Regression tool can be used to perform a complete regression analysis, including statistical tests of significance for the Armand's Pizza Parlor's data in Table 12.1.

Using Excel's Regression Tool for the Armand's Pizza Parlors Problem

Refer to Figure 12.10 and the dialog box in Figure 12.11 as we describe the tasks involved in using Excel's Regression tool to perform the regression analysis for the Armand's data.

Enter Data: The labels Restaurant, Population, and Sales are entered into cells A1:C1 of the worksheet. To identify each of the 10 observations, we enter the numbers 1 through 10 into cells A2:A11 and then enter the sample data into cells B2:C11.

FIGURE 12.10   REGRESSION TOOL OUTPUT FOR ARMAND'S PIZZA PARLORS

	A	B	C	D	E	F	G	H	I	J
1	Restaurant	Population	Sales							
2	1	2	58							
3	2	6	105							
4	3	8	88							
5	4	8	118							
6	5	12	117							
7	6	16	137							
8	7	20	157							
9	8	20	169							
10	9	22	149							
11	10	26	202							
12										
13	SUMMARY OUTPUT									
14										
15	*Regression Statistics*									
16	Multiple R	0.9501								
17	R Square	0.9027								
18	Adjusted R Square	0.8906								
19	Standard Error	13.8293								
20	Observations	10								
21										
22	ANOVA									
23		*df*	*SS*	*MS*	*F*	*Significance F*				
24	Regression	1	14200	14200	74.2484	2.55E-05				
25	Residual	8	1530	191.25						
26	Total	9	15730							
27										
28		*Coefficients*	*Standard Error*	*t Stat*	*P-value*	*Lower 95%*	*Upper 95%*	*Lower 99.0%*	*Upper 99.0%*	
29	Intercept	60	9.2260	6.5033	0.0002	38.7247	81.2753	29.0431	90.9569	
30	Population	5	0.5803	8.6167	2.55E-05	3.6619	6.3381	3.0530	6.9470	
31										

FIGURE 12.11   REGRESSION DIALOG BOX FOR THE ARMAND'S PIZZA
PARLORS PROBLEM

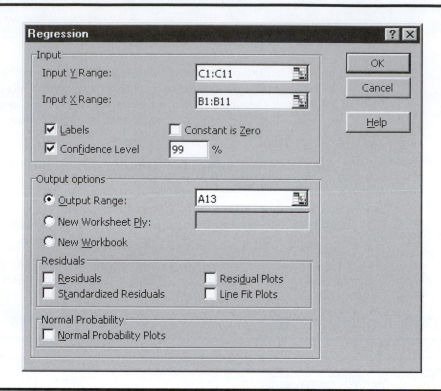

Apply Tools: The following steps describe how to use Excel to perform the regression
analysis computations.

Step 1. Select the **Tools** menu
Step 2. Choose the **Data Analysis** option
Step 3. Choose **Regression** from the list of Analysis Tools
Step 4. When the Regression dialog box appears (see Figure 12.11):
  Enter C1:C11 in the **Input Y Range** box
  Enter B1:B11 in the **Input X Range** box
  Select **Labels**
  Select **Confidence Level**
  Enter 99 in the **Confidence Level** box
  Select **Output Range**
  Enter A13 in the **Output Range** box (to identify the upper left corner of
  the section of the worksheet where the output will appear)
  Click **OK**

*The Excel output can be
reformatted to improve
readability.*

The regression output, titled SUMMARY OUTPUT, begins with row 13 in Figure 12.10. Because Excel initially displays the output using standard column widths, many of the row
and column labels are unreadable. In several places we have reformatted them to improve
readability. We have also reformatted cells displaying numerical values to a maximum of
four decimal places. Numbers displayed using scientific notation were not modified. Regression output in future figures will be similarly reformatted to improve readability.

The first section of the SUMMARY OUTPUT, titled *Regression Statistics*, contains summary statistics such as the coefficient of determination (R Square). The second section of the output, titled ANOVA, contains the analysis of variance table. The last section of the output, which is not titled, contains the estimated regression coefficients and related information. Let us begin our interpretation of the regression output with the information contained in cells A28:I30.

Interpretation of Estimated Regression Equation Output

Row 29 contains information about the y intercept of the estimated regression line. Row 30 contains information about the slope of the estimated regression line. The y intercept of the estimated regression line, $b_0 = 60$, is shown in cell B29, and the slope of the estimated regression line, $b_1 = 5$, is shown in cell B30. The label Intercept in cell A29 and the label Population in cell A30 identify these two values.

In Section 12.5 we showed that the estimated standard deviation of b_1 is $s_{b_1} = .5803$. Cell C30 contains the estimated standard deviation of b_1. As we indicated previously, the standard deviation of b_1 is also referred to as the standard error of b_1. Thus, s_{b_1} provides an estimate of the standard error of b_1. The label Standard Error in cell C28 is Excel's way of indicating that the value in cell C30 is the estimate of the standard error, or standard deviation, of b_1.

In Section 12.5 we stated that the form of the null and alternative hypotheses needed to test for a significant relationship between population and sales are as follows:

$$H_0: \beta_1 = 0$$
$$H_a: \beta_1 \neq 0$$

Recall that the t test for a significant relationship required the computation of the t statistic, $t = b_1/s_{b_1}$. For the Armand's data, the value of t that we computed was $t = 5/.5803 = 8.62$. Note that after rounding, the value in cell D30 is 8.62. The label in cell D28, t *Stat*, reminds us that cell D30 contains the value of the t test statistic.

t **Test**   The p-value in cell E30 provides a means for conducting a test of significance. Excel displays the p-value using scientific notation. To obtain the decimal equivalent, we move the decimal point 5 places to the left; we obtain a p-value of .0000255. Given the level of significance α, the decision of whether to reject H_0 can be made as follows:

$$\text{Reject } H_0 \text{ if } p\text{-value} < \alpha$$

Because the p-value = .0000255 < α = .01, we can reject H_0 and conclude that we have a significant relationship between student population and sales. Because p-values are provided as part of the computer output for regression analysis, the p-value approach is most often used for hypothesis tests in regression analysis.

The information in cells F28:I30 can be used to develop confidence interval estimates of the y intercept and slope of the estimated regression equation. Excel always provides the lower and upper limits for a 95% confidence interval. Recall that in the Regression dialog box (see Figure 12.11) we selected Confidence Level and entered 99 in the Confidence Level box. As a result, Excel's Regression tool also provides the lower and upper limits for a 99% confidence interval. For instance, the value in cell H30 is the lower limit for the 99% confidence interval estimate of β_1 and the value in cell I30 is the upper limit. Thus, after rounding, the 99% confidence interval estimate of β_1 is 3.05 to 6.95. The values in cells F30 and G30 provide the lower and upper limits for the 95% confidence interval. Thus, the 95% confidence interval is 3.66 to 6.34.

Interpretation of ANOVA Output

The information in cells A22:F26 summarizes the analysis of variance computations for the Armand's data. The three sources of variation are labeled Regression, Residual, and Total. The label *df* in cell B23 stands for degrees of freedom, the label *SS* in cell C23 stands for sum of squares, and the label *MS* in cell D23 stands for mean square. Looking at cells C24:C26, we see that the regression sum of squares is 14200, the residual or error sum of squares is 1530, and the total sum of squares is 15730. The values in cells B24:B26 are the degrees of freedom corresponding to each sum of squares. Thus, the regression sum of squares has 1 degree of freedom, the residual, or error sum of squares, has 8 degrees of freedom, and the total sum of squares has 9 degrees of freedom. As we discussed previously, the regression degrees of freedom plus the residual degrees of freedom is equal to the total degrees of freedom, and the regression sum of squares plus the residual sum of squares is equal to the total sum of squares.

Excel refers to the error sum of squares as the residual sum of squares.

In Section 12.5 we stated that the mean square error, obtained by dividing the error or residual sum of squares by its degrees of freedom, provides an estimate of σ^2. The value in cell D25, 191.25, is the mean square error. We also stated that the mean square regression is the sum of squares due to regression divided by the regression degrees of freedom. The value in cell D24, 14200, is the mean square regression.

F Test   In Section 12.5 we showed that an *F* test, based upon the *F* probability distribution, could be used to test for significance in regression. The value in cell F24, .0000255, is the *p*-value associated with the *F* test for significance. Because the *p*-value = .0000255 < α = .01, we can reject H_0 and conclude that a significant relationship exists between student population and sales. Note that this is the same conclusion that we reached using the *p*-value approach for the *t* test for significance. In fact, because the *t* test for significance is equivalent to the *F* test for significance in simple linear regression, the *p*-values provided by both approaches are identical. The label Excel uses to identify the *p*-value for the *F* test for significance, shown in cell F23, is *Significance F*. In Chapter 9 we also stated that the *p*-value is often referred to as the observed level of significance. Thus, the label *Significance F* may be more meaningful if you think of the value in cell F24 as the observed level of significance for the *F* test.

Interpretation of Regression Statistics Output

The output in cells A15:B20 summarizes the regression statistics. The number of observations in the data set, 10, is shown in cell B20. The coefficient of determination, .9027, appears in cell B17; the corresponding label, R Square, is shown in cell A17. The square root of the coefficient of determination provides the sample correlation coefficient of 0.9501 shown in cell B16. Note that Excel uses the label Multiple R (cell A16) to identify this value. In cell A19, the label Standard Error is used to identify the value of *s*, the estimate of σ. Cell B19 shows that the value of *s* is 13.8293. We caution the reader to keep in mind that in the Excel output, the label Standard Error appears in two different places. In the Regression Statistics section of the output the label Standard Error in cell A19 refers to *s*, the estimate of σ. In the Estimated Regression Equation section of the output, the label Standard Error in cell C28 reminds us that the value in cell C30 is the estimated standard deviation of the sampling distribution of b_1.

EXERCISES

Applications

32. Following is a portion of the Excel output for a regression analysis relating maintenance expense (dollars per month) to usage (hours per week) for a particular brand of computer terminal.

ANOVA

	df	SS
Regression	1	1575.76
Residual	8	349.14
Total	9	1924.90

	Coefficients	Standard Error	t Stat
Intercept	6.1092	.9361	
Usage	0.8951	.149	

  a. Write the estimated regression equation.
  b. Use the t test to determine whether monthly maintenance expense is related to usage at the .05 level of significance.
  c. Did the estimated regression equation provide a good fit? Explain.

33. The commercial division of a real estate firm conducted a study to determine the extent of the relationship between annual gross rents ($1000s) and the selling price ($1000s) for apartment buildings. Data were collected on several properties sold, and Excel's Regression tool was used to develop an estimated regression equation. A portion of the Excel output follows.

ANOVA

	df	SS	MS	F
Regression	1	41587.3		
Residual	7			
Total	8	51984.1		

	Coefficients	Standard Error	t Stat
Intercept	20.000	3.2213	6.21
Annual Gross Rents	7.210	1.3626	5.29

  a. How many apartment buildings were in the sample?
  b. Write the estimated regression equation.
  c. Use the t test to determine whether the selling price is related to annual gross rents.
  d. Use the F test to determine whether the selling price is related to annual gross rents.
  e. Estimate the selling price of an apartment building with annual gross rents of $50,000.

34. To determine whether the annual sales at a branch office are related to the number of salespersons at the branch office, a firm used the data from a sample of 30 branch offices to develop an estimated regression equation relating these two variables. A portion of the Excel output that was obtained follows.

ANOVA

	df	SS	MS	F
Regression		6828.6		
Residual				
Total		9127.4		

	Coefficients	Standard Error	t Stat	P-value
Intercept	80.0	11.333		
Number of Salespersons	50.0	5.482		

a. Write the estimated regression equation.
b. Compute the F statistic and test the significance of the relationship at the .05 level of significance.
c. Compute the t statistic and test the significance of the relationship at the .05 level of significance.
d. Compute the p-value associated with the t test for significance.

35. A sample of 15 companies taken from the *Stock Investor Pro* database was used to obtain the following data on the price/earnings (P/E) ratio and the gross profit margin for each company (*Stock Investor Pro*, American Association of Individual Investors, August 21, 1997).

StockPro

Firm	Gross Profit Margin (%)	P/E Ratio
Abbott Laboratories	23.7	22.3
American Home Products	21.1	22.6
Amoco	11.0	16.7
Bristol Meyers Squibb Co.	26.6	25.9
Chevron	11.6	18.3
Exxon	9.8	18.7
General Electric Company	13.4	13.1
Hewlett-Packard	9.7	23.3
IBM	11.5	17.3
Merck & Co. Inc.	25.6	26.2
Mobil	8.2	18.7
Pfizer	25.1	34.6
Pharmacia & Upjohn, Inc.	15.0	22.3
Texaco	7.3	12.3
Travelers Group Inc.	17.8	28.7

a. Determine the estimated regression equation that can be used to predict the price/earnings ratio given the gross profit margin.
b. Use the F test to determine whether the gross profit margin and the P/E ratio are related. What is your conclusion at the .05 level of significance?

    c. Use the *t* test to determine whether the gross profit margin and the P/E ratio are related. What is your conclusion at the .05 level of significance? Is the conclusion that you reached here the same as in part (b)? Explain.

    d. Did the estimated regression equation provide a good fit to the data? Explain.

36. A 10-year study conducted by the American Heart Association provided data on how age related to the risk of strokes. Suppose that the following data were obtained in a follow-up study. Risk is interpreted as the probability (times 100) that the patient will have a stroke over the next 10-year period.

Heart

Patient	Risk	Age
1	12	57
2	24	67
3	13	58
4	56	86
5	28	59
6	51	76
7	18	56
8	31	78
9	37	80
10	15	78
11	22	71
12	36	70
13	15	67
14	48	77
15	15	60
16	36	82
17	8	66
18	34	80
19	3	62
20	37	59

    a. Develop an estimated regression equation that can be used to relate the risk of a stroke to the person's age.

    b. Is the relationship between risk and age significant at the .05 level of significance?

    c. Did the estimated regression equation provide a good fit to the data? Explain.

37. The National Association of Home Builders ranks the most and least affordable housing markets, based on the proportion of homes that a family earning the median income in that market could afford to buy. Data showing the median income ($1000s) and the median sale price ($1000s) for a sample of 12 housing markets that appeared on the list of most affordable markets follow (*The Wall Street Journal Almanac 1998*).

HomeBldg

Market	Income ($1000s)	Price ($1000s)
Syracuse, NY	41.8	76
Springfield, IL	47.7	91
Lima, OH	40.0	65
Dayton, OH	44.3	88

(continued)

Market	Income ($1000s)	Price ($1000s)
Beaumont, TX	37.3	70
Lakeland, FL	35.9	73
Baton Rouge, LA	39.3	85
Nashua, NH	56.9	118
Racine, WI	46.7	81
Des Moines, IA	48.3	89
Minneapolis–St. Paul, MN	54.6	110
Wilmington, DE–MD	55.5	110

a. Use these data to develop an estimated regression equation that could be used to predict the median price for a market given the median income for the market.
b. Use the t test to determine whether the median sale price is related to the median income. What is your conclusion at the .05 level of significance?
c. Did the estimated regression equation provide a good fit? Explain.

38. Cushman & Wakefield, Inc., collects data showing the office building vacancy rates and rental rates for markets in the United States. The following data show the overall vacancy rates (%) and the average rental rates (per square foot) for the central business district for 18 selected markets (*The Wall Street Journal Almanac 1998*).

CD file

OffRates

Market	Vacancy Rate (%)	Average Rental Rate ($)
Atlanta	21.9	18.54
Boston	6.0	33.70
Hartford	22.8	19.67
Baltimore	18.1	21.01
Washington	12.7	35.09
Philadelphia	14.5	19.41
Miami	20.0	25.28
Tampa	19.2	17.02
Chicago	16.0	24.04
San Francisco	6.6	31.42
Phoenix	15.9	18.74
San Jose	9.2	26.76
West Palm Beach	19.7	27.72
Detroit	20.0	18.20
Brooklyn	8.3	25.00
Downtown, NY	17.1	29.78
Midtown, NY	10.8	37.03
Midtown South, NY	11.1	28.64

a. Develop a scatter diagram for these data; plot the vacancy rate on the horizontal axis.
b. Does there appear to be any relationship between these two variables?
c. Develop the estimated regression equation that could be used to predict the average rental rate given the overall vacancy rate.
d. Test the significance of the relationship at the .05 level of significance.
e. Did the estimated regression equation provide a good fit? Explain.

12.7   USING THE ESTIMATED REGRESSION EQUATION FOR ESTIMATION AND PREDICTION

The simple linear regression model is an assumption about the relationship between x and y. Using the least squares method, we obtained the estimated simple linear regression equation. If the results show a statistically significant relationship between x and y, and the fit provided by the estimated regression equation appears to be good, the estimated regression equation should be useful for estimation and prediction.

Point Estimation

In the Armand's Pizza Parlors example, the estimated regression equation $\hat{y} = 60 + 5x$ provides an estimate of the relationship between the size of the student population x and quarterly sales y. We can use the estimated regression equation to develop a point estimate of the mean value of y for a particular value of x or to predict an individual value of y corresponding to a given value of x. For instance, suppose Armand's managers want a point estimate of the mean quarterly sales for all restaurants located near college campuses with 10,000 students. Using the estimated regression equation $\hat{y} = 60 + 5x$, we see that for $x = 10$ (or 10,000 students), $\hat{y} = 60 + 5(10) = 110$. Thus, a point estimate of the mean quarterly sales for all restaurants located near campuses with 10,000 students is $110,000.

Now suppose Armand's managers want to predict sales for an individual restaurant located near Talbot College, a school with 10,000 students. In this case we are not interested in the mean value for all restaurants located near campuses with 10,000 students; we are just interested in predicting quarterly sales for one individual restaurant. As it turns out, the point estimate is the same as the point estimate for the mean value of y. Hence, we would predict quarterly sales of $\hat{y} = 60 + 5(10) = 110$ or $110,000 for this one restaurant.

Interval Estimation

Confidence intervals and prediction intervals indicate the precision of the regression results. Narrower intervals indicate a higher degree of precision.

Point estimates do not provide any information about the precision associated with the estimates. For that we must develop interval estimates much like those in Chapters 8, 10, and 11. The first type of interval estimate, a **confidence interval estimate,** is an interval estimate of the *mean value of y* for a given value of x. The second type of interval estimate, a **prediction interval estimate,** is used whenever we want an interval estimate of an *individual value of y* corresponding to a given value of x. The point estimate of the mean value of y is the same as the point estimate of an individual value of y. But, the interval estimates we obtain for the two cases are different.

Confidence Interval Estimate of the Mean Value of y

The estimated regression equation provides a point estimate of the mean value of y for a given value of x. In describing the confidence interval estimation procedure, we will use the following notation.

$$x_p = \text{the particular or given value of the independent variable } x$$
$$E(y_p) = \text{the mean or expected value of the dependent variable } y$$
$$\text{when } x = x_p$$
$$\hat{y}_p = b_0 + b_1 x_p = \text{the point estimate of } E(y_p) \text{ when } x = x_p$$

Suppose we want to estimate the mean quarterly sales for all Armand's restaurants located near a campus with 10,000 students. In this case, $x_p = 10$ and $E(y_p)$ denotes the unknown mean value of sales for all restaurants where $x_p = 10$. The point estimate of $E(y_p)$ is $\hat{y}_p = 60 + 5(10) = 110$.

In general, we cannot expect $\hat{y}_p$ to equal $E(y_p)$ exactly. If we want to make an inference about how close $\hat{y}_p$ is to the true mean value $E(y_p)$, we must estimate the variance of $\hat{y}_p$. The formula for estimating the variance of $\hat{y}_p$ given x_p, denoted by $s_{\hat{y}_p}^2$, is

$$s_{\hat{y}_p}^2 = s^2\left[\frac{1}{n} + \frac{(x_p - \bar{x})^2}{\Sigma(x_i - \bar{x})^2}\right] \tag{12.22}$$

The estimate of the standard deviation of $\hat{y}_p$ is given by the square root of equation (12.22).

$$s_{\hat{y}_p} = s\sqrt{\frac{1}{n} + \frac{(x_p - \bar{x})^2}{\Sigma(x_i - \bar{x})^2}} \tag{12.23}$$

The computational results for Armand's Pizza Parlors in Section 12.5 provided $s = 13.829$. With $x_p = 10$, $\bar{x} = 14$, and $\Sigma(x_i - \bar{x})^2 = 568$, we can use equation (12.23) to obtain

$$s_{\hat{y}_p} = 13.829\sqrt{\frac{1}{10} + \frac{(10 - 14)^2}{568}}$$
$$= 13.829\sqrt{.1282} = 4.95$$

The general expression for a confidence interval estimate of the mean value of y follows.

Confidence Interval Estimate of the Mean Value of y

The margin of error associated with this internal estimate is $t_{\alpha/2}s_{\hat{y}_p}$.

$$\hat{y}_p \pm t_{\alpha/2}s_{\hat{y}_p} \tag{12.24}$$

where the confidence coefficient is $1 - \alpha$ and $t_{\alpha/2}$ is based on a t distribution with $n - 2$ degrees of freedom.

Using expression (12.24) to develop a 95% confidence interval estimate of the mean quarterly sales for all Armand's restaurants located near campuses with 10,000 students, we need the value of t for $\alpha/2 = .025$ and $n - 2 = 10 - 2 = 8$ degrees of freedom. Using Table 2 of Appendix B, we have $t_{.025} = 2.306$. Thus, with $\hat{y}_p = 110$ and a margin of error of $t_{\alpha/2}s_{\hat{y}_p} = 2.306(4.95) = 11.415$, the 95% confidence interval estimate is

$$110 \pm 11.415$$

In dollars, the 95% confidence interval for the mean quarterly sales of all restaurants near campuses with 10,000 students is $\$110,000 \pm \$11,415$. Therefore, the confidence interval estimate for the mean quarterly sales when the student population is 10,000 is $\$98,585$ to $\$121,415$.

Note that the estimated standard deviation of $\hat{y}_p$ given by equation (12.23) is smallest when $x_p = \bar{x}$ and the quantity $x_p - \bar{x} = 0$. In this case, the estimated standard deviation of $\hat{y}_p$ becomes

$$s_{\hat{y}_p} = s\sqrt{\frac{1}{n} + \frac{(\bar{x} - \bar{x})^2}{\Sigma(x_i - \bar{x})^2}} = s\sqrt{\frac{1}{n}}$$

This result implies that we can make the best or most precise estimate of the mean value of y whenever $x_p = \bar{x}$. In fact, the further x_p is from $\bar{x}$, the larger $x_p - \bar{x}$ becomes. As a result, confidence intervals for the mean value of y will become wider as x_p deviates more from $\bar{x}$. This pattern is shown graphically in Figure 12.12.

Prediction Interval Estimate of an Individual Value of y

Suppose that instead of estimating the mean value of quarterly sales for all Armand's restaurants located near campuses with 10,000 students, we want to estimate the quarterly sales for an individual restaurant located near Talbot College, a school with 10,000 students. As noted previously, the point estimate of an individual value of y given $x = x_p$ is provided by the estimated regression equation $\hat{y}_p = b_0 + b_1 x_p$. For the restaurant at Talbot College, we have $x_p = 10$ and a corresponding estimated quarterly sales of $\hat{y}_p = 60 + 5(10) = 110$, or $110,000. Note that this value is the same as the point estimate of the mean quarterly sales for all restaurants located near campuses with 10,000 students.

To develop a prediction interval estimate, we must first estimate the variance associated with using $\hat{y}_p$ as an estimate of an individual value of y when $x = x_p$. This variance is made up of the sum of the following two components.

1. The variance of individual y values about the mean $E(y_p)$, an estimate of which is given by s^2.
2. The variance associated with using $\hat{y}_p$ to estimate $E(y_p)$, an estimate of which is given by $s_{\hat{y}_p}^2$.

FIGURE 12.12   CONFIDENCE INTERVALS FOR THE MEAN QUARTERLY SALES y AT GIVEN VALUES OF STUDENT POPULATION x

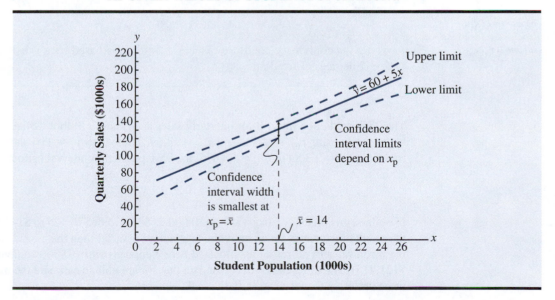

The formula for estimating the variance of an individual value of y, denoted by s_{ind}^2, is

$$
\begin{aligned}
s_{\text{ind}}^2 &= s^2 + s_{\hat{y}_p}^2 \\
&= s^2 + s^2\left[\frac{1}{n} + \frac{(x_p - \bar{x})^2}{\Sigma(x_i - \bar{x})^2}\right] \\
&= s^2\left[1 + \frac{1}{n} + \frac{(x_p - \bar{x})^2}{\Sigma(x_i - \bar{x})^2}\right]
\end{aligned}
\tag{12.25}
$$

Hence, an estimate of the standard deviation of an individual value of y is given by

$$
s_{\text{ind}} = s\sqrt{1 + \frac{1}{n} + \frac{(x_p - \bar{x})^2}{\Sigma(x_i - \bar{x})^2}}
\tag{12.26}
$$

For Armand's Pizza Parlors, the estimated standard deviation corresponding to the prediction of quarterly sales for one specific restaurant located near a campus with 10,000 students is computed as follows.

$$
\begin{aligned}
s_{\text{ind}} &= 13.829\sqrt{1 + \frac{1}{10} + \frac{(10 - 14)^2}{568}} \\
&= 13.829\sqrt{1.1282} \\
&= 14.69
\end{aligned}
$$

The general expression for a prediction interval estimate of an individual value of y follows.

Prediction Interval Estimate of an Individual Value of y

$$
\hat{y}_p \pm t_{\alpha/2}s_{\text{ind}}
\tag{12.27}
$$

where the confidence coefficient is $1 - \alpha$ and $t_{\alpha/2}$ is based on a t distribution with $n - 2$ degrees of freedom.

The margin of error associated with this interval estimate is $t_{\alpha/2}s_{\text{ind}}$.

The 95% prediction interval for quarterly sales at Armand's Talbot College restaurant can be found by using $t_{.025} = 2.306$ and $s_{\text{ind}} = 14.69$. Thus, with $\hat{y}_p = 110$ and a margin of error of $t_{\alpha/2}s_{\text{ind}} = 2.306(14.69) = 33.875$, the 95% prediction interval estimate is

$$
110 \pm 33.875
$$

In dollars, this prediction interval is $110,000 \pm 33,875 or $76,125 to $143,875. Note that the prediction interval for an individual restaurant is wider than the confidence interval for the mean sales of all restaurants located near campuses with 10,000 students ($98,585 to $121,415). The difference reflects the fact that we are able to estimate the mean value of y more precisely than we can an individual value of y.

FIGURE 12.13   CONFIDENCE AND PREDICTION INTERVALS FOR QUARTERLY SALES y
AT GIVEN VALUES OF STUDENT POPULATION x

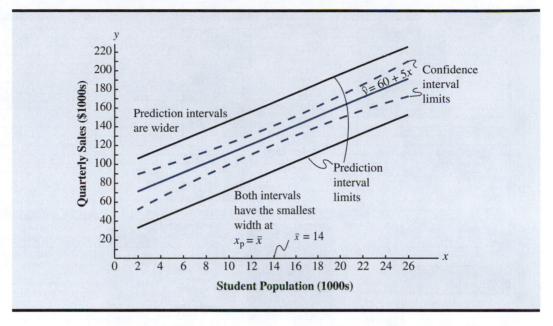

Both confidence interval estimates and prediction interval estimates are most precise when the value of the independent variable is $x_p = \bar{x}$. The general shapes of confidence intervals and the wider prediction intervals are shown together in Figure 12.13.

Using Excel to Develop Confidence and Prediction Interval Estimates

The PredInt.xls macro included on the data disk can be used to develop confidence and prediction intervals.

Excel's Regression tool does not have an option for computing confidence and prediction intervals. But, for simple linear regression, formulas can be designed to compute these intervals using equations (12.24) and (12.27) along with the output provided by the Regression tool. The general expression for a confidence or prediction interval is: point estimate ± margin of error. Thus, we must develop formulas for computing a point estimate and the margin of error.

We begin by showing how to develop a 95% confidence interval estimate of the mean quarterly sales for all Armand's restaurants located near a campus with 10,000 students. In Section 12.6, we showed how Excel's Regression tool could be applied to the Armand's problem. The output provided by the Regression tool is shown again in cells A13:I30 of Figure 12.14. Now refer to cells E1:F13 of that figure as we describe the tasks involved in developing a confidence interval. The formula worksheet is in the background; the value worksheet is in the foreground.

Enter Data: The data (cells B2:C11) and regression output (cells A13:I30) initially developed in Figure 12.10 are used as a starting point here.

Enter Functions and Formulas: Because we want to develop a 95% confidence interval estimate of the mean quarterly sales for restaurants near campuses with 10,000 students, $x_p = 10$ and we enter a value of 10 into cell F2. Excel's AVERAGE function is used to compute $\bar{x}$ in cell F3, the formula =F2−F3 is entered into cell F4 to compute the value of

FIGURE 12.14 USING EXCEL TO COMPUTE CONFIDENCE AND PREDICTION INTERVALS

	A	B	C	D	E	F	G	H	I
1	Restaurant	Population	Sales		Confidence Interval				
2	1	2	58		Given value of x	10			
3	2	6	105		xbar	=AVERAGE(B2:B11)			
4	3	8	88		x-xbar	=F2-F3			
5	4	8	118		(x-xbar)sq	=F4^2			
6	5	12	117		Sum of (x-xbar)sq	=DEVSQ(B2:B11)			
7	6	16	137		Var of yhat	=D25*(1/B20+F5/F6)			
8	7	20	157		Stdev of yhat	=SQRT(F7)			
9	8	20	169		t value	=TINV(0.05,8)			
10	9	22	149		Margin of Error	=F9*F8			
11	10	26	202		Point Estimate	=B29+B30*F2			
12					Lower Limit	=F11-F10			
13	SUMMARY OUTPUT				Upper Limit	=F11+F10			
14									
15	*Regression Statistics*				Prediction Interval				
16	Multiple R	0.95012295520			Var of yind	=D25+F7			
17	R Square	0.90273363000			Stdev of yind	=SQRT(F16)			
18	Adjusted R Square	0.89057533375			Margin of Error	=F9*F17			
19	Standard Error	13.8293166859			Lower Limit	=F11-F18			
20	Observations	10			Upper Limit	=F11+F18			
21									
22	ANOVA								
23		*df*							
24	Regression	1							
25	Residual	8							
26	Total	9							
27									
28		*Coefficients*							
29	Intercept	60							
30	Population	5							
31									

	A	B	C	D	E	F	G	H	I	J
1	Restaurant	Population	Sales		Confidence Interval					
2	1	2	58		Given value of x	10				
3	2	6	105		xbar	14				
4	3	8	88		x-xbar	-4				
5	4	8	118		(x-xbar)sq	16				
6	5	12	117		Sum of (x-xbar)sq	568				
7	6	16	137		Var of yhat	24.5123				
8	7	20	157		Stdev of yhat	4.9510				
9	8	20	169		t value	2.3060				
10	9	22	149		Margin of Error	11.4170				
11	10	26	202		Point Estimate	110				
12					Lower Limit	98.5830				
13	SUMMARY OUTPUT				Upper Limit	121.4170				
14										
15	*Regression Statistics*				Prediction Interval					
16	Multiple R	0.9501			Var of yind	215.7623				
17	R Square	0.9027			Stdev of yind	14.6889				
18	Adjusted R Square	0.8906			Margin of Error	33.8726				
19	Standard Error	13.8293			Lower Limit	76.1274				
20	Observations	10			Upper Limit	143.8726				
21										
22	ANOVA									
23		*df*	*SS*	*MS*	*F*	*Significance F*				
24	Regression	1	14200	14200	74.2484	2.55E-05				
25	Residual	8	1530	191.25						
26	Total	9	15730							
27										
28		*Coefficients*	*Standard Error*	*t Stat*	*P-value*	*Lower 9.5%*	*Upper 9.5%*	*Lower 99.0%*	*Upper 99.0%*	
29	Intercept	60	9.2260	6.5033	0.0002	38.7247	81.2753	29.0431	90.9569	
30	Population	5	0.5803	8.6167	2.55E-05	3.6619	6.3381	3.0530	6.9470	
31										

$x_p - \bar{x}$, and the formula =F4^2 is entered into cell F5 to compute the value of $(x_p - \bar{x})^2$. Excel's DEVSQ function can be used to compute $\Sigma(x_i - \bar{x})^2$ by entering the following formula into cell F6:

$$=DEVSQ(B2:B11)$$

To identify this sum of squares we enter the label "Sum of (x − xbar)sq" into cell E6.

We can now compute $s_{\hat{y}_p}^2$ using equation (12.22) by entering the formula =D25*(1/B20+F5/F6) into cell F7. We then enter the formula =SQRT(F7) into cell F8 to compute $s_{\hat{y}_p}$, the estimate of the standard deviation of $\hat{y}_p$. To compute the t value required by equation (12.24), we entered the formula =TINV(0.05,8) into cell F9. Finally, the margin of error $t_{\alpha/2}s_{\hat{y}_p}$ is computed by entering the formula =F9*F8 into cell F10. To compute $\hat{y}_p$, the point estimate of $E(y_p)$, we enter the formula =B29+B30*F2 into cell F11. The lower and upper limits of the 95% confidence interval are then computed by entering the formulas =F11−F10 and =F11+F10 into cells F12 and F13 respectively.

The value worksheet shows that the 95% confidence interval estimate is 98.583 to 121.417. In dollars, the 95% confidence interval for the mean quarterly sales of restaurants located near campuses with 10,000 students is $98,583 to $121,417. To develop confidence intervals for other values of x_p we simply use this worksheet as a template and enter another value for student population in cell F2. The new confidence interval will appear in cells F12 and F13. If a confidence interval for another value of α is desired, we can just insert the new value of α for the first argument of the TINV function in cell F9.

The confidence interval formulas developed here cannot be applied directly as a template for other regression problems because the number of observations will likely be different and the location of the regression output will not be in the same worksheet cells. The same cells (E1:F13) can be used to develop the confidence interval but the cell references used in cells F3, F6, F7, and F11 will need to be modified to reflect the location of the data and the regression output. The level of significance and the degrees of freedom used for TINV in cell F9 may also need to be changed.

The design of formulas to compute a prediction interval requires some of the same information used to develop a confidence interval. However, equation (12.27) shows that s_{ind}, instead of $s_{\hat{y}_p}$, is used in computing the margin of error. Refer to cells E15:F20 of the worksheet in Figure 12.14 as we describe the tasks involved in computing a 95% prediction interval for Armand's Pizza.

Enter Functions and Formulas: To compute $s_{ind}^2 = s^2 + s_{\hat{y}_p}^2$ we enter the formula =D25+F7 into cell F16. Then, in cell F17 we enter the formula =SQRT(F16) to compute s_{ind}. The labels "Var of yind" and "Stdev of yind" in cells E16 and E17 identify these values. The formula =F9*F17 in cell F18 computes the margin of error. The formulas =F11−F18 and =F11+F18 were entered into cells F19 and F20 respectively to compute the lower and upper limits.

The 95% prediction interval is 76.127 to 143.873. In dollars, the 95% prediction interval is $76,127 to $143,873. To develop prediction intervals for other values of x_p we simply enter another value for student population in cell F2 and the new prediction interval will appear in cells F19 and F20. If a prediction interval for another value of α is desired, we can just insert the new value of α for the first argument of the TINV function in cell F9.

EXERCISES

Methods

39.   The data from Exercise 1 follow.

x_i	1	2	3	4	5
y_i	3	7	5	11	14

a.   Use equation (12.23) to estimate the standard deviation of $\hat{y}_p$ when $x = 4$.

b.   Use equation (12.24) to develop a 95% confidence interval estimate of the expected value of y when $x = 4$.

c.   Use equation (12.26) to estimate the standard deviation of an individual value of y when $x = 4$.

d.   Use equation (12.27) to develop a 95% prediction interval for y when $x = 4$.

40. The data from Exercise 2 follow.

x_i	2	3	5	1	8
y_i	25	25	20	30	16

a. Estimate the standard deviation of $\hat{y}_p$ when $x = 3$.
b. Develop a 95% confidence interval estimate of the expected value of y when $x = 3$.
c. Estimate the standard deviation of an individual value of y when $x = 3$.
d. Develop a 95% prediction interval for y when $x = 3$.

41. The data from Exercise 3 follow.

x_i	2	4	5	7	8
y_i	2	3	2	6	4

Develop the 95% confidence and prediction intervals when $x = 3$. Explain why these two intervals are different.

Applications

42. In Exercise 18, the data on grade point average x and monthly salary y provided the estimated regression equation $\hat{y} = 1790.5 + 581.1x$.
a. Develop a 95% confidence interval estimate of the mean starting salary for all students with a 3.0 GPA.
b. Develop a 95% prediction interval estimate of the starting salary for Joe Heller, a student with a GPA of 3.0.

PCs

43. In Exercise 10, data on the performance score (x) and the overall rating (y) for notebook PCs provided the estimated regression equation $\hat{y} = 51.82 + .1452x$ (*PC World*, February 2000).
a. Develop a point estimate of the overall rating for a PC with a performance score of 200.
b. Develop a 95% confidence interval estimate of the mean overall score for all PCs with a performance score of 200.
c. Suppose that a new PC developed by Dell has a performance score of 200. Develop a 95% prediction interval estimate of the overall score for this new PC.
d. Discuss the differences in your answers to parts (b) and (c).

44. In Exercise 13, data were given on the adjusted gross income x and the amount of itemized deductions taken by taxpayers. Data were reported in thousands of dollars. With the estimated regression equation $\hat{y} = 4.68 + .16x$, the point estimate of a reasonable level of total itemized deductions for a taxpayer with an adjusted gross income of $52,500 is $13,080.
a. Develop a 95% confidence interval estimate of the mean amount of total itemized deductions for all taxpayers with an adjusted gross income of $52,500.
b. Develop a 95% prediction interval estimate for the amount of total itemized deductions for a particular taxpayer with an adjusted gross income of $52,500.
c. If the particular taxpayer referred to in part (b) has claimed total itemized deductions of $20,400, would the IRS agent's request for an audit appear to be justified?
d. Using your answer to part (b), give the IRS agent a guideline as to the amount of total itemized deductions a taxpayer with an adjusted gross income of $52,500 should take before an audit is recommended.

45. Refer to Exercise 21, where data on the production volume x and total cost y for a particular manufacturing operation were used to develop the estimated regression equation $\hat{y} = 1246.67 + 7.6x$.
a. The company's production schedule shows that 500 units must be produced next month. What is the point estimate of the total cost for the next month?

b. Develop a 99% prediction interval estimate of the total cost for next month.

c. If an accounting cost report at the end of next month shows that the actual production cost during the month was $6000, should managers be concerned about incurring such a high total cost for the month? Discuss.

46. Nielsen Media Research collects data showing the number of households tuned in to shows that carry a particular advertisement. This information is useful to advertisers because it tells them how many consumers they are reaching. The following data show the number of times the ad was aired and the number of household exposures in millions for the week of October 27–November 2, 1997 (*USA Today*, November 17, 1997).

CD file

Nielsen

Advertised Brand	Times Ad Aired	Household Exposures
McDonald's	49	359.6
Burger King	42	296.1
HBO	30	271.6
Red Corner movie	26	251.1
Pizza Hut	31	229.3
Sears	20	186.9
Isuzu Rodeo	21	186.3
MCI	24	172.7
Sprint	15	166.0
JCPenney	19	162.1

a. Use these data to develop an estimated regression equation that could be used to predict the number of household exposures given the number of times the ad is aired.

b. Did the estimated regression equation provide a good fit? Explain.

c. Develop a 95% confidence interval estimate of the mean number of household exposures for all ads that are aired 35 times.

d. Suppose that Wendy's was considering airing a particular ad 35 times. Develop a 95% prediction interval estimate for the number of household exposures for this particular ad.

12.8   RESIDUAL ANALYSIS: VALIDATING MODEL ASSUMPTIONS

Residual analysis is the primary tool for determining whether the assumed regression model is appropriate.

As we previously noted, the *residual* for observation i is the difference between the observed value of the dependent variable (y_i) and the estimated value of the dependent variable ($\hat{y}_i$).

Residual for Observation i

$$y_i - \hat{y}_i \qquad (12.28)$$

where

y_i is the observed value of the dependent variable

$\hat{y}_i$ is the estimated value of the dependent variable

In other words, the ith residual is the error resulting from using the estimated regression equation to predict the value of y_i. The residuals for the Armand's Pizza Parlors example are computed in Table 12.7. The observed values of the dependent variable are in the second

TABLE 12.7   RESIDUALS FOR ARMAND'S PIZZA PARLORS

Student Population x_i	Sales y_i	Estimated Sales $\hat{y}_i = 60 + 5x_i$	Residuals $y_i - \hat{y}_i$
2	58	70	−12
6	105	90	15
8	88	100	−12
8	118	100	18
12	117	120	−3
16	137	140	−3
20	157	160	−3
20	169	160	9
22	149	170	−21
26	202	190	12

column and the estimated values of the dependent variable, obtained using the estimated regression equation $\hat{y}_i = 60 + 5x_i$, are in the third column. The corresponding residuals are in the fourth column. An analysis of these residuals will help determine whether the assumptions made about the regression model are appropriate.

Let us now review the regression assumptions for the Armand's Pizza Parlors example. A simple linear regression model was assumed.

$$y = \beta_0 + \beta_1 x + \epsilon$$

This model indicates that we assumed sales (y) to be a linear function of the size of the student population (x) plus an error term ϵ. In Section 12.4 we made the following assumptions about the error term ϵ.

1. $E(\epsilon) = 0$.
2. The variance of ϵ, denoted by σ^2, is the same for all values of x.
3. The values of ϵ are independent.
4. The error term ϵ has a normal probability distribution.

These assumptions provide the theoretical basis for the t test and the F test used to determine whether the relationship between x and y is significant, and for the confidence and prediction interval estimates presented in Section 12.7. If the assumptions about the error term ϵ appear questionable, the hypothesis tests about the significance of the regression relationship and the interval estimation results may not be valid.

The residuals provide the best information about ϵ; hence residual analysis is an important step in determining whether the assumptions for ϵ are appropriate. Much of residual analysis is based on an examination of graphical plots. In this section, we discuss a plot of the residuals against values of the independent variable x, and a plot of the residuals against the predicted values of the dependent variable $\hat{y}$.

Residual Plot Against x

A residual plot against the independent variable x is a graph in which the values of the independent variable are represented by the horizontal axis and the corresponding residual values are represented by the vertical axis. A point is plotted for each residual. The first coordinate for each point is given by the value of x_i and the second coordinate is given by the corresponding value of the residual $y_i - \hat{y}_i$. To develop a residual plot against x with the Armand's Pizza Parlors data from Table 12.7, the coordinates of the first point are $(2, -12)$, corresponding to $x_1 = 2$ and $y_1 - \hat{y}_1 = -12$; the coordinates of the second point are $(6, 15)$, corresponding to $x_2 = 6$ and $y_2 - \hat{y}_2 = 15$, and so on. Figure 12.15 is the resulting residual plot.

Before interpreting the results for this residual plot, let us consider some general patterns that might be observed in any residual plot. Three examples are shown in Figure 12.16. If the assumption that the variance of ϵ is the same for all values of x and the assumed regression model is an adequate representation of the relationship between the variables, the residual plot should give an overall impression of a horizontal band of points such as the one in panel A of Figure 12.16. However, if the variance of ϵ is not the same for all values of x—for example, if variability about the regression line is greater for larger values of x—a pattern such as the one in panel B of Figure 12.16 could be observed. In this case, the assumption of a constant variance of ϵ is violated. Another possible residual plot is shown in panel C. In this case, we would conclude that the assumed regression model is not an adequate representation of the relationship between the variables. A curvilinear regression model or multiple regression model should be considered.

Now let us return to the residual plot for Armand's Pizza Parlors shown in Figure 12.15. The residuals appear to approximate the horizontal pattern in panel A of Figure 12.16. Hence, we conclude that the residual plot does not provide evidence that the assumptions made for Armand's regression model should be challenged. At this point, we are confident in the conclusion that Armand's simple linear regression model is valid.

FIGURE 12.15   PLOT OF THE RESIDUALS AGAINST THE INDEPENDENT VARIABLE x FOR ARMAND'S PIZZA PARLORS

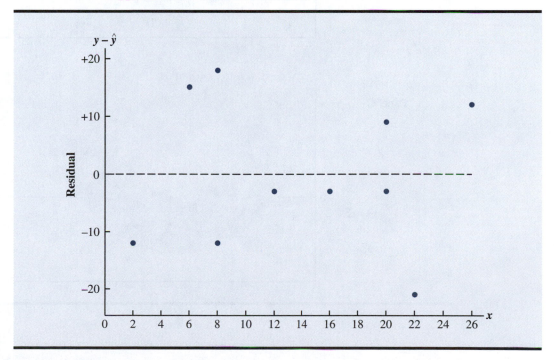

FIGURE 12.16   GENERAL PATTERNS FOR RESIDUAL PLOTS

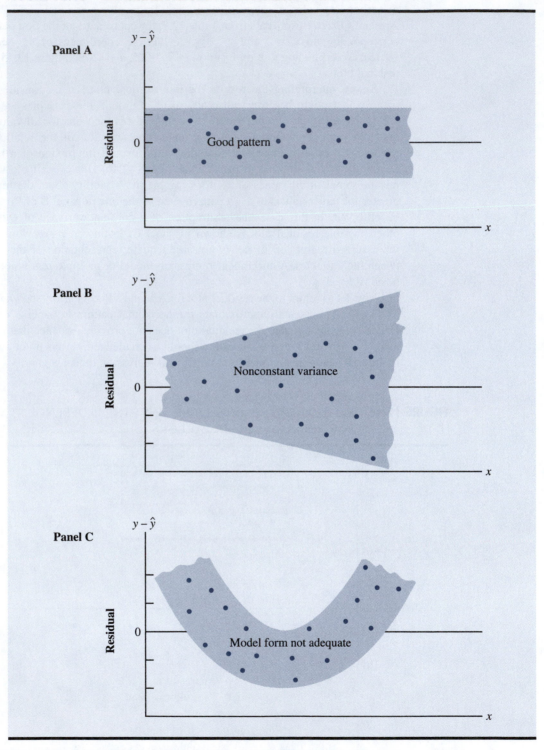

Experience and good judgment are always factors in the effective interpretation of residual plots. Seldom does a residual plot conform precisely to one of the patterns shown in Figure 12.16. Yet analysts who frequently conduct regression studies and frequently review residual plots become adept at understanding the differences between patterns that are reasonable and patterns that indicate the assumptions of the model should be questioned. A residual plot as shown here is one of the techniques for assessing the validity of the assumptions for a regression model.

Residual Plot Against $\hat{y}$

Another residual plot represents the predicted values of the dependent variable $\hat{y}$ on the horizontal axis and the corresponding residual values on the vertical axis. A point is plotted for each residual. The first coordinate for each point is given by $\hat{y}_i$ and the second coordinate is given by the corresponding value of the ith residual $y_i - \hat{y}_i$. With the Armand's data from Table 12.7, the coordinates of the first point are $(70, -12)$, corresponding to $\hat{y}_1 = 70$ and $y_1 - \hat{y}_1 = -12$; the coordinates of the second point are $(90, 15)$, and so on. Figure 12.17 is the residual plot. Note that the pattern of this residual plot is the same as the pattern of the residual plot against the independent variable x. It is not a pattern that would lead us to question the model assumptions. For simple linear regression, both the residual plot against x and the residual plot against $\hat{y}$ provide the same pattern. For multiple regression analysis, the residual plot against $\hat{y}$ is more widely used because of the presence of more than one independent variable.

FIGURE 12.17 PLOT OF THE RESIDUALS AGAINST THE PREDICTED VALUES $\hat{y}$ FOR ARMAND'S PIZZA PARLORS

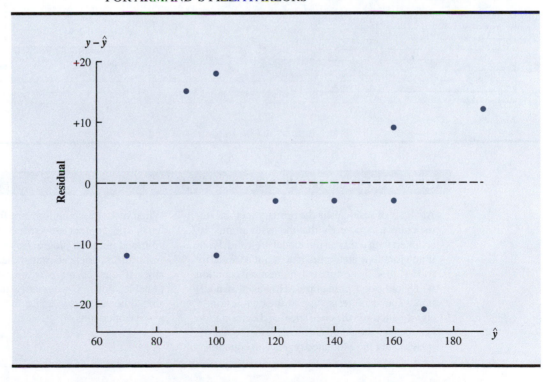

Using Excel's Regression Tool to Construct a Residual Plot

In Section 12.6 we showed how Excel's Regression tool could be used for regression analysis. The Regression tool also provides the capability to obtain a residual plot. To obtain a residual plot, the steps that we described in Section 12.6 in order to obtain the regression output are performed with one change. When the Regression dialog box appears (see Figure 12.11) we must also select the Residual Plots option. The regression output will appear as described previously, and the worksheet will also contain a chart showing a plot of the residuals against the independent variable Population. In addition, a list of predicted values of y and the corresponding residual values is provided below the regression output. Figure 12.18 shows the residual output for the Armand's Pizza problem. We see that the shape of this plot is the same as shown previously in Figure 12.15.

FIGURE 12.18   EXCEL RESIDUAL OUTPUT FOR THE ARMAND'S PIZZA PARLORS PROBLEM

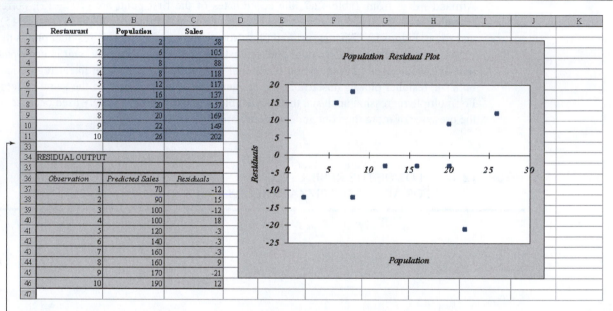

Note: Rows 12–32 are hidden.

NOTES AND COMMENTS

1. Analysis of residuals is the primary method statisticians use to verify that the assumptions associated with a regression model are valid. Even if no violations are found, it does not necessarily follow that the estimated regression equation will yield good predictions. However, if additional statistical tests support the conclusion of significance and the coefficient of determination is large, we should be able to develop good estimates using the estimated regression equation.

2. When model assumptions are found to be violated, the appropriate corrective action must be based on good judgment; recommendations from an experienced statistician can be valuable. If one or more assumptions are questionable, but not necessarily invalid, the user should be cautious in using and interpreting the regression results.

EXERCISES

Methods

47. Given are data for two variables, x and y.

x_i	6	11	15	18	20
y_i	6	8	12	20	30

    a. Develop an estimated regression equation for these data.

    b. Compute the residuals.

    c. Construct a residual plot against the independent variable x. Do the assumptions about the error terms seem to be satisfied?

48. The following data were used in a regression study.

Observation	x_i	y_i	Observation	x_i	y_i
1	2	4	6	7	6
2	3	5	7	7	9
3	4	4	8	8	5
4	5	6	9	9	11
5	7	4			

    a. Develop an estimated regression equation for these data.

    b. Construct a residual plot against x. Do the assumptions about the error term seem to be satisfied?

Applications

49. Data on advertising expenditures ($1000s) and revenue ($1000s) for the Four Seasons Restaurant follow.

Advertising Expenditures	Revenue
1	19
2	32
4	44
6	40
10	52
14	53
20	54

    a. Let x equal advertising expenditures ($1000s) and y equal revenue ($1000s). Use the method of least squares to develop a straight-line approximation of the relationship between the two variables.

    b. Test whether revenue and advertising expenditures are related at a .05 level of significance.

    c. Construct a residual plot against $\hat{y}$.

    d. What conclusions can you draw from residual analysis? Should this model be used, or should we look for a better one?

50. Refer to Exercise 9, where an estimated regression equation relating years of experience and annual sales was developed.

   a. Compute the residuals and construct a residual plot for this problem.

   b. Do the assumptions about the error terms seem reasonable in light of the residual plot?

51. American depository receipts (ADRs) are certificates traded on the NYSE representing shares of a foreign company held on deposit in a bank in its home country. The following table shows the price/earnings (P/E) ratio and the percentage return on equity (ROE) for 10 Indian companies that are likely new ADRs (*Bloomberg Personal Finance*, April 2000).

ADRs

Company	ROE	P/E
Bharti Televentures	6.43	36.88
Gujarat Ambuja Cements	13.49	27.03
Hindalco Industries	14.04	10.83
ICICI	20.67	5.15
Mahanagar Telephone Nigam	22.74	13.35
NIIT	46.23	95.59
Pentamedia Graphics	28.90	54.85
Satyam Computer Services	54.01	189.21
Silverline Technologies	28.02	75.86
Videsh Sanchar Nigam	27.04	13.17

   a. Use Excel to develop an estimated regression equation relating y = P/E and x = ROE.

   b. Construct a residual plot against the independent variable.

   c. Do the assumptions about the error terms and model form seem reasonable in light of the residual plot?

SUMMARY

In this chapter we first showed how regression analysis can be used to determine how a dependent variable y is related to an independent variable x. In simple linear regression, the regression model is $y = \beta_0 + \beta_1 x + \epsilon$. The simple linear regression equation $E(y) = \beta_0 + \beta_1 x$ describes how the mean or expected value of y is related to x. We used sample data and the least squares method to develop the estimated regression equation $\hat{y} = b_0 + b_1 x$. In effect, b_0 and b_1 are the sample statistics used to estimate the unknown model parameters β_0 and β_1.

The coefficient of determination was presented as a measure of the goodness of fit for the estimated regression equation; it can be interpreted as the proportion of the variation in the dependent variable y that can be explained by the estimated regression equation. We reviewed correlation as a descriptive measure of the strength of a linear relationship between two variables.

The assumptions about the regression model and its associated error term ϵ were discussed, and t and F tests, based on those assumptions, were presented as a means for determining whether the relationship between two variables is statistically significant. We showed how to use the estimated regression equation to develop confidence interval estimates of the mean value of y and wider prediction interval estimates of individual values of y.

We used Excel extensively in simple linear regression. We showed how the Chart Wizard could be used to develop a scatter diagram and to fit a trend line to data, and in Section 12.6, we introduced the use of Excel's Regression tool for performing a comprehensive analysis of a regression problem. In Section 12.8 we showed how the Regression tool could also be used to develop a residual plot and how we could use the residuals to validate the regression model assumptions.

GLOSSARY

Dependent variable   The variable that is being predicted. It is denoted by y.

Independent variable   The variable that is being used to predict the value of the dependent variable. It is denoted by x.

Simple linear regression   Regression analysis involving one independent variable and one dependent variable in which the relationship between the variables is approximated by a straight line.

Simple linear regression model   The equation that describes how y is related to x and an error term ϵ: $y = \beta_0 + \beta_1 x + \epsilon$.

Simple linear regression equation   The equation that describes how the mean or expected value of the dependent variable is related to the independent variable: $E(y) = \beta_0 + \beta_1 x$.

Estimated simple linear regression equation   The estimate of the regression equation developed from sample data by using the least squares method: $\hat{y} = b_0 + b_1 x$.

Least squares method   The procedure used to develop the estimated regression equation. The objective is to minimize $\Sigma(y_i - \hat{y}_i)^2$.

Scatter diagram   A graph of bivariate data in which the independent variable is on the horizontal axis and the dependent variable is on the vertical axis.

Coefficient of determination   A measure of the goodness of fit of the estimated regression equation. It can be interpreted as the proportion of the variability in the dependent variable y that is explained by the estimated regression equation.

ith residual   The difference between the observed value of the dependent variable, y_i, and the estimated value of the dependent variable, $\hat{y}_i$.

Correlation coefficient   A measure of the strength of the linear association between two variables.

Mean square error   The estimate of σ^2, the variance of the error term ϵ. It is denoted by MSE or s^2. It is SSE divided by its degrees of freedom.

ANOVA table   The analysis of variance table used to summarize the computations associated with the F test for significance.

Confidence interval estimate   The interval estimate of the mean value of y for a given value of x.

Prediction interval estimate   The interval estimate of an individual value of y for a given value of x.

Residual analysis   The primary tool for determining whether the assumed regression model is appropriate.

KEY FORMULAS

Simple Linear Regression Model

$$y = \beta_0 + \beta_1 x + \epsilon \tag{12.1}$$

Simple Linear Regression Equation

$$E(y) = \beta_0 + \beta_1 x \tag{12.2}$$

Estimated Simple Linear Regression Equation

$$\hat{y} = b_0 + b_1 x \tag{12.3}$$

Least Squares Criterion

$$\min \Sigma(y_i - \hat{y}_i)^2 \tag{12.5}$$

Slope and *y*-Intercept for the Estimated Regression Equation

$$b_1 = \frac{\Sigma(x_i - \bar{x})(y_i - \bar{y})}{\Sigma(x_i - \bar{x})^2} \tag{12.6}$$

$$b_0 = \bar{y} - b_1 \bar{x} \tag{12.7}$$

Sum of Squares Due to Error

$$SSE = \Sigma(y_i - \hat{y}_i)^2 \tag{12.8}$$

Total Sum of Squares

$$SST = \Sigma(y_i - \bar{y})^2 \tag{12.9}$$

Sum of Squares Due to Regression

$$SSR = \Sigma(\hat{y}_i - \bar{y})^2 \tag{12.10}$$

Relationship Among SST, SSR, and SSE

$$SST = SSR + SSE \tag{12.11}$$

Coefficient of Determination

$$r^2 = \frac{SSR}{SST} \tag{12.12}$$

Sample Correlation Coefficient

$$r_{xy} = (\text{sign of } b_1)\sqrt{\text{Coefficient of Determination}}$$
$$= (\text{sign of } b_1)\sqrt{r^2} \tag{12.13}$$

Estimate of σ^2

$$s^2 = MSE = \frac{SSE}{n - 2} \tag{12.15}$$

Estimate of σ

$$s = \sqrt{MSE} = \sqrt{\frac{SSE}{n - 2}} \tag{12.16}$$

Standard Deviation of b_1

$$\sigma_{b_1} = \frac{\sigma}{\sqrt{\Sigma(x_i - \bar{x})^2}} \tag{12.17}$$

Estimated Standard Deviation of b_1

$$s_{b_1} = \frac{s}{\sqrt{\Sigma(x_i - \bar{x})^2}} \tag{12.18}$$

t Test Statistic

$$t = \frac{b_1}{s_{b_1}} \tag{12.19}$$

Mean Square Due to Regression

$$MSR = \frac{SSR}{\text{Number of Independent Variables}} \tag{12.20}$$

F Test Statistic

$$F = \frac{MSR}{MSE} \tag{12.21}$$

Estimated Standard Deviation of $\hat{y}_p$

$$s_{\hat{y}_p} = s\sqrt{\frac{1}{n} + \frac{(x_p - \bar{x})^2}{\Sigma(x_i - \bar{x})^2}} \tag{12.23}$$

Confidence Interval Estimate of the Mean Value of y

$$\hat{y}_p \pm t_{\alpha/2}s_{\hat{y}_p} \tag{12.24}$$

Estimated Standard Deviation of an Individual Value of y

$$s_{ind} = s\sqrt{1 + \frac{1}{n} + \frac{(x_p - \bar{x})^2}{\Sigma(x_i - \bar{x})^2}} \tag{12.26}$$

Prediction Interval Estimate of an Individual Value of y

$$\hat{y}_p \pm t_{\alpha/2}s_{ind} \tag{12.27}$$

Residual for Observation i

$$y_i - \hat{y}_i \tag{12.28}$$

SUPPLEMENTARY EXERCISES

52. Does a high value of r^2 imply that two variables are causally related? Explain.

53. In your own words, explain the difference between an interval estimate of the mean value of y for a given value of x and an interval estimate for an individual value of y for a given value of x.

54. What is the purpose of testing whether $\beta_1 = 0$? If we reject $\beta_1 = 0$, does it imply a good fit?

55. The data in the following table show the number of shares being sold (millions) and the expected price (average of projected low price and projected high price) for 10 selected initial public stock offerings (*USA Today*, November 17, 1997).

Company	Shares Being Sold	Expected Price ($)
American Physician	5.0	15
Apex Silver Mines	9.0	14
Dan River	6.7	15
Franchise Mortgage	8.75	17
Gene Logic	3.0	11
International Home Foods	13.6	19
PRT Group	4.6	13
Rayovac	6.7	14
RealNetworks	3.0	10
Software AG Systems	7.7	13

a. Develop an estimated regression equation with the number of shares being sold as the independent variable and the expected price as the dependent variable.
b. At the .05 level of significance, is there a significant relationship between the two variables?
c. Did the estimated regression equation provide a good fit? Explain.
d. Use the estimated regression equation to estimate the expected price for a firm considering an initial public offering of 6 million shares.

56. Corporate share repurchase programs are often touted as a benefit for shareholders. But Robert Gabele, director of insider research for First Call/Thomson Financial, has noted that many of these have been undertaken solely to acquire stock for a company's incentive options for top managers. Across all companies, existing stock options in 1998 represented 6.2 percent of all common shares outstanding. The following data show the number of shares covered by option grants and the number of shares outstanding for 13 companies (*Bloomberg Personal Finance*, January/February 2000).

Company	Shares Covered by Option Grants (millions)	Common Shares Outstanding (millions)
Adobe Systems	20.3	61.8
Apple Computer	52.7	160.9
Applied Materials	109.1	375.4
Autodesk	15.7	58.9
Best Buy	44.2	203.8
Fruit of the Loom	14.2	66.9
ITT Industries	18.0	87.9
Merrill Lynch	89.9	365.5
Novell	120.2	335.0
Parametric Technology	78.3	269.3
Reebok International	12.8	56.1
Silicon Graphics	52.6	188.8
Toys R Us	54.8	247.6

a. Develop the estimated regression equation that could be used to estimate the number of shares covered by option grants given the number of common shares outstanding.

b. Use the estimated regression equation to estimate the number of shares covered by option grants for a company that has 150 million shares of common stock outstanding.

c. Do you believe the estimated regression equation would provide a good prediction of the number of shares covered by option grants? Use r^2 to support your answer.

57. *Bloomberg Personal Finance* (July/August 2001) reported the market beta for Texas Instruments was 1.46. Market betas for individual stocks are determined by simple linear regression. For each stock, the dependent variable is its quarterly percentage return (capital appreciation plus dividends) minus the percentage return that could be obtained from a risk-free investment (the Treasury Bill rate is used as the risk-free rate). The independent variable is the quarterly percentage return (capital appreciation plus dividends) for the stock market (S&P 500) minus the percentage return from a risk-free investment. An estimated regression equation is developed with quarterly data; the market beta for the stock is the slope of the estimated regression equation (b_1). The value of the market beta is often interpreted as a measure of the risk associated with the stock. Market betas greater than 1 indicate that the stock is more volatile than the market average; market betas less than 1 indicate that the stock is less volatile than the market average. Suppose that the following figures are the differences between the percentage return and the risk-free return for 10 quarters for the S&P 500 and Horizon Technology.

S&P 500	Horizon
1.2	−0.7
−2.5	−2.0
−3.0	−5.5
2.0	4.7
5.0	1.8
1.2	4.1
3.0	2.6
−1.0	2.0
.5	−1.3
2.5	5.5

a. Develop an estimated regression equation that can be used to determine the market beta for Horizon Technology. What is Horizon Technology's market beta?

b. Test for a significant relationship at the .05 level of significance.

c. Did the estimated regression equation provide a good fit? Explain.

d. Use the market betas of Texas Instruments and Horizon Technology to compare the risk associated with the two stocks.

58. The daily high and low temperatures for 20 cities follow (*USA Today*, May 9, 2000).

High-Low

City	Low	High
Athens	54	75
Bangkok	74	92
Cairo	57	84
Copenhagen	39	64
Dublin	46	64

(continued)

City	Low	High
Havana	68	86
Hong Kong	72	81
Johannesburg	50	61
London	48	73
Manila	75	93
Melbourne	50	66
Montreal	52	64
Paris	55	77
Rio de Janeiro	61	80
Rome	54	81
Seoul	50	64
Singapore	75	90
Sydney	55	68
Tokyo	59	79
Vancouver	43	57

a. Develop a scatter diagram with low temperature on the horizontal axis and high temperature on the vertical axis.

b. What does the scatter diagram developed in part (a) indicate about the relationship between the two variables?

c. Develop an estimated regression equation that could be used to predict the high temperature given the low temperature.

d. Test for a significant relationship at the .05 level of significance.

e. Did the estimated regression equation provide a good fit? Explain.

f. What is the value of the sample correlation coefficient?

59. Jensen Tire & Auto is in the process of deciding whether to purchase a maintenance contract for its new computer wheel alignment and balancing machine. Managers feel that maintenance expense should be related to usage and have collected the following information on weekly usage (hours) and annual maintenance expense ($100s).

Weekly Usage (hours)	Annual Maintenance Expense
13	17.0
10	22.0
20	30.0
28	37.0
32	47.0
17	30.5
24	32.5
31	39.0
40	51.5
38	40.0

a. Develop the estimated regression equation that relates annual maintenance expense to weekly usage.

b. Test the significance of the relationship in part (a) at a .05 level of significance.

c. Jensen expects to use the new machine 30 hours per week. Develop a 95% prediction interval for the company's annual maintenance expense.

d. If the maintenance contract costs $3000 per year, would you recommend purchasing it? Why or why not?

60. In a manufacturing process the assembly line speed (feet per minute) was thought to affect the number of defective parts found during the inspection process. To test this theory, managers devised a situation in which the same batch of parts was inspected visually at a variety of line speeds. The following table lists the collected data.

Line Speed	Number of Defective Parts Found
20	21
20	19
40	15
30	16
60	14
40	17

   a. Develop the estimated regression equation that relates line speed to the number of defective parts found.

   b. At a .05 level of significance, determine whether line speed and number of defective parts found are related.

   c. Did the estimated regression equation provide a good fit to the data?

   d. Develop a 95% confidence interval to predict the mean number of defective parts for a line speed of 50 feet per minute.

61. A sociologist was hired by a large city hospital to investigate the relationship between the number of unauthorized days that employees are absent per year and the distance (miles) between home and work for the employees. From a sample of 10 employees, the following data were collected.

Distance to Work	Number of Days Absent
1	8
3	5
4	8
6	7
8	6
10	3
12	5
14	2
14	4
18	2

   a. Develop a scatter diagram for these data. Does a linear relationship appear reasonable? Explain.

   b. Develop the least squares estimated regression equation.

   c. Is there a significant relationship between the two variables? Use $\alpha = .05$.

   d. Did the estimated regression equation provide a good fit? Explain.

   e. Use the estimated regression equation in part (b) to develop a 95% confidence interval estimate of the expected number of days absent for employees living 5 miles from the company.

62. The regional transit authority for a major metropolitan area wants to determine whether any relationship can be found between the age of a bus and the annual maintenance cost. A sample of 10 buses resulted in the following data.

Age of Bus (years)	Maintenance Cost ($)
1	350
2	370
2	480
2	520
2	590
3	550
4	750
4	800
5	790
5	950

a. Develop the least squares estimated regression equation.
b. Test to see whether the two variables are significantly related. Use $\alpha = .05$.
c. Did the least squares line provide a good fit to the observed data? Explain.
d. Develop a 95% prediction interval for the maintenance cost for a specific bus that is 4 years old.

63. A marketing professor at Givens College is interested in the relationship between hours spent studying and total points earned in a course. Data collected on 10 students who took the course last quarter follow.

Hours Spent Studying	Total Points Earned
45	40
30	35
90	75
60	65
105	90
65	50
90	90
80	80
55	45
75	65

a. Develop an estimated regression equation showing how total points earned is related to hours spent studying.
b. Test the significance of the model. Use $\alpha = .05$.
c. Predict the total points earned by Mark Sweeney. He spent 95 hours studying.
d. Develop a 95% prediction interval for the total points earned by Mark Sweeney.

64. The Transactional Records Access Clearinghouse at Syracuse University reported data showing the odds of an Internal Revenue Service audit. The following table shows the average adjusted gross income reported and the percent of the returns that were audited for 20 selected IRS districts (*The Wall Street Journal Almanac 1998*).

District	Adjusted Gross Income ($)	Percent Audited
Los Angeles	36,664	1.3
Sacramento	38,845	1.1
Atlanta	34,886	1.1
Boise	32,512	1.1
Dallas	34,531	1.0
Providence	35,995	1.0
San Jose	37,799	0.9
Cheyenne	33,876	0.9
Fargo	30,513	0.9
New Orleans	30,174	0.9
Oklahoma City	30,060	0.8
Houston	37,153	0.8
Portland	34,918	0.7
Phoenix	33,291	0.7
Augusta	31,504	0.7
Albuquerque	29,199	0.6
Greensboro	33,072	0.6
Columbia	30,859	0.5
Nashville	32,566	0.5
Buffalo	34,296	0.5

IRSAudit

a. Develop the estimated regression equation that could be used to predict the percent audited given the average adjusted gross income reported.

b. At the .05 level of significance, determine whether the adjusted gross income and the percent audited are related.

c. Did the estimated regression equation provide a good fit? Explain.

d. Use the estimated regression equation developed in part (a) to calculate a 95% confidence interval estimate of the expected percent audited for all districts with an average adjusted gross income of $35,000.

Case Problem 1   SPENDING AND STUDENT ACHIEVEMENT

Is the educational achievement level of students related to how much the state in which they reside spends on education? In many communities taxpayers are asking this important question as their school districts increase the amount of tax revenue spent on education. In this case, you will be asked to analyze data on spending and achievement scores in order to determine whether there is any relationship between spending and student achievement in the public schools.

The federal government's National Assessment of Educational Progress (NAEP) program is frequently used to measure the educational achievement of students. Table 12.8 shows the total current spending per pupil per year, and the composite NAEP test score for 35 states that participated in the NAEP program. These data are available on the data disk in the file named NAEP. The composite score is the sum of the math, science, and reading scores on the 1996 (1994 for reading) NAEP test. Pupils tested are in grade 8, except for reading, which is given to fourth-graders only. The maximum possible score is 1300. Table 12.9 shows the spending per pupil for 13 states that did not participate in relevant NAEP surveys. These data were reported in an article on spending and achievement level appearing in *Forbes* (November 3, 1997).

TABLE 12.8   SPENDING PER PUPIL AND COMPOSITE SCORES FOR STATES
THAT PARTICIPATED IN THE NAEP PROGRAM

NAEP

State	Spending per Pupil ($)	Composite Score
Louisiana	4049	581
Mississippi	3423	582
California	4917	580
Hawaii	5532	580
South Carolina	4304	603
Alabama	3777	604
Georgia	4663	611
Florida	4934	611
New Mexico	4097	614
Arkansas	4060	615
Delaware	6208	615
Tennessee	3800	618
Arizona	4041	618
West Virginia	5247	625
Maryland	6100	625
Kentucky	5020	626
Texas	4520	627
New York	8162	628
North Carolina	4521	629
Rhode Island	6554	638
Washington	5338	639
Missouri	4483	641
Colorado	4772	644
Indiana	5128	649
Utah	3280	650
Wyoming	5515	657
Connecticut	7629	657
Massachusetts	6413	658
Nebraska	5410	660
Minnesota	5477	661
Iowa	5060	665
Montana	4985	667
Wisconsin	6055	667
North Dakota	4374	671
Maine	5561	675

Managerial Report

1. Develop numerical and graphical summaries of the data.
2. Use regression analysis to investigate the relationship between the amount spent per pupil and the composite score on the NAEP test. Discuss your findings.
3. Do you think that the estimated regression equation developed for these data could be used to estimate the composite scores for the states that did not participate in the NAEP program?
4. Suppose that you only considered states that spend at least $4000 per pupil but not more than $6000 per pupil. For these states, does the relationship between the two

TABLE 12.9   SPENDING PER PUPIL FOR STATES THAT DID NOT PARTICIPATE
IN THE NAEP PROGRAM

State	Spending per Pupil ($)
Idaho	3602
South Dakota	4067
Oklahoma	4265
Nevada	4658
Kansas	5164
Illinois	5297
New Hampshire	5387
Ohio	5438
Oregon	5588
Vermont	6269
Michigan	6391
Pennsylvania	6579
Alaska	7890

variables appear to be any different from the complete data set? Discuss the results
of your findings and whether you think deleting states with spending less than $4000
per pupil and more than $6000 per pupil is appropriate.

5. Develop estimates of the composite scores for the states that did not participate in
the NAEP program.

6. Based upon your analyses, do you think that the educational achievement level of
students is related to how much the state spends on education?

Case Problem 2   U.S. DEPARTMENT OF TRANSPORTATION

As part of a study on transportation safety, the U.S. Department of Transportation collected
data on the number of fatal accidents per 1000 licenses and the percentage of licensed
drivers under the age of 21 in a sample of 42 cities. Data collected over a one-year period follow. These data are available on the data disk in the file named Safety.

CD file

Safety

Percent Under 21	Fatal Accidents per 1000 Licenses	Percent Under 21	Fatal Accidents per 1000 Licenses
13	2.962	17	4.100
12	0.708	8	2.190
8	0.885	16	3.623
12	1.652	15	2.623
11	2.091	9	0.835
17	2.627	8	0.820
18	3.830	14	2.890
8	0.368	8	1.267
13	1.142	15	3.224
8	0.645	10	1.014

(*continued*)

Percent Under 21	Fatal Accidents per 1000 Licenses	Percent Under 21	Fatal Accidents per 1000 Licenses
9	1.028	10	0.493
16	2.801	14	1.443
12	1.405	18	3.614
9	1.433	10	1.926
10	0.039	14	1.643
9	0.338	16	2.943
11	1.849	12	1.913
12	2.246	15	2.814
14	2.855	13	2.634
14	2.352	9	0.926
11	1.294	17	3.256

Managerial Report

1. Develop numerical and graphical summaries of the data.
2. Use regression analysis to investigate the relationship between the number of fatal accidents and the percentage of drivers under the age of 21. Discuss your findings.
3. What conclusion and/or recommendations can you derive from your analysis?

Case Problem 3   ALUMNI GIVING

Alumni donations are an important source of revenue for colleges and universities. If administrators could determine the factors that influence increases in the percentage of alumni who make a donation, they might be able to implement policies that could lead to increased revenues. Research shows that students who are more satisfied with their contact with teachers are more likely to graduate. As a result, one might suspect that smaller class sizes and lower student-faculty ratios might lead to a higher percentage of satisfied graduates, which in turn might lead to increases in the percentage of alumni who make a donation. Table 12.10 shows data for 48 universities (*America's Best Colleges*, Year 2000 Edition). The column labeled % of Classes Under 20 shows the percentage of classes offered with fewer than 20 students. The column labeled Student/Faculty Ratio is the number of students enrolled divided by the total number of faculty. Finally, the column labeled Alumni Giving Rate is the percentage of alumni who made a donation to the university.

Managerial Report

1. Develop numerical and graphical summaries of the data.
2. Use regression analysis to develop an estimated regression equation that could be used to predict the alumni giving rate given the percentage of classes with fewer than 20 students.
3. Use regression analysis to develop an estimated regression equation that could be used to predict the alumni giving rate given the student-faculty ratio.
4. Which of the two estimated regression equations provides the best fit? For this estimated regression equation, perform an analysis of the residuals and discuss your findings and conclusions.
5. What conclusions and/or recommendations can you derive from your analysis?

TABLE 12.10   DATA FOR 48 NATIONAL UNIVERSITIES

Alumni

School	% of Classes Under 20	Student/Faculty Ratio	Alumni Giving Rate
Boston College	39	13	25
Brandeis University	68	8	33
Brown University	60	8	40
California Institute of Technology	65	3	46
Carnegie Mellon University	67	10	28
Case Western Reserve University	52	8	31
College of William and Mary	45	12	27
Columbia University	69	7	31
Cornell University	72	13	35
Dartmouth College	61	10	53
Duke University	68	8	45
Emory University	65	7	37
Georgetown University	54	10	29
Harvard University	73	8	46
Johns Hopkins University	64	9	27
Lehigh University	55	11	40
Massachusetts Inst. of Technology	65	6	44
New York University	63	13	13
Northwestern University	66	8	30
Pennsylvania State University	32	19	21
Princeton University	68	5	67
Rice University	62	8	40
Stanford University	69	7	34
Tufts University	67	9	29
Tulane University	56	12	17
U. of California–Berkeley	58	17	18
U. of California–Davis	32	19	7
U. of California–Irvine	42	20	9
U. of California–Los Angeles	41	18	13
U. of California–San Diego	48	19	8
U. of California–Santa Barbara	45	20	12
U. of Chicago	65	4	36
U. of Florida	31	23	19
U. of Illinois–Urbana Champaign	29	15	23
U. of Michigan–Ann Arbor	51	15	13
U. of North Carolina–Chapel Hill	40	16	26
U. of Notre Dame	53	13	49
U. of Pennsylvania	65	7	41
U. of Rochester	63	10	23
U. of Southern California	53	13	22
U. of Texas–Austin	39	21	13
U. of Virginia	44	13	28
U. of Washington	37	12	12
U. of Wisconsin–Madison	37	13	13
Vanderbilt University	68	9	31
Wake Forest University	59	11	38
Washington University–St. Louis	73	7	33
Yale University	77	7	50

CHAPTER 13

Multiple Regression

CONTENTS

STATISTICS IN PRACTICE

International Paper*

PURCHASE, NEW YORK

International Paper is the world's largest paper and forest products company. The company employs more than 117,000 people in its operations in nearly 50 countries, and exports its products to more than 130 nations. International Paper produces building materials such as lumber and plywood; consumer packaging materials such as disposable cups and containers; industrial packaging materials such as corrugated boxes and shipping containers; and a variety of papers for use in photocopiers, printers, books, and advertising materials.

To make paper products, pulp mills process wood chips and chemicals to produce wood pulp. The wood pulp is then used at a paper mill to produce paper products. In the production of white paper products, the pulp must be bleached to remove any discoloration. A key bleaching agent used in the process is chlorine dioxide, which, because of its combustible nature, is usually produced at a pulp mill facility and then piped in solution form into the bleaching tower of the pulp mill. To improve one of the processes used to produce chlorine dioxide, researchers studied the process's control and efficiency. One aspect of the study looked at the chemical-feed rate for chlorine dioxide production.

To produce the chlorine dioxide, four chemicals flow at metered rates into the chlorine dioxide generator. The chlorine dioxide produced in the generator flows to an absorber where chilled water absorbs the chlorine dioxide gas to form a chlorine dioxide solution. The solution is then piped into the paper mill. A key part of controlling the process involves the chemical-feed rates. Historically, experienced operators set the chemical-feed rates, but this approach led to overcontrol by the operators. Consequently, chemical engineers at the mill requested that a set

Multiple regression analysis assisted in the development of a better bleaching process for making white paper products.

of control equations, one for each chemical feed, be developed to aid the operators in setting the rates.

Using multiple regression analysis, statistical analysts developed an estimated multiple regression equation for each of the four chemicals used in the process. Each equation related the production of chlorine dioxide to the amount of chemical used and the concentration level of the chlorine dioxide solution. The resulting set of four equations was programmed into a microcomputer at each mill. In the new system, operators enter the concentration of the chlorine dioxide solution and the desired production rate; the computer software then calculates the chemical feed needed to achieve the desired production rate. After the operators began using the control equations, the chlorine dioxide generator efficiency increased, and the number of times the concentrations fell within acceptable ranges increased significantly.

This example shows how multiple regression analysis can be used to develop a better bleaching process for producing white paper products. In this chapter we will discuss how statistical computer packages such as Excel are used for such purposes. Most of the concepts introduced in Chapter 12 for simple linear regression can be directly extended to the multiple regression case.

*The authors are indebted to Marian Williams and Bill Griggs for providing this Statistics in Practice. This application was originally developed at Champion International Corporation, which became part of International Paper in 2000.

In Chapter 12 we presented simple linear regression and demonstrated its use in developing an equation that describes the relationship between two variables. Recall that the variable being predicted or explained by the equation is called the dependent variable and the variable being used to predict or explain the dependent variable is called the independent variable. In this chapter we continue our study of regression analysis by considering situations involving two or more independent variables. This subject area is called **multiple regression analysis**. It enables us to consider more factors and thus obtain better estimates than are possible with simple linear regression.

13.1   MULTIPLE REGRESSION MODEL

Multiple regression analysis is the study of how a dependent variable y is related to two or more independent variables. In the general case, we will use p to denote the number of independent variables.

Regression Model and Regression Equation

The concepts of a regression model and a regression equation introduced in the preceding chapter are applicable in the multiple regression case. The equation that describes how the dependent variable y is related to the independent variables $x_1, x_2, \ldots x_p$ and an error term ϵ is called the **multiple regression model.** We begin with the assumption that the multiple regression model takes the following form.

Multiple Regression Model

$$y = \beta_0 + \beta_1 x_1 + \beta_2 x_2 + \cdots + \beta_p x_p + \epsilon \qquad (13.1)$$

In the multiple regression model, $\beta_0, \beta_1, \beta_2, \ldots, \beta_p$ are the parameters and ϵ (the Greek letter epsilon) is a random variable. A close examination of this model reveals that y is a linear function of $x_1, x_2, \ldots, x_p$ (the $\beta_0 + \beta_1 x_1 + \beta_2 x_2 + \ldots + \beta_p x_p$ part) plus an error term ϵ. The error term accounts for the variability in y that cannot be explained by the linear effect of the p independent variables.

In Section 13.4 we will discuss the assumptions for the multiple regression model and ϵ. One of the assumptions is that the mean or expected value of ϵ is zero. A consequence of this assumption is that the mean or expected value of y, denoted $E(y)$, is equal to $\beta_0 + \beta_1 x_1 + \beta_2 x_2 + \ldots + \beta_p x_p$. The equation that describes how the mean value of y is related to $x_1, x_2, \ldots, x_p$ is called the **multiple regression equation.**

Multiple Regression Equation

$$E(y) = \beta_0 + \beta_1 x_1 + \beta_2 x_2 + \cdots + \beta_p x_p \qquad (13.2)$$

Estimated Multiple Regression Equation

If the values of $\beta_0, \beta_1, \beta_2, \ldots, \beta_p$ were known, equation (13.2) could be used to compute the mean value of y at given values of $x_1, x_2, \ldots, x_p$. Unfortunately, these parameter values will not, in general, be known and must be estimated from sample data. A simple random sample is used to compute sample statistics $b_0, b_1, b_2, \ldots, b_p$ that are used as the point estimators of the parameters $\beta_0, \beta_1, \beta_2, \ldots, \beta_p$. These sample statistics provide the following **estimated multiple regression equation**.

Estimated Multiple Regression Equation

$$\hat{y} = b_0 + b_1x_1 + b_2x_2 + \cdots + b_px_p \tag{13.3}$$

where

$b_0, b_1, b_2, \ldots, b_p$ are the estimates of $\beta_0, \beta_1, \beta_2, \ldots, \beta_p$

$\hat{y} = $ estimated value of the dependent variable

The estimation process for multiple regression is shown in Figure 13.1.

FIGURE 13.1   THE ESTIMATION PROCESS FOR MULTIPLE REGRESSION

In simple linear regression, b_0 and b_1 were the sample statistics used to estimate the parameters β_0 and β_1. Multiple regression parallels this statistical inference process, with b_0, $b_1, b_2, \ldots, b_p$ denoting the sample statistics used to estimate $\beta_0, \beta_1, \beta_2, \ldots, \beta_p$.

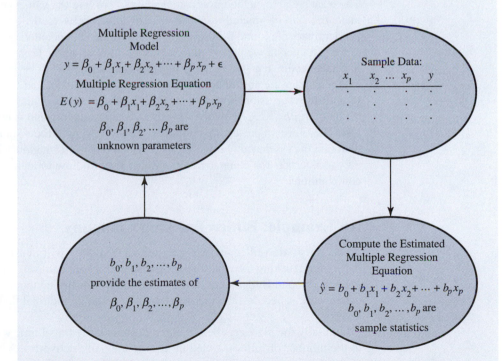

13.2　LEAST SQUARES METHOD

In Chapter 12, we used the **least squares method** to develop the estimated regression equation that best approximated the straight-line relationship between the dependent and independent variables. This same approach is used to develop the estimated multiple regression equation. The least squares criterion is restated as follows.

Least Squares Criterion

$$\min \Sigma(y_i - \hat{y}_i)^2 \tag{13.4}$$

where

y_i = observed value of the dependent variable for the ith observation

$\hat{y}_i$ = estimated value of the dependent variable for the ith observation

---

The estimated values of the dependent variable are computed by using the estimated multiple regression equation,

$$\hat{y} = b_0 + b_1 x_1 + b_2 x_2 + \cdots + b_p x_p$$

The least squares method uses sample data to provide the values of $b_0, b_1, b_2, \ldots, b_p$ that make the sum of squared residuals (the deviations between the observed values of the dependent variable y_i and the estimated values of the dependent variable $\hat{y}_i$) a minimum.

In Chapter 12 we presented formulas for computing the least squares estimators b_0 and b_1 for the estimated simple linear regression equation $\hat{y} = b_0 + b_1 x$. With relatively small data sets, we were able to use those formulas to compute b_0 and b_1 by manual calculations. In multiple regression, however, the presentation of the formulas for the regression coefficients $b_0, b_1, b_2, \ldots, b_p$ involves the use of matrix algebra and is beyond the scope of this text. Therefore, in presenting multiple regression, we will focus on how Excel can be used to obtain the estimated regression equation and other information. The emphasis will be on how to interpret the computer output rather than on how to make the multiple regression computations.

An Example: Butler Trucking Company

As an illustration of multiple regression analysis, we will consider a problem faced by the Butler Trucking Company, an independent trucking company in southern California. A major portion of Butler's business involves deliveries throughout its local area. To develop better work schedules, the managers want to estimate the total daily travel time for their drivers.

Initially the managers believed that the total daily travel time would be closely related to the number of miles traveled in making the daily deliveries. A simple random sample of 10 driving assignments provided the data shown in Table 13.1 and the scatter diagram shown in Figure 13.2. After reviewing this scatter diagram, the managers hypothe-

TABLE 13.1   PRELIMINARY DATA FOR BUTLER TRUCKING

Butler

Driving Assignment	x_1 = Miles Traveled	y = Travel Time (hours)
1	100	9.3
2	50	4.8
3	100	8.9
4	100	6.5
5	50	4.2
6	80	6.2
7	75	7.4
8	65	6.0
9	90	7.6
10	90	6.1

sized that the simple linear regression model $y = \beta_0 + \beta_1 x_1 + \epsilon$ could be used to describe the relationship between the total travel time (y) and the number of miles traveled (x_1). To estimate the parameters β_0 and β_1, the least squares method was used to develop the estimated regression equation.

$$\hat{y} = b_0 + b_1 x_1 \qquad (13.5)$$

FIGURE 13.2   SCATTER DIAGRAM OF PRELIMINARY DATA FOR BUTLER TRUCKING

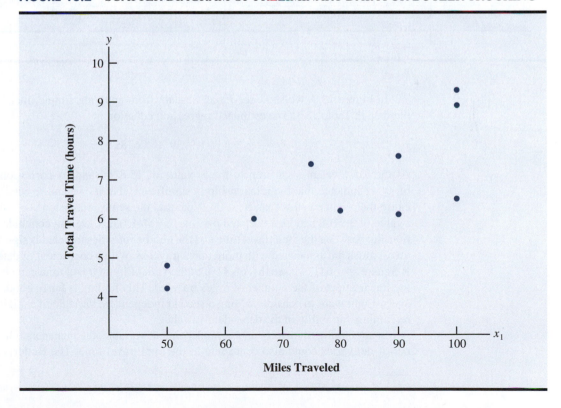

FIGURE 13.3   EXCEL OUTPUT FOR BUTLER TRUCKING WITH ONE INDEPENDENT VARIABLE

	A	B	C	D	E	F	G	H	I	J
1	Assignment	Miles	Time							
2	1	100	9.3							
3	2	50	4.8							
4	3	100	8.9							
5	4	100	6.5							
6	5	50	4.2							
7	6	80	6.2							
8	7	75	7.4							
9	8	65	6							
10	9	90	7.6							
11	10	90	6.1							
12										
13	SUMMARY OUTPUT									
14										
15	*Regression Statistics*									
16	Multiple R	0.8149								
17	R Square	0.6641								
18	Adjusted R Square	0.6221								
19	Standard Error	1.0018								
20	Observations	10								
21										
22	ANOVA									
23		*df*	*SS*	*MS*	*F*	*Significance F*				
24	Regression	1	15.8713	15.8713	15.8146	0.0041				
25	Residual	8	8.0287	1.0036						
26	Total	9	23.9							
27										
28		*Coefficients*	*Standard Error*	*t Stat*	*P-value*	*Lower 95%*	*Upper 95%*	*Lower 99.0%*	*Upper 99.0%*	
29	Intercept	1.2739	1.4007	0.9095	0.3897	-1.9562	4.5040	-3.4261	5.9739	
30	Miles	0.0678	0.0171	3.9768	0.0041	0.0285	0.1072	0.0106	0.1251	
31										

In Figure 13.3, we show the Excel output* from applying simple linear regression to the data in Table 13.1. The estimated regression equation is

$$\hat{y} = 1.2739 + .0678x_1$$

At the .05 level of significance, the F value of 15.8146 and its corresponding p-value of .0041 indicate that the relationship is significant; that is, we can reject H_0: $\beta_1 = 0$ because the p-value is less than $\alpha = .05$. Note that the same conclusion is obtained from the t value of 3.9768 and its associated p-value of .0041. Thus, we can conclude that the relationship between the total travel time and the number of miles traveled is significant; longer travel times are associated with more miles traveled. With a coefficient of determination of R Square = .6641, we see that 66.41% of the variability in travel time can be explained by the linear effect of the number of miles traveled. This finding is fairly good, but the managers might want to consider adding a second independent variable to explain some of the remaining variability in the dependent variable.

In attempting to identify another independent variable, the managers felt that the number of deliveries could also contribute to the total travel time. The Butler Trucking data,

---

*Excel's Regression tool was used to obtain the output. Section 12.6 describes the tasks used for simple linear regression.

with the number of deliveries added, are shown in Table 13.2. To develop the estimated multiple regression equation with both miles traveled (x_1) and number of deliveries (x_2) as independent variables, we will use Excel's Regression tool.

Using Excel's Regression Tool to Develop the Estimated Multiple Regression Equation

In Section 12.6 we showed how Excel's Regression tool could be used to determine the estimated regression equation for the Armand's Pizza Parlors problem. We can use the same procedure with minor modifications to develop the estimated multiple regression equation for the Butler Trucking problem. Refer to Figure 13.4 as we describe the tasks involved.

Enter Data: The labels Assignment, Miles, Deliveries, and Time are entered into cells A1:D1 of the worksheet, and the sample data into cells B2:D11. The numbers 1–10 in cells A2:A11 identify each observation.

Apply Tools: The following steps describe how to use the Regression tool for the multiple regression analysis.

Step 1. Select the **Tools** menu
Step 2. Choose the **Data Analysis** option
Step 3. Choose **Regression** from the list of Analysis Tools
Step 4. When the Regression dialog box appears (see Figure 13.5):
  Enter D1:D11 in the **Input Y Range** box
  Enter B1:C11 in the **Input X Range** box
  Select **Labels**
  Select **Confidence Level**
  Enter 99 in the **Confidence Level** box
  Select **Output Range**
  Enter A13 in the **Output Range** box (to identify the upper left corner of the section of the worksheet where the output will appear)
  Click **OK**

TABLE 13.2   DATA FOR BUTLER TRUCKING WITH MILES TRAVELED (x_1) AND NUMBER OF DELIVERIES (x_2) AS THE INDEPENDENT VARIABLES

CD file
Butler

Driving Assignment	$x_1 = $ Miles Traveled	$x_2 = $ Number of Deliveries	$y = $ Travel Time (hours)
1	100	4	9.3
2	50	3	4.8
3	100	4	8.9
4	100	2	6.5
5	50	2	4.2
6	80	2	6.2
7	75	3	7.4
8	65	4	6.0
9	90	3	7.6
10	90	2	6.1

FIGURE 13.4 EXCEL OUTPUT FOR BUTLER TRUCKING WITH TWO INDEPENDENT VARIABLES

	A	B	C	D	E	F	G	H	I	J
1	Assignment	Miles	Deliveries	Time						
2	1	100	4	9.3						
3	2	50	3	4.8						
4	3	100	4	8.9						
5	4	100	2	6.5						
6	5	50	2	4.2						
7	6	80	2	6.2						
8	7	75	3	7.4						
9	8	65	4	6						
10	9	90	3	7.6						
11	10	90	2	6.1						
12										
13	SUMMARY OUTPUT									
14										
15	*Regression Statistics*									
16	Multiple R	0.9507								
17	R Square	0.9038								
18	Adjusted R Square	0.8763								
19	Standard Error	0.5731								
20	Observations	10								
21										
22	ANOVA									
23		*df*	*SS*	*MS*	*F*	*Significance F*				
24	Regression	2	21.6006	10.8003	32.8784	0.0003				
25	Residual	7	2.2994	0.3285						
26	Total	9	23.9							
27										
28		*Coefficients*	*Standard Error*	*t Stat*	*P-value*	*Lower 95%*	*Upper 95%*	*Lower 99.0%*	*Upper 99.0%*	
29	Intercept	-0.8687	0.9515	-0.9129	0.3916	-3.1188	1.3813	-4.1986	2.4612	
30	Miles	0.0611	0.0099	6.1824	0.0005	0.0378	0.0845	0.0265	0.0957	
31	Deliveries	0.9234	0.2211	4.1763	0.0042	0.4006	1.4463	0.1496	1.6972	
32										

In the Excel output shown in Figure 13.4 the label for the independent variable x_1 is Miles (see cell A30), and the label for the independent variable x_2 is Deliveries (see cell A31). The estimated regression equation is

$$\hat{y} = -.8687 + .0611x_1 + .9234x_2 \tag{13.6}$$

Note that using Excel's Regression tool for multiple regression is almost the same as using it for simple linear regression. The major difference is that in the multiple regression case a larger range of cells is required in order to identify the independent variables.

Note on Interpretation of Coefficients

Compare the relationship between the estimated regression equation with only the miles traveled as an independent variable and the estimated regression equation that includes the number of deliveries as a second independent variable. Note that the value of b_1 is not the same in both cases. In simple linear regression, we interpret b_1 as an estimate of the change in y for a 1-unit change in the independent variable. For example, in the Butler Trucking Company problem involving only one independent variable, number of miles traveled,

FIGURE 13.5   REGRESSION DIALOG BOX FOR THE BUTLER TRUCKING PROBLEM

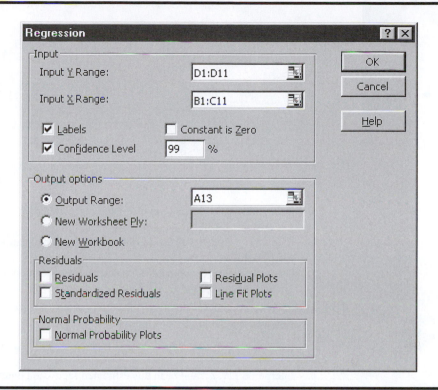

$b_1 = .0678$. Thus, .0678 is an estimate of the expected increase in travel time correspond-ing to an increase of 1 mile in the distance traveled. In multiple regression analysis, this in-terpretation must be modified somewhat; that is, in multiple regression analysis, we interpret each regression coefficient as follows: b_i represents an estimate of the change in y corresponding to a 1-unit change in x_i when all other independent variables are held con-stant. In the Butler Trucking example involving two independent variables, $b_1 = .0611$. Thus, .0611 hours is an estimate of the expected increase in travel time corresponding to an increase of 1 mile in the distance traveled when the number of deliveries is held constant. Similarly, because $b_2 = .9234$, an estimate of the expected increase in travel time corre-sponding to an increase of one delivery when the number of miles traveled is held constant is .9234 hours.

EXERCISES

Methods

1. The estimated regression equation for a problem involving two independent variables and 10 observations follows.

$$\hat{y} = 29.1270 + .5906x_1 + .4980x_2$$

    a. Interpret b_1 and b_2 in this estimated regression equation.
    b. Estimate y when $x_1 = 180$ and $x_2 = 310$.

2. Consider the following data for a dependent variable y and two independent variables, x_1 and x_2.

Exer2

x_1	x_2	y
30	12	94
47	10	108
25	17	112
51	16	178
40	5	94
51	19	175
74	7	170
36	12	117
59	13	142
76	16	211

a. Using these data, develop an estimated regression equation relating y to x_1. Estimate y if $x_1 = 45$.

b. Using these data, develop an estimated regression equation relating y to x_2. Estimate y if $x_2 = 15$.

c. Using these data, develop an estimated regression equation relating y to x_1 and x_2. Estimate y if $x_1 = 45$ and $x_2 = 15$.

3. In a regression analysis involving 30 observations, the following estimated regression equation was obtained.

$$\hat{y} = 17.6 + 3.8x_1 - 2.3x_2 + 7.6x_3 + 2.7x_4$$

a. Interpret b_1, b_2, b_3, and b_4 in this estimated regression equation.

b. Estimate y when $x_1 = 10$, $x_2 = 5$, $x_3 = 1$, and $x_4 = 2$.

Applications

4. A shoe store developed the following estimated regression equation relating sales to inventory investment and advertising expenditures.

$$\hat{y} = 25 + 10x_1 + 8x_2$$

where

$$x_1 = \text{inventory investment (\$1000s)}$$
$$x_2 = \text{advertising expenditures (\$1000s)}$$
$$y = \text{sales (\$1000s)}$$

a. Estimate sales resulting from a $15,000 investment in inventory and an advertising budget of $10,000.

b. Interpret b_1 and b_2 in this estimated regression equation.

5. The owner of Showtime Movie Theaters, Inc., would like to estimate weekly gross revenue as a function of advertising expenditures. Historical data for a sample of eight weeks follow.

Showtime

Weekly Gross Revenue ($1000s)	Television Advertising ($1000s)	Newspaper Advertising ($1000s)
96	5.0	1.5
90	2.0	2.0

Weekly Gross Revenue ($1000s)	Television Advertising ($1000s)	Newspaper Advertising ($1000s)
95	4.0	1.5
92	2.5	2.5
95	3.0	3.3
94	3.5	2.3
94	2.5	4.2
94	3.0	2.5

a. Develop an estimated regression equation with television advertising expenditures as the independent variable.
b. Develop an estimated regression equation with both television advertising expenditures and newspaper advertising expenditures as the independent variables.
c. Is the estimated regression equation coefficient for television advertising expenditures the same in parts (a) and (b)? Interpret the coefficient in each case.
d. What is the estimate of the weekly gross revenue for a week when $3500 is spent on television advertising and $1800 is spent on newspaper advertising?

6. The following table reports the horsepower, curb weight, and the speed at ¼ mile for 16 sports and GT cars (*1998 Road & Track Sports & GT Cars*).

Auto1

Sports & GT Car	Curb Weight (lbs.)	Horsepower	Speed at ¼ mile (mph)
Acura Integra Type R	2577	195	90.7
Acura NSX-T	3066	290	108.0
BMW Z3 2.8	2844	189	93.2
Chevrolet Camaro Z28	3439	305	103.2
Chevrolet Corvette Convertible	3246	345	102.1
Dodge Viper RT/10	3319	450	116.2
Ford Mustang GT	3227	225	91.7
Honda Prelude Type SH	3042	195	89.7
Mercedes-Benz CLK320	3240	215	93.0
Mercedes-Benz SLK230	3025	185	92.3
Mitsubishi 3000GT VR-4	3737	320	99.0
Nissan 240SX SE	2862	155	84.6
Pontiac Firebird Trans Am	3455	305	103.2
Porsche Boxster	2822	201	93.2
Toyota Supra Turbo	3505	320	105.0
Volvo C70	3285	236	97.0

a. Use curb weight as the independent variable and the speed at ¼ mile as the dependent variable. What is the estimated regression equation?
b. Use curb weight and horsepower as two independent variables and the speed at ¼ mile as the dependent variable. What is the estimated regression equation?
c. The 1999 Porsche 911 Carrera was advertised as having a curb weight of 2910 pounds and an engine with 296 horsepower. Use the results of part (b) to predict the speed at ¼ mile for the Porsche 911.

7. Designers of backpacks use exotic material such as supernylon Delrin, high-density poly-
    ethylene, aircraft aluminum, and thermomolded foam to make packs that fit comfortably
    and distribute weight to eliminate pressure points. The following data show the capacity
    (cubic inches), comfort rating, and price for 10 backpacks tested by *Outside Magazine.*
    Comfort was measured using a rating from 1 to 5, with a rating of 1 denoting average com-
    fort and a rating of 5 denoting excellent comfort (*Outside Buyer's Guide,* 2001).

Backpack

Manufacturer and Model	Capacity	Comfort	Price
Camp Trails Paragon II	4330	2	$190
EMS 5500	5500	3	219
Lowe Alpomayo 90+20	5500	4	249
Marmot Muir	4700	3	249
Kelly Bigfoot 5200	5200	4	250
Gregory Whitney	5500	4	340
Osprey 75	4700	4	389
Arc'Teryx Bora 95	5500	5	395
Dana Design Terraplane LTW	5800	5	439
The Works @ Mystery Ranch Jazz	5000	5	525

   a. Determine the estimated regression equation that can be used to predict the price of a
       backpack given the capacity and the comfort rating.
   b. Interpret b_1 and b_2.
   c. Predict the price for a backpack with a capacity of 4500 cubic inches and a comfort
       rating of 4.

8. The following table gives the annual return, the safety rating (0 = riskiest, 10 = safest),
    and the annual expense ratio for 20 foreign funds (*Mutual Funds,* March 2000).

ForFunds

	Safety Rating	Annual Expense Ratio (%)	Annual Return (%)
Accessor Int'l Equity "Adv"	7.1	1.59	49
Aetna "I" International	7.2	1.35	52
Amer Century Int'l Discovery "Inv"	6.8	1.68	89
Columbia International Stock	7.1	1.56	58
Concert Inv "A" Int'l Equity	6.2	2.16	131
Dreyfus Founders Int'l Equity "F"	7.4	1.80	59
Driehaus International Growth	6.5	1.88	99
Excelsior "Inst" Int'l Equity	7.0	0.90	53
Julius Baer International Equity	6.9	1.79	77
Marshall International Stock "Y"	7.2	1.49	54
MassMutual Int'l Equity "S"	7.1	1.05	57
Morgan Grenfell Int'l Sm Cap "Inst"	7.7	1.25	61
New England "A" Int'l Equity	7.0	1.83	88
Pilgrim Int'l Small Cap "A"	7.0	1.94	122
Republic International Equity	7.2	1.09	71
Sit International Growth	6.9	1.50	51
Smith Barney "A" Int'l Equity	7.0	1.28	60
State St Research "S" Int'l Equity	7.1	1.65	50
Strong International Stock	6.5	1.61	93
Vontobel International Equity	7.0	1.50	47

a. Using these data, develop an estimated regression equation relating the annual return to the safety rating and the annual expense ratio.

b. Estimate the annual return for a firm that has a safety rating of 7.5 and annual expense ratio of 2%.

9. Two experts provided subjective lists of school districts that they think are among the best in the country. For each school district the average class size, the combined SAT score, and the percentage of students who attended a four-year college were provided.

Schools

District	Average Class Size	Combined SAT Score	% Attend Four-Year College
Blue Springs, MO	25	1083	74
Garden City, NY	18	997	77
Indianapolis, IN	30	716	40
Newport Beach, CA	26	977	51
Novi, MI	20	980	53
Piedmont, CA	28	1042	75
Pittsburg, PA	21	983	66
Scarsdale, NY	20	1110	87
Wayne, PA	22	1040	85
Weston, MA	21	1031	89
Farmingdale, NY	22	947	81
Mamaroneck, NY	20	1000	69
Mayfield, OH	24	1003	48
Morristown, NJ	22	972	64
New Rochelle, NY	23	1039	55
Newtown Square, PA	17	963	79
Omaha, NE	23	1059	81
Shaker Heights, OH	23	940	82

a. Using these data, develop an estimated regression equation relating the percentage of students who attend a four-year college to the average class size and the combined SAT score.

b. Estimate the percentage of students who attend a four-year college if the average class size is 20 and the combined SAT score is 1000.

10. *Auto Rental News* provided the following data, which show the number of cars in service (1000s), the number of locations, and the rental revenue ($ millions) for 15 car rental companies (*The Wall Street Journal Almanac 1998*).

CarRent

Company	Cars	Locations	Revenue
Alamo	130	171	1180
Avis	190	1130	1500
Budget	126	1052	1500
Dollar	63.5	450	560
Enterprise	315.1	2636	2060
FRCS (Ford)	55.25	1784	312.5
Hertz	250	1200	2400
National	135	935	1200

(continued)

Company	Cars	Locations	Revenue
Payless	15	100	47
PROP (Chrysler)	27	1500	160
Rent-A-Wreck	10.9	460	78
Snappy	15.5	259	85
Thrifty	34	480	340
U-Save	13.5	500	95
Value	18	45	150.1

a. Determine the estimated regression equation that can be used to predict the rental revenue given the number of cars in service.

b. Provide an interpretation for the slope of the estimated regression equation developed in part (a).

c. Determine the estimated regression equation that can be used to predict the rental revenue given the number of cars in service and the number of locations.

13.3 MULTIPLE COEFFICIENT OF DETERMINATION

In simple linear regression we showed that the total sum of squares can be partitioned into two components: the sum of squares due to regression and the sum of squares due to error. The same partition applies to the sum of squares in multiple regression.

Relationship Among SST, SSR, and SSE

$$SST = SSR + SSE \qquad (13.7)$$

where

$$SST = \text{total sum of squares} = \Sigma(y_i - \bar{y})^2$$
$$SSR = \text{sum of squares due to regression} = \Sigma(\hat{y}_i - \bar{y})^2$$
$$SSE = \text{sum of squares due to error} = \Sigma(y_i - \hat{y}_i)^2$$

Because computing the three sums of squares is very tedious, we rely on computer packages to determine these values. The analysis of variance part of the Excel output in Figure 13.4 shows the three sums of squares for the Butler Trucking problem with two independent variables: SST = 23.9, SSR = 21.6006, and SSE = 2.2994. With only one independent variable (number of miles traveled), the Excel output in Figure 13.3 shows that SST = 23.9, SSR = 15.8713, and SSE = 8.0287. The value of SST is the same in both cases because it does not depend on $\hat{y}$, but SSR increases and SSE decreases when a second independent variable (number of deliveries) is added. The implication is that the estimated multiple regression equation provides a better fit for the observed sample data.

In Chapter 12, we used the coefficient of determination, $r^2 = SSR/SST$, to measure the goodness of fit for the estimated regression equation. The same concept applies to multiple regression. The term **multiple coefficient of determination** indicates that we are measuring the goodness of fit for the estimated multiple regression equation. The multiple coefficient of determination, denoted R^2, is computed as follows.

Multiple Coefficient of Determination

$$R^2 = \frac{\text{SSR}}{\text{SST}} \qquad (13.8)$$

The multiple coefficient of determination can be interpreted as the proportion of the variability in the dependent variable that can be explained by the estimated multiple regression equation. Hence, when multiplied by 100, it can be interpreted as the percentage of the variability in y that can be explained by the estimated regression equation.

In the two-independent-variable Butler Trucking example, with SSR = 21.6006 and SST = 23.9, we have

$$R^2 = \frac{21.6006}{23.9} = .9038$$

Therefore, 90.38% of the variability in travel time y is explained by the estimated multiple regression equation with miles traveled and number of deliveries as the independent variables. In Figure 13.4, we see that the multiple coefficient of determination is also provided by the Excel output; it is denoted by R Square = .9038.

Figure 13.3 shows that the R Square value for the estimated regression equation with only one independent variable, number of miles traveled (x_1), is .6641. Thus, the percentage of the variability in travel times that is explained by the estimated regression equation increases from 66.41% to 90.38% when number of deliveries is added as a second independent variable. In general, R^2 always increases as independent variables are added to the model.

Many analysts prefer adjusting R^2 for the number of independent variables to avoid overestimating the impact of adding an independent variable on the amount of variability explained by the estimated regression equation. With n denoting the number of observations and p denoting the number of independent variables, the **adjusted multiple coefficient of determination** is computed as follows.

The adjusted multiple coefficient of determination adjusts for the number of independent variables in the model.

Adjusted Multiple Coefficient of Determination

$$R_a^2 = 1 - (1 - R^2)\frac{n - 1}{n - p - 1} \qquad (13.9)$$

For the Butler Trucking example with $n = 10$ and $p = 2$, we have

$$R_a^2 = 1 - (1 - .9038)\frac{10 - 1}{10 - 2 - 1} = .8763$$

Thus, after adjusting for the two independent variables, we obtain an adjusted multiple coefficient of determination of .8763. This value is provided by the Excel output in Figure 13.4 as Adjusted R Square = .8763.

EXERCISES

Methods

11. Exercise 1 used the following estimated regression equation based on 10 observations.

$$\hat{y} = 29.1270 + .5906x_1 + .4980x_2$$

The values of SST and SSR are 6724.125 and 6216.375, respectively.
a. Find SSE.
b. Compute R^2.
c. Compute R_a^2.
d. Comment on the goodness of fit.

12. In Exercise 2, 10 observations provided data for a dependent variable y and two independent variables x_1 and x_2 that resulted in SST = 15,182.9, and SSR = 14,052.2.
a. Compute R^2.
b. Compute R_a^2.
c. Does the estimated regression equation explain a large amount of the variability in the data? Explain.

13. Exercise 3 used the following estimated regression equation based on 30 observations.

$$\hat{y} = 17.6 + 3.8x_1 - 2.3x_2 + 7.6x_3 + 2.7x_4$$

The values of SST and SSR are 1805 and 1760, respectively.
a. Compute R^2.
b. Compute R_a^2.
c. Comment on the goodness of fit.

Applications

14. Exercise 4 used the following estimated regression equation relating sales to inventory investment and advertising expenditures.

$$\hat{y} = 25 + 10x_1 + 8x_2$$

The data to develop the estimated regression equation came from a survey of 10 stores and resulted in SST = 16,000 and SSR = 12,000.
a. For the estimated regression equation given, compute R^2.
b. Compute R_a^2.
c. Does the model appear to explain a large amount of variability in the data? Explain.

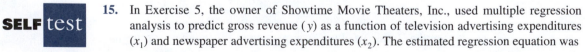

15. In Exercise 5, the owner of Showtime Movie Theaters, Inc., used multiple regression analysis to predict gross revenue (y) as a function of television advertising expenditures (x_1) and newspaper advertising expenditures (x_2). The estimated regression equation was

$$\hat{y} = 83.2 + 2.29x_1 + 1.30x_2$$

The computer solution provided SST = 25.5 and SSR = 23.435.
a. Compute and interpret R^2 and R_a^2.
b. When television advertising expenditures was the only independent variable, $R^2 = .653$ and $R_a^2 = .595$. Do you prefer the multiple regression results? Explain.

16. Exercise 6 provided data for curb weight, horsepower, and speed at ¼ mile for 16 sports and GT cars (*1998 Road & Track Sports & GT Cars*).
    a. Did the estimated regression equation that uses only curb weight to predict the speed at ¼ mile provide a good fit? Explain.
    b. Discuss the benefits of using both the curb weight and the horsepower to predict the speed at ¼ mile.

17. In Exercise 9 an estimated regression equation was developed to relate the percentage of students who attend a four-year college to the average class size and the combined SAT score.
    a. Compute and interpret R^2 and R_a^2.
    b. Does the estimated regression equation provide a good fit to the data? Explain.

18. Exercise 10 provided data on the number of cars in service (1000s), the number of locations, and the rental revenue ($ millions) for 15 car rental companies (*The Wall Street Journal Almanac 1998*).
    a. In part (c) of Exercise 10, an estimated regression equation was developed relating the rental revenue to the number of cars in service and the number of locations. What are the values of R^2 and R_a^2?
    b. Does the estimated regression equation provide a good fit to the data? Explain.

13.4   MODEL ASSUMPTIONS

In Section 13.1 we introduced the following multiple regression model.

Multiple Regression Model

$$y = \beta_0 + \beta_1 x_1 + \beta_2 x_2 + \cdots + \beta_p x_p + \epsilon \qquad (13.10)$$

The assumptions about the error term ϵ in the multiple regression model parallel those for the simple linear regression model.

Assumptions About the Error Term ϵ in the Multiple Regression Model
$y = \beta_0 + \beta_1 x_1 + \cdots + \beta_p x_p + \epsilon$

1. The error term ϵ is a random variable with mean or expected value of zero; that is, $E(\epsilon) = 0$.
   Implication: For given values of $x_1, x_2, \ldots, x_p$, the mean or expected value of y is given by

   $$E(y) = \beta_0 + \beta_1 x_1 + \beta_2 x_2 + \cdots + \beta_p x_p. \qquad (13.11)$$

   Equation (13.11) is the multiple regression equation we introduced in Section 13.1. In this equation, $E(y)$ represents the average of all possible values of y that might occur for the given values of $x_1, x_2, \ldots, x_p$.
2. The variance of ϵ is denoted by σ^2 and is the same for all values of the independent variables $x_1, x_2, \ldots, x_p$.
   Implication: The variance of y equals σ^2 and is the same for all values of $x_1, x_2, \ldots, x_p$.

---

3. The values of ϵ are independent.
   Implication: The size of the error for a particular set of values for the independent variables is not related to the size of the error for any other set of values.
4. The error ϵ is a normally distributed random variable reflecting the deviation between the y value and the expected value of y given by $\beta_0 + \beta_1 x_1 + \beta_2 x_2 + \cdots + \beta_p x_p$.
   Implication: Because $\beta_0, \beta_1, \ldots, \beta_p$ are constants for the given values of $x_1, x_2, \ldots, x_p$, the dependent variable y is also a normally distributed random variable.

To obtain more insight about the form of the relationship given by equation (13.11), consider the following two-independent-variable multiple regression equation.

$$E(y) = \beta_0 + \beta_1 x_1 + \beta_2 x_2$$

The graph of this equation is a plane in three-dimensional space. Figure 13.6 is such a graph. Note that ϵ is shown as the difference between the actual y value and the expected value of y, $E(y)$, when $x_1 = x_1^*$ and $x_2 = x_2^*$.

In regression analysis, the term *response variable* is often used in place of the term *dependent variable.* Furthermore, because the multiple regression equation generates a plane or surface, its graph is called a *response surface.*

FIGURE 13.6   GRAPH OF THE REGRESSION EQUATION FOR MULTIPLE REGRESSION ANALYSIS WITH TWO INDEPENDENT VARIABLES

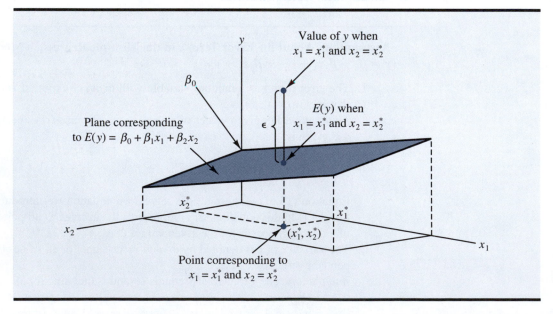

13.5   TESTING FOR SIGNIFICANCE

In this section we show how to conduct significance tests for a multiple regression relationship. The significance tests we used in simple linear regression were a t test and an F test. In simple linear regression, both tests provide the same conclusion; that is, if the null hypothesis is rejected, we conclude that $\beta_1 \neq 0$. In multiple regression, the t test and the F test have different purposes.

1. The F test is used to determine whether a significant relationship exists between the dependent variable and the set of all the independent variables in the model; we will refer to the F test as the test for *overall significance*.
2. If the F test shows an overall significance, the t test is used to determine whether each of the individual independent variables is significant. A separate t test is conducted for each of the independent variables in the model; we refer to each of these t tests as a test for *individual significance*.

In the material that follows, we will explain the F test and the t test and apply each to the Butler Trucking Company example.

F Test

The multiple regression model as defined in Section 13.4 is

$$y = \beta_0 + \beta_1 x_1 + \beta_2 x_2 + \cdots + \beta_p x_p + \epsilon$$

The hypotheses for the F test involve the parameters of the multiple regression model.

$$H_0: \beta_1 = \beta_2 = \cdots = \beta_p = 0$$
$$H_a: \text{One or more of the parameters is not equal to zero}$$

If H_0 is rejected, we have sufficient statistical evidence to conclude that one or more of the parameters is not equal to zero and that the overall relationship between y and the set of independent variables $x_1, x_2, \ldots, x_p$ is significant. However, if H_0 cannot be rejected, we do not have sufficient evidence to conclude that a significant relationship is present.

Before describing the steps of the F test, we need to review the concept of *mean square*. A mean square is a sum of squares divided by its corresponding degrees of freedom. In the multiple regression case, the total sum of squares (SST) has $n - 1$ degrees of freedom, the sum of squares due to regression (SSR) has p degrees of freedom, and the sum of squares due to error (SSE) has $n - p - 1$ degrees of freedom. Hence, the mean square due to regression (MSR) is SSR/p and the mean square due to error (MSE) is SSE/$(n - p - 1)$.

$$MSR = \frac{SSR}{p} \tag{13.12}$$

and

$$MSE = \frac{SSE}{n - p - 1} \tag{13.13}$$

As discussed in Chapter 12, MSE provides an unbiased estimate of σ^2, the variance of the error term ϵ. If H_0: $\beta_1 = \beta_2 = \cdots = \beta_p = 0$ is true, MSR also provides an unbiased estimate of σ^2, and the value of MSR/MSE should be close to 1. However, if H_0 is false, MSR overestimates σ^2 and the value of MSR/MSE becomes larger. To determine how large the value of MSR/MSE must be to reject H_0, we make use of the fact that if H_0 is true and the assumptions about the multiple regression model are valid, the sampling distribution of MSR/MSE is an F distribution with p degrees of freedom in the numerator and $n - p - 1$ degrees of freedom in the denominator. A summary of the F test for significance in multiple regression follows.

F Test for Overall Significance

$$H_0\text{: } \beta_1 = \beta_2 = \cdots = \beta_p = 0$$

H_a: One or more of the parameters is not equal to zero

F Test Statistic

$$F = \frac{\text{MSR}}{\text{MSE}} \tag{13.14}$$

Rejection Rule

Using test statistic: Reject H_0 if $F > F_\alpha$

Using p-value: Reject H_0 if p-value $< \alpha$

where F_α is based on an F distribution with p degrees of freedom in the numerator and $n - p - 1$ degrees of freedom in the denominator.

Let us apply the F test to the Butler Trucking Company multiple regression problem. With two independent variables, the hypotheses are written as follows.

$$H_0\text{: } \beta_1 = \beta_2 = 0$$
$$H_a\text{: } \beta_1 \text{ and/or } \beta_2 \text{ is not equal to zero}$$

Figure 13.7 shows a portion of the Excel output shown previously in Figure 13.4, with miles traveled (x_1) and number of deliveries (x_2) as the two independent variables. In the analysis of variance part of the output, we see that MSR $= 10.8003$ and MSE $= .3285$. Using equation (13.14), we obtain the test statistic.

$$F = \frac{10.8003}{.3285} = 32.9$$

With a level of significance $\alpha = .01$, Table 4 of Appendix B shows that with two degrees of freedom in the numerator and seven degrees of freedom in the denominator, $F_{.01} = 9.55$. With $32.9 > 9.55$, we reject H_0: $\beta_1 = \beta_2 = 0$ and conclude that a significant relationship is present between travel time y and the two independent variables, miles traveled and number of deliveries. The Significance F or p-value $= .0003$ in the last column of the analysis of variance table (Figure 13.7) also indicates that we can reject H_0: $\beta_1 = \beta_2 = 0$ because the p-value is less than α.

FIGURE 13.7   PARTIAL EXCEL OUTPUT FOR THE BUTLER TRUCKING PROBLEM
WITH TWO INDEPENDENT VARIABLES

	A	B	C	D	E	F	G	H	I
13	SUMMARY OUTPUT								
14									
15	*Regression Statistics*								
16	Multiple R	0.9507							
17	R Square	0.9038							
18	Adjusted R Square	0.8763							
19	Standard Error	0.5731							
20	Observations	10							
21									
22	ANOVA								
23		*df*	*SS*	*MS*	*F*	*Significance F*			
24	Regression	2	21.6006	10.8003	32.8784	0.0003			
25	Residual	7	2.2994	0.3285					
26	Total	9	23.9						
27									
28		*Coefficients*	*Standard Error*	*t Stat*	*P-value*				
29	Intercept	-0.8687	0.9515	-0.9129	0.3916				
30	Miles	0.0611	0.0099	6.1824	0.0005				
31	Deliveries	0.9234	0.2211	4.1763	0.0042				
32									
33									
34									
35									

The *Significance F* value in cell F24 is the *p*-value used to test for overall significance.

The *p*-value in cell E30 is used to test for the individual significance of Miles.

The *p*-value in cell E31 is used to test for the individual significance of Deliveries.

Note: Rows 1–12 are hidden.

As noted previously, the mean square error provides an unbiased estimate of σ^2, the variance of the error term ϵ. Referring to Figure 13.7, we see that the estimate of σ^2 is MSE = .3285. The square root of MSE is the estimate of the standard deviation of the error term. This standard deviation is called the standard error of the estimate and is denoted s. Hence, we have $s = \sqrt{\text{MSE}} = \sqrt{.3285} = .5731$. Note that the value of the standard error of the estimate appears in cell B19 of the Excel output in Figure 13.7.

Table 13.3 is the general analysis of variance (ANOVA) table that provides the F test results for a multiple regression model. The test statistic F appears in the last column and

TABLE 13.3   ANOVA TABLE FOR A MULTIPLE REGRESSION MODEL
WITH p INDEPENDENT VARIABLES

Source	Sum of Squares	Degrees of Freedom	Mean Square	F
Regression	SSR	p	$\text{MSR} = \dfrac{\text{SSR}}{p}$	$F = \dfrac{\text{MSR}}{\text{MSE}}$
Error	SSE	$n - p - 1$	$\text{MSE} = \dfrac{\text{SSE}}{n - p - 1}$	
Total	SST	$n - 1$		

can be compared to F_α with p degrees of freedom in the numerator and $n - p - 1$ degrees of freedom in the denominator to make the hypothesis testing conclusion. By reviewing the Excel output for Butler Trucking Company in Figure 13.7, we see that Excel's analysis of variance table contains this information as well as the p-value for the F test.

t Test

If the F test shows that the multiple regression relationship is significant, a t test can be conducted to determine the significance of each of the individual parameters. The t test for individual significance follows.

---

t Test for Individual Significance

For any parameter β_i

$$H_0: \beta_i = 0$$
$$H_a: \beta_i \neq 0$$

t Test Statistic

$$t = \frac{b_i}{s_{b_i}} \qquad (13.15)$$

Rejection Rule

Using test statistic: Reject H_0 if $t < -t_{\alpha/2}$ or if $t > t_{\alpha/2}$

Using p-value: Reject H_0 if p-value $< \alpha$

where $t_{\alpha/2}$ is based on a t distribution with $n - p - 1$ degrees of freedom.

In the test statistic, s_{b_i} is the estimate of the standard deviation or standard error of b_i. The value of s_{b_i} will be provided by the computer software package.

Let us conduct the t test for the Butler Trucking regression problem. Refer to cells B30:E31 in the Excel output shown in Figure 13.7. Values of b_1, b_2, s_{b_1}, and s_{b_2} are as follows.

$$b_1 = .0611 \quad s_{b_1} = .0099$$
$$b_2 = .9234 \quad s_{b_2} = .2211$$

Using equation (13.15), we obtain the test statistic for the hypotheses involving parameters β_1 and β_2.

The t values in the Excel output are 6.1824 and 4.1763. The difference is due to rounding.

$$t = .0611/.0099 = 6.1717$$
$$t = .9234/.2211 = 4.1764$$

Note that both of these t test values are provided by the Excel output in Figure 13.7. Using $\alpha = .01$ and $n - p - 1 = 10 - 2 - 1 = 7$ degrees of freedom, we can use Table 2 of Appendix B to find $t_{.005} = 3.499$. With $6.1717 > 3.499$, we reject $H_0: \beta_1 = 0$. Similarly, with

$4.1764 > 3.499$, we reject H_0: $\beta_2 = 0$. Note that the p-values of .0005 and .0042 on the Excel output also indicate rejection of these hypotheses at the $\alpha = .01$ level of significance. Hence, both parameters are statistically significant.

Multicollinearity

We have used the term *independent variable* in regression analysis to refer to any variable being used to predict or explain the value of the dependent variable. The term does not mean, however, that the independent variables themselves are independent in any statistical sense. On the contrary, most independent variables in a multiple regression problem are correlated to some degree with one another. For example, in the Butler Trucking example involving the two independent variables x_1 (miles traveled) and x_2 (number of deliveries), we could treat the miles traveled as the dependent variable and the number of deliveries as the independent variable to determine whether those two variables are themselves related. We could then compute the sample correlation coefficient $r_{x_1 x_2}$ to determine the extent to which the variables are related. Doing so yields $r_{x_1 x_2} = .16$. Thus, we find some degree of linear association between the two independent variables. In multiple regression analysis, **multicollinearity** refers to the correlation among the independent variables.

To provide a better perspective of the potential problems of multicollinearity, let us consider a modification of the Butler Trucking example. Instead of x_2 being the number of deliveries, let x_2 denote the number of gallons of gasoline consumed. Clearly, x_1 (the miles traveled) and x_2 are related; that is, we know that the number of gallons of gasoline used depends on the number of miles traveled. Hence, we would conclude logically that x_1 and x_2 are highly correlated independent variables.

Assume that we obtain the equation $\hat{y} = b_0 + b_1 x_1 + b_2 x_2$ and find that the F test shows the relationship to be significant. Then suppose we conduct a t test on β_1 to determine whether $\beta_1 \neq 0$, and we cannot reject H_0: $\beta_1 = 0$. Does this mean that travel time is not related to miles traveled? Not necessarily. What it probably means is that with x_2 already in the model, x_1 does not make a significant contribution to determining the value of y. This interpretation makes sense in our example; if we know the amount of gasoline consumed, we do not gain much additional information useful in predicting y by knowing the miles traveled. Similarly, a t test might lead us to conclude $\beta_2 = 0$ on the grounds that, with x_1 in the model, knowledge of the amount of gasoline consumed does not add much.

When the independent variables are highly correlated, it is not possible to determine the separate effect of any particular independent variable on the dependent variable.

To summarize, in t tests for the significance of individual parameters, the difficulty caused by multicollinearity is that it is possible to conclude that none of the individual parameters are significantly different from zero when an F test on the overall multiple regression equation indicates a significant relationship. This problem is avoided when there is little correlation among the independent variables.

A sample correlation coefficient greater than $+0.7$ or less than -0.7 for two independent variables is a rule of thumb warning of potential problems with multicollinearity.

Statisticians have developed several tests for determining whether multicollinearity is high enough to cause problems. According to the rule of thumb test, multicollinearity is a potential problem if the absolute value of the sample correlation coefficient exceeds .7 for any two of the independent variables. The other types of tests are more advanced and beyond the scope of this text.

If possible, every attempt should be made to avoid including independent variables that are highly correlated. In practice, however, strict adherence to this policy is rarely possible. When decision makers have reason to believe substantial multicollinearity is present, they must be aware that separating the effects of the individual independent variables on the dependent variable is difficult.

NOTES AND COMMENTS

Ordinarily, multicollinearity does not affect the way in which we perform our regression analysis or interpret the output from a study. However, when multicollinearity is severe—that is, when two or more of the independent variables are highly correlated with one another—we can have difficulty interpreting the results of t tests on the individual parameters. In addition to the type of problem illustrated in this section, severe cases of multicollinearity have been shown to result in least squares estimates that have the wrong sign. That is,

in simulated studies where researchers created the underlying regression model and then applied the least squares technique to develop estimates of β_0, β_1, β_2, and so on, it has been shown that under conditions of high multicollinearity the least squares estimates can have a sign opposite that of the parameter being estimated. For example, β_2 might actually be $+10$ and b_2, its estimate, might turn out to be -2. Thus, little faith can be placed in the individual coefficients if multicollinearity is present to a high degree.

EXERCISES

Methods

19. Exercise 1 used the following estimated regression equation based on 10 observations.

$$\hat{y} = 29.1270 + .5906x_1 + .4980x_2$$

Here SST = 6724.125, SSR = 6216.375, s_{b_1} = .0813, and s_{b_2} = .0567.
   a. Compute MSR and MSE.
   b. Compute F and perform the appropriate F test. Use $\alpha = .05$.
   c. Perform a t test for the significance of β_1. Use $\alpha = .05$.
   d. Perform a t test for the significance of β_2. Use $\alpha = .05$.

20. Refer to the data presented in Exercise 2. The estimated regression equation for these data is

$$\hat{y} = -18.4 + 2.01x_1 + 4.74x_2$$

Here SST = 15,182.9, SSR = 14,052.2, s_{b_1} = .2471, and s_{b_2} = .9484.
   a. Test for a significant relationship among x_1, x_2, and y. Use $\alpha = .05$.
   b. Is β_1 significant? Use $\alpha = .05$.
   c. Is β_2 significant? Use $\alpha = .05$.

21. The following estimated regression equation was developed for a model involving two independent variables.

$$\hat{y} = 40.7 + 8.63x_1 + 2.71x_2$$

After x_2 was dropped from the model, the least squares method was used to obtain an estimated regression equation involving only x_1 as an independent variable.

$$\hat{y} = 42.0 + 9.01x_1$$

   a. Give an interpretation of the coefficient of x_1 in both models.
   b. Could multicollinearity explain why the coefficient of x_1 differs in the two models? If so, how?

Applications

22. Exercise 4 used the following estimated regression equation relating sales to inventory investment and advertising expenditures.

$$\hat{y} = 25 + 10x_1 + 8x_2$$

The data to develop the estimated regression equation came from a survey of 10 stores and resulted in SST = 16,000 and SSR = 12,000.

a. Compute SSE, MSE, and MSR.

b. Use an F test and a .05 level of significance to determine whether there is a relationship among the variables.

23. Refer to Exercise 5.

a. Use $\alpha = .01$ to test the hypotheses

$$H_0: \beta_1 = \beta_2 = 0$$
$$H_a: \beta_1 \text{ and/or } \beta_2 \text{ is not equal to zero}$$

for the model $y = \beta_0 + \beta_1 x_1 + \beta_2 x_2 + \epsilon$, where

$$x_1 = \text{television advertising expenditures (\$1000s)}$$
$$x_2 = \text{newspaper advertising expenditures (\$1000s)}$$

b. Use $\alpha = .05$ to test the significance of β_1. Should x_1 be dropped from the model?

c. Use $\alpha = .05$ to test the significance of β_2. Should x_2 be dropped from the model?

24. Refer to the data in Exercise 6. Use curb weight and horsepower to predict the speed of a sports and GT car at ¼ mile.

a. Use the F test to determine the overall significance of the relationship. What is your conclusion at the .05 level of significance?

b. Use the t test to determine the significance of each independent variable. What is your conclusion at the .05 level of significance?

25. A sample of 16 companies taken from the *Stock Investor Pro* database provided the following data on the price/earnings (P/E) ratio, the gross profit margin, and the sales growth for each company (*Stock Investor Pro*, American Association of Individual Investors, August 21, 1997).

Stocks

Firm	P/E Ratio	Gross Profit Margin (%)	Sales Growth (%)
Abbott Laboratories	22.3	23.7	10.0
American Home Products	22.6	21.1	5.3
Amoco	16.7	11.0	16.5
Bristol Meyers Squibb Co.	25.9	26.6	9.4
Chevron	18.3	11.6	18.4
Exxon	18.7	9.8	8.3
General Electric Company	13.1	13.4	13.1
Hewlett-Packard	23.3	9.7	21.9
IBM	17.3	11.5	5.6
Merck & Co., Inc.	26.2	25.6	18.9

(continued)

Firm	P/E Ratio	Gross Profit Margin (%)	Sales Growth (%)
Mobil	18.7	8.2	8.1
Pfizer	34.6	25.1	12.8
Pharmacia & Upjohn, Inc.	22.3	15.0	2.7
Procter & Gamble Co.	5.4	14.9	5.4
Texaco	12.3	7.3	23.7
Travelers Group, Inc.	28.7	17.8	28.7

a. Determine the estimated regression equation that can be used to predict the price/earnings ratio given the gross profit margin and the sales growth.

b. Use the F test to determine the overall significance of the relationship. What is your conclusion at the .05 level of significance?

c. Use the t test to determine the significance of each independent variable. What is your conclusion at the .05 level of significance?

d. Remove any independent variable that is not significant from the estimated regression equation. What is your recommended estimated regression equation? Compare the R^2 with the value of R^2 from part (a). Discuss the differences.

26. In Exercise 10 an estimated regression equation was developed to relate the rental revenue ($ millions) to the number of cars in service (1000s) and the number of locations.

a. Test for a significant relationship between the dependent variable and the two independent variables. Use $\alpha = .05$.

b. Is the number of cars in service significant? Use $\alpha = .05$.

c. Is the number of locations significant? Use $\alpha = .05$.

13.6 USING THE ESTIMATED REGRESSION EQUATION FOR ESTIMATION AND PREDICTION

The procedures for estimating the mean value of y and predicting an individual value of y in multiple regression are similar to those in simple linear regression. First, recall that in Chapter 12 we showed that the point estimate of the expected value of y for a given value of x was the same as the point estimate of an individual value of y. In both cases, we used $\hat{y} = b_0 + b_1 x$ as the point estimate.

In multiple regression we use the same procedure; that is, we substitute the given values of $x_1, x_2, \ldots, x_p$ into the estimated regression equation and use the corresponding value of $\hat{y}$ as the point estimate. Suppose that for the Butler Trucking example we want to use the estimated regression equation involving x_1 (miles traveled) and x_2 (number of deliveries) to develop two estimates:

1. A *confidence interval estimate* of the mean travel time for all trucks that travel 100 miles and make two deliveries.

2. A *prediction interval estimate* of the travel time for *one specific* truck that travels 100 miles and makes two deliveries.

Using the estimated regression equation $\hat{y} = -.8687 + .0611x_1 + .9234x_2$ with $x_1 = 100$ and $x_2 = 2$, we obtain the following value of $\hat{y}$.

$$\hat{y} = -.8687 + .0611(100) + .9234(2) = 7.09$$

Hence, the point estimate of travel time in both cases is approximately 7 hours.

TABLE 13.4   THE 95% CONFIDENCE AND PREDICTION INTERVAL ESTIMATES
FOR BUTLER TRUCKING

Value of x_1	Value of x_2	Value of $\hat{y}$	Confidence Interval		Prediction Interval	
			Lower Limit	**Upper Limit**	**Lower Limit**	**Upper Limit**
50	2	4.035	3.146	4.924	2.414	5.656
50	3	4.958	4.127	5.789	3.369	6.548
50	4	5.882	4.815	6.948	4.157	7.606
100	2	7.092	6.258	7.925	5.500	8.683
100	3	8.015	7.385	8.645	6.520	9.510
100	4	8.938	8.135	9.742	7.363	10.514

The PredInt.xls macro included on the data disk can be used to develop confidence and prediction intervals.

To develop interval estimates for the mean value of y and for an individual value of y, we use a procedure similar to that for regression analysis involving one independent variable. The formulas required are beyond the scope of the text, but computer packages for multiple regression analysis often provide confidence intervals once the values of x_1, $x_2, \ldots, x_p$ are specified by the user. Unfortunately, Excel's Regression tool does not have this capability. However, by running the PredInt.xls macro included on the data disk, you will be able to develop confidence and prediction interval estimates. In Table 13.4 we show 95% confidence and prediction interval estimates for the Butler Trucking example for selected values of x_1 and x_2; these values were obtained by using the PredInt macro. Note that the interval estimate for an individual value of y is wider than the interval estimate for the expected value of y. This difference simply reflects the fact that for given values of x_1 and x_2 we can estimate the mean travel time for all trucks with more precision than we can predict the travel time for one specific truck.

EXERCISES

Methods

27. Exercise 1 used the following estimated regression equation based on 10 observations.

$$\hat{y} = 29.1270 + .5906x_1 + .4980x_2$$

a. Develop a point estimate of the mean value of y when $x_1 = 180$ and $x_2 = 310$.
b. Develop a point estimate for an individual value of y when $x_1 = 180$ and $x_2 = 310$.

28. Refer to the data in Exercise 2. The estimated regression equation for those data is

$$\hat{y} = -18.4 + 2.01x_1 + 4.74x_2$$

a. Develop a 95% confidence interval estimate of the mean value of y when $x_1 = 45$ and $x_2 = 15$.
b. Develop a 95% prediction interval estimate of y when $x_1 = 45$ and $x_2 = 15$.

Applications

29. In Exercise 5, the owner of Showtime Movie Theaters, Inc., used multiple regression analysis to predict gross revenue (y) as a function of television advertising expenditures (x_1) and newspaper advertising expenditures (x_2). The estimated regression equation was

$$\hat{y} = 83.2 + 2.29x_1 + 1.30x_2$$

a. What is the gross revenue expected for a week when $3500 is spent on television advertising ($x_1 = 3.5$) and $1800 is spent on newspaper advertising ($x_2 = 1.8$)?

b. Provide a 95% confidence interval estimate for the mean revenue of all weeks with the expenditures listed in part (a).

c. Provide a 95% prediction interval estimate for next week's revenue, assuming that the advertising expenditures will be allocated as in part (a).

30. Exercise 6 provided data for curb weight, horsepower, and speed at ¼ mile for 16 sports and GT cars (*1998 Road and Track Sports & GT Cars*).

a. Estimate the ¼-mile speed of a 1999 Porsche 911 Carrera with a curb weight of 2910 pounds and a horsepower of 296.

b. Provide a 95% confidence interval estimate for the ¼-mile speed of all sports and GT cars with the characteristics listed in part (a).

c. Provide a 95% prediction interval estimate for the 1999 Porsche 911 Carrera described in part (a).

31. In Exercise 9 an estimated regression equation was developed to relate the percentage of students who attend a four-year college to the average class size and the combined SAT score.

a. Develop a 95% confidence interval estimate of the mean percentage of students who attend a four-year college for a school district with an average class size of 25 and whose students have a combined SAT score of 1000.

b. Suppose that a school district in Conway, South Carolina, has an average class size of 25 and a combined SAT score of 950. Develop a 95% prediction interval estimate of the percentage of students who attend a four-year college.

13.7   QUALITATIVE INDEPENDENT VARIABLES

Independent variables may be qualitative or quantitative.

Thus far, the examples given involved quantitative independent variables such as student population, distance traveled, and number of deliveries. In many situations, however, we must work with **qualitative independent variables** such as gender (male, female), method of payment (cash, credit card, check), and so on. The purpose of this section is to show how qualitative independent variables are handled in regression analysis. To illustrate the use and interpretation of a qualitative independent variable, we will consider a problem facing the managers of Johnson Filtration, Inc.

An Example: Johnson Filtration, Inc.

Johnson Filtration, Inc., provides maintenance service for water-filtration systems throughout southern Florida. Customers contact Johnson with requests for maintenance service on their water-filtration systems. To estimate the service time and the service cost, Johnson's managers want to predict the repair time necessary for each maintenance request. Hence, repair time in hours is the dependent variable. Repair time is believed to be related to two factors, the number of months since the last maintenance service and the type of repair problem (mechanical or electrical). Data for a sample of 10 service calls are reported in Table 13.5.

Let y denote the repair time in hours and x_1 denote the number of months since the last maintenance service. The regression model that uses only x_1 to predict y is

$$y = \beta_0 + \beta_1 x_1 + \epsilon$$

Using Excel's Regression tool to develop the estimated regression equation, we obtained the partial Excel output shown in Figure 13.8. The estimated regression equation is

$$\hat{y} = 2.1473 + .3041 x_1 \tag{13.16}$$

TABLE 13.5   DATA FOR THE JOHNSON FILTRATION EXAMPLE

Service Call	Months Since Last Service	Type of Repair	Repair Time in Hours
1	2	electrical	2.9
2	6	mechanical	3.0
3	8	electrical	4.8
4	3	mechanical	1.8
5	2	electrical	2.9
6	7	electrical	4.9
7	9	mechanical	4.2
8	8	mechanical	4.8
9	4	electrical	4.4
10	6	electrical	4.5

At the .05 level of significance, the p-value of .0163 for the t (or F) test indicates that the number of months since the last service is significantly related to repair time. R Square = .5342 indicates that x_1 alone explains 53.42% of the variability in repair time.

To incorporate the type of failure into the regression model, we define the following variable.

$$x_2 = \begin{cases} 0 \text{ if the type of repair is mechanical} \\ 1 \text{ if the type of repair is electrical} \end{cases}$$

FIGURE 13.8   PARTIAL EXCEL OUTPUT FOR THE JOHNSON FILTRATION PROBLEM WITH MONTHS SINCE LAST SERVICE CALL AS THE INDEPENDENT VARIABLE

The Excel regression output appears in a new worksheet because we selected New Worksheet Ply as the Output option in the Regression dialog box.

	A	B	C	D	E	F	G
1	SUMMARY OUTPUT						
2							
3	*Regression Statistics*						
4	Multiple R	0.7309					
5	R Square	0.5342					
6	Adjusted R Square	0.4759					
7	Standard Error	0.7810					
8	Observations	10					
9							
10	ANOVA						
11		*df*	*SS*	*MS*	*F*	*Significance F*	
12	Regression	1	5.5960	5.5960	9.1739	0.0163	
13	Residual	8	4.8800	0.6100			
14	Total	9	10.476				
15							
16		*Coefficients*	*Standard Error*	*t Stat*	*P-value*		
17	Intercept	2.1473	0.6050	3.5493	0.0075		
18	Months	0.3041	0.1004	3.0288	0.0163		
19							

In regression analysis x_2 is called a **dummy** or *indicator* **variable.** Using this dummy variable, we can write the multiple regression model as

$$y = \beta_0 + \beta_1 x_1 + \beta_2 x_2 + \epsilon$$

Table 13.6 is the revised data set that includes the values of the dummy variable. Using Excel and the data in Table 13.6, we can develop estimates of the model parameters. The Excel output in Figure 13.9 shows that the estimated multiple regression equation is

$$\hat{y} = .9305 + .3876x_1 + 1.2627x_2 \tag{13.17}$$

At the .05 level of significance, the Significance F or p-value of .001 associated with the F test ($F = 21.357$) indicates that the regression relationship is significant. The t test part of the output in Figure 13.9 shows that both months since last service (p-value $= .0004$) and type of repair (p-value $= .0051$) are statistically significant. In addition, R Square $= .8592$ and Adjusted R Square $= .8190$ indicate that the estimated regression equation does a good job of explaining the variability in repair times. Thus, equation (13.17) should prove helpful in estimating the repair time necessary for the various service calls.

Interpreting the Parameters

The multiple regression equation for the Johnson Filtration example is

$$E(y) = \beta_0 + \beta_1 x_1 + \beta_2 x_2 \tag{13.18}$$

To understand how to interpret the parameters $\beta_0, \beta_1,$ and β_2 when a qualitative independent variable is present, consider the case when $x_2 = 0$ (mechanical repair). Using $E(y \mid \text{mechanical})$ to denote the mean or expected value of repair time *given* a mechanical repair, we have

$$E(y \mid \text{mechanical}) = \beta_0 + \beta_1 x_1 + \beta_2(0) = \beta_0 + \beta_1 x_1 \tag{13.19}$$

TABLE 13.6   DATA FOR THE JOHNSON FILTRATION EXAMPLE WITH TYPE OF REPAIR
INDICATED BY A DUMMY VARIABLE ($x_2 = 0$ FOR MECHANICAL; $x_2 = 1$
FOR ELECTRICAL)

Customer	Months Since Last Service (x_1)	Type of Repair (x_2)	Repair Time in Hours (y)
1	2	1	2.9
2	6	0	3.0
3	8	1	4.8
4	3	0	1.8
5	2	1	2.9
6	7	1	4.9
7	9	0	4.2
8	8	0	4.8
9	4	1	4.4
10	6	1	4.5

CD file

Johnson

FIGURE 13.9   PARTIAL EXCEL OUTPUT FOR THE JOHNSON FILTRATION PROBLEM WITH MONTHS SINCE LAST SERVICE CALL AND TYPE OF REPAIR AS THE INDEPENDENT VARIABLE

	A	B	C	D	E	F	G
1	SUMMARY OUTPUT						
2							
3	*Regression Statistics*						
4	Multiple R	0.9269					
5	R Square	0.8592					
6	Adjusted R Square	0.8190					
7	Standard Error	0.4590					
8	Observations	10					
9							
10	ANOVA						
11		*df*	*SS*	*MS*	*F*	*Significance F*	
12	Regression	2	9.0009	4.5005	21.357	0.0010	
13	Residual	7	1.4751	0.2107			
14	Total	9	10.476				
15							
16		*Coefficients*	*Standard Error*	*t Stat*	*P-value*		
17	Intercept	0.9305	0.4670	1.9926	0.0866		
18	Months	0.3876	0.0626	6.1954	0.0004		
19	Type	1.2627	0.3141	4.0197	0.0051		
20							

Similarly, for an electrical repair ($x_2 = 1$), we have

$$E(y \mid \text{electrical}) = \beta_0 + \beta_1 x_1 + \beta_2(1) = \beta_0 + \beta_1 x_1 + \beta_2$$
$$= (\beta_0 + \beta_2) + \beta_1 x_1 \tag{13.20}$$

Comparing equations (13.19) and (13.20), we see that the expected value of repair time is a linear function of x_1 for both mechanical and electrical repairs. The slope of both equations is β_1, but the y-intercept differs. The y-intercept is β_0 in equation (13.19) for mechanical repairs and ($\beta_0 + \beta_2$) in equation (13.20) for electrical repairs. The interpretation of β_2 is that it indicates the difference between the expected value of repair time for an electrical repair and the expected value of repair time for a mechanical repair.

If β_2 is positive, the expected value of repair time for an electrical repair will be greater than that for a mechanical repair; if β_2 is negative, the expected value of repair time for an electrical repair will be less than that for a mechanical repair. Finally, if $\beta_2 = 0$, there is no difference in the expected value of repair time between electrical and mechanical repairs and thus the type of repair is not related to the repair time.

Using the estimated multiple regression equation $\hat{y} = .9305 + .3876x_1 + 1.2627x_2$, we see that .9305 is the estimate of β_0 and 1.2627 is the estimate of β_2. Thus, when $x_2 = 0$ (mechanical repair)

$$\hat{y} = .9305 + .3876x_1 \tag{13.21}$$

and when $x_2 = 1$ (electrical repair)

$$\hat{y} = .9305 + .3876x_1 + 1.2627(1)$$
$$= 2.1932 + .3876x_1 \qquad (13.22)$$

In effect, the use of a dummy variable for type of repair provides two equations that can be used to predict the repair time, one corresponding to mechanical repairs and one corresponding to electrical repairs. In addition, with $b_2 = 1.2627$, we learned that, on average, electrical repairs require 1.2627 hours longer than mechanical repairs.

Figure 13.10 is the plot of the Johnson data from Table 13.6. Repair time in hours (y) is represented by the vertical axis, and months since last service (x_1) is represented by the horizontal axis. A data point for a mechanical repair is indicated by an M and a data point for an electrical repair is indicated by an E. Equations (13.21) and (13.22) are plotted on the graph to show graphically the two equations that can be used to predict the repair time, one corresponding to mechanical repairs and one corresponding to electrical repairs.

More Complex Qualitative Variables

Because the qualitative independent variable for the Johnson Filtration example consisted of two levels (mechanical and electrical), defining a dummy variable with zero indicating a mechanical repair and one indicating an electrical repair was easy. However, for a qualitative independent variable with more than two levels, care is required in both defining and

FIGURE 13.10   SCATTER DIAGRAM FOR THE JOHNSON FILTRATION REPAIR DATA
FROM TABLE 13.6

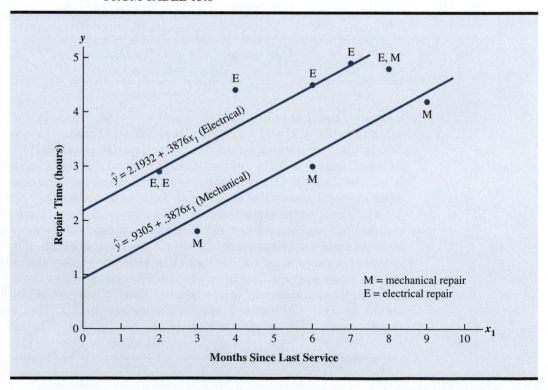

interpreting the dummy variables. As we will show, if a qualitative independent variable has k levels, $k - 1$ dummy variables are needed, with each dummy variable being coded as 0 or 1.

For example, suppose a manufacturer of copy machines organized the sales territories for a particular state into three regions: A, B, and C. The managers want to use regression analysis to help predict the number of copiers sold per week using several independent variables such as the number of sales personnel, advertising expenditures, and so on. Suppose the managers believe sales region is also an important factor in predicting the number of copiers sold. Because sales region is a qualitative variable with three levels, A, B, and C, we need $3 - 1 = 2$ dummy variables to represent the sales region. Each variable can be coded 0 or 1 as follows.

$$x_1 = \begin{cases} 1 \text{ if sales region B} \\ 0 \text{ otherwise} \end{cases}$$

$$x_2 = \begin{cases} 1 \text{ if sales region C} \\ 0 \text{ otherwise} \end{cases}$$

This definition provides the following values of x_1 and x_2.

Region	x_1	x_2
A	0	0
B	1	0
C	0	1

Observations corresponding to region A would be coded $x_1 = 0$, $x_2 = 0$; observations corresponding to region B would be coded $x_1 = 1$, $x_2 = 0$; and observations corresponding to region C would be coded $x_1 = 0$, $x_2 = 1$.

The regression equation relating the expected value of the number of units sold, $E(y)$, to the dummy variables would be written as

$$E(y) = \beta_0 + \beta_1 x_1 + \beta_2 x_2$$

To help us interpret the parameters β_0, β_1, and β_2, consider the following three variations of the regression equation.

$$E(y \mid \text{region A}) = \beta_0 + \beta_1(0) + \beta_2(0) = \beta_0$$
$$E(y \mid \text{region B}) = \beta_0 + \beta_1(1) + \beta_2(0) = \beta_0 + \beta_1$$
$$E(y \mid \text{region C}) = \beta_0 + \beta_1(0) + \beta_2(1) = \beta_0 + \beta_2$$

Thus, β_0 is the mean or expected value of sales for region A; β_1 is the difference between the mean number of units sold in region B and the mean number of units sold in region A; and β_2 is the difference between the mean number of units sold in region C and the mean number of units sold in region A.

Two dummy variables were required because sales region is a qualitative independent variable with three levels. But, the assignment of $x_1 = 0$, $x_2 = 0$ to indicate region A, $x_1 = 1$, $x_2 = 0$ to indicate region B, and $x_1 = 0$, $x_2 = 1$ to indicate region C was arbitrary. For example, we could have chosen $x_1 = 1$, $x_2 = 0$ to indicate region A, $x_1 = 0$, $x_2 = 0$ to indicate region B, and $x_1 = 0$, $x_2 = 1$ to indicate region C. In that case, β_1 would have been interpreted as the mean difference between regions A and B and β_2 as the mean difference between regions C and B.

The important point to remember is that a qualitative independent variable with k levels requires $k - 1$ dummy variables in the multiple regression analysis. Thus, if the sales territory contained a fourth region, labeled D, three dummy variables would be necessary with x_3 defined as follows.

$$x_3 = \begin{cases} 1 \text{ if sales region D} \\ 0 \text{ otherwise} \end{cases}$$

EXERCISES

Methods

32. Consider a regression study involving a dependent variable y, a quantitative independent variable x_1, and a qualitative independent variable with two levels (level 1 and level 2).
   a. Write a multiple regression equation relating x_1 and the qualitative variable to y.
   b. What is the expected value of y corresponding to level 1 of the qualitative variable?
   c. What is the expected value of y corresponding to level 2 of the qualitative variable?
   d. Interpret the parameters in your regression equation.

33. Consider a regression study involving a dependent variable y, a quantitative independent variable x_1, and a qualitative independent variable with three possible levels (level 1, level 2, and level 3).
   a. How many dummy variables are required to represent the qualitative variable?
   b. Write a multiple regression equation relating x_1 and the qualitative independent variable to y.
   c. Interpret the parameters in your regression equation.

Applications

34. The following regression model was proposed to predict sales at a fast-food outlet.

$$y = \beta_0 + \beta_1 x_1 + \beta_2 x_2 + \beta_3 x_3 + \epsilon$$

where

$$x_1 = \text{number of competitors within 1 mile}$$
$$x_2 = \text{population within 1 mile (1000s)}$$
$$x_3 = \begin{cases} 1 \text{ if drive-up window present} \\ 0 \text{ otherwise} \end{cases}$$
$$y = \text{sales (\$1000s)}$$

The following estimated regression equation was developed using the data from a survey of 20 outlets.

$$\hat{y} = 10.1 - 4.2x_1 + 6.8x_2 + 15.3x_3$$

   a. What is the expected amount of sales attributable to the drive-up window?
   b. Predict sales for a store with two competitors, a population of 8000 within 1 mile, and no drive-up window.
   c. Predict sales for a store with one competitor, a population of 3000 within 1 mile, and a drive-up window.

35. Refer to the Johnson Filtration problem introduced in this section. Suppose that in addition to information on the number of months since the machine was serviced and whether a mechanical or an electrical failure had occurred, the managers obtained a list showing which repairperson performed the service. The revised data follow.

Repair

Repair Time in Hours	Months Since Last Service	Type of Repair	Repairperson
2.9	2	Electrical	Dave Newton
3.0	6	Mechanical	Dave Newton
4.8	8	Electrical	Bob Jones
1.8	3	Mechanical	Dave Newton
2.9	2	Electrical	Dave Newton
4.9	7	Electrical	Bob Jones
4.2	9	Mechanical	Bob Jones
4.8	8	Mechanical	Bob Jones
4.4	4	Electrical	Bob Jones
4.5	6	Electrical	Dave Newton

a. Ignore for now the months since the last maintenance service (x_1) and the repairperson who performed the service. Develop the estimated simple linear regression equation to predict the repair time (y) given the type of repair (x_2). Recall that $x_2 = 0$ if the type of repair is mechanical and 1 if the type of repair is electrical.

b. Does the equation you developed in part (a) provide a good fit for the observed data? Explain.

c. Ignore for now the months since the last maintenance service and the type of repair associated with the machine. Develop the estimated simple linear regression equation to predict the repair time given the repairperson who performed the service. Let $x_3 = 0$ if Bob Jones performed the service and $x_3 = 1$ if Dave Newton performed the service.

d. Does the equation you developed in part (c) provide a good fit for the observed data? Explain.

36. Refer to Exercise 35 as you answer the following questions.

a. Develop the estimated regression equation to predict the repair time given the number of months since the last maintenance service, the type of repair, and the repairperson who performed the service.

b. At the .05 level of significance, test whether the estimated regression equation developed in part (a) represents an overall significant relationship between the independent variables and the dependent variable.

c. Is the addition of the independent variable x_3, the repairperson who performed the service, statistically significant? Use $\alpha = .05$. What explanation can you give for the results observed?

37. The National Football League rates prospects position by position on a scale that ranges from 5 to 9. The ratings are interpreted as follows: 8.0–9.0 should start the first year; 7.0–7.9 should start; 6.0–6.9 will make the team as backup; and 5.0–5.9 can make the club and contribute. The following table shows the position, weight, speed (for 40 yards), and ratings for 25 NFL prospects (*USA Today*, April 14, 2000).

Football

Name	Position	Weight (pounds)	Speed (seconds)	Rating
Cosey Coleman	Guard	322	5.38	7.4
Travis Claridge	Guard	303	5.18	7.0
Kaulana Noa	Guard	317	5.34	6.8

(*continued*)

Name	Position	Weight (pounds)	Speed (seconds)	Rating
Leander Jordan	Guard	330	5.46	6.7
Chad Clifton	Guard	334	5.18	6.3
Manula Savea	Guard	308	5.32	6.1
Ryan Johanningmeir	Guard	310	5.28	6.0
Mark Tauscher	Guard	318	5.37	6.0
Blaine Saipaia	Guard	321	5.25	6.0
Richard Mercier	Guard	295	5.34	5.8
Damion McIntosh	Guard	328	5.31	5.3
Jeno James	Guard	320	5.64	5.0
Al Jackson	Guard	304	5.20	5.0
Chris Samuels	Offensive tackle	325	4.95	8.5
Stockar McDougle	Offensive tackle	361	5.50	8.0
Chris McIngosh	Offensive tackle	315	5.39	7.8
Adrian Klemm	Offensive tackle	307	4.98	7.6
Todd Wade	Offensive tackle	326	5.20	7.3
Marvel Smith	Offensive tackle	320	5.36	7.1
Michael Thompson	Offensive tackle	287	5.05	6.8
Bobby Williams	Offensive tackle	332	5.26	6.8
Darnell Alford	Offensive tackle	334	5.55	6.4
Terrance Beadles	Offensive tackle	312	5.15	6.3
Tutan Reyes	Offensive tackle	299	5.35	6.1
Greg Robinson-Ran	Offensive tackle	333	5.59	6.0

a. Develop a dummy variable that will account for the player's position.
b. Develop an estimated regression equation to show how rating is related to position, weight, and speed.
c. At the .05 level of significance, test whether the estimated regression equation developed in part (b) indicates an overall significant relationship between the independent variables and the dependent variable.
d. Does the estimated regression equation provide a good fit for the observed data? Explain.
e. Is position a significant factor in the player's rating? Use $\alpha = .05$. Explain.
f. Suppose a new offensive tackle prospect who weighs 300 pounds ran the 40 yards in 5.1 seconds. Use the estimated regression equation developed in part (b) to estimate the rating for this player.

38. A 10-year study conducted by the American Heart Association provided data on how age, blood pressure, and smoking relate to the risk of strokes. Assume that the following data are from a portion of this study. Risk is interpreted as the probability (times 100) that the patient will have a stroke over the next 10-year period. For the smoking variable, define a dummy variable with 1 indicating a smoker and 0 indicating a nonsmoker.

CD file

Stroke

Risk	Age	Blood Pressure	Smoker
12	57	152	No
24	67	163	No
13	58	155	No
56	86	177	Yes
28	59	196	No

Risk	Age	Blood Pressure	Smoker
51	76	189	Yes
18	56	155	Yes
31	78	120	No
37	80	135	Yes
15	78	98	No
22	71	152	No
36	70	173	Yes
15	67	135	Yes
48	77	209	Yes
15	60	199	No
36	82	119	Yes
8	66	166	No
34	80	125	Yes
3	62	117	No
37	59	207	Yes

a. Using these data, develop an estimated regression equation that relates risk of a stroke to the person's age, blood pressure, and whether the person is a smoker.

b. Is smoking a significant factor in the risk of a stroke? Explain. Use $\alpha = .05$.

c. What is the probability of a stroke over the next 10 years for Art Speen, a 68-year-old smoker who has blood pressure of 175? What action might the physician recommend for this patient?

SUMMARY

In this chapter, we introduced multiple regression analysis as an extension of simple linear regression analysis presented in Chapter 12. Multiple regression analysis enables us to understand how a dependent variable is related to two or more independent variables. The regression equation $E(y) = \beta_0 + \beta_1 x_1 + \beta_2 x_2 + \cdots + \beta_p x_p$ shows that the mean or expected value of the dependent variable y is related to the values of the independent variables x_1, $x_2, \ldots, x_p$. Sample data and the least squares method are used to develop the estimated regression equation $\hat{y} = b_0 + b_1 x_1 + b_2 x_2 + \cdots + b_p x_p$. In effect $b_0, b_1, b_2, \ldots, b_p$ are sample statistics used to estimate the unknown model parameters $\beta_0, \beta_1, \beta_2, \ldots, \beta_p$. Excel output used throughout the chapter emphasizes the fact that statistical software packages are the only realistic means of performing the numerous computations required in multiple regression analysis.

The multiple coefficient of determination provides a measure of the goodness of fit of the estimated regression equation. It determines the proportion of the variation of y that can be explained by the estimated regression equation. The adjusted multiple coefficient of determination, a similar measure of goodness of fit, adjusts for the number of independent variables and thus avoids overestimating the impact of adding more independent variables.

An F test and a t test offer ways to determine statistically whether the relationship among the variables is significant. The F test determines whether a significant overall relationship can be demonstrated between the dependent variable and the set of all the independent variables used. The t test determines whether a significant relationship exists between the dependent variable and a single independent variable given the other independent variables in the regression model. Correlation among the independent variables is known as multi-collinearity. Highly correlated independent variables should not be used in a regression model.

The chapter concluded with a section that showed how dummy variables can be used to incorporate qualitative independent variables into multiple regression analysis.

GLOSSARY

Multiple regression analysis   Regression analysis involving two or more independent variables.

Multiple regression model   The mathematical equation that describes how the dependent variable y is related to the independent variables $x_1, x_2, \ldots, x_p$ and an error term ϵ; it is $y = \beta_0 + \beta_1 x_1 + \beta_2 x_2 + \cdots + \beta_p x_p + \epsilon$.

Multiple regression equation   The mathematical equation that describes how the mean or expected value of the dependent variable y is related to the independent variables $x_1, x_2, \ldots, x_p$; it is $E(y) = \beta_0 + \beta_1 x_1 + \beta_2 x_2 + \cdots + \beta_p x_p$.

Estimated multiple regression equation   The estimate of the multiple regression equation based on sample data and the least squares method; it is $\hat{y} = b_0 + b_1 x_1 + b_2 x_2 + \cdots + b_p x_p$.

Least squares method   The method used to develop the estimated regression equation. It minimizes the sum of squared residuals (the deviations between the observed values of the dependent variable y_i and the estimated values of the dependent variable $\hat{y}_i$).

Multiple coefficient of determination   A measure of the goodness of fit of the estimated multiple regression equation. It can be interpreted as the proportion of the variability in the dependent variable that is explained by the estimated regression equation.

Adjusted multiple coefficient of determination   A measure of the goodness of fit of the estimated multiple regression equation that adjusts for the number of independent variables in the model and thus avoids overestimating the impact of adding more independent variables.

Multicollinearity   The term used to describe the correlation among the independent variables.

Qualitative independent variable   An independent variable with qualitative data.

Dummy variable   A variable, coded as 0 or 1, used to model the effect of qualitative independent variables. A dummy variable is also called an indicator variable.

KEY FORMULAS

Multiple Regression Model

$$y = \beta_0 + \beta_1 x_1 + \beta_2 x_2 + \cdots + \beta_p x_p + \epsilon \tag{13.1}$$

Multiple Regression Equation

$$E(y) = \beta_0 + \beta_1 x_1 + \beta_2 x_2 + \cdots + \beta_p x_p \tag{13.2}$$

Estimated Multiple Regression Equation

$$\hat{y} = b_0 + b_1 x_1 + b_2 x_2 + \cdots + b_p x_p \tag{13.3}$$

Multiple Coefficient of Determination

$$R^2 = \frac{SSR}{SST} \tag{13.8}$$

Adjusted Multiple Coefficient of Determination

$$R_a^2 = 1 - (1 - R^2)\frac{n-1}{n-p-1} \tag{13.9}$$

Mean Square Due to Regression

$$MSR = \frac{SSR}{p} \tag{13.12}$$

Mean Square Due to Error

$$MSE = \frac{SSE}{n-p-1} \tag{13.13}$$

F Test Statistic for Overall Significance

$$F = \frac{MSR}{MSE} \tag{13.14}$$

t Test Statistic for Individual Significance

$$t = \frac{b_i}{s_{b_i}} \tag{13.15}$$

SUPPLEMENTARY EXERCISES

39. The personnel director for Electronics Associates developed the following estimated regression equation relating an employee's score on a job satisfaction test to his or her length of service and wage rate.

$$\hat{y} = 14.4 - 8.69x_1 + 13.5x_2$$

where

$$x_1 = \text{length of service (years)}$$
$$x_2 = \text{wage rate (dollars)}$$
$$y = \text{job satisfaction test score (higher scores}$$
$$\text{indicate greater job satisfaction)}$$

    a. Interpret the coefficients in this estimated regression equation.
    b. Develop an estimate of the job satisfaction test score for an employee who has 4 years of service and makes $6.50 per hour.

40. The admissions officer for Clearwater College developed the following estimated regression equation relating the final college GPA to the student's high-school GPA and SAT mathematics score.

$$\hat{y} = -1.41 + .0235x_1 + .00486x_2$$

where

$$x_1 = \text{high-school grade point average}$$
$$x_2 = \text{SAT mathematics score}$$
$$y = \text{final college grade point average}$$

a. Interpret the coefficients in this estimated regression equation.
b. Estimate the final college GPA for a student who has a high-school GPA of 84 and a score of 540 on the SAT mathematics test.

41. Recall that in Exercise 40, the admissions officer for Clearwater College developed estimated regression equation relating final college GPA to the student's SAT mathematics score and high-school GPA.

$$\hat{y} = -1.41 + .0235x_1 + .00486x_2$$

where

$$x_1 = \text{high-school grade point average}$$
$$x_2 = \text{SAT mathematics score}$$
$$y = \text{final college grade point average}$$

A portion of the Excel Regression tool output follows.

	A	B	C	D	E	F	G
1	SUMMARY OUTPUT						
2							
3	*Regression Statistics*						
4	Multiple R						
5	R Square						
6	Adjusted R Square						
7	Standard Error						
8	Observations						
9							
10	ANOVA						
11		*df*	*SS*	*MS*	*F*	*Significance F*	
12	Regression		1.76209				
13	Residual						
14	Total	9	1.88				
15							
16		*Coefficients*	*Standard Error*	*t Stat*	*P-value*		
17	Intercept	-1.4053	0.4848				
18	X1	0.023467	0.0086666				
19	X2	0.00486	0.001077				
20							

a. Complete the missing entries in this output.
b. Using $\alpha = .05$, test for overall significance.

   c. Did the estimated regression equation provide a good fit to the data? Explain.

   d. Use the t test and $\alpha = .05$ to test H_0: $\beta_1 = 0$ and H_0: $\beta_2 = 0$.

42. Recall that in Exercise 39 the personnel director for Electronics Associates developed the following estimated regression equation relating an employee's score on a job satisfaction test to length of service and wage rate.

$$\hat{y} = 14.4 - 8.69x_1 + 13.5x_2$$

where

$$x_1 = \text{length of service (years)}$$
$$x_2 = \text{wage rate (dollars)}$$
$$y = \text{job satisfaction test score (higher scores}$$
$$\text{indicate greater job satisfaction)}$$

A portion of Excel's Regression tool output follows.

	A	B	C	D	E	F	G
1	SUMMARY OUTPUT						
2							
3	*Regression Statistics*						
4	Multiple R						
5	R Square						
6	Adjusted R Square						
7	Standard Error	3.773					
8	Observations						
9							
10	ANOVA						
11		*df*	*SS*	*MS*	*F*	*Significance F*	
12	Regression						
13	Residual		71.17				
14	Total		720				
15							
16		*Coefficients*	*Standard Error*	*t Stat*	*P-value*		
17	Intercept	14.4	8.191				
18	X1	-8.69	1.555				
19	X2	13.517	2.085				
20							

   a. Complete the missing entries in this output.

   b. Using $\alpha = .05$, test for overall significance.

   c. Did the estimated regression equation provide a good fit to the data? Explain.

   d. Use the t test and $\alpha = .05$ to test H_0: $\beta_1 = 0$ and H_0: $\beta_2 = 0$.

43. A sample of 30 computer hardware companies taken from the *Stock Investor Pro* provided the following data on the price per share, book value per share, and the return on equity for each company (*Stock Investor Pro*, American Association of Individual Investors, August 21, 1997).

Computer

Company	Price per Share	Book Value per Share	Return on Equity (%)
Amdahl Corporation	12.31	4.94	−49.7
Apple Computer, Inc.	21.75	9.46	−71.8
Auspex Systems, Inc.	11.00	4.95	17.2
Capital Associates	3.25	4.33	5.1
Compaq Computer Corp.	65.50	9.58	20.8
Data General Corporation	35.94	8.46	13.3
Dell Computer Corporation	82.06	2.33	74.5
Digi International	15.00	7.35	−11.9
Digital Equipment Corp.	43.00	22.40	−12.9
En Pointe Technologies	14.25	4.11	18.8
Equitrac Corporation	16.25	6.83	10.7
Franklin Electronic Pbls.	12.88	9.13	9.0
Gateway 2000, Inc.	39.13	6.07	28.8
Hewlett-Packard Company	61.50	14.14	18.7
IBM	101.38	20.12	29.9
Ingram Micro, Inc.	28.75	6.35	15.1
Maxwell Technologies, Inc.	30.50	3.78	11.8
MicroAge, Inc.	27.19	12.59	9.8
Micron Electronics, Inc.	16.31	3.64	28.3
Network Computing Devices	11.88	3.56	4.0
Pomeroy Computer Resources	33.00	10.03	16.5
Sequent Computer Systems	28.19	10.64	3.3
Silicon Graphics, Inc.	27.44	9.12	−4.3
Southern Electronics Corp.	15.13	6.15	16.1
Stratus Computer, Inc.	55.50	22.38	11.1
Sun Microsystems, Inc.	48.00	6.40	26.2
Tandem Computers, Inc.	34.24	9.49	8.7
Tech Data Corporation	38.94	10.25	14.3
Unisys Corporation	11.31	0.68	1.6
Vitech America, Inc.	14.63	3.48	24.3

a. Develop an estimated regression equation that can be used to predict the price per share given the book value per share. At the .05 level of significance, test for a significant relationship.

b. Did the estimated regression equation developed in part (a) provide a good fit to the data? Explain.

c. Develop an estimated regression equation that can be used to predict the price per share given the book value per share and the return on equity. At the .05 level of significance, test for overall significance.

44. Following are data on price, curb weight, horsepower, time to go from 0 to 60 miles per hour, and the speed at ¼ mile for 16 sports and GT cars (*1998 Road & Track Sports & GT Cars*).

Auto2

Sports & GT Car	Price ($1000s)	Curb Weight (lbs.)	Horse-power	0 to 60 (seconds)	Speed at ¼ mile (mph)
Acura Integra Type R	25.035	2577	195	7.0	90.7
Acura NSX-T	93.758	3066	290	5.0	108.0
BMW Z3 2.8	40.900	2844	189	6.6	93.2

Sports & GT Car	Price ($1000s)	Curb Weight (lbs.)	Horse-power	0 to 60 (seconds)	Speed at ¼ mile (mph)
Chevrolet Camaro Z28	24.865	3439	305	5.4	103.2
Chevrolet Corvette Convertible	50.144	3246	345	5.2	102.1
Dodge Viper RT/10	69.742	3319	450	4.4	116.2
Ford Mustang GT	23.200	3227	225	6.8	91.7
Honda Prelude Type SH	26.382	3042	195	7.7	89.7
Mercedes-Benz CLK320	44.988	3240	215	7.2	93.0
Mercedes-Benz SLK230	42.762	3025	185	6.6	92.3
Mitsubishi 3000GT VR-4	47.518	3737	320	5.7	99.0
Nissan 240SX SE	25.066	2862	155	9.1	84.6
Pontiac Firebird Trans Am	27.770	3455	305	5.4	103.2
Porsche Boxster	45.560	2822	201	6.1	93.2
Toyota Supra Turbo	40.989	3505	320	5.3	105.0
Volvo C70	41.120	3285	236	6.3	97.0

a. Develop an estimated regression equation with price, curb weight, horsepower, and time to go from 0 to 60 mph as four independent variables to predict the speed at ¼ mile.

b. Use the F test to determine the significance of the regression results. At a .05 level of significance, what is your conclusion?

c. Use the t test to determine the significance of each independent variable. At a .05 level of significance, what is your conclusion?

d. Delete any independent variable that is not significant and provide your recommended estimated regression equation.

45. Nielsen Media Research collects data showing which advertisers get the most exposure during prime time TV on ABC, CBS, NBC, Fox, UPN, and WB networks. Data showing the number of household exposures in millions and the number of times the ad was aired for the week of April 28–May 4, 1997, follow (*USA Today*, May 5, 1997).

Nielsen

Advertised Brand	Times Ad Aired	Household Exposures
Burger King	86	616.7
McDonald's	54	439.2
Sears	33	338.0
Wendy's	28	191.7
Ford Escort	20	174.6
Austin Powers movie	14	161.3
Nissan	16	161.1
Pizza Hut	16	147.7
Saturn	16	146.3
Father's Day movie	11	138.2

a. Develop a scatter diagram with number of times the ad is aired as the independent variable and household exposures as the dependent variable. Is there anything unusual about the pattern of the points in this scatter diagram? Explain.

b. Develop the estimated regression equation showing how the number of times an ad is aired is related to the number of household exposures. Is the relationship between the two variables significant? Use a .05 level of significance.

   c. Consider the addition of the independent variable BigAds, where the value of BigAds is 1 if the number of times an ad is aired is greater than 30, and 0 otherwise. Develop an estimated regression equation that can be used to predict household exposures given the number of times an ad is aired and the dummy variable BigAds.

   d. Using $\alpha = .05$, is the dummy variable added in part (c) significant?

   e. What role does the dummy variable play in modeling the relationship between the number of times an ad is aired and household exposures?

46. Today's marketplace offers a wide choice to buyers of sport utility vehicles (SUVs) and pickup trucks. An important factor to many buyers is the resale value of the vehicle. The following table shows the resale value (%) after two years and the suggested retail price for 10 SUVs, 10 small pickup trucks, and 10 full-size pickup trucks (*Kiplinger's New Cars & Trucks 2000 Buyer's Guide*).

Trucks

Vehicle	Type of Vehicle	Suggested Retail Price ($)	Resale Value (%)
Chevrolet Blazer LS	sport utility	19,495	55
Ford Explorer Sport	sport utility	20,495	57
GMC Yukon XL 1500	sport utility	26,789	67
Honda CR-V	sport utility	18,965	65
Isuzu VehiCross	sport utility	30,186	62
Jeep Cherokee Limited	sport utility	25,745	57
Mercury Mountaineer Monterrey	sport utility	29,895	59
Nissan Pathfinder XE	sport utility	26,919	54
Toyota 4Runner	sport utility	22,418	55
Toyota RAV4	sport utility	17,148	55
Chevrolet S-10 Extended Cab	small pickup	18,847	46
Dodge Dakota Club Cab Sport	small pickup	16,870	53
Ford Ranger XLT Regular Cab	small pickup	18,510	48
Ford Ranger XLT Supercab	small pickup	20,225	55
GMC Sonoma Regular Cab	small pickup	16,938	44
Isuzu Hombre Spacecab	small pickup	18,820	41
Mazda B4000 SE Cab Plus	small pickup	23,050	51
Nissan Frontier XE Regular Cab	small pickup	12,110	51
Toyota Tacoma Xtracab	small pickup	18,228	49
Toyota Tacoma Xtracab V6	small pickup	19,318	50
Chevrolet K2500	full-size pickup	24,417	60
Chevrolet Silverado 2500 Ext	full-size pickup	24,140	64
Dodge Ram 1500	full-size pickup	17,460	54
Dodge Ram Quad Cab 2500	full-size pickup	32,770	63
Dodge Ram Regular Cab 2500	full-size pickup	23,140	59
Ford F150 XL	full-size pickup	22,875	58
Ford F-350 Super Duty Crew Cab XL	full-size pickup	34,295	64
GMC New Sierra 1500 Ext Cab	full-size pickup	27,089	68
Toyota Tundra Access Cab Limited	full-size pickup	25,605	53
Toyota Tundra Regular Cab	full-size pickup	15,835	58

   a. Develop an estimated regression equation that can be used to predict the resale value given the suggested retail price. At the .05 level of significance, test for a significant relationship.

   b. Did the estimated regression equation developed in part (a) provide a good fit to the data? Explain.

c.   Develop an estimated regression equation that can be used to predict the resale value given the suggested retail price and the type of vehicle.
d.   Use the F test to determine the significance of the regression results. At a .05 level of significance, what is your conclusion?

Case Problem 1   CONSUMER RESEARCH, INC.

Consumer Research, Inc., is an independent agency that conducts research on consumer attitudes and behaviors for a variety of firms. In one study, a client asked for an investigation of consumer characteristics that can be used to predict the amount charged by credit card users. Data were collected on annual income, household size, and annual credit card charges for a sample of 50 consumers. The data follow and are on the data disk in the data set named Consumer.

Consumer

Income ($1000s)	Household Size	Amount Charged ($)	Income ($1000s)	Household Size	Amount Charged ($)
54	3	4016	54	6	5573
30	2	3159	30	1	2583
32	4	5100	48	2	3866
50	5	4742	34	5	3586
31	2	1864	67	4	5037
55	2	4070	50	2	3605
37	1	2731	67	5	5345
40	2	3348	55	6	5370
66	4	4764	52	2	3890
51	3	4110	62	3	4705
25	3	4208	64	2	4157
48	4	4219	22	3	3579
27	1	2477	29	4	3890
33	2	2514	39	2	2972
65	3	4214	35	1	3121
63	4	4965	39	4	4183
42	6	4412	54	3	3730
21	2	2448	23	6	4127
44	1	2995	27	2	2921
37	5	4171	26	7	4603
62	6	5678	61	2	4273
21	3	3623	30	2	3067
55	7	5301	22	4	3074
42	2	3020	46	5	4820
41	7	4828	66	4	5149

Managerial Report

1.   Use methods of descriptive statistics to summarize the data. Comment on the findings.
2.   Develop estimated regression equations, first using annual income as the independent variable and then using household size as the independent variable. Which variable is the better predictor of annual credit card charges? Discuss your findings.
3.   Develop an estimated regression equation with annual income and household size as the independent variables. Discuss your findings.

4. What is the predicted annual credit card charge for a three-person household with an annual income of $40,000?

5. Discuss the need for other independent variables that could be added to the model. What additional variables might be helpful?

Case Problem 2   NFL QUARTERBACK RATING

The National Football League (NFL) records weekly performance statistics for individuals and teams. These data can be obtained by accessing the homepage for the NFL (*www.nfl.com*). For many fans, one of the most interesting statistics is the rating used to evaluate the passing performance of quarterbacks. Four categories are used as a basis for compiling a passing rating:

1. Percentage of touchdown passes per attempt
2. Percentage of completions per attempt
3. Percentage of interceptions per attempt
4. Average yards gained per attempt

To illustrate how to compute the rating, consider the performance for Steve Young, the highest rated quarterback in the NFL in 1997. For the 1997 season, Steve Young attempted 356 passes, completed 241 passes for a total of 3029 yards, and had 19 touchdown passes and 6 interceptions. Five steps are needed to compute the passing rating for Steve Young.

Step 1. Compute the ratio of the number of touchdowns (19) to the number of passes attempted (356); the value obtained is $19/356 = 0.0534$. Divide this result by 0.05 to obtain the value for the touchdown component of the rating; the value obtained is $0.0534/0.05 = 1.0680$.

Step 2. Compute the ratio of the number of passes completed (241) to the number of passes attempted (356); the value obtained is $241/356 = 0.6770$. Subtract 0.3 from this result and divide by 0.2 to obtain the value for the second component of the rating; the value obtained is $(0.6770 - 0.3)/0.2 = 1.8850$.

Step 3. Compute the ratio of the number of interceptions (6) to the number of passes attempted (356); the value obtained is $6/356 = 0.0169$. Subtract this value from 0.095 and divide the result by 0.04 to obtain the value for the interceptions component of the rating; the value obtained is $(0.095 - 0.0169)/0.04 = 1.9525$.

Step 4. Compute the ratio of the number of passing yards (3029) to the number of passes attempted (356); the value obtained is $3029/356 = 8.5084$. Subtract 3 from this result and divide by 4 to obtain the value for the yards component of the rating; the value obtained is $(8.5084 - 3)/4 = 1.3771$.

Step 5. Add the results of steps 1 through 4, multiply by 100 and divide by 6. The sum of steps 1 through 4 is $1.0680 + 1.8850 + 1.9525 + 1.3771 = 6.2826$. After multiplying by 100 and dividing by 6 we obtain 104.7100 or 104.7; this figure is the passing rating reported by the NFL for Steve Young.

CD file

NFL

The passing data reported by the NFL for the 1997 season are available on the data disk in the data set named NFL. The labels for the columns are defined as follows:

Att   Number of passes attempted
Comp   Number of passes completed
Comp%   Number of passes completed divided by the number of passes attempted
        times 100
Yds   Number of yards obtained passing

Yds/Att	Number of yards obtained passing divided by the number of passes attempted
TD	Number of touchdowns obtained passing
TD%	Number of touchdowns divided by the number of passes attempted times 100
Long	Longest pass completed
Int	Number of interceptions thrown
Int%	Number of interceptions divided by the number of passes attempted
Rating	The quarterback passing rating

Managerial Report

1. Use methods of descriptive statistics to summarize the data. Comment on the findings.
2. Develop an estimated regression equation that can be used to predict Int% given the value of Comp%. Discuss your findings.
3. Develop an estimated regression equation that can be used to predict Rating. Discuss your findings and comment on how your estimated regression equation relates to the previous discussion of computing passing ratings.
4. If the NFL hired you to compute the passing ratings for next year, what approach would you use? Explain.

Case Problem 3   PREDICTING STUDENT PROFICIENCY TEST SCORES

In order to predict how a school district would have scored when accounting for poverty and other income measures, *The Cincinnati Enquirer* gathered data from the Ohio Department of Education's Education Management Services and the Ohio Department of Taxation (*The Cincinnati Enquirer*, November 30, 1997). First, the newspaper obtained passage-rate data on the math, reading, science, writing, and citizenship proficiency exams given to fourth-, sixth-, ninth-, and twelfth-graders in early 1996. By combining these data, they computed an overall percentage of students who passed the tests for each district.

The percentage of a school district's students on Aid for Dependent Children (ADC), the percentage who qualify for free or reduced-price lunches, and the district's median family income were also recorded. A portion of the data collected for the 608 school districts follows. The complete data set is available on the data disk in the data set named Enquirer.

CD file

Enquirer

Rank	School District	County	% Passed	% on ADC	% Free Lunch	Median Income ($)
1	Ottawa Hills Local	Lucas	93.85	0.11	0.00	48231
2	Wyoming City	Hamilton	93.08	2.95	4.59	42672
3	Oakwood City	Montgomery	92.92	0.20	0.38	42403
4	Madeira City	Hamilton	92.37	1.50	4.83	32889
5	Indian Hill Ex Vill	Hamilton	91.77	1.23	2.70	44135
6	Solon City	Cuyahoga	90.77	0.68	2.24	34993
7	Chagrin Falls Ex Vill	Cuyahoga	89.89	0.47	0.44	38921
8	Mariemont City	Hamilton	89.80	3.00	2.97	31823
9	Upper Arlington City	Franklin	89.77	0.24	0.92	38358
10	Granville Ex Vill	Licking	89.22	1.14	0.00	36235

The data are ranked based on the values in the column labeled % Passed; these data are the overall percentage of students passing the tests. Data in the column labeled % on ADC are the percentage of each school district's students on ADC, and the data in the column labeled % Free Lunch are the percentage of students who qualify for free or reduced-price lunches. The column labeled Median Income shows each district's median family income. Also shown for each school district is the county in which the school district is located. Note that in some cases the value in the % Free Lunch column is 0, indicating that the district did not participate in the free lunch program.

Managerial Report

Use the methods presented in this and previous chapters to analyze this data set. Present a summary of your analysis, including key statistical results, conclusions, and recommendations, in a managerial report. Include any technical material you feel is appropriate in an appendix.

Case Problem 4   ALUMNI GIVING

Alumni donations are an important source of revenue for colleges and universities. If administrators could determine the factors that increase the percentage of alumni who make a donation, they might be able to implement policies that increase revenues. Research shows that students who are more satisfied with their contact with teachers are more likely to graduate. As a result, one might suspect that smaller class sizes and lower student-faculty ratios might lead to a higher percentage of satisfied alumni, which in turn might lead to increases in the percentage of alumni who make a donation. Table 13.7 shows data for 48 national universities (*America's Best Colleges*, Year 2000 Edition). The column labeled Graduation Rate is the percentage of students who initially enrolled at the university and graduated. The column labeled % of Classes Under 20 shows the percentage of classes offered with fewer than 20 students. The column labeled Student-Faculty Ratio is the number of students enrolled divided by the total number of faculty. Finally, the column labeled Alumni Giving Rate is the percentage of alumni who made a donation to the university.

Managerial Report

1. Use methods of descriptive statistics to summarize the data.
2. Develop an estimated regression equation that can be used to predict the alumni giving rate given the percentage of students who graduate. Discuss your findings.
3. Develop an estimated regression equation that could be used to predict the alumni giving rate using any or all of the data provided.
4. What conclusion and recommendations can you derive from your analysis?

TABLE 13.7   ALUMNI DATA FOR 48 NATIONAL UNIVERSITIES

Alumni

Schools	State	Graduation Rate	% of Classes Under 20	Student-Faculty Ratio	Alumni Giving Rate
Boston College	MA	85	39	13	25
Brandeis University	MA	79	68	8	33
Brown University	RI	93	60	8	40
California Institute of Technology	CA	85	65	3	46
Carnegie Mellon University	PA	75	67	10	28
Case Western Reserve Univ.	OH	72	52	8	31
College of William and Mary	VA	89	45	12	27
Columbia University	NY	90	69	7	31
Cornell University	NY	91	72	13	35
Dartmouth College	NH	94	61	10	53
Duke University	NC	92	68	8	45
Emory University	GA	84	65	7	37
Georgetown University	PA	91	54	10	29
Harvard University	MA	97	73	8	46
Johns Hopkins University	MD	89	64	9	27
Lehigh University	PA	81	55	11	40
Massachusetts Inst. of Technology	MA	92	65	6	44
New York University	NY	72	63	13	13
Northwestern University	IL	90	66	8	30
Pennsylvania State Univ.	PA	80	32	19	21
Princeton University	NJ	95	68	5	67
Rice University	TX	92	62	8	40
Stanford University	CA	92	69	7	34
Tufts University	MA	87	67	9	29
Tulane University	LA	72	56	12	17
U. of California–Berkeley	CA	83	58	17	18
U. of California–Davis	CA	74	32	19	7
U. of California–Irvine	CA	74	42	20	9
U. of California–Los Angeles	CA	78	41	18	13
U. of California–San Diego	CA	80	48	19	8
U. of California–Santa Barbara	CA	70	45	20	12
U. of Chicago	IL	84	65	4	36
U. of Florida	FL	67	31	23	19
U. of Illinois–Urbana Champaign	IL	77	29	15	23
U. of Michigan–Ann Arbor	MI	83	51	15	13
U. of North Carolina–Chapel Hill	NC	82	40	16	26
U. of Notre Dame	IN	94	53	13	49
U. of Pennsylvania	PA	90	65	7	41
U. of Rochester	NY	76	63	10	23
U. of Southern California	CA	70	53	13	22
U. of Texas–Austin	TX	66	39	21	13
U. of Virginia	VA	92	44	13	28
U. of Washington	WA	70	37	12	12
U. of Wisconsin–Madison	WI	73	37	13	13
Vanderbilt University	TN	82	68	9	31
Wake Forest University	NC	82	59	11	38
Washington University–St. Louis	MO	86	73	7	33
Yale University	CT	94	77	7	50

CHAPTER 14

Statistical Methods for Quality Control

CONTENTS

Dow Chemical*

FREEPORT, TEXAS

Dow Chemical, Texas Operations, began in 1940 when The Dow Chemical Company purchased 800 acres of Texas land on the Gulf Coast to build a magnesium production facility. That original site, expanded to cover more than 5000 acres, holds one of the largest petrochemical complexes in the world. Among the products from Texas Operations are magnesium, styrene, plastics, adhesives, solvent, glycol, and chlorine. Some products are made solely for use in other processes, but many end up as essential ingredients in products such as pharmaceuticals, toothpastes, dog food, water hoses, ice chests, milk cartons, garbage bags, shampoos, and furniture.

Dow's Texas Operations produce more than 30% of the world's magnesium, an extremely lightweight metal used in products ranging from tennis rackets to suitcases to "mag" wheels. The Magnesium Department was the first group in Texas Operations to train its technical people and managers in the use of statistical quality control. Some of the earliest successful applications of statistical quality control were in chemical processing.

In one application involving the operation of a drier, samples of the output were taken at periodic intervals; the average value for each sample was computed and recorded on a chart called an $\bar{x}$ chart. Such a chart enabled Dow analysts to monitor trends in the output that might indicate the process was not operating correctly. In one instance, analysts began to observe values for the

Statistical quality control has enabled Dow Chemical to improve its processing methods and output. © PhotoDisc, Inc.

sample mean that were not indicative of a process operating within its design limits. On further examination of the control chart and the operation itself, the analysts found that the variation could be traced to problems involving one operator. The $\bar{x}$ chart recorded after retraining of the operator showed a significant improvement in the process quality.

Dow Chemical achieves quality improvements everywhere statistical quality control is applied. Documented savings of several hundred thousand dollars per year are realized, and new applications are continually being discovered.

In this chapter we will show how an $\bar{x}$ chart such as the one used by Dow Chemical can be developed. Such charts are a part of statistical quality control known as statistical process control. We will also discuss methods of quality control for situations in which a decision to accept or reject a group of items is based on a sample.

---

*The authors are indebted to Clifford B. Wilson, Magnesium Technical Manager, The Dow Chemical Company, for providing this Statistics in Practice.

The American Society for Quality (ASQ) defines *quality* as "the totality of features and characteristics of a product or service that bears on its ability to satisfy given needs." In other words, quality measures how well a product or service meets customer needs. Organizations recognize that to be competitive in today's global economy, they must strive for high levels of quality. As a result, they continue to emphasize methods for monitoring and maintaining quality.

Quality assurance refers to the entire system of policies, procedures, and guidelines established by an organization to achieve and maintain quality. Quality assurance consists of two principal functions: quality engineering and quality control. The objective of *quality engineering* is to include quality in the design of products and processes and to identify potential quality problems prior to production. **Quality control** consists of a series of inspections and measurements used to determine whether quality standards are being met. If quality standards are not being met, corrective and/or preventive action can be taken to achieve and maintain conformance. As we will show in this chapter, statistical techniques are extremely useful in quality control.

Dr. W. Edwards Deming is credited with being the person who convinced top managers in Japan to use the methods of statistical quality control.

Traditional manufacturing approaches to quality control are being replaced by improved managerial tools and techniques. Competition with high-quality Japanese products provided the impetus for this evolution. Ironically, it was two U.S. consultants, Dr. W. Edwards Deming and Dr. Joseph Juran, who helped educate the Japanese in quality management.

Although quality is everybody's job, Deming stressed that quality improvements must be led by managers. He developed a list of 14 points that he believed are the key responsibilities of managers. For instance, Deming stated that managers must cease dependence on mass inspection; must end the practice of awarding business solely on the basis of price; must seek continual improvement in all production processes and services; must foster a team-oriented environment; and must eliminate numerical goals, slogans, and work standards that prescribe numerical quotas. Perhaps most important, managers must create a work environment in which a commitment to quality and productivity is maintained at all times.

In 1987, the U.S. Congress enacted Public Law 107, the Malcolm Baldrige National Quality Improvement Act. The Baldrige Award is given annually to U.S. firms that excel in quality. This award, along with the perspectives of individuals such as Dr. Deming and Dr. Juran, has helped top managers recognize that improving service quality and product quality poses the most critical challenge to their companies. Winners of the Malcolm Baldrige Award include Motorola, IBM, Xerox, and FedEx. In this chapter we present two statistical methods used in quality control. The first method, *statistical process control,* uses graphical displays known as *control charts* to monitor a production process; the goal is to determine whether the process can be continued or whether it should be adjusted to achieve a desired quality level. The second method, *acceptance sampling,* is used in situations where a decision to accept or reject a group of items must be based on the quality found in a sample.

The most important use of a control chart is in improving the process.

14.1   STATISTICAL PROCESS CONTROL

In this section we consider quality control procedures for a production process whereby goods are manufactured continuously. On the basis of sampling and inspection of production output, a decision will be made to either continue the production process or adjust it to bring the items or goods being produced up to acceptable quality standards.

Despite high standards of quality in manufacturing and production operations, machine tools invariably wear out, vibrations throw machine settings out of adjustment, purchased materials contain defects, and human operators make mistakes. Any or all of these factors can result in poor quality output. Fortunately, procedures available to monitor production output help detect poor quality early, which allows for the adjustment and correction of the production process.

If the variation in the quality of the production output is due to **assignable causes** such as tools wearing out, incorrect machine settings, poor quality raw materials, or operator error, the process should be adjusted or corrected as soon as possible. Alternatively, if the variation results from **common causes**—that is, randomly occurring variations in materials, temperature, humidity, and so on, which the manufacturer cannot possibly control—the process does not need to be adjusted. The main objective of statistical process control is to determine whether variations in output are due to assignable causes or common causes.

Whenever assignable causes are detected, we conclude that the process is *out of control.* In that case, corrective action should be taken to bring the process back to an acceptable level of quality. However, if the variation in the output of a production process is due only to common causes, we conclude that the process is in *statistical control,* or simply *in control;* in such cases, no changes or adjustments are necessary.

Process control procedures are closely related to hypothesis testing procedures discussed earlier in this text. Control charts provide an ongoing test of the hypothesis that the process is in control.

The statistical procedures for process control are based on the hypothesis testing methodology presented in Chapter 9. The null hypothesis H_0 is formulated in terms of the production process being in control. The alternative hypothesis H_a is formulated in terms of the production process being out of control. Table 14.1 shows that correct are decisions to continue an in-control process and adjust an out-of-control process. However, as with other hypothesis testing procedures, both a Type I error (adjusting an in-control process) and a Type II error (allowing an out-of-control process to continue) are possible.

Control Charts

A **control chart** provides a basis for deciding whether the variation in the output is due to common causes (in control) or assignable causes (out of control). Whenever an out-of-control situation is detected, adjustments and/or other corrective action will be taken to bring the process back into control.

Control charts based on data that can be measured on a continuous scale are called variables control charts. The $\bar{x}$ chart is a variables control chart.

Control charts can be classified by the type of data they contain. An $\bar{x}$ **chart** is used if the quality of the output is measured in terms of a variable such as length, weight, temperature, and so on. In that case, the decision to continue or to adjust the production process will be based on the mean value found in a sample of the output. To introduce some of the concepts common to all control charts, let us consider some specific features of an $\bar{x}$ chart.

Figure 14.1 shows the general structure of an $\bar{x}$ chart. The center line of the chart corresponds to the mean of the process when the process is in control. The vertical line measures

TABLE 14.1   DECISIONS AND STATES OF THE PROCESS

		State of Production Process	
		H_0 True Process in Control	H_0 False Process Out of Control
Decision	**Continue Process**	Correct decision	Type II error (allowing an out-of-control process to continue)
	Adjust Process	Type I error (adjusting an in-control process)	Correct decision

FIGURE 14.1 $\bar{x}$ CHART STRUCTURE

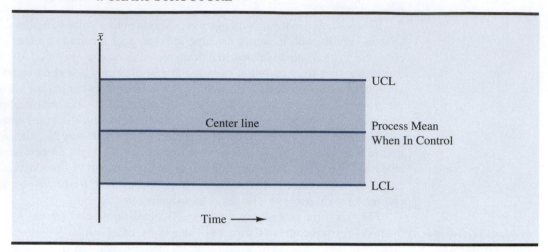

$\bar{x}$ for the variable of interest. Each time a sample is taken from the production process, a value of the sample mean $\bar{x}$ is computed and a data point showing the value of $\bar{x}$ is plotted on the control chart.

The two lines labeled UCL and LCL are important in determining whether the process is in control or out of control. The lines are called the *upper control limit* and the *lower control limit,* respectively. They are chosen so that when the process is in control, there will be a high probability that the value of $\bar{x}$ will be between the two control limits. Values outside the control limits provide strong statistical evidence that the process is out of control and corrective action should be taken.

Over time, more and more data points ($\bar{x}$ values) will be added to the control chart. The order of the data points will be from left to right as the process is sampled. In essence, every time a point is plotted on the control chart, we are carrying out a hypothesis test to determine whether the process is in control.

In addition to the $\bar{x}$ chart, other control charts can be used to monitor the range of the measurements in the sample (R chart), the proportion of defective items in the sample (p chart), and the number of defective items in the sample (np chart). In each case, the control chart contains an LCL line, a center line, and a UCL line similar to the $\bar{x}$ chart in Figure 14.1. The major difference among the charts is what the vertical axis measures; for instance, in a p chart the vertical axis denotes the proportion of defective items in the sample instead of the sample mean. In the following discussion, we will illustrate the construction and use of the $\bar{x}$ chart, R chart, p chart, and np chart.

$\bar{x}$ Chart: Process Mean and Standard Deviation Known

To illustrate the construction of an $\bar{x}$ chart, let us consider the situation at KJW Packaging. This company operates a production line that fills cereal cartons. Suppose KJW has designed the process so that when it is operating correctly—and hence the system is in control—the mean filling weight is $\mu = 16.05$ ounces, and the process standard deviation is $\sigma = .10$ ounces. In addition, assume the filling weights (x) are normally distributed. The normal probability distribution of filling weights is shown in Figure 14.2.

The sampling distribution of $\bar{x}$, as presented in Chapter 7, can be used to determine the expected variation in $\bar{x}$ values for a process that is in control. Let us first briefly review the properties of the sampling distribution of $\bar{x}$. First, recall that the expected value or mean of

FIGURE 14.2   NORMAL PROBABILITY DISTRIBUTION OF CEREAL CARTON
FILLING WEIGHTS

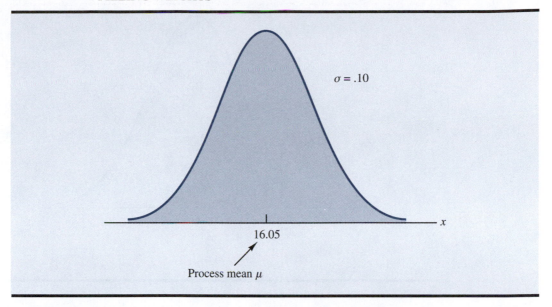

$\bar{x}$, $E(\bar{x})$, is equal to μ; in this case μ is the mean filling weight when the production process is in control. For samples of size n, the formula for the standard deviation of $\bar{x}$, called the *standard error of the mean,* is

$$\sigma_{\bar{x}} = \frac{\sigma}{\sqrt{n}} \qquad (14.1)$$

In addition, because the filling weights (x) are normally distributed, the sampling distribution of $\bar{x}$ is normal for any sample size. Thus, the sampling distribution of $\bar{x}$ is a normal probability distribution with mean μ and standard deviation $\sigma_{\bar{x}}$. This probability distribution is shown in Figure 14.3. Note that the sampling distribution of $\bar{x}$ has the same mean (16.05) as the probability distribution of individual filling weights.

The sampling distribution of $\bar{x}$ is used to determine what values of $\bar{x}$ are reasonable if the process is in control. The general practice in quality control is to define as reasonable any value of $\bar{x}$ that is within 3 standard deviations above or below the mean value μ. Recall from the study of the normal probability distribution, that approximately 99.7% of the values of a normally distributed random variable are within ± 3 standard deviations of its mean value. Thus, if a value of $\bar{x}$ is within the interval $\mu - 3\sigma_{\bar{x}}$ to $\mu + 3\sigma_{\bar{x}}$, we will assume that the process is in control. In summary, then, the control limits for an $\bar{x}$ chart are as follow.

Control Limits for an $\bar{x}$ Chart: Process Mean and Standard Deviation Known

$$UCL = \mu + 3\sigma_{\bar{x}} \qquad (14.2)$$
$$LCL = \mu - 3\sigma_{\bar{x}} \qquad (14.3)$$

Reconsider the KJW Packaging example with the normal probability distribution of filling weights shown in Figure 14.2 and the sampling distribution of $\bar{x}$ shown in Figure 14.3. Assume

FIGURE 14.3   SAMPLING DISTRIBUTION OF $\bar{x}$ FOR A SAMPLE OF n FILLING WEIGHTS

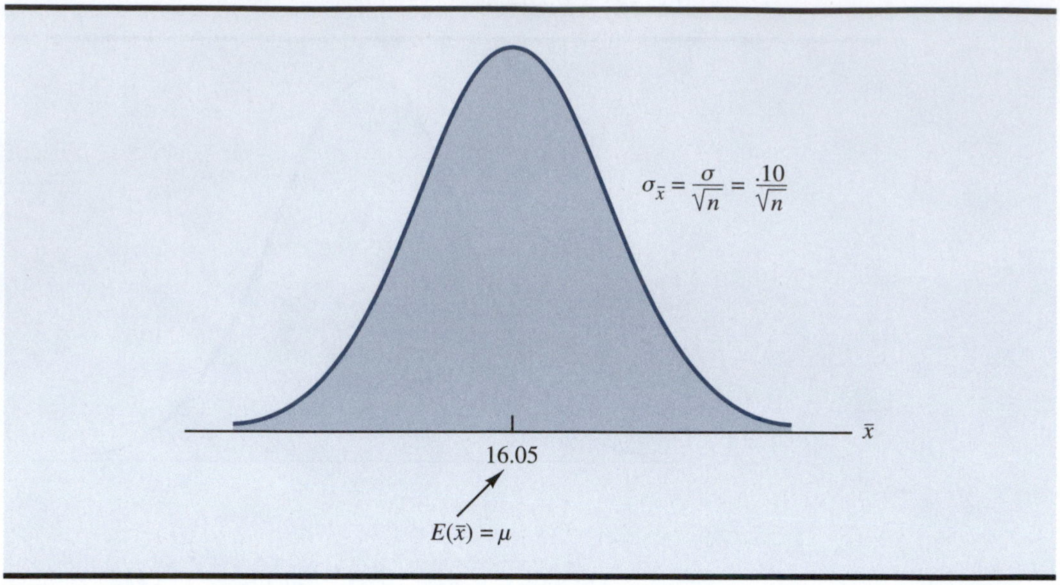

$$\sigma_{\bar{x}} = \frac{\sigma}{\sqrt{n}} = \frac{.10}{\sqrt{n}}$$

16.05

$\bar{x}$

$E(\bar{x}) = \mu$

that a quality control inspector periodically samples six cartons and uses the sample mean filling weight to determine whether the process is in control or out of control. Using equation (14.1), we find that the standard error of the mean is $\sigma_{\bar{x}} = \sigma/\sqrt{n} = .10/\sqrt{6} = .04$. Thus, with the process mean at $\mu = 16.05$, the control limits are UCL = $16.05 + 3(.04) = 16.17$ and LCL = $16.05 - 3(.04) = 15.93$. Figure 14.4 is a control chart showing the results of 10 samples taken over a 10-hour period. For ease of reading, the sample numbers 1 through 10 are listed below the chart.

Note that the mean for the fifth sample in Figure 14.4 shows that the process is out of control. The fifth sample mean is below the LCL indicating that underfilling is occurring and that

FIGURE 14.4 $\bar{x}$ CHART FOR THE CEREAL CARTON FILLING PROCESS

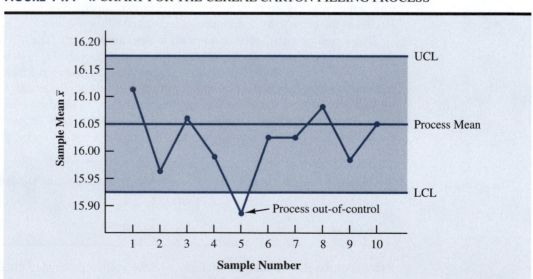

assignable causes of output variation are present. As a result, corrective action was taken at this point to bring the process back into control. The fact that the remaining points on the $\bar{x}$ chart are within the upper and lower control limits indicates that the corrective action was successful.

$\bar{x}$ Chart: Process Mean and Standard Deviation Unknown

In the KJW Packaging example, we showed how an $\bar{x}$ chart can be developed when the mean and standard deviation of the process are known before sampling. In many situations, the process mean and standard deviation must be estimated by using samples that are selected from the process when it is assumed to be operating in control. For instance, KJW might select a random sample of five boxes each morning and five boxes each afternoon for 10 days of operation. For each subgroup, or sample, the mean and standard deviation of the sample are computed. The overall averages of both the sample means and the sample standard deviations can then be used to construct control charts for both the process mean and the process standard deviation.

In practice, it is common to monitor the variability of a production process by using the range instead of the standard deviation because the range is easier to compute. The range can then be used to provide good estimates of the process standard deviation; thus it can be used to construct upper and lower control limits for the $\bar{x}$ chart with little computational effort. To illustrate, let us consider the problem facing Jensen Computer Supplies, Inc.

Jensen Computer Supplies (JCS) manufactures 3.5-inch-diameter computer disks; they have just finished adjusting their production process so that it is operating in control. Suppose random samples of five disks are taken during the first hour of operation, during the second hour of operation, and so on, until 20 samples have been selected. Table 14.2 provides the diameter of each disk sampled as well as the mean $\bar{x}_j$ and range R_j for each of the samples.

TABLE 14.2   DATA FOR JENSEN COMPUTER SUPPLIES

CD file

Jensen

Sample Number	Observations					Sample Mean $\bar{x}_j$	Sample Range R_j
1	3.5056	3.5086	3.5144	3.5009	3.5030	3.5065	.0135
2	3.4882	3.5085	3.4884	3.5250	3.5031	3.5026	.0368
3	3.4897	3.4898	3.4995	3.5130	3.4969	3.4978	.0233
4	3.5153	3.5120	3.4989	3.4900	3.4837	3.5000	.0316
5	3.5059	3.5113	3.5011	3.4773	3.4801	3.4951	.0340
6	3.4977	3.4961	3.5050	3.5014	3.5060	3.5012	.0099
7	3.4910	3.4913	3.4976	3.4831	3.5044	3.4935	.0213
8	3.4991	3.4853	3.4830	3.5083	3.5094	3.4970	.0264
9	3.5099	3.5162	3.5228	3.4958	3.5004	3.5090	.0270
10	3.4880	3.5015	3.5094	3.5102	3.5146	3.5047	.0266
11	3.4881	3.4887	3.5141	3.5175	3.4863	3.4989	.0312
12	3.5043	3.4867	3.4946	3.5018	3.4784	3.4932	.0259
13	3.5043	3.4769	3.4944	3.5014	3.4904	3.4935	.0274
14	3.5004	3.5030	3.5082	3.5045	3.5234	3.5079	.0230
15	3.4846	3.4938	3.5065	3.5089	3.5011	3.4990	.0243
16	3.5145	3.4832	3.5188	3.4935	3.4989	3.5018	.0356
17	3.5004	3.5042	3.4954	3.5020	3.4889	3.4982	.0153
18	3.4959	3.4823	3.4964	3.5082	3.4871	3.4940	.0259
19	3.4878	3.4864	3.4960	3.5070	3.4984	3.4951	.0206
20	3.4969	3.5144	3.5053	3.4985	3.4885	3.5007	.0259

The estimate of the process mean μ developed using k samples of size n is given by the overall sample mean.

Overall Sample Mean

$$\bar{\bar{x}} = \frac{\bar{x}_1 + \bar{x}_2 + \cdots + \bar{x}_k}{k} \qquad (14.4)$$

where

$$\bar{x}_j = \text{mean of the } j\text{th sample } j = 1, 2, \ldots, k$$
$$k = \text{number of samples}$$

For the JCS data in Table 14.2, $k = 20$ and the overall sample mean is $\bar{\bar{x}} = 3.4995$. This value will be the center line for the $\bar{x}$ chart. The range of each sample, denoted R_j, is simply the difference between the largest and smallest values in each sample. The average range for k samples is computed as follows.

Average Range

$$\bar{R} = \frac{R_1 + R_2 + \cdots + R_k}{k} \qquad (14.5)$$

where

$$R_j = \text{range of the } j\text{th sample}, j = 1, 2, \ldots, k$$
$$k = \text{number of samples}$$

For the JCS data in Table 14.2, the average range is $\bar{R} = .0253$.

In the preceding section we showed that the upper and lower control limits for the $\bar{x}$ chart are

$$\mu \pm 3 \frac{\sigma}{\sqrt{n}} \qquad (14.6)$$

The overall sample mean $\bar{\bar{x}}$ is used to estimate μ and the sample ranges are used to develop an estimate of σ.

Hence, to construct the control limits for the $\bar{x}$ chart, we need to estimate μ and σ, the mean and standard deviation of the process. An estimate of μ is given by $\bar{\bar{x}}$. An estimate of σ can be developed by using the range data.

It can be shown that an estimator of the process standard deviation σ is the average range divided by d_2, a constant that depends on the sample size n. That is,

$$\text{Estimator of } \sigma = \frac{\bar{R}}{d_2} \qquad (14.7)$$

The *American Society for Testing and Materials Manual on Presentation of Data and Control Chart Analysis* provides values for d_2 as shown in Table 14.3. For instance, when $n = 5$, $d_2 = 2.326$, and the estimate of σ is the average range divided by 2.326. If we substitute $\bar{\bar{x}}$ for μ and $\bar{R}/d_2$ for σ in equation (14.6), we can write the control limits for the $\bar{x}$ chart as

$$\bar{\bar{x}} \pm 3\,\frac{\bar{R}/d_2}{\sqrt{n}} = \bar{\bar{x}} \pm \frac{3}{d_2\sqrt{n}}\,\bar{R} = \bar{\bar{x}} \pm A_2\bar{R} \qquad (14.8)$$

Note that $A_2 = 3/(d_2\sqrt{n})$ is a constant that depends only on the sample size. Values for A_2 are also provided in Table 14.3. For $n = 5$, $A_2 = .577$; thus, the control limits for Jensen's $\bar{x}$ chart are

$$3.4995 \pm (.577)(.0253) = 3.4995 \pm .0146$$

Hence, UCL = 3.514 and LCL = 3.485.

TABLE 14.3 FACTORS FOR $\bar{x}$ AND R CONTROL CHARTS

Observations in Sample, n	d_2	A_2	d_3	D_3	D_4
2	1.128	1.880	0.853	0	3.267
3	1.693	1.023	0.888	0	2.574
4	2.059	0.729	0.880	0	2.282
5	2.326	0.577	0.864	0	2.114
6	2.534	0.483	0.848	0	2.004
7	2.704	0.419	0.833	0.076	1.924
8	2.847	0.373	0.820	0.136	1.864
9	2.970	0.337	0.808	0.184	1.816
10	3.078	0.308	0.797	0.223	1.777
11	3.173	0.285	0.787	0.256	1.744
12	3.258	0.266	0.778	0.283	1.717
13	3.336	0.249	0.770	0.307	1.693
14	3.407	0.235	0.763	0.328	1.672
15	3.472	0.223	0.756	0.347	1.653
16	3.532	0.212	0.750	0.363	1.637
17	3.588	0.203	0.744	0.378	1.622
18	3.640	0.194	0.739	0.391	1.608
19	3.689	0.187	0.734	0.403	1.597
20	3.735	0.180	0.729	0.415	1.585
21	3.778	0.173	0.724	0.425	1.575
22	3.819	0.167	0.720	0.434	1.566
23	3.858	0.162	0.716	0.443	1.557
24	3.895	0.157	0.712	0.451	1.548
25	3.931	0.153	0.708	0.459	1.541

Source: Adapted from Table 27 of ASTM STP 15D, *ASTM Manual on Presentation of Data and Control Chart Analysis.* Copyright 1976 American Society of Testing and Materials, Philadelphia, PA. Reprinted with permission.

Figure 14.5 shows the $\bar{x}$ chart for Jensen Computer Supplies. We used the data in Table 14.2 and Excel's Chart Wizard to construct the chart. We added the labels for the control limits and center line. The center line is shown at the overall sample mean $\bar{\bar{x}} = 3.499$. The upper control limit (UCL) is 3.514, which is 3 "sigma limits" above $\bar{\bar{x}}$. The lower control limit (LCL) is 3.485, which is 3 "sigma limits" below $\bar{\bar{x}}$. The $\bar{x}$ chart shows the 20 sample means plotted over time. Because all 20 sample means fall within the control limits, our assumption is confirmed that the data were collected during a period the process was in control. This chart can now be used to monitor the process mean on an ongoing basis.

R Chart

Let us now consider a range chart or **R chart** that can be used to control the variability of a process. To develop the R chart, we need to think of the range of a sample as a random variable with its own mean and standard deviation. The average range $\bar{R}$ provides an estimate of the mean of this random variable. Moreover, it can be shown that an estimate of the standard deviation of the range, denoted $\hat{\sigma}_R$, is

$$\hat{\sigma}_R = d_3 \frac{\bar{R}}{d_2} \qquad (14.9)$$

FIGURE 14.5 $\bar{x}$ CHART FOR JENSEN COMPUTER SUPPLIES

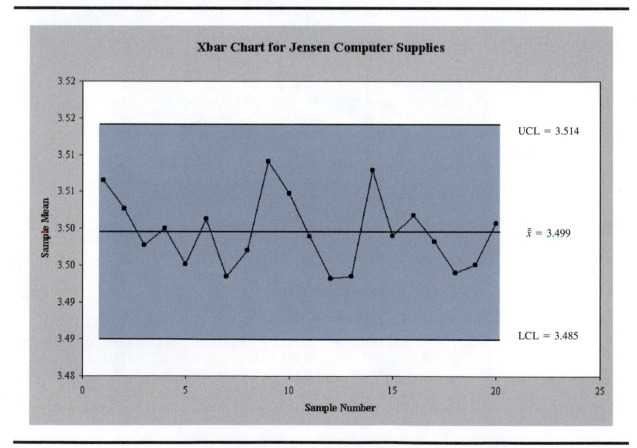

where d_2 and d_3 are constants that depend on the sample size; values of d_2 and d_3 are provided in Table 14.3. Thus, the UCL for the R chart is given by

$$\bar{R} + 3\hat{\sigma}_R = \bar{R} + 3d_3\frac{\bar{R}}{d_2} = \bar{R}\left(1 + 3\frac{d_3}{d_2}\right) \qquad (14.10)$$

and the LCL is

$$\bar{R} - 3\hat{\sigma}_R = \bar{R} - 3d_3\frac{\bar{R}}{d_2} = \bar{R}\left(1 - 3\frac{d_3}{d_2}\right) \qquad (14.11)$$

If we let

$$D_4 = 1 + 3\frac{d_3}{d_2} \qquad (14.12)$$

$$D_3 = 1 - 3\frac{d_3}{d_2} \qquad (14.13)$$

we can write the control limits for the R chart as

$$UCL = \bar{R}D_4 \qquad (14.14)$$
$$LCL = \bar{R}D_3 \qquad (14.15)$$

Values for D_3 and D_4 are also provided in Table 14.3. Note that for $n = 5$, $D_3 = 0$, and $D_4 = 2.114$. Thus, with $\bar{R} = .0253$, the control limits are

$$UCL = .0253(2.114) = .0535$$
$$LCL = .0253(0) = 0$$

Figure 14.6 shows the R chart for Jensen Computer Supplies. We used the data in Table 14.2 and Excel's Chart Wizard to construct the chart. The center line is shown at the overall mean of the 20 sample ranges, $\bar{R} = .0253$. The UCL is .0535 or 3 sigma limits above $\bar{R}$. The LCL is 0.0 or 3 sigma limits below $\bar{R}$. The R chart shows the 20 sample ranges plotted over time. Because all 20 sample ranges are within the control limits, we confirm that the process was in control during the sampling period.

If the R chart indicates that the process is out of control, the $\bar{x}$ chart should not be interpreted until the R chart indicates the process variability is in control.

Using Excel to Construct an R Chart and an $\bar{x}$ Chart

The $\bar{x}$ chart in Figure 14.5 and the R chart in Figure 14.6 were constructed using Excel. Here we show how the data in Table 14.2 can be used to construct an R chart and an $\bar{x}$ chart using Excel. Figure 14.7 is an Excel worksheet containing the Jensen Computer Supplies data. The average value for the range is needed to compute the lower and upper control limits for the $\bar{x}$ chart. So we will construct the R chart first. Our approach will be to first develop a worksheet with the needed data. Then the Chart Wizard will be used to develop the R chart. A similar procedure is followed to construct the $\bar{x}$ chart. Figure 14.8 contains the data developed for the R chart. The formula worksheet is in the background; the value worksheet is in the foreground.

FIGURE 14.6 *R* CHART FOR JENSEN COMPUTER SUPPLIES

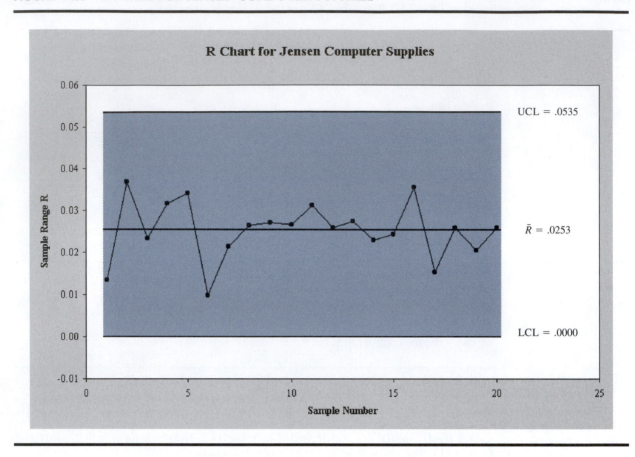

FIGURE 14.7   EXCEL WORKSHEET OF 20 SAMPLES OF SIZE 5 FOR JENSEN COMPUTER SUPPLIES

	A	B	C	D	E	F	G
1	Sample	Observation 1	Observation 2	Observation 3	Observation 4	Observation 5	
2	1	3.5056	3.5086	3.5144	3.5009	3.5030	
3	2	3.4882	3.5085	3.4884	3.5250	3.5031	
4	3	3.4897	3.4898	3.4995	3.5130	3.4969	
5	4	3.5153	3.5120	3.4989	3.4900	3.4837	
6	5	3.5059	3.5113	3.5011	3.4773	3.4801	
19	18	3.4959	3.4823	3.4964	3.5082	3.4871	
20	19	3.4878	3.4864	3.4960	3.5070	3.4984	
21	20	3.4969	3.5144	3.5053	3.4985	3.4885	
22							

Note: Rows 7–18 (samples 6–16) are hidden.

FIGURE 14.8   EXCEL WORKSHEET SHOWING RANGE DATA AND COMPUTATION OF LCL, MEAN, AND UCL FOR AN *R* CHART

	A	B	C	D	E	F
1	Sample	R	LCL	Mean	UCL	
2	1	=MAX(Data!B2:F2)-MIN(Data!B2:F2)	=$D$23*$B$22	=$B$22	=$D$24*$B$22	
3	2	=MAX(Data!B3:F3)-MIN(Data!B3:F3)	=$D$23*$B$22	=$B$22	=$D$24*$B$22	
4	3	=MAX(Data!B4:F4)-MIN(Data!B4:F4)	=$D$23*$B$22	=$B$22	=$D$24*$B$22	
5	4	=MAX(Data!B5:F5)-MIN(Data!B5:F5)	=$D$23*$B$22	=$B$22	=$D$24*$B$22	
6	5	=MAX(Data!B6:F6)-MIN(Data!B6:F6)	=$D$23*$B$22	=$B$22	=$D$24*$B$22	
19	18	=MAX(Data!B19:F19)-MIN(Data!B19:F19)	=$D$23*$B$22	=$B$22	=$D$24*$B$22	
20	19	=MAX(Data!B20:F20)-MIN(Data!B20:F20)	=$D$23*$B$22	=$B$22	=$D$24*$B$22	
21	20	=MAX(Data!B21:F21)-MIN(Data!B21:F21)	=$D$23*$B$22	=$B$22	=$D$24*$B$22	
22	Mean(Rbar)	=AVERAGE($B$2:$B$21)				
23			D3	0		
24			D4	2.114		
25						

	A	B	C	D	E	F
1	Sample	R	LCL	Mean	UCL	
2	1	0.0135	0.0000	0.0253	0.0534	
3	2	0.0368	0.0000	0.0253	0.0534	
4	3	0.0233	0.0000	0.0253	0.0534	
5	4	0.0316	0.0000	0.0253	0.0534	
6	5	0.0340	0.0000	0.0253	0.0534	
19	18	0.0259	0.0000	0.0253	0.0534	
20	19	0.0206	0.0000	0.0253	0.0534	
21	20	0.0259	0.0000	0.0253	0.0534	
22	Mean(Rbar)	0.0253				
23			D3	0.0000		
24			D4	2.1140		
25						

Note: Rows 7–18 (samples 6–17) are hidden.

Enter Data: The data for the diameter measurements for the 20 samples selected by Jensen Computer Supplies are contained in the worksheet in Figure 14.7. We will use the data in this worksheet to construct the worksheets shown in Figures 14.8 and 14.9. For future reference, the worksheet in Figure 14.7 is named Data. The only values entered directly into the worksheets in Figures 14.8 and 14.9 are the sample numbers 1–20 in column A, the heading in cells A1:E1, and cells C23 and C24.

Enter Functions and Formulas: The worksheet in Figure 14.8 contains the formulas needed to construct an *R* chart using the Chart Wizard. Here we describe how this worksheet was constructed. Column A contains the sample numbers 1–20 as noted. Column B contains the Excel formulas needed to compute the range for each sample from the data in cells B2:F21 of the Data worksheet shown in Figure 14.7. Excel's MAX and MIN functions are used. The cell references in the formulas are to cells in the Data worksheet; note that the

FIGURE 14.9   EXCEL WORKSHEET SHOWING $\bar{x}$ DATA AND COMPUTATION OF LCL, MEAN, AND UCL

	A	B	C	D	E	F
1	Sample	xbar	LCL	Mean	UCL	
2	1	=AVERAGE(Data!B2:F2)	=$B$22-$D$23*$D$24	=$B$22	=$B$22+$D$23*$D$24	
3	2	=AVERAGE(Data!B3:F3)	=$B$22-$D$23*$D$24	=$B$22	=$B$22+$D$23*$D$24	
4	3	=AVERAGE(Data!B4:F4)	=$B$22-$D$23*$D$24	=$B$22	=$B$22+$D$23*$D$24	
5	4	=AVERAGE(Data!B5:F5)	=$B$22-$D$23*$D$24	=$B$22	=$B$22+$D$23*$D$24	
6	5	=AVERAGE(Data!B6:F6)	=$B$22-$D$23*$D$24	=$B$22	=$B$22+$D$23*$D$24	
19	18	=AVERAGE(Data!B19:F19)	=$B$22-$D$23*$D$24	=$B$22	=$B$22+$D$23*$D$24	
20	19	=AVERAGE(Data!B20:F20)	=$B$22-$D$23*$D$24	=$B$22	=$B$22+$D$23*$D$24	
21	20	=AVERAGE(Data!B21:F21)	=$B$22-$D$23*$D$24	=$B$22	=$B$22+$D$23*$D$24	
22		Mean	=AVERAGE(B2:B21)			
23			A2	0.577		
24			Rbar	0.025275		
25						

	A	B	C	D	E	F
1	Sample	xbar	LCL	Mean	UCL	
2	1	3.5065	3.4849	3.4995	3.5141	
3	2	3.5026	3.4849	3.4995	3.5141	
4	3	3.4978	3.4849	3.4995	3.5141	
5	4	3.5000	3.4849	3.4995	3.5141	
6	5	3.4951	3.4849	3.4995	3.5141	
19	18	3.4940	3.4849	3.4995	3.5141	
20	19	3.4951	3.4849	3.4995	3.5141	
21	20	3.5007	3.4849	3.4995	3.5141	
22	Mean	3.4995				
23			A2	0.577		
24			Rbar	0.0253		
25						

Note: Rows 7–18 (samples 6–17) are hidden.

worksheet name followed by an exclamation point must precede a cell reference when the cells referenced are in another worksheet of the same workbook. We see, in the value worksheet, that the ranges computed are the same as in Table 14.2. The AVERAGE function used in cell B22 computes the average of the ranges for the 20 samples.

In order to compute the LCL and UCL we must know D_3 and D_4. These values are obtained from Table 14.3 and placed into cells D23 and D24, respectively. The formulas in cells C2:C21 are identical; they compute the LCL by multiplying D_3 (cell D23) times the average range (cell B22). The formulas in cells D2:D21 are also identical; they provide the average range. Finally, the formulas in cells E2:E21 (also identical) compute the UCL by multiplying D_4 (cell D24) times the average range (cell B22).

Apply Tools: The following steps describe how to use Excel's Chart Wizard to construct the R chart from the data in cells A2:E21 of Figure 14.8.

Step 1. Select cells A2:E21
Step 2. Click the **Chart Wizard** button on the standard toolbar (or select the **Insert** menu and choose the **Chart** option)
Step 3. When the **Chart Wizard—Step 1 of 4—Chart Type** dialog box appears:
Choose **XY (Scatter)** in the **Chart type** list
Choose **Scatter with data points connected by Lines** from the **Chart sub-type** display
Click **Next>**
Step 4. When the **Chart Wizard—Step 2 of 4—Chart Source Data** dialog box appears:
Click **Next>**
Step 5. When the **Chart Wizard—Step 3 of 4—Chart Options** dialog box appears:
Select the **Titles** tab and then
Type **R Chart for Jensen Computer Supplies** in the **Chart title** box
Type **Sample Number** in the **Value (X)** axis box
Type **Sample Range R** in the **Value (Y)** axis box
Select the **Legend** tab and remove the check in the **Show Legend** Box
Select the **Gridlines** tab and remove the check in the **Major gridlines** box
Click **Next>**
Step 6. When the **Chart Wizard—Step 4 of 4—Chart Location** dialog box appears:
Specify a location for the chart (we chose the **As new sheet** option)
Click **Finish**

The resulting R chart will appear in a new sheet entitled "Chart 1" in your workbook.

You will need to do some editing of your chart to make it look like Figure 14.6. To make the UCL line a solid line like it is in Figure 14.6 follow these steps:

Step 1. Right click on the UCL line at one of the data points and select **Format Data Series**
Step 2. When the Format Data Series dialog box appears:
In the **Line** section:
Choose black for **Color**
Choose the second line from the bottom for **Weight**
In the **Marker** section:
Choose the "long dash" for **Style**
Choose black for **Foreground**
Click **OK**

The UCL line will now appear as a solid black line. You should then follow the same steps for the average and LCL lines to make them look as they do in Figure 14.6. As a final step you will need to right click on the vertical axis to format the axis labels as shown in Figure 14.6. You will probably also want to resize the chart to satisfy your own preference. Just select the chart and move the drag handles until the chart looks the way you want it.

The procedure for constructing an $\bar{x}$ chart is similar. Figure 14.9 shows the worksheet developed to provide the data needed to construct an $\bar{x}$ chart. It is analogous to the worksheet developed for the R chart in Figure 14.8. We used the Chart Wizard with this worksheet to construct the $\bar{x}$ chart shown in Figure 14.5. The steps followed are almost identical to those we just described for the R chart, so we will not repeat them here.

p Chart

Control charts based on data indicating the presence of a defect or the number of defects are called attributes control charts. A p chart is an attributes control chart.

Let us consider the case in which the output quality is measured in terms of the items being either nondefective or defective. The decision to continue or to adjust the production process will be based on $\bar{p}$, the proportion of defective items found in a sample of the output. The control chart used to monitor the proportion of defective items is called a **p chart**.

To illustrate the construction of a *p* chart, consider the use of automated mail-sorting machines in a post office. These automated machines scan the zip codes on letters and divert each letter to its proper carrier route. Even when a machine is operating properly, some letters are diverted to incorrect routes. Suppose that when a machine is operating correctly, or in a state of control, 3% of the letters are incorrectly diverted. Thus *p*, the proportion of letters incorrectly diverted when the process is in control, is .03.

The sampling distribution of $\bar{p}$, as presented in Chapter 7, can be used to determine the variation that can be expected in $\bar{p}$ values for a process that is in control. Recall that the expected value or mean of $\bar{p}$ is *p*, the proportion defective when the process is in control. With samples of size *n*, the formula for the standard deviation of $\bar{p}$, called the standard error of the proportion, is

$$\sigma_{\bar{p}} = \sqrt{\frac{p(1-p)}{n}} \tag{14.16}$$

We also learned in Chapter 7 that the sampling distribution of $\bar{p}$ can be approximated by a normal probability distribution whenever the sample size is large. With $\bar{p}$, the sample size can be considered large whenever the following two conditions are satisfied.

$$np \geq 5$$
$$n(1-p) \geq 5$$

In summary, whenever the sample size is large, the sampling distribution of $\bar{p}$ can be approximated by a normal probability distribution with mean *p* and standard deviation $\sigma_{\bar{p}}$. This distribution is shown in Figure 14.10.

To establish control limits for a *p* chart, we follow the same procedure we used to establish control limits for an $\bar{x}$ chart. That is, the limits for the control chart are set at 3 standard errors above and below the proportion defective when the process is in control. Thus, we have the following control limits.

Control Limits for a *p* Chart

$$\text{UCL} = p + 3\sigma_{\bar{p}} \tag{14.17}$$
$$\text{LCL} = p - 3\sigma_{\bar{p}} \tag{14.18}$$

FIGURE 14.10   SAMPLING DISTRIBUTION OF $\bar{p}$

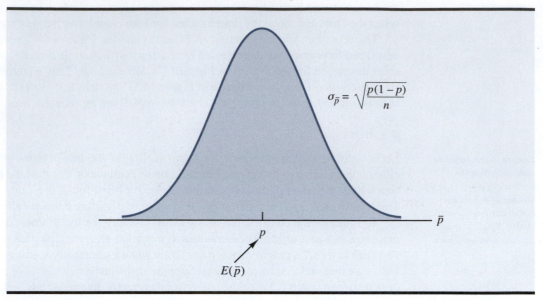

With $p = .03$ and samples of size $n = 200$, equation (14.16) shows that the standard error is

$$\sigma_{\bar{p}} = \sqrt{\frac{.03(1 - .03)}{200}} = .0121$$

Hence, the control limits are UCL $= .03 + 3(.0121) = .0663$, and LCL $= .03 - 3(.0121) = -.0063$. Whenever equation (14.18) provides a negative value for LCL, LCL is reset to zero in the control chart.

Figure 14.11 is the control chart for the mail-sorting process. The points plotted show the sample proportion defective found in samples of letters taken from the process. All points are within the control limits, and the sorting process shows no evidence of being out of control. In fact, the p chart indicates that the process should continue to operate.

If the proportion of defective items for a process that is in control is not known, that value is first estimated by using sample data. Suppose, for example, that k different samples, each of size n, are selected from a process that is in control. The fraction or proportion of defective items in each sample is then determined. Treating all the data collected as one large sample, we can determine the average number of defective items for all the data; that value can then be used to provide an estimate of p, the proportion of defective items observed when the process is in control. Note that this estimate of p also enables us to estimate the standard error of the proportion; upper and lower control limits can then be established.

np Chart

An ***np* chart** is a control chart developed for the number of defective items observed in a sample. In this case, n is the sample size and p is the probability of observing a defective item when the process is in control. Whenever the sample size is large, that is when $np \geq 5$ and $n(1 - p) \geq 5$, the distribution of the number of defective items observed in a sample size n can be approximated by a normal probability distribution with mean np and standard deviation $\sqrt{np(1 - p)}$. Thus, for the mail-sorting example, with $n = 200$ and $p = .03$, the

FIGURE 14.11   *p* CHART FOR THE PROPORTION DEFECTIVE IN A MAIL-SORTING
PROCESS

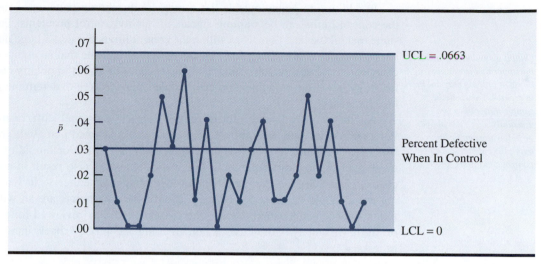

number of defective items observed in a sample of 200 letters can be approximated by a
normal probability distribution with a mean of 200(.03) = 6 and a standard deviation of
$\sqrt{200(.03)(.97)}$ = 2.4125.

The control limits for an *np* chart are set at 3 standard deviations above and below the
expected number of defective items observed when the process is in control. Thus, we have
the following control limits.

Control Limits for an *np* Chart

$$\text{UCL} = np + 3\sqrt{np(1 - p)} \tag{14.19}$$

$$\text{LCL} = np - 3\sqrt{np(1 - p)} \tag{14.20}$$

For the mail-sorting process example, with *p* = .03 and *n* = 200, the control limits are
UCL = 6 + 3(2.4125) = 13.2375, and LCL = 6 − 3(2.4125) = − 1.2375. Because equation (14.20) provides a negative value for LCL, it is reset to zero in the control chart. Hence,
if the number of letters diverted to incorrect routes is greater than 13, the process is concluded to be out of control.

The information provided by an *np* chart is equivalent to the information provided by
the *p* chart; the only difference is that the *np* chart is a plot of the number of defective items
observed whereas the *p* chart is a plot of the proportion of defective items observed. Thus,
if we were to conclude that a particular process is out of control on the basis of a *p* chart,
the process would also be concluded to be out of control on the basis of an *np* chart.

Interpretation of Control Charts

*Control charts are designed
to identify when assignable
causes of variation are
present. Managers must
then authorize action to
eliminate the assignable
cause and return the process
to an in-control state.*

The location and pattern of points in a control chart enable us to determine, with a small
probability of error, whether a process is in statistical control. A primary indication that a
process may be out of control is a data point outside the control limits, such as point 5 in

Figure 14.4. Such a point is statistical evidence that the process is out of control; in such cases, corrective action should be taken as soon as possible.

In addition to points outside the control limits, certain patterns of the points within the control limits can be warning signals of quality control problems. For example, assume that all the data points are within the control limits but that a large number of points are on one side of the center line. This pattern may indicate that an equipment problem, a change in materials, or some other assignable cause of a shift in quality occurred. Careful investigation of the production process should be undertaken to determine whether quality has changed.

Even if all points are within the upper and lower control limits, a process may not be in control. Trends in the sample data points or unusually long runs above or below the center line may also indicate out-of-control conditions.

Another pattern to watch for in control charts is a gradual shift, or trend, over time. For example, as tools wear out, the dimensions of machined parts will gradually deviate from their designed levels. Gradual changes in temperature or humidity, general equipment deterioration, dirt buildup, or operator fatigue may also result in a trend pattern in control charts. Six or seven points in a row that indicate either an increasing or decreasing trend should be cause for concern, even if the data points are all within the control limits. When such a pattern occurs, the process should be reviewed for possible changes or shifts in quality. Corrective action to bring the process back into control may be necessary.

NOTES AND COMMENTS

1. Because the control limits for the $\bar{x}$ chart depend on the value of the average range, these limits will not have much meaning unless the process variability is in control. In practice, the R chart is usually constructed before the $\bar{x}$ chart; if the R chart indicates that the process variability is in control, then the $\bar{x}$ chart is constructed.

2. The p and np control charts can also be constructed using Excel's Chart Wizard. For instance, to develop a p chart, start by organizing the data for $\bar{p}$, LCL, mean, and UCL in a worksheet similar to Figures 14.8 or 14.9. Then use the Chart Wizard in the same way we did earlier to construct an R chart.

3. An np chart is used to monitor a process in terms of the number of defects. The Motorola Six-Sigma Quality Level sets a goal of producing no more than 3.4 defects per million operations (*American Production and Inventory Control*, July 1991); this goal implies $p = .0000034$.

EXERCISES

Methods

1. A process that is in control has a mean of $\mu = 12.5$ and a standard deviation of $\sigma = .8$.
   a. Construct an $\bar{x}$ chart if samples of size 4 are to be used.
   b. Repeat part (a) for samples of size 8 and 16.
   c. What happens to the limits of the control chart as the sample size is increased? Discuss why this change is reasonable.

2. Twenty-five samples, each of size 5, were selected from a process that was in control. The sum of all the data collected was 677.5 pounds.
   a. What is an estimate of the process mean (in terms of pounds per unit) when the process is in control?
   b. Develop the control chart for this process if samples of size 5 will be used. Assume that the process standard deviation is .5 when the process is in control, and that the mean of the process is the estimate developed in part (a).

3. Twenty-five samples of 100 items each were inspected when a process was considered to be operating satisfactorily. In the 25 samples, 135 items were found to be defective.
   a. What is an estimate of the proportion defective when the process is in control?
   b. What is the standard error of the proportion if samples of size 100 will be used for statistical process control?
   c. Compute the upper and lower control limits for the control chart.

4. An in-control process sampled 20 times with a sample of size 8 resulted in $\bar{\bar{x}} = 28.5$ and $\bar{R} = 1.6$. Compute the upper and lower control limits for the $\bar{x}$ and R charts for this process.

Applications

5. Temperature is used to measure the output of a production process. When the process is in control, the mean of the process is $\mu = 128.5$ and the standard deviation is $\sigma = .4$.
   a. Construct an $\bar{x}$ chart if samples of size 6 are to be used.
   b. Is the process in control for a sample providing the following data?

   | 128.8 | 128.2 | 129.1 | 128.7 | 128.4 | 129.2 |

   c. Is the process in control for a sample providing the following data?

   | 129.3 | 128.7 | 128.6 | 129.2 | 129.5 | 129.0 |

6. A quality control process monitors the weight per carton of laundry detergent. Control limits are set at UCL = 20.12 ounces and LCL = 19.90 ounces. Samples of size 5 are used for the sampling and inspection process. What are the process mean and process standard deviation for the manufacturing operation?

7. The Goodman Tire and Rubber Company periodically tests its tires for tread wear under simulated road conditions. To study and control the manufacturing process, 20 samples, each containing three radial tires, were chosen from different shifts over several days of operation; the data collected are shown below. Assuming that these data were collected when the manufacturing process was believed to be operating in control, develop the R and $\bar{x}$ charts.

Tires

Sample	Tread Wear*		
1	31	42	28
2	26	18	35
3	25	30	34
4	17	25	21
5	38	29	35
6	41	42	36
7	21	17	29
8	32	26	28
9	41	34	33
10	29	17	30
11	26	31	40
12	23	19	25
13	17	24	32
14	43	35	17
15	18	25	29
16	30	42	31
17	28	36	32
18	40	29	31
19	18	29	28
20	22	34	26

*Hundredths of an inch

8. Over several weeks of normal, or in-control, operation, 20 samples of 150 packages each of synthetic-gut tennis strings were tested for breaking strength. A total of 141 packages of the 3000 tested failed to conform to the manufacturer's specifications.
    a. What is an estimate of the process proportion defective when the system is in control?
    b. Compute the upper and lower control limits for a p chart.
    c. With the results of part (b), what conclusion should be drawn about the process if tests on a new sample of 150 packages find 12 defective? Do there appear to be assignable causes in this situation?
    d. Compute the upper and lower control limits for an np chart.
    e. Answer part (c) using the results of part (d).
    f. Which control chart would be preferred in this situation? Explain.

9. An automotive industry supplier produces pistons for several models of automobiles. Twenty samples, each consisting of 200 pistons, were selected when the process was known to be operating in control. The numbers of defective pistons found in the samples follow.

8	10	6	4	5	7	8	12	8	15
14	10	10	7	5	8	6	10	4	8

   a. What is an estimate of the proportion defective for the piston manufacturing process when it is in control?
   b. Construct a p chart for the manufacturing process, assuming each sample has 200 pistons.
   c. With the results of part (b), what conclusion should be made if a sample of 200 has 20 defective pistons?
   d. Compute the upper and lower control limits for an np chart.
   e. Answer part (c) using the results of part (d).

14.2   ACCEPTANCE SAMPLING

In acceptance sampling, the items of interest can be incoming shipments of raw materials or purchased parts as well as finished goods from final assembly. Suppose we want to decide whether to accept or reject a group of items on the basis of specified quality characteristics. In quality control terminology, the group of items is a **lot**, and **acceptance sampling** is a statistical method that enables us to make an accept-reject decision based on the sample of items from the lot.

Acceptance sampling has the following advantages over 100% inspection:
1. *Usually less expensive*
2. *Less product damage due to less handling and testing*
3. *Fewer inspectors required*
4. *Provides only approach possible if destructive testing must be used.*

The general steps of acceptance sampling are shown in Figure 14.12. After a lot is received, a sample is selected for inspection. The results of the inspection are compared to specified quality characteristics. If the quality is satisfactory, the lot is accepted and sent to production or shipped to customers. If the quality is not satisfactory, the lot is rejected. Managers must then decide on the disposition of the lot. In some cases, the decision may be to keep the lot and remove the unacceptable or nonconforming items. In other cases, the lot may be returned to the supplier at the supplier's expense; the extra work and cost placed on the supplier can motivate the supplier to provide high-quality lots. Finally, if the rejected lot consists of finished goods, the goods must be scrapped or reworked to meet acceptable quality standards.

The statistical procedure of acceptance sampling is based on the hypothesis testing methodology presented in Chapter 9. The null and alternative hypotheses are stated as follows.

$$H_0: \text{Good-quality lot}$$
$$H_a: \text{Poor-quality lot}$$

Table 14.4 shows the outcomes of the hypothesis testing procedure. Note that correct decisions correspond to accepting a good-quality lot and rejecting a poor-quality lot. However, as with

FIGURE 14.12   ACCEPTANCE SAMPLING PROCEDURE

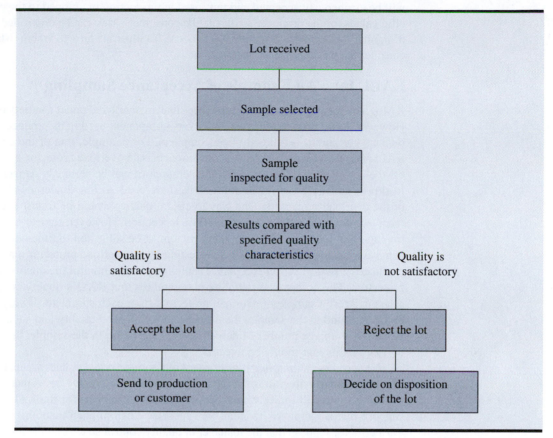

other hypothesis testing procedures, we need to be aware of the possibilities of making a Type I error (rejecting a good-quality lot) or a Type II error (accepting a poor-quality lot).

Because the probability of a Type I error creates a risk for the producer of the lot, it is known as the **producer's risk.** For example, a producer's risk of .05 indicates a 5% chance that a good-quality lot will be erroneously rejected. Because the probability of a Type II error creates a risk for the consumer of the lot, it is known as the **consumer's risk.** For

TABLE 14.4   THE OUTCOMES OF ACCEPTANCE SAMPLING

		State of the Lot	
		H_0 True Good-Quality Lot	H_0 False Poor-Quality Lot
Decision	**Accept the Lot**	Correct decision	Type II error (accepting a poor-quality lot)
	Reject the Lot	Type I error (rejecting a good-quality lot)	Correct decision

example, a consumer's risk of .10 means that there is a 10% chance that a poor-quality lot will be erroneously accepted and thus used in production or shipped to the customer. Specific values for the producer's risk and the consumer's risk can be controlled by the person designing the acceptance sampling procedure. To illustrate how to assign risk values, let us consider the problem faced by KALI, Inc.

KALI, Inc.: An Example of Acceptance Sampling

KALI, Inc., manufactures home appliances that are marketed under a variety of trade names. However, KALI does not manufacture every component used in its products. Several components are purchased directly from suppliers. For example, one of the components that KALI purchases for use in home air conditioners is an overload protector, a device that turns off the compressor if it overheats. The compressor can be seriously damaged if the overload protector does not function properly, therefore KALI is concerned about the quality of the overload protectors. One way to ensure quality would be to test every component received; this approach is known as 100% inspection. However, to determine proper functioning of an overload protector, the device must be subjected to time-consuming and expensive tests, and KALI cannot justify testing every overload protector it receives.

Instead, KALI uses an acceptance sampling plan to monitor the quality of the overload protectors. The acceptance sampling plan requires that KALI's quality control inspectors select and test a sample of overload protectors from each shipment. If very few defective units are found in the sample, the lot is probably of good quality and should be accepted. However, if a large number of defective units are found in the sample, the lot is probably of poor quality and should be rejected.

An *acceptance sampling plan* consists of a sample size n and an acceptance criterion c. The **acceptance criterion** is the maximum number of defective items that can be found in the sample and still indicate an acceptable lot. For example, for the KALI problem let us suppose that a sample of 15 items will be selected from each incoming shipment or lot. Furthermore, suppose that the manager of quality control states that the lot can be accepted only if no defective items are found. In this case, the acceptance sampling plan established by the quality control manager is $n = 15$ and $c = 0$.

This acceptance sampling plan is easy for the quality control inspector to implement. The inspector simply selects a sample of 15 items, performs the tests, and reaches a conclusion based on the following decision rule.

- *Accept the lot* if zero defects are found.
- *Reject the lot* if one or more defects are found.

Before implementing this acceptance sampling plan, the quality control manager wants to evaluate the risks or errors possible under the plan. The plan will be implemented only if both the producer's risk (Type I error) and the consumer's risk (Type II error) are controlled at reasonable levels.

Computing the Probability of Accepting a Lot

The key to analyzing both the producer's risk and the consumer's risk is a what-if type of analysis; that is, we assume that a lot has some known percentage of defective items and compute the probability of accepting the lot for a given sampling plan. By varying the assumed percentage of defective items, we can examine the effect of the sampling plan on both types of risks.

Let us begin by assuming that in a large shipment of overload protectors 5% of the overload protectors are defective. For a shipment or lot with 5% of the items defective, what is the probability that the $n = 15$, $c = 0$ sampling plan will lead us to accept the lot? Because each overload protector tested will be either defective or nondefective and because the lot size is large, the number of defective items in a sample of 15 has a *binomial probability distribution*. The binomial probability function, which was presented in Chapter 5, follows.

Binomial Probability Function for Acceptance Sampling

$$f(x) = \frac{n!}{x!(n-x)!} p^x (1-p)^{(n-x)} \tag{14.21}$$

where

n = the sample size
p = the proportion of defective items in the lot
x = the number of defective items in the sample
$f(x)$ = the probability of x defective items in the sample

For the KALI acceptance sampling plan, $n = 15$; thus, for a lot with 5% defective ($p = .05$), we have

$$f(x) = \frac{15!}{x!(15-x)!} (.05)^x (1-.05)^{(15-x)} \tag{14.22}$$

Using equation (14.22), $f(0)$ will provide the probability that zero overload protectors will be defective and the lot will be accepted. In using equation (14.22), recall that $0! = 1$. Thus, the probability computation for $f(0)$ is

$$f(0) = \frac{15!}{0!(15-0)!} (.05)^0 (1-.05)^{(15-0)}$$

$$= \frac{15!}{0!(15)!} (.05)^0 (.95)^{15} = (.95)^{15} = .4633$$

We now know that the $n = 15$, $c = 0$ sampling plan has a .4633 probability of accepting a lot with 5% defective items. Hence, a corresponding probability of rejecting a lot with 5% defective items is $1 - .4633 = .5367$.

Excel's BINOMDIST function can also be used to compute these probabilities. See Chapter 5.

In Table 14.5 we show the probability that the $n = 15$, $c = 0$ sampling plan will lead to the acceptance of lots with 1%, 2%, 3%, ... defective items. The probabilities in the table were computed by using $p = .01$, $p = .02$, $p = .03$, ... in the binomial probability function (14.21).

With the data in Table 14.5, a graph of the probability of accepting the lot versus the percent defective in the lot can be drawn as shown in Figure 14.13. This graph, or curve, is called the **operating characteristic (OC) curve** for the $n = 15$, $c = 0$ acceptance sampling plan.

Perhaps we should consider other sampling plans, ones with different sample sizes n and/or different acceptance criteria c. First consider the case in which the sample size remains $n = 15$ but the acceptance criterion increases from $c = 0$ to $c = 1$; that is, we will

TABLE 14.5 PROBABILITY OF ACCEPTING THE LOT FOR THE KALI PROBLEM
WITH $n = 15$ AND $c = 0$

Percent Defective in the Lot	Probability of Accepting the Lot
1	.8601
2	.7386
3	.6333
4	.5421
5	.4633
10	.2059
15	.0874
20	.0352
25	.0134

now accept the lot if zero or one defective item is found in the sample. For a lot with 5% defective items ($p = .05$), the binomial probability function in equation (14.21) can be used to compute $f(0)$ and $f(1)$. Summing these two probabilities provides the probability that the $n = 15$, $c = 1$ sampling plan will accept the lot. We find that with $n = 15$ and $p = .05$, $f(0) = .4633$ and $f(1) = .3658$. Thus, we find a $.4633 + .3658 = .8291$ probability that the $n = 15$, $c = 1$ plan will lead to the acceptance of a lot with 5% defective items.

Figure 14.14 shows the operating characteristic curves for four alternative acceptance sampling plans for the KALI problem. Samples of size 15 and 20 are considered. Note that

FIGURE 14.13 OPERATING CHARACTERISTIC CURVE FOR THE $n = 15$, $c = 0$
ACCEPTANCE SAMPLING PLAN

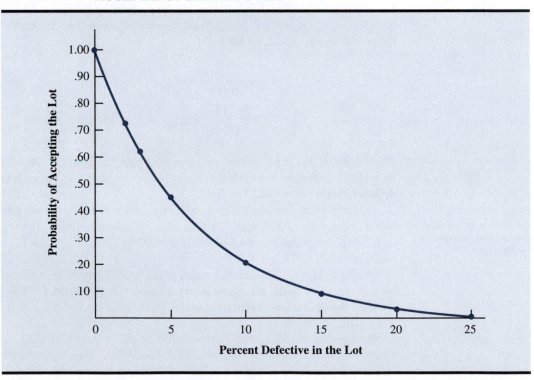

FIGURE 14.14   OPERATING CHARACTERISTIC CURVES FOR FOUR ACCEPTANCE
SAMPLING PLANS

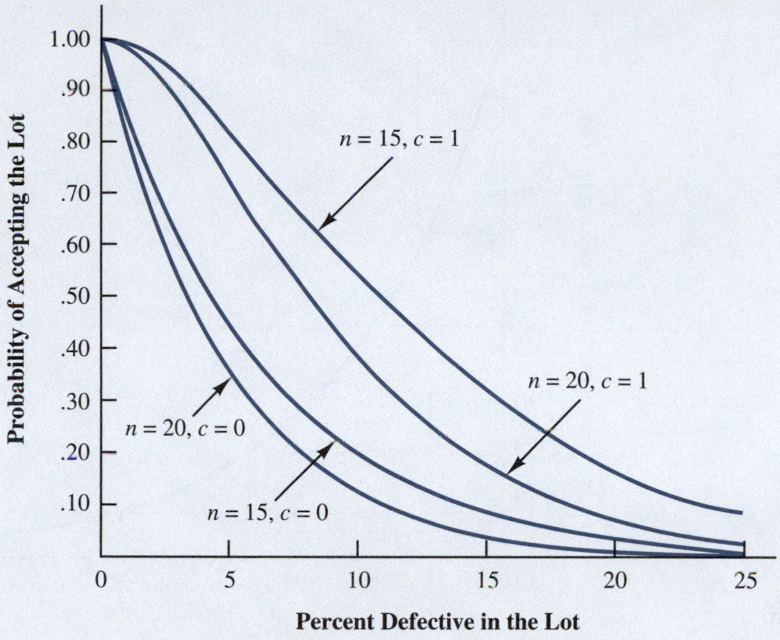

regardless of the proportion defective in the lot, the $n = 15, c = 1$ sampling plan provides the highest probabilities of accepting the lot. The $n = 20, c = 0$ sampling plan provides the lowest probabilities of accepting the lot; however, that plan also provides the highest probabilities of rejecting the lot.

Selecting an Acceptance Sampling Plan

Now that we know how to use the binomial probability distribution to compute the probability of accepting a lot with a given proportion defective, we are ready to select the values of n and c that determine the desired acceptance sampling plan for the application being studied. In formulating an acceptance plan, managers must specify two values for the fraction defective in the lot. One value, denoted p_0, will be used to control for the producer's risk, and the other value, denoted p_1, will be used to control for the consumer's risk.

In showing how this formulation can be done, we will use the following notation.

α = the producer's risk; the probability that a lot with p_0 defective will be rejected

β = the consumer's risk; the probability that a lot with p_1 defective will be accepted

Suppose that for the KALI problem, the managers specify that $p_0 = .03$ and $p_1 = .15$. From the OC curve for $n = 15, c = 0$ in Figure 14.15, we see that $p_0 = .03$ provides a producer's risk of approximately $1 - .63 = .37$, and $p_1 = .15$ provides a consumer's risk of approximately $.09$. Thus, if the managers are willing to tolerate both a .37 probability of rejecting a lot with 3% defective items (producer's risk) and a .09 probability of accepting a lot with 15% defective items (consumer's risk), the $n = 15, c = 0$ acceptance sampling plan would be acceptable.

FIGURE 14.15   OPERATING CHARACTERISTIC CURVE FOR $n = 15$, $c = 0$ WITH $p_0 = .03$ AND $p_1 = .15$

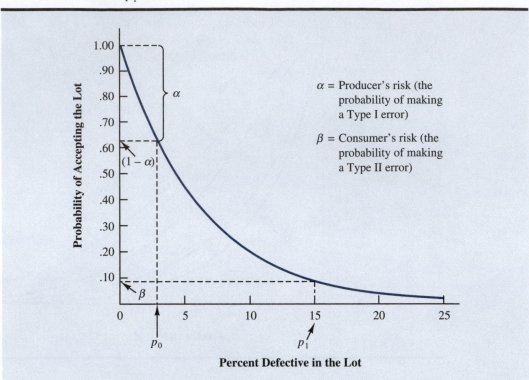

Suppose, however, that the managers request a producer's risk of $\alpha = .10$ and a consumer's risk of $\beta = .20$. We see that now the $n = 15$, $c = 0$ sampling plan offers a better-than-desired consumer's risk but an unacceptably large producer's risk. The fact that $\alpha = .37$ indicates that 37% of the lots will be erroneously rejected when only 3% of the items in them are defective. The producer's risk is too high, and a different acceptance sampling plan should be considered.

Using $p_0 = .03$, $\alpha = .10$, $p_1 = .15$, and $\beta = .20$ in Figure 14.14 shows that the acceptance sampling plan with $n = 20$ and $c = 1$ comes closest to meeting both the producer's and the consumer's risk requirements. Exercise 13 at the end of this section will ask you to compute the producer's risk and the consumer's risk for the $n = 20$, $c = 1$ sampling plan.

As shown in this section, several computations and several operating characteristic curves may need to be considered to determine the sampling plan with the desired producer's and consumer's risks. Fortunately, tables of sampling plans are published. For example, the American Military Standard Table, MIL-STD-105D, provides information helpful in designing acceptance sampling plans. More advanced texts on quality control, such as those listed in the bibliography, describe the use of such tables. The advanced texts also discuss the role of sampling costs in determining the optimal sampling plan.

Multiple Sampling Plans

The acceptance sampling procedure presented for the KALI problem is called a *single-sample plan*, because only one sample or sampling stage is used. After the number of defective components in the sample is determined, a decision must be made to accept or reject the lot. An alternative to the single-sample plan is a **multiple sampling plan,** in which two or more stages of sampling are used. At each stage a decision is made among three possibilities: stop sampling and accept the lot, stop sampling and reject the lot, or continue sampling. Although more complex, multiple sampling plans often result in a smaller total sample size than single-sample plans with the same α and β probabilities.

The logic of a two-stage, or double-sample, plan is shown in Figure 14.16. Initially a sample of n_1 items is selected. If the number of defective components x_1 is less than or equal to c_1, accept the lot. If x_1 is greater than or equal to c_2, reject the lot. If x_1 is between c_1 and c_2 ($c_1 < x_1 < c_2$), select a second sample of n_2 items. Determine the combined, or

FIGURE 14.16   A TWO-STAGE ACCEPTANCE SAMPLING PLAN

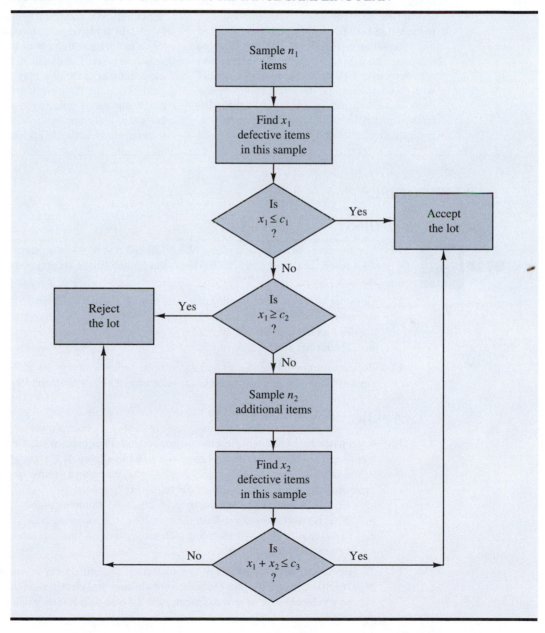

total number of defects from the first sample (x_1) and the second sample (x_2). If $x_1 + x_2 \leq c_3$, accept the lot; otherwise reject the lot. The development of the double-sample plan is more difficult because the sample sizes n_1 and n_2 and the acceptance numbers c_1, c_2, and c_3 must meet acceptable levels of both the producer's and consumer's risks.

NOTES AND COMMENTS

1. The use of the binomial probability distribution for acceptance sampling is based on the assumption of large lots. If the lot size is small, the hypergeometric probability distribution is the appropriate distribution.

2. In the MIL-ST-105D sampling tables, p_0 is called the acceptable quality level (AQL). In some sampling tables, p_1 is called the lot tolerance percent defective (LTPD) or the rejectable quality level (RQL). Many of the published sampling plans also use quality indexes such as the indifference quality level (IQL) and the average outgoing quality limit (AOQL). The more advanced texts listed in the bibliography provide a complete discussion of these other indexes.

3. In this section we provided an introduction to *attributes sampling plans*. In these plans each item sampled is classified as nondefective or defective. In *variables sampling plans*, a sample is taken and a measurement of the quality characteristic is taken. For example, for gold jewelry a measurement of quality may be the amount of gold it contains. A simple statistic such as the average amount of gold in the sample jewelry is computed and compared with an allowable value to determine whether to accept or reject the lot.

EXERCISES

Methods

10. For an acceptance sampling plan with $n = 25$ and $c = 0$, find the probability of accepting a lot when the defect rate is 2%. What is the probability of accepting the lot if the defect rate is 6%?

11. Consider an acceptance sampling plan with $n = 20$ and $c = 0$. Compute the producer's risk for each of the following cases.
   a. The lot has a defect rate of 2%.
   b. The lot has a defect rate of 6%.

12. Repeat Exercise 11 for the acceptance sampling plan with $n = 20$ and $c = 1$. What happens to the producer's risk as the acceptance number c is increased? Explain.

Applications

13. Refer to the KALI problem presented in this section. The quality control manager requested a producer's risk of .10 or less when p_0 was .03 and a consumer's risk of .20 or less when p_1 was .15. Consider the acceptance sampling plan based on a sample size of 20 and an acceptance criterion of $c = 1$. Answer the following questions.
   a. What is the producer's risk for the $n = 20$, $c = 1$ sampling plan?
   b. What is the consumer's risk for the $n = 20$, $c = 1$ sampling plan?
   c. Does the $n = 20$, $c = 1$ sampling plan satisfy the risk limits as requested by the quality control manager? Discuss.

14. To inspect incoming shipments of raw materials, a manufacturer is considering samples of sizes 10, 15, and 20. Use binomial probabilities to select a sampling plan that provides a producer's risk of $\alpha = .03$ when p_0 is .05 and a consumer's risk of $\beta = .12$ when p_1 is .30.

15. A domestic manufacturer of watches purchases quartz crystals from a Swiss firm. The crystals are shipped in lots of 1000. The acceptance sampling procedure uses 20 randomly selected crystals.

    a. Construct operating characteristic curves for acceptance criteria of 0, 1, and 2.

    b. If p_0 is .01 and $p_1 = .08$, what are the producer's and consumer's risks for each sampling plan in part (a)?

SUMMARY

In this chapter we discussed how statistical methods can be used to assist in the control of quality. We first presented the $\bar{x}$, R, p, and np control charts as graphical aids in monitoring process quality. Control limits are established for each chart; samples are selected periodically and the data plotted on the control chart. Data outside the control limits indicate that the process is out of control and that corrective action should be taken. Patterns of data within the control limits can also indicate potential quality control problems and suggest that corrective action may be warranted.

We also considered the technique known as acceptance sampling. With this procedure, a sample is selected and inspected. The number of defective items in the sample provides the basis for accepting or rejecting the lot. The sample size and the acceptance criterion can be adjusted to control both the producer's risk (Type I error) and the consumer's risk (Type II error).

GLOSSARY

Quality control   A series of inspections and measurements used to determine whether quality standards are being met.

Assignable causes   Variations in process outputs that are due to factors such as machine tools wearing out, incorrect machine settings, poor-quality raw materials, operator error, and so on. Corrective action should be taken whenever assignable causes are detected.

Common causes   Normal or natural variations in process outputs that are due purely to chance. No corrective action is necessary when output variations are due to common causes.

Control chart   A graphical tool used to help determine whether a process is in control or out of control.

$\bar{x}$ chart   A control chart used to monitor the mean value of a variable such as a length, weight, temperature, and so on.

R chart   A control chart used to control the variability of a process.

p chart   A control chart used to monitor the proportion of defective items generated by a process.

np chart   A control chart used to monitor the number of defective items generated by a process.

Lot   A group of items such as an incoming shipment of raw materials, a shipment of purchased parts, or a batch of finished goods from final assembly.

Acceptance sampling   A statistical procedure in which the number of defective items found in a sample is used to determine whether a lot should be accepted or rejected.

Producer's risk   The risk of rejecting a good-quality lot; a Type I error.

Consumer's risk   The risk of accepting a poor-quality lot; a Type II error.

Acceptance criterion   The maximum number of defective items that can be found in the sample and still indicate an acceptable lot.

Operating characteristic curve   A graph showing the probability of accepting the lot as a function of the percent defective in the lot. This curve can be used to determine whether a particular acceptance sampling plan meets both the producer's and the consumer's risk requirements.

Multiple sampling plan   A form of acceptance sampling in which more than one sample or stage is used. On the basis of the number of defective items found in a sample, a decision will be made to accept the lot, reject the lot, or continue sampling.

KEY FORMULAS

Standard Error of the Mean

$$\sigma_{\bar{x}} = \frac{\sigma}{\sqrt{n}} \tag{14.1}$$

Control Limits for an $\bar{x}$ Chart: Process Mean and Standard Deviation Known

$$\text{UCL} = \mu + 3\sigma_{\bar{x}} \tag{14.2}$$
$$\text{LCL} = \mu - 3\sigma_{\bar{x}} \tag{14.3}$$

Overall Sample Mean

$$\bar{\bar{x}} = \frac{\bar{x}_1 + \bar{x}_2 + \cdots + \bar{x}_k}{k} \tag{14.4}$$

Average Range

$$\bar{R} = \frac{R_1 + R_2 + \cdots + R_k}{k} \tag{14.5}$$

Control Limits for an $\bar{x}$ Chart: Process Mean and Standard Deviation Unknown

$$\bar{\bar{x}} \pm A_2 \bar{R} \tag{14.8}$$

Control Limits for an R Chart

$$\text{UCL} = \bar{R}D_4 \tag{14.14}$$
$$\text{LCL} = \bar{R}D_3 \tag{14.15}$$

Standard Error of the Proportion

$$\sigma_{\bar{p}} = \sqrt{\frac{p(1-p)}{n}} \tag{14.16}$$

Control Limits for a p Chart

$$\text{UCL} = p + 3\sigma_{\bar{p}} \tag{14.17}$$
$$\text{LCL} = p - 3\sigma_{\bar{p}} \tag{14.18}$$

Control Limits for an np Chart

$$\text{UCL} = np + 3\sqrt{np(1-p)} \tag{14.19}$$
$$\text{LCL} = np - 3\sqrt{np(1-p)} \tag{14.20}$$

Binomial Probability Function for Acceptance Sampling

$$f(x) = \frac{n!}{x!(n-x)!} p^x(1-p)^{(n-x)} \tag{14.21}$$

SUPPLEMENTARY EXERCISES

16. Samples of size 5 provided the following 20 sample means for a production process that is believed to be in control.

95.72	95.24	95.18
95.44	95.46	95.32
95.40	95.44	95.08
95.50	95.80	95.22
95.56	95.22	95.04
95.72	94.82	95.46
95.60	95.78	

    a. Based on these data, what is an estimate of the mean when the process is in control?
    b. Assuming that the process standard deviation is $\sigma = .50$, develop a control chart for this production process. Assume that the mean of the process is the estimate developed in part (a).
    c. Are any of the 20 sample means outside the control limits?

17. Product filling weights are normally distributed with a mean of 350 grams and a standard deviation of 15 grams.
    a. Develop the control limits for samples of size 10, 20, and 30.
    b. What happens to the control limits as the sample size is increased?
    c. What happens when a Type I error is made?
    d. What happens when a Type II error is made?
    e. What is the probability of a Type I error for samples of size 10, 20, and 30?
    f. What is the advantage of increasing the sample size for control chart purposes? What error probability is reduced as the sample size is increased?

18. Twenty-five samples of size 5 resulted in $\bar{\bar{x}} = 5.42$ and $\bar{R} = 2.0$. Compute control limits for the $\bar{x}$ and R charts, and estimate the standard deviation of the process.

19. The following quality control data for a manufacturing process at Kensport Chemical Company show the temperature in degrees centigrade at five points in time during a manufacturing cycle. The company is interested in using control charts to monitor the temperature of its manufacturing process. Construct the $\bar{x}$ chart and R chart. What conclusions can be made about the quality of the process?

Sample	$\bar{x}$	R	Sample	$\bar{x}$	R
1	95.72	1.0	11	95.80	.6
2	95.24	.9	12	95.22	.2
3	95.18	.8	13	95.56	1.3
4	95.44	.4	14	95.22	.5
5	95.46	.5	15	95.04	.8
6	95.32	1.1	16	95.72	1.1
7	95.40	.9	17	94.82	.6
8	95.44	.3	18	95.46	.5
9	95.08	.2	19	95.60	.4
10	95.50	.6	20	95.74	.6

20. The following data were collected for the Master Blend Coffee production process. The data show the filling weights based on samples of 3-pound cans of coffee. Use these data to construct the $\bar{x}$ and R chart. What conclusions can be made about the quality of the production process?

Coffee

	Observations				
Sample	1	2	3	4	5
1	3.05	3.08	3.07	3.11	3.11
2	3.13	3.07	3.05	3.10	3.10
3	3.06	3.04	3.12	3.11	3.10
4	3.09	3.08	3.09	3.09	3.07
5	3.10	3.06	3.06	3.07	3.08
6	3.08	3.10	3.13	3.03	3.06
7	3.06	3.06	3.08	3.10	3.08
8	3.11	3.08	3.07	3.07	3.07
9	3.09	3.09	3.08	3.07	3.09
10	3.06	3.11	3.07	3.09	3.07

21. Consider the following situations. Comment on whether the sample results might cause concern about the quality of the process.
   a. A p chart has LCL = 0 and UCL = .068. When the process is in control, the proportion defective is .033. Plot the following seven sample results: .035, .062, .055, .049, .058, .066, and .055. Discuss.
   b. An $\bar{x}$ chart has LCL = 22.2 and UCL = 24.5. The mean is μ = 23.35 when the process is in control. Plot the following seven sample results: 22.4, 22.6, 22.65, 23.2, 23.4, 23.85, and 24.1. Discuss.

22. Managers of 1200 different retail outlets make twice-a-month restocking orders from a central warehouse. Past experience shows 4% of the orders contain one or more errors such as wrong item shipped, wrong quantity shipped, and item requested but not shipped. Random samples of 200 orders are selected monthly and checked for accuracy.
   a. Construct a control chart for this situation.
   b. Six months of data show the following numbers of orders with one or more errors: 10, 15, 6, 13, 8, and 17. Plot the data on the control chart. What does your plot indicate about the order process?

23. An n = 10, c = 2 acceptance sampling plan is being considered; assume that p_0 = .05 and p_1 = .20.
   a. Compute both the producer's and the consumer's risks for this acceptance sampling plan.
   b. Would the producer, the consumer, or both be unhappy with the proposed sampling plan?
   c. What change in the sampling plan, if any, would you recommend?

24. An acceptance sampling plan with n = 15 and c = 1 was designed with a producer's risk of .075.
   a. Was the value of p_0 equal to .01, .02, .03, .04, or .05? What does this value mean?
   b. What is the consumer's risk associated with this plan if p_1 is .25?

25. A manufacturer produces lots of a canned food product. Let p denote the proportion of the lots that do not meet the product quality specifications. An n = 25, c = 0 acceptance sampling plan will be used.
   a. Compute points on the operating characteristic curve when p = .01, .03, .10, and .20.
   b. Plot the operating characteristic curve.
   c. What is the probability that the acceptance sampling plan will reject a lot that has .01 defective?

Appendix A   References and Bibliography

General

Bowerman, B. L., and R. T. O'Connell, *Applied Statistics: Improving Business Processes*, Irwin, 1996.

Freedman, D., R. Pisani, and R. Purves, *Statistics*, 3rd ed., W. W. Norton, 1997.

Hogg, R. V., and A. T. Craig, *Introduction to Mathematical Statistics*, 5th ed., Prentice Hall, 1994.

Hogg, R. V., and E. A. Tanis, *Probability and Statistical Inference*, 6th ed., Prentice Hall, 2001.

Miller, I., and M. Miller, *John E. Freund's Mathematical Statistics*, Prentice Hall, 1998.

Tanur, J. M., *Statistics: A Guide to the Unknown*, 4th ed., Brooks/Cole, 2002.

Probability

Hogg, R. V., and E. A. Tanis, *Probability and Statistical Inference*, 6th ed., Prentice Hall, 2001.

Ross, S. M., *Introduction to Probability Models*, 7th ed., Academic Press, 2000.

Wackerly, D. D., W. Mendenhall, and R. L. Scheaffer, *Mathematical Statistics with Applications*, 6th ed., Duxbury, 2002.

Quality Control

Deming, W. E., *Quality, Productivity, and Competitive Position*, MIT, 1982.

Evans, J. R., and W. M. Lindsay, *The Management and Control of Quality*, 4th ed., South-Western, 1998.

Gryna, F. M., and I. M. Juran, *Quality Planning and Analysis: From Product Development Through Use*, 3rd ed., McGraw-Hill, 1993.

Ishikawa, K., *Introduction to Quality Control*, Kluwer Academic, 1991.

Montgomery, D. C., *Introduction to Statistical Quality Control*, 3rd ed., Wiley, 1996.

Regression Analysis

Chatterjee, S., and B. Price, *Regression Analysis by Example*, 3rd ed., Wiley, 1999.

Draper, N. R., and H. Smith, *Applied Regression Analysis*, 3rd ed., Wiley, 1998.

Graybill, F. A., and H. Iyer, *Regression Analysis: Concepts and Applications*, Duxbury Press, 1994.

Kleinbaum, D. G., L. L. Kupper, and K. E. Muller, *Applied Regression Analysis and Other Multivariate Methods*, 3rd ed., Duxbury Press, 1997.

Kutner, M. H., C. J. Nachtschiem, W. Wasserman, and J. Neter, *Applied Linear Statistical Models*, 4th ed., Irwin, 1996.

Mendenhall, M., and T. Sincich, *A Second Course in Statistics: Regression Analysis*, 5th ed., Prentice Hall, 1996.

Appendix B   Tables

TABLE 1   CUMULATIVE PROBABILITIES FOR THE STANDARD NORMAL DISTRIBUTION

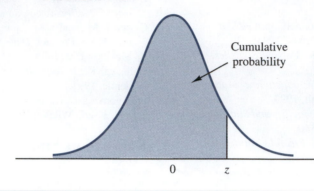

Cumulative probability

Entries in the table give the area under the curve to the left of the z value. For example, for $z = 1.25$ the cumulative probability is .8944.

z	.00	.01	.02	.03	.04	.05	.06	.07	.08	.09
.0	.5000	.5040	.5080	.5120	.5160	.5199	.5239	.5279	.5319	.5359
.1	.5398	.5438	.5478	.5517	.5557	.5596	.5636	.5675	.5714	.5753
.2	.5793	.5832	.5871	.5910	.5948	.5987	.6026	.6064	.6103	.6141
.3	.6179	.6217	.6255	.6293	.6331	.6368	.6406	.6443	.6480	.6517
.4	.6554	.6591	.6628	.6664	.6700	.6736	.6772	.6808	.6844	.6879
.5	.6915	.6950	.6985	.7019	.7054	.7088	.7123	.7157	.7190	.7224
.6	.7257	.7291	.7324	.7357	.7389	.7422	.7454	.7486	.7517	.7549
.7	.7580	.7611	.7642	.7673	.7704	.7734	.7764	.7794	.7823	.7852
.8	.7881	.7910	.7939	.7967	.7995	.8023	.8051	.8078	.8106	.8133
.9	.8159	.8186	.8212	.8238	.8264	.8289	.8315	.8340	.8365	.8389
1.0	.8413	.8438	.8461	.8485	.8508	.8531	.8554	.8577	.8599	.8621
1.1	.8643	.8665	.8686	.8708	.8729	.8749	.8770	.8790	.8810	.8830
1.2	.8849	.8869	.8888	.8907	.8925	.8944	.8962	.8980	.8997	.9015
1.3	.9032	.9049	.9066	.9082	.9099	.9115	.9131	.9147	.9162	.9177
1.4	.9192	.9207	.9222	.9236	.9251	.9265	.9279	.9292	.9306	.9319
1.5	.9332	.9345	.9357	.9370	.9382	.9394	.9406	.9418	.9429	.9441
1.6	.9452	.9463	.9474	.9484	.9495	.9505	.9515	.9525	.9535	.9545
1.7	.9554	.9564	.9573	.9582	.9591	.9599	.9608	.9616	.9625	.9633
1.8	.9641	.9649	.9656	.9664	.9671	.9678	.9686	.9693	.9699	.9706
1.9	.9713	.9719	.9726	.9732	.9738	.9744	.9750	.9756	.9761	.9767
2.0	.9772	.9778	.9783	.9788	.9793	.9798	.9803	.9808	.9812	.9817
2.1	.9821	.9826	.9830	.9834	.9838	.9842	.9846	.9850	.9854	.9857
2.2	.9861	.9864	.9868	.9871	.9875	.9878	.9881	.9884	.9887	.9890
2.3	.9893	.9896	.9898	.9901	.9904	.9906	.9909	.9911	.9913	.9913
2.4	.9918	.9920	.9922	.9925	.9927	.9929	.9931	.9932	.9934	.9936
2.5	.9938	.9940	.9941	.9943	.9945	.9946	.9948	.9949	.9951	.9952
2.6	.9953	.9955	.9956	.9957	.9959	.9960	.9961	.9962	.9963	.9964
2.7	.9965	.9966	.9967	.9968	.9969	.9970	.9971	.9972	.9973	.9974
2.8	.9974	.9975	.9976	.9977	.9977	.9978	.9979	.9979	.9980	.9981
2.9	.9981	.9982	.9982	.9983	.9984	.9984	.9985	.9985	.9986	.9986
3.0	.9987	.9987	.9987	.9988	.9988	.9989	.9989	.9989	.9990	.9990

TABLE 2   *t* DISTRIBUTION

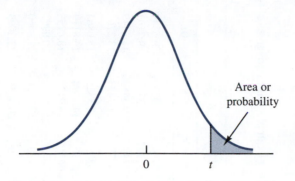

Area or probability

Entries in the table give *t* values for an area or probability in the upper tail of the *t* distribution. For example, with 10 degrees of freedom and a .05 area in the upper tail, $t_{.05} = 1.812$.

Degrees of Freedom	Area in Upper Tail				
	.10	.05	.025	.01	.005
1	3.078	6.314	12.706	31.821	63.656
2	1.886	2.920	4.303	6.965	9.925
3	1.638	2.353	3.182	4.541	5.841
4	1.533	2.132	2.776	3.747	4.604
5	1.476	2.015	2.571	3.365	4.032
6	1.440	1.943	2.447	3.143	3.707
7	1.415	1.895	2.365	2.998	3.499
8	1.397	1.860	2.306	2.896	3.355
9	1.383	1.833	2.262	2.821	3.250
10	1.372	1.812	2.228	2.764	3.169
11	1.363	1.796	2.201	2.718	3.106
12	1.356	1.782	2.179	2.681	3.055
13	1.350	1.771	2.160	2.650	3.012
14	1.345	1.761	2.145	2.624	2.977
15	1.341	1.753	2.131	2.602	2.947
16	1.337	1.746	2.120	2.583	2.921
17	1.333	1.740	2.110	2.567	2.898
18	1.330	1.734	2.101	2.552	2.878
19	1.328	1.729	2.093	2.539	2.861
20	1.325	1.725	2.086	2.528	2.845
21	1.323	1.721	2.080	2.518	2.831
22	1.321	1.717	2.074	2.508	2.819
23	1.319	1.714	2.069	2.500	2.807
24	1.318	1.711	2.064	2.492	2.797
25	1.316	1.708	2.060	2.485	2.787
26	1.315	1.706	2.056	2.479	2.779
27	1.314	1.703	2.052	2.473	2.771
28	1.313	1.701	2.048	2.467	2.763
29	1.311	1.699	2.045	2.462	2.756
30	1.310	1.697	2.042	2.457	2.750
40	1.303	1.684	2.021	2.423	2.704
60	1.296	1.671	2.000	2.390	2.660
120	1.289	1.658	1.980	2.358	2.617
∞	1.282	1.645	1.960	2.326	2.576

TABLE 3 CHI-SQUARE DISTRIBUTION

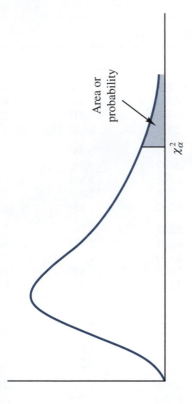

Area or probability

χ_α^2

Entries in the table give χ_α^2 values, where α is the area or probability in the upper tail of the chi-square distribution. For example, with 10 degrees of freedom and a .01 area in the upper tail, $\chi_{.01}^2 = 23.2093$.

Degrees of Freedom	Area in Upper Tail											
	.995	.99	.975	.95	.90	.10	.05	.025	.01	.005
1	$392,704 \times 10^{-10}$	$157,088 \times 10^{-9}$	$982,069 \times 10^{-9}$	$393,214 \times 10^{-8}$	.0157908	2.70554	3.84146	5.02389	6.63490	7.87944
2	.0100251	.0201007	.0506356	.102587	.210720	4.60517	5.99147	7.37776	9.21034	10.5966
3	.0717212	.114832	.215795	.351846	.584375	6.25139	7.81473	9.34840	11.3449	12.8381
4	.206990	.297110	.484419	.710721	1.063623	7.77944	9.48773	11.1433	13.2767	14.8602
5	.411740	.554300	.831211	1.145476	1.61031	9.23635	11.0705	12.8325	15.0863	16.7496
6	.675727	.872085	1.237347	1.63539	2.20413	10.6446	12.5916	14.4494	16.8119	18.5476
7	.989265	1.239043	1.68987	2.16735	2.83311	12.0170	14.0671	16.0128	18.4753	20.2777
8	1.344419	1.646482	2.17973	2.73264	3.48954	13.3616	15.5073	17.5346	20.0902	21.9550
9	1.734926	2.087912	2.70039	3.32511	4.16816	14.6837	16.9190	19.0228	21.6660	23.5893
10	2.15585	2.55821	3.24697	3.94030	4.86518	15.9871	18.3070	20.4831	23.2093	25.1882
11	2.60321	3.05347	3.81575	4.57481	5.57779	17.2750	19.6751	21.9200	24.7250	26.7569
12	3.07382	3.57056	4.40379	5.22603	6.30380	18.5494	21.0261	23.3367	26.2170	28.2995
13	3.56503	4.10691	5.00874	5.89186	7.04150	19.8119	22.3621	24.7356	27.6883	29.8194
14	4.07468	4.66043	5.62872	6.57063	7.78953	21.0642	23.6848	26.1190	29.1413	31.3193
15	4.60094	5.22935	6.26214	7.26094	8.54675	22.3072	24.9958	27.4884	30.5779	32.8013
16	5.14224	5.81221	6.90766	7.96164	9.31223	23.5418	26.2962	28.8454	31.9999	34.2672
17	5.69724	6.40776	7.56418	8.67176	10.0852	24.7690	27.5871	30.1910	33.4087	35.7185
18	6.26481	7.01491	8.23075	9.39046	10.8649	25.9894	28.8693	31.5264	34.8053	37.1564
19	6.84398	7.63273	8.90655	10.1170	11.6509	27.2036	30.1435	32.8523	36.1908	38.5822

TABLE 3   CHI-SQUARE DISTRIBUTION (*continued*)

Degrees of Freedom	Area in Upper Tail									
	.995	.99	.975	.95	.90	.10	.05	.025	.01	.005
20	7.43386	8.26040	9.59083	10.8508	12.4426	28.4120	31.4104	34.1696	37.5662	39.9968
21	8.03366	8.89720	10.28293	11.5913	13.2396	29.6151	32.6705	35.4789	38.9321	41.4010
22	8.64272	9.54249	10.9823	12.3380	14.0415	30.8133	33.9244	36.7807	40.2894	42.7958
23	9.26042	10.19567	11.6885	13.0905	14.8479	32.0069	35.1725	38.0757	41.6384	44.1813
24	9.88623	10.8564	12.4011	13.8484	15.6587	33.1963	36.4151	39.3641	42.9798	45.5585
25	10.5197	11.5240	13.1197	14.6114	16.4734	34.3816	37.6525	40.6465	44.3141	46.9278
26	11.1603	12.1981	13.8439	15.3791	17.2919	35.5631	38.8852	41.9232	45.6417	48.2899
27	11.8076	12.8786	14.5733	16.1513	18.1138	36.7412	40.1133	43.1944	46.9630	49.6449
28	12.4613	13.5648	15.3079	16.9279	18.9392	37.9159	41.3372	44.4607	48.2782	50.9933
29	13.1211	14.2565	16.0471	17.7083	19.7677	39.0875	42.5569	45.7222	49.5879	52.3356
30	13.7867	14.9535	16.7908	18.4926	20.5992	40.2560	43.7729	46.9792	50.8922	53.6720
40	20.7065	22.1643	24.4331	26.5093	29.0505	51.8050	55.7585	59.3417	63.6907	66.7659
50	27.9907	29.7067	32.3574	34.7642	37.6886	63.1671	67.5048	71.4202	76.1539	79.4900
60	35.5346	37.4848	40.4817	43.1879	46.4589	74.3970	79.0819	83.2976	88.3794	91.9517
70	43.2752	45.4418	48.7576	51.7393	55.3290	85.5271	90.5312	95.0231	100.425	104.215
80	51.1720	53.5400	57.1532	60.3915	64.2778	96.5782	101.879	106.629	112.329	116.321
90	59.1963	61.7541	65.6466	69.1260	73.2912	107.565	113.145	118.136	124.116	128.299
100	67.3276	70.0648	74.2219	77.9295	82.3581	118.498	124.342	129.561	135.807	140.169

Reprinted from E. S. Pearson and H. O. Hartley, Table 8, "Percentage Points of the χ^2 Distribution," *Biometrika Tables for Statisticians*, Vol. 1, 3rd ed., 1966, by permission of the Biometrika Trustees.

TABLE 4 F DISTRIBUTION

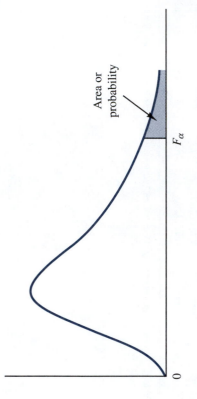

Area or probability

F_α

Entries in the table give F_α values, where α is the area or probability in the upper tail of the F distribution. For example, with 12 numerator degrees of freedom, 15 denominator degrees of freedom, and a .05 area in the upper tail, $F_{.05} = 2.48$.

Table of $F_{.05}$ Values

Denominator Degrees of Freedom	Numerator Degrees of Freedom																		
	1	2	3	4	5	6	7	8	9	10	12	15	20	24	30	40	60	120	∞
1	161.4	199.5	215.7	224.6	230.2	234.0	236.8	238.9	240.5	241.9	243.9	245.9	248.0	249.1	250.1	251.1	252.2	253.3	254.3
2	18.51	19.00	19.16	19.25	19.30	19.33	19.35	19.37	19.38	19.40	19.41	19.43	19.45	19.45	19.46	19.47	19.48	19.49	19.50
3	10.13	9.55	9.28	9.12	9.01	8.94	8.89	8.85	8.81	8.79	8.74	8.70	8.66	8.64	8.62	8.59	8.57	8.55	8.53
4	7.71	6.94	6.59	6.39	6.26	6.16	6.09	6.04	6.00	5.96	5.91	5.86	5.80	5.77	5.75	5.72	5.69	5.66	5.63
5	6.61	5.79	5.41	5.19	5.05	4.95	4.88	4.82	4.77	4.74	4.68	4.62	4.56	4.53	4.50	4.46	4.43	4.40	4.36
6	5.99	5.14	4.76	4.53	4.39	4.28	4.21	4.15	4.10	4.06	4.00	3.94	3.87	3.84	3.81	3.77	3.74	3.70	3.67
7	5.59	4.74	4.35	4.12	3.97	3.87	3.79	3.73	3.68	3.64	3.57	3.51	3.44	3.41	3.38	3.34	3.30	3.27	3.23
8	5.32	4.46	4.07	3.84	3.69	3.58	3.50	3.44	3.39	3.35	3.28	3.22	3.15	3.12	3.08	3.04	3.01	2.97	2.93
9	5.12	4.26	3.86	3.63	3.48	3.37	3.29	3.23	3.18	3.14	3.07	3.01	2.94	2.90	2.86	2.83	2.79	2.75	2.71
10	4.96	4.10	3.71	3.48	3.33	3.22	3.14	3.07	3.02	2.98	2.91	2.85	2.77	2.74	2.70	2.66	2.62	2.58	2.54
11	4.84	3.98	3.59	3.36	3.20	3.09	3.01	2.95	2.90	2.85	2.79	2.72	2.65	2.61	2.57	2.53	2.49	2.45	2.40
12	4.75	3.89	3.49	3.26	3.11	3.00	2.91	2.85	2.80	2.75	2.69	2.62	2.54	2.51	2.47	2.43	2.38	2.34	2.30
13	4.67	3.81	3.41	3.18	3.03	2.92	2.83	2.77	2.71	2.67	2.60	2.53	2.46	2.42	2.38	2.34	2.30	2.25	2.21
14	4.60	3.74	3.34	3.11	2.96	2.85	2.76	2.70	2.65	2.60	2.53	2.46	2.39	2.35	2.31	2.27	2.22	2.18	2.13

TABLE 4 *F* DISTRIBUTION (*continued*)

Table of $F_{.05}$ Values

Denominator Degrees of Freedom	Numerator Degrees of Freedom																		
	1	2	3	4	5	6	7	8	9	10	12	15	20	24	30	40	60	120	∞
15	4.54	3.68	3.29	3.06	2.90	2.79	2.71	2.64	2.59	2.54	2.48	2.40	2.33	2.29	2.25	2.20	2.16	2.11	2.07
16	4.49	3.63	3.24	3.01	2.85	2.74	2.66	2.59	2.54	2.49	2.42	2.35	2.28	2.24	2.19	2.15	2.11	2.06	2.01
17	4.45	3.59	3.20	2.96	2.81	2.70	2.61	2.55	2.49	2.45	2.38	2.31	2.23	2.19	2.15	2.10	2.06	2.01	1.96
18	4.41	3.55	3.16	2.93	2.77	2.66	2.58	2.51	2.46	2.41	2.34	2.27	2.19	2.15	2.11	2.06	2.02	1.97	1.92
19	4.38	3.52	3.13	2.90	2.74	2.63	2.54	2.48	2.42	2.38	2.31	2.23	2.16	2.11	2.07	2.03	1.98	1.93	1.88
20	4.35	3.49	3.10	2.87	2.71	2.60	2.51	2.45	2.39	2.35	2.28	2.20	2.12	2.08	2.04	1.99	1.95	1.90	1.84
21	4.32	3.47	3.07	2.84	2.68	2.57	2.49	2.42	2.37	2.32	2.25	2.18	2.10	2.05	2.01	1.96	1.92	1.87	1.81
22	4.30	3.44	3.05	2.82	2.66	2.55	2.46	2.40	2.34	2.30	2.23	2.15	2.07	2.03	1.98	1.94	1.89	1.84	1.78
23	4.28	3.42	3.03	2.80	2.64	2.53	2.44	2.37	2.32	2.27	2.20	2.13	2.05	2.01	1.96	1.91	1.86	1.81	1.76
24	4.26	3.40	3.01	2.78	2.62	2.51	2.42	2.36	2.30	2.25	2.18	2.11	2.03	1.98	1.94	1.89	1.84	1.79	1.73
25	4.24	3.39	2.99	2.76	2.60	2.49	2.40	2.34	2.28	2.24	2.16	2.09	2.01	1.96	1.92	1.87	1.82	1.77	1.71
26	4.23	3.37	2.98	2.74	2.59	2.47	2.39	2.32	2.27	2.22	2.15	2.07	1.99	1.95	1.90	1.85	1.80	1.75	1.69
27	4.21	3.35	2.96	2.73	2.57	2.46	2.37	2.31	2.25	2.20	2.13	2.06	1.97	1.93	1.88	1.84	1.79	1.73	1.67
28	4.20	3.34	2.95	2.71	2.56	2.45	2.36	2.29	2.24	2.19	2.12	2.04	1.96	1.91	1.87	1.82	1.77	1.71	1.65
29	4.18	3.33	2.93	2.70	2.55	2.43	2.35	2.28	2.22	2.18	2.10	2.03	1.94	1.90	1.85	1.81	1.75	1.70	1.64
30	4.17	3.32	2.92	2.69	2.53	2.42	2.33	2.27	2.21	2.16	2.09	2.01	1.93	1.89	1.84	1.79	1.74	1.68	1.62
40	4.08	3.23	2.84	2.61	2.45	2.34	2.25	2.18	2.12	2.08	2.00	1.92	1.84	1.79	1.74	1.69	1.64	1.58	1.51
60	4.00	3.15	2.76	2.53	2.37	2.25	2.17	2.10	2.04	1.99	1.92	1.84	1.75	1.70	1.65	1.59	1.53	1.47	1.39
120	3.92	3.07	2.68	2.45	2.29	2.17	2.09	2.02	1.96	1.91	1.83	1.75	1.66	1.61	1.55	1.50	1.43	1.35	1.25
∞	3.84	3.00	2.60	2.37	2.21	2.10	2.01	1.94	1.88	1.83	1.75	1.67	1.57	1.52	1.46	1.39	1.32	1.22	1.00

Reprinted from E. S. Pearson and H. O. Hartley, Table 18, "Percentage Points of the χ^2 Distribution," *Biometrika Tables for Statisticians*, Vol. 1, 3rd ed., 1966, by permission of the Biometrika Trustees.

TABLE 4 F DISTRIBUTION (*Continued*)

Table of $F_{.025}$ Values

Denominator Degrees of Freedom	Numerator Degrees of Freedom																		
	1	2	3	4	5	6	7	8	9	10	12	15	20	24	30	40	60	120	∞
1	647.80	799.50	864.20	899.60	921.80	937.10	948.20	956.70	963.30	968.60	976.70	984.90	993.10	997.20	1,001	1,006	1,010	1,014	1,018
2	38.51	39.00	39.17	39.25	39.30	39.33	39.36	39.37	39.39	39.40	39.41	39.43	39.45	39.46	39.46	39.47	39.48	39.49	39.50
3	17.44	16.04	15.44	15.10	14.88	14.73	14.62	14.54	14.47	14.42	14.34	14.25	14.17	14.12	14.08	14.04	13.99	13.95	13.90
4	12.22	10.65	9.98	9.60	9.36	9.20	9.07	8.98	8.90	8.84	8.75	8.66	8.56	8.51	8.46	8.41	8.36	8.31	8.26
5	10.01	8.43	7.76	7.39	7.15	6.98	6.85	6.76	6.68	6.62	6.52	6.43	6.33	6.28	6.23	6.18	6.12	6.07	6.02
6	8.81	7.26	6.60	6.23	5.99	5.82	5.70	5.60	5.52	5.46	5.37	5.27	5.17	5.12	5.07	5.01	4.96	4.90	4.85
7	8.07	6.54	5.89	5.52	5.29	5.21	4.99	4.90	4.82	4.76	4.67	4.57	4.47	4.42	4.36	4.31	4.25	4.20	4.14
8	7.57	6.06	5.42	5.05	4.82	4.65	4.53	4.43	4.36	4.30	4.20	4.10	4.00	3.95	3.89	3.84	3.78	3.73	3.67
9	7.21	5.71	5.08	4.72	4.48	4.32	4.20	4.10	4.03	3.96	3.87	3.77	3.67	3.61	3.56	3.51	3.45	3.39	3.33
10	6.94	5.46	4.83	4.47	4.24	4.07	3.95	3.85	3.78	3.72	3.62	3.52	3.42	3.37	3.31	3.26	3.20	3.14	3.08
11	6.72	5.26	4.63	4.28	4.04	3.88	3.76	3.66	3.59	3.53	3.43	3.33	3.23	3.17	3.12	3.06	3.00	2.94	2.88
12	6.55	5.10	4.47	4.12	3.89	3.73	3.61	3.51	3.44	3.37	3.28	3.18	3.07	3.02	2.96	2.91	2.85	2.79	2.72
13	6.41	4.97	4.35	4.00	3.77	3.60	3.48	3.39	3.31	3.25	3.15	3.05	2.95	2.89	2.84	2.78	2.72	2.66	2.60
14	6.30	4.86	4.24	3.89	3.66	3.50	3.38	3.29	3.21	3.15	3.05	2.95	2.84	2.79	2.73	2.67	2.61	2.55	2.49
15	6.20	4.77	4.15	3.80	3.58	3.41	3.29	3.20	3.12	3.06	2.96	2.86	2.76	2.70	2.64	2.59	2.52	2.46	2.40
16	6.12	4.69	4.08	3.73	3.50	3.34	3.22	3.12	3.05	2.99	2.89	2.79	2.68	2.63	2.57	2.51	2.45	2.38	2.32
17	6.04	4.62	4.01	3.66	3.44	3.28	3.16	3.06	2.98	2.92	2.82	2.72	2.62	2.56	2.50	2.44	2.38	2.32	2.25
18	5.98	4.56	3.95	3.61	3.38	3.22	3.10	3.01	2.93	2.87	2.77	2.67	2.56	2.50	2.44	2.38	2.32	2.26	2.19
19	5.92	4.51	3.90	3.56	3.33	3.17	3.05	2.96	2.88	2.82	2.72	2.62	2.51	2.45	2.39	2.33	2.27	2.20	2.13
20	5.87	4.46	3.86	3.51	3.29	3.13	3.01	2.91	2.84	2.77	2.68	2.57	2.46	2.41	2.35	2.29	2.22	2.16	2.09
21	5.83	4.42	3.82	3.48	3.25	3.09	2.97	2.87	2.80	2.73	2.64	2.53	2.42	2.37	2.31	2.25	2.18	2.11	2.04
22	5.79	4.38	3.78	3.44	3.22	3.05	2.93	2.84	2.76	2.70	2.60	2.50	2.39	2.33	2.27	2.21	2.14	2.08	2.00
23	5.75	4.35	3.75	3.41	3.18	3.02	2.90	2.81	2.73	2.67	2.57	2.47	2.36	2.30	2.24	2.18	2.11	2.04	1.97
24	5.72	4.32	3.72	3.38	3.15	2.99	2.87	2.78	2.70	2.64	2.54	2.44	2.33	2.27	2.21	2.15	2.08	2.01	1.94
25	5.69	4.29	3.69	3.35	3.13	2.97	2.85	2.75	2.68	2.61	2.51	2.41	2.30	2.24	2.18	2.12	2.05	1.98	1.91
26	5.66	4.27	3.67	3.33	3.10	2.94	2.82	2.73	2.65	2.59	2.49	2.39	2.28	2.22	2.16	2.09	2.03	1.95	1.88
27	5.63	4.24	3.65	3.31	3.08	2.92	2.80	2.71	2.63	2.57	2.47	2.36	2.25	2.19	2.13	2.07	2.00	1.93	1.85
28	5.61	4.22	3.63	3.29	3.06	2.90	2.78	2.69	2.61	2.55	2.45	2.34	2.23	2.17	2.11	2.05	1.98	1.91	1.83
29	5.59	4.20	3.61	3.27	3.04	2.88	2.76	2.67	2.59	2.53	2.43	2.32	2.21	2.15	2.09	2.03	1.96	1.89	1.81
30	5.57	4.18	3.59	3.25	3.03	2.87	2.75	2.65	2.57	2.51	2.41	2.31	2.20	2.14	2.07	2.01	1.94	1.87	1.79
40	5.42	4.05	3.46	3.13	2.90	2.74	2.62	2.53	2.45	2.39	2.29	2.18	2.07	2.01	1.94	1.88	1.80	1.72	1.64
60	5.29	3.93	3.34	3.01	2.79	2.63	2.51	2.41	2.33	2.27	2.17	2.06	1.94	1.88	1.82	1.74	1.67	1.58	1.48
120	5.15	3.80	3.23	2.89	2.67	2.52	2.39	2.30	2.22	2.16	2.05	1.94	1.82	1.76	1.69	1.61	1.53	1.43	1.31
∞	5.02	3.69	3.12	2.79	2.57	2.41	2.29	2.19	2.11	2.05	1.94	1.83	1.71	1.64	1.57	1.48	1.39	1.27	1.00

TABLE 4 *F* DISTRIBUTION (*Continued*)

Table of $F_{.01}$ Values

Numerator Degrees of Freedom

Denominator Degrees of Freedom	1	2	3	4	5	6	7	8	9	10	12	15	20	24	30	40	60	120	∞
1	4,052	4,999.5	5,403	5,625	5,764	5,859	5,928	5,982	6,022	6,056	6,106	6,157	6,209	6,235	6,261	6,287	6,313	6,339	6,366
2	98.50	99.00	99.17	99.25	99.30	99.33	99.36	99.37	99.39	99.40	99.42	99.43	99.45	99.46	99.47	99.47	99.48	99.49	99.50
3	34.12	30.82	29.46	28.71	28.24	27.91	27.67	27.49	27.35	27.23	27.05	26.87	26.69	26.60	26.50	26.41	26.32	26.22	26.13
4	21.20	18.00	16.69	15.98	15.52	15.21	14.98	14.80	14.66	14.55	14.37	14.20	14.02	13.93	13.84	13.75	13.65	13.56	13.46
5	16.26	13.27	12.06	11.39	10.97	10.67	10.46	10.29	10.16	10.05	9.89	9.72	9.55	9.47	9.38	9.29	9.20	9.11	9.06
6	13.75	10.92	9.78	9.15	8.75	8.47	8.26	8.10	7.98	7.87	7.72	7.56	7.40	7.31	7.23	7.14	7.06	6.97	6.88
7	12.25	9.55	8.45	7.85	7.46	7.19	6.99	6.84	6.72	6.62	6.47	6.31	6.16	6.07	5.99	5.91	5.82	5.74	5.65
8	11.26	8.65	7.59	7.01	6.63	6.37	6.18	6.03	5.91	5.81	5.67	5.52	5.36	5.28	5.20	5.12	5.03	4.95	4.86
9	10.56	8.02	6.99	6.42	6.06	5.80	5.61	5.47	5.35	5.26	5.11	4.96	4.81	4.73	4.65	4.57	4.48	4.40	4.31
10	10.04	7.56	6.55	5.99	5.64	5.39	5.20	5.06	4.94	4.85	4.71	4.56	4.41	4.33	4.25	4.17	4.08	4.00	3.91
11	9.65	7.21	6.22	5.67	5.32	5.07	4.89	4.74	4.63	4.54	4.40	4.25	4.10	4.02	3.94	3.86	3.78	3.69	3.60
12	9.33	6.93	5.95	5.41	5.06	4.82	4.64	4.50	4.39	4.30	4.16	4.01	3.86	3.78	3.70	3.62	3.54	3.45	3.36
13	9.07	6.70	5.74	5.21	4.86	4.62	4.44	4.30	4.19	4.10	3.96	3.82	3.66	3.59	3.51	3.43	3.34	3.25	3.17
14	8.86	6.51	5.56	5.04	4.69	4.46	4.28	4.14	4.03	3.94	3.80	3.66	3.51	3.43	3.35	3.27	3.18	3.09	3.00
15	8.68	6.36	5.42	4.89	4.56	4.32	4.14	4.00	3.89	3.80	3.67	3.52	3.37	3.29	3.21	3.13	3.05	2.96	2.87
16	8.53	6.23	5.29	4.77	4.44	4.20	4.03	3.89	3.78	3.69	3.55	3.41	3.26	3.18	3.10	3.02	2.93	2.84	2.75
17	8.40	6.11	5.18	4.67	4.34	4.10	3.93	3.79	3.68	3.59	3.46	3.31	3.16	3.08	3.00	2.92	2.83	2.75	2.65
18	8.29	6.01	5.09	4.58	4.25	4.01	3.84	3.71	3.60	3.51	3.37	3.23	3.08	3.00	2.92	2.84	2.75	2.66	2.57
19	8.18	5.93	5.01	4.50	4.17	3.94	3.77	3.63	3.52	3.43	3.30	3.15	3.00	2.92	2.84	2.76	2.67	2.58	2.49
20	8.10	5.85	4.94	4.43	4.10	3.87	3.70	3.56	3.46	3.37	3.23	3.09	2.94	2.86	2.78	2.69	2.61	2.52	2.42
21	8.02	5.78	4.87	4.37	4.04	3.81	3.64	3.51	3.40	3.31	3.17	3.03	2.88	2.80	2.72	2.64	2.55	2.46	2.36
22	7.95	5.72	4.82	4.31	3.99	3.76	3.59	3.45	3.35	3.26	3.12	2.98	2.83	2.75	2.67	2.58	2.50	2.40	2.31
23	7.88	5.66	4.76	4.26	3.94	3.71	3.54	3.41	3.30	3.21	3.07	2.93	2.78	2.70	2.62	2.54	2.45	2.35	2.26
24	7.82	5.61	4.72	4.22	3.90	3.67	3.50	3.36	3.26	3.17	3.03	2.89	2.74	2.66	2.58	2.49	2.40	2.31	2.21
25	7.77	5.57	4.68	4.18	3.85	3.63	3.46	3.32	3.22	3.13	2.99	2.85	2.70	2.62	2.54	2.45	2.36	2.27	2.17
26	7.72	5.53	4.64	4.14	3.82	3.59	3.42	3.29	3.18	3.09	2.96	2.81	2.66	2.58	2.50	2.42	2.33	2.23	2.13
27	7.68	5.49	4.60	4.11	3.78	3.56	3.39	3.26	3.15	3.06	2.93	2.78	2.63	2.55	2.47	2.38	2.29	2.20	2.10
28	7.64	5.45	4.57	4.07	3.75	3.53	3.36	3.23	3.12	3.03	2.90	2.75	2.60	2.52	2.44	2.35	2.26	2.17	2.06
29	7.60	5.42	4.54	4.04	3.73	3.50	3.33	3.20	3.09	3.00	2.87	2.73	2.57	2.49	2.41	2.33	2.23	2.14	2.03
30	7.56	5.39	4.51	4.02	3.70	3.47	3.30	3.17	3.07	2.98	2.84	2.70	2.55	2.47	2.39	2.30	2.21	2.11	2.01
40	7.31	5.18	4.31	3.83	3.51	3.29	3.12	2.99	2.89	2.80	2.66	2.52	2.37	2.29	2.20	2.11	2.02	1.92	1.80
60	7.08	4.98	4.13	3.65	3.34	3.12	2.95	2.82	2.72	2.63	2.50	2.35	2.20	2.12	2.03	1.94	1.84	1.73	1.60
120	6.85	4.79	3.95	3.48	3.17	2.96	2.79	2.66	2.56	2.47	2.34	2.19	2.03	1.95	1.86	1.76	1.66	1.53	1.38
∞	6.63	4.61	3.78	3.32	3.02	2.80	2.64	2.51	2.41	2.32	2.18	2.04	1.88	1.79	1.70	1.59	1.47	1.32	1.00

Appendix C   Summation Notation

Summations

Definition

$$\sum_{i=1}^{n} x_i = x_1 + x_2 + \cdots + x_n \qquad \text{(C.1)}$$

Example for $x_1 = 5, x_2 = 8, x_3 = 14$:

$$\sum_{i=1}^{3} x_i = x_1 + x_2 + x_3$$
$$= 5 + 8 + 14$$
$$= 27$$

Result 1

For a constant c:

$$\sum_{i=1}^{n} c = \underbrace{(c + c + \cdots + c)}_{n \text{ times}} = nc \qquad \text{(C.2)}$$

Example for $c = 5, n = 10$:

$$\sum_{i=1}^{10} 5 = 10(5) = 50$$

Example for $c = \bar{x}$:

$$\sum_{i=1}^{n} \bar{x} = n\bar{x}$$

Result 2

$$\sum_{i=1}^{n} cx_i = cx_1 + cx_2 + \cdots + cx_n$$
$$= c(x_1 + x_2 + \cdots + x_n) = c\sum_{i=1}^{n} x_i \qquad \text{(C.3)}$$

Example for $x_1 = 5, x_2 = 8, x_3 = 14, c = 2$:

$$\sum_{i=1}^{3} 2x_i = 2\sum_{i=1}^{3} x_i = 2(27) = 54$$

Result 3

$$\sum_{i=1}^{n} (ax_i + by_i) = a\sum_{i=1}^{n} x_i + b\sum_{i=1}^{n} y_i \qquad \text{(C.4)}$$

Example for $x_1 = 5, x_2 = 8, x_3 = 14, a = 2, y_1 = 7, y_2 = 3, y_3 = 8, b = 4$:

$$\sum_{i=1}^{3} (2x_i + 4y_i) = 2 \sum_{i=1}^{3} x_i + 4 \sum_{i=1}^{3} y_i$$
$$= 2(27) + 4(18)$$
$$= 54 + 72$$
$$= 126$$

Double Summations

Consider the following data involving the variable x_{ij}, where i is the subscript denoting the row position and j is the subscript denoting the column position:

		Column		
		1	**2**	**3**
Row	**1**	$x_{11} = 10$	$x_{12} = 8$	$x_{13} = 6$
	2	$x_{21} = 7$	$x_{22} = 4$	$x_{23} = 12$

Definition

$$\sum_{i=1}^{n} \sum_{j=1}^{m} x_{ij} = (x_{11} + x_{12} + \cdots + x_{1m}) + (x_{21} + x_{22} + \cdots + x_{2m})$$
$$+ (x_{31} + x_{32} + \cdots + x_{3m}) + \cdots + (x_{n1} + x_{n2} + \cdots + x_{nm}) \qquad \text{(C.5)}$$

Example:

$$\sum_{i=1}^{2} \sum_{j=1}^{3} x_{ij} = x_{11} + x_{12} + x_{13} + x_{21} + x_{22} + x_{23}$$
$$= 10 + 8 + 6 + 7 + 4 + 12$$
$$= 47$$

Definition

$$\sum_{i=1}^{n} x_{ij} = x_{1j} + x_{2j} + \cdots + x_{nj} \qquad \text{(C.6)}$$

Example:

$$\sum_{i=1}^{2} x_{i2} = x_{12} + x_{22}$$
$$= 8 + 4$$
$$= 12$$

Shorthand Notation

Sometimes when a summation is for all values of the subscript, we use the following shorthand notations:

$$\sum_{i=1}^{n} x_i = \sum x_i \qquad \text{(C.7)}$$

$$\sum_{i=1}^{n} \sum_{j=1}^{m} x_{ij} = \sum \sum x_{ij} \qquad \text{(C.8)}$$

$$\sum_{i=1}^{n} x_{ij} = \sum_i x_{ij} \qquad \text{(C.9)}$$

Chapter 1

2. a. 9
 b. 4
 c. Qualitative: country and room rate
   Quantitative: number of rooms and overall score
 d. Country is nominal; room rate is ordinal; number of rooms is ratio; overall score is interval

3. a. Average number of rooms = 808/9 = 89.78 or approximately 90 rooms
 b. Average overall score = 732.1/9 = 81.3
 c. 2 of 9 are located in England; approximately 22%
 d. 4 of 9 have a room rate of $$; approximately 44%

4. a. 10
 b. All brands and models of minisystems manufactured
 c. $314
 d. $314

6. Questions a, c, and d are quantitative
  Questions b and e are qualitative

8. a. 1005
 b. Qualitative
 c. Percentages
 d. Approximately 291

10. a. Quantitative; ratio
 b. Qualitative; nominal
 c. Qualitative; ordinal
 d. Qualitative; nominal
 e. Quantitative; ratio

12. a. All visitors to Hawaii
 b. Yes
 c. Questions 1 and 4 provide quantitative data
   Questions 2 and 3 provide qualitative data

13. a. Quantitative
 b. Time series with 6 observations
 c. Earnings for Volkswagen
 d. An increase would be expected in 2003, but it appears that the rate of increase is slowing

14. a. Qualitative

16. a. Product taste tests and test marketing
 b. Specially designed statistical studies

18. a. 40%
 b. Qualitative

20. a. 56% and $387,325
 b. 3.73
 c. $387,325

22. a. All adult viewers reached by the station
 b. Viewers contacted in the telephone survey
 c. Too difficult and costly to reach the entire population

24. a. Correct
 b. Incorrect
 c. Correct
 d. Incorrect
 e. Incorrect

Chapter 2

2. a. .20
 b. 40
 c/d.

Class	Frequency	Percent Frequency
A	44	22
B	36	18
C	80	40
D	40	20
Total	200	100

3. a. $360° \times 58/120 = 174°$
 b. $360° \times 42/120 = 126°$
 c.

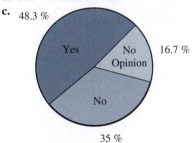

 d.

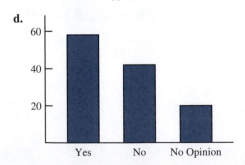

4. a. Qualitative

b.

TV Show	Frequency	Percent Frequency
Millionaire	24	48
Frasier	15	30
Chicago Hope	7	14
Charmed	4	8
Total	50	100

d. Millionaire has the largest market share; Frasier is second

6. a.

Book	Frequency	Percent Frequency
7 Habits	10	16.66
Millionaire	16	26.67
Motley	9	15.00
Dad	13	21.67
WSJ Guide	6	10.00
Other	6	10.00
Total	60	100.00

b. First 5: *Millionaire, Dad, 7 Habits, Motley, WSJ Guide*

c. 48.33%

7.

Rating	Frequency	Relative Frequency
Outstanding	19	.38
Very good	13	.26
Good	10	.20
Average	6	.12
Poor	2	.04

Management should be pleased with these results: 64% of the ratings are very good to outstanding, and 84% of the ratings are good or better; comparing these ratings to previous results will show whether the restaurant is making improvements in its customers' ratings of food quality

8. a.

Position	Frequency	Relative Frequency
P	17	.309
H	4	.073
1	5	.091
2	4	.073
3	2	.036
S	5	.091
L	6	.109
C	5	.091
R	7	.127
Totals	55	1.000

b. Pitcher

c. 3rd base

d. Right field

e. Infielders 16 to outfielders 18

10. a. Quality classifications

b.

Response	Frequency	Relative Frequency
3	2	.03
4	4	.07
5	12	.20
6	24	.40
7	18	.30
Totals	60	1.00

12.

Class	Cumulative Frequency	Cumulative Relative Frequency
≤19	10	.20
≤29	24	.48
≤39	41	.82
≤49	48	.96
≤59	50	1.00

14. a/b.

Class	Frequency	Percent Frequency
6.0–7.9	4	20
8.0–9.9	2	10
10.0–11.9	8	40
12.0–13.9	3	15
14.0–15.9	3	15
Totals	20	100

15. a/b.

Waiting Time	Frequency	Relative Frequency
0–4	4	.20
5–9	8	.40
10–14	5	.25
15–19	2	.10
20–24	1	.05
Totals	20	1.00

c/d.

Waiting Time	Cumulative Frequency	Cumulative Relative Frequency
≤4	4	.20
≤9	12	.60
≤14	17	.85
≤19	19	.95
≤24	20	1.00

e. 12/20 = .60

16. a.

Stock Price ($)	Frequency	Relative Frequency	Percent Frequency
10.00–19.99	10	.40	40
20.00–29.99	4	.16	16
30.00–39.99	6	.24	24
40.00–49.99	2	.08	8
50.00–59.99	1	.04	4
60.00–69.99	2	.08	8
Total	25	1.00	100

b.

Earnings per Share ($)	Frequency	Relative Frequency	Percent Frequency
−3.00 to −2.01	2	.08	8
−2.00 to −1.01	0	.00	0
−1.00 to −0.01	2	.08	8
0.00 to 0.99	9	.36	36
1.00 to 1.99	9	.36	36
2.00 to 2.99	3	.12	12
Total	25	1.00	100

18. a. Lowest salary: $93,000
Highest salary: $178,000

b.

Salary ($1000s)	Frequency	Relative Frequency	Percent Frequency
91–105	4	0.08	8
106–120	5	0.10	10
121–135	11	0.22	22
136–150	18	0.36	36
151–165	9	0.18	18
166–180	3	0.06	6
Total	50	1.00	100

c. 20/50
d. 24%

20. a. 48.9%
b. 51.1%
c. 43.4%
d. 97.075 million
e. 46.6125 million

22.
```
5 | 7  8
6 | 4  5  8
7 | 0  2  2  5  5  6  8
8 | 0  2  3  5
```

23. Leaf unit = .1
```
 6 | 3
 7 | 5  5  7
 8 | 1  3  4  8
 9 | 3  6
10 | 0  4  5
11 | 3
```

24. Leaf Unit = 10
```
11 | 6
12 | 0  2
13 | 0  6  7
14 | 2  2  7
15 | 5
16 | 0  2  8
17 | 0  2  3
```

25.
```
 9 | 8  9
10 | 2  4  6  6
11 | 4  5  7  8  8  9
12 | 2  4  5  7
13 | 1  2
14 | 4
15 | 1
```

26. Leaf Unit = .1
```
0 | 4  7  8  9  9
1 | 1  2  9
2 | 0  0  1  3  5  5  6  8
3 | 4  9
4 | 8
5 |
6 |
7 | 1
```

28. a.
```
0 | 5  8
1 | 1  1  3  3  4  4
1 | 5  6  7  8  9  9
2 | 2  3  3  3  5  5
2 | 6  8
3 |
3 | 6  7  7  9
4 | 0
4 | 7  8
5 |
5 |
6 | 0
```

b.

2000 P/E Forecast	Frequency	Relative Frequency
5–9	2	6.7
10–14	6	20.0
15–19	6	20.0
20–24	6	20.0
25–29	2	6.7
30–34	0	0.0
35–39	4	13.3
40–44	1	3.3
45–49	2	6.7
50–54	0	0.0
55–59	0	0.0
60–64	1	3.3
Total	30	100.0

30. a.

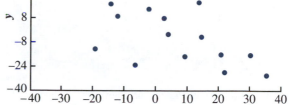

b. There is a negative relationship between x and y; y decreases as x increases

29. a.

		y		
		1	**2**	**Total**
	A	5	0	5
x	**B**	11	2	13
	C	2	10	12
	Total	18	12	30

b.

		y		
		1	**2**	**Total**
	A	100.0	0.0	100.0
x	**B**	84.6	15.4	100.0
	C	16.7	83.3	100.0

c.

		y	
		1	**2**
	A	27.8	0.0
x	**B**	61.1	16.7
	C	11.1	83.3
	Total	100.0	100.0

d. *A* values are always in $y = 1$
    B values are most often in $y = 1$
    C values are most often in $y = 2$

32. a.

Sales/ Margins/ ROE	EPS Rating					
	0– 19	**20– 39**	**40– 59**	**60– 79**	**80– 100**	**Total**
A				1	8	9
B		1	4	5	2	12
C	1		1	2	3	7
D	3	1		1		5
E		2	1			3
Total	4	4	6	9	13	36

b.

Sales/ Margins/ ROE	EPS Rating					
	0– 19	**20– 39**	**40– 59**	**60– 79**	**80– 100**	**Total**
A				11.11	88.89	100
B		8.33	33.33	41.67	16.67	100
C	14.29		14.29	28.57	42.86	100
D	60.00	20.00		20.00		100
E		66.67	33.33			100

Higher EPS ratings seem to be associated with higher ratings on Sales/Margins/ROE

34. b. No apparent relationship

36. a.

Vehicle	Frequency	Percent Frequency
F-Series	17	34
Silverado	12	24
Taurus	8	16
Camry	7	14
Accord	6	12
	50	100

b. Ford F-Series Pickup and Chevrolet Silverado

38. a.

Response	Frequency	Percent Frequency
Accuracy	16	16
Approach shots	3	3
Mental approach	17	17
Power	8	8
Practice	15	15
Putting	10	10
Short game	24	24
Strategic decisions	7	7
Total	100	100

b. Poor short game, poor mental approach, lack of accuracy, and limited practice

40. a/b.

Closing Price	Freq.	Rel. Freq.	Cum. Freq.	Cum. Rel. Freq.
0–9.99	9	.225	9	.225
10–19.99	10	.250	19	.475
20–29.99	5	.125	24	.600
30–39.99	11	.275	35	.875
40–49.99	2	.050	37	.925
50–59.99	2	.050	39	.975
60–69.99	0	.000	39	.975
70–79.99	1	.025	40	1.000
Totals	40	1.000		

42.

Income ($)	Frequency	Relative Frequency
18,000–21,999	13	0.255
22,000–25,999	20	0.392
26,000–29,999	12	0.235
30,000–33,999	4	0.079
34,000–37,999	2	0.039
Total	51	1.000

44. a. High Temperature

```
3 |
4 |
5 | 7
6 | 1 4 4 4 4 6 8
7 | 3 5 7 9
8 | 0 1 1 4 6
9 | 0 2 3
```

b. Low Temperature

```
3 | 9
4 | 3 6 8
5 | 0 0 0 2 4 4 5 5 7 9
6 | 1 8
7 | 2 4 5 5
8 |
9 |
```

c. The range of low temperatures is below the range of high temperatures

d. 8 cities

e.

Temperature	Frequency	
	High Temp.	Low Temp.
30–39	0	1
40–49	0	3
50–59	1	10
60–69	7	2
70–79	4	4
80–89	5	0
90–99	3	0
Total	20	20

46. a.

Occupation	Satisfaction Score 30–39	40–49	50–59	60–69	70–79	80–89	Total
Cabinetmaker			2	4	3	1	10
Lawyer	1	5	2	1	1		10
Physical Therapist			5	2	1	2	10
Systems Analyst		2	1	4	3		10
Total	1	7	10	11	8	3	40

b.

Occupation	Satisfaction Score 30–39	40–49	50–59	60–69	70–79	80–89	Total
Cabinetmaker			20	40	30	10	100
Lawyer	10	50	20	10	10		100
Physical Therapist			50	20	10	20	100
Systems Analyst		20	10	40	30		100

c. Cabinetmakers seem to have the highest job satisfaction scores; lawyers seem to have the lowest

48. a. Row totals: 247; 54; 82; 121
Column totals: 149; 317; 17; 7; 14

b.

Year	Freq.	Fuel	Freq.
1973 or before	247	Elect.	149
1974–79	54	Nat. Gas	317
1980–86	82	Oil	17
1987–91	121	Propane	7
Total	504	Other	14
		Total	504

c. Crosstabulation of Column Percentages

Year Constructed	Fuel Type Elect.	Nat. Gas	Oil	Propane	Other
1973 or before	26.9	57.7	70.5	71.4	50.0
1974–1979	16.1	8.2	11.8	28.6	0.0
1980–1986	24.8	12.0	5.9	0.0	42.9
1987–1991	32.2	22.1	11.8	0.0	7.1
Total	100.0	100.0	100.0	100.0	100.0

d. Crosstabulation of row percentages.

Year Constructed	Fuel Type Elect.	Nat. Gas	Oil	Propane	Other	Total
1973 or before	16.2	74.1	4.9	2.0	2.8	100.0
1974–1979	44.5	48.1	3.7	3.7	0.0	100.0
1980–1986	45.1	46.4	1.2	0.0	7.3	100.0
1987–1991	39.7	57.8	1.7	0.0	0.8	100.0

50. a. Crosstabulation of market value and profit

Market Value ($1000s)	Profit ($1000s) 0–300	300–600	600–900	900–1200	Total
0–8000	23	4			27
8000–16,000	4	4	2	2	12
16,000–24,000		2	1	1	4
24,000–32,000		1	2	1	4
32,000–40,000		2	1		3
Total	27	13	6	4	50

b. Crosstabulation of row percentages

Market Value ($1000s)	Profit ($1000s) 0–300	300–600	600–900	900–1200	Total
0–8000	85.19	14.81	0.00	0.00	100
8000–16,000	33.33	33.33	16.67	16.67	100
16,000–24,000	0.00	50.00	25.00	25.00	100
24,000–32,000	0.00	25.00	50.00	25.00	100
32,000–40,000	0.00	66.67	33.33	0.00	100

c. A positive relationship is indicated between profit and market value; as profit goes up, market value goes up

52. b. A positive relationship is demonstrated between market value and stockholders' equity

Chapter 3

2. 16, 16.5

3. Arrange data in order: 15, 20, 25, 25, 27, 28, 30, 34

$i = \dfrac{20}{100}(8) = 1.6$; round up to position 2

20th percentile = 20

$i = \dfrac{25}{100}(8) = 2$; use positions 2 and 3

25th percentile $= \dfrac{20 + 25}{2} = 22.5$

$i = \dfrac{65}{100}(8) = 5.2$; round up to position 6

65th percentile = 28

$$i = \frac{75}{100}(8) = 6; \text{ use positions 6 and 7}$$

$$75\text{th percentile} = \frac{28 + 30}{2} = 29$$

4. 59.727, 57, 53

6. a. 92.25; 80.5; multimodal
 b. 66.7; 68; 70
 c. 500 @ $50
 d. Yes

8. a. $\bar{x} = \dfrac{\Sigma x_i}{n} = \dfrac{695}{20} = 34.75$

 Mode = 25 (appears three times)
 b. Data in order: 18, 20, 25, 25, 25, 26, 27, 27, 28, 33, 36, 37, 40, 40, 42, 45, 46, 48, 53, 54

 Median (10th and 11th positions)

 $$\frac{33 + 36}{2} = 34.5$$

 At home workers are slightly younger

 c. $i = \dfrac{25}{100}(20) = 5;$ use positions 5 and 6

 $$Q_1 = \frac{25 + 26}{2} = 25.5$$

 $$i = \frac{75}{100}(20) = 15; \text{ use positions 15 and 16}$$

 $$Q_3 = \frac{42 + 45}{2} = 43.5$$

 d. $i = \dfrac{32}{100}(20) = 6.4;$ round up to position 7

 32nd percentile = 27
 At least 32% of the people are 27 or younger

10. a. 48.33, 49; do not report a mode
 b. 45, 55

12. a. $639
 b. 98.8 pictures
 c. 110.2 minutes

14. 16, 4

15. Range = 34 − 15 = 19
 Arrange data in order: 15, 20, 25, 25, 27, 28, 30, 34

 $$i = \frac{25}{100}(8) = 2; \quad Q_1 = \frac{20 + 25}{2} = 22.5$$

 $$i = \frac{75}{100}(8) = 6; \quad Q_3 = \frac{28 + 30}{2} = 29$$

 $$IQR = Q_3 - Q_1 = 29 - 22.5 = 6.5$$

 $$\bar{x} = \frac{\Sigma x_i}{n} = \frac{204}{8} = 25.5$$

x_i	$(x_i - \bar{x})$	$(x_i - \bar{x})^2$
27	1.5	2.25
25	−.5	.25
20	−5.5	30.25
15	−10.5	110.25
30	4.5	20.25
34	8.5	72.25
28	2.5	6.25
25	−.5	.25
		242.00

$$s^2 = \frac{\Sigma(x_i - \bar{x})^2}{n - 1} = \frac{242}{8 - 1} = 34.57$$

$$s = \sqrt{34.57} = 5.88$$

16. a. Range = 190 − 168 = 22

 b. $\bar{x} = \dfrac{\Sigma x_i}{n} = \dfrac{1068}{6} = 178$

 $$s^2 = \frac{\Sigma(x_i - \bar{x})^2}{n - 1}$$

 $$= \frac{4^2 + (-10)^2 + 6^2 + 12^2 + (-8)^2 + (-4)^2}{6 - 1}$$

 $$= \frac{376}{5} = 75.2$$

 c. $s = \sqrt{75.2} = 8.67$

 d. $\dfrac{s}{\bar{x}}(100) = \dfrac{8.67}{178}(100) = 4.87$

18. a. Mainland: 115.13; 111.56
 Asia: 36.62; 36.695
 b. Mainland: 86.24; 26.82; 23.30
 Asia: 42.97; 11.40; 31.13
 c. Greater mean and standard deviation for Mainland

20. *Dawson:* range = 2, s = .67
 Clark: range = 8, s = 2.58

22. a. 161, 92.5; 56, 19.5
 b. 2705.3816, 52.01; 290.8526, 17.05
 c. 56.38, 25.56
 d. Greater for 500 @ $50

24. *Quarter-milers:* s = .0564, Coef. of Var. = 5.8
 Milers: s = .1295, Coef. of Var. = 2.9

26. .20, 1.50, 0, −.50, −2.20

27. Chebyshev's theorem: *at least* $(1 - 1/z^2)$

 a. $z = \dfrac{40 - 30}{5} = 2; \ 1 - \dfrac{1}{(2)^2} = .75$

 b. $z = \dfrac{45 - 30}{5} = 3; \ 1 - \dfrac{1}{(3)^2} = .89$

 c. $z = \dfrac{38 - 30}{5} = 1.6; \ 1 - \dfrac{1}{(1.6)^2} = .61$

d. $z = \dfrac{42 - 30}{5} = 2.4; \; 1 - \dfrac{1}{(2.4)^2} = .83$

e. $z = \dfrac{48 - 30}{5} = 3.6; \; 1 - \dfrac{1}{(3.6)^2} = .92$

28. a. 95%
   b. Almost all
   c. 68%

30. a. 34%
   b. 81.5%
   c. 16%

32. a. $-.95$
   b. 3.90
   c. Labor cost in part (b) is an outlier

34. a. 100; 13.88 or approximately 14
   b. 16%
   c. 11.1 and 10.77; no outliers

36. 15, 22.5, 26, 29, 34

38. Arrange data in order: 5, 6, 8, 10, 10, 12, 15, 16, 18

$i = \dfrac{25}{100}(9) = 2.25;$ round up to position 3

$Q_1 = 8$

Median (5th position) $= 10$

$i = \dfrac{75}{100}(9) = 6.75;$ round up to position 7

$Q_3 = 15$

5-number summary: 5, 8, 10, 15, 18

40. a. 5, 9.6, 14.5, 19.2, 52.7
   b. Limits: -4.8, 33.6
   c. 41.6 is an outlier
   52.7 is an outlier

41. a. Arrange data in order low to high

$i = \dfrac{25}{100}(21) = 5.25;$ round up to 6th position

$Q_1 = 1872$

Median (11th position) $= 4019$

$i = \dfrac{75}{100}(21) = 15.75;$ round up to 16th position

$Q_3 = 8305$

5-number summary: 608, 1872, 4019, 8305, 14,138
   b. IQR $= Q_3 - Q_1 = 8305 - 1872 = 6433$
   Lower limit: $1872 - 1.5(6433) = -7777$
   Upper limit: $8305 + 1.5(6433) = 17{,}955$
   c. No; data are within limits
   d. $41{,}138 > 27{,}604;$ 41,138 would be an outlier; data value would be reviewed and corrected

e.

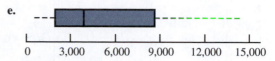

42. a. 105.7933, 52.7
   b. 15.7, 78.3
   c. Silicon Graphics, Toys R Us
   d. 26.73; much greater

44. a. 37.48, 23.67
   b. 7.91, 51.92
   c. Limits: -58.11, 117.94
   Russia and Turkey are outliers

45. b. There appears to be a negative linear relationship between x and y
   c.

x_i	y_i	$x_i - \bar{x}$	$y_i - \bar{y}$	$(x_i - \bar{x})(y_i - \bar{y})$
4	50	-4	4	-16
6	50	-2	4	-8
11	40	3	-6	-18
3	60	-5	14	-70
16	30	8	-16	-128
40	230	0	0	-240

$\bar{x} = 8; \; \bar{y} = 46$

$s_{xy} = \dfrac{\Sigma(x_i - \bar{x})(y_i - \bar{y})}{n - 1} = \dfrac{-240}{4} = -60$

The sample covariance indicates a negative linear association between x and y

   d. $r_{xy} = \dfrac{s_{xy}}{s_x s_y} = \dfrac{-60}{(5.43)(11.40)} = -.969$

The sample correlation coefficient of $-.969$ is indicative of a strong negative linear relationship

46. b. There appears to be a positive linear relationship between x and y
   c. $s_{xy} = 26.5$
   d. $r_{xy} = .693$

48. $-.91$; negative relationship

50. a. .92
   b. Strong positive linear relationship

52. a. 3.69
   b. 3.175

53. a.

f_i	M_i	$f_i M_i$
4	5	20
7	10	70
9	15	135
5	20	100
25		325

$\bar{x} = \dfrac{\Sigma f_i M_i}{n} = \dfrac{325}{25} = 13$

b.

f_i	M_i	$(M_i - \bar{x})$	$(M_i - \bar{x})^2$	$f_i(M_i - \bar{x})^2$
4	5	-8	64	256
7	10	-3	9	63
9	15	2	4	36
5	20	7	49	245
25				600

$$s^2 = \frac{\Sigma f_i(M_i - \bar{x})^2}{n - 1} = \frac{600}{25 - 1} = 25$$

$$s = \sqrt{25} = 5$$

54. a.

Grade x_i	Weight w_i
4 (A)	9
3 (B)	15
2 (C)	33
1 (D)	3
0 (F)	0
	60 credit hours

$$\bar{x} = \frac{\Sigma w_i x_i}{\Sigma w_i} = \frac{9(4) + 15(3) + 33(2) + 3(1)}{9 + 15 + 33 + 3}$$

$$= \frac{150}{60} = 2.5$$

b. Yes

56. 10.74, 25.63, 5.06; Estimate = 1288.8

58. a. 138.52, 129, 0
b. No, much more
c. 95, 169
d. 467, 74
e. 9271.01, 96.29
f. Yes, the $467 value

60. a. 18.57, 16.5
b. 53.49, 7.31
c. Quantex
d. 1.15
e. $-.90$
f. No

62. a. $\bar{x} = 83.135 \; s = 16.173$
b. $50,789 to $115,481
c. Same range as in part (b); higher probability
d. Danbury, CT is an outlier

64. a. 502.67; positive linear relationship
b. .933

66. b. .9856, strong positive relationship

68. a. 817
b. 833

70. a. 60.68
b. $s^2 = 31.23$; $s = 5.59$

Chapter 4

2. $\binom{6}{3} = \frac{6!}{3!3!} = \frac{6 \cdot 5 \cdot 4 \cdot 3 \cdot 2 \cdot 1}{(3 \cdot 2 \cdot 1)(3 \cdot 2 \cdot 1)} = 20$

ABC	ACE	BCD	BEF
ABD	ACF	BCE	CDE
ABE	ADE	BCF	CDF
ABF	ADF	BDE	CEF
ACD	AEF	BDF	DEF

4. b. (H,H,H), (H,H,T), (H,T,H), (H,T,T),
(T,H,H), (T,H,T), (T,T,H), (T,T,T)
c. $\frac{1}{8}$

6. $P(E_1) = .40, P(E_2) = .26, P(E_3) = .34$
The relative frequency method was used

8. a. 4: Commission Positive—Council Approves
Commission Positive—Council Disapproves
Commission Negative—Council Approves
Commission Negative—Council Disapproves

9. $\binom{50}{4} = \frac{50!}{4!46!} = \frac{50 \cdot 49 \cdot 48 \cdot 47}{4 \cdot 3 \cdot 2 \cdot 1} = 230,300$

10. a. Use the relative frequency approach
$P(\text{California}) = 1,434/2,374 = .60$
b. Number not from four states
$$= 2,374 - 1,434 - 390 - 217 - 112$$
$$= 221$$
$P(\text{Not from 4 states}) = 221/2,374 = .09$
c. $P(\text{Not in early stages}) = 1 - .22 = .78$
d. Estimate of number of Massachusetts' companies in early stage of development = $(.22)390 \approx 86$
e. If we assume the size of the awards did not differ by state, we can multiply the probability an award went to Colorado by the total venture funds disbursed to get an estimate

Estimate of Colorado funds = $(112/2374)(\$32.4)$
$$= \$1.53 \text{ billion}$$

Authors' Note: The actual amount going to Colorado was $1.74 billion

12. a. 1,906,884
b. 1/1,906,884
c. 1/80,089,128

14. a. $\frac{1}{4}$
b. $\frac{1}{2}$
c. $\frac{3}{4}$

15. a. $S = $ (ace of clubs, ace of diamonds, ace of hearts, ace of spades)
b. $S = $ (2 of clubs, 3 of clubs, . . . , 10 of clubs, J of clubs, Q of clubs, K of clubs, A of clubs)
c. There are 12; jack, queen, or king in each of the four suits
d. For (a): 4/52 = 1/13 = .08
For (b): 13/52 = 1/4 = .25
For (c): 12/52 = .23

16. a. 36

c. $\frac{1}{6}$

d. $\frac{5}{18}$

e. No; $P(\text{odd}) = P(\text{even}) = \frac{1}{2}$

f. Classical

17. a. (4, 6), (4, 7), (4, 8)

b. .05 + .10 + .15 = .30

c. (2, 8), (3, 8), (4, 8)

d. .05 + .05 + .15 = .25

e. .15

18. a. $P(0) = .05$

b. $P(4 \text{ or } 5) = .20$

c. $P(0, 1, \text{ or } 2) = .55$

20. a. .112

b. .086

c. .49

22. a. .40, .40, .60

b. .80, yes

c. $A^c = (E_3, E_4, E_5)$; $C^c = (E_1, E_4)$;
$P(A^c) = .60$; $P(C^c) = .40$

d. (E_1, E_2, E_5); .60

e. .80

23. a. $P(A) = P(E_1) + P(E_4) + P(E_6)$
$= .05 + .25 + .10 = .40$
$P(B) = P(E_2) + P(E_4) + P(E_7)$
$= .20 + .25 + .05 = .50$
$P(C) = P(E_2) + P(E_3) + P(E_5) + P(E_7)$
$= .20 + .20 + .15 + .05 = .60$

b. $A \cup B = \{E_1, E_2, E_4, E_6, E_7\}$;
$P(A \cup B) = P(E_1) + P(E_2) + P(E_4) + P(E_6) + P(E_7)$
$= .05 + .20 + .25 + .10 + .05$
$= .65$

c. $A \cap B = \{E_4\}$; $P(A \cap B) = P(E_4) = .25$

d. Yes, they are mutually exclusive

e. $B^c = \{E_1, E_3, E_5, E_6\}$;
$P(B^c) = P(E_1) + P(E_3) + P(E_5) + P(E_6)$
$= .05 + .20 + .15 + .10$
$= .50$

24. a. .05

b. .70

26. a. .30, .23

b. .17

c. .64

28. Let B = rented a car for business reasons
P = rented a car for personal reasons

a. $P(B \cup P) = P(B) + P(P) - P(B \cap P)$
$= .540 + .458 - .300$
$= .698$

b. $P(\text{Neither}) = 1 - .698 = .302$

30. a. $P(A \mid B) = \dfrac{P(A \cap B)}{P(B)} = \dfrac{.40}{.60} = .6667$

b. $P(B \mid A) = \dfrac{P(A \cap B)}{P(A)} = \dfrac{.40}{.50} = .80$

c. No, because $P(A \mid B) \neq P(A)$

32. a.

	Single	Married	Total
Under 30	.55	.10	.65
30 or Over	.20	.15	.35
Total	.75	.25	1.0

b. Higher probability of under 30

c. Higher probability of single

d. .55

e. .8462

f. No

33. a.

	Reason for Applying			
	Quality	**Cost/ Convenience**	**Other**	**Total**
Full-time	.218	.204	.039	.461
Part-time	.208	.307	.024	.539
Total	.426	.511	.063	1.000

b. A student is most likely to cite cost or convenience as the first reason (probability = .511); school quality is the reason cited by the second largest number of students (probability = .426)

c. $P(\text{quality} \mid \text{full-time}) = .218/.461 = .473$

d. $P(\text{quality} \mid \text{part-time}) = .208/.539 = .386$

e. For independence, we must have $P(A)P(B) = P(A \cap B)$; from the table

$P(A \cap B) = .218$, $P(A) = .461$, $P(B) = .426$
$P(A)P(B) = (.461)(.426) = .196$

Because $P(A)P(B) \neq P(A \cap B)$, the events are not independent

34. a. .44

b. .15

c. .0225

d. .0025

e. .136

f. .106

36. b. .075

c. .20

d. .25

e. .15

f. .60

g. .275

38. a. 52/1035
  b. .0004
  c. .0676

39. a. Yes, because $P(A_1 \cap A_2) = 0$
  b. $P(A_1 \cap B) = P(A_1)P(B \mid A_1) = .40(.20) = .08$
  $P(A_2 \cap B) = P(A_2)P(B \mid A_2) = .60(.05) = .03$
  c. $P(B) = P(A_1 \cap B) + P(A_2 \cap B) = .08 + .03 = .11$
  d. $P(A_1 \mid B) = \dfrac{.08}{.11} = .7273$

  $P(A_2 \mid B) = \dfrac{.03}{.11} = .2727$

40. a. .10, .20, .09
  b. .51
  c. .26, .51, .23

42. M = missed payment
  D_1 = customer defaults
  D_2 = customer does not default
  $P(D_1) = .05, P(D_2) = .95, P(M \mid D_2) = .2, P(M \mid D_1) = 1$
  a. $P(D_1 \mid M) = \dfrac{P(D_1)P(M \mid D_1)}{P(D_1)P(M \mid D_1) + P(D_2)P(M \mid D_2)}$

  $= \dfrac{(.05)(1)}{(.05)(1) + (.95)(.2)}$

  $= \dfrac{.05}{.24} = .21$

  b. Yes, the probability of default is greater than .20

44. .6754

46. a. .68
  b. 52
  c. 10

48. a. .61
  b. 18–34 and 65+
  c. .30

50. a. 76
  b. .24

52. b. .2022
  c. .4618
  d. .4005

54. a. .49
  b. .44
  c. .54
  d. No
  e. Yes

56. a. .25
  b. .125
  c. .0125
  d. .10
  e. No

58. 3.44%

60. a. .0625
  b. .0132
  c. Three

Chapter 5

1. a. Head, Head (H, H)
  Head, Tail (H, T)
  Tail, Head (T, H)
  Tail, Tail (T, T)
  b. x = number of heads on two coin tosses
  c.

Outcome	Values of x
(H, H)	2
(H, T)	1
(T, H)	1
(T, T)	0

  d. Discrete; it may assume 3 values: 0, 1, and 2

2. a. x = time in minutes to assemble product
  b. Any positive value: $x > 0$
  c. Continuous

3. Let: Y = position is offered
  N = position is not offered
  a. $S = \{(Y, Y, Y), (Y, Y, N), (Y, N, Y), (Y, N, N), (N, Y, Y),$
  $(N, Y, N), (N, N, Y), (N, N, N)\}$
  b. Let N = number of offers made; N is a discrete random variable
  c.

Experimental Outcome	(Y, Y, Y)	(Y, Y, N)	(Y, N, Y)	(Y, N, N)	(N, Y, Y)	(N, Y, N)	(N, N, Y)	(N, N, N)
Value of N	3	2	2	1	2	1	1	0

4. $x = 0, 1, 2, \ldots, 12$

6. a. $0, 1, 2, \ldots, 20$; discrete
  b. $0, 1, 2, \ldots$; discrete
  c. $0, 1, 2, \ldots, 50$; discrete
  d. $0 \le x \le 8$; continuous
  e. $x > 0$; continuous

7. a. $f(x) \ge 0$ for all values of x
  $\Sigma f(x) = 1$; therefore, it is a valid probability distribution
  b. Probability $x = 30$ is $f(30) = .25$
  c. Probability $x \le 25$ is $f(20) + f(25) = .20 + .15 = .35$
  d. Probability $x > 30$ is $f(35) = .40$

8. a.

x	$f(x)$
1	3/20 = .15
2	5/20 = .25
3	8/20 = .40
4	4/20 = .20
Total	1.00

b. $f(x)$

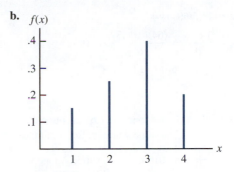

c. $f(x) \geq 0$ for $x = 1, 2, 3, 4$
   $\Sigma f(x) = 1$

10. a.

x	1	2	3	4	5
$f(x)$	.05	.09	.03	.42	.41

b.

x	1	2	3	4	5
$f(x)$	.04	.10	.12	.46	.28

c. .83
d. .28
e. Senior executives more satisfied

12. a. Yes
b. .65

14. a. .05
b. .70
c. .40

16. a.

y	$f(y)$	$yf(y)$
2	.20	.40
4	.30	1.20
7	.40	2.80
8	.10	.80
Totals	1.00	5.20

$$E(y) = \mu = 5.20$$

b.

y	$y - \mu$	$(y - \mu)^2$	$f(y)$	$(y - \mu)^2 f(y)$
2	−3.20	10.24	.20	2.048
4	−1.20	1.44	.30	.432
7	1.80	3.24	.40	1.296
8	2.80	7.84	.10	.784
			Total	4.560

$$\text{Var}(y) = 4.56$$
$$\sigma = \sqrt{4.56} = 2.14$$

18. a/b.

x	$f(x)$	$xf(x)$	$(x - \mu)$	$(x - \mu)^2$	$(x - \mu)^2 f(x)$
0	.01	.00	−2.3	5.29	.0529
1	.23	.23	−1.3	1.69	.3887
2	.41	.82	−0.3	0.09	.0369
3	.20	.60	0.7	0.49	.0980
4	.10	.40	1.7	2.89	.2890
5	.05	.25	2.7	7.29	.3645

$$E(x) = 2.30 \qquad\qquad \text{Var}(x) = 1.2300$$
$$\sigma = 1.11$$

The expected value, $E(x) = 2.3$, of the probability distribution is the same as the average reported in the *1997 Statistical Abstract of the United States*

$$\text{Var}(x) = 1.23 \text{ television sets squared}$$

$$\sigma = \sqrt{1.23} = 1.11 \text{ television sets}$$

20. a. 166
b. −94; concern is to protect against the expense of a big accident

22. a. 445
b. 1250 loss

24. a. Medium: 145; large: 140
b. Medium: 2725; large: 12,400

25. a.

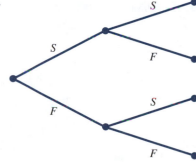

b. $f(1) = \binom{2}{1}(.4)^1(.6)^1 = \dfrac{2!}{1!1!}(.4)(.6) = .48$

c. $f(0) = \binom{2}{0}(.4)^0(.6)^2 = \dfrac{2!}{0!2!}(1)(.36) = .36$

d. $f(2) = \binom{2}{2}(.4)^2(.6)^0 = \dfrac{2!}{2!0!}(.16)(.1) = .16$

e. $P(x \geq 1) = f(1) + f(2) = .48 + .16 = .64$
f. $E(x) = np = 2(.4) = .8$
   $\text{Var}(x) = np(1 - p) = 2(.4)(.6) = .48$
   $\sigma = \sqrt{.48} = .6928$

26. a. $f(0) = .3487$
b. $f(2) = .1937$
c. .9298
d. .6513

e. 1

f. $\sigma^2 = .9000, \sigma = .9487$

28. a. .3292

    b. .6422

    c. .0182

30. a. Probability of a defective part being produced must be .03 for each trial; trials must be independent

    b. Let D = defective

        G = not defective

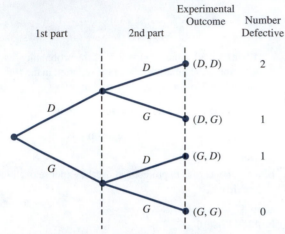

    c. Two outcomes result in exactly one defect

    d. $P(\text{no defects}) = (.97)(.97) = .9409$

       $P(1 \text{ defect}) = 2(.03)(.97) = .0582$

       $P(2 \text{ defects}) = (.03)(.03) = .0009$

32. a. .90

    b. .99

    c. .999

    d. Yes

34. a. .0634

    b. .0634

    c. .9729

38. a. $f(x) = \dfrac{3^x e^{-3}}{x!}$

    b. .2241

    c. .1494

    d. .8008

39. a. $f(x) = \dfrac{2^x e^{-2}}{x!}$

    b. $\mu = 6$ for 3 time periods

    c. $f(x) = \dfrac{6^x e^{-6}}{x!}$

    d. $f(2) = \dfrac{2^2 e^{-2}}{2!} = \dfrac{4(.1353)}{2} = .2706$

    e. $f(6) = \dfrac{6^6 e^{-6}}{6!} = .1606$

    f. $f(5) = \dfrac{4^5 e^{-4}}{5!} = .1563$

40. a. $\mu = 48(5/60) = 4$

    $f(3) = \dfrac{4^3 e^{-4}}{3!} = \dfrac{(64)(.0183)}{6} = .1952$

    b. $\mu = 48(15/60) = 12$

    $f(10) = \dfrac{12^{10} e^{-12}}{10!} = .1048$

    c. $\mu = 48(5/60) = 4$; one can expect four callers to be waiting after 5 minutes

    $f(0) = \dfrac{4^0 e^{-4}}{0!} = .0183$; the probability none will be waiting after 5 minutes is .0183

    d. $\mu = 48(3/60) = 2.4$

    $f(0) = \dfrac{2.4^0 e^{-2.4}}{0!} = .0907$; the probability of no interruptions in 3 minutes is .0907

42. a. $f(0) = \dfrac{7^0 e^{-7}}{0!} = e^{-7} = .0009$

    b. probability $= 1 - [f(0) + f(1)]$

    $f(1) = \dfrac{7^1 e^{-7}}{1!} = 7e^{-7} = .0064$

    probability $= 1 - [.0009 + .0064] = .9927$

    c. $\mu = 3.5$

    $f(0) = \dfrac{3.5^0 e^{-3.5}}{0!} = e^{-3.5} = .0302$

    probability $= 1 - f(0) = 1 - .0302 = .9698$

    d.

probability $= 1 - [f(0) + f(1) + f(2) + f(3) + f(4)]$

            $= 1 - [.0009 + .0064 + .0223 + .0521 + .0912]$

            $= .8271$

44. a. $\mu = 1.25$

    b. .2865

    c. .3581

    d. .3554

46. a. $f(1) = \dfrac{\binom{3}{1}\binom{10-3}{4-1}}{\binom{10}{4}} = \dfrac{\left(\frac{3!}{1!2!}\right)\left(\frac{7!}{3!4!}\right)}{\frac{10!}{4!6!}}$

          $= \dfrac{(3)(35)}{210} = .50$

    b. $f(2) = \dfrac{\binom{3}{2}\binom{10-3}{2-2}}{\binom{10}{2}} = \dfrac{(3)(1)}{45} = .067$

    c. $f(0) = \dfrac{\binom{3}{0}\binom{10-3}{2-0}}{\binom{10}{2}} = \dfrac{(1)(21)}{45} = .4667$

d. $f(2) = \dfrac{\binom{3}{2}\binom{10-3}{4-2}}{\binom{10}{4}} = \dfrac{(3)(21)}{210} = .30$

48. a. .50
  b. .3333

50. $N = 60, n = 10$
  a. $r = 20, x = 0$

$$f(0) = \dfrac{\binom{20}{0}\binom{40}{10}}{\binom{60}{10}} = \dfrac{(1)\left(\dfrac{40!}{10!30!}\right)}{\dfrac{60!}{10!50!}}$$

$$= \left(\dfrac{40!}{10!30!}\right)\left(\dfrac{10!50!}{60!}\right)$$

$$= \dfrac{40 \cdot 39 \cdot 38 \cdot 37 \cdot 36 \cdot 35 \cdot 34 \cdot 33 \cdot 32 \cdot 31}{60 \cdot 59 \cdot 58 \cdot 57 \cdot 56 \cdot 55 \cdot 54 \cdot 53 \cdot 52 \cdot 51}$$

$$\approx .01$$

  b. $r = 20, x = 1$

$$f(1) = \dfrac{\binom{20}{1}\binom{40}{9}}{\binom{60}{10}} = 20\left(\dfrac{40!}{9!31!}\right)\left(\dfrac{10!50!}{60!}\right)$$

$$\approx .07$$

  c. $1 - f(0) - f(1) = 1 - .08 = .92$
  d. Same as the probability one will be from Hawaii; in part (b) it was equal to approximately .07

52. a. .5333
  b. .6667
  c. .7778
  d. $n = 7$

54. a. $f(x) \geq 0$ and $\Sigma f(x) = 1$
  b. 3.64, .6704
  c. Appears overvalued

56. a. .0364
  b. .4420
  c. 48
  d. 6.7882

58. a. .9510
  b. .0480
  c. .0490

60. a. 328
  b. 13.91
  c. 13.91

62. .1912

64. a. .2240
  b. .5767

66. a. .4667
  b. .4667
  c. .0667

Chapter 6

1. a.

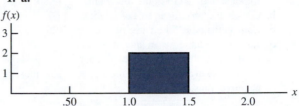

  b. $P(x = 1.25) = 0$; the probability of any single point is zero because the area under the curve above any single point is zero
  c. $P(1.0 \leq x \leq 1.25) = 2(.25) = .50$
  d. $P(1.20 < x < 1.5) = 2(.30) = .60$

2. b. .50
  c. .60
  d. 15
  e. 8.33

4. a.

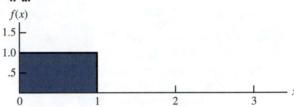

  b. $P(.25 < x < .75) = 1(.50) = .50$
  c. $P(x \leq .30) = 1(.30) = .30$
  d. $P(x > .60) = 1(.40) = .40$

6. a. .40
  b. .64
  c. .68

10. a. .9332
  b. .8413
  c. .0919
  d. .4938

12. a. .2967
  b. .4418
  c. .3300
  d. .5910
  e. .8849
  f. .2389

13. a. $.6879 - .0239 = .6640$
  b. $.8888 - .6985 = .1903$
  c. $.9599 - .8508 = .1091$

14. a. $z = 1.96$
  b. $z = 1.96$
  c. $z = .61$
  d. $z = 1.12$
  e. $z = .44$
  f. $z = .44$

15. a. Look in the table for an area of $1.000 - .2119 = .7881$; $z = .80$ cuts off an area of $.2119$ in the upper tail. Thus, for an area of $.2119$ in the lower tail, $z = -.80$

  b. Look in the table for an area of $.9515$; $z = 1.66$

  c. Look in the table for an area of $.6026$; $z = .26$

  d. Look in the table for an area of $.9948$; $z = 2.56$

  e. Look in the table for an area of $.6915$; because the value we are seeking is below the mean, the z value must be negative; thus, $z = -.50$

16. a. $z = 2.33$

  b. $z = 1.96$

  c. $z = 1.645$

  d. $z = 1.28$

18. a. Find $P(x \geq 60)$

  At $x = 60$, $z = \dfrac{60 - 49}{16} = \dfrac{11}{16} = .69$

  $P(x < 60) = .7549$

  $P(x \geq 60) = 1 - P(x < 60) = 1 - .7549 = .2451$

  b. Find $P(x \leq 30)$

  At $x = 30$, $z = \dfrac{30 - 49}{16} = -1.19$

  $P(x \leq 30) = 1.000 - .8830$

  $ = .1170$

  c. Find z-value so that $P(z \geq z\text{-value}) = .10$

  A z-value of 1.28 cuts off 10% in upper tail

  Now, solve for corresponding value of x

  $1.28 = \dfrac{x - 49}{16}$

  $x = 49 + (16)(1.28)$

  $ = 69.48$

  So, 10% of subscribers spend 69.48 minutes or more reading *The Wall Street Journal*

20. a. $.025$

  b. 5.16%

  c. 33.72 or more

22. a. $.4194$

  b. $\$517.44$ or more

  c. $.0166$

24. a. 902.75, 114.185

  b. $.1841$

  c. $.1977$

  d. $1{,}091$ million

26. a. $.5276$

  b. $.3935$

  c. $.4724$

  d. $.1341$

27. a. $P(x \leq x_0) = 1 - e^{-x_0/3}$

  b. $P(x \leq 2) = 1 - e^{-2/3} = 1 - .5134 = .4866$

  c. $P(x \geq 3) = 1 - P(x \leq 3) = 1 - (1 - e^{-3/3})$

  $ = e^{-1} = .3679$

d. $P(x \leq 5) = 1 - e^{-5/3} = 1 - .1889 = .8111$

e. $P(2 \leq x \leq 5) = P(x \leq 5) - P(x \leq 2)$

  $ = .8111 - .4866 = .3245$

28. a. $.3935$

  b. $.2231$

  c. $.3834$

29. a.

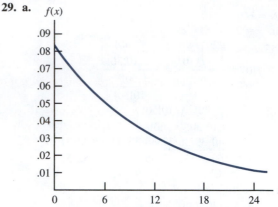

  b. $P(x \leq 12) = 1 - e^{-12/12} = 1 - .3679 = .6321$

  c. $P(x \leq 6) = 1 - e^{-6/12} = 1 - .6065 = .3935$

  d. $P(x \geq 30) = 1 - P(x < 30)$

  $ = 1 - (1 - e^{-30/12})$

  $ = .0821$

30. a. 50 hours

  b. $.3935$

  c. $.1353$

32. a. $f(x) = 30e^{-30x}$

  b. $.0821$

  c. $.7135$

34. a. $\$63{,}000$

  b. $\$43{,}800$ or less

  c. 12.92%

  d. $\$87{,}675$

36. a. 3229.18

  b. $.2245$

  c. $\$12{,}385$ or more

38. a. $.0228$

  b. $\$50$

40. a. 38.3%

  b. 3.59% better, 96.41% worse

  c. 38.21%

42. $\mu = 19.23$ ounces

44. a. $\frac{1}{7}$ minute

  b. $7e^{-7x}$

  c. $.0009$

  d. $.2466$

46. a. 2 minutes

  b. $.2212$

  c. $.3935$

  d. $.0821$

Chapter 7

1. **a.** AB, AC, AD, AE, BC, BD, BE, CD, CE, DE
   b. With 10 samples, each has a $\frac{1}{10}$ probability
   c. E and C because 8 and 0 do not apply; 5 identifies E; 7 does not apply; 5 is skipped because E is already in the sample; 3 identifies C; 2 is not needed because the sample of size 2 is complete

2. 22, 147, 229, 289

3. 459, 147, 385, 113, 340, 401, 215, 2, 33, 348

4. **a.** Number companies: 1-AT&T, 2-IBM, ..., 10-Pfizer
   Sample: Microsoft, Motorola, Cisco, Johnson & Johnson, AT&T
   b. America Online, Johnson & Johnson, General Electric, Motorola, Intel
   c. 252

6. 2782, 493, 825, 1807, 289

8. **a.** Wisconsin, Clemson, Washington, USC, Oklahoma, Colorado; 21 random numbers used
   b. Nebraska, Florida State, Michigan, Texas, Washington, TCU; 25 random numbers used

10. **a.** Finite
    b. Infinite
    c. Infinite
    d. Infinite
    e. Finite

11. **a.** $\bar{x} = \dfrac{\Sigma x_i}{n} = \dfrac{54}{6} = 9$

    b. $s = \sqrt{\dfrac{\Sigma(x_i - \bar{x})^2}{n - 1}}$

    $\Sigma(x_i - \bar{x})^2 = (-4)^2 + (-1)^2 + 1^2 + (-2)^2 + 1^2 + 5^2$
    $= 48$

    $s = \sqrt{\dfrac{48}{6 - 1}} = 3.1$

12. **a.** .50
    b. .3667

13. **a.** $\bar{x} = \dfrac{\Sigma x_i}{n} = \dfrac{465}{5} = 93$

    b.

x_i	$(x_i - \bar{x})$	$(x_i - \bar{x})^2$
94	+1	1
100	+7	49
85	−8	64
94	+1	1
92	−1	1
Totals 465	0	116

    $s = \sqrt{\dfrac{\Sigma(x_i - \bar{x})^2}{n - 1}} = \sqrt{\dfrac{116}{4}} = 5.39$

14. **a.** .19
    b. .32
    c. .79

16. .80

19. **a.** The sampling distribution is normal with:
    $$E(\bar{x}) = \mu = 200$$
    $$\sigma_{\bar{x}} = \frac{\sigma}{\sqrt{n}} = \frac{50}{\sqrt{100}} = 5$$

    For $+5$, $(\bar{x} - \mu) = 5$,
    $$z = \frac{\bar{x} - \mu}{\sigma_{\bar{x}}} = \frac{5}{5} = 1$$
    $$P(0 \le z \le 1) = .3413$$
    $$\text{Area} = .3413 \times 2 = .6826$$

    b. For ± 10, $(\bar{x} - \mu) = 10$,
    $$z = \frac{\bar{x} - \mu}{\sigma_{\bar{x}}} = \frac{10}{5} = 2$$
    $$P(0 \le z \le 2) = .4772$$
    $$\text{Area} = .4772 \times 2 = .9544$$

20. 3.54, 2.50, 2.04, 1.77
    $\sigma_{\bar{x}}$ decreases as n increases

22. **a.** Only for $n = 30$ and $n = 40$
    b. $n = 30$; normal with $E(\bar{x}) = 400$
    and $\sigma_{\bar{x}} = 9.13$
    $n = 40$; normal with $E(\bar{x}) = 400$
    and $\sigma_{\bar{x}} = 7.91$

24. **a.** Normal with $E(\bar{x}) = 51,800$ and $\sigma_{\bar{x}} = 516.40$
    b. $\sigma_{\bar{x}}$ decreases to 365.15
    c. $\sigma_{\bar{x}}$ decreases as n increases

25. **a.**

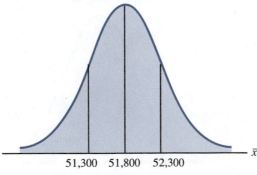

$$\sigma_{\bar{x}} = \frac{\sigma}{\sqrt{n}} = \frac{4000}{\sqrt{60}} = 516.40$$
$$z = \frac{52,300 - 51,800}{516.40} = +.97$$
$$\text{Area} = .3340 \times 2 = .6680$$

b. $\sigma_{\bar{x}} = \dfrac{\sigma}{\sqrt{n}} = \dfrac{4000}{\sqrt{120}} = 365.15$

$$z = \frac{52,300 - 51,800}{365.15} = +1.37$$
$$P(0 \le z \le 1.37) = .4147$$
$$\text{Area} = .4147 \times 2 = .8294$$

26. a. Normal with $E(\bar{x}) = 1.20$ and $\sigma_{\bar{x}} = .014$
   b. .8414
   c. .5224

28. a. .5034, .6212, .7888, .9232, .9876
   b. Smaller standard error

30. a. Normal with $E(\bar{x}) = 166,500$ and $\sigma_{\bar{x}} = 4200$
   b. .9826
   c. .7660, .4514, .1896
   d. Increase the sample size

32. a. No, 40/4000 < .05
   b. With: 1.2902
       Without: 1.2965
   c. .8764

34. a. $E(\bar{p}) = .40$

$$\sigma_{\bar{p}} = \sqrt{\frac{p(1-p)}{n}} = \sqrt{\frac{(.40)(.60)}{200}} = .0346$$

$$z = \frac{\bar{p} - p}{\sigma_{\bar{p}}} = \frac{.03}{.0346} = .87$$

$$P(0 \le z \le .87) = .3078$$
$$\text{Area} = .3078 \times 2 = .6156$$

   b. $z = \dfrac{\bar{p} - p}{\sigma_{\bar{p}}} = \dfrac{.05}{.0346} = 1.45$

$$P(0 \le z \le 1.45) = .4265$$
$$\text{Area} = .4265 \times 2 = .8530$$

36. a. .6156
   b. .7814
   c. .9488
   d. .9942
   e. Higher probability with larger n

37. a.

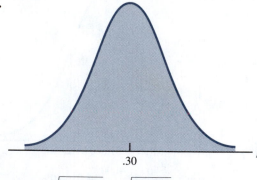

$$\sigma_{\bar{p}} = \sqrt{\frac{p(1-p)}{n}} = \sqrt{\frac{.30(.70)}{100}} = .0458$$

The normal distribution is appropriate because $np = 100(.30) = 30$ and $n(1-p) = 100(.70) = 70$ are both greater than 5.

   b. $P(.20 \le \bar{p} \le .40) = ?$

$$z = \frac{.40 - .30}{.0458} = 2.18$$

$$P(0 \le z \le 2.18) = .4854$$
$$\text{Area} = .4854 \times 2 = .9708$$

c. $P(.25 \le \bar{p} \le .35) = ?$

$$z = \frac{.35 - .30}{.0458} = 1.09$$

$$P(0 \le z \le 1.09) = .3621$$
$$\text{Area} = .3621 \times 2 = .7242$$

38. a. Normal with $E(\bar{p}) = .76$ and $\sigma_{\bar{p}} = .0214$
   b. .8384
   c. .9452

40. a. Normal with $E(\bar{p}) = .25$ and $\sigma_{\bar{p}} = .0306$
   b. .6730
   c. .8968

42. a. Normal with $E(\bar{p}) = .15$ and $\sigma_{\bar{p}} = .0505$
   b. .4448
   c. .8389

44. 112, 145, 73, 324, 293, 875, 318, 618

46. a. Normal with $E(\bar{x}) = 31.5$ and $\sigma_{\bar{x}} = 1.70$
   b. .4448
   c. .9232

48. a. 707.11
   b. .50
   c. .8427
   d. Increase to .95

50. a. 625
   b. .7888

52. a. Normal with $E(\bar{p}) = .305$ and $\sigma_{\bar{p}} = .0326$
   b. .7802
   c. .4605

54. a. .9606
   b. .0495

56. a. 48
   b. Normal, $E(\bar{p}) = .25$, $\sigma_{\bar{p}} = .0625$
   c. .2119

Chapter 8

2. Use $\bar{x} \pm z_{\alpha/2}(\sigma/\sqrt{n})$ with the sample standard deviation s used to estimate σ
   a. $32 \pm 1.645 (6/\sqrt{50})$
       32 ± 1.4; (30.6 to 33.4)
   b. $32 \pm 1.96(6/\sqrt{50})$
       32 ± 1.66; (30.34 to 33.66)
   c. $32 \pm 2.58(6/\sqrt{50})$
       32 ± 2.19; (29.81 to 34.19)

4. 62

5. a. $\sigma_{\bar{x}} = \sigma/\sqrt{n} = 5.00/\sqrt{49} = .7143$
   b. $1.96\sigma/\sqrt{n} = 1.96 (5.00/\sqrt{49}) = 1.4$
   c. 34.80 ± 1.4 or (33.40 to 36.20)

6. a. $\bar{x} = 381$
   b. $s = 50$
   c. 374.8 to 387.2

8. a. 11,769 to 12,231
   b. 11,725 to 12,275
   c. 11,638 to 12,362
   d. Width increases to be more confident

10. 7.25 to 8.25

12. a. 3.8 minutes
   b. .81
   c. 2.99 to 4.61

14. a. 1.734
   b. -1.321
   c. 3.365
   d. -1.761 and 1.761
   e. -2.048 and 2.048

15. a. $\bar{x} = \dfrac{\Sigma x_i}{n} = \dfrac{80}{8} = 10$

   b. $s = \sqrt{\dfrac{\Sigma(x_i - \bar{x})^2}{n-1}} = \sqrt{\dfrac{84}{8-1}} = 3.46$

   c. With 7 degrees of freedom, $t_{.025} = 2.365$

   $$\bar{x} \pm t_{.025}\dfrac{s}{\sqrt{n}}$$

   $$10 \pm 2.365\dfrac{3.46}{\sqrt{8}}$$

   $$10 \pm 2.90;\ 7.10 \text{ to } 12.90$$

16. a. 15.97 to 18.53
   b. 15.71 to 18.79
   c. 15.14 to 19.36

17. At 90%, $80 \pm t_{.05}(s/\sqrt{n})$ with degrees of freedom = 17
   $t_{.05} = 1.740$
   $80 \pm 1.740(10/\sqrt{18})$
   $80 \pm 4.10;\ (75.90 \text{ to } 84.10)$

   At 95%, $80 \pm t_{.025}(10/\sqrt{18})$ with degrees of freedom = 17
   $t_{.025} = 2.110$
   $80 \pm 2.110\ (10/\sqrt{18})$
   $80 \pm 4.97;\ (75.03 \text{ to } 84.97)$

18. a. 1.58
   b. .1474
   c. 1.49 to 1.67

20. a. 21.15 to 23.65
   b. 21.12 to 23.68
   c. Intervals are essentially the same

22. a. 6.86
   b. 6.54 to 7.18

24. a. Planning value of $\sigma = \dfrac{\text{Range}}{4} = \dfrac{36}{4} = 9$

   b. $n = \dfrac{z_{.025}^2 \sigma^2}{E^2} = \dfrac{(1.96)^2(9)^2}{(3)^2} = 34.57;$ use $n = 35$

   c. $n = \dfrac{(1.96)^2(9)^2}{(3)^2} = 77.79;$ use $n = 78$

25. a. Use $n = \dfrac{z_{\alpha/2}^2 \sigma^2}{E^2}$

   $n = \dfrac{(1.96)^2(6.82)^2}{(1.5)^2} = 79.41;$ use $n = 80$

   b. $n = \dfrac{(1.645)^2(6.82)^2}{(2)^2} = 31.47;$ use $n = 32$

26. a. 340
   b. 1358
   c. 8487

28. a. 53
   b. 75
   c. 129
   d. Must increase n

30. 59

31. a. $\bar{p} = \dfrac{100}{400} = .25$

   b. $\sqrt{\dfrac{\bar{p}(1 - \bar{p})}{n}} = \sqrt{\dfrac{.25(.75)}{400}} = .0217$

   c. $\bar{p} \pm z_{.025}\sqrt{\dfrac{\bar{p}(1 - \bar{p})}{n}}$

   $.25 \pm 1.96(.0217)$
   $.25 \pm .0424;\ (.2076 \text{ to } .2924)$

32. a. .6733 to .7267
   b. .6682 to .7318

34. 1068

35. a. $\bar{p} = 562/814 = .6904$

   b. $1.645\sqrt{\dfrac{.6904(1 - .6904)}{814}} = .0267$

   c. $.6904 \pm .0267;\ (.6637 \text{ to } .7171)$

36. a. .4393
   b. .3870 to .4916

38. a. .0430
   b. .2170 to .3030
   c. 822

39. a. $n = \dfrac{1.96^2 p(1 - p)}{E^2}$

   $n = \dfrac{1.96^2(.33)(.67)}{(.03)^2} = 943.75;$ use $n = 944$

   b. $n = \dfrac{2.576^2(.33)(.67)}{(.03)^2} = 1630.19;$ use $n = 1631$

40. a. .2505
   b. .0266

42. 601, 1068, 2401, 9604

44. a. 2009
   b. 47,991 to 52,009

46. a. 49.8
  b. 15.99
  c. 47.58 to 52.02
48. a. 13.2
  b. 7.8
  c. 7.62 to 18.78
  d. Wide interval; large n desirable
50. 37
52. 176
54. a. .5420
  b. .0508
  c. .4912 to .5928
56. a. 1267
  b. 1509
58. a. .68
  b. .6391 to .7209
60. a. .3101
  b. .2898 to .3304
  c. 8219; No, this sample size is unnecessarily large

Chapter 9

2. a. $H_0: \mu \leq 14$
    $H_a: \mu > 14$
  b. No evidence that the new plan increases sales
  c. The research hypothesis $\mu > 14$ is supported; the new plan increases sales
4. a. $H_0: \mu \geq 220$
    $H_a: \mu < 220$
  b. No evidence new method reduces cost
  c. New method reduces cost
5. a. Rejecting $H_0: \mu \leq 8.6$ when it is true
  b. Accepting $H_0: \mu \leq 8.6$ when it is false
6. a. $H_0: \mu \leq 1$
    $H_a: \mu > 1$
  b. Claiming $\mu > 1$ when it is not true
  c. Claiming $\mu \leq 1$ when it is not true
8. a. $H_0: \mu \geq 220$
    $H_a: \mu < 220$
  b. Claiming $\mu < 220$ when it is not true
  c. Claiming $\mu \geq 220$ when it is not true
10. a. $z = 2.05$
    Reject H_0 if $z > 2.05$
  b. $z = \dfrac{\bar{x} - \mu}{s/\sqrt{n}} = \dfrac{16.5 - 15}{7/\sqrt{40}} = 1.36$
  c. Area for $z = 1.36 = .9131$
    p-value $= 1 - .9131 = .0869$
  d. Do not reject H_0
12. a. .0344; reject H_0
  b. .3264; do not reject H_0
  c. .0668; do not reject H_0
    Approximately 0; reject H_0
    .13; do not reject H_0

13. a. $H_0: \mu \geq 1056$
    $H_a: \mu < 1056$
  b. Reject H_0 if $z < -1.645$
  c. $z = \dfrac{\bar{x} - \mu}{s/\sqrt{n}} = \dfrac{910 - 1056}{1600/\sqrt{400}} = -1.83$
  d. Reject H_0; conclude $\mu < 1056$
  e. p-value $= 1 - .9664 = .0336$
14. a. Reject if $z > 2.33$
  b. 3.11
  c. Reject H_0
16. $z = -2.74$; reject H_0
  p-value $= .0031$
18. a. $H_0: \mu \leq 5.72$
    $H_a: \mu > 5.72$
  b. 2.12
  c. .0170
  d. Reject H_0
20. a. $H_0: \mu \leq 37,000$
    $H_a: \mu > 37,000$
  b. $z = \dfrac{\bar{x} - \mu}{s/\sqrt{n}} = \dfrac{38,100 - 37,000}{5200/\sqrt{48}} = 1.47$
  c. p-value $= 1.0000 - .9292 = .0708$
  d. p-value $> \alpha$; do not reject H_0
    Cannot conclude population mean salary increased in June 2001
22. a. Reject H_0 if $z < -2.33$ or $z > 2.33$
  b. -1.13
  c. .2584
  d. Do not reject H_0
24. a. .0718; do not reject H_0
  b. .6528; do not reject H_0
  c. .0404; reject H_0
  d. Approximately 0; reject H_0
  e. .3174; do not reject H_0
25. a. Reject H_0 if $z < -1.96$ or $z > 1.96$
  b. $z = \dfrac{\bar{x} - \mu_0}{s/\sqrt{n}} = \dfrac{38.5 - 39.2}{4.8/\sqrt{112}} = -1.54$
  c. Do not reject H_0
  d. p-value $= 2(1.0000 - .9382) = .1236$
26. a. $z = -1.06$; do not reject H_0
  b. .0872
28. $z = 6.37$; reject H_0
30. a. $H_0: \mu = 1075$
    $H_a: \mu \neq 1075$
  b. $z = 1.43$
  c. .1528
  d. Do not reject H_0
32. a. $\bar{x} = \dfrac{\Sigma x_i}{n} = \dfrac{108}{6} = 18$
  b. $s = \sqrt{\dfrac{\Sigma(x_i - \bar{x})}{n-1}} = \sqrt{\dfrac{10}{6-1}} = 1.414$

c. Reject H_0 if $t < -2.571$ or $t > 2.571$

d. $t = \dfrac{\bar{x} - \mu}{s/\sqrt{n}} = \dfrac{18 - 20}{1.41/\sqrt{6}} = -3.46$

e. Reject H_0; conclude H_a is true

34. a. .01; reject H_0
   b. .10; do not reject H_0
   c. .03; reject H_0
   d. .15; do not reject H_0
   e. .003; reject H_0

35. a. $H_0: \mu = 3.00$
      $H_a: \mu \neq 3.00$
   b. Reject H_0 if $t < -2.262$ or if $t > 2.262$
   c. $\bar{x} = \Sigma x_i/n = {}^{28}/_{10} = 2.80$

   d. $s = \sqrt{\dfrac{\Sigma(x_i - \bar{x})^2}{n - 1}} = .70$

   e. $t = \dfrac{\bar{x} - \mu_0}{s/\sqrt{n}} = \dfrac{2.80 - 3.00}{.70/\sqrt{10}} = -.90$

   f. Do not reject H_0
   g. $t_{.10} = 1.383$; p-value greater than $2(.10) = .20$

36. a. $t = -1.90$; do not reject H_0
   b. Approximately .07

38. a. $\mu = 4000$
      $\mu \neq 4000$
   b. Reject H_0 if $t < -2.160$ or if $t > 2.160$
   c. 1.63
   d. Do not reject H_0
   e. Between .10 and .20

40. $t = 2.45$; reject H_0

42. a. Reject H_0 if $z < -1.96$ or $z > 1.96$

   b. $\sigma_{\bar{p}} = \sqrt{\dfrac{.20(.80)}{400}} = .02$

   $z = \dfrac{\bar{p} - p}{\sigma_{\bar{p}}} = \dfrac{.175 - .20}{.02} = -1.25$

   c. p-value $= 2(1 - .8944) = .2112$
   d. Do not reject H_0

44. a. $H_0: p \leq .4$
      $H_a: p > .4$
   b. Reject H_0 if $z > 1.645$
   c. 1.99
   d. Reject H_0

45. $H_0: p \geq .64$
    $H_a: p < .64$
    Reject H_0 if $z < -1.645$
    $\bar{p} = {}^{52}/_{100} = .52$

    $z = \dfrac{.52 - .64}{\sqrt{\dfrac{.64(.36)}{100}}} = -2.5$

    Reject H_0

46. a. .57
   b. $z = 3.13$; reject H_0
   c. Yes; it shows Burger King is preferred

48. a. .6381
   b. 2.83
   c. .0046
   d. Reject H_0

50. a. -1.20
   b. .1151
   c. Do not reject H_0

52. a. $H_0: \mu \leq 45{,}250$
      $H_a: \mu > 45{,}250$
   b. 2.71
   c. .0034
   d. Reject H_0

54. $z = 2.26$; p-value $= .0119$
    Reject H_0

56. a. $z = 1.80$; do not reject H_0
   b. .0718
   c. 549 to 575

58. $z = -3.84$; reject H_0

60. a. Show $p < .50$
   b. $z = -6.62$; reject H_0

62. a. .6502
   b. $-.98$
   c. .3270
   d. Do not reject H_0

64. a. .352
   b. -2.64
   c. .0041
   d. Reject H_0

Chapter 10

1. a. $\bar{x}_1 - \bar{x}_2 = 13.6 - 11.6 = 2$

   b. $s_{\bar{x}_1 - \bar{x}_2} = \sqrt{\dfrac{s_1^2}{n_1} + \dfrac{s_2^2}{n_2}} = \sqrt{\dfrac{(2.2)^2}{50} + \dfrac{3^2}{35}} = .595$

      $2 \pm 1.645(.595)$
      $2 \pm .98$ or 1.02 to 2.98
   c. $2 \pm 1.96(.595)$
      2 ± 1.17, or $.83$ to 3.17

2. a. 2.4
   b. 5.27
   c. .09 to 4.71

4. a. .60
   b. .56 to .64

6. $-.51$ to 1.27

8. a. $\bar{x}_1 - \bar{x}_2 = 45{,}700 - 44{,}500 = 1200$

b. Pooled variance

$$s^2 = \frac{7(700)^2 + 11(850)^2}{18} = 632{,}083$$

$$s_{\bar{x}_1-\bar{x}_2} = \sqrt{632{,}083\left(\frac{1}{8} + \frac{1}{12}\right)} = 362.88$$

With 18 degrees of freedom $t_{.025} = 2.101$,

$1200 \pm 2.101(362.88)$

1200 ± 762, or 438 to 1962

c. Populations are normally distributed with equal variances

10. a. 2.18

b. 4.41

c. .71 to 3.65

d. Yes, confidence interval does not contain 0

11. a. $s_{\bar{x}_1-\bar{x}_2} = \sqrt{\dfrac{s_1^2}{n_1} + \dfrac{s_2^2}{n_2}} = \sqrt{\dfrac{(5.2)^2}{40} + \dfrac{6^2}{50}} = 1.18$

$$z = \frac{(\bar{x}_1 - \bar{x}_2) - (\mu_1 - \mu_2)}{s_{\bar{x}_1-\bar{x}_2}}$$

$$= \frac{(25.2 - 22.8)}{1.18} = 2.03$$

Reject H_0 if $z > 1.645$; therefore reject H_0; conclude H_a is true and $\mu_1 > \mu_2$

b. p-value $= 1 - .9788 = .0212$

12. a. $z = -1.53$; do not reject H_0

b. .1260

14. a. $H_0: \mu_1 - \mu_2 = 0$
$H_a: \mu_1 - \mu_2 \neq 0$

b. Reject if $z < -1.96$ or $z > 1.96$

c. 2.18

d. Reject H_0

e. .0292

16. $H_0: \mu_1 - \mu_2 = 0$
$H_a: \mu_1 - \mu_2 \neq 0$
Reject H_0 if $z < -1.96$ or if $z > 1.96$

$$z = \frac{(\bar{x}_1 - \bar{x}_2) - 0}{\sqrt{s_1^2/n_1 + s_2^2/n_2}} = \frac{40 - 35}{\sqrt{(9)^2/36 + (10)^2/49}}$$

$= 2.41$

p-value $= 2(1.000 - .9920) = .0160$

Reject H_0; customers at the two stores differ in terms of mean ages

18. $z = 3.88$, Reject H_0

20. a. 1.08

b. .2802

c. Do not reject H_0

22. a. $H_0: \mu_1 - \mu_2 \leq 0$
$H_a: \mu_1 - \mu_2 > 0$

b. Reject H_0 if $t > 1.711$
$t = 2.07$, Reject H_0

23. a. 1, 2, 0, 0, 2

b. $\bar{d} = \dfrac{\Sigma d_i}{n} = \dfrac{5}{5} = 1$

c. $s_d = \sqrt{\dfrac{\Sigma(d_i - \bar{d})^2}{n - 1}} = \sqrt{\dfrac{4}{5 - 1}} = 1$

d. With 4 degrees of freedom, $t_{.05} = 2.132$; reject H_0 if $t > 2.132$

$$t = \frac{\bar{d} - \mu_d}{s_d/\sqrt{n}} = \frac{1 - 0}{1/\sqrt{5}} = 2.24$$

Reject H_0; conclude $\mu_d > 0$

24. a. 3, −1, 3, 5, 3, 0, 1

b. 2

c. 2.082

d. 2

e. .07 to 3.93

25. $d =$ rating after − rating before
$H_0: \mu_d \leq 0$
$H_a: \mu_d > 0$
With 7 degrees of freedom, reject H_0 if $t > 1.895$
$\bar{d} = .625$ and $s_d = 1.3025$,

$$t = \frac{\bar{d} - \mu_d}{s_d/\sqrt{n}} = \frac{.63 - 0}{1.3025/\sqrt{8}} = 1.36$$

Do not reject H_0; we cannot conclude that seeing the commercial improves the potential to purchase

26. .16 to .35

28. $t = 1.63$; do not reject H_0

30. a. Cannot reject the hypothesis that a $10 price differential exists

b. 6.45 to 11.27

32. a. $\bar{\bar{x}} = (30 + 45 + 36)/3 = 37$

$$\text{SSTR} = \sum_{j=1}^{k} n_j(\bar{x}_j - \bar{\bar{x}})^2$$
$$= 5(30 - 37)^2 + 5(45 - 37)^2 + 5(36 - 37)^2$$
$$= 570$$

$$\text{MSTR} = \frac{\text{SSTR}}{k - 1} = \frac{570}{2} = 285$$

b. $\text{SSE} = \displaystyle\sum_{j=1}^{k} (n_j - 1)s_j^2$
$$= 4(6) + 4(4) + 4(6.5) = 66$$

$$\text{MSE} = \frac{\text{SSE}}{n_T - k} = \frac{66}{15 - 3} = 5.5$$

c. $F = \dfrac{\text{MSTR}}{\text{MSE}} = \dfrac{285}{5.5} = 51.82$

$F_{.05} = 3.89$ (2 degrees of freedom numerator and 12 denominator)

Because $F = 51.82 > F_{.05} = 3.89$, we reject the null hypothesis that the means of the three populations are equal

d.

Source of Variation	Sum of Squares	Degrees of Freedom	Mean Square	F
Treatments	570	2	285	51.82
Error	66	12	5.5	
Total	636	14		

34. a. 510

b. 38.17

c. Reject H_0

d.

Source of Variation	Sum of Squares	Degrees of Freedom	Mean Square	F
Treatments	1020	2	510	13.36
Error	458	12	38.17	
Total	1478	14		

36. a.

Source of Variation	Sum of Squares	Degrees of Freedom	Mean Square	F
Treatments	120	2	60	20
Error	216	72	3	
Total	336	74		

b. $F_{.05} = 3.12$

c. Reject H_0

37.

	Mfg 1	Mfg 2	Mfg 3
Sample mean	23	28	21
Sample variance	6.67	4.67	3.33

$$\bar{\bar{x}} = (23 + 28 + 21)/3 = 24$$

$$\text{SSTR} = \sum_{j=1}^{k} n_j(\bar{x}_j - \bar{\bar{x}})^2$$
$$= 4(23 - 24)^2 + 4(28 - 24)^2$$
$$+ 4(21 - 24)^2 = 104$$

$$\text{MSTR} = \frac{\text{SSTR}}{k - 1} = \frac{104}{2} = 52$$

$$\text{SSE} = \sum_{j=1}^{k} (n_j - 1)s_j^2$$
$$= 3(6.67) + 3(4.67) + 3(3.33) = 44.01$$

$$\text{MSE} = \frac{\text{SSE}}{n_T - k} = \frac{44.01}{12 - 3} = 4.89$$

$$F = \frac{\text{MSTR}}{\text{MSE}} = \frac{52}{4.89} = 10.63$$

$F_{.05} = 4.26$ (2 degrees of freedom numerator and 9 denominator)

Because $F = 10.63 > F_{.05} = 4.26$, we reject the null hypothesis that the mean time needed to mix a batch of material is the same for each manufacturer

38. $F = 10.63$, $F_{.05} = 4.26$
Reject H_0

40. $F = 1.19$, $F_{.05} = 3.22$
Do not reject H_0

42. $10,000 \pm 1066$

44. a. $H_0: \mu_1 - \mu_2 \leq 0$
$H_a: \mu_1 - \mu_2 > 0$

b. $z = .59$, $z_{.05} = 1.645$
Do not reject H_0

c. p-value $= 1.0000 - .7224 = .2776$

46. a. $H_0: \mu_1 - \mu_2 \leq 0$
$H_a: \mu_1 - \mu_2 > 0$

b. $t = 1.42$, p-value $= .09$
Do not reject H_0

48. From Excel: $F = 18.59$, $F_{.05} = 3.35$
p-value ≈ 0
Reject the null hypothesis

50. $F = 4.87$, $F_{.05} = 2.87$
Difference is significant

52. $F = 8.74$, $F_{.05} = 2.87$
Mean salaries differ by region

54. From Excel: $F = 93.16$, $F_{.05} = 3.14$
Download times differ by country

Chapter 11

2. a. $\bar{p} = \dfrac{n_1\bar{p}_1 + n_2\bar{p}_2}{n_1 + n_2} = \dfrac{200(.22) + 300(.16)}{200 + 300} = .184$

$$s_{\bar{p}_1 - \bar{p}_2} = \sqrt{(.184)(.816)\left(\frac{1}{200} + \frac{1}{300}\right)} = .0354$$

Reject H_0 if $z > 1.645$

$$z = \frac{(.22 - .16) - 0}{.0354} = 1.69$$

Reject H_0

b. p-value $= (1 - .9545) = .0455$

4. a. .2206

b. $.2206 \pm .0418$

6. a. $\bar{p}_1 = .93$, $\bar{p}_2 = .85$

b. Reject H_0

c. $.08 \pm .05$

8. a. $z = -3.42 < -1.96$
Reject H_0

b. $.15 \pm .0863$

10. p-value $= .0226$; Reject H_0

12. Expected frequencies: $e_1 = 200(.40) = 80$
$e_2 = 200(.40) = 80$
$e_3 = 200(.20) = 40$

Actual frequencies: $f_1 = 60, f_2 = 120, f_3 = 20$

$$\chi^2 = \frac{(60 - 80)^2}{80} + \frac{(120 - 80)^2}{80} + \frac{(20 - 40)^2}{40}$$

$$= \frac{400}{80} + \frac{1600}{80} + \frac{400}{40}$$

$$= 5 + 20 + 10 = 35$$

$\chi^2_{.01} = 9.21034$, with $k - 1 = 3 - 1 = 2$ degrees of freedom

Because $\chi^2 = 35 > 9.21034$, reject the null hypothesis; that is, the population proportions are not as stated in the null hypothesis

14. H_0: $p_{ABC} = .29, p_{CBS} = .28, p_{NBC} = .25, p_{Other} = .18$
H_a: The proportions are not
$p_{ABC} = .29, p_{CBS} = .28, p_{NBC} = .25, p_{Other} = .18$
Expected frequencies: $300(.29) = 87, 300(.28) = 84$
$\qquad\qquad\qquad 300(.25) = 75, 300(.18) = 54$
$e_1 = 87, e_2 = 84, e_3 = 75, e_4 = 54$
Actual frequencies: $f_1 = 95, f_2 = 70, f_3 = 89, f_4 = 46$
$\chi^2_{.05} = 7.81$ (3 degrees of freedom)

$$\chi^2 = \frac{(95 - 87)^2}{87} + \frac{(70 - 84)^2}{84} + \frac{(89 - 75)^2}{75}$$

$$+ \frac{(46 - 54)^2}{54} = 6.87$$

Do not reject H_0; there is no significant change in the viewing audience proportions

16. $\chi^2 = 2.65, \chi^2_{.10} = 4.61$
No significant difference

18. $\chi^2 = 2.31, \chi^2_{.05} = 5.99$
No significant difference

20. H_0: The column variable is independent of the row variable

H_a: The column variable is not independent of the row variable

Expected frequencies:

	A	B	C
P	28.5	39.9	45.6
Q	21.5	30.1	34.4

$$\chi^2 = \frac{(20 - 28.5)^2}{28.5} + \frac{(44 - 39.9)^2}{39.9} + \frac{(50 - 45.6)^2}{45.6}$$

$$+ \frac{(30 - 21.5)^2}{21.5} + \frac{(26 - 30.1)^2}{30.1} + \frac{(30 - 34.4)^2}{34.4}$$

$$= 7.86$$

$\chi^2_{.025} = 7.37776$, with $(2 - 1)(3 - 1) = 2$ degrees of freedom

Because $\chi^2 = 7.86 > 7.37776$, reject H_0; that is, conclude that the column variable is not independent of the row variable

22. H_0: Type of ticket purchased is independent of the type of flight

H_a: Type of ticket purchased is not independent of the type of flight

Expected frequencies:

$e_{11} = 35.59 \qquad e_{12} = 15.41$
$e_{21} = 150.73 \qquad e_{22} = 65.27$
$e_{31} = 455.68 \qquad e_{32} = 197.32$

Ticket	Flight	Observed Frequency (f_i)	Expected Frequency (e_i)	$(f_i - e_i)^2/e_i$
First	Domestic	29	35.59	1.22
First	International	22	15.41	2.82
Business	Domestic	95	150.73	20.61
Business	International	121	65.27	47.59
Full-fare	Domestic	518	455.68	8.52
Full-fare	International	135	197.32	19.68
Totals		920		100.43

$\chi^2_{.05} = 5.99$ with $(3 - 1)(2 - 1) = 2$ degrees of freedom

Because $100.43 > 5.99$ we reject H_0; type of ticket purchased is not independent of the type of flight

24. $\chi^2 = 12.39, \chi^2_{.01} = 11.3449$
Major and industry type are not independent

26. $\chi^2 = 3.41, \chi^2_{.01} = 15.09$
Do not reject H_0

28. $\chi^2 = 7.96, \chi^2_{.05} = 9.4877$
Do not reject H_0

30. $\chi^2 = 45.36, \chi^2_{.01} = 13.28$
Ratings are not independent

32. a. H_0: $p_1 - p_2 \leq 0$
$\qquad H_a$: $p_1 - p_2 > 0$
b. p-value ≈ 0
c. Reject H_0

34. p-value $= .0174$
Reject H_0

36. a. $\bar{p}_1 - \bar{p}_2 = .16$
b. H_0: $p_1 - p_2 \leq 0$
$\qquad H_a$: $p_1 - p_2 > 0$
c. Reject H_0; expectations have diminished

38. $\chi^2 = 41.69, \chi^2_{.01} = 13.2767$
Attitudes differ

40. $\chi^2 = 7.44, \chi^2_{.05} = 9.48773$
Assumption cannot be rejected

42. $\chi^2 = 8.11, \chi^2_{.05} = 5.99147$
Shift and quality are not independent

44. $\chi^2 = 2.21, \chi^2_{.05} = 7.81473$
Cannot reject assumption of independence

46. $\chi^2 = 9.76$, $\chi^2_{.05} = 9.48773$

Reject; industry type and P/E ratio are related

48. $\chi^2 = 7.78$, $\chi^2_{.05} = 7.81473$

Do not reject; cannot conclude dependence

Chapter 12

1. a.

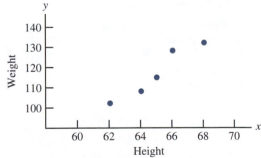

b. There appears to be a linear relationship between x and y

c. Many different straight lines can be drawn to provide a linear approximation of the relationship between x and y; in part (d) we will determine the equation of a straight line that "best" represents the relationship according to the least squares criterion

d. Summations needed to compute the slope and y-intercept:

$\Sigma x_i = 15$, $\Sigma y_i = 40$, $\Sigma(x_i - \bar{x})(y_i - \bar{y}) = 26$,
$\Sigma(x_i - \bar{x})^2 = 10$

$$b_1 = \frac{\Sigma(x_i - \bar{x})(y_i - \bar{y})}{\Sigma(x_i - \bar{x})^2} = \frac{26}{10} = 2.6$$

$b_0 = \bar{y} - b_1\bar{x} = 8 - (2.6)(3) = 0.2$

$\hat{y} = 0.2 - 2.6x$

e. $\hat{y} = .2 + 2.6x = .2 + 2.6(4) = 10.6$

2. b. There appears to be a linear relationship between x and y

d. $\hat{y} = 30.33 - 1.88x$

e. 19.05

4. a.

b. It indicates there may be a linear relationship between the variables

c. Many different straight lines can be drawn to provide a linear approximation of the relationship between x and y; in part (d) we will determine the equation of a straight line that "best" represents the relationship according to the least squares criterion

d. Summations needed to compute the slope and y-intercept:

$\Sigma x_i = 325$, $\Sigma y_i = 585$, $\Sigma(x_i - \bar{x})(y_i - \bar{y}) = 110$,
$\Sigma(x_i - \bar{x})^2 = 20$

$$b_1 = \frac{\Sigma(x_i - \bar{x})(y_i - \bar{y})}{\Sigma(x_i - \bar{x})^2} = \frac{110}{20} = 5.5$$

$b_0 = \bar{y} - b_1\bar{x} = 117 - (5.5)(65) = -240.5$

$\hat{y} = -240.5 + 5.5x$

e. $\hat{y} = -240.5 + 5.5(63) = 106$

The estimate of weight is 106 pounds

6. c. $\hat{y} = 6.02 - .07x$

e. .42

8. b. Yes

c. $\hat{y} = 490.2143 + 204.2449x$

d. $1307

10. b. $\hat{y} = 51.82 + .145x$

c. 84.4

12. c. $\hat{y} = 1293 + .3165x$

d. 25,031

14. b. $\hat{y} = 49.63 + 2.455x$

c. 69.3%

15. a. $\hat{y}_i = .2 + 2.6x_i$ and $\bar{y} = 8$

x_i	y_i	$\hat{y}_i$	$y_i - \hat{y}_i$	$(y_i - \hat{y}_i)^2$	$y_i - \bar{y}$	$(y_i - \bar{y})^2$
1	3	2.8	.2	.04	−5	25
2	7	5.4	1.6	2.56	−1	1
3	5	8.0	−3.0	9.00	−3	9
4	11	10.6	.4	.16	3	9
5	14	13.2	.8	.64	6	36
				SSE = 12.40		SST = 80

SSR = SST − SSE = 80 − 12.4 = 67.6

b. $r^2 = \dfrac{\text{SSR}}{\text{SST}} = \dfrac{67.6}{80} = .845$

The least squares line provided a good fit; 84.5% of the variability in y has been explained by the least squares line

c. $r_{xy} = \sqrt{.845} = +.9192$

16. a. SSE = 6.33, SST = 114.80, SSR = 108.47

b. $r^2 = .945$

c. $r_{xy} = -.9721$

18. a. The estimated regression equation and the mean for the dependent variable:

$\hat{y} = 1790.5 + 581.1x$, $\bar{y} = 3650$

The sum of squares due to error and the total sum of squares:

SSE $= \Sigma(y_i - \hat{y}_i)^2 = 85{,}135.14$,
SST $= \Sigma(y_i - \bar{y})^2 = 335{,}000$

Thus, SSR = SST − SSE
$= 335{,}000 - 85{,}135.14 = 249{,}864.86$

b. $r^2 = \dfrac{\text{SSR}}{\text{SST}} = \dfrac{249,864.86}{335,000} = .746$

The least squares line accounted for 74.6% of the total sum of squares

c. $r_{xy} = \sqrt{.746} = +.8637$

20. a. $\hat{y} = -48.11 + 2.3325x$

b. $r^2 = .82$

c. $173,500

22. a. $\hat{y} = -1.0183 + .1258x$

b. $r^2 = .3631$

c. $r_{xy} = +.6026$

23. a. $s^2 = \text{MSE} = \dfrac{\text{SSE}}{n-2} = \dfrac{12.4}{3} = 4.133$

b. $s = \sqrt{\text{MSE}} = \sqrt{4.133} = 2.033$

c. $\Sigma(x_i - \bar{x})^2 = 10$

$s_{b_1} = \dfrac{s}{\sqrt{\Sigma(x_i - \bar{x})^2}} = \dfrac{2.033}{\sqrt{10}} = .643$

d. $t = \dfrac{b_1 - \beta_1}{s_{b_1}} = \dfrac{2.6 - 0}{.643} = 4.04$

$t_{.025} = 3.182$ (3 degrees of freedom)

Because $t = 4.04 > t_{.05} = 3.182$, we reject $H_0: \beta_1 = 0$

e. $\text{MSR} = \dfrac{\text{SSR}}{1} = 67.6$

$F = \dfrac{\text{MSR}}{\text{MSE}} = \dfrac{67.6}{4.133} = 16.36$

$F_{.05} = 10.13$ (1 degree of freedom numerator and 3 denominator)

Because $F = 16.36 > F_{.05} = 10.13$, we reject $H_0: \beta_1 = 0$

Source of Variation	Sum of Squares	Degrees of Freedom	Mean Square	F
Regression	67.6	1	67.6	16.36
Error	12.4	3	4.133	
Total	80	4		

24. a. 2.11

b. 1.453

c. .262

d. Significant

$t = -7.18 < -t_{.025} = -3.182$

e. Significant

$F = 51.41 > F_{.05} = 10.13$

26. a. $s^2 = \text{MSE} = \dfrac{\text{SSE}}{n-2} = \dfrac{85,135.14}{4} = 21,283.79$

$s = \sqrt{\text{MSE}} = \sqrt{21,283.79} = 145.89$

$\Sigma(x_i - \bar{x})^2 = .74$

$s_{b_1} = \dfrac{s}{\sqrt{\Sigma(x_i - \bar{x})^2}} = \dfrac{145.89}{\sqrt{.74}} = 169.59$

$t = \dfrac{b_1 - \beta_1}{s_{b_1}} = \dfrac{581.08 - 0}{169.59} = 3.43$

$t_{.025} = 2.776$ (4 degrees of freedom)

Because $t = 3.43 > t_{.025} = 2.776$, we reject $H_0: \beta_1 = 0$

b. $\text{MSR} = \dfrac{\text{SSR}}{1} = \dfrac{249,864.86}{1} = 249,864.86$

$F = \dfrac{\text{MSR}}{\text{MSE}} = \dfrac{249,864.86}{21,283.79} = 11.74$

$F_{.05} = 7.71$ (1 degree of freedom numerator and 4 denominator)

Because $F = 11.74 > F_{.05} = 7.71$, we reject $H_0: \beta_1 = 0$

c.

Source of Variation	Sum of Squares	Degrees of Freedom	Mean Square	F
Regression	29,864.86	1	29,864.86	11.74
Error	85,135.14	4	21,283.79	
Total	335,000	5		

28. They are related because $F = 20.17 > F_{.05} = 4.67$

30. No significant relationship

32. a. $\hat{y} = 6.1092 + .8951x$

b. Significant relationship

c. $r^2 = .82$; a good fit

34. a. $\hat{y} = 80.0 + 50.0x$

b. $F = 83.17 > F_{.05} = 4.20$; reject $H_0: \beta_1 = 0$

c. $t = 9.12 > t_{.025} = 2.048$; reject $H_0: \beta_1 = 0$

d. p-value $= .000$

36. a. $\hat{y} = -42.7965 + 1.0043x$

b. Significant

c. 0.4288; not a good fit

38. b. There appears to be a linear relationship between the two variables

c. $\hat{y} = 37.0747 - 0.7792x$

d. Significant relationship

e. 0.43; not a good fit

39. a. $s = 2.033$

$\bar{x} = 3, \Sigma(x_i - \bar{x})^2 = 10$

$s_{\hat{y}_p} = s\sqrt{\dfrac{1}{n} + \dfrac{(x_p - \bar{x})^2}{\Sigma(x_i - \bar{x})^2}}$

$= 2.033\sqrt{\dfrac{1}{5} + \dfrac{(4-3)^2}{10}} = 1.11$

b. $\hat{y} = .2 + 2.6x = .2 + 2.6(4) = 10.6$

$\hat{y}_p \pm t_{\alpha/2}s_{\hat{y}_p}$

$10.6 \pm 3.182(1.11)$

10.6 ± 3.53, or 7.07 to 14.13

c. $s_{ind} = s\sqrt{1 + \dfrac{1}{n} + \dfrac{(x_p - \bar{x})^2}{\Sigma(x_i - \bar{x})^2}}$

$= 2.033\sqrt{1 + \dfrac{1}{5} + \dfrac{(4 - 3)^2}{10}} = 2.32$

d. $\hat{y}_p \pm t_{\alpha/2}s_{ind}$
$10.6 \pm 3.182(2.32)$
10.6 ± 7.38, or 3.22 to 17.98

40. a. 1.453
  b. 22.53 to 26.85
  c. 1.61
  d. 19.57 to 29.81

42. a. $s = 145.89$, $\bar{x} = 3.2$, $\Sigma(x_i - \bar{x})^2 = .74$
$\hat{y} = 1790.5 + 581.1x = 1790.5 + 581.1(3)$
$= 3533.8$

$s_{\hat{y}_p} = s\sqrt{\dfrac{1}{n} + \dfrac{(x_p - \bar{x})^2}{\Sigma(x_i - \bar{x})^2}}$

$= 145.89\sqrt{\dfrac{1}{6} + \dfrac{(3 - 3.2)^2}{.74}} = 68.54$

$\hat{y}_p \pm t_{\alpha/2}s_{\hat{y}_p}$
$3533.8 \pm 2.776(68.54)$
3533.8 ± 190.27, or \$3343.53 to \$3724.07
  b. $\hat{y} = 1790.5 + 581.1x = 1790.5 + 581.1(3)$
$= 3533.8$

$s_{ind} = s\sqrt{1 + \dfrac{1}{n} + \dfrac{(x_p - \bar{x})^2}{\Sigma(x_i - \bar{x})^2}}$

$= 145.89\sqrt{1 + \dfrac{1}{6} + \dfrac{(3 - 3.2)^2}{0.74}} = 161.19$

$\hat{y}_p \pm t_{\alpha/2}s_{ind}$
$3533.8 \pm 2.776(161.19)$
3533.8 ± 447.46, or \$3086.34 to \$3981.26

44. a. \$11,740 to \$14,420
  b. \$9,300 to \$16,860
  c. Yes, \$20,400 is much larger than anticipated
  d. Any deductions exceeding \$16,800

46. a. $\hat{y} = 67.0476 + 5.8167x$
  b. $r^2 = .894$; very good fit
  c. 250.59 to 290.67
  d. 215.39 to 325.87

47. a. Using Excel's Regression tool the estimated
regression equation is $\hat{y} = -7.0222 + 1.5873x$
or $\hat{y} = -7.02 + 1.59x$
  b.

x_i	y_i	$\hat{y}_i$	$y_i - \hat{y}_i$
6	6	2.52	3.48
11	8	10.47	−2.47
15	12	16.83	−4.83
18	20	21.60	−1.60
20	30	24.78	5.22

c.

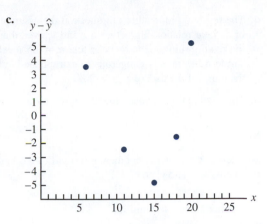

With only five observations, it is difficult to determine whether the assumptions are satisfied; however, the plot does suggest curvature in the residuals, which would indicate that the error term assumptions are not satisfied; the scatter diagram for these data also indicates that the underlying relationship between x and y may be curvilinear

48. a. $\hat{y} = 2.322 + .6366x$
  b. Assumption that variance is the same for all values of x is questionable; the variance appears to increase for larger values of x

49. Using Excel's Regression tool the estimated regression equation is $\hat{y} = 29.39911 + 1.547458x$ or $\hat{y} = 29.40 + 1.55x$
  b. Significant relationship: Significance F (or p-value) $< \alpha = .05$
  c.

x_i	y_i	$\hat{y}_i = 29.40 + 1.55x_i$	$y_i - \hat{y}_i$
1	19	30.95	−11.95
2	32	32.50	−.50
4	44	35.60	8.40
6	40	38.70	1.30
10	52	44.90	7.10
14	53	51.10	1.90
20	54	60.40	−6.40

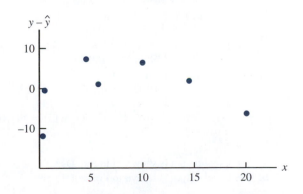

d. The residual plot leads us to question the assumption of a linear relationship between x and y; even though the relationship is significant at the $\alpha = .05$ level, it would be extremely dangerous to extrapolate beyond the range of the data (e.g., $x > 20$)

50. b. The assumptions concerning the error terms appear reasonable

52. No

54. To determine whether or not there is a significant relationship between x and y; no

56. a. $\hat{y} = -3.8338 + .2957x$
   b. Approximately 40.6 million
   c. Yes; $r^2 = .919$

58. b. There appears to be a positive linear relationship between the two variables
   c. $\hat{y} = 23.8987 + .8980x$
   d. Significant relationship
   e. $r^2 = .781$; good fit
   f. $r_{xy} = +.88$

60. a. $\hat{y} = 22.1739 - .1478x$
   b. Significant relationship
   c. $r^2 = .739$; good fit
   d. 12.294 to 17.271

62. a. $\hat{y} = 220 + 131.6667x$
   b. Significant relationship
   c. $r^2 = .873$; good fit
   d. 559.3 to 933.9

64. a. $\hat{y} = -.4710 + .00004x$
   b. Significant relationship; p-value $= .0384$
   c. $r^2 = .217$; not a good fit
   d. .7729 to .9927

Chapter 13

2. a. The estimated regression equation is
   $\hat{y} = 45.0594 + 1.9436x_1$
   An estimate of y when $x_1 = 45$ is
   $\hat{y} = 45.0594 + 1.9436(45) = 132.52$
   b. The estimated regression equation is
   $\hat{y} = 85.2171 + 4.3215x_2$
   An estimate of y when $x_2 = 15$ is
   $\hat{y} = 85.2171 + 4.3215(15) = 150.04$
   c. The estimated regression equation is
   $\hat{y} = -18.3683 + 2.0102x_1 + 4.7378x_2$
   An estimate of y when $x_1 = 45$ and $x_2 = 15$ is
   $\hat{y} = -18.3683 + 2.0102(45) + 4.7378(15) = 143.16$

4. a. $255,000

5. a. The Excel output is shown in Figure D13.5a
   b. The Excel output is shown in Figure D13.5b

c. It is 1.6039 in part (a) and 2.2902 in part (b); in part (a) the coefficient is an estimate of the change in revenue due to a one-unit change in television advertising expenditures; in part (b) it represents an estimate of the change in revenue due to a one-unit change in television advertising expenditures when the amount of newspaper advertising is held constant
   d. Revenue $= 83.2301 + 2.2902(3.5) + 1.3010(1.8)$
   $= 93.59$ or $93,590

6. a. Speed $= 49.78 + .0151$ Weight
   b. Speed $= 80.4873 - .0031$ Weight $+ .1047$ Horsepower
   c. 102

8. a. Return $= 247.3579 - 32.8445$ Safety $+ 34.5887$ ExpRatio
   b. 70.2

10. a. Revenue $= 33.3352 + 7.9840$ Cars
   b. Increase of 1000 cars will increase revenue by $7.984 million
   c. Revenue $= 105.9727 + 8.9427$ Cars $- .1914$ Locations

12. a. $R^2 = \dfrac{\text{SSR}}{\text{SST}} = \dfrac{14{,}052.2}{15{,}182.9} = .926$
   b. $R_a^2 = 1 - (1 - R^2)\dfrac{n - 1}{n - p - 1}$
   $= 1 - (1 - .926)\dfrac{10 - 1}{10 - 2 - 1} = .905$
   c. Yes; after adjusting for the number of independent variables in the model, we see that 90.5% of the variability in y has been accounted for

14. a. .75
   b. .68

15. a. $R^2 = \dfrac{\text{SSR}}{\text{SST}} = \dfrac{23.435}{25.5} = .919$
   $R_a^2 = 1 - (1 - R^2)\dfrac{n - 1}{n - p - 1}$
   $= 1 - (1 - .919)\dfrac{8 - 1}{8 - 2 - 1} = .887$
   b. Multiple regression analysis is preferred because both R^2 and R_a^2 show an increased percentage of the variability of y explained when both independent variables are used

16. a. No, $R^2 = .3112$
   b. Multiple regression analysis

18. a. $R^2 = .9416$, $R_a^2 = .9318$
   b. The fit is very good

19. a. $\text{MSR} = \dfrac{\text{SSR}}{p} = \dfrac{6216.375}{2} = 3108.188$
   $\text{MSE} = \dfrac{\text{SSE}}{n - p - 1} = \dfrac{507.75}{10 - 2 - 1} = 72.536$

FIGURE D13.5a

Regression Statistics	
Multiple R	0.8078
R Square	0.6526
Adjusted R Square	0.5946
Standard Error	1.2152
Observations	8

ANOVA

	df	SS	MS	F	Significance F
Regression	1	16.6401	16.6401	11.2688	0.0153
Residual	6	8.8599	1.4767		
Total	7	25.5			

	Coefficients	Standard Error	t Stat	P-value
Intercept	88.6377	1.5824	56.0159	2.174E-09
Television Advertising ($1000s)	1.6039	0.4778	3.3569	0.0153

FIGURE D13.5b

Regression Statistics	
Multiple R	0.9587
R Square	0.9190
Adjusted R Square	0.8866
Standard Error	0.6426
Observations	8

ANOVA

	df	SS	MS	F	Significance F
Regression	2	23.4354	11.7177	28.3778	0.0019
Residual	5	2.0646	0.4129		
Total	7	25.5			

	Coefficients	Standard Error	t Stat	P-value
Intercept	83.2301	1.5739	52.8825	4.57E-08
Television Advertising ($1000s)	2.2902	0.3041	7.5319	0.0007
Newspaper Advertising ($1000s)	1.3010	0.3207	4.0567	0.0098

b. $F = \dfrac{MSR}{MSE} = \dfrac{3108.188}{72.536} = 42.85$

$F_{.05} = 4.74$ (2 degrees of freedom numerator and 7 denominator)

Because $F = 42.85 > F_{.05} = 4.74$, the overall model is significant

c. $t = \dfrac{b_1}{s_{b_1}} = \dfrac{.5906}{.0813} = 7.26$

$t_{.025} = 2.365$ (7 degrees of freedom)

With $t = 7.26 > t_{.025} = 2.365$, β_1 is significant

d. $t = \dfrac{b_2}{s_{b_2}} = \dfrac{.4980}{.0567} = 8.78$

With $t = 8.78 > t_{.025} = 2.365$, β_2 is significant

20. a. Significant; p-value $= .0001$

b. Significant; p-value $= .000$

c. Significant; p-value $= .0016$

22. a. SSE $= 4000$, MSE $= 571.43$,
MSR $= 6000$

b. Significant; $F = 10.50 > F_{.05} = 4.74$

23. a. $F = 28.38$

$F_{.01} = 13.27$ (2 degrees of freedom numerator and 1 denominator)

Because $F > F_{.01} = 13.27$, reject H_0

Alternatively, the p-value of .002 leads to the same conclusion

b. $t = 7.53$

$t_{.025} = 2.571$

Because $t > t_{.025} = 2.571$, β_1 is significant and x_1 should not be dropped from the model

c. $t = 4.06$

$t_{.025} = 2.571$

With $t > t_{.025} = 2.571$, β_2 is significant and x_2 should not be dropped from the model

24. a. Reject H_0: $\beta_1 = \beta_2 = 0$; p-value $= .000$

b. Weight: Cannot reject H_0: $\beta_1 = 0$; p-value $= .3861$
Horsepower: Reject H_0: $\beta_2 = 0$; p-value $= .000$

26. a. Significant; p-value $= .000$

b. Significant; p-value $= .000$

c. Not significant; p-value $= .0868$

28. a. Using the PredInt macro, the 95% confidence interval is 132.16 to 154.16

b. Using the PredInt macro, the 95% prediction interval is 111.13 to 175.18

29. a. See Excel output in Figure D13.5b

$\hat{y} = 83.2301 + 2.2902(3.5) + 1.3010(1.8) = 93.588$
or $93,588$

b. Using the PredInt macro: 92.840 to 94.335, or $92,840 to $94,335

c. Using the PredInt macro: 91.774 to 95.401, or $91,774 to $95,401

30. a. 101.29

b. 99.490 to 103.089

c. 94.596 to 107.984

32. a. $E(y) = \beta_0 + \beta_1 x_1 + \beta_2 x_2$

where $x_2 = \begin{cases} 0 \text{ if level 1} \\ 1 \text{ if level 2} \end{cases}$

b. $E(y) = \beta_0 + \beta_1 x_1 + \beta_2(0) = \beta_0 + \beta_1 x_1$

c. $E(y) = \beta_0 + \beta_1 x_1 + \beta_2(1) = \beta_0 + \beta_1 x_1 + \beta_2$

d. $\beta_2 = E(y \mid \text{level 2}) - E(y \mid \text{level 1})$
β_1 is the change in $E(y)$ for a 1-unit change in x_1 holding x_2 constant

34. a. $15,300, because $b_3 = 15.3$

b. $\hat{y} = 10.1 - 4.2(2) + 6.8(8) + 15.3(0)$
$= 10.1 - 8.4 + 54.4$
$= 56.1$
Sales prediction: $56,100

c. $\hat{y} = 10.1 - 4.2(1) + 6.8(3) + 15.3(1)$
$= 10.1 - 4.2 + 20.4 + 15.3$
$= 41.6$
Sales prediction: $41,600

36. a. $\hat{y} = 1.8602 + 0.2914 \text{ Months} + 1.1024 \text{ Type} - 0.6091 \text{ Person}$

b. Significant; p-value $= .0021 < \alpha = .05$

c. Person is not significant

38. a. $\hat{y} = -91.7595 + 1.0767 \text{ Age} + .2518 \text{ Pressure} + 8.7399 \text{ Smoker}$

b. Significant; p-value $= .0102 < \alpha = .05$

c. 95% prediction interval is 21.35 to 47.18 or a probability of .2135 to .4718; quit smoking and begin some type of treatment to reduce his blood pressure

40. b. 3.19

42. b. Significant; $F = 22.79 > F_{.05} = 5.79$

c. $R_a^2 = .861$; good fit

d. Both are significant

44. a. Speed $= 97.5702 + .0693 \text{ Price} - .0008 \text{ Weight} + .0590 \text{ Horsepwr} - 2.4836 \text{ Zero60}$

b. Significant relationship

c. Price and Weight are not significant

d. Speed $= 103.1028 + .0558 \text{ Horsepwr} - 3.1876 \text{ Zero60}$

46. a. Resale% $= 38.7718 + .0008 \text{ Price}$

b. Not a good fit; R Square $= .3671$

c. Resale% $= 42.5539 + 9.0903 \text{ Type 1} + 7.9172 \text{ Type 2} + .0003 \text{ Price}$
where Type 1 $= 1$ if a full-size pickup and Type 2 $= 1$ if a sport utility vehicle

d. Significant relationship; p-value corresponding to $F = 14.7892 = .000 < \alpha = .05$

Chapter 14

2. a. 5.42
   b. UCL = 6.09, LCL = 4.75

4. *R chart:*
   UCL = $\bar{R}D_4$ = 1.6(1.864) = 2.98
   LCL = $\bar{R}D_3$ = 1.6(.136) = .22
   $\bar{x}$ chart:
   UCL = $\bar{\bar{x}} + A_2\bar{R}$ = 28.5 + .373(1.6) = 29.10
   LCL = $\bar{\bar{x}} - A_2\bar{R}$ = 28.5 − .373(1.6) = 27.90

6. 20.01, .082

8. a. .0470
   b. UCL = .0989, LCL = −.0049 (use LCL = 0)
   c. $\bar{p}$ = .08; in control
   d. UCL = 14.826, LCL = −0.726 (use LCL = 0)
      Process is out of control if more than 14 defective
   e. In control with 12 defective
   f. *np* chart

10. $f(x) = \dfrac{n!}{x!(n - x)!} p^x(1 - p)^{n-x}$

   When p = .02, the probability of accepting the lot is

   $f(0) = \dfrac{25!}{0!(25 - 0)!}(.02)^0(1 - .02)^{25} = .6035$

   When p = .06, the probability of accepting the lot is

   $f(0) = \dfrac{25!}{0!(25 - 0)!}(.06)^0(1 - .06)^{25} = .2129$

12. p_0 = .02; producer's risk = .0599
   p_0 = .06; producer's risk = .3396
   Producer's risk decreases as the acceptance criterion c is increased

14. n = 20, c = 3

16. a. 95.4
   b. UCL = 96.07, LCL = 94.73
   c. No

18.

	R Chart	$\bar{x}$ Chart
UCL	4.23	6.57
LCL	0	4.27

Estimate of standard deviation = .86

20.

	R Chart	$\bar{x}$ Chart
UCL	.1121	3.112
LCL	0	3.051

22. a. UCL = .0817, LCL = −.0017 (use LCL = 0)

24. a. .03
   b. β = .0802

Excel provides a wealth of functions for data management and statistical analysis. If we know what function is needed, and how to use it, we can simply enter the function into the appropriate worksheet cell. However, if we are not sure what functions are available to accomplish a task or are not sure how to use a particular function, Excel can provide assistance.

Finding the Right Excel Function

*In earlier versions of Excel, the **Paste Function** dialog box serves the same purpose as the **Insert Function** dialog box in Excel 2002.*

To identify the functions available in Excel, select the **Insert** menu and then choose **Function** from the list of options. Alternatively, select the f_x button on the formula bar. Either approach provides the **Insert Function** dialog box shown in Figure 1.

The **Search for a function** box at the top of the Insert Function dialog box enables us to type a brief description of what we want to do. After doing so and clicking **Go**, Excel will search for and display, in the **Select a function** box, the functions that may accomplish our task. In many situations, however, we may want to browse through an entire category of functions to see what is available. For this task, the **Or select a category** box is helpful. It contains a drop-down list of several categories of functions provided by Excel. Figure 1 shows that we selected the **Statistical** category. As a result, Excel's statistical functions appear in alphabetic order in the **Select a function** box. We see the AVEDEV function listed first, followed by the AVERAGE function, and so on.

The AVEDEV function is highlighted in Figure 1, indicating it as the function currently selected. The proper syntax for the function and a brief description of the function appear below the Select a function box. We can scroll through the list in the Select a function box to display the syntax and a brief description for each of the statistical functions available. For instance, scrolling down further, we select the COUNTIF function. See Figure 2. Note

FIGURE 1 INSERT FUNCTION DIALOG BOX

Insert Function   ? ✕

Search for a function:

| Type a brief description of what you want to do and then click Go | Go |

Or select a category: Statistical ▾

Select a function:

AVEDEV
AVERAGE
AVERAGEA
BETADIST
BETAINV
BINOMDIST
CHIDIST

AVEDEV(number1,number2,...)
Returns the average of the absolute deviations of data points from their mean. Arguments can be numbers or names, arrays, or references that contain numbers.

Help on this function   OK   Cancel

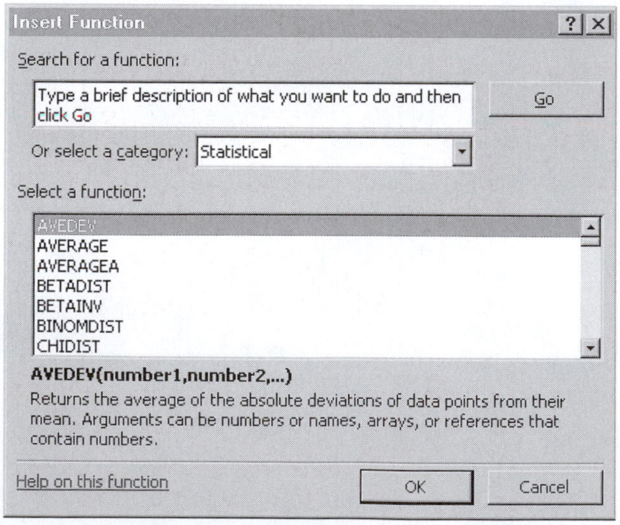

FIGURE 2   DESCRIPTION OF THE COUNTIF FUNCTION IN THE INSERT FUNCTION
DIALOG BOX

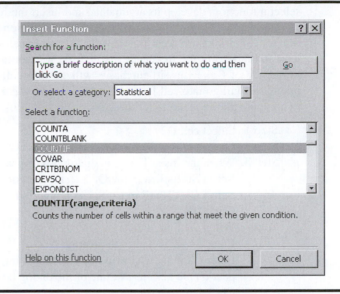

that COUNTIF is now highlighted, and that immediately below the **Select a function** box
we see **COUNTIF(range,criteria)**, which indicates that the COUNTIF function contains
two arguments, range and criteria. In addition, we see that the description of the COUNTIF
function is "Counts the number of cells within a range that meet the given condition."

In earlier versions of Excel,   If the function selected (highlighted) is the one we want to use, we click **OK**; the **Func-**
a similar dialog box will   **tion Arguments** dialog box then appears. The Function Arguments dialog box for the
appear. It serves the same   COUNTIF function is shown in Figure 3. This dialog box assists in creating the appropri-
*purpose as the **Function***   ate arguments for the function selected. When finished entering the arguments, we click
Arguments dialog box in   **OK**; Excel then inserts the function into a worksheet cell.
Excel 2002.

FIGURE 3   FUNCTION ARGUMENTS DIALOG BOX FOR THE COUNTIF FUNCTION

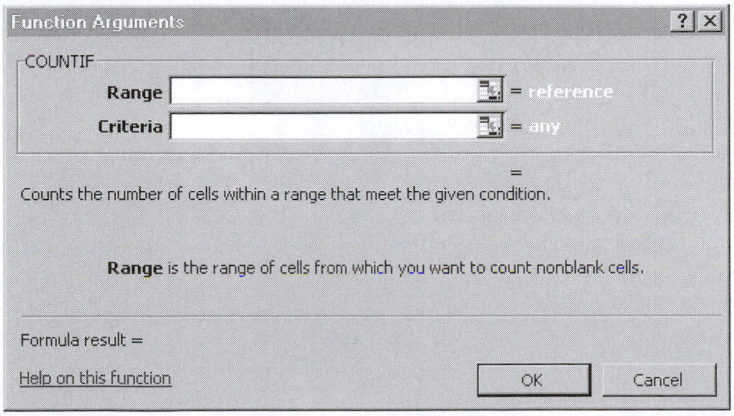

Inserting a Function into a Worksheet Cell

We will now show how to use the Insert Function and Function Arguments dialog boxes to select a function, develop its arguments, and insert the function into a worksheet cell.

In Section 2.1, we used Excel's COUNTIF function to construct a frequency distribution for soft drink purchases. Figure 4 displays an Excel worksheet containing the soft drink data and labels for the frequency distribution we would like to construct. We see that the frequency of Coke Classic purchases will go into cell D2, the frequency of Diet Coke purchases will go into cell D3, and so on. Suppose we want to use the COUNTIF function to compute the frequencies for these cells and would like some assistance from Excel.

Step 1. Select cell D2
Step 2. Click on f_x on the formula bar (or select **Insert** and then choose **Function**)
Step 3. When the Insert Function dialog box appears:
Select **Statistical** in the Or select a category box
Select **COUNTIF** in the Select a function box
Click **OK**
Step 4. When the Function Arguments box appears (see Figure 5):
Enter $A$2:$A$51 in the **Range** box
Enter C2 in the **Criteria** box (At this point, the value of the function will appear on the next-to-last line of the dialog box. Its value is 19.)
Click **OK**
Step 5. Copy cell D2 to cells D3:D6

The worksheet then appears as in Figure 6. The formula worksheet is in the background; the value worksheet is in the foreground. The formula worksheet shows that the COUNTIF function was inserted into cell D2. We copied the contents of cell D2 into cells D3:D6. The value worksheet shows the proper class frequencies as computed.

We illustrated the use of Excel's capability to provide assistance in using the COUNTIF function. The procedure is similar for all Excel functions. This capability is especially helpful if you do not know what function to use or forget the proper name and/or syntax for a function.

FIGURE 4　EXCEL WORKSHEET WITH SOFT DRINK DATA AND LABELS
FOR THE FREQUENCY DISTRIBUTION

CD file

SoftDrink

Note: Rows 11–44 are hidden.

	A	B	C	D	E
1	Brand Purchased		Soft Drink	Frequency	
2	Coke Classic		Coke Classic		
3	Diet Coke		Diet Coke		
4	Pepsi-Cola		Dr. Pepper		
5	Diet Coke		Pepsi-Cola		
6	Coke Classic		Sprite		
7	Coke Classic				
8	Dr. Pepper				
9	Diet Coke				
10	Pepsi-Cola				
45	Pepsi-Cola				
46	Pepsi-Cola				
47	Pepsi-Cola				
48	Coke Classic				
49	Dr. Pepper				
50	Pepsi-Cola				
51	Sprite				
52					

FIGURE 5   COMPLETED FUNCTION ARGUMENTS DIALOG BOX
FOR THE COUNTIF FUNCTION

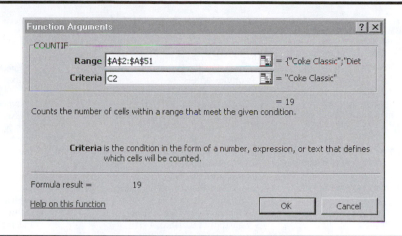

FIGURE 6   EXCEL WORKSHEET SHOWING THE USE OF EXCEL'S COUNTIF FUNCTION
TO CONSTRUCT A FREQUENCY DISTRIBUTION

	A	B	C	D	E
1	**Brand Purchased**		**Soft Drink**	**Frequency**	
2	Coke Classic		Coke Classic	=COUNTIF($A$2:$A$51,C2)	
3	Diet Coke		Diet Coke	=COUNTIF($A$2:$A$51,C3)	
4	Pepsi-Cola		Dr. Pepper	=COUNTIF($A$2:$A$51,C4)	
5	Diet Coke		Pepsi-Cola	=COUNTIF($A$2:$A$51,C5)	
6	Coke Classic		Sprite	=COUNTIF($A$2:$A$51,C6)	
7	Coke Classic				
8	Dr. Pepper				
9	Diet Coke				
10	Pepsi-Cola				
45	Pepsi-Cola				
46	Pepsi-Cola				
47	Pepsi-Cola				
48	Coke Classic				
49	Dr. Pepper				
50	Pepsi-Cola				
51	Sprite				
52					

	A	B	C	D	E
1	**Brand Purchased**		**Soft Drink**	**Frequency**	
2	Coke Classic		Coke Classic	19	
3	Diet Coke		Diet Coke	8	
4	Pepsi-Cola		Dr. Pepper	5	
5	Diet Coke		Pepsi-Cola	13	
6	Coke Classic		Sprite	5	
7	Coke Classic				
8	Dr. Pepper				
9	Diet Coke				
10	Pepsi-Cola				
45	Pepsi-Cola				
46	Pepsi-Cola				
47	Pepsi-Cola				
48	Coke Classic				
49	Dr. Pepper				
50	Pepsi-Cola				
51	Sprite				
52					

Index